Social Psychology
Twelfth Edition

Robert A. Baron
Rensselaer Polytechnic Institute

Nyla R. Branscombe
University of Kansas

Donn Byrne
University at Albany,
State University of New York

PEARSON

Boston   New York   San Francisco
Mexico City   Montreal   Toronto   London   Madrid   Munich   Paris
Hong Kong   Singapore   Tokyo   Cape Town   Sydney

Editor-in-Chief: Susan Hartman
Acquisitions Editor: Michelle Limoges
Editorial Assistant: Christina Manfroni
Executive Marketing Manager: Karen Natale
Production Supervisor: Liz Napolitano
Editorial Production Service: NK/Black Dot
Composition Buyer: Linda Cox
Manufacturing Buyer: JoAnne Sweeney
Electronic Composition: NK/Black Dot
Interior Design: Gina Hagen
Photo Researcher: Annie Pickert, Naomi Rudov
Cover Designer: Linda Knowles

For related titles and support materials, visit our online catalog at www.ablongman.com.

Between the time website information is gathered and then published, it is not unusual for some sites to have closed. Also, the transcription of URLs can result in typographical errors. The publisher would appreciate notification where these errors occur so that they may be corrected in subsequent editions.

ISBN-13: 978-0-205-58149-8   ISBN-10: 0-205-58149-8

Library of Congress Cataloging-in-Publication Data

Baron, Robert A.
  Social psychology / Robert A. Baron, Nyla R. Branscombe, Donn Byrne.—12th ed.
    p. cm.
  ISBN 978-0-205-58149-8 (alk. paper)
  1. Social psychology. I. Branscombe, Nyla R. II. Byrne, Donn Erwin. III. Title.
  HM1033.B35 2009   302—dc22   2007045159

Printed in the United States of America

10 9 8 7 6 5 4 3 2 1   Q-WC-V   11 10 09 08 07

To the founders of social psychology whose research and thought strongly shaped the nature of the field—and, of course!—the contents of this book.

And to Rebecca, who not only lights up my life with her wit, charm, and warmth, but also regularly provides me with many of my very best ideas; and to Jessica, who always has had, and always will have, a special place in my heart.

—RAB

And to Rose Croxall, Howard Branscombe, Marlene Boyd, Leona Endall, Gerald Branscombe, and Elaine Haase—my siblings and oldest support group.

—NRB

And to my mother, Rebecca Singleton Byrne, and my father, Bernard Byrne. They offered unconditional love and support throughout most of my life, and they are truly missed.

—DB

Brief Contents

1 Social Psychology   2
THE SCIENCE OF THE SOCIAL SIDE OF LIFE

2 Social Cognition   36
HOW WE THINK ABOUT THE SOCIAL WORLD

3 Social Perception   72
PERCEIVING AND UNDERSTANDING OTHERS

4 The Self   110
ANSWERING THE QUESTION "WHO AM I?"

5 Attitudes   146
EVALUATING AND RESPONDING TO THE SOCIAL WORLD

6 Stereotyping, Prejudice, and Discrimination   184
THE CAUSES, EFFECTS, AND CURES

7 Interpersonal Attraction and Close Relationships   224

8 Social Influence   270
CHANGING OTHERS' BEHAVIOR

9 Prosocial Behavior   304
HELPING OTHERS

10 Aggression   336
ITS NATURE, CAUSES, AND CONTROL

11 Groups and Individuals   376
THE CONSEQUENCES OF BELONGING

12 Social Psychology   416
APPLYING ITS PRINCIPLES TO LAW, HEALTH, AND BUSINESS

Contents

Special Features   xxi
Preface   xxiii
About the Authors   xxxi
Foreword   xxxiii

1 Social Psychology
THE SCIENCE OF THE SOCIAL SIDE OF LIFE   2

Social Psychology: What It Is and What It Does   5
Social Psychology Is Scientific in Nature   6
Social Psychology Focuses on the Behavior of Individuals   8
Social Psychology Seeks to Understand the
 Causes of Social Behavior and Thought   8
Social Psychology: Summing Up   13

Social Psychology: Its Cutting Edge   14
Cognition and Behavior: Two Sides of the Same Social Coin   14
Social Neuroscience: Where Social Psychology and Brain Research Meet   14
The Role of Implicit (Nonconscious) Processes   16
Taking Full Account of Social Diversity   18

**A Brief Look at History: The Origins and Early Development of
Social Psychology   19**
The Early Years: Social Psychology Emerges   19
Social Psychology's Youth: The 1940s, 1950s, and 1960s   19
The 1970s, 1980s, and 1990s: A Maturing Field   20

**How Social Psychologists Answer the Fascinating Questions They Raise: Research
as the Route to Increased Knowledge   21**
Systematic Observation: Describing the World around Us   21
Correlation: The Search for Relationships   23
The Experimental Method: Knowledge through Systematic Intervention   25
Further Thoughts on Causality: The Role of Mediating Variables   27

The Role of Theory in Social Psychology   28

**The Quest for Knowledge and Rights of Individuals:
Seeking an Appropriate Balance   31**

Getting the Most Out of This Book: A User's Guide   32
Summary and Review   34
Key Terms   35

2 Social Cognition
HOW WE THINK ABOUT THE SOCIAL WORLD　36

Schemas: Mental Frameworks for Organizing—and Using—Social Information　39

The Impact of Schemas on Social Cognition:
Attention, Encoding, and Retrieval　40

Priming: Which Schemas Guide Our Thought?　41

Schema Persistence: Why Even Discredited Schemas Can Sometimes Influence Our
Thought and Behavior　42

Heuristics: How We Reduce Our Effort in Social Cognition　43

BUILDING THE SCIENCE: Classics of Social Psychology　The Self-
Confirming Nature of Schemas: When—and Why—Beliefs Shape Reality　44

Representativeness: Judging by Resemblance　46

Availability: "If I Can Think of It, It Must Be Important"　46

Anchoring and Adjustment: Where You Begin Makes a Difference　47

Automatic and Controlled Processing: Two Basic Modes of Social Thought　49

Automatic Processing and Automatic Social Behavior　49

The Benefits of Automatic Processing: Beyond Mere Efficiency　51

**Potential Sources of Error in Social Cognition: Why Total Rationality Is
Rarer Than You Think　54**

Basic "Tilts" in Social Thought: The Negativity Bias and Our Powerful Tendency
to Be Overly Optimistic　54

Situation-Specific Sources of Error in Social Cognition: Counterfactual Thinking,
Thought Suppression, and Magical Thinking　57

SOCIAL PSYCHOLOGY: What It Tells Us About . . . The War in Iraq: Did the
Optimistic Bias Play a Role?　58

Social Cognition: Some Optimistic Conclusions　62

**Affect and Cognition: How Feelings Shape Thought and
Thought Shapes Feelings　63**

The Influence of Affect on Cognition　64

The Influence of Cognition on Affect　65

Affect and Cognition: Social Neuroscience Evidence for Two Separate Systems　67

MAKING SENSE OF COMMON SENSE: A Social Psychological Perspective
Is Being in a Good Mood Always Beneficial? The Potential Downside of
Being Up　68

Summary and Review　69

Key Terms　70

Connections: Integrating Social Psychology　71

3 Social Perception
PERCEIVING AND UNDERSTANDING OTHERS   72

Nonverbal Communication: The Unspoken Language of Expressions, Gazes, and Gestures   75

Nonverbal Communication: The Basic Channels   76

Deception: Recognizing It through Nonverbal Cues and Its Effects on Social Relations   80

MAKING SENSE OF COMMON SENSE: A Social Psychological Perspective Are Men Really "Clueless" When It Comes to Nonverbal Cues? Fiction—and Fact—about Gender Differences in Nonverbal Communication   83

Attribution: Understanding the Causes of Others' Behavior   85

Theories of Attribution: Frameworks for Understanding How We Attempt to Make Sense of the Social World   85

Attribution: Some Basic Sources of Error   89

BUILDING THE SCIENCE: Classics of Social Psychology The Fundamental Attribution Error: Stronger Than You Might Guess   91

Applications of Attribution Theory: Insights and Interventions   96

Impression Formation and Impression Management: Combining Information about Others   97

The Beginning of Research on First Impressions: Asch's Research on Central and Peripheral Traits   98

How Quickly Are Impressions Formed?   99

Implicit Personality Theories: Schemas That Shape First Impressions   100

Impression Formation: A Cognitive Perspective   101

Is Accuracy Always Best in Social Perception? Evidence That Illusions, Too, Can Sometimes Be Helpful   102

Impression Management: The Fine Art of Looking Good   103

SOCIAL PSYCHOLOGY: What It Tells Us About . . . Speed Dating—Can We Really Choose the One We Might Love in a Few Minutes?   107

Summary and Review   108

Key Terms   109

Connections: Integrating Social Psychology   109

4 The Self
ANSWERING THE QUESTION "WHO AM I?" 110

Self-Presentation: Managing the Self in Different Social Contexts 114
Self-Presentation Tactics 114
MAKING SENSE OF COMMON SENSE: A Social Psychological Perspective
The Internet: Presenting Your Online Identity 115

Self-Knowledge: How Do We Know Who We Are? 117
Introspection: Looking Inward to Discover the Causes of Our Own Behavior 117
The Self from the Other's Standpoint 119

Thinking about the Self: Personal versus Social Identity 120
Who I Am Depends on the Situation 121
Who I Am Depends on Others' Treatment 123
SOCIAL PSYCHOLOGY: What It Tells Us About . . . How We Manage When
There Is Conflict Among Our Identities 124
Possible Selves: The Self over Time 126
Self-Control 127

Self-Esteem: Attitudes toward Ourselves 129
The Measurement of Self-Esteem 129
Is High Self-Esteem Always Beneficial? 131
Do Women and Men Differ in Their Level of Self-Esteem? 131

Social Comparison: How We Evaluate Ourselves 133
Self-Serving Biases 136
BUILDING THE SCIENCE: Classics of Social Psychology Is Being Unrealistic
Good for You? Can That Be Realistic? 137

The Self as Target of Prejudice 138
Emotional Consequences: How Well-Being Can Suffer 138
Cognitive Consequences: Performance Deficits 139
Behavioral Consequences: Stereotype Threat 140
Summary and Review 143
Key Terms 145
Connections: Integrating Social Psychology 145

5 Attitudes
EVALUATING AND RESPONDING TO THE SOCIAL WORLD   146

Attitude Formation: How Attitudes Develop   150
   Classical Conditioning: Learning Based on Association   150
   Instrumental Conditioning: Rewards for the "Right" Views   153
   Observational Learning: Learning by Exposure to Others   154

When and Why Do Attitudes Influence Behavior?   156
   Role of the Social Context in the Link between Attitudes and Behavior   156
   MAKING SENSE OF COMMON SENSE: A Social Psychological Perspective
      Are Attitudes Consistently Related to Behavior?   157
   Situational Constraints That Affect Attitude Expression   158
   Strength of Attitudes   158
   Attitude Extremity: Role of Vested Interests   159
   Attitude Certainty: Importance of Clarity and Correctness   160
   Role of Personal Experience   161

How Do Attitudes Guide Behavior?   162
   Attitudes Arrived at through Reasoned Thought   162
   Attitudes and Spontaneous Behavioral Reactions   164

The Fine Art of Persuasion: How Attitudes Are Changed   165
   Persuasion: Communicators, Messages, and Audiences   165
   The Cognitive Processes Underlying Persuasion   168

Resisting Persuasion Attempts   170
   Reactance: Protecting Our Personal Freedom   170
   SOCIAL PSYCHOLOGY: What It Tells Us About . . . The Effects of Caffeine on
      Persuasion   171
   Forewarning: Prior Knowledge of Persuasive Intent   172
   Selective Avoidance of Persuasion Attempts   173
   Actively Defending Our Attitudes: Counterarguing Against the Competition   173
   Individual Differences in Resistance to Persuasion   174
   Ego Depletion Can Undermine Resistance   175

Cognitive Dissonance: What It Is and How Do We Manage It?   176
   Dissonance and Attitude Change: The Effects of Induced Compliance   177
   BUILDING THE SCIENCE: Classics of Social Psychology   Famous Cognitive
      Dissonance Studies: When Less Leads to More Self-Persuasion   178
   When Dissonance Is a Tool for Beneficial Changes in Behavior   179
Summary and Review   181
Key Terms   183
Connections: Integrating Social Psychology   183

6 Stereotyping, Prejudice, and Discrimination
THE CAUSES, EFFECTS, AND CURES 184

How Members of Different Groups Perceive Inequality 188

The Nature and Origins of Stereotyping 190

    Stereotyping: Beliefs about Social Groups 191

    MAKING SENSE OF COMMON SENSE: A Social Psychological Perspective
The Gender or Race Card: Too Easy to Play, or Harder Than You Think? 195

    Can We Conclude that Stereotyping Is Absent When Members of Different Groups
Are Rated the Same? 196

    Can We Be Victims of Stereotyping and Not Even Recognize It?: The Case of Single
People 198

    Why Do People Form and Use Stereotypes? 200

Prejudice and Discrimination: Feelings and Actions toward Social Groups 202

    The Origins of Prejudice: Contrasting Perspectives 204

    BUILDING THE SCIENCE: Classics of Social Psychology What Causes
Groups to Be Prejudiced toward Other Groups and Is Prejudice Inevitable? 207

    Discrimination: Prejudice in Action 211

    SOCIAL PSYCHOLOGY: What It Tells Us About . . . When Our Group Has
Done Harm to Others 212

Why Prejudice Is Not Inevitable: Techniques for Countering Its Effects 214

    On Learning Not to Hate 215

    The Potential Benefits of Contact 215

    Recategorization: Changing the Boundaries 216

    The Benefits of Guilt for Prejudice Reduction 217

    Can We Learn to "Just Say No" to Stereotypes? 218

    Social Influence as a Means of Reducing Prejudice 219

Summary and Review 221

Key Terms 222

Connections: Integrating Social Psychology 223

7 Interpersonal Attraction and Close Relationships 224

Internal Determinants of Attraction: The Need to Affiliate and the Basic Role of Affect 226
The Importance of Affiliation for Human Existence 226
Affect and Attraction: Feelings as a Basis for Liking 228
The Affect-Attraction Relationship and Social Influence 229

External Determinants of Attraction: Proximity and Others' Observable Characteristics 230
The Power of Proximity: Unplanned Contacts 231
Observable Characteristic of Others: Liking—or Disliking—What We See 233

Factors Based on Interacting with Others: Similarity and Mutual Liking 238
Similarity: Birds of a Feather Actually Do Flock Together 238
MAKING SENSE OF COMMON SENSE: A Social Psychological Perspective Complementarity or Similarity: Which Is the Basis for Attraction? 239
Reciprocal Liking or Disliking: Liking Those Who Like Us 242
What Do We Desire in Others? Designing Ideal Interaction Partners 242

Close Relationships: Family, Friends, Lovers, and Spouses 244
The Cultural Foundations of Relationships: Seeing the Social World through the Lens of Our Culture 245

Interdependent Relationships: Family and Friends 245
Family: Where Relationships and Attachment Styles Begin 246
Friendships: Relationships beyond the Family 248
Loneliness: Life without Close Relationships 249

Romantic Relationships and Falling in Love 252
Romance: Beyond Friendship—Far beyond! 252
Selecting a Potential Mate: Different Criteria for Women and Men 253
Love: Who Can Explain It? Who Can Tell You Why? Just Maybe, Social Psychologists! 254
Jealousy: An Internal Threat to Relationships—Romantic and Otherwise 258

Marriage: Happily Ever After—or Not? 260
BUILDING THE SCIENCE: Classics of Social Psychology Terman's Early Research on Similarity and Marital Happiness 261
Marital Happiness: What Factors Affect It? 261
SOCIAL PSYCHOLOGY: What It Tells Us About . . . The Role of Positive Illusions in Marital Happiness 263
Why Relationships Fail—and Why, Sometimes, They Succeed 264
Summary and Review 267
Key Terms 268
Connections: Integrating Social Psychology 269

8 Social Influence
CHANGING OTHERS' BEHAVIOR 270

Conformity: Group Influence in Action   274

Asch's Research on Conformity: Social Pressure—The Irresistible Force?   275

Sherif's Research on the Autokinetic Phenomenon: How Norms Emerge   277

Factors Affecting Conformity: Variables that Determine the Extent to which We "Go Along"   277

Situational Norms: Automaticity in Normative Behavior   279

The Social Roots of Conformity: Why We Often Choose to Go Along   280

The Downside of Conformity: When Pressures to Go Along Can Produce Harmful Effects   280

BUILDING THE SCIENCE: Classics of Social Psychology   Why Good People Sometimes Do Evil Things: The Powerful—But Not Invincible—Effects of Norms, Situations, and Conformity Pressure   282

Resisting Pressures to Conform: Why, Sometimes, We Choose Not to Go Along   284

Minority Influence: Does the Majority Always Rule?   286

MAKING SENSE OF COMMON SENSE: A Social Psychological Perspective   Do Women and Men Differ in the Tendency to Conform?   287

Compliance: To Ask—Sometimes—Is to Receive   288

Compliance: The Underlying Principles   288

Tactics Based on Friendship or Liking: Ingratiation   290

Tactics Based on Commitment of Consistency: The Foot-in-the-Door and the Lowball   290

Tactics Based on Reciprocity: The Door-in-the-Face and the "That's-Not-All" Approach   292

Tactics Based on Scarcity: Playing Hard to Get and the Fast-Approaching-Deadline Technique   293

Symbolic Social Influence: How We Are Influenced by Others Even When They Are Not There   294

SOCIAL PSYCHOLOGY: What It Tells Us About . . . The Epidemic of Eating Disorders   296

Obedience to Authority: Would You Harm an Innocent Stranger If Ordered to Do So?   298

Obedience in the Laboratory   298

Destructive Obedience: Why It Occurs   299

Destructive Obedience: Resisting Its Effects   300

Summary and Review   302

Key Terms   303

Connections: Integrating Social Psychology   303

9 Prosocial Behavior
HELPING OTHERS 304

Why People Help: Motives for Prosocial Behavior 306

Empathy-Altruism: It Feels Good to Help Others 306

Negative-State Relief: Sometimes, Helping Reduces Unpleasant Feelings 308

Empathic Joy: Helping as an Accomplishment 308

Why Nice People Sometimes Finish First: Competitive Altruism 308

Kinship Selection Theory: Helping Ourselves by Helping People Who Share
Our Genes 310

Responding to an Emergency: Will Bystanders Help? 312

Helping in Emergencies: Apathy—or Action? 312

Five Crucial Steps Determine Helping versus Not Helping 312

BUILDING THE SCIENCE: Classics of Social Psychology Is There Safety in
Numbers? Not Always! 313

External and Internal Influences on Helping Behavior 318

Situational (External) Factors That Enhance or Inhibit Helping Behavior 318

Emotions and Prosocial Behavior 320

Empathy: An Important Foundation for Helping 321

Social Exclusion: When Being Left out Reduces Helping 323

Personality and Helping 325

SOCIAL PSYCHOLOGY: What It Tells Us About . . . The Downside of Being
Helped: Why, Often, It May Actually Be Better to Give than to Receive 326

Long-Term Commitment to Prosocial Acts 328

Volunteering: Helping as an Ongoing Commitment 328

Self-Interest, Moral Integrity, and Moral Hypocrisy 331

MAKING SENSE OF COMMON SENSE: A Social Psychological Perspective
Are Helping (Prosocial Behavior) and Hurting (Aggression) Really Opposites? 333

Summary and Review 334

Key Terms 335

Connections: Integrating Social Psychology 335

10 Aggression
ITS NATURE, CAUSES, AND CONTROL 336

Perspectives on Aggression: In Search of the Roots of Violence 338

The Role of Biological Factors: From Instincts to the Evolutionary Perspective 338

Drive Theories: The Motive to Harm Others 339

Modern Theories of Aggression: The Social Learning Perspective and the General Aggression Model 340

Causes of Human Aggression: Social, Cultural, Personal, and Situational 342

Social Determinants of Aggression: Frustration, Provocation, and Heightened Arousal 343

Exposure to Media Violence: The Effects of Violence in Films, on Television, and in Video Games 347

BUILDING THE SCIENCE: Classics of Social Psychology Bandura's Famous "Bobo Doll" Studies: Televised Violence Visits the Laboratory 348

Violent Pornography: When Sex and Aggression Mix—and Perhaps Explode! 351

SOCIAL PSYCHOLOGY: What It Tells Us About . . . The Effects of Sexually Aggressive Song Lyrics 352

Cultural Factors in Aggression: "Cultures of Honor" and Sexual Jealousy 352

Personality and Aggression: Why Some People Are More Aggressive than Others 355

Situational Determinants of Aggression: The Effects of Heat and Alcohol 360

Aggression in Ongoing Relationships: Bullying and Aggression at Work 364

Bullying: Singling Out Others for Repeated Abuse 364

Workplace Aggression: Harming Others at Work 365

Abusive Supervision: Bosses Who Make Workplaces Unbearable 367

The Prevention and Control of Aggression: Some Useful Techniques 368

Punishment: Just Desserts or Deterrence? 368

Self-Regulation: Internal Mechanisms for Controlling Aggression 370

Forgiveness: Compassion Instead of Revenge 371

MAKING SENSE OF COMMON SENSE: A Social Psychological Perspective Catharsis: Does "Blowing Off Steam" Really Help? 372

Summary and Review 374

Key Terms 375

Connections: Integrating Social Psychology 375

11 Groups and Individuals
THE CONSEQUENCES OF BELONGING   376

Groups: When We Join . . . And When We Leave   380
Groups: Key Components   382
SOCIAL PSYCHOLOGY: What It Tells Us About . . . Is YouTube Just a Website, or Is It a Real Group?   382
The Benefits—and Costs—of Joining   388

The Benefits of Joining: What Groups Do for Us   389

Effects of the Presence of Others: From Task Performance to Behavior in Crowds   394
Social Facilitation: Performing in the Presence of Others   394
BUILDING THE SCIENCE: Classics of Social Psychology   Does the Presence of Others Have an Effect on Performance? Ask Any Cockroach!   396

Social Loafing: Letting Others Do the Work   396
Effects of Being in a Crowd   399

Coordination in Groups: Cooperation or Conflict?   401
Cooperation: Working with Others to Achieve Shared Goals   401
Conflict: Its Nature, Causes, and Effects   402
Resolving Conflicts: Some Useful Techniques   403

Perceived Fairness in Groups: Its Nature and Effects   405
Basic Rules for Judging Fairness: Distributive, Procedural, and Transactional Justice   406
Reactions to Perceived Unfairness: Tactics for Dealing with Injustice   407

Decision Making by Groups: How It Occurs and the Pitfalls It Faces   408
The Decision-Making Process: How Groups Attain Consensus   408
The Downside of Group Decision Making   409
MAKING SENSE OF COMMON SENSE: A Social Psychological Perspective   Does Brainstorming in a Group Result in More and Higher Quality Inventive Ideas?   412
Summary and Review   414
Key Terms   415
Connections: Integrating Social Psychology   415

12 Social Psychology
APPLYING ITS PRINCIPLES TO LAW, HEALTH, AND BUSINESS 416

Social Psychology and the Legal System 420

Social Influence and the Legal System 420

Social Cognition and the Legal System: Why Eyewitness Testimony Is Often Inaccurate 425

BUILDING THE SCIENCE: Classics of Social Psychology Early Evidence that Even "Expert" Eyewitnesses Are Inaccurate: Munsterberg's Ingenious Research 426

The Influence of Prejudice and Stereotypes on the Legal System 429

Social Psychology and Health 432

The Role of Attitudes in Personal Health: Promoting a Healthy Lifestyle 433

Obesity: A Social Psychological Perspective on a Major Threat to Health 435

Stress: Its Causes, Effects, and Control 436

Social Psychology and the World of Work 442

Work-Related Attitudes: The Nature and Effects of Job Satisfaction 442

MAKING SENSE OF COMMON SENSE: A Social Psychological Perspective Are Happy Employees Productive Employees? The Attitude-Behavior Link Revisited 445

Organizational Citizenship Behavior: Prosocial Behavior at Work 446

Leadership: Influence in Group Settings 449

SOCIAL PSYCHOLOGY: What It Tells Us About . . . How to Make a Good First Impression in Job Interviews 454

Summary and Review 456

Key Terms 457

Connections: Integrating Social Psychology 457

Glossary 459

References 469

Name Index 519

Subject Index 528

Photo Credits 539

Special Features

BUILDING THE SCIENCE: Classics of Social Psychology

The Self-Confirming Nature of Schemas: When—and Why—Beliefs Shape Reality   44

The Fundamental Attribution Error: Stronger Than You Might Guess   91

Is Being Unrealistic Good for You? Can That Be Realistic?   137

Famous Cognitive Dissonance Studies: When Less Leads to More Self-Persuasion   178

What Causes Groups to Be Prejudiced toward Other Groups and Is Prejudice Inevitable?   207

Terman's Early Research on Similarity and Marital Happiness   261

Why Good People Sometimes Do Evil Things: The Powerful—But Not Invincible—Effects of Norms, Situations, and Conformity Pressure   282

Is There Safety in Numbers? Not Always!   313

Bandura's Famous "Bobo Doll" Studies: Televised Violence Visits the Laboratory   348

Does the Presence of Others Have an Effect on Performance? Ask Any Cockroach!   396

Early Evidence that Even "Expert" Eyewitnesses Are Inaccurate: Munsterberg's Ingenious Research   426

SOCIAL PSYCHOLOGY: What it Tells Us About . . .

The War in Iraq: Did the Optimistic Bias Play a Role?   58

Speed Dating—Can We Really Choose the One We Might Love in a Few Minutes?   107

How We Manage When There Is Conflict Among Our Identities   124

The Effects of Caffeine on Persuasion   171

When Our Group Has Done Harm to Others   212

The Role of Positive Illusions in Marital Happiness   263

The Epidemic of Eating Disorders   296

The Downside of Being Helped: Why, Often, It May Actually Be Better to Give Than to Receive   326

The Effects of Sexually Aggressive Song Lyrics   352

Is YouTube Just a Website, or Is It a Real Group?   382

How to Make a Good First Impression in Job Interviews   454

MAKING SENSE OF COMMON SENSE: A Social Psychological Perspective

Is Being in a Good Mood Always Beneficial? The Potential Downside of Being Up   68

Are Men Really "Clueless" When It Comes to Nonverbal Cues? Fiction—and Fact—about Gender Differences in Nonverbal Communication   83

The Internet: Presenting Your Online Identity   115

Are Attitudes Consistently Related to Behavior?   157

The Gender or Race Card: Too Easy to Play, or Harder Than You Think?   195

Complementarity or Similarity: Which Is the Basis for Attraction?   239

Do Women and Men Differ in the Tendency to Conform?   287

Are Helping (Prosocial Behavior) and Hurting (Aggression) Really Opposites?   333

Catharsis: Does "Blowing Off Steam" Really Help?   372

Does Brainstorming in a Group Result in More and Higher Quality Inventive Ideas?   412

Are Happy Employees Productive Employees? The Attitude-Behavior Link Revisited   445

Preface

Social Psychology As . . . The Fountain of Youth!

O f all the dreams that human beings have pursued over the centuries, one of the most enticing—and persistent—has been that of finding the fabled Fountain of Youth. According to legend, this magical spring restores the youth and vigor of anyone lucky enough to drink from its waters. This alluring dream has launched many voyages of exploration.

Sadly, the fountain—in a literal sense—has remained only a dream. Despite amazing advances in medicine and other health sciences, we remain destined to grow older. Yet, as you'll find in the pages of this book, *you* already have access to one remarkable source of renewal and restoration, if not an actual fountain of youth: **the field of social psychology**.

These words may sound like exaggeration or excessive enthusiasm on the part of "true believers" (which we are!), but in an important sense, they are accurate. We have been participating in social psychology for several decades and if there's one thing we have learned, it is this: Our field is, in fact, *forever new*. It perpetually reinvents itself; the field offers new ideas and insights concerning the social side of life. **Social psychology**—the focus of this book—never grows old, because there are always new and exciting findings to report. In each decade, social psychologists have grappled with the issues of the day, researching the psychological processes underlying our responses to events, and in this way have kept their field fresh, vigorous, and challenging.

One of the key goals we set for ourselves in writing this new twelfth edition was representing this basic fact—presenting social psychology as the ever-changing field it is. Another was illustrating, as clearly and accurately as possible, how *useful* social psychology continues to be: The insights it provides on current social issues and trends can help us adapt to a rapidly changing social world. To achieve these objectives, we took many concrete steps to assure that this new edition truly represents what's *newest*, most *current*, and most *exciting* in our field—its authentic "cutting edge." We've gone out of our way to ensure treatment of new technologies that deliver the results of the social psychological research. We cover the cutting-edge changes in information that we as faculty adapt to, and our students take for granted and embrace. At the same time, though, we have also taken vigorous steps to assure that that the *foundations* of all the new work we cover are also clearly represented. In science, nothing new appears suddenly and without a foundation in earlier theorizing, so we've made certain to address the classics along with the fresh and new.

But enough generalities. Here we describe the specific steps that we took to reach our two goals of presenting what's new and current, *and*, at the same time, representing the strong and lasting foundations of our field.

Changes in the Structure of the Book: Presenting the Cutting Edge

New patterns of research in social psychology have shaped the following major changes in the structure of the book.

- Paralleling increased interest in the *self*, we have moved this chapter earlier in the book, so it is now Chapter 4 (instead of Chapter 5).
- Representing increasing integration of research on attraction and interpersonal relationships, we have combined these topics in a single, integrated chapter (Chapter 7).
- Responding to the growing interest in applying the basic principles of social psychology to practical issues in fields such as law, medicine, and business, we now treat all these topics in a single integrated chapter (Chapter 12). This chapter emphasizes the ways in which social psychology's knowledge of basic processes (e.g., social cognition, social influence, attitudes) provide invaluable insights into a wide range of practical questions and issues.

Changes in Content Within Chapters: New Topics and Lines of Research

Continuing a long tradition for this book, we have included literally dozens of new topics. In fact, every chapter presents new lines of research, new findings, and new theoretical perspectives. Here is a partial list of the new topics included:

- Recent research on social neuroscience and on the role of implicit (nonconscious) processes as examples of "cutting edge" work in the field (Chapter 1)
- The effects of automatic processing on social behavior (Chapter 2)
- The benefits of automatic thought (Chapter 2)
- Social neuroscience research on the interplay between affect and cognition (Chapter 2)
- The role of level of construals in attributing events to fate or our own actions (Chapter 3)
- The role of action identification in attributions concerning other's intentions, cognition, and motives (Chapter 3)
- The role of magical thought in attribution (Chapter 3)
- Self-presentation on the internet (Chapter 4)
- How conflicts among multiple identities are managed (Chapter 4)
- The role of attitude certainty in the attitude-behavior relationship (Chapter 5)
- The effects of caffeine on persuasion (Chapter 5)
- Consequences of ego-depletion for our ability to resist persuasion (Chapter 5)
- How members of different racial groups perceive inequality (Chapter 6)
- Is playing the race- or gender-card as easy as you think? (Chapter 6)
- A new form of stereotyping—singlism—and why singles don't even realize they are victims (Chapter 6)

- Appearance rejection-sensitivity (Chapter 7)
- The effects of culture on relationships (Chapter 7)
- What we desire in others—the traits of "ideal" partners (Chapter 7)
- The role of positive illusions in marital happiness (Chapter 7)
- The "downside" of conformity, including the effects of conformity to gender roles on sexual enjoyment and the acceptance of rape myths (Chapter 8)
- Norms that encourage individuality instead of conformity (Chapter 8)
- Empathy and helping across different social groups (Chapter 9)
- Effects of social exclusion (Chapter 9)
- Reactions to being helped by others (Chapter 9)
- Effects of *teasing* as a potential cause of aggression (Chapter 10)
- The effects of playing violent video games on aggression (Chapter 10)
- Neuroscience evidence for desensitization stemming from exposure to media violence (Chapter 10)
- How alcohol can increase aggression even when it is not actually consumed (Chapter 10)
- Self-regulatory mechanisms helpful in reducing aggression. (Chapter 10)
- How YouTube activity reflects group processes (Chapter 11)
- New findings concerning maintaining our individuality in groups (Chapter 11)
- The role of "fuzzy trace theory" in memory distortion among eyewitnesses to a crime (Chapter 12)
- New findings concerning "anti-fat" prejudice (Chapter 12)
- New models and theories of leadership (Chapter 12)

New Themes: Emotion, Culture, Gender, Social Neuroscience, Evolutionary Perspective

In every chapter, research and findings relating to several basic themes are presented. These themes relate to *emotion*, the effects of *culture*, *social neuroscience*, the pervasive influence of *gender*, the role of the internet and other technologies on social interaction, and the *evolutionary perspective*. These themes are presented where appropriate; they are in no way forced or introduced artificially; rather they are presented when they reflect current work in the field.

New Special Features

To clearly illustrate the foundations of modern research, we have added a new type of special feature titled **Building the Science: Classics of Social Psychology**. These sections cover truly classic work in the field—research and theory that exerted a powerful effect on work that followed. A few examples:

- The Self-Confirming Nature of Schemas: When—and Why—Beliefs Shape Reality (Chapter 2)
- The Fundamental Attribution Error: Stronger Than You Might Guess (Chapter 3)
- Is Being Unrealistic Good for You? Can That Be Realistic? (Chapter 4)
- Famous Cognitive Dissonance Studies: When Less Leads to More Self-Persuasion (Chapter 5)

BUILDING THE SCIENCE
CLASSICS OF SOCIAL PSYCHOLOGY

What Causes Groups to Be Prejudiced toward Other Groups and Is Prejudice Inevitable?

- What Causes Groups to Be Prejudiced toward Other Groups, and Is Prejudice Inevitable? (Chapter 6)
- Terman's Early Research on Similarity and Marital Happiness (Chapter 7)
- Why Good People Sometimes Do Evil Things: The Powerful—But Not Invincible—Effects of Norms, Situations, and Conformity Pressure (Chapter 8)
- Is There Safety in Numbers? Not Always! (Chapter 9)
- Bandura's Famous "Bobo Doll" Studies: Televised Violence Visits the Laboratory (Chapter 10)
- Does the Presence of Others Have an Effect on Performance? Ask any Cockroach! (Chapter 11)

To illustrate the tremendous relevance of social psychology—the important ways in which it helps us understand events and trends occurring in the world around us—we have added another type of special section entitled **Social Psychology: What It Tells Us About . . .** Here are a few examples:

- The War in Iraq: Did the Optimistic Bias Play a Role? (Chapter 2)
- Speed Dating—Can We Really Choose the One We Might Love in a Few Minutes? (Chapter 3)
- How We Manage When There Is Conflict Among Our Identities (Chapter 4)
- The Effects of Caffeine on Persuasion (Chapter 5)
- When Our Group Has Done Harm to Others (Chapter 6)
- The Role of Positive Illusions in Marital Happiness (Chapter 7)
- The Epidemic of Eating Disorders (Chapter 8)
- The Downside of Being Helped: Why, Often, It May Actually Be Better to Give Than to Receive (Chapter 9)
- The Effects of Sexually Aggressive Song Lyrics (Chapter 10)
- Is YouTube Just a Website, or Is It a Real Group? (Chapter 11)
- How to Make a Good First Impression in Job Interviews (Chapter 12)

Finally, to illustrate how social psychology helps refine and correct "common sense" ideas about the social side of life, we have retained a feature included in the previous edition, **Making Sense of Common Sense: A Social Psychological Perspective.** However, virtually all of these sections are new to this edition. A few examples:

- The Internet: Presenting your Online Identity (Chapter 4)
- Are Attitudes Consistently Related to Behavior? (Chapter 5)
- Complementarity or Similarity: Which Is the Basis for Attraction? (Chapter 7)
- Do Women and Men Differ in the Tendency to Conform? (Chapter 8)
- Are Helping (Prosocial Behavior) and Hurting (Aggression) Really Opposites? (Chapter 9)
- Catharsis: Does "Blowing Off Steam" Really Help? (Chapter 10)

New Student Aids

Any textbook is good only to the extent it is both useful and interesting to students. To make this edition even better on these two dimensions, we have included several new student aids. Included among these features are the following:

Chapter openings linked to important trends and events in society: Most chapters begin with examples or anecdotes closely linked to current trends and events in society—for instance, popular films, television shows, events in the news. This helps relate the topics covered to events with which readers are already very familiar.

Key Points: Every major section ends with a brief review of key points covered, and a **critical-thinking question (Think About It)**

Principles to Remember: At the end of each major section, a key principle that students should retain is presented and highlighted.

End-of-Chapter Summaries: Each chapter ends with a summary, which recaps the key points covered.

Special labels on all graphs and charts: To make these easy to understand, we have continued to use the "special labels" that are a unique feature of this book.

Connections: Finally, to help students recognize links between the various chapters and lines of research in social psychology, we include, once more, **Connections** tables that call attention to such links.

Supplementary Materials

Excellent texts are supported by a complete package of supplementary material, both for the students and the instructor. This text offers a full array of such aids including *PowerPoint®* lectures, a fully revised *Test Bank,* and an *Instructor's Manual* with great lecture and discussion ideas. The major components of this teaching-learning package are:

For Instructors:

The following are available for qualified instructors only. Please contact your Pearson representative.

- **Instructor's Manual** (ISBN:0-205-58186-2)
  Daniel A Miller, Indiana University—Purdue University, Fort Wayne
  Prepared by Daniel A. Miller of Indiana University—Purdue University, Fort Wayne, the *Instructor's Manual* has been reorganized and updated to be even easier to use, with Chapter Learning Objectives, key terms, a detailed chapter outline, both classic and innovative lecture launchers, and out-of-class assignments with appropriate handouts. Each lecture and activity idea is linked to a specific learning objective.

- **Test Bank and Computerized Test Bank**
  (Test Bank ISBN: 0-205-58178-1; Computerized Test Bank ISBN: 0-205-58187-0)
  Greg Nichols, University of Kansas
  Fully updated by Greg Nichols of the University of Kansas, the *Test Bank* is composed of approximately 2,000 fully referenced multiple-choice, completion (fill-in-the-blank), short-answer, and essay questions. Each question may be viewed by level of difficulty and skill types. To help instructors follow through with the dynamic resources offered in *MyPsychLab* in assessments, this edition of the *Test Bank* offers one essay question per chapter that tests a relevant *MyPsychLab* asset! This supplement is also available in the *TestGen Computerized Test Bank* version, an easy way to create polished, hard-copy tests.

- **PowerPoint® Presentation** (ISBN: 0-205-58179-X)
  Amy Schaffer, University of Miami
  New to this Edition! Amy Schaffer of the University of Miami has prepared two versions of the *PowerPoint® Presentation*: a *Lecture* version with text and select art, and an *Art-Only* version, which includes all of the figures from the book, so professors can easily customize their lecture presentations.

- **Allyn & Bacon Transparencies for Social Psychology, ©2005** (ISBN: 0-205-43958-6)
  Contains approximately 100 revised, full-color acetates to enhance classroom lectures and discussions. Includes images from Allyn & Bacon's major Social Psychology texts.

- **MyPsychLab for Social Psychology**
  MyPsychLab is a state-of-the-art interactive and instructive solution for Social Psychology, designed to be used as a supplement to a traditional lecture course, or to completely administer an online course. *MyPsychLab* includes over 200 embedded video clips (2 to 4 minutes in length, close-captioned and with post-viewing activities) and over 100 embedded animations and simulations that dynamically illustrate chapter concepts. With over 100 text-specific practice test questions per chapter, *MyPsychLab* also helps students master the concepts from the text and prepare for exams. *MyPsychLab* gives instructors and students access to a wealth of resources all geared to meet the individual teaching and learning needs of every instructor and every student. Combining an E-book, video, audio, multimedia simulations, research support, practice tests, exams, and more, *MyPsychLab* engages students and gives them the tools they need to enhance their performance in the course.

- **ABC Video for Social Psychology © 2005** (ISBN: 0-205-44199-8)
  A wonderful tool, including 7 video clips. Clips cover topics such as self-esteem, plastic surgery, philanthropy, bullying, sororities, age discrimination, and more.

  1. Becoming Barbie
  2. The Hope Scale: How to Tell if You're Negative or Positive
  3. For Better or For Worse
  4. The Philanthropists
  5. Soothing the Savage Beast
  6. America in Black and White on Prom Night
  7. Sorority Hazing: Tales of Abusive Initiation Rituals

- **Contemporary Videos in Social Psychology DVD © 2007**
  Adopters can receive this new video that includes short clips covering all major topics in Social Psychology. Please contact your Pearson representative to obtain a copy.

For Students:

- **GradeAid Student Workbook with Practice Tests** (ISBN: 0-205-58180-3)
  Virginia Gills Centanni, Oakwood College and Virginia College
  Prepared by Virginia Centanni of Oakwood College and Virginia College, the *GradeAid Student Workbook with Practice Tests* has been designed as the go-to resource for preparing students for the material in the chapter (Before You Read . . .), helping them retain the information they are gathering (As You Read . . .), testing what they remember (After You Read . . .), and finally, taking them deeper into the material (When You Have Finished . . .). **New to this Edition,** the *GradeAid* has a section titled "When You Have Finished . . . You be the Researcher" a feature that encourages students to apply and expand their knowledge with a dynamic activity.

- **MyPsychLab for Social Psychology**
  MyPsychLab is the online all-in-one study resource that offers a dynamic, electronic version of *Social Psychology, 12th Edition,* with over 200 embedded video clips (2 to 4 minutes in length, closed-captioned and with post-viewing activities) and over 100 embedded animations and simulations that dynamically illustrate chapter concepts. With over 100 text-specific practice test questions per chapter, *MyPsychLab* helps students master the concepts from the text and prepare for exams. To access *MyPsychLab* or to take a tour of its features, visit *www.MyPsychLab.com.*
- **Social Psychology Study Site (Open Access)**
  This open access website offers *Learning Objectives, Flashcards, Weblinks,* and *Practice Tests* for a comprehensive list of topics covering Social Psychology to assess knowledge and comprehension in the coursework. To access this site go to: *www.absocialpsychology.com.*

Some Concluding Words

Looking back over the book's changes and its enhanced supplement package, we truly believe that we have done everything we could to make this new edition the best one yet! But, as we have said many times in the past, only you—our colleagues and the students who use this text—can tell us whether, and to what extent, we have succeeded. So please do send us your comments, reactions, and suggestions. As in the past, we will listen to them very carefully, and do our best to use them constructively in planning the next edition.

Our warm regards and thanks!

Nyla R. Branscombe   Robert A. Baron   Donn Byrne
nyla@ku.edu   baronr@rpi.edu   vyaduckdb@aol.com

Acknowledgments

WORDS OF THANKS

Now that the hard work of preparing a new edition is over, we want to take this opportunity to thank the many talented and dedicated people whose help throughout the process has been truly invaluable.

First, our sincere thanks to the following colleagues, who responded to our survey regarding how the Twelfth Edition could be improved. Their input was invaluable to us in planning this new edition: Michele Breault, Truman State University; Tina M. Burns, Florida International University; Gail Ditkoff, California University of Pennsylvania; Susan E. O. Field, Georgian Court University; Marcia A. Finkelstein, University of South Florida; Brian Johnson, University of Tennessee, Martin; James Johnson, University of North Carolina, Wilmington; Greg Nichols, University of Kansas; Paul Rose, Southern Illinois University, Edwardsville; Samuel R. Sommers, Tufts University; Rowena Tan, University of Northern Iowa.

Second, we wish to offer our personal thanks to Michelle Limoges, our editor at Allyn & Bacon. It is a true pleasure to work with her, and her intelligence and good judgment are matched only by her friendliness and enthusiasm. We look forward to working with her for many years (and editions!) to come.

Third, our thanks to Claudia Frigo for very careful and constructive copyediting. Her comments were insightful and thought-provoking, thus providing valuable help in improving and clarifying our words.

Fourth, our thanks to all of those others who contributed to various aspects of the production process: to Annie Pickert for photo research, to Gina Hagen for interior design work, and to Linda Knowles for the cover design. Thanks, too, to Diana Chamberlain and Stephen Reysen for the photos they provided. We also want to thank Liz Napolitano who oversaw the entire production process and kept her expert and firm hand on the tiller, and Katie Ostler, for an excellent job in handling all aspects of the proof and correcting errors she or we noticed.

We also wish to offer our thanks to the many colleagues who provided reprints and preprints of their work, and to the many students who kindly shared their thoughts about the book with us. These individuals are too numerous to list here, but their input is gratefully acknowledged.

Finally, our sincere thanks to Daniel Miller of Indiana University-Purdue University, Fort Wayne, for outstanding work on the *Instructor's Manual;* to Virginia Centanni of Virginia College for the help in preparing the *GradeAid* workbook; to Greg Nichols of the University of Kansas for preparing the *Test Bank;* and to Amy Schaffer of the University of Miami for her work on the *PowerPoint®* presentation. To all of these truly outstanding people, and to many others, too, our warmest personal regards and thanks.

RAB, NRB, & DB
August, 2007

About the Authors

Robert A. Baron is Wellington Professor of Management and Psychology at Rensselaer RPI. He received his PhD in Social Psychology from the University of Iowa (1968). Prof. Baron has held faculty appointments at Purdue, the Universities of Minnesota, Texas, South Carolina, Washington, Princeton University, and Oxford University. From 1979–1981 he served as Program Director for Social and Developmental Psychology at NSF. In 2001 he was appointed as a Visiting Senior Research Fellow by the French Ministry of Research (Universite de Toulouse). Baron is a Fellow of APA and a Charter Fellow of APS. He has published more than one hundred articles and forty chapters, and is the author of 48 books in management and psychology. He holds three U.S. patents and was founder and CEO of IEP, Inc. (1993–2000). His current research interests focus on social and cognitive factors in entrepreneurship.

Nyla R. Branscombe is Professor of Psychology at University of Kansas. She received her B.A. from York University in Toronto in 1980, an M.A. from the University of Western Ontario in 1982, and her Ph.D. from Purdue University in 1986. Professor Branscombe has held visiting appointments at the University of Illinois at Urbana-Champaign, Free University of Amsterdam, and Australian National Univeristy. She has served as Associate Editor for *Personality and Social Psychology Bulletin,* as well as *Group Processes and Intergroup Relations.*

Professor Branscombe has published more than one hundred articles and chapters in professional journals and edited books. In 1999, she was a co-recipient of the Otto Klienberg prize for research on Intercultural and International Relations from the Society for the Psychological Study of Social Issues, and the 1996 and 2001 *Society of Personality and Social Psychology Publication Award.* She coedited the 2004 volume *Collective Guilt: International Perspectives,* published by Cambridge University Press, and the 2007 volume *Commemorating Brown: The Social Psychology of Racism and Discrimination,* published by the American Psychological Association.

Professor Branscombe's current research focuses primarily on two main issues: the psychology of historically privileged groups, in particular when and why they may feel collective guilt for their advantages and harmful actions toward other social groups, and the psychology of disadvantaged groups, especially how they cope with prejudice and discrimination.

Donn Byrne holds the rank of Distinguished Professor Emeritus at the University at Albany, State University of New York. He received his Ph.D. degree in 1958 from Stanford University and has held academic positions at the San Francisco State University, the University of Texas, and Purdue University as well as visiting professorships at the University of Hawaii and Stanford University. He was elected president of the Midwestern Psychological Association and of the Society for the Scientific Study of Sexuality. He headed the personality program at Texas, the social-personality programs at Purdue and Albany, and was chair of the psychology department at Albany. Professor Byrne is a fellow of the American Psychological Association and a Charter Fellow of the American Psychological Society.

During his career, Professor Byrne has published over 150 articles in psychological journals, and twenty-nine of them have been republished in books of readings. He has authored or co-authored thirty-seven chapters in edited volumes, and fourteen books, including *Psychology: An Introduction to a Behavioral Science, An Introduction to Personality, The Attraction Paradigm,* and *Exploring Human Sexuality.*

He has served on the editorial boards of fourteen professional journals and has directed the doctoral work of fifty-two Ph.D. students. He was invited to deliver a G. Stanley Hall lecture at the 1981 meeting of the American Psychological Association in Los Angeles and a state of the science address at the 1981 meeting of the Society for the Scientific Study of Sexuality in New York City. He was invited to testify at Attorney General Meese's Commission on Obscenity and Pornography in Houston in 1986 and to participate in Surgeon General Koop's Workshop on Pornography and Health in 1986 in Arlington, Virginia. He received an Excellence in Research Award from the University at Albany in 1987 and the Distinguished Scientific Achievement Award from the Society for the Scientific Study of Sexuality in 1989. In 2002, he attended a Festschrift at the University of Connecticut honoring his scientific contributions organized by his graduate students (past and present) from Texas, Purdue, and Albany. He delivered the William Griffitt Memorial Lecture at Kansas State University in 2004. Professor Byrne's current research interests focus on the determination of interpersonal attraction, adult attraction styles, and sexually coercive behavior.

Foreword

Personal Brushes with History: Reflections on Getting to Know Ned Jones, Solomon Asch, Stanley Milgram, Leon Festinger, and Stan Schachter

Every career—and every life—has its peaks and valleys. For me, a definite peak occurred during the 1977–78 academic year. After six years at Purdue, I had earned a sabbatical, and—much to my delight—was invited by an outstanding and gracious colleague—John Darley—to spend it at Princeton University. When I arrived late in the summer, John, Joel Cooper, and many other colleagues made me feel welcome. (Nancy Cantor joined the department near the end of my stay, and getting to know her was another great pleasure.) Princeton is a beautiful town, and I was lucky enough to rent a house overlooking scenic Lake Carnegie. The graduate students, too, were outstanding, and many went on to make major contributions to social psychology—people whose names you will see on the pages of this book, among them Roy Baumeister and Russ Fazio to mention just two. Overall, the whole year was virtually perfect. What made it really special, though, was the opportunity to get to know three people who shaped the history of social psychology: Ned Jones, Solomon Asch, and Stanley Milgram.

Ned Jones had just moved to Princeton when I arrived, and was still settling in. We had many personal conversations and I soon realized what a truly brilliant—and nice—person he was. He kindly invited me to meetings, research seminars, and parties, and spent hours talking with me about his new theories and research, especially his research on *self-handicapping* and attribution. I had previously had little experience with the cognitive side of social psychology, but under Ned's instruction, I learned to appreciate it and its implications for the entire field. As a result, by the time the year was over and I returned to Purdue, my understanding of important areas of social psychology had been greatly enhanced. The effects of our conversations are still visible in this book (see Chapters 2 and 3), and in my own research, which often focuses on cognitive factors and processes (e.g., Baron, 2006).

During that same year, I also met Solomon Asch (see photo). He visited Princeton regularly because he was still actively involved in research. (Some

Solomon Asch

of his groundbreaking studies on impression management and conformity are described in Chapters 3 and 6). When I met Solomon, one of the first things I noticed was his great modesty. When I told him how highly I valued his work and how much I loved talking about it in class, he thanked me, but added: "Truly . . . it was nothing. It's young people like you who will carry the field forward . . ." (Remember: This was 1977 and I *was* young!). The second thing I noticed was his amazing intellectual curiosity. He was interested in everything, and asked me all about my research and my textbook (the second edition of this book had just been published). We discussed trends I saw in the field and many other topics (such as food and fine wine—interests we both shared). My understanding of social psychology,was enriched by interacting with this wonderful colleague, whose work has had such a major and lasting impact on social psychology.

After I had been at Princeton for a few months, I received an invitation to visit the Graduate Center of the City of New York—the university where Stanley Milgram then worked (see photo). I had known about Milgram's research for a long time: when I was in high school, his niece was one of my classmates. She would often tell us all about her famous uncle's research experiences. Princeton is only an hour from New York City by train, so I happily accepted. When I arrived, Stanley explained to me that he saw many connections between his research on obedience and my own work on aggression (some of which is discussed in Chapter 10). He took me to his laboratory and demonstrated the famed apparatus he used to show that our tendency to obey authority—sometimes blindly—can have dangerous effects. (This machine is shown on page 299.) When I left the building and headed for the train back to Princeton, I knew that once again, I had learned a lot from someone I admired greatly.

Yes, 1977–78 was an enchanted academic year for me, and provided a series of opportunities and experiences that changed my thinking forever. I had entered graduate school at Stanford in 1954, young, inexperienced, and naïve. At the beginning, I had not really appreciated the fact that I was interacting with an array of illustrious psychologists. At Stanford, small seminars, the department lunch room, and social gatherings were opportunities to meet individuals such as Paul Farnsworth, usually seen only from a distance in a large auditorium where he taught introductory psychology using the text authored by Ernest Hilgard. After I became a graduate student, the department hired a kindly and amusing new Ph.D. from Iowa named Al Bandura, who soon became a superstar. During this same period, they also added an eminent social psychologist to the faculty, Leon Festinger.

Stanley Milgram

Festinger was already well known (see photo), but after his book on cognitive dissonance was published in 1957, his name became a household word (among psychologists, at least), and his work is covered in detail in Chapter 4. He was brilliant but sufficiently caustic that I was literally afraid to take one of his classes. Instead, I only observed him from across the room playing cribbage with various individuals and trading sardonic insults. Some of his humor was directed at himself, as when he estimated that *A Theory of Cognitive Dissonance* earned him about $1.79 an hour for his labor. When I joined the faculty at Texas, I was invited to return to Palo Alto to become a visiting professor at Stanford, and suddenly individuals such as Leon Festinger were my colleagues. I no longer feared him, and I will always remember an evening at a Greek restaurant near the campus: The music played and several of us joined Leon to dance in a circle around the table and then smash wine glasses in the fireplace.

A few years after that, Texas was given funds to hire a number of new faculty, starting with Gardner Lindsay as department chair. Among the many possible candidates was Leon. At this point, he was no longer interested in

Leon Festinger

cognitive dissonance but was involved in work on perception and other new areas of research. I have a lasting memory of one afternoon after he had given a talk and he had a couple of hours before a planned party and dinner. I offered to drive him to his hotel to rest, but, as a steadfast New Yorker, he said that he would just go outside, stand by the fountain, and hail a cab. I politely suggested that taxis were not as likely to be cruising the streets of Austin as would be true in Manhattan, so he traveled instead in my car. Texas did not succeed in recruiting him, and unfortunately, Leon and I did not cross paths again.

When I was a new faculty member at Texas, a group of us were having lunch and somehow the research of Stanley Schachter came up. We were all impressed by his work with Festinger and Back dealing with college dorms and the effect of proximity on social interactions. He also conducted the first experimental work on similar and dissimilar attitudes and how they affected interpersonal rejection and communication. His new (at the time) book dealt with fear and anxiety as motivators of affiliation along with the effect of birth order on this relationship.

Stanley Schachter

In the years to follow, Stan Schachter continued to investigate new areas of human behavior, bringing his unique insight to diverse subjects, as in his study of the way in which we perceive our emotional state as a function of physiological arousal, cognitive interpretation, and the social context in which this takes place (see photo). He was always able to surprise the social psychological world with new and original topics, such as how obesity affects eating peanuts in the shell versus out of the shell.

Though I was aware of and influenced by his work throughout my career, we did not meet until the mid 1980s. At that time, I was department chair at Albany, and the university was surprised when I discovered that there were fewer psychologists in the "psych" department than in other areas of the institution, including education, business, social welfare, criminal justice, gerontology, biology, and several other settings. Given this information, the administrators decided to bring all of us together; to effect this, they made funds available for a series of prominent psychologists to be invited to give lectures of interest to the entire psychological community. Stan Schachter was the first individual to be invited, and I was asked to transport him and his wife from their hotel to lunch before his presentation. I had no idea what to expect, but found both Schachters to be interesting and personable, and I regretted not having met him sooner.

Robert A. Baron
Donn Byrne

Social Psychology

1

Social Psychology
The Science of the Social Side of Life

CHAPTER OUTLINE

- **Social Psychology: What It Is and What It Does**
  Social Psychology Is Scientific in Nature
  Social Psychology Focuses on the Behavior of
    Individuals
  Social Psychology Seeks to Understand the Causes
    of Social Behavior and Social Thought
  Social Psychology: Summing Up

- **Social Psychology: Its Cutting Edge**
  Cognition and Behavior: Two Sides of the Same
    Social Coin
  Social Neuroscience: Where Social Psychology and
    Brain Research Meet
  The Role of Implicit (Nonconscious) Processes
  Taking Full Account of Social Diversity

- **A Brief Look at History: The Origins and Early
  Development of Social Psychology**

- **How Social Psychologists Answer the Fascinating
  Questions They Raise: Research as the Route to
  Increased Knowledge**
  Systematic Observation: Describing the World
    around Us
  Correlation: The Search for Relationships
  The Experimental Method: Knowledge through
    Systematic Intervention
  Further Thoughts on Causality: The Role of
    Mediating Variables

- **The Role of Theory in Social Psychology**

- **The Quest for Knowledge and Rights of Individuals:
  Seeking an Appropriate Balance**

- **Getting the Most Out of this Book: A User's Guide**

The social side of life is perhaps the most central aspect of our daily lives. How many times each day do you interact with other people—family, friends, roommates, romantic partners, neighbors, professors, sales staff in stores, or waitstaff in restaurants? And how many times do you think about other people? The correct answer is, probably, "Who can possibly count that high?" Similarly, it is clear that other people shape our lives in crucial ways. They are the source of our most intense pleasure and, sadly, our deepest pain; they offer vast amounts of useful information; and they are the mirror through which we come to know and understand ourselves. So yes, the social side of life—which is the core of social psychology—is a key aspect of our lives and our existence. This fact could readily be illustrated in many ways, but a description of a recent, popular film highlights many of the topics we'll examine in this book.

The movie is *Legally Blonde,* and when it opens, the heroine, Elle Woods (played by Reese Witherspoon; see Figure 1.1 on page 4), is shopping for a dress with the help of two friends. She is certain that her boyfriend Warner is going to propose to her that night, so she wants to look her best on their date. Much to her surprise, however, he throws her a curve: He has been accepted to Harvard Law School and tells her that he will be too busy to keep their relationship going. She is devastated but decides to win him back by gaining entry to the same prestigious school. Although she seems to be an unlikely candidate for law school (shopping, parties, and the like, not studying, are her specialties), she works hard and does gain admission, partly by acing the entrance test. But when she arrives on campus, she seems totally out of place: Her clothes, her appearance, and her lifestyle all seem totally wrong for this serious academic environment. Even worse, she discovers that Warner is engaged to another woman. However Elle doesn't give up; she decides, instead, to become a brilliant student and win him back with her outstanding achievements.

She gets her opportunity to shine when she is invited by a faculty member (a famous

Figure 1.1
The Social Side of Life as Shown in the Movies
In the recent film, Legally Blonde, *the heroine's, Elle Woods, life is changed in dramatic ways by her relationships with other people and where these relationships lead her. Even though the producers of this movie didn't intend to do so, Elle's actions throughout the film illustrate many of the processes and topics studied by social psychologists (impression management, social cognition, helping, group processes, aggression, and so on).*

attorney) to join his team in defending a rich young woman accused of murdering her husband. Elle quickly assists the team by recognizing that one of the witnesses for the prosecution, who claims that he was having an affair with the young wife, is actually gay. (She bases this on the fact that he recognizes famous brands of women's clothes—something, she suggests, no heterosexual male can do.) Even more importantly, the accused wife happens to belong to the same sorority as Elle, and as a result, she quickly comes to trust Elle totally. Ultimately, she asks Elle to replace the famous attorney in representing her, and Elle miraculously wins the case by asking the murdered husband's daughter where she was when her father was shot. The daughter replies, "In the shower, washing my hair." Elle points out to the jury that the daughter had previously reported that she had a perm that day, and as Elle notes: "No woman would ever wash her hair the same day she had a permanent." When Elle makes this statement, the daughter breaks down and confesses that she shot her father by accident, intending to shoot his young wife instead. Elle becomes the heroine of the day and wins high praise from everyone—the judge, the other attorneys on her team, and even the prosecutor. Along the way to this legal triumph, Elle has used her new knowledge of the law to help her beautician friend by forcing this woman's ex-boyfriend to return their pet dog. At the end of the movie, Warner tries to win her back, but he is too late: She has changed and no longer wants him; in fact, she has her eye on a much better man.

ertainly, this is not one of the greatest films of all time (even though it led to a sequel). But in many ways, it clearly illustrates the central importance of the social side of life. The heroine's experiences are powerfully shaped by the people around her—her boyfriend, the people she meets in law school, her clients, and many others. In fact, she is changed in fundamental and important ways by her relationships with these people and by her new life as a law school student. Her self-image changes, and she is, in many ways, a truly different person than when she began law school. As she experiences these shifts, Elle not only engages in acts of kindness toward others, but also shows strong verbal aggression toward Warner's new fiancée and others who treat her rudely, which is something that she would not have done at the beginning of the story

All of these events and processes illustrate major topics we will discuss in future chapters. In trying to understand her boyfriend and win back his love, Elle engages in complex social thought (see Chapter 2). The first impression she makes on other law school students is very bad, and this has important consequences for her (see Chapter 3). She is strongly influenced in her manner of dress, behavior, and even ways of thinking by the other law students and professors (social influence; see Chapter 8), and her image and understanding of herself are radically changed by these experiences (Chapter 5). She is clearly the target of sexism and negative stereotypes suggesting that women—and especially attractive women—can't be highly intelligent and therefore will not make successful law students (Chapter 6). Further, her efforts to overcome these stereotypes provide a clear illustration of how such views can be challenged. Her efforts to help the beautician recover her pet dog provide a good example of what social psychologists term *prosocial behavior* (Chapter 9). Her verbal barbs against Warner's new fiancée are clearly aggressive (Chapter 10), and Elle's ability to recognize that the daughter of the murder victim was lying and her skill in getting her to admit this lie reflect ways in which social psychology finds application in practical settings (Chapter 12). Overall, this movie illustrates the key point we have already made and will repeat throughout this book: The topics and questions studied by social psychologists are truly central to our lives. In other words, we live social psychology even if we don't realize it.

After that passionate endorsement of our field, you might expect us to turn, at once, to the fascinating topics it studies. That will come, but we feel it is important to provide you with some background information about the scope, nature, and methods of our field. This information will be useful to you in reading the entire book (and succeeding in your course), so it is crucial that we provide it here.

First, we'll present a more formal definition of social psychology—what it is and what it seeks to accomplish. Second, we'll describe some major, current trends in social psychology. These will be reflected throughout this book, so knowing about them at the start will help you recognize them and understand why they are important. Third, we'll examine some of the methods used by social psychologists to answer questions about the social side of life. A working knowledge of these basic methods will help you to understand how social psychologists add to our understanding of social thought and social behavior and will also be useful to you outside the context of this course.

Social Psychology: What It Is and What It Does

Providing a formal definition of almost any field is a complex task. In the case of social psychology, this difficulty is increased by two factors: the field's broad scope and its rapid rate of change. As you will see in every chapter of this book, social psychologists have a wide range of interests. Despite this, most social psychologists focus mainly on the following task: understanding how and why individuals behave, think, and feel as they do in social situations—ones involving the actual or imagined presence of other people. Consistent with this basic fact, we define **social psychology** as the scientific field that seeks to understand the nature and causes of individual behavior and thought in social situations. Another way to put this is to say that social psychology investigates the ways in which our thoughts, feelings, and actions are influenced by the social environments in which we live—by other people or even by our thoughts about them. For example, we imagine how other people would react to actions we might perform. We'll now clarify this definition by taking a closer look at several aspects of it.

Social Psychology Is Scientific in Nature

What is *science?* Many people seem to believe that this term refers only to fields such as chemistry, physics, and biology—ones that use the kind of equipment shown in Figure 1.2. If you share that view, you may find our suggestion that social psychology is a scientific discipline somewhat puzzling. How can a field that seeks to study the nature of love, the causes of aggression, and everything in between be scientific in the same sense as physics, biochemistry, or computer science? The answer is surprisingly simple.

In reality, the term *science* does not refer to a special group of highly advanced fields. Rather, it refers to two things: (1) a set of values and (2) several methods that can be used to study a wide range of topics. In deciding whether a given field is scientific or not, the critical question is: Does it adopt these values and methods? To the extent it does, it is scientific in nature. To the extent it does not, it falls outside the realm of science. We'll examine the procedures used by social psychologists in their research in a future section, so for now, we'll focus on the core values that all fields must adopt to be considered scientific in nature. Four of these are most important:

1. **Accuracy** is a commitment to gathering and evaluating information about the world (including social behavior and thought) in as careful, precise, and error-free a manner as possible.

2. **Objectivity** is a commitment to obtaining and evaluating such information in a manner that is as free from bias as humanly possible.

3. **Skepticism** is a commitment to accepting findings as accurate only to the extent they have been verified again.

4. **Open-mindedness** is a commitment to changing one's views—even views that are strongly held—if existing evidence suggests that these views are inaccurate.

Social psychology, as a field, is deeply committed to these values and applies them in its efforts to understand the nature of social behavior and social thought. For this reason, it makes sense to describe social psychology as scientific in orientation. In contrast, fields that are not scientific make assertions about the world and about people that are not subjected to the careful test and analysis required by the values listed above. In such fields—like astrology and aromatherapy—intuition, faith, and unobservable forces are considered to be sufficient for reaching conclusions—the opposite of what is true in social psychology (see Figure 1.2).

"But why adopt the scientific approach? Isn't social psychology just common sense?" Having taught for many years, we can almost hear you asking this question. And we understand why you might feel this way; we have all spent our entire lives interacting with other people and thinking about them, so in a sense, we are all amateur social psychologists. Why not rely on our own experience and intuition—or even on "the wisdom of the ages"—as a basis for understanding the social side of life? Our answer is straightforward: Because such sources provide an inconsistent and unreliable guide.

social psychology
The scientific field that seeks to understand the nature and causes of individual behavior and thought in social situations.

Figure 1.2
What Is Science, Really?
Many people seem to believe that only fields that use sophisticated equipment like that shown (left) *can be viewed as scientific. In fact, though, the term* science *simply refers to adherence to a set of basic values (e.g., accuracy, objectivity) and use of a set of basic methods that can be applied to almost any aspect of the world around us—including the social side of life. In contrast, fields that are not scientific in nature* (right) *do not accept these values or use these methods.*

For instance, consider the following statement, suggested by common sense: "Absence makes the heart grow fonder." Do you agree? Is it true that when people are separated from those they love that they miss them and so experience increased longing for them? Many people would agree. They would answer "Yes, that's right. Let me tell you about the time I was separated from . . ." But now consider the following statement "Out of sight, out of mind." How about this one? Is it true? When people are separated from those they love, do they quickly find another romantic interest? (Many popular songs suggest that this so—for instance "If you can't be with the one you love, love the one you're with," by Crosby, Stills, Young, and Nash.) As you can see, these two views—both suggested by common sense and popular culture—are contradictory. The same is true for many other informal observations about human behavior—they seem plausible but often suggest opposite conclusions. How about these: "Two heads are better than one," and "Too many cooks spoil the broth." One suggests that when people work together, they perform better (e.g., make better decisions). The other suggests that when they work together, they may get in each other's way resulting in reduced performance. And is it, "Familiarity breeds content" (as we come to know others better, we tend to like them more—we feel more comfortable with them) or "Familiarity breeds contempt" (as we come to know others better, we tend to like them less)? Common sense suggests that more is more when liking is concerned—the more familiar we are with others, the more we tend to like them, and there is some support for this view (see Chapter 7). On the other hand, recent findings indicate that the more we know about others (the better we come to know them), the less we like them (Norton, Frost, & Ariely, 2006). Why? Because as we learn more about others, we recognize more ways in which we are dissimilar to them, and this growing awareness of dissimilarity cascades, causing us to notice other ways in which we are dissimilar and that leads to disliking.

There are many more examples, but the main point should be clear: Common sense often suggests a confusing and inconsistent picture of human behavior. This is one important reason why social psychologists put their faith in the scientific method: It yields much more conclusive evidence. In fact, it is designed to help us determine not only which of the opposite sets of predictions discussed is correct, but also when and why one or the other might apply. We think this principle is so important that we will call attention to it throughout the book in special sections designed to show how careful research by social psychologists has helped to refine—and in some cases, to refute—the conclusions offered by common sense. These sections are titled, *Making Sense of Common Sense: A Social Psychological Perspective,* and they will give you a true appreciation of just why the scientific field of social psychology is so important and so valuable.

However this is not the only reason for being suspicious of common sense. Another reason relates to the fact that we are not perfect information-processing machines. On the contrary, as we'll note over and over again (e.g., Chapters 2, 3, 4, and 6), our thinking is subject to several forms of error that can lead us badly astray. Here's one example: Think back over major projects on which you have worked in the past (writing term papers, cooking a complicated dish, or painting your room). Now try to remember two things: (1) your initial estimates about how long it would take you to complete these jobs and (2) how long it actually took. Is there a gap between these two numbers? In all likelihood there is because most of us fall victim to the planning fallacy—a strong tendency to believe that projects will take less time than they actually do or that we can accomplish more in a given period of time than is really true. Moreover, we fall victim to this bias in our thoughts over and over again, despite repeated experiences that tell us "everything takes longer than we think it will." Why are we subject to this kind of error? Research by social psychologists indicates that part of the answer involves a tendency to think about the future when we are estimating how long a job will take. This prevents us from remembering how long similar tasks took in the past, and that, in turn, leads us to underestimate the time we will need now (e.g., Buehler, Griffin, & Ross, 1994). This is just one of the many ways in which we can—and often do—make errors in thinking about other people (and ourselves); we'll consider many others in Chapter 2. Because we are prone to such errors in our informal thinking about the social world, we cannot rely on it—or on common sense—to solve the mysteries of social behavior. Rather, we need scientific evidence, and that, in essence, is what social psychology is all about.

Social Psychology Focuses on the Behavior of Individuals

Societies differ greatly in terms of their views concerning courtship and marriage; yet it is still individuals who fall in love. Similarly, societies vary greatly in terms of their overall levels of violence; yet, it is still individuals who perform aggressive actions or refrain from doing so. The same argument applies to virtually all other aspects of social behavior, from prejudice to helping: the actions are performed by, and the thoughts occur in, the minds of individuals. Because of this basic fact, the focus in social psychology is strongly on individuals. Social psychologists realize, of course, that we do not exist in isolation from social and cultural influences—far from it. As we will see throughout the book, much social behavior occurs in group settings, and these can exert powerful effects on us. But the field's major interest lies in understanding the factors that shape the actions and thoughts of individuals in social settings.

Social Psychology Seeks to Understand the Causes of Social Behavior and Thought

In a key sense, the heading of this section states the most central aspect of our definition of social psychology: Social psychologists are primarily interested in understanding the many factors and conditions that shape the social behavior and thought of individuals—their actions, feelings, beliefs, memories, and inferences concerning other people. Obviously, a huge number of variables play a role in this regard. Most, though, fall under the five major headings described below.

Social Interactions

Imagine the following events: You are at a party when you notice that an attractive person is looking at you and smiling. In fact, this person is looking at you in a way that leaves little room for interpretation: They are sending clear signals saying "Wow! I like the way you look!"

You are in a hurry and notice that you are driving faster than you usually do—above the speed limit, in fact. Suddenly, up ahead, you see the blinking lights of a state trooper who is in the process of pulling another driver over to the side of the road.

Will these actions by others have any effect on your behavior and thoughts? Absolutely. Depending on your own personality, you may either blush with pleasure when you see someone looking at you in a "let's-get-acquainted" kind of way, or you may simply go over and say hello. And when you spot the state trooper's blinking light, you will almost certainly slow down—a lot. Instances like these, which occur hundreds of times each day, indicate that other people's behavior often has a powerful impact on us (see Figure 1.3).

In addition, we are also often affected by other people's appearance. Be honest: Don't you behave differently toward highly attractive people than toward less attractive ones? Toward old people compared to young ones? Toward people who belong to racial and ethnic groups different from your own? Your answer to some of these questions is probably yes because we do often react to the visible characteristics, such as appearance, of others (e.g., McCall, 1997; Twenge & Manis, 1998). In fact, research findings (e.g., Hassin & Trope, 2000) indicate that we cannot ignore the appearance of other people even when we consciously try to do so. So despite warnings to avoid "judging books by their covers," we are often strongly affected by other people's outward appearance—even if we are unaware of such effects and might deny their existence (see Chapter 7).

Cognitive Processes

Suppose that you have arranged to meet a friend, and this person is late. In fact, after thirty minutes you begin to suspect that your friend will never arrive. Finally, she or he does appear and says "Sorry . . . I forgot

Figure 1.3
Reacting to the Actions of Other People
As shown in these scenes, the behavior of other people often exerts powerful effects on our own behavior and thought.

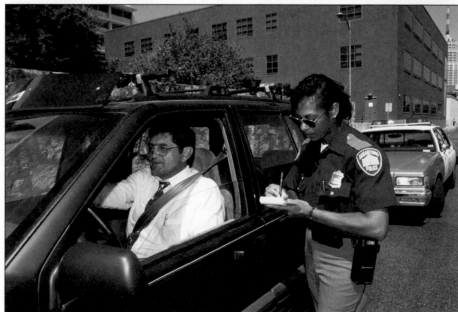

all about meeting you until a few minutes ago." How will you react? Probably with annoyance. Imagine that instead, however, your friend said: "I'm so sorry to be late ... There was a big accident, and the traffic was tied up for miles." Now how will you react? Probably with less annoyance, but not necessarily. If your friend is often late and has used this excuse before, you may be suspicious about whether this explanation is true. In contrast, if this is the first time your friend has been late or if your friend has never used such an excuse in the past, you may accept it as true. In other words, your reactions in this situation will depend strongly on your memories of your friend's past behavior and your *inferences* about whether her or his explanation is really true. Situations like this one call attention to the fact that *cognitive processes* play a crucial role in social behavior and social thought. We are always trying to make sense out of the social world, and this leads us to engage in lots of social cognition—to think long and hard about other people—what they are like, why they do what they do, how they might react to our behavior, and so on (e.g., Shah, 2003). Social psychologists are well aware of the importance of such processes, and in fact, social cognition is one of the most important areas of research in the field (e.g., Killeya & Johnson, 1998; Swann & Gill, 1997).

Environmental Variables: Impact of the Physical World

Are people more prone to wild impulsive behavior during the full moon than at other times (Rotton & Kelley, 1985)? Do we become more irritable and aggressive when the weather is hot and steamy than when it is cool and comfortable (Anderson, Bushman, & Groom, 1997; Rotton & Cohn, 2000)? Does exposure to a pleasant smell in the air make people more helpful to others (Baron, 1997)? Research findings indicate that the physical environment does indeed influence our feelings, thoughts, and behavior, so ecological variables certainly fall within the realm of modern social psychology.

Cultural Context

Social behavior and social thought are certainly strongly influenced by the actions or characteristics of the people around us, but they do not occur in a cultural vacuum. On the contrary, our relations with others and how we think about them are often strongly affected by events, beliefs, and trends in our own culture. For instance, in the past, people in the United States dressed in certain ways when they attended a concert, went to church, or dined in a fine restaurant: Men wore jackets and ties, and women wore dresses or skirts. Now, however, casual is definitely in, and many people dress casually in these settings. That trend toward casual dress, however, has not progressed to the same level in all cultures. For instance, in Europe and many Asian countries, casual dress is still not acceptable in many settings (see Figure 1.4).

In a sense, this is a trivial example: Cultural beliefs and norms (rules governing behavior) influence much more important aspects of behavior, such as when people should marry and whom, how many children they should have, whether it is OK to "fudge" one's income taxes, to be in debt, or to live with one's romantic partner (see Chapter 7). So clearly, social behavior and social thought can be, and often are, strongly affected by cultural factors. (The term *culture* refers to the system of shared meanings, perceptions, and beliefs held by people belonging to some group [Smith & Bond, 1993].) And attention to the effects of cultural factors is an important trend in social psychology as the field attempts to take account of the growing cultural diversity in many different countries.

evolutionary psychology
A new branch of psychology that seeks to investigate the potential role of genetic factors in various aspects of human behavior.

Biological Factors

Is social behavior influenced by biological processes and genetic factors? In the past, most social psychologists would have answered no, at least to the genetic part of this question. Now, however, many have come to believe that our preferences, behaviors, emotions, and even attitudes are affected, to some extent, by our biological inheritance (Buss, 1999; Nisbett, 1990; Schmitt, 2004).

The view that biological factors play an important role in social behavior comes from the field of **evolutionary psychology** (e.g., Buss, 2004; Buss & Shackelford, 1997). This new branch of psychology suggests that our species, like all others on the planet, has been subject to the process of biological evolution throughout its history, and that as a result of this process, we now possess a large number of evolved psychological mechanisms that help (or once helped) us to deal with important problems relating to survival. How do these become part of our biological inheritance? Through the process of evolution, which, in turn, involves three basic components: *variation, inheritance,* and *selection*. Variation refers to the fact that organisms belonging to a given species vary in many different ways; indeed, such variation is a basic part of life on our planet. Human beings, as you already know, come in a wide variety of shapes and sizes and vary on what sometimes seems to be an almost countless number of dimensions.

Inheritance refers to the fact that some of these variations can be passed from one generation to the next through complex mechanisms that we are only now beginning to fully understand. Selection refers to the fact that some variations give the individuals who possess them an "edge" in terms of reproduction: They are more likely to survive, find mates, and pass these variations on to succeeding generations. The result is that over time, more and more members of the species possess these vari-

ations. This change in the characteristics of a species over time—immensely long periods of time—is the concrete outcome of evolution. (See Figure 1.5 on page 12 for a summary of this process.)

Social psychologists who adopt the evolutionary perspective suggest that this process applies to at least some aspects of social behavior. For instance, consider the question of mate preference. Why do we find some people attractive? According to the evolutionary perspective, the characteristics they show—symmetrical facial features, well-toned, shapely bodies, clear skin, and lustrous hair—are associated with "good genes;" they suggest that the people who possess them are likely to be healthy and vigorous, and therefore good mates (e.g., Schmitt & Buss, 2001; Tesser & Martin, 1996). For instance, these characteristics—the ones we find attractive—indicate that the people who show them have strong immune systems that protect them from many illnesses (e.g., Li & Kenrick, 2006). Presumably, a preference for characteristics associated with good health and vigor among

Figure 1.4
Culture: An Important Determinant of Social Behavior
In the past, most people in the United States dressed up when they went to a concert or dined in a fine restaurant. However, cultural beliefs about dress have changed greatly, and many people now dress casually in these settings. But in some countries, casual dress is still not acceptable in these settings.

Figure 1.5
Evolution: An Overview
Evolution involves three major components: variation, inheritance, and selection.

```
   ┌─────────────┐              ┌──────────────┐
   │  Variation  │ ───────────▶ │ Inheritance  │
   │ Organisms   │              │ Some of these│
   │ vary in     │              │ variations   │
   │ many ways   │              │ are heritable│
   └─────────────┘              └──────────────┘
                                        │
                                        ▼
   ◇ This is the ◇              ┌──────────────┐
     crucial       ───────────▶ │  Selection   │
     outcome of                 │ Variations   │
     evolution                  │ that are     │
                                │ adaptive     │
                                │ become       │
                                │ increasingly │
                                │ common in the│
                                │ population   │
                                └──────────────┘
```

our ancestors increased the chances that they would reproduce successfully; this, in turn, contributed to our preference for people who possess these aspects of appearance.

Here's another example, and one that is perhaps a little less obvious. All parents would like their children to resemble themselves, at least to some extent. But do men and women differ in this respect? The evolutionary perspective suggests that they might and offers one reason why. Women can be certain that any child they have is theirs; but for men this is never totally certain. Are they the father, or was some other male involved? In stable long-term relationships, fathers can be 99.99 percent certain that a child is theirs, but there is always some chance, however, small, that they are not the biological father. For this reason, it has been suggested that early in life, children closely resemble their fathers; this helps reduce the doubts we just mentioned and thereby elicit love from male parents. Later, however, this difference may fade, and the children may come to resemble their mothers to a greater extent (e.g., Buss, 2004). If that's true, men might well like the device shown in Figure 1.6 even more than women.

Other topics have been studied from the evolutionary perspective (e.g., helping others; aggression; preferences for various ways of attracting persons who are already in a relationship), and we'll describe this research in other chapters. Here, however, we emphasize the following fact: The evolutionary perspective does not suggest that we inherit specific patterns of social behavior; rather, it contends that we inherit tendencies or predispositions that may or may not be apparent in our overt actions, depending on the environments in which we live.

Figure 1.6
Parent–Child Resemblance: An Evolutionary Perspective That May Be More Important to Males
According to an evolutionary perspective, men may be more concerned than women, at least initially, that their children resemble them. Although women can always be certain that a new baby is theirs, men can never enjoy the same total certainty. For this reason, they might like the invention shown here even more than women.

(*Source:* 1997 John McPherson/ Dist. by Universal Press Syndicate, 7/24/2005.)

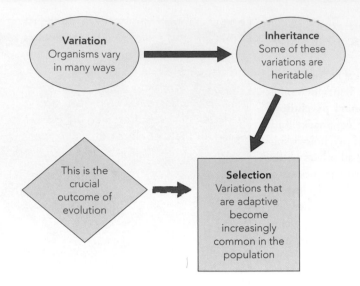

New technology for parents.

Similarly, this perspective does not suggest that we are "forced" or driven by our genes to act in specific ways. Rather, it merely suggests that because of our genetic inheritance, we have tendencies to behave in certain ways that, at least in the past, enhanced the chances that our ancestors would survive and pass their genes on to us. These tendencies, can be—and often are—overridden by cognitive factors and the effects of experience (i.e., learning [Pettijohn & Jungeberg, 2004]). For instance, what is viewed as attractive changes over time and is often very different in diverse cultures. So yes, genetic factors play some role in our behavior and thought, but they are clearly only one factor among many that influence how we think and act.

Social Psychology: Summing Up

In sum, social psychology focuses mainly on understanding the causes of social behavior and social thought—on identifying factors that shape our feelings, behavior, and thought in social situations. It seeks to accomplish this goal through the use of scientific methods, and it takes careful note of the fact that social behavior and thought are influenced by a wide range of social, cognitive, environmental, cultural, and biological factors.

The remainder of this text is devoted to describing some of the key findings of social psychology. This information is truly fascinating, so we're certain that you will find it of interest. We're equally sure, however, that you will also find some of it surprising, and that it will challenge many of your ideas about people and social relations. So please get ready for some new insights. We predict that after reading this book, you'll never think about the social side of life in quite the same way as before.

KeyPoints

- Social psychology is the scientific field that seeks to understand the nature and causes of individual behavior and thought in social situations.

- It is scientific in nature because it adopts the values and methods used in other fields of science.

- Social psychologists adopt the scientific method because common sense provides an unreliable guide to social behavior and because our thought is influenced by many potential sources of bias.

- Social psychology focuses on the behavior of individuals and seeks to understand the causes of social behavior and thought, which can involve social interaction, cognitive processes, environmental factors, cultural values, and biological factors.

Think About It

Do you think it's really possible to have a scientific field of social psychology? Or do you believe that topics, such as love, aggression, and prejudice, are ones that can't be studied by scientific methods?

Social Psychology: Its Cutting Edge

We feel strongly that any textbook should reflect the field it covers in an accurate and up-to-date manner. Consistent with this belief, we will now describe several major trends in modern social psychology—themes and ideas that appear to be on the cutting edge of our field and that we will describe throughout this book.

Cognition and Behavior: Two Sides of the Same Social Coin

In the not-so-distant past, social psychologists could be divided into two distinct groups: those who were primarily interested in social behavior—how people act in social situations—and those who were primarily interested in social thought—how people attempt to make sense out of the social world and to understand themselves and others. This division has now largely disappeared. In modern social psychology, behavior and cognition are seen as intimately and continuously linked. In other words, there is virtually universal agreement in the field that we cannot hope to understand how and why people behave in certain ways in social situations without considering their thoughts, memory, intentions, emotions, attitudes, and beliefs. Similarly, virtually all social psychologists agree that there is a continuing and complex interplay between social thought and social behavior. What we think about others influences our actions toward them, and the consequences of these actions then affect our social thought. So, the loop is continuous, and in trying to understand the social side of life, modern social psychology integrates both. That will be our approach throughout the book, and it will be present in virtually every chapter.

Social Neuroscience: Where Social Psychology and Brain Research Meet

Do you understand these words as you read them? If so, it is the result of activity in your brain. Do you feel happy? Sad? Excited? Calm? Again, whatever you are feeling right now derives from activity in your brain and other biological events. Can you remember what your psychology professor looks like? What it felt like to have your first kiss? Do you have plans? Goals? Intentions? In every case, these psychological events and processes are the result of activity in several areas of your brain. In recent years, powerful new tools, such as magnetic resonance imaging (MRI) and positron emission tomography (PET) scans, have allowed psychologists and other scientists to peer into the human brain as people engage in various activities (e.g., while solving problems, looking at emotion-provoking photos or films, and so on). The result is that we now know much more about the complex relationships between neural events and psychological ones—feelings, thoughts, and overt actions.

Recently, social psychologists, too, have begun to search for the neural foundations of social thought and social behavior. In fact, the volume of research on this topic has increased greatly (e.g., Harris, Todorov, & Fiske, 2005; Harmon-Jones & Devine, 2003). In conducting such research, social psychologists use the same basic tools as other scientists—they study events in the brain (through the use of MRI and other kinds of brain scans), other neural activity, and even changes in the immune system (e.g., Taylor, Lerner, Sherman, Sage, & McDowell, 2003) to determine how these events are related to important social processes. The findings of this research have been truly fascinating. Here's one example of what we mean.

Recent findings indicate that prejudice—a topic we'll examine in detail in Chapter 6—actually has two underlying dimensions (e.g., Cuddy, Fiske, & Glick, in press). One refers to the extent to which we see others as friend or foe (groups toward whom we are prejudiced tend to be seen as foe or enemy). This dimension is *warmth*. The other refers to *competence*—can others (members of various groups) do what they set out to do? (Friends, presumably, would want to help us; enemies would want to harm us.) Combining these two dimensions suggests that four kinds of prejudice can exist: high warmth–high competence (we react positively to such people, with pride, because they are our own group), high warmth–low competence (we react with pity to such groups, which includes disabled people or elderly people), low warmth–high competence (we react with envy to people in such groups, which includes extremely rich people), and low warmth–low competence (we react with disgust to such people and perceive them as the worst of all; these groups include homeless people and drug addicts).

Recently, two social psychologists hypothesized that when exposed to people from the first three groups, people would show activity in areas of the brain often involved in social thought (Harris & Fiske, 2006). They would be actively thinking about these people. But people in the fourth category—the groups we truly dislike—might show a different pattern. Such people might be viewed as "less than human"; they would be dehumanized, and as a result, would not trigger much in the way of social thought. To test this prediction, the researchers had participants in their study look at photos of members of groups known from previous studies to represent the four combinations of warmth and competence previously described (high–high, high–low, low–high, and low–low). While looking at the photos, participants were asked to rate how much of each of four emotions (pride, envy, pity, and disgust) they were experiencing. Participants' brains were scanned while they performed these tasks, and the results offered clear support for the hypothesis: Areas of the brain known to be involved in social thought were indeed active for the first three groups (ones high in warmth and competence, high in warmth but low in competence, or low in warmth and high in competence), but they were not active for the fourth—groups that were low in both warmth and competence—the groups participants truly despise (see Figure 1.7 on page 16). In fact, activity in response to members of the fourth group was as low as it was in response to disgusting physical objects (e.g., an overflowing toilet). In short, when participants truly disliked certain groups, they dehumanized them in the sense that their brains did not even show the kind of activity usually produced by other people. As less than human, in other words, these people were not even worth thinking about.

Research in the rapidly expanding field of **social neuroscience** is clearly at the forefront of advances in social psychology, and we will represent it fully—and often—in this text. We should insert one warning, however. As noted by several experts in this field (e.g., Cacioppo, Hawkley, and Berntson, 2003), social neuroscience cannot provide the answer to every question we have about social thought or behavior. There are many aspects of social thought that cannot easily be related to activity in specific areas of the brain—aspects such as attitudes, attributions, and reciprocity (e.g., Willingham & Dunn, 2003). In principle, all of these components of social thought reflect activity in the brain, but this does not necessarily mean that it is best to try to study them in this way. In fact, the situation may be similar to that one that exists between chemistry and physics. All chemists agree that ultimately, every chemical reaction can be explained in terms of physics. But the principles of chemistry are still so useful that chemists continue to use them in their research and do not all rush out and become physicists. The same may well be true for social psychology: It does not have to seek to understand all of its major topics in terms of activities in the brain or nervous system; other approaches that we will describe in later chapters are still useful and can provide important new insights. Throughout this book, therefore, we will describe research that uses a wide range of methods, from brain scans on the one hand, to direct observations of social behavior on the other. This reflects the current, eclectic nature of social psychology and is, therefore, the most appropriate content for this book.

social neuroscience
An area of research in social psychology that seeks knowledge about the neural and biological bases of social processes.

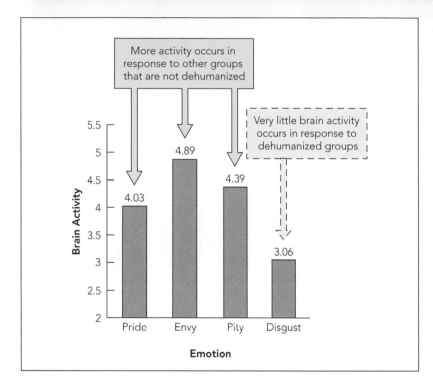

Figure 1.7
The Neural Face of Prejudice: Absence of Brain Activity as a Sign of Dehumanizing Others
In the study represented here, participants saw photos of people belonging to various groups that varied in terms of their perceived warmth (then friend or foe) and competence (Row A). Activity occurred in regions of the brain known to be active during social thought for all of the groups except ones low on both dimensions, which were groups the participants truly disliked and that elicited disgust. In fact, as shown in the photos in Row B, brain activity was as low as when individuals looked at disgusting physical objects, such as an overflowing toilet.

(*Source:* Based on data from Harris & Fiske, 2006; photos courtesy of Dr. Susan T. Fiske.)

The Role of Implicit (Nonconscious) Processes

Have you ever had the experience of meeting someone for the first time and taking an immediate liking—or disliking—to that person? Afterward, you may have wondered, "Why do I like (dislike) this person?" But probably, you didn't wonder for long because we are all experts at finding good reasons to explain our own actions or feelings. This speed in no way implies that we really do understand why we behave or think in certain ways.

And in fact, a growing theme of recent research in social psychology has been just this: In many cases we really don't know why we think or behave as we do in social contexts. On the contrary, our thought and actions are shaped by factors and processes of which we are only dimly aware, at best, and which often take place in an automatic manner without any conscious thought or intentions on our part. This is one more reason why social psychologists are reluctant to trust common sense as a basis for reliable information about social behavior or social thought; we are unaware of many of the factors that influence how we think and how we behave and so cannot report on them accurately. An intriguing illustration of this basic principle is provided by research conducted by Pelham, Mirenberg, and Jones (2002).

In this research, the authors argued that as a result of our strong tendencies to enhance ourselves and our self-image, our feelings about almost anything in the world around us will be influenced by its relationship to our self-concept. The closer it is to our self-concept, the more we will tend to like it. As a result, people will tend to live—at a higher rate than chance would predict—in places (cities or states) whose names resemble their own (e.g., people named Louis are more likely to live in St. Louis). Similarly, they will tend to live, at a greater than expected rate, in cities whose names begin with the numbers of their birthday (e.g., Three Corners; Seven Springs) and will tend to choose careers whose names resemble their own (e.g., people named Dennis or Denise will be overrepresented among dentists, while people named Lawrence or Laura will be overrepresented among lawyers). In ten separate studies, they found evidence for these predictions. While questions have been raised about the validity of these findings (Gallucci, 2003), additional evidence offers support for the original conclusion: Our preferences for the places in which we live and the careers we choose can be influenced by reactions and feelings we don't even realize we have (Pelham et al., 2003).

Here's another and more serious illustration of the impact of nonconscious processes, one involving babies. It has been found in studies with adults that people are more accurate at recognizing faces from their own racial group than faces from other groups. In other words, it is as if people from groups other than their own "all look alike" to them (e.g., Richson & Shelton, 2003). Presumably, with adults, such preference for one's own group is at least partly conscious; individuals may have preferences for people in their own groups and realize that this is so. But what about babies only three months old? Obviously, they aren't verbal beings, so they can't really be conscious of such racial preferences. But recent findings indicate that these exist anyway. In a study by Bar-Haim, Ziv, Lamy, and Hodes (2006), three-month-old infants were shown photos of people in their own race or another race, and the amount of time they spent looking at the photos was recorded. The children were from three groups: African children living in Africa who saw predominantly African faces around them; African children living in Israel who saw a mixture of Caucasian and African faces; and Caucasian children living in Israel, who saw primarily Caucasian faces. Would the babies show preferences for their own group even at this young age? As seen in Figure 1.8 on page 18, they did. The Caucasian children looked more at Caucasian faces than at African faces, and the African children living in Africa looked more at African than Caucasian faces. The African children living in Israel, however, showed no clear preference. This is not surprising because unlike the other two groups, they saw a real mixture of faces around them. Because the babies were so young, it is clear that their preferences for faces of people in their own racial group were not something of which they were conscious; yet, these preferences certainly existed and strongly influenced their behavior, so once again, the powerful effects of nonconscious processes are clear.

Research on the role of implicit (nonconscious) processes in our social behavior and thought has examined many other topics, such as the impact of our moods on what we tend to remember about other people or complex issues (e.g., Ruder & Bless, 2003); how negative attitudes toward members of social groups other than our own which we deny having can still influence our reactions toward them (e.g., Fazio & Hilden, 2001); how we automatically evaluate people belonging to various social groups once we have concluded that they belong to that group (Castelli, Zobmaster, & Smith, 2004); and how our tendency to assume that other's people's behavior reflects their underlying traits rather than their reactions to the present situation can interfere with our ability to tell when they are lying (O'Sullivan, 2003). In short, the more deeply social psychologists delve into this topic, the broader the effects of nonconscious factors in our social behavior and thought seem to be. We will examine such effects in several chapters because they are clearly on the cutting edge of progress in our field (see Chapters 2 and 6).

Figure 1.8
Nonconscious Processes at Work in Three-Month-Old Babies

Infants only three months old showed clear preferences for faces of their own racial group: Caucasian children looked more at Caucasian faces than African faces, and African children living in Africa looked more at African faces. However, African children living in an environment with many Caucasian people did not show any preference for either group. Because the infants could not speak, these findings illustrate—in a unique way—the powerful role of nonconscious processes in what, for these infants, are the beginnings of social thought.

(*Source:* Based on data from Bar-Haim, Ziv, Lamy, & Hodes, 2006.)

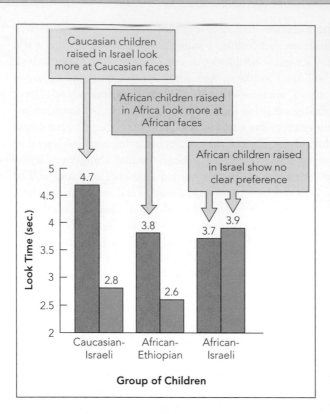

Taking Full Account of Social Diversity

There can be no doubt that the United States—like many other countries—is undergoing a major social and cultural transformation. Recent figures indicate that 64 percent of the population identifies itself as Caucasian (of European heritage), while fully 36 percent identifies itself as belonging to some other group (13 percent African American, 4.5 percent American Indian, 14 percent Hispanic, 4.5 percent Asian or Pacific Islander, and 7 percent some other group). This represents a tremendous change from the 1960s, when approximately 90 percent of the population was of European descent. Indeed, in several states (e.g., California, New Mexico, Texas, and Arizona), people of European heritage are no longer a clear majority. In response to these tremendous shifts, psychologists have increasingly recognized the importance of taking cultural factors and differences into careful account in everything they do—teaching, research, counseling, and therapy; and social psychologists are certainly no exception to this rule. They have been increasingly sensitive to the fact that an individual's cultural, ethnic, and racial heritage often play a key role in self-identity and that this, in turn, can exert important effects on behavior. This is in sharp contrast to the point of view that prevailed in the past, which suggested that cultural, ethnic, and gender differences are relatively unimportant. In contrast to that perspective, social psychologists currently believe that such differences are quite important and must be taken carefully into account in efforts to understand human behavior. As a result, psychology in general, and social psychology too, now adopts a **multicultural perspective**—one which carefully and clearly recognizes the potential importance of gender, age, ethnicity, sexual orientation, disability, socioeconomic status, religious orientation, and many other social and cultural dimensions. This perspective has led to important changes in focus of social psychological research, and this trend seems likely to continue. So clearly, increased recognition of diversity is a hallmark of modern social psychology, and we will discuss research highlighting the importance of such factors at many points in this book.

Now that we have described social psychology as it exists today, we think it's important to say just a few words about how it got to this point. Nothing—especially scientific fields as rich in content and broad in perspective as modern social psychology—arises abruptly. Rather, scientific fields emerge gradually and develop and change in many different ways on the way to their current forms. To take note of that fact, we'll now present a very abbreviated glance at the history of social psychology—how it emerged and progressed toward its current form. We hope that you will also read the Foreword, "Personal Brushes with History," on page xxxiii, because it describes some of our personal experiences with individuals who were truly social psychology's founders and who helped make it into the kind of field it is at present.

multicultural perspective
A focus on understanding the cultural and ethnic factors that influence social behavior.

A Brief Look at History: The Origins and Early Development of Social Psychology

When, precisely, did social psychology begin? This question is difficult to answer, because speculation about social behavior stretches back to ancient times (Allport, 1985). For this reason, we'll focus here on the emergence of social psychology as an independent field and on its growth in recent decades. We have already described in the preceding pages major trends that have shaped its current, fully modern form.

The Early Years: Social Psychology Emerges

Fields of science don't mark their beginnings with formal ribbon-cutting ceremonies. Instead, they develop gradually as growing numbers of scientists become interested in specific topics or develop new methods for studying existing ones. This pattern applies to social psychology: No bottles of champagne were uncorked to mark its launch, so it is difficult to choose a specific date for its official launching. Perhaps the years between 1908 and 1924 qualify because that is the period during which social psychology became an independent field. In both of these years, important texts containing the words social psychology in their titles were published. The first, by William McDougall (1908), was based largely on the view that social behavior stems from innate tendencies or *instincts*. While many modern social psychologists accept the fact that genetic factors play a role in some aspects of social behavior, almost all reject the idea of fixed, unchanging instincts as important causes of social behavior. Thus, it is clear that the field had *not* reached its modern form in McDougall's early book.

The second volume, by Floyd Allport (1924), is a different matter. That book is much closer to the modern orientation of our field. Allport argued that social behavior stems from many different factors, including the presence of other persons and their specific actions. Further, his book emphasized the value of experimentation and contained discussions of actual research that had already been conducted on such topics as conformity, the ability to recognize others' emotions from their facial expressions, and the impact of audiences on task performance. All of these topics have been studied by social psychologists in recent years, so the following conclusion seems justified: By the middle of the Roaring Twenties, social psychology had appeared on the scene and had begun to investigate many of the topics it still studies today.

The two decades following publication of Allport's text (the 1930s and early 1940s) were marked by rapid growth. New issues were studied and new methods for investigating them were devised. Important milestones in the development of the field during this period include research by two of its founders: Muzafer Sherif and Kurt Lewin. Sherif (1935) studied the nature and impact of *social norms*—rules indicating how individuals ought to behave—and so contributed basic insights to our understanding of pressures toward *conformity*. Kurt Lewin and his colleagues (e.g., Lewin, Lippitt, & White, 1939; see Figure 1.9) carried out revealing research on the nature of leadership and other group processes.

Quite apart from this research, Lewin's influence on social psychology was profound, because many of his students went on to become very prominent contributors to the field. Their names—Leon Festinger, Harold Kelley, Morton Deutsch, Stanley Schachter, John Thibaut—read like a "Who's Who" of famous social psychologists during the 1950s, 1960s, and even 1970s. In short, by the close of the 1930s, social psychology was a growing field that had already contributed much to our knowledge of social behavior.

Social Psychology's Youth: The 1940s, 1950s, and 1960s

After a pause resulting from World War II, social psychology continued its growth. During the 1940s and 1950s, the field expanded its scope in several directions. For instance, social psychologists focused attention on the influence that groups and group membership

Figure 1.9
Kurt Lewin
Kurt Lewin was one of many Euopean social psychologists who came to the United States to escape from Nazi persecution. He conducted important studies on many topics, including leadership, and trained many students who went on to become famous social psychologists themselves.

exert on individual behavior (Forsyth, 1991). And they examined the link between various personality traits and social behavior, for example, in research on the authoritarian personality—a cluster of traits that seem to predispose individuals toward acceptance of extreme political views such as Nazism (Adorno et al., 1959).

One of the most important events of this period was the development of the theory of *cognitive dissonance* (Festinger, 1957). This theory proposed that human beings dislike inconsistency and strive to reduce it. Specifically, the theory argues that people seek to eliminate inconsistency between various attitudes that they hold, or between their attitudes and their behavior. While this theory may strike you as being quite sensible, it actually leads to many unexpected predictions. For example, dissonance theory suggests that offering individuals small rewards for stating views they don't really hold is often more effective in getting them to change these opinions than offering them larger rewards for the same actions. Why? Because when people say something they don't believe and they realize that they had few reasons for engaging in such behavior, they experience strong pressure to change their views to agree with what they've just said—stronger pressure than when they are offered large rewards and, therefore, have many good reasons for stating such views. We'll examine this, and other surprising predictions derived from the theory of cognitive dissonance in Chapter 5.

In an important sense the 1960s can be viewed as the time when social psychology came of age. During this turbulent decade of rapid social change, the number of social psychologists rose dramatically, and the field expanded to include practically every aspect of social interaction you might imagine. So many lines of research either began or expanded during these years that it is impossible to list them all here, but among the most important were these: *interpersonal attraction* and *romantic love, impression formation, attribution,* and other aspects of *social perception;* many different aspects of *social influence,* such as *obedience, conformity,* and *compliance; the causes and prevention of human aggression;* and *effects of the physical environment* on many forms of social behavior.

The 1970s, 1980s, and 1990s: A Maturing Field

The rapid pace of change did not slacken during the 1970s; if anything, it accelerated. Many lines of research begun during the 1960s were expanded, and several new topics rose to prominence. Among the most important of these were *attribution* (the process through which we seek to understand the causes of others' behavior—*why* they act as they do; see Chapter 3); *gender differences* and *sex discrimination* (investigation of the extent to which the behavior of women and men actually differs, and the impact of negative stereotypes concerning the traits supposedly possessed by both genders; see Chapters 4 and 6); and *environmental psychology* (investigations of the effects of the physical environment—noise, heat, crowding, air quality—on social behavior).

In addition, two larger-scale trends took shape during the 1980s: growing influence of a cognitive perspective and growing influence on application. Because we discussed both of these trends, plus several others in earlier sections, we'll simply mention them again here and close this brief discussion of social psychology's history with two points. First, we offer this brief historical overview primarily to help you appreciate the fact that social psychology, like many other fields, has evolved and changed throughout its existence. Second, because we realize that names and dates are always somewhat abstract, we have described our own personal experiences with founders of the field—the people who truly shaped modern social psychology—in the Foreword on pages xxxiii–1 ("Personal Brushes with History"). Our conversations with these true "giants" of social psychology shaped our thinking in important ways, and contributed to our own research in many respects. But more important, the insights we gained helped us adopt the very broad and eclectic perspective on social psychology we represent in this book. We feel very fortunate that, during our own careers, we actually got to know Ned Jones, Solomon Asch, Stanley Milgram, Stan Schachter, Leon Festinger, and other founders of the field, and we hope you enjoy reading about our experiences with these brilliant colleagues.

KeyPoints

- Social psychologists currently recognize that social thought and social behavior are two sides of the same coin and that there is a continuous complex interplay between them.

- Another major direction in the field involves growing interest in social neuroscience—efforts to relate activity in the brain and other biological events to key aspects of social thought and behavior.

- Our behavior and thought is often shaped by factors of which we are unaware. Growing attention to such implicit (nonconscious) processes is another major theme of modern social psychology.

- Social psychology currently adopts a multicultural perspective. This perspective recognizes the importance of cultural factors in social behavior and social thought and notes that research findings obtained in one culture do not necessarily generalize to other cultures.

Think About It

How important do you think nonconscious processes are in determining your own thinking and behavior? And if they are nonconscious, how can we ever really understand the effects of such factors?

How Social Psychologists Answer the Fascinating Questions They Raise: Research as the Route to Increased Knowledge

Now that we've described the current state of social psychology, we can turn to the third major task mentioned at the start of this chapter: explaining how social psychologists attempt to answer questions about social behavior and social thought. Because social psychology is scientific in orientation, social psychologists usually seek to accomplish this task through systematic research. To provide you with basic information about the specific techniques used, we'll examine three related topics. First, we will describe several methods of research in social psychology. Next, we will consider the role of theory in such research. And finally, we'll touch on some of the complex ethical issues relating to social psychological research.

Systematic Observation: Describing the World around Us

One basic technique for studying social behavior involves **systematic observation**— carefully observing behavior as it occurs. Such observation is not the kind of informal observation we all practice from childhood on; rather, in a scientific field, such as social psychology, it is observation accompanied by careful, accurate measurement. For example, suppose that a social psychologist wanted to find out how frequently people touch each other in different settings. The researcher could study this topic by going to shopping malls, airports, college campuses, and many other locations and by observing, in those settings, who touches whom, how they touch, and with what frequency. Such research, which has actually been conducted, (see Chapter 3), would be employing what is known as *naturalistic observation,* which is observation of behavior in natural settings (Linden, 1992). Note that in such observation, the researcher would simply notice what is happening in various contexts; they would make no attempt to change the behavior of the people being observed. In fact, such observation requires that the researcher take great pains to avoid influencing the people being observed in any way. Thus the psychologist would try to remain as inconspicuous as possible and might even try to hide behind natural barriers, such as telephone poles, walls, or even bushes.

systematic observation
A method of research in which behavior is systematically observed and recorded.

Figure 1.10
Surveys on the Internet: An Example
Have you ever visited the Web site shown here? If so, you know that it presents the results of online ratings of professors by students in their classes. This is just one example of how the survey method is now being used on the Internet.

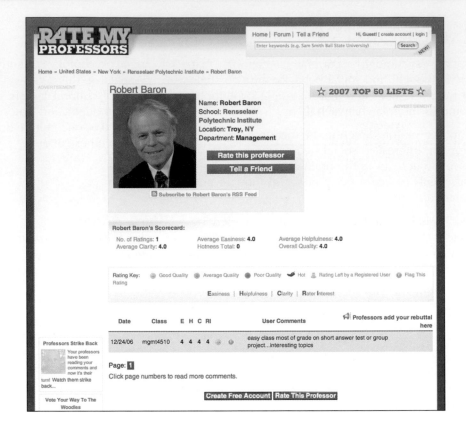

Another technique that is often included under the heading of systematic observation is known as the **survey method.** Here, researchers ask large numbers of people to respond to questions about their attitudes or behavior. Surveys are used for many purposes—to measure attitudes toward specific issues, to find out how voters feel about various political candidates, and even to assess student reactions to professors; your own university probably uses a form on which you rate your professors each semester. Social psychologists sometimes use this method to measure attitudes concerning social issues—for instance, national health care or affirmative action programs. Scientists and practitioners in other fields use the survey method to measure everything from political views to consumer reactions to new products.

Surveys offer several advantages. Information can be gathered about thousands or even hundreds of thousands of people with relative ease. In fact, surveys are now often conducted online. For instance, have you ever visited Ratemyprofessors.com? It is a Web site that presents students' ratings of their professors, and that's just one example of how the survey method is now being used on the internet (see Figure 1.10).

To be useful as a research tool, though, surveys must meet certain requirements. First, the people who participate must be representative of the larger population about which conclusions are to be drawn—the issue of sampling. If this condition is not met, serious errors can result. For instance, CNN conducts a poll on some current issue every day; the next day, they present the results. One recent topic, for instance, was "Should parents permit their adult children to move in with them?" Results indicated that a majority said "Yes." Can we have confidence in these results? Yes, but only to the extent that the people who responded to the survey were representative of the entire population. Suppose, for instance, that only adult children planning to move back in with their parents had responded. Clearly, this would not reflect the parents' views, which could be quite different.

survey method
A method of research in which a large number of people answer questions about their attitudes or behavior.

Yet another issue that must be carefully addressed with respect to surveys is this: The way in which the items are worded can exert strong effects on the outcomes obtained. For example, suppose a survey asked "Do you think that people convicted of multiple murders should be executed?" Many people might agree; after all, the convicted criminals have murdered several victims. But if, instead, the survey asked: "Are you in favor of the death penalty?" a smaller percent might agree. So, the way in which questions are posed can strongly affect the results.

In sum, the survey method can be a useful approach for studying some aspects of social behavior, but the results obtained are accurate only to the extent that issues relating to sampling and wording are carefully addressed.

Correlation: The Search for Relationships

At various times, you have probably noticed that some events appear to be related to the occurrence of others; as one changes, the other changes, too. For example, perhaps you've noticed that people who drive new, expensive cars tend to be older than people who drive old, inexpensive cars or that when interest rates rise, the stock market often falls. When two events are related in this way, they are said to be correlated or that a correlation exists between them. The term *correlation* refers to a tendency for one event to change as the other changes. Social psychologists refer to such changeable aspects of the natural world as *variables* because they can take different values.

From a scientific point of view, the existence of a correlation between two variables can be useful. When a correlation exists, it is possible to predict one variable from information about one or more other variables. The ability to make such predictions is one important goal of all branches of science, including social psychology. Being able to make accurate predictions can be quite helpful. For instance, imagine that a correlation is observed between certain attitudes on the part of individuals (one variable) and the likelihood that they will later engage in workplace violence against coworkers or their boss (another variable). This correlation could be useful in identifying potentially dangerous people so that companies can avoid hiring them. Similarly, suppose that a correlation is observed between certain patterns of behavior in married couples (e.g., the tendency to criticize each other harshly) and the likelihood that they will later divorce. Again, this information might be helpful in counseling the people involved and perhaps, if it was what they desired, in saving their relationship (see Chapter 7 for a discussion of why long-term relationships sometimes fail.)

How accurately can such predictions be made? The stronger the correlation between the variables in question are, the more accurate the predictions are. Correlations can range from 0 to −1.00 or +1.00; the greater the departure from 0, the stronger the correlation. Positive numbers mean that as one variable increases, the other increases, too. Negative numbers indicate that as one variable increases, the other decreases. For instance, there is a negative correlation between age and the amount of hair on the heads of some males: The older they are, the less hair they have.

These basic facts underlie an important method of research sometimes used by social psychologists: the **correlational method.** In this approach, social psychologists attempt to determine whether, and to what extent, different variables are related to each other. This involves making careful observations of each variable and then performing appropriate statistical tests to determine whether and to what degree the variables are correlated. Perhaps a concrete example will help.

Imagine that a social psychologist wants to find out if, as common sense seems to suggest, people who are in a good mood are more likely to be helpful to others than people who are in a bad mood. How could research on this **hypothesis**—an as yet unverified prediction— be conducted? One basic approach would go something like this: The researcher might ask people to complete a questionnaire that measures their typical mood—how they usually feel

correlational method
A method of research in which a scientist systematically observes two or more variables to determine whether changes in one are accompanied by changes in the other.

hypothesis
An as yet unverified prediction concerning some aspect of social behavior or social thought.

Figure 1.11

Why Correlation Does *Not* Necessarily Mean Causation

Suppose that a correlation is found between mood and helping: The better people's moods are, the more instances of helping others they report. Does this mean that being in a good mood causes increased helpfulness? (Upper path) Not necessarily. As shown here, this finding may stem from the fact that people who are often in a good mood also tend to be friendlier than other people. This, in turn, encourages others to ask them for help. So they are more helpful not because they are in a good mood, but because of this other factor (their increased friendliness; Lower path). And to add yet another complication, helping others may cause boosts in our mood rather than vice versa (dotted arrow).

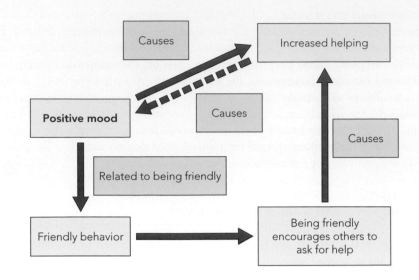

during the course of the day. (Our moods fluctuate greatly over time, in response to events in our lives; but there are also differences between people in how they feel most of the time, when nothing very good or bad is happening to them). Participants in the research would also be asked to report how many times they are helpful to others each day—how many times they do favors for them, make a donation to charity, and so on. If positive correlations are obtained between these two factors—between mood and helpfulness—this would provide evidence for the hypothesis that being in a good mood is indeed related to helping.

Suppose that this was the finding actually obtained in the research (e.g., a correlation of +0.51 between mood and helpfulness), what could we now conclude? That being in a good mood causes people to help others? Although it's tempting to jump to this conclusion, it may be totally false. Here's why: The fact that two variables are correlated in no way guarantees that changes in one cause changes in the other. On the contrary, the relationship between them may be the result of the fact that changes in both variables are related to a third variable (see Figure 1.11). For instance, in this case, it is possible that being in a good mood doesn't really make people more helpful; rather, it may simply be that people who are often in a good mood are friendlier than people who are not, and it is *this* factor that results in their showing higher levels of helpfulness. Why? Because their friendliness encourages others to ask them for favors or other kinds of help. After all, would you be more likely to ask a smiling person for a favor or one who is frowning? Thus the fact that people in a good mood engage in more helping than people not in a good mood may stem from this factor and not from any direct connection between mood and helpfulness.

There is still one further complication: It is also possible that helping others puts us in a good mood. In other words, it's not that being in a good mood causes increased helpfulness, but rather, helping produces boosts in our mood. Correlations simply tell us that two variables are related; they do not indicate the direction of these effects.

Despite this major drawback, the correlational method of research is sometimes useful to social psychologists. It can be used in natural settings, and it is often highly efficient: A large amount of information can be obtained in a relatively short period of time. However, the fact that it is generally not conclusive with respect to cause-and-effect relationships is a serious one, and one that leads social psychologists to prefer another method in many instances. It is to this approach that we turn next.

The Experimental Method: Knowledge through Systematic Intervention

As we have just seen, the correlational method of research is quite useful from the point of view of one important goal of science: making accurate predictions. It is less useful, though, from the point of view of attaining another important goal: explanation. This is sometimes known as the "why" question because scientists do not merely wish to describe the world and relationships between variables in it; they want to be able to explain these relationships, too.

To attain the goal of explanation, social psychologists employ a method of research known as **experimentation** or the **experimental method.** As the heading of this section suggests, experimentation involves the following strategy: One variable is changed systematically, and the effects of these changes on one or more other variables are carefully measured. If systematic changes in one variable produce changes in another variable (and if two additional conditions we'll describe next are also met), it is possible to conclude with reasonable certainty that there is indeed a causal relationship between these variables: that changes in one do indeed cause changes in the other. Because the experimental method is so valuable in answering this kind of question, it is frequently the method of choice in social psychology. But please bear in mind that there is no single "best" method of research. Rather, social psychologists, like all other scientists, choose the method that is most appropriate for studying a particular topic.

Experimentation: Its Basic Nature

In its most basic form, the experimental method involves two key steps: (1) the presence or strength of some variable believed to affect an aspect of social behavior or thought is systematically changed, and (2) the effects of such changes (if any) are carefully measured. The factor systematically varied by the researcher is termed the **independent variable,** while the aspect of behavior studied is termed the **dependent variable.** In a simple experiment, then, different groups of participants are exposed to contrasting levels of the independent variable (such as low, moderate, and high). The researcher then carefully measures their behavior to determine whether it does in fact vary with these changes in the independent variable. If it does—and if two other conditions are also met—the researcher can tentatively conclude that the independent variable does indeed cause changes in the aspect of behavior being studied.

To illustrate the basic nature of experimentation in social psychology, we'll use the following example. Suppose that a social psychologist is interested in the following question: Does exposure to guns increase the likelihood that people will aggress against others—not by using the guns, but in any way (e.g., verbally or by hitting them with one's hands)? Such a relationship has been suggested, especially by people who support strict regulation of firearms. How can this possibility be investigated by using the experimental method? Here is one possibility.

Participants in the experiment could be asked to examine either a gun or some other neutral object (e.g., a puzzle). An appropriate explanation for these activities could be readily provided; for instance, the experimenter might explain to participants that the study is designed to find out how readily people can write instructions for assembling or disassembling an object after examining it. After examining either the gun or the neutral object, participants in the research would be placed in a situation where they could, if they wished, aggress against another person. For instance, they could be told that the next part of the study is concerned with taste sensitivity and asked to add as much hot sauce as they wish to a glass of water that another person will drink. Participants would taste a sample in which only one drop of sauce has been placed in the glass, so they would know how hot the drink would be if they added more than one drop. Lots of sauce would make the drink so hot that it would truly hurt the person who consumed it.

If simple exposure to guns increases aggression against others, then participants who examine the weapon would use more hot sauce—and so inflict more pain on another

experimentation (experimental method)
A method of research in which one or more factors (the independent variables) are systematically changed to determine whether such variations affect one or more other factors (dependent variables).

independent variable
The variable that is systematically changed (i.e., varied) in an experiment.

dependent variable
The variable that is measured in an experiment.

random assignment of participants to experimental conditions
A basic requirement for conducting valid experiments. According to this principle, research participants must have an equal chance of being exposed to each level of the independent variable.

person—than participants who examined the puzzle. If results indicate that this is the case, then the researcher could conclude, at least tentatively, that mere exposure to guns does increase aggression. The researcher can offer this conclusion because if the study was done correctly, the only difference between the experiences of the two groups in the study is that one handled a gun, while the other handled a puzzle for the same amount of time. As a result, any difference in their behavior (in their aggression) must be as a result of this factor. It's important to note that in experimentation, the independent variable—in this case, exposure to a gun or puzzle—is systematically changed by the researcher. In the correlational method, in contrast, variables are not altered in this manner; rather, naturally occurring changes in them are simply observed and recorded.

Experimentation: Two Key Requirements for Its Success

Previously, we referred to two conditions that must be met before a researcher can conclude that changes in an independent variable have caused changes in a dependent variable. Let's consider these conditions now. The first involves what is termed **random assignment of participants to experimental conditions.** This means that all participants in an experiment must have an equal chance of being exposed to each level of the independent variable. The reason for this rule is simple: If participants are not randomly assigned to each condition, it may later be impossible to determine if differences in their behavior stem from differences they brought with them to the study, from the impact of the independent variable, or both. For instance, imagine that in the study on handling guns, all the people assigned to handle the gun come from a Judo club—they practice martial arts regularly—while all those assigned to handle the puzzle come from a knitting club. If those who handle the gun show higher levels of aggression, what does this tell us? Not much. The difference between the two groups could come from the fact that individuals who already show strong tendencies toward aggression handled the guns, while individuals who show weaker tendencies toward aggression handled the puzzle. As result, we can't tell why any differences between them occurred; we have violated random assignment of participants to experimental treatments and that makes the results virtually meaningless.

Figure 1.12
Confounding of Variables: A Fatal Flaw in Experimentation
In a hypothetical experiment designed to investigate the effects of handling a gun or a toy on aggression, the independent variable is confounded with another variable, the behavior of the assistants conducting the study. One assistant is kind and polite, and the other is rude and surly. The friendly assistant collects most of the data in the toy condition, while the rude assistant collects most of the data in the gun condition. The result is that if the participants who handle the gun are more aggressive, we can't tell whether this is a result of handling the gun or the assistant's rude treatment. The two variables are confounded, and the experiment doesn't provide useful information on the issue it is designed to study.

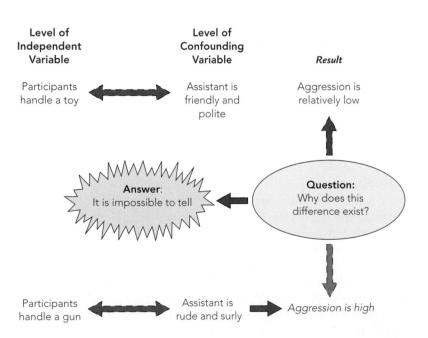

The second condition essential for successful experimentation is as follows: Insofar as possible, all factors, other than the independent variable, that might also affect participants' behavior must be held constant. To see why this is so, consider what will happen if, in the study on handling guns or puzzles, two assistants collect the data. One is kind and friendly, and the other is rude and surly. By random luck, the rude assistant collects most of the data for the gun condition, and the polite one collects most of the data for the puzzle condition. Again, suppose that participants who handle the gun are more aggressive toward another person. What do the findings tell us? Again, virtually nothing because we can't tell whether it was handling the gun or the rude treatment they received from the assistant that produced higher aggression. In situations like this, the independent variable is said to be *confounded* with another variable—one that is not under systematic investigation in the study. When such confounding occurs, the findings of an experiment may be largely uninterpretable (see Figure 1.12).

In sum, experimentation is, in several respects, the crown jewel among social psychologist's methods. It certainly isn't perfect; for example, because it is often conducted in laboratory settings that are quite different from the locations in which social behavior actually occurs, the question of **external validity** often arises: To what extent can the findings of experiments be generalized to real-life social situations and perhaps people different from those who participated in the research? And there are situations where it can't be used because of ethical or legal considerations. For instance, it would clearly be unethical to expose certain individuals to a kind of television programming that we believe will cause them to harm themselves or randomly assign people to marry someone. But in situations in which it is appropriate and is used with skill and care, the experimental method can yield results that help us to answer complex questions about social behavior and social thought. However, please keep the following basic point in mind: there is no single best method of conducting research in social psychology. Rather, all methods offer advantages and disadvantages, so the guiding principle is that the method that is most appropriate to answering the questions being investigated is the one that should be used.

Further Thoughts on Causality: The Role of Mediating Variables

We noted previously that social psychologists often use experimentation because it is helpful in answering questions about causality: Do changes in one variable produce (cause) changes in another? That is a valuable kind of information to have because it helps us understand what events, thoughts, or situations lead to various outcomes—more or less helping, more or less aggression, more or less prejudice. Often, though, social psychologists take experimentation one step further in their efforts to answer the question *why?*— to understand why one variable produces changes in another. For instance, returning to the study in handling a gun or puzzle, it is reasonable to ask "Why does handling a gun increase aggression?" Because it induces increased thoughts about harming others? Reminds people of real or imagined wrongs they have suffered at the hands of other people? Or is something else involved?

To get at this question of underlying processes, social psychologists often conduct studies in which they measure not only a single dependent variable, but also other factors that they believe to be at work—factors that are influenced by the independent variable and then, in turn, affect the dependent measures. Actually, the study in handling guns just described provides a clear example of such research because in a recent study, these procedures have been precisely used to determine if handling guns generates an increase in testosterone (a male sexual hormone that has been found to be related to aggression). Increases in testosterone, in turn, increase aggression. If this is so, then testosterone level

external validity
The extent to which findings of an experiment can be generalized to real-life social situations and perhaps to people different from those who participated in the research.

mediating variable
A variable that is affected by an independent variable and then influences a dependent variable. Mediating variables help explain why or how specific variables influence social behavior or thought in certain ways.

is a **mediating variable** that helps explain why handling a gun leads to increased aggression against others.

To test this hypothesis, researchers conducted a study in which a participant's level of testosterone was measured at the start of the study and then again after handling either a gun or a toy (Klinesmith, Kasser, & McAndrew, 2006). (This is easy to do because testosterone level can be assessed from a sample of saliva.) Results provided clear support for the mediating role of testosterone. Participants who handled a gun for fifteen minutes showed an increase in testosterone and also an increase in aggression. All male participants who handled a toy for the same amount of time showed no increase in testosterone and a lower level of aggression (see Figure 1.13).

Through procedures like these, social psychologists attempt to determine not only which variables influence specific aspects of social behavior, but also why and how they produce such effects. By extending experimentation in this manner, in other words, they can gain added insights into many aspects of social behavior and social thought—and that is certainly the central goal of the entire field.

The Role of Theory in Social Psychology

There is one more aspect of social psychological research we should consider before concluding. As we noted previously, in their research, social psychologists seek to do more than simply describe the world: They want to be able to explain it, too. For instance, social psychologists don't want to merely state that racial prejudice is common in the United States; they want to be able to explain why some people are more prejudiced toward a particular group than are others. In social psychology, as in all branches of sci-

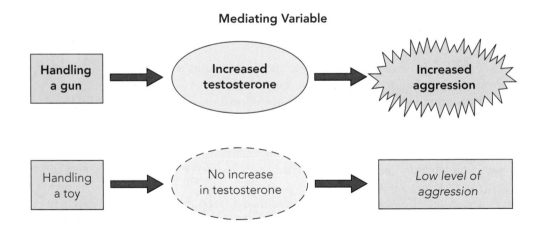

Figure 1.13
Mediation: Insights into How One Variable Affects Another
To find out how an independent variable influences some aspect of social behavior or social thought (a dependent variable), social psychologists often conduct research designed to identify mediating variables. In one recent study, it was found that handling a gun produced increments in testosterone; testosterone, in turn, increased aggression among male participants. In contrast, handling a toy did not produce an increase in testosterone, so aggression was lower.

(*Source:* Based on findings reported by Klinesmith, Kasser, & McAndrew, 2006).

ence, explanation involves the construction of **theories**—frameworks for explaining various events or processes. The procedure involved in building a theory goes something like this:

1. On the basis of existing evidence, a theory that reflects this evidence is proposed.

2. This theory, which consists of basic concepts and statements about how these concepts are related, helps to organize existing information and makes predictions about observable events. For instance, the theory might predict the conditions under which individuals acquire racial prejudice.

3. These predictions, known as hypotheses, are then tested by actual research.

4. If results are consistent with the theory, confidence in its accuracy is increased. If they are not, the theory is modified and further tests are conducted.

5. Ultimately, the theory is either accepted as accurate or rejected as inaccurate. Even if it is accepted as accurate, however, the theory remains open to further refinement as improved methods of research are developed and additional evidence relevant to the theory's predictions is obtained.

This may sound a bit abstract, so let's turn to a concrete example. Suppose that a social psychologist formulates the following theory: When people believe that they hold a view that is in the minority, they will be slower to state it (something known as

theories
Efforts by scientists in any field to answer the question "Why?" Theories involve attempts to understand why certain events or processes occur as they do.

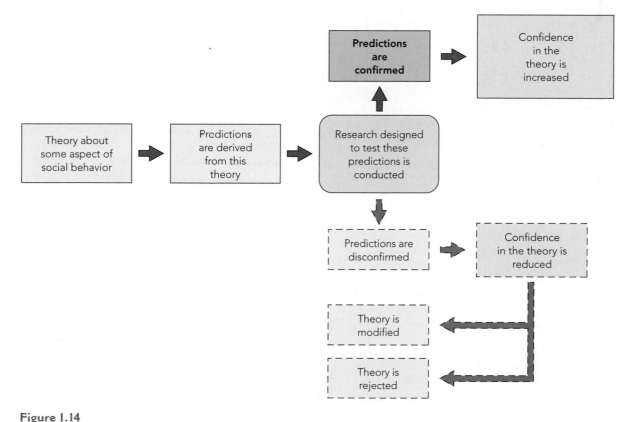

Figure 1.14
The Role of Theory in Social Psychological Research
Theories both organize existing knowledge and make predictions about how various events or processes will occur. Once a theory is formulated, hypotheses derived logically from it are tested through careful research. If results agree with the predictions, confidence in the theory is increased. If results disagree with such predictions, the theory may be modified or ultimately rejected as false.

the *minority slowness* effect), and this stems not only from the strength of their views, but also from reluctance to state minority opinions publicly where others will hear and perhaps disapprove of them for holding those views. This theory would lead to specific predictions; for instance, the minority slowness effect will be reduced if people can state their opinions privately (e.g., Bassili, 2003). If research findings are consistent with this prediction and with others derived from the theory, confidence in the theory is increased. If findings are not consistent with the theory, it will be modified or perhaps rejected.

This process of formulating a theory, testing it, modifying the theory, testing it again, and so on lies close to the core of the scientific method, so it is an important aspect of social psychological research (see Figure 1.14 on page 29). Thus many different theories relating to important aspects of social behavior and social thought will be presented in this book.

Two final points: First, theories are never proven in any final, ultimate sense. Rather, they are always open to test and are accepted with more or less confidence depending on the weight of available evidence. Second, research is not undertaken to prove or verify a theory; it is performed to gather evidence relevant to the theory. If a researcher sets out to prove their pet theory, this is a serious violation of the principles of scientific skepticism, objectivity, and open-mindedness described on page 6.

> **⌒Principles to Remember**
>
> The fact that two variables are correlated does not necessarily mean that changes in one cause changes in the other. In fact, both could be related to a third variable and may not be directly linked to each other.

⌒KeyPoints

- With systematic observation, behavior is carefully observed and recorded. In naturalistic observation, such observations are made in settings where the behavior naturally occurs.

- Survey methods often involve large numbers of people who are asked to respond to questions about their attitudes or behavior.

- When the correlational method of research is employed, two or more variables are measured to determine how they might be related to one another.

- The existence of even strong correlations between variables does not indicate that they are causally related to each other.

- Experimentation involves systematically altering one or more variables (independent variables) to determine whether changes in this variable affect some aspect of behavior (dependent variables).

- Successful use of the experimental method requires random assignment of participants to conditions and holding all other factors that might

also influence behavior constant so as to avoid confounding of variables.

- Although it is a very powerful research tool, the experimental method is not perfect—questions concerning the external validity of findings so obtained often arise. Further, it cannot be used in some situations because of practical or ethical considerations.

- Research designed to investigate mediating variables adds to understanding of how specific variables influence certain aspects of social behavior or social thought.

- Theories are frameworks for explaining various events or processes. They play a key role in social psychological research.

Think About It

Why does the experimental method of research often provide evidence about social behavior and thought that is more informative than systematic observation or the correlational approach?

The Quest for Knowledge and the Rights of Individuals: Seeking an Appropriate Balance

In their use of experimentation, correlation, and systematic observation, social psychologists do not differ from researchers in other fields. One technique, however, does seem to be unique to research in social psychology: **deception.** This technique involves efforts by researchers to withhold or conceal information about the purposes of a study from participants. The reason for doing so is simple: Many social psychologists believe that if participants know the true purposes of a study, their behavior in it will be changed by that knowledge. Thus the research will not yield valid information about social behavior or social thought.

Some kinds of research do seem to require the use of temporary deception. For example, consider, the minority slowness effect previously described. If participants know that the purpose of a study is to investigate this effect, isn't it likely that they might lean over backwards to avoid showing it? Similarly, consider a study of the effects of physical appearance on attraction between strangers. Again, if participants know that the researcher is interested in this topic, they might work hard to avoid being influenced by a stranger's appearance. In this and many other cases, social psychologists feel compelled to employ temporary deception in their research (Suls & Rosnow, 1988). However the use of deception raises important ethical issues that cannot be ignored.

First, there is the chance, however, slim, that deception may result in some kind of harm to the persons exposed to it. They may be upset by the procedures used or by their own reactions to them. For example, in several studies concerned with helping in emergencies, participants were exposed to seemingly real emergency situations. For instance, they overheard what seemed to be a medical emergency—another person having an apparent seizure (e.g., Darley & Latané, 1968). Many participants were strongly upset by these staged events, and others were disturbed by the fact that although they recognized the need to help, they failed to do so. Clearly, the fact that participants experienced emotional upset raises complex ethical issues about just how far researchers can go when studying even very important topics such as this one.

We should hasten to emphasize that such research represents an extreme use of deception: Generally, deception takes much milder forms. For example, participants may receive a request for help from a stranger who is actually an assistant of the researchers; or they may be informed that most other students in their university hold certain views when in fact they do not. Still, even in such cases, the potential for some kind of harmful effects to participants exists, and this is a potentially serious drawback to the use of deception.

Second, there is the possibility that participants will resent being "fooled" during a study, and as a result, they will acquire negative attitudes toward social psychology and psychological research in general; for instance, they may become suspicious about information presented by researchers (Kelman, 1967). To the extent such reactions occur—and recent findings indicate, at least to a degree, that they do (Epley & Huff, 1998)—they have disturbing implications for the future of social psychology, which places so much emphasis on scientific research.

Because of such possibilities, the use of deception poses something of a dilemma to social psychologists. On the one hand, it seems essential to their research. On the other, its use raises serious problems. How can this issue be resolved? While opinion remains somewhat divided, most social psychologists agree on the following points. First, deception should never be used to persuade people to take part in a study; withholding information about what will happen in an experiment or providing misleading information to induce people to take part in it is definitely not acceptable (Sigall, 1997). Second, most social psychologists agree that temporary deception may sometimes be acceptable provided

deception
A technique whereby researchers withhold information about the purposes or procedures of a study from people participating in it.

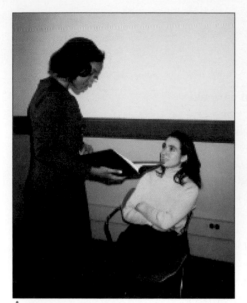

Figure 1.15
Career Debriefing: A
Requirement in Studies
Using Deception
*After an experimental session
is completed, participants
should be provided with
thorough debriefing—full
information about the
experiment's goals and the
reasons why temporary
deception was used. Thorough
debriefing should also be
provided even if deception
was not used.*

informed consent
A procedure in which research
participants are provided with as
much information as possible
about a research project before
deciding whether to participate
in it.

debriefing
Procedures at the conclusion
of a research session in which
participants are given full
information about the nature of
the research and the hypothesis
or hypotheses under
investigation.

two basic safeguards are employed. One of these is **informed consent**—giving participants as much information as possible about the procedures to be followed before they make their decision to participate. In short, this is the opposite of withholding information to persuade people to participate. The second is careful **debriefing**—providing participants with a full description of the purposes of a study after they have participated in it (see Figure 1.15). Such information should also include an explanation of deception and why it was necessary to employ it.

Fortunately, existing evidence indicates that together informed consent and thorough debriefing can substantially reduce the potential dangers of deception (Smith & Richardson, 1985). For example, most participants report that they view temporary deception as acceptable, provided that potential benefits outweigh potential costs and if there is no other means of obtaining the information sought (Rogers, 1980; Sharpe, Adair, & Roese, 1992). However, as we noted previously, there is some indication that they do become somewhat more suspicious about what researchers tell them during an experiment; even worse, such increased suspiciousness seems to last over several months (Epley & Huff, 1998).

Overall, then, it appears that most research participants do not react negatively to temporary deception as long as its purpose and necessity are clear. However, these findings do not mean that the safety or appropriateness of deception should be taken for granted (Rubin 1985). On the contrary, the guiding principles for all researchers planning to use this procedure should be: (1) Use deception only when it is absolutely essential to do so—when no other means for conducting the research exists; (2) always proceed with caution; and (3) make certain that every possible precaution is taken to protect the rights, safety, and well-being of research participants. In terms of the latter, all universities in the United States that receive federal funding must have an institutional review board to review the ethics, including a cost-benefit analysis when deception is to be employed, for all proposed research involving human participants.

Getting the Most Out of This Book: A User's Guide

A textbook that is hard to read or understand is like a dull tool: It really can't do what it is designed to do well. Being well aware of this fact, we have tried our best to make this book easy to read and have included a number of features designed to make it more enjoyable—and useful—for you. Here is an overview of the steps we've taken to make reading this book a pleasant and informative experience.

First, each chapter begins with an outline of the topics to be covered. This is followed by a chapter-opening story that "sets the stage" and explains how the topics to be covered are related to important aspects of our everyday lives. Within each chapter, key terms are printed in **dark type like this** and are followed by a definition. These terms are also defined in a running glossary in the margins and in a glossary at the end of the book. To help you understand what you have read, each major section is followed by a list of *Key Points,* which is a brief summary of major points and one or more critical thinking questions (*Think About It*). All figures and tables are clear and simple, and most contain special labels and notes designed to help you understand them (see Figure 1.8 for an example). Finally, each chapter ends with a *Summary and Review*. Reviewing this section can be an important aid to your studying.

Second, this book has an underlying theme that can be stated as follows: Social psychology is much more than just a collection of interesting findings to be enjoyed for the moment, recalled on tests, and then quickly forgotten. On the contrary, it provides a new way of looking at the social world that everyone should use long after the course is over. To emphasize this theme, we have included two special features, which appear in each chapter. One of these is *What Social Psychology Tells Us about . . .* These sections illustrate how the findings and principles of social psychology are all around us and relate to everything from current events in the news, to popular movies, television shows, and the Internet.

The second type of special section is *Making Sense of Common Sense: A Social Psychological Perspective.* These sections are designed to highlight how the scientific approach taken by social psychology has helped to resolve—or at least clarify—the contradictions often contained in common sense. Does absence make the heart grow fonder or is it a case of out of sight out of mind? Does blowing off steam (expressing anger and aggressive impulses) help reduce these feelings? When a judge says to a jury: "Disregard that information," can the jurors really do that? We'll examine these and many other instances in which social psychology has helped resolve questions that have persisted down through the ages.

A third feature included in every chapter is designed to highlight classic work in the field—research and theory that had a strong and lasting impact on later work. Such sections are *Building the Science: Classics of Social Psychology.* Understanding the past, it has often been said, is a key to knowing the present and predicting the future. We agree, and for this reason, want to highlight these important past contributions—ones that truly *did* provide the foundations of modern social psychology.

Yet another feature that we believe will help enhance the benefits you derive from your first contact with social psychology is *Principles to Remember*. These are key ideas that you will take with you—and use—in your own lives. In this way, we believe, you will continue to benefit from your first exposure to social psychology long after this course is over.

Finally, to help you understand how research in each area of social psychology is related to research in other areas, we've included a special *Connections* table at the end of each chapter. These tables provide a kind of global review, reminding you of related topics discussed elsewhere in the book. In addition, they emphasize the fact that many aspects of social behavior and thought are closely linked; they do not occur in isolation from each other.

We think that together, these features will help you get the most out of this book and from your first contact with social psychology. Good luck! And may your first encounter with our field prove to be a rich, informative, and valuable experience—and also, we hope—fun!

KeyPoints

- Deception involves efforts by social psychologists to withhold or conceal information about the purposes of a study from participants.

- Most social psychologists believe that temporary deception is often necessary to obtain valid research results.

- However, they view deception as acceptable only when important safeguards are employed: informed consent and thorough debriefing.

Think About It

Have you ever participated in a psychological experiment? If so, what was the debriefing like? Did it provide you with a clear understanding of the purposes of the study?

SUMMARY AND REVIEW

- Social psychology is the scientific field that seeks to understand the nature and causes of individual behavior and thought in social situations. It is scientific in nature because it adopts the values and methods used in other fields of science. Social psychologists adopt the scientific method because common sense provides an unreliable guide to social behavior and because our thought is influenced by many potential sources of bias. Social psychology focuses on the behavior of individuals and seeks to understand the causes of social behavior and thought, which can involve social interaction, social cognition, environmental factors, cultural values, and biological factors.

- Social psychologists currently recognize that social thought and social behavior are two sides of the same coin, and that there is a continuous complex interplay between them. Another major direction in the field involves growing interest in social neuroscience— efforts to relate activity in the brain and other biological events to key aspects of social thought and behavior. Our behavior and thought is often shaped by factors of which we are unaware. Growing attention to such implicit (nonconscious) processes is another major theme of modern social psychology. Social psychology currently adopts a multicultural perspective. This perspective recognizes the importance of cultural factors in social behavior and social thought.

- To answer questions about social behavior and social thought, social psychologists use a variety of research methods. In systematic observation, behavior is carefully observed and recorded. In the survey method, large numbers of people respond to questions about their attitudes or behavior. In the correlational method of research, two or more variables are measured to determine if they are related to one another in any way.

- The existence of even strong correlations between variables does not indicate that they are causally related to each other. Experimentation involves systematically altering one or more variables (independent variables) to determine whether changes in this variable affect some aspect of behavior (dependent variables). Successful use of the experimental method requires random assignment of participants to conditions and holding all other factors that might also influence behavior constant so as to avoid confounding of variables. Although it is a very powerful research tool, the experimental method is not perfect—questions concerning its external validity often arise. Research designed to investigate mediating variables adds to understanding of how specific variables influence certain aspects of social behavior or social thought. Theories are frameworks for explaining various events or processes.

- Deception involves efforts by social psychologists to withhold or conceal information about the purposes of a study from participants. Most social psychologists believe that temporary deception is often necessary to obtain valid research results. However, they view deception as acceptable only when important safeguards are employed: informed consent and thorough debriefing.

Key Terms

correlational method (p. 23)

debriefing (p. 32)

deception (p. 31)

dependent variable (p. 25)

evolutionary psychology (p. 11)

experimentation (experimental method) (p. 25)

external validity (p. 27)

hypothesis (p. 23)

independent variable (p. 25)

informed consent (p. 32)

mediating variable (p. 28)

multicultural perspective (p. 18)

random assignment of participants to experimental conditions (p. 26)

social neuroscience (p. 15)

social psychology (p. 6)

survey method (p. 22)

systematic observation (p. 21)

theories (p. 29)

Social Cognition
How We Think about the Social World

2

CHAPTER OUTLINE

- **Schemas: Mental Frameworks for Organizing—and Using—Social Information**
  The Impact of Schemas on Social Cognition: Attention, Encoding, and Retrieval
  Priming: Which Schemas Guide Our Thought?
  Schema Persistence: Why Even Discredited Schemas Can Sometimes Influence Our Thought and Behavior
  BUILDING THE SCIENCE: CLASSICS OF SOCIAL PSYCHOLOGY—THE SELF-CONFIRMING NATURE OF SCHEMAS: WHEN—AND WHY—BELIEFS SHAPE REALITY

- **Heuristics: How We Reduce Our Effort in Social Cognition**
  Representativeness: Judging by Resemblance
  Availability: "If I Can Think of It, It Must Be Important"
  Anchoring and Adjustment: Where You Begin Makes a Difference

- **Automatic and Controlled Processing: Two Basic Modes of Social Thought**
  Automatic Processing and Automatic Social Behavior

The Benefits of Automatic Processing: Beyond Mere Efficiency

- **Potential Sources of Error in Social Cognition: Why Total Rationality Is Rarer Than You Think**
  Basic "Tilts" in Social Thought: The Negativity Bias and Our Powerful Tendency to Be Overly Optimistic
  SOCIAL PSYCHOLOGY: WHAT IT TELLS US ABOUT . . . THE WAR IN IRAQ: DID THE OPTIMISTIC BIAS PLAY A ROLE?
  Situation-Specific Sources of Error in Social Cognition: Counterfactual Thinking, Thought Suppression, and Magical Thinking
  Social Cognition: Some Optimistic Conclusions

- **Affect and Cognition: How Feelings Shape Thought and Thought Shapes Feelings**
  The Influence of Affect on Cognition
  The Influence of Cognition on Affect
  Affect and Cognition: Social Neuroscience Evidence for Two Separate Systems
  MAKING SENSE OF COMMON SENSE: A SOCIAL PSYCHOLOGICAL PERSPECTIVE—IS BEING IN A GOOD MOOD ALWAYS BENEFICIAL? THE POTENTIAL DOWNSIDE OF BEING UP

More than twenty years ago, I decided to sell an old car that was beginning to be more trouble than it was worth. The car in question was a Toyota, and although Toyota has a reputation for producing amazingly reliable cars, this one had become a perpetual problem. It broke down on several long trips, and even worse, the car was rusting badly, and the paint was peeling in many spots. As a result, I spent many hours filling in small rust holes as they developed and applying touch-up paint to the repairs. After many months of this repeated chore, I had enough and decided to sell the car. I placed an ad in the local newspaper (the Internet didn't exist yet), and soon I received several phone inquiries. Without any detailed thinking, I set the asking price higher than what I really hoped to get, to leave me some room for negotiation. But the first person who came to look at the car threw me a major curve. After driving it and listening to my explanation about the rust, paint, and other problems, he said: "OK, I'll take it." Without thinking, I blurted out: "You mean, you'll pay the full price?" When he said yes, I again responded quickly and without any careful thought, "No, that's too much," I said. "It's really only worth [and I named a reduced figure]—that's all I really want." His response, too, was immediate; I could literally see the doubt and worry creep onto his face, and after a moment, he said: "Well . . . I don't know . . . Now, I think I have to get the car inspected by my mechanic." In other words, he responded to my effort to be fair and honest with mistrust!

Ultimately, the story had a happy ending: He had the car inspected and because I had been honest about all its problems, the mechanic gave him the "OK," and he bought the car for a price several hundred dollars less than what I had asked. But I'll never forget the look of doubt and worry on his face when he handed me his check and took the keys . . .

social cognition
The manner in which we interpret, analyze, remember, and use information about the social world.

Selling a used car . . . what, you may be wondering, does this have to do with the major focus of this chapter, **social cognition**—how we think about the social world, try to understand it, and understand ourselves and our place in it (e.g., Bargh, 1999; Higgins & Kruglanski, 1996). The answer is simple: This incident actually captures many of the key issues relating to social cognition that we will examine in the rest of this chapter. First, it suggests strongly that often our thinking about the social world proceeds on "automatic"—quickly, effortlessly, and without lots of careful reasoning or logic. For instance, when I chose an asking price, I didn't sit down and do any careful mathematical calculations; I simply asked a little more than I really hoped to get from a buyer. And when a potential buyer agreed to this price, I didn't have to stop and think carefully about what to do: I *knew*, instantly, that it would be wrong to accept this much from him; it would violate my own personal standards of fairness. As we'll see later, such automatic thought or automatic processing offers important advantages; it requires little or no effort and can be efficient. But as the cartoon in Figure 2.1 suggests, there are situations in which it occurs, and we are not sure that this is beneficial.

This incident also illustrates another important fact about social thought: Often it is guided by cognitive frameworks we have acquired through past experience. I already had such a framework (these are called schemas) for selling something to a stranger, and it guided my thinking (e.g., my asking a higher price than I really expected to receive) and my actions (placing an ad, letting potential buyers take the car for a test drive, and so on). The buyer, too, was guided in his thinking by cognitive frameworks—although, as we'll note later, his frameworks were different from mine in important ways.

A third point this used car incident illustrates is perhaps a very central one: Although we do lots of social thought on automatic, we do sometimes stop and think much more carefully and logically about it. Such controlled processing, as social psychologists term it, tends to occur when a situation is important to us or when something unexpected happens—something that jolts us out of automatic, effortless thought. When the buyer offered me the full asking price and I said "No, that's too much . . ." I certainly jolted him out of automatic modes of thought. He stopped, considered my action carefully, and quickly decided that this was a warning signal, that he could not really trust me, and should think carefully about the present situation. As we'll see in later sections, unexpected events often trigger such careful, effortful thought.

Figure 2.1
Social Cognition: Often, It Proceeds on Automatic
As suggested by this cartoon, our thinking about the social world often proceeds in a relatively effortless, automatic manner. That offers important advantages of speed and efficiency, but in some situations—such as the one shown here—it may not be the best course or the one we really want to follow.

(*Source: The New Yorker*, December 19, 2005.)

"I can't remember what we're arguing about, either. Let's keep yelling, and maybe it will come back to us."

Finally, the fact that the buyer and I had somewhat different cognitive frameworks, or expectations, for this situation illustrates another important point: People from different cultures often have different schemas (cognitive frameworks) for the same situation and so tend to understand them differently. I grew up in a large city where everyone bargained about everything, so I fully expected that the buyer would suggest a lower price than the one advertised in my ad. I later learned, however, that he had grown up in a small, rural town where people did not typically bargain. As a result, he expected that he would either pay the price asked or look for another car.

In the remainder of this chapter, we'll examine each of these ideas in detail and describe the careful research conducted by social psychologists on which they are based. Specifically, we'll proceed as follows. First, we'll return to the basic component of social thought mentioned above—schemas. **Schemas** are mental frameworks that allow us to organize large amounts of information in an efficient manner. Once formed, these frameworks exert strong effects on social thought; effects that are not always beneficial from the point of view of accuracy. Second, we'll consider **heuristics,** which are simple rules of thumb we often use to make decisions or draw inferences quickly and with minimal effort. In other words, heuristics are another means of reducing cognitive effort, the mental work we must do to make sense out of the social world (e.g., Kunda, 1999). After discussing heuristics, we'll return to the fact that often social thought occurs in an automatic manner. In other words, it often unfolds in a quick and relatively effortless manner rather than in a careful, systematic, and effortful one. After considering that point, we'll examine several specific tendencies or "tilts" in social thought—tendencies that can lead us to false conclusions about others or to additional errors in our efforts to understand the social world. Finally, we'll focus on the complex interplay between **affect**—our current feelings or moods—and various aspects of social cognition (e.g., Forgas, 1995a; 2000). Note that we will also examine important aspects of social thought in Chapter 3, which considers several aspects of person perception (how we perceive others and try to understand them), and in Chapter 5, which examines key aspects of our social self.

Schemas: Mental Frameworks for Organizing— and Using—Social Information

What happens when you visit your doctor? Probably something like this: You enter and sign in. Then you sit and wait. If you are lucky, the wait is not long, and a nurse takes you into an examining room. Once there, you wait some more. Eventually, the doctor enters, talks to you about how you're feeling, and likely examines you. Finally, you leave and perhaps pay some part of your bill (the co-pay) on the way out. It doesn't matter who your doctor is or where you live—this sequence of events, or something like it, will take place. None of this surprises you; in fact, you expect these events to occur—including the waiting. Why? Because through past experience, you have built up a mental structure or framework for this kind of situation—visiting a doctor. Similarly, you have other mental structures for going to restaurants, working in the library, shopping for groceries, going to the movies (see Figure 2.2 on page 40), or as noted in the chapter opening example, for selling a used car.

But you don't simply have such frameworks for specific situations; you also have them for people, occupations, social roles, specific social groups, and many other aspects of the social world. In each case, your experience has allowed you to build up a mental framework that helps you to organize your knowledge and assumptions about each of these subjects or themes—about the situations, people, or social groups in question. Social psychologists term such frameworks as schemas and define them as mental structures that help us to organize social information and that guide the processing of such information. Because your personal experience is probably similar to that of other people in your culture in many respects, all people in a given society tend to share certain basic schemas. For instance, in the United States, most people have similar schemas for eating in a restaurant; they all expect a similar sequence of events in this setting. But in other ways, schemas may vary from one person to the next, reflecting unique life experiences. Once they are formed,

schemas
Mental frameworks centering on a specific theme that help us to organize social information.

heuristics
Simple rules for making complex decisions or drawing inferences in a rapid manner and seemingly effortless manner.

affect
Our current feelings and moods.

Figure 2.2

Schemas: Mental Frameworks for Organizing Information about the Social World

Through experience, we acquire schemas—mental frameworks for organizing, interpreting, and processing social information. For instance, you almost certainly have well-developed schemas for such events as going to the doctor (left) and going to the movies (right). In other words, you know what to expect in these and many other situations and are prepared to behave in them in certain ways.

schemas play a role in determining what we notice about the social world, what information we remember, and how we use and interpret such information. Let's take a closer look at these effects because they exert an important impact on our understanding of the social world and ultimately our relations with other people.

The Impact of Schemas on Social Cognition: Attention, Encoding, and Retrieval

How do schemas influence social thought? Research findings suggest that they influence three basic processes: attention, encoding, and retrieval. Attention refers to what information we notice. Encoding refers to the processes through which information we notice gets stored in memory. Finally, retrieval refers to the processes through which we recover information from memory to use it in some manner—for example, in making judgments about other people.

Schemas have been found to influence all of these aspects of social cognition (Wyer & Srull, 1994). With respect to attention, schemas often act as a kind of filter: Information consistent with them is more likely to be noticed and to enter our consciousness. Information that does not fit with our schemas is often ignored (Fiske, 1993), unless it is so extreme that we can't help but notice it. And even then, it is often discounted as the "exception that proves the rule."

Turning to encoding, which refers to the specific information that is entered into memory, the information that becomes the focus of our attention is much more likely to be stored in long-term memory. So again, in general, it is information that is consistent with our schemas that is encoded. However information that is sharply inconsistent with our schemas—information that does not agree with our expectations in a given situation—may sometimes be encoded into a separate memory location and marked with a unique "tag." After all, it is so unexpected that it literally seizes our attention and almost forces us to make a mental note of it (Stangor & McMillan, 1992). Here's an example: You have a well-developed schema for the role of professor. You expect professors to come to class, to lecture, to answer questions, to give and grade exams, and so on. Suppose that one of your professors comes to class and instead of lecturing, does magic tricks. You will certainly remember these experiences because they are so inconsistent with your schema for professors—your mental framework for what professors do and say.

That leads to the third process: retrieval from memory. What information is most readily remembered? Is it information that is consistent with our schemas or information that is inconsistent with these mental frameworks? This is a complex question that has been investigated in many different studies (e.g., Stangor & McMillan, 1992). Overall, this research suggests that people tend to report remembering and using information that is consistent with schemas to a greater extent than information that is inconsistent. This could potentially stem from differences in actual memory, or alternatively, from simple response tendencies. In other words, information that is inconsistent with schemas might be present in memory as strongly or even more strongly than information consistent with schemas, but people simply tend to report (describe) information consistent with their schemas. In fact, the latter appears to be the case. When measures of memory are corrected for this response tendency or when individuals are asked to actually recall information rather than simply use it or indicate whether they recognize it, a strong tendency to remember information that is incongruent (i.e., does not fit) with schemas appears. So, there is no simple answer to the question—Which do we remember better—information consistent or inconsistent with our schemas or expectations? Rather, this depends on the measure of memory employed. In general, people report information consistent with their schemas, but in fact, information inconsistent with schemas may be strongly present in memory, too.

At this point, it's important to note that the effects of schemas on social cognition (e.g., how we then use the information we notice and remember to make decisions or judgments) are strongly influenced by several other factors. For instance, such effects are stronger when schemas are themselves strong and well developed (e.g., Stangor & McMillan, 1992; Tice, Bratslavky, & Baumeiseter, 2000) and stronger when cognitive load—how much mental effort we are expending at a given time—is high rather than low (e.g., Kunda, 1999). In other words, when we are trying to handle a lot of information at one time, we rely on our schemas because they help us process this information efficiently.

Priming: Which Schemas Guide Our Thought?

As a result of our rich and varied experiences, we all develop a large array of schemas—cognitive frameworks that help us interpret and use social information. That raises an interesting question: Which of these frameworks influence our thought at any given point in time? One answer involves the strength of various schemas: The stronger and more well developed schemas are, the more likely they are to influence our thinking and especially our memory for social information (e.g., Stangor & McMillan, 1992; Tice et al., 2000).

Second, schemas can be temporarily activated by what is known as **priming**—transitory increases in the ease which specific schemas can be activated produced by experiences relevant to the schemas (e.g., Sparrow & Wegner, 2006). For instance, suppose you have just seen a violent movie. Now, you are looking for a parking spot near a shopping mall. You notice a spot, but another driver turns in front of you and takes it first. Do you perceive her behavior as aggressive? Because you have just had an experience that activated your schema for aggressive actions, you may, in fact, be more likely to perceive the driver taking the parking spot as aggressive, more so than if you had seen a comedy film instead. This illustrates the effects of priming; recent experiences make some schemas more active than they would otherwise be, and as a result, they exert stronger effects on current thinking.

How powerful is priming? One recent study suggests that priming effects are not temporary; in fact, in this study, people who had seen specific black-and-white drawings as part of a psychology experiment were actually more likely to recognize portions of these drawings *fully seventeen years later* more so than people who had never seen the original drawings (Mitchell, 2006)! This study and similar findings in other studies—ones that used somewhat shorter period of time (e.g., Budson & Price, 2005)—suggest that priming tends to have long lasting effects once it occurs. Fortunately, however, other evidence indicates that it *can* be deactivated by something social psychologists describe as **unpriming.** What unpriming means is that if some thoughts or actions are primed by a

priming
It is a situation that occurs when stimuli or events increase the availability in memory or consciousness of specific types of information held in memory.

unpriming
Refers to the fact that the effects of the schemas tend to persist until they are somehow expressed in thought or behavior and only then do their effects decrease.

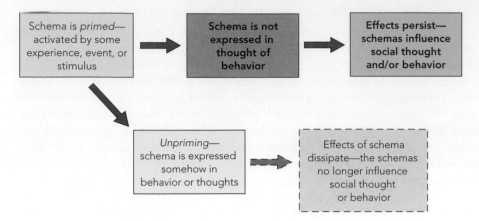

Figure 2.3

Unpriming of Schemas: Bringing the Effects of Priming to an End

When schemas are primed—activated by experiences, events, or stimuli—their effects tend to persist. In fact, they have been observed over months or even years. If the schema is somehow expressed in thought or behavior, however, unpriming may occur, and the impact of the schema may decrease or even disappear.

(*Source:* Based on findings reported by Sparrow & Wegner, 2006).

recent experience, this priming only persists until it somehow finds expression. Once it does, the effect dissipates.

Unpriming effects are clearly demonstrated in the study by Sparrow and Wegner (2006). Participants were given a series of easy yes-or-no questions (e.g., Does a triangle have three sides). One group of participants was told to try to answer the questions randomly—not correctly. Another responded to the questions twice; the first time, they were told to try to answer them correctly, while the second time, they were to try to answer them randomly. It was predicted that participants in the first group would not be able to answer the questions randomly; their schema for answering correctly would be activated and lead them to provide the correct answers. In contrast, participants who answered the questions twice—first correctly and then randomly—would do better at responding randomly. Their first set of answers would provide expression for the schema answer questions correctly and so permit them to answer randomly the second time around. That's precisely what happened; those who only answered the question once and were told to try to do so randomly were actually correct 58 percent of the time—their activated schema prevented them from replying in a truly random manner. The participants who first answered the questions correctly and then randomly did much better: Their answers the second time around were correct only 49 percent of the time. They did show random performance. These findings indicate that once primed, schemas are somehow expressed, then unpriming occurs, and the influence of the primed schemas disappears. So although priming is a powerful effect, it does not in fact, last forever. (Figure 2.3 summarizes the nature of unpriming.) If primed schemas are not expressed, however, their effects may persist for long periods of time—even years—as we noted above.

Schema Persistence: Why Even Discredited Schemas Can Sometimes Influence Our Thoughts and Behavior

Although schemas are based on our past experience and are often helpful because they permit us to make sense out of a vast array of social information, they have an important "downside" too. By influencing what we notice, enter into memory, and later remember, schemas can produce distortions in our understanding of the social world. For example, as we'll see in Chapter 6, schemas play an important role in prejudice, forming one basic component of stereotypes about specific social groups. And, unfortunately, once they are formed, schemas are often resistant to change; they show a strong **perseverance effect,** remaining unchanged even in the face of contradictory information (e.g., Kunda & Oleson, 1995). For instance, when we encounter information inconsistent with our schemas, such as an engineer who is a wonderful cook and extremely charming (traits we don't expect in engineers, as a rule), we do not alter our schema for engineers. Rather, we may place such people in a special category or subtype consisting of people who do not confirm the schema or stereotype (e.g., Richards & Hewstone, 2001). Perhaps even worse, schemas can sometimes be self-fulfilling: They influence our responses to the social world in ways that make it consistent with the schema. Such self-confirming effects of schemas have been established by the findings of many different studies, but perhaps the most famous research pointing to such effects is a true "classic" of social psychology; for that reason, we highlight it in *Building the Science: Classics of Social Psychology* (see pages 44–45).

> ### ◆Principles to Remember
> Schemas help us make sense of the social world but watch out: Once they are formed, they tend to persist even in the face of disconfirming information and can exert self-fulfilling effects on our behavior.

perseverance effect
The tendency for beliefs and schemas to remain unchanged even in the face of contradictory information.

◆KeyPoints

- Because we have limited cognitive capacity, we often attempt to reduce the effort we expend on social cognition—how we think about other people. This can increase efficiency but reduce our accuracy with respect to this important task.

- One basic component of social cognition is schemas—mental frameworks developed through experience that, once formed, help us to organize social information.

- Once formed schemas exert powerful effects on what we notice (attention), enter into memory (encoding), and later remember (retrieval). Individuals report remembering more information consistent with their schemas than information inconsistent with them, but in fact, inconsistent information, too, is strongly represented in memory.

- Schemas are often primed—activated by experiences, events, or stimuli. Once they are primed, the effects of the schemas tend to persist until they

are somehow expressed in thought or behavior; such expression (known as unpriming) then reduces the likelihood they will influence thought or behavior.

- Schemas help us to process information, but they often persist even in the face of disconfirming information, thus distorting our understanding of the social world.

- Schemas can also exert self-confirming effects, causing us to behave in ways that create confirmation of them.

Think About It

Do you believe it is possible to influence the kind of schemas we develop? Or are they simply an unavoidable part of our life experience? If we could influence them, what kind of schemas should we seek to develop?

◆Heuristics: How We Reduce Our Effort in Social Cognition

Several states have passed or are considering adopting laws that ban talking on hand-held cell phones while driving. Why? Because it has been found over and over again that when drivers are distracted, they are more likely to get into accidents, and talking on the phone

BUILDING THE SCIENCE
CLASSICS OF SOCIAL PSYCHOLOGY

The Self-Confirming Nature of Schemas: When—and Why—Beliefs Shape Reality

Do our cognitive frameworks—our schemas—actually shape the social world and reflect it? A large body of evidence suggests that this is definitely so (e.g., Madon, Jussim, & Eccles, 1997; Smith, Jussim, & Eccles, 1999). Perhaps the most dramatic evidence that schemas can be self-fulfilling, however, was provided by Robert Rosenthal and Lenore Jacobson (1968), in a famous and well-known study of teachers and the unintended effects of their beliefs on students.

During the turbulent 1960s, there was growing concern over the possibility that teachers' beliefs about minority students—their schemas for such social groups—were causing them to treat these children differently (less favorably) than students in the majority group, and that as a result, the minority group students were falling further and further behind.

To gather evidence on the possible occurrence of such effects, Rosenthal and Jacobson conducted an ingenious study that exerted a powerful effect on subsequent research in social psychology. They went to an elementary school in San Francisco and administered an IQ test to all students. They then told the teachers that some of the students had scored high and were about to "bloom" academically. In fact, this was not true: They chose the names of these students randomly. But Rosenthal and

Figure 2.4
The Self-Fulfilling Influence of Schemas
Teachers' schemas concerning different groups of students can strongly affect the teachers' behavior toward these students and so start a process in which the teachers' schemas become self-fulfilling. For instance, in classic research (Rosenthal & Jacobson, 1968), teachers gave more attention and help to students they expected to "bloom" academically than to ones they expected to show no gains in performance. These findings have important implications: Because many teachers tend to believe that minority students would not excel academically, they often give such students less help and attention and actually tend to confirm these mistaken views.

can often be highly distracting. And what about global position systems (GPSs) that show maps to drivers; do you think that they, too, can lead to distraction and so cause accidents (see Figure 2.5 on page 45)? This illustrates a basic principle concerning some of our basic cognitive systems—they are definitely limited. At any given time, we are capable of handling a certain amount of information; additional input beyond this level puts us into a state of **information overload:** The demands on our cognitive system are greater than its capacity. In addition, our processing capacity can be depleted by high levels of stress or other demands on us (e.g., Chajut & Algom, 2003). To deal with such situations, we adopt various strategies designed to "stretch" our cognitive resources—to let us do more, with less effort, than would otherwise be the case. This is one major reason why so much of our social thought occurs on automatic—in a quick and effortless way. We'll discuss the costs and potential benefits of such thought later. Here, however, we'll focus on other techniques that we use to deal quickly with large amount of information. While many strategies for accomplishing this task exist, one the most useful tactics involves the use of heuristics—simple rules for making complex decisions or drawing inferences in a rapid and efficient manner.

information overload
Instances in which our ability to process information is exceeded.

Jacobson predicted that this information might change teachers' expectations (and schemas) about these children and hence their behavior toward them. Teachers were not given such information about other students, who constituted a control group.

To find out if this was true, they returned eight months later and tested both groups of children once again. Results were clear—and dramatic: Those who had been described as "bloomers" to their teachers showed significantly larger gains on the IQ test than those in the control group. In short, teachers' beliefs about the students had operated in a self-fulfilling manner: The students whose teachers believed would bloom academically, actually did.

How did such effects occur? In part through the impact of schemas on the teachers' behavior. Further research (Rosenthal, 1994) indicated that teachers gave the students they expected to bloom more attention, more challenging tasks, more and better feedback, and more opportunities to respond in class (see Figure 2.4 on page 44). In short, the teachers acted in ways that benefited the students they expected to bloom, and as a result, these youngsters really did.

As a result of this early research, social psychologists began to search for other self-confirming effects of schemas in many settings—education, therapy, and business, to name just a few. They soon uncovered much evidence that schemas do often shape behavior in ways that lead to their confirmation. For example, they observed that teachers' lower expectations for success by minority students or females undermined the confidence of these groups and actually contributed to poorer performance by them (e.g., Sadker & Sadker, 1994). Further, many studies indicated that the self-confirming effects of schemas do not result from deliberate attempts by people to confirm these mental frameworks (Chen & Bargh, 1997). On the contrary, they occur even when individuals attempt to avoid letting their expectations shape their behavior toward others. Thus schemas are definitely a two-edged sword: They help us make sense out of the social world and to process vast amounts of information quickly and with minimal effort, but they can also lock us into perceiving the world in ways that may not, in fact, be accurate. We'll consider these effects again in the discussion of prejudice in Chapter 6.

Figure 2.5
Information Overload:
A Potential Cause of
Accidents
Our capacity to process incoming information is definitely limited and can easily be exceeded. This can happen when drivers talk on the phone or pay attention to a GPS while driving in heavy traffic. If they exceed their capacity to process information and enter into a state of information overload, serious accidents may result.

Representativeness: Judging by Resemblance

Suppose that you have just met your next-door neighbor for the first time. While chatting with her, you notice that she is dressed conservatively, is very neat in her personal habits, has a large library in her home, and seems to be gentle and a little shy. Later you realize that she never mentioned what she does for a living. Is she a business manager, a physician, a waitress, an attorney, a dancer, or a librarian? One quick way of making a guess is to compare her with other members of each of these occupations. How well does she resemble people you have met in each of these fields or, perhaps, the typical member of these fields? If you proceed in this manner, you may quickly conclude that she is probably a librarian; her traits seem closer to those associated with this profession than to the traits associated with being a physician, dancer, or executive. If you made your judgment about your neighbor's occupation in this manner, you would be using the **representativeness heuristic.** In other words, you would make your judgment on the basis of a relatively simple rule: The more similar an individual is to typical members of a given group, the more likely she or he is to belong to that group.

Are such judgments accurate? Often they are because belonging to certain groups does affect the behavior and style of people in them and because people with certain traits are attracted to particular groups in the first place. But sometimes, judgments based on representativeness are wrong mainly because decisions or judgments made on the basis of this rule tend to ignore base rates, which refer to the frequency with which given events or patterns (e.g., occupations) occur in the total population (Kahneman & Tversky, 1982; Koehler, 1993). In fact, there are many more business managers than librarians—perhaps fifty times as many. Thus, even though your neighbor seemed more similar to librarians than managers in her personal traits, the chances are actually higher that she is a manager than a librarian. Yet because of our strong tendency to use the representativeness heuristic, we tend to ignore such base rate information and to base our judgments on similarity to typical members of a group or category. In this and related ways, the representativeness heuristic can lead to errors in our thinking about others.

Availability: "If I Can Think of It, It Must Be Important"

Are you safer in a huge sport utility vehicle (SUV) or in a smaller, lighter car? Many people would answer: "In the big SUV—if you are an accident, you are less likely to get hurt." While that may be true, actual data indicate that death rates (number of deaths per 1,000,000 vehicles on the road) are actually higher for SUV (e.g., Gladwell, 2004). So why do so many people conclude, falsely, that they are safer in a bulky SUV? The answer seems to involve what we remember when we think about this question. Most people can recall scenes in which a huge SUV had literally crushed another vehicle in an accident. Because such scenes are dramatic, we can readily bring these memories to mind. But this "ease of retrieval" effect may mislead us: We assume that because we can easily recall such scenes, they accurately reflect the overall situation when, in fact, they don't. For instance, they don't remind us of the fact that huge SUVs are involved in accidents more often than smaller, lighter cars, that large SUVs tip over much more frequently, and that they are— quite simply—much larger targets. This, and many similar errors in our thinking, illustrate of the operation of another heuristic—the **availability heuristic,** another cognitive rule of thumb suggesting that the easier it is to bring information to mind, the greater its impact on subsequent judgments or decisions. This heuristic, too, makes good sense: After all, the fact that we can bring some information to mind quite easily suggests that it must be frequent or important and should influence our judgments and decisions. But relying on availability in making social judgments can also lead to errors. For instance, it can lead us to overestimate the likelihood of events that are dramatic but rare because they are easy

representativeness heuristic
A strategy for making judgments based on the extent to which current stimuli or events resemble other stimuli or categories.

availability heuristic
A strategy for making judgments on the basis of how easily specific kinds of information can be brought to mind.

to bring to mind. Consistent with this principle, many people fear travel in airplanes more than travel in automobiles, even though the chances of dying in an auto accident are hundreds of times higher. Here's another example: Physicians who examine the same patient often reach different diagnoses about the patient's illness. Why? One possibility is that the physicians have had different experiences in their medical practices and so find different kinds of diseases easier to bring to mind. Their diagnoses then reflect these differences in ease-of-retrieval or their reliance on the availability heuristic.

Interestingly, research suggests that there is more to the availability heuristic than merely the subjective ease with which relevant information comes to mind. In addition, the amount of information we can bring to mind seems to matter, too (e.g., Schwarz et al., 1991). The more information we can think of, the greater its impact on our judgments. Which of these two factors is more important? The answer appears to involve the kind of judgment are making. If it is one involving emotions or feelings, we tend to rely on the "ease" rule, while if it is one involving facts or information, we tend to rely more on the "amount" rule (e.g., Rothman & Hardin, 1997; Ruder & Bless, 2003).

Anchoring and Adjustment: Where You Begin Makes a Difference

Remember the used car example from the start of the chapter? Let's revisit it briefly. The price in the paper was higher than the seller really hoped to get, and that's a fairly common practice. Why? Partly because sellers want to give themselves some room for bargaining. Often the selling price is the starting point for discussions; the buyer offers less, the seller counters, and the process continues until an agreement is reached, or the buyer gives up. It turns out that when a seller sets a starting price, this is an important advantage because of another heuristic that strongly influences our thinking: the **anchoring and adjustment heuristic.** This heuristic involves the tendency to deal with uncertainty in many situations by using something we do know as a starting point and then making adjustments to it. The seller's price provides such a starting point, to which buyers try to make adjustments to lower the price they pay. Such lowering makes the buyer feel that, by comparison to the original asking price, they are getting a good deal.

In a sense, the existence of the anchoring and adjustment heuristic is far from surprising. In uncertain situations we have to start somewhere. What is more surprising, however, is how powerful this effect is even in situations where, rationally, it should not operate. For instance, consider an unsettling study by Englich, Mussweiler, and Strack (2006), research indicating that even court decisions and sentences can be strongly influenced by anchoring and adjustment, and that, moreover, this occurs even for experienced judges.

In this research, the participants were highly experienced legal professionals in Germany—people who were either judges or experienced prosecutors. They were asked to read a realistic court case and then learned of sentences recommended for the defendant. In one study, these recommendations were from a journalist—someone with no legal training. In another study, the recommended sentences were actually generated by throwing dice—randomly and with no connection to the crime itself. Finally, in another, they were from an experienced prosecutor. Some of the recommendations were lenient (e.g., one month of probation), and others were harsh (e.g., three years in prison for the same crime). After receiving this information, the experienced legal participants make their own sentencing recommendations. Clearly, the recommendations of these experts should not be influenced by the anchors they received, especially when the sources were either irrelevant or purely random in two conditions (lenient or harsh recommendations from a journalist or ones generated by the throw of dice). As you can see in Figure 2.6 (page 48), however, these anchors did have significant effects: Sentences were harsher when participants learned of a harsh anchor but more lenient when they received a lenient anchor. And it didn't matter whether the source of the anchor was a journalist, an experienced prosecutor, or merely

anchoring and adjustment heuristic
A heuristic that involves the tendency to use a number of value as a starting point to which we then make adjustments.

Figure 2.6
Anchoring and Adjustment in Legal Decisions

When experienced legal experts (judges, prosecutors) learned of the sentences recommended by an irrelevant source (someone with no legal training—a journalist), their own recommendations were strongly influenced by these anchors. They recommended harsher sentences when the anchors were harsh but more lenient sentences when the anchors were lenient. The same effects were found when the source of the anchor was relevant—an experienced prosecutor. These findings, and those of many other studies, indicate that the anchor-and-adjustment heuristic often exerts powerful effects on social thought.

(*Source:* Based on data from Englich, Mussweiler, & Strack, 2006).

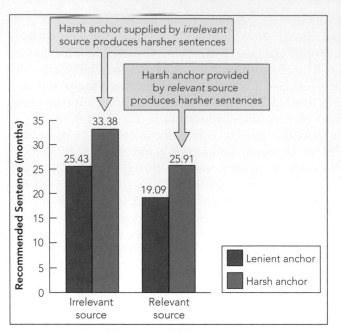

the throw of dice. These findings are, in a sense, quite disturbing. If even experienced and highly trained legal experts can be influenced by anchoring and adjustment, it seems clear that this is indeed a powerful effect; one kind of shortcut to social thought that can have important effects in important contexts.

Why are the effects of the anchoring and adjustment heuristic so powerful? Recent findings indicate that one reason is that although we do make adjustments to anchors when they are provided, these adjustments are often not sufficient to overcome the initial impact of the anchors. In other words, we seem to stop as soon as a value we consider plausible is reached (Epley & Gilovich, 2006). In a sense, this is yet another example of the "save mental effort" principle that we tend to follow in many contexts and across many different aspects of social thought. Interestingly, the tendency to make insufficient judgments is greater when individuals are in a state in which they are less capable of engaging in effortful thought—for instance, after consuming alcohol or when people are busy doing other tasks (Epley & Gilovich, 2006). Overall, then, it appears that our tendency to let initial anchors influence our judgments—even in important situations—does stem, to an important degree, from a tendency to avoid the effortful work involved in making adjustments to this anchor.

KeyPoints

- Because our capacity to process information is limited, we often experience information overload. To avoid this, we make use of heuristics—rules for making decisions in a quick and relatively effortless manner.

- One such heuristic is representativeness, which suggests that the more similar an individual is to typical members of a given group, the more likely she or he is to belong to that group.

- Another heuristic is availability, which suggests that the easier it is to bring information to mind, the greater its impact on subsequent decisions or judgments. In some cases, availability may also involve the amount of information we bring to mind.

- A third heuristic is anchoring and adjustment, which leads us to use a number or value as a starting point from which we then make adjustments. These adjustments may not be sufficient to reflect actual social reality, perhaps, because once we attain a plausible value, we stop the process.

Think About It

Heuristics offer "mental shortcuts" that save us effort in attempting to understand the social world. While this is often useful, can you think of situations in which following this principle is inappropriate? Why?

Automatic and Controlled Processing: Two Basic Modes of Social Thought

At several points in this chapter, we have referred to the fact that social thought can occur in either of two distinctly different ways: in a systematic, logical, careful, and highly effortful manner known as controlled processing, or in a fast, relatively effortless, and intuitive manner known as **automatic processing.** This distinction has been confirmed in literally hundreds of different studies, and it is now recognized by social psychologists as an important aspect of social thought. But please note: this doesn't mean that these two kinds of thought are totally independent; in fact, recent evidence suggests that automatic and controlled processing may often occur together, especially in situations involving some uncertainty (Ferrita, Garcia-Marques, Sherman, & Sherman, 2006). Still, the distinction between them is important and worth considering carefully.

While a great deal of evidence supports the existence of these two different modes of social thought, perhaps the most convincing support is provided by the kind of social neuroscience research, which is research that examines activity in the human brain as an individual processes social information, described briefly in Chapter 1. The findings of such research indicate that we actually possess two different neural systems for processing social information—one that operates in an automatic manner and another that operates in a systematic and controlled manner. Moreover, these two systems appear to be centered in different regions of the brain. For instance, consider research on evaluative reactions—a basic kind of social judgment relating to whether we like or dislike something (a person, idea, object, whatever). Such evaluations can occur in two distinct ways: simple good—bad judgments that occur in a rapid and seemingly automatic manner (Phelps et al., 2001) or through more effortful thought in which we think carefully and logically, weighing all the relevant points fully and systematically (e.g., Duncan & Owen, 2000). The first kind of reaction seems to occur primarily in the amygdala, while the second seems to involve portions of the prefrontal cortex (especially the medial prefrontal cortex and ventrolateral prefrontal cortex (e.g., Cunningham et al., 2003). In addition, as we'll note in a later discussion of the relationship between cognition and affect (between thought and feelings or moods), we also seem to possess two distinct brain systems for processing these types of information, with controlled processing (reasoning, logic) occurring primarily in areas of the brain we mentioned previously (i.e., the cortex), and emotion-related, automatic reactions occurring mainly in the limbic system, structures deep inside the brain (e.g., Cohen, 2005).

Overall, the results of many social neuroscience studies and more traditional methods of social psychological research suggest that the distinction between automatic and controlled processing is indeed real—and important. We'll be illustrating this fact in many places throughout this book, but here, we'll try to clarify why it is so important by examining two specific issues relating to automatic processing: the effects of automatic processing on social behavior and the benefits provided by such processing.

Automatic Processing and Automatic Social Behavior

As we have already seen, schemas, once activated, exert important effects on social thought. That they exert equally powerful effects on actual social behavior is also clear. Often, people act in ways that are consistent with their schemas, even if they are not aware of these frameworks, do not intend to do so, and are unaware that they are acting in this manner. For example, consider well-known research by Bargh, Chen, and Burrows (1996). In one of their studies, these researchers first activated either the schema for the trait of

automatic processing
This occurs when, after extensive experience with a task or type of information, we reach the stage where we can perform the task or process the information in a seemingly effortless, automatic, and nonconscious manner.

rudeness or the schema for the trait of politeness through priming. To prime these schemas, participants in the study worked on unscrambling scrambled sentences containing words related either to rudeness (e.g., bold, rude, impolitely, bluntly) or words related to politeness (cordially, patiently, polite, courteous, discreetly). Exposure to words related to schemas has been found, in past research, to prime (activate) these mental frameworks. People in a third (control) group unscrambled sentences containing words unrelated to either trait (e.g., exercising, flawlessly, occasionally, rapidly, normally). After completing these tasks, participants in the study were asked to report back to the experimenter who would give them additional tasks. When they approached the experimenter, they were engaged in a conversation with another person (an accomplice). The experimenter continued this conversation, ignoring the participant. The major dependent measure was whether the participant interrupted the conversation to receive further instructions. The researchers predicted that people for whom the trait rudeness had been primed would be more likely to interrupt than those for whom the trait politeness had been primed, and this is precisely what happened. Further findings indicated that these effects occurred despite the fact that participants' ratings of the experimenter in terms of politeness did not differ across the three experimental conditions. Thus, these differences in behavior seemed to occur in a nonconscious, automatic manner.

In a second study, Bargh, Chen, and Burrows (1996) either primed the stereotype for elderly (again through exposure to words related to this schema) or did not prime it. Then they timed the number of seconds it took participants to walk down a hallway at the end of the study. As predicted, those for whom the stereotype elderly had been primed actually walked slower! Together, the results of these and many other studies (e.g., Djiksterhuis & Bargh, 2001) indicate that activating stereotypes or schemas can exert seemingly automatic effects on behavior—effects that occur in the absence of intention or conscious awareness. These findings have important implications. For instance, they suggest that once stereotypes are activated (stereotypes are one type of schema) individuals not only think in terms of these mental frameworks, they may actually behave in ways consistent with them as well, even if they are unaware of such cognitive activation. For instance, negative stereotypes of minority groups may lead the people possessing them to act in hostile ways toward members of these groups, even if they do not intend to do so. Clearly, then, automatic processing is an important aspect of social thought and one that may often become visible in outward, overt behavior.

But additional research suggests that the effects of automatic processing may be even more general than that of triggering particular forms of behavior. Once automatic processing is initiated (e.g., through priming), individuals may—again unconsciously—begin to prepare for future interactions with the people or groups who are the focus of this automatic processing. As noted by Cesario, Plaks, and Higgins (2006), activating a schema may not merely trigger behaviors consistent with this schema, it may also activate behaviors that, in a sense, "get the people involved ready" to actually interact with others. One study conducted by Cesario and others (2006) clearly illustrates such effects clearly. Participants were primed with photos of men labeled gay or straight These photos were shown so quickly that they could not actually see the images; but as in many other studies, it was expected that the photos would prime (activate) schemas for these two groups. Then, in what seemed to be unrelated procedures, the computer on which the study was being conducted locked up, and participants were instructed to get the experimenter to help get it started. When the experimenter entered, he acted in a hostile manner. The key question was: Would participants whose negative stereotype (schemas) of gays had been primed behave in more hostile manner than those whose stereotypes of heterosexuals had been primed? If so, this would be directly contrary to the stereotype of gays, which generally suggests that such people are passive and nonaggressive. However, it would be consistent with the view that priming this schema motivates individuals to prepare to interact with members of the people or group who are the focus of the schema—in this case, a group

Stereotypes (Schemas) Trigger Schema-Consistent Behaviors

Stereotypes (Schemas) Trigger Preparation for Interacting with Persons or Groups Who are the Focus of the Schemas

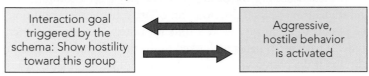

Figure 2.7
Automatic Processing Initiates Preparations for Future Interactions

In previous research, activation of schemas has been shown to trigger behaviors consistent with these cognitive frameworks. Recent research suggests that in addition, schemas, once activated, may also trigger motivated efforts to prepare for interacting with the people or groups who are the focus of these schemas. In the case of gay men, for instance, this enhances tendencies for heterosexuals to act in a hostile, aggressive manner.

(*Source:* Based on suggestions by Cesario, Plaks, & Higgins, 2006.)

they do not like. Results offered clear support for this prediction: When interacting with the experimenter, participants did in fact show greater hostility if they had been primed with faces labeled gay than with faces labeled straight. Remember this activation was automatic because participants could not consciously report seeing these photos; they were presented for only eleven milliseconds. The different predictions of these two views— (1) schemas trigger behaviors consistent with the schemas or (2) schemas trigger motivated preparation to interact with the people or groups who are the subject of the schemas—are summarized in Figure 2.7.

Related results have been obtained in several other studies (e.g, Jonas & Sassenberg, 2006). Overall, it appears that automatic processing not only sometimes triggers automatic social behavior, but it also often initiates a more general process in which the people involved prepare for future social interactions with the people or groups who are the focus of their automatic (and usually unconscious) processing.

The Benefits of Automatic Processing: Beyond Mere Efficiency

One kind of automatic processing with which most people are familiar occurs when we try to remember something (someone's name or a thought we previously had) but don't succeed. When that happens, we often turn to doing something else while the search for the information we want goes on automatically and without our conscious awareness. Often, this kind of memory search is successful, and the missing name or fact pops into mind. In such cases, we are dimly aware that something was happening, but can't really describe it. Research on this aspect of automatic processing confirms that it does really occur: We often attempt to deal with problems, and even complex decisions, while our attention is directed elsewhere (e.g., Dijksterhuis & Nordgren, 2007). Perhaps even more surprising, recent evidence indicates that sometimes, it may be superior to careful, conscious thought in terms of making excellent decisions. To the extent this is true, then, we can conclude that automatic processing is not merely quick, effortless and efficient: It may also sometimes yield other important benefits, too.

A clear illustration of these advantages is provided by research conducted by Dijksterhuis and van Olden (2006). These social psychologists asked students who participated in their research to look at various posters and indicate the one they liked most. In one condition (immediate decision), the posters were all shown on a computer screen simultaneously, and students made their decision immediately. In another condition (conscious thought), the posters were shown one at a time for ninety seconds, and after looking at them, the students were given paper and asked to list their thoughts and evaluations—to think carefully about the posters and their preferences for them. Finally, in a third condition (unconscious thought), participants worked on another task (solving anagrams) after seeing the posters. Then, several minutes later, they indicated which poster they liked. The anagrams task prevented them from thinking actively and consciously about their preferences for the various posters.

When these events were completed, the participants received a surprise: They were given their favorite poster to take home. Three to five weeks later, they were phoned and asked how satisfied they were with the poster they had received and how much they would want (in Euros) if they sold their poster. The researchers predicted that participants would actually be most satisfied with their choice in the unconscious condition, where they made the choice without an opportunity to think consciously about it, and as you can see from Figure 2.8, this is precisely what happened. This suggests—surprisingly—that participants

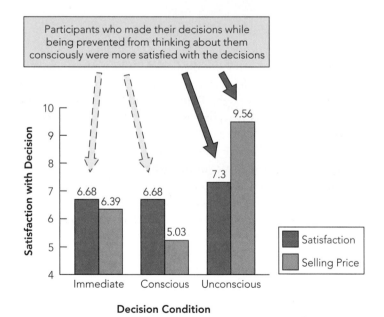

Figure 2.8

The Benefits of Automatic (Unconscious) Thought

Participants who were prevented from thinking consciously about their preferences for various posters (unconscious condition) were more satisfied with the choices they made than participants who could engage in careful, systematic thought (conscious) or than participants who made their choice immediately after seeing the poster (immediate). These findings suggest that automatic processing offers more benefits than simply being quick and efficient.

(*Source:* Based on data from Dijksterhuis & van Olden, 2006).

actually made better decisions, in terms of being satisfied with them, when they did so on automatic rather than when they had a chance to think about them carefully.

Why is this so? Perhaps because as we noted earlier, conscious thought has strict limits in terms of the amount of information it can handle, so when we think actively about decisions we may not be unable to take account of all available information. In contrast, unconscious, automatic thought has much greater capacity. Similarly, when we think about decisions consciously, we may fail to weigh the various dimensions or elements accurately and thinking about these dimensions may get us confused about which were actually the most important. Unconscious, automatic processing is more natural in this respect and so may reflect our real preferences more clearly. Whatever the precise reason, these findings and those of many related studies (e.g., Ito, Chiao, Devine, Lorig, & Cacioppo, 2006) suggest that automatic processing offers important advantages beyond those of merely being quick and efficient. In a sense, therefore, it is not at all surprising that much of our thought about the social world occurs in this manner, and not only is it less effortful than systematic thought, but it also often works by producing the results and outcomes we desire. Certainly, there are real risks to such thought—ones we'll describe in detail in our discussion of prejudice (Chapter 6). But there are important benefits, too, so it's important to take full account of this mode of thought in our efforts to understand how we seek to understand the social world.

KeyPoints

- A large amount of evidence indicates that the distinction between automatic and controlled processing is a basic one. In fact, different regions of the brain appear to be involved in these two types of processing, especially with respect to evaluations of various aspects of the social world.

- When schemas or other cognitive frameworks are activated (even without our conscious awareness of such activation), they strongly influence our behavior, triggering actions consistent with the frameworks and also preparing us to interact with the people or groups who are the focus of these schemas.

- Automatic processing is clearly quick and efficient; in addition, however, it may also sometimes offer other advantages, too—such as decisions with which we are more satisfied.

Think About It

If automatic processing is so efficient and so effective, why do we ever bother to engage in more systematic controlled thinking? Are there situations in which such thought is required or likely to yield superior results?

Potential Sources of Error in Social Cognition: Why Total Rationality Is Rarer Than You Think

Human beings are definitely not computers. While we can imagine being able to reason in a perfectly logical way, we know from our own experience that often, we fall short of this goal. This is true for many aspects of social thought. In our efforts to understand others and make sense out of the social world, we are subject to a wide range of tendencies that, together, can lead us into serious error. We'll now consider several of these tilts in social cognition. Before doing so, however, we emphasize the following point: While these aspects of social thought do sometimes result in errors, they are also often quite adaptive. They help us to focus on the kinds of information that are most useful to us, and they reduce the effort required for understanding the social world. So they are definitely something of a mixed bag, supplying us with tangible benefits and exacting important costs.

As we'll soon see, there are many different ways in which our social thought departs from rationality. To acquaint you with a wide range of these effects, we'll start with two basic tendencies that seem to occur in a wide range of situations and often produce important errors in our social thought: Our tendency to devote special attention to negative information and our counterbalancing tendency to be optimistic—often, overly optimistic—in a wide range of situations. After considering these general tendencies, we'll turn to several other ways in which social thought departs from rationality, ones that are important but tend to occur in specific situations rather than generally.

Basic "Tilts" in Social Thought: The Negativity Bias and Our Powerful Tendency to Be Overly Optimistic

If we were completely rational in the ways in which we think about the social world, we would simply gather information, process it, and then use it to make various decisions, judgments, and inferences. In fact, however, we seem to be especially sensitive to certain kinds of information, so that the information plays an especially important role in much of our social thought.

Negativity Bias: The Tendency to Pay Extra Attention to Negative Information

Imagine that you meet someone for the first time and—as we'll describe in more detail in Chapter 3—are forming a first impression of this person. Most of the information you notice is positive: This person is pleasant, friendly, and seems intelligent. But in addition, you notice that he is also somewhat conceited; he has what appears to be an excessively positive view of his own characteristics. What kind of impression do you form? Research indicates that probably it will be quite negative (Kunda, 1999). Why? Because it appears that we pay more attention to negative information than we do to positive information about another person, an event, or almost anything (e.g., Cacioppo, Gardner, & Brentson, 1997). Social psychologists refer to this effect as **negativity bias,** and it seems to be both general and powerful, strongly influencing our social thought in many different situations.

From an evolutionary perspective, this tendency makes a great deal of sense. Negative information reflects features of the external world that may, potentially, be threatening to our safety or well-being. For this reason, it is especially important that we be sensitive to such stimuli and thus able to respond to them quickly. Research findings offer support for this reasoning. For instance, consider our ability to recognize facial expressions in others. It appears that we are faster and more accurate in detecting negative facial expressions (e.g., ones showing anger or hostility) than positive facial expressions (e.g., ones showing friendliness [Ohman, Lundqvist, & Esteves, 2001]).

negativity bias
Refers to the fact that we show greater sensitivity to negative information than to positive information.

Negativity bias is not universal, however—and with good reason. While it makes a lot of sense to be highly sensitive to negative information in many situations, there are at least some in which paying attention to positive information might be more useful—ones in which there is little or no danger. For instance, it might be more adaptive for males of many different species to be highly sensitive to information suggesting that a female finds them attractive and perhaps acceptable as a mate. That the negativity bias can be overcome by such situational factors is clearly illustrated by research carried out by Smith and colleagues (Smith et al., 2006). These researchers exposed participants in their study to pictures that were positive or negative in content. In one condition, mostly positive pictures were shown (positive priming) while in another, mostly negative picture were presented. Next, using methods from social neuroscience, the researchers measured signs of attention in brain activity. Results indicated that the negativity bias was in fact eliminated when positive stimuli had been frequent—when positive reactions were primed. In follow-up research, other methods were used to prime positive or negative reactions (participants were shown positive or negative words rather than pictures). Again, despite the change in methods, the negativity bias was eliminated by priming positive reactions.

These findings indicate that while we do have a strong tendency to pay more attention to negative than positive information, this tendency is not set in stone; it can be reduced, or even eliminated, if we find ourselves in situations in which paying attention to positive information is useful. In other words, as we'll see throughout this chapter and this entire book, social thought—like people are—is adaptable and often flows along channels that help us deal effectively with the complex social world in which we live.

The Optimistic Bias: Our Tendency to See the World through Rose-Colored Glasses

While the tendency to notice negative information is strong one, we also have a seemingly opposite tendency known as the **optimistic bias**—a powerful predisposition to expect things to turn out well overall. In fact, research findings indicate that most people believe that they are more likely than others to experience positive events, and less likely to experience negative events (e.g., Shepperd, Ouellette, & Fernandez, 1996). Similarly, we often have greater confidence in our beliefs or judgments than is justified—an effect known as the **overconfidence barrier** (Vallone, Ross, & Lepper, 1985). Our strong leaning toward optimism is seen in many other contexts, too: Most people believe that they are more likely than others to get a good job, have a happy marriage, and live to a ripe old age but are less likely to experience negative outcomes, such as being fired, getting seriously ill, or getting divorced (e.g., Schwarzer, 1994). And when entrepreneurs start a new business, they believe that the chances of making it successful are much higher than is actually true (Baron & Shane, 2007).

Yet another illustration of optimism is the **planning fallacy**—our tendency to believe that we can get more done in a given period of time than we actually can or that a given job will take less time than it really will. Because of this aspect of the optimistic bias, governments frequently announce overly optimistic schedules for public works (e.g., new roads, new airports, new bridges; see Figure 2.9 on page 56), and individuals adopt unrealistically optimistic schedules for their own work. If you have ever estimated that a project would take you a certain amount of time but then found that it took much longer, you are already familiar with this effect, and with the planning fallacy.

Why do we fall prey to this particular kind of optimism? According to Buehler, Griffin, and Ross (1994), social psychologists who have studied this tendency in detail, several factors play a role. One is that when individuals make predictions about how long it will take them to complete a given task, they enter a planning or narrative mode of thought in which they focus primarily on the future and how they will perform the task. This, in turn, prevents them from looking backward in time and remembering how long similar tasks

optimistic bias
Our predisposition to expect things to turn out well overall.

overconfidence barrier
The tendency to have more confidence in the accuracy of our own judgments than is reasonable.

planning fallacy
The tendency to make optimistic predictions concerning how long a given task will take for completion.

Figure 2.9
The Planning Fallacy
in Action
*Construction of a major
tunnel in Boston took several
years longer, and cost billions
of dollars more than original
projections. This is far from a
rare occurrence: Public projects
routinely take much longer to
complete than originally
planned. This may reflect
effects of the planning
fallacy—the tendency to
believe that we can accomplish
more than we actually can in
a given period of time.*

took them in the past. As a result, one important reality check that might help them avoid being overly optimistic is removed. In addition, when individuals do consider past experiences in which tasks took longer than expected, they tend to attribute such outcomes to factors outside their control. The result is that they tend to overlook important potential obstacles when predicting how long a task will take and fall prey to the planning fallacy. These predictions have been confirmed in several studies (e.g., Buehler et al., 1994), and they provide important insights into the origins of the tendency to make optimistic predictions about task completion.

These cognitive factors are not the entire story, though. Additional findings suggest that another factor, motivation to complete a task, also plays an important role in the planning fallacy. When predicting what will happen, individuals often guess that what will happen is what they want to happen (e.g., Johnson & Sherman, 1990). In cases where they are strongly motivated to complete a task, therefore, they make overoptimistic predictions about when they will attain this desired state of affairs. Research findings offer support for this reasoning, too (e.g., Buehler, Griffin, & MacDonald, 1997). It appears, then, that our estimates of when we will complete a task are indeed influenced by our hopes and desires; we want to finish early or on time, so we predict that we will. The result? Unfounded optimism strikes again!

The Rocky Past versus the Golden Future: Optimism at Work

Think back over your past life. Did it have peaks—times when things were going great for you—and valleys   times when things were not good? Now, in contrast, try to imagine your future: How do you think it will unfold? If you are like most people, you may notice a difference in these descriptions. While most of us recognize that our past has been mixed in terms of highs and lows, we tend to forecast a rosy or golden future—one in which we will be quite happy and in which few negative events happen to us. In fact, research by Newby-Clark and Ross (2003) indicates that this tendency is so strong that it occurs even when people have just recalled negative episodes from their own pasts. What accounts for this difference? One possibility is that when we think about the past, we can recall failures, unpleasant events, and other disappointments, while these unexpected possibilities are not salient when we think about our future. When we think about the future, in contrast, we tend to concentrate on desirable goals, personal happiness, and doing things we have always wanted to do—such as engaging in travel to exotic places. The result? Because our thinking is dominated by these positive thoughts, we make highly optimistic predictions about the future and tend to perceive it as indeed golden, at least in its promise or potential for us. In short, the optimistic bias seems to occur for people not just for specific tasks or situations but also in our projections of our entire future lives as well.

> **Principles to Remember**
> We have strong tendencies to pay special attention to negative information and at the same time, powerful tendencies to expect things to turn out well. Beware of both because they can generate serious errors in social thought.

How powerful is the optimistic bias? So strong that it can actually distort even the judgments of people who are expert in a given domain and who should—therefore—know better. As an illustration of the pervasive impact of the optimistic bias, read *Social Psychology: What It Tells Us About . . .* on pages 58–59.

Situation-Specific Sources of Error in Social Cognition: Counterfactual Thinking, Thought Suppression, and Magical Thinking

The negativity and optimistic biases are general in nature; they occur in a wide range of social situations and contexts. Other important forms of "error" or bias in our social thought are somewhat more restricted in the sense that they tend to occur only in certain kinds of situations. We'll now examine several of these—counterfactual thinking, thought suppression, and what is sometimes termed magical thinking.

Counterfactual Thinking: Imagining What Might Have Been

Suppose that you take an important exam; when you receive your score, it is a C—much lower than you had hoped. What thoughts will enter your mind as you consider your grade? If you are like most people, you may quickly begin to imagine what might have been—receiving a higher grade—along with thoughts about how you could have obtained that better outcome. "If only I had studied more," or "If only I had come to class more often," you may think to yourself. And then, perhaps you may begin to formulate plans for actually doing better on the next test.

Such thoughts about what might have been—known in social psychology as **counterfactual thinking**—occur in a wide range of situations, not just ones in which we experience disappointments For instance, suppose you read an article in the newspaper about someone who left work at the normal time and was injured in an automobile accident in which another driver ran a stop sign. Certainly, you would feel sympathy for this

counterfactual thinking
The tendency to imagine other outcomes in a situation than the ones that actually occurred ("What might have been").

SOCIALPSYCHOLOGY

The War in Iraq: Did The Optimistic Bias Play a Role?

On September 11, 2001, a group of terrorists flew commercial jet airplanes into the World Trade Center and the Pentagon; and only the heroic efforts of passengers on a fourth plane prevented it from heading directly for—and possibly destroying—the White House. As a result, President Bush launched a "war on terrorism," which soon led to the invasion of Afghanistan and in 2003, to the invasion of Iraq. The stated purpose of the invasion of Iraq was to destroy a vast arsenal of weapons of mass destruction that, presumably, the government of Saddam Hussein had created and might use. Secondarily, the United States invaded Iraq to end the atrocities that Hussein's government was committing against the people of Iraq. The invasion went largely according to plan, so within a few months, President Bush was able to stand on the deck of a warship and proclaim victory. But now, several years later, it is clear that this war did not end in 2003. Rather, it continued with an ever-rising toll of deaths both to Iraqis and to U.S. troops; in fact, by 2006, more than three thousand U.S. troops had been killed in Iraq. This is definitely not a book about politics, and we would never dream of taking take sides on this complex issue. What we can state is that today experts from all sides of the political spectrum generally agree that (1) weapons of mass destruction did not exist, (2) Iraq was not a direct threat to the United States, and (3) far from improving the life of the people of Iraq, the war has unleashed forces that threaten to tear the country apart and plunge it into bitter civil war (see Figure 2.10).

All these tragic events raise a key question: How could highly experienced military and government officials ever support this war? Why did they go along with President Bush's claim that it was necessary, just, and vital to the safety of the United States?

The answer to this question is, of course, complex. But it is likely that these errors in judgment stemmed, at least in part, from the kind of cognitive biases we have been describing—especially, the optimistic bias. Remember, this bias suggests that everyone (experts and nonexperts alike) have a powerful tendency to assume that good things will happen—that events will turn out well. Furthermore, people tend to believe that use of coercion on enemies will be successful, while simultaneously being aware that such coercion would not be successful in persuading our own group. Such thinking, we believe, is clearly present in statements by President Bush and many others to the effect that "The people of

person and would probably recommend compensation for him. But now imagine the same story with a slight difference: The same person was injured in the same kind of accident, but in this case, he had left work early to run an errand. Because the accident is the same, you should rationally feel the same amount of sympathy for the victim. But in fact, you may not because given that he left work earlier than usual, it is easy to imagine him *not* being in the accident. In other words, counterfactual thoughts about what might have happened instead of what did happen can influence your sympathy—as well as your recommendations concerning compensation for the victim (e.g., Miller & McFarland, 1987).

Because counterfactual thoughts seem to occur automatically in many situations, we can't help imagining that things might have turned out differently. To overcome these automatic tendencies, therefore, we must try to correct for their influence, and this requires both active processing in which we suppress the counterfactual thoughts or discount them. Evidence that this is indeed the case is provided by studies demonstrating that anything that reduces our information-processing capacity actually strengthens the impact of counterfactual thoughts on our judgments and behavior (Goldinger et al., 2003). Together, this research indicates that counterfactual thinking—imagining what did not actually happen—is a strong tendency of our social thought.

When counterfactual thinking does occur, a wide range of effects can follow—some of which are beneficial and some of which are costly to the people involved (e.g., Kray,

Figure 2.10

The War in Iraq: The Optimistic Bias Gone Wild?

The war in Iraq has not produced the kind of positive results many military and government officials in the United States predicted. Were these leaders victims of the optimistic bias—a basic error in social thought that led them to anticipate unrealistically favorable outcomes? While we'll never know for sure, it seems possible that this bias and other cognitive errors too (e.g., escalation of commitment) played a role.

Iraq will welcome us with open arms, and we will rescue them from the evils of the regime headed by Saddam Hussein." It is also seen in what now seem to be wildly optimistic beliefs that the Iraqi people would quickly adopt a democratic form of government—one that protects their human rights. Even more disturbing, however, is the excessively optimistic belief that the major groups living in Iraq—Sunnis, Shiites, Kurds, and others—would quickly put aside their grudges and suspicions and—in an instant—overcome decades or even centuries of anger and mistrust.

In addition, another kind of cognitive bias—something known as sunk costs or the escalation of commitment—was likely to be at work. Sunk costs refers to the fact that once we make a decision or invest in a strategy, we often stick to it, even in the face of negative outcomes. Why? Because backing away from it means that we must admit that we might have made a mistake in the first place, and that's something most people are reluctant to do (in any situation). This cognitive error may have contributed to the Bush administration's plan to send more troops to Iraq to continue this costly and distressing war.

So what's the bottom line of all this? The principles and findings of social psychology are truly visible everywhere, even on the stage of world events and conflict and can help us not only to understand many aspects of the social world in which we live—including the origins of history-shaping events. (And let us add that in this belief, we do not feel that we are being overly optimistic!)

Galinsky, & Wong, 2006; Nario-Redmond & Branscombe, 1996; Roese & Olson). Depending on its focus, counterfactual thinking can yield either boosts to, or reductions in, our current moods. If individuals imagine *upward counterfactuals,* comparing their current outcomes with more favorable ones than they experienced, the result may be strong feelings of dissatisfaction or envy, especially if they do not feel capable of obtaining better outcomes in the future (Sanna, 1997). Olympic athletes who win a silver medal but who can easily imagine winning a gold one, experience such reactions (e.g., Medvec, Madey, & Gilovich, 1995). Alternatively, if individuals compare their current outcomes with less favorable ones—it might have been worse—they may experience positive feelings of satisfaction or hopefulness. Such reactions have been found among Olympic athletes who win bronze medals and who can easily imagine what it would be like to have not won any medal whatsoever (e.g., Gleicher et al., 1995). In sum, engaging in counterfactual thought can strongly influence affective states (Medvec & Savitsky, 1997).

In addition, it appears that we often use counterfactual thinking to mitigate the bitterness of disappointments. After tragic events, such as the death of a loved one, people often find solace in thinking: "Nothing more could be done; the death was inevitable." In other words, they adjust their view concerning the inevitability of the death so as to make it seem more certain and therefore unavoidable. In contrast, if they have different counterfactual thoughts—"If only the illness had been diagnosed sooner . . ." or "If only

Figure 2.11
Thought Suppression:
Can We Really Avoid
Thinking about Things
We Don't Want to Think
about? Yes, But It's Not
Easy!

*In many situations, we engage
in thought suppression; we try
not to think about things that
we don't want to influence our
behavior. For instance, people
on a diet may avoid looking at
a display of delicious desserts
because they don't want to
think about these temptations.*

we had gotten him to the hospital quicker . . . ," their suffering may be increased. So by assuming that negative events or disappointments were inevitable, we tend to make these events more bearable (Tykocinski, 2001). We'll have more to say about such effects in a later section.

Finally, we should note that counterfactual thinking can sometimes help us to perform better—to do a better job at various tasks. Why? Because by imagining how we might have done better, we may come up with improved strategies and ways of using our effort more effectively. So, sometimes—for instance, when we expect to repeat various tasks—engaging in counterfactual thought can enhance performance on important tasks (e.g., Kray et al., 2006).

In sum, imagining what might have been in a given situation can yield many effects, ranging from despair and intense regret on the one hand to hopefulness and increased determination to do better in the future on the other hand. Our tendency to think not only about what is, but also about what *might* have been, therefore, can have far-reaching effects on many aspects of our social thought and social behavior.

> ### Principles to Remember
>
> When we imagine outcomes different from those that actually occurred, we engage in counterfactual thinking. This can boost our moods if we imagine worse outcomes but impair them if we imagine even better outcomes.

Thought Suppression: Why Efforts to Avoid Thinking Certain Thoughts Sometimes Backfire

In our discussion of counterfactual thinking, we noted that such thoughts occur automatically in many situations, and that to prevent them from influencing our judgments, we must often try to suppress them. You have probably tried to do this—to suppress certain thoughts—in many other contexts, too. For example, if you have ever been on a diet, you probably tried to avoid thinking about delicious desserts or other forbidden foods (see Figure 2.11). And if you have ever felt nervous about giving a speech in front of others, you probably tried to avoid thinking about all the ways in which you could fail at this task.

How do we accomplish such **thought suppression,** and what are the effects of this process? According to Daniel Wegner (1992a; Wegner & Gold, 1995), a social psychologist who has studied thought suppression in detail, efforts to keep certain thoughts out of consciousness involve two components. First, there is an automatic monitoring process, which searches for evidence that unwanted thoughts are about to intrude. When such thoughts are detected by the first process, a second one, which is more effortful and less automatic (i.e., more controlled), swings into operation. This operating process involves effortful, conscious attempts to distract oneself by finding something else to think about. In a sense, the monitoring process is an "early warning" system that tells the person unwanted thoughts are present, and the second one is an active prevention system that keeps such thoughts out of consciousness through distraction.

thought suppression
Our efforts to prevent certain thoughts from entering consciousness.

Under normal circumstances, the two processes do a good job of suppressing unwanted thoughts. When information overload occurs or when individuals are fatigued, however, the monitoring process continues to identify unwanted thoughts, but the operating process no longer has the resources to keep them from entering consciousness. The result is that the individual actually experiences a pronounced rebound effect in which the unwanted thoughts occur at an even higher rate than was true before efforts to suppress them began. As we'll soon see, this can have serious consequences for the people involved.

The operation of the two processes described by Wegner (1992b, 1994) has been confirmed in many different studies (e.g., Wegner & Zanakos, 1994) and with respect to thoughts ranging from strange or unusual images (e.g., a white elephant) to thoughts about former lovers (Wegner & Gold, 1995). So this model of thought suppression appears to be an accurate one.

What are the effects of engaging in thought suppression—and of failing to accomplish this task? Generally, people engage in thought suppression as a means of influencing their own feelings and behavior. For example, if you want to avoid feeling angry, it's best not to think about incidents that cause you to feel resentment toward others. Similarly, if you want to avoid feeling depressed, it's useful to avoid thinking about events or experiences that make you feel sad. But sometimes, people engage in thought suppression because they are told to do so by someone else—for instance a therapist who is trying to help them cope with a personal problem. For example, a therapist may tell an individual with a drinking problem to avoid thinking about the pleasures of alcohol (e.g., how good drinking makes them feel). If the individual succeeds in suppressing such thoughts, this might help them overcome this problem. But consider what happens if the individual fails in these efforts at thought suppression. This may lead the patient to think: "What a failure I am—I can't even control my thoughts!" As a result, this person's motivation to continue these efforts—or even to continue therapy—may decline, which is a negative outcome (e.g., Kelly & Kahn, 1994).

In sum, thought suppression is as tricky and complex process. Although we all engage in it from time to time, it is sometimes difficult to perform, and while it can certainly be a help when we are trying to regulate our own behavior, it can sometimes go badly astray and generate effects that we don't desire and do not anticipate. So clearly, it is one aspect of social thought we should engage in with considerable care.

Magical Thinking, Terror Management, and Belief in the Supernatural

Please answer truthfully:

If you are in class and don't want the professor to call on you, do you try to avoid thinking about being called on?

Imagine that someone offered you a piece of chocolate shaped like a cockroach—would you eat it?

On the basis of purely rational considerations, you know what your answers should be: no and yes. But are those the answers you actually gave? Probably not, if you are like most people. In fact, research findings indicate that as human beings, we are quite susceptible to what has been termed **magical thinking** (Rozin & Nemeroff, 1990). Such thinking makes assumptions that don't hold up to rational scrutiny but which are compelling nonetheless. One principle of such magical thinking assumes that someone's thoughts can influence the physical world in a manner not governed by the laws of physics; if you think about being called on by your professor, it does not change the probability that you actually will be! Another is the law of similarity, which suggests that things that resemble one another share basic properties. So people won't eat a chocolate shaped like a cockroach even though they know, rationally, that its shape has nothing to do with how it tastes (see Figure 2.12 on page 62).

magical thinking
Thinking involving assumptions that don't hold up to rational scrutiny—for example, the belief that things that resemble one another share fundamental properties.

Figure 2.12
Magical Thinking:
An Example
*Would you eat the candy
shown here? Many people
would not, even though they
realize that the shape of the
candy has nothing to do with
its taste. This illustrates the
law of similarity—one aspect
of what social psychologists
term magical thinking.*

Surprising as it may seem, our thinking about many situations—including social ones—is frequently influenced by such magical thinking. And some thinking of this has, surprisingly, a logical basis. As human beings, we are uniquely aware of the fact that will certainly die; this, in turn, causes us to engage in what is known as **terror management**—efforts to come to terms with this certainty and its unsettling implications. One kind of thinking that helps is belief in the supernatural—powers outside our understanding and certainly control—that can influence our lives. Recent research indicates that when we are reminded of our own mortality, such beliefs are strengthened (Norenzayan & Hansen, 2006). In short, when we come face-to-face with the certainty of our own deaths, we try to manage the strong reactions this produces, and one way of doing this is to engage in thinking that is largely outside of what we consider to be rational or logical thought.

So, the next time you are tempted to make fun of someone's superstitious belief (e.g., fear of the number thirteen or of black cats crossing one's path), think again: Your own thinking is almost certainly not totally free from the kind of magical (i.e., nonrational) assumptions that seem to underlie a considerable portion of our social thought.

Social Cognition: Some Optimistic Conclusions

Having discussed the sources of error in social thought—the negativity bias, the optimistic bias, counterfactual thinking, magical thinking, and thought suppression—you may be ready to lose hope: Can we ever get it right? The answer, in fact, is absolutely. Although we are definitely not perfect information-processing machines, we do have limited cognitive capacities, and we can't increase these by buying pop-in memory chips, our judgments do seem to "suffice" much of the time. And yes, we are somewhat lazy where social thought is concerned: We generally do the least amount of cognitive work possible in any situation. Despite these limitations, though, we frequently do an impressive job in thinking about others. While we're flooded by truly enormous amounts of social information, we manage to sort, store, remember, and use a large portion of this input in an intelligent and highly efficient manner. Our thinking is indeed subject to many potential sources of bias, and we do make errors. But by and large, we do a good job of processing social information and making sense out of the social world around us. So, while we can imagine being even better at these tasks than we are, there's no reason to be discouraged. On the contrary, we can take pride in the fact that we accomplish so much with the limited tools at our disposal.

terror management
Our efforts to come to terms
with certainty of our own death
and its unsettling implications.

KeyPoints

- We show a strong negativity bias—a tendency to be highly sensitive to negative stimuli or information. This tendency appears to be basic and may be built into the functioning of our brains. Thus, it may be the result of evolutionary factors.

- However, it can be overcome by situational factors indicating that paying attention to positive information is adaptive.

- We also show a strong optimistic bias, which is expecting positive events and outcomes in many contexts. In addition, we tend to make overly optimistic predictions about how long it will take to complete a given task, an effect known as the planning fallacy. The optimistic bias also shows up in our tendency to assume that we are more likely than other people to experience positive outcomes but are less likely than others to experience negative ones.

- In many situations, individuals imagine what might have been, when they engage in counterfactual thinking. Such thought can affect our sympathy for people who have experienced negative outcomes and can cause us to experience strong regret over missed opportunities.

- Individuals often engage in thought suppression, trying to prevent themselves from thinking about certain topics (e.g., delicious desserts, alcohol, cigarettes). These efforts are often successful, but sometimes they result in a rebound effect, in which such thoughts actually increase in frequency.

- There are important limits on our ability to think rationally about the social world. One involves magical thinking—thinking based on assumptions that don't hold up to rational scrutiny. For instance, we may believe that if two objects are in contact, properties can pass from one to the other.

- One form of such thinking—belief in the supernatural—stems, at least in part, from terror management—our efforts to cope with the knowledge that we will die. While social cognition is subject to many sources of error, we generally do an excellent job of understanding the social world.

Think About It

Do you think we can learn to use counterfactual thinking so that it provides mainly benefits—boosts in our current moods, better task performance—rather than negative outcomes, such as bitter regrets? How could we learn to do this?

Affect and Cognition: How Feelings Shape Thought and Thought Shapes Feelings

Think of a time in your own life when you were in a good mood—something good had happened and you were feeling happy. Now, in contrast, remember a time when you were in a bad or negative mood—something bad had occurred, and you were feeling down and blue. Was your thinking different at these two times? In other words, did you perceive the world differently, remember different kinds of events or experiences, reason differently, and perhaps think about other people in contrasting ways? In all likelihood you did, because a large body of research findings indicate that there is a continuous and complex interplay between affect—our current moods or feelings—and cognition—various aspects of the ways in which people think, process, store, remember, and use information (e.g., Forgas, 2000; Isen, 2002; Isen & Labroo, 2003). We don't use the word *interplay* lightly because in fact, existing evidence strongly suggests that the relationship between affect and cognition is a two-way street: Our feelings and moods strongly influence several aspects of cognition, and cognition, in turn, exerts strong effects on our feelings and moods (e.g., Baron, In press; McDonald & Hirt, 1997; Seta, Hayes, & Seta, 1994). We'll now take a closer look at the nature of these effects.

The Influence of Affect on Cognition

First, and perhaps most obviously, our current moods often strongly influence our perceptions of the world around us. When we are in a good mood (experiencing positive affect), we tend to perceive almost everything—situations, other people, ideas, even new inventions—in more positive terms than we do when we are in a negative mood (e.g., Clore, Schwarz, & Conway, 1993). Indeed, this effect is so strong and so pervasive, that we are even more likely to judge statements as true if we encounter them while in a positive mood than if we read or hear them while in a neutral or negative mood (Garcia-Marques, et al., 2004).

Such effects have important practical implications. For instance, consider their impact on job interviews—a context in which interviewers meet many people for the first time. A growing body of evidence indicates that even experienced interviewers can't avoid being influenced by their current moods: They assign higher ratings to the people they interview when they are in a good mood than when they are in a bad mood (e.g., Baron, 1993; Robbins & DeNisi, 1994).

Another way in which affect influences cognition involves its impact on memory. Here, two different, but related, kinds of effects seem to occur. One is known as **mood congruence effects.** This refers to the fact that current moods strongly determine which information in a given situation is noticed and entered into memory. In other words, current moods serve as a kind of filter, permitting primarily information consistent with these moods to enter into long-term storage. Second, affect also influences what specific information is retrieved from memory, an effect known as **mood dependent memory** (e.g., Baddeley, 1990; Eich, 1995). When experiencing a particular mood, individuals are more likely to remember information they acquired in the past while in a similar mood than information they acquired while in a different mood. Current moods, in other words, serve as a kind of retrieval cue, prompting recall of information consistent with these moods. Here's an illustration of the difference between these two effects. Suppose that you a meet two people for the first time. You meet one when you are in a good mood but meet the other one when you are in a bad mood (e.g., you just learned that you did poorly on an important exam). Because of mood congruence effects, you will probably notice and store in memory mainly positive information about the first person, but you are more likely to notice and store in memory mainly negative information about the second person. Your mood when you meet these people determines what you notice and remember about them.

Now, imagine that at a later time, you are in a good mood. Which person comes to mind? Probably, the one you met while in a similar (good) mood. Here, your current mood serves to trigger memories of information you acquired (and stored in memory) when you were in a similar mood in the past. Together, mood congruence and mood dependent memory strongly influence the information we store in memory. Because this is the information we can later remember, the impact of affect on memory has important implications for many aspects of social thought and social behavior. (See Figure 2.13 on page 65 for a summary of these points).

Our current moods also influence another important component of cognition—creativity. The results of several studies suggest that being in a happy mood can increase creativity, perhaps because being in a happy mood activates a wider range of ideas or associations than being in a negative mood, and creativity consists, in part, of combining such associations into new patterns (e.g., Estrada, Isen, & Young, 1995; Isen, 2000).

A third way in which affect influences cognition involves the tendency to engage in heuristic processing, thinking that relies heavily on mental shortcuts (heuristics) and knowledge acquired through past experience. For instance, if we choose to buy a product because a famous celebrity we like endorses it, even though the celebrity has no special

mood congruence effects
The fact that we are more likely to store or remember positive information when in a positive mood and negative information when in a negative mood.

mood dependent memory
The fact that what we remember while in a given mood may be determined, in part, by what we learned when previously in that mood.

expertise concerning this product, we are engaging in heuristic thinking: We buy the product simply because someone we like uses it. The tendency to engage in heuristic thinking, in turn, has important implications for decision making and problem solving—activities we all perform frequently. Research findings indicate that people experiencing positive affect are more likely than people experiencing negative affect to engage in

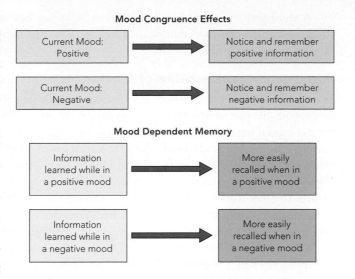

Mood Congruence Effects

Current Mood: Positive → Notice and remember positive information

Current Mood: Negative → Notice and remember negative information

Mood Dependent Memory

Information learned while in a positive mood → More easily recalled when in a positive mood

Information learned while in a negative mood → More easily recalled when in a negative mood

Figure 2.13
The Effects of Mood on Memory
Our moods influence what we remember through two mechanisms: mood congruence effects, which refer to the fact that we are more likely to store or remember information consistent with our current mood, and mood dependent memory, which refers to the fact that we tend to remember information consistent with our current moods.

heuristic thought (i.e., to rely on previously acquired rules of thumb and previously gathered information) in dealing with current problems or decisions (e.g., Mackie & Worth, 1989; Park & Banaji, 2000; Wegner & Petty, 1994). This tendency, in turn, offers a mixed pattern of advantages and disadvantages. One potential benefit is the capacity to make decisions faster and more efficiently (Erez & Isen, 2002).

On the other hand, an enhanced tendency to engage in heuristic thought can interfere with effective decision making and problem solving when individuals face novel tasks to which previous knowledge is not applicable or relevant (Isen, 2000). In such cases, detailed, analytical thinking is required, and heuristic processing may prove detrimental.

Finally, we should mention that our current moods (affect) often influence our interpretations of other people's behavior and the motives behind it. Positive affect tends to promote attributions of positive motives on the part of other people, while negative affect tends to encourage attributions of negative motives (e.g., Forgas, 2000). As we'll note in Chapter 3, our thoughts about the cause of others' behavior play an important role in many situations, so this is another way in which the interplay between affect and cognition can have important effects.

The Influence of Cognition on Affect

Most research on the relationship between affect and cognition has focused on how feelings influence thought. However, there is also strong evidence for the reverse—the impact of cognition on affect. One aspect of this relationship is described in what is known as the two-factor theory of emotion (Schachter, 1964). This theory suggests that often, we don't know our own feelings or attitudes directly. Rather, because these internal reactions are often somewhat ambiguous, we infer their nature from the external world—from the kinds of situations in which we experience these reactions. For example, if we experience increased arousal in the presence of an attractive person, we may conclude that we are in love. In contrast, if we experience increased arousal after being cut off in traffic by another driver, we may conclude that what we feel is anger.

A second way in which cognition can influence emotions is by activating schemas containing a strong affective component. For example, if we label an individual as belonging to some group, the schema for this social category may suggest what traits they probably possesses. In addition, it may tell us how we feel about such people. Thus, activation of a strong racial, ethnic, or religious schema or stereotype may exert powerful effects on our current feelings. (We'll return to this topic in Chapter 6.)

A third way in which our thoughts can influence our affective states involves our efforts to regulate our own emotions and feelings. This topic has important practical implications, so we'll examine it carefully.

Cognition and the Regulation of Affective States

Learning to regulate our emotions is an important task; negative events and outcomes are an unavoidable part of life, so learning to cope with the negative feelings these events generate is crucial for effective personal adjustment—and for good social relations with others. For example, individuals who lose their tempers often usually find it difficult to get along with others and may, in fact, be avoided by them. Among the most important techniques we use for regulating our moods and emotions are ones involving cognitive mechanisms. In other words, we use our thoughts to regulate our feelings. Many techniques for accomplishing this goal exist, but here, we'll consider one that is especially common—giving in to temptation as a means of improving our current mood.

When we feel "down" or distressed, we often engage in activities that we know are bad for us but which make us feel better, at least temporarily (e.g., eating fattening snacks, wasting time watching television; see Figure 2.14). These actions make us feel better, but we know full well that have an important downside. Why, then, do we choose to do them? In the past it was assumed that we engage in such actions because the emotional distress we are experiencing reduces either our capacity or motivation to control our impulses to do things that are enjoyable but potentially bad for us. However, Tice and others (2000) argue that in fact, cognitive factors play a role in such behavior. They argue that we often consciously choose to yield to temptations at times when we are experiencing negative affect. In other words, this is not an automatic behavior or a sign of weakness; rather it is a strategic choice that we make. We yield to temptation because it does help us deal with strong negative feelings.

To test this prediction, Tice et al. (2000) conducted a study in which participants were first put into a good or bad mood (by reading stories in which they either saved a child's life or ran a red light and so caused the death of a child). Then, they were either told that their moods could change over time or that because of an aromatherapy candle the experimenter lit, their moods were "frozen" and could not change much. Participants were then told that they would work on an intelligence test and would receive feedback on their performance. Before doing the test, though, they would have a fifteen-minute practice session to prepare for it. The experimenter then left them in a room containing materials for practicing for the test and distracters—other tasks on which they could work. For half the participants these tasks were attractive and tempting (e.g., a challenging puzzle, a video game, and popular magazines). For the

Figure 2.14
Regulating Our Own Affective States: Conscious Choice or Yielding to Temptation?
When they are feeling down, many people engage in activities designed to boost their moods—they eat, watch television, consume alcohol, and so on. In the past, it was assumed that such actions were the result of yielding to temptation. Research findings now suggest, however, that engaging in such actions is the result of conscious cognitive strategies for regulating our emotions.

others, they were less attractive (a preschool-level plastic puzzle and out-of-date technical journals). The main question was this: Would people in a bad mood spend more of the practice time than people in a good mood playing with the distracters (procrastinating)? More importantly, would this occur only in the condition in which participants believed they could change their own moods? After all, there would be no use in playing with the distracters if participants believed that their moods were frozen and could not be altered. Ticc and others (2000) predicted that this would be the case: People in a bad mood would procrastinate more, but only when they believed doing so would enhance their moods.

Results offered clear support for the prediction. These findings indicate that the tendency to yield to temptation and engage in forbidden pleasures is one technique we use to reduce negative feelings of distress. Further, it appears that such actions may represent a strategic and conscious choice and not a simple lapse in the ability to control our own impulses. Through this and other techniques, we use various aspects of cognition to influence our moods, so truly, the interface between affect and cognition is very much a two-way street.

Affect and Cognition: Social Neuroscience Evidence for Two Separate Systems

So far we have argued that affect and cognition are intimately linked, and in fact, existing evidence suggests that this is certainly the case. However, we should also note that recent findings using neuroscience techniques (e.g., scanning of human brains as individuals perform various activities) indicate that actually two distinct systems for processing social information may exist within the human brain (e.g., Cohen, 2005). One system is concerned with what might be termed reason—logical thought—while the other deals primarily with affect or emotion. These two systems, although distinct in certain respects, interact in many ways during problem solving, decision making, and other important forms of cognition. For instance, consider research employing what is known as an "ultimatum" paradigm.

In such research, two people are told that they can divide a given sum (e.g., ten dollars) between them. One person can suggest an initial division, and the second can accept or reject it. Because any division provides the second person with positive payoffs, total rationality (and classic economic theory) suggests that acceptance of any division offered is the most rational (and best) course of action. In fact, however, most people reject divisions that give them less than three dollars, and many reject division that offer them less than five dollars. Magnetic resonance imaging (MRI) scans of the brains of people performing this task reveal that when they receive offers they view as unfair, brain regions related both to reasoning (e.g., the dorsolateral prefrontal cortex) and to emotion (e.g., the limbic system) are active. However the greater the amount of activity in the emotion-processing regions is, the greater the likelihood that individuals will reject the offers and act in ways that are, in a sense, contrary to their own economic interests (e.g., Sanfey, Rilling, Aronson, Nystrum, & Cohen, 2003). These findings, and those of many other studies, provide concrete evidence for the existence of two distinct systems (reason and emotion) that interact in complex ways during decision-making and other cognitive processes (e.g., Gabaix & Laibson, 2006).

Additional research indicates that the neural system for emotion (affect) tends to be impulsive, preferring immediate rewards, while the system for reason is more forward-looking and accepting of delays that ultimately yield larger rewards. For instance, when offered the choice between an immediate gain (a fifteen-dollar Amazon.com gift now) and a larger one in two weeks (a twenty-dollar gift voucher), increased activity again occurs in both emotion and reason-processing regions of the brain. The immediate option, however,

MAKING SENSE OF COMMON SENSE
A SOCIAL PSYCHOLOGICAL PERSPECTIVE
Is Being in a Good Mood Always Beneficial?
The Potential Downside of Being Up

Everyone wants to feel happy, and there is no doubt that for most of us, being in a good mood is more pleasant than being in a bad one. So common sense strongly suggests that we should do everything we can to enhance our current moods. Consistent with this belief, research findings indicate that when people are in a good mood they tend to be more creative and to be more helpful to others than when they are in a negative mood (e.g., Baron, 1997; Isen, 1984; Isen & Levin, 1972). But is being in a good mood always a plus? Does it always produce positive effects? In fact, growing evidence suggests that in this respect, as in many others, common sense may be throwing us a curve. Constantly being in a good mood, in fact, may have some real drawbacks well worth considering.

First, there is no doubt that being in a good mood increases our willingness to help others—that has been demonstrated in many different studies (e.g., Isen, 1984). But the other side of the coin is that when we are in a good mood, we are more susceptible to others' efforts to get us to do what they want. In other words, as the cartoon in Figure 2.15 suggests, we are more susceptible to social influence from other people. We'll discuss such influence in detail in Chapter 8, but here, we should note that others who want to change our behavior or our attitudes don't always have our best interests at heart. Advertisers, salespeople, and sometimes politicians, too, want to influence us because doing so is beneficial to them, not us. So in this respect, being in a good mood can be quite risky: It increases our tendency to say yes to requests or other forms of influence from others and that can sometimes be downright dangerous!

An additional important disadvantage to being in a good mood relates to the effects of such positive feelings on social cognition. As we noted earlier, existing evidence suggests that one effect of being in a good mood is that it tends to encourage heuristic thinking—a reliance on mental shortcuts that reduce effort. Why would this

"A.T.&T. sent this drink over in the hope that you'll consider switching your long-distance provider."

Figure 2.15
One Potential Cost of Being in a Good Mood
When we experience positive affect, this often increases our willingness to accept influence from others. Executives at the large company named here hope to turn that effect to their advantage by enhancing the current mood of one potential customer.

(*Source: The New Yorker,* October 17, 2005.)

be the case? Several possibilities exist. First, being in a happy mood may decrease our capacity to process information, thus increasing our reliance on heuristics (Mackie & Worth, 1989). Second, happy moods may reduce our motivation to process information carefully; we are feeling too good to put out this kind of effort (e.g., Wegner & Petty, 1994). In fact, recent findings (Wilson, Centerbar, Kermer, & Gilbert, 2005) indicate that thinking systematically about pleasant events—ones that make us feel happy—can reduce the pleasure we obtain from such events. This, too, may lead us to prefer heuristic (automatic) thinking to controlled processing, at least with respect to events that make us feel good.

A closely related effect of being in a good mood involves dependence on an aspect of the availability heuristic—the ease-of-use heuristic. This mental shortcut suggests that the easier it is to use information in some way, the more influential or important it is viewed as being (e.g., Bless, 2001). Research findings indicate that when people are in a good mood, they are more likely to rely on this heuristic than when they are in a neutral mood, and that when they are in a bad mood, they are more likely to pay careful attention to the content of such information and not just how easily they can remember it (e.g., Ruder & Bless, 2003).

What does all this mean in practical terms? Although being in a good mood is certainly pleasant, such feelings are not always beneficial where the quality or effectiveness of our social cognition is concerned. In fact, feeling happy can lead us to ignore important information and to think in ways that can result in serious errors. Overall, then, careful research by social psychologists has helped us to qualify the commonsense suggestion that "feeling good is always a plus" and to understand that where social thought is concerned, this suggestion is not always correct.

induces greater activity in the emotion-related areas than the delayed option (e.g., the limbic system [McClure, Laibson, Lowenstein, & Cohen, 2004]).

Overall, then, evidence from research using modern techniques for scanning brain activity during cognitive processes suggests that affect plays a fundamental role in human thought, and that if we wish to fully understand the complex ways in which we think about the social world and our place in it, we must take this fact into careful account because truly, feelings shape our thoughts, and certain aspects of our thoughts influence our feelings.

Common sense suggests that feeling happy is a good thing, and as we saw earlier, positive affect does tend to enhance creativity and to increase efficiency in decision making. But is being in a good mood always beneficial? For a discussion of this intriguing issue and what social psychologists have to say about it, please read *Making Sense of Common Sense: A Social Psychological Perspective* on page 68.

> ### Principles to Remember
>
> Our moods strongly influence many aspects of our thinking (e.g., memory, decision making), and our thinking, in turn, can strongly influence our moods. So affect and cognition are closely and continuously linked.

KeyPoints

- Affect influences cognition in several ways. Our current moods can cause us to react positively or negatively to new stimuli, including other people, the extent to which we think systematically or heuristically, and can influence memory through mood dependent memory and mood congruence effects.

- Affect can also influence creativity. Recent findings indicate that emotion-provoking information can strongly influence judgments and decisions even if we try to ignore it.

- When we are in a positive mood, we tend to think heuristically to a greater extent than when we are a negative mood. Specifically, we show increased reliance on stereotypes and other mental short-cuts.

- Cognition influences affect through our interpretation of emotion-provoking events and through the activation of schemas containing a strong affective component.

- Research in social neuroscience indicates that we may actually possess two distinct systems for processing social information—one concerned with logical thought and the other with affect or emotion.

- We employ several cognitive techniques to regulate our emotions or feelings. For instance, when distressed, we can consciously choose to engage in activities that, while damaging in the long run, make us feel better in the short run.

- While experiencing positive feelings is certainly pleasant, there is definitely a downside to positive affect in which social cognition is concerned.

Think About It

Why should we possess two systems for processing social information—one relating to logical thought and the other to emotion? Can you think of ways in which this might be useful or adaptive?

SUMMARY AND REVIEW

- Because we have limited cognitive capacity, we often attempt to reduce the effort we expend on social cognition—how we think about other people and the social world. One basic component of social cognition is schemas—mental frameworks developed through experience that, once formed, help us to organize social information. Once formed, schemas exert powerful effects on what we notice (attention), enter into memory (encoding), and later remember (retrieval). Individuals report remembering more information consistent with their schemas than information inconsistent with them, but in fact, inconsistent information, too, is strongly represented in memory. Schemas are often primed—activated by experiences, events, or stimuli. Once they are primed, the effects of the schemas tend to persist until they are somehow expressed in thought or behavior; such expression (known as unpriming) then reduces their effects. Schemas help us to process information, but they often persist even in the face of disconfirming information. Schemas can also exert self-confirming effects, causing us to behave in ways that confirm them.

- Because our capacity to process information is limited, we often experience information overload. To avoid this, we make use of heuristics—rules for making decisions in a quick and relatively effortless manner. One such heuristic is representativeness, which suggests that the more similar an individual is to typical members of a given group, the more likely she or he is to belong to that group. Another heuristic is availability, which suggests that the easier it is to bring information to mind, the greater its impact on subsequent decisions or judgments. A third heuristic is anchoring and adjustment, which leads us to use a number or value as a starting point from which we then make adjustments. These adjustments may not be sufficient to reflect actual social reality because, perhaps, once we attain a plausible value, we stop the process.

- A large amount of evidence indicates that the distinction between automatic and controlled processing is a basic one. In fact, different regions of the brain appear to be involved in these two types of processing, especially with respect to evaluations of various aspects of the social world. When schemas or other cognitive frameworks are activated (even without our conscious awareness of such activation), they strongly influence our behavior, triggering actions consistent with the frameworks and also preparing us to interact with the people or groups who are the focus of these schemas. Automatic processing is quick and efficient; in addition, however, it may also sometimes offer other advantages, too—such as increased satisfaction with decisions.

- We show a strong negativity bias—a tendency to be highly sensitive to negative stimuli or information. However, this tendency can be overcome by situational factors indicating that paying attention to positive information is adaptive. We also show a strong optimistic bias, expecting positive events and outcomes in many contexts. In many situations, individuals imagine what might have been when they engage in counterfactual thinking. Such thought can affect our sympathy for people who have experienced negative outcomes and can cause us to experience strong regret over missed opportunities. Counterfactual thoughts seem to occur automatically in many situations, and their effects can only be reduced through hard, cognitive work in which they are suppressed is discounted. Individuals often engage in thought suppression, which is trying to prevent themselves from thinking about certain topics (e.g., delicious desserts, alcohol, cigarettes). These efforts are often successful, but sometimes they result in a rebound effect, in which such thoughts actually increase in frequency.

- There are important limits on our ability to think rationally about the social world. One involves magical thinking—thinking based on assumptions that don't hold up to rational scrutiny. For instance, we may believe that if two objects are in contact, properties can pass from one to the other. One form of such thinking—belief in the supernatural—stems, at least in part, from terror management, which are our efforts to cope with the knowledge that we will die. While social cognition is subject to many sources of error, we generally do an excellent job of understanding the social world.

- Affect influences cognition in several ways. Our current moods influence our perceptions of the world around us, the extent to which we think systematically or heuristically, and influence memory through mood congruence effects and mood dependent memory, Affect can also influence creativity, and our interpretations of others' behavior. Cognition influences affect through our interpretation of emotion-provoking events and through the activation of schemas containing a strong affective component. In addition, we employ several cognitive techniques to regulate our emotions or feelings (e.g., consciously giving into temptation to reduce negative feelings). Although affect and cognition are closely related, social neuroscience research indicates that they involve distinct systems within the brain.

Key Terms

affect (p. 39)

anchoring and adjustment heuristic (p. 47)

automatic processing (p. 49)

availability heuristic (p. 46)

counterfactual thinking (p. 57)

heuristics (p. 39)

information overload (p. 44)

magical thinking (p. 61)

mood congruence effects (p. 64)

mood dependent memory (p. 64)

negativity bias (p. 54)

optimistic bias (p. 55)

overconfidence barrier (p. 55)

planning fallacy (p. 55)

perseverance effect (p. 43)

priming (p. 41)

representativeness heuristic (p. 46)

schemas (p. 39)

social cognition (p. 38)

terror management (p. 62)

thought suppression (p. 60)

unpriming (p. 41)

Connections
INTEGRATING SOCIAL PSYCHOLOGY

In this chapter, you read about . . .	In other chapters, you will find related discussions of . . .
schemas	the effects of schemas on other aspects of social behavior such as attitudes (Chapter 4) and prejudice (Chapter 6).
potential sources of error in social cognition	the role of these errors in first impressions (Chapter 2), persuasion (Chapter 4), long-term relationships (Chapter 8), and the legal system (Chapter 13).
the interplay between affect and cognition	the role of such these links in many forms of social behavior, including prejudice (Chapter 6), attraction (Chapter 7), helping (Chapter 10), aggression (Chapter 11), and behavior in work settings (Chapter 13).

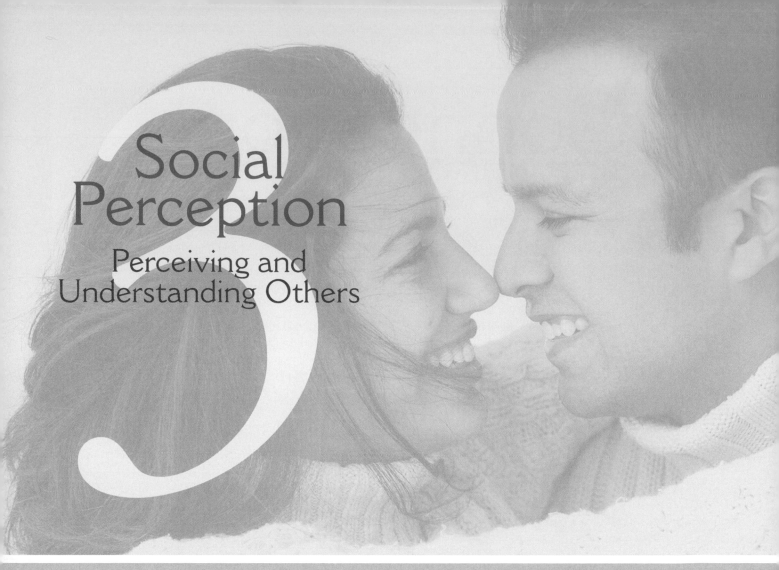

3 Social Perception

Perceiving and Understanding Others

CHAPTER OUTLINE

- **Nonverbal Communication: The Unspoken Language of Expressions, Gazes, and Gestures**
  Nonverbal Communication: The Basic Channels
  Deception: Recognizing It through Nonverbal Cues and Its Effects on Social Relations
  MAKING SENSE OF COMMON SENSE: A SOCIAL PSYCHOLOGICAL PERSPECTIVE—ARE MEN REALLY "CLUELESS" WHEN IT COMES TO NONVERBAL CUES? FICTION—AND FACT—ABOUT GENDER DIFFERENCES IN NONVERBAL COMMUNICATION

- **Attribution: Understanding the Causes of Others' Behavior**
  Theories of Attribution: Frameworks for Understanding How We Attempt to Make Sense of the Social World
  Attribution: Some Basic Sources of Error
  BUILDING THE SCIENCE: CLASSICS OF SOCIAL PSYCHOLOGY—THE FUNDAMENTAL ATTRIBUTION ERROR: STRONGER THAN YOU MIGHT GUESS
  Applications of Attribution Theory: Insights and Interventions

- **Impression Formation and Impression Management: Combining Information about Others**
  The Beginning of Research on First Impressions: Asch's Research on Central and Peripheral Traits
  How Quickly Are First Impressions Formed?
  Implicit Personality Theories: Schemas That Shape First Impressions
  Impression Formation: A Cognitive Perspective
  Is Accuracy Always Best in Social Perception? Evidence That Illusions, Too, Can Sometimes Be Helpful
  Impression Management: The Fine Art of Looking Good
  SOCIAL PSYCHOLOGY: WHAT IT TELLS US ABOUT . . . SPEED DATING—CAN WE REALLY CHOOSE THE ONE WE MIGHT LOVE IN A FEW MINUTES?

One of the most complex mysteries we face in life—and one we can't leave unsolved—is other people. We spend a lot of time thinking about others, trying to understand why they do what they do, whether they mean what they say, and how they feel about us. Social psychologists refer to this process as social perception, and it is a very central aspect of our existence as social beings. Are we good at this process? The answer suggested by decades of research is "Yes—and no." Sometimes we do it well, but at other times, we reach false conclusions about others and really don't understand them as well as we would prefer. Here are a couple of examples from my own life—first, an instance in which I did a good job at social perception and then another in which I did not.

I'll never forget the night I met my wife. I was attending a conference in Florida and was invited to dinner by friends who were also attending. When I arrived, one of my friends introduced me to a new faculty member from his department—and as soon as I looked at her, I felt as though I had been struck by lighting. Although I was a little dazed, I struck up a conversation with her and sat next to her at dinner. And then, gradually, I began to perceive that, wonder of wonders, she liked me, too! There was something in her eyes, in the way she smiled, and the fact that we seemed to lean toward each other as we spoke. . . . All this encouraged me, so I asked her to take a walk with me after dinner. When she agreed, I remember thinking "Wow! For some reason, this beautiful, intelligent, charming woman likes *me*!" The rest is history—our history because we are now a happily married couple. So, that night, my social perception worked well and gave me accurate information—thank goodness! But now consider the following experience, when I didn't do it well at all. . . .

I was selling a used car (an old Volkswagen, this time). I placed an ad in the local newspaper, and the first person who came to see it drove all the way from a city about sixty miles away. He took the car for a test drive, and then quickly offered me a figure close to the asking price. "Sold!" I said and felt happy about the transaction. He wrote me a check, and then after the documents were signed, he drove off in my old car. Can you guess what happened next? When I tried to cash his check, it bounced. Apparently, he had closed his account and moved out of the state, leaving behind a pile of unpaid bills, including the bad check he wrote to me. As I thought about what had happened, I realized that there were clear signs that I should have noticed. He never looked me in the eye as we spoke and seemed a little nervous throughout the entire transaction. Also, his wife, who had come with him, stood far away and seemed a little upset when he handed me the check. And he seemed in a hurry from the moment he arrived and didn't really check out the car carefully. . . . So in fact, there had been clear signs that he was not to be trusted. But somehow, I overlooked them— and paid the price. In this case, my efforts at social perception failed and led me to the wrong conclusions about the buyer; I assumed that he was a legitimate buyer, when, in fact, he had larceny in mind from the start. (As we'll soon see, determining whether another person is telling the truth or lying is one of the trickiest tasks we face with respect to social perception.)

As these examples illustrate, **social perception** is indeed a complex and tricky business. In the rest of this chapter, we'll explain why social perception is often so difficult and the times when we are most likely to get it right. Unfortunately, no machine, like the one in the cartoon in Figure 3.1, exists (at least not yet), so we have to rely on our own skills and abilities in our efforts to understand others. In fact, this is an important task because other people play such a central role in our lives that we have no choice but to try to understand them as well as we can. As you can probably guess, social perception is a complex process and involves many different tasks. Here, however, we'll focus on three of its most central aspects. First, we'll consider **nonverbal communication**—valuable information about others' current feelings and reactions provided by their facial expressions, eye contact, body movements, and postures (e.g., Ekman, 2003; Zebrowitz, 1997). Next, we'll examine **attribution,** the process through which we attempt to understand the reasons behind others' behavior—why they have acted as they have in a given situation, what goals they are seeking, and what intentions they have (e.g., Burrus & Roese, 2006). Third, we'll examine the nature of **impression formation**—how we form first impressions of others—and **impression management (or self-presentation)**—how we try to assure that these impressions are favorable ones.

social perception
The process through which we seek to know and understand other people.

nonverbal communication
Communication between individuals that does not involve the content of spoken language. It relies instead on an unspoken language of facial expressions, eye contact, and body language.

attribution
The process through which we seek to identify the causes of others' behavior and so gain knowledge of their stable traits and dispositions.

impression formation
The process through which we form impressions of others.

impression management (self-presentation)
Efforts by individuals to produce favorable first impressions on others.

Nonverbal Communication: The Unspoken Language of Expressions, Gazes, and Gestures

Are other people more likely to do favors for you when they are in a good mood or a bad one? And when are they more likely to lose their temper and lash out at you, when they are feeling happy and content or when they are feeling tense and irritable? The answers are obvious, and they suggest that often, social actions—our own and those of other people—are affected by temporary factors or causes. Changing moods, shifting emotions, fatigue, illness, or drugs—all of these other variables, too—can influence the ways in which we think and behave.

Because such temporary factors exert important effects on social behavior and thought, we are often interested in them: We try to find out how others are feeling right now. How do we go about this process? Sometimes, in a straightforward way: We ask other people directly. Unfortunately, this strategy often fails because others are unwilling to reveal their inner feelings to us. On the contrary, they may actively seek to conceal such information or even lie to us about their current emotions (e.g., DePaulo et al., 2003; Forrest & Feldman, 2000).

Figure 3.1
A Machine for Social Perception? Not Yet
No machine for measuring the truthfulness of others' words—or their motives, intentions, or traits—yet exists. So, contrary to what this cartoon suggests, we must rely on our own skills rather than electronic equipment in our efforts to understand others.

(*Source:* Universal Press syndicate, November 13, 1998.)

For example, negotiators often hide their reactions from their opponents; and salespeople frequently show more liking and friendliness toward potential customers than they really feel.

In situations like these, we often fall back on another, less direct method for gaining information about others' reactions: We pay careful attention to nonverbal cues provided by changes in their facial expressions, eye contact, posture, body movements, and other expressive actions. As noted by De Paulo et al. (2003), such behavior is relatively irrepressible—difficult to control—so that even when people try to conceal their inner feelings from us, these feelings often "leak out" in many ways through nonverbal cues. The information conveyed by such cues, and our efforts to interpret this input, are often described as nonverbal communication. In this section, we'll first examine the basic means through which nonverbal communication takes place. (This is known as the basic channels of nonverbal communication.) Then we'll turn to some interesting findings concerning how we use nonverbal cues to cut through deception—efforts by other people to mislead us about their true feelings or beliefs (e.g., DePaulo, 1994). Before beginning, though, we should make one more point: Nonverbal cues emitted by others can affect our own feelings even if we are not consciously paying attention to these cues or trying to figure out how these people feel (Ko, Judd, & Blair, 2006). For instance, when individuals hear feminine-sounding voices (ones that are high in pitch), they tend to attribute stereotypic female traits to the speaker even if they don't expect to meet these people or interact with them (Ko et al., 2006). In contrast, if they hear masculine-sounding voices (ones that are lower in pitch and greater in resonance), they attribute masculine traits to these speakers. In other words, they jump to important conclusions about others on the basis of subtle nonverbal cues (voice pitch is, in a sense, a *nonverbal cue* because it is unrelated to the words being spoken.) Having made that point, let's now examine the basic channels of nonverbal communication.

Nonverbal Communication: The Basic Channels

Think for a moment: Do you act differently when you are feeling happy than when you are feeling sad? Most likely, you do. People tend to behave differently when experiencing different emotional states. But precisely how do differences in your inner states—your emotions, feelings, and moods—show up in your behavior? This question relates to the basic channels through which such communication takes place. Research findings indicate that there are five of these channels: *facial expressions*, *eye contact*, *body movements*, *posture, and touching*.

Unmasking the Face: Facial Expressions as Clues to Others' Emotions

More than two thousand years ago, the Roman orator Cicero stated: "The face is the image of the soul." By this he meant that human feelings and emotions are often reflected in the face and can be read there in specific expressions. Modern research suggests that Cicero was correct: It is possible to learn a great deal about others' current moods and feelings from their facial expressions. In fact, it appears that five different basic emotions are represented clearly on the human face, even from an early age: *anger, fear, happiness, sadness,* and *disgust* (Izard, 1991; Rozin, Lowery, & Ebert, 1994). Surprise is another emotion that has also been suggested as a basic one reflected clearly in facial expressions, but recent evidence concerning this suggestions is mixed, so it may not be as basic or as clearly represented in facial expressions as other emotions (Reisenzein, Bordgen, Holtbernd, & Matz, 2006).

It's important to realize that the fact that only five different emotions are represented on our faces does not imply that human beings can show only a small number of facial expressions. On the contrary, emotions occur in many combinations (e.g., joy together with sorrow, fear combined with anger), and each of these reactions can vary greatly in strength. Thus, while there may be only a small number of basic themes in facial expressions, the number of variations on these themes is immense (see Figure 3.2 on page 77).

Figure 3.2
Facial Expressions: The Range Is Huge
Although only five basic emotions are represented in distinct facial expressions, these emotions can occur in many combinations and be shown to varying degrees. The result is that the number of unique facial expressions any one person can show is truly immense.

Now for another important question: Are facial expressions universal? In other words, if you traveled to a remote part of the world and visited a group of people who had never before met an outsider, would their facial expressions in various situations resemble your own? Would they smile in reaction to events that made them happy, frown when exposed to conditions that made then angry, and so on? Further, would you be able to recognize these distinct expressions as readily as the ones shown by people belonging to your own culture? Early research on this question seemed to suggest that facial expressions are universal in both respects (e.g., Ekman & Friesen, 1975), and with few exceptions, these results have been confirmed in more recent research (Elfenbein & Ambady, 2002). In fact, it has been found that certain facial expressions—smiles, frowns and other signs of sadness—occur and are recognized as representing basic underlying emotions (e.g., happiness, anger, sadness) in many different cultures (e.g., Shaver, Murdaya, & Fraley, 2001). This overall pattern of findings is not entirely consistent (e.g., Russell, 1994), but it seems reasonable to conclude that some facial expressions provide clear signals of underlying emotional states and are recognized as doing so all over the world. Cultural differences certainly do exist with respect to the precise meaning of facial expressions, but unlike spoken languages, they do not seem to require much in the way of translation.

While many different studies provide clear evidence for these conclusions, research conducted with athletes competing in the Olympics are especially interesting in this respect. When photos of the faces of these athletic stars are taken at various times (on winning or losing their matches, when receiving their medals, while posing for photographers), clear evidence of recognizable facial expressions—ones reflecting the athletes' underlying emotional states—is obtained (Matsumoto & Willingham, 2006). For instance, almost all gold medal winners smile clearly and openly when they win their matches and also when they receive their medals. Most bronze medalists, too, smile although not as high a percentage as among gold medal winners. In contrast, few silver medal winners smile. Why does this difference between bronze and silver medal winners exist? Because the bronze medal winners are happy to have won *any* medal, their facial expressions show this. In contrast, silver medalists torture themselves with (counterfactual) thoughts about how they could have received the gold "if only . . ." (see Chapter 2; Figure 3.3 on page 78).

Additional findings indicate that when posing for photographers, gold and bronze medal winners show true (real) smiles; silver medal winners, in contrast, show the kind of "social smiling" everyone can show when a smile is required, but the smiles do not reflect underlying happiness. These findings, and those of many other studies, indicate that others' facial

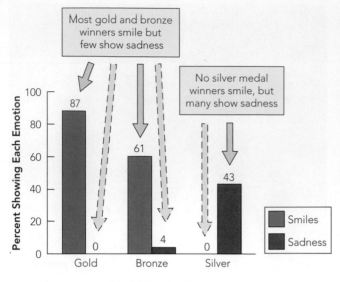

Figure 3.3
Facial Expressions among Gold, Silver, and Bronze Medal Olympic Medal Winners

As shown here, gold medal winners and bronze medal winners smiled frequently (at the conclusion of their matches and when receiving their medals). In contrast, silver medal winners did not smile; they showed sadness instead. These findings reflect the underlying emotions of these athletes: Gold and bronze medal winners are happy with their results; silver medal winners, in contrast, are unhappy because they imagine getting the gold.

(*Source:* Based on data from Matsumoto & Willingham, 2006).

staring
A form of eye contact in which one person continues to gaze steadily at another regardless of what the recipient does.

body language
Cues provided by the position, posture, and movement of others' bodies or body parts.

expressions are often a useful guide to their feelings. Thus it is not at all surprising that we rely on such information as a basis for forming accurate perceptions of others—or at least, perceptions of how they are feeling at a given moment.

Gazes and Stares: Eye Contact as a Nonverbal Cue

Have you ever had a conversation with someone wearing vary dark or mirrored sunglasses? If so, you realize that this can be an uncomfortable situation. Because you can't see the other person's eyes, you are uncertain about how she or he is reacting. Taking note of the importance of cues provided by others' eyes, ancient poets often described the eyes as "windows to the soul." In one important sense, they were correct: We do often learn much about others' feelings from their eyes. For example, we interpret a high level of gazing from another as a sign of liking or friendliness (Kleinke, 1986). In contrast, if others avoid eye contact with us, we may conclude that they are unfriendly, don't like us, or are simply shy.

While a high level of eye contact with others is usually interpreted as a sign of liking or positive feelings, there is one exception to this general rule. If another person gazes at us continuously and maintains such contact regardless of what we do, that person can be said to be **staring.** A stare is often interpreted as a sign of anger or hostility—as in cold stare—and most people find this particular nonverbal cue disturbing (Ellsworth & Carlsmith, 1973). In fact, we may quickly terminate social interaction with someone who stares at us and may even leave the scene (Greenbaum & Rosenfield, 1978). This is one reason why experts on "road rage"—highly aggressive driving by motorists, sometimes followed by actual assaults—recommend that drivers avoid eye contact with people who are disobeying traffic laws and rules of the road (e.g., Bushman, 1998). Apparently, such people, who are already in a highly excitable state, interpret anything approaching a stare from another driver as an aggressive act and react accordingly.

Body Language: Gestures, Posture, and Movements

Try this simple demonstration for yourself:

First, remember some incident that made you angry—the angrier the better. Think about it for a minute.

Now, try to remember another incident, one that made you feel sad—again, the sadder the better.

Compare your behavior in the two contexts. Did you change your posture or move your hands, arms, or legs as your thoughts shifted from the first event to the second? There is a good chance that you did because our current moods or emotions are often reflected in the position, posture, and movement of our bodies. Together, such nonverbal behaviors are termed **body language,** and they, too, can provide useful information about others.

First, body language often reveals others' emotional states. Large numbers of movements—especially ones in which one part of the body does something to another part (touching, rubbing, scratching) —suggest emotional arousal. The greater the frequency of such behavior is, the higher the level of arousal or nervousness is.

Larger patterns of movements, involving the whole body, can also be informative. Such phrases as "she adopted a *threatening posture*" and "he greeted her with *open arms*" suggest that different body orientations or postures indicate contrasting emotional states. In fact, research by Aronoff, Woike, and Hyman (1992) confirms this possibility. These researchers first identified two groups of characters in classical ballet: ones who played a dangerous or threatening role (e.g., Macbeth, the Angel of Death, Lizzie Borden) and ones who played warm, sympathetic roles (Juliet, Romeo). Then they examined examples of dancing by these characters in actual ballets to see if they adopted different kinds of postures.

Figure 3.4
Gestures: One Form of Nonverbal Communication
Do you recognize the gestures shown here? Can you tell what they mean? In the United States and other Western cultures, each of these gestures has a clear meaning. However they might well have no meaning or entirely different meanings, in other cultures.

Aronoff and his colleagues predicted that the dangerous, threatening characters would show more diagonal or angular postures, while the warm sympathetic characters would show more rounded postures, and results strongly confirmed this hypothesis. These and related findings indicate that large-scale body movements or postures can sometimes provide important information about others' emotions and even about their apparent traits.

More specific information about others' feelings is often provided by gestures. These fall into several categories, but perhaps the most important are emblems, which are body movements carrying specific meanings in a given culture. Do you recognize the gestures shown in Figure 3.4? In the United States and several other countries, these movements have clear and definite meanings. However in other cultures, they might have no meaning or even a different meaning. For this reason, it is wise to be careful about using gestures while traveling in cultures different from your own: You may offend the people around you without meaning to do so.

Interestingly, other findings (e.g., Schubert, 2004) indicate that specific gestures can have different meanings for women and men. For instance, gestures associated with bodily force, such a clenched fist, seem to signal increased power (or efforts to obtain it) for men; for women, such bodily actions seem to signal loss of power or reduced hope of gaining it. This, in turn, may reflect the fact that men are considerably stronger than women and so often seek to gain power through force, while for women, force is more often defensive and has much less chance of success. Whatever the precise mechanisms involved, gender differences in the use and perception of various gestures do appear to exist.

Touching: Is a Firm Handshake Really a "Plus"?

Suppose that during a brief conversation with another person, she or he touched you briefly. How would you react? What information would this behavior convey? The answer to both questions is *it depends*. And what it depends on is several factors relating to who does the touching (a friend, a stranger, or a member of your own or the other gender); the nature of this physical contact (brief or prolonged, gentle or rough, what part of the body is touched); and the context in which the touching takes place (a business or social setting, a doctor's office). Depending on such factors, touch can suggest affection, sexual interest, dominance, caring, or even aggression. Despite such complexities, existing evidence indicates that when touching is considered appropriate, it often produces positive reactions in the person being touched (e.g., Alagna, Whitcher, & Fisher, 1979; Smith, Gier, & Willis, 1982). But remember it must be viewed as appropriate to produce such reactions.

One acceptable way in which people in many different cultures touch strangers is through handshaking. "Pop psychology" and even books on etiquette (e.g., Vanderbilt, 1957) suggest that handshakes reveal much about other people—for instance, their personalities—and that a firm handshake is a good way to make a favorable first impression on others. Are such observations true? Is this form of nonverbal communication actually revealing? Research findings (e.g., Chaplin, Phillips, Brown, Clanton, & Stein, 2000) suggest that it is. The firmer, longer, and more vigorous others' handshakes are, the higher we tend to rate them in terms of extraversion and openness to experience, and our first impressions of them tend to be more favorable.

In sum, we use this particular kind of touching as a basis for forming social perceptions of others. In this respect, popular books about the road to success are correct: A firm handshake *is* a valuable asset, at least in cultures in which handshakes are used for greetings and departures.

Deception: Recognizing It through Nonverbal Cues, and Its Effects on Social Relations

Shakespeare once wrote: "Though I am not naturally honest, I am so sometimes by chance." As usual, he was a keen observer of human behavior because research findings indicate that most people tell one or more lies every day (DePaulo & Kashy, 1998). In fact, diary studies in which individuals describe their own behavior indicate that people use deception in almost 20 percent of their social interactions, and experiments indicate that a majority of strangers lie to each other at least once during a brief first encounter (Feldman, Forrest, & Happ, 2002; Tyler & Feldman, 2004). Why do people lie? For many reasons: to avoid hurting others' feelings, to conceal their real feelings or reactions, to avoid punishment for misdeeds. In short, lying is an all-too-common part of social life. This sad fact raises two important questions: (1) How good are we at recognizing deception by others? And (2) how can we do a better job at this task? The answer to the first question is somewhat discouraging. In general, we do only a little better than chance in determining whether others are lying or telling the truth (e.g., Ekman 2001; Malone & DePaulo, 2003). There are many reasons why this so, including the fact that we tend to perceive others as truthful and so don't search for clues to deception (Ekman, 2001). These include our desire to be polite, which makes us reluctant to discover or report deception by others, and our lack of attention to nonverbal cues that might reveal deception (e.g., Etcoff, Ekman, Magee, & Frank, 2000). Recently, another explanation—and a compelling one at that—has been added to this list: We tend to assume that if people are truthful in one situation or context, they will be truthful in others, and this can prevent us from realizing that they might indeed lie on some occasions (e.g., O'Sullivan, 2003). We'll return to this possibility in more detail in our later discussion of attribution. We should add that trying to "read" others' nonverbal cues accurately does not always center on efforts to determine whether they are telling the truth. Research findings (e.g., Pickett, Gardner, & Knowles, 2004) indicate that accuracy in decoding nonverbal cues is also related to the desire to be liked and accepted by other people—the higher a individual's need to belong is, the better they tend to be at reading nonverbal cues because they pay careful attention to others and want to understand them.

Given that nearly everyone engages in deception at least occasionally, it seems important to be able to identify lies when they occur. How can we accomplish this especially tricky aspect of social perception? The answer seems to involve careful attention to both nonverbal and verbal cues that can reveal the fact that others are trying to deceive us.

With respect to nonverbal cues, the following information has been found to be helpful (e.g., DePaulo et al., 2003):

microexpressions
Fleeting facial expressions lasting only a few tenths of a second.

1. **Microexpressions:** These are fleeting facial expressions lasting only a few tenths of a second. Such reactions appear on the face quickly after an emotion-provoking event and are difficult to suppress. As result, they can be quite revealing about others' true feelings or emotions. For instance, if you ask another person whether they like something (e.g., an idea you have expressed, something you have just purchased), watch their faces closely as they respond. If you see one expression (e.g., a frown), which is followed quickly by another (e.g., a smile), this can be a useful sign that they are lying; they are stating one opinion or reaction when in fact, they really have another.

2. **Interchannel discrepancies:** A second nonverbal cue revealing of deception is known as interchannel discrepancies. (The term *channel* refers to type of nonverbal cues; for instance, facial expressions are one channel, body movements are another.) These are inconsistencies between nonverbal cues from different basic channels. These result from the fact that people who are lying often find it difficult to control all these channels at once. For instance, they may manage their facial expressions well but may have difficulty looking you in the eye as they tell their lie.

3. **Eye contact:** Efforts at deception are often revealed by certain aspects of eye contact. People who are lying often blink more often and show pupils that are more dilated than people who are telling the truth. They may also show an unusually low level of eye contact or—surprisingly—an unusually high one, as they attempt to fake being honest by looking others right in the eye.

4. **Exaggerated facial expressions:** Finally, people who are lying sometimes show exaggerated facial expressions. They may smile more—or more broadly—than usual or may show greater sorrow than is typical in a given situation. A prime example: Someone says no to a request you've made and then shows exaggerated regret. This is a good sign that the reasons the person has supplied for saying "no" may not be true.

In addition to these nonverbal cues, other signs of deception are sometimes present in nonverbal aspects of what people actually say or in the words they choose. When people are lying, the pitch of their voices often rises—especially when they are highly motivated to lie. Similarly, they often take longer to begin or to respond to a question or describe events. And they may show a greater tendency to start sentences, stop them, and begin again. In other words, certain aspects of people's **linguistic style** can be revealing of deception.

In sum, through careful attention to nonverbal cues and to various aspects of the way people speak (e.g., the pitch of their voices), we *can* often tell when others are lying or merely trying to hide their feelings from us. Success in detecting deception is far from certain; some people are skillful liars. But if you pay careful attention to the cues described, you will make their task of "pulling the wool over your eyes" much more difficult and may become as successful at this task as a group of people identified by Paul Ekman—a leading expert on facial expressions—who can reliability distinguish lies from the truth more than 80% percent of the time (Coniff, 2004). (These people, by the way, did not belong to a particular profession; they were simply a heterogeneous group of individuals who were exceptionally good at detecting deception.) Is this a useful skill? Absolutely; imagine the benefits if we could hire—or train—such people to work at airports or other locations, identifying terrorists. Clearly, then, understanding how we can learn to recognize deception has important implications not just for individuals but also for society as a whole.

The Effects of Deception on Social Relations

Assuming that deception is an all-too-common aspect of social life, what are its effects? As you might guess, they are largely negative. First, recent findings (e.g., Tyler, Feldman, & Reichert, 2006), indicate that when people find themselves on the receiving end of lies, they react with mistrust of, and disliking toward, the liar. In fact, the more lies a stranger tells, the more these people are disliked and the less they are trusted. Further, and perhaps of even greater interest, after being exposed to someone who has lied, most people are more willing to engage in such behavior themselves. Evidence for such effects is provided by research conducted by Tyler, Feldman, and Reichert (2006).

These researchers gave participants in their studies information about another person—information indicating that this person had lied during a videotaped interview. (Participants watched the videotape, so they knew the stranger had lied.) Some lies involved exaggerations (e.g., the liar said that he had been an honor student in high school when this was not true) and others involved minimizations (e.g., the liar indicated that his

linguistic style
Aspects of speech apart from the meaning of the words employed.

academic record was worse than it really was). Moreover, they varied the frequency of lying, so that the liars engaged in deception only once or four times. When participants rated the liars, they gave lower scores for likeability and trustworthiness to the frequent liars and to the liars who had exaggerated rather than minimized their own achievements. This suggests that some lies are indeed worse than others. Now, here's the most disturbing finding of all. After these procedures, participants in the study had a brief conversation with another person (an assistant of the researchers). During this discussion, participants who had observed frequent lying on the videotape now showed stronger tendencies to lie themselves than those who had observed only one lie or no lies at all. Together, these findings indicate that lying is not only ethically wrong, but it also undermines the quality of social relations perhaps because it tends to spread from one person to another. It seems possible that such effects contribute to the kind of scandals that rock large corporations from time to time. Lying by the top people in these companies encourages unethical behavior by many others, sometimes with disastrous results (see Figure 3.5).

Now, before concluding this discussion of nonverbal communication, we'll address one additional question: Do women and men differ in their ability to use and interpret such cues? Common sense suggests that they do and that women are vastly superior. Is this actually true? To see what social psychological research has to say about these ideas, read *Making Sense of Common Sense: A Social Psychological Perspective* on page 83.

> **◯Principles to Remember**
>
> Nonverbal cues can provide us with useful information about others' internal states, but they occur quickly and are easy to miss or misinterpret. Use caution when employing them as guides to social perception.

Figure 3.5
Lying: It Can Create an Unethical and Dangerous Social Environment
Do you know about the Enron scandal? It involved unethical behavior—including overt lying—by the company's top officials. This behavior, in turn, created an environment in which many kinds of unethical or illegal behavior was tolerated, and that, ultimately, led to the collapse of the company. Jeffrey Skilling, CEO at the time of Enron's collapse, received a sentence of twenty-four years, four months in prison for his unprincipled behavior.

MAKING SENSE OF COMMON SENSE
A SOCIAL PSYCHOLOGICAL PERSPECTIVE
Are Men Really "Clueless" When It Comes to Nonverbal Cues? Fiction—and Fact—about Gender Differences in Nonverbal Communication

Folklore is filled with references to "feminine intuition." According to such beliefs, women possess a special "sixth sense" that allows them to understand social situations that remain mysterious to males who are often described as being totally "clueless" when it comes to sending and using subtle nonverbal cues. Translated into the language of modern social psychology, these beliefs suggest that women are far better at key aspects of social perception than men and that this gives them a big edge in a wide range of situations.

Is this really true? Do women actually demonstrate superior capabilities where social perception—and especially nonverbal communication—is concerned? The answer, as revealed by systematic research on gender differences in social perception, is somewhat mixed. Overall, there is no clear evidence that women are better than men at *all* aspects of social perception. But they *do* seem to be superior in performing several important tasks, such as judging other people with respect to specific personality characteristics (e.g., Vogt & Colvin, 2003), recognizing

"Know what I think?"
"Of course."

Figure 3.6
Gender Differences in Nonverbal Communication: Do They Really Exist?
This cartoon presents a widely accepted view about social perception: Women are much better than men at understanding others and perceiving them accurately. In fact, men are often portrayed as being totally clueless in this regard. Are these beliefs accurate? Research conducted by social psychologists suggests that they may contain a large grain of truth, although the reasons why such differences exist remain unclear.

(*Source: The New Yorker*, July 10, 2000.)

their current moods (e.g., Hall & Matsumoto, 2004), and in both sending and interpreting nonverbal cues (e.g., Mayo & Henley, 1981; Rosenthal & DePaulo, 1979). The advantage for women is greatest with respect to reading facial expressions—women are clearly superior at this—and is also quite large with respect to interpreting body movements and gestures (Rosenthal & DePaulo, 1979). However it is smaller for interpreting voice tone and for noticing discrepancies between different nonverbal cues—for instance, inconsistencies between facial expressions and body cues.

Recent research adds to this picture by suggesting that women are also much better than men at remembering others' appearance—how they look, dress, comb their hair, and so on (Horgan, Schmid Mast, Hall, & Carter, 2004). In fact, in a series of carefully conducted studies, Schmid Mast and Hall (2006) found that women were significantly better than men at remembering others' appearance regardless of general motivation to do well on this task, general memory abilities, and even whether participants were instructed to gaze at the other person or to pay careful attention to themselves. In other words, this gender difference in one aspect of person perception—memory for various nonverbal aspects of others' appearance—was strong and general and occurred under a wide range of circumstances.

This leaves us with a puzzling question: *Why* do such differences in social perception—and especially, in the use of nonverbal cues—exist? One possibility, noted by Schmid, Mast, and Hall (2006), is that it may be related to the evolutionary perspective. According to this approach, appearance is more important for women than men because women's appearance is more closely related to their social status than is true for men. Over the course of human history, more attractive women obtained higher-status mates, and so acquired higher status themselves (e.g., Cashdan 1998). As a result, women are now more sensitive than men to this particular aspect—to their own and others' appearance—of social perception.

Another possibility is that because women have less power and status in many societies, they find it essential to pay attention to nonverbal cues indicating others' moods or feelings. Accurate knowledge of these states and reactions is necessary for them to attain their goals because they don't have the power or status to achieve them more directly (e.g., Eagly and Karau, 2002). Some evidence that this is true exists because other socially devalued groups also show greater accuracy compared to ones who are powerful (Fiske & Berdahl, 2007). Regardless of the specific mechanisms at work, it appears that overall, women are indeed much better at using nonverbal communication—much better at sending and interpreting the subtle cues this aspect of person perception involves. There is one exception to this general pattern, though. Women are *not* better, overall, at telling when others are lying (Ekman, O'Sullivan, & Frank, 1999).

In sum, research conducted by social psychologists has served to clarify and refine the suggestions of common sense concerning women's intuition and men's "cluelessness" in terms of what kinds of gender differences actually exist with respect to nonverbal communication. The findings of this work suggest that in fact, women are better than men at several aspects of social perception. While such research has not yet clarified the origins of these differences, it does point to several intriguing possibilities, ones that, together, may help explain women's superior abilities in perceiving others' accurately, understanding their feelings, traits, and motives more fully and—perhaps—interacting with them more effectively than their male counterparts.

⌒KeyPoints

- Social perception involves the processes through which we seek to understand other people. It plays a key role in social behavior and social thought.

- To understand others' emotional states, we often rely on nonverbal communication—an unspoken language of facial expressions, eye contact, and body movements and postures.

- While facial expressions for all basic emotions may not be as universal as once believed, they do often provide useful information about others' emotional states. Useful information on this issue is also provided by eye contact, body language, and touching.

- Recent findings indicate that handshaking provides useful nonverbal cues about others' personality and can influence a person's first impressions of strangers.

- If we pay careful attention to certain nonverbal cues, we can recognize efforts at deception by others, even if these people are from a culture other than our own.

- Women are better than men at both sending and interpreting nonverbal cues and also better at remembering details of others' appearance. This gives them an important advantage in many situations and may account for widespread belief in women's intuition.

Think About It

Do you think people can be trained to be better at sending and reading nonverbal cues? If so, how could they then benefit from these improved skills?

Attribution: Understanding the Causes of Others' Behavior

Accurate knowledge of others' current moods or feelings can be useful in many ways. Yet, where social perception is concerned, this knowledge is often only the first step. In addition, we usually want to know more, to understand others' lasting traits, and to know the causes behind their behavior—for instance, to understand their motives, goals, and intentions. Social psychologists believe that our interest in such questions stems, in large measure, from our basic desire to understand cause-and-effect relationships in the social world (Pittman, 1993; Van Overwalle, 1998). In other words, we don't simply want to know *how* others have acted, we want to understand *why* they have done so, too, because we realize that this knowledge can help us to predict how they will act in the future. The process through which we seek such information and draw inferences is known as attribution. More formally, attribution refers to our efforts to understand the causes behind others' behavior and on some occasions, the causes behind *our* behavior, too. Social psychologists have studied attribution for several decades, and their research has yielded many intriguing insights (e.g., Graham & Folkes, 1990; Heider, 1958; Read & Miller, 1998).

Theories of Attribution: Frameworks for Understanding How We Attempt to Make Sense of the Social World

Because attribution is complex, many theories have been proposed to explain its operation. Here, we will focus on two classic views that continue to be especially influential.

From Acts to Dispositions: Using Others' Behavior as a Guide to Their Lasting Traits

The first of these classic theories—Jones and Davis's (1965) theory of **correspondent inference**—asks how we use information about others' behavior as a basis for inferring that they possess various traits. In other words, the theory is concerned with how we decide, on the basis of others' overt actions, that they possess specific traits or dispositions likely to remain fairly stable over time.

At first glance, this might seem to be a simple task. Others' behavior provides us with a rich source on which to draw, so if we observe it carefully, we should be able to learn a lot about them. Up to a point, this is true. The task is complicated, however, by the following fact: Often, individuals act in certain ways not because doing so reflects their own preferences or traits but rather because *external factors* leave them little choice. For example, suppose you go to restaurant and the young woman who greets you at the "Please Wait to Be Seated" sign smiles and acts in a friendly manner. Does this mean that she is a friendly person who simply likes people? It's possible, but perhaps she is acting in this way because that is what her job requires; she has no choice. Her boss has told her: "We are always friendly to our customers; I won't tolerate anything else." Situations like this are common, and in them, using others' behavior as a guide to their lasting traits or motives can be misleading.

How do we cope with such complications? According to Jones and Davis's theory (Jones & Davis, 1965; Jones & McGillis, 1976), we accomplish this task by focusing our attention on certain types of actions: those most likely to prove informative.

First, we consider only behavior that seems to have been freely chosen, while largely ignoring ones that were somehow forced on the person in question. Second, we pay careful attention to actions that show what Jones and Davis term **noncommon effects**—effects that can be caused by one specific factor but not by others. (Don't confuse this word with *uncommon,* which simply means infrequent.) Why are actions that produce noncommon effects informative? Because they allow us to zero in on the causes of others' behavior. For example, imagine that one of your friends has just gotten engaged. His future

correspondent inference
A theory describing how we use others' behavior as a basis for inferring their stable dispositions.

noncommon effects
Effects produced by a particular cause that could not be produced by any other apparent cause.

spouse is attractive, has a great personality, is wildly in love with your friend, and is rich. What can you learn about your friend from his decision to marry this woman? Not much. There are so many good reasons that you can't choose among them. In contrast, imagine that your friend's fiancé is attractive but that she treats him with indifference and is known to be extremely boring; also, she is deeply in debt and known to be someone who usually lives far beyond her means. Does the fact that your friend is marrying this woman tell you anything about him under these conditions? Definitely. You can probably conclude that he cares more about physical beauty than about personality or wealth. As you can see from this example, then, we can usually learn more about others from actions on their part that yield noncommon effects than from ones that do not.

Finally, Jones and Davis (1965) suggest that we also pay greater attention to actions by others that are low in social desirability than to actions that are high on this dimension. In other words, we learn more about others' traits from actions they perform that are somehow out of the ordinary than from actions that are much like those of most other people.

In sum, according to the theory proposed by Jones and Davis (1965), we are most likely to conclude that others' behavior reflects their stable traits (that is, we are likely to reach correspondent inferences about them), when that behavior (1) is freely chosen; (2) yields distinctive, noncommon effects, and (3) is low in social desirability.

Kelley's Theory of Causal Attributions: How We Answer the Question "Why"

Consider the following events:

You arrange to meet an acquaintance outside a movie theater, but he doesn't show.

You leave several messages for a friend, but she doesn't call back.

You expect a promotion in your job, but you don't receive it.

In all of these situations, you would probably wonder why these events occurred: Why didn't your acquaintance show up at the movie theater—did he forget? Did he do it on purpose? Why has your friend failed to return your messages—is she angry at you? Is her answering machine or cell phone not working? Why didn't you get the promotion—is your boss disappointed in your performance? Were you the victim of some kind of discrimination? In many situations, this is the central attributional task we face. We want to know why other people have acted as they have or why events have turned out in a specific way. Such knowledge is crucial because if we understand the causes behind others' actions or events that occur we can hope to make sense out of the social world (and potentially prevent those bad outcomes from coming our way again in the future). Obviously, the number of specific causes behind others' behavior is large. To make the task more manageable, therefore, we often begin with a preliminary question: Did others' behavior stem mainly from internal causes (their own traits, motives, intentions), mainly from external causes (some aspect of the social or physical world); or from a combination of the two? For example, you might wonder whether you didn't receive the promotion because you really haven't worked hard (an internal cause), because your boss is unfair and biased against you (an external cause), or perhaps because of both factors. How do we attempt to answer this question? A theory proposed by Kelley (Kelley, 1972; Kelley & Michela, 1980) provides important insights into this process.

According to Kelley (1972), in our attempts to answer the question why about others' behavior, we focus on three major types of information. First, we consider **consensus**—the extent to which other people react to a given stimulus or event in the same manner as the person we are considering. The higher the proportion of people who react in the same way, the higher the consensus is. Second, we consider **consistency**—the extent to which the person in question reacts to the stimulus or event in the same way on other occasions over time. And third, we examine **distinctiveness**—the extent to which this person reacts in the same manner to other, different stimuli or events.

---

consensus
The extent to which other people react to some stimulus or even in the same manner as the person we are considering.

consistency
The extent to which an individual responds to a given stimulus or situation in the same way on different occasions (i.e., across time).

distinctiveness
The extent to which an individual responds in the same manner to different stimuli or events.

According to Kelley's (1972) theory, we are most likely to attribute another's behavior to internal causes under conditions in which consensus and distinctiveness are low, but consistency is high. In contrast, we are most likely to attribute another's behavior to external causes when consensus, consistency, and distinctiveness are all high. Finally, we usually attribute another's behavior to a combination of internal and external factors when consensus is low, but consistency and distinctiveness are high. Perhaps a concrete example will help illustrate the reasonable nature of these ideas.

Imagine that you see a server in a restaurant flirt with a customer. This behavior raises an interesting question: Why does the server act this way? Because of internal causes or external causes? Is he simply someone who likes to flirt (an internal cause)? Or is the customer extremely attractive (an external cause). According to Kelley's (1972) theory, your decision (as an observer of this scene) would depend on information relating to the three factors mentioned previously. First, assume that the following conditions prevail: (1) You observe other servers flirting with this customer; (consensus is high); (2) You have seen this server flirt with the same customer on other occasions (consistency is high); and (3) You have *not* seen this server flirt with other customers (distinctiveness is high). Under these conditions—high consensus, consistency, and distinctiveness—you would probably attribute the clerk's behavior to external causes—this customer is attractive and that's why the server flirts with her.

Now, in contrast, assume these conditions exist: (1) No other servers flirt with the customer (consensus is low); (2) You have seen this server flirt with the same customer on other occasions (consistency is high); and (3) You have seen this server flirt with many other customers, too (distinctiveness is low). In this case, Kelley's (1972) theory suggests that you would attribute the server's behavior to internal causes: The server is simply a person who likes to flirt (see Figure 3.7).

The basic assumptions of Kelley's theory have been confirmed in a wide range of social situations, so it seems to provide important insights into the nature of causal attributions. However research on the theory also suggests the need for certain modifications or extensions, as described next.

Other Dimensions of Causal Attribution

While we are often interested in knowing whether others' behavior stemmed mainly from internal or external causes, this is not the entire story. In addition, we are also concerned with two other questions: (1) Are the causal factors that influenced their behavior likely to be stable over time or to change? Or (2) are these factors controllable—can the individual change or influence them if she or he wishes to do so (Weiner, 1993, 1995)? These dimensions are independent of the internal-external dimension we have just considered. For instance, some internal causes of behavior tend to be quite stable over time, such as personality traits or temperament (e.g., Miles & Carey, 1997). In contrast, other internal causes can, and often do, change greatly, for instance, motives, health, or fatigue. Similarly, some internal causes are controllable; individuals can, if they wish, learn to hold their tempers in check, and other internal causes, such as chronic illnesses or disabilities,

Figure 3.7
Kelley's Theory of Causal Attribution: An Example
Under the conditions shown in the top part of this figure, we would attribute the server's behavior to external causes; for example, the attractiveness of this customer. Under the conditions shown in the bottom part, however, we would attribute the server's behavior to internal causes, for instance, this person likes to flirt.

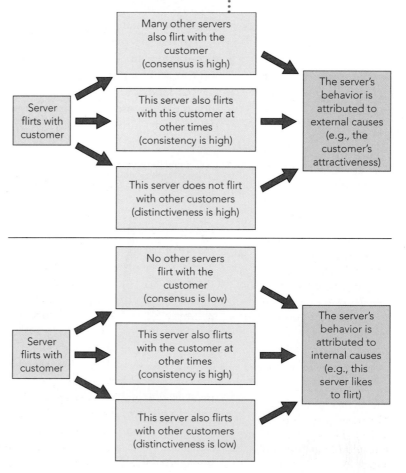

are not. The same is true for external causes of behavior: Some are stable over time (e.g., laws or social norms telling how we should behave in various situations), while others are not (e.g., bad luck). A large body of evidence indicates that in trying to understand the causes behind others' behavior, we do take note of all three of these dimensions—internal-external, stable-unstable, and controllable-uncontrollable (Weiner, 1985, 1995).

Fate versus Personal Actions

Another fascinating question concerning attribution is this: Do we perceive the events in our own lives (and perhaps, in other people's lives, too) as stemming primarily from fate—forces outside our control that, in a sense, predetermine our destiny—or from our own actions—in which case, the outcomes we experience will depend on what we freely choose to do. This is a complex question, and in fact, although these two explanations for events might seem to be contradictory, research findings suggest that we actually accept both—we believe that both fate outside *and* our own actions shape our lives. However we don't give these two possible causes equal weight at all times. Rather, we tend to swing back and forth between them depending on what social psychologists describe as the level of construal—whether we think about such events abstractly or in more concrete terms (e.g., Trope & Lieberman, 2003). Here's an example of what this means: Suppose you are asked to describe some past accomplishment from your own life (e.g., you made it onto a team; you won a prize for some activity). You can think about this accomplishment abstractly—for instance, wondering why you sought that goal or what good came from attaining it. Or you can think about it more concretely, asking yourself: What did you have to do to attain that goal? What techniques or skills did you use to achieve it? As you can see, the first kind of thinking considers the ultimate meaning of your actions and various events, while the latter considers smaller details—how it occurred and not why it occurred. Two researchers (Burrus & Roese, 2006) have recently proposed that thinking in abstract terms (high levels of construals) leads us to emphasize the importance of fate as a factor in our lives while thinking in more concrete terms leads us to downplay the influence of fate.

To test this prediction, they asked participants in their study to describe a past life accomplishment. Then they asked them to think about it either abstractly ("Why did you want to achieve this goal?" "What does achieving it mean for your life?") or concretely ("What kinds of tasks did you have to perform in completing this goal?" "What techniques did you use in completing the goal?") Participants then rated the extent to which the goal was caused by themselves or by fate. In addition, they also rated the extent to which their own actions could have changed these events. As expected, results showed that participants rated fate as a more important determinant of their experiences when they thought abstractly than when they thought about the same events concretely. However they also showed strong belief in the effects of their own actions regardless of level of construal (abstract versus concrete; see Figure 3.8).

These results suggest that while we do often see fate as a powerful causal factor in our lives, we mix such beliefs with faith in our own abilities to influence our outcomes and

Figure 3.8

Fate as a Cause of Events in Our Lives

When individuals think about events in their lives abstractly (e.g., the ultimate goals or effects of these events), they tend to emphasize the impact of fate on these events relative to when they think more concretely. However regardless of mode of thought, most people tend to perceive their own actions as an important factor in their experiences.

(*Source:* Based on data from Burrus & Roese, 2006).

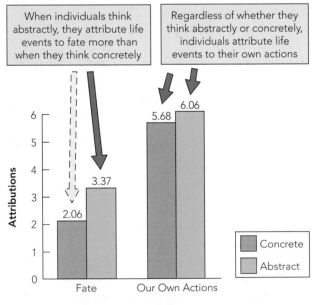

our lives. In other words, while recognizing the importance of fate and other forces beyond our control, we also seem to accept these words, spoken by a character in one of Shakespeare's plays (Brutus, in *Julius Caesar*, Act I, Scene 2): "Men at some time are masters of their fates. . . ."

Action Identification and the Attribution Process

When we see other people perform some action and try to understand it, why they are doing it and what they want to accomplish, we have a wide range of interpretations open to us. For instance, suppose you saw someone putting loose change into a jar. You could conclude: "She wants to avoid losing the change so she puts it into the jar." Alternatively, you could conclude: "She is trying to save so that she can to contribute to her own education." The first is a low-level interpretation that focuses on the action itself and attributes little in the way of planning or long-range goals to the person involved; the second, in contrast, attributes such plans, intentions, and goals to this person. The action is the same (putting changes into a jar), but our interpretation of it—and of why it occurs—is different. The level of interpretation we use is known as **action identification.**

Recent findings indicate that this is a basic aspect of attribution. When we view others' actions as involving little more than the actions themselves, we also tend to make few attributions about their intentions, goals, or higher-order cognition. When, instead, we view others' actions as having greater meaning, we attribute much greater mental activity to them. We see their actions not only as produced by the present situation, but also as reflecting much more—the person's goals, characteristics, and intentions—their "mind," if you will. Research conducted by Kozak, Marsh, and Wegner (2006) provide strong support for this reasoning. Across several studies, they found that the more others' actions are interpreted at higher levels (as reflecting more than the action itself), the actors are also seen as possessing more complex motives, goals, and thought processes. So, where attribution is concerned, it is not only what other people do that counts, but also our interpretations of these actions is crucial, too, and can shape our perceptions of the people in question.

Attribution: Some Basic Sources of Error

A basic theme we'll develop throughout this book is that although we generally do a good job of thinking about the social world, we are far from perfect in this respect. In fact, our efforts to understand other people—and ourselves—are subject to several types of errors that can lead us to false conclusions about why others have acted as they have and how they will act in the future. We now describe several of these errors.

The Correspondence Bias: Overestimating the Role of Dispositional Causes

Imagine that you witness the following scene. A man arrives at a meeting one hour late. On entering, he drops his notes on the floor. While trying to pick them up, his glasses fall off and break. Later, he spills coffee all over his tie. How would you explain these events? The chances are good that you would reach conclusions such as "This person is disorganized and clumsy." Are such attributions accurate? Perhaps, but it is also possible that the man was late because of unavoidable delays at the airport; he drops his notes because they were printed in slick paper; and he spilled his coffee because the cup was too hot to hold. The fact that you would be less likely to consider such potential external causes of his behavior illustrates what Jones (1979) labeled **correspondence bias**—the tendency to explain others' actions as stemming from (corresponding to) dispositions even in the presence of clear situational causes (e.g., Gilbert & Malone, 1995). This bias seems to be so general in scope that many social psychologists refer to as the **fundamental attribution error.** In short, we tend to perceive others as acting as they do because they are "that kind of person," rather than because of the many external factors that may influence their behavior. This tendency occurs in a wide range of contexts but appears to be strongest in

action identification
The level of interpretation we place on an action; low-level interpretations focus on the action itself, while higher-level interpretations focus on its ultimate goals.

correspondence bias (fundamental attribution error)
The tendency to explain others' actions as stemming from dispositions even in the presence of clear situational causes.

fundamental attribution error (correspondence bias)
The tendency to overestimate the impact of dispositional cues on others' behavior.

situations in which both consensus and distinctiveness are low, as predicted by Kelley's (1972) theory and when we are trying to predict others' behavior in the far-off future rather than the immediate future (Nussbaum, Trope, & Liberman, 2003; Van Overwalle, 1997). Why? Because when we think of the far-off future we tend to do so in abstract terms and this leads us to think about others in terms of global traits, and as a result, we tend to overlook potential external causes of their behavior. While this fundamental attribution error has been demonstrated in many studies, it was first reported in truly classic research—studies conducted by Jones and Harris (1967) and then, a few years later, by Nisbett, Caputo, Legbant, and Marecek (1973). This research had such a strong effect on subsequent efforts to understand attribution, that we describe it in *Building the Science: Classics of Social Psychology* on page 91.

Social psychologists have conducted many studies to find out why this bias occurs (e.g., Robins, Spranca, & Mendelsohn, 1996), but the issue is still somewhat in doubt. One possibility is that when we observe another person's behavior, we tend to focus on his or her actions—the context in which the person behaves—and hence potential situational causes of his or her behavior, often fade into the background. As a result, dispositional causes (internal causes) are easier to notice (they are more salient) than situational ones. In other words, from our perspective, the person we are observing is high in perceptual salience and is the focus of our attention, while situational factors that might also have influenced this person's behavior are less salient and so seem less important to us. Another explanation is that we notice such situational causes but give them insufficient weight in our attributions. Still another explanation is when we focus on others' behavior, we tend to begin by assuming that their actions reflect their underlying characteristics. Then we attempt to correct for any possible effects of the external world—the current situation—by taking these into account. (This involves the mental shortcut known as anchoring and adjustment, which we discussed in Chapter 2.) This correction, however, is often insufficient—we don't make enough allowance for the impact of external factors. We don't give enough weight to the possibility of delays at the airport or a slippery floor when reaching our conclusions (Gilbert & Malone, 1995).

Evidence for this two-step process—quick, automatic reactions followed by a slower, more controlled corrections—has been obtained in many studies (e.g., Chaiken & Trope, 1999; Gilbert, 2002), so it seems to offer a compelling explanation for the correspondence bias (i.e., fundamental attribution error). In fact, it appears that most people are aware of this process or at least aware of the fact they start by assuming that other people behave as they do because of internal causes (e.g., their personality, their true beliefs) but then correct this assumption, at least to a degree, by taking account of situational constraints.

Perhaps even more interesting, we tend to assume that *we* adjust our attributions to take account situational constraints more than other people do. In other words, we perceive that we are less likely to fall victim to the correspondence bias than others.

Cultural Factors in the Fundamental Attribution Error

Is the tendency to emphasize dispositional causes truly universal, or is it influenced, like many other aspects of social behavior and thought, by cultural factors? Research findings indicate that they do. Specifically, the fundamental attribution error appears to be more common or stronger in cultures that emphasize individual freedom—individualistic cultures, such as those in Western Europe or the United States and Canada, than in collectivistic cultures that emphasize group membership, conformity, and interdependence (e.g., Triandis, 1990). This difference seems to reflect the fact that in individualistic cultures, there is a norm of internality—the view that people should accept responsibility for their own outcomes. In collectivistic cultures, in contrast, this norm is weaker or absent (Jellison & Green, 1981). For example, consider one interesting study on this effect by Morris and Pang (1994). They analyzed newspaper articles about two mass murders—ones committed by a Chinese graduate student and ones committed by a Caucasian postal worker. The articles were published in English in the *New York Times* and in Chinese in

BUILDING THE SCIENCE
CLASSICS OF SOCIAL PSYCHOLOGY

The Fundamental Attribution Error: Stronger Than You Might Guess

Suppose that you read a short essay written by another person—an essay dealing with an important topic. On the basis of this essay, you would get an idea of where the writer stands with respect to this issue—is she "pro" or "anti"? So far, so good. But now assume that before reading the essay, you learned that the author had been instructed to write it so as to support a particular position—again, pro or anti. From a purely rational perspective, you should realize that in this case, the essay tells you nothing about the writer's true views; after all, the writer is merely following instructions. But two social psychologists—Jones and Harris (1967)—reasoned that in fact, the fundamental attribution error is so strong, that even in the second case, we would assume that we can determine the writer's views from the essay—even though this person was told to write it in a particular way.

To test this reasoning, they asked research participants to read short essay that either supported or opposed Fidel Castro's rule in Cuba (remember, the research was conducted in 1967). In one condition, participants were told that the essay writer had free choice as to what position to take. In another, they were told that the writer was instructed to write the essay in a pro-Castro or anti-Castro manner. After reading the essay, participants were asked to estimate the essay writer's true beliefs. Results were clear: Even in the condition where the writer had been instructed to take one position or the other, research participants assumed that they could tell the writer's real views from the essay. In other words, they attributed the essay writer's actions to internal factors (her or his true beliefs), even though they knew that this was not the case. Clearly, this was a dramatic demonstration of the fundamental attribution error in action.

Subsequent research that can also be viewed as classic in the field reached the same conclusions. For instance, in a revealing study by Nisbett et al. (1973), participants were shown a series of twenty paired traits (e.g., quiet-talkative, lenient-firm) and were asked to decide which of these traits were true of themselves, their best friend, their father, a casual acquaintance, or Walter Cronkite (a famous newscaster at the time). The participants were also offered a third choice: They could choose "depends on the situation." Results again offered strong evidence for

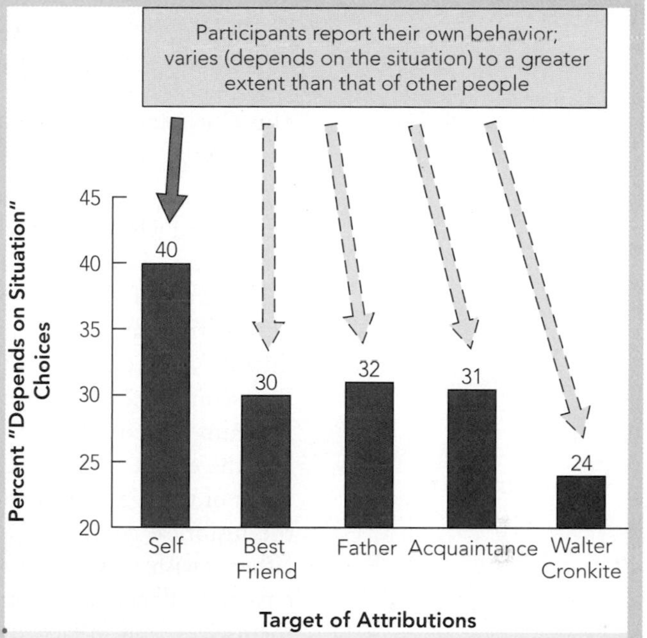

Figure 3.9

The Fundamental Attribution Error in Action: Classic Evidence

Participants in the study shown here were asked to indicate which of the traits in twenty pairs of traits were true of themselves and several other people (their best friend, fathers, and so on) They also had the option of choosing another response: depends on the situation. As shown here, they were much more likely to do this with respect to their own behavior than that of other people. In other words, they recognized that their own actions were strongly influenced by external causes but assumed that the actions of other people stem primarily from internal causes, such as their own traits.

(*Source:* Based on data from Nisbett, Caputo, Legbant, and Marecek, 1973).

the fundamental attribution error: The participants in the study chose "depends on the situation" much more often for themselves than for the other people. In other words, they reported that their own behavior varied from situation to situation, while that of other people (their best friend, father, or even a famous news anchor), reflected primarily personal traits (see Figure 3.9).

Together, early studies like these provided powerful evidence for the fact that our efforts to understand others' behavior—and our own actions—are not totally rational. On the contrary, they are influenced by number of "tilts" or biases, and among these, the fundamental attribution error is one of the strongest.

the *World Journal*, newspaper published in the United States. Careful analysis of the articles indicated that those written in English attributed both murderers' actions to dispositional factors (characteristics of the murderers) to a greater extent than the articles written in Chinese.

Similar findings—a correspondence bias in Western, individualistic countries than in Asian and more collectivistic ones—have been reported in several others studies (e.g., Choi & Nisbett, 1998; van Boven, White, Kamada, & Gilovich, 2003). In sum, there seems little doubt that cultural factors play a role even in this basic aspect of attribution.

The Correspondence Bias in Attributions about Groups

Not only do we make attributions about the behavior of individual persons, but we also sometimes make attributions about the behavior of groups, too. For instance, we try to understand why one group seems to dislike or even hate another—why, for example, did the Tutsis and Hutus (groups living in Rwanda) hate each other to the point where this hatred erupted into widespread genocide? And why did so many Germans hate Jews in pre–World War II Germany? Are our attributions about why various groups behave as they do also subject to the correspondence bias? Research conducted by Doosje and Branscombe (2003) suggests that it is. These researchers asked people who visited a museum related to events during the Holocaust (Anne Frank's home in Amsterdam) to rate the extent to which German atrocities against Jews during World War II were the result of the aggressive nature of Germans (an internal cause) or to external factors (e.g., the historical context in which these actions occurred). Participants in the study were either Jewish or German. The researchers predicted that Jewish people would show a greater tendency to attribute German atrocities to internal causes than would Germans themselves, and in fact, this is what was found (see Figure 3.10). While neither group showed a strong tendency to explain these events in terms of internal causes, Jewish people—whose group had been harmed—showed this tendency to a greater extent than Germans, thus demonstrating that attributions can be strongly affected by group membership—an effect we will consider again in our discussion of prejudice (Chapter 6) and other group processes (Chapter 12). In any case, it seems clear that attributional processes—and errors—can operate with respect to social groups or even entire nations as well with respect to perceptions of individuals.

The Actor-Observer Effect: "You Fell; I Was Pushed"

The fundamental attribution error, powerful as it is, applies mainly to attributions we make about others; we don't tend to overly attribute our own actions to external causes. This

Figure 3.10

Attributions about Groups: The Correspondence Bias Revisited

As shown here, Jewish research participants attributed German atrocities during World War II to internal causes (Germans' aggressiveness) to a greater extent than did German research participants. Germans, in contrast, tended to explain these atrocities more in terms of external causes (e.g., historical events and contexts).

(*Source:* Based on data from Doosje & Branscombe, 2006).

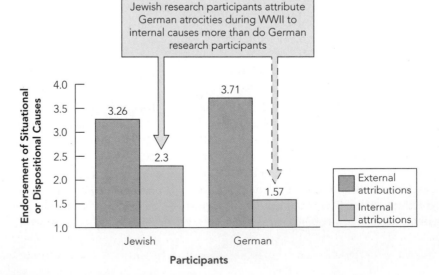

fact helps explain another and closely related type of attributional bias known as the **actor-observer effect** (Jones & Nisbett, 1971), which is the tendency to attribute our own behavior to situational (external) causes but that of others to dispositional (internal) ones. Thus when we see another person trip and fall, we tend to attribute this event to his or her clumsiness. If we trip, however, we are more likely to attribute this event to situational causes, such as ice on the sidewalk.

Why does the actor-observer effect occur? In part because we are quite aware of the many external factors affecting our own actions but are less aware of such factors when we turn our attention to the actions of other people. Thus we tend to perceive our own behavior as arising largely from situational causes but that of others as deriving mainly from their traits or dispositions.

The Self-Serving Bias: "I'm Good; You Are Lucky"

Suppose that you write a paper and when you get it back, you find the following comment on the first page: "An outstanding paper—one of the best I've see in years. A+." To what will you attribute this success? Probably, you will explain it in terms of internal causes: your high level of talent, the effort you invested in writing the paper, and so on.

Now, in contrast, imagine that when you get the paper back, and these comments are written on it. "Unsatisfactory paper—one of the worst I've seen in years. D-." How will you interpret this outcome? The chances are good that you will be tempted to focus mainly on external (situational factors): the difficulty of the task, your professor's unfairly harsh grading standards, the fact that you didn't have enough time to do a good job, and so on.

This tendency to attribute our own positive outcomes to internal causes but negative ones to external factors is known as the **self-serving bias,** and it appears to be both general in scope and powerful in its effects (Brown & Rogers, 1991; Miller & Ross, 1976).

Why does this tilt in our attributions occur? Several possibilities have been suggested, but most of these fall into two categories: cognitive and motivational explanations. The cognitive model suggests that the self-serving bias stems mainly from certain tendencies in the way we process social information (see Chapter 2; Ross, 1977). Specifically, it suggests that we attribute positive outcomes to internal causes, but negative ones to external causes because we expect to succeed and have a tendency to attribute expected outcomes to internal causes more than to external causes. In contrast, the motivational explanation suggests that the self-serving bias stems from our need to protect and enhance our self-esteem or the related desire to look good to others (Greenberg, Pyszczynski, & Solomon, 1982). While both cognitive and motivational factors may well play a role in this kind of attributional error, research evidence seems to offer more support for the motivational view (e.g., Brown & Rogers, 1991).

Regardless of the origins of the self-serving bias, it can be the cause of a great deal of interpersonal friction. It often leads people working with others on a joint task to perceive that they, not their partners, have made the major contributions and to blame others in the group for negative outcomes (see Figure 3.11 on page 94).

Interestingly, the results of several studies indicate that the strength of the self-serving bias varies across cultures (e.g., Oettingen, 1995; Oettingen & Seligman, 1990). In particular, it is weaker in cultures, such as those in Asia, that place a greater emphasis on group outcomes and group harmony, than it is in Western cultures, in which individual accomplishments are emphasized and it is considered appropriate for winners to gloat (at least a little) over their victories. For example, Lee and Seligman (1997) found that Americans of European descent showed a larger self-serving bias than either Chinese Americans or mainland Chinese. Once again, therefore, we see that cultural factors often play an important role even in basic aspects of social behavior and social thought.

Before concluding the discussion of the many ways in which our attributions depart from the original "perfectly logical person" described by Kelley (1972), we should note that despite all the errors described here, growing evidence suggests that social perception

actor-observer effect
The tendency to attribute our own behavior mainly to situational causes but the behavior of others mainly to internal (dispositional) causes.

self-serving bias
The tendency to attribute positive outcomes to internal causes (e.g., one's own traits or characteristics) but negative outcomes or events to external causes (e.g., chance, task difficulty).

Figure 3.11
The Self-Serving Bias in Action: Taking Credit for Success, Blaming Others for Failure
The self-serving bias leads us to take credit for positive outcomes—perhaps more credit than we deserve—but to blame others for negative results. This is one reason why after experiencing failure, the members of teams (whether athletic teams or business teams) often blame each other for the negative outcomes they have experienced.

can be quite accurate; we do, in many cases, reach accurate conclusions about others' traits and motives from observing their behavior. We'll examine some of the evidence pointing to this conclusion as part of our future discussion of the process of impression formation.

Magical Thinking Revisited: Why We Sometimes Believe (Irrationally) That Our Thoughts Influence Events

Be truthful: Do you ever imagine that your thoughts can influence the external world? For instance, if you imagine harm to another person, do you believe—even just a little— that your wishes might come true? And when you root for your favorite team, do you ever imagine that by thinking the "right" thoughts, you can help them win? If so, welcome to the club: As we saw in our discussion of magical thinking in Chapter 2, most of us do indeed believe to at least a minimal degree, that our thoughts can influence the physical world or that other events that cannot possibly influence each other do so. Does such thinking play a role in our attributions? In fact, growing evidence indicates that it does. Basically, these beliefs lead us to conclude that we have produced events or effects that, in fact, we really did not influence. In a sense, then, magical thinking leads us to overesti- mate our influence on the external world—an effect that can be viewed as another kind of attributional error (e.g., Wegner, 2003). What is the basis of such false beliefs about the impact of our thoughts on the external world? Perhaps it's the fact that our thoughts pre- cede some physical event, coupled with the fact that we can't see any other clear potential cause of this event. The result: We jump to the (false) conclusion that our thoughts, wishes, or intentions caused it (Aarts, Custers, & Wegner, 2005).

Figure 3.12
Magical Thinking in Our Attributions
When participants in a study stuck pins in the head of a voodoo doll similar to this one, they concluded that they had caused another person (an assistant of the researchers) to experience a headache that he reported having. This was especially true when the assistant had acted in a rude and irritating manner, thus giving participants in the study a good reason to think angry thoughts about him.

(Photo Courtesy Dr. Daniel M. Wegner.)

Convincing evidence for this reasoning—and for the fact that we do often believe our thoughts have influenced events—is provided by research conducted by Pronin, Wegner, McCarthy, and Rodriguez (2006). In one of their studies, these researchers had participants stick pins in a voodoo doll at many locations, including the head, presumably as part of a study of psychological factors in producing physical symptoms (see Figure 3.12). The doll represented another person (an assistant of the experimenters) who had either acted in a rude and irritating manner or in a more neutral manner. After the pins had been stuck in the doll, the assistant reported that he had a slight headache, and in fact, participants had been asked to stick one of the pins into the voodoo doll's head. When asked to rate the extent to which they had produced the victim's headache, people who had seen him act in a rude and irritating manner actually reported stronger beliefs that they had produced this symptom than people who had seen him act in a neutral manner. In short, when they had a reason to dislike the assistant and to think negative thoughts about him, participants believed that they had actually produced his headache. (In fact, of course, the assistant did not have a headache; he just pretended that he did.)

These findings were confirmed in several other studies, including ones involving actual sports events. For instance, in one study, participants were asked how much they had thought about a recent Super Bowl game and various plays during it. Results indicated that the more they reported thinking about the game and their team's performance in it, the more they felt responsible for the game's outcome. In other words, they believed—to some extent—that their thoughts had influenced the outcomes of a game they saw on television and that took place hundreds of miles away. Together, the results of these studies strongly suggest that attributions, like other aspects of social thought, can sometimes be influenced by magical thinking.

Applications of Attribution Theory: Insights and Interventions

Kurt Lewin, one of the founders of modern social psychology, often remarked: "There's nothing as practical as a good theory." By this he meant that once we obtain scientific understanding of some aspect of social behavior or social thought, we can, potentially, put this knowledge to practical use. Where attribution theory is concerned, this has definitely been the case. As basic knowledge about attribution has grown, so too has the range of practical problems to which such information has been applied (Graham & Folkes, 1990; Miller & Rempel, 2004). As an example of such research, we'll examine how attribution theory has been applied to understanding one key aspect of mental health—depression.

Attribution and Depression

Depression is the most common psychological disorder. In fact, it has been estimated that almost half of all human beings experience such problems at some time during their lives (e.g., Blazer, Kessler, McGonagle, & Swartz, 1994). Although many factors play a role in depression, one that has received increasing attention is what might be termed a *self-defeating* pattern of attributions. In contrast to most people, who show the self-serving bias previously described, depressed individuals tend to adopt an opposite pattern. They attribute negative outcomes to lasting, internal causes, such as their own traits or lack of ability, but attribute positive outcomes to temporary, external causes, such as good luck or special favors from others. As a result, such people perceive that they have little or no control over what happens to them; they are simply being blown about by the winds of unpredictable fate (see Figure 3.13). Little wonder that they become depressed and tend to give up on life. And once they are depressed, the tendency to engage in this self-defeating pattern is strengthened, and a vicious cycle is often initiated.

Fortunately, several forms of therapy that focus on changing such attributions have been developed and appear to be quite successful (e.g., Bruder, et al., 1997; Robinson, Berman, & Neimeyer, 1990). These new forms of therapy focus on getting depressed people to change their attributions, to take personal credit for successful outcomes, to stop

Figure 3.13

Attribution and Depression
While most people trend to attribute positive events to lasting internal causes (e.g., their own talent) and negative events to external, temporary causes (e.g., bad luck), depressed people exhibit the opposite pattern. They attribute negative outcomes to lasting internal causes (e.g., their own lack of ability) and attribute positive outcomes to temporary external causes (e.g., good luck). New forms of therapy attempt to treat depression by changing these harmful patterns of attributions.

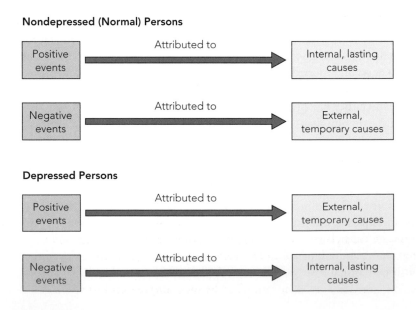

Nondepressed (Normal) Persons

Positive events — Attributed to → Internal, lasting causes

Negative events — Attributed to → External, temporary causes

Depressed Persons

Positive events — Attributed to → External, temporary causes

Negative events — Attributed to → Internal, lasting causes

blaming themselves for negative outcomes (especially ones that can't be avoided), and to view at least some failures as the result of external factors beyond their control. Because attribution theory provides the basis for these new forms of treatment, it has certainly proven useful in this respect.

KeyPoints

- To obtain information about others' lasting traits, motives, and intentions, we often engage in attribution, which are efforts to understand why people have acted as they have.

- According to Jones and Davis's theory of correspondent inference, we attempt to infer others' traits from observing certain aspects of their behavior, especially behavior that is freely chosen, produces noncommon effects, and is low in social desirability.

- According to another theory, Kelley's theory of causal attribution, we are interested in the question of whether others' behavior stemmed from internal or external causes. To answer this question, we focus on information relating to consensus, consistency, and distinctiveness.

- Two other important dimensions of causal attribution relate to whether specific causes of behavior are stable over time and controllable or not controllable.

- When we think abstractly about the events in our lives, we assign fate a powerful role in determining them. When we think more concretely, however, we tend to perceive fate as less important. Regardless of mode of thought, we also view our own actions as important factors in shaping our lives.

- Attribution is subject to many potential sources of bias. One of the most important of these is the correspondence bias, which is the tendency to

explain others' actions as stemming from dispositions even in the presence of situational causes. This tendency seems to be stronger in Western cultures than in Asian cultures and can occur for attributions for groups as well as individuals.

- Two other attributional errors are the actor-observer effect—the tendency to attribute our own behavior to external (situational causes) but that of others to internal causes, and the self-serving bias—the tendency to attribute positive outcomes to internal causes but negative ones to external causes.

- The strength of the self-serving bias varies across various cultures and is stronger in Western societies such as the United States than in Asian cultures, such as China.

- Attribution has been applied to many practical problems, often with great success. For instance, it has been applied to understanding the causes of depression and to treating this important form of mental disorder.

Think About It

Do you see any relationship between attribution and the legal system? For instance, is the reason why someone commits a crime important in determining what kind of punishment they should receive? Can you think of examples when it is?

Impression Formation and Impression Management: Combining Information about Others

When we meet another person for the first time, we are—quite literally—flooded with information. We can see, at a glance, how they look and dress, how they speak, and how they behave. Although the amount of information reaching us is large, we somehow manage to combine it into an initial first impression of this person—a mental representation of this person and our reactions to her or him. Clearly, then, impression formation is an important aspect of social perception. This fact raises several important questions: What, exactly, are first impressions? How are they formed and how quickly? Are they accurate? And perhaps most intriguing of all, is accuracy always best in forming first and more lasting impressions of others? We'll now examine what research by social psychologists tells us about each of these issues. To do so, we'll first begin with some famous and classic research in the field and then move on to more recent research and its findings.

The Beginning of Research on First Impressions: Asch's Research on Central and Peripheral Traits

As we have already seen, some aspects of social perception, such as attribution, require lots of hard mental work: It's not always easy to draw inferences about others' motives or traits from their behavior. In contrast, forming first impressions seems to be relatively effortless. As Solomon Asch (1946), one of the founders of experimental social psychology, put it: "We look at a person and immediately a certain impression of his character forms itself in us. A glance, a few spoken words are sufficient to tell us a story about a highly complex matter . . ." (1946, p. 258). How do we manage to do this? How, in short, do we form unified impressions of others in the quick and seemingly effortless way that we often do? This is the question Asch set out to study.

At the time Asch conducted his research, social psychologists were heavily influenced by the work of Gestalt psychologists, specialists in the field of perception. A basic principle of Gestalt psychology was this: "The whole is often greater than the sum of its parts." This means that what we perceive is often more than the sum of individual sensations. To illustrate this point for yourself, simply look at any painting (except a modern one). What you see is not individual splotches of paint on the canvas, rather, you perceive an integrated whole—a portrait, a landscape, a bowl of fruit—whatever the artist intended. So as Gestalt psychologists suggested, each part of the world around us is interpreted and understood, only in terms of its relationships to other parts or stimuli—in effect, as a totality.

Asch applied these ideas to understanding impression formation, suggesting that we do not form impressions simply by adding together all of the traits we observe in other people. Rather, we perceive these traits in relation to one another, so that the traits cease to exist individually and become, instead, part of an integrated, dynamic whole. How could these ideas be tested? Asch came up with an ingenious answer. He gave individuals lists of traits supposedly possessed by a stranger and then asked them to indicate their impressions of this person by putting check marks next to traits (on a much longer list) that they felt fit their overall impression of the stranger.

For example, in one study, participants read one of the following two lists:

intelligent—skillful—industrious—warm—determined—practical—cautious

intelligent—skillful—industrious—cold—determined—practical—cautious

As you can see, the lists differ only with respect to two words: *warm* and *cold*. Thus if people form impressions merely by adding together individual traits, the impressions formed by people exposed to these two lists shouldn't differ much. However this was not the case. People who read the list containing *warm* were much more likely to view the stranger as generous, happy, good natured, sociable, popular, and altruistic than were people who read the list containing *cold*. The words *warm* and *cold*, Asch concluded, were central traits—ones that strongly shaped overall impressions of the stranger and colored the other adjectives in the lists. Asch obtained additional support for this view by substituting the words *polite* and *blunt* for *warm* and *cold*. When he did this, the two lists yielded highly similar impressions of the stranger. So, polite and blunt it appeared were not central traits that colored the entire impressions of the stranger.

On the basis of many studies such as this one, Asch concluded that forming impressions of others involves more than simply combining individual traits. As he put it: "There is an attempt to form an impression of the *entire* person. . . . As soon as two or more traits are understood to belong to one person they cease to exist as isolated traits, and come into immediate . . . interaction. . . . The subject perceives not this *and* that quality, but the two entering into a particular relation . . ." (1946, p. 284). While research on impression formation has become far more sophisticated since Asch's early work, many of his basic ideas about impression formation have withstood the test of time. Thus his research exerted a lasting impact and is still worthy of careful attention even today.

How Quickly Are First Impressions Formed?

That we form first impressions in a seemingly effortless manner seems clear: When we meet other people for the first time, we seem to form a cognitive picture of them easily and without a lot of mental work. How quickly do we perform this task? The answer offered by the findings of recent research is "Very quickly!" For instance, in one ingenious study (Todorov, Mandisodza, Goren, & Hall, 2005), participants saw the faces of candidates for the U.S. Senate for just one second. Then they were asked to rate these candidates on a number of different traits—attractiveness, trustworthiness, likeability, and competence. These ratings were then related to the outcome of the elections, and what emerged was fascinating, to say the least: Ratings of competence based one a one-second exposure to the faces of the candidates were significant predictors of the election results! This suggests that not only do we form first impressions of others quickly, but also that these impressions then play a strong role in our overt actions, including the important behavior of choosing between candidates for political office.

Even more impressive findings have been reported recently in research in which exposure times to the faces of strangers were even shorter (Willis & Todorov, 2006). In these studies, participants saw the faces of male and female actors for brief periods of time: one-tenth of a second, half a second, or a second. Then they rated these people on several traits: trustworthiness, competence, likeability, aggressiveness, attractiveness, and indicated their confidence in these ratings. These ratings were compared with ratings provided by another group of people who examined photos of the same actors without any time constraints; they could examine them as long as they wished. If we really do form first impressions quickly, then the ratings of the two groups should be similar (i.e., they should be highly correlated). In other words, whether we can look at others' faces for as long as we wish or just for a fraction of a second, the ratings assigned to each stranger should be the same. This is exactly what was found; in fact, correlations between the two sets of ratings (the ones done without any time limits and the ones completed at short exposure times) ranged from about 0.60 to about 0.75, indicating that we do indeed form impressions of others quickly.

Perhaps even more surprising, whether participants saw the photos for one-tenth of a second, half a second, or a full second made little difference: Confidence in the judgments increased, but across the five traits, agreement between the impressions based on short exposure times and those based on much longer examination of the photos did not change (see Figure 3.14).

So what's the bottom line of this research? We form impressions of others

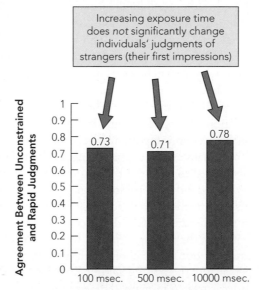

Increasing exposure time does *not* significantly change individuals' judgments of strangers (their first impressions)

Figure 3.14

First Impressions: Evidence that We Form Them *Very* Rapidly

When shown faces of strangers (female and male actors), individuals form first impressions of these people rapidly. In fact, even exposure times of one-tenth of a second are sufficient, and increasing exposure times do not change the first impressions significantly.

(*Source:* Based on data from Willis & Todorov, 2006).

very, very quickly and often on the basis of limited amounts of information (e.g., their facial appearance). As Willis and Todorov (2006, p. 597) put it, "Inferences about other persons may be effortless. . . . Person impressions are created effortlessly on-line from minimal information."

Implicit Personality Theories: Schemas that Shape First Impressions

Suppose one of your friends described someone they had just met as *helpful* and *kind*. Would you now assume that this person is also sincere? Probably. And what if your friend described this stranger as *practical* and *intelligent*; would you now assume that she or he is also ambitious? Again, the chances are good that you might. But why, in the absence of information on these specific traits, would you assume that this person possesses them? In part because we all possess what social psychologists describe as **implicit personality theories**—beliefs about what traits or characteristics tend to go together (e.g., Sedikes & Anderson, 1994). These theories, which can be viewed as a specific kind of schema, suggest that when individuals possess some traits, they are likely to possess others, too. Such expectations are strongly shaped by the cultures in which we live. For instance, in many societies, but not all, it is assumed that "what is beautiful is good"—that people who are attractive also possess other positive traits, such as good social skills and an interest in enjoying good times and the good things in life (e.g., Wheeler & Kim, 1997). Similarly, in some cultures, but again, not in all, there is a schema for "the jock"—a young male who loves sports, prefers beer to wine, and can, on occasions (e.g., during an important game), be loud and coarse. Again, once an individual is seen as having one of these traits, he or she is seen as possessing others because typically, we expect them to covary (to go together).

These tendencies to assume that certain traits or characteristics go together are common and can be observed in many contexts. For instance, you may well have implicit beliefs about the characteristics related to birth order. A large body of research findings indicates that we expect firstborns to be high achievers who are aggressive, ambitious, dominant, and independent, while we expect middle-born children to be caring, friendly, outgoing, and thoughtful. Only children, in contrast, are expected to be independent, self-centered, selfish, and spoiled (e.g., Nyman, 1995).

The strength and generality of these implicit beliefs about the effects of birth order are illustrated clearly in research conducted recently by Herrera, Zajonc, Wierczorkowska, and Cichomski (2003). These researchers asked participants to rate firstborns, only children, middle-born children, last-born children, and themselves on various trait dimensions: agreeable-disagreeable, bold-timid, creative-uncreative, emotional-unemotional, extraverted-introverted, responsible-irresponsible, and several others. Results indicated clear differences in expectations about the traits supposedly shown by each group. First-borns were seen as being more intelligent, responsible, obedient, stable, and unemotional; only children were seen as being the most disagreeable; middle-born children were expected to be envious and the least bold; and last-born children were seen as the most creative, emotional, disobedient, and irresponsible. So clearly, implicit beliefs about links between birth order and important traits exist.

Perhaps even more surprising, additional findings indicated that birth order was actually related to important life outcomes: In a large sample of people living in Poland, the earlier individuals' position in their family's birth order, the higher their occupational status and the more education they completed. This illustrates an important point we made in Chapter 2: Beliefs and expectations are often self-fulfilling, at least to a degree. More generally, the findings reported by Herrera et al. (2003) and many other researchers indicate that our beliefs about birth order can be viewed as one important kind of implicit personality theory: We *do* strongly believe that an individual's place in their family's birth order is related to many different traits.

In sum, our impressions of others are often strongly shaped by our beliefs about what

implicit personality theories
Beliefs about what traits or characteristics tend to go together.

traits or characteristics go together. Indeed, these beliefs are often so strong that we will sometimes bend our perceptions of other people to be consistent with them. The result? We can form impressions of others that reflect our implicit beliefs more than their actual traits (e.g., Gawronski, 2003).

Impression Formation: A Cognitive Perspective

Since Asch's classic research, social psychologists have made a great deal of progress toward understanding the nature of impression formation—the process through which we form impressions of others (e.g., Fiske, Lin, & Neuberg, 1999). A major reason for this progress has been adoption of a cognitive perspective on this topic. Briefly, social psychologists have found it useful to examine impression formation in terms of basic cognitive processes. For instance, when we meet others for the first time, we don't pay equal attention to all kinds of information about them, rather, we focus on certain kinds—the kinds of input we view as being most useful (e.g., DeBruin & Lange, 2000). Further, to form lasting first impressions, we must enter various kinds of information into memory so that we can recall it at later times. And of course, our first impressions of others will depend, to a degree, on our own characteristics. In fact, we can't help but see others through the lens of our own traits, motives, and desires (Vinokur & Schul, 2000).

Early work that adopted a cognitive perspective grappled with the following question: How do we mange to combine diverse information about other people into unified impressions of them? Two possibilities seemed to exist: We could form unified impressions of others by adding discrete pieces of information about them, or alternatively, we might form our impressions by averaging available information in some way (e.g., Anderson, 1965, 1968). Results were complex but generally pointed to the conclusion that averaging was the better explanation. The findings that led to this conclusion went something like this: If research participants were given information suggesting that a stranger possessed two highly favorable traits (e.g., truthful and reasonable), they formed a more favorable impression of this person than if they were given information suggesting that he or she possessed two highly favorable traits and two moderately favorable ones (e.g. truthful-reasonable and painstaking-persuasive). Researchers reasoned that if people combine the information they received simply by adding it together, they would like the second person more than first one because he was described as possessing a greater number of positive characteristics (two favorable traits and two moderately favorable traits). If, in contrast, they combined the information through averaging, they would like the first one better because the average of two highly favorable traits is higher than the average of two highly favorable and two moderately favorable traits. On the basis of these and related results, it was concluded that we form our impressions of others on the basis of a relatively simple kind of "cognitive algebra" (e.g., Anderson, 1973). Although some traits may have more influence than others (Asch's central traits, for instance), the process seemed to be largely one involving a cognitive averaging of information.

More recent research on impression formation has gone far beyond this initial approach and has, for instance, addressed the question "What are the specific contents of first impressions?" (e.g., Ruscher & Hammer, 1994; Wyer, Budesheim, Lambert, & Swan, 1994). The answer that has emerged from such research is that impressions of others involve two major components: concrete examples of behaviors they have performed that are consistent with a given trait—exemplars of this trait—and mental summaries that are abstracted from repeated observations of others' behavior—abstractions as they are usually termed (e.g., Klein, Loftus, & Plog, 1992; Smith & Zarate, 1992). Some models of impression formation stress the role of behavioral exemplars. These models suggest that when we make judgments about others, we recall examples of their behavior and base our judgments—and our impressions—on these. In contrast, other models stress the role of abstractions (sometimes referred to as categorical judgments). Such views suggest that when we make judgments about others, we simply bring our previously formed abstractions to mind and then use these as the basis for our impressions and our decisions. For instance, we recall that we have previously judged a person to be kind or unkind, friendly or hostile, optimistic or pessimistic, and then combine these traits into an impression of this individual. Both of these views recognize the fact that often, we interact with others on many different occasions, and our impressions of them are based on these repeated exposures rather than just one. That is quite different from the early research described previously, which did not directly address this basic fact.

Existing evidence suggests that both exemplars and mental abstractions play a role in impression formation (e.g., Budesheim & Bonnel, 1998; Klein & Loftus, 1993; Klein, Loftus, & Plog, 1992). In fact, it appears that the nature of impressions may shift as we gain increasing experience with others. At first, our impression of someone we have just met consists largely of exemplars. Later, as our experience with this person increases, our impression comes to consist mainly of mental abstractions derived from many observations of the person's behavior (Sherman & Klein, 1994).

The cognitive perspective has also shed new light on another important issue—the influence of our motives (what we are trying to accomplish in a given situation) on the kind of impressions we form and even the processes through which we form them. As we noted in Chapter 2, people generally do the least cognitive work they can, and impression formation is no exception to this rule. So usually, we form impressions in the simplest and easiest way possible, by placing people into large social categories with which we are already familiar (e.g., "she is an engineer," "he is an Irish American," and so on). Then, we base our impressions, at least in part, on what we know about these social groups. If we are motivated to be more accurate, though, we may focus on people we meet more as individuals possessing a unique collection of traits (e.g., Fiske et al., 1999; Stevens & Fiske, 2000).

In sum, a cognitive perspective on impression formation has provided many valuable insights into the nature of this process. Such research suggests that although we seem to form impressions of others in a rapid and seemingly effortless manner, these impressions actually emerge out of the operation of cognitive processes relating to the storage, recall, and interpretation of social information. In short, there is a lot more going on beneath the surface than you might at first suspect.

Is Accuracy Always Best in Social Perception? Evidence That Illusions, Too, Can Sometimes Be Helpful

Throughout this discussion of first impressions, and really, throughout this entire chapter, we have suggested that a key goal of social perception is accuracy—perceiving others as accurately as possible. In general, this is a good guiding principle: We do want to understand others without a minimum of error and distortion. But, is accuracy always best? Aren't there times when it would be helpful to perceive others as better than they are or as showing even more desirable traits than they really do? For instance, should parents seek to perceive their children with 100 percent accuracy? Or is it better for their own mental health and happiness to emphasize the positive and, perhaps, see their offspring as better than they really are? And what about romantic relationships? Is it really better to perceive the people we love in a completely accurate manner? Or can positive illusions about them be beneficial?

We'll discuss romantic and other long-term relationships in detail in Chapter 7, but here, we want to call attention to the fact that a growing body of evidence indicates that in social perception, as in many other areas of life, some degree of inaccuracy—some illusions—may actually be beneficial (e.g., Murray, Holmes, Dolderman, & Griffin,, 2000). Specifically, recent research findings indicate that when romantic partners perceive each other as better than they really are, this can have important positive implications for their relationships and can enhance their personal happiness over a period of many years. A clear example of such research is provided by a study conducted by Miller, Niehuis, and Huston (2006), who studied recently married couples over a thirteen-year period.

The researchers began by having the couples rate each others' behavior in two major categories: agreeable actions (e.g., expressing approval of their partner, complimenting the partner, expressing physical affection) and disagreeable actions (e.g., criticizing the partner, showing anger and impatience, seeming uninterested or bored with the partner). From the participants' responses, they could form an estimate of the extent to which each member of a couple showed agreeable or disagreeable behaviors. Positive illusions referred to the extent to which each member of a couple viewed their partner more favorably than their ratings of the partner's behavior would suggest. In other words, positive illusions, in this research, referred to perceiving one's partner as better than she or he was in terms of the extent to which the partner showed agreeable rather than disagreeable behaviors.

Data concerning the partners' behavior and marital love (how loving and close each couple was) were gathered through interviews and questionnaires at several points in time: when the couples were newlyweds (married two months), after they were married for one year, two years, and again after they had been married for about thirteen years.

What did Miller et al. (2006) find? First, that positive illusions—perceiving one's partner as better than she or he is objectively—did have beneficial effects. Couples who had such positive illusions for each other maintained their feelings of love and closeness better than those who did not. Moreover, they maintained these for many years—throughout the first thirteen years of their marriage. Such illusions did not predict divorce, but overall, they seemed to be an important "plus" for the couples in the study.

In sum, while in most situations, accuracy should indeed be a key goal in social perception, there seem to be instances in which some degree of inaccuracy—in the form of positive illusions about one's lover or spouse—are beneficial. To put is simply: To keep that "loving feeling" mentioned in so many popular songs, allow yourself to see your loved ones as better than they actually are. The result may actually be enhanced personal relationships and increased personal happiness (see Figure 3.15 on page 104).

Impression Management: The Fine Art of Looking Good

The desire to make a favorable impression on others is a strong one, so most of us do our best to "look good" to others when we meet them for the first time. Social psychologists use the term impression management (or self-presentation) to describe these efforts to make a good impression on others, and the results of their research on this process suggest that it is well worth the effort: People who perform impression management successfully *do* often gain important advantages in many situations (e.g., Sharp & Getz, 1996; Wayne & Liden, 1995). What tactics do people use to create favorable impressions on others? Which work best? Let's see what research findings indicate about these intriguing questions.

Tactics of Impression Management and Their Relative Success

While individuals use many different techniques for boosting their image, most of these fall into two major categories: self-enhancement—efforts to increase their appeal to others, and other-enhancement—efforts to make the target person feel good in various ways.

With respect to self-enhancement, specific strategies include efforts to boost one's physical appearance through style of dress and personal grooming. In addition, people sometimes use various "props" to enhance their appeal (see Figure 3.16 on page 105). For instance, they carry the "right" kind of handbag or, in the case of male professors, sometimes, hold a pipe while lecturing, even if they really don't like to smoke it (Terry & Krantz, 1993). Additional tactics of self-enhancement involve efforts to appear highly skilled or describing oneself in positive terms, explaining, for instance, how they (the person engaging in

Figure 3.15
Should We Always Strive for Accuracy in Person Perception? Perhaps Not!
Research findings indicate that although accuracy is generally desirable in social perception, positive illusions about others, too, can be beneficial. Specifically, perceiving people we love as better than they really are can enhance our relationships with them and so contribute to our personal happiness. In such cases, total accuracy is not necessarily best.

impression management) overcame daunting obstacles (Stevens & Kristoff, 1995). Other findings (e.g., Rowatt, Cunningham, & Druen, 1998) indicate that many people use this tactic to increase their appeal to potential dating partners; they describe themselves in favorable terms (more favorable than they really deserve) to impress people they want to date. In short, they bend the truth to enhance their own appeal. Many good examples of this can be found in online dating services (Match.com, Yahoo Personals, etc.) and on Facebook or MySpace—sites where people can keep up with old friends and make new ones. The descriptions of themselves offered by at least some people are—to say the least—not totally accurate. In fact, some people describe themselves in flattering terms because they realize that this is a good way to win more contacts or dates. So clearly, impression management now occurs in cyberspace and in face-to-face meetings.

Turning to other enhancement, individuals use many different tactics to induce positive moods and reactions in others. A large body of research findings suggests that such reactions, in turn, play an important role in generating liking for the person responsible for them (Byrne, 1992). The most commonly used tactic of other enhancement is flattery, which is making statements that praise the target person, his or her traits, or accomplishments, or the organization with which the target person is associated (Kilduff & Day, 1994). Such tactics are often highly successful, provided they are not overdone. Additional tactics of other enhancement involve expressing agreement with the target person's views, showing a high degree of interest in this person, doing small favors for them, asking for their advice and feedback in some manner (Morrison & Bies, 1991), or expressing liking for them nonverbally (e.g., through high levels of eye contact, nodding in agreement, and smiling [Wayne & Ferris, 1990]).

That individuals often employ such tactics is obvious: You can probably recall many instances in which you either used, or were the target of, such strategies. A key question, however, is: Do they work? Do these tactics of impression management succeed in generating positive feelings and reactions on the part of the people toward whom they are directed? The answer provided by a growing body of literature is clear: Yes, provided they are used with skill and care. For example, in one large-scale study involving more than fourteen hundred employees, Wayne, Liden, Gran, and Ferris (1997) found that several social skills (including impression management) were the single best predictor of job performance ratings and assessments of potential for promotion for employees in a wide range of jobs. These findings, and those of many related studies (e.g., Paulhus, Bruce, & Trapnell, 1995; Wayne & Kacmar, 1991; Witt & Ferris, 2003), indicate that impression management tactics often do succeed in enhancing the appeal of people who use them effectively. However we should hasten to add that the use of these tactics involves potential pitfalls: If they are overused or used ineffectively, they can backfire and produce negative rather than positive reactions from others. For instance, in one interesting study, Vonk (1998) found strong evidence for what she terms the *slime effect*, which is a tendency to form negative impressions of others who "lick upward but kick downward." That is, people in a work setting who play up to their superiors but treat subordinates with disdain and contempt. The moral of these findings is clear: While tactics of impression management often succeed this is not always the case, and sometimes, they can boomerang, adversely affecting reactions to the people who use them.

Figure 3.16
Props as a Tactic of Impression Management
Sometimes individuals seeking to make a favorable impression on others carry the right props and display them prominently. Women are certain to carry the "right" kind of handbag to demonstrate that they are en vogue while young male professors may hold a pipe to appear older and wiser than they actually are.

Impression Management: The Role of Cognitive Load

That we try to make a favorable impression on others in many situations is obvious; and this makes a great deal of sense. We have strong reasons for wanting to look good to others in job interviews, on first dates, when attempting to gain membership in a fraternity or sorority, and in many other contexts. Generally, we can do quite a good job in this respect because we have practiced impression management skills for many years. As a result, we can engage in positive self-presentation in a relatively automatic and effortless manner; we are just following well-practiced scripts (see Schlenker & Pontari, 2001). Some situations in which we try to make a good first impression on others, however, are demanding ones: A lot is going on, so we don't have the luxury of concentrating solely or entirely on making a good first impression. For instance, consider the situation faced by politicians seeking the nomination of their party. Often, they face a grueling schedule of meetings, speeches, and travel as they move from one location and one audience to another. As a result, they often become fatigued and experience cognitive overload; they are trying to handle more tasks and information than they can. How does such extra cognitive load influence our ability to present ourselves in a favorable light?

At first, you might guess that the effects would always be harmful: When we are busy performing other tasks, we can't do as good a job at presenting ourselves, and in general, this appears to be true (e.g., Tice, Butler, Muraven, & Stillwell, 1995). And in fact, political candidates often do make serious blunders when fatigued or otherwise overloaded. But consider this: Some people are uncomfortable in social situations because they feel anxious and tend to worry about how others will perceive them. For such people, being busy with other tasks may distract them from such feelings and thoughts and so actually enhance their ability to present themselves favorably. Research by Pontari and Schlenker (2000) confirms these seemingly counterintuitive predictions. They had people who were extroverts (outgoing, friendly, sociable) and people who were introverts (reserved, shy, withdrawn) take part in a mock job interview in which they tried to present themselves either as they were (extroverted or introverted) or as the opposite kind of person. During the interview, participants were either busy performing another task (trying to remember an eight-digit number) or were not busy. Results indicated that for the extroverts, cognitive busyness interfered with their ability to present themselves as introverts (i.e., to appear shy, withdrawn, etc.) For introverts, however, the opposite was true: trying to remember the eight-digit number actually improved their ability to appear to be extroverts. Pontari and Schlenker (2000) interpret these findings as indicating that being busy with other tasks prevented introverts from feeling anxious and focusing on their fear of doing poorly. In short, for such people, cognitive distraction was actually a plus; it helped them to do a better job at self-presentation. But interesting as this finding is, it does not negate the fact that in most situations, and for most people, cognitive overload can interfere with their efforts to look good in the eyes of others. Now let's consider another situation in which individuals try to look good while under considerable pressure—speed dating. (This topic is discussed in *Social Psychology: What It Tells Us About . . .* on page 107.)

> ### ∂Principles to Remember
>
> First impressions are important and often exert lasting effects on social relationships. For this reason it is important to make a good first impression on others when we care about their evaluations of us.

KeyPoints

- Most people are concerned with making good first impressions on others because they believe that these impressions will exert lasting effects.

- Research on impression formation—the process through which we form impressions of others—suggests that this is true. Asch's classic research on impression formation indicated that impressions of others involve more than simple summaries of their traits and that some traits (central traits) can influence the interpretation of other traits.

- More modern research indicates impressions of others consist both of examples of behavior relating to specific traits (exemplars) and mental abstractions based on observations of many instances of behavior.

- While accuracy is generally a good guiding principle for impression formation (and social perception generally), recent findings indicate that positive illusions about people we love may strengthen intimate relationships and contribute to personal happiness.

- To make a good impression on others, individuals often engage in impression management (self-presentation).

- Many techniques are used for this purpose, but most fall under two major headings: self-enhancement—efforts to boost one's appeal others, and other-enhancement—efforts to induce positive moods or reactions in others.

- Impression management is something we practice throughout life, so we can usually engage it in a fairly effortless manner. When other tasks require our cognitive resources, however, impression management can sometimes suffer, unless such tasks distract us from anxiety and fears over performing poorly.

- Speed dating allows single people to form first impressions of many potential romantic partners in a single evening.

Think About It

What techniques do you use to make a good first impression on others? Do they work? What else might you do that would be more effective?

SOCIALPSYCHOLOGY

WHAT IT TELLS US ABOUT . . .

Speed Dating—Can We Really Choose the One We Might Love in a Few Minutes?

Imagine the following scene: In a restaurant, twenty small tables have been set up with two chairs facing each other (see Figure 3.17). At a signal, men and women sit down on opposite sides of the table and begin conversations. Three minutes later, a loud bell rings, and everyone shifts to another table, where they begin talking to someone else. At the end of the evening, they turn in cards on which they indicate whether they want to see each person they have met again.

What we have just described is a popular trend known as speed dating. This has become a widespread means of meeting other people among young adults—especially, those who have graduated from school and are now working. Such people often find that they have little time or opportunity to meet potential partners, so for them, speed dating has great appeal. Some of its advantages are obvious: Each participant can meet many new people in a single evening instead of only one, as usually happens in arranged blind dates. And the costs are relatively low, both in terms of time and money spent on meals, theater tickets, and so on. But such procedures raise an intriguing question: Are they actually useful? Can we really make useful decisions about how much we might like people in such a rapid manner and on the basis of so little information?

A few years ago, we would probably have answered "no." But now, in light of new evidence indicating that we can form stable and perhaps relatively accurate impressions of others quickly (e.g., Willis & Todorov, 2006), it seems possible that speed dating may actually succeed. Specifically, many people may in fact be able to form useful first impressions of potential romantic partners in just a few minutes.

In addition, other evidence also offers convincing support for this possibility. Such research has examined the question of how quickly we can form accurate impressions of others' personalities—where they stand on key dimensions of personality (e.g., what is known as the "the Big Five" dimensions [Mount & Barrick, 1995]). The results of such studies indicate that we can form fairly accurate impressions of others' personalities on the basis of short meetings with them (e.g., Barrick Stewart, & Piotrowski, 2002). For instance, even from a brief first encounter lasting only a few minutes, we can tell whether other people are friendly and sociable or shy and withdrawn (a basic dimension of personality known as extraversion). Similarly, we can tell whether they are cooperative and trusting on the one hand or uncooperative and mistrustful on the other (a basic dimension of personality known as agreeableness).

In view of these findings, it appears that speed dating may not be as overly optimistic as we might assume: Perhaps we can determine, quite quickly, whether we would be interested in another person as a potential romantic partner. On the other hand, though, speed dating does have important limitations: In a few minutes we can observe only a small sample of others' behavior—just enough, perhaps, to notice those aspects of their personality and behavior that are the most obvious. Many other, more subtle aspects are not readily apparent. But because attraction (a topic we'll consider in detail in Chapter 7) does often involve intangibles such as "chemistry" and because we can't like or date people we never meet, speed dating may well succeed in its major goal: giving single people a wider range of potential romantic partners than they might otherwise have.

Figure 3.17

Speed Dating: Can it Really Work?

In speed dating, individuals meet many potential romantic partners and have brief conversations with them (five minutes or even less) during one evening. They rate each person they have met, and pairs who rate each other highly can then arrange to meet again in a more traditional way (e.g., on a date). Can we really form accurate impressions of people we meet for just a few minutes and tell whether we might want them as a romantic partner? Some research findings indicate that we can, so speed dating may actually work, at least to some extent.

SUMMARY AND REVIEW

- Social perception involves the processes through which seek to understand other people. It plays a key role in social behavior and social thought. To understand others' emotional states, we often rely on nonverbal communication—an unspoken language of facial expressions, eye contact, and body movements and postures. While facial expressions may not be as universal as once believed, they do often provide useful information about others' emotional states. Useful information on this issue is also provided by eye contact, body language, and touching. Recent findings indicate that handshaking provides nonverbal cues about others' personality and can influence first impressions of strangers. If we pay careful attention to certain nonverbal cues, we can recognize efforts at deception by others. Women are better than men at both sending and interpreting nonverbal cues and also better at remembering details of others' appearance. This gives them an important advantage in many situations.

- To obtain information about others' lasting traits, motives, and intentions, we often engage in attribution—efforts to understand why people have acted as they have. According to Jones and Davis's theory of correspondent inference, we attempt to infer others' traits from observing certain aspects of their behavior, especially behavior that is freely chosen, produces noncommon effects, and is low in social desirability. Another theory, Kelley's theory of causal attribution, states that we are interested in the question of whether others' behavior stemmed from internal or external causes. To answer this question, we focus on information relating to consensus, consistency, and distinctiveness. Two other important dimensions of causal attribution relate to whether specific causes of behavior are stable over time and controllable or not controllable. When we think abstractly about the events in our lives, we assign fate a powerful role in determining them. When we think more concretely, however, we tend to perceive fate as less important. Attribution is subject to many potential sources of error. One of the most important of these is the correspondence bias—the tendency to explain others' actions as stemming from dispositions even in the presence of situational causes. This tendency seems to be stronger in Western cultures than in Asian cultures and can occur for attributions for groups as well as individuals. Two other attributional errors are the actor-observer effect—the tendency to attribute our own behavior to external (situational causes) but that of others to internal causes, and the self-serving bias—the tendency to attribute positive outcomes to internal causes but negative ones to external causes. Attribution has been applied to many practical problems. For instance, it has been applied to treating depression—perhaps the most common important form of mental disorder.

- Most people are concerned with making good first impressions on others because they believe that these impressions will exert lasting effects. Asch's classic research on impression formation indicated that impressions of others involve more than simple summaries of their traits. More modern research indicates impressions of others consist both of examples of behavior relating to specific traits (exemplars) and mental abstractions based on observations of many instances of behavior. While accuracy is generally a good guiding principle for impression formation (and social perception generally), recent findings indicate that positive illusions about people we love may strengthen intimate relationships and contribute to personal happiness. To make a good impression on others, individuals often engage in impression management (self-presentation). Many techniques are used for this purpose, but most fall under two major headings: self-enhancement—efforts to boost one's appeal to others, and other-enhancement—efforts to induce positive moods or reactions in others. Impression management is something we practice throughout life, so we can usually engage it in a fairly effortless manner. When other tasks require our cognitive resources, however, impression management can sometimes suffer. Speed dating allows single people to form first impressions of many potential romantic partners in a single evening, and some evidence indicates that these impressions are relatively accurate.

Key Terms

action identification (p. 89)

actor-observer effect (p. 93)

attribution (p. 75)

body language (p. 78)

consensus (p. 86)

consistency (p. 86)

correspondence bias (p. 89)

correspondent inference (p. 85)

distinctiveness (p. 86)

fundamental attribution error (p. 89)

implicit personality theories (p. 100)

impression formation (p. 75)

impression management (p. 75)

linguistic style (p. 81)

microexpressions (p. 80)

noncommon effects (p. 85)

nonverbal communication (p. 75)

self-serving bias (p. 93)

social perception (p. 75)

staring (p. 78)

Connections
INTEGRATING SOCIAL PSYCHOLOGY

In this chapter, you read about . . .	In other chapters, you will find related discussions of . . .
basic channels of nonverbal communication	the role of nonverbal cues in interpersonal persuasion (Chapter 4), prejudice (Chapter 6), attraction (Chapter 7), and charismatic leadership (Chapter 12).
theories of attribution	the role of attribution in persuasion (Chapter 4), social identity and self-perception (Chapter 5), prejudice (Chapter 6), long-term relationships (Chapter 8), prosocial behavior (Chapter 10), and aggression (Chapter 11).
first impressions and impression management	the role of first impressions in interpersonal attraction (Chapter 7) and the role of impressions management in job interviews (Chapter 12).

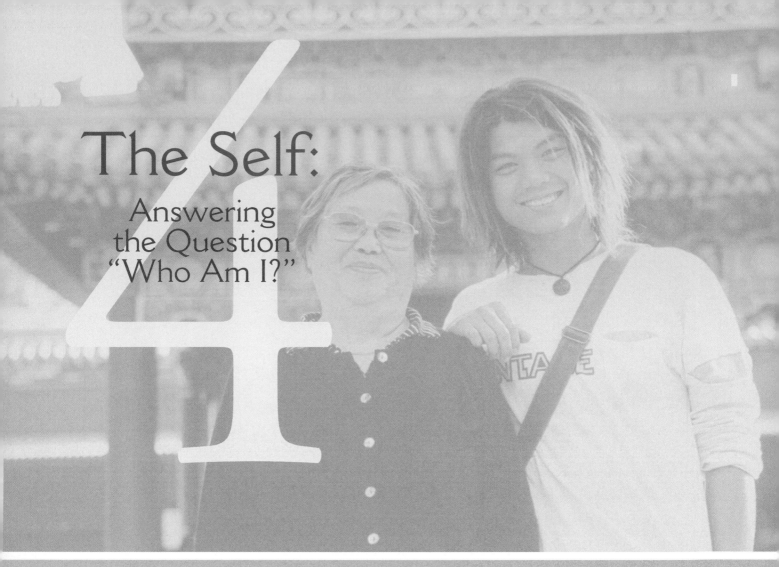

The Self:
Answering the Question "Who Am I?"

CHAPTER OUTLINE

- **Self-Presentation: Managing the Self in Different Social Contexts**
  Self-Presentation Tactics
    MAKING SENSE OF COMMON SENSE: A SOCIAL PSYCHOLOGICAL PERSPECTIVE—THE INTERNET: PRESENTING YOUR ONLINE IDENTITY

- **Self-Knowledge: How Do We Know Who We Are?**
  Introspection: Looking Inward to Discover the Causes of Our Own Behavior
  The Self from the Other's Standpoint

- **Thinking about the Self: Personal versus Social Identity**
  Who I Am Depends on the Situation
    SOCIAL PSYCHOLOGY: WHAT IT TELLS US ABOUT ... HOW WE MANAGE WHEN THERE IS CONFLICT AMONG OUR IDENTITIES
  Who I Am Depends on Others' Treatment

- Possible Selves: The Self over Time
  Self-Control

- **Self-Esteem: Attitudes toward Ourselves**
  The Measurement of Self-Esteem
  Is High Self-Esteem Always Beneficial?
  Do Women and Men Differ in Their Level of Self-Esteem?

- **Social Comparison: How We Evaluate Ourselves**
  Self-Serving Biases
    BUILDING THE SCIENCE: CLASSICS OF SOCIAL PSYCHOLOGY—IS BEING UNREALISTIC GOOD FOR YOU? CAN THAT BE REALISTIC?

- **The Self as Target of Prejudice**
  Emotional Consequences: How Well-Being Can Suffer
  Cognitive Consequences: Performance Deficits
  Behavioral Consequences: Stereotype Threat

My identity as a social psychology professor requires me to be clued in to how university students spend their time. It is important to keep up with changes in their social world, and students' involvement with the Internet is one of those changes, so I felt it would be useful for me to become familiar with myspace.com, facebook.com, and the countless other Web sites my students visit. For my first online foray I decided to simply observe some chat room behavior. By doing so, I hoped to gain insight into why so many people engage in this form of social interaction and at the same time get the hang of netiquette, that is, the "proper" way to behave in the online world.

After entering a chat room sponsored by a big Internet company, I soon found myself wanting to interact with the other chatters. I can't remember exactly what I contributed to the ongoing conversation, but it was clearly unacceptable (perhaps I offered some insufferable psychological analysis of an issue being discussed). In any case, within a few seconds, the moderator of the room announced that I had been banned from that chat room for twenty-four hours. What? I was outraged!

How could he so quickly pass judgment on me? How dare he cut off the meaningful bonds that I had formed with my fellow chatters! Well no, wait, I hardly knew my fellow chatters, having exchanged only a few moments of inane banter with any of them. It didn't matter why I'd been banished, the exclusion was painful.

Shortly after that first experience, I entered a different chat room, determined to be more careful. I didn't announce my entry into the room, hanging back to see what the current conversation was about. After some period of observation, one of the more frequent contributors to the conversation called me a "troll." Troll? Was he referring to me? I'm a good person, and I certainly don't live under a bridge. One of his buddies then referred to me as a "lurker," meaning one of those who merely watches, too afraid to say anything. Goaded by my wish to avoid further condemnation, I spoke up with some sort of vague pleasantry—only to endure instantaneous replies: "Noob!" and "Please go kill yourself!"

Things were not going well for me or my online identity. Within the space of one week, I had been excluded, scorned, and urged to commit suicide, in each case by people with whom I'd hardly spent more than a few virtual minutes. How is it possible that the comments of a few anonymous people had caused me such hurt feelings, an intense wish for justice, and against all common sense, a renewed wish to belong—in a chat room?

I continued to wonder why I had been rejected after only a few words. I decided that on the Web, just as in real life, knowing the "ropes," the nuances of speech and timing, might make a lot of difference in people's first impression. However, it also occurred to me that maybe gender had something to do with it (I was using a female online name)—were the "bits of wisdom" I'd offered less palatable because they were coming from a female? I never found out exactly why my novice experiences resulted in this rejection, but I had no further troubles in subsequent chat rooms I visited. Maybe gaining practice in dealing with social life on the Web is like becoming accustomed to any other unfamiliar culture—it just takes some getting used to. Could the person in Figure 4.1 be you?

Figure 4.1
Online Interaction or Live Interaction: What's Your Preference?
Is the nature of social life to be divided into before online and after online?

You might wonder whether considering those chat room experiences as potentially the result of my gender reflects, as social psychologist Pinel (2004) refers to it, **stigma consciousness**—a readiness to see negative outcomes as due to discrimination. That's possible. Or, perhaps, you think that gender based exclusion and discrimination is a thing of the past—not something you would see on the Internet today. You might even consider it possible that gender discrimination played a role in my exclusion experience but, because discrimination can be sufficiently subtle, it is not always easy to tell whether what happens to us is really a result of our gender. Certainly the many legal barriers that once prevented women from entering various occupations have been dismantled. But, as you'll see in this chapter as well as Chapter 6, differential treatment based on gender is not history although its operation is considerably more subtle than it was in the past when women were overtly excluded from certain occupations.

Stereotypes about women have certainly changed over time, and this reflects the real changes that have occurred in women's roles (Dasgupta & Asgari, 2004; Eagly, 2007). Although it may be amusing to take a look at how previous generations thought about women's work, as illustrated in Figure 4.2, it would be incorrect to conclude that women no longer experience discrimination. As we'll illustrate, there are negative emotional, cognitive, and behavioral consequences of perceiving ourselves to be the target of prejudice (Schmitt & Branscombe, 2002a). In fact, merely considering the possibility that sexism might play a role in the outcomes we receive can affect our self-esteem and our subsequent academic performance (Adams, Garcia, Purdie-Vaughns, & Steele, 2006).

The nature of the self and how we present ourselves to others has been a central topic of research in social psychology. In this chapter, we'll look at the impact of Internet technology on how we experience and present ourselves to others. As the cartoon in Figure 4.3 on page 114 suggests, we can choose to withhold some crucial information about ourselves when communicating over the Internet.

We'll then consider methods that people use to gain self-knowledge, examine whether people have just one self or many selves, and investigate whether one aspect of the self is more true or predictive of behavior than another. Does our sense of self stay the same all the time, or does it vary with the circumstances and the feedback we get? What role does social comparison play in how we evaluate ourselves? Then we'll turn to the issue of self-esteem: How do we get it, and how do we lose it? Are there group differences in average level of self-esteem? Specifically, we'll consider whether men and women differ in self-esteem. Finally, we'll look in depth at the effects of being a target of prejudice including the emotional, cognitive, and performance consequences of rejection by others because of our group membership.

Figure 4.2
The 1945 Stereotype of a Good Woman: How the Times Have Changed

Looking back more than a half century, it might be difficult to believe that these were the nonnative expectations for women. Clearly, employment outside of the home was not expected for married women particularly, although today most college-educated women in the United States will be in the labor force for much of their adult lives.

The Good Wife's Guide

- Have dinner ready. Plan ahead, even the night before, to have a delicious meal ready, on time for his return. This is a way of letting him know that you have been thinking about him and are concerned about his needs. Most men are hungry when they come home and the prospect of a good meal (especially his favorite dish) is part of the warm welcome needed.
- Prepare yourself. Take 15 minutes to rest so you'll be refreshed when he arrives. Touch up your makeup, put a ribbon in your hair and be fresh-looking. He has just been with a lot of work-weary people.
- Clear away the clutter. Make one last trip through the main part of the house just before your husband arrives.
- Gather up schoolbooks, toys, paper, etc., and then run a dustcloth over the tables.
- Be happy to see him.
- Listen to him. You may have a dozen important things to tell him, but the moment of his arrival is not the time. Let him talk first—remember, his topics of conversation are more important than yours.
- Make him comfortable. Have him lean back in a comfortable chair or have him lie down in the bedroom. Have a cool or warm drink ready for him.
- Don't ask him questions about his actions or question his judgment or integrity. Remember, he is the master of the house and as such will always exercise his will with fairness and truthfulness. You have no right to question him.
- A good wife always knows her place.

stigma consciousness
A readiness to perceive negative outcomes as a result of our devalued group membership.

Self-Presentation: Managing the Self in Different Social Contexts

Shakespeare's maxim, "All the world's a stage, and all the men and women merely players," conveys the social psychological scenario in which we all participate: presenting who we are to a constantly observing and potentially ever-changing audience. As we noted in Chapter 3, we have some choices to make when deciding how to put our best foot forward and present ourselves to others.

Self-Presentation Tactics

We can try to ensure that others form impressions of us based on our most favorable self-aspects; that is, we can engage in **self-promotion.** If we want others to think we're smart, we can emphasize our intelligence "credentials"—grades obtained, awards won, and degrees sought. If we want others to conclude we are fun, we can choose to tell them about the great parties we attend or those we've hosted. Sometimes this works. If we say we're really good at something, people will often believe us, and saying so may even help convince ourselves that it's true.

Considerable research from a **self-verification perspective**—the processes we use to lead others to agree with our self-views—suggests that negotiation occurs with others to ensure they agree with our self-claims (Swann, 2005). For example, while trading self-relevant information with a potential roommate, you might stress the student part of your self-concept—emphasize your good study habits and pride in your good grades, and underplay your fun qualities. This potential roommate might even note that "You don't sound like you're very interested in having fun here at college." To gain that person's agreement with your most central self-perception—serious student—you may even be willing to entertain a negative assessment of your fun quotient, as long as the other person is willing to go along with your self-assessment of the dimension most critical to you. Indeed, in this interaction, the potential roommate might wish to emphasize his or her party side. In this instance, it may be especially useful for you to downplay your own partying skills so that the other can achieve distinctiveness on this dimension. Through this sort of self-presentational exchange process, you may "buy" their self-assessment as a party type, to the extent that it helps you to "sell" your own self-assessment as an excellent student.

So, according to the self-verification view, even if it means potentially receiving information that is negative about ourselves, we may still wish to have other people see us as we see ourselves. Suppose you are certain that you lack athletic ability, are shy, or that you lack math skills. Even though these attributes might be seen as relatively negative compared to their alternatives—athletic star, extroverted, or math whiz—you might prefer to have people see you in a way that is consistent with how you see yourself. Research has revealed that, when given a choice, we prefer to be with other people who verify our views about ourselves rather than with those who fail to verify our dearly held self-views—even if they are not flattering (Chen, Chen, & Shaw, 2004).

We can also choose to create a favorable self-presentation by conveying our positive regard for others. We like to feel that others respect us, and we appreciate those who convey it to us (Tyler & Blader, 2000). To achieve this end, you can present yourself to others as someone who particularly values or respects them. In general, as we discussed in Chapter 3, when we want to make a good impression on others, it can be useful to employ **ingratiation** tactics. That is, we can make others like us by praising them. This is generally quite effective, unless we overdo it, and people suspect our sincerity (Vonk, 1999). To achieve the same

Figure 4.3
Not All Aspects of Ourselves Are Equally Available When We Communicate over the Internet
As shown in this cartoon, it may be easier to conceal important information about ourselves on the Internet than in face-to-face encounters.

(*Source:* Peter Steiner, *The New Yorker*, page 61 of July 5, 1993)

"On the Internet, nobody knows you're a dog."

self-promotion
Attempting to present ourselves to others as having positive attributes.

self-verification perspective
Theory that addresses the processes by which we lead others to agree with our views of ourselves; wanting others to agree with how we see ourselves.

ingratiation
When we try to make others like us by conveying that we like them; praising others to flatter them.

end, we can be **self-deprecating**—imply that we are not as good as someone else—to communicate admiration or to simply lower the audience's expectations of our abilities.

Are our self-presentations always honest? Or are they at times strategic and occasionally less than straightforward? Research indicates that college students report telling lies to other people about twice a day (Kashy & DePaulo, 1996), frequently to advance their own interests but sometimes to help protect the other person. Consistent with the latter possibility, those people who tell more lies have more friends. For more on the complexities of self-presentation, read *Making Sense of Common Sense: A Social Psychological Perspective.*

> ## 〜 Principles to Remember
> Self-presentation tactics vary depending on the medium—face-to-face interaction or those lacking nonverbal cues—and people's goals.

self-deprecating
Putting ourselves down or implying that we are not as good as someone else.

MAKING SENSE OF COMMON SENSE:
A SOCIAL PSYCHOLOGICAL PERSPECTIVE
The Internet: Presenting Your Online Identity

The Internet is a place where we can seek out general information about the world—"google" it—and become anyone we want to be—catch up with old friends on facebook.com or make new friends. But does being online change the rules of self-presentation? Do we manage the impressions we leave on other people in the same way as we do when interacting in person? Common sense might suggest that people are people, so the processes of social interaction online are likely to be largely the same as in face-to-face interaction settings. To address the accuracy of this common sense claim, we first consider recent research about how people choose to present themselves on the Web and then whether there are differences in how our online and face-to-face social interactions are regulated.

In what way might access to Internet technology affect people differently? Some people may put information about themselves on the Web (e.g., myspace.com) because they believe such information better represents who they are than does the "live" impression they leave in the "real world." Marcus, Machilek, and Schütz (2006) confirmed that the "self and other" agreement about what a person is like was higher for Web-based social interactions than for real-world interactions. That is, when interacting with another person via their self-constructed Web page, viewers infer attributes that agree with the self-image of the person who constructed the page. Of course, this might just mean that people who present themselves on the Web can more easily manage others' impressions of them than they can when the interaction is face to face because they have total control over what information is being conveyed on the Internet.

Another online versus offline difference is experienced by shy people (Stritzke, Nguyen, & Durkin, 2004). In the real world, shy and non-shy people vary in the constraints they feel in their interactions: Sensitivity to rejection, difficulties initiating contact, or problems with self-disclosure are experienced in different degrees. These researchers concluded that the absence of visual and auditory feedback enabled the shyer participants to be more like their non-shy counterparts when interacting online. The absence of paralinguistic cues such as gestures and tone of voice that typically benefit the non-shy, results in a more level playing field for the shy online.

Online interaction allows more latitude for deception than the real world. For example, Yahoo instant-messenging accounts allow you to create up to five profiles: you can describe yourself differently for various roles as dad, business manager, or little league coach. People *can* use these different profile possibilities to change their age, race, gender, income, or any number of factors on which they might be judged when making an initial impression on others. So what happens if you're found out? Are there any consequences? It has long been known that when we behave disloyally or dishonestly, people who are like us—members of our own group—are harsher in their criticism than they would be of someone they perceive as not like us—not a member of our group (Branscombe, Wann, Noel, & Coleman, 1993; Marques, Abrams, & Serôdio, 2001). Such "black sheep" come to be regarded with disdain or distrust. In one study (Birchmeier, Joinson, & Dietz-Uhler, 2005), a member of an online group was found to have been deceptive. Reactions of the group members were mostly negative, that is, they were angry and wanting to exclude the deceptive member from the group.

Continued on page 116

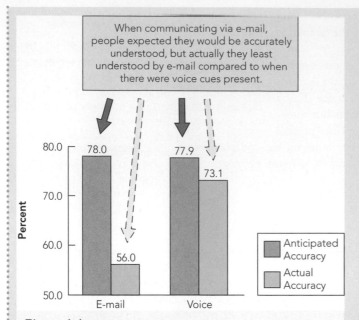

When communicating via e-mail, people expected they would be accurately understood, but actually they least understood by e-mail compared to when there were voice cues present.

Figure 4.4
Communication Clarity: Accuracy of Emotion Content Is Low via E-mail
When people had to send a message to their friend with sarcastic content, it was least well understood when sent via e-mail, although people believed it would be accurately interpreted by their friend. Messages sent over the phone with the same sarcasm were more likely to be accurately detected.

(*Source:* Based on data from Kruger, Epley, Parker & Ng, 2005).

So why might some people prefer the online world to the real one? Many people prefer text messaging or instant messaging over talking on the phone or face-to-face communication. A focus-group study (Madell & Muncer, 2007) revealed that people feel a greater level of control in asynchronous communication (such as text messaging or instant messaging) than in synchronous communication (responding to others immediately). Because asynchrony allows us to contemplate our responses, it offers greater control over how fast we carry on a conversation, which enables us to present ourselves as we would like to be perceived.

The apparent advantage of using forms of **asynchronous communication**—including e-mail and other forms of text messaging—can cause some problems with people being understood by others. Consider recent research by Kruger, Epley, Parker, and Ng (2005) who found that the recipients of e-mails frequently failed to understand the sender's expressions of sarcasm or humor. Pairs of friends were separated and told their task was to identify which of their friend's twenty statements about college, the weather, food, and the world were sarcastic or serious. The statements were then sent either via e-mail or over the phone. Because nonverbal expressions (such as tone of voice) used to detect sarcasm are absent in e-mail, but e-mail writers fail to appreciate this, they will think others understand them when they do not. As shown in Figure 4.4, this is exactly what was found—the message sender thought they were equally likely to be understood, regardless of method of communication, but the message's sarcasm was less likely to be accurately detected in the e-mail condition compared to the voice condition.

Is there a downside to controlling our self-presentation through technology? An investigation into Internet use by Caplan (2005) showed that individuals who lack self-presentational skills are more likely to be attracted to online social interaction relative to face-to-face or other forms of synchronous communication. Obviously, a dependency on the Internet for one's social interactions cannot help but detract from building skills for dealing with people in the real world. One of the primary seductions of the Web is the ability to present those aspects of ourselves we wish to present and to more easily control our responses to others. But consistent with common sense and the message shown in Figure 4.5, as long as we balance our online interactions with offline communications, we're likely to maintain a healthy relationship with this constantly developing technology.

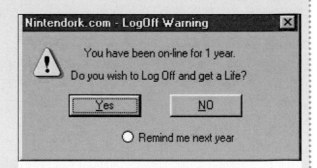

Figure 4.5
Is Online Living Equivalent to Having a Satisfying "Real-Life"?
To what extent are our "virtual selves" different or the same as our "real-life" selves?

KeyPoints

- People who are high in stigma consciousness—a readiness to see negative outcomes as stemming from their devalued group membership—may attribute exclusion or other negative social outcomes that they experience to discrimination.

- We can choose various self-presentational strategies, including self-promotion and ingratiation tactics. We can also agree with others' preferred self-presentations so that they will concur with our own attempts to self-verify.

- Differences between shy and non-shy people are reduced when interactions take place over the Internet. This can result in compulsive Internet use for some and take away from developing skills for dealing with people in the real world.

- If caught, dishonesty online breeds disdain and distrust, just as it does in face-to-face interaction—

especially by those who see us as members of their group.

- People like asynchronous forms of communication—e-mail and text-messaging—in part because it affords them greater feelings of control in terms of how and when to respond to others. We often think we are communicating accurately in text formats, particularly when it involves sarcasm or humor, but others frequently misunderstand our intentions.

Think About It

Are you aware of adjusting how you present yourself to others in different social contexts? Or do you think most people are so good at it, and do so automatically, that they are no longer aware of the shifts they make in their self-presentation?

Self-Knowledge: How Do We Know Who We Are?

We now turn to some of the ways in which we seek to gain self-knowledge. One straightforward method is to attempt to directly analyze ourselves. Another method is to try to see ourselves as we think others see us—to take an observer's perspective on the self. Both of these approaches have consequences for self-appraisal and we will consider each in turn.

Introspection: Looking Inward to Discover the Causes of Our Own Behavior

One important method that people have assumed is useful for learning about the self is to engage in **introspection**—to privately think about who we are. In a whole host of self-help books that sell millions of copies per year, we are told time and again that the best way to get to know ourselves is by looking inwardly. Indeed, many people in our society believe that the more a person introspects about the self, the greater the self-understanding they will achieve. As shown in Figure 4.6 on page 118, pop psychology authors repeatedly tell us that the road to self-knowledge runs through such self-inspection. Is this really the best way to accurately understand ourselves?

First of all, we should note that often we do not know or have conscious access to the reasons for our actions, although we can certainly generate—after the fact—what might seem to be logical theories of why we acted as we did (Nisbett & Wilson, 1977). However, thinking about reasons for our actions can misdirect our quest for self-knowledge when our behavior is really driven by our feelings. Because we often genuinely don't know why we feel or act in a particular way, generating reasons (that are likely to be inaccurate) could cause us to arrive at false conclusions. Wilson and Kraft (1993) illustrated this process in a series of studies concerning introspection on topics ranging from "why I feel as I do about my romantic partner" to "why I like one type of jam over another." They found that, after introspecting about the reasons for their feelings, people changed their attitudes, at least temporarily, to match their stated reasons. As you might imagine, this

asynchronous communication
Use of text, which allows greater control over what we say to others, visual and voice cues are absent.

introspection
To privately contemplate "who we are." It is a method for attempting to gain self-knowledge.

Figure 4.6
Self-Help Books Recommend Introspection
The titles of these pop psychology books imply that the route to self-knowledge lies in introspection, but recent research reveals that self-reflection can be misleading. Depending on the nature of the factors that are actually driving our behavior, introspection may misdirect us about why we respond as we do.

can lead to regrettable choices because the original feelings—based on other factors entirely—are still there.

Introspection can also mislead us when we attempt to predict how we will feel about a particular event in the future. Try imagining how you would feel living in a new city, being fired from your job, or living with another person for many years. When we are not in these specific circumstances, we might not be able to accurately predict how we would respond when we are in them. This applies to both positive and negative future circumstances.

When we think about something terrible happening to us and try to predict how we would feel one year after the event, we focus exclusively on the awfulness of that event and neglect all the other factors that will almost certainly contribute to our happiness level as the year progresses (Gilbert & Wilson, 2000). Consequently, people predict that they would feel much worse than they actually would when the future arrives. Likewise, for positive events, if we focus on only that occurrence, we will mispredict our happiness as being considerably higher than the actual moderate feelings that are likely one year later. Again, this miscalculation would occur because we fail to consider the daily hassles we are likely to experience in the future, and those would most likely moderate how we actually feel.

Does all this mean that introspection is inevitably misleading? No. It depends on *what* we introspect about. When the behavior in question is actually based on a conscious decision-making process—and is not based on unconscious emotional factors—thinking about those reasons might well lead to accurate self-judgments. On the other hand, when we fail to take into account factors that really do influence how we feel, our introspections may not lead to accurate self-inferences. So, while looking inward can be helpful, it may not be under all circumstances. When asked, people can easily generate reasons for why they do what they do, but those reasons may be based on self-theories about the causes of behavior. By relying on such theories, we may remain unaware of the real reasons, for example emotional factors, that cause our behavior. Gaining insight into one's own emotions and motivations can be tricky indeed.

The Self from the Other's Standpoint

Another attempt to learn about ourselves involves taking an "observer" perspective on our own past. As discussed in Chapter 3, when we analyze our own actions, we tend to attribute our behavior to more situational (external) causes, whereas when we observe others, we tend to attribute the same behavior to more dispositional (internal) causes. If we therefore take an observer's perspective on ourselves, we will be more likely to characterize ourselves in dispositional or trait terms. Pronin and Ross (2006) found this to be true when people were asked to describe themselves as they were five years ago or as they are today. The self in the present was seen as varying with different situations and was therefore characterized less frequently in terms of general dispositions or traits than was the past self. As shown in Figure 4.7, this was the case regardless of the actual age of the participant. Both the middle-aged and college-aged participants saw themselves in terms of consistent traits (as observers tend to) when they were describing themselves in the past compared to when they were describing their present selves.

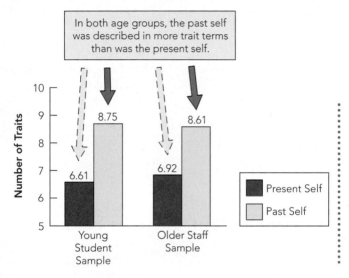

Figure 4.7
Selves across Time: Taking an Observer's Perspective on One's Past Self
In both college students and middle-aged staff members, the past self was described in more trait terms—as observers do— than was the present self.

(*Source:* Based on data from Pronin & Ross, 2006.)

How does considering ourselves from an observer's perspective rather than our own change the way we characterize ourselves? Pronin and Ross (2006) illustrated the effects of different perspectives by employing different types of acting techniques. The participants were divided into two groups and were given "acting" instructions using one of two methods. In the "method-acting" condition, they were told that the goal was to "feel as if you are this other person." In the "standard-acting" condition, they were told that the goal was to "put on a performance so that you appear to others as though you are this person." After practicing various scenes using their assigned method, the participants were then told to enact a family dinner when they were fourteen years old. In this case, everyone played their past self from one of two perspectives: One group was told to play their past self from the perspective of someone experiencing it, and the other group was told to play their past self as if they were an outside observer. Again, the number of consistent dispositions or traits used to describe their fourteen-year-old self was the central measure of interest: Did taking an observer stance on the self lead to greater trait consistency perceptions of the self? The answer was a clear yes. Those who performed with the method-actor technique were more actor-like and saw themselves in terms of few consistent traits, whereas those who played themselves from a more "observer-acting" perspective saw themselves in consistent trait terms. So, when we try to learn about the self from the vantage point of another, we are likely to see ourselves as observers do— in terms of consistent traits.

> **Principles to Remember**
> By introspecting about ourselves we can focus on factors that are not the central ones that drive our responses. Likewise, we may neglect factors that will moderate our reactions to extreme events in the future, which results in mispredicting our own likely responses.

KeyPoints

- One common method by which we attempt to gain self-knowledge is through introspection—looking inwardly to assess and understand why we do what we do.

- When it comes to self-queries about why we acted as we did, mistaken results can occur if we do not have conscious access to the factors that actually influenced our responses, although after the fact we can and do construct explanations that seem plausible to us.

- When it comes to predicting how we might feel in the future, we fail to take into account other events that will moderate how we will feel besides the extreme and isolated event being judged.

- When we think about our past selves we often take an observer's stand point on it, and this leads us to see our past selves in more trait-like consistent terms.

Think About It

If looking inwardly toward our past selves or projecting ourselves into the future can result in biased self-inferences, then how do people ever achieve accurate self-knowledge?

Thinking about the Self: Personal versus Social Identity

social identity theory
Addresses how we respond when our group identity is salient. Suggests that we will move closer to positive others with whom we share an identity but distance from other ingroup members who perform poorly or otherwise make our social identity negative.

personal-versus-social identity continuum
This signifies the two distinct ways that we can categorize ourselves. At the personal level, we can be thought of as a unique individual, whereas at the social identity level, we think of the self as a member of a group.

salience
When someone or some object stands out from its background or is the focus of attention.

intragroup comparisons
Judgments that result from comparisons between individuals who are members of the same group.

According to **social identity theory** (Tajfel & Turner, 1986), we can perceive ourselves differently at any given moment in time, depending on where we are on the **personal-versus-social identity continuum.** At the personal end of this continuum, we think of ourselves primarily as individuals. At the social end, we think of ourselves as members of specific social groups. We do not experience all aspects of our self-concept simultaneously; where we place ourselves on this continuum at any given moment will influence how we think about ourselves. This momentary **salience**—the part of our identity that is the focus of our attention—can affect much in terms of how we perceive and respond to others. When our personal identity is salient and we think of ourselves as unique individuals, our self-descriptions emphasize how we differ from other individuals. For example, you might describe yourself as fun when thinking of yourself at the personal identity level—to emphasize your self-perception as having more of this attribute than other individuals you are using as the comparison. Personal identity self-description can be thought of as an **intragroup comparison**—involving comparisons with other individuals who share our group membership. For this reason, when describing the personal self, which group is the referent can affect the content of our self-descriptions (Oakes, Haslam, & Turner, 1994). Consider how you might characterize yourself if you were asked to describe how you are different from other U.S. citizens. You might describe yourself as particularly liberal in that case, but if you were indicating how you are different from other college students you might say that you are rather conservative. The point is that even for personal identity, the content we generate to describe ourselves depends on some comparison, and this can result in describing ourselves differently—as either liberal or conservative—depending on the comparative context.

At the social identity end of the continuum, perceiving ourselves as members of a group means we emphasize what we share with other group members. We describe ourselves in terms of the attributes that differentiate our group from another comparison group. Descriptions of the self at the social identity level are **intergroup comparisons** in nature—they involve contrasts between groups. For example, your social identity as a fraternity or sorority group member may lead you to ascribe traits to yourself that you share with other members of your group. Attributes of athleticism and self-motivation might, for example, differentiate your group from other fraternities or sororities that you see as being more studious and scholarly than your group. Your gender group is another social identity. If you are female, you might emphasize the attributes that you share with other women (e.g., warm and caring) and that you perceive as differentiating women from men. If you are male, you might emphasize qualities that you are stereotyped as sharing with men (e.g., rational, independent) in contrast to women.

What's important to note here is that when you think of yourself as an individual, the content of your self-description is likely to differ from when you are thinking of yourself as a member of a category that you share with others. Of course, as these examples indicate, most of us are members of a variety of different groups (e.g., occupation, age group, sexual orientation, nationality, sports teams), but all of these will not be salient at the same time. According to social identity theory, people are likely to act in ways that reflect the aspect of their self-concept that is salient at any given moment. Because there may be a number of situational factors that will alter how we define ourselves, the actions that stem from those self-definitions will differ accordingly. Figure 4.8 summarizes the processes involved and consequences of experiencing the self in personal rather than social identity terms.

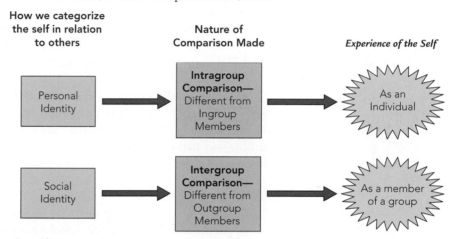

So, at any given time we can define ourselves differently, thus creating many "selves." Can we say that one of these is the true self—either the personal self or any one of a person's potential social identities? Not really. All of these could be correct portraits of the self and accurately predict behavior, depending on the context and comparison dimension (Oakes & Reynolds, 1997). Note, too, how some ways of thinking about ourselves could even imply behaviors that are opposite to those that would result from other self-descriptions (e.g., fun versus scholarly; liberal versus conservative).

Despite such potential variability in self-definition, most of us manage to maintain a coherent image of ourselves, while realizing that we may define ourselves and behave differently in different situations. This can occur either because the domains in which we see ourselves as inconsistent are deemed to be relatively unimportant, or they simply are not salient when we think of ourselves in terms of any particular identity (Patrick, Neighbors, & Knee, 2004).

Figure 4.8
The Personal versus Social Identity Continuum
Depending on how we define ourselves—in terms of our personal or a social identity—the self will be defined in terms of the content that results from either an intragroup or intergroup comparison. The resulting salient identity experience will be either as an individual or as a member of a social group.

(*Source:* Based on Oakes, Haslam, & Turner, 1994.)

Who I Am Depends on the Situation

People do describe themselves differently depending on whether the question they are asked implies situational specificity or not. This effect was illustrated by Mendoza-Denton, Ayduk, Mischel, Shoda, and Testa (2001). In their study, participants were given one of two different types of sentence completion tasks. When the prompt was open ended, such as "I am a (an) . . . person," self-definition as an individual is implied. In this condition, participants' responses were primarily trait-like and global (e.g., "I am an ambitious person"). When, however, the prompt implied particular settings, "I am a (an) . . . when . . ." then the responses were more contingent on the situation considered by the participant (e.g., "I am an ambitious person when a professor provides me with a challenge"). Our

intergroup comparisons
Judgments that result from comparisons between our group and another group.

tendency to see ourselves differentially depending on what relationships with others we consider and according to the context increases with age (Byrne & Shavelson, 1996; Roccas & Brewer, 2002).

We also differ across the lifespan in the extent to which we have multiple aspects of our self-concepts that are important to us (Settles, 2004). For example, people who are experienced with both Asian and Western cultural traditions, might express their "Asianness" in contexts that cue that aspect of the self, but express their "Western-ness" in contexts that cue that aspect. This notion that bicultural individuals possess both Asian and Western identities and can respond according to either was tested with students in Hong Kong who were fluent in both Chinese and English (Trafimow, Silverman, Fan, & Law, 1997). These students were asked to answer the question, "Who am I?" in either one language or the other. The Hong Kong students who responded to the question in English described themselves in terms of personal traits that differentiated them from others, which reflected an individualistic self-construal. In contrast, those who answered the question in Chinese described themselves in terms of group memberships that they shared with others, reflecting a more interdependent self-construal. Thus important group-based differences in the self-concept emerge primarily when that group identity is activated, as it was in this example, when using a particular language.

Such context shifts in self-definition can influence how we categorize ourselves in relation to other people, which in turn, affect how we respond to others (Ryan, David, & Reynolds, 2004). When participants categorize a person in need as a fellow university student—so that person is seen as a member of the same category as the participant— then men and women were equally likely to display care-oriented responses toward that person. In contrast, when the participants categorized themselves in terms of their gender, then women displayed significantly more care-oriented responses than did men. In fact, men reduced their care-oriented responses to the person in need in the gender salient condition compared to the shared university-identity condition. Thus gender differences in caring responses toward another individual depended on gender being a salient category at the time the response was made. Of course, gender is a powerful social category that is likely to be activated a great deal of the time (Fiske & Stevens, 1993). This means it can influence perceptions of the self and our responses to others with some frequency.

Not only must gender be salient for gender differences in self-construal to emerge, but recent research (Guimond et al., 2007) has also revealed that how we perceive ourselves depends on which gender group we compare ourselves to. In a five-nation study, these investigators found that only when men and women were asked to compare themselves to members of the other gender group did they display the expected gender difference in rated self-insecurity. That is, when women compared themselves to men they said they were insecure, and when men compared themselves to women they said they were not insecure. In this case, people saw themselves as consistent with their own gender group's stereotype. However as shown in Figure 4.9, when the same self judgments were made in an intragroup group context—where women compared their standing to other women and men compared their standing to other men—no reliable gender differences in perceived insecurity of the self were found. So, how we see ourselves—in terms of what traits we have— depends on the comparison we use in assessing ourselves.

What determines which aspect of the self will be most influential at any given moment, if how we define ourselves can differ according to the context? First, one aspect of the self might be especially relevant to a particular context (e.g., thinking of ourselves as fun when at a party but as hard working when we are at work). Second, features of the context can make one aspect of the self highly distinctive, with that aspect of identity forming the basis of self-perception. For example, suppose an office is composed of only one woman among several men. In this context, the woman's gender distinguishes her from her colleagues and is therefore likely to be frequently salient. Thus the lone woman is particularly likely to feel "like a woman," and she may be treated as representative of that group (Fuegen & Biernat, 2002; Yoder & Berendsen, 2001). Similarly, African American students at predominantly Caucasian universities where other minority group members are rare are likely to think of themselves in terms of their race (Pollak & Niemann, 1998; Postmes & Branscombe, 2002). Third, some people may be more ready to categorize themselves in terms of a particular personal trait (e.g., intelligence) or group identity (e.g., gender) because of their importance to the self. Fourth, other people, including how they refer to us linguistically, can cue us to think of ourselves in personal versus social identity terms.

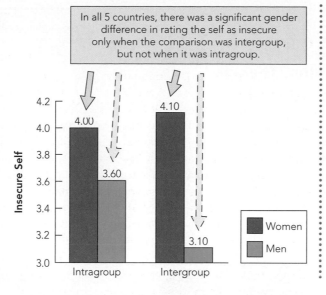

Figure 4.9
Measuring Gendered Self-Perceptions around the World
In a cross-cultural study of 950 participants from five nations (France, Belgium, Malaysia, the Netherlands, and United States), gender differences in perceiving the self as anxious, fearful, and insecure were present only when people compared themselves to members of the other gender group, but no significant gender difference was found when the self was compared to members of their own gender group.

(*Source:* Based on data from Guimond et al., 2007.)

Aspects of the self-concept that are referred to as nouns (e.g., woman, student) are particularly likely to activate social identities (Simon, 2004). Nouns suggest discrete categories, which trigger perceptions of members of those categories as sharing a fundamental nature or essence that is different from members of other categories (Lickel, Hamilton, & Sherman, 2001). In contrast, aspects of the self that are referred to with either adjectives or verbs (e.g., weak, taller, extremely supportive) reference perceived differences between people within a category (Turner & Onorato, 1999) and are especially likely to elicit self-perceptions at the personal identity level. To understand how people manage when different aspects of their identity are in conflict, read *Social Psychology: What It Tells Us About . . .* on page 124.

Who I Am Depends on Others' Treatment

How others treat us, and how we believe they will treat us in the future, have important implications for how we think about ourselves. When it comes to the self, no one is truly an island. If we expect that others will reject us because of some aspect of ourselves, there are a few response options available to us (Tajfel, 1978). To the extent that it is possible to change an aspect of ourselves and avoid being rejected, we could potentially choose to do that. In fact, we could choose to only change that particular feature when we anticipate being in the presence of others who will reject us because of it. In other words, for some aspects of ourselves, we can attempt to hide them from disapproving others. As we discussed, the U.S. military policy of "don't ask, don't tell" implies there are group identities we can choose to reveal or not. However this option will be practically impossible for some social identities. We can't easily hide or change our race, gender, or age. In some cases, even if we could alter the part of the self that brings rejection, we may rebel against those rejecting us by making that feature even more self-defining. That is, we may emphasize that feature as a method of contrasting ourselves from those who reject us—in effect, we can publicly communicate that we value something different than those who might judge us negatively because of it.

This point was illustrated in research conducted by Jetten, Branscombe, Schmitt, and Spears (2001). These researchers studied young people who elect to get body piercings in visible parts of the body other than earlobes (e.g., navel, tongue, eyebrow), a practice that has

SOCIALPSYCHOLOGY

How We Manage When There Is Conflict among Our Identities

"I wonder if I could ask God to forgive me if I pretended not to believe in Him," wonders a teenager in her myspace blog. She wants to join the Art Club at her high school—unfortunately, the group's members claim to be atheists. This is a dilemma for this teen because her personal identity—who she is as an individual—will be inconsistent with the values overtly expressed in the group that she would like to join.

Sometimes, trying to accommodate our personal self-concept to a social identity cannot be managed by simply foregoing that group membership because we may already be a member of the group before the conflict between its norms and our personal beliefs is perceived. In that case, giving up the group by leaving it may be seen as undesirable. Consider Crandall's (2004) research involving binge-eating norms in college sororities. Any individual member's bingeing habits could be predicted from the level of bingeing of her best friends in the sorority. Thus a person who joined the sorority without knowing about the bingeing habits of its members might find it difficult to pull away from the group once involved. Managing the identity conflict between personal values of eating sparingly and one's sorority sisters' norm might require compromising what identity to be "true to."

Sometimes, it is two social identities that are in conflict. Calling it quits with either social identity could be extremely difficult. Consider people who are both homosexual and members of an Orthodox Jewish group (Halbertal & Koren, 2006). In this case, achieving an identity synthesis might be impossible; homosexual and fundamentalist religious identities may be irreconcilable. In a similar vein, Young (2005) describes her struggle to reconcile inconsistent policies and values as a member of

the U.S. military. Many people, she argues, join the military in large part because they hold as personal values those that are also expressed by the organization as core institutional values. That is, living honestly was both highly important to her personally, and, she thought, also to the branch of the military she chose to join. But the policy called "don't ask, don't tell" concerning homosexuals in the military brings these two values into conflict. By requiring homosexual soldiers to treat their sexuality as a secret that they must hide from the world, and at the same time believing that a soldier never lies, makes it difficult to honor both values. Put simply, were such military members to honestly express their homosexual social identities, they would be forced to leave a valued institution and their valued identity as a member of it.

Consider a related identity conflict. U.S. Vice-President Dick Cheney's daughter, Mary, who is a lesbian, describes her father's reaction when she told him of her sexual orientation in her book *Now It's My Turn.* He reportedly emphasized that she was his daughter and that he loved her and wanted her to be happy, whatever her orientation. His identity as a supportive father is, however, in conflict with his identity as a Republican Party member who supports the Federal Marriage Amendment, which would bar Mary and her partner from marrying and even from forming a civil union—along with the partner benefits that union would bring (see Figure 4.10). Vice-President Cheney himself has been guarded and doesn't comment when questioned about how he can loyally support Republican Party policy that is incompatible with his daughter's identity. The vice president's situation, then, is similar to that described by Young: His political identity would appear to violate his identity as a good father.

Figure 4.10
When Two Important Social Identities Clash
U.S. Vice President Dick Cheney supports Republican Party policies that are widely perceived to be antigay; they would bar marriage or civil unions between members of the same sex. Yet he is loyal to and supportive of his daughter Mary, who is a lesbian. Mr. Cheney simply refuses to publicly discuss the clash that exists between his two social identities as a father and a Republican.

gained in popularity. How we dress and alter our bodies can be conceptualized as important identity markers—ways of communicating to the world who we are. Although some identity markers may bring acceptance into peer groups, they may be perceived by other groups as weird or antinormative. Today, body piercings may be comparable to the wearing of blue jeans and men having long hair in the 1960s. These identity markers were the visible indicator of a "hippie" identity, reflecting a self-perception as a rebel against the establishment. Like their 1960s counterparts, today's young people who opt for visible body piercings appear to be engaged in a similar form of rebel identity construction.

People who get such piercings often know that they are likely to be discriminated against because of them. This expectation can lead to stronger self-definition in terms of a group dynamic perceived to be actively rejecting the dominant culture's standards of beauty. An expectation of rejection and devaluation on the part of the culture as a whole can result in increasingly strong identification with a newly forming cultural group. Indeed, those with body piercings, who were led to expect rejection from the mainstream because of their piercings, identified more strongly with other people who have body piercings than did those who were led to expect acceptance from the mainstream. As Figure 4.11 illustrates, people with body piercings seem to be creating an identity that communicates to all that "we are different from the mainstream." If, however, over time, the practice of getting body piercings ultimately becomes diffused throughout the culture, with almost everyone adopting the practice—as happened in the 1960s as everyone started wearing blue jeans—then those who are attempting to convey their collective difference from the mainstream may be compelled to become increasingly more extreme to achieve the same identity end.

This sort of identity dilemma—whether to increasingly emphasize and take pride in an identity or, in contrast, discard and distance ourselves from it—may be especially likely to be provoked when a person moves from one social context to another. Consider the dilemma experienced by Latino(a) students as they leave their home environment to attend a primarily Caucasian university. Social psychologists have examined the different strategies that such students can employ during their first year at college (Ethier & Deaux, 1994). People facing this identity dilemma can use one of two strategies—psychologically moving away from the identity or increased movement toward it. Among those for whom a Latino(a) identity was initially not important, when they moved to a non-Latino environment, they de-emphasized their Latino(a) identity. In contrast, for those who initially valued their Latino(a) identity, in the new context where they know they may be excluded based on that identity, they increased the emphasis they placed on their ethnic identity as indicated by joining Latino(a) student associations. Interestingly, those students who increasingly emphasized their Latino(a) identity and took pride in their differences from others in this new environment had higher self-esteem during their transition to college.

Figure 4.11
Claiming an Identity That Is "Nonmainstream"
Many forms of body adornment and body modification are visual indicators of social identity. This young woman may be conveying to the mainstream that she is not one of them, and that she fits in with other members of her peer group.

Those who chose to distance themselves from their Latino(a) identity suffered reduced self-esteem when they faced rejection based on that identity. So, as we saw with the body piercing research, whether others devalue an identity one might hold is not necessarily correlated with how important that identity is to the self (Ashmore, Deaux, & McLaughlin-Volpe, 2004).

Possible Selves: The Self over Time

Although most of us experience ourselves as relatively consistent over time, it is nonetheless true that sometimes we perceive ourselves as having changed. Studies of **autobiographical memory** show that when we compare our past self with our present self, to the extent that it suggests that there has been improvement over time, we feel good about ourselves (Wilson & Ross, 2001). How might the past be used to bolster our present selves? Ross and Wilson (2003) performed a series of studies in which they asked participants to describe their past self—which they were induced to perceive as far in the past or not so long ago—on either important or unimportant characteristics. Criticism of the "distant" past self was greater than when the same self was perceived as "nearer" to the present, and this was especially the case for important aspects of the self. By derogating our past selves, we can feel better (like we have really grown) about the aspects of ourselves that we care most about. Likewise, these researchers found that people who feel close in time to some self-failure, view their current self less positively than those who are able to see that same failure as far in the distant past.

What are the consequences of thinking about future **possible selves**? If it is a positively valued possible self, it can inspire you to forego current activities that are enjoyable but will not help, or might even hinder, bringing about this improved self (Markus & Nurius, 1986). In this instance, we may forego immediately enjoyable activities to achieve the goal of becoming our desired possible self.

Think about what is involved in attaining a variety of valued social identities. We give up years of "having fun" to attain the status of being a college graduate, complete years of schooling and long internships to be able to call ourselves doctors, and we put in grueling hours at law school and studying for state bar exams to become lawyers. Lockwood and Kunda (1999) found that role models—other people we wish to imitate or be like—can inspire us to invest in such long-term achievements but, to do so, we must see the possible self that the role model represents as being potentially attainable. The image of a possible future self has been found to influence people's motivation to study harder, give up smoking, or invest in parenting classes, to the extent that they can imagine that a new and improved self will result from such changes. We may suffer pain in the present in the hopes of obtaining a more desired future possible self. As the photos in Figure 4.12 illustrate, like those seen on the TV program "Extreme Makeover," rather dramatic changes in the self are possible.

We often consider new possible selves of this sort and how to avoid negative and feared future possible selves, when we are making New Year's resolutions. Polivy and Herman (2000) suggest that envisioning such self-changes can induce feelings of control and optimism, but failing to keep those resolutions is a common experience and repeated failures can lead to unhappiness. When people feel they want to change but cannot succeed in doing so, they may be tempted to reduce this uncomfortable state of self-awareness by distracting themselves—either in mundane ways such as getting lost in a novel or in more damaging ways such as consuming heavy amounts of alcohol (Baumeister, 1991).

Of course, having efficacy in our ability to change is important for doing so, but overconfidence in our ability to do so can lead to false hope and ultimately, disappointment. As we pointed out in Chapter 3, recent research suggests that people often overestimate their ability to influence outcomes (Pronin et al., 2006). In this research, people seemed to imagine they had control over events even when it was objectively impossible. When the situation is indeed uncontrollable, it may not be adaptive to perceive ourselves as hav-

autobiographical memory
Concerned with memory of the ourselves in the past, sometimes over the life course as a whole.

possible selves
Image of how we might be in the future—either a "dreaded" potential to be avoided or "desired" potential that can be strived for.

Figure 4.12
There May Be Limits to Our Ability to Change Ourselves, But Some Extreme Makeovers Suggest that Major Change Is Possible
These photos make the point that if we make extreme enough changes to ourselves, there might not seem to be much of our original self left.

ing control. Consider an instance where you might have wished a negative outcome on another person, and then a few days later something terrible befalls that person. Would you feel responsible—and perceive that your "evil" thoughts actually brought about your enemy's suffering? Or, conversely, suppose you were watching your favorite sports game and you thought about how your favorite player might score some big points. Then, shortly thereafter, you see that player do exactly what you'd imagined. Would you feel you had influenced the outcome of the game? When stated this bluntly, many of us are likely to deny believing we have such "magical powers." But, in a series of studies, Pronin and others (2006) showed we really do believe we are able to control outcomes like these, even when no such control could exist.

Our successful performance in physical, academic, and job tasks is enhanced by feelings of **self-efficacy** (Huang, 1998; Sanna & Pusecker, 1994). It is necessary to believe that we can achieve a goal as a result of our own actions to even try (Bandura, 1997). Indeed, people high in self-efficacy in a domain tend to prefer to allocate their time and effort to tasks that can be solved, and they stop working on tasks that cannot be solved more quickly than those who are low in self-efficacy. A defining feature of people who are entrepreneurs (those who start new businesses) is their high levels of perceived self-efficacy (Markman, Balkin, & Baron, 2002). Indeed, high self-efficacy seems to lead people to select more effective negotiation tactics, which ultimately results in their obtaining better deals than people low in self-efficacy (Sullivan, O'Connor, & Burris, 2006).

Self-Control

As we have noted, we often want to change ourselves—for example, quit smoking, go on a diet, study more effectively—but find it difficult to stick with such long-range goals. Instead, we often succumb to the lure of an immediate reward and break with our prior commitment. In other words, we fail to control ourselves in some meaningful way.

How does the way we think about ourselves affect our success in such **self-control** endeavors—in which long-term goals are pursued even though short-term outcomes might be more immediately gratifying? In a series of studies, Fujita, Trope, Liberman and Levin-Sagi (2006) illustrated the important role of how we construe our ability to successfully control ourselves. By a high level of self-construal, these authors mean thinking in relatively abstract terms, whereas a low level of self-construal involves considering the same event or action in more concrete terms. For example, thinking about why you do something activates a higher level self-construal than does thinking about how you do it. The results of

self-efficacy
The belief that we can achieve a goal as a result of our own actions.

self-control
Foregoing short-term rewards and instead waiting for long-term rewards.

several studies have revealed that after people think about why they engage in a task versus how they physically accomplish that same task, people stay engaged in difficult tasks longer, are willing to wait longer for a reward, have stronger behavioral intentions to withstand the costs required to obtain a valued benefit, and evaluate goal-inconsistent temptations negatively. So, if you wish to control yourself to obtain more distant goals, this research suggests you would be best able to do so (and resist impulsively breaking your deal with yourself) by construing your goals in the most abstract way possible.

Let's consider what the research on level of self-construal suggests about how we might most successfully stick with a new diet, even when confronted with temptation in the form of chocolate cake. This line of research suggests that we'd be wise to actively remind ourselves about why we went on the diet in the first place—focus on our abstract level goals—health, looks, or whatever. From this perspective, we need not spend a lot of time thinking about the "mechanics" of dieting—for that is close to construing the task at the most concrete level.

Research suggests that the act of controlling ourselves is taxing and makes exercising subsequent self-control more difficult. Vohs and Heatherton (2000) propose that we have a limited ability to regulate ourselves. If we use our control resources on unimportant tasks, there will be less available for the important ones. Studies where participants are first required to control themselves in some way (e.g., not think about a particular topic, engage in two tasks simultaneously, or control their emotional expression) do less well on later self-control tasks than those who have not had to recently control themselves. Consider Vohs and Heatherton's study of chronic dieters who have a long history of attempting to resist temptation in the interests of achieving long-term weight loss. When these participants were first placed close to a dish of appealing candy, their ability to self-regulate on a second task was reduced—so they ate more ice cream than those who had not had to first control themselves. So, not only is controlling ourselves sometimes difficult to do in the first place, but after doing so successfully, it can impair our ability to do so again.

> ### Principles to Remember
>
> The context can make our different selves differentially salient. Both our personal self and our social selves are equally true. When our different selves come into conflict, it can be an extremely difficult and painful matter to reconcile them.

KeyPoints

- Our self-conceptions can vary in terms of their emphasis on the personal self or the social self, with the resulting behavior stemming from intragroup or intergroup comparisons. We have multiple social identities, each of which could have rather different implications for behavior, depending on whether it is activated in a particular context.

- The context that we find ourselves in can alter the aspect of the self that is salient. Gender differences will be exhibited most when our gender group identity is salient, and they may be absent entirely when another group identity is salient. Likewise, gender differences in perceived insecurity of the self across five different nations have been shown to occur when the self is compared to members of the other gender group but not when the self is compared to members of one's own gender group.

- Several different factors can influence what aspect of the self is salient and influential for our behavior: when the context makes one relevant, when the context makes one distinctive, when one is of greater importance to us, and may also be influenced by others' treatment or language.

- When there is conflict among our identities, we can compromise, forego membership in the group that conflicts with our personal values, or find it difficult to reconcile when it involves two valued but incompatible identities—being homosexual and in the military or a member of an orthodox religious group.

- A frequent response to perceived rejection by others is to choose to emphasize the aspect of one's identity that differentiates the self from those rejecting us. To create a self-perception as a rebel one can take on a feature that differentiates members of one's peer group from the mainstream.

- Images of future possible selves can inspire us to make difficult changes in the present to achieve this more desirable self. Self-control is most likely to be achieved when the self is construed at the

most abstract level. Ability to self-control can be depleted by prior attempts at control.

- To succeed in changing something about ourselves, we need to have self-efficacy or feelings that we can accomplish a goal.

Think About It

Given the potential conflicts we can have between different parts of our identity, how do most of us, most of the time, manage to feel that we have a coherent self?

Self-Esteem: Attitudes toward Ourselves

For the most part, **self-esteem** has been conceptualized by social psychologists as our overall attitude toward ourselves. What kind of attitude do you have toward yourself—is it positive or negative? Is your attitude toward yourself stable, or does your degree of self-esteem vary across contexts?

The Measurement of Self-Esteem

The most common method of measuring self-esteem as a general trait-like self-evaluation using the ten-item Rosenberg (1965) scale. As shown in Figure 4.13, the items on this scale are rather straightforward. Given that most people can guess what is being assessed with these items, it is not surprising that this measure correlates highly with responses to the simple item, "I have high self-esteem" (Robins, Hendin, & Trzesniewski, 2001). On this measure, people are asked to provide their own explicit attitude toward themselves. There are also more specific measures of self-esteem that are used to assess self-esteem in particular domains, such as academics, personal relationships, appearance, and athletics, with scores on these more specific types of self-esteem being predicted by performance indicators in those domains (Swann, Chang-Schneider, & McClarty, 2007).

self-esteem
The degree to which we perceive ourselves positively or negatively; our overall attitude toward ourselves. It can be measured explicitly or implicitly.

1. I feel that I am a person of worth, at least on an equal basis with others.
2. I feel that I have a number of good qualities.
3. All in all, I am inclined to feel that I am a failure.*
4. I am able to do things as well as most other people.
5. I feel I do not have much to be proud of.*
6. I take a positive attitude toward myself.
7. On the whole, I am satisfied with myself.
8. I wish I could have more respect for myself.*
9. I certainly feel useless at times.*
10. At times I think I am no good at all.*

Figure 4.13
Measurement: The Rosenberg Self-Esteem Scale
Each of the items with an asterisk is reverse scored and then an average of all ten items is computed so that higher numbers indicate greater self-esteem.

(*Source:* Based on Rosenberg, 1965.)

Self-esteem is responsive to life events. As Figure 4.14 illustrates, when we achieve important goals self-esteem can increase, while failures can temporarily harm self-esteem. For example, when people are reminded of the ways they fall short of their ideals, self-esteem decreases (Eisenstadt & Leippe, 1994). When people with low self-esteem experience negative feedback, their self-esteem suffers further declines (DeHart & Pelham, 2007). Being ostracized, excluded, or ignored by other people—even in chat rooms on the Internet, as we noted in the opening of this chapter—can lower self-esteem (Williams, 2001).

Researchers have recently attempted to measure self-esteem with more subtlety. Attitudes toward the self might be biased by self-presentation concerns with the existing explicit measures such as the Rosenberg scale. As an alternative, Dijksterhuis (2004) used the logic of classical conditioning procedures to test whether implicit self-esteem can be improved without the participant's conscious awareness. After repeatedly pairing representations of the self (I or me) with positive trait terms (e.g., nice, smart, warm) that were presented subliminally (too quickly for participants to consciously recognize them), implicit self-esteem was found to be significantly higher compared to those in a control group who were not exposed to such self-positive trait pairings. This subliminal conditioning prevented participants from suffering a self-esteem reduction when they were later given negative false feedback about their intelligence. Thus consistent with research on explicit self-esteem (such as studies using the Rosenberg scale) that shows people with high self-esteem are less vulnerable to threat following a failure experience, this subliminal training procedure appears to provide similar self-protection at the implicit level when faced with a threat to the self.

Consistent with this analysis concerning nonconscious influences on self-esteem, DeHart, Pelham, and Tennen (2006) found that young adults whose parents were consistently nurturing of them reported higher implicit self-esteem than those whose parents were less nurturing. Conversely, young adults whose parents were overprotective of them showed lower implicit self-esteem than those whose parents displayed trust in them during their teenage years. Such implicit messages—based on our experiences with our parents—may lay the foundation for implicit associations between the self and positive attributes.

Figure 4.14

Self-Esteem: Attitudes toward the Self

One's self-esteem, or attitude about oneself, can range from positive to negative. At least temporarily, the individuals shown here would seem to be expressing a negative and positive attitude about themselves.

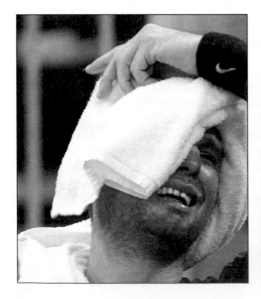

Is High Self-Esteem Always Beneficial?

Given the many techniques that have been developed for raising self-esteem, it is reasonable to ask whether high self-esteem is a crucial goal for which we should all strive. Indeed, some social scientists have suggested that the lack of high self-esteem (or presence of low self-esteem) is the root of many social ills, including drug abuse, poor school performance, depression, and various forms of violence including terrorism. In fact, some have argued that low self-esteem might be an important cause of aggression and general negativity toward others (Baumeister, Campbell, Krueger, & Vohs, 2003). However strong evidence has now accumulated in favor of the opposite conclusion—that high self-esteem is associated with bullying, narcissism, exhibitionism, self-aggrandizing, and interpersonal aggression (Baumeister, Campbell, Krueger, & Vohs, 2005). For example, it is men with high self-esteem, not those with low self-esteem, who are most likely to commit violent acts when someone disputes their favorable view of themselves.

Why might this be the case? To the extent that high self-esteem implies superiority to others, that view of the self may need to be defended with some frequency—whenever the individual's pride is threatened. It may even be that high self-esteem coupled with instability (making for greater volatility) results in the most hostility and defensive responding (Kernis, Cornell, Sun, Berry, & Harlow, 1993). When unstable high self-esteem people experience failure, their underlying self-doubt is reflected in physiological responses indicative of threat (Seery, Blascovich, Weisbuch, & Vick, 2004). Thus while there are clear benefits for individuals to have a favorable view of themselves, there also appears to be a potential downside.

Do Women and Men Differ in Their Level of Self-Esteem?

Who do you think, on average, has higher or lower self-esteem—women or men? Most people might guess that the men in panel A of Figure 4.15 on page 132 will have higher self-esteem than the women in panel B. Why might social psychologists predict this too? Because women occupy positions of lower status and are frequently targets of prejudice, their social structural position should have negative consequences for their self-esteem. Beginning with George Herbert Mead (1934), who first suggested that self-esteem is affected by how important others in our environment see us, women have been expected to have lower self-esteem overall compared to men because self-esteem is responsive to the treatment received from others. How important the dimensions are on which women are devalued in the larger society, and how aware women are of their devalued status, will influence the extent to which a gender-based self-esteem difference is observed.

To test this idea, Williams and Best (1990) conducted a fourteen-nation study of the self-concepts of women and men. In nations, such as India and Malaysia, where women are expected to remain in the home in their roles as wives and mothers, women have the most negative self-concepts. In contrast, in nations such as England and Finland, where women are most active in the labor force and the status difference between women and men is less, members of each gender tend to perceive themselves equally favorably. This research suggests that when women are excluded from important life arenas, they will have worse self-concepts than men. Longitudinal research with employed women in the United States finds that women in jobs in which gender discrimination is most frequent exhibit increasingly poorer emotional and physical health over time (Pavalko, Mossakowski, & Hamilton, 2003). Harm to women—as a function of employment in a discriminatory work environment—can be observed in comparison to health status before their employment began.

A meta-analysis comparing the global self-esteem of women and men in 226 samples collected in the U.S. and Canada from 1982 to 1992 has likewise found that men have reliably higher self-esteem than women (Major, Barr, Zubek, & Babey, 1999). Although

Figure 4.15
Which of These Groups of People Are More Likely to Have Higher Self-Esteem? *Research indicates that many socially disadvantaged groups do have, on average, somewhat lower self-esteem than groups that are socially advantaged.*

the size of the effect obtained across all these studies was not large, as Prentice and Miller (1992) point out, small differences between groups can be quite impressive. Precisely because there are substantial differences within each gender group in level of self-esteem, being able to detect reliable group differences in self-esteem at all is remarkable. Consistent with the reasoning of the previous cross-nation research, Major et al. (1999) found that the self-esteem difference between men and women was less among those in the professional class and greatest among those in the middle and lower classes. Again, those women who have attained culturally desirable positions suffer less self-esteem loss than those who are more likely to experience the greatest devaluation. Interestingly, it was among Caucasian North Americans that the largest overall difference in level of self-esteem between men and women was observed, while no reliable difference in self-esteem by gender was obtained for ethnic minority Americans. For ethnic minority groups, members of both genders are likely to experience broad social devaluation based on their ethnicity, while only among Caucasians are women likely to be discriminated against in important aspects of life. Consistent with the idea that the degree of gender discrimination matters, there was no reliable gender difference in self-esteem among preadolescents, but beginning in puberty when discrimination experiences are more likely, a reliable self-esteem difference emerges that continues through adulthood, with women's self-esteem levels being lower than men's. So, is the common sense notion correct after all—does overall self-esteem suffer for groups that are devalued in a given society? The research findings offer a straightforward answer for gender: Yes. How badly self-esteem suffers appears to depend on how much discrimination and devaluation the group that is the subject of such treatment experiences (Hansen & Sassenberg, 2006).

KeyPoints

- Self-esteem is our overall attitude toward ourselves. Self-esteem is most frequently measured with explicit items that capture our perceptions of our level of self-esteem. Other more implicit measures assess the strength of the positive or negative association between ourselves and stimuli associated with us, including trait terms such as warm and honest.

- Self-esteem is responsive to life experiences, and more specific forms of self-esteem depend on how we perform in those domains.

- Low self-esteem may not be predictive of the social ills many had thought. In fact, high self-esteem—especially when it is unstable—is associated with violent reactions when our superior view of ourself is threatened.

- There is a small but reliable gender-based difference in self-esteem. Women's self-esteem is worse than men's to the extent that they live in a nation with more exclusion of women from public life compared to women who live in a nation with higher labor force participation by women. Among those U.S. women who work in occupations in which discrimination is frequent and pervasive, lower self-esteem is more prevalent than those in occupations in which discrimination is encountered less often.

Think About It

If high self-esteem is predictive of negative social behaviors—in contrast to most of our intuitions—should schools and other institutions work so hard to improve students' self-esteem? Clearly, implicit self-esteem can be conditioned and improved but might there be social costs of doing so without simultaneously raising students' skills?

Social Comparison: How We Evaluate Ourselves

How do we evaluate ourselves and decide whether we're good or bad in various domains, what our best and worst traits are, and how likable we are to others? Social psychologists believe that all human judgment is relative to some comparison standard (Kahneman & Miller, 1986). So, how we think and feel about ourselves will depend on the standard of comparison we use. To take a simple example, if you compare your ability to complete a puzzle to a child's ability to solve it, you'll probably feel pretty good about your ability. This would represent a **downward social comparison**—where your own performance is compared with someone who is less capable than yourself. On the other hand, if you compare your performance on the same task to a puzzle expert you might not fare so well and not feel so good about yourself. This is the nature of **upward social comparisons,** which

downward social comparison
A comparison of the self to another who does less well than or is inferior to us.

upward social comparison
A comparison of the self to another who does better than or is superior to us.

tend to be threatening to our self-image. As the amateur musician in the cartoon in Figure 4.16 suggests, being able to evaluate ourselves positively depends on choosing the right standard of comparison.

You might be wondering why we compare ourselves to other people at all. Festinger's (1954) **social comparison theory** suggests that we compare ourselves to others because for many domains and attributes, there is no objective yardstick to evaluate ourselves against; other people are therefore highly informative. Indeed, feeling uncertain about ourselves in a particular domain is one of the central conditions that lead people to engage in social comparison (Wood, 1989).

To whom do we compare ourselves, or how do we decide what standard of comparison to use? It depends on our motive for the comparison. Do we want an accurate assessment of ourselves, or do we want to simply feel good about ourselves? In general, the desire to see ourselves positively appears to be more powerful than either the desire to accurately assess ourselves or to verify strongly held beliefs about ourselves (Sedikides & Gregg, 2003). But, suppose, for the moment, that we really do want an accurate assessment. Festinger (1954) originally suggested we can gauge our abilities most accurately by comparing our performance with someone who is similar to us. But what determines similarity? Do we base it on age, gender, nationality, occupation, year in school, or something else entirely? In general, similarity tends to be based on broad social categories, such as gender, race, or experience in a particular task domain (Goethals & Darley, 1977; Wood, 1989).

Often, by using comparisons with others who share a social category with us, we can judge ourselves more positively than when we compare ourselves with others who are members of a different social category (especially one that is more advantaged than our own). This is partly because there are different performance expectations for members of different categories in particular domains (e.g., children versus adults, men versus women). To the extent that the context encourages us to categorize ourselves as a member of a category with relatively low expectations in a particular domain, we will be able to conclude that we measure up rather well. For example, a woman could console herself by thinking that her salary is "pretty good for a woman," while she would feel considerably worse if she made the same comparison to men, who on average, are paid more (Reskin & Padavic, 1994; Vasquez, 2001). Self-judgments are often less negative when the standards of our in-group are used (Biernat, Eidelman, & Fuegen, 2002). Indeed, such in-group comparisons may protect members of disadvantaged groups from painful social comparisons with members of more advantaged groups (Crocker & Major, 1989; Major, 1994).

Some suggest that the goal of perceiving the self positively is the "master motive" of human beings

Figure 4.16
Choosing the Right Standard of Comparison Helps Protect Self-Esteem
If we can induce others to use a low standard when evaluating us, we can have higher self-esteem.

(*Source:* Jeff Stahler reprinted by permission of Newspaper Enterprise Association, Inc., 2004.)

social comparison theory
Festinger (1954) suggested that people compare themselves to others because for many domains and attributes there is no objective yardstick to evaluate ourselves against, and other people are therefore highly informative.

(Baumeister, 1998). How we achieve the generally positive self-perception that most of us have of ourselves depends on how we categorize ourselves in relation to comparison others (Wood & Wilson, 2003). Such self-categorization influences how particular comparisons affect us by influencing the *meaning* of the comparison. Two influential perspectives on the self—the **self-evaluation maintenance model** and social identity theory—both build on Festinger's (1954) original social comparison theory to describe the consequences of social comparison in different contexts.

Self-evaluation maintenance (Tesser, 1988) applies when we categorize the self at the personal level and we compare ourselves as an individual to another individual. Social identity theory (Tajfel & Turner, 1986) applies when we categorize ourselves at the group level (e.g., as a woman), and the comparison other is categorized as sharing the same category as ourselves. When the context encourages comparison at the group level, the same other person will be responded to differently than when the context suggests a comparison between individuals. For example, another member of our gender group who performs poorly might be embarrassing to our gender identity when we categorize ourselves as also belonging to that group. In contrast, that same poor performing in-group member could be flattering if we were to compare ourselves personally to that other individual.

Let's consider first what happens in an interpersonal comparison context. When someone with whom you compare yourself outperforms you in an area that is important to you, you will be motivated to distance yourself from the person because it evokes a relatively painful interpersonal comparison. After all, this other person has done better than you have on something that matters to you. Conversely, when you compare yourself to another person who performs even worse than you, then you will be more likely to align yourself with that other person because the comparison is positive. By performing worse than you, this person makes you look good by comparison. Such psychological movement toward and away from a comparison other who performs better or worse than us illustrates an important means by which positive self-evaluations are maintained when our personal identities are salient.

So, will we always dislike others who do better than us? No—it depends on how we categorize ourselves in relation to the other. According to social identity theory, we are motivated to perceive our groups positively, and this should especially be the case for those who most strongly value a particular social identity. Other people, when categorized as a member of the same group as ourselves, can help make our group more positive when they perform well. Therefore when we think of ourselves at the social identity level, say in terms of a sports team, then a strong performing teammate will enhance our group's identity instead of threatening it.

Either disliking or liking of the same high performing other person can occur, depending on whether you think of that person as another individual or as someone who shares your group identity. The other's excellent performance has negative implications for you when you compare as an individual but positive implications for you when you compare the members of your group to those of another group.

To investigate this possibility, Schmitt, Silvia, and Branscombe (2000) first selected participants for whom the performance dimension was relevant to the self. This was achieved by selecting people for the study who said that being creative was important to them. Responses to another person who performs better or equally poorly as the self will depend on how you are categorizing yourself—at the individual level or at the social identity level. As shown in Figure 4.17 on page 136, when participants believed their performance as an individual would be compared to the other person, they liked the poor performing target more than the high-performing target who represented a threat to their positive personal self-image. In contrast, when participants categorized themselves in terms of the gender group that they shared with that person and the expected comparison was intergroup in nature (between women and men), then the high performing other woman was evaluated more positively than the similar-to-self poor performing other. Why? Because this talented person made the participants' group—women—look good. Because different contexts can induce us to categorize ourselves as an individual or as a member

self-evaluation maintenance model
This perspective suggests that to maintain a positive view of ourselves, we distance ourselves from others who perform better than we do on valued dimensions and move closer to others who perform worse than us. This view suggests that doing so will protect our self-esteem.

Figure 4.17
How Do We Evaluate Another Who Performs Better or Worse than Us?
Research findings indicate that it depends on whether the context is interpersonal, in which the personal self is at stake, or intergroup, in which the social self is at stake. As illustrated here, the low-performing target is liked best in an interpersonal context. The high-performing target is liked best in an intergroup context.

(*Source:* Based on data from Schmitt, Silvia, & Branscombe, 2000.)

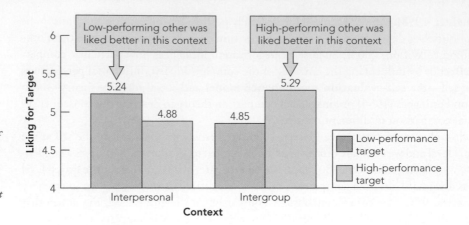

of a group, it has important implications for the effects that upward and downward social comparisons will have on self-evaluation.

Self-Serving Biases

We want to feel positively about ourselves, and there are a number of strategies that we can use to ensure we see ourselves favorably much of the time. Many of us show the **above average effect**—we think we are better than the average person on almost every dimension imaginable (Alicke, Vredenburg, Hiatt, & Govorun, 2001; Klar, 2002). Indeed, people's tendency to see themselves as better than their peers (in terms of both their traits and abilities) predicts increases in self-esteem during the subsequent 6 months (Zuckerman & O'Loughlin, 2006).

Even when we are directly provided with negative social feedback that contradicts our typically rosy view of ourselves, we show evidence of forgetting such instances and emphasizing information that supports our favored positive self-perceptions (Sanitioso & Wlodarski, 2004). Likewise, information that might imply we are responsible for negative outcomes is assessed critically, and our ability to refute such arguments appears to be rather remarkable (Greenwald, 2002).

In contrast to our resistance to accepting responsibility for negative outcomes, we easily accept information that suggests we are responsible for our successes. Not only do people show self-serving biases for their personal outcomes, but they do so also for their group's achievements. Fans of sports teams often believe that their presence and cheering was responsible for their team's success (Wann & Branscombe, 1993). People in groups that perform well tend to claim primary responsibility for those outcomes, while those assigned to groups that failed do not assume responsibility for the outcomes.

There are, however, culture-based limits on people's willingness to "grab the credit" and reactions to others who are more successful than the self (White, Lehman, & Cohen, 2006). For example, in China, modesty is an important basis for self-esteem (Bond, 1996). Accordingly, Chinese students attribute their success in school to their teachers, whereas U.S. students attribute it to their own skills. Conversely, when it comes to failure, Chinese students are more likely to explain their failure as stemming from their own flaws, whereas U.S. students tend to explain their failures as being the result of someone else.

People's positive self-assessments are particularly important as they relate to their capacities for getting things done. It turns out that, on the whole, we are unrealistically optimistic, and this has implications for our mental and physical health, a topic we'll take up in *Building the Science: Classics of Social Psychology.*

Principles to Remember

People generally manage to evaluate themselves positively. They do so by comparing themselves to others who are worse off, showing self-serving biases of responsibility for outcomes, unrealistic optimism, and discrediting negative feedback.

---

above average effect
The tendency for people to rate themselves as above the average on most positive social attributes.

positive illusions
Beliefs we hold about ourselves that are not entirely accurate—that we can do more than is the case, that negative events aren't as likely to befall us as they are others, and the chances for success are higher for the self than others.

BUILDING THE SCIENCE
CLASSICS OF SOCIAL PSYCHOLOGY

Is Being Unrealistic Good for You? Can That Be Realistic?

A classic paper by Taylor and Brown (1988) documented the many forms of positive illusions that people hold. Of course, it might not seem surprising to you that people are not particularly accurate about themselves, but the implications of such illusions about the self for well-being is a great deal less obvious. What exactly is an illusion? It is not grandiose beliefs about the self—as might be found in some forms of psychopathology. And, unlike the biases and errors of judgment that were described in Chapter 3, **positive illusions** about the self are both pervasive and difficult to eliminate. We consider here a key idea developed by Taylor and Brown that was counterintuitive—that such positive illusions about ourselves are adaptive.

It might seem perfectly sensible to assume that being "realistic" is a critical sign of mental health. Not true, according to these researchers. "Unrealistic optimism," including seeing our chances for success in life as higher than our peers' chances, appears to be healthier than realism. Of course, it can't be true that all of us have higher likelihoods of successful life outcomes than our peers—this is not Lake Wobegon, and "the children" can't all be above average.

Another consequence of unrealistic optimism is to imagine that we can get something done in less time than it actually ends up taking—an everyday phenomenon we referred to in Chapter 2 as the planning fallacy. Virtually everyone appears to show this effect, including university students who were asked to estimate when they would complete their honors' thesis and to give their worst case prediction. The students, on average, took twenty-two days longer than they had estimated and were a week later than their prediction for the worst case scenario (Buehler, Griffin, & Ross, 1994). Moreover, about two-thirds of students readily admitted that they routinely finished assignments late, although they confidently predicted they would finish their current assignment by the due date. This phenomenon is not limited to students but was also found to be true for Canadian taxpayers' completion of their tax returns. Additionally, Sorrentino and colleagues (2005) showed such optimism was not limited to North Americans but was also true for Japanese as well. Taylor (1989) notes that people's daily things-to-do lists are a "poignant example" of the unrealistic optimism phenom-

enon. We will routinely fail to get even half of what's on our list accomplished (that's certainly true for my life!), but we repeat the same behavior day after day, oblivious to how unrealistic our plans are.

Taylor and Brown's (1988) contribution is a theoretical classic because of the linkage they draw between optimistic illusions and psychological and physical well-being. They document connections between positive illusions and contentment, confidence, and feelings of personal control. People who believe they can somehow finish their to-do lists are more likely to proceed with feelings of self-efficacy (Bandura, 1977) and high motivation than people who are more realistic. Thus higher motivation and greater persistence are associated with unrealistic optimism—and these lead to higher levels of performance on average and greater feelings of satisfaction.

But surely, you might wonder, isn't there a downside? Poor decisions must end up producing bad consequences when reality doesn't match up to those expectations. Despite the many reasons you might generate for why unrealistic optimism could be embarrassing, dangerous, or unwise, the most disconcerting one is the question of physical health (Armor & Taylor, 2002). Could unrealistic expectations cause one to forego a useful medical test? This classic line of research has, however, consistently failed to obtain a significant relationship between optimistic expectations and risky behavior. Having said that, your boss at work might not appreciate unrealistic planning when she or he is still waiting for the completion of a task you predicted would be finished weeks ago.

Among entrepreneurs, undue optimism appears to be a dangerous illusion (Baron & Shane, 2008). Every entrepreneur believes that he or she will succeed, yet 80 percent of all new business ventures fail within three years. Perhaps their over optimism leads entrepreneurs to begin with insufficient resources and take excessive risks. Such well-founded challenges to Taylor and Brown's classic assertions about the benefits of unrealistic optimism are not in short supply. And yet, the long-term economic strength of the United States appears to rest, in part, on a bedrock of optimism, much of which is admittedly naïve and unrealistic. Unrealistic optimism may be then overall adaptive, especially if it is coupled with good luck!

KeyPoints

- Social comparison is a central means by which we evaluate ourselves. Downward social comparison refers to instances in which we compare to someone of lesser ability than ourselves. Such comparisons can be flattering, as long as we are not worried that the worse off other represents our own future. Upward social comparisons, in contrast, refer to someone who outperforms us in areas central to the self.

- We often find people who outperform us to be threatening when we compare ourselves to them as individuals, but they are experienced more positively when we categorize ourselves and them together as members of the same group.

- Social comparison theory spawned two perspectives on the consequences of negative or upward social comparisons for the self—the self-evaluation maintenance model and social identity theory. When we are categorized at the individual level, we distance from a better performing other, but when we are categorized at the social identity level, we distance from the poor performing other.

- Most people show unrealistic optimism when it comes to their outcomes relative to others. We are also subject to the planning fallacy—where we overestimate how quickly and how much we can accomplish. Such positive illusions are, however, linked with various adaptive outcomes.

- We maintain our positive view of ourselves, in part, with self-serving biases in the explanations they provide for their outcomes. North Americans especially accept credit for positive outcomes and refute responsibility for negative outcomes, whereas Asians tend to show the reverse pattern.

Think About It

Virtually all of the evidence we examined suggests that people are biased about themselves in ways that flatter them. Despite inaccuracy in the unrealistic plans we create, we continue to do so again the next day. How can such inaccuracy be the route to mental health?

The Self as Target of Prejudice

Although the experience of not getting what you want is generally negative, how you explain such undesirable outcomes has important implications for how you feel about yourself, and by extension, how you cope with them. As you saw in Chapter 3, attributions affect the meaning derived from events; as a result, some attributions for a negative outcome are more psychologically harmful than others, for example, they can cause depression and undermine self-esteem (Weiner, 1985). We will consider in turn the emotional, cognitive, and behavioral consequences of perceiving the self as a target of prejudice.

Emotional Consequences: How Well-Being Can Suffer

Suppose your performance on some task is negative. Figure 4.18 on page 139 illustrates several different possible attributions that a person could make for that unfavorable outcome. Different types of attributions result in different feelings about ourselves. The worst possible attribution for psychological well-being is when the outcome is attributed to an internal and stable factor that is likely to apply to many situations (e.g., you conclude your performance on this task means you're uniquely unintelligent for a college student). The next, slightly better attribution is an attribution to prejudice (e.g., you were rated poorly on the task because the grader is biased against your group) because it is unlikely to be applicable across so many situations. Making an attribution to prejudice will be better for psychological well-being when such prejudice is thought to be rare compared to when you believe you may encounter it frequently. True external attributions, which could come in

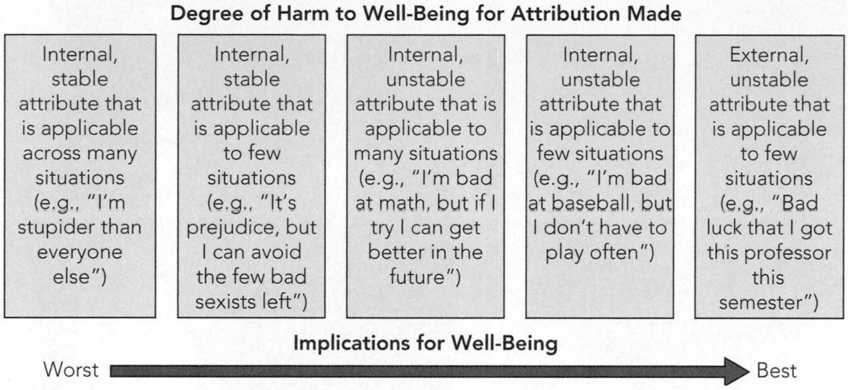

Degree of Harm to Well-Being for Attribution Made

Internal, stable attribute that is applicable across many situations (e.g., "I'm stupider than everyone else")	Internal, stable attribute that is applicable to few situations (e.g., "It's prejudice, but I can avoid the few bad sexists left")	Internal, unstable attribute that is applicable to many situations (e.g., "I'm bad at math, but if I try I can get better in the future")	Internal, unstable attribute that is applicable to few situations (e.g., "I'm bad at baseball, but I don't have to play often")	External, unstable attribute that is applicable to few situations (e.g., "Bad luck that I got this professor this semester")

Implications for Well-Being

Worst ➡ Best

Figure 4.18

Attributions for an Outcome Can Differ in How Harmful They Are for Well-Being

As this figure illustrates, the worst attribution a person can make for a bad performance for well-being is that there is something unique about themselves that is stable and applicable to many situations. The best attribution—for well-being—will be that the outcome is the result of something entirely external that is unstable and is one that will be encountered rarely.

many different forms (e.g., the other person is a jerk to all, is having a bad day, bad luck), are the most likely to be protective of the attributor's self and well-being.

An attribution to prejudice, and its effect on psychological well-being, depends on its frequency. Any prejudice-based outcome can reflect pervasive discriminatory treatment that is likely to be encountered repeatedly, or it can be perceived as reflecting a rare or unusual instance. In effect, a discriminatory experience could be seen as reflecting "what also happens in other contexts," or it could be seen as an encounter with a "lone bigot." Schmitt, Branscombe, and Postmes (2003) illustrated the importance of the perceived pervasiveness of prejudice for psychological well-being in women. In their experiment, all participants received the identical negative feedback from one of twenty male interviewers. However while waiting for their interviewing feedback, the experimenter "confided" to the participant either that: (1) "your interviewer is a real jerk and seems to give everyone a negative evaluation" (the non-sexist external attribution); (2) "your *particular* interviewer is really sexist and gives the women negative evaluations but is positive toward the men" (the lone sexist); or (3) "*all* of the interviewers, including yours, are really sexist" (pervasive sexism). Feelings of self-esteem and mood were worse when the prejudicial outcome was seen as reflecting pervasive discrimination, that is, all twenty interviewers were sexist, compared to either the lone sexist or no prejudice conditions. When discrimination was seen as a result of a lone sexist, self-esteem was no worse than when a non-sexist jerk delivered the negative feedback. Thus all attributions to prejudice are not "equal." What is fundamentally important for whether psychological well-being will be harmed is how likely it is that you can expect to encounter discriminatory treatment in the future.

Cognitive Consequences: Performance Deficits

Perceived prejudice not only affects psychological well-being, but it can also interfere with our ability to learn and acquire new skills. Several studies have found that when people fear that others will discover their devalued group membership, as might be the case for concealable stigmas (think of gays and lesbians in the military), this fear can negatively affect people's ability to learn (Frable, Blackstone & Scherbaum, 1990; Lord & Saenz, 1985). Feeling we need to hide our identity can be distracting; studies measuring attention allocation reveal that when such distractions weigh on disadvantaged group members, their cognitive abilities are impaired, and performance suffers.

Figure 4.19
A Stigmatized Identity Depends on the Larger Cultural Context
Is "elderly" a positive or negative social identity? It depends on the cultural context. In the United States, the elderly are often perceived as irrelevant and are negatively stereotyped as forgetful. However in China, the elderly are valued and viewed as having wisdom and not denigrated as incompetent. Where would you rather be a member of this social category?

Cognitive deficits stemming from concerns about a given social identity are only found when it is an identity that is devalued by the larger culture. Levy and Langer (1994) showed that this is the case for cognitive tasks involving memory. As the photos in Figure 4.19 reveal, the elderly are devalued in the United States, while in China the elderly are a revered social category. When the memory abilities of older adults in the United States and China were compared, the older Americans showed deficits in memory, while this was not the case for elderly Chinese.

How might these deficits in the stigmatized be prevented (assuming the stigma itself can't be removed)? Recent research suggests that a critical issue is the extent to which people can affirm themselves in other ways. Martens, Johns, Greenberg, and Schimel (2006) examined whether first having people affirm their most valued attribute, perhaps a talent for art or other accomplishment, would eliminate cognitive deficits in those who were later reminded of their stigmatized group membership; this was exactly what they found. Thus it appears it is the extent to which a negative stereotype may define a person's entire worth that leads to underperformance.

Behavioral Consequences: Stereotype Threat

stereotype threat
Can occur when people believe that they might be judged in light of a negative stereotype about their group or that, because of their performance, they may in some way confirm a negative stereotype of their group.

Stereotype threat occurs when people believe they might be judged in light of a negative stereotype about their social identity or that they may inadvertently act in some way to confirm a negative stereotype of their group (Steele, 1997). When people value their ability in a certain domain (e.g., math), but it is one in which their group is stereotyped as performing poorly (e.g., women), stereotype threat may occur. When those who are vulnerable to stereotype threat are reminded in some overt or subtle way that the stereotype might apply to them, then performance in that domain may be undermined.

Stereotype threat effects are fairly difficult to control. For example, simply telling women before they take a math test that men do better on math than women do (Spencer, Steele, & Quinn, 1999) or having African Americans indicate their race before taking a difficult verbal test (Steele & Aronson, 1995) is sufficient to evoke stereotype threat and hurt their performance. Indeed, because women are negatively stereotyped as being worse at math than men, women tend to perform more poorly when they simply take a difficult math test in the presence of men, whereas they tend to perform better when the same test is taken in the presence of only other women (Inzlicht & Ben-Zeev, 2000). It is worth noting that these decrements in performance occur only with respect to stereotype-relevant dimensions that are applicable to the self—it is not all types of performances that are harmed (Marx & Stapel, 2006). Thus women are vulnerable on math, while African Americans are vulnerable on tests of verbal ability.

Precisely because such stereotype threat effects have been quite difficult to eliminate, investigators have considered the response options that are available to devalued group members when they are in settings in which they experience stereotype threat. One option that has been suggested is disidentification with the domain (Steele, Spencer, & Aronson, 2002). That is, people could try to distance themselves from situations in which they are stereotypically vulnerable. Such an option, though, is likely to be problematic for people who strongly value performing well in a given area to begin with. Women in this research are strongly concerned about doing well in math; likewise, African Americans who participate are keen to do well in occupations requiring strong verbal skills. Another option that might be used in a stereotype threat situation is to attempt to distance the self from the group identity as a whole. That is, women could decrease how much they identify with their gender group, or African Americans might do the same with their race. However this option also comes with long-term risks—minority group identification is known to be important for psychological well-being (Postmes & Branscombe, 2002).

Research has revealed a third option that is available to people who are vulnerable to stereotype threat, which allows them to maintain their overall level of identification with their group and distance themselves only from the stereotypic dimensions that represent a threat to their performance in a particular valued domain. Consider the dilemma of women who have taken a lot of math classes and who perceive math to be an important aspect of their self-concept. They also value their identity as women. When they then find themselves exposed to information that suggests there are reliable sex differences in math ability, with men doing better than women, these women experience threat. How then do they manage to cope with such threat, without simultaneously distancing from either the domain or their group as a whole? Pronin, Steele, and Ross (2004) found that high math-identified women distanced themselves only from gender stereotypic dimensions that are deemed to be incompatible with math success (e.g., leaving work to raise children, being flirtatious) but did not do so for gender stereotypic dimensions deemed to be irrelevant to math success (e.g., being empathic, being fashion conscious). Disidentification from such aspects of their gender group occurred only in the stereotype threat condition but not when it was absent, suggesting it was a motivated process designed to alleviate the threat experienced.

Why do stereotype threat-based performance decrements occur? Some researchers suggest that anxiety is evoked in women, African Americans, and Latinos when their group membership is portrayed as predictive of poor performance (Osborne, 2001). As a result of such anxiety, their actual performance on the relevant test is disrupted. Some studies have, however, failed to find increased self-reported anxiety among stigmatized group members in stereotype threat conditions (Aronson et al., 1999). This could be because members of stigmatized groups are reluctant to admit their feelings of anxiety in conditions in which they realize they will be compared to dominant group members, or it may be that they do not actually realize they are feeling anxious or aroused and so cannot accurately report those feelings.

Research that has examined nonverbal measures of anxiety illustrates how anxiety plays a crucial role in stereotype threat effects. In a clever test of the hypothesis that anxiety causes stereotype threat performance deficits, Bosson, Haymovitz, and Pinel (2004) first either reminded or did not remind gay and straight participants of their category membership before videotaping their interactions with young children in a nursery school. Participants were reminded of their sexual orientation by asking them to indicate their sexual orientation on a form just before they interacted with the children. After this subtle reminder that their group is stereotyped as one that is dangerous to children, the gay participants' childcare skills (as rated by judges unaware of the hypotheses and procedure) suffered compared to when they were not so reminded of their category membership and its associated stereotype. This same group membership reminder had no effect on the straight participants because there is no associated stereotype of danger to children. Consequently, straight participants were not at risk of potentially confirming a negative stereotype in the performance situation they faced.

Was increased anxiety in the gay men the cause of the reduction in their rated childcare skills? On standard self-report measures of anxiety and evaluation apprehension, the answer would seem to be no—Bosson et al. (2004) did not obtain differences in these self-reports as a function of either sexual orientation or stereotype threat condition. Importantly, however, independent judges' ratings of nonverbal anxiety—as indicated by various behaviors revealing discomfort during the interaction with the children—were affected by sexual orientation and stereotype threat. Among the gay men who were reminded of their category membership, their anxiety was discernible in their nonverbal behavior compared to the gay men who were not experiencing stereotype threat. That is, although the gay men experiencing stereotype threat did not rate themselves as more anxious than those not experiencing stereotype threat, they were visibly more fidgety, they averted their eyes and otherwise exhibited signs of discomfort. This nonverbal anxiety disrupted their interactions with the children. However among heterosexual men, reminders of their category membership tended to result in fewer nonverbal symptoms of anxiety compared to when their category was not made relevant.

Is it only for groups that are historically devalued in the culture as a whole that stereotype threat effects have been observed? No. Such effects occur with men who are not a devalued group as a whole but who are stereotyped as being less emotional than women (Leyens, Désert, Croizet, & Darcis, 2000). When men were reminded of the stereotype concerning their emotional deficits, their performance on a task requiring them to identify emotions suffered. In an even more dramatic way, Stone, Lynch, Sjomeling, and Darley (1999) illustrated a similar point. They found that stereotype threat effects can occur among dominant group members as long as their group is expected to perform less favorably than the comparison group. In their research, Caucasian men who expected to be compared to African American men performed more poorly on an athletic performance task when they believed it reflected "natural athletic ability." The reverse occurred when Caucasian men believed the exact same task reflected "sports intelligence," which is a dimension on which they expect to excel as compared with African American men. Likewise, although there is no stereotype that Caucasians perform poorly on math, when they are threatened by a potentially negative comparison to Asians who are stereotyped as performing better than Caucasians, then they show math performance deficiencies (Aronson et al., 1999). Thus expecting to do poorly in comparison to another group can undermine performance, even in members of historically advantaged groups. Stereotype threat effects illustrate the importance of group membership for the experience of threat to the self, and how such threat can easily disrupt performance.

> ### Principles to Remember
>
> All attributions to prejudice are not equivalent. When we can convince ourselves that the discrimination our devalued group faces is rare, psychological harm is lessened.

KeyPoints

- Emotional responses to a negative outcome depend on the attribution made for it.

- When outcomes are attributed to prejudice, if that prejudice is seen as pervasive, then well-being will be harmed more than if it is seen as isolated or rare.

- The fear of being found out by others in terms of having a negatively valued group identity can disrupt performance. Such monitoring can consume cognitive resources and make it difficult to learn new skills. Such deficits only occur when the identity is devalued in the culture as a whole and are absent when the same identity is valued.

- Stereotype threat effects occur in capable people in a domain they value. Stereotype threat effects have been observed in historically devalued group members (African Americans, women) and in dominant groups (Caucasians, men) when they believe they might negatively compare on an important dimension with members of another group.

- Stereotype threat effects are difficult to control, and they can be induced easily. Simply requiring people to indicate their group membership before taking a test in a domain in which they are vulnerable is enough to undermine performance.

- If people can first affirm their most important value, before being subjected to stereotype threat, underperformance is less likely.

- When people experience stereotype threat, they can distance themselves from the task domain, or they can distance themselves from the group as a whole. However both of these options present long-term problems. One option that has received support is distancing the self from only the negative part of the stereotype about one's group.

- Anxiety appears to be the mechanism by which stereotype threat effects occur. However self-report measures of anxiety often fail to reveal its importance, but nonverbal measures have illustrated its important role.

Think About It

Our position in the social world—whether we are members of a devalued or dominant group—has important consequences including the experience of discrimination and stereotype threat. Even though we may be unaware that thinking of ourselves in terms of these social categories affects our behavioral responses, considerable research indicates that it does.

SUMMARY AND REVIEW

- We face many audiences and how we present ourselves to others can vary. We might attempt to engage in self-promotion—present our most favorable self-aspects. On other occasions, we may be motivated to present ourselves in ways that induce others to agree with our own self-views. That is, we may engage in self-verification, even if it means having others perceive negative qualities we believe we possess. We may also create a favorable self-presentation by using ingratiation tactics that convey respect for others.

- When we communicate with others online, many paralinguistic cues that help with accuracy are absent. Shy people and those who desire greater control over their self-presentations may prefer asynchronous forms of communication, such as text-messaging over face-to-

face interactions. There is, however, a greater risk of others not understanding us—especially emotional or sarcastic content—with this medium of communication.

- Self-knowledge is sought through two primary methods—introspection and considering ourselves from others' vantage point. Introspection is tricky because we often don't have conscious access to the emotional factors that affect our behavioral choices. We also may have difficulty predicting how we will feel in the future because we neglect to consider other events that will also occur besides the focal ones considered. When we think of ourselves by taking an observer's perspective, we see the self in more trait terms and less responsive to situations as observers do.

- How we think about ourselves varies depending on where we are on personal-versus-social identity continuum at any given moment in time. At the personal identity level we can think of ourselves in terms of attributes that differentiate our selves from other individuals, and therefore will be based on intragroup comparison. At the social identity level, perceptions of our selves are based on attributes that are shared with other group members; perception of the self at the social identity level stems from intergroup comparison processes.

- Self-definitions can vary across situations, with each being valid predictors of behavior in those settings. How we conceptualize ourselves can also depend on how others expect us to be and how we believe they will treat us. Context shifts that change whether or not we define ourselves in terms of our gender can result in gender differences in self-construal appearing or disappearing. What aspect of the self is influential at any moment in time depends on: context, distinctiveness of the attribute, importance of the identity, and how others refer to us.

- Different aspects of our selves can be in conflict, and this can be emotionally difficult. Conflicts can be between two personal values, the personal self and a social identity, or between two social identities that are fundamentally incompatible, such as religious fundamentalism and homosexuality. When other people reject us because of some aspect of our identity, people often rebel against those doing the rejecting and make that feature even more self-defining.

- Other selves, besides who we are currently, can motivate us to attempt self-change. Dreaded possible selves can lead us to give up certain behaviors (e.g., smoking), while desired possible selves can lead us to work long hours to attain them. When people compare their present self to their past self, the further in the past that self is the more we downgrade it relative to our present self. This approach to autobiographical memory allows us to feel good about our current self.

- Feeling a strong sense of self-efficacy is important for changing ourselves. However we often overestimate our ability to influence outcomes—sometimes even see ourselves as affecting the objectively uncontrollable. Self-control is necessary if we are to forego immediate pleasures in exchange for larger long-term goals. How the self is construed affects our ability to resist temptation. Self-control may be a resource that can be depleted.

- How we feel about ourselves can be assessed directly, as well as with more implicit or indirect methods. High self-esteem comes with risks. It is correlated with an increased likelihood of interpersonal aggression, which appears to be in response to the greater need to defend one's superior self-view. Thus while there are clear benefits to high self-esteem, there appears to be also a downside.

- Women do, on average, have lower self-esteem than men. This is particularly the case in nations where women do not participate in the labor force, and in the United States among middle-class and lower-class women who work in environments in which gender-based devaluation is most frequent.

- Social comparison is a vital means by which we judge ourselves. Upward social comparisons at the personal level can be painful, and downward social comparisons at this level of identity can be comforting. The reverse is true when one's social identity is salient. Most people show self-serving biases, such as the above average effect, where we see ourselves more positively (and less negatively) than we see most other people. We consistently hold positive illusions about ourselves and are unrealistically optimistic about our ability to avoid negative outcomes. We consistently show the planning fallacy in which we imagine we can accomplish more in less time than is typically feasible. Such unrealistic optimism is, however, predictive of positive mental health.

- Attributions for negative outcomes can differ in their implications for psychological well-being. When the self is seen as a target of pervasive discrimination, it is more harmful for self-esteem than when it is seen as reflecting a single instance or lone bigot.

- Suspecting that prejudice might be operating and affecting one's outcomes can be distracting, deplete cognitive resources, and create anxiety. Stereotype threat effects can occur in historically devalued groups when they are simply reminded of their group membership and fear they might confirm negative expectancies about their group. Stereotype threat can undermine performance in dominant group members as well, when they fear a negative comparison with members of another group that is expected to outperform them. This undermining of performance only occurs on dimensions relevant to the stereotype.

- People cope with stereotype threat by distancing themselves from the performance domain (e.g., math) or from their group as a whole (e.g., women), but both of these options are emotionally costly. Distancing from only the stereotypic dimensions relevant to high performance in a domain appears to be preferable. Stereotype threat research reveals how our group memberships can affect our self-concepts and performance on tasks we care deeply about.

Key Terms

above average effect (p. 136)

asynchronous communication (p. 117)

autobiographical memory (p. 126)

downward social comparison (p. 133)

ingratiation (p. 114)

intergroup comparisons (p. 121)

intragroup comparisons (p. 120)

introspection (p. 117)

personal-versus-social identity continuum (p. 120)

positive illusions (p. 137)

possible selves (p. 126)

salience (p. 120)

self-control (p. 127)

self-deprecating (p. 115)

self-efficacy (p. 127)

self-esteem (p. 129)

self-evaluation maintenance model (p. 135)

self-promotion (p. 114)

self-verification perspective (p. 114)

social comparison theory (p. 134)

social identity theory (p. 120)

stereotype threat (p. 140)

stigma consciousness (p. 113)

upward social comparison (p. 133)

Connections
INTEGRATING SOCIAL PSYCHOLOGY

In this chapter, you read about . . .	In other chapters, you will find related discussions of . . .
the role of norms in social functioning	the nature of norms and their role in social influence (Chapter 9) and aggression (Chapter 11).
the nature of attribution and social explanation	self-serving biases in attribution (Chapter 3).
individuals' concern with others' evaluations of their performance	the effects of others' evaluations on our liking for others (Chapter 7) and self-presentation (Chapter 3).
unrealistic optimism and the planning fallacy	biases and errors in social cognition (Chapter 2).
the importance of the situation or context for judgment	audience effects on attitudes (Chapter 5).
the role of stereotyping and discrimination	the nature of prejudice (Chapter 6) and various forms of social influence (Chapter 9).

Attitudes
Evaluating and Responding to the Social World

CHAPTER OUTLINE

- **Attitude Formation: How Attitudes Develop**
  Classical Conditioning: Learning Based on
  Association
  Instrumental Conditioning: Rewards for the
  "Right" Views
  Observational Learning: Learning by Exposure to
  Others

- **When and Why Do Attitudes Influence Behavior?**
  Role of the Social Context in the Link between
  Attitudes and Behavior
  MAKING SENSE OF COMMON SENSE: A SOCIAL
  PSYCHOLOGICAL PERSPECTIVE—ARE ATTITUDES
  CONSISTENTLY RELATED TO BEHAVIOR?
  Situational Constraints that Affect Attitude
  Expression
  Strength of Attitudes
  Attitude Extremity: Role of Vested Interests
  Attitude Certainty: Importance of Clarity and
  Correctness
  Role of Personal Experience

- **How Do Attitudes Guide Behavior?**
  Attitudes Arrived at through Reasoned Thought
  Attitudes and Spontaneous Behavioral Reactions

- **The Fine Art of Persuasion: How Attitudes Are Changed**

Persuasion: Communicators, Messages, and
  Audiences
The Cognitive Processes Underlying Persuasion

- **Resisting Persuasion Attempts**
  Reactance: Protecting Our Personal Freedom
  SOCIAL PSYCHOLOGY: WHAT IT TELLS US ABOUT . . .
  THE EFFECTS OF CAFFEINE ON PERSUASION
  Forewarning: Prior Knowledge of Persuasive
  Intent
  Selective Avoidance of Persuasion Attempts
  Actively Defending Our Attitudes:
  Counterarguing Against the Competition
  Individual Differences in Resistance to Persuasion
  Ego Depletion Can Undermine Resistance

- **Cognitive Dissonance: What It Is and How Do We
  Manage It?**
  Dissonance and Attitude Change: The Effects of
  Induced Compliance
  BUILDING THE SCIENCE: CLASSICS OF SOCIAL
  PSYCHOLOGY—FAMOUS COGNITIVE DISSONANCE
  STUDIES: WHEN LESS LEADS TO MORE SELF-
  PERSUASION
  When Dissonance Is a Tool for Beneficial Changes
  in Behavior

How do you feel about high school and university students who cheat on their exams or who plagiarize essays? Do you have a negative or positive attitude toward these people? Do you see such behaviors as acceptable and widespread, or wrong and infrequent? How do you think your friends and peers would feel about such behaviors? Does your response to these questions depend on how extreme the cheating is—lifting a few phrases without attributing them to the correct source as opposed to buying an entire essay and turning it in as one's own? Would you cheat, if you thought you would not get caught?

If you're anything like the students in several recent national surveys conducted in Britain, Canada, and the United States (BBC News, 2004; Gulli, Kohler, & Patriquin, 2007), you may have done some of these actions, or been tempted to do so. Estimates vary widely in terms of the percentage of students who admit to having cheated—depending on the question asked and the severity of the offense, anywhere from 9 to 70 percent say yes they have done so on at least one occasion. What might cheating on an exam as a student imply about a person's willingness to commit other dishonest behaviors in another context? Do students' attitudes toward cheating in college predict their later behavior in the workplace? Are students who cheat today, likely to become tomorrow's Ken Lay and Jeffrey Skilling of Enron fame? What techniques might be effective in persuading students not to cheat, regardless of what their peers do?

In this chapter we'll explore the factors that shape the attitudes we hold. We'll address the key question, When do attitudes predict our behavior? Along the way we'll consider whether all attitudes are equal or if some attitudes are more strongly linked to behavior than others. Lastly, we'll discuss the process of persuasion and how attitudes can be changed, including self-persuasion—how our behavior can lead us to change our own attitudes.

Social psychologists use the term **attitude** to refer to people's evaluation of virtually any aspect of their social world (e.g., Olson & Maio, 2003; Petty, Wheeler, & Tormala, 2003). People can have favorable or unfavorable reactions to issues, ideas, objects, a specific behavior (such as cheating on an exam), or entire social groups. Some attitudes are quite stable and resistant to change, while others may be unstable and show considerable variability depending on the situation (Schwarz & Bohner, 2001). We may hold some attitudes with great certainty, while other attitudes may be relatively unclear or uncertain. What is your attitude toward the topic depicted in Figure 5.1? Is your attitude toward student cheating likely to depend on whether you yourself have done so, and what other people you know think about cheating? Alternatively, might there be a discrepancy between your actual attitude toward cheating and the attitude you (or your parents) wish you held? Do you think that if this discrepancy between your actual and ideal attitudes were to become known, you would feel a push toward some type of resolution or change (Higgins & Spiegel, 2004)? Later in this chapter we'll consider how our own actions can influence our attitudes. The act of having cheated on a test might lead us to change our own attitudes about cheating—illustrating the process through which we manage to persuade ourselves (Maio & Thomas, 2007).

The study of attitudes is central to the field of social psychology because they are capable of coloring virtually every aspect of our experience. As we saw in Chapter 2, the tendency to evaluate stimuli as positive or negative—something we like or dislike—appears to be an initial step in our efforts to make sense out of the world. In fact, such reactions, which can range from "awesome" to "eew," occur almost immediately, even before we can fully integrate a new stimulus into our previous experience. Responding to a stimulus in terms of our attitudes—on an immediately evaluative basis—produces different brain waves from a response on a nonevaluative basis (Crites & Cacioppo, 1996). Our brains operate differently whether we are engaged in evaluative perception or thoughtful examination of our world.

Attitudes can influence our thoughts, even if they are not always reflected in our overt behavior. Moreover, while many of our attitudes are **explicit attitudes**—conscious and reportable—other attitudes may be **implicit attitudes**—uncontrollable and perhaps not consciously accessible to us. Consider this distinction as it applies to racial attitudes. Many color-blind or self-perceived egalitarian people will report positive explicit attitudes toward African Americans. However they may also display negative involuntary evaluative reactions—implicit attitudes—because it is almost impossible to grow up in the United States without acquiring such negative racial associations (Fazio & Olson, 2003).

While social psychologists can learn people's attitudes about many objects from their conscious reports of the thoughts and feelings they have about them, another approach is required if we want to learn someone's implicit attitudes. A method for assessing these is the Implicit Association Test (IAT; Greenwald, McGhee & Schwarz, 1998). The IAT is based on the the degree of readiness with which we may associate various social objects with positive or negative descriptive words. When a person has a close association between a social group—say, Canadians—and some evaluative word such as *polite*, the person's reaction in identifying this connection is faster than if the social object was paired with a word that the person does not readily associate with Canadians, perhaps *rude*. Quicker reactions to negative words such as *lazy* and some social groups would be taken as evidence of negative implicit attitudes toward that group. If you dare, the Web site at http://implicit.harvard.edu/implicit offers a wide-ranging set of IATs about groups that you can take to learn your implicit attitudes about those groups.

Before doing so, though, consider one warning: Although the IAT is viewed by some investigators as an important way to "get inside your head," a criticism that has been leveled at this test is that it really assesses commonly known connections between social groups and various adjectives, even though the respondent might not actually endorse the

attitude
Evaluation of various aspects of the social world.

explicit attitudes
Consciously accessible attitudes that are controllable and easy to report.

implicit attitudes
Unconscious associations between objects and evaluative responses.

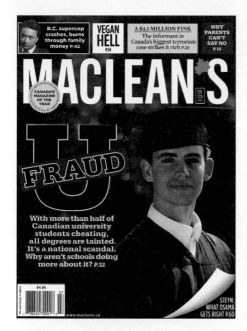 

Figure 5.1
Do Attitudes Predict Behavior?
Have attitudes toward cheating changed in our society? Do we accept it as normal that students cheat on exams, people cheat on their tax returns, or employees lift company goods? Do we now live in a cheating culture, in which student cheating, as shown in the photos above, is but the tip of the iceberg (Callahan, 2004)?

validity of those connections. That is, one might be fully aware of a common negative stereotype regarding a particular social group but not personally concur with that negative belief. Consider the possibility raised by Arkes and Tetlock (2004). Because well-known African American leader Jesse Jackson is likely to have knowledge of the negative stereotypic attributes associated with African Americans, he might fail the IAT! That is, this measure might indicate that he holds negative attitudes toward his own group, African Americans. This implies that such implicit measures assess familiarity with the culture rather than an individual's actual attitudes. Moreover, recent research has revealed that the IAT is susceptible to deliberate faking (Fiedler, Messner, & Bluemke, 2006) and that it becomes easier to do so as people gain experience with the IAT (Blair, 2002). Thus the meaning that we should attribute to IAT scores remains controversial. Taken together, though, it is clear from the considerable research on implicit and explicit attitudes that they reflect evaluations of the world around us, and therefore represent a basic aspect of social cognition. So, in a sense, attitudes truly are an essential building block of social thought (Eagly & Chaiken, 2005).

Another reason that social psychologists view attitudes as important is that they do often affect our behavior. This is especially likely to be true when attitudes are strong and accessible (Ajzen, 2001; Bizer, Tormala, Rucker, & Petty, 2006; Fazio, 2000). What is your attitude toward Lindsay Lohan, Britney Spears, and Paris Hilton? If positive, you may enjoy hearing about events in their lives on "Entertainment Tonight" or the many Web sites devoted to each of them. Do you like Reality TV? If so, we might safely predict that you will probably choose to watch *Survivor*, *America's Next Top Model*, *The Real World*, or *America's Got Talent*.

Because attitudes influence behavior, knowing something about them can help us to predict people's overt actions in a wide range of contexts. Recent research found that advertisements resulting in formation of a positive attitude and inducing willingness to purchase a product had persuasive slogans that matched participants' goal orientation (Werth & Foerster, 2007). Knowing how a person generally approaches situations—whether in terms of the gains to be had or the possible losses to be prevented—can determine the most effective route to attitude change.

For people whose goals are **prevention focused**—concerned about avoiding losses— a persuasive message that focuses on safety is most effective. On the other hand, for people who are **promotion focused**—concerned with not missing an opportunity to benefit—a

prevention focus
When people are concerned about avoiding losses and focused on preventing negative events from occurring.

promotion focus
When people are concerned with promoting or gaining outomes; when they focus on not missing an opportunity to benefit.

Figure 5.2
Changing Attitudes by
Matching the Message to
the Goals of the
Audience
*The most positive attitudes
toward a new product
(washing machine) were
formed when the persuasive
message slogan matched the
orientation of the audience.
For those focused on promoting
their ideals—they are said to
have a promotion focus—
attitudes were more positive
when the message was
promoting (comfort slogan). In
contrast, for those focused on
prevention, a safety slogan
resulted in more positive
attitudes toward the product.*

(*Source:* Based on data from
Werth & Foerster, 2007).

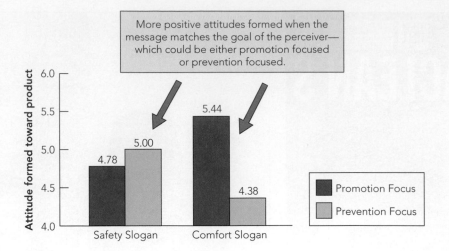

persuasive message that focuses on comforts is most effective. As shown in Figure 5.2, what
attitude people formed about a single product depended on a stable aspect of themselves—
whether the ad they received matched their general orientation or not. Their prevention
versus promotion orientation affected whether they were persuaded by ads that emphasized possible gains or those that focused on potential risks.

In this chapter, we'll first consider the ways in which attitudes are formed. Next, we'll
address a question we have already raised: When do attitudes influence behavior? Third,
we'll turn to the important question of how attitudes are changed—the process of persuasion. Fourth, we'll examine some reasons why attitudes are often resistant to change.
Finally, we'll consider the intriguing fact that on some occasions our own actions shape
our attitudes rather than vice versa: This process is known as cognitive dissonance, and it
has fascinating implications not just for attitude change, but for many aspects of social
behavior as well.

Attitude Formation: How Attitudes Develop

How do you feel about the U.S. role in the war in Iraq, peanut butter, people who cover
their body in tattoos, condoms, telemarketers, cats, sushi, or people who talk on their cell
phones while driving? Most people hold attitudes about these aspects of our culture. But
where, precisely, do these views come from? Are they acquired as a result of firsthand experiences or exposure to the opinions of others? Are such attitudes stable over time or are
they likely to change with circumstances in which we find ourselves? Many of our views
are acquired in situations in which we interact with or observe the behavior of others, called
social learning. Such learning can be acquired through several processes, and our attitudes are affected by different forms of influence.

Classical Conditioning: Learning Based on Association

The first process uses a basic principle of psychology—the evoking of an attitude by the
association of an **unconditioned stimulus** with a neutral or **conditioned stimulus.** When
a stimulus that is capable of producing a positive response (the unconditioned stimulus)
regularly precedes a second stimulus (the conditioned stimulus), the first becomes a signal for the second. Advertisers and other persuasion agents have considerable expertise in

social learning
The process through which we
acquire new information, forms
of behavior, or attitudes from
other people.

unconditioned stimulus
A stimulus that evokes a positive
or negative response without
substantial learning.

conditioned stimulus
The stimulus that comes to
stand for or signal a prior
unconditioned stimulus.

using this principle to create positive attitudes toward their products. Although tricky in the details, it is actually a fairly straightforward method for creating new attitudes. To start with, you need to know what your potential audience already responds positively toward (what to use as the unconditioned stimulus). If you are marketing a new beer, and your target audience is young adult males, you might safely assume that attractive young women will produce a positive response. Next, your product (in the form of your beer logo, the neutral or conditioned stimulus) is repeatedly paired with images of beautiful women. Before long, positive attitudes will develop toward your new beer. See how the manufacturer in Figure 5.3 has used this principle to beneficially affect sales of its product.

Figure 5.3
Classical Conditioning of Attitudes
Initially people may be neutral toward this product and its packaging. However after repeatedly pairing this product's logo with an unconditioned stimulus of an attractive female for the targeted group of young males, seeing the beer logo may come to elicit positive attitudes on its own.

This process, known as **classical conditioning,** has important implications for attitude formation. Consider how this process might affect not only consumer preferences but also social attitudes. A young child sees her mother frown and show other signs of displeasure each time a member of a particular ethnic group is encountered. At first, the child is neutral toward members of this group and their visible characteristics (e.g., skin color, style of dress, accent). The child has not yet learned to categorize these variations in terms of group membership. However once these cues are paired repeatedly with the mother's negative emotional reactions, then classical conditioning occurs, and the child comes to react negatively to members of a particular ethnic group (see Figure 5.4. on page 152). This can occur without the child having conscious access to the role that her mother's subtle facial changes have had on the attitudes formed (De Houwer, Thomas, & Baeyens, 2001). The result is that the child acquires a negative attitude that is generalized to members of that group as a whole (Walther, 2002), an attitude that may ultimately form the core of prejudice, which we'll examine in detail in Chapter 6.

Not only can classical conditioning contribute to shaping our attitudes as we saw in the child's example, but often we may not be aware of the stimuli that affects the conditioning. For instance, in one experiment (Krosnick, Betz, Jussim, & Lynn, 1992), students were shown photos of a stranger engaged in routine daily activities, such as shopping in a grocery store or walking into her apartment. While viewing these photos, other pictures associated with either positive or negative feelings were exposed for brief periods of time—so brief that participants were not aware of their presence. Participants who were nonconsciously exposed to photos that induced positive feelings (e.g., a newlywed couple, people playing cards and laughing) liked the stranger better than participants who had been exposed to photos that nonconsciously induced negative feelings (e.g., open-heart surgery, a werewolf). Even though participants were not consciously aware that they had been exposed to the second group of photos while viewing the stranger, the photos did significantly influence the attitudes that were formed toward the stranger. Those exposed to the positive photos reported more favor-

classical conditioning
A basic form of learning in which one stimulus, initially neutral, acquires the capacity to evoke reactions through repeated pairing with another stimulus. In a sense, one stimulus becomes a signal for the presentation or occurrence of the other.

Figure 5.4
Classical Conditioning
of Attitudes
*Initially, young children may
have little or no emotional
reaction to the visible
characteristics of members of
different social groups. If,
however, a person sees others
showing signs of negative
reactions when in their
presence, gradually negative
reactions toward them will be
acquired, as a result of the
process of classical conditioning.*

able attitudes toward the person than those exposed to the negative photos. These findings suggest that attitudes can be influenced by **subliminal conditioning**—classical conditioning that occurs in the absence of conscious awareness of the stimuli involved.

Indeed, **mere exposure**—having seen an object before, but not remembering having seen it—can result in attitude formation. In fact, the effects of mere exposure on attitudes are stronger when the stimuli are presented subliminally compared to when they are consciously perceived (Bornstein & D'Agostino, 1992). Conscious memory for the stimuli is definitely not required; patients with advanced Alzheimer's disease, who therefore cannot remember the stimuli, show evidence of having formed new attitudes as a result of mere exposure (Winograd, Goldstein, Monarch, Peluso, & Goldman, 1999).

Once formed, such attitudes can influence behavior—even when those attitudes are inconsistent with how we are explicitly expected to behave. Consider the child whose attitudes toward an ethnic or religious group, such as Arabs or Muslims, have been classically conditioned to be negative and who later is in a multicultural classroom in which such negative attitudes are nonnormative (i.e., they are viewed negatively or as being unacceptable). Recent research has revealed that when the norms in a setting such as a classroom are antidiscriminatory, it is only when feelings of threat from that group are low is prejudice expression reduced. If, however, the child feels threatened by that group, the child is likely to continue to show prejudice even when the norms are antidiscriminatory. As shown in Figure 5.5, this is exactly what happens—only when threat is absent are attempts to change negative responses effective.

subliminal conditioning
Classical conditioning of
attitudes by exposure to stimuli
that are below individuals'
threshhold of conscious
awareness.

mere exposure
By having seen before, but not
necessarily remembering having
done so, attitudes toward an
object can become more
positive.

Figure 5.5
Feelings of Threat Can
Result in Prejudiced
Action toward
Foreigners, Even
When Norms are
Antidiscriminatory
*In this study, an
antidiscrimination norm
against showing prejudice
toward foreigners was only
effective at reducing
favoritism toward members
of one's own group when
people were feeling little
threat. Regardless of feelings
of threat, if a pro-
discrimination norm is
present, people discriminate
by showing favoritism
toward their own group
members*

(Based on data from Falomir-
Pichastor, Munoz-Rojas,
Invernizzi, & Mugny, 2004).

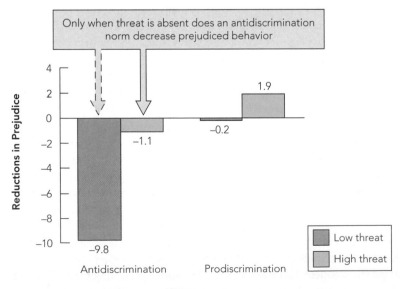

Instrumental Conditioning: Rewards for the "Right" Views

When we asked you to think about your attitudes toward cheating, many of you are likely to have immediately thought, "Oh, that's wrong!" This is because most children have been repeatedly praised or rewarded by their parents for stating such views concerning both the rightness of honesty and the wrongness of dishonesty. As a result, individuals learn which views are seen as the "right" attitudes to hold by virtue of being rewarded for voicing those attitudes by the people they identify with and want to be accepted by. Attitudes that are followed by positive outcomes tend to be strengthened and are likely to be repeated, while attitudes that are followed by negative outcomes are weakened so their likelihood of being expressed again is reduced. Thus another way in which attitudes are acquired is through this process of **instrumental conditioning,** which is a process of rewards and punishments tied to our attitudes and actions. Sometimes the conditioning process is rather subtle, with the reward being psychological acceptance. Parents reward children with smiles, approval, or hugs for stating the right views. As a result of this form of conditioning, most children express political, religious, and social views that are highly similar to those of their parents and other family members, until the teen years when peer influences become especially strong (Oskamp & Schultz, 2005).

As adults, we may be aware that different groups we belong to will reward (or punish) us for expressing support for a particular attitude position. We may even find ourselves expressing one view on a topic to one audience and another view to a different audience. Indeed, elections are sometimes won or lost on a candidate's success at delivering the right view to the right audience. But politicians (and ordinary people) who are perceived as shifting their responses to accommodate the views of different audiences may hurt themselves, if caught, by looking as though they are not taking a firm stand on anything. Fortunately for most of us, not only is it implausible that our every word might be replayed to another audience with a different view, but our potentially incompatible audiences tend to remain physically separated (Goffman, 1959). What this means is that we are less likely than politicians to be caught expressing different attitudes to different audiences. In your own life, consider the attitudes that your parents would appreciate versus those that your peers would reward. You may assure your parents that you will eat healthy food and limit your consumption of alcohol. Yet at school, you might join your friends in praising late night pizza binges and beer such that your parents would see your at-school attitudes as incompatible with the views you had only recently expressed to them.

One way that social psychologists assess the extent to which people's reported attitudes depend on the expected audience is by varying who can be expected to learn of their attitude position. For example, people seeking membership in a fraternity or sorority (e.g., pledges) express different attitudes about other fraternities and sororities depending on whether they believe their attitudes will remain private or will become known to the powerful members of their group who will be controlling their admittance (Noel, Wann, & Branscombe, 1995). When they believe that other members will learn of their responses, they express derogatory opinions of other fraternities or sororities; this communicates to decision makers of their desired organization that they belong with their group. Yet when they believe their responses will be private, they do not disparage other fraternities or sororities. Thus both the attitudes we form and the ones we express can depend on the responses given for holding them—rewards received in the past and those we expect to receive in the future.

The effect on our attitudes of others as potential audiences can be both powerful and subtle. Consider a study conducted by Baldwin and Holmes (1987), in which they first asked women to think about either two of their friends on campus or two of their older relatives. They then exposed the women to sexually explicit stimuli as a pretext of a separate study. The attitudes the women formed about those stimuli related to the group of people they had previously been thinking about. The women who had been thinking of their friends had attitudes toward the sexual materials that were more positive than those

instrumental conditioning
A basic form of learning in which responses that lead to positive outcomes or which permit avoidance of negative outcomes are strengthened.

Figure 5.6
Observational Learning in Action

We acquire attitudes toward different dance styles by watching how others are rewarded or not rewarded on "Dancing with the Stars." Likewise, we learn how different types of music styles are evaluated—either positively or negatively—by watching the judges and listening to their comments on "American Idol." Indeed, we may even put what we've learned into practice when the audience gets to vote and have our say in the outcome.

of the women who had been thinking about older members of their family. Although the participants expressed their attitudes toward the sexual materials in private, the audience they had in mind when forming their attitudes had a substantial effect.

Observational Learning: Learning by Exposure to Others

A third means by which attitudes are formed can operate even in the absence of direct rewards for acquiring or expressing those attitudes. This process is **observational learning,** and it occurs when individuals acquire attitudes or behaviors simply by observing others (Bandura, 1997). For example, as illustrated in Figure 5.6, many people have acquired attitudes toward (and learn how to judge) different types of dances from watching "Dancing with the Stars," and different musical styles from exposure to "American Idol." Just think about how much observational learning most of us are doing as we watch television.

Why do people often adopt the attitudes that they hear others express or imitate the behaviors they observe in others? One answer involves the mechanism of **social comparison**—our tendency to compare ourselves with others to determine whether our view of social reality is correct or not (Festinger, 1954). That is, to the extent that our views agree with those of other people, we tend to conclude that our ideas and attitudes are accurate; after all, if others hold the same views, these views must be right. But are we equally likely to adopt all others' attitudes, or does it depend on our relationship to those others?

People often adjust their attitudes so as to hold views closer to those of others who they value and identify with—their **reference groups.** For example, Terry and Hogg (1996) found that the adoption of favorable attitudes toward wearing sunscreen depended on the extent to which the respondents identified with the group advocating this change. Thus, as a result of social comparison with others whom we value, new attitudes can be formed. Consider how this could affect the attitudes we form toward a new social group with whom you have personally had no contact. Imagine that you heard someone you like and respect expressing negative views about this group. Would this influence your attitudes? While it might be tempting to say "Absolutely not," research findings indicate otherwise. Hearing others whom we see as similar to ourselves state negative views about the group can lead us to adopt similar attitudes, without ever meeting any members

observational learning
A basic form of learning in which individuals acquire new forms of behavior as a result of observing others.

social comparison
The process through which we compare ourselves to others to determine whether our view of social reality is, or is not, correct.

reference groups
Groups of people with whom we identify and whose opinions we value.

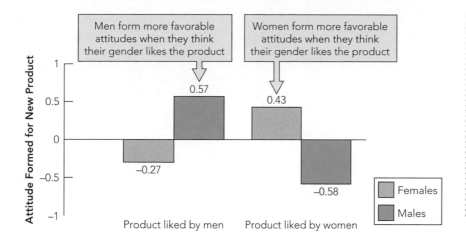

Figure 5.7

Attitude Formation among Those Who Are Highly Identified with Their Gender Group

Men formed more positive attitudes toward the new product when they thought other men liked it, and women formed more positive attitudes toward the product when they thought other women liked it.

(*Source:* Based on data in Fleming & Petty, 2000).

of that group (e.g., Maio, Esses, & Bell, 1994; Terry, Hogg, & Duck, 1999). In such cases, attitudes are being shaped by our own desire to be similar to people we like. Now imagine that you heard someone you dislike and see as dissimilar to yourself expressing negative views toward this group. In this case, you might indeed be unlikely to adopt this person's attitude position. People are not troubled by disagreement with people whom they categorize as different from themselves; in fact, they expect to hold different attitudes from them. It is, however, uncomfortable to differ on important attitudes from people whom we see as similar to ourselves and therefore with whom we expect to agree (Turner, 1991).

Not only are we influenced by other people's attitude positions depending on how much we identify with them, but we also expect to be influenced by other people's attitude positions depending on how much we identify with those people. A message concerning safe sex and acquired immune deficiency syndrome (AIDS) prevention was created for university students and delivered by a student group. The listeners who identified with their university's student group believed that they would be personally influenced by the position advocated in the message, while those who were low in identification with their university's student group did not expect to be personally influenced by the message (Duck, Hogg, & Terry, 1999). Thus when we identify with a group, we expect to be influenced by those others and in fact, are likely to take on the attitudes advocated by that group.

To see this process in action, suppose you were asked to evaluate a new product you've not encountered before. How might the identity relevance of the message influence your attitude? To address this question, Fleming and Petty (2000) first selected students who were either high or low in identification with their gender group to participate in the study. Then they introduced a new snack product ("Snickerdoodles") to men and women as either "women's favorite snack food" or "men's favorite snack food." As Figure 5.7 illustrates, a more favorable attitude toward this product was formed when the message was framed in terms of their own group liking that food among those who highly identified with their gender group. In contrast, among the men and women who were low in identification with their gender group, no differences in the attitudes they formed toward the new food was found as a function of which group was said to favor that food.

Principles to Remember

Attitudes are learned using the same mechanisms as any other form of knowledge acquisition. For this reason, those same techniques can be applied to changing attitudes.

KeyPoints

- Attitudes are evaluations of any aspect of the social world; attitudes help us understand people's responses to new stimuli. Knowing that a person is prevention focused or promotion focused helps us predict what kind of advertisement for a new product they will find persuasive.

- Attitudes can be explicit, that is, conscious and easy to report, or implicit, which implies they are uncontrollable and potentially not consciously accessible.

- Attitudes are acquired from other people through social learning processes.

- Such learning can involve classical conditioning, instrumental conditioning, or observational learning.

- Attitudes can be classically conditioned even without our awareness—via subliminal conditioning and mere exposure.

- Attitudes that are acquired through instrumental conditioning stem from differential rewards and punishments for adopting particular views.

- Because we compare ourselves with others to determine whether our view of social reality is correct or not, we often adopt the attitudes that others hold. As a result of the process of social comparison, we tend to adopt the attitude position of those we see as similar to ourselves but not of those we see as dissimilar.

- When we identify with a group, we expect to be influenced by messages that are aimed at our group. We do not expect to be influenced when we do not identify with the group that message is aimed at.

Think About It

All of the processes described so far suggest that our attitudes result from various types of social influence—that is, other people. Does this mean that our attitudes, which often feel subjectively so personal, might not really be so unique after all?

When and Why Do Attitudes Influence Behavior?

So far we have considered the processes responsible for the attitudes we form. But we haven't addressed another important question: Why would we bother to acquire attitudes toward all sorts of objects and topics, if these attitudes aren't consistently related to behavior? Many factors can alter the degree to which attitudes and behavior are related. For an in-depth look at this, read *Making Sense of Common Sense: A Social Psychological Perspective* on page 157.

Role of the Social Context in the Link between Attitudes and Behavior

You have probably experienced a gap between your own attitudes and behavior on many occasions—this is because the social context can directly affect the attitude-behavior connection. For instance, what would you say if one of your friends shows you a new tattoo of which he or she is proud and asks for your opinion? Would you state that you think it is not attractive, if that was your view? Perhaps, but the chances are quite good that you would try to avoid hurting your friend's feelings by saying that you like it even though your actual attitude is negative. In such cases, we are often clearly aware of our conscious choice not to act on our true attitude. As this example illustrates, social contextual factors can limit the extent to which attitudes alone determine behavior.

In contrast to your attitude–behavior inconsistency in responding to your friend's tattoo, your attitude might be a good predictor of whether you would get a tattoo or not. Consider another example: If you like pepperoni pizza, but dislike pizza with anchovies,

MAKING SENSE OF COMMON SENSE
A SOCIAL PSYCHOLOGICAL PERSPECTIVE
Are Attitudes Consistently Related to Behavior?

Perhaps you expect that people's social attitudes will directly predict their behaviors? If so, you are not alone: We generally believe, for example, that those who hold bigoted attitudes will consistently behave in a prejudicial fashion and that nonbigoted people will not do so. Is this common sense really accurate?

More than seventy years ago, a classic study concerning ethnic attitudes and discriminatory behavior was conducted by Richard LaPiere (1934). He wondered whether people with negative attitudes toward a specific social group would, in fact, act in line with their attitudes. To find out, he spent two years traveling around the United States with a young Chinese couple. During these travels, they stopped at 184 restaurants and sixty-six hotels and motels. In the majority of the cases, they were treated courteously. In fact, they were refused service only once, and LaPiere reported that they had, in fact, received above average service in most instances.

Six months after his travels were completed, LaPiere wrote to all the businesses where he and the Chinese couple had stayed or dined, asking whether they would or would not offer service to Chinese visitors. The results were startling: Of the 128 businesses that responded, 92 percent of the restaurants and 91 percent of the hotels said "no to Chinese customers!" In short, LaPiere's results seemed to indicate that there is often a sizeable gap between attitudes and behavior—that is, what a person says is his or her attitude, and what he or she actually does when confronted with the object of that attitude may be quite different.

Does this mean that attitudes don't predict behavior? Not necessarily. Subsequent research has revealed that people are more complex than that; framing the question as an either-or question overlooks that complexity. To understand why attitudes toward an ethnic group might not straightforwardly predict behavior, we need to recognize that there are a host of norms and laws that make many forms of discriminatory behavior unacceptable or illegal. So, even the most prejudiced people will not always act on their attitudes when there are strong situational pressures to do otherwise. Likewise, there are social conditions under which people who do not think of themselves as prejudiced may find themselves discriminating against others based on their group membership.

Consider the radio personality, Don Imus, who was fired from CBS for his racist (and sexist) statements about the African American women on Rutgers University's basketball team. A video of his commentary was quickly posted on Youtube.com, and more than 500,000 views of it and 4,000 comments soon followed. On numerous blogs, in just a matter of days, thousands of Imus-related comments were made, many of them arguing about whether his behavior did or did not reflect his actual racial attitudes. Like Michael Richards (the actor who played Kramer on "Seinfeld"), who had earlier publicly behaved in a racially abhorrent way, Imus acknowledged his behavior was wrong but says it wasn't an accurate reflection of his true racial attitudes. And, in fact, he argued that CBS hired him to push the envelope and be controversial while on the air.

What these examples make clear is that attitudes and behavior can be inconsistent. Although it might seem reasonable or common sense to expect that a favorable attitude toward a given ethnic group will directly predict nondiscriminatory behaviors and that discriminatory behaviors necessarily reflect a prejudiced attitude the matter is often considerably more complicated than that.

which one are you most likely to order? Again, your attitude toward anchovies will affect your behavior. But what if you are with friends who love anchovies—will you express your hatred of anchovies? Maybe not—it may be preferable to swallow a couple of anchovies rather than risk offending your friends. Thus as suggested in Figure 5.8 on page 158, depending on the degree to which the action is public and there are potential social consequences, attitudes will do not always predict behavior.

Because of the important role that the social context plays in determining when attitudes and behavior will be related, recent research has focused on the factors that determine when consistency can be expected and the issue of how attitudes influence behavior. Several factors determine the extent to which attitudes and behavior correspond, although a meta-analysis of eighty-eight studies assessing this relationship has found there

Figure 5.8
Attitudes: They May
Predict Our Behavior
Better When We're
Alone Than with a
Potentially Disapproving
Audience
*We may be inhibited from
expressing our true attitudes
toward some object or topic in
the presence of other people
who would disapprove. In the
photos shown here, the person
in panel A expresses disgust at
anchovies on the pizza, but
with other people looking on,
the person's true attitude is
inhibited and in fact pleasure
appears to be expressed.*

(*Source:* Stephen Reysen.)

is overall a reliable relationship between the two (Kraus, 1995). However as we have already discussed, aspects of the situation can strongly influence the extent to which attitudes determine our behavior. In addition, features of the attitudes themselves are also important—for example, how certain are you of your own attitude? Attitudes that we hold with greater clarity or certainty are more strongly linked to behavior (Tormala & Petty, 2004) than are attitudes about which we feel some uncertainty. After considering situational influences on the attitude-behavior relationship, we'll examine the question of how attitudes influence behavior—the underlying mechanisms involved in this process.

Situational Constraints that Affect Attitude Expression

Have you ever been worried about what others would think of you if you expressed your true attitude toward an issue? If so, you will understand the dilemma that Princeton University students experienced in a study conducted by Miller, Monin, and Prentice (2000). The private attitudes of those students toward heavy alcohol consumption were relatively negative. But they believed that other students' attitudes toward heavy alcohol consumption were more positive than their own (an instance of **pluralistic ignorance,** in which we erroneously believe others have different attitudes than ourselves). When these students were placed in a discussion about alcohol use with other students, they expressed greater comfort with campus drinking than they actually felt, and their beliefs about what others would think about them predicted their behavior in the group discussion better than their actual attitudes.

Such constraints on revealing our private attitudes can occur even when we are with other people with whom we highly identify. For example, members of groups that were either pro-choice or pro-life in their stance toward abortion have been studied (Robinson, Keltner, Ward, & Ross, 1995). In both groups, the participants were reluctant to publicly reveal the ambivalence they actually felt about their political position for fear that members of their own group would see them as disloyal. Thus important forms of situational constraints of this sort can prevent attitudes from being expressed in overt behavior (Fazio & Roskos-Ewoldsen, 1994; Olson & Maio, 2003).

Strength of Attitudes

pluralistic ignorance
When we collectively
misunderstand what attitudes
others hold and believe
erroneously that others have
different attitudes than us.

Consider the following situation: A large company markets a dangerous product to the public for decades, while internally sharing memos about the addictiveness of the product and how to manipulate that addictiveness. Along the way, an executive of the company has serious moral qualms about the rightness of these actions. Eventually, the concerned employee tips off the news media about these practices and an investigation is

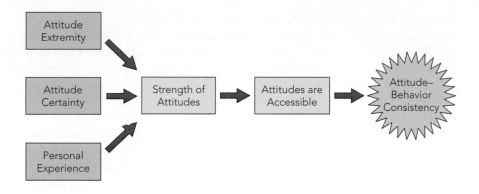

Figure 5.9
How Attitude Strength
Influences Attitude-
Behavior Consistency
*Attitudes that are extreme,
certain, and formed on the
basis of personal experience
with the attitude object tend to
be strong attitudes. Stronger
attitudes are more likely to be
accessible when a behavioral
response is made, which results
in greater attitude-behavior
consistency than when attitudes
are weak.*

(*Source:* Based on suggestions by
Petrocelli, Tormala, & Rucker,
2007; Petty & Krosnick, 1995).

begun. The whistle-blower is eventually found out and is even sued by his former employer (although the lawsuit that was initiated against him is ultimately dropped).

You may recognize the person and company being described here because these events were ultimately made into a movie, *The Insider.* It was Jeffrey Wigand who blew the whistle on the practices of the tobacco industry in general and his former employer, Brown & Williamson, in particular. Why might people take such drastic and potentially risky action (i.e., informing on their employer)? The answer is clear: Such people are passionately committed to the notion that corporations must be honest, especially when there is the potential for damage to the public. In other words, people who become whistle-blowers have strong attitudes, which are important determinants of their behavior. Indeed, Wigand is now a consultant with various state agencies working to help reduce tobacco use. Such incidents call attention to the fact that whether attitudes will predict sustained and potentially costly behavior is strongly dependent on the strength of the attitudes. Let's consider why attitude strength has this effect.

The term *strength* captures the extremity of an attitude (how strong the emotional reaction is), the degree of certainty with which an attitude is held (the sense that you know what your attitude is and the feeling that it is the correct position to hold) and the extent to which the attitude is based on personal experience with the attitude object. These three factors can affect attitude accessibility (how easily the attitude comes to mind in various situations), which ultimately determines the extent to which attitudes drive our behavior (Fazio, Ledbetter, & Towles-Schwen, 2000). As shown in Figure 5.9, recent findings indicate that all of these components of attitude strength are interrelated and that each plays a role in the likelihood that attitudes will be accessible and affect behavior (Petty & Krosnick, 1995).

Attitude Extremity: Role of Vested Interests

Let's consider first attitude extremity, which is the extent to which an individual feels strongly in one direction or the other, about an issue (Giner-Sorolla, 2001; Krosnick, 1988). One of the key determinants of this is what social psychologists term *vested interest*, which is the extent to which the attitude is relevant to the concerns of the individual who holds it. This typically amounts to whether the object or issue might have important consequences for this person. The results of many studies indicate that the greater such vested interest is, the stronger the impact of the attitude on behavior is (Crano, 1995; Visser, Krosnick, & Simmons, 2003). For example, when students at a large university were telephoned and asked if they would participate in a campaign against increasing the legal age for drinking alcohol from eighteen to twenty-one, their responses depended on whether they would be affected by the policy change or not (Sivacek & Crano, 1982). Students who would be affected by this new law—those younger than twenty-one—have a stronger stake in this issue than those who would not be affected by the law because they were already twenty-one or would reach this age before the law took effect. Thus it was predicted that those in the first group—whose interests were at stake—would be much more likely to join a rally against the proposed policy change than those in the second group. This is exactly what happened: While more than 47 percent of those with high vested interest agreed to take part in the campaign, only 12 percent of those in the low vested interest group did so.

Not only do people with a vested interest behave in a way that supports their cause, but they are also likely to elaborate on arguments that favor their position. By doing so, attitude-consistent thoughts come to mind when an issue is made known. For example, Haugtvedt and Wegener (1994) found that when participants were asked to consider a nuclear power plant being built in their own state (high personal relevance), they developed more counterarguments against the plan than when the power plant might be potentially built in a distant state (low personal relevance). Thus attitudes based on vested interest are more likely to be thought about carefully, be resistant to change, and be an accessible guide for behavior.

Attitude Certainty: Importance of Clarity and Correctness

Research has identified two important components of attitude certainty: attitude clarity, which is being clear about what one's attitude is, and attitude correctness, which is feeling one's attitude is the valid or the proper one to hold. Recent research by Petrocelli, Tormala, and Rucker (2007) provides evidence for the distinction between these two components of attitude certainty by showing how different factors affect them.

Petrocelli and others (2007) first determined their participants felt negatively about a specific attitude issue: requiring students to carry identification cards with them at all times. Then to manipulate the perception of consensus concerning their attitude position, half of the participants were given feedback that most other students (89 percent) agreed with their attitude toward the identification card issue, while the other half were told that most other students disagreed (only 11 percent agreed) with them. Although attitude clarity was equivalent in both the high and low consensus conditions, perceived correctness was greater when consensus was high (the 89 percent condition) rather than low (only 11 percent). So, when we learn that others share our attitudes, it acts as justification for that attitude and thereby increases certainty.

Clarity, the other component of attitude certainty, reflects a lack of ambivalence about an attitude issue. The more often you are asked to report on your attitude, the more it will facilitate clarity and thereby certainty. Attitude restatement appears to work by increasing our subjective sense that we really do know how we feel about an object or issue. When Petrocelli and others (2007) had their participants express their attitudes toward gun control either several times or only once, attitude certainty differed. Those in the group that expressed their view more had greater certainty about their attitude toward gun control than those in the group that expressed their view once.

What happens when both the clarity and correctness components are varied simultaneously? Returning to the identification card example, Petrocelli and others (2007) gave students with negative attitudes toward the policy manipulations that were designed to affect both correctness (consensus) and clarity (repeated expression). The students were then given a persuasive message with strong arguments in favor of the policy but against their initial attitudes, that is, why the policy would enhance student safety. More attitude change resulted in the low clarity case than the high clarity condition (single versus repeated expression), and more attitude change occurred in the low correctness versus the high correctness condition (low versus high consensus). Both components of attitude certainty, when they are high, can increase resistance to a persuasive message; each independently contributed to resistance to persuasion.

The social context too is important in assessing the relative effects of attitude clarity and correctness. High clarity will be more predictive of behavior in private but not public where correctness concerns are likely to be greater. Moreover, when people's attitudes are attacked, successfully resisting those attacks may well increase perceptions of attitude certainty because mounting and expressing counterarguments will increase perceptions of attitude correctness. In terms of attitude-behavior consistency, an attitude that is high on both clarity and correctness is most likely to reliably predict behavior in public and in private.

How is attitude certainty likely to play out in the real world? High attitude certainty can, of course, be found in many people, but it is often quite notable in the public expressions of politicians. For example, U.S. President George W. Bush is a person who claims to be sure of his views on the Iraq War. What psychological factors might play into the creation of that certainty? In terms of consensus information, the president is surrounded by many people who represent strong support for his views; this president's inner circle is limited to those whose views are similar to his own. In addition, his duties involve him repeatedly stating his attitudes in speeches. Such repeated expressions are likely to increase clarity about his attitude concerning the war.

It is also interesting to note that attitude certainty can also have an effect on listeners, not just the people who express them. Many people believe that certainty is diagnostic of accuracy. Because the president's attitudes are typically conveyed to his listeners with great confidence, this may have an impact on perceived accuracy (see Chapter 12 in which we discuss juror biases and witness credibility). Additionally, his listeners may perceive him as having clear attitudes, partially because statements of his views are often accompanied by a kind of folksy wisdom which, for some, may suggest a straightforward "plain folks" clarity.

Role of Personal Experience

Depending on how attitudes are formed initially, the link between attitudes and behavior can differ. Considerable evidence indicates that attitudes formed on the basis of direct experience with the object about which we hold a particular attitude can exert stronger effects on behavior than ones formed indirectly. This is because attitudes formed on the basis of direct experience are likely to be stronger and be more likely to come to mind when in the presence of the attitude object (Tormala, Petty, & Brinol, 2002). Similarly, attitudes based on personal relevance are more likely to be elaborated on in terms of supporting arguments, and this makes them resistant to change (Wegener, Petty, Smoak, & Fabrigar, 2004). Consider the difference between having a friend tell you that a particular car model is a lemon versus having experienced some failures with this brand yourself. When looking at new models of that brand, would your friend's opinion even come to mind? Maybe not. Would your own experiences come to mind? Probably. Thus when you have direct experience with an attitude object it is likely to be quite personally relevant and strong, and your attitude toward it is likely to predict your behavior toward it in the future.

In sum, existing evidence suggests that attitudes really do affect behavior (Eagly & Chaiken, 1993; Petty & Krosnick, 1995). However the strength of this link is strongly determined by a number of different factors. First of all, situational constraints may not permit us to overtly express our attitudes. Second, attitude extremity, which is a function of whether we have a vested interest in the issue or not, influences whether our attitudes translate into behavior. Third, attitudes, which are clear and experienced as correct, are more likely to affect behavior than are those that lack clarity or that we are uncertain about their correctness. Fourth, whether or not we have personal experience with the attitude object can affect the accessibility of the attitude, and attitudes that are more accessible are more likely to determine behavior compared to those that are not accessible.

> ### Principles to Remember
> Attitudes do guide behavior if they are accessible. Strong attitudes—based on extremity, certainty, and personal experience—predict behaviors that are consistent with them.

KeyPoints

- Attitudes toward a group, issue, or object do not always directly predict behavior. Rather, there are situational constraints that affect our willingness to express our true attitudes. Concerns about what others, especially those with whom we identify, may think of us can limit the extent to which our attitudes and behavior are consistent.

- People often show pluralistic ignorance—erroneously believing that others have different attitudes than us. This can limit the extent to which we express our attitudes in public.

- Strong attitudes are ones we are committed to, and we typically have elaborate arguments available to support them. For this reason, they are more likely to be accessible at the time we take action and are particularly likely to influence behavior.

- Attitude strength subsumes several factors: extremity, certainty, and degree of personal experience.

Those attitudes that are more extreme, certain (both in terms of clarity and perceived correctness), and based on personal experience are more likely to be accessible and guide behavior than are less extreme, unclear, and indirectly formed attitudes.

Think About It

Suppose you wanted to design a campaign to increase condom use. You believe that many young adults have positive attitudes toward safe sex, but the problem is getting them to act on those attitudes. Given the factors that are important for a close link between attitudes and behaviors, how can they be used to ensure that attitudes about safe sex are accessible and translate into behavior when they are really needed?

How Do Attitudes Guide Behavior?

When it comes to the question of how attitudes guide behavior, it should come as no surprise that researchers have found that there is more than one basic mechanism through which attitudes shape behavior. We'll first consider behaviors that are driven by attitudes based on reasoned thought and then examine the role of attitudes in more spontaneous behavioral responses.

Attitudes Arrived at through Reasoned Thought

theory of reasoned action
A theory suggesting that the decision to engage in a particular behavior is the result of a rational process in which behavioral options are considered, consequences or outcomes of each are evaluated, and a decision is reached to act or not to act. That decision is then reflected in behavioral intentions, which strongly influence overt behavior.

theory of planned behavior
An extension of the theory of reasoned action, suggesting that in addition to attitudes toward a given behavior and subjective norms about it, individuals also consider their ability to perform the behavior.

In some situations we give careful, deliberate thought to our attitudes and their implications for our behavior. Insight into the nature of this process is provided by the **theory of reasoned action,** a theory that was later refined and termed the **theory of planned behavior,** first proposed by Icek Ajzen and Martin Fishbein in 1980. This theoretical view starts with the notion that the decision to engage in a particular behavior is the result of a rational process. Various behavioral options are considered, the consequences or outcomes of each are evaluated, and a decision is reached to act or not act. That decision is then reflected in behavioral intentions, which are often strong predictors of whether we act on our attitudes in a given situation (Ajzen, 1987). Indeed, for a number of behavioral domains—from condom use to engaging in regular exercise—intentions are moderately correlated with behavior (Albarracin, Johnson, Fishbein, & Muellerleile, 2001).

Recent research has made it clear that the intention–behavior relationship is even stronger when people have formed a plan for how and when they will translate their intentions into behavior (Webb & Sheeran, 2007). Suppose for example you form the intention to go to your college gym to work out. If you develop a plan for how you will translate your intention into actual behavior—beginning with setting your alarm, preparing your exercise clothes, and so forth—you will be more likely to succeed at doing so. In my own case, because I formed the intention to walk three mornings a week, I made a commitment to do so with my next door neighbor. The reason why this is a particularly effective **implementation plan** is that I no longer have to assess whether I really want to go out today—in the cold, rain, or rely on having my attitude toward getting more exercise be accessible at that time of the morning—because I made a commitment to my neighbor and she will be ready to go and expect that I will be also. As Gollwitzer (1999) has noted, such a plan to implement our intentions is effective because it involves delegating control of one's

"I don't usually go to parties, but I'm very fond of Aaron."

Figure 5.10
Thwarting Our Best Intentions
As this cartoon illustrates, by wanting to please our friends, even our best intentions can be undermined.

(*Source: The New Yorker,* August 2, 1993.)

behavior to the situation—in my case, my alarm clock beeping and, if that doesn't work, my neighbor ringing my doorbell.

But how do you form an intention to change some aspect of your behavior? According to the theory, intentions, are determined by two factors: Attitudes toward the behavior— positive or negative evaluations of performing the behavior (whether we think it will yield positive or negative consequences), and subjective norms— perceptions of whether other people will approve or disapprove of this behavior. A third factor: perceived behavioral control— appraisals of our ability to perform the behavior—was subsequently added to the theory (Ajzen, 1991). Perhaps a specific example will help illustrate the nature of these ideas.

Suppose a young woman is considering getting a body piercing—for instance, wearing a nose ornament. Will she actually go to the shop and take this action? First, the answer will depend on her intentions, which will be strongly influenced by her attitude toward body piercings. Her decision to get one or not will also be based on perceived norms and the extent to which she has control over the decision. If the young woman believes that a body piercing will be relatively painless and it will make her look fashionable (she has positive attitudes toward the behavior), she also believes that people whose opinions she values will approve of this action (subjective norms) and that she can readily do it (she knows an expert who does body piercing), her intentions to carry out this action may be quite strong. On the other hand, if she believes that getting the piercing will be painful, it might not improve her appearance, her friends will disapprove of this behavior, and she will have trouble finding an expert to do it safely, then her intentions to get the nose ornament will be weak. Her intentions are more likely to translate into behavior, as we noted previously, if she formulates a plan for when and how to get the piercing (e.g., "on Friday when I get my pay check, I'll take the bus to the shop and get it done"). Of course, even the best of intentions can be thwarted by situational factors (see the cartoon in Figure 5.10 for an amusing instance of this) but, in general, intentions are an important predictor of behavior.

Reasoned action and planned behavior ideas have been applied to predicting behavior in many settings with considerable success. Indeed, research suggests that these theories are useful for predicting such divergent behaviors as soldiers' conduct on the battlefront (Ajzen & Fishbein, 2005) and whether individuals drive a vehicle after they have consumed alcohol (MacDonald, Zanna, & Fong, 1995). Other behaviors, including use of the recreational drug ecstasy, can be predicted with careful measurement of the components suggested by these theories. For example, Orbell, Blair, Sherlock, and Conner (2001) approached young people in various locations and asked them to complete a question-

implementation plan
A plan for how to implement our intentions to carry out some action.

naire designed to measure (1) their attitudes toward ecstasy (e.g., is this drug enjoyable-unenjoyable, pleasant-unpleasant, beneficial-harmful, and so forth), (2) their intention to use it in the next two months, (3) subjective norms (whether their friends would approve of their using it), and (4) two aspects of perceived control over using this drug (whether they could obtain it and whether they could resist taking it if they had some). Two months later, the same people were contacted and asked whether they had actually used ecstasy. The results indicated that having a positive attitude toward ecstasy, seeing its use as normatively accepted by one's peer group, and having perceived control over using it were all significant predictors of intentions to use this drug. In fact, attitudes, subjective norms, and intentions were all significant predictors of actual ecstasy use.

Attitudes and Spontaneous Behavioral Reactions

Our ability to predict behavior in situations in which we have the time and opportunity to reflect carefully on various possible actions that we might undertake is quite good. However in many situations, we have to act quickly and our reactions are more spontaneous.

Figure 5.11
Spontaneous Attitude-to-Behavior Process Effects
According to the attitude-to-behavior process view, events trigger our attitudes and, simultaneously, the appropriate norms for how people should or typically do behave in a given situation. In this case, being cut off in traffic by another driver triggers our attitudes toward such people and our knowledge that this action is atypical. This interpretation, in turn, determines how we behave. Thus attitudes are an important factor in shaping our overt behavior.

(*Source:* Based on Fazio, 2000.)

Suppose another driver cuts in front of you on the highway without signaling. In such cases, attitudes seem to influence behavior in a more direct and seemingly automatic manner, with intentions playing a less important role. According to one theoretical view—the **attitude-to-behavior process model** (Fazio & Roskos-Ewoldsen, 1994)—the process works as follows: Some event activates an attitude; that attitude, once activated, influences how we perceive the attitude object. At the same time, our knowledge about what's appropriate in a given situation (our knowledge of various social norms) is also activated. Together, the attitude and the previously stored information about what's appropriate or expected shape our definition of the event. This perception, in turn, influences our behavior. Let's consider a concrete example.

Imagine that someone cuts into your traffic lane as you are driving (see Figure 5.11). This event triggers your attitude toward people who engage in such dangerous and discourteous behavior and your understanding of how people are expected to behave on expressways. As a result, you perceive this behavior as nonnormative, which influences your definition of and your response to that event. You might think, "Who does this person think they are? What nerve!" Or perhaps your response is more situational, "Gee, this person must be in a big hurry; or maybe he or she is a foreigner who doesn't know that you should signal before pulling in the lane in front of someone." Whichever of these interpretations of the event is given, it will shape your behavior. Several studies provide support for this perspective on how attitudes can influence behavior by affecting the interpretation given to the situation.

In short, attitudes affect our behavior through at least two mechanisms, and these operate under somewhat contrasting conditions. When we have time to engage in careful, reasoned thought, we can weigh all the alternatives and decide how we will act. Under the hectic conditions of everyday life, however, we often don't have time for this kind of deliberate weighing of alternatives, and often our responses appear to be much faster than

attitude-to-behavior process model
A model of how attitudes guide behavior that emphasizes the influence of attitudes and stored knowledge of what is appropriate in a given situation on an individual's definition of the present situation. This definition, in turn, influences overt behavior.

such deliberate thought processes can account for. In such cases, our attitudes seem to spontaneously shape our perceptions of various events—often with little conscious cognitive processing—and thereby shapes our immediate behavioral reactions (e.g., Bargh & Chartrand, 2000; Dovidio, Brigham, Johnson, & Gaertner, 1996). To the extent that a person repeatedly performs a specific behavior—and a **habit** is formed—that person's responses may become relatively automatic whenever that same situation is encountered (Wood, Quinn, & Kashy, 2002).

> ### Principles to Remember
> Attitudes can guide behavior either through a reasoned conscious process or because our attitudes spontaneously come to mind and shape our immediate behavioral reactions.

KeyPoints

- Several factors affect the strength of the relationship between attitudes and behavior; some of these relate to the situation in which the attitudes are activated and some to aspects of the attitudes themselves.

- Attitudes seem to influence behavior through two different mechanisms. When we can give careful thought to our attitudes, intentions derived from our attitudes, norms, and perceived control over the behavior all predict behavior. In situations in which we do not engage in such deliberate thought, attitudes may be automatically activated and influence behavior by shaping our perceptions of the situation, which in turn dictates our behavior.

Think About It

If attitudes can affect behavior through a conscious reasoning process and the formation of intentions to act in a new way, why, despite this, is it often so difficult to change our habits even though our attitudes have changed?

The Fine Art of Persuasion: How Attitudes Are Changed

How many times in the last few days has someone tried to change your attitudes about something or other? If you stop and think for a moment, you may be surprised at the answer, for it is clear that each day we are literally bombarded with such attempts, some of which are illustrated in Figure 5.12 on page 166. Billboards, television commercials, magazine ads, pop-up ads on your computer, and even our friends may all attempt to change our attitudes. The list of potential "would-be persuaders" seems almost endless. To what extent are such attempts at **persuasion**—efforts to change our attitudes through the use of various kinds of messages—successful? And what factors determine if they succeed or fail? Social psychologists have studied these issues for decades, and as we'll soon see, their efforts have yielded important insights into the cognitive processes that play a role in persuasion (e.g., Petty et al., 2003; Wegener & Carlston, 2005).

Persuasion: Communicators, Messages, and Audiences

Early research efforts aimed at understanding persuasion involved the study of the following elements: Some source directs some type of message to some person or group of people (the audience). Following World War II, persuasion research conducted by Hovland, Janis, and Kelley (1953) focused on these key elements, asking: "*Who* says *what* to *whom* with what effect?" This approach yielded a number of important findings, with the following being the most consistently obtained.

habit
Repeatedly performing a specific behavior so responses become relatively automatic whenever that situation is encountered.

persuasion
Efforts to change others' attitudes through the use of various kinds of messages.

 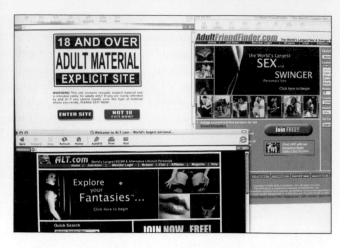

Figure 5.12

Persuasion: A Part of Daily Life

Each day we are bombarded with dozens of messages designed to change our attitudes or our behavior. Clearly, if they weren't effective some of the time, advertisers would not pay the sums that they do for these opportunities to try and persuade us to do what they are promoting.

- Communicators who are credible—who seem to know what they are talking about or who are expert with respect to the topics or issues they are presenting—are more persuasive than those who are seen as lacking expertise. For instance, in a famous study on this topic, Hovland and Weiss (1951) asked participants to read communications dealing with various issues (e.g., atomic submarines, the future of movie theaters— remember, this was back in 1950). The supposed source of these messages was varied so as to be high or low in credibility. For instance, for atomic submarines, a highly credible source was the famous scientist Robert J. Oppenheimer, while the low credibility source was *Pravda*, the newspaper of the Communist party in the Soviet Union (notice how the credible source was an in-group member for these U.S. participants, while the low credible source was an out-group source). Participants expressed their attitudes toward these issues a week before the experiment and then immediately after receiving the communications. Those who were told that the source of the messages they read was a highly credible in-group member showed significantly greater attitude change than those who thought the message was from the out-group, which lacked trustworthiness and credibility. Indeed, members of our own group are typically seen as more credible and therefore are likely to influence us more than those with whom we do not share a group membership and with whom we might even expect to disagree (Turner, 1991).

  Communicators can, though, lose their credibility and therefore their ability to persuade. One means by which credibility can be undermined is if you learn that a communicator has a personal stake (financial or otherwise) in persuading you to adopt a particular position. Consequently, communicators are seen as most credible and, therefore persuasive, when they are perceived as arguing against their self-interests (Eagly, Chaiken, & Wood, 1981).

- Communicators who are attractive in some way (e.g., physically) are more persuasive than communicators who are not attractive (Hovland & Weiss, 1951). This is one reason why advertisements often include attractive models. Frequently, advertisers are attempting to suggest to us that if we buy their product, we, too, will be perceived as attractive. Another way that communicators can be seen as attractive is via their perceived likeability (Eagly & Chaiken, 1993). We are more likely to be persuaded by a communicator we like than one we dislike. This is one reason why famous sports figures, such as Tiger Woods, musicians, such as Fergie or Beyonce Knowles, and even actors or models are selected as spokespersons for various products; we already like them so are more readily persuaded by them. If we apply these findings to the couple shown in Figure 5.13, which partner is more likely to persuade the other?

- Messages that do not appear to be designed to change our attitudes are often more successful than those that seem to be designed to achieve this goal (Walster & Festinger, 1962). Indeed, a recent meta-analysis of the existing research on this issue has revealed that forewarning does typically lessen the extent to which attitude change occurs (Benoit, 1998). So, simply knowing that a sales pitch is coming your way undermines its persuasiveness.

- One aspect of message content that has received considerable research attention is whether those that contain emotional information, specifically **fear appeals,** which are messages that arouse fear in the recipient, are persuasive or not. For example, Janis and Feshbach (1953) gave people one of three messages about the tooth decay that can result from not brushing one's teeth. They found that the message that induced mild fear resulted in the greatest subsequent tooth brushing, while the message that induced the most fear resulted in the least increase in brushing. When the message is so fear arousing that people genuinely feel threatened, they are likely to react defensively and argue against the threat or else dismiss its applicability to themselves (Liberman & Chaiken, 1992; Taylor & Shepperd, 1998).

In the case of fear appeals that have been directed toward people who smoke tobacco, research has revealed that people are likely to say to themselves: "The evidence isn't that strong," "I'll quit before those consequences will occur," or "It just won't happen to me," all of which can undermine the effectiveness of truly frightening messages. Despite the evidence that using fear appeals effectively can be a tricky business, many government campaigns are predicated on the idea that you can induce people to change with fear. In Canada, for example, all tobacco products carry large warnings of the sort, "Smoking KILLS." As shown in Figure 5.14 on page 168, millions of dollars have been spent creating fear-based commercials showing diseased lungs and other grotesque long-term consequences of smoking and mangled bodies stemming from auto accidents in which passengers failed to wear their seat belts.

Might inducing more moderate levels of fear work better? There is some evidence that this is the case, but the fear needs to be paired with specific methods of behavioral change that will allow the negative consequences to be avoided (Leventhal, Watts, & Pagano, 1967). If people do not know how to change or do not believe that they can succeed in doing so, then fear will do little except induce avoidance and defensive responses.

Research findings (Broemer, 2004) suggest that health messages of various sorts can be more effective if they are framed in a positive manner (e.g., how to attain good health) rather than in a negative manner (e.g., risks and the undesirable consequences that can follow from a particular behavior). For example, any health message can be framed positively as "do this and you will feel better." Negative framings for the same message might be: "If you don't do this you will shorten your life." The point is that the same health information can be framed either positively in terms of potential benefits of taking a particular action or in terms of the negative consequences that can ensue if you don't take that action.

Positively framed messages can be even more effective persuasion devices when they are used to address potentially fatal health matters. Consider how message framing and

Figure 5.13
Role of Attractiveness in Persuasion: Who Would Be More Successful at Persuading the Other Person?
Research reveals that we are more persuaded by someone we view as attractive. Because the fellow in this cartoon sees the woman as more attractive than she sees him, we would predict that she will be more persuasive than he will be.

(*Source: The New Yorker,* June 4, 1990).

fear appeals
Attempting to change people's behaviors by use of a message that induces fear.

Figure 5.14
Using Fear as a Means of Encouraging Change
Many government messages use frightening images in an attempt to scare people into changing their attitudes and behavior, including the sorts of warnings illustrated here that are aimed at getting people to not drink and drive.

perceived risk of having a serious outcome can affect persuasion following exposure to a message designed to encourage low income ethnic minority women to be tested for human immunodeficiency virus (HIV; Apanovitch, McCarthy, & Salovey, 2003). Those women who perceived themselves as unlikely to test positive for HIV (but not those who saw themselves as at high risk) were more likely to be persuaded to be tested (and they actually got tested) when the message was framed in terms of the gains to be had by doing so (e.g., "the peace of mind you'll get or you won't have to worry that you could spread the virus") than when the message was framed in terms of potential losses they would otherwise experience (e.g., "you won't have peace of mind or you could spread the virus unknowingly to those you care about"). It would appear that positive framing can be effective in inducing change—in the population that is disproportionately affected by this health threat—especially when those individuals fail to perceive themselves as especially at risk.

Early research on persuasion certainly provided important insights into the factors that influence persuasion. What such work didn't do, however, was offer a comprehensive account of how persuasion occurs. For instance, why, precisely, are highly credible or attractive communicators more effective in changing attitudes than less credible or attractive ones? Why might positive message framing (rather than negative or fear based) produce more attitude change? In recent years, social psychologists have recognized that to answer such questions, it is necessary to carefully examine the cognitive processes that underlie persuasion; in other words, what goes on in people's minds while they listen to a persuasive message. It is to this highly sophisticated work that we turn next.

The Cognitive Processes Underlying Persuasion

systematic processing
Processing of information in a persuasive message that involves careful consideration of message content and ideas.

central route (to persuasion)
Attitude change resulting from systematic processing of information presented in persuasive messages.

heuristic processing
Processing of information in a persuasive message that involves the use of simple rules of thumb or mental shortcuts.

peripheral route (to persuasion)
Attitude change that occurs in response to peripheral persuasion cues, which is often based on information concerning the expertise or status of would-be persuaders.

What happens when you are exposed to a persuasive message—for instance, when you watch a television commercial or see ads pop up on your screen as you surf the Internet? Your first answer might be something like: "I think about what's being said and shown," and in a sense, that's correct. But as we saw in Chapter 2, we often do the least amount of cognitive work that we can in a given situation. Indeed, we may want to avoid listening to such commercial messages (and thanks to VCRs, DVDs, DVRs, and TiVo, people can sometimes skip commercials entirely). But when we are subjected to a message, the central issue—the one that seems to provide the key to understanding the entire process of persuasion—is really, "How do we process (absorb, interpret, and evaluate) the information contained in such messages?" The answer that has emerged from hundreds of separate studies is that basically, we can process persuasive messages in two distinct ways.

Systematic versus Heuristic Processing

The first type of processing we can employ is known as **systematic processing** or the **central route** to persuasion, and it involves careful consideration of message content and the ideas it contains. Such processing requires effort, and it absorbs a great deal of our information-processing capacity. The second approach, known as **heuristic processing** or the **peripheral route** to persuasion, involves the use of simple rules of thumb or mental

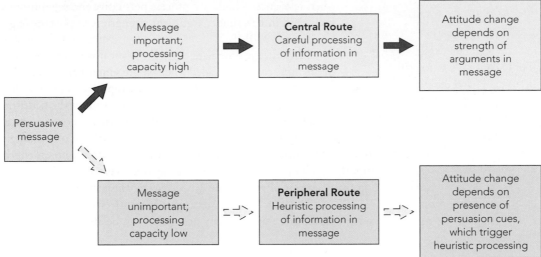

Figure 5.15
The ELM Model: A Cognitive Theory of Persuasion
According to the elaboration-likelihood model (ELM), persuasion can occur in one of two ways. First, we can be persuaded by carefully and systematically processing the information contained in the persuasive messages (the central route), or second, by use of heuristics or mental shortcuts (the peripheral route). Systematic processing occurs when the message is important to us, and we have the cognitive resources available to think about it carefully. Heuristic processing is most likely when the message is not important to us or we do not have the cognitive resources (or time) to engage in careful thought.

(Source: Based on suggestions by Petty & Cacioppo, 1986).

shortcuts, such as the belief that experts' statements can be trusted, or the idea that "if it makes me feel good, I'm in favor of it." This kind of processing requires less effort and allows us to react to persuasive messages in an automatic manner. It occurs in response to cues in the message or situation that evoke various mental shortcuts (e.g., beautiful models evoke the "What's beautiful is good and worth listening to" heuristic).

When do we engage in each of these two distinct modes of thought? Modern theories of persuasion such as the **elaboration-likelihood model** (ELM; e.g., Petty & Cacioppo, 1986; Petty, Wheeler, & Tormala, 2003) and the heuristic-systematic model (e.g., Chaiken, Liberman, & Eagly, 1989; Eagly & Chaiken, 1998) provide the following answer. We engage in the most effortful and systematic processing when our motivation and capacity to process information relating to the persuasive message is high. This type of processing occurs if we have a lot of knowledge about the topic, we have a lot of time to engage in careful thought, or the issue is sufficiently important to us and we believe it is essential to form an accurate view (Maheswaran & Chaiken, 1991; Petty & Cacioppo, 1990).

In contrast, we engage in the type of processing that requires less effort (heuristic processing) when we lack the ability or capacity to process more carefully (we must make up our minds quickly or we have little knowledge about the issue) or when our motivation to perform such cognitive work is low (the issue is unimportant to us or has little potential effect on us). Advertisers, politicians, salespeople, and others wishing to change our attitudes prefer to push us into the heuristic mode of processing because, for reasons we'll describe, it is often easier to change our attitudes when we think in this mode than when we engage in more careful and systematic processing. Strong arguments in favor of the position being advocated aren't needed when people do not process those arguments carefully! The two routes to persuasion suggested by the ELM model are shown in Figure 5.15.

The discovery of these two contrasting modes of processing provided an important key to understanding the process of persuasion. This is because the existence of these two modes of thought helps us to solve several intriguing puzzles. For instance, when persuasive messages are not interesting or relevant to us, the degree of persuasion they produce are not strongly influenced by the strength of the arguments these messages contain. When such messages are highly relevant to us, however, we are much more successful in inducing persuasion when the arguments they contain are strong and convincing. Can you see why this so? According to modern theories, such as the ELM and heuristic-systematic model, when relevance is low, we tend to process messages through the heuristic mode by means of cognitive shortcuts. Thus argument strength has little impact on us. In contrast,

elaboration-likelihood model (ELM)
A theory suggesting that persuasion can occur in either of two distinct ways, differing in the amount of cognitive effort or elaboration it requires.

when relevance is high, we process persuasive messages more systematically, and in this mode, argument strength is important (e.g., Petty & Cacioppo, 1990).

Similarly, the systematic versus heuristic distinction helps explain why we are more easily persuaded when we are somewhat distracted than when we are not. Under these conditions, the capacity to process the information in a persuasive message is limited, so we adopt the heuristic mode of thought. If the message contains the right cues that will induce heuristic processing (e.g., communicators who are attractive or seemingly expert), persuasion may occur because we respond to these cues and not to the arguments being presented. In sum, the modern cognitive approach really does seem to provide a crucial key to understanding many aspects of persuasion. In *Social Psychology: What It Tells Us About . . .* on pages 171–172, we illustrate how consuming caffeine affects how we will process messages more systematically and therefore why persuasion can be affected.

KeyPoints

- Early research on persuasion—efforts to change attitudes through the use of messages—focused primarily on characteristics of the communicator (e.g., expertise, attractiveness), message (e.g., fear appeals, one-sided versus two-sided arguments), and audience.

- Modern theories of persuasion include the elaboration-likelihood model (ELM) and the heuristic-systematic model. Research based on these models has sought to understand the cognitive processes that play a role in persuasion.

- Persuasive messages can be processed in two distinct ways: through systematic processing or central route to persuasion, which involves careful attention to message content, or through heuristic processing or peripheral route to persuasion, which involves the use of mental shortcuts (e.g., experts are usually right).

- Argument strength only affects persuasion when more systematic processing is engaged, whereas peripheral cues, such as features of the communicator's attractiveness or expertise, only affect persuasion when more heuristic processing occurs.

- Substances, such as caffeine, can affect persuasion because of their effects on systematic processing of the information in a message.

Think About It

Given the frequency with which we are exposed to persuasive messages and the two distinct routes by which we can be persuaded, when and why might our opinions remain stable?

Resisting Persuasion Attempts

As we have been discussing, people can be persuaded to change their attitudes and behavior, either because they think systematically about a compelling message or because they are influenced by more peripheral cues. Why then might people sometimes be a "tough sell," in which efforts to change attitudes are concerned? The answer involves several factors that, together, enhance our ability to resist even highly skilled efforts at persuasion.

Reactance: Protecting Our Personal Freedom

Few of us like being told what to do, but in a sense that is precisely what advertisers and other would-be persuaders do. You have probably experienced another individual who increasingly pressures you to get you to change your attitude on some issue. In both of

SOCIALPSYCHOLOGY

The Effects of Caffeine on Persuasion

Does that cup of java many of us seem to *need* to consume every morning, make us more or less persuadable? Although many of us get our jolt of caffeine from coffee, sodas are another popular source, especially among adolescents. Regardless of how we get our caffeine dose, a substantial percentage of North Americans—approximately 80 percent—consume moderate amounts of caffeine each day. This means that even if caffeine were to have mild effects, they might be of considerable social importance, given how much potential there is for its impact to be widespread. Besides helping the person in Figure 5.16 wake up, what implications might the caffeine being consumed by her have for the likelihood that her attitudes will be changed by the persuasive messages she is being exposed to?

Caffeine primarily activates the brain and central nervous system, so it affects people's ability to focus their attention on a task (Weinberg & Bealer, 2002). Therefore you might expect even moderate caffeine intake would act as a performance-enhancing drug for complex information processing tasks. As for persuasion, recall the ELM and its description of the peripheral and central routes to persuasion (see page 169). The peripheral route produces persuasion through such cues as communicator attractiveness or credibility (i.e., peripheral cues) that don't rely on close attention to the message itself. The central route, on the other hand, produces persuasion by asking people to attend to a message and to systematically process its contents. Given that caffeine intake should increase people's ability to systematically process the contents of a message, if people have the opportunity to focus on a persuasive message, they should be more persuaded by that message after consuming caffeine than after not consuming any. On the other hand, placing people under conditions of significant distraction when they are exposed to a persuasive message should prevent them from systematically processing that message, regardless of their caffeine consumption, and thereby lessen the extent to which they are persuaded by the message.

To test this hypothesis, Martin, Hamilton, McKimmie, Terry, and Martin (2007) first selected students whose attitudes were inconsistent with the persuasive message that they would be receiving later in an experiment. These individuals were then invited to the laboratory, where they were randomly assigned to receive a drink containing caffeine or a placebo without caffeine. The students were then exposed to a strongly argued message in favor of voluntary euthanasia under conditions of low or high distraction.

Figure 5.16
Drinking Beverages Containing Caffeine Can Increase Persuasion
According to recent research, the person shown here getting a dose of caffeine is more likely to be persuaded by the message than someone who has not consumed caffeine, to the extent that the information given is systematically processed.

(*Source:* Based on data from Martin, Hamilton, McKimmie, Terry, & Martin, 2007).

As expected, in the low distracter condition, those who had consumed caffeine agreed more with the message (so they were persuaded away from their original opinion) than those who had received the placebo. In contrast, in the high distraction condition—in which systematic processing of the message content was impossible—there was no difference in the attitudes of those who had consumed caffeine and those who had not.

People in both the high and low distraction conditions were then asked to recall the thoughts they had when processing the persuasive message. When the message-congruent thoughts that people reported were analyzed, they mapped perfectly on to the hypothesis: Those in the low distracter condition who had received caffeine reported a greater proportion of message-congruent thoughts than those in the placebo condition. Thus it was the increased thinking about the message

(continued on page 172)

The Effects of Caffeine on Persuasion, *cont.*

that occurred in the caffeine drinkers that produced the subsequent increased level of persuasion. In the high distraction case though, thinking about the message was prevented, and so few message-relevant thoughts were reported, and having consumed caffeine therefore failed to result in increased attitude change.

In another study, these same investigators (Martin et al., 2007) found evidence that people in the caffeine con-dition whose attitudes had been changed were then better able to resist subsequent persuasion attempts to the extent that the initial persuasive message had induced systematic processing of its contents. Perhaps, then, the next time you find yourself drinking coffee and watching TV, you'll keep in mind how susceptible to persuasion you might be if you take the time to listen and think carefully about the commercial messages you are receiving.

---

these instances, you are on the receiving end of threats to your freedom to decide for yourself. As a result, you may experience a growing level of annoyance and resentment. The final outcome: Not only do you resist their persuasion attempts, but you may also actually lean over backwards to adopt views opposite to those the would-be persuader wants you to adopt. Such behavior is an example of what social psychologists call **reactance**—a negative reaction to efforts by others to reduce our freedom by getting us to believe or do what they want (Brehm, 1966). Research indicates that in such situations, we really do often change our attitudes and behavior in the opposite direction from what we are being urged to believe or to do. Indeed, when we are feeling reactance, strong arguments in favor of attitude change can increase opposition compared to moderate or weak arguments (Fuegen & Brehm, 2004). The existence of reactance is one reason why hard-sell attempts at persuasion often fail. When individuals perceive such appeals as direct threats to their personal freedom (or their image of being an independent person), they are strongly motivated to resist.

Forewarning: Prior Knowledge of Persuasive Intent

When we watch television, we fully expect there to be commercials, and we know full well that these messages are designed to persuade us to purchase various products. Similarly, we know that when we listen to a political speech that the person delivering it is attempting to persuade us to vote for him or her. Does the fact that we know in advance about the persuasive intent behind such messages help us to resist them? Research on the effects of such advance knowledge—known as **forewarning**—indicates that it does (e.g., Cialdini & Petty, 1979; Johnson, 1994). When we know that a speech, taped message, or written appeal is designed to alter our views, we are often less likely to be affected by it than when we do not possess such knowledge. Why? Because forewarning influences several cognitive processes that play an important role in persuasion.

First, forewarning provides us with more opportunity to formulate counterarguments—those that refute the message—and that can lessen the message's impact. In addition, forewarning provides us with more time in which to recall relevant facts and information that may prove useful in refuting the persuasive message. Wood and Quinn (2003) found that forewarning was generally effective at increasing resistance and that simply expecting to receive a persuasive message (without actually even receiving it) can influence attitudes in a resistant direction. In many cases, then, it appears that to be forewarned is indeed to be forearmed where persuasion is concerned. But what if you are distracted between the time of the warning and receipt of the message to such an extent that it prevents you from forming counterarguments? Research has revealed that forewarning does not prevent persuasion when we are distracted; in this case, we are no more likely to resist the message than those not forewarned of the upcoming persuasive appeal.

reactance
Negative reactions to threats to one's personal freedom. Reactance often increases resistance to persuasion and can even produce negative attitude change or opposite to what was intended.

forewarning
Advance knowledge that one is about to become the target of an attempt at persuasion. Forewarning often increases resistance to the persuasion that follows.

There are instances, though, in which forewarnings can encourage attitude shifts toward the position being advocated in a message, but this effect appears to be a temporary response to our desire to defend our view of ourselves as not gullible or easily influenced (Quinn & Wood, 2004). In this case, because people make the attitude shift before they receive the persuasive appeal, they can convince themselves that they were not in fact influenced at all! We can be assured that this effect is motivated because people are especially likely to show it when they know that the "future persuader" is an expert or will be highly persuasive. Thus when people fully expect to be convinced, they prepare themselves by becoming "preconvinced" before being subjected to the persuasion attempt itself. Furthermore, in such cases, distraction after forewarning has been received, which presumably would inhibit thought, has no effect on the extent to which attitudes are changed in the direction of the expected message. Thus in this type of forewarning situation, people appear to be using a simple heuristic (e.g., I'll look stupid if I don't agree with what this expert says) and change their attitudes before they even receive the message.

Selective Avoidance of Persuasion Attempts

Still another way in which we resist attempts at persuasion is through **selective avoidance,** which is a tendency to direct our attention away from information that challenges our existing attitudes. Television viewing provides a clear illustration of the effects of selective avoidance. We do not simply sit in front of the television passively absorbing whatever the media decides to dish out. Instead, we channel surf, mute the commercials, tape our favorite programs, or simply cognitively tune out when confronted with information contrary to our views. The opposite effect occurs as well. When we encounter information that supports our views, we tend to give it our full attention. Such tendencies to ignore information that contradicts our attitudes, while actively attending to information consistent with them constitute two sides of what social psychologists term *selective exposure.* Such selectivity in what we make the focus of our attention helps ensure that many of our attitudes remain largely intact for long periods of time.

Actively Defending Our Attitudes: Counterarguing against the Competition

Ignoring or screening out information incongruent with our current views is certainly one way of resisting persuasion. But growing evidence suggests that in addition to this kind of passive defense of our attitudes, we also use a more active strategy as well: We actively counterargue against views that are contrary to our own (e.g., Eagly, Chen, Chaiken, & Shaw-Barnes, 1999). By doing so, it makes the opposing views more memorable than they would be otherwise, but it reduces their impact on our attitudes.

Eagly, Kulesa, Brannon, Shaw, and Hutson-Comeaux (2000) identified students as either pro-choice or pro-life in their attitudes toward abortion. These students were then exposed to persuasive messages that were either consistent with their attitudes or were contrary to their views. After hearing the messages, participants reported their attitudes toward abortion, the strength of their attitudes, and listed all the arguments in the message they could recall (a measure of memory). In addition, they listed the thoughts they had while listening to the message; this provided information on the extent to which they counterargued against the message when it was contrary to their own views.

As expected, the results indicated that the counterattitudinal message and the proattitudinal message were equally memorable. However participants reported thinking more systematically about the counterattitudinal message and reported having more oppositional thoughts about it—a clear sign that they were indeed counterarguing against this message.

selective avoidance
A tendency to direct attention away from information that challenges existing attitudes. Such avoidance increases resistance to persuasion.

Figure 5.17

Counterarguing against Counterattitudinal Messages

Participants reported having more oppositional thoughts about a counterattitudinal message, but they reported having more supportive thoughts about a proattitudinal message. These findings are consistent with the view that one reason we are so good at resisting persuasion is that we actively defend our attitudes against opposing views by counterarguing against them.

(*Source:* Based on data from Eagly, Kulesa, Brannon, Shaw, & Hutson-Comeaux, 2000.)

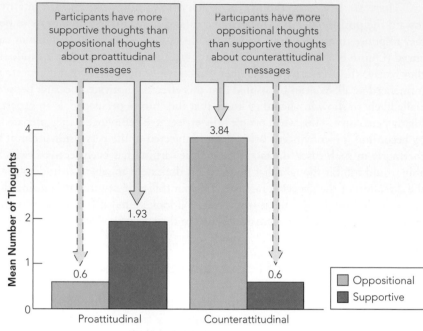

In contrast, they reported more supportive thoughts in response to the proattitudinal message (see Figure 5.17). Therefore one reason we are so good at resisting persuasion is that we not only ignore information that is inconsistent with our current views, but we also carefully process counterattitudinal input and argue actively against it. In a sense, we provide our own, strong defense against efforts to change our attitudes. In other words, exposure to arguments opposed to our attitudes can serve to strengthen the views we already hold, making us more resistant to subsequent efforts to change them.

Individual Differences in Resistance to Persuasion

We differ in their vulnerability to persuasion (Brinol, Rucker, Tormala, & Petty, 2004). Some people may be resistant because they are motivated to engage in counterarguing; they, therefore, would agree with items such as: "When someone challenges my beliefs, I enjoy disputing what they have to say," and "I take pleasure in arguing with those who have opinions that differ from my own." On the other hand, some people are relatively resistant to persuasion because they attempt to bolster their own beliefs when they encounter counterattitudinal messages. Those individuals would be likely to agree with items such as: "When someone has a different perspective on an issue, I like to make a mental list of the reasons in support of my perspective," and "When someone gives me a point of view that conflicts with my attitudes, I like to think about why my views are right for me." To determine whether scores on these two measures of resistance to persuasion were in fact predictive of attitude change in a persuasion situation, Brinol and others (2004) measured these self-beliefs and then gave participants an advertisement for "Brown's Department Store." These researchers found that indeed, scores on both these measures assessing different approaches to resisting persuasion predicted successful resistance to the message in the advertisement. Furthermore, the types of thoughts people have when they are confronted with a counterattitudinal message are predicted by their self-perceived preference for resisting persuasion by either counterarguing or bolstering their initial attitude position. So, apparently we do know something about how we deal with attempts to persuade us, and we use our favored techniques quite effectively.

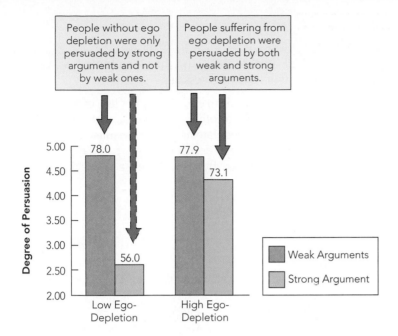

Figure 5.18
Evidence That Ego Depletion Can Make Weak Ideas Persuasive
When we're not ego depleted, we can differentiate between weak and strong arguments and can only be persuaded by strong arguments. In contrast, when we're suffering from ego depletion, we fail to differentiate between strong and weak arguments and can therefore be persuaded by both.

(*Source:* Based on data from Wheeler, Brinol, & Hermann, 2007).

Ego Depletion Can Undermine Resistance

As we just described, your ability to resist persuasion can result from successful counter-arguing against a persuasive message or consciously considering why your initial attitude is better than the position you are being asked to adopt. Factors that make either of these strategies more difficult—because they undermine our ability to engage in **self-regulation**—could certainly undermine our ability to resist persuasion. To the extent that we have a limited capacity to self-regulate (i.e., to engage our willpower in controlling our own thinking), prior expenditure of these limited resources could leave us vulnerable to persuasion. For example, when we are tired, have failed to self-regulate on a prior task, or otherwise are in a state of **ego depletion,** we may simply acquiesce when confronted with a counterattitudinal message—that is, we will show attitude change.

To test this possibility, Wheeler, Brinol, and Hermann (2007) gave participants an easy or difficult first task, with the difficult task being designed to deplete their self-regulation resources. Subsequently, participants were given a weak or strong message arguing in favor of mandatory comprehensive examinations for graduation—a topic all of these students were initially strongly against. Did ego depletion result in people being more persuaded by bad (weak) arguments? The answer, as shown in Figure 5.18, was a resounding yes. The weak arguments were unpersuasive to the people with no ego depletion, but they were just as persuasive to those who suffered from ego depletion as were the strong arguments. For participants in the nondepleted condition, strong arguments were more persuasive than weak ones, as you might expect.

Examination of the participants' thoughts in response to the message verified that the participants who were nondepleted had more favorable thoughts about the message when the arguments were strong compared to when it was weak. In contrast, the thoughts of the participants who were ego depleted were equally as favorable in the strong and weak arguments case. This research implies that we are more vulnerable to persuasion when our self-regulatory resources have been depleted. Perhaps we especially need to watch out for would-be persuaders when we're depressed, have failed on some task, or have generally had a bad day trying to diet because that may be precisely when we'll agree with their weak message that chocolate is a health food.

> ℭ*Principles to Remember*
> We show the greatest resistance to persuasion when we're aware that we're targets, and we either avoid or systematically argue against the message we're presented with.

self-regulation
Limited capacity to engage our willpower and control our own thinking and emotions.

ego depletion
When our capacity to self-regulate has been reduced because of prior expenditures of limited resources.

KeyPoints

- Several factors contribute to our ability to resist persuasion. One such factor is reactance—negative reactions to efforts by others to reduce or limit our personal freedom, which can produce greater overall opposition to the message content.

- Resistance to persuasion is often increased by forewarning, which is the knowledge that someone will be trying to changes our attitudes, and by selective avoidance, which is the tendency to avoid exposure to information that contradicts our views.

- In addition, when we are exposed to persuasive messages that are contrary to our existing views, we actively counterargue against the information they contain. This is a critical means by which our resistance to persuasion is increased.

- There are also individual differences in ability to resist persuasion. Those include consciously counterarguing messages we receive and bolstering our

initial attitude position when confronted with a counterattitudinal message.

- Ego depletion from attempts to exert our willpower on another task can undermine our ability to self-regulate and resist persuasion. When suffering from ego depletion, we are equally likely to be persuaded by both strong and weak messages.

Think About It

Ego depletion can undermine resistance to persuasion—by decreasing our scrutiny of the quality of a message. It may be the case then that we're exposed to the most persuasion—TV watching—precisely when many of us are least equipped to resist, that is, at the end of the day, when we are likely to be suffering from ego depletion the most.

Cognitive Dissonance: What It Is and How Do We Manage It?

When we first introduced the question of whether, and to what extent, attitudes and behavior are linked, we noted that in many situations, there is a sizeable gap between what we feel on the inside (positive or negative reactions to some object or issue) and what we show on the outside. For instance, I have a neighbor who recently purchased a huge SUV. I have strong negative attitudes toward such giant vehicles because they get low gas mileage, add to pollution, and block my view while driving. But when my neighbor asked how I liked her new vehicle, I hesitated and then said "Nice, very nice," with as much enthusiasm as I could muster. She is a good neighbor who looks after my cats when I'm away, and I did not want to offend her. But I certainly felt uncomfortable when I uttered these words. Why? Because in this situation I was aware that my behavior was not consistent with my attitudes (e.g., that essentially I was lying), and this is an uncomfortable state to find ourselves in. Social psychologists term my negative reaction **cognitive dissonance**—an unpleasant state that occurs when we notice that various attitudes we hold or our attitudes and our behavior are somehow inconsistent. As you will see, when we cannot justify our attitude-inconsistent behavior (but note that I could do so by saying how important it was to not offend my neighbor) we may end up changing our own attitudes.

Most people experience cognitive dissonance each day. Any time you become aware of saying what you don't really believe (e.g., praise something you don't actually like, "just to be polite"), make a difficult decision that requires you to reject an alternative you find attractive, or discover that something you've invested effort or money in is not as good as you expected, you are likely to experience dissonance. In all these situations, there is a gap between your attitudes and your actions, and such gaps tend to make us uncomfortable. Most important from the present perspective, cognitive dissonance can sometimes lead us to change our own attitudes, to shift them so that they are consistent with our overt behav-

cognitive dissonance
An internal state that results when individuals notice inconsistency between two or more attitudes or between their attitudes and their behavior.

ior, even in the absence of any strong external pressure to do so. We'll look closely at cognitive dissonance and its intriguing implications for attitude change, but first we'll describe the origins of this perspective in *Building the Science: Classics of Social Psychology* on page 178.

As we have described, dissonance theory began with a reasonable idea: We often find inconsistency between our actions and attitudes uncomfortable. But how does any resulting dissonance get resolved? First, we can change either our attitudes or alter our behavior so that they are more consistent with each other. Second, we can reduce cognitive dissonance by acquiring new information (justifications) that supports our behavior. Recall our chapter opening involving students potentially cheating on an exam. If students were induced to do so and thereby violate their attitudes toward themselves as honest people, there might be considerable need to justify their actions. Many possible justifications could be used: "I did it just this once so my behavior doesn't really violate my attitude toward myself," "If I don't pass this course, some terrible outcome will befall me," "It was really my roommate's fault, because her party kept me up so I couldn't study," or "Everybody else is doing it, so they'll have an unfair advantage in the final grading." To the extent that they are unable to sufficiently justify their own behavior, students' attitude toward cheating might be modified (and become more favorable). Or many different forms of justifications for the cheating behavior could be used to cope with the dissonance that is aroused when confronted with the fact that our behavior is inconsistent with our moral principles. The third option for managing dissonance is to decide that the inconsistency actually doesn't matter; in other words, we can engage in trivialization, concluding that the attitudes or behaviors in question are not important so any inconsistency between them is of no importance (Simon, Greenberg, & Brehm, 1995).

All of these strategies can be viewed as direct methods of dissonance reduction: They focus on the attitude-behavior-discrepancy that is causing the dissonance. Research by Steele (1988) and others (e.g., Steele & Lui, 1983) also indicates that dissonance can be reduced via indirect means, which means that the basic discrepancy between the attitude and behavior are left intact, but the unpleasant or negative feelings generated by dissonance are still reduced. Adoption of indirect tactics to reduce dissonance is most likely when the attitude-behavior discrepancy involves important attitudes or self-beliefs (so trivialization isn't feasible). Under these conditions, when we experience dissonance we may not focus so much on reducing the gap between our attitudes and behavior, but instead on other methods that will allow us to feel good about ourselves despite the gap (Steele, Spencer, & Lynch, 1993).

Specifically, we engage in self-affirmation—restoring positive self-evaluations that are threatened by the dissonance (e.g., Elliot & Devine, 1994; Tesser, Martin, & Cornell, 1996). This can be accomplished by focusing on positive self-attributes—good things about ourselves. For instance, when I experienced dissonance as a result of saying nice things about my neighbor's giant new SUV, even though I am strongly against such vehicles, I could remind myself that I am a considerate person. By contemplating positive aspects of myself, it can help to reduce the discomfort produced by my failure to act in a way that was consistent with my pro-environmental (and anti-SUV) attitudes. However we choose to reduce dissonance, whether it be through indirect tactics or direct strategies that are aimed at reducing the attitude-behavior discrepancy, we all find strategies to help us deal with the discomfort that comes from being aware of discrepancies between our attitudes and behavior.

Dissonance and Attitude Change: The Effects of Induced Compliance

We can engage in attitude-discrepant behavior for many reasons, and some of these are more compelling than others. When will our attitudes change more: When there are good reasons for engaging in attitude-discrepant behavior or when there is little justification for

BUILDING THE SCIENCE
CLASSICS OF SOCIAL PSYCHOLOGY

Famous Cognitive Dissonance Studies: When Less Leads to More Self-Persuasion

The ideas reflected in cognitive dissonance theory first came to Leon Festinger as he read about a group in Chicago who were convinced that the end of the world was near, and in fact, a date was set a for its demise. Festinger speculated about what would happen when the group's prophecy failed, and the world did not end on the specified date. According to cognitive dissonance theory, the group was faced with two dissonant cognitions: "we predicted the end of the world on a certain date" and "that date has undeniably passed, and the world has not ended." After disconfirmation of the prophecy, if cognitive dissonance theory was correct, the group members would not conclude their belief in the prophecy had been wrong, but instead they would seek to add followers to reaffirm the rightness of their beliefs.

Festinger reasoned that adding followers to the group would provide a consonant cognition: Great numbers of faithful believers couldn't be wrong. As we saw previously in the section on attitude certainty, adding numbers of believers is likely to heighten consensus, thereby increasing the perceived correctness of their attitudes toward the prophecy. When the date had passed, the group reported that the Earth had been spared because of their strong faith, and that they should begin an urgent search to add people to the group of believers (Festinger, Riecken, & Schachter, 1956).

The first formal test of his theory of cognitive dissonance gave rise to a classic paper in social psychology (Festinger & Carlsmith, 1959). Participants in this experiment were first asked to engage in an extremely boring series of tasks—such as turning pegs in a board full of holes. After the task was over, the experimenter made an unusual request: He told participants that one of the research assistants had not shown up that day and asked if they would please "fill in" by greeting the next participant and telling that person that the task to be performed was an interesting one. Festinger told half of these participants that they would be paid twenty dollars if they would tell this fib to the waiting participant, and the other half were told that they would receive one dollar for doing so. After doing the favor of telling the person waiting the fib about the experiment, the participants were asked to report their own attitudes toward the boring tasks (i.e., rate how interesting the tasks were).

The participants who were paid twenty dollars rated the task as less interesting than participants who were paid one dollar. If you were rewarded more generously for praising the task, shouldn't you feel more positively about it? No! To understand why not, let's look at the psychological forces at play in this situation: Most people don't think of themselves as liars, but the participants had indeed been induced to lie to a peer. And, though they were lured into it, they nevertheless endured some discomfort over the conflict between two inconsistent cognitions. When you were paid twenty dollars, you would have had a justification for your lying but not if you were paid one dollar to tell that same fib. So, the problem is that, if given insufficient justification for your behavior, a situation that was more true in the one-dollar condition (than the twenty-dollar condition) of the experiment, there is a greater need to reduce your dissonance. In the one-dollar case, the money explanation for your behavior is not convincing to yourself.

What do people do to reduce their greater cognitive dissonance in the one-dollar condition? Easy. They change the cognition that is causing the problem. Because in this example, you can't change the lie you told (i.e., deny your behavior), you can decide it wasn't really a lie at all by "making" the boring task more interesting and reporting your attitude as being more positive in the one-dollar condition than in the twenty-dollar condition.

Why is this rather simple experiment such a classic in social psychology? If you believed that there is no such thing as cognitive dissonance, you would have to expect that a larger reward would produce a more positive response on the questionnaire than would the small reward. So, why was it so surprising that some unseen mental process might be operating here and produce the opposite result? Because, at that time, B. F. Skinner's (1938) behaviorism perspective claimed behavior is controlled solely by rewards and that punishments reigned. Cognitive operations that were not directly observable were not considered valid causes of behavior. But Festinger's research showed just the opposite of what a simple operant conditioning model would have predicted, and with this study, he ushered in an era in which mental operations involving people's self-images could be postulated and studied.

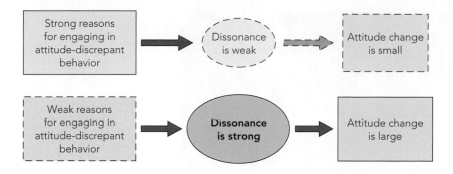

Figure 5.19
Why Smaller
Inducements Often Lead
to More Attitude
Change after Attitude-
Discrepant Behavior
*When we have strong reasons
for engaging in attitude-
discrepant behavior, we
experience relatively weak
dissonance and do not change
our attitudes. In contrast,
when we have little apparent
justification for engaging in the
attitude-discrepant behavior,
we will experience stronger
dissonance and greater pressure
to change our attitudes. The
result is that less justification
leads to more dissonance and
more attitude change following
attitude-discrepant behavior.*

doing so? As we already noted, cognitive dissonance theory argues that dissonance will be stronger when we have few reasons for engaging in attitude-discrepant behavior. This is so because when we have little justification and therefore cannot explain away our actions to ourselves, dissonance will be quite intense.

As Figure 5.19 illustrates, cognitive dissonance theory predicts that it will be easier to change our attitudes by offering us just barely enough to get us to engage in the attitude-discrepant behavior. This ensures that we will feel there is little justification for our behavior, while additional reasons or rewards would help to reduce dissonance and result in little subsequent attitude change. Social psychologists sometimes refer to this surprising prediction as the **less-leads-to-more effect,** that is, less reasons or rewards for an action often leads to greater attitude change, and it has been confirmed in many studies (Harmon-Jones, 2000; Leippe & Eisenstadt, 1994). Because such conditions do often exist, the strategy of offering us just barely enough to induce us to say or do things contrary to our true attitudes can often be an effective technique for inducing attitude change. Indeed, the more money or other rewards that are offered to us to behave in a particular way provides a justification for our actions and can undermine the likelihood that attitude change will occur. Thus strong forms of coercion will undermine dissonance. In addition, small rewards lead to greater attitude change only when we believe that we were personally responsible for both the chosen course of action and any negative effects it produced. For instance, when ordered by an authority to do a particular behavior we may not feel either responsible for our actions or dissonance when the action we performed is inconsistent with our personal attitudes.

When Dissonance Is a Tool for Beneficial Changes in Behavior

- People who don't wear safety belts are much more likely to die in auto accidents than those who do.

- People who smoke are much more likely to suffer from lung cancer and heart disease than those who don't.

- People who engage in unprotected sex are much more likely than those who engage in safe sex to contract dangerous diseases, including AIDS.

Most of us know these statements are true, and our attitudes are generally favorable toward using seatbelts, quitting smoking, and engaging in safe sex (Carey, Morrison-Beedy, & Johnson, 1997). Despite having positive attitudes, they are often not translated into overt actions: Some people continue to drive without seatbelts, to smoke, and to have unprotected sex. To address these major social problems, what's needed is not so much a change in attitudes as shifts in overt behavior. Can dissonance be used to promote beneficial

less-leads-to-more effect
The fact that offering
individuals small rewards for
engaging in counterattitudinal
behavior often produces more
dissonance, and so more
attitude change, than offering
them larger rewards.

Figure 5.20
Using Hypocrisy to
Change Behavior
*When we are made to confront
our own hypocrisy, most choose
to reduce such dissonance
through direct means (by
changing our behavior). In
contrast, when we are asked to
think about reasons why people
in general do not act according
to their own beliefs, many
choose to reduce dissonance
and feel better about ourselves
via an indirect route, and we
do not change our behavior.*

(*Source:* Based on data provided
by Stone, Wiegand, Cooper, &
Aronson, 1997.)

behavioral changes? A growing body of evidence suggests that it can (Batson, Kobrynowicz, Dinnerstein, Kampf, & Wilson, 1997; Gibbons, Eggleston, & Benthin, 1997; Stone et al., 1994), especially when it is used to generate feelings of **hypocrisy**—publicly advocating some attitude and then making known to the person that they have acted in a way that is inconsistent with their own attitudes. Such feelings might be sufficiently intense that only actions that reduce dissonance directly, by inducing behavioral change, may be effective. These predictions concerning the possibility of dissonance-induced behavior change have been tested in several studies.

Stone, Wiegand, Cooper, and Aronson (1997) asked participants to prepare a videotape advocating the use of condoms (safe sex) to avoid contracting AIDS. Next participants were asked to think about reasons why they themselves hadn't used condoms in the past (personal reasons) or reasons why people in general sometimes fail to use condoms (normative reasons that didn't center on their own behavior). The researchers predicted that dissonance would be maximized in the personal reasons condition, where participants had to come face-to-face with their own hypocrisy. Then all the people in the study were given a choice between a direct means of reducing dissonance—purchasing condoms at a reduced price—or an indirect means of reducing dissonance—making a donation to a program designed to aid homeless people. The results indicated that when participants had been asked to focus on the reasons why they didn't engage in safe sex in the past, an overwhelming majority chose to purchase condoms, suggesting that their behavior in the future will be different—the direct route to dissonance reduction. In contrast, when asked to think about reasons why people in general didn't engage in safe sex, more actually chose the indirect route to dissonance reduction—a donation to an aid-the-homeless project—and didn't change their behavior (see Figure 5.20).

These findings suggest that using dissonance to make our own hypocrisy known can indeed be a powerful tool for changing our behavior in desirable ways. For maximum effectiveness, however, such procedures must involve several elements: The people in question must publicly advocate the desired behaviors (e.g., using condoms, wearing safety belts), must be induced to think about their own behavioral failures in the past, and they must be given access to direct means for reducing their dissonance (i.e., a method for changing their behavior). When these conditions are met, dissonance can bring about beneficial changes in behavior.

> **Principles to Remember**
> Inconsistency in our attitudes and our behavior can induce self-persuasion, unless there is a perception that our behavioral inconsistency was justified.

hypocrisy
Publicly advocating some
attitudes or behavior and then
acting in a way that is
inconsistent with these attitudes
or behavior.

KeyPoints

- Cognitive dissonance is an arousing state that occurs when we notice discrepancies between our attitudes and our behavior. Experiencing dissonance does indeed produce negative affect and attitude change.

- Dissonance often occurs in situations involving forced compliance, in which we are minimally induced by external factors to say or do things that are inconsistent with our true attitudes. Dissonance can lead to attitude change when we have reasons that are barely sufficient to get us to engage in attitude-discrepant behavior. Stronger reasons (or larger rewards) produce less attitude change: This is sometimes referred to as the less-leads-to-more effect.

- Dissonance can be reduced directly (e.g., changing our attitudes) or via an indirect method, such as self-affirmation on some other dimension.

- Dissonance induced through hypocrisy—inducing individuals to advocate certain attitudes or behaviors and then reminding them that their own behavior has not always been consistent with these attitudes—can be a powerful tool for inducing beneficial changes in behavior.

Think About It

How can we use cognitive dissonance to persuade others to change their attitudes? As you saw in the induced-compliance paradigm, the "soft touch" is most likely to prevent people from justifying their behavior and thereby avoiding attitude change. This implies that, whether as teacher, parent, or boss, we are seeking to change the attitude of our student, child, or coworker, using the weakest inducement possible to get them to comply will be the most effective at bringing about change.

SUMMARY AND REVIEW

- Attitudes are evaluations of any aspect of the social world. Often, attitudes are explicit—consciously accessible and easy to report. Attitudes can be implicit though, and therefore not consciously reportable or controllable. Attitudes are acquired from other people through social learning. Such learning can involve classical conditioning, instrumental conditioning, or observational learning. In fact, attitudes can be formed via subliminal conditioning, which occurs in the absence of conscious awareness of the stimuli involved, and mere exposure. Attitudes are also formed on the basis of social comparison—our tendency to compare ourselves with others to determine whether our view of social reality is or is not correct. To be similar to others we like, we accept the attitudes that they hold, to the extent that we identify with that group.

- Several factors affect the strength of the relationship between attitudes and behavior. Situational constraints may prevent us from expressing our attitudes overtly, including concerns about what others may think of us. People often show pluralistic ignorance, that is, erroneously believing that others have different attitudes than we do, which can limit our willingness to express our attitudes in public. Several aspects of attitudes themselves also moderate the attitude-behavior link. These include factors related to attitude strength: including the extremity of our attitude position, the certainty with which our attitudes are held, and whether we have personal experience with the attitude object. All of these factors can make our attitudes more accessible and therefore likely to guide our behavior.

- Attitudes can influence behavior through two different mechanisms. According to the theory of reasoned action and theory of planned behavior, when we can give careful thought to our attitudes, intentions derived from our attitudes strongly predict behavior. According to the attitude-to-behavior process model, in situations where our behavior is more spontaneous and we don't engage

In such deliberate thought, attitudes influence behavior by shaping our perception and interpretation of the situation.

- Early research on persuasion—efforts to change attitudes through the use of messages—focused primarily on the source (e.g., communicator credibility, attractiveness), the message (e.g., fear appeals; one-sided versus two-sided argument presentation), and the audience (e.g., young versus elderly). More recent research has sought to understand the cognitive processes that play a role in persuasion. Such research suggests that we process persuasive messages in two distinct ways: through systematic processing, which involves careful attention to message content, or through heuristic processing, which involves the use of mental shortcuts (e.g., experts are usually right). Recent research suggests that consuming caffeine increases the extent to which people are persuaded by increasing their ability to systematically process the message contents.

- Several factors contribute to such people's ability to resist persuasion. One such factor is reactance—negative reactions to efforts by others to reduce or limit our personal freedom. When we feel reactance, we often change their attitudes in the opposite direction from that advocated. This is one reason why the hard sell can be counterproductive.

- Resistance to persuasion is often increased by forewarning—the knowledge that someone is trying to change our attitudes. This typically gives us a chance to counterargue against the expected persuasive appeal and thereby resist the message content when it is presented. Forewarning does not prevent persuasion though when we are distracted and therefore unable to expend effort refuting the message in advance.

- We also maintain our current attitudes by selective avoidance—the tendency to overlook or disregard information that contradicts our existing views. Likewise, we give close attention to information that supports our views, and by means of selective exposure, we will actively seek out information that is consistent with our existing attitudes.

- When exposed to information that is inconsistent with our views, we can actively counterargue against them. The more we have oppositional thoughts when exposed to a counterattitudinal message, the more we are able to resist being persuaded by it. In a sense, we provide our own defense against persuasion attempts. We also differ in our vulnerability to persuasion. Some are aware that they use counterarguing, and others know they attempt to bolster their original views when they are in persuasion situations.

- Our ability to resist persuasion can depend on our own psychological state—whether we are ego depleted or not. When we suffer from ego depletion, we experience greater difficulty self-regulating, which can undermine our ability to resist persuasion. Recent research has revealed that when we're ego depleted, we do not differentiate between messages with strong and weak arguments and are equally persuaded by both. In contrast, when we're not ego depleted, we're not persuaded by weak arguments only by strong arguments.

- Cognitive dissonance is an unpleasant state that occurs when we notice discrepancies between our attitudes and our behavior. Recent findings indicate that dissonance does indeed produce negative affect. Festinger and Carlsmith's (1959) classic study—in contrast to the radical behaviorism, which was the prominent theoretical perspective of the day—revealed that cognitive inconsistency itself could instigate change. In contrast, to a behavioral perspective, stronger reasons (or larger rewards) can produce less attitude change—the less-leads-to-more effect—and smaller rewards (because they leave us feeling less justified in our inconsistency) could produce more attitude change.

- Dissonance often occurs in situations involving forced compliance—ones in which we are induced by external factors to say or do things that are inconsistent with our true attitudes. In such situations, attitude change is maximal when we have reasons that are barely sufficient to get us to engage in attitude-discrepant behavior. Other means of coping with dissonance, besides changing our attitudes, include adding justifications, trivialization, or concluding that the inconsistency doesn't matter. Dissonance can also be dealt with by use of indirect strategies, that is, to the extent that we can be affirmed by focusing on some other positive feature of ourselves, then dissonance can be reduced without changing our attitudes. Dissonance that is induced by making us aware of our own hypocrisy can result in behavioral changes.

Key Terms

attitude-to-behavior process model (p. 164)

attitudes (p. 148)

central route (to persuasion) (p. 168)

classical conditioning (p. 151)

cognitive dissonance (p. 176)

conditioned stimulus (p. 150)

ego depletion (p. 175)

elaboration-likelihood model (ELM) (p. 169)

explicit attitudes (p. 148)

fear appeals (p. 167)

forewarning (p. 172)

habit (p. 165)

heuristic processing (p. 168)

hypocrisy (p. 180)

implicit attitudes (p. 148)

implementation plan (p. 163)

instrumental conditioning (p. 153)

less-leads-to-more effect (p. 179)

mere exposure (p. 152)

observational learning (p. 154)

peripheral route (to persuasion) (p. 168)

persuasion (p. 165)

pluralistic ignorance (p. 158)

prevention focus (p. 149)

promotion focus (p. 149)

reactance (p. 172)

reference groups (p. 154)

selective avoidance (p. 173)

self-regulation (p. 175)

social comparison (p. 154)

social learning (p. 150)

subliminal conditioning (p. 152)

systematic processing (p. 168)

theory of planned behavior (p. 162)

theory of reasoned action (p. 162)

unconditioned stimulus (p. 150)

Connections
INTEGRATING SOCIAL PSYCHOLOGY

In this chapter, you read about . . .	In other chapters, you will find related discussions of . . .
the role of social learning in attitude formation	the role of social learning in several forms of social behavior—attraction (Chapter 8), helping (Chapter 10), and aggression (Chapter 11).
persuasion and resistance to persuasion	other techniques for changing attitudes and behavior and why they are effective or ineffective (Chapter 9), the use of persuasive techniques in health-related messages, and leadership (Chapter 12).
cognitive dissonance	the role of cognitive dissonance in various attitudes and forms of social behavior, for example job satisfaction (Chapter 12).
the role of automatic and controlled or systematic information processing	effects on impression formation (Chapter 3) and prejudice and discrimination (Chapter 6).

Stereotyping, Prejudice, and Discrimination:
The Causes, Effects, and Cures

CHAPTER OUTLINE

- **How Members of Different Groups Perceive Inequality**
- **The Nature and Origins of Stereotyping**
  Stereotyping: Beliefs about Social Groups
  MAKING SENSE OF COMMON SENSE: A SOCIAL PSYCHOLOGICAL PERSPECTIVE—THE GENDER OR RACE CARD: TOO EASY TO PLAY, OR HARDER THAN YOU THINK?
  Can We Conclude that Stereotyping Is Absent When Members of Different Groups Are Rated the Same?
  Can We Be Victims of Stereotyping and Not Even Recognize It?: The Case of Single People
  Why Do People Form and Use Stereotypes?
- **Prejudice and Discrimination: Feelings and Actions toward Social Groups**
  The Origins of Prejudice: Contrasting Perspectives

BUILDING THE SCIENCE: CLASSICS OF SOCIAL PSYCHOLOGY—WHAT CAUSES GROUPS TO BE PREJUDICED TOWARD OTHER GROUPS AND IS PREJUDICE INEVITABLE?
  Discrimination: Prejudice in Action
  SOCIAL PSYCHOLOGY: WHAT IT TELLS US ABOUT...WHEN OUR GROUP HAS DONE HARM TO OTHERS
- **Why Prejudice Is Not Inevitable: Techniques for Countering Its Effects**
  On Learning Not to Hate
  The Potential Benefits of Contact
  Recategorization: Changing the Boundaries
  The Benefits of Guilt for Prejudice Reduction
  Can We Learn to Just Say "No" to Stereotypes?
  Social Influence as a Means of Reducing Prejudice

Many in the United States believe that we've moved some distance away from blatant expressions of racial prejudice. In fact, some contend that we've made considerable strides toward being a "color-blind" society. But there's evidence that some features of prejudice have become woven into the fabric of our culture and are therefore still with us. The content of stereotypes and the targets of prejudice may have changed, but the origins of these psychological phenomena may not be so different at all.

Consider the 2007 incident involving six Imams—Islamic religious leaders who are also U.S. citizens—attempting to return home to Phoenix on a U.S. Airways flight out of Chicago O'Hare airport. According to newspaper reports, some of the Imams were wearing religious garments, and they prayed together in the concourse before their flight. On the airplane, they split into pairs to take their seats, and a couple of them asked for seat-belt extensions. Some passengers became concerned about these behaviors and told the flight attendants. As the word spread throughout the airplane, concern escalated to fear. These behavioral cues seemed indicative of terrorists, and possibly reminiscent of the 9/11 hijackers. Because we've had time to reflect, these behaviors may seem less associated with terrorists and more likely typical of Muslims or religious leaders (and of being overweight, hence the request for seatbelt extensions).

As we'll make clear, beliefs about groups can affect perceptual processes when we encounter members of those groups. We are vulnerable to psychological processes that occur spontaneously and nonconsciously, causing us to see and hear things that on videotape replay would show were ambiguous at best.

On September 12, 2002, a year and a day after 9/11, Eunice Stone was sitting with her son in a Shoney's restaurant in Georgia. She heard three men of Middle-Eastern descent talking about 9/11, laughing about those deaths, and mentioning another attack planned for the next day. Stone recounts the exchange:

> The bearded man said, "They mourned on 9/11, and they are going to mourn again on 9/13." One of the men asked, "Do you think we have enough to bring it down?" Another replied, "If we don't have enough to bring it down, I have contacts and we can get enough to bring it down."

To Stone, "That meant they were planning to blow up something."

Later, the three men, who were medical students traveling to Miami, told police that they had been talking about bringing a car down to Miami but denied saying anything about 9/11 or 9/13, whether in jest or seriously. During that first anniversary of 9/11, anyone watching TV was subjected to twenty-four-hour imagery of the World Trade Center and Pentagon sites and photos of the nineteen 9/11 hijackers. Stone, primed with those images and encountering those young Arab American men, really did think she heard what she reported. But the facts are compelling that the three young medical students did not say what she reported.

So are Eunice Stone and the U.S. Airways passengers all anti-Arab racists? We can't know. But we can be almost positive that before 9/11, none of these Arab Americans would have been objects of suspicion to be forcibly detained. After 9/11, they were associated with terrorist hijackers. Might we assume their accusers were vulnerable to misperceptions because of their negative emotions toward that particular group—is this what current research suggests? Current research confirms this, but psychological theory also leads us to consider whether these were ordinary people responding to social cues provided by their culture.

A cursory look at U.S. culture suggests that we are currently concerned about Latino illegal immigrants (a threat to jobs), rappers (a threat to morals), or gays (a threat to marriage), and especially the threat of foreign terrorists. Images like those in Figure 6.1 of the twin towers aflame, pictures of the nineteen Arab hijackers, and anti-American sentiment in the Arab world may help to construct a reality that in both the cases we've described was one that caused genuine anxiety. These images and one-year anniversary tributes created a scenario that subconsciously put people on edge and primed them to categorize people in that context based on these images (Adams, Biernat, Branscombe, Crandall, & Wrightsman, 2007).

Figure 6.1
Does Perceiving Threat toward Us Increase Our Prejudice toward Them?
These vivid images of the devastating effects of prejudice against the United States, and the 9/11 Al Qaeda perpetrators in particular, are highly memorable and become linked in our minds to all people of Middle-Eastern descent or even all nine hundred million Muslims around the world.

At some time or other, everyone comes face to face with **prejudice**—dislike based on group membership. We can experience prejudice as its targets; we can observe it in the treatment of members of another group as in the opening examples; or we can recognize prejudice in ourselves as we realize our actions toward some groups are less positive compared to how we respond to members of our own group. We know that people are more concerned about prejudice and injustice when it is directed toward "innocent victims," which almost always is how we'll see members of our own group compared to those who suffer but are members of out-groups (Correia, Vala, & Aguiar, 2007). As you'll see in this chapter, the roots of such prejudice can be found in the cognitive and emotional processes that social psychologists have measured with reference to a number of different social groups.

Prejudice is not limited to extreme forms, such as what motivated Al Qaeda's attack on the World Trade Center on September 11, 2001. Even if less extreme, prejudice based on category memberships, including age, marital status, occupation, gender, religion, language spo-

prejudice
Negative emotional responses based on group membership.

ken, sexual orientation, or body weight, to name just a few, can have important effects on its victims. Discriminatory treatment based on such category memberships can be blatant, or it can be relatively subtle (Devine, Plant, & Blair, 2001; Swim & Campbell, 2001). Prejudice may be perceived by its perpetrators as legitimate and justified (Crandall, Eshleman, & O'Brien, 2002), or it can be seen as illegitimate and something that individuals should actively strive to prevent, both in themselves and others (Maddux, Barden, Brewer, & Petty, 2005; Monteith, Ashburn-Nardo, Voils, & Czopp, 2002). In other words, all forms of differential treatment based on group membership are not perceived and responded to in the same way.

In this chapter we begin by considering how our own group membership affects our perceptions of social events. Then we examine the nature of **stereotypes** and consider how it is related to **discrimination.** We'll emphasize gender stereotyping in that discussion, in part because it is a group membership in which we all have a stake. Although there is a high degree of interpersonal contact between men and women, which tends to be absent in other cases such as racial and religious groups (Jackman, 1994), gender-based discrimination continues to affect a substantial proportion of the population by blocking women's progress in the workplace. We then turn to perspectives on the origins and nature of prejudice and consider why it so persistent across time and social groups. Last we'll explore various strategies that have been used to successfully change stereotypes and reduce prejudice.

How Members of Different Groups Perceive Inequality

The perception of prejudice depends on whether we are a member of the targeted group or the group perpetrating the unequal treatment. These groups significantly differ in their assessments of the severity and legitimacy of discrimination and the degree of progress they think has been made towards its reduction. For example, Caucasians and African Americans show substantial differences in how much discrimination they perceive to be operating in housing and employment settings (Sigelman & Welch, 1991), with Caucasians tending to perceive less racism in many everyday events than do African Americans (Johnson, Simmons, Trawalter, Ferguson, & Reed, 2003). Likewise, in terms of perceptions of how much progress has been made in moving toward equality, national surveys consistently find that Caucasian respondents perceive there to have been "a lot of progress," whereas African American respondents are more likely to perceive that there has been "not much progress." In this sense, there continues to be a racial divide in the United States. Is one group correct and one group incorrect in their perceptions? How are we to explain such different subjective perceptions and evaluations of the same events and outcomes?

Accounting for these differences involves consideration of the implications that the groups see in any potential change in relations between them. According to Kahneman and Tversky's (1984) prospect theory (for which the 2002 Nobel Prize in economics was awarded), people are **risk averse:** We weigh possible losses more heavily than equivalent potential gains. For example, we see losing one dollar as more negative than we see gaining one dollar is positive.

How might being risk averse affect racial perceptions of social changes that could result in greater racial equality? Let's assume that Caucasians will perceive greater equality from the standpoint of a potential loss for their group, as compared to their historically privileged position. Caucasians will therefore respond more negatively to additional movement toward equality and will also suppose that more change has already occurred, than will African Americans. In contrast, if we assume that African Americans are likely to see greater equality as a potential gain for them, as compared to their historically disadvantaged position, then change toward increased equality will be experienced as a positive. But if a possible loss evokes more intense emotion than a possible gain does, then increased equality should be more negative for Caucasians than the same increased equality is positive for

---

stereotypes
Beliefs about social groups in terms of the traits or characteristics that they are believed to share. Stereotypes are cognitive frameworks that influence the processing of social information.

discrimination
Differential (usually negative) behaviors directed toward members of different social groups.

risk averse
We weigh possible losses more heavily than equivalent potential gains. As a result, we respond more negatively to changes that are framed as potential losses than positively to changes that are framed as potential gains.

Figure 6.2
Hate Groups on the
Internet Claim Their
Group Is Losing Ground
*Hate groups incite concerns about
their own group by claiming they
are "losing ground," and that the
targeted group is illegitimately
gaining (and conspiring) to
undermine them.*

African Americns. Recent research has revealed that Caucasians, who are highly identified with their racial group, do respond negatively when confronted with a possible loss of their race-based privileges, and may respond with increased modern racism (Branscombe, Schmitt, & Schiffhauer, 2007). Indeed, even a cursory look at racist Web sites, such as that shown in Figure 6.2, reveals that such hate groups do consistently frame the state of existing race relations as "White people are losing ground." This is, of course, not unlike how the Nazis and other anti-Semitic groups (again, all too easily found on the Internet) framed German, and now Christian, losses (and Jewish gains).

Although racist hate group members are not typical Caucasians, perhaps this tendency to see social change as a zero-sum outcome in which "we are losing" plays a role in explaining the consistent discrepancies that are observed between minority and majority perceptions. To test this explanation, Eibach and Keegan (2006) had Caucasian and minority participants create a graph depicting change in the racial composition of students in U.S. universities from 1960 to the present, in one of three forms. In the "minority gains and Caucasian losses" form, the percentages they were asked to insert showed the percent of Caucasians going down and the exact same percentage increase in favor of minorities. In a "Caucasian losses only" form, the students simply showed a reduction in the percentage of Caucasians, and in the "Minorities gain" form, they only showed an increase in the percentage of minorities at U.S. universities.

In both conditions in which Caucasian losses were the focus, Caucasian participants saw race relations in a more zero-sum fashion than when minority gains alone were considered. What impact did this have on judged progress toward equality? As shown in Figure 6.3 on page 190, in the two conditions that focused on Caucasian losses, there were racial group differences in judged progress, which consistently mirrored the obtained national survey findings. Caucasian participants perceived greater progress toward equality for minorities than did minority participants. However when only minority gains were considered, Caucasians perceived less progress toward equality; in fact, in that case, their perceptions were no different than the minority participants. So, the racial divide in public perceptions of events seems to stem in part from Caucasians framing social change as involving losses in status and negative outcomes for their own group.

It's worth considering whether a similar tendency to frame affirmative action as a loss of Caucasian privilege or as a gain for minorities can account for racial differences in support for that social change policy, too (Crosby, 2004). Recent research reveals that by focusing on possible losses their own racial group could experience, Caucasians expect that affirmative action procedures will negatively affect their chances to obtain jobs and promotions, and therefore they oppose affirmative action policies, regardless of what impact it might have on minority groups (Lowery, Unzueta, Goff, & Knowles, 2006).

> **Principles to Remember**
> Group differences in perception of social change can stem solely from one group considering the change reflecting a loss for their group and the other considering the change a gain for their group.

Figure 6.3
Opportunities in U.S. Society Can Be Framed as Gains or Losses
When admissions to U.S. universities were framed as minorities' gains, Caucasian participants judged overall progress toward equality in the United States as less than when those same changes were framed as Caucasian losses. Only in the minorities' gains condition, did Caucasian and non-Caucasian participants not differ from each other. For minority participants, the framing had no effect on judged progress.

(*Source:* Based on data from Eibach & Keegan, 2006.)

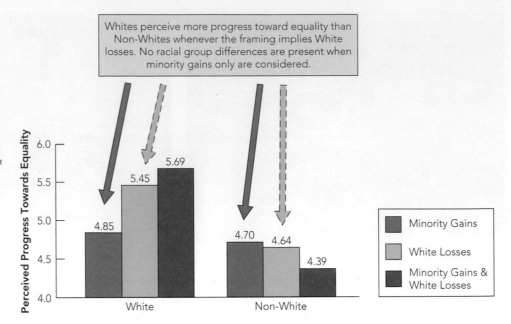

KeyPoints

- Discriminatory treatment can be based on many different category memberships, including age, race, marital status, occupation, gender, religion, language spoken, sexual orientation, and body weight.

- All forms of prejudice based on group membership are not perceived and responded to in the same way. Some forms are perceived as legitimate, while people actively strive to eliminate others.

- Prospect theory argues that we are risk averse, and we therefore weigh possible losses more heavily than equivalent potential gains.

- When change is seen as a potential loss, those who are privileged respond more negatively to further change, and suppose that more change has already occurred, than those who do not see it as a loss for them.

- Social groups differ in the value they accord equality. When equality is framed as a loss for Caucasians, they perceive that more progress has already occurred than do African Americans and show less support for affirmative action.

Think About It

Accuracy in social judgments may be difficult to determine when those judgments can vary depending on whether they are framed as stemming from potential losses or gains. Consider how politicians might manipulate our perceptions by altering how social change is framed.

The Nature and Origins of Stereotyping

In everyday conversation, the terms *stereotyping, prejudice,* and *discrimination* are often used interchangeably. However, social psychologists have traditionally drawn a distinction between these terms as different components of attitudes. As we saw in Chapter 5, we can think of stereotypes as the cognitive component of attitudes toward a social group, beliefs about what a particular group is like. Prejudice is considered the affective component—the feelings we have about particular groups. Discrimination concerns the behavioral component or differential actions taken toward members of specific social groups. According to this paradigm, negative stereotyped beliefs lead to general feelings of hostility, which then result in a conscious intention to act against members of the targeted group. However, hostility might actually be only one of several emotions involved in prejudice toward different groups. As we consider these components in the light of current research, ask yourself: How well does the attitude approach capture the phenomena of interest (Adams et al., 2007a)?

Stereotyping: Beliefs about Social Groups

Stereotypes about groups are the beliefs and expectations that we have concerning what members of those groups are like. Stereotypes can include more than just traits; physical appearance, activity preferences, and behaviors are all common components of stereotypic expectancies (Biernat & Thompson, 2002; Deaux & LaFrance, 1998). The traits thought to distinguish between the groups can be either positive or negative attributes, they can be accurate or inaccurate, and they can be agreed with or rejected by members of the stereotyped group.

Gender stereotypes—beliefs concerning the characteristics of women and men—contain both positive and negative traits (see Table 6.1). Stereotypes of each gender are typically the converse of one another. For instance, on the positive side of the gender stereotype for women, they are viewed as being kind, nurturing, and considerate. On the negative side, they are viewed as being dependent, weak, and overly emotional. Thus our collective portrait of women is that they are high on warmth but low on competence (Fiske, Cuddy, Glick, & Xu, 2002). Indeed, perceptions of women on these two dimensions are similar to other groups who are seen as relatively low in status and nonthreatening (Eagly, 1987; Stewart, Vassar, Sanchez, & David, 2000). Contrast this to a group perceived as a threat to the high-status group, such as Jews in Nazi Germany and perhaps Asian Americans at present in the United States, both of whom may be perceived as a threat to the high-status group, at least on some dimensions. This is referred to as "envious prejudice," and such groups are frequently stereotyped as low in warmth but high in competence (see Glick, 2002).

Table 6.1 Common Traits Stereotypically Associated with Women and Men

As this list of stereotypic traits implies, women are seen as "nicer and warm," whereas men are seen as more "competent and independent."

FEMALE TRAITS	MALE TRAITS
Warm	Competent
Emotional	Stable
Kind/polite	Tough/coarse
Sensitive	Self-confident
Follower	Leader
Weak	Strong
Friendly	Accomplished
Fashionable	Nonconformist
Gentle	Aggressive

(*Source:* Compiled based on Deaux & Kite, 1993; Eagly & Mladinic, 1994; Fiske, Cuddy, Glick, & Xu, 2002).

gender stereotypes
Stereotypes concerning the traits possessed by females and males and that distinguish the two genders from each other.

Men are also assumed to have both positive and negative stereotypic traits (i.e., they are viewed as decisive, assertive, and accomplished but also as aggressive, insensitive, and arrogant). Such a portrait, being perceived as high on competence but low on communal attributes, reflects men's relatively high status. Interestingly, because of the strong emphasis on warmth in the stereotype for women, people tend to feel somewhat more positively about women on the whole compared to men, which is a finding described by Eagly and Mladinic (1994) as the "women are wonderful" effect.

Despite this greater perceived likeability, women face a key problem: The traits they supposedly possess tend to be viewed as less appropriate for high-status positions than the traits supposedly possessed by men. Women's traits tend to make them seem appropriate for support roles, which is reflected in the actual occupational roles of women in the United States today. The vast majority of working women are in clerical, nursing, or service occupations, all of which bring less status and monetary compensation than comparably skilled male-dominated occupations (Jacobs & Steinberg, 1990; Peterson & Runyan, 1993). Although women are more than half the population in the United States, the power structure remains heavily male dominated: Men own and control most of the wealth and hold the political power (Center for the American Woman and Politics, 2005).

Stereotypes and the Glass Ceiling

As of 2005 in the United States, women occupy 37 percent of all management positions (U.S. Bureau of Labor Statistics, 2006). However, their proportion of high-level managers remains low—under 5 percent, with only about 1 percent of CEO positions in Fortune 500 companies being occupied by women (Catalyst, 2002). Many authors have suggested that a **glass ceiling,** that is, a final barrier that prevents women, as a group, from reaching top positions in the workplace, can explain these differential outcomes. Several studies have confirmed that a "think manager, think male" bias helps to maintain the glass ceiling (Schein, 2001). Because the stereotypic attributes of a typical manager overlap considerably with the typical man and share few attributes with the typical woman, this leads to a perception that women do not fit in positions of organizational leadership (Heilman, 2001). As the cartoon in Figure 6.4 illustrates, people lacking the attributes of the powerful group can experience a visit to their environment as "foreign" territory.

glass ceiling
Barriers based on attitudinal or organizational bias that prevent qualified females from advancing to top-level positions.

Figure 6.4
Progress toward Gender Equality in Management Remains a Worthy But Unfulfilled Goal
As this cartoon illustrates, women's (or the dragon's) presence in male-dominated professions (the knights' domain) represents a good start, but it can hardly be said to represent a warm and welcoming environment.

(*Source: The New Yorker,* 1983.)

"To begin with, I would like to express my sincere thanks and deep appreciation for the opportunity to meet with you. While there are still profound differences between us, I think the very fact of my presence here today is a major breakthrough."

Even when women do break through the glass ceiling, they experience less favorable outcomes in their careers because of their gender than do men (Heilman & Okimoto, 2007; Stroh, Langlands, & Simpson, 2004). For example, when women serve as leaders, they tend to receive lower evaluations from subordinates than males, even when they act similarly (Eagly, Makhijani, & Klonsky, 1992; Lyness & Heilman, 2006). Indeed, those women who have been rather successful in competitive, male-dominated work environments are more likely to report experiencing gender discrimination compared to those in gender stereotypic occupations (Redersdorff, Martinot, & Branscombe, 2004), and they are especially likely to be evaluated negatively when their leadership style is task focused or authoritarian (Eagly & Karau, 2002).

In other words, when women violate stereotypic expectancies concerning warmth and nurturance, and instead act according to the prototype of a leader, particularly in masculine domains, they are likely to be rejected. For example, between 1978 and 1998, in 1,696 state executive office elections, Fox and Oxley (2003) found women were less successful when they ran for offices that were inconsistent with the stereotype of women (e.g., financial comptroller or attorney general) than if they ran for offices that were consistent with the stereotype of women (e.g., education or human services). Violations of stereotype-based expectancies by women in the workplace appear to evoke threat in some men, particularly among those inclined to sexually harass (Maass, Cadinu, Guarnieri, & Grasselli, 2003).

The overlap of stereotypes about men and stereotypes about leaders leads to the converse of the glass ceiling effect for men when they enter predominantly female occupations. In such cases, men tend to be given a ride to the top on a "glass escalator" (Williams, 1992) and rapidly become managers and executives in nursing and other traditionally female-dominated fields after entering them. Thus the bias against people rising to the top when they enter work roles that are inconsistent with gender stereotypes appears to be primarily a bias against women.

Gender Stereotypes and Differential Respect

Although gender stereotypes are an important part of the glass ceiling, they are not the only factor affecting women's progress in the workplace. Jackson, Esses, and Burris (2001) suggest that another variable—differential **respect**—is critical for women attaining high status positions. Because men do, at present, occupy positions of greater power and status in society, people may simply infer that men are more deserving of respect than are women who are more likely to be found in lower status positions.

To determine if differential respect actually does play a role in discrimination against women, Jackson and others (2001) conducted a series of studies in which male and female participants evaluated applicants for relatively high-status or low-status jobs (e.g., regional director of a real estate company versus short-order cook). The applicants were either men or women, and participants rated these people on the basis of information contained in job applications they had, supposedly, completed. In addition to rating the applicants in terms of whether they should be hired, participants also completed a standard measure of gender stereotyping. Finally, they indicated their level of respect for the applicants.

Males received higher ratings in terms of both hiring recommendations and respect, and this was the case particularly for the higher status jobs. Ratings of respect for the job applicants significantly predicted hiring recommendations. The more respect participants in the study expressed for each applicant, the more likely they were to recommend hiring that person. However, the extent to which participants rated the applicants as having traits consistent with gender stereotypes did not predict hiring recommendations. Because across the board males received higher ratings of respect, the results suggested that this factor plays an important role in some forms of discrimination against women. In sum, although gender stereotypes certainly contribute to the persistence of discrimination against women, they are not the entire story. Differential respect for the two genders contributes substantially.

respect
Being seen positively and as having worth.

Figure 6.5
Do Visible and High Status Women Lead Us to Believe that Discrimination Is a Thing of the Past?
Condoleeza Rice (left), U.S. Secretary of State, was the first minority woman in such a top government position. Likewise, Congresswoman Nancy Pelosi (right) is the first female leader of the U.S. House of Representatives. Does their presence in these visible positions suggest that group membership is no longer important, even though research illustrates that gender and racial discrimination are alive and well in the U.S. workplace?

tokenism
Tokenism can refer to hiring based on group membership. It can concern a numerically infrequent presence of members of a particular category or it can refer to instances where individuals perform trivial positive actions for members of out-groups that are later used as an excuse for refusing more meaningful beneficial actions for members of these groups.

Consequences of Token Women in High Places.

Some individual women, like Condoleeza Rice or Nancy Pelosi, do manage to break through the glass ceiling in business or politics (see Figure 6.5 for examples). Does their success make discrimination seem less plausible as an explanation for other women's relative lack of success? Yes and no. To the extent that their success is taken as evidence that gender no longer matters, people may infer that the relative absence of women in high places is a result of women lacking the necessary qualities or motivation to succeed. For this reason, the success of a few women may obscure the systemic nature of the disadvantages that women on the whole still face. Thus the presence of a few successful women can lead those who do not achieve similar success to believe that they only have themselves to blame (Schmitt, Ellemers, & Branscombe, 2003). A number of laboratory experiments have confirmed that **tokenism,** a situation in which only a few members of a previously excluded group are admitted, can be a highly effective strategy for deterring collective protest in disadvantaged groups. For instance, allowing even a small percentage (e.g., 2 percent) of low status group members to advance into a higher status group deters collective resistance and leads disadvantaged group members to favor individual attempts to overcome barriers (Lalonde & Silverman, 1994; Wright, Taylor, & Moghaddam, 1990).

There are other negative consequences of tokenism, especially when the subsequent performance and well-being of the person selected is considered. First, people who are hired as token representatives of their groups are perceived quite negatively by other members of the organization (Yoder & Berendsen, 2001). In a sense then, such tokens are set up to be marginalized and disliked by their coworkers (Fuegen & Biernat, 2002). Job applicants who are identified as affirmative action hirees are perceived as less competent by people reviewing their files than applicants who are not identified in this manner (Heilman, Block, & Lucas, 1992). Second, people's confidence in their role is diminished by the awareness of tokenism. When Brown, Charnsangavej, Keough, Newman, and Rentfrow (2000) told some women that they were selected to lead a group because there was a quota for their gender, the women's performance in that role was undermined compared to that of the women who were led to believe that they were selected based on their qualifications and their gender (see Figure 6.6).

Hiring people as token members of their group is just one form of tokenism; it can be manifested in other ways as well. Making symbolic gestures of goodwill toward targets of prejudice can later serve to rationalize discriminatory treatment (Wright, 2001). For practioners of this form of tokenism, prior positive actions serve as a credential that indicates their nonprejudiced identity (Monin & Miller, 2001), which in turn frees them to later discriminate. In whatever form it occurs, research indicates that tokenism can have at least two negative effects. First, it lets prejudiced people off the hook; they can point to the token as as evidence of their open-mindedness and the fairness of the system even among members of the disadvantaged group (see Ellemers, 2001). Second, tokenism when realized can be damaging to the self-esteem and confidence of the targets of prejudice, including those few people who are selected as tokens. What happens when tokens or other targets of discrimination complain about their treatment? We discuss this issue in *Making Sense of Common Sense: A Social Psychological Perspective.*

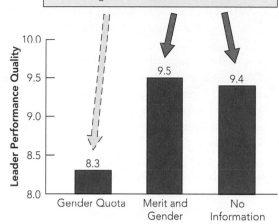

Only when selected solely on the basis of their gender does leadership performance decline. When merit played a role also, performance is as strong as when no information was given for basis of selection.

Figure 6.6
Believing You Are Selected Strictly Based on Group Membership Leads to Underperformance as a Leader
When women were told that they were selected because of a quota, their leadership performance was reduced compared to when they believed their qualifications also played a role in their selection or when no information was given about why they were made leader.

(*Source:* Based on data from Brown, Charnsangavej, Keough, Newman, & Rentfrow, 2000.)

MAKING SENSE OF COMMON SENSE
A SOCIAL PSYCHOLOGICAL PERSPECTIVE
The Gender or Race Card:
Too Easy to Play or Harder Than You Think?

Complaining about unjust circumstances can serve a useful function (Kowalski, 1996). It draws people's attention to undesirable conditions and can ultimately bring about improved future outcomes. But complaining can be also construed as attempting to escape personal responsibility, and that is one reason why we as observers might be suspicious of it. In Western cultures, those who attribute their outcomes to internal factors rather than to external ones are perceived more favorably (Beauvois & Dubois, 1988; Dubois & Beauvois, 1996). More specifically, we don't like people who blame others for their misfortunes (Jellison & Green, 1981), and a discrimination complaint frequently involves pointing the finger at a particular perpetrator. But what if someone's negative outcome is, in fact, a result of something outside themselves, would we still want them to accept responsibility? In an experiment (Kaiser and Miller, 2001) participants heard one of two scenarios about an African American student who got a poor grade on an essay. One group was told that the student attributed his negative results to racial discrimination (the complaint condition); the other group was told that he accepted responsibility for his bad outcome. Participants were also asked to consider a probability that the grader was actually racist, by being given likelihoods of 0, 50, or 100 percent that the grader was prejudiced.

Did the likelihood of discrimination have a propor-

tional effect on Caucasian participants' evaluations of the student complaint? That is, the more likely the racism, the more sympathy the participant would bring to evaluations? In fact, the degree of the grader's prejudice did not factor into their judgment. Regardless of whether the Caucasian perceivers in the study thought the bad grade was a result of discrimination or not, they evaluated the student more negatively in the complaining condition than in the taking responsibility condition. Thus even when we as observers recognize that another person's negative outcome is not their fault, we disapprove when that individual attributes it (even accurately) to discrimination rather than accepting responsibility for the outcome!

Moreover, Garcia, Horstman Reser, Amo, Redersdorff, and Branscombe (2005) demonstrated that members of the complainer's own in-group may disapprove most of complaining about discrimination when they believe it could suggest to out-group members that the in-group is given to unjustified griping. But even allowing for these negative aspects of complaining, common sense might suggest that playing the race or gender card is, in the mind of a stigmatized group member, an attractive option, even if only to themselves.

Crocker and Major (1989) suggested that among those

(continued on page 196)

The Gender or Race Card, *cont.*

who are stigmatized attributing negative outcomes to prejudice is protective of self-esteem. They argued that if the target of prejudice could attribute the cause of a negative outcome to another person's discrimination, then the target could view the cause as an external one (i.e., having little or nothing to do with them personally). The problem with this idea, and indeed the problem for anyone whose first thought is to perceive a gender or race discrimination complaint as the stigmatized trying to avoid responsibility, is that an attribution to prejudice is not simply, for the person making it, a psychologically external one.

That is, my social identity as a female is an important and stable aspect of myself. Schmitt and Branscombe (2002b) have shown that an attribution to prejudice is perceived as having a substantial internal component by the person experiencing the discrimination. If discrimination is seen as internal, being about me or my group membership, then it cannot provide self-protection by discounting myself as a cause of the discriminatory outcome. Therefore if I was African American and my race was, analogously, an important social identity to me, it hardly seems reasonable that I would think of racial discrimination as not about me. Worse, keep in mind how pervasively prejudice may be experienced. As we saw in Chapter 4, the most psychologically harmful effects for a stigmatized group member occur when an outcome is attributed to internal and stable factors, that is, it's the result of something about me, and it is not going to change. Therefore

concluding that important outcomes are the result of discrimination that stems from a key group membership (one that honors my childhood and my family) will be rather painful. Research has illustrated that disadvantaged group members who perceive themselves as experiencing more discrimination have worse well-being than those who report experiencing less discrimination. This relationship has been found in numerous devalued groups: women, African Americans, homosexuals, Jewish Canadians, and people who are overweight (see Branscombe, Schmitt, & Harvey, 1999; Crocker, Cornwell, & Major, 1993; Dion & Earn, 1975; Herek, Gillis, & Cogan, 1999; Schmitt, Branscombe, Kobrynowicz, & Owen, 2002).

To summarize, members of the socially dominant group see those who play the gender or race card as blaming their negative outcomes on others. But targeted group members attempting to explain their disadvantages as the result of discrimination and to place the problem outside themselves, discover that the process has a substantial internal element. Attributing problems to prejudice tends to be a painful attribution, and one that its victims are well aware can bring social condemnation from both one's in-group and the out-group if voiced and acted on (Crangle, 2007; Hopkins, 2007). Therefore social psychological research has revealed that the common sense notion that publicly playing the race or gender card is an easy way of avoiding responsibility for negative outcomes is not borne out from the victims' perspective.

Can We Conclude that Stereotyping Is Absent When Members of Different Groups Are Rated the Same?

Most of us would be quick to answer this question with a definite, "Of course," but we would be wrong! Biernat's (2005) work on **shifting standards** indicates that, although the same evaluation ratings can be given to members of different groups, stereotypes may have, nevertheless, influenced those ratings. Further, those identical evaluation ratings given to members of different groups will not necessarily translate into the same behavioral expectations for the people rated.

We can use different standards but the same words to describe different objects. For example, I may say that I have a large cat and a small car, but I don't mean that my large cat is anywhere near the size of my small car! When I use the word *large* to describe both a car and a cat, I am using different comparisons (large as cats go and small compared to other cars) and therefore referencing different meanings. I know that in feet and inches small cars and large cats are not close to the same size.

Likewise, for judgments of people, I may use the same sort of language to describe two basketball players whom I believe will actually perform quite differently. Take a ten-year-old basketball player whom I might refer to as "good," but that good does not mean the same thing as when I say my favorite NBA player is good. The ten-year old is good in

shifting standards
When we use one group as the standard but shift to another group as the comparison standard when judging members of a different group.

A subjective scale for ratings of management potential

1	2	3	4	5	6	7
highly incompentent	very incompetent	somewhat incompetent	neither competent nor incompetent	somewhat competent	very competent	highly competent

An objective scale showing likely sales decreases/increases after a year of management leadership

1	2	3	4	5	6	7	8	9	10
−25	−20	−15	−10	−5	+5 %	+10	+15	+20	+25

Below are the mental representations based on a stereotype of differing management potential
(1) A within-group (subjective) scale for females

1	2	3	4	5	6	7	
hi inc	very inc	some inc	neither comp nor inc	some comp	**very comp**	hi comp	mental representation of female competence as a group ("for a female")

(2) A within-group (subjective) scale for males

	1	2	3	4	5	6	7
mental representation of male competence as a group ("for a male")	hi inc	very inc	some inc	neither comp nor inc	some comp	**very comp**	hi comp

(3) A real-world (objective) scale that encompasses both mental representations

1	2	3	4	5	6	7	8	9	10
−25	−20	−15	−10	−5	+5 %	+10	+15	+20	+25

Figure 6.7

Shifting Standards: Do Similar Ratings of Males and Females Always Mean the Same Thing?

Subjective and objective scales (top) are what participants use to rate job applicants. The scales labeled (1) and (2) reflect the mental representations based on stereotypes of male and female management potential. A 6 rating for Ann ("very competent—for a female") on scale (1) means a 5 percent expected increase in sales under her leadership, on the objective scale (3). A 6 rating for Andrew ("very competent—for a male") on scale (2) translates into an expected 20 percent increase in sales for him on the objective scale (3). The result: We get to call each one "very competent," but Andrew has a better chance than Ann of getting the offer in a real hiring situation.

(*Source:* Based on Biernat, 2005.)

comparison to other child players, whereas the NBA player is good in comparison to other professional players. Terms, such as good–bad and small–large, are, in effect, "slippery language," which can mask our actual use of different mental representations as standards of comparison (i.e., stereotypes). But other standards are available that will always mean the same thing no matter what is being referred to. That is, when rating a basketball player, I might use a standard such as percentage of free throws made over the course of a season; such a standard is the same no matter if the ten-year old or the NBA player is attempting to sink those shots from the free-throw line. These standards are referred to as **objective scales** because the meaning is the same no matter who they are applied to, while standards that can take on different meanings, depending on who they are applied to, are called **subjective scales.** This ease of shifting the meaning of subjective standards allows for real stereotyping effects, even when the same rating is given to two quite different targets.

Let's see how this would play out when a person has to evaluate a male and a female and decide which should be appointed to a management position. Let's assume a belief that males are more capable in business management than are females. Although both the female and male candidates might receive a similarly good rating on their likelihood of business success, that good rating will mean different things on measures whose meaning is the same no matter who is rated. So, when asked to rate the male and female applicants on their potential sales capabilities in dollars they will sell per year, the male may be rated higher on this objective measure of dollars than the female applicant. Thus the use of subjective rating scales can conceal the presence of stereotypical judgments, whereas use of objective scales will tend to expose them. Numerous studies have supported the process, which is illustrated in Figure 6.7. In this research, the "same" ratings on subjective scales do not necessarily mean equal on objective scales or the absence of stereotyping.

objective scales
Those with measurement units that are tied to external reality so that they mean the same thing regardless of category membership (e.g., dollars earned, feet and inches, chosen or rejected).

subjective scales
Response scales that are open to interpretation and lack an externally grounded referent, including scales labeled from good to bad or weak to strong. They are said to be subjective because they can take on different meanings depending on the group membership of the person being evaluated.

Can We Be Victims of Stereotyping and Not Even Recognize It?: The Case of Single People

Do we always recognize when we stereotype ourselves and others? Or are there circumstances in which we might unconsciously concur with widely held stereotypes, even ones that harm ourselves? DePaulo (2006) points out one intriguing instance of this in her research on **singlism,** which is the negative stereotyping and discrimination that is directed toward people who are single. In a study of over one thousand undergraduates, DePaulo and Morris (2006) measured how single and married people are characterized. As shown in Table 6.2, the attributes these primarily single participants used to describe singles are fairly negative, particularly in contrast to how they described married people. And the differences in the descriptions spontaneously used to describe these groups were often quite substantial: Fifty percent of the time, married people were described as kind, giving, and caring, but those attributes were applied to single people only 2 percent of the time. Furthermore, this difference in how married and single people are stereotyped is even greater when the targets are described as over forty years old compared to when they were said to be twenty-five years of age.

There is no shortage of evidence of discrimination against singles (DePaulo & Morris, 2006). When asked to indicate whom they would prefer to rent property to, undergraduates overwhelmingly chose a married couple (70 percent) over a single man (12 percent) or single woman (18 percent). There are also a variety of legal privileges that come with married status: employer-subsidized health benefits for spouses, discounts on auto insurance, club memberships, travel, and tax and social security benefits. So, why is this inequality not pointed out (and protested) by its victims? One reason seems to be that it isn't even noticed by single people. When singles are asked if they are members of any groups that might be targets of discrimination, DePaulo and Morris report that only 4 percent spontaneously mention single as such a category. When asked directly if singles might be stigmatized, only 30 percent of singles say that could be the case. In contrast, almost all members of other stigmatized groups, including those based on race, weight, and sexual orientation agree they could be discriminated against.

Table 6.2   Traits Stereotypically Associated with Single and Married People

As this list of stereotypic traits illustrates, single people are stereotyped in largely negative terms, whereas those who are married are characterized in terms of more positive attributes.

TRAITS OF SINGLE PEOPLE	TRAITS OF MARRIED PEOPLE
Immature	Mature
Insecure	Stable
Self-centered	Kind
Unhappy	Happy
Ugly	Honest
Lonely	Loving
Independent	Giving

(*Source:* Compiled based on DePaulo & Morris, 2006).

singlism
Negative stereotyping and discrimination directed toward people who are single.

So, a lack of awareness of the negative stereotyping and discrimination they face does appear to be part of the explanation for why singles themselves fail to acknowledge singlism. But might it also be a case in which people (even its victims) feel that such discrimination is warranted and therefore it is legitimate to treat certain groups differently than others? As we'll discuss in the next section on prejudice, there are groups toward whom we seem to feel we can justify prejudice (although it is not typical for members of those groups to agree!).

Depaulo and Morris (2006) suggest that negative stereotyping and discrimination against singles serves to protect and glorify an important social institution—marriage— and this is a central reason why it is so widespread and heavily legitimized. Singles, by definition, challenge the existing belief system that finding and marrying one's soul mate is crucial to having a meaningful life. By derogating those who challenge that idea, we can all believe in vital cultural myths. Consider how knowing the marital status of the people shown in Figure 6.8 affects the inferences we make about what they are like.

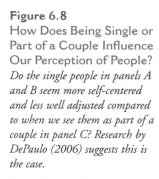

Figure 6.8
How Does Being Single or Part of a Couple Influence Our Perception of People?
Do the single people in panels A and B seem more self-centered and less well adjusted compared to when we see them as part of a couple in panel C? Research by DePaulo (2006) suggests this is the case.

(*Source:* Stephen Reysen.)

Why Do People Form and Use Stereotypes?

Stereotypes often function as schemas—cognitive frameworks for organizing, interpreting, and recalling information (Wyer & Srull, 1994). As we noted in Chapter 2, we often act like "cognitive misers," investing the least amount of cognitive effort possible in many situations. Thus one important reason we hold stereotypes is that doing so can conserve the cognitive effort that would be required to perceive the person as an individual. As discussed in Chapter 5, we can simply rely on quicker, heuristic-driven processing and use our preconceived beliefs when making behavioral choices. The results of several studies offer support for this view of stereotyping (Bodenhausen, 1993; Macrae, Milne, & Bodenhausen, 1994). However as you'll see, stereotypes can serve important motivational purposes; in addition to providing us with a sense that we understand the world, they can help us feel positive about our own group identity in comparison to other social groups. For now though, let's consider what the cognitive miser perspective illustrates in terms of how stereotypes are used.

Stereotypes: How They Operate

Consider the following groups: homosexuals, American Indians, artists, U.S. soldiers, homeless people, professors, and dog lovers. Suppose you were asked to list the traits most characteristic of each. You would probably not find this a difficult task. Most people can easily construct a list for each group, and moreover, they could probably do so even for groups with whom they have had limited personal contact. Stereotypes provide us with information about the typical traits possessed by people belonging to these groups (Judd, Ryan, & Park, 1991), and once activated, these traits come automatically to mind. It's this fact that explains the ease with which you can construct such lists, even though you may not have had much direct experience with American Indians, artists, or homeless people.

Stereotypes act as theories, guiding what we attend to and exerting strong effects on how we process social information (Yzerbyt, Rocher, & Schradron, 1997). Information relevant to an activated stereotype is often processed more quickly and remembered better than information unrelated to it (Dovidio, Evans, & Tyler, 1986; Macrae, Bodenhausen, Milne, & Ford, 1997). Similarly, stereotypes lead us to pay attention to specific types of information—usually, information consistent with our stereotypes. When information inconsistent with stereotypes does manage to enter consciousness, it may be actively refuted or changed in subtle ways that makes it seem consistent with those stereotypes (Kunda & Oleson, 1995; Locke & Walker, 1999; O'Sullivan & Durso, 1984).

Research findings also indicate that when we encounter someone who belongs to a group about whom we have a stereotype, and this person does not seem to fit the stereotype (e.g., a highly intelligent and cultivated person who is also a member of a low status occupational group), we do not necessarily alter our stereotype about what is typical of members of that group. Rather, we place such people into a special category or **subtype** consisting of people who do not confirm the schema or stereotype (Richards & Hewstone, 2001; Queller & Smith, 2002). Subtyping acts to protect the stereotype of the group as a whole (Park, Wolsko, & Judd, 2001). It's only when the person who disconfirms the stereotype in one specific way but is otherwise seen as typical that stereotype revision will occur (Locke & Johnston, 2001). When the disconfirming target is seen as atypical of the group as a whole though, stereotypes are not revised.

Do Stereotypes Ever Change?

If stereotypes are automatically activated, and we interpret information inconsistent with them in ways that allow us to maintain our stereotypes, the question is raised: Do stereotypes ever change? Many theorists have suggested that stereotyping will be stable as long as the nature of the relationship that exists between our group and the stereotyped group is stable (e.g., Eagly, 1987; Oakes et al., 1994; Tajfel, 1981). That's because we construct stereotypes that reflect how we see members of different groups actually behaving, stereotype change should only occur when the relations between the groups change (so the behaviors we observe change accordingly). In addition, we generally hold stereotypes that are

subtype
A subset of a group that is not consistent with the stereotype of the group as a whole.

favorable to our own group in comparison to another group. Unless social conditions shift so that we no longer see in-group favoritism as acceptable, unfavorable stereotypes of groups we are not members of can be expected to persist (Spears, Jetten, & Doosje, 2001).

Because stereotypes support existing social arrangements, they will only change when values and the categorizations used shift, or our stake in the present status relations are altered (Haslam, 2001). We can see this process in action when people change group memberships and move up within the status hierarchy. Research suggests that those with power are especially inclined to attend to information that is consistent with negative stereotypes about members of subordinate groups (Brauer, 2001; Goodwin, Gubin, Fiske, & Yzerbyt, 2000). In contrast, members of subordinate groups— because they need to be accurate and individuate members of the powerful group—tend to stereotype them less (Fiske, 2000). This does not mean that disadvantaged groups do not have stereotypes about powerful groups because they do. For example, African Americans stereotype Caucasians as relatively greedy, spiteful, and selfish (Johnson & Lecci, 2003; Monteith & Spicer, 2000), which reflects their experiences with the more powerful racial group.

> ### Principles to Remember
> Stereotypes can serve cognitive functions such as efficiency, but they also have motivational properties. We tend to stereotype groups in ways that serve our own group's interests.

KeyPoints

- Gender stereotypes, which are beliefs about the different attributes that males and females possess, play an important role in the differential outcomes that men and women receive. Women are stereotyped as high on warmth dimensions but low on competence, whereas men are viewed as possessing the reverse combination of traits.

- A glass ceiling exists such that women encounter more barriers than men in their careers and as a result find it difficult to move into top positions. Women are especially likely to be affected in the workplace by the think manager, think male bias.

- Both women and men express greater respect for men, and this plays an important role in biases in employee selection.

- Tokenism, which is the hiring or acceptance of only a few members of a particular group, has two effects: It maintains perceptions that the system is not discriminatory, and it harms how tokens are perceived by others and can undermine performance when they believe their appointment to leadership positions was without regard to their merit.

- Making an attribution to discrimination tends to be psychologically painful for disadvantaged group members. Publicly claiming discrimination as a cause of one's outcomes can produce negative responses in both out-group and in-group members, albeit for different reasons.

- Stereotypes can influence behavior, even in the absence of different subjective scale ratings. When objective scale measures are employed, where shifting standards cannot be used and the meaning of the response is constant, women receive worse outcomes than do men.

- In the case of singlism, which is negative stereotyping and discrimination directed toward people who are single, both single and married people show the effect. Singlism may stem from the targets being unaware of the discrimination they face or because they too see it as legitimate to be biased against their group.

- Stereotypes lead us to attend to information that is consistent with them and to construe inconsistent information in ways that allow us to maintain our stereotypes. When a person's actions are highly discrepant from a stereotype, we are likely to subtype that person as a special case that proves the rule and not change our stereotype.

- Stereotypes change as the relations between the groups are altered. Those in positions of power are especially likely to negatively stereotype those with lesser status, whereas those with little power are motivated to attend to and individuate the powerful.

Think About It
When we give members of two different groups the same good athletic rating, could our stereotypes about one group being more athletic than the other mean that we actually have different expectations about how fast members of each of those groups can run?

Prejudice and Discrimination: Feelings and Actions toward Social Groups

Prejudice reflects our negative response to another person based solely on that person's membership in a particular group. In that sense, prejudice is not personal, it is an affective reaction toward the category as a whole. In other words, when we are prejudiced toward some social group, we are predisposed to evaluate its members negatively because they belong to that group and not to our group. The individual's behaviors play little role (Turner, Hogg, Oakes, Reicher, & Wetherell, 1987). Discrimination has been traditionally defined as less favorable treatment or negative actions directed toward members of disliked groups. Whether or not prejudice will be expressed in overt discrimination will depend on the perceived norms or acceptability of doing so (Crandall et al., 2002; Jetten, Spears, & Manstead, 1997; Turner et al., 1987). Indeed, as we'll see in the final section of this chapter, changing the perceived norms for treatment of a particular group is sufficient to alter prejudice expression.

Research has illustrated that individuals who score higher on measures of prejudice toward a particular group do tend to process information about that group differently than individuals who score lower on measures of prejudice. For example, information relating to the targets of the prejudice is often given more attention or is processed more carefully than information not relating to them (Hugenberg & Bodenhausen, 2003). Indeed, those who are high in prejudice toward a particular social group are concerned with learning the group membership of a person (when that is ambiguous). This is because they believe the groups have underlying **essences,** that is, often some biologically based feature that distinguishes that group from other groups and can serve as justification for their differential treatment (Yzerbyt, Corneille, & Estrada, 2001). For example, the "one drop of blood rule" for racial classification means that if our great-grandparent was African American that would be enough to categorize us as a member of that racial group. As a result of such attention to categorizing people in terms of their group membership and processing information in ways that confirms our feelings about that group, prejudice becomes a kind of closed loop that can increase in strength over time. By seeing such groups as completely different from our own, expectations develop so that interactions with members of that group provoke anxiety and are awkward, which, in turn, produces further avoidance of cross-group contact (Plant & Butz, 2006; Vorauer, Hunter, Main, & Roy, 2000).

As an attitude, prejudice is the negative feelings experienced on the part of the prejudiced when they are in the presence of, or merely think about, members of the groups they dislike (Brewer & Brown, 1998). However some theorists have suggested that all prejudices are not the same, or at least they are not based on the same type of negative affect. According to this view, we may not be able to speak of prejudice as a generic negative emotional response at all. Instead, we may need to distinguish between prejudices that are associated with specific intergroup emotions, including fear, anger, envy, guilt, or disgust (Glick, 2002; Mackie & Smith, 2002). As depicted in Figure 6.9, even when the level of prejudice toward different groups (in terms of overall negative feelings toward that group) is similar, distinct emotions can form the primary basis of prejudicial responses. For example, these respondents' primary emotional response toward American Indians was pity, but their primary emotional response toward gay men was disgust (Cottrell & Neuberg, 2005).

Depending on what emotion underlies prejudice toward a particular group, the discriminatory actions that might be expected could be different. For example, when our prejudice primarily reflects anger, we may attempt to harm the out-group directly. In contrast, prejudice based on pity or guilt might lead to avoidance of the out-group because of the distress their plight can evoke (Miron, Branscombe, & Schmitt, 2006). From this perspective, prejudice reduction efforts may need to tackle the specific intergroup emotions on which that prejudice is based. For example, to the extent that anxiety and fear are reduced when prejudice is based on that emotion, then prejudice is reduced (Miller, Smith, & Mackie,

essence
Typically some biologically based feature that is used to distinguish one group and another; frequently can serve as justification for the differential treatment of those groups.

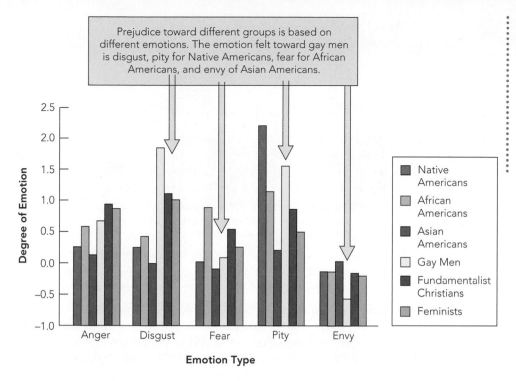

Figure 6.9
Different Social Groups Evoke Different Emotional Responses

Various social groups, even when prejudice level is similar, evoke quite different emotional profiles, relative to the participants' own in-group.

(*Source:* Based on data from Cottrell & Neuberg, 2005.)

2004). When prejudice toward a specific group is based on another emotion entirely (e.g., disgust), then different techniques for lessening prejudice toward that group might be needed. Reminders of how members of that out-group are like the in-group might lessen prejudice by undermining the emotion on which it is based.

Research suggests that inducing some negative emotions can lead directly to prejudice responses (DeSteno, Dasgupta, Bartlett, & Cajdric, 2004). In two experiments, these researchers found that after experiencing anger but not sadness or a neutral state more negative attitudes toward an out-group occurred. In these studies, participants were first assigned to **minimal groups;** they were falsely told that they belong to a social group that was created in the context of the study. Specifically, participants were told there were over-estimaters or underestimaters of event frequencies, and they were members of one of those groups. Once participants were categorized in this way, they were given a writing task to induce emotions (e.g., to write in detail about when they felt angry, sad, or neutral in the past). Finally, participants were asked to evaluate other members of their in-group (e.g., those wearing the same colored wristband) or the out-group (e.g., those wearing another color wristband).

As shown in Figure 6.10 on page 204, reaction times to associate positive or negative evaluation words with the in-group and out-group differed depending on the type of negative emotion participants experienced. When feeling angry, they more rapidly associated the out-group with negative evaluations and the in-group with positive evaluations, whereas it took considerably longer to learn to associate the out-group with positive evaluations and the in-group with negative evaluations. When either feeling sad or neutral, in contrast, no difference in time to associate the in-group and out-group with positive or negative evaluations was obtained. This suggests that even **incidental feelings** of anger, those caused by factors other than the out-group per se (in this case, the writing task), can generate automatic prejudice toward members of groups to which we do not belong.

As you can see, such **implicit associations**—links between group membership and evaluative responses—can be triggered in a seemingly automatic manner as a result of in-group and out-group categorization. As we discussed in Chapter 5, such implicit attitudes

minimal groups
When we are categorized into different groups based on some "minimal" criteria we tend to favor others who are categorized in the same group as ourselves compared to those categorized as members of a different group.

incidental feelings
Those feelings induced separately or before a target is encountered; as a result, those feelings are irrelevant to the group being judged but can still affect judgments of the target.

implicit associations
Links between group membership and trait associations or evaluations that the perceiver may be unaware of. They can be activated automatically based on the group membership of a target.

Figure 6.10
One Way Prejudice
Can Develop

When feeling angry for incidental reasons, we take longer to learn to associate positive evaluations about members of an out-group than to learn to associate positive evaluations with members of our in-group. Likewise, it takes us longer to develop negative associations between our in-group when angry, although negative associations about the out-group develop rapidly. These differences in time to develop associations were only present when anger was induced and not when sadness or a neutral mood preceded the evaluation pairing task.

(*Source:* Based on data from DeSteno, Dasgupta, Bartlett, & Cajdric, 2004.)

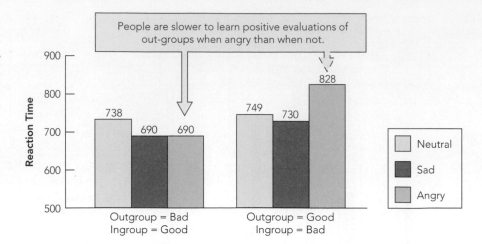

can influence overt behavior even when the people involved are largely unaware of their prejudiced views (Fazio & Hilden, 2001; Greenwald et al., 2002). Numerous studies indicate that implicit stereotyping and prejudice toward African Americans can be automatically activated (Kawakami, Dion, & Dovidio, 1998), as well many other groups, including soccer hooligans, child abusers, skinheads, and even professors (Dijksterhuis & Van Knippenberg, 1996; Kawakami, Dovidio, Moll, Hermsen, & Russin, 2000).

The important thing about such implicit stereotyping and prejudice is this: We may not be aware it is occurring, although our judgments and decisions about other people and how we interact with them can be influenced. Consider the decisions made by Caucasian participants in a simple video game about whether to shoot or not shoot either African American or Caucasian targets who were armed or unarmed (Correll, Urland, & Ito, 2006). Overall, participants were quicker in deciding to shoot armed African American targets than armed Caucasian targets, and they were faster in deciding not to shoot unarmed Caucasian compared to unarmed African Americans. Indeed, those who had stronger implicit associations between African Americans and violence were especially likely to show these decision biases. Such automatic prejudice effects are more difficult to inhibit following alcohol consumption (Bartholow, Dickter, & Sestir, 2006). In these studies, participants' ability to stop responding in a fashion that was consistent with stereotypes was lower when they drank alcohol compared to when no alcohol was consumed.

Before turning to a discussion of the many ways that prejudice can be expressed in overt behavior, we'll first address the important questions: What motivations might affect the extent to which prejudice is felt? What psychological benefits might people get from expressing prejudice toward particular groups?

The Origins of Prejudice: Contrasting Perspectives

Several important perspectives have been developed to answer the question: Where does prejudice come from, and why does it persist? The most general response to this question has focused on **threat,** whether it's material or symbolic, to a valued in-group. We consider first how perceptions of threat to self-esteem and group interests are critical for prejudice. Then we'll discuss how competition for scarce resources can increase prejudice. At the end of this section, we'll examine whether categorizing ourselves as a member of a group and others as members of a different group is a sufficient condition for prejudice to occur. Based on a cross-cultural study of 186 different societies, it's clear that the more important loyalty toward our in-group is, the greater the support there is for prejudice

threat

It primarily concerns fear that our group interests will be undermined or our self-esteem is in jeopardy.

toward out-groups (Cohen, Montoya, & Insko, 2006). So, feelings about our group are related to feelings about out-groups.

Threats to Self-Esteem

It is certainly true that prejudice cannot be understood, unless threat and how it affects people is taken into account. We want to see our own group positively (Tajfel & Turner, 1986), which in practice means more positively than some other group. When an event threatens our perceptions of our group's value, we may retaliate by derogating the source of the threat. It is also the case that perceiving a threat to our group can lead us to identify more with our in-group. Several studies, using reminders of the terrorist attacks of September 11, 2001, as the threatening event, have found increases in identification with the nation and representatives of it, such as President George W. Bush (Landau et al., 2004).

For prejudiced responses to occur, does the event that threatens our group identity need to involve possible death, or is it sufficient that it simply implies our group is not as positive as we would like to see it? To test this idea, U.S. college students, who differed in the extent to which they placed value on their identity as U.S. citizens, were shown one of two six-minute videos based on the movie *Rocky IV* (Branscombe & Wann, 1994). In one clip, Rocky (a U.S. boxer played by Sylvester Stallone) won the match against Ivan (a Russian contender played by Dolph Lundgren). This version was not threatening, for it supports the view of Americans as winners. In the other clip, Rocky loses the fight to Ivan. This version was threatening, particularly to those who highly value their identity as U.S. citizens, and it lowered feelings of self-esteem based on group membership. The question is: Can exposure to such a minor threat to identity in the laboratory result in prejudice? The answer obtained was yes; those who were highly identified as U.S. citizens and who saw the film clip with Rocky as loser showed increased prejudice toward Russians and advocated they be kept out of the United States in the future. In fact, the more these participants negatively evaluated Russians, the more their self-esteem based on their group membership subsequently increased. This research suggests that holding prejudiced views of an out-group allows group members to bolster their own group's image, particularly when it has been threatened. As the cartoon in Figure 6.11 suggests, it may not be sufficient to perceive our own group positively, we may need to see the other group negatively to feel good about ourselves. By putting down members of another group, we can affirm our own group's comparative value, and such prejudice may be most strongly expressed when threat is experienced.

Experiencing threat can affect men's actions toward women they perceive as a threat to their group's position. Rudman and Fairchild (2004) hypothesized that men would be particularly likely to sabotage a woman who beat them at a computer game task when it was one that men expected to be good at compared to one that women might be expected to do well at. Thus when women seem to be "moving in" on males' traditional territory, women will be more likely to be sabotaged in ways that affect their subsequent performance, which in turn serves to rationalize future prejudice toward them. Evidence for each step in this process,

"It's not enough that we succeed. Cats must also fail."

Figure 6.11
People and (Dogs) Can Feel Good about Their Own Group by Derogating the Other Group
The experience of threat to our own group can encourage derogation of the other group.

(*Source:* Leo Cullum, *The New Yorker,* 1997.)

Figure 6.12
Prejudice Persists When It Serves Our Group's Interests
When self-esteem is threatened, people are most likely to derogate the groups representing the threat. Indeed, doing so helps to boost or restore threatened self-esteem. Through this mechanism, groups can maintain their dominant positions.

(*Source:* Based on data from Branscombe & Wann, 1994; Rudman & Fairchild, 2004.)

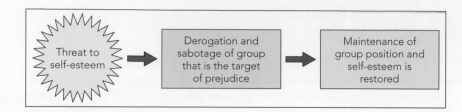

illustrated in Figure 6.12, has been obtained in several experiments. Indeed, the threatened males knew they were compromising the "deviant" target's ability to perform well in the future, and these "backlash" responses against the threatening target were associated with increased self-esteem.

Perceived threat can also have consequences for prejudice against immigrants. To test this idea, a new fictitious immigrant group was created and described to Canadian participants (Esses, Jackson, Nolan, & Armstrong, 1999). In the threat condition, participants read that the new immigrant group would be competition for Canadians in the job market because of their strong skills. This fictitious immigrant group was responded to more negatively, and more severe immigration policies were advocated, when this threatening information was provided compared to when it was not. Similarly, when an immigrant group is seen as a threat to the in-group culture, Caucasians express more negative attitudes toward Hispanic immigrants, and harsher policies are advocated (Zarate, Garcia, Garza, & Hitlan, 2004). Overall, then, these studies suggest that advantaged groups exhibit prejudice toward out-groups most strongly when they are experiencing a threat to their group's image and interests.

realistic conflict theory
The view that prejudice stems from direct competition between various social groups over scarce and valued resources.

superordinate goals
Those that can only be achieved by cooperation between groups.

Competition for Resources as a Source of Prejudice

It's sad but true that the things people want most—good jobs, nice homes—are in short supply. Quite frequently, these are zero-sum outcomes; if one group gets them, the other group can't. Consider the conflict between the Israelis and Palestinians, which has been ongoing since the creation of the state of Israel in 1948. Both want to control Jerusalem. This sort of conflict over desirable territory has been considered within **realistic conflict theory** to be a major cause of prejudice (Bobo, 1983). The theory further suggests that as competition escalates, the members of the groups involved will come to view each other in increasingly negative terms. They may label each other as enemies, view their own group as morally superior, draw the boundaries between themselves and their opponents more firmly, and under extreme conditions, may come to see the opposing group as not even human (Bar-Tal, 2003). From this perspective, what starts out as simple competition can gradually escalate into full scale prejudice (see Figure 6.13).

Evidence from several different studies confirms that competition can increase intergroup conflict. A dramatic demonstration of such effects is described in *Building the Science: Classics of Social Psychology* on page 207.

Figure 6.13
Intergroup Competition as a Source of Prejudice
When groups compete with each other for valued resources (e.g., land), they may come to view each other in increasingly negative terms. Ultimately, full-scale hate toward the group they are in competition with may develop. As shown here, both Israelis and Palestinians are in competition for Jerusalem.

BUILDING THE SCIENCE
CLASSICS OF SOCIAL PSYCHOLOGY

What Causes Groups to Be Prejudiced toward Other Groups and Is Prejudice Inevitable?

One might reasonably ask: What can eleven-year old boys who were sent to a summer camp in a remote area of Oklahoma possibly tell us about intergroup conflict? Sherif, Harvey, White, Hood, and Sherif (1961) conducted just such a study, which resulted in great insight into how prejudice between groups can develop. It all began when the boys arrived at the camp, called Robber's Cave. The boys were, unbeknownst to them, randomly assigned to two different groups and placed in well-separated cabins. Initially, the boys in each cabin engaged in enjoyable activities, hiking, swimming, and other sports, unaware that the other group even existed.

The boys rapidly developed strong attachments to their own group, choosing names (Rattlers and Eagles) and making up flags with their groups' symbols on them. In the second phase of the study, the groups were brought together, and they began a series of competitions. They were told that the winning team would receive a trophy and various desirable prizes, because the boys wanted the prizes badly, the stage was set for intense competition.

Would such conflict generate prejudice? As the boys competed, the tension between the groups rose. At first it was limited to verbal taunts but soon escalated into direct acts—such as those shown in Figure 6.14—when the Eagles burned the Rattlers' flag. After that, the Rattlers broke into the Eagles' cabin, overturning beds, tearing out mosquito netting, and generally wreaking havoc. The two groups voiced increasingly negative views of each other, while heaping praise on their own group members. In short, strong prejudice developed.

In the final phase, Sherif and others attempted to reduce the negative reactions the competition had instilled. Increasing the amount of contact between the groups seemed to only fan the flames of the boys' hostility. But when conditions were altered so that the groups found it necessary to work together to reach **superordinate goals**—ones they both desired but neither group could achieve alone—dramatic changes occurred. The boys worked cooperatively together to restore their water supply (secretly sabotaged by the researchers), combined funds

Figure 6.14
Prejudice Can Escalate under Conditions of Competition
The two groups of boys at Robber's Cave developed strong in-group identities. When competition between the groups for resources was added, the conflict you see here rapidly escalated.

(*Source:* Photo from Sherif, Harvey, White, Hood, & Sherif, 1961, University of Oklahoma Press.)

to rent a movie, and jointly repaired a broken down truck so they could all go into town. The tensions between the groups gradually decreased, and many cross-group friendships developed.

Because the researchers selected normal middle-class, well-adjusted boys to participate in the study, they could rule out pathological personality as an explanation for the prejudice that developed. Despite what the research showed about factors that can instigate and calm intergroup conflict, what it did not show is whether or not competition is necessary for prejudice to develop. In fact, the researchers note that, before the introduction of the competition, the mere knowledge of the presence of the other group was sufficient to generate name-calling among the two groups of boys. Perhaps simply being a member of a group and identifying with it, is sufficient for prejudice to emerge. This is the idea that Tajfel and Turner (1986) developed further in their social identity theory, which we turn to next.

Role of Social Categorization: The Us-versus-Them Effect

How is genocide possible? was a question that preoccupied Henri Tajfel throughout his life, in part because he was a Jew who had lived through the Nazi Holocaust. Unlike some who believed that the source of such intergroup violence lay in irrationality, Tajfel (1982) believed that there were important cognitive processes involved. He argued that a history of conflict, personal animosity, individual self-interest, or competition was not needed to create group behavior. If people were merely categorized into different groups, then you would see the beginnings of in-group loyalty and out-group discrimination. Indeed, he was searching for a baseline condition in which prejudice would be lacking, when he stumbled onto the most basic condition needed to create it. Tajfel, Billing, Bundy, and Flament (1971) originated a paradigm for studying intergroup behavior in which participants were categorized into groups on some trivial basis. At first he had participants view images of a large number of dots and then estimate how many dots there were. In other studies, they viewed a set of pictures, as shown in Figure 6.15, by the artists Klee and Kandinsky. In all instances, participants were assigned to one group or the other randomly but were told that it was based on whether they had overestimated or underestimated the number of dots or shared a preference for Klee or Kandinsky paintings. Each group that was so created had no purpose, no history, no contact among its members, no leader, that is, nothing whatsoever that would cause it to be a real group.

The task of the participants was simply to allocate points or money between two other participants—one of whom was an in-group member and one of whom was an out-group member. Participants on average awarded members of their own group more money than members of the other group. Furthermore, when participants could choose to allocate more money in absolute terms to members of their own group, they chose to allocate smaller absolute amounts if that would also mean allocating relatively less to members of the other group, suggesting that the participants were attempting to maximize the difference between the rewards given to the two groups, as opposed to focusing on benefiting their own group members. The results of these experiments were shocking at the time because they illustrated how people could be divided into distinct categories on almost any basis, even seemingly trivial ones, and doing so could result in different perceptions of, and actions toward, us (members of the in-group) versus them (members of the out-group).

Figure 6.15

Social Categorization: In-Groups and Out-Groups

Which painting do you prefer? In panel A, the artist Paul Klee's work is shown, and a Kandinsky painting is shown in panel B. A "minimal" categorization can be created by telling participants that they share a preference for one artist over the other.

 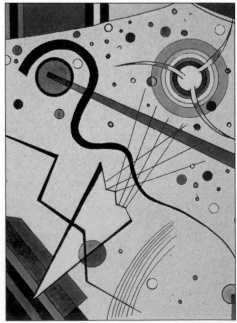

Once the social world is divided into us and them, it takes on emotional significance. Some differences are granted social importance and have meaning for our identities (Oakes et al., 1994). People in the us category are viewed in more favorable terms, whereas those in the them category are perceived more negatively. Indeed, it may be widely expected that some groups should be disliked, although prejudice toward other groups is seen as not justified (Crandall et al., 2002). For example, college students who were asked to rate the extent to which it was appropriate or legitimate to express prejudice toward 105 different social groups did so easily. They formulated the top ten groups it is acceptable to display prejudice toward and the top ten for whom it is least legitimate to express prejudice against. The results are shown in Table 6.3.

How, precisely, does social categorization result in prejudice? **Social identity theory** suggests that we seek to feel positively about the groups we belong to and part of our self-esteem is derived from our social group memberships. Because people who are identified with our group are most likely to express favoritism toward own own group and a corresponding bias against out-groups, valuing our own group will have predictable consequences for prejudice (Spears, Doosje, & Ellemers, 1999).

When, then, will we be most likely to express tolerance toward other groups or cultures? When we feel secure with respect to our own group identity (e.g., its goodness or superiority), more positive attitudes toward other groups, or conversely, reduced prejudice

Table 6.3   Who Do We Believe It Is OK or Not OK to Express Prejudice toward?

The "top 10" list on the left indicates what groups college students perceive it to be acceptable and legitimate to feel prejudice toward. The "top 10" list on the right indicates what groups they perceive it to be unacceptable and illegitimate to feel prejudice toward. How do you think these lists would differ for people living in other regions of the United States besides the Midwest? How might they differ for people who are members of different ethnic groups?

PREJUDICE LEGITIMIZED	PREJUDICED SEEN AS ILLEGITIMATE
Rapists	Blind people
Child abusers	Women homemakers
Child molesters	People who are deaf
Wife beaters	People who are mentally impaired
Terrorists	Family men
Racists	Farmers
Ku Klux Klan members	Male nurses
Drunk drivers	Librarians
Nazi party members	Bowling league members
Pregnant women who drink alcohol	Dog owners

(*Source:* Based on data provided by Crandall, Eshleman, & O'Brien, 2002.)

social identity theory
A theory concerned with the consequences of perceiving ourselves as a member of a social group and identifying with it.

is most likely (Hornsey & Hogg, 2000). Conversely, when we feel that the distinctiveness (superiority) of our own group or culture is somehow threatened because our group is lumped together with another, we will react most negatively to the other group, and moreover, these reactions will be intensified by perceived similarity between the in-group and the other group. Why? Such similarity threatens our group's distinctiveness. In contrast, when we do not feel that the distinctiveness of our own group is threatened or challenged, similarity to other groups has the opposite effect: The greater the similarity between the in-group and another group, the more positive the reactions to the out-group will be.

To test these predictions, Hornsey and Hogg (2000) recruited science and humanities students at a large university in Australia as participants in a study. They were asked to read short written passages indicating either that science students and humanities students are different in their ideas and attitudes (the low similarity condition) or that they are actually quite similar (the high similarity condition). After reading these passages, half of the participants were induced to think that they are all members of the same category—students, a procedure designed to threaten the distinctiveness of their own subgroup, whether humanities or science students; this was the threat to subgroup distinctiveness condition. The remaining participants were induced to think both about being in the same student category and about their subgroup identity as either a science or humanities student; this was the no threat to subgroup distinctiveness condition. In this case, participants were made aware of their membership in one of the two subgroups and also of their membership in the entire university community.

The students were then asked to rate the extent to which they would enjoy working with humanities or science students and how difficult working with those students would be. Participants rated both their own group and the other group in this manner. It was predicted that in the condition where the distinctiveness of their own subgroup was not threatened, participants would express less bias toward the other group when it was described as similar rather than dissimilar to their own. In contrast, in the threat to subgroup distinctiveness condition, the opposite should be true: Participants would actually express more bias against an out-group described as similar to their own because this would pose an even bigger threat to their group's distinctiveness. As you can see from Figure 6.16, both of these predictions were confirmed.

Figure 6.16
Social Identity Processes in Action
When the distinctiveness of their own subgroup was not threatened, individuals reported less bias toward an out-group when it was similar to their own group compared to when it was dissimilar. However when the distinctiveness of their subgroup had been threatened, participants expressed more bias toward an out-group that was described as similar to their own.

(*Source:* Hornsey & Hogg, 2000.)

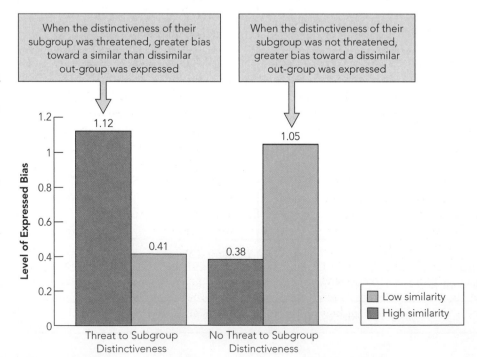

These findings suggest that efforts to reduce prejudice by breaking down the distinction between us and them can succeed but only if doing so does not threaten each subgroup's unique identity. Our tendency to divide the social world into opposing categories seems to serve important esteem-boosting functions for us; if these motives are overlooked, efforts to reduce prejudice by urging distinct cultural or ethnic groups to view themselves as one, and not distinct, could backfire.

Discrimination: Prejudice in Action

Attitudes, as we noted in Chapter 5, are not always reflected in overt actions, and prejudice is no exception to this. In many cases, people with negative attitudes toward various groups cannot express their views directly. Laws, social pressure, fear of retaliation all serve to deter them from putting their prejudiced views into practice. For these reasons, blatant forms of discrimination have decreased in recent years in the United States and many other countries (Devine et al., 2001; Swim & Campbell 2001). Thus actions, such as restricting members of various groups to certain seats on buses or in movie theaters, barring them from public schools, or neighborhoods, which were all common in the past, have now largely vanished in many countries. This is not to suggest that extreme expressions of prejudice have totally vanished, however. On the contrary, dramatic instances of hate crimes, which are crimes based on racial, ethnic, and other types of prejudice, continue to occur. For instance, college student Matthew Shepard was murdered in Wyoming in 1998 because of his sexual preference (he was homosexual), and anti-gay Web sites, like Web sites for other hate groups, present such violent crimes as desirable. Despite these extreme incidents, prejudice, in general, often finds expression in much more subtle forms of behavior. We turn now to these subtle or disguised forms of discrimination.

Modern Racism: More Subtle But Just as Deadly

At one time, many people felt no qualms about expressing openly racist beliefs (Sears, 2007). Now, few North Americans openly state such anti-African American sentiments. Does this mean that racism has disappeared or is on the wane? Although this is certainly plausible, many social psychologists believe that "old-fashioned racism," encompassing blatant feelings of superiority, has been replaced by more subtle forms, which they term **modern racism** (McConahay, 1986; Swim, Aikan, Hall, & Hunter, 1995).

What is such racism like? It can involve concealing prejudice from others in public settings, but expressing bigoted attitudes when it is safe to do so, for instance, in the company of friends known to share these views. It might also involve attributing various bigoted views to sources other than prejudice, whenever another explanation for potentially biased behavior is feasible. It could also involve attempting to appear color-blind and refusing to acknowledge race as a means of suggesting one isn't a true racist. In an interesting demonstration of the latter strategy (Norton, Sommers, Apfelbaum, Pura, & Ariely, 2006), Caucasian participants who were concerned about appearing racist were placed in a setting where they had to describe other individuals to either an African Americna partner or a Caucasian partner. When their partner in this game was African American, these participants were reluctant to use race as a descriptive term, even when highly diagnostic of the people they were asked to describe. In contrast, when their partner was Caucasian, the same people the participant was to describe were referred to in terms of their race because it was so diagnostic (e.g., the only African American person in a group of Caucasians). Precisely because many people want to conceal their racist attitudes—both from others and from themselves—and failing to even notice race might seem to be one way of doing so, social psychologists have had to develop unobtrusive means of studying such attitudes. Let's take a look at how such attitudes can be detected.

modern racism
More subtle beliefs than blatant feelings of superiority. It consists primarily of thinking minorities are seeking and receiving more benefits than they deserve and a denial that discrimination affects their outcomes.

bona fide pipeline
A technique that uses priming to measure implicit racial attitudes.

collective guilt
The emotion that can be experienced when we are confronted with the harmful actions done by our in-group against an out-group. It is most likely to be experienced when the harmful actions are seen as illegitimate.

Measuring Implicit Racial Attitudes: Finding a Bona Fide Pipeline

The most straightforward approach to measuring prejudice is to simply ask people to express their views toward various racial, ethnic, or gender groups. But many people are not willing to admit to holding prejudiced views, so alternative ways of assessing their actual views have been developed. In recent years, as we discussed in Chapter 5, social psychologists have recognized that many attitudes people hold are implicit, that is, they exist and can influence several forms of behavior, but the people holding them may not be aware of doing so. In fact, in some cases, they might vigorously deny that they have such views and instead proclaim their color blindness (Dovidio & Gaertner, 1999; Greenwald & Banaji, 1995). How then can such subtle forms of prejudice be measured? Several different methods have been developed (Kawakami & Dovidio, 2001), but most are based on priming, in which exposure to certain stimuli or events, prime information held in memory, making it easier to bring to mind or more available to influence our current reactions.

One technique that makes use of priming to study implicit or automatically activated racial attitudes is known as the **bona fide pipeline** (Banaji & Hardin, 1996; Towles-Schwen & Fazio, 2001). With this procedure, participants see various adjectives and are asked to indicate whether they have a good or bad meaning by pushing one of two but-

SOCIAL PSYCHOLOGY

WHAT IT TELLS US ABOUT . . .

When Our Group Has Done Harm to Others

In June 2004, the *Washington Post* reported that U.S. soldiers stripped Muslim detainees, beat them, covered them in excrement, photographed them in humiliating sexual poses, and used unmuzzled dogs to frighten and intimidate them during interrogations at Abu Ghraib prison in Iraq. Photographs of these actions, like that shown in Figure 6.17, revealed that U.S. military personnel were deeply involved in tactics deemed by a U.S. Army general to be "sadistic, blatant and wanton criminal abuses." The treatment of the prisoners at Abu Ghraib, according to the conclusions of the U.S. Senate hearing on the matter, violated long-standing tenets of how prisoners and civilians under the control of an occupying force are to be treated, including the U.S. Army's field manual, which prohibits "acts of violence or intimidation" by U.S. soldiers.

Figure 6.17
Shocking Photos of Abuse by U.S. Personnel at Abu Ghraib Prison in Iraq
How do we respond when we see members of our own group behaving in such an abusive and prejudicial fashion? There are a variety of strategies we can use when confronted with such damaging information about our own in-group.

How do we respond when we learn about the harmful and prejudicial actions of members of our own group?

There are a number of protective strategies that we can use when we are exposed to information that implies our group has perpetrated injustice. First, we can deny the possibility of collective responsibility (Branscombe, Slugoski, & Kappen, 2004) and see it all as quite irrelevant to ourselves. Another way we can avoid the aversive feelings of **collective guilt,** which is an emotional response that we can experience when we are confronted with the wrongdoings of members of our own group (Branscombe & Miron, 2004), is to argue that it isn't the whole nation, or even the U.S. army, that has behaved immorally but rather that there were just a "few bad apples" who did so. This method of limiting guilt when the Abu Ghraib abuses came to light was that selected by the Pentagon and White House—it isn't about us or our institutions, it's a handful of individuals who will be prosecuted.

When the in-group's responsibility for the harmful actions cannot be denied, we can blame the victims for

tons. Before seeing each adjective, however, they are briefly exposed to faces of people belonging to various racial groups (African Americans, Caucasians, Asian Americans, and Hispanic Americans). It is reasoned that implicit racial attitudes will be revealed by how quickly participants respond to the words that have a negative meaning. In contrast, participants will respond more slowly to words with a positive meaning after being primed with the faces of those same minority group members because the positive meaning is inconsistent with the negative attitude elicited by the priming stimulus.

Research findings using this procedure indicate that we do indeed have implicit racial attitudes that are automatically elicited by seeing members of racial groups and that such automatically elicited attitudes, in turn, can influence important forms of behavior, such as decisions concerning others and the degree of friendliness that is expressed in interactions with them (Fazio & Hilden, 2001; Towles-Schwen & Fazio, 2001). The important point to note is this: Despite the fact that blatant forms of racism and sexism have decreased from public life, automatic prejudice is alive, and through more subtle kinds of reactions, continues to represent a serious problem. We turn to now how people respond when members of their own group display prejudicial behaviors toward members of another group. We'll consider that question in *Social Psychology: What It Tells Us About . . .* below.

> ### Principles to Remember
>
> People have many strategies available to protect their group's identity, even when they are confronted with their group's discriminatory treatment of others.

its occurrence by suggesting that they deserved the outcomes they received; derogation of victims helps perpetrators to be "less burdened" when faced with their harm doing (Bandura, 1990). Toward this end, we may choose to believe that the prisoners at Abu Ghraib were not primarily civilians but terrorists. At its most extreme, the victims can even be excluded from the human category entirely so they are seen as not deserving humane treatment at all, which will permit any harm done to them to be seen as justified (Bar-Tal, 1990). As Aquino, Reed, Thau, and Freeman (2006) illustrate in their research, dehumanization of the victims helps to justify our group's actions as having served a righteous purpose: that of retaliating against our enemy's evil.

If the actions at Abu Ghraib can be perceived as legitimate, there will be no basis for guilt—either personal on the part of the perpetrators or collective on the part of group members who learn of those actions. With legitimization, we can accept that other's actions did result in harmful outcomes, but because it is seen as necessary to achieve larger moral purposes, (e.g., to get important information that would prevent the loss of U.S. lives) little guilt may be felt. Moral disengagement from the victims following legitimization could make it okay for our military personnel to maltreat prisoners in Abu Ghraib or at Guantanamo Bay, if doing so will somehow protect the in-group.

There are other ways that people can deal with their group's harm doing, such as motivated forgetting. Sah-

dra and Ross (2007) have shown that people's memory for harmful behaviors committed by their in-group is not equivalent to their memory of instances in which their in-group was victimized by another group. In their research, Sikh and Hindu Canadian residents were asked about their memories concerning events that were committed in India by Sikhs and Hindus, in which each group had targeted innocent and unarmed members of the other group for violent acts. Members of both religious groups admitted they were not proud of the violence perpetrated by their side. However when asked to recall three incidents from the 1980s (a period of heavy intergroup violence), incidents in which their group had been perpetrators of violence were less likely to be remembered compared to incidents in which their group members were the victims of violence.

About two-thirds of participants recalled at least one in-group victim event, whereas only about half recalled at least one in-group perpetrated event. Those who were more highly identified with their in-group recalled the fewest instances of in-group harm doing to others. Members of both the groups involved in this religious conflict tailored their memories so that events in which their group perpetrated harm to others were more difficult to bring to mind than events in which the other group victimized their own group. Thus we have available to us a variety of motivated mental strategies that help us maintain a favorable view of our in-group despite its harm to others.

KeyPoints

- Prejudice is the feelings component of attitudes toward members of a group based solely on their group membership. It can be triggered in a seemingly automatic manner and can be implicit and explicit.

- Research indicates that prejudice may reflect more specific underlying emotional responses to different out-groups, including fear, anger, guilt, pity, and disgust. Different behaviors are likely depending on the emotional basis of the prejudice.

- Prejudice persists because derogating out-groups can protect our self-esteem. Threat to our group's interests can motivate prejudice, and perceived competition between groups for resources can escalate conflict. Superordinate goals, in which desired outcomes can only be obtained if the groups work together, can help to decrease conflict.

- According to social identity theory, prejudice is derived from our tendency to divide the world into us and them and to view our own group more favorably than various out-groups.

- People may feel it is legitimate to display prejudice toward some groups, but it is seen as highly illegitimate to express prejudice toward other groups.

- Feeling secure in one's subgroup distinctiveness results in less prejudice toward similar out-groups. In contrast, feeling insecure about the distinctiveness of one's subgroup leads to greater prejudice toward similar out-groups.

- Discrimination involves differential actions toward members of various social groups. Although blatant racial discrimination has clearly decreased, more subtle forms, such as modern racism, persist.

- Those high in modern racism may want to hide their prejudice. The bona fide pipeline is based on the assumption that people are unaware of their prejudices, but they can be revealed with implicit measures in which priming a category to which the individual has negative attitudes will result in faster responses to words with negative meanings.

- When we are exposed to instances in which members of our own group have behaved in a prejudicial fashion, we can distance ourselves and not feel collective guilt to the extent that we can conclude the harmful acts were performed by a small few or the acts were not so severe. Additionally, we may conclude that the acts were legitimate either because the people harmed do not warrant concern or because doing so serves the in-group's higher goals. People may also show evidence of motivated forgetting of their own group's harm doing.

Think About It

Prejudice toward out-groups appears to serve important social purposes. If so, then how likely is it that simply changing people's emotions toward different groups is going to achieve real social change?

Why Prejudice Is Not Inevitable: Techniques for Countering Its Effects

Prejudice, in some form, appears to be an all-too-common aspect of life in most, if not all, societies (Sidanius & Pratto, 1999). Does this mean that it is inevitable? As we explained throughout this chapter, prejudice certainly has some regular properties (e.g., it will escalate under competition or when one's group identity has been threatened by a negative comparison with another group). Yet under the right conditions, prejudice toward particular groups can be reduced. We turn now to some of the techniques that social psychologists have developed in their attempts to reduce prejudice.

On Learning Not to Hate

According to the **social learning view,** children acquire negative attitudes toward various social groups because they hear such views expressed by significant others and because they are directly rewarded (with love, praise, and approval) for adopting these views. In addition, people's own direct experience with people belonging to other groups also shapes attitudes. Evidence for the strong impact of both these types of childhood experiences on several aspects of racial prejudice has been reported (Towles-Schwen & Fazio, 2003). That is, the more Caucasian participants' parents are prejudiced and the less positive participants' own interactions with minority group persons were, the greater restraint participants felt when interacting with African Americans. To the extent that such restraint reflects feelings of social awkwardness and anticipation of potential conflict, these findings support the role of parents in training children to be prejudiced.

The question of whether all children are equally influenced by their parents' explicit racial attitudes has been examined (Sinclair, Dunn, & Lowery, 2005). Perhaps the degree to which parents' racial attitudes and their children's are related depends on the extent to which those children identify with their parents. Children who care about making their parents proud of them should show the greatest parental influence. In a sample of fourth and fifth graders, it was found that parental and children's racial attitudes were positively related only among children with relatively high identification with their parents.

How might parents be encouraged to teach racial tolerance to their children? Research has revealed that highly prejudiced people experience everyday activities and life itself as lower in enjoyment than do people low in prejudice (Feagin & McKinney, 2003). Because it is clear that people holding intense racial and ethnic prejudices suffer harmful effects from their intolerant views, these findings might well be used to encourage change in parents. Because most parents want to do everything they can to further their children's well-being, calling these costs to their attention may be effective in discouraging them from transmitting, at least explicitly, prejudiced views to their children.

However, we continue to be socialized in terms of ethnic attitudes well beyond childhood. What are the consequences of joining institutions that subtly support either diversity or prejudice toward particular out-groups? Guimond (2000) investigated this issue among Canadian military personnel. He found that English Canadians became significantly more prejudiced toward specific out-groups (e.g., French Canadians, immigrants, and civilians) and internalized justifications for the economic gap between their own group and these out-groups as they progressed through the four-year officer training program. Further, he found that the more they identified with the military and the category they aspired to join within it (e.g., Canadian Forces Officers), the more they showed increases in prejudice over time. It would seem therefore that institutions, which can be molded to value diversity or prejudice, can exert considerable influence on the adults who identify with them.

The Potential Benefits of Contact

At the present time many U.S. cities have a disintegrating and crime-ridden core that is inhabited primarily by minority groups, surrounded by relatively affluent suburbs inhabited mainly by Caucasians. Such segregation, which at present has almost returned to the levels that existed before the *Brown v. Topeka Board of Education* public school desegregation order by the U.S. Supreme Court in 1954 (see Pettigrew, 2007), raises an intriguing question. Could racial prejudice be reduced by increasing the degree of contact between different groups? The idea that it can do so is known as the **contact hypothesis,** and there are several good reasons for predicting that such a strategy can be effective (Pettigrew, 1981; 1997). Increased contact between people from different groups can lead to a growing

social learning view (of prejudice)
The view prejudice is acquired through direct and vicarious experiences in much the same manner as other attitudes.

contact hypothesis
The view that increased contact between members of various social groups can be effective in reducing prejudice between them.

recognition of similarities between them, which can change the categorizations that people employ. As we saw previously, those who are categorized as us are responded to more positively than those categorized as them. Increased contact or merely having knowledge that other members of our group have such contact with out-group members can signal that the norms of the group are not so "anti-out-group" as individuals might initially have believed. The existence of cross-group friendships suggests that members of the out-group do not necessarily dislike members of our in-group, and this knowledge can reduce intergroup anxiety.

Consider, for example, the situation of Catholics and Protestants in Northern Ireland. Members of these groups live in highly segregated housing districts, and contact between the members of the two groups is often perceived negatively. Social psychologists there (Paolini, Hewstone, Cairns, & Voci, 2004) have, however, found that direct contact between members of these two religious groups and indirect contact (through knowledge of other in-group members' friendships with out-group members) can reduce prejudice by reducing anxiety about future encounters with out-group members.

Other research has likewise suggested that among groups throughout Europe, positive contact that is seen as important, when it reflects increased cooperation between the groups, can change norms so that group equality is favored and, thereby, reduce prejudice (Van Dick et al., 2004). Moreover, the beneficial effects of such cross-group friendships can readily spread to other people who have not themselves experienced such contacts, simply knowing about them can be enough.

In a series of studies involving heterosexuals who were friends with gay men, Vonofakou, Hewstone, and Voci (2007) found that degree of perceived closeness with the friend and the extent to which the gay friend was seen as typical of that group predicted lower prejudice toward gay men as a whole. Perceived closeness lessened anxiety about interacting with gay people, and perceiving the friend as typical ensured that the friend was not subtyped (an optimal condition for generalization of contact and stereotype revision, as we discussed previously in this chapter).

Recategorization: Changing the Boundaries

Think back to your high school days. Imagine that your school's basketball team was playing an important game against a rival school from a nearby town. In this case, you would certainly view your own school as us and the other school as them. But now imagine that the other school's team won and went on to play against a team from another state in a national tournament. Now how would you view them? The chances are good that under these conditions, you would view the other school's team (the team you lost to) as us; after all, they now represent your state. And of course, if a team from a state other than your own was playing against teams from other countries, you might then view them as us relative to the foreign team.

Situations like this, in which we shift the boundary between us and them, are quite common in everyday life, and they raise an interesting question: Can such shifts, or **recategorization** as it's termed by social psychologists, be used to reduce prejudice? The **common in-group identity model** suggests that it can (Dovidio, Gaertner, & Validzic, 1998; Gaertner, Rust, Dovidio, Bachman, & Anastasio, 1994). To the extent that individuals who belong to different social groups come to view themselves as members of a single social entity, their attitudes toward each other become more positive. So, although us and them categorical distinctions can produce prejudice, when them becomes us, prejudice should be eliminated.

How can we induce people, who belong to different groups, to perceive themselves as members of a single group? As Sherif and others (1961), observed at the Robber's Cave boys camp, when individuals belonging to initially distinct groups work together toward

recategorization
Shifts in the boundaries between our in-group ("us") and some out-group ("them"). As a result of such recategorization, people formerly viewed as out-group members may now be viewed as belonging to the in-group and consequently are viewed more positively.

common in-group identity model
A theory suggesting that to the extent individuals in different groups view themselves as members of a single social entity, intergroup bias will be reduced.

shared or superordinate goals, they come to perceive themselves as a single social entity. Then feelings of hostility toward the former out-group—toward them—seem to fade away. Such effects have been demonstrated in several studies, both in the laboratory and in the field (Gaertner, Mann, Murrell, & Dovidio, 1989; Gaertner, Mann, Dovidio, Murrell, & Potmare, 1990). When recategorization can be induced successfully, it has proven to be a useful technique for reducing prejudice toward those who were previously categorized as out-group members.

The power of shifting to a more inclusive category for reductions in negative feelings toward an out-group has been shown even among groups with a long history, including one group's brutality toward another. Consider how Jews in the present are likely to feel about Germans, given the Holocaust history. Although that conflict has long been terminated, to the extent that the victim group continues to categorize Jews and Germans as separate and distinct groups, contemporary Germans are likely to be responded to with prejudice, even though they were not alive during the time of the Nazi atrocities against the Jews. In a strong test of the recategorization hypothesis, Jewish Americans were induced to either think about Jews and Germans as separate groups or to categorize them as members of a single and maximally inclusive group—that of humans (Wohl & Branscombe, 2005). Following this manipulation of whether the two groups were considered separate groups or both were included in the same group, Jewish participants were asked to indicate the extent to which they were willing to forgive Germans for the past. In the condition, in which Germans and Jews were thought about as separate groups, participants reported less forgiveness of Germans compared to when the two groups were included in one social category (humans). Including members of an out-group in the same category as the in-group has important consequences for prejudice reduction and willingness to have social contact, even with members that were once considered enemies.

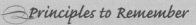

> **Principles to Remember**
>
> Changing how we categorize people is crucial to reducing prejudice and discrimination.

The Benefits of Guilt for Prejudice Reduction

When we have egalitarian self-images, we may be motivated to suppress prejudice (Monteith, Devine, & Zuwerink, 1993). Indeed, failing to do so, and subsequently being confronted with instances in which we have personally behaved in a prejudiced fashion can lead to feelings of guilt for having violated our personal standards (Plant & Devine, 1998). But what about when we are a member of a group that has a history of being prejudiced toward another group, might we feel guilt by association, even if we have not personally behaved in a prejudiced fashion? Considerable research has now revealed that people can feel collective guilt, based on the actions of other members of their group, when they are confronted with the harm that their group's prejudice toward another group has produced (Branscombe, 2004). Can such feelings of collective guilt be used as a means of reducing racism?

In a set of studies, Powell, Branscombe, and Schmitt (2005) found evidence that feeling collective guilt can reduce racism. First, these researchers recognized that the difference between two groups can be framed either in terms of the disadvantages experienced by one group or the advantages experienced by the other. Moreover, how existing inequality is framed can have important implications for whether the self, defined at the collective level, is seen as playing a role in maintaining that inequality. It was hypothesized that when the self, through one's membership in a group, is perceived as playing a role in racial inequality, then prejudice might be reduced to the extent that guilt is induced.

In their research, college students were first asked to think about the racial inequality that exists in the United States. Then in one condition, Caucasian participants were asked to write down all the advantages they receive because of their race. In the other condition, participants were asked to write down all the disadvantages that African Americans receive because of their race. This simply varied how the existing racial inequality was framed. As expected, the Caucasian advantage framing resulted in significantly more collective guilt than did the African American disadvantage framing. Furthermore, as shown in Figure 6.18, the more collective guilt was experienced in the Caucasian advantage condition, the lower subsequent racism. This research suggests that reflecting on racial inequality can be an effective means of lowering racism, to the extent that the problem is seen as one involving the in-group as beneficiary.

Can We Learn to "Just Say No" to Stereotypes?

Throughout this chapter, we have noted that the tendency to think about others in terms of their group membership is a vital factor in the occurrence and persistence of several forms of prejudice. To the extent that people want to be egalitarian, it may be possible to train them so that the automatic activation of stereotypes is reduced, and they can therefore behave according to their egalitarian principles. As we described previously, we acquire stereotypes by learning to associate certain characteristics (e.g., negative traits, such as hostile or dangerous) with various racial or ethnic groups; once such automatic associations are formed, members of these groups can serve as primes for racial or ethnic stereotypes, which are then automatically activated. Can we actively break the stereotype habit by saying "no" to the stereotypic traits we associate with a specific group? Kawakami and others (2000) reasoned that people can learn to not rely on stereotypes they already possess.

To test this idea, the researchers conducted several studies where participants' stereotypic associations were first assessed. After this, participants were divided into two groups. In one group—those in the stereotype maintaining condition—participants were instructed to respond "yes" when they were presented with a photograph of a Caucasian person and a Caucasian stereotype word (e.g., ambitious or uptight) or a photograph of a African American person and a African American stereotype word (e.g., athletic or poor). They were told to respond "no" to pairings that were not consistent with stereotypes (e.g., a word consistent with the stereotype for Caucasian but paired with a photo of a African American individual). Those in a second group, the stereotype negation condition, were told to respond "no" when presented with a photo of a Caucasian person and a word consistent with this stereotype or a photo of a African American person and a word consistent with this stereotype. On the other hand, they were told to respond "yes" to pairings that were not consistent with the stereotype. In others words, they practiced negating their

Figure 6.18
Collective Guilt Can Reduce Racism
The same inequality between groups can be framed as either reflecting the advantages of one group or the disadvantages of the other. Having Caucasians think about inequality as Caucasian advantage led to increased feelings of collective guilt, and this, in turn, resulted in lowered racism. A little collective guilt may then have social benefits.

(*Source:* Based on data from Powell, Branscombe, & Schmitt, 2005).

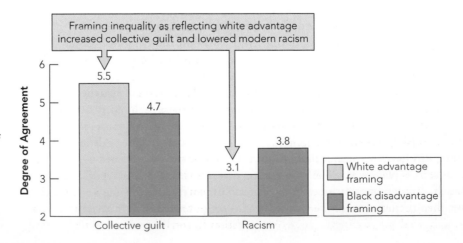

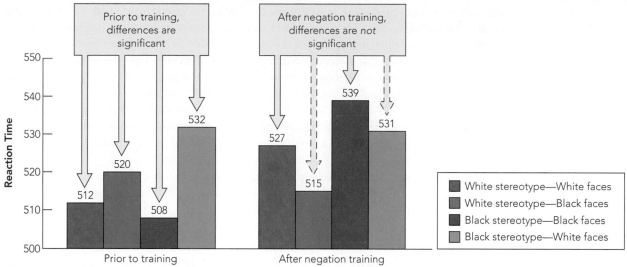

Figure 6.19
Saying "No" to Stereotypes: One Promising Technique for Combating Prejudice

Before negation training, during which participants responded "no" to racial stereotypes, participants categorized Caucasian faces more quickly than African American faces after seeing words related to the stereotype for Caucasians; African American faces were categorized more quickly after seeing words related to the stereotype for African Americans. After negation training, which was designed to weaken these implicit stereotypes, these differences disappeared.

(*Source:* Based on data from Kawakami, Dovidio, Moll, Hermsen, & Russn, 2000).

own implicit racial stereotypes. Participants in both groups performed these procedures several hundred times.

The results were clear. Reliance on stereotypes can be reduced through the process of repeatedly saying "no" to them. As shown in Figure 6.19, before negation training, participants categorized Caucasian faces more quickly than African American faces after seeing Caucasian stereotype words but African American faces more quickly after seeing African American stereotype words. After negation training designed to weaken these implicit stereotypes, however, these differences disappeared. Although we do not yet know how reduced stereotype activation influences actual interactions with group members, the possibility that people can learn to say "no" to racial and ethnic stereotypes, with practice in doing so, is encouraging.

Social Influence as a Means of Reducing Prejudice

Being provided with evidence that members of our own group like people belonging to another group that is typically the target of prejudice can sometimes serve to weaken such negative reactions (Pettigrew, 1997; Wright, Aron, McLaughlin-Volpe, & Ropp, 1997). In contrast, when stereotypic beliefs are said to be endorsed by our in-group and our membership in that group is salient, then the in-group's beliefs are more predictive of prejudice than are our personal beliefs about the out-group (Haslam & Wilson, 2000). This suggests that stereotypes that we believe to be widely shared within our own group play a critical role in the expression of prejudice.

Evidence that social influence processes can be used to reduce prejudice was reported by Stangor, Sechrist, and Jost (2001). Caucasian students were first asked to estimate the percentage of African Americans possessing various stereotypical traits. After completing these estimates, participants were given information suggesting that other students in their university disagreed with their ratings. In one condition (favorable feedback), they learned that other students held more favorable views of African Americans than they did (i.e., the other students estimated a higher incidence of positive traits and a lower incidence of negative traits than they did). In another condition (unfavorable feedback), they learned that other students held less favorable views of African Americans than they did (i.e., these people estimated a higher incidence of negative traits and a lower incidence of positive traits). After receiving this information, participants again estimated the percentage of African Americans possessing positive and negative traits. Participants' racial attitudes were indeed affected by social influence. Endorsement of negative stereotypes increased in the unfavorable feedback condition, whereas endorsement of such stereotypes decreased in the favorable feedback condition.

Together, these findings indicate that racial attitudes certainly do not exist in a social vacuum; on the contrary, the attitudes that individuals hold are influenced not only by their early experience but also by current information indicating how closely their views match other members of their group. The moral is clear: If we can be induced to believe that our prejudiced views are out of line with those of most other people, especially those we admire or respect, we may well change those views toward a less prejudiced position.

KeyPoints

- Social psychologists believe that stereotyping and prejudice are not inevitable; a variety of reduction techniques have been successfully employed.

- Children acquire prejudiced attitudes from their parents, and this is especially the case for children who strongly identify with their parents. Pointing out the costs of prejudice and undermining the justifications for prejudice are two methods that can be used to encourage less prejudice.

- Another technique, suggested by the contact hypothesis, involves bringing previously segregated groups into contact. This can reduce prejudice, especially when the contact is with out-group members who are seen as typical of their group, the contact is seen as important, it results in cross-group friendships, and anxiety about interacting with out-group members is reduced.

- As suggested by the common in-group identity model, prejudice can also be reduced through recategorization, which is shifting the boundary between us and them to include former out-groups in the us category. This is the case even for long-standing enemy groups when the maximal category—humans—is used.

- Emotional techniques for reducing prejudice are also effective. People with egalitarian standards can feel guilty when they violate those beliefs and personally behave in a prejudicial fashion.

- We can also feel collective guilt for our group's prejudiced history. By framing inequality as a result of the in-group's advantages, collective guilt can be induced, and this in turn can reduce racism.

- Reductions in prejudiced responses can also be accomplished by training individuals to say "no" to associations between stereotypes and specific social groups.

- Social influence plays an important role in both the maintenance and reduction of prejudice. We want to hold beliefs that we see as normative of our group; our prejudices are often predicted by what beliefs we think other members of our own group hold. Providing individuals with evidence suggesting that members of their group hold less prejudiced views than them can reduce prejudice.

Think About It

There are a variety of strategies that have been effectively used to lower prejudice. Are they all equally likely to be employed, and will their effects on changed attitudes continue over time?

SUMMARY AND REVIEW

- Discriminatory treatment can be based on many different types of category memberships—from those that are temporary and based on minimal criteria to long-term group memberships, such as marital status, gender, religion, sexual orientation, and age. Discrimination based on all these types of group memberships are not perceived and responded to in the same way; some forms of discrimination are seen as legitimate, whereas others are seen as illegitimate.

- Members of different groups are likely to perceive discrimination and the relations between those groups rather differently. When changes to the existing relations between racial groups are assessed, Caucasians see more progress toward equality than do African Americans. Research suggests that this is partly a result of Caucasians perceiving change and equality as a potential loss for them, whereas African Americans perceive the same increases in egalitarianism as gains. We are risk averse, with potential losses having greater psychological impact than potential gains.

- Gender stereotypes are beliefs about the different attributes that males and females possess. Women are stereotyped as high on warmth dimensions but low on competence, whereas men are viewed as possessing the reverse combination of traits. People express greater respect for men than women, and this factor plays an important role in discrimination against women in the workplace. The glass-ceiling effect is when qualified women have disproportionate difficulty attaining high-level positions. Women are most likely to be sabotaged when men are experiencing threat and women behave in a manner that is inconsistent with the stereotype. Stereotypes lead us to attend to information that is consistent with them and to construe inconsistent information in ways that allow us to maintain our stereotypes.

- Tokenism, which is the hiring or acceptance of only a few members of a particular group, has two effects: It maintains perceptions that the system is not discriminatory, and it can harm the token person's self-esteem and how they are perceived by others. For disadvantaged group members to publicly complain about discrimination, it can result in negative evaluations on the part of both in-group and out-group members.

- Stereotypes can influence behavior even in the absence of different subjective scale evaluations of men and women. When objective scale measures are employed, in which shifting standards cannot be used and the meaning of the response is constant, women are likely to receive worse outcomes than men.

- Singlism is negative stereotyping and discrimination directed toward people who are single. Both those who are single and those who are married show this bias, which may arise either because it is seen by them as legitimate or because they lack an awareness of the bias.

- Prejudice can be considered an attitude (usually negative) toward members of a social group. It can be triggered in a seemingly automatic manner and can be implicit and explicit in nature. Prejudice may reflect more specific underlying emotional responses to different out-groups including fear, anger, guilt, and disgust.

- According to social identity theory, prejudice is derived from our tendency to divide the world into us and them and to view our own group more favorably than various out-groups. Prejudice persists because disparaging out-groups can protect our self-esteem. Threat to our group's interests can motivate prejudice, and perceived competition between groups for resources can escalate conflict.

- We may feel it is legitimate to display prejudice toward some social groups—that it is normative to do so, whereas for other groups it is seen as highly illegitimate to express prejudice. Although blatant discrimination has clearly decreased, more subtle forms such as modern racism persist. The bona fide pipeline uses implicit measures to assess prejudices that we may be unaware we have.

- When we are exposed to instances in which members of our own group have behaved in a prejudicial fashion we can feel collective guilt to the extent that we do not engage in strategies that minimize collective responsibility or that allow us to conclude our group's harmful acts were legitimate. We also show evidence of motivated forgetting, in which instances of our group's harm doing toward others are more difficult to recall than are instances in which our group was harmed by an enemy out-group.

- Social psychologists believe that prejudice can be reduced by several techniques. Pointing out the costs of prejudice and undermining the justifications subscribed to for prejudice are two methods that can be used to encourage less prejudice. Another technique involves direct contact between people from different groups. Particularly when an out-group member is seen as typical of their group, the contact is viewed as important, and it results in cross-group friendships then intergroup anxiety can be lessened and result in lower prejudice. In fact, simply knowing that members of one's own group have formed friendships with members of an out-group may be sufficient to reduce prejudice.

- As suggested by the common in-group identity model, prejudice can be also reduced through recategorization, which is shifting the boundary between us and them so as to include former out-groups in the us category. This is the case even for long-standing enemy groups when the more inclusive category is that of human. Prejudice reduction can be also accomplished by training individuals to say "no" to associations between stereotypes and specific social groups. Emotions can be used to motivate others to be nonprejudiced, and feeling collective guilt can result in reductions in racism when the in-group is focused on as a cause of existing racial inequality. Beliefs that are believed to be held by other members of one's own group predict prejudice. When we are provided with evidence suggesting that our in-group has less prejudiced views than ourselves, it can be used to effectively reduce prejudice.

Key Terms

bona fide pipeline (p. 212)

collective guilt (p. 212)

common in-group identity model (p. 216)

contact hypothesis (p. 215)

discrimination (p. 188)

essence (p. 202)

gender stereotypes (p. 191)

glass ceiling (p. 192)

implicit associations (p. 203)

incidental feelings (p. 203)

minimal groups (p. 203)

modern racism (p. 211)

objective scales (p. 197)

prejudice (p. 187)

realistic conflict theory (p. 206)

recategorization (p. 216)

respect (p. 193)

risk averse (p. 188)

shifting standards (p. 196)

singlism (p. 198)

social identity theory (p. 209)

social learning view (of prejudice) (p. 215)

stereotypes (p. 188)

subjective scales (p. 197)

subtype (p. 200)

superordinate goals (p. 206)

threat (p. 204)

tokenism (p. 194)

Connections
INTEGRATING SOCIAL PSYCHOLOGY

In this chapter, you read about . . .	**In other chapters, you will find related discussions of . . .**
stereotypes as mental shortcuts	heuristics (Chapters 2, 3, and 5).
the role of competition in prejudice	the role of frustration in aggression (Chapter 10).
how stereotypes and prejudice can be changed	the processes involved in attitude change (Chapter 5).
the tendency to divide the social world into us and them and its effects	other effects of group membership (Chapter 11).
evaluations of women in positions of authority or leadership	Other aspects of leadership (Chapter 12).
the effects of prejudice on its targets	Coping when the self is a target of prejudice (Chapter 4).
the effects of perceived similarity on prejudice	The effects of perceived similarity on attraction (Chapter 7).

Interpersonal Attraction and Close Relationships

CHAPTER OUTLINE

- **Internal Determinants of Attraction: The Need to Affiliate and the Basic Role of Affect**
  The Importance of Affiliation for Human Existence
  Affect and Attraction: Feelings as a Basis for Liking
  The Affect-Attraction Relationship and Social Influence

- **External Determinants of Attraction: Proximity and Others' Observable Characteristics**
  The Power of Proximity: Unplanned Contacts
  Observable Characteristic of Others: Liking—or Disliking—What We See

- **Factors Based on Interacting with Others: Similarity and Mutual Liking**
  Similarity: Birds of a Feather Actually Do Flock Together
  MAKING SENSE OF COMMON SENSE: A SOCIAL PSYCHOLOGICAL PERSPECTIVE—COMPLEMENTARITY OR SIMILARITY: WHICH IS THE BASIS FOR ATTRACTION?
  Reciprocal Liking or Disliking: Liking Those Who Like Us
  What Do We Desire in Others? Designing Ideal Interaction Partners

- **Close Relationships: Family, Friends, Lovers, and Spouses**

The Cultural Foundations of Relationships: Seeing the Social World through the Lens of Our Culture

- **Interdependent Relationships: Family and Friends**
  Family: Where Relationships and Attachment Styles Begin
  Friendships: Relationships beyond the Family
  Loneliness: Life without Close Relationships

- **Romantic Relationships and Falling in Love**
  Romance: Beyond Friendship—Far beyond!
  Selecting a Potential Mate: Different Criteria for Women and Men
  Love: Who Can Explain It? Who Can Tell You Why? Just Maybe, Social Psychologists!
  Jealousy: An Internal Threat to Relationships— Romantic and Otherwise

- **Marriage: Happily Ever After—or Not?**
  BUILDING THE SCIENCE: CLASSICS OF SOCIAL PSYCHOLOGY—TERMAN'S EARLY RESEARCH ON SIMILARITY AND MARITAL HAPPINESS
  Marital Happiness: What Factors Affect It?
  SOCIAL PSYCHOLOGY: WHAT IT TELLS US ABOUT . . . THE ROLE OF POSITIVE ILLUSIONS IN MARITAL HAPPINESS
  Why Relationships Fail—and Why, Sometimes, They Succeed

When my grandmother passed away in 1980, she and my grandfather had been married for sixty-seven years; and from everything I could observe, they had been very happy together throughout those long decades. My grandfather truly lit up when my grandmother entered the room, and he always called her "Mommy," a term he used with obvious affection. She in turn, called him "Daddy," and often, I saw them holding hands as they walked down the street, even when they were in their seventies and eighties.

When my father passed away, just a few years ago, he and my mother had been married for sixty-three years. But I can't say with confidence that they were happy together most of that time. I rarely saw them exchange signs of affection, and my childhood memories are dotted with images of angry arguments that often ended with my mother in tears. Near the end, when my father was ill, they seemed to get along better, but they were never the model of marital bliss that my grandparents provided. In fact, looking back, I now believe these two couples were very different right from the start. My grandfather told me several times that he fell in love with my grandmother the first time he saw her. "She was so beautiful, so warm, so intelligent," he said, "one look, and I was gone." In contrast, my mother told me that when she met my father, she didn't find him particularly attractive despite the fact that several of her friends thought he was a living "dream." In fact, she had little or no romantic interest in him until, when, as a soldier during World War II, he wrote her beautiful letters. "His letters were pure poetry," she told me, "They were so moving and so sensitive, that I fell in love with him as I read them. . . ." Whatever the basis for their relationship, they didn't waste any time in starting a family: I was born only nine months and two weeks after their marriage!

Think for a moment: What do you want most in life? What would make you truly happy? Different people give very different answers to this question, but a large proportion include in their answers something like this: "A close, long-term relationship with someone I truly love and who loves me." Similarly, many also mention their desire to have good friends—ones they can really trust and to whom they can reveal their deepest thoughts and desires. Clearly, then, this aspect of our social lives—forming and maintaining long-term, intimate relationships with others—is truly a crucial one. Social psychologists have long recognized this fact and have sought, in their research, to answer questions such as these: "Why do people like or dislike each other—in other words, what are the causes of interpersonal attraction?" "Why do some relationships continue and gradually move toward deeper and deeper levels of commitment, while others fizzle out and end?" "Why do people fall in love—and with whom?" and "What *is* love?" No, we don't have full or perfect answers to these and many other questions about attraction, love, and relationships; but based on decades of careful research by social psychologists, we do have some very good ones—and we'll share that knowledge with you in this chapter. Our discussion of these critical aspects of social life will proceed as follows.

First, we'll examine the nature of interpersonal attraction, examining the many factors that influence whether, and to what extent, people like or dislike each other. As we'll soon see, many factors play a role, and these range from the basic need to affiliate with others, through similarity to them and their physical appearance. After considering interpersonal attraction, we'll turn to the close relationships that often develop when attraction is high. These are lasting social bonds we form with family, friends, lovers, and spouses, and we'll examine how such relationships form, the nature of love—the "social cement" that holds them together—and factors that sometimes cause these relationships to end—sometimes, prematurely (see Figure 7.1). While the risk of painful endings to even the closest relationships is always present, it is a risk almost everyone is willing to bear because life without such bonds and without love is—for most of us—truly unthinkable.

"Well, if you can't walk through walls this is where I say goodbye."

Figure 7.1
A Relationship about to End
While this cartoon shows an extreme example, research findings indicate that romantic relationships end for many different reasons, including the discovery, by one or both partners, that they are incompatible in various ways.

(*Source: The New Yorker*, April 2, 2007.)

Internal Determinants of Attraction: The Need to Affiliate and the Basic Role of Affect

Much of our life is spent interacting with other people, and this tendency to affiliate (i.e., associate with them) seems to have a neurobiological basis (Rowe, 1996). In fact, the need to affiliate with others and to be accepted by them may be just as basic to our psychological well-being as hunger and thirst are to our physical well-being (Baumeister & Leary, 1995; Koole, Greenberg, & Pyszczynski, 2006).

The Importance of Affiliation for Human Existence

From an evolutionary perspective, it would almost certainly have been an advantage to our ancestors to interact socially and to cooperate with one another in obtaining food and protecting one another from danger. Human infants are apparently born with the motivation and the ability to seek contact with their interpersonal world (Baldwin, 2000), and even newborns are predisposed to look toward faces in preference to other stimuli (Mondloch et al., 1999), so our need to affiliate with others appears to be present even in the earliest days of our lives.

Individual Differences in the Need to Affiliate

People are not all the same, of course, and they differ in the strength of their **need for affiliation.** These differences, whether based on genetics or experience, constitute a relatively stable trait (or disposition). Basically, we tend to seek the amount of social contact that is optimal for us, preferring to be alone some of the time and in social situations some of the time (O'Connor & Rosenblood, 1996).

When their affiliation needs are not met, how do people react? When, for example, other people ignore you, the experience is unpleasant. Being ignored can occur at any age (Faulkner & Williams, 1999) and in many, quite different cultures (Williams, Cheung, & Choi, 2000). When you are left out by others, it hurts, leaves you with the sense that you have lost control, and makes you feel both sad and angry because you simply don't belong (Buckley, Winkel, & Leary, 2003). Social exclusion leads to increased sensitivity to interpersonal information (Gardner, Pickett, & Brewer, 2000) and actually results in less effective cognitive functioning (Baumeister, Twenge, & Nuss, 2002).

Situational Influences on the Need to Affiliate

In addition to individual differences in affiliation need, external events can elicit temporary states reflecting an increase in the need to affiliate. When people are reminded of their own mortality, for example, a common response is the desire to affiliate with others (Wisman & Koole, 2003). Newspaper and television stories frequently describe affiliation as one consequence of natural disasters. Following such disasters as a flood, earthquake, or blizzard, strangers come together and interact in a positive way to help and comfort one another (Benjamin, 1998; Byrne, 1991). These disaster-induced interactions are described as friendly and cheerful, with people doing their best to help one another.

One basic reason for responding to stress with friendliness and affiliation was first identified by Schachter (1959). His early work revealed that participants in an experiment who were expecting to receive an electric shock preferred to spend time with others facing the same unpleasant prospect rather than being alone. Those in the control group, not expecting shock, preferred to be alone or didn't care whether they were with others or not. One conclusion from this line of research was that "misery doesn't just love any kind of company, it loves only miserable company" (Schachter, 1959, p. 24).

Why should real life threats and laboratory manipulations that induce anxiety arouse the need to affiliate? Why should frightened, anxious people want to interact with other frightened, anxious people? One answer is that such affiliation provides the opportunity for social comparison. People want to be with others—even strangers—to communicate about what is going on, to compare their perceptions, and to make decisions about what to do. Arousing situations lead us to seek "cognitive clarity" to know what is happening and "emotional clarity—better understanding of our own current feelings (Gump & Kulik, 1997; Kulik, Mahler, & Moore, 1996). Contact with other humans that is likely to include both conversations and hugs can be a real source of comfort.

Individual Differences in the Need to Affiliate: Are There People Who Don't Need Other People?

One old song you may have heard begins with the words: "People who need people are luckiest people in the world. . . ." The message of the song was clear: We all need each other, and therefore, have a strong desire to affiliate with others. Decades of research by social psychologists indicate that this is generally true: The need to affiliate is indeed a strong one, and a need almost all people have (e.g., Baumeister & Twenge, 2003). In fact, it has recently been suggested that it is one of our most basic needs or concerns (Koole, Greenberg, & Pyszczynski, 2006). Yet, there are people who show what is known as the dismissing avoidant attachment *style*—a pattern in which they claim to have little or no need for emotional attachments to others, and who, in fact, tend to avoid close relationships (e.g., Collins & Feeney, 2000). Are such people really an exception to the general rule that as human

need for affiliation
The basic motive to seek and maintain interpersonal relationships.

beings we have a strong need to affiliate with others? This is a difficult question to answer because such people strongly proclaim that they do not have these needs. Social psychologists are ingenious, though, and in a recent study, Carvallo and Gabriel (2006) designed procedures for obtaining evidence on the question of whether such people do or do not really have affiliation needs. Here's how they accomplished this task.

A large group of participants (students) took part in a study in which they exchanged information about themselves with three other people. Then the participants rated each other and ranked their preferences for working with each other on another task. In fact, all participants received the same information about the other participants. In addition, they received information indicating either that they had received the highest ranking and could choose any of the other participants as a future partner (i.e., they were accepted by the other participants), or they were not given this information about being accepted by the other participants; they were merely told that they would be assigned to work with one of them (a control condition). After these procedures, participants in both groups (acceptance by others and control) were asked to complete questionnaires that measured their current mood, their self-esteem, and their attachment style—the extent to which they claimed to have no need for close relationships with others. (A sample item: "I am comfortable without close emotional relationships.") The researchers reasoned that if people scoring high on the measure of dismissing attachment style really had little or no need for affiliation, their mood and self-esteem would not be affected by learning that they were preferred as a future partner by the other participants. However if such people really do have a need for affiliation, their mood and self-esteem would be higher after receiving this "accepted" information than when they did not receive it. As you can see from Figure 7.2, the results supported the view that even people who claim to have little or no affiliation need do have such needs. Participants high in dismissing attachment style showed significant increases in both self-esteem and current mood (positive affect) when they learned that they had been chosen (accepted) by the other participants.

These findings indicate that in fact all human beings—even people who claim otherwise—have strong needs for affiliation and to feel connected to others. They may conceal these needs under a mask of seeming indifference, but in fact, the needs are still there no matter how much such people try to deny them.

Figure 7.2
The Need for Affiliation: Evidence that We All Have It
Some individuals claim that they have little or no need for affiliation—for connections to other people. But research findings indicate that even such people really do have affiliation needs. After learning that they have been accepted by others, both the moods and self-esteem of such people (those high in dismissing attachment style) increase relative to a control condition in which they did not learn of such acceptance.

(*Source:* Based on data from Carvallo & Gabriel, 2006).

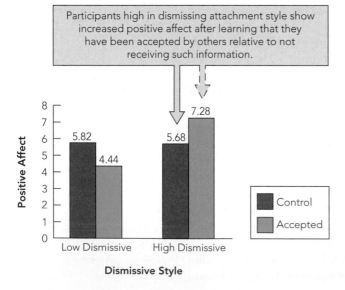

Participants high in dismissing attachment style show increased positive affect after learning that they have been accepted by others relative to not receiving such information.

Affect and Attraction: Feelings as a Basis for Liking

However complex positive and negative affect may turn out to be, a basic principle remains: The presence of positive affect often leads to positive evaluations of other people, that is, liking, while negative affect often leads to negative evaluations, that is, disliking (Byrne, 1997a; Dovidio, Gaertner, Isen, & Lowrance, 1995).

The Direct Effect of Emotions on Attraction

Emotions have a direct effect on attraction when another person says or does something that makes you feel good or bad. It probably does not come as a surprise to be informed that you like someone who makes you feel good and dislike someone who makes you feel bad (Ben-Porath, 2002). Many experiments have confirmed just such an effect. For example, attraction toward another person is less if he or she provides punishments in rating one's performance on a task rather than rewards (McDonald, 1962) and less toward a stranger who annoyingly invades one's personal space than one who remains at a comfortable distance (Fisher & Byrne, 1975). Many such findings allow us to predict with confidence that a stranger will like you better if you do or say something pleasant (e.g., "That's a beautiful dog you've got.") as opposed to something unpleasant (e.g., "Where did you find such an ugly mutt?").

The Associated Effect of Emotions on Attraction

A phenomenon that is perhaps more surprising than the direct effect of emotions on attraction is what is known as the associated effect of emotions on attraction. This occurs when another person is simply present at the same time that one's emotional state is aroused by something or someone else. Though the individual toward whom you express like or dislike is not in any way responsible for what you are feeling, you nevertheless tend to evaluate him or her more positively when you are feeling good and more negatively when you are feeling bad. For example, if you come in contact with a stranger shortly after you receive a low grade on an exam, you tend to like that person less than someone you meet shortly after you receive a check in the mail.

These associated (or indirect) influences of one's affective state have been demonstrated in many experiments involving emotional states based on a variety of quite diverse external causes. Examples include the subliminal presentation of pleasant versus unpleasant pictures—for example, kittens versus snakes (Krosnick et al., 1992)—the presence of background music that college students perceived as pleasant versus unpleasant—for example rock and roll versus classical jazz (May & Hamilton, 1980)—and the positive versus negative mood states that the research participants report before the experiment began (Berry & Hansen, 1996).

The general explanation for the influence of affect on attraction (and on other attitudes) rests on classical conditioning, a process we described in Chapter 5. When a neutral stimulus is paired with a positive stimulus, it is evaluated more positively than a neutral stimulus that has been paired with a negative stimulus, even when the person is not aware that the pairing occurred (Olson & Fazio, 2001). Figure 7.3 illustrates both direct and associated effects of emotion on attraction as examples of conditioning.

Figure 7.3
Affect and Attraction: Direct Effects and Associated Effects
When any stimulus (including another person) arouses positive affect, the stimulus is liked. If it arouses negative affect, it is disliked. These constitute direct effects of affect on attraction. Indirect effects occur when any neutral stimulus (including another person) is present at the same time that affect is aroused by some unrelated source. The neutral stimulus becomes associated with the affect and is therefore either liked or disliked as a result. An indirect or associated effect is a form of classical conditioning.

The Affect-Attraction Relationship and Social Influence

The fact that interpersonal evaluations are strongly influenced both directly and indirectly by emotional states can be, and often is, used in attempts to influence our behavior. Can we really be persuaded to purchase specific products, vote for specific political candidates, and support particular issues just because the right emotions have been aroused? The answer is yes. And, such manipulation has become a familiar aspect of our lives. In addition to the relatively simple attempts of a salesperson to evoke a positive response with a free sample or a compliment, all branches of the media attempt to arouse our emotions. The goal is make us like whatever or whoever is being sold and, sometimes, dislike whatever the alternative may be. In the movie theater, before the film begins, we are exposed to bright images and happy music with the general message, "let's all go to the lobby" to buy popcorn, candy, and soda. Similarly, the people in political advertisements smile because we believe that smiling people are better and more likeable human beings (Glaser & Salovey, 1998; Harker & Keltner, 2001). Every attempt is made to associate the candidate being "sold"

> **Principles to Remember**
> One reason why we often don't know why we like or don't like others is that our attraction toward them is the result of classical conditioning—a process of which we are usually unaware.

Figure 7.4
Positive Affect =
Attraction = Increased
Sales
In advertising, positive affect is used to sell the product, and sometimes negative affect is used to discourage interest in the competition. For instance, in this ad, the people shown using the product are both attractive and happy; exposure to them causes people exposed to the ad to experience positive affect—and so increases (advertisers hope)—their willingness to buy the product shown.

with positive words, such as moral, courageous, strong, and caring, while associating the opponent with negative words, such as destructive, radical, incompetent, and corrupt (Weisberg, 1990). And of course, many products are presented in ads along with people who are highly attractive and who are having a wonderful time (see Figure 7.4).

Are such attempts to influence our behavior by influencing our moods (affect) really effective? Research findings indicate that they are (e.g., Pentony, 1995). Overall, it seems clear that irrelevant affective states—ones induced by factors unrelated to the candidates, products, or items being sold—can indeed influence our liking for them and hence our overt actions (our votes, our purchase decisions). Keep this point in mind the next time you are exposed to any kind of message that is clearly designed to cause you to experience positive or negative feelings: The ultimate goal may be persuasion or influence and not merely making you feel good.

KeyPoints

- Interpersonal attraction refers to the evaluations we make of other people—the positive and negative attitudes we form about them.

- Human beings are apparently born with a need for affiliation and the motivation to interact with other people in a cooperative way. The strength of this need differs among individuals and across situations, but even people who claim they do not have it show evidence that they do.

- Positive and negative affective states influence attraction both directly and indirectly. Direct effects occur when another person is responsible for arousing the emotion. Indirect effects occur when the source of the emotion is elsewhere,

and another person is simply associated with its presence.

- The application of associated affect is a common element in both commercial and political advertising. This approach is most effective when directed at an audience that is relatively unaware and uninformed.

Think About It

Do you think that cognitive factors—what we know or believe about other people—can ever outweigh affect (our moods or feelings) in shaping our liking or disliking for them? When would this be most likely to occur?

External Determinants of Attraction: Proximity and Others' Observable Characteristics

Whether or not two specific people ever come in contact is quite often determined by accidental, unplanned aspects of their physical environment. For example, two students assigned to adjoining classroom seats are more likely to interact than those two given seats several rows apart. Once physical proximity brings about contact, their first impressions of one another are often determined by preexisting beliefs and attitudes—stereotypes they hold about such observable factors as race, gender, physical attractiveness, accent, height, and so forth. We'll now describe just how proximity and observable characteristics, such as physical appearance, influence attraction.

The Power of Proximity: Unplanned Contacts

More than 6.3 billion people now live on our planet, but you are likely to come into contact with only a very small percentage of them in your lifetime. Without some kind of contact, you obviously can't become acquainted or have any basis on which to decide which individuals you like or dislike.

Though it is not exactly surprising, most of us are not really conscious of the way our interpersonal behavior is shaped by our physical surroundings. Many seemingly unimportant details of the setting in which we live, work, and go to school can have a powerful influence on our interpersonal lives. Basically, two people are likely to become acquainted if external factors, such as the location of their classroom seats, dormitory rooms, office desks, or whatever, bring them into repeated contact. Such contacts occur on the basis of physical **proximity.** This is less true in the age of the Internet, when people can meet and become acquainted online, but it is still an important principle in many contexts. As suggested in Figure 7.5 below, people ordinarily become aware of one another and begin to interact in settings that bring them into close proximity. That may seem simple enough, but what is it about being brought into physical contact that influences social behavior?

Why Does Proximity Matter? Repeated Exposure Is the Key

Picture yourself in a large lecture class on the first day of school. Let's say that you don't see anyone you know and that the instructor has a chart that assigns students to seats alphabetically. At first, this roomful of strangers is a confusing blur of unfamiliar faces. Once you find your assigned seat, you probably notice the person sitting on your right and the one on your left, but you may or may not speak to one another. By the second or third day of class, however, you recognize your seat "neighbors" when you see them and may even say, "Hi." In the weeks that follow, you may have bits of conversation about the class or about something that is happening on campus. If you see either of these two individuals at some other location, there is mutual recognition, and you are increasingly likely to interact. After all, it feels good to see a familiar face. Numerous early studies in the United States and in Europe revealed that students are most likely to become acquainted if they are seated in adjoining chairs (Byrne, 1961a; Maisonneuve, Palmade, & Fourment, 1952; Segal, 1974). In addition to proximity in the classroom, investigations conducted throughout the twentieth century

proximity
In attraction research, the physical closeness between two individuals with respect to where they live, where they sit in a classroom, where they work, and so on. The smaller the physical distance, the greater the probability that the two people will come into repeated contact experiencing repeated exposure to one another, positive affect, and the development of mutual attraction.

Figure 7.5
Proximity: Repeated Contacts as a Basic for Attraction
At school, at work, or where you live, proximity results in repeated contact with other people. Such contact (repeated exposure to them) usually leads to recognition, an increasingly positive evaluation of them, and a greater likelihood that people involved will become acquainted.

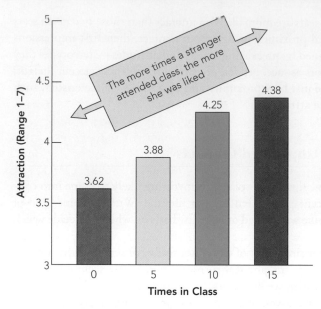

Figure 7.6
Frequency of Exposure and Liking in the Classroom
To test the repeated exposure effect in a college classroom, Moreland and Beach (1992) employed four female research assistants who pretended to be members of a class. One of them did not attend class all semester, another attended class five times, a third attended ten times, and a fourth came to class fifteen times. None of them interacted with the actual students. At the end of the semester, the students were shown photos of the assistants and were asked to indicate how much they liked each one. It was found that the more times the students had been exposed to an assistant, the more they liked her.

(*Source:* Based on data from Moreland & Beach, 1992.)

indicated that people who live or work in close proximity are likely to become acquainted, form friendships, and even marry one another (Bossard, 1932; Festinger, Schachter, & Back, 1950). Despite the many examples of proximity resulting in attraction, you might wonder why proximity results in attraction.

The answer has been provided by numerous experiments showing that **repeated exposure** to a new stimulus results in an increasingly positive evaluation of that stimulus (Zajonc, 1968). This finding is sometimes called the mere exposure effect because the positive response to a stranger, a drawing, a word in an unknown language, or whatever that is observed multiple times occurs simply on the basis of exposure. Even infants tend to smile at a photograph of someone they have seen before but not at a photograph of someone they are seeing for the first time (Brooks-Gunn & Lewis, 1981).

A clear demonstration of such effects is provided by a study conducted in a classroom setting (Moreland & Beach, 1992). In a college course, one female assistant attended class fifteen times during the semester, a second assistant attended class ten times, a third attended five times, and a fourth did not attend the class at all. None of the assistants interacted with the other class members. At the end of the semester, the students were shown slides of the four assistants and asked to indicate how much they liked each one. As shown in Figure 7.6, the more times a particular assistant attended class, the more she was liked. In this and many other experiments, repeated exposure was found to have a positive effect on attraction.

Zajonc (2001) explains the effect of repeated exposure by suggesting that we ordinarily respond with at least mild discomfort when we encounter anyone or anything new and unfamiliar. It is reasonable to suppose that it was adaptive for our ancestors to be wary of approaching anything or anyone for the first time. Whatever is unknown and unfamiliar is always at least potentially dangerous. With repeated exposure, however, negative emotions decrease and positive emotions increase (Lee, 2001). A familiar face, for example, elicits positive affect, is evaluated positively, and activates facial muscles and brain activity in ways associated with positive emotions (Harmon-Jones & Allen, 2001). Not only does familiarity elicit positive affect, but positive affect elicits the perception of familiarity (Monin, 2003). For example, even when it is seen for the first time, a beautiful face is perceived as being more familiar than an unattractive one.

Many animals, too, appear to categorize specific individuals in their social encounters as friends or foes (Schusterman, Reichmuth, & Kastak, 2000). It may be helpful to remember that the word *familiar* is related to the word *family*. In a way, repeated exposure allows us to include new individuals and new aspects of the world in our expanded "family."

As powerful as the repeated exposure effect has been found to be, it fails to operate when a person's initial reaction to the stimulus is very negative. Repeated exposure in this instance not only fails to bring about a more positive evaluation, it can even lead to greater dislike (Swap, 1977). You may have experienced this yourself when a song or a commercial you disliked at first seems even worse when you hear it over and over again. So sometimes, increasing familiarity can result in contempt rather than attraction.

repeated exposure
Zajonc's finding that frequent contact with any mildly negative, neutral, or positive stimulus results in an increasingly positive evaluation of that stimulus.

Observable Characteristics of Others: Liking—or Disliking— What We See

Though positive affect from any source and the positive affect aroused by repeated exposure tend to result in attraction, it doesn't always work out that way. Sometimes people do not interact with the person sitting next to them all semester or the person living in the next apartment. And sometimes you may be attracted to someone who is not in close proximity and with whom you do not have repeated contact. What might account for such effects? In other words, how can a person we don't know elicit a kind of instantaneous emotional reaction?

Whenever we like—or dislike—someone at first sight (the way my grandfather did when he met my grandmother for the first time), our reaction strongly suggests that something about that person has produced the positive or negative affect that, as we have already noted, is often the basis for liking or disliking. Presumably, this kind of reaction is based on past experiences, stereotypes, and attributions that are often both inaccurate and irrelevant (Andreoletti, Zebrowitz, & Lachman, 2001). For example, if a stranger reminds you of someone you know and like, you probably will respond positively to that person (Andersen & Baum, 1994). Or if the stranger belongs to a category of people about whom you hold an attitude (e.g., individuals from a particular ethnic group), you may tend to like the stranger if you have a positive attitude toward that group or dislike the stranger if you hold a negative attitude.

One pervasive factor that influences our initial responses to others is their **physical attractiveness** (Maner et al., 2003). Despite warnings to avoid "judging books by their covers," other's appearance has been found to be a powerful determinant of initial attraction to them, so we'll now take a closer look at the effects of this factor.

Physical Attractiveness: Beauty May Be Only Skin Deep, But We Pay A Lot of Attention to Skin

Certainly, at some point in your life, you have heard the saying "Don't judge a book by its cover," or the equivalent "Beauty is only skin deep." Both expressions warn us to avoid assigning too much weight to outward appearance—how people or objects (books) look. Nevertheless, physical appearance has been found to be a powerful factor in our liking for others (Collins & Zebrowitz, 1995).

Both in experiments and in the real world, physical appearance determines many types of interpersonal evaluations, including judgments of guilt or innocence in the courtroom (see Chapter 12). People even respond more positively to attractive infants than to unattractive ones (Karraker & Stern, 1990). Moreover, as we'll see later in this chapter, appearance plays an important role in mate selection.

One of the reasons we focus on appearance is that we hold stereotypes based on how people look. Before you read any further, take a look at Figure 7.7 and follow the instructions it contains.

Most people tend to believe that attractive men and women are more poised, interesting, sociable, independent, dominant, exciting, sexy, well adjusted, socially skilled, successful, and more masculine (men) and more feminine (women) than unattractive individuals (Dion & Dion, 1991; Hatfield & Sprecher, 1986a). Altogether, as social psychologists have repeatedly found in their research, most people assume that "what is beautiful is good" (Dion, Berscheid, & Hatfield, 1972).

Despite widespread acceptance of attractiveness as an important cue to personality and character, most of the appearance stereotypes are incorrect (Feingold, 1992,

physical attractiveness
The combination of characteristics that are evaluated as beautiful or handsome at the positive extreme and as unattractive at the negative extreme.

Figure 7.7
How Would You Describe These People?
Make a list of the personality characteristics that you think might best describe each of these individuals. For example, what do you think about each person's sociability, adjustment, intelligence, poise, independence, masculinity-femininity, popularity, vanity, potential for success, integrity, concern for others, sexual appeal, and other qualities? When you are finished, find out whether your perceptions of them are similar to those of most other people, as indicated by findings described in this section.

Kenealy, Gleeson, Frude, & Shaw, 1991). For instance, extremely evil people (e.g., Saddam Hussein's sons) may be good looking, and many people who do not look like movie stars—for instance, Bill Gates—are often intelligent, interesting, kind, and generous. Though stereotypes about attractive people tend to be invalid, attractiveness is associated with popularity, good interpersonal skills, and high self-esteem (Diener, Wolsic, & Fujita, 1995; Johnstone, Frame, & Bouman, 1992). A possible reason is that very attractive people have spent their lives being liked and treated well by other people who are responding to their appearance (Zebrowitz, Collins, & Dutta, 1998). And, those who are attractive to others are often aware that they are pretty or handsome (Marcus & Miller, 2003). In other words, appearance does not create social skills and self-esteem but such characteristics are developed because of the way other people have reacted to appearance.

Though people who are beautiful are usually seen as "good," attractiveness is also associated with some negative assumptions. For example, beautiful women are sometimes perceived as vain and materialistic (Cash & Duncan, 1984). Also handsome male political candidates are more likely to be elected than unattractive ones, but an attractive female candidate is not helped by her appearance (Sigelman, Thomas, Sigelman & Robich, 1986), possibly because being "too feminine" can be assumed to be detrimental for someone in a legislative, judicial, or executive position.

What, Exactly, Constitutes "Attractiveness"?

Judgments of one's own attractiveness may not match the judgments of others well, but there is surprisingly good agreement when two people are asked to rate a third person (Cunningham, Roberts, Wu, Barbee, & Druen, 1995; Fink & Penton-Voak, 2002). The greatest agreement occurs when men are judging the attractiveness of women (Marcus & Miller, 2003). Despite general agreement about who is and is not attractive, it is not easy to identify the precise cues that determine these judgments.

In attempting to discover just what these cues might be, investigators have used two quite different procedures. One approach is to identify a group of individuals who are rated as attractive and then to determine what they have in common. Cunningham (1986) asked male undergraduates to rate photographs of young women. The women who were judged to be most attractive fell into one of two groups, as shown in Figure 7.8. Some had "childlike features" consisting of large, widely spaced eyes and a small nose and chin. Women like Eva Longoria fit this category and are considered "cute" (Johnston & Oliver-Rodriguez, 1997; McKelvie, 1993a). The other category of attractive women had mature features with prominent cheekbones, high eyebrows, large pupils, and a big smile—Angelina Jolie is an example. These same two general facial types are found among fashion models, and they are commonly seen among Caucasian, African American, and Asian American women (Ashmore, Solomon, & Longo, 1996).

A second approach to the determination of what is meant by attractiveness was taken by Langlois and Roggman (1990). They began with several facial photographs and then used computer digitizing to combine multiple faces into one face. The image in each photo is divided into microscopic squares, and each square is translated into a number that represents a specific shade. Then the numbers are averaged across two or more pictures, and the result is translated back into a composite image.

Figure 7.8
Two Types of Attractive Women: Cute or Mature
The study of physical attractiveness has identified two types of women who are rated most attractive. One category is considered cute—childlike features, large widely spaced eyes, with a small nose and chin—for example, Eva Longoria. The other category of attractiveness is the mature look—prominent cheekbones, high eyebrows, large pupils, and a big smile—for example, Angelina Jolie.

You might reasonably guess that a face created by averaging would be rated as average in attractiveness. Instead, composite faces are rated as more attractive than most of the individual faces used to make the composite (Langlois, Roggman, & Musselman, 1994; Rhodes & Tremewan, 1996). In addition, the more faces that are averaged, the more beautiful the resulting face. As shown in Figure 7.9, when you combine as many as thirty-two faces, "you end up with a face that is pretty darned attractive" (Judith Langlois quoted in Lemley, 2000, p. 47). As a note, you might find it interesting to visit *http://campaignforrealbeauty.com/flat4.asp?id=6909;* it shows how personal beauty can be enhanced by technology. As shown in this site, the faces presented in ads and on billboards are not nearly as attractive in reality as they appear when advertisers— and beauty specialists—get through "enhancing" them.

Why should composite faces be especially attractive? It is possible that each person's schema of women and of men is created in our cognitions in much the same way that the averaged face is created. That is, we form such schemas on the basis of our experiences with many different images, so a composite face is closer to that schema than is any specific face. If this is an accurate analysis, a composite of other kinds of images should also constitute the most attractive alternative, but this does not work with composite dogs or composite birds (Halberstadt & Rhodes, 2000). It may be that our perception of human composites is different because it was historically more important to our species to recognize potential friends, enemies, and mates than to recognize dogs and birds.

In addition to the details of facial features, perceptions of attractiveness are also influenced by the situation. When research participants are shown pictures of very attractive people, they rate a stranger as less attractive than do participants who have not been looking at such pictures (Kenrick, Montello, Gutierres, & Trost, 1993). Why? The difference between the attractiveness of the people in the photographs and the stranger creates what is known as a contrast effect. In a similar way, men rate their own female partners less positively if they have just been looking at photos of especially attractive women (Kenrick & Gutierres, 1980) or perhaps at a Web site like the one mentioned previously, where normal women are converted— almost as if by magic—into something approaching supermodels.

Other aspects of context also matter. As suggested by Mickey Gilley's song about searching for romance in bars, "the girls all get prettier at closing time." In fact, both "girls" and "boys" are perceived as more attractive by members of the opposite sex as the evening progresses—an effect some describe using the term "beer goggles" (Nida & Koon, 1983; Pennebaker et al., 1979). Ratings of same-sex strangers do not improve as closing time approaches, so alcohol consumption (which might impair judgment) does not explain the effects (Gladue & Delaney, 1990). Rather, as people pair off, and the number of available partners decreases, the resulting scarcity results in a more positive evaluation of those who remain unattached.

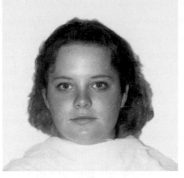

2 Faces

4 Faces

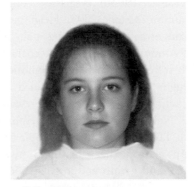

8 Faces

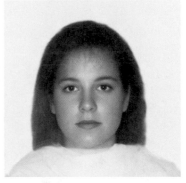

16 Faces

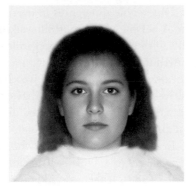

32 Faces

Figure 7.9
Averaging Multiple Faces Results in an Attractive Face
When computer images of several different faces are combined to form a composite, the resulting average face is seen as more attractive than the individual faces that were averaged. As the number of faces contributing to the average increases, the attractiveness of the composite increases.

(*Source:* Lemley, 2000, p. 47.)

Other Aspects of Appearance and Behavior that Influence Attraction

When we meet someone for the first time, we usually react to a variety of factors. Any observable cue, no matter how superficial, may evoke a stereotype, and the resulting emotional reactions lead to instant likes and dislikes. One of the factors that have been studied is clothing (Cheverton & Byrne, 1998; Jarrell, 1998). Beyond such factors as neatness (Mack & Rainey, 1990), clothing colors seem to have an effect. People make an automatic association between brightness and affect; specifically, bright equals good and dark equals bad (Meier, Robinson, & Clore, 2004). However cultural factors play a role. I have lived in France (in the beautiful city of Toulouse), and there, dark colors are seen as quite attractive. In fact, there is a French saying to the effect that "Black or grey is always in style." Attraction is also influenced by the presence of observable disabilities (Fichten & Amsel, 1986), behavioral cues that suggest mental illness (Schumacher, Corrigan, & Dejong, 2003), perceived age (McKelvie, 1993b), eyeglasses (Lundberg & Sheehan, 1994), and the presence of a beard (Shannon & Stark, 2003). Height, too, plays a role, and in political elections, the taller candidates often win (Zebrowitz et al., 2003).

Among other observable characteristics is a person's physique and is also associated with stereotypes that trigger emotional reactions and differential attraction. It was once thought that body type provided information about personality (Sheldon, Stevens, & Tucker, 1940), but decades of research indicated that this assumption was an inaccurate one. Nevertheless, people do respond to others as if physique provided useful information. Though it is untrue, people believe that a round and fat body indicates a sad and sloppy person, that a hard and muscular body indicates good health and lack of intelligence, and a thin and angular body indicates intelligence and fearfulness (Gardner & Tockerman, 1994; Ryckman, Robbins, Kaczor, & Gold, 1989). We'll return to the potentially damaging effects that can stem from "anti-fat" attitudes and beliefs in Chapter 12.

Observable differences in overt behavior also elicit stereotypes that influence attraction. A person with a youthful walking style elicits a more positive response than one who walks with an elderly style, regardless of gender or actual age (Montepare & Zebrowitz-McArthur, 1988). A person with a firm handshake is perceived as being extroverted and emotionally expressive—positive characteristics (Chaplin et al., 2000). People respond positively to someone whose behavior is animated (Bernieri, Gillis, Davis, & Grahe, 1996), who actively participates in class discussions (Bell, 1995), and who acts modestly rather than arrogantly (Hareli & Weiner, 2000).

In initial encounters, men who behave in a dominant, authoritative, competitive style are preferred to submissive, noncompetitive, less masculine styles (Friedman, Riggio, & Casella, 1988). If there are additional interactions that provide more information about the individual, however, the preference shifts to men who are prosocial and sensitive (Jensen-Campbell, West, & Graziano, 1995; Morey & Gerber, 1995). It might be said that over the long haul, nice guys finish first.

Perhaps the most surprising influence on interpersonal perceptions is a person's first name. Familiar names activate a category of experience and information that provides us with a stereotype (Macrae, Mitchell, & Pendy, 2002). And various male and female names elicit widely shared positive and negative stereotypes (Mehrabian & Piercy, 1993), as shown in Table 7.1. In addition, a distinctive first name attached to a highly publicized individual (real or fictional) becomes associated with some of the characteristics of that individual; the resulting stereotype then transfers to anyone else who happens to have that name. What do you think your first thought would be if you met someone named Osama, Keanu, Rosie, Orlando, Beyonce, or Gisele?

Concern about One's Appearance—and Rejection because of It

Given that physical appearance plays an important role in interpersonal attraction, it is not at all surprising that most of us do everything we can to enhance it—to be as physically attractive as possible. That's one reason why the sales of cosmetics, clothing, and various grooming aids often continue to boom even during economic downturns. It's probably safe to say that everyone—even people who are extremely attractive—worry about their own

Table 7.1   What's in a Name? The Answer Is Stereotypes

Initial impressions are sometimes based on a person's first name. Once again, stereotypes lead to inaccurate assumptions, and the assumptions influence interpersonal behavior.

MALE NAMES	FEMALE NAMES	ATTRIBUTIONS ABOUT THE INDIVIDUAL
Alexander	Elizabeth	Successful
Otis	Mildred	*Unsuccessful*
Joshua	Mary	Moral
Roscoe	Tracy	*Immoral*
Mark	Jessica	Popular
Norbert	Harriet	*Unpopular*
Henry	Ann	Warm
Ogden	Freida	*Cold*
Scott	Brittany	Cheerful
Willard	Agatha	*Not cheerful*
Taylor	Rosalyn	Masculine
Eugene	Isabella	*Feminine*

(*Source:* Based on information in Mehrabian and Piercy, 1993.)

appearance from time to time. After all, there is a real possibility that if others don't like the way we look, they may reject us on this basis. In other words, most people experience what is known as **appearance-rejection sensitivity** from time to time: They worry about their appearance and fear that others may snub them because they don't quite measure up on this dimension (Park & Pelham, 2006).

As you can readily guess, people differ greatly with respect to how often and how intensely they experience such concerns, and such differences can be measured by a recently developed scale (Park, 2007). Further, individuals who score high on the appearance-rejection sensitivity scale react much more negatively to experiences that threaten their confidence in their own appearance. Such reactions are clearly illustrated in a study conducted by Park. She asked participants in her research to either think about aspects of their own bodies and physical appearance that they do not like or simply to think about objects in the room where the research took place. The first condition, of course, was designed to threaten their confidence in their own appearance, and it was predicted that participants asked to think about their own perceived flaws would report feeling rejected by others more than those who performed the neutral, think-about-objects task. As shown in Figure 7.10, this is

appearance-rejection sensitivity
From time to time these people worry about their appearance and fear that others may snub them because they don't quite measure up on this dimension.

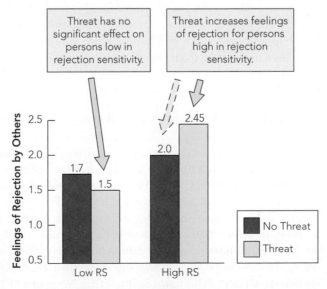

Figure 7.10
Concern over Our Physical Appearance: The Effects Can Be Negative
When individuals high in concern that they will be rejected by others because of their appearance (people high in appearance-based rejection sensitivity) think about the aspects of their own appearance they don't like (threat condition), their feelings of rejection by others increase. People low in appearance-based rejection sensitivity, in contrast, don't show such effects.

(*Source:* Based on data from Park, 2007).

precisely what occurred. These findings, and those of related studies (e.g., Park & Pelham, 2006), indicate that concern about physical appearance is an important matter for many people—one that affects their self-esteem and their capacity to form satisfying relationships with others. So is beauty only skin deep? Perhaps, but its effects seem to go far deeper than what can be directly seen with our eyes.

KeyPoints

- The initial contact between two people is often based on the proximity, that is, they are near each other in physical space.

- Proximity, in turn, leads to repeated exposure, and that often produces positive affect and increased attraction (the mere exposure effect).

- Interpersonal attraction and judgments based on stereotypes are strongly affected by various observable characteristics of those we meet, including physical attractiveness. People like and make positive attributions about attractive men and women of all ages, despite the fact that assumptions based on appearance are usually inaccurate.

- In addition to attractiveness, many other observable characteristics influence initial interpersonal evaluations, including physique, weight, behavioral style, food preferences, first names, and other superficial characteristics.

- Individuals differ in their concern that they will be rejected by others because of their appearance, and people high in such concern often feel rejected by others and experience reduced self-esteem.

Think About It

If initial attraction between people is a result of factors such as proximity, repeated exposure, and physical appearance, how do people ever choose someone who is "right" for them—someone with whom they can form a stable, happy, long-term relationship? In other words, how do we overcome the powerful initial influence of factors that are not predictive of happy relationships?

Factors Based on Interacting with Others: Similarity and Mutual Liking

Although our own need for affiliation, proximity, repeated exposure, and others' physical appearance can exert strong effects on interpersonal attraction, they are far from the entire story. Some important factors that affect attraction only emerge as we interact with others—communicate with them and acquire more information about them. Among these, two have been found to be the most influential: our degree of similarity to others and the extent to which they like us.

Similarity: Birds of a Feather Actually Do Flock Together

The role of similarity in generating interpersonal attraction is now widely accepted. This phenomenon has been observed and discussed for well over two thousand years, beginning with Aristotle's (330 B.C./1932) essay on friendship. Empirical support for the "similarity hypothesis" was not provided, however, until Sir Francis Galton (1870/1952) obtained correlational data on married couples, indicating that spouses resembled one another in many respects. In the first half of the twentieth century, additional correlational studies continued to find that friends and spouses expressed a greater than chance degree of similarity (e.g., Hunt, 1935). The positive correlations could have meant either that liking led to similarity or vice versa, but in well-known early research, Newcomb (1956) found that similar attitudes predicted subsequent liking between students. In his research, he reasoned that if attitudes were measured before people had even met and it was found that later, the more similar their attitudes the more they liked each other, it could be concluded that similarity produced such attraction. To test this hypothesis, he studied two groups of transfer students—students who had not met each other before coming to the university. He measured their attitudes about issues, such as the family, religion, public affairs, and race relations by mail, before the students reached campus. Then their liking for one another was assessed weekly after they came to campus. Results indicated that in fact, the more similar the students were initially, the more they liked each other by the end of the semester. This was strong evidence that similarity produced attraction rather than vice versa. Newcomb's initial findings were confirmed in many later studies (Byrne, 1961b; Schachter, 1951), so just as Aristotle and others had speculated, research findings indicated that two people who find that they are similar like each other because they are similar.

Now, before we go on to describe the research that justifies this conclusion, we'll pause to address a question about which you may already be wondering: "If similarity is a cause of attraction, what about opposites? Don't they also attract? For a discussion of this intriguing—and complex issue—read *Making Sense of Common Sense: A Social Psychological Perspective* below.

MAKING SENSE OF COMMON SENSE
A SOCIAL PSYCHOLOGICAL PERSPECTIVE
Complementarity or Similarity: Which Is the Basis for Attraction?

The idea that opposites attract is nearly as ancient as the idea that birds of a feather flock together and as new as the last movie you saw in which two different people become friends, roommates, or romantic partners. In plays, movies, and television series, a familiar story line is one in which two quite different people are attracted to one another, in part because they are so different. Think, for example, of Marge and Homer Simpson or a movie such as *Shrek*. In contrast, such real life pairings are relatively rare (Angier, 2003; Buston & Emlen, 2003). Even when opposites do form a relationship (e.g., a married couple like Democratic strategist James Carville and Republican strategist Mary Matalin; see Figure 7.11) one can guess that despite their opposing political views, they have a great deal in common. For example, both are intensely interested in the political process.

In the early days of research on this topic, the proposed attraction of opposites was often phrased in terms of complementarities. That is, it was suggested that dominant individuals would be attracted to submissive ones, talkative people to quiet ones, sadists to masochists, etc. The idea was that such complementary characteristics would be mutually reinforcing and hence a good basis for a relationship. Direct tests of these propositions failed to support complementarity as a determinant of attraction, even with respect to dominance and submissiveness (Palmer & Byrne, 1970). With respect to attitudes, values, personality characteristics, bad habits, intellectual ability, income level, and even minor preferences, such as choos-

ing the right-hand versus left-hand aisle in a movie theater, similarity was found to result in attraction (Byrne, 1971). On the basis of multiple experiments over the past

Figure 7.11
With Rare Exceptions, Opposites Don't Attract
Though the belief that opposites attract is a familiar one in fiction, similarity is a much better predictor of attraction. Even when seemingly opposite people do attract one another (as with Democrat James Carville and his wife Republican Mary Matalin) they are usually found to have a great deal in common.

several decades, one can only conclude that there is no evidence that opposites attract.

(continued on page 240)

Complementarity or Similarity: Which Is the Basis for Attraction?, *cont.*

There is, however, consistent evidence that complementarity sometimes does operate when a male and a female are interacting. Specifically, when one person engages in dominant behavior, the other then responds in a submissive fashion (Markey, Funder, & Ozer, 2003; Sadler & Woody, 2003). And this specific kind of complementarity leads to greater attraction than when the second person copies the first person (Tiedens & Fragale, 2003). Given these findings, we must add that the opposites may, in fact, attract, at least with respect to dominance versus submission in male–female interactions. With respect to other kinds of interaction (e.g., a person who is verbally withdrawn and unresponsive interacting with someone who is verbally expressive and critical) opposite styles not only fail to attract, but they are also quite incompatible and more likely to lead to rejection and avoidance than liking and attraction (Swann, Rentfrow, & Gosling, 2003). Overall, then, the evidence is both strong and consistent: similarity—not complementarity (opposites)—seems to be the basis for attraction across many kinds of situations and many kinds of relationships.

Similarity–Dissimilarity: A Consistent Predictor of Attraction

attitude similarity
The extent to which two individuals share the same attitudes.

similarity–dissimilarity effect
The consistent finding that people respond positively to indications that another person is similar to themselves and negatively to indications that another person is dissimilar from themselves.

proportion of similarity
The number of specific indicators that two people are similar divided by the number of specific indicators that two people are similar plus the number of specific indicators that they are dissimilar.

Much of the early work on the **similarity–dissimilarity effect** focused on **attitude similarity,** but this phrase was generally used as a shorthand term that included not only similarity of attitudes, but also of beliefs, values, and interests. The initial laboratory experiments on this topic consisted of two steps: First, the attitudes of the participants were assessed and second, these individuals were exposed to the attitudes and such of a stranger and asked to evaluate this person (Byrne, 1961b). The results were straightforward in that people consistently indicated that they liked similar strangers much better than they liked dissimilar ones. Not only do we like people who are similar to ourselves, but we also judge them to be more intelligent, better informed, more moral, and better adjusted than people who are dissimilar. As you might suspect on the basis of our discussion of affect previously in this chapter, similarity arouses positive feelings and dissimilarity arouses negative feelings.

Many such investigations with a variety of populations, procedures, and topics, revealed that people respond to similarity–dissimilarity in a surprisingly precise way. Attraction is determined by the **proportion of similarity.** That is, when the number of topics on which two people express similar views is divided by the total number of topics on which they have communicated, the resulting proportion can be inserted in a simple formula that allows us to predict attraction (Byrne & Nelson, 1965) The higher the proportion of similarity is, the greater the liking is, as illustrated in Figure 7.12. No one knows exactly how attitudinal information is processed to produce that outcome, but it is as if

Figure 7.12
As Attitude Similarity Increases, So, Too, Does Attraction
The relationship between proportion of similar attitudes and attraction is a consistent and highly predictable one. The greater the proportion of similar attitudes, the greater is the attraction. This relationship can be expressed in a simple linear formula, and it holds true for both genders and across different age groups, different cultures, and different educational levels.

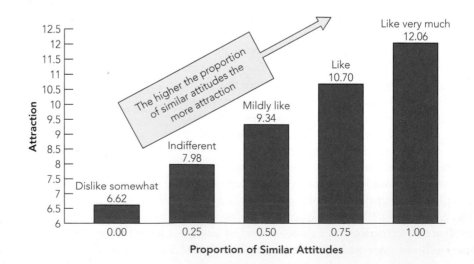

people automatically engage in some kind of cognitive addition and division, manipulating the units of positive and negative affect they experience.

The effect of attitude similarity on attraction is a strong one, and it holds true regardless of the number of topics on which people express their views and regardless of how important or trivial the topics may be. It holds equally true for males and females, regardless of age, educational, or cultural differences (Byrne, 1971). The general level of attraction may vary and the total impact of proportion may vary based on dispositional factors, but the basic proportion effect remains true (Kwan, 1998).

The most serious challenge to the validity of such findings was offered by Rosenbaum (1986) when he proposed that using proportion as the independent variable made it impossible to separate the effect of similarity from the effect of dissimilarity. Based on some data he gathered, the **repulsion hypothesis** was put forth as an alternative to the similarity–dissimilarity effect. The basic idea is that information about similarity has no effect on attraction; people are simply repulsed by information about dissimilarity. Later research was able to show that the idea is wrong (Smeaton, Byrne, & Murnen, 1989), but there was a grain of truth in the repulsion hypothesis. Specifically, under most circumstances, information about dissimilarity has a slightly stronger effect on attraction than the same amount of information about similarity (Chen & Kenrick, 2002; Singh & Ho, 2000; Tan & Singh, 1995).

Beyond attitudes and values, many kinds of similarity–dissimilarity have been investigated, and in each instance people prefer those similar to themselves rather than dissimilar. Examples include similarity–dissimilarity with respect to physical attractiveness (Zajonc, Adelmann, Murphy, & Niedenthal, 1987), smoking marijuana (Eisenman, 1985), religious practices (Kandel, 1978), self-concept (Klohnen & Luo, 2003), being a "morning person" versus an "evening person" (Watts, 1982), and finding the same jokes amusing (Cann, Calhoun, & Banks, 1995). Together, these diverse findings indicate that similarity is indeed an important determinant of attraction. But why is this so? Why do we like others who are similar to ourselves but tend to dislike others who are different? That's a key question and one to which we turn next.

Explaining the Effect of Similarity–Dissimilarity on Attraction

To ask the same question in a slightly different way, *why* does similarity elicit positive affect while dissimilarity elicits negative affect? The oldest explanation—**balance theory**—was proposed independently by Newcomb (1961) and by Heider (1958). This framework suggests that people naturally organize their likes and dislikes in a symmetrical way (Hummert, Crockett, & Kemper, 1990). When two people like each other and discover that they are similar in some specific respect, this constitutes a state of balance, and balance is emotionally pleasant. When two people like each other and find out that they are dissimilar in some specific respect, the result is imbalance. Imbalance is emotionally unpleasant, causing the individuals to strive to restore balance by inducing one of them to change and thus create similarity or by misperceiving the dissimilarity or simply by deciding to dislike one another. Whenever two people dislike one another, their relationship involves nonbalance. This is not especially pleasant or unpleasant because each individual is indifferent about the other person's similarities or dissimilarities.

These aspects of balance theory are correct, but they do not deal with the question of why similarity should matter in the first place. So, a second level of explanation is needed. Why should you care if someone differs from you with respect to musical preferences, belief in God, or anything else? One answer is provided by Festinger's (1954) **social comparison theory.** Briefly stated, you compare your attitudes and beliefs with those of others because the only way you can evaluate your accuracy and normality is by finding that other people agree with you. This is not a perfect way to determine the truth, but it is often the best we can do. For example, if you are the only one who believes that invisible Martians have landed and are living in your attic, the odds are that you are incorrect. No one wants to be in that position, so we turn to others to obtain consensual validation—

repulsion hypothesis
Rosenbaum's provocative proposal that attraction is not increased by similar attitudes but is simply decreased by dissimilar attitudes. This hypothesis is incorrect as stated, but it is true that dissimilar attitudes tend to have negative effects that are stronger than the positive effects of similar attitudes.

balance theory
The formulations of Heider and of Newcomb that specify the relationships among (1) an individual's liking for another person, (2) his or her attitude about a given topic, and (3) the other person's attitude about the same topic. Balance (liking plus agreement) results in a positive emotional state. Imbalance (liking plus disagreement) results in a negative state and a desire to restore balance. Nonbalance (disliking plus either agreement or disagreement) leads to indifference.

social comparison theory
Festinger (1954) suggested that people compare themselves to others because, for many domains and attributes, there is no objective yardstick with which to evaluate the self, so we compare ourselves to others to gain this information.

evidence that others share our views. When you learn that someone else holds the same attitudes and beliefs that you do, it feels good because such information at least suggests that you have sound judgment, are in contact with reality, and so forth. Dissimilarity suggests the opposite, and that creates negative affect, unless such dissimilarity comes from out-group members, whom we expect to be different from ourselves.

A third approach to an explanation of the similarity–dissimilarity effect rests on an evolutionary perspective as an **adaptive response** to potential danger. Gould (1996) suggests that our negative reaction to dissimilar others may have originated when humans were living in small groups of hunters and gatherers on the savannas of Africa. It seems that a great deal (perhaps most) of human animosity is based on reactions to dissimilarity. In the words of Howard Stern, "If you're not like me, I hate you" (Zoglin, 1993), and such reactions, in turn, may be based, at least in part, on the evolutionary history of our species.

Imagine what it was like when a band of our primitive ancestors accidentally encountered humans from a different band. If, the strangers are good and kind, a friendly approach could benefit both groups. If, however, the strangers posed a threat (perhaps the most likely possibility), then greeting them with friendliness and trust would be the most dangerous and least adaptive response that could be made. Survival, and hence reproduction, would best be enhanced by either retreating or attacking, and the latter is probably the most effective way to survive.

This general account at least seems plausible, so we may have strong, inherited tendencies to fear and hate anyone (especially of the same gender) who is different from ourselves. Though such reactions may have once been crucial to survival and reproductive success for our species, today they form the basis for prejudice, hate crimes, and a general dislike of anyone who differs from ourselves.

Reciprocal Liking or Disliking: Liking Those Who Like Us

Everyone (or at least, nearly everyone) wants to be liked. Not only do we enjoy being evaluated positively, we even welcome such input when it is inaccurate or even if it is an insincere attempt at flattery. To an outside observer, false flattery may be perceived accurately for what it is, but to the person being flattered, it is likely to appear accurate, even if not completely honest (Gordon, 1996; Vonk, 1998, 2002). Using this type of ingratiation technique to deal with a boss or supervisor may annoy one's coworkers, but it often pays off in raises and promotions (Orpen, 1996). Only if someone is totally obvious does flattery fail.

Research findings offer strong support for the powerful effects of others' liking for us on our liking for them (e.g., Condon & Crano, 1988), so overall, it appears that the rule of reciprocity—which applies to many aspects of social life—operates with respect to attraction, too. In general, we tend to like those who express liking toward us and dislike others who indicate that as far as they are concerned, we don't really measure up.

What Do We Desire In Others? Designing Ideal Interaction Partners

In this discussion so far, we have focused on the factors that lead individuals to like—or dislike—each other. But now, consider a different but closely related question: What do people desire in others? In other words, suppose you could design the perfect person for a particular kind of relationship—a romantic interest, a work group member, someone to play sports with, whatever. Can you think of the characteristics you'd most want this person to have? In other words, what would make you like this person a great deal—more, perhaps, than anyone else you have actually met? That question has recently been addressed by social psychologists (e.g., Kurzbaum & Neuberg, 2005), and in a sense, it serves as a good bridge to the discussion of relationships that forms the next major portion of this chapter.

While many studies have addressed this issue, perhaps the most revealing is research conducted by Cottrell, Neuberg, and Li (2007). These researchers began by asking under-

adaptive response
Any physical characteristic or behavioral tendency that enhances the odds of reproductive success for an individual or for other individuals with similar genes.

graduate students to "create an ideal person" and rating thirty-one positive characteristics in terms of how important it is for their ideal person to have. Included among the characteristics were trustworthiness, cooperativeness, agreeableness, extraversion (outgoing, sociable), emotionally stable, physical health, and physical attractiveness. Results were clear: trustworthiness and cooperativeness were viewed as the most important traits, followed by agreeableness (being kind, interpersonally warm) and extraversion (being outgoing and sociable). These initial findings indicate that overall, there are indeed characteristics that most people desire in others. They do not, however, address another question: Do these characteristics vary with the kind of relationship in question? In other words, do we desire different traits in friends, work-partners, lovers, friends, or employees?

To find out, the researchers asked undergraduate students of both genders to imagine creating ideal members of several different groups and relationships—work project team members, final exam study group members, golf team members, sorority members, fraternity members, close friends, and employees. For each task or relationship, they rated the extent to which seventy-five different traits were important for this ideal person to possess. As shown in Table 7.2, results were revealing. First, across all seven relationships, trustworthiness and cooperativeness were rated as most important. Agreeableness followed closely. As you might expect, though, other traits were viewed as more or less important, depending on the kind of relationship participants had with this imaginary ideal person. For instance, intelligence was rated as quite important for project teams and study groups but much less important for fraternity or sorority members. Similarly, humor was rated as quite important for close friends but less important for employees or project team and study group members. In other words, overall, the results pointed to two major conclusions. First, there are several traits (trustworthiness, cooperativeness, and agreeableness) that we value in everyone—no matter what kind of relationship we have with them. Second, we value other traits differentially—that is, to a greater or lesser degree—depending on the kind of relationship we have with the other person.

In sum, although we can't always explain why we like or dislike other people, it seems clear that our reactions in these respects are somewhat predictable. They are influenced by

Table 7.2 What Do We Desire in Others? It Depends on the Context

As shown here, several traits (trustworthiness, cooperativeness, and agreeableness) are viewed as important in ideal partners across many different kinds of relationships (project teams, employees, friends, and so on). The importance of other traits, however, varies with the kind of relationship in question. For instance, attractiveness is important in a sorority member but not in a project team or study group member. (High ratings for various traits are shown in boldface and indicate that the traits in question were rated as very important by research participants.)

TRAIT	PROJECT TEAM	STUDY GROUP	GOLD TEAM	SORORITY	FRATERNITY	CLOSE FRIEND	EMPLOYEE
Trustworthiness	7.35	6.87	7.74	7.45	7.33	7.68	7.78
Cooperativeness	6.39	5.93	5.70	6.51	6.29	6.79	6.28
Agreeableness	6.36	5.65	5.38	6.99	6.50	7.14	6.76
Attractiveness	2.84	2.68	3.17	6.36	5.24	4.73	3.74
Intelligence	7.67	7.74	5.52	6.04	5.97	6.51	7.39
Humor	5.17	4.48	5.02	6.61	6.92	7.53	5.49
Wealth	3.43	2.17	3.70	4.82	4.92	3.94	4.45

(*Source:* Based on data from Cottrell et al., 2007).

a number of factors, including our similarity to other people, their liking for us, their appearance, how frequently we interact with them, and their possession of certain key traits. Viewed through the lens of social psychological research, then, interpersonal attraction loses some of its mystery, but at the same time, becomes much more understandable and predictable. And as we noted in Chapter 1, understanding and prediction are key goals of all branches of science, regardless of whether they study the nature of galaxies and atoms, the biochemistry of life, or the social side of life.

KeyPoints

- One of the many factors determining attraction toward another person is similarity of attitudes, beliefs, values, and interests.

- Despite the continuing popularity of the idea that opposites attract (complementarity), it rarely occurs in the real world.

- Though dissimilarity tends to have a greater impact on attraction than similarity, we respond to both, and the larger the proportion of similar attitudes is, the greater the attraction is.

- The similarity–dissimilarity effect has been explained by balance theory, social comparison theory, and by an evolutionary perspective as an adaptive response to potential danger.

- We especially like other people who indicate that they like us. We dislike quite a bit those who dislike and negatively evaluate us.

Think About It

If we tend to like others who are similar to ourselves and who indicate that they like us, doesn't this put us at risk for surrounding ourselves with people who never challenge our beliefs or views and who express positive evaluations of us regardless of whether we deserve these?

Close Relationships: Family, Friends, Lovers, and Spouses

Social psychologists began investigating the nature and causes of interpersonal attraction almost one hundred years ago, although they did not turn their attention to interpersonal or close relationships until recent decades. Once it got started, however, such research has literally exploded in volume, with the result that we now know much more about the formation and nature of close relationships than was true before (e.g., Adams, 2006; Arriaga, Reed, Goodfriend, & Agnew, 2006; Berscheid & Reis, 1998; Lehmiller & Agnew, 2006), In the sections that follow, we'll describe what has been learned about such relationships, beginning with relationships with family members, and turning to romantic relationships and what is meant by love. Finally, we'll consider marriage, a relationship that exerts profound effects on our lives, and sometimes (as in the case of my grandparents and parents), lasts for many decades. Before turning to the nature of these relationships and the factors that affect them, however, we'll first comment briefly on the fact that all relationships are strongly influenced by the cultures in which they develop.

The Cultural Foundations of Relationships: Seeing the Social World through the Lens of Our Culture

Initially, you might assume that close relationships are much the same all over the world: family ties, friendships, love—these are relationships all human beings experience. To an extent, of course, that's true; these relationships, and the feelings that accompany them, are somewhat universal (Adams, Anderson, & Adonu, 2004). On the other hand, the nature and form of such relationships is also strongly affected by cultural factors. In other words, the cultures in which we live often tell us what to expect in various relationships (marriage, friendship, family ties), what are obligations are in those relationships, and how these close social ties should be formed and then develop. For instance, consider how different expectations concerning marriage tend to be in countries that accept only monogamous marriages and those in which people can be married to several partners at the same time. Similarly, consider family responsibilities. In many cultures, once children are grown, they are not required to care for their parents as they age. In others, in contrast, children who fail to take ill or aging parents into their homes to care for them would be strongly condemned. So, clearly, cultural factors often play a powerful role in determining the nature of important social relationships.

One especially intriguing illustration of such effects is provided by research conducted by Adams (2005) on a kind of relationship that seems to vary tremendously across cultures: **enemyship.** This refers to a personal relationship based on hatred and malice in which one person wishes to produce another person's downfall and attempts to sabotage that person's life progress (Femlee & Sprecher, 2000). In many African countries, individuals are familiar with this concept and believe that they often experience such relationships, while in North American cultures the concept is much less familiar. Thus when asked if they are the target of interpersonal enemies, fully 79 percent of research participants in Ghana indicate they are, while only 17 percent of North American students answer yes. Similarly, while North Americans generally believe that such personal enemies should be ignored (54 percent), Ghanaians are more likely to indicate that it is better to confront them (23 percent) or to seek protection against such person (26 percent) by purchasing amulets or through the help of a sorcerer (see Figure 7.13).

While these findings are interesting in themselves, they also illustrate an important principle: Our perceptions of social relationships—what they should be like, what they involve, and how we should behave in them—are strongly shaped by the cultures in which we live. To paraphrase Adams (2006), relationships are not context-free expressions of human nature; rather, they reflect the constructions of reality provided to us by our cultures and do, indeed, vary greatly around the globe.

Interdependent Relationships: Family and Friends

While close relationships are indeed strongly influenced by cultural factors, they share one common characteristic: **interdependence.** This term refers to an interpersonal association in which two people consistently influence each other's lives (Holmes, 2002). They often focus their thoughts and emotions on one another and

enemyship
This refers to a personal relationship based on hatred and malice in which one person wishes to produce another person's downfall and attempts to sabotage that person's life progress.

interdependence
Refers to an interpersonal association in which two people influence each others' lives. They often focus their thoughts on one another and regularly engage in joint activities.

Figure 7.13
Enemyship: A Culturally Linked Type of Relationships
In several African cultures (e.g., Ghana), a type of relationship known as enemyship is widely perceived to exist. This is a relationship in which one person wants to produce another's downfall or block their progress in life. To cope with this culturally defined problem, individuals often purchase amulets (special charms) or seek the help of sorcerers who specialize in reducing the harmful effects of enemies.

regularly engage in joint activities. Interdependent relationships with family members, friends, and romantic partners include a sense of commitment to the relationship itself (Fehr, 1999). Interdependence occurs across age groups and across different kinds of interactions. The importance of forming such bonds with other people is emphasized by Ryff and Singer (2000, p. 30), who propose that "Quality ties to others are universally endorsed as central to optimal living."

Family: Where Relationships and Attachment Styles Begin

Parent-child interactions are of basic importance because this is usually one's first contact with another person. We come into the world ready to interact with other humans, but the specific characteristics of those interactions differ from person to person and family-to-family. It is those details that seem to have important implications for our later interpersonal behavior.

During the first year of life, when the range of possible behaviors is obviously limited, human infants are extremely sensitive to facial expressions, body movements, and the sounds people make. The person taking care of the baby is typically the mother, and she, in turn, is equally sensitive to what the infant does (Kochanska, Friesenborg, Lange, & Martel, 2004). As they interact, the two individuals communicate and reinforce the actions of one another (Murray & Trevarthen, 1986; Trevarthen, 1993). The adult shows interest in the infant's communication in various ways, such as engaging in baby talk and displaying exaggerated facial expressions. The infant, in turn, shows interest in the adult by attempting to make appropriate sounds and expressions. Such reciprocal interactions tend to be a positive educational experience for both participants (see Figure 7.14). There is even evidence that a mother's "baby talk" is "incredibly systematic and rhythmical"— much like that found in poetry and song lyrics (Miall & Dissanayake, quoted in Selim, 2004, p. 16). In addition to interpersonal bonding, these interactions may also form the basis for the emotional response to music and other artistic expressions.

attachment style
The degree of security experienced in interpersonal relationships. Differential styles initially develop in the interactions between infant and caregiver when the infant acquires basic attitudes about self-worth and interpersonal trust.

interpersonal trust
An attitudinal dimension underlying attachment styles that involves the belief that other people are generally trustworthy, dependable, and reliable as opposed to the belief that others are generally untrustworthy, undependable, and unreliable. This is the most successful and most desirable attachment style.

Figure 7.14
Infant-Mother Connection
Beginning in early infancy, babies are sensitive to the sounds, facial expressions, and bodily movements of their mothers or other caregivers. Caregivers, in turn, are equally sensitive to the infants' sounds, expressions, and movements. Such two-way communication constitutes the earliest form of social interaction.

The Lasting Importance of Parent-Child Interactions
Early relationships have primarily been studied by developmental psychologists, but the fact that these relationships affect the nature of later interpersonal behavior has led social psychologists to look more closely at what happens in early childhood.

As a brief overview, it appears that the quality of the interaction between a mother (or other caregiver) and infants determines their future interpersonal attitudes and actions as they progress into childhood, adolescence, and beyond (Oberlander, 2003). People are found to be consistent with respect to their interaction patterns in quite different relationships—parent-child, friends, and romantic partners (Foltz, Barber, Weinryb, Morse, & Chittams, 1999).

Bowlby's (1969, 1973) studies of mothers and infants led him to the concept of **attachment style,** which is the degree of security an individual feels in interpersonal relationships. It is assumed that an infant acquires two basic attitudes during its earliest interactions with an adult. The first is an attitude about self that we label self-esteem. The behavior and the emotional reactions of the caregiver provide information to the infant that he or she is a valued, important, loved individual, or at the other extreme, someone who is without value, unimportant, and unloved. The second basic attitude acquired by an infant is about other people, involving general expectancies and beliefs. This attitude is labeled **interpersonal trust.** It is based on whether the caregiver is perceived as trustworthy, dependable, and reliable or as relatively untrustworthy, undependable, and unreliable. Research findings suggest that we develop these basic attitudes about self and about others long before we acquire language skills.

Based on the two basic attitudes, infants, children, adolescents, and adults can be roughly classified as having a particular style involving interactions with others. There is some disagreement in the field as to the number of attachment styles, but there is general agreement about their effects (Bartholomew & Horowitz, 1991; Bowlby, 1982). If you conceptualize self-esteem as one dimension and interpersonal trust as another, it follows that a person could be high on both dimensions, low on both, or high on either one and low on the other. This yields four attachment styles. A person with a **secure attachment style** is high in both self-esteem and trust. Secure individuals are best able to form lasting, committed, satisfying relationships throughout life (Shaver & Brennan, 1992). In many respects, a secure style is ideal not only with respect to relationships, but it is also associated with a high need for achievement, low fear of failure, and strong curiosity about their environment (Elliot & Reis, 2003; Green & Campbell, 2000). Someone low in both self-esteem and interpersonal trust has a **fearful-avoidant attachment style.** Fearful-avoidant individuals tend not to form close relationships or to have unhappy ones (Mikulincer, 1998; Tidwell, Reis, & Shaver, 1996). A negative self-image combined with high interpersonal trust produces a **preoccupied attachment style.** These individuals want closeness (sometimes excessively so), and they readily form relationships. They cling to others but expect eventually to be rejected because they believe themselves to be unworthy (Lopez et al., 1997; Whiffen, Aube, Thompson, & Campbell, 2000). Those with a **dismissing attachment style** are high in self-esteem and low in interpersonal trust. This combination leads to the belief that one is deserving of good relationships; but people with a dismissing style expect the worst of others, so they fear genuine closeness, and as we noted previously in discussing research by Carvallo and Gabriel (2006), these people often state that they don't really need or want close relationships with others (Onishi, Gjerde, & Block, 2001).

It is sometimes assumed that the attachment style one develops in infancy and childhood remains constant throughout life (Klohnen & Bera, 1998), and styles frequently are stable from infancy through childhood and beyond (Fraley, 2000). Nevertheless, there is considerable evidence that very good or very bad relationship experiences can lead to a change in style (Brennan & Bosson, 1998; Cozzarelli, Karafa, Collins, & Tagler, 2003; Davila & Cobb, 2003). For example, a relationship breakup is likely to reduce secure attachment, while a positive, lasting relationship is likely to increase secure attachment (Ruvolo, Fabin, & Ruvolo, 2001).

The Role of Other Family Members

Besides the mother (or caregiver), other family members also interact with infants and young children. Research is beginning to reveal the importance of fathers, mothers, grandparents, and others (Lin & Harwood, 2003; Maio, Fincham, & Lycett, 2000). Because these people differ in personality characteristics, children can be influenced in a variety of ways (Clark, Kochanska, & Ready, 2000). For example, the negative effects of having a withdrawn, unreliable mother can be partly offset by the presence of an outgoing, dependable grandfather. Every interaction is potentially important as the young person is developing attitudes about the meaning and value of such factors as trust, affection, self-worth, competition, and humor (O'Leary, 1995). When an older person plays games with a youngster, learning involves not only the game itself, but also how people interact in a social situation, follow a set of rules, behave honestly or cheat, and how they deal with disagreements. All of this affects the way the child interacts with other adults and with peers (Lindsey, Mize, & Pettit, 1997).

Relationships between and among Siblings

Approximately 80 percent of us grow up in a household with at least one sibling, and sibling interactions contribute to what we learn about interpersonal behavior (Dunn, 1992).

secure attachment style
A style characterized by high self-esteem and high interpersonal trust. This is the most successful and most desirable attachment style.

fearful-avoidant attachment style
A style characterized by low self-esteem and low interpersonal trust. This is the most insecure and least adaptive attachment style.

preoccupied attachment style
A style characterized by low self-esteem and high interpersonal trust. This is a conflicted and somewhat insecure style in which the individual strongly desires a close relationship but feels that he or she is unworthy of the partner and is thus vulnerable to being rejected.

dismissing attachment style
A style characterized by high self-esteem and low interpersonal trust. This is a conflicted and somewhat insecure style in which the individual feels that he or she deserves a close relationship but is frustrated because of mistrust of potential partners. The result is the tendency to reject the other person at some point in the relationship to avoid being the one who is rejected.

Figure 7.15
Relationships with Siblings: Usually—But Not Always—Positive
I generally got along well with my two younger brothers (all three of us are shown in this photo), and I'm sure that the positive relationships I formed with them served as a good model for relationships I formed with other people outside my family. (Left to Right: Richard, Randy, and Robert Baron.)

close friendship
A relationship in which two people spend a great deal of time together, interact in a variety of situations, and provide mutual emotional support.

Among elementary school children, those who have no siblings are found to be less liked by their classmates and to be more aggressive or to be more victimized by aggressors than those with siblings, presumably because having brothers or sisters provides useful interpersonal learning experiences (Kitzmann, Cohen, & Lockwood, 2002). Sibling relationships, unlike those between parent and child, often combine feelings of affection, hostility, and rivalry (Boer, Westenberg, McHale, Updegraff, & Stocker, 1997). A familiar theme is some version of "Mom always liked you best" or "They took a hundred pictures of you for every one they took of me." Parents, though, seldom admit that they feel any such favoritism.

Most of us have experienced (or observed in others) multiple examples of sibling rivalry, and we have heard a great many adults complain about events involving competition between siblings that occurred in the distant past. In fact, though, most siblings get along fairly well, and I can remember many occasions on which I was helped by my younger brothers and watched over them while my parents were away (see Figure 7.15). The result? We are close and still help each other whenever the need arises. An affectionate relationship between siblings is most likely if each has a warm relationship with the parents and if the mother and father are satisfied with their marriage (McGuire, McHale, & Updegraff, 1996).

Friendships: Relationships beyond the Family

Beginning in early childhood, most of us establish casual friendships with peers who share common interests. They generally begin on the basis of proximity, as described previously, or because of parental friendships. Such relationships are maintained in part by mutual interests and by positive rather than negative experiences together.

Close Friendships

Many childhood friendships simply fade away. At times, however, a relationship begun in early childhood can mature into a **close friendship** (see Figure 7.16) that involves increasingly mature types of interaction. What, exactly, is involved in close friendships?

Such friendships have several distinctive characteristics. For example, many people tend to engage in self-enhancing behavior (such as bragging) when interacting with a wide range of others, but they exhibit modesty when interacting with their friends (Tice et al., 1995). Friends are less likely to lie to one another, unless the lie is designed to make the friend feel better (DePaulo & Kashy, 1998). And friends begin to speak of "we" and "us" rather than "she and I" or "he and I" (Fitzsimmons & Kay, 2004).

Once established, a close relationship results in the two individuals spending increasing amounts of time together, interacting in varied situations, self-disclosing, and providing mutual emotional support (Laurenceau, Barrett, & Pietromonaco, 1998; Matsushima & Shiomi, 2002). A close friend is valued for his or her generosity, sensitivity, and honesty—someone with whom you can relax and be yourself (Urbanski, 1992). But cultural differences exist with respect to friendship, too. Japanese college students, describe a best friend as someone in a give-and-take relationship, a person with whom it is easy to get along, who does not brag, and is considerate and not short-tempered (Maeda & Ritchie, 2003). U.S. students describe friends in a similar way, except they also value as friends individuals who are spontaneous and active.

Gender and Friendships

Women report having more close friends than men do (Fredrickson, 1995). Women also place more importance on intimacy (e.g., self-disclosure and emotional support) than is true for men (Fehr, 2004).

There are many benefits to having close friends, but there can also be pain when you lose a friend or have to separate. For example, when a friendship is interrupted by college graduation, the two individuals must adapt to the emotional threat of separation. As a result, graduating seniors, especially women, report more intense emotional involvement when interacting with close friends than is true for students not facing graduation (Fredrickson, 1995). The importance of friendships extends far beyond the undergraduate years and even plays a role in the social position of professionals in the world of business (Gibbons & Olk, 2003).

Loneliness: Life without Close Relationships

Despite a biological need to establish relationships and the many rewards of being in a relationship, many individuals are unable to achieve that goal. The result is **loneliness**—an individual's emotional and cognitive reaction to having fewer and less satisfying relationships than he or she desires (Archibald, Bartholomew, & Marx, 1995).

Figure 7.16
Friendships: Sometimes, It Lasts
Children are often brought together by proximity—living in the same neighborhood or attending the same school. If they enjoy interacting with each other, they often become friends. Childhood friendships often end as interests change or families move, but in some cases, they last. The two young women shown in these photos (Lindsey Byrne and Chanda Brown), lived across the street from each other and played together from the time they were toddlers. They are still friends, more than two decades later.

In contrast, those people who simply do not want friends do not experience loneliness (Burger, 1995). Some simply desire solitude for positive reasons (Long, Seburn, Averill, & More, 2003). Loneliness appears to be a common human experience, occurring in many cultures all around the world (Goodwin, Cook, & Yung, 2001; Rokach & Neto, 2000; Shams, 2001).

The Consequences of Being Lonely

Not surprisingly, people who feel lonely tend to spend their leisure time in solitary activity, to have few dates, and to have only casual friends or acquaintances (Berg & McQuinn, 1989). Lonely individuals feel left out and believe they have little in common with those they meet (Bell, 1993). Even if a child only has only one friend, that is enough to reduce such reactions (Asher & Paquette, 2003).

Loneliness is unpleasant, and the negative affect includes feelings of depression, anxiety, unhappiness, dissatisfaction, pessimism about the future, self-blame, and shyness (Anderson, Miller, Riger, Dill, & Sedikides, 1994; Jackson, Soderlind, & Weiss, 2000). From the perspective of others, lonely individuals are perceived as maladjusted (Lau & Gruen, 1992; Rotenberg & Kmill, 1992). Even worse, loneliness is associated with poor health and with how long an individual is expected to live (Cacioppo, Hawkley, & Berntson, 2003; Hawkley, Burleson, Berntson, & Cacioppo, 2003). A possible reason for these negative effects has been provided by Cacioppo and others (2002). They found that in both the laboratory and at home, lonely individuals exhibit sleep problems. People need an appropriate amount of sleep to restore the daily wear and tear on the body.

Why Are Some People Lonely?

The origins of dispositional loneliness include a combination of genetic factors, attachment style, and the opportunity for early social experiences with peers. In an intriguing study designed to examine the possible role of genetic factors in loneliness, McGuire and Clifford

loneliness
The unpleasant emotional and cognitive state based on desiring close relationships but being unable to attain them.

(2000) conducted a behavioral genetic investigation of loneliness among children aged nine to fourteen. The participants included pairs of biological siblings, pairs of unrelated siblings raised in adoptive homes, and pairs of identical and fraternal twins. The data consistently indicated that loneliness is based in part on inherited factors. For example, identical twins are more similar in loneliness than are fraternal twins, indicating that greater genetic similarity is associated with greater similarity with respect to loneliness. Nevertheless, loneliness was also found to be influenced by environmental factors, as indicated by the fact that unrelated siblings raised in adoptive homes are more similar in loneliness than random pairs of children. As the investigators point out, the fact that there is a genetic component to loneliness does not fully explain just how it operates. For example, the relevant genes could affect feelings of depression or hostility; if so, differences in loneliness could be the result of rejection based on genetically determined differences in interpersonal behavior.

Another possible source of loneliness can be traced to attachment style (Duggan & Brennan 1994). Both dismissing and fearful-avoidant individuals fear intimacy and so tend to avoid establishing relationships (Sherman & Thelen, 1996). Such individuals do not have sufficient trust in other people to risk seeking closeness. In general, insecure attachment is associated with social anxiety and loneliness (Vertue, 2003). A study of Dutch students by Buunk and Prins (1998) suggests that certain kinds of attachment style may also lead to loneliness, especially when individuals perceive themselves to be giving more than they receiving. This perceived lack of reciprocity also leads to feelings of loneliness and not being sufficiently appreciated.

A third possible factor that results in loneliness is a failure to develop social skills, and this can occur for a variety of reasons (Braza, Braza, Carrera, & Munoz, 1993). In part, children learn interpersonal skills by interacting with peers. As a result, children who have attended preschool or otherwise had the opportunity to engage in play-related interactions with multiple peers are liked better in elementary school than those lacking such experiences (Erwin & Letchford, 2003). Without appropriate social skills, a child may engage in self-defeating behaviors, such as avoidance of others, or engaging in verbal aggression, such as teasing or in physical aggression. As a result of such actions, he or she may be rejected as a playmate, and seeds for loneliness can be planted (Johnson, Poteat, & Ironsmith, 1991; Ray, Cohen, Secrist, & Duncan, 1997). Factors that influence loneliness are summarized in Figure 7.17.

Without some form of intervention to alter this behavior, interpersonal difficulties typically continue throughout childhood and adolescence and into adulthood; they do not simply go away with the passage of time (Asendorpf, 1992; Hall-Elston & Mullins, 1999).

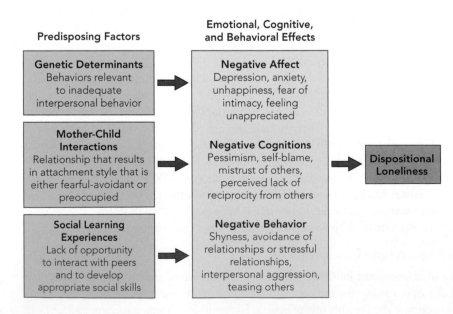

Figure 7.17
Factors Affecting Loneliness
As shown here, the tendency to experience loneliness (dispositional loneliness) appears to stem from several different factors: genetic factors, certain aspects of an attachment style, and early social learning experience.

Reducing Loneliness

Those who function badly in social interactions are usually well aware that there is a problem (Duck, Pond, & Leatham, 1994). They know that they are unhappy, dissatisfied, and unpopular (Furr & Funder, 1998; Meleshko & Alden, 1993). Are there any satisfactory ways to reduce this problem and the pain it produces?

Once loneliness develops, it's obviously not possible to change the individual's history by providing different genes or by altering what occurred during early mother-child interactions. It is, however, possible to acquire new and more appropriate social skills. Such intervention concentrates on a number of fairly specific behaviors. The major intervention procedures are cognitive therapy (Salmela-Aro & Nurmi, 1996) and social skills training (Hope, Holt, & Heimberg, 1995), and they can be used simultaneously. The goal of cognitive therapy is to disrupt the pattern of negativity and to encourage new thoughts, perceptions, and expectations about social interactions. In social skills training, the lonely person is provided with examples of socially appropriate behavior on videotape and then given the opportunity to copy the observed behavior in role play. Finally, there are instructions to practice the new skills in actual social situations. A person can learn to interact with others in a friendly way, to avoid expressing anger and hostility, and to make casual conversation (Keltner, Young, Heerey, Oemig, & Monarch, 1998; Reisman, 1984), to express interest in the other person and to make fewer self-references (Kowalski, 1993), and to self-disclose in an appropriate way (Bell, 1991; Rotenberg, 1997). Just as people can be taught mathematics, table manners, and how to drive a car, they can also be taught social skills and how to interact with other people and learning these skills can go a long way toward reducing loneliness. Overall, while it is not easy to change long-established patterns of thought and behavior, they can be altered, and to the extent they are (often with the help of a trained psychologist), the factors that cause people to lead lives of lonely desperation can be changed.

> ### Principles to Remember
> The attachment styles people acquire as children often persist and can strongly influence their relationships with others throughout life.

KeyPoints

- Close relationships are characterized by interdependence, in which two people influence each other's lives, share their thoughts and emotions, and engage in joint activities.

- The first relationships are within the family, and we acquire an attachment style (a combination of level of self-esteem and degree of interpersonal trust) based on interactions with a caregiver. Children also learn what to expect from other people and how to interact with them as a result of their interactions with parents, siblings, grandparents, and other family members.

- Friendships outside of the family begin in childhood and are initially based simply on such factors as common interests and other sources of positive affect, resulting in attraction. With increasing maturity, it becomes possible to form close friendships that involve spending time together, interacting in many different situations, providing mutual social support, and engaging in self-disclosure.

- Loneliness occurs when a person has fewer and less satisfying relationships than he or she desires. The result is depression and anxiety. Dispositional loneliness originates in a combination of genetics, an insecure attachment style based on caregiver-child interactions, and the lack of early social experiences with peers. A helpful intervention involves a combination of cognitive therapy and social skills training.

Think About It

If families are really a kind of "training ground" for learning about relationships and how to form them, can we predict how someone will be as a boyfriend, girlfriend, or marriage partner from observing their relationships with their parents and siblings?

Romantic Relationships and Falling in Love

"I will love you all my life

Always be by your side

And I will give you all I have

Cause you gave me peace and joy . . . again, again, again . . ." Jennifer Lopez

"Love is life. All, everything that I understand, I understand only because I love.
Everything is, everything exists, only because I love. . . ." Leo Tolstoy

Love, most people would agree that this is one of the most important parts—if not the most important part—of their lives. But what, precisely, *is* love? And how does it develop? Does it flow naturally from other relationships, or is it something special and occurs when the "right" two people meet—the "bolt of lighting" that strikes unexpectedly and without warning? Given its importance in the social side of life, social psychologists have attempted to unravel these and other mysteries concerning love. We'll now provide a summary of some of their most important—and interesting—findings. But please get ready for some surprises, because scientific efforts to study love have yielded answers that are, in some respects, quite different from those provided by poets, philosophers, or popular singers.

Romance: Beyond Friendship—Far beyond!

Among the most obvious differences between friendship and romance are sexual attraction and at least some level of physical intimacy. Depending on what is acceptable in one's culture, the sexual attraction may or may not lead to some form of sexual behavior and the physical intimacy may be limited to hand holding, hugging, and kissing, or it can include more explicitly sexual interactions. At least one of the partners is likely to believe that he or she is in love and that the relationship may lead to marriage (Hendrick & Hendrick, 2002).

Similarities and Differences between Friendship and Romance

Most often, romantic attraction begins in the same way that all interpersonal attraction begins: a combination of affiliation need, affect arousal, proximity, reactions to observable characteristics, similarity, and mutual liking. But it differs from friendship in several ways. Among college students, an ideal romantic partner is one who is similar to oneself and most importantly, one with a secure attachment style (Dittmann, 2003; Klohnen & Luo, 2003). Another key factor is the belief that one's partner is committed to the relationship and wants it to last. In contrast, if one partner in a budding romantic relationship perceives their partner's commitment to it fluctuates greatly, that is a good predictor that the relationship will, in fact, end (Arriaga et al., 2006).

A primary feature of romance is the interpretation of one's emotional arousal in the presence of another person as strong attraction that includes at least the potential for love and sex. In addition, both men and women set higher standards for romantic partners than for friends with respect to physical attractiveness, social status, and characteristics, such as warmth and intelligence (Sprecher & Regan, 2002). Playfulness also plays a special role in romantic relationships (Aune & Wong, 2002).

Researchers who have studied romantic relationships suggest that it is often helpful to think about them in terms of three overlapping schemas (Fletcher, Simpson, Thomas, & Giles, 1999). There is a self schema, a schema that is one's perception of the partner, and a third schema that encompasses the relationship between self and partner (see Figure 7.18 on page 253).

The schema involving one's partner is often an unrealistic and inaccurate one. Each wants to believe that the other person represents the perfect partner, and each wants uncomplicated, totally positive feedback from that partner (Katz & Beach, 2000; Simpson, Ickes, & Blackstone, 1995). The closer the partner is to one's ideal, the better the relationship is perceived to be and the longer it is expected to last (Campbell, Simpson, Kashy, & Fletcher, 2001; Fletcher, Simpson, & Thomas, 2000). That person's virtues are emphasized, and possible faults are dismissed as unimportant (Murray & Holmes, 1999).

As unrealistic as this may appear to an outsider, romance is built in part on fantasies and illusions, and these illusions may even be crucial in creating the relationship and helping it to survive. In fact, as we'll see in our discussion of marriage, idealizing one's partner can be one factor that contributes to the survival of love over decades or even throughout an entire life (Miller, Niehuis, & Huston, 2006; Murray & Holmes, 1997).

The shared illusions present in the relationship schema are frequently based on the belief in romantic destiny—the conviction that two people are meant for each other—"It was written in the stars." In fact, to the extent that two people like one another and believe that they are meant to be together, such views concerning destiny may actually help maintain the relationship (Franiuk, Cohen, & Pomerantz, 2002; Knee, 1998).

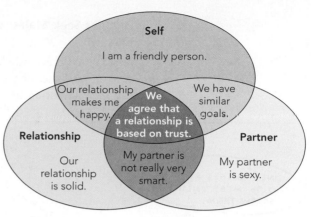

Figure 7.18
The Role of Schemas in Romantic Relationships
Romantic relationships often involve three overlapping schemas: self, one's partner, and the relationships. The three schemas overlap, and the thoughts and ideas at this intersection of the schemas play an important role in the nature and success of the relationship.

Selecting a Potential Mate: Different Criteria for Women and Men

Dreams of romance may not include the desire to become a parent, but evolutionary psychologists suggest that our genetic history plays a key role in romantic attraction (Geary, Vigil, & Byrd-Craven, 2004). We may not be consciously aware of the fact, but our search for a suitable romantic partner involves something different than the search for a suitable friend. What matters most in a romantic partner? This differs to some extent by gender. Males tend to stress the physical attractiveness of a potential mate, while women tend to stress a mate's status and resources; both genders prefer a mate who is kind and intelligent (Li, Bailey, Kenrick, & Lisenmeier, 2002).

Males Seek Female Attractiveness: Youth and Beauty Equal Reproductive Fitness

From the perspective of evolutionary determinants, female beauty may be sexually attractive to men because they are associated with fertility. The basic principle is that the reproductive success of our male ancestors was enhanced by selecting female mates on the basis of such cues. Though men in a dating relationship are not ordinarily interested in reproduction (sex perhaps, but not reproduction), they are predisposed to respond positively to beauty. This preference was adaptive because beauty is indicative of youth (fertility) and good health (enough strength to endure childbirth and to raise offspring). Over hundreds of thousands of years, males who were attracted to youthful beauty were more likely to pass on their genes to the next generation than were males for whom youth and beauty were irrelevant.

Men are attracted not only to beauty but also to other specific characteristics that indicate youth and health. A woman's long hair is one example (Jacobi & Cash, 1994), presumably because healthy, shiny hair is a sign of youth and health (Etcoff, 1999). Another positive cue is a face that exhibits **bilateral symmetry** (having identical left and right sides). A symmetrical face is perceived as more attractive than an unsymmetrical one (Hughes, Harrison, & Gallup, 2002). Beyond that, bodily symmetry, too, is associated with genetic fitness, health, and fertility (Manning, Koukourakis, & Brodie, 1997; Scutt, Manning, Whitehouse, Leinster, & Massey, 1997).

bilateral symmetry
When the left and the right side of the body (or parts of a body) are alike.

Females Seek Males with Resources: Power Equals Ability to Raise and Protect Offspring

As we noted previously both women and men respond positively to an attractive physical appearance. In seeking a romantic partner, however, research findings indicate that women pay more attention to a male's resources, whether that consists of a warm cave and the ability to fight off predators or of economic and interpersonal power. According to an evolutionary perspective, the reason that females are less concerned about male youth and attractiveness is explained by the fact that while women have a relatively limited age span during which reproduction is possible, men are usually able to reproduce from puberty well into old age. For prehistoric females, reproductive success was enhanced by choosing a mate who had the ability to protect and care for her and for their offspring (Kenrick, Neuberg, Zierk, & Krones, 1994; Kenrick, Sundie, Nicastle, & Stone, 2001).

Many studies of contemporary men and women suggest that even today, mate preferences are consistent with this evolutionary description. For example, a study in the Netherlands of men and women from twenty to sixty years of age reported that men preferred women who were more attractive than themselves, while women preferred men who were higher in income, education, self-confidence, intelligence, dominance, and social position than themselves (Buunk, Dukstra, Fetchenhauer, & Kenrick, 2002). These differential preferences often result in couples consisting of a younger, attractive woman and an older, wealthier man both in movies and in real life.

As compelling as this evolution-based explanation of gender differences may be, it is not universally accepted (see Miller, Putcha-Bhagavatula, & Pedersen, 2002). Cultural factors are important, and research findings indicate that both men and women prefer a wealthy and healthy mate (Miller et al., 2002). The fact that they do makes more sense in terms of cultural values than genetic influences (Hanko, Master, & Sabini, 2004). With this point in mind, it is interesting to note that both George Washington and Thomas Jefferson chose to marry wealthy widows (Wood, 2004), even though, we imagine, they had a large choice of potential mates.

Figure 7.19
Finding a Mate: Cupid or the Internet?
Finding a suitable mate is a challenging task—especially when, as is now true in many societies, individuals must do this for themselves. Recent developments such as speed dating and Internet-based dating services can help, but this doesn't necessarily mean that Cupid is permanently out of a job.

(*Source: The New Yorker,* October 27, 2003.)

Finding a Mate: Families, Friends . . . or the Internet?

Whatever the basis of mating preferences, people face a practical obstacle to romance: How can they find a suitable partner? Historically, the answer was simply to enter a marriage arranged by the two sets of parents. In contrast, throughout much of the world, this process is left largely up to the two individuals directly involved. This has led to the development of many aids to finding a mate—speed dating, and Internet-based services that help people with similar interests and backgrounds meet. Does that mean that cupid is out of a job (see Figure 7.19)? Perhaps, but we doubt it because even if people find each other through Internet dating services, they must still meet and interact—and even today, that seems to be essential to finding partners for serious and lasting romantic relationships.

Love: Who Can Explain It? Who Can Tell You Why? Just Maybe, Social Psychologists!

love
A combination of emotions, cognitions, and behaviors that often play a crucial role in intimate relationships.

Love is one of the most popular themes in our songs, movies, and everyday lives. Most people in many different cultures accept love as a familiar human experience, and a 1993 poll found that almost three out of four North Americans said they were currently "in love." In part, love is an emotional reaction that seems as basic as anger, sadness, happiness, and fear (Shaver, Morgan, & Wu, 1996). Maybe love is even good for you. Aron, Paris, and Aron (1995) found that falling in love leads to an increase in self-efficacy and self-esteem (see Chapter 4). So, what do we mean by the word *love*?

Some clues to the meaning of love can be found in the spontaneous definitions people offer when asked what it means. When asked, "What is love?" a group of college students (Harrison, 2003) offered answers like this: "Love is offering the last bite"; "Love when you look at your partner when they first wake up and still think they are beautiful"; "Love is like an elevator; you can ride it to the top or end up in the basement, but eventually you'll choose which floor to get off." You probably have your own answer, and it is probably quite different from these.

Interestingly, social psychologists did not attempt to study love systematically until the 1970s, when one researcher (Rubin, 1970) developed a measure of romantic love, and others (Berscheid & Hatfield, 1974) proposed a psychological theory of love. Since that time, however, love has become a major research interest. At the least, we know what it is not. Love is definitely something more than a close friendship, and something different from merely being romantically or sexually interested in another person. The specific details may vary from culture to culture (Beall & Sternberg, 1995), but there is reason to believe that the basic phenomenon we call love is a universal one (Hatfield & Rapson, 1993). Here's an overview of its major cognitive and emotional aspects as based on research findings.

Passionate Love

Aron, Dutton, Aron, and Iverson (1989) pointed out that many people fall in love, but no one ever seems to have "fallen in friendship." Unlike attraction, or even romance, **passionate love** involves an intense and often unrealistic emotional reaction to another person. Passionate love usually begins as an instant, overwhelming, surging, all-consuming positive reaction to another person—a reaction that feels as if it's beyond your control, like an unpredictable accident. It often occurs suddenly, as captured by the saying, "falling head over heels in love." A person in love is preoccupied with the loved one and can think about little else (see Figure 7.20 above).

Meyers and Berscheid (1997) propose that sexual attraction is a necessary but not sufficient condition for being in love with another person. That is, you can be sexually attracted without being in love, but you aren't likely to be in love in the absence of sexual attraction (Regan, 2000). Surveys indicate that college students agree (Regan, 1998). For many people, love makes sex more acceptable; and sexual activity tends to be romanticized (Goldenberg et al., 1999). That's why it is more acceptable for two people to "make love" than simply to copulate like animals in heat.

In addition to sex, passionate love includes strong emotional arousal, the desire to be physically close, and an intense need to be loved as much as you love the other person. Loving and being loved are positive experiences, but they are accompanied by a recurring fear that something may happen to end the relationship. Hatfield and Sprecher (1986b) developed the Passionate Love Scale to measure the various elements, and it contains items such as "For me, _____ is the perfect romantic partner" and "I would feel deep despair if _____ left me."

Figure 7.20
Falling in Love
Passionate love often begins suddenly and without warning as an all-encompassing emotional reaction to another person. The couples shown here appear to be experiencing this overwhelming surge of feelings.

passionate love
An intense and often unrealistic emotional response to another person. When this emotion is experienced, it is usually perceived as an indication of true love, but to outside observers it appears to be infatuation.

Though it sounds like something that only happens in movies, most people, when asked, report having had the experience of suddenly falling in love with a stranger—love at first sight (Averill & Boothroyd, 1977). Often, sadly, just one person falls in love, and their feelings are not returned by the partner; that's known as **unrequited love.** Such one-way love is most common among people with a conflicted attachment style (Aron, Aron, & Allen, 1998). In one large survey investigation, about 60 percent of the respondents said that they had experienced this kind of love within the past two years (Bringle & Winnick, 1992).

According to Hatfield and Walster (1981), passionate love requires the presence of three factors. First, you have to learn about love, and most of us are exposed from childhood on to love-related images in fairy tales, songs about love, and romantic movies. These images motivate us to experience love and provide a script that tells us how to act when it happens (Sternberg, 1996). Second, an appropriate love object must be present. "Appropriate" tends to mean a physically attractive person of the opposite sex who is not currently married or otherwise attached. Third, the individual must be in a state of physiological arousal (sexual excitement, fear, anxiety, or whatever) that can then be interpreted as the emotion of love (Dutton & Aron, 1974; Istvan, Griffitt, & Weidner, 1983).

What Is the Origin of Love?

The answer is that no one knows for sure. It is possible that love is only a pleasant fantasy that we share, much like Santa Claus and the Tooth Fairy. Another explanation involved the fact that when our early hominid ancestors first began to walk in an upright position, they hunted for meat and gathered edible vegetables that could be carried back to a place of shelter (Lemonick & Dorfman, 2001). The survival of these few, relatively frail beings, and later of the entire species, depended on their reproductive success (Buss, 1994). Among many factors, such success was more likely if heterosexual pairs were erotically attracted to one another and if they were willing to invest time and effort in feeding and protecting any offspring they produced. These two important characteristics (lust and interpersonal commitment) are presumably based in biology. We experience sexual desire and the desire to bond with both mate and children because such motivations were adaptive (Rensberger 1993). Our ancestors were more than simply sex partners. It was an advantage if they liked and trusted one another and if they could divide up tasks such as hunting and child care. Altogether, bonding with a mate and with one's offspring was important to the success of the species. As a consequence, today's humans may be genetically primed to seek sex (for the purpose of reproduction), fall in love, and become loving parents. Monogamy may depend in part on brain chemistry (Insel & Carter, 1995), and most young adults say they expect to have a monogamous relationship with the person they love (Wiederman & Allgeier, 1996). Keep in mind that cultural influences can affect both lust and commitment by way of religious teachings, civil laws, and the way we depict love and marriage in our songs and stories (Allgeier & Wiederman, 1994).

The Components of Love

Though passionate love is a common occurrence, it is too intense and too overwhelming to be maintained as a permanent emotional state. There are other kinds of love, however, that can be long lasting. Hatfield (1988, p. 205) describes **companionate love** as the "affection we feel for those with whom our lives are deeply entwined." Unlike passionate love, companionate love is based on an extremely close friendship in which two people are sexually attracted, have a great deal in common, care about each other's well-being, and express mutual liking and respect (Caspi & Herbener, 1990). It's not exactly as exciting as passionate love nor as interesting a theme for music and fiction, but it is able to sustain a satisfying and lasting relationship.

In addition to these two aspects of love, four other styles have been identified. Game

unrequited love
Love felt by one person for another who does not feel love in return.

companionate love
Love that is based on friendship, mutual attraction, shared interests, respect, and concern for one another's welfare.

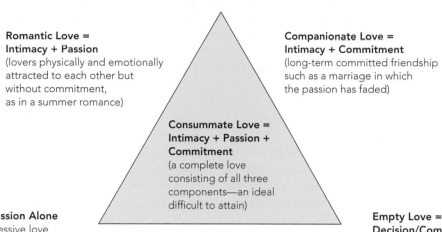

Liking = Intimacy Alone
(true friendship without passion or long-term commitment)

**Romantic Love =
Intimacy + Passion**
(lovers physically and emotionally attracted to each other but without commitment, as in a summer romance)

**Companionate Love =
Intimacy + Commitment**
(long-term committed friendship such as a marriage in which the passion has faded)

**Consummate Love =
Intimacy + Passion +
Commitment**
(a complete love consisting of all three components—an ideal difficult to attain)

Infatuation = Passion Alone
(passionate, obsessive love at first sight without intimacy or commitment)

**Empty Love =
Decision/Commitment Alone**
(decision to love another without intimacy or passion)

Fatuous Love = Passion + Commitment
(commitment based on passion but without time for intimacy to develop—shallow relationship such as a whirlwind courtship)

Figure 7.21
Sternberg's Triangular Model of Love

Sternberg suggests that love has three basic components: intimacy, passion, and decision (commitment). For a given couple, love can be based on any one of these three components, on a combination of any two of them, or on all three. These various possibilities yield seven types of relationships, including the ideal (consummate love) that consists of all three basic components equally represented.

playing love includes such behavior as having two lovers at once; possessive love concentrates on the fear of losing one's lover; logical love is based on decisions as to whether a partner is suitable; and selfless love is a rare phenomenon in which an individual would rather suffer than have a lover suffer (Hendrick & Hendrick, 1986). Among the many findings with respect to style differences, men are more likely to engage in game playing love than women, but the reverse is true for logical and possessive love (Hendrick, Hendrick, Foote, & Slapion-Foote, 1984). In general, people agree that companionate love and selfless love are the most desirable, while game-playing is the least desirable (Hahn & Blass, 1997).

A different conception of the meaning of love is provided by Sternberg's (1986) **triangular model of love,** as shown in Figure 7.21. This formulation suggests that each love relationship is made up of three basic components that are present in varying degrees in different couples (Aron & Westbay, 1996). One component is **intimacy**—the closeness two people feel and the strength of the bond that holds them together. Intimacy is essentially companionate love. Partners high in intimacy are concerned with each other's welfare and happiness, and they value, like, count on, and understand one another. The second component, **passion,** is based on romance, physical attraction, and sexuality—in other words, passionate love. Men are more likely to stress this component than women (Fehr & Broughton, 2001). The third component, **decision (commitment)** represents cognitive factors such as the decision that you love and want to be with the other person plus a commitment to maintain the relationship on a permanent basis. When all three angles of the triangle are equally strong and balanced, the result is **consummate love**—defined as the ideal form, but something difficult to attain (and maintain).

Though research on attraction has long stressed the effects of physical attractiveness on liking, its effect on love have been somewhat overlooked until recently. In Spain, almost two thousand individuals ranging in age from eighteen to sixty-four were asked questions about physical attractiveness, falling in love, and each of the components of Sternberg's

triangular model of love
Sternberg's conceptualization of love relationships.

intimacy
In Sternberg's triangular model of love, the closeness felt by two people—the extent to which they are bonded.

passion
In Sternberg's triangular model of love, the sexual motives and sexual excitement associated with a couple's relationship.

model (Sangrador & Yela, 2000). The findings suggest that appearance is not only important with respect to passion, but also with respect to intimacy and decision (commitment) as well. Also attractiveness is as important in the later stages of a relationship as it is at the beginning. In the words of these Spanish psychologists, "What is beautiful is loved." This focus on external appearance may not be wise, but these investigators suggest that we should at least acknowledge the reality of the influence of physical attractiveness on relationships.

Jealousy: An Internal Threat to Relationships—Romantic and Otherwise

Jealousy has often been described as "the green-eyed monster," and with good reason. Feelings of jealousy—concerns that a romantic partner or other person about whom we care deeply might transfer their affection or loyalty to another—are deeply distressing. While most people think about jealousy primarily in connection with romantic relationships, it can occur in other contexts too: All that is essential is that a valued relationship with another person is threatened by a rival (e.g., DeSteno, 2004). But despite this fact, it seems clear that jealousy may exert its strongest and most dangerous effects in the context of romantic triads: One person becomes jealous over the possibility that her or his partner is interested in a rival (Harris, 2003). For instance, in 2006, astronaut Lisa Nowak became jealous over the possibility that her romantic partner, William Oefelein, was involved with another woman. She drove more than one thousand miles to confront this rival, Colleen Shipman, and then attacked her by squirting her with what police believe was pepper spray. Nowak was charged with attempted murder because she had brought several weapons with her and seemed intent on removing her rival, even if this involved murdering her. Clearly, this is a dramatic and frightening illustration of jealousy in action.

Government statistics indicate that jealousy is a major factor in a large proportion of homicides, especially against women; women are most likely to be murdered by current or former jealous partners (U.S. Department of Justice, 2003). But why, precisely, does jealousy occur? Is it "built into" our emotional reactions by genetic factors (Buss, Larsen, Westen, & Semmelroth, 1992)? Or are other factors involved? In fact, growing evidence now points to the conclusion that jealousy is largely the result of threats to one's self-esteem. In other words, we experience jealousy because anticipated or actual social rejection threatens our self-esteem.

Clear evidence for this view is provided by research conducted by DeSteno, Valdesolo, and Bartlett (2006). These researchers arranged for participants in their study to perform a problem-solving task with a partner, who was actually an assistant of the researchers. This person praised the real subject's work, smiled at her (participants were all females), and provided lots of encouragement. The result was that the assistant and the real subject formed a pleasant working relationship. Then this relationship was threatened by a rival—a third person who entered the room, apologizing for being late. The three people (two assistants and the one real subject) then worked on another task and during this activity, the experimenter informed them that they could work either as pairs or alone. That meant that one person would be "out"—she would have to work alone. In the jealousy inducing condition, the partner—with whom the real subject had previously worked so well—chose to work with the newly arrived rival. In a control condition, not designed to induce jealousy, the partner suddenly remembered that she had another appointment and had to leave. In this condition, too, she ended the enjoyable working relationship with the real subject, but in a way that would not be expected to produce jealousy.

After these procedures were over, participants in both conditions (jealousy and no jealousy) completed measures of their jealousy and their self-esteem. The researchers predicted that those exposed to the conditions meant to induce jealousy would experience stronger jealousy than those in the control group, and this is precisely what was found. In addi-

decision (commitment)
In Sternberg's triangular model of love, these are the cognitive processes involved in deciding that you love another person and are committed to maintain the relationship.

consummate love
In Sternberg's triangular model of love, a complete and ideal love that combines intimacy, passion, and decision (commitment).

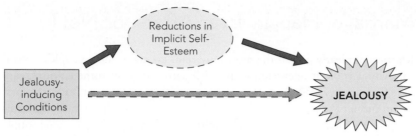

Figure 7.22
Jealousy and Threats to
Self-Esteem
*Research findings indicate that
jealousy stems primarily from
threats to self-esteem* (thick,
upper arrows). *These threats
involve the possibility that
someone we care about (a
romantic partner, a work
partner, etc.) may desert us
for a rival.*

(*Source:* Based on suggestions by
DeSteno, Valdesolo, & Bartlett,
2006.)

tion, and more importantly, these feelings of jealousy stemmed from reductions in self-esteem (which was measured explicitly through a questionnaire, and implicitly through procedures based on the IAT—see Chapter 5). In fact, as shown in Figure 7.22, it appeared that jealousy operated largely through reductions in self-esteem.

So jealousy, it appears, stems largely from threats to self-esteem—threats that occur whenever someone we care about (a lover, work partner, good friend) seems ready to desert us for a rival. As we'll see in Chapter 10, such feelings are not merely unpleasant and distressing: They can sometimes lead to overt violence against others, especially in cultures that emphasize the importance of protecting one's "honor." In this respect, the green-eyed monster really is a monster and can pose a serious threat not only to personal happiness, but also to safety and even life as well.

> **Principles to Remember**
>
> Love—one of the most powerful feelings of which we are capable—involves much more than passion; it involves caring and commitment too.

KeyPoints

- One defining characteristic of romantic relationships is some degree of physical intimacy, ranging from holding hands to sexual interactions.

- As is true for attraction and friendship, romantic attraction is influenced by factors such as physical proximity, appearance, and similarity. In addition, romance includes sexual attraction and the desire for total acceptance by the other person.

- The reproductive success of our ancient ancestors was enhanced by male attraction to young, fertile females, female attraction to males with resources, and by bonding between mates and between parents and their offspring.

- Love consists of multiple components. For example, passionate love is a sudden, overwhelming emotional response to another person. Companionate love resembles a close friendship that includes caring, mutual liking, and respect. Sternberg's triangular model of love includes these two components plus a third—decision (commitment)—that is a cognitive decision to love and to be committed to a relationship.

- Jealousy is a powerful emotion, and research findings suggest that it is often triggered by threats to our self-esteem—threats arising when we fear that someone we love or care about will desert us for a rival.

Think About It

Do you think that even extreme reactions to jealousy—for instance, "crimes of passion"—result from threats to self-esteem? Or could other factors, too, be involved?

Marriage: Happily Ever After—or Not?

Marriage is clearly one of the most important events in most people's lives; that's one reason why it is often celebrated with lavish parties that, in some cultures, can continue for days (see Figure 7.23). And that's hardly surprising: In almost all cultures, marriage involves a commitment to remain in a close relationship forever—throughout the remainder of one's life. Clearly, that's a very serious commitment and although only some couples maintain it (remember my grandparents and my parents—both of whom were married for more than sixty years?), the goal of remaining married to one person throughout life is still one accepted by most people.

Any relationship this important is certainly worthy of careful attention, and in recent decades, social psychologists have joined researchers in other branches of psychology in seeking to understand important aspects of marriage—how we choose our marriage partners, what factors contribute to marital happiness or unhappiness, and the overall impact of marriage on our lives and health (e.g., Ruiz, Matthews, Scheier, & Schulz, 2006). While most of this research is quite recent, it's also important to note that marriage was first studied from a social psychological perspective as long ago as the 1930s. Because this early research had a lasting impact on subsequent research, we'll pause here to examine it briefly in *Building the Science: Classics of Social Psychology*.

Figure 7.23
Marriage: It Is Celebrated around the World
As shown here, marriage is celebrated with parties, feasts, and other events in almost all cultures. That's not surprising because marriage is one of the most important relationships we ever enter.

BUILDING THE SCIENCE
CLASSICS OF SOCIAL PSYCHOLOGY

Terman's Early Research on Similarity and Marital Happiness

Lewis M. Terman is best known for his research on intelligence and ways to measure it. But he was also interested in identifying the factors that contribute to marital happiness—those factors that make couples compatible—in his research. In the 1930s, he performed a series of studies designed to apply what was already known about the relationship between similarity and attraction to understanding the differences between happy and unhappy couples (Terman & Buttenwieser, 1935a, 1935b).

In this research, Terman and Buttenwieser proposed that if similarity results in mutual attraction, highly similar spouses should be more satisfied with their marriages than less similar spouses. To test this hypothesis, hundreds of couples completed a measure of marital happiness, and the one hundred most happy and one hundred least happy couples (ones who had already divorced) were chosen. The couples were matched in terms of age, education, and occupational status. Then, they were asked to complete a psychological inventory consisting of more than five hundred items on which each person individually indicated whether they felt positively or negatively about various activities, occupations, kinds of people, and famous individuals.

The results were striking. First, it was found that across all couples—happy and unhappy—people tended to marry someone similar to themselves, at least with respect to their answers on the five-hundred-item inventory. Second, and more important, the degree to which members of each couples were similar or dissimilar was associated with the couple's happiness. For instance, the more couples agreed on the importance of avoiding arguments, contributing to charity, and getting attention when ill, the happier they were. Similarly, the more they agreed in their feelings about other people (dentists, insurance salesman, etc.), the happier they were.

Because the research was correlational in nature, we can't draw the firm conclusion that similarity leads to marital happiness. For instance, it's possible that the longer couples lived together, the more similar they became so that similarity might be a result of happiness, rather than a cause. But as we described previously, more recent research using more modern methods points to the same conclusion. So Terman's early research was definitely on track in terms of its conclusions and started a research tradition that has continued in social psychology up until the present time; in that sense, it clearly helped to build the new and rapidly developing field of social psychology.

Marital Happiness: What Factors Affect It?

Given the fact that most people get married and that half or more of these marriages fail, it would be helpful if each of us knew as much as possible about the factors that contribute to long-term relationship happiness or unhappiness. Though the importance of commitment to the relationship is often stressed, commitment based on fear of a breakup is not as effective as commitment based on the positive rewards of a continuing relationship (Frank & Brandstatter, 2002). In a long-term relationship, many problems can arise over time—financial problems, family-related problems, and issues relating to children. But aside from such problems, research findings indicate that there are several factors present even before the wedding that are useful in predicting whether, and to what extent, marriages will succeed or fail. We'll now examine some of these.

Similarity and Assumed Similarity

We have already described early research suggesting that similarity between potential spouses is an important predictor of marital happiness—Terman's classic studies (Terman & Buttenwieser, 1935a; 1935b). More recent research has confirmed the importance of this factor and extended our understanding of its effects. For instance, longitudinal research that followed couples from the time they became engaged through twenty years of marriage indicated that couples are generally quite similar in many respects (attitudes, values, and goals [Caspi, Herbener, & Ozer, 1992]). Further, such similarity does not change much over time. In short, people tend to marry others similar to themselves, and they remain similar—or even become more similar—with the passage of years. So as we noted previously in this chapter (in *Making Sense of Common Sense: A Social Psychological Perspective* on page 239), opposites don't attract; rather, similarity is an important cause of attraction. With these findings in mind, it seems reasonable to suggest that couples contemplating making a long-term commitment might benefit from paying close attention to their similarities and dissimilarities—and perhaps, less attention to attractiveness and sexuality. Although that may be hard to do, it may contribute to having a happy long-term relationship, in marriage or outside of it.

Not only do similar people marry, but in happy marriages, the partners *believe* they are even more similar than they actually are; they show high levels of **assumed similarity** (Byrne & Blaylock, 1963; Schul & Vinokur, 2000). Moreover, both actual and assumed similarity appear to contribute to marital satisfaction. Interestingly, dating couples show higher assumed similarity than married couples with respect to assumed similarity, perhaps reflecting the romantic illusions we discussed previously. As we'll see in *Social Psychology: What It Tells Us About . . .* on page 263, these and other illusions (biases would probably be a better term) may actually play an important role in marital happiness.

Dispositional Factors

Beyond similarity, marital success is affected by specific personality dispositions. In other words, some individuals are better able to maintain a positive relationship than others, and they are better bets as marriage partners than others.

For example, **narcissism** refers to an individual who feels superior to most other people, someone who seeks admiration, and lacks empathy (American Psychiatric Association, 1994). Narcissists report feeling less commitment to a relationship (Campbell & Foster, 2002). As an exception to the similarity rule, two narcissists are not likely to have a happy relationship (Campbell, 1999). Other important personality dispositions that affect the success of a relationship are those associated with interpersonal behavior and attachment styles. Thus individuals with preoccupied or fearful-avoidant styles have less satisfying relationships than those with secure or dismissing styles (Murray, Holmes, Griffin, Bellavia, & Rose, 2001).

Additional personality characteristics, such as anxiety, negativity, and neuroticism, (assessed when couples were newlyweds) are associated with later relationship problems (Caughlin, Huston, & Houts, 2000; Huston, Caughlin, Houts, Smith, & George, 2001). These characteristics not only influence marital happiness, they also appear to influence the health of marriage partners. For instance, in situations in which one partner has had major surgery and needs help and support to recover at home, a partner's neuroticism (lack of emotional stability) can be harmful and lead to depression on the part of the patient (e.g., Ruiz et al., 2006). The same study also reported that such effects were stronger when couples had low marital satisfaction than when they had high levels of satisfaction. In other words, personal health and recovery from serious illnesses are influenced both by a spouse's personality traits and by the couple's overall marital satisfaction. These findings are real to me because when I had serious brain surgery several years ago, it was clearly the love, concern, and support of my wife Rebecca that pulled me through. She made sure that I received attention while in the hospital, brought me food (I was slowly starving on hospital fare), and nursed me attentively when I came home. So, do I believe in a connection between marital happiness and personal health? Absolutely! (Now, let's take a closer look at the role of illusions in marriage in *Social Psychology: What It Tells Us About . . .* on page 263.)

assumed similarity
The extent to which two people believe they are similar.

narcissism
A personality disposition characterized by unreasonably high self-esteem, a feeling of superiority, a need for admiration, sensitivity to criticism, a lack of empathy, and exploitative behavior.

SOCIALPSYCHOLOGY

WHAT IT TELLS US ABOUT . . .

The Role of Positive Illusions in Marital Happiness

Most married couples start their relationships with positive feelings about their chosen partners; after all, they are in love. In addition, they often hold positive beliefs concerning each other—beliefs that are, in a sense inflated. In other words, they view each other as possessing more positive characteristics, and being much closer to perfect than is actually the case (see Figure 7.24). Do such positive illusions lead to disaster—to becoming disillusioned with and disappointed in one's spouse? While some early research suggested this might be so, more recent evidence points strongly to the opposite conclusion: Couples who begin their marriages with idealized views of each other usually develop more satisfying and happier relationships than those who do not (e.g., Miller, Caughlin, & Huston, 2003). Why would this be the case? Perhaps because when couples start with idealized views of one another, they use several cognitive strategies to maintain these favorable illusions. For instance, they tend to focus on their partner's strengths while downplaying weaknesses, and interpret their partner's actions—even ones that are not supportive or pleasant—in a positive way. "Yes, Joe was late, but he couldn't help it; they kept him late at the office." "Chris loses her temper sometimes, but really, it's usually my fault . . ."

Do such illusions predict marital happiness, and perhaps the survival of love? Growing evidence suggests that they do (e.g., Miller et al., 2003). For instance, in one longitudinal study, newly married couples were studied for thirteen years. The research occurred in four phases: after the couples had been married for two months, one year, two years, and after approximately thirteen years. During each phase, the researchers conducted face-to-face interviews with the 168 couples in the study, obtaining measures of the agreeableness or disagreeableness of their spouse's behavior, ratings of their spouse's overall agreeableness, and their love for their spouses. Agreeable behaviors included such actions as expressing approval or complimenting the spouse,

Figure 7.24
Idealizing One's Mate: How Many Relationships Begin
Early in their relationships, most couples have a strong tendency to idealize their new mates. Couples who hold onto such positive illusions over the years appear to experience greater happiness and love than those who let them fade.

saying "I love you," kissing, hugging, and cuddling the spouse. Disagreeable behaviors included yelling, snapping, raising his/her voice, criticizing or complaining about something the spouse did, or seeming bored and uninterested in the partner. During the first phase of the study, participants kept diaries in which they reported such actions by their partners on a daily basis. During this and later phases, they also rated the extent to which their partners showed traits related to agreeableness (cheerful, pleasant, friendly, happy, easygoing, and patient). Positive illusions were measured in terms of the extent to which partners perceived each other to be more agreeable (in terms of the trait ratings) than would be expected on the basis of actual agreeable or disagreeable behavior (as reported in the daily diaries).

Results indicated that the stronger the tendency of the couples to hold positive illusions about each other (to perceive their partners are more agreeable than their actual behavior indicated), the greater love they reported and the smaller the declines in love they experienced during the period studied (thirteen years). In short, positive illusions about one's spouse predicted marital happiness well beyond the newlywed period. There was no clear evidence that such illusions protected the couples from divorce, but overall, the results of this study and many others (e.g., Miller et al., 2003) suggest that viewing our marriage partners as better than they really are can provide an important boost to continued love and happiness. This is one context, therefore, in which illusions may actually be better than the cold light of reality!

Why Relationships Fail—and Why, Sometimes, They Succeed

As we just saw, most people enter marriage with high hopes and positive views of their partners; yet, more than 50 percent of marriages in the United States and many other countries end in divorce (McNulty & Karney, 2004). Despite these statistics, unmarried respondents estimate for themselves only a 10 percent chance of a divorce when they marry (Fowers, Lyons, Montel, & Shaked, 2001). In other words, people expect their own marriages to succeed, despite the fact that most marriages fail. Why is it, then, that so many marriages fail? As you can probably guess, the answer is complex and involves many different factors.

Costs and Benefits of Marital Interactions

Before we discuss specific problems, it may be useful to consider each interaction in a marriage in terms of costs and benefits. Presumably, the greater the number of benefits relative to the number of costs there are, the higher the quality of the relationship is.

Clark and Grote (1998) identified several types of costs and benefits, some of which are intentionally positive or negative, and some of which are unintentional. From the viewpoint of attempting to maintain a good relationship, it is potentially possible to engage in intentionally positive acts and to avoid intentionally negative acts, but both partners have to be conscious of what they say and do and to be motivated to exercise self-control. Instead of emphasizing the positive aspects of their relationship, some individuals actually work to obtain negative, threatening information (Ickes, Hutchison, & Mashek, 2004). Altogether, marital satisfaction depends strongly on maximizing benefits and minimizing costs, so what happens in relationships that fail? What makes the costs rise and the benefits fall?

Problems between Spouses

One factor is the failure to understand the reality of a relationship. That is, no spouse (including oneself) is perfect. No matter how ideal the other person may have seemed through the mist of romantic images, it eventually becomes obvious that he or she has negative qualities and positive ones. For example, there is the disappointing discovery that the actual similarity between spouses is less than the assumed similarity (Sillars et al., 1994). Also over time the negative personality characteristics that we discussed previously become less and less tolerable. Minor personality and behavioral flaws that once seemed cute can come to be perceived as annoying and unlikable (Femlee, 1995; Pines, 1997). If you are initially drawn to someone because that person is quite different from you or perhaps even unique, chances are good that disenchantment will eventually set in (Femlee, 1998).

Some marital problems are universal, and probably unavoidable, because being in any kind of close relationship involves some degree of compromise. When you live alone, you can do as you wish. When two people are together, however, they must somehow decide what to eat for dinner, who prepares it, and when and how to serve the meal. Similar decisions must be made about whether to watch TV and which programs to watch, whether to wash the dishes after dinner or let them wait until the next day, where to set the thermostat, whether to have sex right now or some other time: The list of decisions—and compromises—is endless. Because both partners have needs and preferences, there is an inevitable conflict between the desire for independence and the need for closeness (Baxter, 1990). As a consequence, 98.8 percent of married couples report that they have disagreements, and most indicate that serious conflicts arise once a month or more often (McGonagle, Kessler, & Schilling, 1992). Because disagreements and conflicts are essentially inevitable, what becomes crucial is how those conflicts are handled.

Perceiving Love—or at Least Approval—as Contingent on Success

Another problem that troubles many marriages (and other long-term relationships) is a growing tendency on the part of one or both partners to perceive that their partner's love and approval is linked to external success—achievements in their careers, jobs, or at school. In other words, spouses come to expect that their partners will be kind and loving, and express approval of them, only when they are successful (Murray, Holmes, & Griffin, 2000). Such beliefs can badly erode even loving relationships. Even worse, such perceptions may be especially likely to develop among people low in self-esteem. This fact is demonstrated clearly in research by Murray, Griffin, Rose, and Bellavia (2006). They asked 173 couples (either married or cohabiting) to complete questionnaires that measured their self-esteem and their satisfaction with their relationship. In addition, the couples completed daily event diaries for twenty-one days, reporting (each day) on their personal successes, personal failures, felt rejection, and felt acceptance by their spouses. The key question was whether members of these couples would report feeling less acceptance from their spouses (and more rejection) on days when they experienced failures than on days when they experienced successes. A related question was whether people low in self-esteem would be more likely to perceive such negative outcomes than ones high in self-esteem. This is precisely what was found. People low in self-esteem felt less accepted and less loved on days when they had failures in their professional lives (i.e., their jobs, careers, or school). People high in self-esteem, however, did not report such effects.

In sum, for people low in self-esteem, personal failures on the job or at school spilled over into their marriages, causing them to feel less accepted and more rejected by their spouses. Clearly, to the extent such effects occur, they can be devastating for marital happiness.

External Pressures: The Effects of Being in a Marginalized Relationship

Do you know any couples in which the two partners are from different ethnic groups? Are the same gender? Different in age? If so, you probably realized that such couples face special problems. They often find themselves the victims of prejudice on the part of people who, for various reasons, disapprove of their relationship or marriage. For instance, even today, same-sex marriage is not legal in most states of the United States and in many other countries, too. Although the situation appears to be changing, recent surveys indicate that even among young people (eighteen to twenty-nine) only 41 percent favor this legal change. Given these current conditions, same-sex couples (and interracial couples or couples in which the partners are different in age) are often marginalized—they experience social disapproval as a result of their union. What are the effects of external pressures on the couples who experience them? One possibility is that this will reduce partners' willingness to invest in their relationships—to invest time and effort in the relationship, or develop joint friendships. This, in turn, may reduce their commitment and so tend to pull them apart. On the other hand, they might react to external disapproval by becoming more committed to their relationship.

Research by Lehmiller and Agnew (2006) provides evidence on these possibilities. These researchers identified several hundred couples—both ones that were marginalized (they included members of the same sex, the partners were of different races, or one partner was ten years older or younger than the other) and couples that would not be expected to receive social disapproval for their union. Both groups of couples reported on their satisfaction with the relationship, investments in it (e.g., "I have put a great deal into our relationship . . ."), their commitment to their relationships (e.g. , "I am committed to maintaining my relationship with my partner . . ."), and the extent to which they received social disapproval from others (e.g., "Most people disapprove of my relationship . . .").

Results indicated that people in these marginalized relationships did report lower investments in their relationships but showed satisfaction equal to that of people in nonmarginalized relationships. Further, and perhaps more surprising, people in marginalized relationships actually expressed greater commitment to their relationships than people in nonmarginalized relationships. They seemed to compensate for their lower investments by perceiving that alternatives to their current relationships were unappealing. This is similar to what is known as the "Romeo-and-Juliet" effect: a tendency for members of a couple that experiences interference or rejections from others to become even more tightly bonded together. Overall, then, available evidence suggests that while external pressures can—and often do—exert negative effects on couples, these effects are by no means impossible to resist and can, sometimes, strengthen rather than weaken the bonds between them.

The Consequences of a Failed Relationship

Friends may drift apart peacefully, but spouses are much more likely to feel intense distress and anger when a marriage fails (Fischman, 1986). In part, spouses find the end of their relationship more difficult than the end of a friendship because they have invested considerable time and effort in one another, engaged in many mutually rewarding activities, planned a future together, and expressed a lasting commitment to the relationship (Simpson, 1987). Suddenly, all of the experiences, the interactions, and the plans seem to have been a waste of time, and, of course, blame is attributed primarily to the other person.

When it has become clear that a relationship has severe problems, each partner can respond either actively or passively to the situation (Rusbult & Zembrodt, 1983). An active response consists of either ending the relationship as quickly as possible (moving out, filing for divorce, etc.) or working to improve it (deliberately trying to behave in a more positive way, seeing a marriage counselor, etc.). A passive response involves simply waiting and hoping that things will get better or waiting for things to get worse. Men and women with a secure attachment style are more likely to work actively to save a relationship, while those with insecure attachment styles are more likely to end the relationship or simply to wait for it to get worse (Rusbult, Morrow, & Johnson, 1990).

It is difficult, though possible, to reverse a deteriorating relationship. A couple is most able to reconcile if (1) the needs of each partner can be satisfied, (2) each is committed to continuing the relationship, and (3) alternative lovers are not readily available (Arriaga & Agnew, 2001; Rusbult, Martz, & Agnew, 1998).

Despite the shattered hopes of living "happily ever after" and despite the emotional and often financial pain of a marital breakup, most divorced individuals marry again, especially men. In fact, almost half of all marriages in the United States are remarriages for one or both partners, and millions of people have been married two, three, or even more times (Koch 1996). The desire for love and happiness in a relationship seems to have a greater influence on what people do than negative experiences with a former spouse. And of course, there are many happy couples—people who, like my grandparents—pass through the decades of life accompanied by their loving, supportive partners. Perhaps it is exposure to these models of happiness that leads such a large proportion of adults to marry—and then, if this fails, to marry again. So, perhaps Samuel Johnson, a philosopher of the nineteenth century, was correct when he remarked: "Remarriage, sir, represents the triumph of hope over experience." The hope springs from our exposure to truly happy couples, whose joy and contentment we hope to match.

> *Principles to Remember*
>
> Marriages usually begin with love, but many factors—some generated by the couples and some produced by external pressures—can drive even happy couples apart.

KeyPoints

- In the United States, about 50 percent of marriages end in divorce, but people do not believe that their own marriages will fail.

- Factors that exert negative effects on couples include beliefs that their partner's love and approval are contingent on success, and external disapproval of the relationships and pressures from outside the marriage, such as social disapproval of the relationships by others.

- Positive illusions about one's partner often appear to strengthen the long-term relationships in which they occur.

- If dissatisfaction becomes too great, individuals tend to respond either actively or passively in the hope of restoring the relationship or ending it through divorce.

Think About It

Given all the factors that can work to undermine love and drive married couples apart, why are some couples able to remain together for their entire lives? What are they doing "right" that others are doing "wrong?"

SUMMARY AND REVIEW

- Interpersonal attraction refers to the evaluations we make of other people—the positive and negative attitudes we form about them. We are apparently born with a need for affiliation and the motivation to interact with other people in a cooperative way. The strength of this need differs among individuals and across situations, but even people who claim they do not have it show evidence that they do. Positive and negative affective states influence attraction both directly and indirectly.

- The initial contact between two people is often based on the proximity, that is, they are near each other in physical space. Proximity, in turn, leads to repeated exposure, and that often produces positive affect and increased attraction (the mere exposure effect).

- Interpersonal attraction and judgments based on stereotypes are strongly affected by various observable characteristics of those we meet, including physical attractiveness. People like and make positive attributions about attractive men and women of all ages, despite the fact that assumptions based on appearance are usually inaccurate. In addition to attractiveness, many other observable characteristics influence initial interpersonal evaluations, including physique, weight, behavioral style, food preferences, first names, and other superficial characteristics. Individuals differ in their concern

that they will be rejected by others because of their appearance, and people high in such concern often feel rejected by others and experience reduced self-esteem.

- One factor that exerts powerful effects on attraction is similarity of attitudes, beliefs, values, and interests. Despite the continuing popularity of the idea that opposites attract (complementarity), it rarely occurs in the real world. Though dissimilarity tends to have a greater impact on attraction than similarity, we respond to both, and the larger the proportion of similar attitudes is, the greater the attraction is. The similarity–dissimilarity effect has been explained by balance theory, social comparison theory, and by an evolutionary perspective as an adaptive response to potential danger from strangers. We especially like other people who indicate that they like us. We dislike those a great deal who dislike and negatively evaluate us.

- Close relationships are characterized by interdependence, in which two people influence each other's lives, share their thoughts and emotions, and engage in joint activities.

- The first relationships are within the family, and we acquire an attachment style (a combination of level of self-esteem and degree of interpersonal trust) based on interactions with a caregiver. Friendships outside of the family begin in childhood and are initially based simply on such factors as common interests and other sources of positive affect, resulting in attraction. With increasing maturity, it becomes possible to form close friendships. Loneliness occurs when a person has fewer and less satisfying relationships than they desire. The result is depression and anxiety. Dispositional loneliness originates in a combination of genetics, an insecure attachment style based on caregiver-child interactions, and the lack of early social experiences with peers. A helpful intervention involves a combination of cognitive therapy and social skills training.

- One defining characteristic of romantic relationships is some degree of physical intimacy, ranging from holding hands to sexual interactions. As is true for attraction and friendship, romantic attraction is influenced by factors such as physical proximity, appearance, and similarity. In addition, romance includes sexual attraction, the desire for total acceptance by the other person, and an acceptance of positive fantasies about such relationships. The reproductive success of our ancient ancestors was enhanced by male attraction to young, fertile females, female attraction to males with resources, and by bonding between mates and between parents and their offspring. Love involves multiple components. For example, passionate love is a sudden, overwhelming emotional response to another person. Companionate love resembles a close friendship that includes caring, mutual liking, and respect. Sternberg's triangular model of love includes these two components plus a third—decision (commitment)—that is a cognitive decision to love and to be committed to a relationship. Jealousy is a powerful emotion, and research findings suggest that it is often triggered by threats to our self-esteem—threats arising when we fear that someone we love or care about will desert us for a rival.

- In the United States, about 50 percent of marriages end in divorce, but people do not believe that their own marriages will fail. Most married couples have some degree of conflict and disagreement. When difficulties can be resolved constructively, the marriage is likely to endure. When the problems are made worse by destructive interactions, the marriage is likely to fail. Positive illusions about one's partner, however, can help to strengthen marriages and other long-term relationships. Other factors that exert negative effects on couples include beliefs that their partner's love and approval are contingent on success, and external pressures from outside the marriage, such as social disapproval of the relationships by others. If dissatisfaction becomes too great, individuals tend to respond either actively or passively in the hope of restoring the relationship or ending it through divorce.

Key Terms

adaptive response (p. 242)

appearance-rejection sensitivity (p. 237)

assumed similarity (p. 262)

attachment style (p. 246)

attitude similarity (p. 240)

balance theory (p. 241)

bilateral symmetry (p. 253)

close friendship (p. 248)

companionate love (p. 256)

consummate love (p. 257)

decision (commitment) (p. 257)

dismissing attachment style (p. 247)

enemyship (p. 245)

fearful-avoidant attachment style (p. 247)

interdependence (p. 245)

interpersonal trust (p. 246)

intimacy (p. 257)

loneliness (p. 249)

love (p. 254)

narcissism (p. 262)

need for affiliation (p. 227)

passion (p. 257)

passionate love (p. 255)

physical attractiveness (p. 233)

preoccupied attachment style (p. 247)

proportion of similarity (p. 240)

proximity (p. 231)

repeated exposure (p. 232)

repulsion hypothesis (p. 241)

secure attachment style (p. 247)

similarity–dissimilarity effect (p. 240)

social comparison theory (p. 241)

triangular model of love (p. 257)

unrequited love (p. 256)

Connections
INTEGRATING SOCIAL PSYCHOLOGY

In this chapter, you read about . . .	In other chapters, you will find related discussions of . . .
attitudes about people	attitudes (Chapter 4).
conditioning of affect and attraction	conditioning of attitudes (Chapter 4).
appearance and stereotypes	prejudice and stereotypes (Chapter 6).
jealousy and its effects on relationships	effects of jealousy on aggression (Chapter 10).
love as emotional misattribution	attribution theory (Chapter 3).
conflict between spouses	conflict as a more general process (Chapter 11).

Social Influence
Changing Others' Behavior

CHAPTER OUTLINE

- **Conformity: Group Influence in Action**
  Asch's Research on Conformity: Social Pressure—
  The Irresistible Force?
  Sherif's Research on the Autokinetic
  Phenomenon: How Norms Emerge
  Factors Affecting Conformity: Variables that
  Determine the Extent to which We "Go
  Along"
  Situational Norms: Automaticity in Normative
  Behavior
  The Social Roots of Conformity: Why We Often
  Choose to Go Along
  The Downside of Conformity: When Pressures
  to Go Along Produce Harmful Effects
  BUILDING THE SCIENCE: CLASSICS OF SOCIAL
  PSYCHOLOGY—WHY GOOD PEOPLE SOMETIMES DO
  EVIL THINGS: THE POWERFUL—BUT NOT
  INVINCIBLE—EFFECTS OF SITUATIONS, NORMS,
  AND CONFORMITY PRESSURE
  Resisting Pressures to Conform: Why, Sometimes,
  We Choose Not to Go Along
  Minority Influence: Does the Majority Always
  Rule?

MAKING SENSE OF COMMON SENSE: A SOCIAL
PSYCHOLOGICAL PERSPECTIVE—DO
WOMEN AND MEN DIFFER IN THE TENDENCY
TO CONFORM?

- **Compliance: To Ask—Sometimes—Is to Receive**
  Compliance: The Underlying Principles
  Tactics Based on Friendship or Liking:
  Ingratiation
  Tactics Based on Commitment of Consistency:
  The Foot-in-the-Door and the Lowball
  Tactics Based on Reciprocity: The Door-in-the-
  Face and the "That's-Not-All" Approach
  Tactics Based on Scarcity: Playing Hard to Get
  and the Fast-Approaching-Deadline Technique

- **Symbolic Social Influence: How We Are Influenced
  by Others Even When They Are Not There**
  SOCIAL PSYCHOLOGY: WHAT IT TELLS US ABOUT . . .
  THE EPIDEMIC OF EATING DISORDERS

- **Obedience to Authority: Would You Harm an
  Innocent Stranger If Ordered to Do So?**
  Obedience in the Laboratory
  Destructive Obedience: Why It Occurs
  Destructive Obedience: Resisting Its Effects

Imagine a time in the future when you are in the midst of your career. You are working for a company everyone admires and you really like your job. Then one day you wake up to find that the company has gone completely bankrupt. You no longer have a job, your pension has vanished, and the stock in the company that you purchased or received as a bonus each year has lost all its value. How would you feel? We don't have to guess because this is exactly what happened to more than 21,000 employees of a large company called Enron a few years ago. One day their company, their jobs, and their pensions were there; the next day, they were gone. As you can guess, these suddenly jobless employees were upset, distressed, and angry. How did this appalling situation develop? For the answer we have to look at the top people in the company and consider the impact of the topic on which we'll focus in this chapter: social influence.

Two of the top people at Enron were Jeffrey Skilling, its chief executive officer (CEO) and Ken Lay, who took over when Skilling suddenly and unexpectedly retired. Both were highly experienced executives; in fact, Lay had founded Enron, which was in the energy business and had been named "America's Most Innovative Company" six years in a row. Sadly, though both of these leaders engaged in unethical and, as indicated by later court decisions, illegal actions. They concealed the fact that the company was piling up huge debts, exaggerated its earnings, benefited from insider trading (using their "inside" knowledge to buy and sell the company's shares at just the right times), and lied to auditors whose job it was to examine the financial condition of the company. They also involved Enron in business deals that were highly questionable and, in some cases, downright illegal. As a result of their actions, and those of other top leaders of the company (e.g., Ken Fastow, Chief Financial Officer [CFO]), Enron became an empty shell: It had huge debts, almost no assets, and no income. This situation developed over several years yet during that period, no one did anything to change the situation, even though literally dozens of employees knew what was happening.

Finally, as is always the case, the truth came out. Sherron Watkins, a trained accountant and a vice president at Enron, was so disturbed by what she saw that she *did* take action. First, she made an appointment to see Skilling. But Skilling resigned as CEO before she could see him. So, undeterred, she went to see his successor, Lay. When she explained her concerns to him, she expected him to take vigorous action, but he did not. Instead, he simply discussed the situation with the company's attorneys, and they began a series of legal actions designed to get Enron out of some of its riskiest activities. Their efforts, plus Watkins's testimony in court, quickly brought matters to a head, and Enron dropped rapidly into bankruptcy. Ultimately, criminal charges were filed against Skilling, Lay, Fastow, and other top people at Enron. In 2006, Skilling received a sentence of twenty-four years in prison for his illegal actions; Lay died of a heart attack while awaiting sentencing; and Fastow received seven years in jail for his actions. While these outcomes could not restore the lost jobs, pensions, or savings of Enron's 21,000 employees, at least they did provide the small satisfaction of seeing the guilty persons punished. And it did nothing for the thousands of thousands of ordinary people who had purchased Enron's shares because they thought they were a good investment. . . .

No, we haven't forgotten: This book is about social psychology, not life in large corporations. But we begin with this sad tale because it clearly illustrates the power of the crucial process we examine in this chapter: **social influence.** A general definition of social influence is that it involves the many ways in which people produce changes in others—in their behavior, attitudes, or beliefs (Cialdini, 2000, 2006; see Figure 8.1). Change with respect to attitudes is usually described as persuasion, a topic we discussed in Chapter 5. In contrast, change in overt behavior, generally produced by a specific request, is termed *compliance*; it involves getting other people to do what we want them to do. Change induced by general rules concerning what behavior is appropriate or required in a given situation is termed *conformity*. Finally, change induced by direct orders or commands from others is described as obedience. In this chapter we'll examine all of these forms of social influence except persuasion (which was discussed in Chapter 5). Before turning to these concepts, let's first consider how they are related to the sad story of Enron.

First, consider the fact that, for several years, no one took strong steps to block the illegal actions of Enron's top management. Was this simply the result of obedience to the orders of these powerful people? Perhaps, but it also involved the development of a "mind-your-own-business" attitude within the company. Employees who questioned what was going on were told that "good employees of Enron keep out of such things." They did, and the situation continued. And when specific people became upset and did threaten to take action, steps were taken (often by their bosses) to assure their continued silence; various tactics of compliance were used, including offering them raises, promotions, or bonuses, or alternatively, threatening them with the loss of their jobs if they didn't comply. In short, we believe that social influence played a key role in the chain of events that produced Enron's bankruptcy—and misery for thousands of innocent victims.

As one well-known social psychologist, Philip Zimbardo (2007), has put it, in cases like this, the powerful impact of social influence helps us understand why basically good people sometimes do bad things and certainly, many of the people who worked for Enron and could have prevented the events that led to its decline were good people who objected to what was going on when they learned about it. Yet they yielded to various kinds of social pressure, and that paved the way for disaster.

social influence
Efforts by one or more individuals to change the attitudes, beliefs, perceptions, or behaviors of one or more others.

"*A fantastic evangelist was on TV, and I sent him everything.*"

Figure 8.1
Social Influence: One Technique
Each day we try to influence others and are on the receiving end of many influence attempts from them. Not all are this effective, but often they do change our actions or beliefs.

(*Source: The New Yorker*, 1987; Drawing by W. Miller.)

To provide you with a broad overview of the nature and power of social influence, we'll proceed as follows. First, we'll examine **conformity**—pressure to behave in ways that are viewed as acceptable or appropriate by a group or society generally. Then we'll turn to **compliance**—direct efforts to get others to change their behavior in specific ways (Cialdini, 2006; Sparrowe, Soetjipto, & Kraimer, 2006).

Third, we'll examine what is, in some ways, the most intriguing form of social influence—influence that occurs when other people are not present and are not making any direct attempts to affect our behavior (e.g., Fitzsimons & Bargh, 2003). We'll refer to such effects as **symbolic social influence** to reflect the fact that it results from our mental representations of other people rather than their actual presence or overt actions. After considering this indirect form of social influence, we'll examine another kind that is, in some respects, its direct opposite: **obedience**—social influence in which one person simply orders one or more others to do what they want.

Conformity: Group Influence in Action

During an exam, another student's cell phone begins to ring loudly. What does this person do?

Your friend has just had a new tattoo and asks you whether you like it.

In a supermarket, a new checkout line suddenly opens, right next to a checkout with a long line of shoppers. Who gets to go first in that new line?

In each of these situations, the people involved could, potentially, behave in many different ways. But probably, you can predict with great certainty what they will do. The student with the loud cell phone will silence it immediately and perhaps apologize to other members of the class sitting nearby. When your friend asks, you will probably say that you like the new tattoo, even if you don't because, after all, we are supposed to make our friends feel good, not bad. The checkout line is a little trickier. People near the front of the long checkout line should get to be first in the new line, but this might not happen. Someone from the back of the long line might beat them to it. In contexts in which norms are more clear cut, greater conformity by most people can be expected compared to contexts like this in which norms are less clear about what action is the "correct" one.

The fact that we can predict others' behavior (and our own) with considerable confidence in these and many other situations illustrates the powerful and general effects of pressures toward conformity—toward doing what we are expected to do in a given situation. Conformity, in other words, refers to pressures to behave in ways consistent with rules indicating how we *should* or *ought to* behave. These rules are known as **social norms,** and they often exert powerful effects on our behavior. The uncertainty you might experience in the checkout line situation stems from the fact that the norms in that situation are not as clear as in the others; it's uncertain whether people in the front or the back of the existing line should go first.

In some instances, social norms are stated explicitly and are quite detailed. For instance, governments generally function through written constitutions and laws; athletic contests are usually regulated by written rules; and signs in many public places (e.g., along highways, in parks, at airports) describe expected behavior in considerable detail (e.g., *Speed Limit: 55; No Swimming; No Parking; Keep off the Grass*). In other situations, norms may be unspoken or implicit, and in fact, may have developed in a totally informal manner. For instance, we all recognize such unstated rules as "Don't stare at strangers on an elevator"; "don't arrive early at parties or other social events"; and "do try to look your best when going on a job interview." Regardless of whether social norms are explicit or implicit, formal or informal, one fact is clear: Most people follow them most of the time. For instance, virtually everyone, regardless of personal political beliefs, stands when the

conformity
A type of social influence in which individuals change their attitudes or behavior to adhere to existing social norms.

compliance
A form of social influence involving direct requests from one person to another.

symbolic social influence
Social influence resulting from the mental representation of others or our relationships with them.

obedience
A form of social influence in which one person simply orders one or more others to perform some action(s).

social norms
Rules indicating how individuals are expected to behave in specific situations.

national anthem of their country is played at sports events or other public gatherings. Similarly, few people visit restaurants without leaving a tip for the waitperson (see Figure 8.2). In fact, so powerful is this social norm that most people leave a tip of around 15 percent *regardless* of the quality of the service they have received (Azar, 2007).

Figure 8.2
Social Norms: A Powerful Influence on Our Behavior
Social norms tell us what we should do (or not do) in a given situation, and most people obey them most of the time. For instance, few people would think of leaving a restaurant without leaving a tip for the waitperson.

At first glance, this strong tendency toward conformity may seem objectionable. After all, it does place restrictions on personal freedom. Actually, though, there is a strong basis for so much conformity: Without it, we would quickly find ourselves facing social chaos. Imagine what would happen outside movie theaters, stadiums, or at supermarket checkout counters if people did not obey the norm "Form a line and wait your turn." And consider the danger to both drivers and pedestrians if there were not clear and widely followed traffic regulations. In many situations, then, conformity serves a useful function. If you have ever driven in a country in which traffic rules are widely ignored or viewed as mere suggestions, you know what we mean: When people don't follow social norms, their actions are unpredictable, and sometimes that can be dangerous (see Figure 8.3).

Figure 8.3
Conformity: Why It's Often Useful
When norms telling people how to behave don't exist—or are largely ignored—chaos can develop. Countries in which traffic regulations are taken lightly provide a clear illustration of this fact and of why conformity can sometimes be very useful.

Given that strong pressures toward conformity exist in many social settings, it is surprising to learn that conformity, as a social process, received relatively little attention in social psychology until the 1950s. At that time, Solomon Asch (1951), whose research on impression formation we considered in Chapter 3, carried out a series of experiments on conformity that yielded dramatic results. Asch's research was clearly a classic of social psychology, and we could certainly feature it in *Building the Science: Classics of Social Psychology*, but in fact, it was so modern in some respects that we'll simply describe it here as part of the overall discussion of conformity.

Asch's Research on Conformity: Social Pressure— The Irresistible Force?

Suppose that just before an important math exam, you discover that your answer to a homework problem—a problem of the type that will be on the test—is different from that obtained by one of your friends. How would you react? Probably with mild concern. Now imagine that you learn that a second person's answer, too, is different from yours. To make matters worse, it agrees with the answer reported by the first person. How would you feel now? The chances are good that your anxiety will increase. Next you discover that

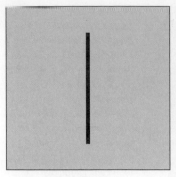

Standard Line

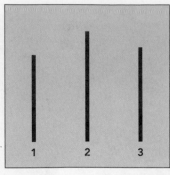

1 2 3

Comparison Lines

Figure 8.4
Asch's Line Judgment Task

Participants in Asch's research were asked to report their judgments on problems such as this one. Their task was to indicate which of the comparison lines (1, 2, or 3) best matched the standard line in length. To study conformity, he had participants make these judgments out loud, only after hearing the answers of several other people—all of whom were Asch's assistants. On certain critical trials the assistants all gave wrong answers. This exposed participants to strong pressures toward conformity.

a third person agrees with the other two. At this point, you know that you are in big trouble. Which answer should you accept? Yours or the one obtained by your three friends? The exam is about to start, so you have to decide quickly.

Life is filled with such dilemmas—instances in which we discover that our own judgments, actions, or conclusions are different from those reached by other people. What do we do in such situations? Important insights into our behavior were provided by studies conducted by Solomon Asch (1951; 1955), research that is viewed as a true classic in social psychology.

Asch created a compelling social dilemma for his participants whose task was ostensibly to simply respond to a series of perceptual problems, such as the one in Figure 8.4. On each of the problems, participants were to indicate which of three comparison lines matched a standard line in length. Several other people (usually six to eight) were also present during the session, but unknown to the real participant, all were assistants of the experimenter. On certain occasions known as critical trials (twelve out of the eighteen problems) the accomplices offered answers that were clearly wrong: they unanimously chose the wrong line as a match for the standard line. Moreover, they stated their answers before the real participants responded. Thus on these critical trials, the people in Asch's study faced precisely the type of dilemma described previously. Should they go along with the other individuals present or stick to their own judgments? The judgments seemed to be simple ones, so the fact that other people agreed on an answer different from the one the participants preferred was truly puzzling. Results were clear: A large majority of the people in Asch's research chose conformity. Across several different studies, fully 76 percent of those tested went along with the group's false answers at least once; and overall, they voiced agreement with these errors 37 percent of the time. In contrast, only 5 percent of the participants in a control group, who responded to the same problems alone, made such errors.

Of course, there were large individual differences in this respect. Almost 25 percent of the participants never yielded to the group pressure. At the other extreme, some people went along with the majority nearly all the time. When Asch questioned them, some of these people stated: "I am wrong, they are right;" they had little confidence in their own judgments. Others, however, said they felt that the other people present were suffering from an optical illusion or were merely sheep following the responses of the first person. Yet, when it was their turn, these people, too, went along with the group.

In further studies, Asch (1956) investigated the effects of shattering the group's unanimity by having one of the accomplices break with the others. In one study, this person gave the correct answer, becoming an "ally" of the real participant; in another study, he chose an answer in between the one given by the group and the correct one; and in a third, he chose the answer that was even more incorrect than that chosen by the majority. In the latter two conditions, in other words, he broke from the group but still disagreed with the real participants. Results indicated that conformity was reduced under all three conditions. However somewhat surprisingly, this reduction was greatest when the dissenting assistant expressed views even more extreme (and wrong) than the majority. Together, these findings suggest that it is the unanimity of the group that is crucial; once it is broken, no matter how, resisting group pressure becomes much easier.

There's one more aspect of Asch's research that is important to mention. In later studies, he repeated his basic procedure but with one important change: Instead of stating their answers out loud, participants wrote them down on a piece of paper. As you might guess, conformity dropped sharply because the participants didn't have to display the fact that they disagreed to the other people present. This finding points to the importance of distinguishing between public conformity—doing or saying what others around us say or do, and private acceptance—actually coming to feel or think as others do. Often, it appears, we follow social norms overtly but don't actually change our private views (Maas & Clark, 1984). This distinction between public conformity and private acceptance is an important one, and we'll refer to it at several points in this book.

Sherif's Research on the Autokinetic Phenomenon: How Norms Emerge

A clear illustration of private acceptance of social influence was provided many years ago by another founder of social psychology—Muzafer Sherif (1937). Sherif was interested in several questions, but among these, two were most important: (1) how do norms develop in social groups? and (2) how strong is their influence on behavior once they (the norms) emerge? To examine these issues, he used an interesting situation, one involving the **autokinetic phenomenon.** Autokinetic phenomenon refers to the fact that when placed in completely dark room and exposed to a single, stationary point of light, most people perceive the light as moving about. This is because in the dark room, there are no clear cues to distance or location. The perceived movement is known as the autokinetic phenomenon.

Sherif (1937) realized that he could use this situation to study the emergence of social norms. This is so because different people perceive the light as moving different distances. Thus when placed in this setting with several others and asked to report what they perceive the light to be doing, they influence one another and soon converge on a particular amount of movement; that agreement, in a sense, constitutes a group norm. If the same individuals are then placed in the situation alone, they continue to give estimates of the light's movement consistent with the group norm, so clearly, the effect of such norms persist. This suggests that these effects reflect changes in what participants in these studies actually believe—private acceptance or commitment; after all, they continue to obey the group norm even if they are no longer in the group.

Sherif's findings also help explain why social norms develop in many situations, especially ambiguous ones. We have a strong desire to be correct—to behave in an appropriate manner—and social norms help us attain that goal. As we'll note, this is one key foundation of social influence; another is the desire to be accepted by others and liked by them. Together, these two factors virtually assure that social influence is a powerful force—one that can often strongly affect our behavior.

Asch's research was the catalyst for a great deal of activity in social psychology because many other researchers sought to investigate the nature of conformity to identify factors that influence it and to establish its limits (e.g., Crutchfield, 1955; Deutsch & Gerard, 1955). Indeed, such research is continuing today and is still adding to our understanding of the factors that affect this crucial form of social influence (e.g., Baron, Vandello, & Brunsman, 1996; Bond & Smith, 1996; Lonnqvist, Leikas, Paunonen, et al., 2006).

Factors Affecting Conformity: Variables that Determine the Extent to which We "Go Along"

Asch's research demonstrated the existence of powerful pressures toward conformity, but even a moment's reflection suggests that conformity does not occur to the same degree in all settings. Why? In other words, what factors determine the extent to which individuals yield to conformity pressure or resist it? Research findings suggest that many factors play a role; here, we'll examine the ones that appear to be most important.

autokinetic phenomenon
The apparent movement of a single, stationary source of light in a dark room. Often used to study the emergence of social norms and social influence.

Cohesiveness and Conformity: Being Influenced by Those We Like

One factor that strongly influences our tendency to conform—to go along with whatever norms are operating in a given situation—is **cohesiveness**—the extent to which we are attracted to a particular social group and want to belong to it (e.g., Turner, 1991). The greater cohesiveness is, the more we tend to follow the norms (i.e., rules) of the group. This is hardly surprising: The more we value being a member of a group and want to be accepted by the other members, the more we want to avoid doing anything that will separate us from them. Similarly, acting and looking like others is often a good way to win their approval. So, in basic terms, the more we like other people and want to belong to the same group as they do, the more we tend to conform (Crandall, 1988; Latané & L'Herrou, 1996; Noel et al., 1995). In other words, cohesiveness and the desire to be accepted can be viewed as factors that intensify the tendency to conform. For instance, someone seeking membership in an exclusive club would probably do their best to conform to the formal and informal rules of the club, including the way its members dress and talk.

Conformity and Group Size: Why More Is Better with Respect to Social Pressure

Another factor that produces similar effects is the size of the group that is exerting influence. Asch (1956) and other early researchers (e.g., Gerard, Wilhelmy, & Conolley, 1968) found that conformity increases with group size but only up to about three or four members, and beyond that point, it appears to level off or even decrease. However more recent research has failed to confirm these early findings concerning group size (e.g., Bond & Smith, 1996). Instead, these later studies found that conformity tended to increase with group size up to eight group members and beyond. In short, the larger the group is—the greater the number of people who behave in some specific way—the greater our tendency to conform, and "do as they do" is.

Descriptive and Injunctive Social Norms: How Norms Affect Behavior

Social norms, we have already seen, can be formal or informal in nature—as different as rules printed on large signs and informal guidelines such as "Don't leave your shopping cart in the middle of a parking spot outside a supermarket." This is not the only way in which norms differ, however. Another important distinction is that between descriptive norms and injunctive norms (e.g., Cialdini, Kallgren, & Reno, 1991; Reno, Cialdini, & Kallgren, 1993). **Descriptive norms** are ones that simply describe what most people do in a given situation. They influence behavior by informing us about what is generally seen as effective or adaptive in that situation. In contrast, **injunctive norms** specify what ought to be done—what is approved or disapproved behavior in a given situation. For instance, there is a strong injunctive norm against cheating on exams; such behavior is considered to be ethically wrong. The fact that some students disobey this norm does not change the moral expectation that they should obey it. Overall, both kinds of norms—descriptive and injunctive—can exert strong effects on our behavior and the fact some people disobey such norms in no way changes this basic principle (e.g., Brown, 1998).

Because people obviously do disobey injunctive norms in many situations (they speed on highways, cut into line in front of others), a key question is this: When, precisely, do injunctive norms influence behavior? When are they likely to be obeyed? One answer is provided by **normative focus theory** (e.g., Cialdini, Reno, & Kallgren, 1990). This theory suggests that norms will influence behavior only to the extent that they are *salient* (i.e., relevant, significant) to the people involved at the time the behavior occurs.

In other words, people will obey injunctive norms only when they think about them and see them as relevant to their own actions. This prediction has been verified in many different studies (e.g., Reno, Cialdini, & Kallgren 1993; Kallgren, Reno, & Cialdini, 2000), so it seems to be a general principle that norms influence our actions primarily when we think about them and view them as relevant to our behavior. When, in contrast, we do not think about them or view them as irrelevant (i.e., as not applying to us, as may

cohesiveness
The extent to which we are attracted to a social group and want to belong to it.

descriptive norms
Norms simply indicating what most people do in a given situation.

injunctive norms
Norms specifying what ought to be done; what is approved or disapproved behavior in a given situation.

normative focus theory
A theory suggesting that norms will influence behavior only to the extent that they are focal for the people involved at the time the behavior occurs.

have been true for the top executives at Enron), their effects are much weaker or even nonexistent. In fact, this is one reason why people (e.g., the Enron executives discussed in the opening example) sometimes disobey even strong injunctive norms: They don't see these norms as applying to them.

Situational Norms: Automaticity in Normative Behavior

When you enter a museum or hospital, do you lower the volume of your voice? And when you are in a sports stadium, do you raise it? If so, you are showing adherence to what social psychologists describe as situational norms—norms that guide behavior in a certain situation or environment (e.g., Cialdini & Trost, 1998). But do we have to be aware of these norms—or any others—for them to influence our behavior? Recent findings indicate that such awareness is not necessary. On the contrary, norms can be activated in an automatic manner without our consciously thinking of them, and when they are, they can still strongly affect our overt actions. A clear illustration of such effects, and of the powerful effects of situational norms, is provided by research conducted by Aarts and Dijksterhuis (2003). These researchers first asked participants to look at photos of a library or an empty railway station. Some of the people who saw the photo of the library were told that they would later be visiting this location; others were not given this information. Then they were instructed to read out loud ten words presented on a computer screen. The volume of their voices was measured as they performed this task. The researchers predicted that when individuals expected to visit the library, the situational norm of being quiet would be activated and that as a result, they would read the words less loudly. Such effects would not occur when they did not expect to visit the library or when they saw a photo of railway station—a place in which the "be quiet" norm does not apply. As you can see from Figure 8.5, this is precisely what was found: Participants lowered the volume of their voices in the expect-to-visit library condition relative to the other two conditions. In additional studies, Aarts and Dijksterhuis found similar effects with respect to acting in a polite manner in a fancy restaurant, thus indicating that situational norms operate in many different locations and that they can automatically influence our behavior in these settings. In fact, participants for whom this norm had been activated actually ate a biscuit more neatly than those for whom this norm had not been primed. Overall, then, two facts seem clear: (1) situational norms that tell us how to behave in a given environments or locations often strongly affect our behavior, and (2) such norms—like other norms—can exert such effects in a relatively automatic manner, even if we do not consciously recognize their impact. In other words, social influence is indeed a powerful and pervasive aspect of daily life— perhaps stronger and more widespread than you would ever guess.

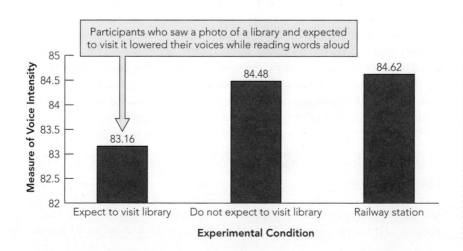

Figure 8.5
The Effects of Situational Norms on Behavior
Participants who saw a photo of a library and expected to visit this location lowered the intensity of their voices relative to people who saw a photo of a library but did not expect to visit it or those who saw a photo of a railway station. This illustrates the effects of situational norms ("Be quiet in libraries") on overt behavior.

(*Source:* Based on data from Aarts & Dijksterhuis, 2003.)

The Social Roots of Conformity: Why We Often Choose to Go Along

As we have just seen, several factors determine whether and to what extent conformity occurs. Yet this does not alter the essential point: Conformity is a basic fact of social life. Most people conform to the norms of their groups or societies much, if not most, of the time. Why is this so? Why do people often choose to go along with these social rules instead of resisting them? The answer seems to involve two powerful motives possessed by all human beings: the desire to be liked or accepted by others and the desire to be right—to have accurate understanding of the social world (Deutsch & Gerard, 1955; Insko, 1985)—plus the impact of cognitive processes that lead us to view conformity as fully justified after it has occurred (e.g., Buehler & Griffin, 1994).

Normative Social Influence: The Desire to Be Liked

How can we get others to like us? This is one of the eternal puzzles of social life. As we saw in Chapters 3 and 7, many tactics can prove effective in this regard. One of the most successful of these is to appear to be as similar to others as possible. From our earliest days, we learn that agreeing with the people around us, and behaving as they do, causes them to like us. Parents, teachers, friends, and others often heap praise and approval on us for showing such similarity (see our discussion of attitude formation in Chapter 5). One important reason we conform, therefore, is this: We have learned that doing so can help us win the approval and acceptance we crave. This source of conformity is known as **normative social influence** because it involves altering our behavior to meet others' expectations.

The Desire to Be Right: Informational Social Influence

If you want to know your weight, you can step onto a scale. If you want to know the dimensions of a room, you can measure them directly. But how can you establish the accuracy of your own political or social views or decide which hairstyle suits you best? There are no simple physical tests or measuring devices for answering these questions. Yet we want to be correct about such matters, too. The solution to this dilemma is obvious: to answer such questions, we refer to other people. We use their opinions and actions as guides for our own. Such reliance on others, in turn, is often a powerful source of the tendency to conform. Other people's actions and opinions define social reality for us, and we use these as a guide for our own actions and opinions. This basis for conformity is known as **informational social influence** because it is based on our tendency to depend on others as a source of information about many aspects of the social world.

Research evidence suggests that because our motivation to be correct or accurate is quite strong, informational social influence is a very powerful source of conformity. However as you might expect, this is more likely to be true in situations in which we are highly uncertain about what is correct or accurate than in situations in which we have more confidence in our own ability to make such decisions (e.g., Baron et al., 1996).

How powerful are the effects of social influence when we are uncertain about what is correct and what is not? Research findings suggest a chilling answer: extremely powerful. Because such effects often operate to encourage negative behaviors—ones with harmful social effects—we'll now describe them in more detail. But please note: before we proceed, we should clearly note that sometimes conformity can be helpful in such situations; for instance, when confronted with an emergency (e.g., a fire), we can sometimes escape from danger by doing what others do—for instance, following them to the nearest safe exit.

The Downside of Conformity: When Pressures to Go Along Produce Harmful Effects

We noted previously that the tendency to conform—to obey social norms—can produce positive effects. The fact that most people comply with most social norms most of the

normative social influence
Social influence based on the desire to be liked or accepted by other people.

informational social influence
Social influence based on the desire to be correct (i.e., to possess accurate perceptions of the social world).

time introduces a large measure of predictability into social relations: We know how we and others are expected to behave and can proceed on the assumption that these expectations will be met. Other motorists will drive on the correct side of the street (whatever that is in our own society) and stop for red lights; people waiting for service in a store will form a line and wait their turn. But as we have already noted, there is definitely a downside to conformity, too. In fact, recent research by social psychologists suggests that pressures to conform, and our tendency to surrender to such pressures, can sometimes result in very harmful effects. In fact, we'll discuss what is the most dramatic research illustrating such effects—Zimbardo and other's (Zimbardo, Haney, Banks, & Jaffe, 1973) famous prison study, which showed, among other things, the powerful impact of norms concerning various social roles—in *Building the Science: Classics of Social Psychology* (pages 282–284). Here, however, we'll first describe other harmful effects of conformity pressures—effects that although perhaps not as dramatic, can be equally harmful to the people involved.

First, consider the strong tendency with which most people conform to gender norms. As described in Chapter 4, such norms indicate how women and men are expected to behave, primarily, in ways consistent with societal beliefs about differences between them. The tendency to conform to such norms can produce negative effects in many ways. As we saw in Chapters 4 and 6, they can place limits on the opportunities and career aspirations of both women and men—and especially on those of women (see Eagly, 2007). For instance, to the extent that women accept and conform to gender norms, they might feel that they are not suited for a career in the physical sciences or mathematics and might conclude that they will not make good leaders in many contexts (e.g., Rudman & Fairchild, 2004). Recent findings suggest that the negative effects of conformity to gender norms may also influence personal happiness in other ways, too. For instance, in a series of intriguing studies, Sanchez and others (e.g., Sanchez, Crocker, & Boike, 2005; Sanchez, Kiefer, & Ybarra, 2006) have found that the tendency to conform to gender norms can interfere with sexual enjoyment among both women and men.

In one revealing study on this topic (Sanchez et al., 2005), the researchers reasoned that to the extent individuals feel it is important to conform to gender norms, they will base their self-esteem on others' approval of their doing so. To the extent this is so, in turn, their sexual autonomy will be reduced: They will be more concerned with "doing the right thing" (as prescribed by gender norms) to win their partner's approval than they will be with their own sexual fulfillment. To test these predictions, students who were sexually active were asked to complete a questionnaire that measured four important variables: (1) their desire to conform to gender norms ("To what extent is being similar to the ideal man or woman an important part of who you are?"), (2) the extent to which they based their self-esteem on others' approval, (3) their sexual autonomy ("When I am having sex with someone, I feel free to be who I am"), and (4) the level of pleasure they derived from their sexual activities.

Results offered strong support for the key hypothesis: The stronger participants' commitment to conforming to gender norms, the stronger was their desire to gain others' approval, and the stronger this desire, the less sexual autonomy they experienced. The lower such autonomy, the lower was their level of sexual pleasure (see Figure 8.6). In other words, where sexual activity is concerned, a tendency to conform to gender norms actually interfered with having a fulfilling and enjoyable sex life.

Figure 8.6
Some Unexpected Costs of Conformity
Research findings indicate that when individuals are committed to complying with gender norms, they tend to base their self-esteem on winning others' approval. Doing that, in turn, reduces their sexual autonomy (expressing themselves freely during sexual activities). This reduced autonomy then lessens their sexual pleasure.

(*Source:* Based on findings reported by Sanchez, Crocker, & Boike, 2005).

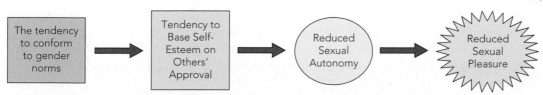

BUILDING THE SCIENCE
CLASSICS OF SOCIAL PSYCHOLOGY

Why Good People Sometimes Do Evil Things: The Powerful—But Not Invincible—Effects of Situations, Norms, and Conformity Pressure

Do good people ever do bad things? The answer, of course, is "Yes." History is filled with atrocities performed by people who, most of the time, were good neighbors, parents, friends, and spouses, and who often showed kindness and concern for others in their daily lives. Yet under some conditions, they seem to surrender all these positive qualities and engage in actions that most of us—and they, too—would find inexcusable. The key question for social psychologists is: Why? What makes good people turn bad—at least sometimes? While there is no single, simple answer, one famous study in social psychology—a true classic in the field—provides at least a partial answer. This research was conducted by Philip Zimbardo and others (Zimbardo et al., 1973) and was unusual in many respects. Here's how it took place:

Imagine that one peaceful Sunday you hear a loud knock on your door. When you go to answer, you find yourself face to face with several police officers. Without any explanation, they arrest you and take you downtown to be photographed, fingerprinted, and booked. Next, you are blindfolded and driven to a prison whose location you can only guess. Once there, you are stripped of all your clothes and are forced to dress in an uncomfortable, loose-fitting gown and a tight nylon cap. All of your personal possessions are removed and you are given an identification number instead of a name. Then you are locked in an empty cell containing only the bare necessities. Guards in the prison wear identical uniforms and reflecting sunglasses. And they carry clubs, whistles, and other signs of their authority.

As a prisoner, you are expected to obey a long set of rules under threat of severe punishment. You must remain silent during rest periods and after lights are turned out each night. You must eat only at mealtimes; you must address other prisoners only by their identification numbers and your guards as "Mr. Correctional Officer." And you must ask their permission to do anything—from reading and writing to going to the bathroom.

How would you react to such conditions? Would you obey? Rebel? Become angry? Depressed? Resentful? And what if you were a guard instead of a prisoner? Would you treat prisoners with respect or would you seek to humiliate them? These are the questions Zimbardo

and his colleagues investigated in the famous Stanford prison study. It was conducted in the basement of the Stanford University psychology building, and all guards and prisoners were paid volunteers. In fact, whether a volunteer became a guard or a prisoner was determined completely at random.

The main purpose of the study was to determine whether participants would come to behave very much like real guards and real prisoners—whether they would, in a sense, conform to the norms established for these respective roles. The answer was clear: They did. The prisoners were rebellious at first but then became increasingly passive and depressed. And the guards grew increasingly brutal and sadistic. They harassed the prisoners constantly, forced them to make fun of one another, and assigned them to difficult, senseless tasks. They also tended to dehumanize the prisoners, coming to perceive them as inferior to themselves, and "less than human." In fact, these changes in behavior were so large that it was necessary to stop the study after only six days; initial plans called for it to last two weeks.

So, what do we learn from this striking and thought-provoking study? Philip Zimbardo, who planned the research and served as "prison warden," contends that it drives home a key point about human behavior: It is the situations in which people find themselves—not their personal traits—that largely determine their behavior. Yes, people do differ in many ways, but place them in a powerful situation like this one, and such differences tend to disappear. Zimbardo (2007) suggests that it is this tendency to yield to situational pressures—including conformity pressures—that is responsible for much evil behavior. As he puts it: "we all like to think that the line between good and evil is impermeable—that people who do terrible things. . .are on the other side of the line—and we could never get over there. . . . My work began by saying no, that line is permeable. The reason some people are on the good side of the line is that they've never been fully tested. . . ." In other words, according to Zimbardo, placed in the wrong kind of situation, virtually all of us—even those who have always been good, upstanding citizens—might commit atrocities. As we'll soon see, not all social psychologists accept this view, although all recognize the powerful impact of situational factors on our social behavior.

Zimbardo leaves some room for personal heroism: He recognizes that some people seem able to resist even powerful situational or conformity pressures. But most of us, he contends, cannot; situations are often stronger than our ability to resist and remain true to our values. Recently, Zimbardo has related his famous study to the disturbing events that occurred in the Abu Ghraib prison in Iraq in 2005—events in which American soldiers humiliated and physically abused Iraqi prisoners. Zimbardo's explanation for these events is much the same as for the findings of the Stanford prison study: The soldiers found themselves in a situation in which prevailing norms pushed them toward viewing the prisoners as less than human, in which they (the soldiers) were anonymous, and in which they could alleviate their boredom by turning the prisoners into playthings.

If Zimbardo is correct, then our tendency to go along with prevailing norms and with requirements of the roles we play in life can indeed sometimes lead good people to perform evil acts. But please take heart; more recent research, including another dramatic prison study (this time conducted jointly by social psychologists and the British Broadcasting Corporation [BBC]) offers a much more optimistic set of conclusions (Reicher & Haslam, 2006). In this research, volunteers were, again, placed in a kind of prison and assigned to be either guards or prisoners. And once more, the guards were given means to enforce their authority over the prisoners (e.g., they could place disobedient prisoners in an isolation cell as punishment). Overall, then, the BBC prison study was similar in many respects to Zimbardo's famous research. Important differences did exist, however.

For instance, it was explained to the guards and prisoners that they had been chosen for these roles on the basis of extensive psychological tests (all volunteers were actually assessed by trained psychologists before their selection as participants in the study). Further, it was explained that the guards could promote prisoners they selected to become guards, and in fact, one prisoner was promoted to become a guard. After this event, however, it was made clear that guards would remain guards, and prisoners would remain prisoners, so no chance of further changes existed. Then, three days later, both guards and prisoners were told that careful observations indicated that in fact, no differences existed between the two groups. However because it would be impractical to change the roles now, they would remain unchanged for the rest of the study. In a sense, this removed any legitimacy of assignments to these roles.

These differences turned out to have dramatic effects on the results. In contrast to the findings of the Stanford prison study, guards and prisoners in the BBC research did not passively accept their roles. Rather, the guards actually rejected their power over the prisoners while the prisoners, in contrast, identified closely with one another and actually took action to gain equal power. They succeeded, and for a time, the prison adopted a democratic structure in which guards and prisoners had relatively equal rights (see Figure 8.7). When this new structure seemed to fail, however, both groups moved toward acceptance of a rigidly authoritarian approach in which the prisoners surrendered almost totally and no longer offered any resistance to their inequality.

These findings point to an important conclusion: Social norms and the social structure from which they arise do not necessarily produce acceptance of inequalities. On the contrary, whether individuals go along with roles (and norms) that impose inequality depends on the extent to which the people involved identify with these roles; if their identification is low, they may resist and seek

(continued on page 284)

Figure 8.7

Conformity: Sometimes, It Leads Good People to Do Evil Things—but Not Always

In a recent study that replicated Zimbardo's famous Stanford prison experiment, volunteers were also placed in a simulated "prison" and played the roles of prisoners and guards. Initially, they showed behavior consistent with these roles, but soon the guards rejected the norms of their assigned roles, and the prisoners rebelled, seizing equal power for themselves.

(*Source:* Photos reproduced with permission from the *British Journal of Social Psychology* © The British Psychological Society.)

Why Good People Sometimes Do Evil Things, *cont.*

social change rather than simply resign themselves to their disadvantaged fate. As noted by one social psychologist (Turner, 2006), this is why social change occurs: People decide to challenge an existing social structure rather than accept it. In sum, the power of social norms and social roles to induce conformity is strong. But as we'll note once again in our discussion of obedience, it is not invincible

and sometimes, under the right conditions, individuals challenge existing social orders and the rules they impose and actively seek social change. As Turner (2006, p. 45) puts it, social psychologists realize that social structures are not set in stone; on the contrary "the future is created in the social present" and change and stability is a common aspect of the social side of life.

This is not the only way in which conformity pressures can produce negative outcomes, however. In addition—and even more disturbingly—they have also been found to influence acceptance of belief of what are known as rape myths by males. Rape myths are false beliefs that women provoke rapes and may even enjoy such assaults when they occur (e.g., Bohner, Jarvis, Eyssel, & Siebler, in press). When men are exposed to false information suggesting that such myths are widely accepted by other men, they show increased acceptance of such myths themselves, and—most chilling of all—an increased acceptance of using force to obtain sexual relations with women (Bohner, Siebler, & Schmelcher, 2006). Truly, this is a disturbing result of the tendency to yield to conformity pressures. But again, please note that conformity is not always negative. For instance, as we noted in Chapter 6, learning that others are less prejudiced than you can lead many people to conform to this pro-social norm and show less discrimination toward others.

Resisting Pressures to Conform: Why, Sometimes, We Choose Not to Go Along

Our discussion so far may have left you with the impression that pressures toward conformity are so strong that they are all but impossible to resist. If so, take heart. In many cases, individuals—or groups of individuals—do resist. This was certainly true in Asch's research in which, as you may recall, most of the participants yielded to social pressure but only part of the time. On many occasions, they stuck to their guns even in the face of a unanimous majority that disagreed with them. If you want other illustrations of resistance to conformity pressures, just look around you: You will find that while most people adhere to social norms most of the time, some do not. And most people do not go along with all social norms, rather they pick and choose, conforming to most but rejecting at least a few (see Figure 8.8). For instance, do you know any men who have shoulder-length

Figure 8.8
Norms: They Are Not Always Obeyed
As shown here, even when clear norms concerning specific behavior exist, people sometimes violate them. This suggests that pressures to "go along" and conform can be resisted.

hair, even though this is typically not in style? Similarly, do you have any friends who hold unpopular political or social views and continue to do so despite strong pressure to conform? As these examples suggest, conformity pressures are not irresistible. What accounts for our ability to resist them? While many factors appear to be important (e.g., Burger, 1992), three seem to be most important: the need to maintain our individuality, the need to maintain control over our own lives, and—paradoxically—certain social norms themselves, norms urge individuals to "be themselves" and not go along with what most other people are doing (Jetten & Postmes, 2006).

The Need to Maintain Individuality, Culture, and Resistance to Conformity

The need to maintain our individuality, in particular, appears to be a powerful one. Yes, we want to be like others but not, it seems, to the extent that we lose our personal identity. In other words, along with the needs to be right and to be liked, most of us possess a desire for **individuation**—for being distinguishable from others in some respects (e.g., Maslach, Santee, & Wade, 1987). In general, we want to be like others—especially others we like or respect—but we don't want to be exactly like these people.

If this is indeed true, then an interesting prediction relating to the impact of culture on conformity—and on the ability to resist it—follows logically: The tendency to conform will be lower in cultures that emphasize individuality (individualistic cultures) than in ones that emphasize being part of the group (collectivist cultures). Research by Bond and Smith (1996) examined this hypothesis by comparing conformity in seventeen different countries. They examined the results of 133 past studies that used the Asch line-judging task to measure conformity. Among these studies, they identified ones conducted in countries with collectivist cultures (e.g., countries in Africa and Asia) and ones with individualistic cultures (ones in North America and Western Europe). Then they compared the amount of conformity shown in these two groups of countries. Results were clear: More conformity did indeed occur in the countries with collectivistic cultures, in which the motive to maintain one's individuality was expected to be lower, and this was true regardless of the size of the influencing group. Similar results have been obtained in other studies (e.g., Hamilton & Sanders, 1995), so it does appear that the need for individuation varies greatly across different cultures, and that these differences, in turn, influence the tendency to conform.

The Desire for Personal Control

Another reason why individuals often choose to resist group pressure involves their desire to maintain control over the events in their lives (e.g., Daubman, 1993). Most people want to believe that they can determine what happens to them and yielding to social pressure sometimes runs counter to this desire. After all, going along with a group implies behaving in ways one might not ordinarily choose, and this can be viewed as a restriction of personal freedom. The results of many studies suggest that the stronger individuals' need for personal control, the less likely they are to yield to social pressure (e.g., Cialdini, 2000), so this factor, too, appears to be an important one when resisting conformity is concerned.

Norms that Encourage Individualism

In our discussion of social norms so far, we have suggested that these rules of social life tell individuals what they should do or ought to do in a given situation. In most cases, such norms suggest that individuals should go along and do what most other people do. Sometimes, though, the norms of a specific group suggest just the opposite; in a sense, such groups have informal rules that say: "Do your own thing—do it your own way." What kind of groups adopt such norms? Ones that are seeking social change and ones that emphasize the importance of individual preferences and choices are just two examples. Research on the effects of individualist norms (e.g., Jetten, McAuliffe, Hornsey, & Hogg, 2006) indicates that they often lead individuals to define themselves as "individualists"—

individuation
The need to be distinguishable from others in some respects.

people who don't simply go along with what's popular or typical and increase their acceptance of unusual or individualistic behavior by others. In short, norms can actually increase conformity and reduce it as well.

In sum, several factors operate to counter the strong tendency to conform. As a result, whether we conform in a given situation depends on the relative strength of several various factors and the complex interplay between them, and conformity—although common—is not the only pattern that can emerge. (Do gender differences in conformity exist? For a discussion of what social psychologists have learned about this issue, see *Making Sense of Common Sense: A Social Psychological Perspective* on page 287.)

Minority Influence: Does the Majority Always Rule?

As we noted previously, individuals can, and often do, resist group pressure. Lone dissenters or small minorities can dig in their heels and refuse to go along. Yet there is more going on in such situations than just resistance; in addition, there are instances in which such people—minorities within their groups—actually turn the tables on the majority and exert rather than merely receive social influence. History provides many examples of such events. Giants of science, such as Galileo Galilei, Louis Pasteur, and Sigmund Freud, faced virtually unanimous majorities who initially rejected their views. Yet over time, these famous people overcame such resistance and won widespread acceptance for their theories.

More recent examples of minorities influencing majorities are provided by the successes of environmentalists. Initially, such people were viewed as wild-eyed radicals with strange ideas. Gradually, however, they succeeded in changing the attitudes of the majority so that today, many of their views are widely accepted. For instance, many people are deeply concerned about global warming, which results in part from the burning of fossil fuels, such as the gasoline we use to run our cars (see Figure 8.9).

But when, precisely, do minorities succeed in influencing majorities? Research findings suggest that they are most likely to do so under certain conditions (Moscovici, 1985). First, the members of such groups must be consistent in their opposition to majority opinions. If they waver, or seem to be divided, their impact is reduced. Second, members of the minority must avoid appearing to be rigid and dogmatic (Mugny, 1975). A minority that merely repeats the same position over and over again is less persuasive than one that demonstrates a degree of flexibility. Third, the general social context in which a minority operates is important. If a minority argues for a position that is consistent with current social trends

Figure 8.9
Minorities Can
Sometimes Rule—or at
Least, Change Public
Opinion
*In the 1960s,
environmentalists were viewed
as weird radicals. Now,
however, the views they stated
are accepted by large numbers
of people throughout the world.*

MAKING SENSE OF COMMON SENSE

A SOCIAL PSYCHOLOGICAL PERSPECTIVE
Do Women and Men Differ in the Tendency to Conform?

Consider the following statement by Queen Victoria of England, one of the most powerful rulers in the history of the world: "We women are not made for governing—and if we are good women, we must dislike these masculine occupations . . ." (Letter dated February 3, 1852). This and many similar quotations suggest that women do not like to be in charge; they would prefer to follow rather than lead. And that idea, in turn, suggests that they may be more conforming than men. As informal evidence for this view, many people who accept it point to the fact that in general, women seem to be more likely than men to adopt new fashions in clothing and hairstyles. But does this mean that they are really more likely to conform in general? Early studies on conformity (e.g., Crutchfield, 1955) seemed to suggest that they are, but more recent—and more sophisticated research—points to a different conclusion.

For instance, Eagly and Carli (1981) conducted a meta-analysis of 145 different studies in which more than 20,000 people participated. Results indicated the existence of a small difference between men and women, with women being slightly more accepting of social influence than men. So if such gender differences existed, they were much smaller than common sense suggested.

But that's not the end of the story. Additional research has further clarified when and why these small differences may exist—if they exist at all. With respect to when, it appears that both genders are more easily influenced when they are uncertain about how to behave or about the correctness of their judgments. And careful examination of many studies on conformity indicates that the situations and materials used were ones more familiar to men than women. The result? Men were more certain about how to behave and so showed less conformity. Direct evidence for this reasoning was obtained by Sistrunk and McDavid (1971) who found that when males and females were equally familiar with the situations or materials employed, differences between them in terms of conformity disappeared.

Turning to why any gender differences in conformity might exist, the answer seems to involve differences in status between men and women. In the past—and even to some extent today—men tend to holder higher status jobs and positions in many societies than do women. And there is a relationship between status and susceptibility to social influence: Lower status leads to greater tendencies to conform (Eagly, 1987). So, when and if gender differences in conformity exist, they seem to be linked to social factors such as differences in status and gender roles—not to any basic, "built-in" differences between the two genders. These are certainly changing, and recent polls indicate that in the United States, a large majority of voters state that they would readily cast their ballots for a woman candidate for president (Eagly, 2007).

In sum, contrary to what common sense—and widespread beliefs once suggested—women are generally not more susceptible to conformity pressures (or social influence) than men. On the contrary, any differences between the two genders that do exist are quite small. And when such factors as confidence in one's own judgments (as determined by familiarity with the situation) and social status are considered, these differences totally disappear. Once again, therefore, we see how the careful, scientific approach adopted by social psychology helps us to clarify and refine common sense views about important social issues.

(e.g., conservative views at a time of growing conservatism), its chances of influencing the majority are greater than if it argues for a position out of step with such trends. Of course, even when these conditions are met, minorities face a tough uphill fight. But both history and research findings (e.g., Kenworthy & Miller, 2001) indicate that they can sometimes prevail. For instance, only a minority of the people living in the United States were in favor of gaining independence from Britain when the Revolutionary War began, but that minority did prevail and founded a new nation that has served as a model for many others over the intervening centuries.

> **Principles to Remember**
>
> Pressures to conform can be truly powerful, so try to avoid situations in which the pressures to go along might overwhelm your personal values.

KeyPoints

- Social influence—the many ways in which people produce changes in other people's behavior, attitudes, or beliefs—is a common part of life.

- Most people behave in accordance with social norms most of the time; in others words, they show strong tendencies toward conformity.

- Conformity was first systematically studied by Asch, whose classic research indicated that many people will yield to social pressure from a unanimous group. Many factors determine whether, and to what extent, conformity occurs. These include cohesiveness—degree of attraction felt by an individual toward some group, group size, and type of social norm operating in that situation—descriptive or injunctive.

- Norms tend to influence our behavior primarily when they are relevant to us.

- However situational norms, like other norms, can influence our behavior in an automatic manner, even when we are not consciously aware of them.

- Two important motives underlie our tendency to conform: the desire to be liked by others and the desire to be right or accurate. These two motives are reflected in two distinct types of social influence, normative and informational social influence.

- The effects of social influence are powerful and pervasive but tend to be magnified in situations in which we are uncertain about our own judgments or what is correct.

- Pressures to conform often produce harmful effects. For instance, pressures to conform to gender norms can interfere with sexual enjoyment by both women and men.

- More dramatic evidence from the Stanford prison study suggests that strong pressures to conform—coupled with other factors—can result in conditions in which good people commit evil acts because their personal values are overwhelmed by strong situational forces.

- Although pressures toward conformity are strong, many people resist them, at least part of the time. This resistance seems to stem from two strong motives: the desire to retain one's individuality and the desire to exert control over one's own life.

- Under some conditions, minorities can induce even large majorities to change their attitudes or behavior.

Think About It

Overall, do you think that our strong tendency to conform—to go along with prevailing social norms—is beneficial or harmful? Why? And when would it produce these opposite effects?

Compliance: To Ask—Sometimes—Is to Receive

Suppose that you wanted someone to do something for you, how would you go about getting this person to agree? If you think about this question for a moment, you'll quickly realize that you have many tactics for gaining compliance—for getting others to say yes to your requests. (One unusual approach is shown in Figure 8.10). What are these techniques and which ones work best? These are among the questions we'll now consider. Before doing so, however, we'll introduce a basic framework for understanding the nature of these techniques and why they often work.

Compliance: The Underlying Principles

Some years ago, Robert Cialdini, a well-known social psychologist, decided that the best way to find out about compliance was to study what he termed *compliance professionals*—people whose success (financial or otherwise) depends on their ability to get others to say yes? Who are such people? They include salespeople, advertisers, political lobbyists, fund-

Figure 8.10
Compliance: Getting Others to Say Yes
We all use—and are exposed to—many different techniques for gaining compliance—for getting others to do what we would like them to do. The one shown here is unusual, but suggests just how varied approaches for gaining compliance can be.

(*Source:* United Feature Syndicate, 12/15/98.)

raisers, politicians, con artists, professional negotiators, and many others. Cialdini's technique for learning from these people was simple: He temporarily concealed his true identity and took jobs in various settings in which gaining compliance is a way of life. In other words, he worked in advertising, direct (door-to-door) sales, fund-raising, and other fields focused on compliance. On the basis of these firsthand experiences, he concluded that although techniques for gaining take many different forms, they all rest to some degree on six basic principles (Cialdini, 1994, 2006):

- *Friendship or liking:* In general, we are more willing to comply with requests from friends or from people we like than with requests from strangers or people we don't like.

- *Commitment or consistency:* Once we have committed ourselves to a position or action, we are more willing to comply with requests for behaviors that are consistent with this position or action than with requests that are inconsistent with it.

- *Scarcity:* In general, we value and try to secure outcomes or objects that are scarce or decreasing in availability. As a result, we are more likely to comply with requests that focus on scarcity than ones that make no reference to this issue.

- *Reciprocity:* We are generally more willing to comply with a request from someone who has previously provided a favor or concession to us than to someone who has not. In other words, we feel obligated to pay people back in some way for what they have done for us.

- *Social validation:* We are generally more willing to comply with a request for some action if this action is consistent with what we believe people similar to ourselves are doing (or thinking). We want to be correct, and one way to do so is to act and think like others.

- *Authority:* In general, we are more willing to comply with requests from someone who holds legitimate authority—or simply appears to do so.

According to Cialdini (2000, 2006), these basic principles underlie many techniques used by professionals—and ourselves—for gaining compliance from others. We'll now examine techniques based on these principles, plus a few others as well.

Tactics Based on Friendship or Liking: Ingratiation

We've already considered several techniques for increasing compliance through liking in our discussion in Chapter 3 of impression management, which are various procedures for making a good impression on others. While this can be an end in itself, impression management techniques are often used for purposes of ingratiation—getting others to like us so that they will be more willing to agree to our requests (Jones, 1964; Liden & Mitchell, 1988).

What ingratiation techniques work best? A review of existing studies on this topic (Gordon, 1996) suggests that flattery—praising others in some manner, is one of the best. Another is known as self-promotion—informing others about our past accomplishments or positive characteristics ("I'm really organized"; or "I'm really easy to get along with" [Bolino & Turnley, 1999]). Other techniques that seem to work are improving one's own appearance, emitting many positive nonverbal cues, and doing small favors for the target people (Gordon, 1996; Wayne & Liden, 1995). Because we described many of these tactics in detail in Chapter 3, we won't repeat that information here. Suffice it to say that many of the tactics used for purposes of impression management are also successful from the point of view of increasing compliance.

Still another means of increasing others' liking for us—and thus increasing the chances that they will agree to requests we make—involves what has been termed *incidental similarity*—calling attention to small and slightly surprising similarities between them and us. In several recent studies, Burger and his colleagues (Burger, Messian, Patel, et al., 2004) found that research participants were more likely to agree to a small request (make a donation to charity) from a stranger when this person appeared to have the same first name or birthday as they did than when the requester was not similar to them in these ways. Apparently, these trivial forms of similarity enhance liking or a feeling of affiliation with the requester and so increase the tendency to comply with this person's requests.

Tactics Based on Commitment or Consistency: The Foot-in-the-Door and the Lowball

foot-in-the-door technique
A procedure for gaining compliance in which requesters begin with a small request and then, when this is granted, escalate to a larger one (the one they actually desired all along).

When you visit the food court of your local shopping mall, are you ever approached by people offering you free samples of food (see Figure 8.11)? If so, why do they do this? The answer is simple: They know that once you have accepted this small, free gift, you will be more willing to buy something from their booth. This is the basic idea behind an approach for gaining compliance known as the **foot-in-the-door technique.** Basically, this involves inducing target people to agree to a small initial request ("Accept this free sample") and then making a larger request—the one desired all along. The results of many studies indicate that this tactic works—it succeeds in inducing increased compliance (e.g., Beaman, Cole, Preston, et al., 1983; Freedman & Fraser, 1966). Why is this the case? Because the foot-in-the-door technique rests on the principle of consistency: Once we have said yes to the small request, we are more likely to say yes to subsequent and larger ones, too, because refusing these would be inconsistent with our previous behavior. For exam-

Figure 8.11
The Foot-in-the-Door Action
Why do many restaurants ask passersby in shopping malls to accept free samples of food? Probably not because they are generous. Rather, they know that once people say "yes" to these small gifts, they may be more likely to agree with requests for more significant and costly actions, such as purchasing meals at the restaurants that gave them the free samples.

ple, imagine that you wanted to borrow one of your friend's class notes since the start of the semester. You might begin by asking for the notes from one lecture. After copying these, you might come back with a larger request: the notes for all the other classes. If your friend complied, it might well be because refusing would be inconsistent with his or her initial yes (e.g., DeJong & Musilli, 1982).

The foot-in-the-door technique is not the only tactic based on the consistency or commitment principle, however. Another is the **lowball procedure.** In this technique, which is often used by automobile salespeople, a good deal is offered to a customer. After the customer accepts, however, something happens that makes it necessary for the salesperson to change the deal and make it less advantageous for the customer—for example, the sales manager rejects the deal. The totally rational response for customers, of course, is to walk away. Yet often they agree to the changes and accept the less desirable arrangement (Cialdini, Cacioppo, Basssett, & Miller, 1978). In instances such as this, an initial commitment seems to make it more difficult for individuals to say no, even though the conditions which led them to say yes in the first place have now been changed.

Clear evidence for the importance of an initial commitment in the success of the lowball technique is provided by research conducted by Burger and Cornelius (2003). These researchers phoned students living in dorms and asked them if they would contribute five dollars to a scholarship fund for underprivileged students. In the lowball condition, the caller indicated that people who contributed would receive a coupon for a free smoothie at a local juice bar. Then if the participant agreed to make a donation, the caller told them that she had just run out of coupons and couldn't offer them this incentive. She then asked if they would still contribute. In another condition (the interrupt condition), the caller made the initial request but before the participants could answer yes or no, interrupted them and indicated that there were no more coupons for people who donated. In other words, this was just like the lowball condition, except that participants had no opportunity to make an initial commitment to donating to the fund. Finally, in a third (control) condition, participants were asked to donate five dollars with no mention of any coupons for a free drink. Results indicated that more people in the lowball condition agreed to make a donation than in either of the other two conditions (see Figure 8.12).

These results indicate that the lowball procedure does indeed rest on the principles of commitment: Only when individuals are permitted to make an initial public commitment—when they say yes to the initial offer—does it work. Having made this initial commitment, they feel compelled to stick with it, even though the conditions that lead them to say yes in the first place no longer exist. Truly, this is a subtle yet powerful technique for gaining compliance.

lowball procedure
A technique for gaining compliance in which an offer or deal is changed to make it less attractive to the target person after this person has accepted it.

Figure 8.12
The Role of Commitment in the Lowball Technique
In the lowball condition, participants were asked to make a donation of five dollars to needy students and then after doing so were told that an incentive for the donation was no longer available (a coupon for a free smoothie). They were then asked if they still wished to contribute. In the interrupt condition, participants learned that the incentive was no longer available before making the initial commitment to donate. As shown here, results indicated that the lowball procedure generated much higher rates of compliance. These findings underscore the importance of an initial commitment in the lowball technique.

(*Source:* Based on data from Burger & Cornelius, 2003.)

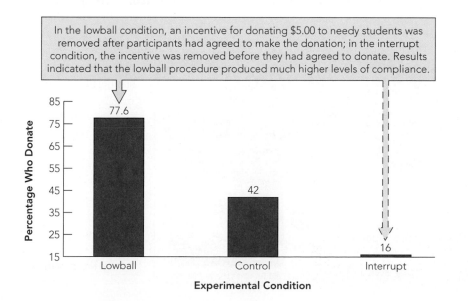

In the lowball condition, an incentive for donating $5.00 to needy students was removed after participants had agreed to make the donation; in the interrupt condition, the incentive was removed before they had agreed to donate. Results indicated that the lowball procedure produced much higher levels of compliance.

Tactics Based on Reciprocity: The Door-in-the-Face and the "That's-Not-All" Approach

Reciprocity is a basic rule of social life: We usually "do unto others as they have done unto us." If they have done a favor for us, therefore, we feel that we should be willing to do one for them in return. While this is viewed by most people as being fair and just, the principle of reciprocity also serves as the basis for several techniques for gaining compliance. One of these is, on the face of it, the opposite of the foot-in-the-door technique. Instead of beginning with a small request and then escalating to a larger one, people seeking compliance sometimes start with a large request and then, after this is rejected, shift to a smaller request—the one they wanted all along. This tactic is known as the **door-in-the-face technique** (because the first refusal seems to slam the door in the face of the requester), and several studies indicate that it can be quite effective. For example, in one well-known experiment, Cialdini and his colleagues (1975) stopped college students on the street and presented a huge request: Would the students serve as unpaid counselors for juvenile delinquents two hours a week for the next two years. As you can guess, no one agreed. When the experimenters then scaled down their request to a much smaller one—would the same students take a group of delinquents on a two-hour trip to the zoo—fully 50 percent agreed. In contrast, less than 17 percent of those in a control group agreed to this smaller request when it was presented cold rather than after the larger request.

The same tactic is often used by negotiators, who may begin with a position that favors them greatly and is quite extreme. When it is rejected by the other side, they retreat to a position much closer to the one they really hope to obtain. This apparent concession on their part puts subtle pressure on the others side to compromise, too, and the result may be favorable for the first side—the one that began with the extreme offer.

A related procedure for gaining compliance is known as the **that's-not-all technique.** Here, an initial request is followed, before the target person can say yes or no, by something that sweetens the deal—a small extra incentive from the people using this tactic (e.g., a reduction in price, "throwing in" something additional for the same price). For example, television commercials for various products frequently offer something extra to induce viewers to pick up the phone and place an order—for instance a "free" knife or a "free" cookbook (see Figure 8.13). Several studies confirm informal observations suggesting that the that's-not-all technique really works (Burger, 1986). Why is this so? One possibility is that this tactic succeeds because it is based on the principle of reciprocity: People on the receiving end of this approach view the extra thrown in by the other side as an added concession and so feel obligated to make a concession themselves. The result: They are more likely to say yes.

door-in-the-face technique
A procedure for gaining compliance in which requesters begin with a large request and then, when this is refused, retreat to a smaller one (the one they actually desired all along).

that's-not-all technique
A technique for gaining compliance in which requesters offer additional benefits to target people before they have decided whether to comply with or reject specific requests.

Figure 8.13
The "That's-Not-All" Technique: An Example
Television commercials sometimes offer potential customers something extra for free if they order the item being promoted. This is an example of the "that's-not-all" technique—a tactic for gaining compliance in which something extra is offered before the target person has a chance to say yes or no. Research findings indicate that this tactic, too, often works: It increases sales of the main item.

Tactics Based on Scarcity: Playing Hard to Get and the Fast-Approaching-Deadline Technique

It's a general rule of life that things that are scarce, rare, or difficult to obtain are viewed as being more valuable than those that are plentiful or easy to obtain. Thus we are often willing to expend more effort or go to greater expense to obtain items or outcomes that are scarce than to obtain ones that are in large supply. This principle serves as the foundation for several techniques for gaining compliance. One of the most common of these is **playing hard to get**—a tactic often used in the area of romance. What it involves is actions by a person using this technique suggesting that they have little interest in the target person—the one toward whom playing hard to get is directed. For instance, a person play-

Figure 8.14
The Deadline Technique: A Procedure Based on Scarcity
In the deadline technique, potential customers or others are lead to believe that if they do not do what the people using this technique want now, it will soon be too late. The result? People do indeed hurry to buy items that are really not in short supply and that will be available for the same or lower price at a later time.

ing hard to get might drop hints to the effect that a potential partner (the target person) has a lot of competition—many rivals. When it works, this tactic can fan the flames of passion in the people who are on the receiving end (e.g., Walster, Walster, Piliavin, & Schmidt, 1973).

The playing hard to get tactic is also not limited to dating and romance, however; research findings indicate that it is also sometimes used by job candidates to increase their attractiveness to potential employers, and hence to increase the likelihood that these employers will offer them a job. People using this tactic let the potential employer know that they have other offers and so are quite a desirable employee. And in fact, research findings indicate that this technique often works (Williams, Radefeld, Binning, & Suadk, 1993).

A related procedure also based on the "what's-scarce-is-valuable" principle is one frequently used by department stores. Ads using this **deadline technique** state that a special sale will end on a certain date, implying that after that, the prices will go up. In many cases, the time limit is false: The prices won't go up after the indicated date and may, in fact, continue to drop if the merchandise remains unsold. Yet many people reading such ads or seeing signs, like the one in Figure 8.14, believe them and hurry down to the store to avoid missing out on a great opportunity. So when you encounter an offer suggesting that "the clock is ticking" and may soon run out, be cautious: This may simply be a technique for boosting sales.

In sum, there are many different tactics for gaining compliance—for changing others' behavior in ways we desire. And remember: Such efforts work both ways. We try to influence others, and they, in turn, often attempt to influence us. Thus it's wise to always remember these words, written by Eric Hofer (1953): "It would be difficult to exaggerate the degree to which we are influenced by those we influence."

playing hard to get
A technique that can be used for increasing compliance by suggesting that a person or object is scarce and hard to obtain.

deadline technique
A technique for increasing compliance in which target people are told that they have only limited time to take advantage of some offer or to obtain some item.

> **Principles to Remember**
> Tactics for gaining compliance are common. For this reason, you should be familiar with them so that you can know when they are being directed at you. In particular, watch out for the foot-in-the-door, flattery, the door-in-the-face, and playing hard to get—they are common in the social side of life.

KeyPoints

- Individuals use many different tactics for gaining compliance, that is, getting others to say yes to various requests. Many of these tactics rest on basic principles well known to social psychologists.

- Two widely used tactics, the foot-in-the-door and the lowball procedure rest on the principle of commitment or consistency. In contrast, the door-in-the-face and that's-not-all techniques rest on the principle of reciprocity.

- Playing hard to get and the deadline technique are based on the principle of scarcity—what is scarce or hard to obtain is valuable.

Think About It

Now that you know about the many different techniques people use to gain compliance with their wishes, do you think this will help you to resist such tactics when used against you? And turning things around, will this knowledge help you to gain compliance from others?

Symbolic Social Influence: How We Are Influenced by Others Even When They Are Not There

That other people can influence us when they are present and trying to do so is not surprising; like us, they have many techniques at their disposal for getting us to say, think, or do what they want. But growing evidence suggests that others can influence us even when they are not present and not trying to change our behavior or thoughts. In a sense, they do not produce such effects: We do. Our mental representations of others—what they want or prefer, our relationships with them, how we think they would evaluate us or our current actions—can exert powerful effects on us and even, it appears, when we are not consciously aware of these effects (e.g., Bargh, Gollwitzer, Lee-Chai, & Barndollar, 2001). For example, in one well-known study—a study that triggered interest in this topic—Baldwin, Carrell, and Lopez (1990) found that graduate students evaluated their own research ideas more negatively after being exposed, subliminally, to the face of their scowling department chair. In other words, the chair's face was shown for so short a period of time that the graduate students were not aware of having seen him. Yet his negative facial expression exerted significant effects on their evaluations of their own work anyway.

How can the psychological presence of others in our mental representations of them influence our behavior and thought? Two mechanisms seem to be involved, and both may involve goals—objectives we wish to attain. First, to the extent other people are present in our thoughts (and even if we are not aware that they are), this may trigger relational schemas—mental representations of people with whom we have relationships and of these relationships themselves. When these relational schemas are triggered, in turn, goals relevant to them may be activated, too. For instance, if we think of a friend, the goal of being helpful may be activated; if we think of our mother or father, the goal of making them proud of us may be triggered. These goals, in turn, can affect our behavior, our thoughts about ourselves, and our evaluations of others. For instance, if the goal of helping others is triggered, then we may become more helpful. If the goal of being physically attractive is activated, we may refuse that delicious dessert when it is offered.

Second, the psychological presence of others may trigger goals with which that person is associated—goals they want us to achieve. This, in turn, can affect our performance on various tasks and our commitment to reaching these goals, among other things (e.g., Shah, 2003). For instance, if we have thoughts about our father, we know that he wants us to do well in school, our commitment to this goal may be increased and we may work harder to attain it, especially if we feel close to him.

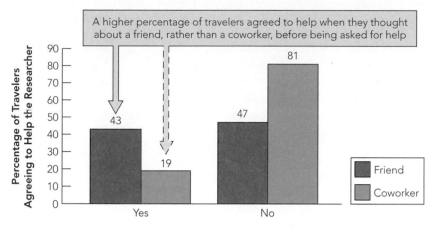

A higher percentage of travelers agreed to help when they thought about a friend, rather than a coworker, before being asked for help

Figure 8.15
Symbolic Social Influence: An Example
People at an airport who thought about a friend before being asked for help were more likely to agree than people who thought about a coworker. This was because thinking about a friend triggered the goal of helping.

(*Source:* Based on data from Fitzsimons & Bargh, 2003.)

In other words, to the extent that others are psychologically present in our thoughts, the nature of our relationships with them, goals we seek in these relationships, or goals these people themselves want us to attain can all be stimulated, and these ideas and knowledge structures, in turn, can strongly affect our behavior.

While many different studies have recently reported such effects, research conducted on this topic by Fitzsimons and Bargh (2003) is especially revealing. In one such study, people at an airport were approached and asked to think either of a good friend or a coworker. Then they were asked to write down the initials of the person of whom they were thinking and to answer a series of questions about that person (e.g., describe his or her appearance, how long they had known this person, his or her age, and so on). Finally participants were asked if they would be willing to help the researcher by answering a longer set of questions. It was predicted that those who thought about a friend would be more willing to help because thinking about a friend would trigger the goal of helping—something we often do for friends. As you can see from Figure 8.15 below, this is precisely what happened: People who thought about a friend rather than a coworker were more willing to help. Note that they were not asked to help their friend; rather, they were asked to assist a stranger—the researcher. But still, thoughts of the friend affected their current behavior.

In another interesting study, the same researchers asked participants to think about and describe their mother or to think about neutral events not involving other people (e.g., the first musical CD they had purchased, vacations they had taken) Next participants were given a set of seven letters and asked to generate as many words as possible from these. It was predicted that participants who thought about their mothers would do better on this task but only if they had the goal of making their mother proud of them. (Information on the extent to which they held this goal had been collected previously.) Results offered clear support for this prediction: People who thought about their mother and wanted to make her proud did better than those who thought about their mother but did not have this goal; for people in the control condition, who thought about neutral events, whether they wanted to make their mothers proud of them had no effect—and why should it? They were not thinking about her as they performed the word task.

Findings such as these, and those reported in a growing number of other studies (e.g., Shah, 2003), suggest that we can be strongly influenced by other people when they are not physically present on the scene and trying to affect us, as long as they are psychologically present (in our thoughts). Such effects can have a strong negative impact on personal health and well-being as well as a positive one. Please see *Social Psychology: What It Tells Us About . . .* on page 296 to learn more information on such effects.

Principles to Remember
We are often influenced by others even when they are not attempting to exert such effects. So, watch out for such symbolic social influence, especially with respect to media celebrities.

SOCIALPSYCHOLOGY

WHAT IT TELLS US ABOUT . . .

The Epidemic of Eating Disorders

There is little doubt that where the fashion industry, movies, and television are concerned, "Thin is in." In fact, it has sometimes been said, "You can never be too thin—or too rich." We don't know about being too rich, but there is no doubt whatsoever that people can be too thin. In fact, psychologists and other mental health professionals have reported a virtual epidemic of **eating disorders**—serious forms of mental disorder in which individuals engage in unhealthy and sometimes downright dangerous, efforts to control their body weight. One of these disorders is known as anorexia nervosa, and involves intense fears of gaining weight coupled with refusal to eat enough to maintain normal body weight. Another, that is even more disturbing, is bulimia nervosa, which is an eating disorder in which individuals engage in repeated episodes of binge eating followed by some form of purging (e.g., they make themselves throw up to get rid of the food they have consumed.)

While these disorders are observed among both sexes, they are far more common among women than men. And that fact suggests one important cause of such disorders: the tremendous emphasis, in the media, on the importance of being thin as a basis for being attractive. Models, movie stars, singers—in fact, nearly everyone in the entertainment and fashion industries, individuals who are held up by the media as being glamorous and people we should try to emulate—are thin. In fact, they are so thin, that some authorities have begun to argue for legislation requiring them to be more normal in weight. In cities such as Milan, Paris, and New York where high-fashion rules, regulators have come up with recommendations for a model's minimum body mass index (BMI). BMI is a widely used measurement of an individual's weight and where it stands on a continuum of underweight, normal, or overweight. The requirement varies from country to country, but it is somewhere between eighteen and nineteen, a level that, according to medical authorities, is still clearly underweight but not as extreme as the fifteen and sixteen scores found among many fashion models and celebrities (see Figure 8.16). (You can calculate your own BMI as follows: BMI = 703 × your weight (lbs)/your height in inches squared. For instance, someone who is 66 inches tall and weights 137 pounds, the BMI is: 703 × (137/4356) = 703 × 0.03 = 22.10—a number that places this person in the ideal weight range (which is 18.5 to 25). Are such standards for models and other media celebrities needed? The results of one recent study of 12,000 aspiring models in Israel indicate that almost 14 percent were so thin that physicians would immediately admit them to the hospital (Mackinnon, 2007). The same study reported that 10 percent of girls between the ages of fourteen and seventeen suffer from eating disorders.

So what does social psychology have to say about these disturbing findings and about eating disorders generally? Quite a lot. As we have tried to show throughout this chapter, social influence is a powerful force. We are strongly influenced by the words and actions of other people—both when they are trying to influence us and even when they are not. So exposing children and teenagers to people who are extremely thin (sometimes dangerously thin), and associating such thinness with being glamorous, causes many people—especially females, for whom attractiveness is emphasized much more than males—to conclude that they must be thin, too, if they want to be liked by others. Because it is almost impossible to be as thin as the models and celebrities shown in the media without drastic action, the result is easy to predict: the epidemic of eating disorders to which we referred earlier.

To the extent that social factors play a role in these serious disorders—and growing evidence suggests that they do (e.g., Stice, 2002; Thompson & Stice, 2001)—there are at least some grounds for optimism: Change what is represented as glamorous and attractive in the media so that it more closely matches what is healthy (and attainable), and the incidence of eating disorders will decrease. Social psychologists, in other words, already know how to reduce the frequency of serious eating disorders. The key question is: Will society listen to their good advice? We certainly hope so.

eating disorders
Serious forms of mental disorder in which individuals engage in unhealthy, and sometimes dangerous, efforts to control their body weight. Research findings indicate that social influence exerted by the media may play an important role in these disorders.

Figure 8.16
You *Can* Be Too Thin

Models and many others held up to young people as being "glamorous"—people they should try to emulate—are so thin that their health is at risk (left). This may be one important cause of the epidemic of eating disorders among teenagers and young adults, especially, young women. To change this unsettling situation, some fashion centers have begun requiring that models have a body mass index (BMI) of at least eighteen or nineteen, numbers that would at least place them closer to what is viewed as normal weight for their height (right).

⊘KeyPoints

- Other people can influence us even when they are not present through our mental representations of them and our relationship with them. This is known as symbolic social influence.

- Such influence often involves goals relevant to our relationships with them or goals with which these people themselves are associated.

- To the extent that others are psychologically present in our thoughts, goals we seek in our relationships with them, or goals these people themselves seek or want us to attain can be stimulated, and these, in turn, can strongly affect our behavior.

- Does exposure to very thin people shown in the mass media contribute to the widespread occurrence of eating disorders among young people? The findings of social psychological research suggest the existence of such a relationship.

Think About It

Can you think of other ways in which implicit or explicit messages presented by the media exert harmful effects on the people exposed to them? Is it ethical for the media to present such content? Or should the government attempt to ban it, just as commercials for cigarettes were banned many years ago?

Obedience to Authority: Would You Harm an Innocent Stranger If Ordered to Do So?

Have you ever been ordered to do something you didn't want to do by someone with authority over you—a teacher, your boss, your parents? If so, you are already familiar with another major type of social influence—obedience—in which one person directly orders one or more others to behave in specific ways. Obedience is less frequent than conformity or compliance because even people who possess authority and could use it often prefer to exert influence in less obvious ways—through requests rather than direct orders (e.g., Yukl & Falbe, 1991). Still, obedience is far from rare and occurs in many settings, ranging from schools through military bases. Obedience to the commands of people who possess authority is far from surprising; they usually have effective means for enforcing their orders. More unexpected is the fact that often, people lacking in such power can also induce high levels of submission from others. The clearest and most dramatic evidence for such effects was reported by Stanley Milgram in a series of famous—and controversial—studies (Milgram, 1963, 1965a, 1974).

Obedience in the Laboratory

In his research, Milgram wished to find out whether individuals would obey commands from a relatively powerless stranger requiring them to inflict what seemed to be considerable pain on another person—a totally innocent stranger. Milgram's interest in this topic derived from tragic events in which seemingly normal, law-abiding people actually obeyed such directives. For example, during World War II, troops in the German army frequently obeyed commands to torture and murder unarmed civilians. In fact, the Nazis established horrible but highly efficient death camps designed to eradicate Jews, Gypsies, and other groups they felt were inferior or a threat to their own racial purity.

In an effort to gain insights into the nature of such events, Milgram designed an ingenious, if unsettling, laboratory simulation. The experimenter informed participants in the study (all males) that they were taking part in an investigation of the effects of punishment on learning. One person in each pair of participants would serve as a learner and would try to perform a simple task involving memory (supplying the second word in pairs of words they had previously memorized after hearing only the first word). The other participant, the teacher, would read these words to the learner and would punish errors by the learner (failures to provide the second word in each pair) through electric shock. These shocks would be delivered by means of the equipment shown in Figure 8.17, and as you can see from the photo, this device contained thirty numbered switches ranging from 15 volts (the first) through 450 volts (the thirtieth). The two people present—a real participant and a research assistant—then drew slips of paper from a hat to determine who would play each role; as you can guess, the drawing was rigged so that the real participant always became the teacher. The teacher was then told to deliver a shock to the learner each time the learner made an error on the task. Moreover—and this is crucial—*teachers were told* to increase the strength of the shock each time the learner made an error. This meant that if the learner made many errors, he or she would soon be receiving strong jolts of electricity. It's important to note that this information was false: In reality, the assistant (the learner) never received any shocks during the experiment. The only real shock ever used was a mild pulse from button number three to convince participants that the equipment was real.

During the session, the learner (following prearranged instructions) made many errors. Thus participants soon found themselves facing a dilemma: Should they continue punishing this person with what seemed to be increasingly painful shocks? Or should they refuse? If they hesitated, the experimenter pressured them to continue with a graded series prods: "Please continue"; "The experiment requires that you continue"; "It is absolutely essential that you continue"; and "You have no other choice; you must go on."

 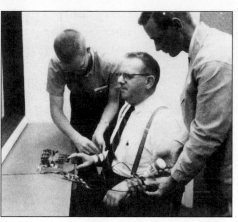

Figure 8.17
Studying Obedience in the Laboratory
The left photo shows the apparatus Stanley Milgram used in his famous experiments on destructive obedience. The right photo shows the experimenter (right front) and a participant (rear) attaching electrodes to the learner's (accomplice's) wrist.

(*Source:* From the film *Obedience*, distributed by the New York University Film Library, Copyright 1965 by Stanley Milgram. Reprinted by permission of the copyright holder.)

Because participants were all volunteers and were paid in advance, you might predict that most would quickly refuse the experimenter's orders. In reality, though, fully 65 percent showed total obedience—they proceeded through the entire series to the final 450-volt level. Many participants, of course, protested and asked that the session be ended. When ordered to proceed, however, a majority yielded to the experimenter's influence and continued to obey. Indeed, they continued doing so even when the victim pounded on the wall as if in protest over the painful shocks (at the 300-volt level), and then no longer responded, as if the victim had passed out. The experimenter told participants to treat failures to answer as errors; so from this point on, many participants believed that they were delivering dangerous shocks to someone who might already be unconscious!

In further experiments, Milgram (1965b, 1974) found that similar results could be obtained even under conditions that might be expected to reduce such obedience. When the study was moved from its original location on the campus of Yale University to a run-down office building in a nearby city, participants' level of obedience remained virtually unchanged. Similarly, a large proportion continued to obey even when the accomplice complained about the painfulness of the shocks and begged to be released. Most surprising of all, many (about 30 percent) obeyed even when they were required to grasp the victim's hand and force it down on a metal shock plate. That these chilling results are not restricted to a single culture is indicated by the act that similar findings were soon reported in several different countries (e.g., Jordan, Germany, and Australia) and with children and adults (e.g., Kilham & Mann, 1974; Shanab & Yanya, 1977). Thus Milgram's findings seemed to be alarmingly general in scope.

I actually went to high school with Milgram's niece and can remember the disbelief with which students in the class reacted when she told us about her uncle's findings, several years before they were published. Psychologists, too, found Milgram's results highly disturbing. His studies seemed to suggest that ordinary people are willing, although with some reluctance, to harm an innocent stranger if ordered to do so by someone in authority—in a sense, echoing the theme stated by Zimbardo in his famous prison study and more recent work (Zimbardo, 2007). This led to an important question: What factors lie behind this tendency to obey, even when obedience results in potential harm to others?

Destructive Obedience: Why It Occurs

As we noted previously, one reason why Milgram's results are so disturbing is that they seem to parallel many real life events involving atrocities against innocent victims such as the murder of millions of Jews and other people by the Nazis and the massacre of more than one million Armenians by Turkish troops in the early years of the twentieth century. To repeat the question we raised above: Why does such destructive obedience occur? Why were participants in these experiments—and many people in tragic situations outside the laboratory—so willing to yield to this form of social influence? Social psychologists have identified several factors that seem to play a role, and several of these are related to other aspects of social influence we have already considered.

First, in many situations, the people in authority relieve those who obey of the responsibility for their own actions. "I was only carrying out orders" is the defense many offer after obeying harsh or cruel commands. In life situations, this transfer of responsibility may be implicit; the person in charge (e.g., the military or police officer) is assumed to have the responsibility for what happens. This seems to be what happened in the tragic events at Abu Ghraib prison camp in Iraq, when U.S. soldiers—both men and women—were filmed abusing and torturing prisoners. The soldiers' defense? "I was only following orders. . . . I was told to do this and a good soldier always obeys!" In Milgram's experiments, this transfer of responsibility was explicit. Participants were told at the start that the experimenter (the authority figure), not they, would be responsible for the learner's well-being. In view of this fact, it is not surprising that many obeyed: after all, they were completely off the hook.

Second, people in authority often possess visible badges or signs of their status. They wear special uniforms or insignia, have special titles, and so on. These serve to remind many individuals of the social norm "Obey the people in charge." This is a powerful norm, and when confronted with it, most people find it difficult to disobey. After all, we do not want to do the wrong thing, and obeying the commands of those who are in charge usually helps us avoid such errors. In Milgram's study, the experimenter wore a white lab coat, which suggested that he was a doctor or someone with authority. So it's not surprising that so many participants obeyed the commands this person issued (e.g., Bushman, 1988; Darley, 1995).

A third reason for obedience in many situations where the targets of such influence might otherwise resist involves the gradual escalation of the authority figure's orders. Initial commands may call for relatively mild actions, such as merely arresting people. Only later do orders come to require behavior that is dangerous or objectionable. For example, police or military personnel may at first be ordered only to question or threaten potential victims. Gradually, demands are increased to the point where these personnel are commanded to beat, torture, or even murder unarmed civilians. In a sense, people in authority use the foot-in-the-door technique, asking for small actions first, but ever-larger ones later. In a similar manner, participants in Milgram's research were first required to deliver only mild and harmless shocks to the victim. Only as the sessions continued did the intensity of these punishments rise to potentially harmful levels.

Finally, events in many situations involving destructive obedience move very quickly: Demonstrations turn into riots, arrests into mass beatings or murder, and so on, quite suddenly. The fast pace of such events gives participants little time for reflection or systematic thought: People are ordered to obey, and—almost automatically—they do so. Such conditions prevailed in Milgram's research; within a few minutes of entering the laboratory, participants found themselves faced with commands to deliver strong electric shocks to the learner. This fast pace, too, may tend to increase obedience.

In sum, the high levels of obedience generated in Milgram's studies are not as mysterious as they may seem. A social psychological analysis of the conditions existing both there and in many real life situations identifies several factors that, together, may make it quite difficult for individuals to resist the commands they receive (these are summarized in Figure 8.18 on page 301). The consequences, of course, can be truly tragic for innocent and often defenseless victims.

Destructive Obedience: Resisting Its Effects

Now that we have considered some of the factors responsible for the strong tendency to obey sources of authority, we will turn to a related question: How can this type of social influence be resisted? Several strategies may be helpful in this respect.

First, individuals exposed to commands from authority figures can be reminded that they—not the authorities—are responsible for any harm produced. Under these condi-

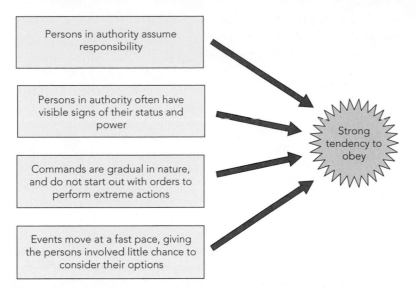

Figure 8.18
Obedience to Authority: Why It Often Occurs
As shown here, several factors combine to make it all to easy to obey orders from people in authority, even if these commands involve harming others and violating our own ethical or moral standards.

tions, sharp reductions in the tendency to obey have been observed (e.g., Hamilton, 1978; Kilham & Mann, 1974).

Second, individuals can be provided with a clear indication that beyond some point, total submission to destructive commands is inappropriate. One procedure that is highly effective in this regard involves exposing individuals to the actions of disobedient models—people who refuse to obey an authority figure's commands. Research findings indicate that such models can greatly reduce unquestioning obedience (e.g., Rochat & Modigliani, 1995). When we see one or more people refuse to obey the commands of an authority figure, we may be strongly encouraged to do the same—with the ultimate result that the power of those in authority is severely weakened.

Third, individuals may find it easier to resist influence from authority figures if they question the expertise and motives of these figures. Are those in authority really in a better position to judge what is appropriate and what is not? What motives lie behind their commands—socially beneficial goals or selfish gains? Dictators always claim that their brutal orders reflect their undying concern for their fellow citizens and are in their best interest, but to the extent large numbers of people question these motives, the power of such dictators can be eroded and perhaps, ultimately, be swept away

Finally, simply knowing about the power of authority figures to command blind obedience may be helpful in itself. Some research findings (e.g., Sherman, 1980) suggest that when individuals learn about the results of social psychological research, they often recognize these as important (Richard, Bond, & Stokes-Zoota, 2001) and sometimes change their behavior to take into account of this new knowledge. With respect to destructive obedience, there is some hope that knowing about this process can enhance individuals' resolve to resist. To the extent this is so, then even exposure to findings as disturbing as those reported by Milgram can have positive social value.

The power of authority figures to command obedience is certainly great, but it is not irresistible. Under appropriate conditions, it can be countered or reduced. As in many other areas of life there is a choice. Deciding to resist the commands of people in authority can, of course, be highly dangerous: They usually control most of the weapons, the army, and the police. Yet history is filled with instances in which the authority of powerful and entrenched regimes has been resisted by courageous people who ultimately triumphed, despite the long odds against them (see Turner, 2006). Indeed, the American Revolution against the British began in just this way: Small bands of poorly armed citizens decided to make a stand against Britain, the most powerful country on earth at the time. Their success in winning their independence became a model for many other people all over the world and changed history. The lesson from this and related events, is clear: Power is never permanent, and ultimately, victory often goes to those who stand for freedom and decency rather than to those who wish to control the lives of their fellow human beings.

KeyPoints

- Obedience is a form of social influence in which one person orders one or more to do something, and they do so. It is, in a sense, the most direct form of social influence.

- Research by Milgram indicates that many people readily obey orders from a relatively powerless source of authority, even if these orders require them to harm another innocent person.

- Such destructive obedience, which plays a role in many real life atrocities, stems from several factors. These include: the shifting of responsibility to the authority figure; outward signs of authority which remind many people of the norm "obey those in authority"; a gradual escalation of the scope of the commands given (related to the foot-in-the-door technique); and the rapid pace with which such situations proceed.

- Several factors can help to reduce the occurrence of destructive obedience. These include reminding individuals that they share in the responsibility for any harm produced, reminding them that beyond some point, obedience is inappropriate, calling the motives of authority figures into question, and informing the general public of the findings of social psychological research on this topic.

Think About It

Suppose you were placed in a situation in which you were ordered to do something you felt was unethical or immoral by someone in authority—for instance a boss or one of your professors. What do you think you would do? Would you have the courage to resist? Be honest—and think about this question carefully; doing so may tell you a lot of things about yourself.

SUMMARY AND REVIEW

- Social influence refers to the many ways in which people produce changes in others—in their behavior, attitudes, or beliefs. Most people show strong tendencies toward conformity; they obey social norms most of the time. Conformity was first systematically studied by Asch, whose classic research indicated that many people will yield to social pressure from a unanimous group. Many factors determine whether, and to what extent, conformity occurs. These include cohesiveness—degree of attraction felt by an individual toward some group; group size, and type of social norm operating in that situation—descriptive or injunctive. Norms tend to influence our behavior primarily when they are relevant to us. However, situational norms, like other norms, can influence our behavior in an automatic manner, even when we are not consciously aware of them.

- Two important motives underlie our tendency to conform: the desire to be liked by others and the desire to be right or accurate. These two motives are reflected in two distinct types of social influence, normative and informational social influence. The effects of social influence are powerful and pervasive but tend to be magnified in situations in which we are uncertain about our own judgments or what is correct. In such situa-

tions, pressures to conform often produce harmful effects. For instance, pressures to conform to gender norms can interfere with sexual enjoyment by both women and men.

- More dramatic evidence from the Stanford prison study suggests that strong pressures to conform coupled with other factors can result in conditions in which good people commit evil acts; their personal values are overwhelmed by strong situational forces. Although pressures toward conformity are strong, many people resist them, at least part of the time. This resistance seems to stem from two strong motives: the desire to retain one's individuality and the desire to exert control over one's own life. Under some conditions, minorities can induce even large majorities to change their attitudes or behavior.

- Individuals use many different tactics for gaining compliance—getting others to do what they want them to do. Many of these tactics rest on basic principles well known to social psychologists. Two widely used tactics, the foot-in-the-door and the lowball procedure rest on the principle of commitment or consistency. In contrast, the door-in-the-face and that's-not-all techniques rest on the principle of reciprocity. Playing hard to get and the deadline technique are based on the principle of scarcity—what is scarce or hard to obtain is valuable.

- Other people can influence us even when they are not present through our mental representations of them and our relationship with them. This is known *as* symbolic social influence. Such influence often involves goals relevant to our relationships with them or goals with which these people themselves are associated. Research findings suggest that exposure to the thin people in the mass media (e.g., models) contributes to the occurrence of eating disorders among young people.

- Obedience is a form of social influence in one person orders one or more to do something, and they do so. It is, in a sense, the most direct form of social influence. Research by Milgram indicates that many people readily obey orders from a relatively powerless source of authority, even if these orders require them to harm another person. Such destructive obedience, which plays a role in many real life atrocities, stems from several factors including the shifting of responsibility to the authority figure, outward signs of authority on the part of these people which remind many people of the norm "obey those in authority," a gradual escalation of the scope of the commands given (related to the foot-in-the-door technique), and the rapid pace with which such situations proceed. Several factors can help to reduce the occurrence of destructive obedience. These include reminding individuals that they share in the responsibility for any harm produced, reminding them that beyond some point, obedience is inappropriate, calling the motives of authority figures into question, and informing the general public of the findings of social psychological research on this topic.

Key Terms

autokinetic phenomenon (p. 277)

cohesiveness (p. 278)

compliance (p. 274)

conformity (p. 274)

deadline technique (p. 293)

descriptive norms (p. 278)

door-in-the-face technique (p. 292)

eating disorders (p. 296)

foot-in-the-door technique (p. 290)

individuation (p. 285)

injunctive norms (p. 278)

informational social influence (p. 280)

lowball procedure (p. 291)

normative focus theory (p. 278)

normative social influence (p. 280)

obedience (p. 274)

playing hard to get (p. 293)

social influence (p. 273)

symbolic social influence (p. 274)

social norms (p. 274)

that's-not-all technique (p. 292)

Connections
INTEGRATING SOCIAL PSYCHOLOGY

In this chapter, you read about . . .	In other chapters, you will find related discussions of . . .
the role of social norms in conformity	the role of social norms in attraction (Chapter 7), helping (Chapter 9), aggression (Chapter 10), and group decision making (Chapter 11).
the basic principles underlying many different techniques for gaining compliance	the role of these principles in other aspects of social behavior: the role of reciprocity in attraction (Chapter 7), aggression (Chapter 10), and cooperation (Chapter 11); the role of the desire to be consistent in attitude change (Chapter 5), the self-concept (Chapter 4), and helping (Chapter 9); the role of liking or friendship in social perception (Chapter 3), social relationships (Chapter 7), leadership (Chapter 11), and the legal process (Chapter 12).
the role of mood in compliance	the effects of mood on social cognition (Chapter 3), attitudes (Chapter 5), and helping (Chapter 9).
the role of automaticity with respect to situational norms	the role of automaticity in attitudes (Chapter 5), prejudice (Chapter 6), and group processes (Chapter 11).

Prosocial Behavior
Helping Others

9

CHAPTER OUTLINE

• **Why People Help: Motives for Prosocial Behavior**
Empathy-Altruism: It Feels Good to Help Others
Negative-State Relief: Sometimes, Helping
Reduces Your Unpleasant Feelings
Empathic Joy: Helping as an Accomplishment
Why Nice People Sometimes Finish First:
Competitive Altruism
Kin Selection Theory: Helping Ourselves by
Helping People Who Share Our Genes

• **Responding to an Emergency: Will Bystanders
Help?**
Helping in Emergencies: Apathy—or Action?
Five Crucial Steps Determine Helping versus Not
Helping
BUILDING THE SCIENCE: CLASSICS OF SOCIAL
PSYCHOLOGY—IS THERE SAFETY IN NUMBERS? NOT
ALWAYS!

• **External and Internal Influences on Helping
Behavior**
Situational (External) Factors that Enhance or
Inhibit Helping

Emotions and Prosocial Behavior
Empathy: An Important Foundation for Helping
Social Exclusion: When Being Left out Reduces
Helping
Personality and Helping
SOCIAL PSYCHOLOGY: WHAT IT TELLS US
ABOUT . . . THE DOWNSIDE OF BEING HELPED:
WHY, OFTEN, IT MAY ACTUALLY BE BETTER
TO GIVE THAN TO RECEIVE

• **Long-Term Commitment to Prosocial Acts**
Volunteering: Helping as an Ongoing
Commitment
Self-Interest, Moral Integrity, and Moral
Hypocrisy
MAKING SENSE OF COMMON SENSE: A SOCIAL
PSYCHOLOGICAL PERSPECTIVE: ARE HELPING
(PROSOCIAL BEHAVIOR) AND HURTING
(AGGRESSION) REALLY OPPOSITES?

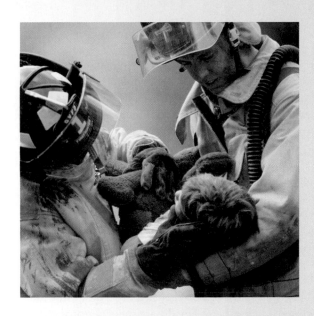

Keith R. Miller was jogging along the beach when he saw Carlos Hernandez struggling to stay afloat in the water. He waded into the ocean—where the temperature was only about forty degrees—and swam the rest of the way to reach Hernandez who was, by then, floating face down. Miller rolled him over and then towed him back to shore. A police officer arrived and helped Miller bring Hernandez to shore. He was hospitalized, as were Miller and the officer, but all recovered. . . .

Jay Johansen saw flames in a building while driving by. He stopped and heard Sandra Stephenson screaming inside. The smoke was so dense that she could not see or breathe and was huddled on some stairs. Johansen entered the building and made his way to Stephenson. He told her to put her arms around his neck and then carried her to safety. Both were treated for smoke inhalation, but soon recovered.

These are dramatic examples of pure heroism—one person risking his or her life to save another. But helping doesn't always take these extreme forms. Consider this incident:

Many years ago, I was traveling in Paris for the first time. I had read many reports suggesting that French people didn't like Americans and were often rude to them, so I was reluctant to ask for help when I lost my way on the Metro (the Paris subway system). I studied my map in what must have been obvious dismay when a young man approached me and asked, in halting English, if I was lost. I told him I was, and he tried to give me directions in French. I couldn't understand so he simply stated, in English: "Follow me—I will show you." And he did: He got off the train we were on and waited with me for another one, rode with me on that one for a few stops, and then said: "Here . . . Exit!" I did and waved as the train pulled away with this truly nice person who must have known, I suppose, that he wasn't supposed to be nice to Americans.

Perhaps you have never been rescued from the ocean or pulled from a burning building, but we're certain that you have been helped by other people who came to your assistance just when you needed help most. In fact, **prosocial behavior**—actions by individuals that help others with no immediate benefit to the helper—are a common part of social life. People rush to the assistance of others who have fallen, give rides to their friends whose cars aren't working or maybe even loan them a car, help graduate students with their dissertations by participating in psychological research, offer directions to lost strangers, and help in countless other ways. From the point of view of personal gains, such behavior might seem strange; after all, the people who engage in such actions often don't receive anything back, and in fact, often don't expect any compensation for their assistance. The young man in Paris who helped me many years ago received nothing tangible from me except my warmest thanks and a handshake. But clearly, he wanted to help and did so without any expectations of gain.

This raises an intriguing question: *Why*, precisely, do people help others so frequently? What are the motives behind such behavior? And *when* do they help? Are they more likely to offer assistance under some conditions than others? Finally, are there personal characteristics that predispose people to be more or less helpful to others? Clearly, the person shown in Figure 9.1 is low in the tendency to help, but others are much more willing to behave in a prosocial manner. We'll examine all of these questions in the present chapter. Specifically, our discussion of prosocial behavior will proceed as follows. First, we'll examine the basic motives behind helpful behavior—why, in short, people do it. Second, we'll consider helping in emergencies—why people sometimes engage in heroic acts like the ones previously described or, more disturbingly, why they don't. Third, we'll examine both situational and personal factors that influence helping. Finally, we'll examine long-term helping—why some people make a life-long commitment to helping others by volunteering or in other ways.

Why People Help: Motives for Prosocial Behavior

Why do people help? As we'll soon see, many factors play a role in determining whether, and to what extent, specific people engage in prosocial actions. Many aspects of the situation are important, and several personal (i.e., dispositional) factors are also influential. We'll examine many of these factors in a later discussion. Here, though, we'll focus on a very basic question: Why do people perform prosocial acts? Several different explanations have been offered, and we'll now briefly describe these contrasting views.

Empathy-Altruism: It Feels Good to Help Others

One explanation of prosocial behavior involves **empathy**—the capacity to be able to experience others' emotional states, feeling sympathetic toward them, and taking their perspective. This perspective suggests that we help others because if we experience empathy toward them, we want their plight to end and also because "it feels good to do good deeds." This is unselfish because it leads us to offer help for no extrinsic reason, but it is also selfish, in one sense, because the behavior of assisting others is rewarding to the helper: It makes this person feel good. Reflecting these basic observations, Batson, Duncan, Ackerman, Buckley, and Birch (1981) offered the **empathy-altruism hypothesis.** They suggest that at least some prosocial acts are motivated solely by the desire to help someone in need (Batson & Oleson, 1991). Such motivation can be sufficiently strong that the helper is willing to engage in unpleasant, dangerous, and even life-threatening

prosocial behavior
Actions by individuals that help others with no immediate benefit to the helper.

empathy
Emotional reactions that are focused on or oriented toward other people and include feelings of compassion, sympathy, and concern.

empathy-altruism hypothesis
The suggestion that some prosocial acts are motivated solely by the desire to help someone in need.

activity (Batson, Batson, et al., 1995). Compassion for other people outweighs all other considerations (Batson, Klein, Highberger, & Shaw, 1995).

To test this view of helping behavior, Batson and his colleagues devised an experimental procedure in which they aroused a bystander's empathy by describing another person who was experiencing unpleasant outcomes as being similar to themselves. Other participants were told that the victim was not similar to themselves, and so pre-

Figure 9.1
The Tendency to Help: Large Individual Differences Exist
While the tendency to help others in need of assistance is both strong and general, not everyone is equally likely to engage in such behavior. The person shown behind the window in this cartoon is clearly low on this dimension.

(*Source: The New Yorker,* February 8, 1988.)

sumably experienced less empathy toward this person. Participants (bystanders to the "victim's" discomfort) were then presented with an opportunity to help (Batson, O'Quin, Fultz, Vanderplas, & Isen, 1983; Toi & Batson, 1982). They were given the role of an observer who watched a fellow student on a TV monitor as she performed a task while (supposedly) receiving electric shocks. The victim was actually a research assistant recorded on videotape. After the task was underway, the assistant said that she was in pain and confided that as a child she had had a traumatic experience with electricity. Though she said that she was willing to continue if necessary, the experimenter asked whether the observer would trade places with her or perhaps whether the experiment should simply be terminated. When empathy was low (victim and participant were dissimilar), the participants preferred to end the experiment rather than engage in a painful prosocial act—taking the other person's place. In contrast, when empathy was high (victim and participant similar), participants were much more likely to take the victim's place and receive the shocks, presumably motivated simply by empathic concern for the victim.

Feelings of empathy complicate matters when there are multiple victims who need help (Figure 9.2). How do you react when you learn that a large number of people are in need? Mailings from charities often mention that many people are in need of assistance. Because it is difficult or impossible to feel empathy for that many individuals at once, this approach might actually reduce helping in some instances. Recognizing this fact, many charitable organizations mention the existence of large number of people in need of help but then prominently feature the photo of a single child or other needy person. This allows individuals to engage in selective altruism, which is helping the individual even though that means neglecting the remaining millions (Batson, Ahmed et al., 1999).

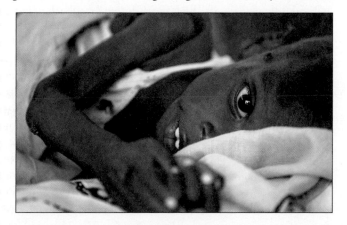

Figure 9.2
Empathy Can Increase Helping—If We Experience It
If we feel empathy toward others, our tendency to help them may be strengthened. But it is impossible to feel empathy toward "starving millions." That's why charitable organizations often include the photo of one or a few victims rather than trying to show the magnitude of the problem. So empathy can increase helping, but we have lots of ways of ensuring that we don't experience it.

Negative-State Relief: Sometimes, Helping Reduces Unpleasant Feelings

Another possible motive for helping others is, in a sense, the mirror image of empathy: Instead of helping because we genuinely care about the welfare of another person, we help because such actions allow us to reduce our own negative, unpleasant emotions. In other words, we do a good thing to stop feeling bad. The knowledge that others are suffering, or more generally, witnessing those in need can be distressing. To decrease this distress in ourselves, we might help others.

This explanation of prosocial behavior is known as the **negative-state relief model** (Cialdini, Baumann, & Kenrick, 1981). Research indicates that it doesn't matter whether the bystander's negative emotions were aroused by something unrelated to the emergency or by the emergency itself. That is, you could be upset about receiving a bad grade or about seeing that a stranger has been injured. In either instance, you engage in a prosocial act primarily as a way to improve your own negative mood (Dietrich & Berkowitz, 1997; Fultz, Schaller, & Cialdini, 1988). In this kind of situation, unhappiness leads to prosocial behavior, and empathy is not a necessary component (Cialdini et al., 1987).

Empathic Joy: Helping as an Accomplishment

It is generally true that it feels good to have a positive effect on the lives of other people. In this way, at least, it can indeed be better to give help than to receive it. Helping can thus be explained on the basis of the **empathic joy hypothesis** (Smith, Keating, & Stotland, 1989). The idea is that a helper responds to the needs of a victim because they want to accomplish something and doing so is rewarding in and of itself.

An important implication of this proposal is that it is crucial for the person who helps to know that his or her actions had a positive impact on the victim. It is argued that if helping were based entirely on empathy, feedback about its effects would be irrelevant because we know we "did good" and that should be enough. But it would not guarantee that empathic joy occurs. To test that prediction, Smith, Keating, and Stotland asked participants to watch a videotape in which a female student said she might drop out of college because she felt isolated and distressed. She was described as either similar to the participant (high empathy) or dissimilar (low empathy). After participants watched the tape, they were given the opportunity to offer helpful advice. Some were told they would receive feedback about the effectiveness of their advice while others were told that they would not be able to learn what the student eventually decided to do. It was found that empathy alone was not enough to produce a prosocial response. Rather, participants were helpful only if there was high empathy *and* feedback about impact on the victim.

Why Nice People Sometimes Finish First: Competitive Altruism

negative state-relief model
The proposal that prosocial behavior is motivated by the bystander's desire to reduce his or her own uncomfortable negative emotions or feelings.

empathic joy hypothesis
The view is that helpers respond to the needs of a victim because they want to accomplish something, and doing so is rewarding in and of itself.

The three theoretical models described so far (summarized in Figure 9.3) suggest that the affective state (feelings) of the person engaging in a prosocial act is a crucial element. All three formulations rest on the assumption that people engage in helpful behavior either because it feels good or because it makes make them feel less bad—it counters negative moods or feelings. This general idea is carried one step further by another perspective on prosocial behavior—the *competitive altruism approach*. This view suggests that one important reason why people help others is that doing so boosts their own status and reputation and, in this way, ultimately brings them large benefits, ones that more than offset the costs of engaging in prosocial actions (e.g., Van Vugt & Van Lange, in press).

Why does helping others confer status? Because often helping others is costly, and

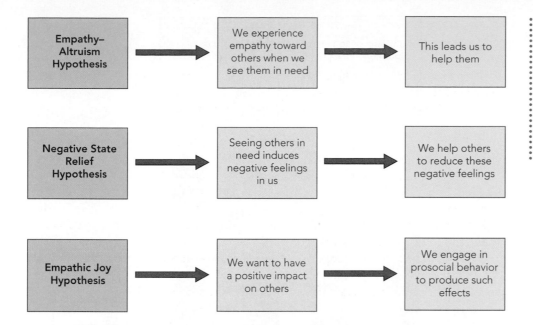

Figure 9.3
The Origins of Prosocial Behavior: Three Different Views
What are the origins of prosocial behavior—actions that help others? The views summarized here are among the explanations offered by social psychologists.

this suggests to other people that the individuals engaging in such behavior have desirable personal qualities; they are definitely the kind of people a group—or society—wants to have around. For the people who engage in prosocial actions, too, the gains may be substantial. High status confers many advantages, and people who engage in prosocial behavior may be well compensated for their kind and considerate actions. For instance, as you probably know, many people who donate large amounts of money to universities are treated like stars when they visit their alma mater, and they may have entire buildings named after them—as is true at the university where I work (see Figure 9.4).

Evidence for this reasoning, and for the competitive altruism perspective, is provided by research conducted by Hardy and Van Vugt (2006). These researchers had high school students participate in a public good dilemma—a game in which players could earn money for themselves or for the entire group. At the start, participants were given one hundred pence (about 175 U.S. cents) and told they could contribute any amount from zero to one hundred pence to a private fund, which they would keep as individuals, and any amount they wished to the group fund, which would be divided equally among the three group members. In one condition, the participants received information on the other players' contributions to the public and private funds and were told that their contributions

Figure 9.4
Competitive Altruism in Action
According to the competitive altruism theory, people sometimes engage in prosocial behavior because doing so provides them with large gains in status. This kind of outcome is visible on many university campuses, where buildings or entire schools are named after people who make large donations.

Figure 9.5
Evidence for the Competitive Altruism Perspective

As shown here, when participants in a public "good dilemma" situation did not know how much each of the other two players had contributed to the shared group fund, the size of the contributions made by these people (low, medium, high) had no effect on status (no reputation condition). When this information was provided to participants, however, the more each player contributed, the higher her or his status.

(*Source:* Based on data from Hardy & Van Vugt, 2006).

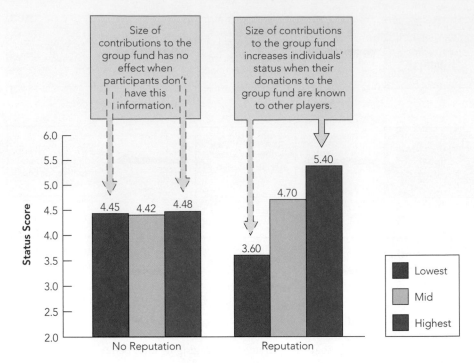

would also be provided to the other players. Thus in this condition (the reputation condition), donating to the group fund could bring enhanced reputation and status to the donors. In another condition (the no reputation condition), participants received no information on the other players' choices, so in this condition, acting in a prosocial manner would not necessarily boost the donor's reputation and status. When later asked to rate the status of each player, results offered clear support for the competitive altruism hypothesis. In the reputation condition, in which prosocial actions were known to the other players, the more each one donated, the higher his or her status. In the no reputation condition, in contrast, prosocial behavior had no impact on status (see Figure 9.5).

In other, closely related studies by the same researchers, it was found that the greater the costs involved in behaving in a prosocial manner, the greater the gains in status to people who behave in this way. This, too, is consistent with the competitive altruism framework. Additional studies also suggest that sometimes, people engage in prosocial behavior as a way of boosting their reputations and status (e.g., Flynn, Reagans, Amanatullah, & Ames, 2006). So, overall, this appears to be an important motive for helping others. Doing so is a signal to others that the people behaving this way have desirable qualities, and this enhances their status. As a result, they receive substantial benefits that more than offset the costs of their generous actions. In short, contrary to cynical beliefs about "nice people finishing last," these results make clear that in many life situations, nice people (ones who are kind, generous, and helpful) actually reap major benefits—in terms of status and others' perceptions of them—from their kind, generous actions.

Kin Selection Theory: Helping Ourselves by Helping People Who Share Our Genes

kin selection theory
A theory suggesting that a key goal for all organisms—including human beings—is getting our genes into the next generation; one way in which individuals can reach this goal is by helping others who share their genes.

A different approach to understanding prosocial behavior is offered by the **kin selection theory** (Cialdini, Brown, Lewis, Luce, & Neuberg, 1997; Pinker, 1998). From an evolutionary perspective, a key goal for all organisms—including humans—is getting our genes into the next generation. Support for this general prediction has been obtained in many studies suggesting that in general we are more likely to help others to whom we are closely related than help people to whom we are not related (e.g., Neyer & Lang, 2003). For example, Burnstein, Crandall, and Kitayama (1994) conducted a series of studies in which participants were asked whom they would choose to help in an emergency. As predicted on the basis of genetic similarity, participants were more likely to say they would help a close relative than either a distant relative or a nonrelative. Further, and also consistent with kin selection theory, they were more likely to help young relatives, who have many years of reproductive life ahead of them, than older ones. For example, given a choice between a female relative young enough to reproduce and a female relative past menopause, help would go to the younger individual.

Overall, then, there is considerable support for kin selection theory. There is one basic problem, though, that you may already have noticed: We don't just help biological relatives; instead, often, we do help people who are unrelated to us. Why do we do so? According to kin selection theory, this would not be useful or adaptive behavior because it would not help us transmit our genes to future generations. One answer is provided by reciprocal altruism theory—a view suggesting that we may be willing to help people unrelated to us because helping is usually reciprocated: If we help them, they help us, so we do ultimately benefit, and our chances of survival are increased.

Whatever the precise mechanisms involved, it seems clear that many different factors and motives contribute to our tendency to help others. In a sense, that's a comforting thought because it implies that prosocial behavior is not an unusual or rare form of behavior, but rather, it is widespread in nature and constitutes an important aspect of the social side of life.

> ❧ **Principles to Remember**
>
> Prosocial behavior stems from several different motives and helps us attain many different goals. For this reason, it is a common and important aspect of everyday social life.

❧ KeyPoints

- The empathy-altruism hypothesis proposes that because of empathy we help those in need because we want their plight to end and also because it feels good to do so.

- The negative-state relief model proposes that people help other people to relieve and make less negative their own emotional discomfort.

- The empathic joy hypothesis bases helping on the positive feelings of accomplishment that arise when the helper knows that they were able to have a beneficial impact on the person in need.

- The competitive altruism theory suggests that we help others as a means of increasing our own status and reputation—and so reaping large rewards in the future.

- Kinship selection theory suggests that we help others who are related to us because this increases the likelihood that our genes will be transmitted to future generations.

Think About It

All of the theories described so far suggest that people have good reasons for offering help to others. Does this mean that there is no such thing as pure altruism—instances in which people help others without any possibility of benefit to themselves?

Responding to an Emergency: Will Bystanders Help?

When an emergency arises, people often rush forward to provide help—as was true in the incidents described at the start of this chapter. But we also often learn of situations in which witnesses to an emergency stand around and do nothing; they stand by while victims suffer or perhaps even die. What can explain such dramatic differences in people's behavior? Let's see what social psychologists have discovered about this important question.

Helping in Emergencies: Apathy—or Action?

Consider the following situation. You are walking across an icy street, lose your footing as you step up on the curb, and fall, injuring your knee. Because of your pain and the slickness of the ice, you find that you can't get back on your feet. Suppose (1) the block is relatively deserted, and only one person is close enough to witness your accident or (2) the block is crowded, and a dozen people can see what happened. Common sense suggests that the more bystanders that are present, the more likely you are to be helped. In the first situation, you are forced to depend on the assistance of just one individual and that person's decision to help or not help you. In the second situation, with twelve witnesses, there would seem to be a much greater chance that at least one of them (and quite possibly more) will be motivated to behave in a prosocial way. So, is there really safety in numbers? The more witnesses present at an emergency, the more likely the victims are to receive help? Reasonable as this may sound, research by social psychologists suggests that it may be wrong—dead wrong.

The reasons why it may be incorrect were first suggested by John Darley and Bibb Latané (1968) two social psychologists who thought long and hard about this issue after learning of a famous murder in New York City. In this tragic crime, a young woman (Kitty Genovese) was assaulted by a man in a location where many people could see and hear what was going on; all they had to do was look out of their apartment windows. Despite the fact that the attacker continued to assault the victim for many minutes, and even left and then returned to continue the assault later, *not a single person reported the crime to the police.* When news of this tragic crime hit the media, there was much speculation about the widespread selfishness and indifference of people in general or at least, of people living in big cities. Darley and Latané, however, raised a more basic question: Common sense suggests that the greater the number of witnesses to an emergency (or in this case, a crime), the more likely it is that someone will help. So why wasn't this the case in the tragic murder of Kitty Genovese? In their efforts to answer this question, Darley and Latané developed several possible explanations and then tested them in research that is certainly a true classic of social psychology. Their ideas—and the research it generated—are described in the *Building the Science: Classics of Social Psychology* on page 313.

Five Crucial Steps Determine Helping versus Not Helping

As the study of prosocial behavior expanded beyond the initial concern with the number of bystanders, Latané and Darley (1970) proposed that the likelihood of a person engaging in a prosocial act is determined by a series of decisions that must be made quickly by those who witness an emergency.

Any one of us can sit in a comfortable chair and figure out instantly what bystanders should do. The witnesses to the assault on Genovese should either have called the police immediately or perhaps even intervened directly by shouting at the attacker or working

BUILDING THE SCIENCE
CLASSICS OF SOCIAL PSYCHOLOGY

Is There Safety in Numbers? Not Always!

In their attempts to understand why no one came to Kitty Genovese's aid—or even phoned the police—Darley and Latané (1968) considered many possible explanations. The one that seemed to be most promising, however, was straightforward: Perhaps no one helped because *all the witnesses assumed that someone else would do it.* In other words, all the people who saw or heard what was happening believed that it was OK for them to do nothing because others would take care of the situation. Darley and Latané referred to this as **diffusion of responsibility** and suggested that according to this principle, the greater the number of witnesses to an emergency, the less likely are the victims to receive help. After all, the greater the number of potential helpers, the less responsible any one individual will feel, and the more each will assume that someone else will do it.

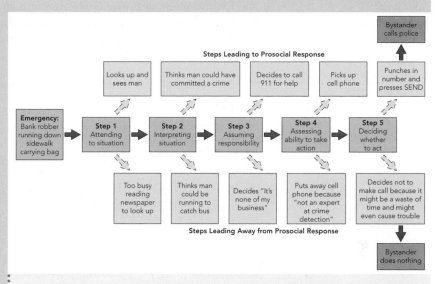

Figure 9.6

Diffusion of Responsibility and Helping in Emergencies

The greater the number of witnesses to a staged emergency, the less likely they were to help the apparent victim. This illustrates the powerful inhibiting effect of diffusion of responsibility in such situations.

(*Source:* Based on data from Darley & Latané, 1968.)

To test this reasoning, they performed an ingenious but disturbing experiment in which male college students were exposed to an apparent—but fictitious—emergency. During an experiment, a fellow student apparently had a seizure, began to choke, and was clearly in need of help. The participants interacted by means of an intercom, and it was arranged that some believed they were the only person aware of the emergency, one of two bystanders, or one of five bystanders. Helpfulness was measured in terms of (1) the percentage of participants in each experimental group who attempted to help and (2) the time that passed before the help began.

Darley and Latané's predictions about diffusion of responsibility were correct. The more bystanders participants believed were present, the lower the percentage who made a prosocial response (offered help to the apparent victim; see Figure 9.6) and the longer they waited before responding. Applying this to the example of a fall on the ice described previously , you would be more likely to be helped if you fell with only one witness present than if twelve witnesses were present.

Over the years, additional research on prosocial behavior has identified a great many additional factors that determine how people respond to an emergency, but the bystander effect is clearly an important basic discovery. More recently, the bystander effect has been extended to include simply thinking about groups. For example, imagining a dinner gathering with a group (versus having dinner with just one person) inhibits prosocial actions (Garcia, Weaver, Moskowitz, & Darley, 2002). Thus the priming (see Chapter 2) of a social context by inducing people to think about the presence of others results in less helping behavior in a subsequent, unrelated situation. Such findings indicate that diffusion of responsibility can be triggered not only by the presence of others but also by cognitive processes, leading to an implicit bystander effect.

diffusion of responsibility
A principle suggesting that the greater the number of witnesses to an emergency the less likely victims are to receive help. This is because each bystander assumes that someone else will do it.

as a group to halt the attack. Indeed, on September 11, 2001, the passengers on one of the hijacked planes apparently responded jointly, thus preventing the terrorists from accomplishing their goal of crashing into the U.S. Capitol. In a similar manner, the students in the laboratory experiment conducted by Darley and Latané (1968) should have rushed out of the cubicle to help their fellow student who was, apparently, having a medical emergency. Why didn't they do so? One answer is that when we are suddenly and unexpectedly faced with an emergency, the situation is often complex and hard to interpret. Before acting, we must first figure out what, if anything is going on, and what we should do about it. This requires a series of decisions, and at each step—and for each decision—many factors determine the likelihood that we will fail to help. Here's a summary of the decisions involved, and the factors that play a role in each one.

(1). Noticing, or Failing to Notice, that Something Unusual Is Happening

An emergency is obviously something that occurs unexpectedly, and there is no sure way to anticipate that it will take place or to plan how best to respond. We are ordinarily doing something else and thinking about other things when we hear a scream outside our window, observe that a fellow student is coughing and unable to speak, or observe that some of the other passengers on our airplane are holding weapons in their hands. If we are asleep, deep in thought, concentrating on something else, we may simply fail to notice that something unusual is happening.

In everyday life, we often ignore many sights and sounds because they are not relevant to our concerns. If we could not screen out most aspects of our surroundings, we would be overwhelmed by the sheer volume of information we encounter. For this reason, we tend to ignore lots of things going on in the social world and may, as a result, not even notice an emergency when it occurs. This kind of effect was observed by Darley and Batson (1973) who conducted a field study to test the importance of this first step in the "decide-to-help-or-not-help" process. Their research was conducted with students who were training to become clergy, individuals who should be especially likely to help a stranger in need. The experimenters instructed each participant to walk to a nearby building on the campus to give a talk. To vary the degree to which they were preoccupied with their own affairs, and so would tend to ignore a developing emergency, the investigators created three different conditions. Some of the students were told that they had plenty of extra time to reach the other building, some were told that they were right on schedule with just enough time to get there, and the third group was told that they were late for the speaking assignment and needed to hurry. Presumably, during their walk across the campus, individuals in the first group would be the least preoccupied by the need to hurry, and those in the third group would be the most preoccupied. Would the degree of preoccupation influence whether or not the participants engaged in prosocial behavior?

Along the route to the building where the talk was to be given, an emergency was staged. A stranger (actually a research assistant) was slumped in a doorway, coughing and groaning. Would the students notice this apparently sick or injured individual? Yes, but even for these clergy-in-training, being preoccupied with their own business reduced helping. Of those who had spare time, 63 percent of the participants provided help. For the group that was on schedule, 45 percent helped. In the most preoccupied group (those in a hurry), only 9 percent responded to the stranger. Many of the preoccupied students paid little or no attention to the person who was coughing and groaning. They simply stepped over the him and continued on their way.

It seems clear that a person who is too busy to pay attention to his or her surroundings simply fails to notice even an obvious emergency. Under these conditions, little help is given because the potential helper is not even aware that an emergency exists.

(2). Correctly Interpreting an Event as an Emergency

Even after we pay attention to an event, we have only limited and incomplete information as to what exactly is happening. Most of the time, whatever catches our attention

Figure 9.7
Is This Really an Emergency? One of the Decisions Potential Helpers Must Make
Suppose you saw a suspicious-looking man enter your neighbor's garage and start checking some duct work or wiring (right photo). *Is he there for a legitimate reason, or is he a burglar? If you call the police, you could be a hero, if the man really is a burglar. But if he turns out to be a repairman hired by your neighbor* (left photo), *you will face a very embarrassing situation: You have called the police for nothing. The fact that most people want to avoid such situations is one reason why many bystanders don't rush to help in real emergencies.*

does not turn out to be an emergency and so does not require immediate action. Whenever potential helpers are not completely sure about what is going on, they tend to hold back and wait for further information. It's quite possible that in the early morning when Genovese was murdered, her neighbors could not clearly see what was happening, even though they heard the screams and knew that a man and a woman were possibly having a dispute. It could have just been a loud argument between a woman and her boyfriend. Or perhaps the couple was just joking with each other. Either of these two possibilities is actually more likely to be true than the fact that a stranger was stabbing a woman to death. With ambiguous information as to whether one is witnessing a serious problem or something inconsequential, most people are inclined to accept a comforting and undemanding interpretation that indicates no need to take action (Wilson & Petruska, 1984).

This suggests that the presence of multiple witnesses may inhibit helping not only because of the diffusion of responsibility, but also because it is embarrassing to misinterpret a situation and to act inappropriately. Making such a serious mistake in front of several strangers might lead them to think you are overreacting in a stupid way. For instance, if you see someone prowling around a neighbor's house, do you immediately phone the police? Perhaps it is a burglar. But it might also be someone there to read the electric meter, or someone who was hired by your neighbor to provide an estimate for some work she wants done (see Figure 9.7). You are not certain, but you know one thing for sure: If the person is there for a legitimate reason and you call the police, you are likely to have an embarrassing experience.

So, uncertain of what to do you do . . . nothing

When others are around, we rely on social comparisons to test our interpretations. If other people show no sign of alarm about the events we are witnessing, it is safer to follow their lead. No one wants to look foolish or to lose his or her "cool." The tendency for an individual surrounded by a group of strangers to hesitate and do nothing is based on what is known as **pluralistic ignorance.** That is, because none of the bystanders knows for sure what is happening, each depends on the others to provide cues. Each

pluralistic ignorance
Refers to the fact that because none of the bystanders respond to an emergency, no one knows for sure what is happening and each depends on the others to interpret the situation.

Figure 9.8
Whose Responsibility Is
It to Help?
*When people feel responsible
for helping in an emergency,
they often spring into action—
like the firefighters shown here.
If responsibility for helping is
less clear, however, bystanders
are uncertain what to do—
and often do nothing.*

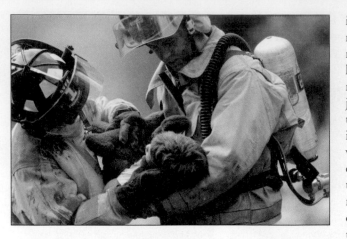

individual is less likely to respond if the others fail to respond. Latané and Darley (1968) provided a dramatic demonstration of just how far people will go to avoid making a possibly inappropriate response to what may or may not be an emergency. The investigators placed students in a room alone or with two other students and asked them to fill out questionnaires. After several minutes had passed, the experimenters secretly and quietly pumped smoke into the research room through a vent. When a participant was working there alone, most (75 percent) stopped what they were doing when the smoke appeared and left the room to report the problem. When three people were in the room, however, only 38 percent reacted to the smoke. Even after it became so thick that it was difficult to see, 62 percent continued to work on the questionnaire and failed to make any response to the smoke-filled room. The presence of other people clearly inhibits responsiveness. It is as if risking death is preferable to making a fool of ourselves.

This inhibiting effect is much less if the group consists of friends rather than strangers, because friends are likely to communicate with one another about what is going on (Rutkowski, Gruder, & Romer, 1983). The same is true of people in small towns who are likely to know one another as opposed to big cities where most people are strangers (Levine, Martinez, Brase, & Sorenson, 1994). Not surprisingly, any anxiety about the reactions of others and thus the fear of doing the wrong thing is reduced by alcohol. As a result, people who have been drinking show an increased tendency to be helpful (Steele, Critchlow, & Liu, 1985). But of course, they sometimes show other changes in behavior that are not so beneficial.

(3). Deciding that It Is Your Responsibility to Provide Help

In many instances, the responsibility for helping is clear. Firefighters are the ones to do something about a blazing building; police officers take charge when cars collide; and medical personnel deal with injuries and illnesses (see Figure 9.8). If responsibility is not clear, people assume that anyone in a leadership role must take responsibility—for instance, adults with children, professors with students. As we have pointed out previously, when there is only one bystander, he or she usually take charge because there is no alternative.

(4). Deciding that You Have the Knowledge or Skills to Act

Even if a bystander progresses as far as step three and assumes responsibility, a prosocial response cannot occur unless the person knows how to be helpful. Some emergencies are sufficiently simple that almost everyone has the necessary skills to help. If someone slips on the ice, most bystanders are able to help that person get up. On the other hand, if you see someone parked on the side of the road, peering under the hood of the car, you can't be of direct help unless you know something about cars and how they function. The best you can do is offer to call for assistance.

When emergencies require special skills, usually only a portion of the bystanders are able to help. For example, only good swimmers can assist a person who is drowning. With a medical emergency, a registered nurse is more likely to be helpful than a history professor (Cramer, McMaster, Bartell, & Dragma, 1988).

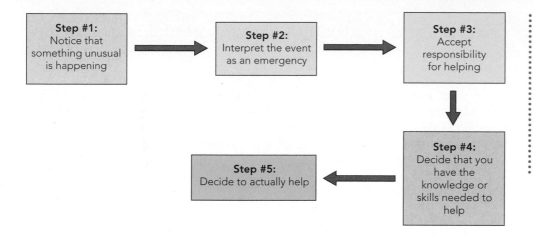

Figure 9.9

Five Steps on the Path to Helping in Emergencies
As shown here, deciding to actually offer help to the victims of emergencies depends on five steps. Only if these steps or decisions are positive does actual helping occur.

(Based on suggestions by Latané & Darley, 1970.)

(5). Making the Final Decision to Provide Help

Even if a bystander passes the first four steps in the decision process, help does not occur unless he or she makes the ultimate decision to engage in a helpful act. Helping at this final point can be inhibited by fears (often realistic ones) about potential negative consequences. In effect, potential helpers engage in "cognitive algebra" as they weigh the positive versus the negative aspects of helping (Fritzsche, Finkelstein, & Penner, 2000). As we will note in a later discussion, the rewards for being helpful are primarily provided by the emotions and beliefs of the helper, but there are a great many varieties of potential costs. For example, if you intervened in the Kitty Genovese attack, you might be stabbed yourself. You might slip while helping a person who has fallen on the ice. A person might be asking for assistance simply as a trick leading to robbery or worse (R. L. Byrne, 2001).

In sum, deciding to help in an emergency situation is not a simple, one-time decision. Rather, it involves a number of steps or decisions and only if all of these decisions are positive, does actual helping occur. (Figure 9.9 summarizes these steps.)

Principles to Remember

Contrary to what common sense suggests, more witnesses to an emergency do not increase the likelihood that the victims will receive help.

KeyPoints

- When an emergency arises and someone is in need of help, a bystander may or may not respond in a prosocial way—responses can range from heroism to apathy.

- In part because of diffusion of responsibility, the more bystanders present as witnesses to an emergency, the less likely each of them is to provide help and the greater the delay before help occurs (the bystander effect).

- When faced with an emergency, a bystander's tendency to help or not help depends in part on decisions made at five crucial steps.
  - First, it is necessary for the bystander to pay attention and be aware that an unusual event is occurring.

- Second, the bystander must correctly interpret the situation as an emergency.

- Third, the bystander must assume responsibility to provide help.

- Fourth, the bystander must have the required knowledge and skills to be able to act.

- Fifth, the bystander must decide to act.

Think About It

If helping in emergencies requires multiple decisions, how do bystanders ever decide to act quickly enough to make a difference?

External and Internal Influences on Helping Behavior

As we noted previously, interest in prosocial behavior by social psychologists was first inspired by the question "Why do bystanders at an emergency sometimes help and sometimes fail to do anything?" We have already considered one important factor to emerge from research on this question—the number of bystanders present. Here, we'll examine additional aspects of the situation that influence the tendency to help others. Then, we'll turn to a number of internal factors (e.g., emotions and personal characteristics) that also influence such behavior.

Situational (External) Factors that Enhance or Inhibit Helping

Are all victims equally likely to receive help? Or are some more likely to get assistance than others? And is the tendency to help others affected by social influence—for instance, by the actions of others who might also help? Let's see what research by social psychologists has revealed about these and other factors that might influence helping.

Helping People We Like

Most of the research we'll now discuss has focused on providing help to strangers because it is obvious that most people are likely to help family members and friends when they need assistance. But the situation is less clear-cut when strangers are involved. Suppose, for instance, that you observe what seems to be an emergency, and the victim is a stranger. If this person is similar to you with respect to age, nationality, or some other factor, are you more likely to help than you would be if the victim were different from yourself—for instance, much older, a member of a group different from your own? The answer provided by careful research is "yes"–we are indeed more likely to help people who are similar to ourselves than people who are dissimilar (Hayden, Jackson, & Guydish, 1984; Shaw, Borough, & Fink, 1994). In fact, any characteristic that affects attraction (see Chapter 7) also increases the probability of a prosocial response (Clark, Oulette, Powell, & Milberg, 1987). Appearance also influences prosocial behavior. Physically attractive victims often receive more help than unattractive ones (Benson, Karabenick, & Lerner, 1976).

Holding similar values also results in a victim's receiving help. If an unemployed individual is known to have violated their religious values with respect to belief in God, sexual orientation, or premarital sex, religious fundamentalists believe they should not be helped; instead, they should first change their lifestyles (Jackson & Esses, 1997). If the victim was unemployed but had not violated religious values, fundamentalists favored aiding them. So, in short, we are often more likely to help people we like than people to whom we have less positive feelings.

Helping Those Who Are Not Responsible for Their Problem

If you were walking down the sidewalk early one morning and passed a man lying unconscious by the curb, would you help him? You know that helpfulness would be influenced by all of the factors we have discussed—from the presence of other bystanders to interpersonal attraction. But there is an additional consideration, too. Why is the man lying there? If his clothing is stained and torn and an empty wine bottle in a paper sack is by his side, what would you assume about his problem? You might well decide that he is a hopeless drunk who passed out on the sidewalk. In contrast, what if he is wearing an expensive suit and has a nasty cut on his forehead? These cues might lead you to decide that this was a man who had been brutally mugged on his way to work. Based on your attributions about the reasons for a man lying unconscious on the sidewalk, you would be less likely to help the victim with the wine bottle than the one with the cut on his head. In general, we are less likely to act if we believe that the victim is to blame (Higgins & Shaw, 1999; Weiner, 1980). The man in the business suit did not choose to be attacked, so we are more inclined to help him.

Figure 9.10
Social Models and Prosocial Behavior
Displays like this one are used by many museums to increase donations by visitors. Seeing this display suggests that other visitors have contributed and puts subtle pressure on people visiting the museum now to do the same.

Exposure to Prosocial Models Increases Prosocial Behavior

You are out shopping and encounter representatives of a charity collecting money for their cause. Do you decide to help by making a contribution? An important factor in this decision is whether you observe someone else make a donation. If others give money, you are more likely to do so (Macaulay, 1970). Even the presence of coins and bills (presumably contributed earlier in the day) may encourage you to respond. Have you ever visited a museum and seen a large container with bills near the entrance (Figure 9.10)? This is done to encourage you to donate as well. Seeing the money, in a sense, exposes you to information suggesting that others have donated; perhaps, you should, too. This and other techniques for gaining compliance (see Chapter 8) are directly relevant to this kind of helping behavior and are often used by charitable organizations, political parties, and many other organizations to increase donations.

In an emergency, we know that the presence of bystanders who fail to respond inhibits helpfulness. It is equally true, however, that the presence of a helpful bystander provides a strong social model, and the result is an increase in helping behavior among the remaining bystanders. An example of such modeling is provided by a field experiment in which a young woman (a research assistant) with a flat tire parked her car just off the road. Motorists were much more inclined to stop and help this woman if they had previously driven past a staged scene in which another woman with car trouble was observed receiving assistance (Bryan & Test, 1967).

In addition to prosocial models in the real world, helpful models in the media also contribute to the creation of a social norm that encourages prosocial behavior. For example, when public television stations conduct fund drives, they often show volunteers answering phones and give reports about how much money callers have donated; the goal is to influence other viewers to pick up the phone and donate, too. Such effects were studied systematically in an investigation of the power of TV conducted by Sprafkin, Liebert, and Poulous (1975). These researchers were able to increase the prosocial responsiveness of six-year-olds. Some of the children were shown an episode of *Lassie* in which there was a rescue scene—thus serving as a model for providing help. A second group of children watched a *Lassie* episode that did not focus on a prosocial theme. A third group watched a humorous episode of *The Brady Bunch*—also without prosocial content. After watching one of these shows, the children played a game, with the winner receiving a prize. During the game, it was arranged that each child would encounter a group of whining, hungry puppies. At that point, the child was faced with a choice between pausing to help the pups (and thereby lose the chance to win a prize) and ignoring the puppies and continue playing the game. The children were clearly influenced by which TV show they had watched. Those who had viewed the *Lassie* rescue episode stopped and spent much more time trying to comfort the little animals than did the children who watched either of the other TV presentations. As predicted, watching prosocial behavior on television increased the incidence of prosocial behavior in real life.

Additional experiments have confirmed the influence of positive TV models. For example, preschool children who watch such prosocial shows as *Sesame Street* or *Barney and Friends* are much more apt to respond in a prosocial way than children who do not watch such shows (Forge & Phemister, 1987). Of course, as we'll see in more detail in Chapter 10, television viewing can also have negative effects on prosocial behavior. As one example, research participants who played violent video games, such as *Mortal Kombat* and *Street Fighter*, showed a subsequent decrease in prosocial behavior (Anderson & Bushman, 2001).

Emotions and Prosocial Behavior

Emotional states are determined by both internal and external factors. On any given day, our moods or feelings shift rapidly and frequently, from happiness to sadness, from anger to contentment, and through many other possibilities. As we saw in Chapters 2 and 7, emotions are often divided into two major categories—positive and negative. Do these contrasting feelings or moods have contrasting effects on helping?

It might seem that being in a good mood would increase the tendency to help others, while being in a bad mood would interfere with helping. There is, in fact, a good deal of evidence supporting this general assumption (Forgas, 1998a). Research indicates, however, that the effects of emotions on prosocial behavior can be more complicated than you might expect (Salovey, Mayer, & Rosenhan, 1991).

Positive Emotions and Prosocial Behavior

Children seem very quick to acquire the idea that it's better to request something from a parent (or a teacher) when they are in a good mood rather than in a bad one. Most often, this is true, and the effect extends to prosocial acts as well. Research indicates that people are more willing to help a stranger when their mood has been elevated by listening to a comedian (Wilson, 1981), finding money in the coin return slot of a public telephone (Isen & Levin, 1972), or spending time outdoors on a pleasant day (Cunningham, 1979).

Emotions are also influenced by environmental conditions. For instance, a pleasant fragrance in the air makes us feel better, and the positive mood that results has been found to influence behavior (Baron, 1990b). Baron and Thomley (1994), for instance, observed that exposure to a pleasant lemon or floral odor increased willingness of research participants to volunteer time to help. In a related field study, shoppers in a mall were more likely to pick up a stranger's dropped pen or to make change for a dollar bill for a stranger when they were near a pleasant smelling shop such as a bakery (Baron, 1997; see Figure 9.11).

Under certain specific circumstances, however, a positive mood

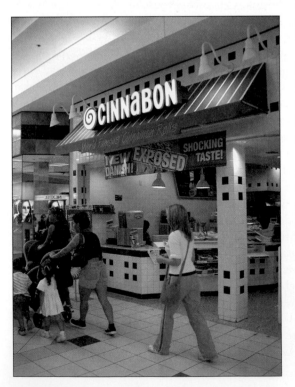

Figure 9.11
Mood and Helping: The Role of Environmental Factors
Research findings indicate that anything that puts us in a good mood—including environmental conditions, such as pleasant smells in the air—can increase helping. Positive moods or emotions don't always enhance prosocial behavior, but often, they do seem to have this effect.

can decrease the probability of responding in a prosocial way (Isen, 1984). A bystander in a positive mood who encounters an ambiguous emergency tends to interpret the situation as a nonemergency. Even if it is clear that an emergency exists, people in a good mood tend to resist helping if doing so involves performing actions that are difficult and unpleasant (Rosenhan, Salovey, & Hargis, 1981). Why? Partly because people in a good mood don't want to do anything that will interfere with or reduce their pleasant feelings. If helping others can, potentially, have such effects, then the people involved are less likely to engage in prosocial actions.

Negative Emotions and Prosocial Behavior

It is commonly assumed that someone in a negative mood is less likely to help others, and some research findings offer support for this view (Amato, 1986). As with positive emotions, however, specific circumstances can strongly influence this general trend. For example, if the act generates positive feelings, people in a bad mood may actually be more likely to help than those in a neutral or even positive mood because they want to make themselves feel better, and helping others can help them accomplish this goal (Cialdini, Kenrick, & Bauman, 1982). This is consistent with the negative-state relief model described previously. A negative mood or emotion is most likely to increase prosocial behavior if the negative feelings are not too intense, if the emergency is clear-cut rather than ambiguous, and if the act of helping is interesting and satisfying rather than dull and unrewarding (Cunningham et al., 1990).

Empathy: An Important Foundation for Helping

Though many factors have been identified as affecting prosocial behavior, people facing the same situation do not respond in an identical way. Some are more helpful than others, and these individual differences are visible in a wide range of contexts. Among such factors—personal factors that influence helping—the one that appears to be most important is the tendency to experience empathy—emotional reactions that are focused on or oriented toward other people and include feelings of compassion, sympathy, and concern (e.g., Batson & Oleson, 1991)—toward others. More formally, empathy consists of affective and cognitive responses to another person's emotional state and includes sympathy, a desire to solve the problem, and taking the perspective of the other person (Batson et al., 2003). An empathetic person feels what another person is feeling and understands why that person feels as he or she does (Azar, 1997; Darley, 1993; Duan, 2000). Individual differences in this respect tend to be relatively consistent over time. For example, children who are prosocial in early childhood behave in a similar way in adolescence (Caprara, Barbaranelli, Pastorelli, et al., 2000; Eisenberg et al., 2002). Thus they are often an important factor in the decision to help or not help others.

The affective component is essential to empathy, and children as young as twelve months seem clearly to feel distress in response to the distress of others (Brothers, 1990; see Figure 9.12). This same characteristic is also observed in other primates (Ungerer et al., 1990) and probably among many animal species (Azar, 1997). For instance, cats and dogs often

Figure 9.12
Empathy: It Emerges Early in Life
Even young infants show empathy—for instance, they will cry when exposed to another infant who is distressed and crying.

hate going to the vet. Why? Perhaps because they hear other animals crying out in pain or fear, and they experience empathy toward these other pets. This is mainly speculation, but seems at least a reasonable possibility.

The cognitive component of empathy appears to be a uniquely human quality that develops only after we progress beyond infancy. Such cognitions include the ability to consider the viewpoint of another person, sometimes referred to as perspective taking—the ability to "put yourself in someone else's shoes." Social psychologists have identified three different types of perspective taking (Batson, Early, & Salvarani, 1997). (1) You can imagine how the other person perceives an event and how he or she must feel as a result—taking the "imagine other" perspective. Those who take this perspective experience relatively pure empathy that motivates altruistic behavior. (2) You can imagine how you would feel if you were in that situation—taking the "imagine self" perspective. Those who take this perspective also experience empathy, but they tend to be motivated by self-interest, and that can interfere with altruism. (3) The third type of perspective taking involves fantasy—feeling empathy for a fictional character. In this instance, there is an emotional reaction to the joys, sorrows, and fears of a person (or an animal) in a book, movie, or TV program. Many children (and adults, too) may cry when Bambi discovers that his mother has been shot or to cringe in fear when the Wicked Witch of the West threatens Dorothy and "your little dog, too."

Empathy and Helping across Group Boundaries

Empathy involves being able to take the perspective of other people, feeling sympathy toward them, and wanting to help solve their problems or reduce their distress. This raises an intriguing question: Is it more difficult to experience empathy toward people outside our own social group than people within it? And if so, could this help explain why people belonging to one social group often fail to help those in other groups when they face emergencies or are in need of assistance for other reasons? Research findings suggest that this may indeed be the case (e.g., Pryor, Reeder, Yeadon, & Hesson-McInnis, 2004; Stuermer, Snyder, & Omoto, 2005).

A clear example of such findings is provided by research conducted by Stuermer, Snyder, Kropp, and Siem (2006). In this study, two groups of male students in Germany—ones of German cultural background and the other of Muslim cultural background—performed a task in which they learned about a serious problem being experienced by another person: He was out of money and could not find a place to live in the city to which he had just moved. This person was presented as being either a member of their own group or of the other group. After learning of the stranger's problem, participants completed a measure of empathy toward this person and also indicated the likelihood that they would help. The researchers predicted that empathy would encourage helping, but that this effect would be much stronger within groups than across groups. In other words, empathy would increase helping for members of one's own group but would have weaker effects in this respect for members of another group. This is exactly what was found.

Overall, these results indicate that empathy does indeed increase prosocial behavior, but that such effects are stronger for people to whom we feel similar than for people we view as being dissimilar to ourselves in various ways. These findings are related to the proposals of kinship selection theory, which is the view suggesting that we are more likely to help people who share our genes than people who do not. In many case, we are more likely to share genes with people in our own ethnic or cultural group than with people from other groups. Of course, such evidence is far from conclusive, but it does suggest that empathy—a factor involving both emotional and cognitive reactions—seems to influence prosocial behavior in ways consistent with predictions based on an evolutionary perspective.

How Does Empathy Develop?

Before concluding this discussion of the role of empathy in helping, it's important to address one additional issue: How does empathy develop? People differ a great deal in how they respond to the emotional distress of others. At one extreme are those willing to risk their lives to help another person. At the other extreme are those who enjoy inflicting pain and humiliation on a helpless victim. As with most individual characteristics, the answer seems to lie in a combination of biological differences and contrasting experiences.

The potential role of genetic factors was first investigated by Davis, Luce, and Kraus (1994). They examined more than eight hundred sets of identical and fraternal twins and found that heredity underlies the two affective aspects of empathy (personal distress and sympathetic concern) but not cognitive empathy. Genetic factors account for about one-third of the variations among people in affective empathy. Presumably, external factors account for differences in cognitive empathy and for two-thirds of the variation in affective empathy. Psychologist Janet Strayer (quoted in Azar, 1997) suggests that we are all born with the biological capacity for empathy, but that our specific experiences determine whether this potential becomes a vital part of ourselves or fails to manifest itself. Children of preschool age are able to differentiate empathic and selfish behavior in others, and those who understand this difference behave in a more prosocial way than those who do not (Ginsburg et al., 2003).

What kinds of specific experiences might enhance or inhibit the development of empathy? Having a secure attachment style facilitates an empathic response to the needs of others (Mikulincer et al., 2001). Previously, we described research indicating the positive effects of brief exposure to prosocial TV models on empathy. It seems likely that prolonged exposure to such models on television and in movies would be of added value. Researchers believe that the influence of parents as models is probably much greater than the influence of the media. In his book *The Moral Intelligence of Children*, Robert Coles (1997) emphasizes the importance of mothers and fathers in shaping such behavior. He suggests that the key is to teach children to be "good" and "kind" and to think about other people rather than just about themselves. Good children are not self-centered, and they are more likely to respond to the needs of others. Moral intelligence is not based on memorizing rules and regulations or on learning abstract definitions. Instead, children learn by observing what their parents do and say in their everyday lives. Coles believes that the elementary school years are the crucial time during which a child develops or fails to develop a conscience. Also, in early adolescence, the positive influence of parents and teachers in some instances is replaced by the negative influence of peers (Ma, Shek, Teung, & Tam, 2002). Without appropriate models and appropriate experiences throughout their development, children can easily grow into selfish and rude adolescents and then into equally unpleasant adults. Coles quotes novelist Henry James, whose nephew asked how he should live his life. James replied, "Three things in human life are important. The first is to be kind. The second is to be kind. And the third is to be kind." Coles agrees and says that those who learn to be kind have a strong commitment to helping others rather than hurting them.

Empathy is most likely to develop if the child's mother is a warm person, if both parents emphasize how other people are affected by hurtful behavior, and if the family is able to discuss emotions in a supportive atmosphere. Parents who use anger as the major way to control their children inhibit the development of empathy (Azar, 1997; Carpenter, 2001a).

Either because of genetic differences or because of different socialization experiences, women express higher levels of empathy than do men (Trobst, Collins, & Embree, 1994). Consistent with that finding, women outnumbered men two to one among those in World War II who helped rescue Jews from the Nazis (Anderson, 1993; see Figure 9.13 on page 324).

Social Exclusion: When Being Left out Reduces Helping

To some extent, engaging in prosocial behavior involves the belief, among the helpers, that they are part of a community—a group or society in which people will engage in mutual help, support, and kindness. Such beliefs can encourage empathy toward others, and as we have already seen, empathy is a powerful force for helping. But what happens when people feel that they have been excluded (**social exclusion**)? One possibility, suggested

social exclusion
Conditions in which individuals feel that they have been excluded from some social group.

Figure 9.13
Prosocial Behavior: One Result of Empathy
Irena Sendler, who is now almost one hundred years old, rescued more than 2,500 Jewish children from the Nazis by smuggling them out of the Warsaw ghetto where they were destined for certain death. She was recently honored by the Polish government for her heroism. Sendler is just one of many women who engaged in similar actions; in fact, many more women than men risked their own lives to rescue Jews from the Nazi death machine, perhaps because women experience higher levels of empathy than men.

recently by Twenge, Baumeister, DeWall, Ciarocco, and Bartels (2007), is that the emotional reactions that make us feel close to others and encourage helping might be reduced or eliminated. Being excluded socially is a painful experience, and one that may leave people who experience it with few emotional resources: They are too busy trying to deal with their own feelings of rejection and abandonment to have much emotion left for experiencing empathy concerning the problems of others.

Evidence for this reasoning has recently been reported by Twenge and others (2007) in a series of carefully conducted studies. In several of these experiments, some participants were made to feel excluded by being told that their responses to a personality test indicated that they would probably be alone later in life. Others, in contrast, were told that their responses predicted that they would probably enjoy a future rich in personal relationships. Participants in two control groups were either given no information about their future social lives or were told that they were likely to experience accidents in the future (a negative outcome unrelated to social exclusion).

The tendency to help others was measured by asking participants how much of their payment for being in the study they wanted to contribute to a fund to help needy students. As you can see from Figure 9.14, those told they would have a rich future social gave much more than those told they would probably be excluded. Participants in the two control conditions (misfortune, no feedback) who were not expected to experience feelings that would block empathy also gave more than those in the social exclusion condition.

In further studies, Twenge and others (2007) obtained evidence indicating that when people experience social exclusion, they adopt a cautious attitude toward social relations. They want to have good relations with others, but because they have recently been rejected, they are reluctant to expose themselves to the risk of even further exclusion. As a result, they are less likely to experience empathy toward others and less likely to use prosocial actions as a way of winning new friends and social support. This suggests that exclusion can sometimes have lasting effects because it effectively prevents people who experience it

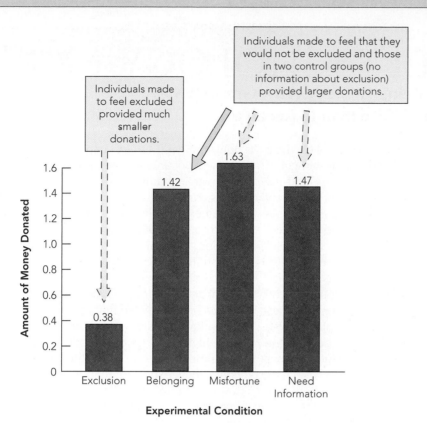

Figure 9.14
Social Exclusion: Negative Effects on Helping
As shown here, people told that they would probably be alone later in life (they would experience social exclusion) were less generous in donating to a student fund than people told that they would experience a full, rich social life in the future. These findings suggest that when individuals feel excluded or rejected, their ability to experience empathy toward others is reduced, thus decreasing their tendency to engage in prosocial behavior.

(*Source:* Based on data from Twenge, Baumeister, DeWall, et al., 2007).

from building the new social relationships they so badly want. Truly, then, social exclusion—which is far from rare—may be damaging not just to individuals but also to groups and societies than was previously suspected. As we noted in Chapter 6, being the target of discrimination is a negative experience, and in several respects, is closely related to feelings of being excluded. In some ways, the opposite of social exclusion is being helped by others—assuming that is taken as an indicator that one is cared about by those others. But is being the recipient of help always a positive experience? Does it make the recipients more likely to be helpful themselves? For some surprising answers read *Social Psychology: What It Tells Us About . . .* on page 326.

Personality and Helping

In addition to empathy, several other aspects of personality are related to prosocial behavior. For instance, people high in interpersonal trust engage in more prosocial acts than do people who distrust others (Cadenhead & Richman, 1996). Similarly, Machiavellianism—an aspect of personality involving distrust, cynicism, egocentricity, and the desire to manipulate and control others—is negatively related to helping; the higher people are in Machiavellianism, the less likely they are to help others in need of their assistance (McHoskey, 1999).

The fact that several aspects of personality are involved in prosocial acts has led some investigators to propose that a combination of relevant factors constitutes what has been designated as the **altruistic personality.** An altruistic person is high on five dimensions that are characteristic of people who engage in prosocial behavior in an emergency situation (Bierhoff, Klein, & Kramp, 1991) and in many other contexts, too:

1. **Empathy.** As we have already seen, people who help are found to be higher in empathy than those who are not. The most altruistic people describe themselves as responsible, socialized, conforming, tolerant, self-controlled, and motivated to make a good impression.

altruistic personality
A cluster of traits (e.g., high in empathy, belief in a just world) that predisposes individuals to behave in a prosocial manner.

SOCIAL PSYCHOLOGY

The Downside of Being Helped: Why, Often, It May Actually Be Better to Give than to Receive

Being helped when we need assistance can be a tremendous relief. When the young stranger in the chapter opening story helped me find my way on the Paris subway, I was deeply and sincerely grateful to him; he had showed me considerable kindness, and I only wished there were some way in which I could repay him. But is this always the case? Do people always react positively to receiving help? If you have ever received a gift you didn't want or had someone insist on doing a favor for you that you really didn't need, you already know that our reactions to help from others are not always positive. So, contrary to widely held cultural beliefs, behaving in a prosocial manner may not always produce positive effects (see Figure 9.15).

In fact, research findings indicate that people who receive help from others may experience negative rather than positive reactions to such assistance. For example, someone with a physical impairment may need help but still feel depressed when help is given (Newsom, 1999); it reminds this person of her or his disability. If these negative feelings are expressed, the one who helps interprets the reaction as a lack of gratitude and is less likely to offer help in the future.

The general problem is that when people receive help, their self-esteem can suffer. This is especially likely to occur when the person on the receiving end is lower in status than the helper because in such cases, receiving help drives home the status difference between them (e.g., Penner, Dovidio, Piliavin, & Schroeder, 2005). For instance, in several studies, Nadler and Halabi (2006) exposed participants—Jewish Israelis and Arab Israelis—to situations in which they received or did not receive help from members of their own group or the other group. The researchers predicted that in general, people belonging to low status groups are reluctant to receive help from high status groups, especially when they trying to gain equality—to boost their own status. Specifically, they expected that Arab-Israelis, who have lower status in Israel than Jewish Israelis, would react negatively to help from Jewish Israelis, especially when they perceived such help as threatening their quest for equality by suggesting that they are dependent on the high status group. This is precisely what was found: Members of the low status group (Arab-Israelis) reacted negatively in several respects—more negative feelings, lower evaluations of the other group (and the helper) to unsolicited help. Findings such as this drive home the key point: Being helped by others is not always a positive experience and in

2. **Belief in a just world.** Helpful individuals perceive the world as a fair and predictable place in which good behavior is rewarded and bad behavior punished. This belief leads to the conclusion that helping those in need is the right thing to do *and* to the expectation that the person who helps will actually benefit from doing a good deed.

3. **Social responsibility.** The most helpful individuals also express the belief that each person is responsible for doing his or her best to assist anyone who needs help.

4. **Internal locus of control.** This is the belief that a person can choose to behave in ways that maximize good outcomes and minimize bad ones. People who fail to help, in contrast, tend to have an external locus of control and believe that their behavior is irrelevant because outcomes are controlled by luck, fate, people with power, and other uncontrollable factors.

5. **Low egocentrism.** Altruistic people do not tend to be self-absorbed and competitive.

In summary, prosocial behavior is found to be influenced in both positive and negative ways by many aspects of the situation, by one's emotional state, and by empathy and other personality dispositions that are based in part on genetic differences and in part on childhood experiences.

> ## Principles to Remember
>
> The tendency to help others is not equal across different people. In fact, it is strongly influenced by emotions, empathy, and by several aspects of personality.

fact, under some conditions, can be viewed negatively by the persons on the receiving end (DePaulo, Brown, Ishii, & Fisher, 1981; Nadler, Fisher, & Itzhak, 1983).

On the other hand, more positive reactions to help often occur when the person receiving assistance believes that the help was offered because of positive feelings on the part of the helper (Ames, Flynn, & Weber, 2004). Such helping evokes the reciprocity norm and the one who was helped is motivated to reciprocate with a kind deed in the future. When the helping is based on the helper's role (e.g., a policeman helping a lost child) or on the helper's cost-benefit analysis (e.g., a helper deciding to help because they would gain more than they would lose from the deed), the desire to reciprocate is weaker.

One positive effect that sometimes results from receiving help—even when it generates negative feelings—is that the recipient experiences increased motivation to avoid similar situations in the future by engaging in self-help—by getting to the point where help from others is unnecessary (Fisher, Nadler, &

Figure 9.15
Does Helping Always Produce Positive Reactions?
As this pet owner has just discovered, engaging in prosocial behavior does not always generate gratitude and thanks from the recipients. Rather, like the fish shown here, they may react negatively and actually "bite the hand that feeds (helps) them."

(Source: The New Yorker.)

Whitcher-Alagna, 1982; Lehman, Daubman, Guarna, Jordan, & Cirafesi, 1995). No one wants to be seen as helpless or incompetent, and self-help can reduce feelings of dependence as well (Daubman, 1995). For instance, I realized, long ago, that a working knowledge of basic carpentry, plumbing, and electricity would allow me to fix things at home myself and not be dependent on the help of friends, family, or neighbors. Even though I like most of my neighbors and realize that my friends are all too willing to help, being dependent on them made me feel uneasy, so I took steps to learn the skills I needed to make such help unnecessary—and in fact, being able to do most minor repairs myself did boost my self-confidence and self-esteem.

In short, there may be a significant grain of truth to the statement "It is better to give than to receive," because help—like gifts—often has some major psychological strings attached, and most people would prefer not to become entangled in them if at all possible.

KeyPoints

- We are more likely to help others who are similar to ourselves than others who are dissimilar. This leads to lower tendencies to help people outside our own social groups.

- Positive and negative emotional states can either enhance or inhibit prosocial behavior, depending on specific factors in the situation and on the nature of the required assistance.

- Empathy is an important determinant of helping behavior. It is weaker across group boundaries than within social groups.

- Social exclusion often reduces prosocial behavior because people who experience it have reduced capacity to feel empathy toward others.

- Several aspects of personality influence helping including belief in a just world, social responsibility, internal locus of control, and low egocentrism.

Think About It

A number of factors influence whether, and to what extent, individuals offer help to others. Does this mean that heroism is simply a result of the "right" combination of such factors? Or are people who engage in truly heroic actions different, in important ways, from most others?

Long-Term Commitment to Prosocial Acts

In addition to responding to an emergency situation by helping someone in need, prosocial behavior takes many other forms. We have mentioned some of these, including picking up pens that someone has dropped, comforting an unhappy puppy, protecting victims of persecution, and giving money to a charity. A somewhat different type of prosocial behavior is represented by volunteering one's time to a worthy cause, often over a long period of time. With respect to all types of prosocial behavior, moral issues arise in making a choice as to whether to act or not, and the individual must balance self-interest with moral integrity, while not engaging in moral hypocrisy. In this section, we'll consider those issues, too.

Volunteering: Helping as an Ongoing Commitment

A special type of prosocial behavior is required when the person in need has a chronic, continuing problem that requires help over a prolonged time period (Williamson & Schulz, 1995). A person who volunteers to provide assistance in this context must commit their time and effort over weeks, months, or even longer. In the United States alone, fully 26.7% of the population volunteered by joining or working for an organization in 2006 (Bureau of Labor Statistics, 2007). Overall, almost one hundred million adults volunteer 20.5 billion hours each year, averaging 4.2 hours of prosocial activity each week (Moore, 1993). It is reasonable to assume that, around the world, people are spending an enormous amount of time engaged in voluntary acts of helpfulness. For example, after hurricane Katrina struck New Orleans and the Gulf coast of the United States, thousands of volunteers went to these locations to help the victims rebuild and deal with a host of medical and legal problems. The devastation was huge, and government agencies seemed unable to cope with it, so these volunteers did a great deal to help (see Figure 9.16).

The five steps required to respond to an emergency that were described previously also apply to volunteering. To help those who are homeless, for example, you must become aware of the problem (usually through the news media), interpret the problem accurately (a major need is for affordable housing), assume personal responsibility to provide help, decide on a course of action that is possible for you (e.g., signing up to work with Habitat for Humanity several hours a week), and then actually engage in the behavior.

Figure 9.16
Volunteering: Long-Term Commitment to Helping
Volunteerism is a form of prosocial behavior that requires a long-term commitment to performing helpful acts. After Hurricane Katrina devastated New Orleans and many other cities, thousands of volunteers went to the devastated area to help the victims of this violent storm. These efforts continue even today.

What motivates people to give up a portion of their ongoing lives to help in this way? One answer is that an individual has to be convinced of the importance of a given need; there are obviously many worthwhile causes, and no one can help all of them. When the people who volunteer time and money are identified by race and ethnic group, different concerns become apparent. In the United States, Caucasians give most to help animals, the environment, and emergency personnel, such as police officers and fire fighters. African Americans are more likely to assist those who are homeless or hungry, groups fighting for minority rights, and religious institutions. Asian Americans prefer helping museums and other artistic and cultural enterprises. Hispanic Americans provide help to immigrants and to people in other countries. It seems that people with different backgrounds are motivated by the specific concerns of their group. On a more personal level, motives also vary, and we will examine some of them.

Motives for Volunteering

Patients with AIDS provide an example of people with a continuing problem, requiring the time-consuming commitment of volunteers. While progress is being made in medical research seeking a way to immunize against HIV infection and to find a cure for AIDS, throughout the world a growing number of individuals simply require assistance as they await death from this disease. Volunteers can work in preventive educational programs or with groups raising money for research and treatment. It is also possible to work directly with patients to provide emotional support and to help with household chores and transportation.

Why would anyone be willing to spend part of his or her life engaged in such activities when most of us have plenty to do as it is? And AIDS provides a special excuse not to help; as we have seen, people have less sympathy for a victim perceived to be responsible for his or her problem. Pullium (1993) found that people have much less empathy for and willingness to help an AIDS patient who has engaged in homosexual acts or who has shared needles than for a patient who contracted the disease from a blood transfusion. Even if one overcomes the issue of blame, there is the fear (however unfounded) of contracting the disease or of being avoided by friends because of association with these patients.

Given these negative considerations, a person must be strongly motivated to volunteer to provide help to patients with this disease. Clary and Snyder (1999) identified six basic functions that are served by working as an AIDS volunteer, and these are summarized in Table 9.1 on page 330. The decision to volunteer can be based on personal values, the need to understand more about this disease, the desire to enhance one's own development, the chance to gain career-related experience, the need to improve one's own personal relationships, or the desire to reduce negative feelings, such as guilt, or escape from personal problems. In other words, volunteers may work side by side doing exactly the same job but for quite different underlying reasons.

One reason for identifying these motivational differences is that efforts to recruit volunteers are most successful when there is an emphasis on multiple reasons to become involved rather than just a single reason. The greatest success occurs when it is possible to match the recruitment message to the recipient's motivation (Clary et al., 1998).

In volunteer work, beyond the task of recruitment is the more difficult problem of turnover. About half of those who volunteer quit within a year (Grube & Piliavin, 2000; Omoto & Snyder, 1995). It is reasonable to suppose that a major reason to continue with volunteer work is the feeling of satisfaction provided by such activity. Those in the first year of a volunteer project who felt the most satisfaction did volunteer more hours per week, but satisfaction was unrelated to continued commitment to the activity (Davis, Hall, & Meyer, 2003). Instead, quitting is directly related to their motivation for volunteering in the first place. People who continue volunteer work for at least two-and-a-half

Table 9.1 Motives for Volunteering

People volunteer (make long-term commitments to helping others) for many reasons. Some of the most important are shown here.

FUNCTION SERVED	DEFINITION	SAMPLE ITEM
Values	To express or act on important values such as humanitarianism	"I feel it is important to help others."
Understanding	To learn more about the world or exercise skills that are often not used	"Volunteering lets me learn through direct, hands-on experience."
Enhancement	To grow and develop psychologically through volunteer activities	"Volunteering makes me feel better about myself."
Career	To gain career-related experiences	"Volunteering can help me to get my foot in the door at a place where I would like to work."
Social	To strengthen social relationships	"People I know share an interest in community service."
Protective	To reduce negative feelings, such as guilt, or to address personal problems	"Volunteering is a good escape from my own problems."

(*Source:* Based on information in Clary & Snyder, 1999)

years tend to be those motivated by the need to gain understanding, enhance self-esteem, and assist their own personal development. These self-centered needs provide better indicators of who will continue volunteer work than the seemingly "selfless" needs centering on humanitarianism and the desire to help others.

Volunteering because of Mandates, Altruism, or Generativity

One way to encourage volunteerism is to mandate it, as when some high schools and colleges require students to spend a specified amount of time in volunteer work to graduate. Though this practice does result in a large number of "volunteers," the sense of being forced to engage in such work decreases interest in future volunteer activity for many students (Stukas, Snyder, & Clary, 1999). College students have a favorable attitude toward volunteering, and some indicate a strong intention to volunteer their time after being exposed to a recruitment message. In fact, however, only one out of three with a high intention score actually enrolled in a volunteer program (Okun & Sloane, 2002).

Do volunteers exhibit the same characteristics as those who engage in other forms of helping? The answer is yes, in that volunteers tend to believe in internal locus of control (Guagnano, 1995) and to be high in empathy (Penner & Finkelstein, 1998), especially with respect to empathic concern, perspective taking, and personal distress (Unger & Thumuluri, 1997).

A different characteristic shown by volunteers—generativity—has been described by McAdams, Diamon, Aubin, and Mansfield (1997). They define **generativity** as an adult's interest in and commitment to the well-being of future generations. Those high in generativity show this interest and commitment by becoming parents, by teaching young people, and by engaging in acts that will have positive effects beyond their own lifetimes. People high in generativity believe that people need to care for one another. They possess

generativity
Refers to an adult's interest in and commitment to the well-being of future generations.

enduring moral values that give purpose and meaning to their lives, perceive bad events as opportunities to create good outcomes, and make an effort to contribute to the progressive development of a better society.

Self-Interest, Moral Integrity, and Moral Hypocrisy

Few people are consciously apathetic or heartless when confronted by someone who is hurt, frightened, lost, or hungry. Sadly, though, many people can be nudged in that direction (toward being apathetic) by convincing them that there is no reason to provide help (Bersoff, 1999). For example, we can choose to ignore a victim for a variety of reasons, many of which we have already discussed. For example, "It's not my responsibility" and "It's her own fault." With a good enough excuse, we can set aside or disengage moral standards (Bandura, 1999b). We tend to overestimate our own moral actions and to believe that we are more likely to engage in selfless and kind behavior than are most people—a "holier than thou" self-assessment (Epley & Dunning, 2000). In fact, it is fairly easy for otherwise good, kind people to find a reason not to act morally in situations as varied as a stranger needing help in an emergency, charities needing help in responding to a natural disaster, and organizations needing volunteers to help care for others. We'll describe some of the motives underlying moral behavior.

Motivation and Morality

Batson and Thompson (2001) suggest that three major motives are relevant when a person is faced with a moral dilemma such as whether to help someone or not, to donate to a worthy cause or not, or to volunteer one's time or not. These motives are: self-interest, moral integrity, and moral hypocrisy. People can be roughly categorized with respect to which motive is primary for them. We'll examine what is meant by each of these motives.

Most of us are motivated, at least in part, by **self-interest (egoism).** This means that much of our behavior is based on seeking whatever provides us with the most satisfaction; we seek rewards and try to avoid punishments. People whose primary motive is self-interest are not concerned about questions of right and wrong or fair and unfair—they simply do what is best for themselves.

Other people are strongly motivated by **moral integrity.** They care about considerations of goodness and fairness when they act and frequently accept some sacrifice of self-interest in order to do "the right thing." For a person primarily motivated by morality, the conflict between self-interest and moral integrity is resolved by making the moral choice. This sometimes painful decision has both internal and external support. For example, a moral decision is enhanced by reflecting on one's values or being reminded of those values by others. At times, of course, moral integrity is overwhelmed by self-interest, and the result is questionable behavior and a feeling of guilt.

A third category of people consists of those who want to appear moral while avoiding the costs of actually being moral. Their behavior is motivated by moral hypocrisy. That is, they are driven by self-interest but are also concerned with outward appearances. It is important for them to seem to care about doing the right thing, while they act to satisfy their own needs.

To investigate these basic motivations, Batson and his co-workers (Batson et al, 1997a) developed a laboratory situation in which undergraduate students were faced with a moral dilemma. Each was given the power to assign himself or herself to one of two experimental tasks. The more desirable task included the chance to win raffle tickets. The less desirable task was described as dull and boring (and involved no raffle tickets). Most participants (over 90 percent) agreed that assigning the dull task to oneself (at least initially) was the moral thing to do and also the polite choice. They seem to have accepted the concept that you should "do unto others as you would have them do unto you." Despite these sentiments, most (70 to 80 percent) actually did the opposite. In this simple situation, most

self-interest (egoism)
The view that a large portion of human behavior is based on seeking whatever provides us with the most satisfaction; we seek rewards and try to avoid punishments.

moral integrity
Refers to the extent which individuals care about considerations of goodness and fairness when they act; moral integrity frequently involves accepting some sacrifice of self-interest to do "the right thing."

people made a choice based on self-interest. Only a minority (20 to 30 percent) behaved in a way they had indicated was the moral thing to do. Subsequent research was designed to determine the effect of varying the strength of moral integrity motivation.

Making Morality More Salient

Using the same experimental situation just described, Batson and his colleagues (Batson, Thompson, Seuferling, Whitney, & Strongman, 1999) made the moral standard of fairness more salient for some participants. They were told, "Most participants feel that giving both people an equal chance—for example, by flipping a coin—is the fairest way to assign themselves and the participant to the tasks." The experimenter then provided a coin for the participants to use if they wished to do so.

Again, there was good agreement about the most moral choice; almost all agreed that a fair procedure involved either tossing the coin or taking the dull procedure themselves. Nevertheless, only about half of the participants tossed the coin. Again, most (80 to 90 percent) of those who did not use the coin, assigned the positive task (raffle ticket, and so on) to themselves. More surprisingly, of those who did toss the coin, the same percentage still took the positive task for themselves. Some of these honestly won the flip (Batson, Thompson, & Chen, 2002), but many others (presumably motivated by self-interest) cheated when the coin toss didn't turn out the way they wanted. A few (presumably motivated by moral integrity) tossed the coin and made the task assignment on that basis even when they did not like the outcome. Others (presumably motivated by moral hypocrisy) tossed the coin to appear fair but then ignored the outcome when it conflicted with what they preferred.

In further research, the moral decision was made even more salient by giving participants the choice of flipping a coin or having the experimenter do it (Batson, Tsang, & Thompson, 2000). Most (80 percent) of those who opted for a coin toss wanted the experimenter to do it. With this procedure, they wouldn't have a chance to cheat, making it easier to behave with moral integrity.

One further variation involved increasing the costs of morality. The experiment now involved giving participants a choice of assigning a positive task and a painful task (receiving electric shock) to themselves and a fellow participant. Under these conditions, almost all of the participants gave the positive task to themselves without even pretending to be fair.

In summary, as shown in Figure 9.17, it seems that some people simply choose to act

Figure 9.17
Effect of Motivation on Behavior
When faced with a moral decision, people make a choice based on their underlying motivation. Some are motivated primarily by self-interest and do what is most rewarding for themselves. Others are motivated by moral integrity and behave in a moral and fair way. Some are motivated primarily by moral hypocrisy and behave so as to appear moral while actually pursuing their own self-interest.

(*Source:* Based on information in Batson & Thompson, 2001).

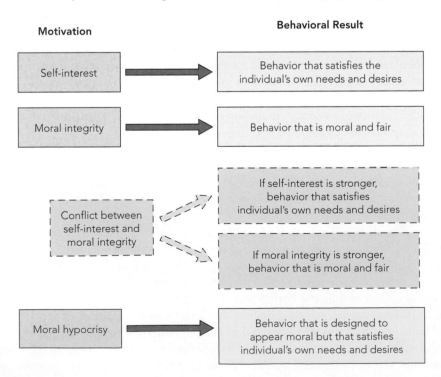

in their own self-interest even though they realize that this is less fair and less moral. Others are motivated to act in a moral way but not when the moral choice is sufficiently unpleasant. Still others make it seem as if they are acting in a moral way, but their actual behavior is based on self-interest even if it requires cheating. (Chapter 10 deals with a different form of social behavior—aggression. So, now seems to be an appropriate point to raise an intriguing question: Are helping and hurting best viewed as opposites? For some thoughts on this issue you may find surprising, please read *Making Sense of Common Sense: A Social Psychological Perspective* below.

MAKING SENSE OF COMMON SENSE
A SOCIAL PSYCHOLOGICAL PERSPECTIVE
Are Helping (Prosocial Behavior) and Hurting (Aggression) Really Opposites?

Helping and hurting: At first glance, they certainly seem to be opposites. Rushing to the aid of victims in emergencies, donating to charity, giving directions to people who are lost—these and countless other helpful actions seem opposite in many ways to aggression, which social psychologists generally define as intentional efforts to harm others in some way. But are helping and aggression really opposites? If you stopped one hundred people at random, showed them a line, and asked them to place helping and aggression along it, almost all of them would in fact place these forms of social behavior at opposite sides.

But get ready for a surprise: Social psychologists have thought long and hard about this issue for many years and reached the conclusion that in many ways, prosocial behavior and aggression are not opposites. In fact, they overlap much more than you might expect. First, consider the motives underlying such actions. The motivation for helping, you might assume is simply to do something beneficial for the recipient; the motivation for aggression, in contrast, is to do something bad—to harm the victim in some way. But look a bit more closely: As we have seen in this chapter, people sometimes engage in prosocial actions not primarily to help the recipients, but rather, to boost their own status, to incur obligations, and to gain a positive reputation. Their motivation, in short, is not necessarily to do something beneficial for the recipients. Certainly, that motive does exist; but it is often not the primary one responsible for helpful actions toward others.

Now consider aggression: Is the motivation behind such behavior always to harm the victim in some way? Perhaps, but consider the following situation: A sports coach, dissatisfied with the effort an athlete is investing in practice and angry at this person, orders the athlete to take ten laps around the field and then also confines the athlete to her or his room that evening: no parties or getting together with friends. Do these actions—which might seem to be

aggressive—stem from a motive to harm the athlete? Far from it. The coach takes these actions to help the athlete improve—or at least, become more motivated. We could offer many other examples, but the main point is clear: The motives behind prosocial behavior and aggression sometimes overlap and can't be easily separated. In this respect, certainly, they are not polar opposites.

Now, consider, the actions involved in prosocial behavior and aggression. These, you might guess, are direct opposites. Prosocial actions help the recipients in some way, while aggressive actions harm them, so they involve different kind of actions. Perhaps. But now imagine the following scene: A young woman takes a sharp needle and uses it to puncture the skin of another person, who cries out in pain. Is she behaving aggressively? Maybe yes, maybe no. What if she is placing a tattoo on the supposed "victim's" body—one she has requested and paid for in advance? So while these actions appear to be aggressive, they may actually have little or nothing to do with harming the victim. Not all aggressive and prosocial actions overlap in this sense, but some do, and this suggests that these two aspects of social behavior are not direct opposites.

Finally, consider the effects of aggression and prosocial behavior. By definition, aggression produces harm and prosocial actions produce benefits, but again, not always. For instance, consider someone who uses a sharp knife to cut into the body of another person. Is this aggression? On the surface it may appear to be. But what if the person performing this action is a skilled surgeon, trying to save the other person's life? The short-term effects might seem harmful (the "victim" bleeds profusely), but the long-term effects are actually beneficial: The patient's health is restored. Similarly, prosocial actions can seem beneficial in the short term but harm the recipient in the long term. Help we don't request or want can undermine our

(continued on page 334)

Are Helping (Prosocial Behavior) and Hurting (Aggression) Really Opposites? *(cont.)*

self-esteem and confidence, so short-term benefits can soon turn into long-term harm.

Finally, we should mention the fact that recent findings (e.g., Hawley, Card, & Little, 2007) indicate that aggression and prosocial behavior are sometimes used by the same people to gain popularity and status. Specifically, such research indicates that individuals who behave aggressively can be highly attractive to others—rather than merely alarming—if they combine such actions with prosocial ones. Such people are "tough" and assertive but also possess social skills that allow them to be charming and helpful; and they know when to "turn" their tough sides on and off. Hawley and others describe this as "the allure of mean friends" (the appeal of people who are indeed aggressive but also have other skills that help them to attain important goals) and have found that this com-

bination of toughness and prosocial action is seductive and far from rare.

As you can see, then, the question of whether helping and aggression are opposites is far more complex than at first meets the eye. The motives underlying these forms of behavior, the behaviors themselves, and effects they produce are complex and overlap much more than you at might initially guess. And that's not really surprising because all social behavior is complex; generally, it stems from many different motives, takes a wide range of forms, and produces many different effects. So yes, indeed, helping and hurting are different in several respects but not, perhaps, as different as common sense suggests. In some instances, then, the words written by British historian Mandell Creighton (1904) do seem to contain a sizeable grain of truth: *"No people do so much harm as those who go about doing good"*

KeyPoints

- People volunteer to provide help on a long-term basis as a function of various selfish and selfless motives. Those most likely to continue working as volunteers are those motivated by relatively selfish concerns.

- People can be differentiated in terms of their primary motivation when faced with making a choice that involves relatively moral versus relatively immoral alternatives. The three primary motives are self-interest, moral integrity, and moral hypocrisy.

- When the helper and the recipient are similar, the person who is helped tends to react negatively and to feel incompetent, to experience decreased self-

esteem, and to resent the helper. These negative reactions also tend to motivate self-help in the future. Help from a dissimilar person elicits a more positive reaction but fails to motivate future self-help.

Think About It

What percent of the time are you motivated by self-interest? When are you likely to behave in ways suggested by principles of moral integrity? Can you think of steps that could be taken to increase the influence of such principles on people's social behavior?

SUMMARY AND REVIEW

- The empathy-altruism hypothesis proposes that because of empathy, we help those in need simply because we value their welfare, and, perhaps, it "feels good to help." The negative-state relief model proposes that people help other people to relieve or lessen their own emotional discomfort. The empathic joy hypothesis bases helping on the positive feelings of accomplishment that arise when the helper knows that they were able to

have a beneficial impact on the person in need. The competitive altruism theory suggests that we help others as a means of increasing our own status and reputation—and thereby reap large rewards in the future. Kinship selection theory suggests that we help others who are related to us because this increases the likelihood that our genes will be transmitted to future generations.

- When an emergency arises and someone is in need of help, a bystander may or may not respond in a prosocial way. Failure to act often stems from diffusion of responsibility, the belief that someone else will do it. When faced with an emergency, a bystander's tendency to help or not help depends in part on decisions made at five crucial steps. First, it is necessary for the bystander to pay attention and be aware that an unusual event is occurring. Second, the bystander must correctly interpret the situation as an emergency. Third, the bystander must assume responsibility to provide help. Fourth, the bystander must have the required knowledge and skills to be able to act. Fifth, the bystander must decide to act. We are more likely to help others who are similar to ourselves than others who are dissimilar. This leads to lower tendencies to help people outside our own social groups.

- Positive and negative emotional states can either enhance or inhibit prosocial behavior, depending on specific factors in the situation and on the nature of the required assistance. Empathy is an important determinant of helping behavior. It is weaker across group boundaries than within social groups. Social exclusion often reduces prosocial behavior because the people who experience it have reduced capacity to feel empathy toward others. Several aspects of personality influence helping, including belief in a just world, social responsibility, internal locus of control, and low egocentrism. People volunteer to provide help on a long-term basis as a function of various selfish and selfless motives. Those most likely to continue working as volunteers are those motivated by relatively selfish concerns.

- People can be differentiated in terms of their primary motivation when faced with making a choice that involves relatively moral versus relatively immoral alternatives. The three primary motives are self-interest, moral integrity, and moral hypocrisy. When the helper and the recipient are similar, the person who is helped tends to react negatively and to feel incompetent, to experience decreased self-esteem, and to resent the helper. These negative reactions also tend to motivate self-help in the future.

Key Terms

altruistic personality (p. 325)

diffusion of responsibility (p. 313)

empathic joy hypothesis (p. 308)

empathy (p. 306)

empathy-altruism hypothesis (p. 306)

generativity (p. 330)

kin selection theory (p. 310)

moral integrity (p. 331)

negative state-relief model (p. 308)

pluralistic ignorance (p. 315)

prosocial behavior (p. 306)

self-interest (egoism) (p. 331)

social exclusion (p. 323)

Connections
INTEGRATING SOCIAL PSYCHOLOGY

In this chapter, you read about . . .	In other chapters, you will find related discussions of . . .
bystanders' response to nonverbal cues of other bystanders	interpretation of nonverbal cues (Chapter 3),
social comparison processes among the witnesses to an emergency	the importance of social comparison in the study of attitudes (Chapter 5), attraction (Chapter 7), and social influence (Chapter 9).
attributions as to the cause of a victim's problem	attribution theory (Chapter 3).
self-concept as a determinant of helping behavior and the effect of receiving help on self-esteem	research and theory on self-concept and self-esteem (Chapter 4).
similarity of victim and bystander as a determinant of empathy and helping	similarity and attraction (Chapters 7 and 8).
affective state and helping	affect as a factor in attitudes (Chapter 5), prejudice (Chapter 6), attraction and relationships (Chapter 7), and aggression (Chapter 10).
genetics and helping	genetics as a factor in attraction and mate selection (Chapter 7).

Aggression

Its Nature, Causes, and Control

10

CHAPTER OUTLINE

- **Perspectives on Aggression: In Search of the Roots of Violence**
  The Role of Biological Factors: From Instincts to the Evolutionary Perspective
  Drive Theories: The Motive to Harm Others
  Modern Theories of Aggression: The Social Learning Perspective and the General Aggression Model

- **Causes of Human Aggression: Social, Cultural, Personal, and Situational**
  Social Determinants of Aggression: Frustration, Provocation, and Heightened Arousal
  Exposure to Media Violence: The Effects of Violence in Films, on Television, and in Video Games
  BUILDING THE SCIENCE: CLASSICS OF SOCIAL PSYCHOLOGY—BANDURA'S FAMOUS "BOBO DOLL" STUDIES: TELEVISED VIOLENCE VISITS THE LABORATORY
  Violent Pornography: When Sex and Aggression Mix—and Perhaps Explode!
  SOCIAL PSYCHOLOGY: WHAT IT TELLS US ABOUT . . . THE EFFECTS OF SEXUALLY AGGRESSIVE SONG LYRICS

Cultural Factors in Aggression: "Cultures of Honor" and Sexual Jealousy
Personality and Aggression: Why Some People Are More Aggressive than Others
Situational Determinants of Aggression: The Effects of Heat and Alcohol

- **Aggression in Ongoing Relationships: Bullying and Aggression at Work**
  Bullying: Singling Out Others for Repeated Abuse
  Workplace Aggression: Harming Others at Work
  Abusive Supervision: Bosses Who Make Workplaces Unbearable

- **The Prevention and Control of Aggression: Some Useful Techniques**
  Punishment: Just Desserts or Deterrence?
  Self-Regulation: Internal Mechanisms for Controlling Aggression
  Forgiveness: Compassion Instead of Revenge
  MAKING SENSE OF COMMON SENSE: A SOCIAL PSYCHOLOGICAL PERSPECTIVE—CATHARSIS: DOES "BLOWING OFF STEAM" REALLY HELP?

It's a Monday evening and throughout the United States—and other countries, too—millions of TVs are tuned to the popular show, *24*. The focus of the show is timely, especially for U.S. citizens. In each episode (and sometimes across several continuing episodes), agents of a fictitious government agency, the counter terrorist unit (CTU) do battle with people who are truly evil: terrorists who want to kill large numbers of unarmed civilians, destroy landmark buildings, and spread fear, unrest, and disorder throughout the land. The agents of CTU take their job seriously and in fact, often adopt extreme measures to defeat the terrorists and block their evil plans. For instance, in one episode, Jack Bauer—one of the show's central characters (see Figure 10.1)—corners a foreign diplomat in his office. Bauer is demanding the whereabouts of the head of a terrorist group that has obtained nuclear warheads and is planning to launch them against U.S. cities. When the answer he seeks is not provided, Bauer pulls out a gun and holds it to the diplomat's head. When the diplomat still claims ignorance, Bauer begins to beat him, soon knocking him almost senseless. Then he changes tactics once again. Pulling out a large knife, he hacks off one of the diplomat's fingers. Only then does this person finally give Bauer the information he seeks. International law, of course, forbids such actions, and Bauer is well aware of this fact. But Bauer feels he is only doing what's necessary to protect this country. The show is so popular that, in all probability, Bauer and other agents of CTU will go on beating, torturing, and killing terrorists on television for years to come. . . .

hy do we begin with a description of a popular television program that, in a sense, glorifies torture and violence—seemingly undertaken for "good" purposes—on a weekly basis? Because it illustrates a key point: **Aggression**—actions that intentionally inflict harm on others—is all around us, especially in the mass media. It is also frighteningly common in the lives of ordinary people who all too often come face-to-face with assault, rape, and murder, and other acts that have occurred on a massive scale throughout human history. Serial killings, wars, invasions, genocide—these are, sadly, a common part of the human story, from ancient times until the present.

Given the pervasiveness of violence, it is not surprising that social psychologists have sought for many years to obtain a greater understanding of aggression—new insights into its nature and causes. The ultimate goal of such research is to use our increased knowledge to develop techniques for reducing aggression in many different contexts (e.g., Anderson & Bushman, 2002b; Baumeister, 2005). To provide you with an overview of this valuable and rapidly expanding body of knowledge, we'll proceed as follows.

First, we'll describe several theoretical perspectives on aggression, contrasting views about its nature and origins. Next, we'll examine several important determinants of human aggression. These include social factors—the words or actions of other people, either "in the flesh" or as shown in the mass media (e.g., Fischer & Greitemeyer, 2006), cultural factors, such as norms, requiring that individuals respond aggressively to insults to their honor; aspects of personality—traits that predispose specific people toward aggressive outbursts; and situational factors—aspects of the external world such as high temperatures and alcohol. After examining the effects of all these factors, we'll turn our attention to two forms of aggression that are especially disturbing because they occur within the context of long-term relationships—bullying (repeated victimization of specific people by one or more other people) and workplace aggression. Finally, to conclude on an optimistic note, we'll examine various techniques for the prevention and control of aggression.

Perspectives on Aggression: In Search of the Roots of Violence

Why do human beings aggress against others? What makes them turn, with savage brutality, on their fellow human beings? Thoughtful people have pondered these questions for centuries and have proposed many contrasting explanations. Here, we'll examine several that have been especially influential, ending with those offered by social psychological research.

The Role of Biological Factors: From Instincts to the Evolutionary Perspective

The oldest and probably most famous explanation for human aggression suggests that human beings are somehow "programmed" for violence by their basic nature. Such theories attribute human violence to built-in (i.e., inherited) urges to aggress against others. The most famous supporter of this theory was Sigmund Freud, who held that aggression stems mainly from a powerful death wish (thanatos) possessed by all people. According to Freud, this instinct is initially aimed at self-destruction but is soon redirected outward toward others. A related view was proposed by Konrad Lorenz, a Nobel Prize-winning ethologist (Lorenz, 1966; 1974), who suggested that aggression springs mainly from an inherited fighting instinct, which assures that only the strongest males will obtain mates and pass their genes on to the next generation.

Until recently, most social psychologists rejected such ideas. Among the many reasons for their objections to the view that human aggression is genetically programmed were

aggression

Behavior directed toward the goal of harming another living being who is motivated to avoid such treatment.

these: (1) human beings aggress against others in many different ways—everything from ignoring them to performing overt acts of violence. How can such a huge range of behaviors all be determined by genetic factors? (2) The frequency of aggressive actions varies tremendously across human societies, so that it is much more likely to occur in some than in others (e.g., Fry, 1998). Again, social psychologists asked, "How can aggressive behavior be determined by genetic factors if such huge differences exist?"

Figure 10.1
Violence All around Us—and Certainly Present on Television
In one popular television show (24) agents of an imaginary federal agency (counter terrorist unit [CTU]) do their best to defeat terrorists. They are often shown using torture to force people who have been captured to reveal the details of their deadly plans.

With the growth of the evolutionary perspective in psychology, however, this situation has changed. While most social psychologists continue to reject the view that human aggression stems largely from innate factors, some now accept the possibility that genetic factors play *some* role in human aggression. For instance, consider the following reasoning based on an evolutionary perspective (see our discussion of this theory in Chapter 1). In the past (and even at present to some extent), males seeking desirable mates found it necessary to compete with other males. One way of eliminating such competition is through successful aggression, which drives such rivals away or even eliminates them entirely. Because males who were adept at such behavior may have been more successful in securing mates and in transmitting their genes to offspring, this may have lead to the development of a genetically influenced tendency for males to aggress against other males. In contrast, males would not be expected to possess a similar tendency to aggress against females; in fact, development of such tendencies might be discouraged because females would tend to reject as mates males who are aggressive toward them. As a result, males may have weaker tendencies to aggress against females than against other males. In contrast, females might aggress equally against males and females or even more frequently against males than other females. Research findings provide some evidence consistent with this reasoning—males tend to be more aggressive toward other males than toward females, while similar differences do not exist (or are weaker) among females (e.g., Hilton, Harris, & Rice, 2000) (As we'll note later in this chapter, though, gender differences in aggression are not nearly as large as many people seem to believe [Hawley, Card, & Little, 2007]). In any case, findings such as these have led some social psychologists to conclude that biological or genetic factors do indeed play a role in human aggression, although the size of this role continues to be the subject of spirited discussion. As we noted in Chapter 1, however, the fact that a given form of behavior is influenced by genetic factors does not mean that such behavior must occur or is an essential part of human nature. It simply means that a potential for engaging in such behavior exists, and is generated, at least in part, by biological factors.

Drive Theories: The Motive to Harm Others

When social psychologists rejected the instinct views of aggression proposed by Freud and Lorenz, they countered with an alternative of their own: the view that aggression stems mainly from an externally elicited drive to harm others. This approach is reflected in several different **drive theories** of aggression (e.g., Berkowitz, 1989; Feshbach, 1984).

drive theories (of aggression)
Theories suggesting that aggression stems from external conditions that arouse the motive to harm or injure others. The most famous of these is the frustration-aggression hypothesis.

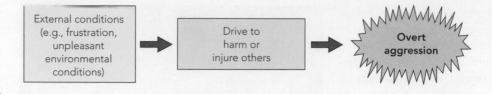

These theories propose that external conditions—especially frustration—arouse a strong motive to harm others. This aggressive drive, in turn, leads to overt acts of aggression (see Figure 10.2).

By far the most famous of these theories is the well-known **frustration-aggression hypothesis** (Dollard, Doob, Miller, Mowerer, & Sears, 1939). According to this view, frustration leads to the arousal of a drive whose primary goal is that of harming some person or object—primarily the perceived cause of frustration (Berkowitz, 1989). As we'll see in a later discussion, the central role assigned to frustration by the frustration-aggression hypothesis has turned out to be largely false: Frustration is only one of many different causes of aggression, and in fact, a relatively weak one. Moreover, aggression stems from many causes others than frustration. While social psychologists have largely rejected this theory, it still enjoys widespread acceptance outside our field, and you may sometimes hear your friends refer to it in such statements as: "He was so frustrated that he finally blew up," or "She was feeling frustrated, so she took it out on her roommate." We'll note in this chapter why such statements are often truly misleading.

Modern Theories of Aggression: The Social Learning Perspective and the General Aggression Model

Unlike earlier views, modern theories of aggression (e.g., Anderson & Bushman, 2002b; Berkowitz, 1993; Zillmann, 1994) do not focus on a single factor (instincts, drives, or frustration) as the primary cause of aggression. Rather, they draw on advances in many areas of psychology to gain added insight into the factors that play a role in the occurrence of such behavior. One such theory, known as the social learning perspective (e.g., Bandura, 1997) begins with a reasonable idea: Human beings are not born with a large array of aggressive responses at their disposal. Rather, they must acquire these in the much the same way that they acquire other complex forms of social behavior: through direct experience or by observing the behavior of others (i.e., social models—live people or characters on television, in movies, or even in video games who behave aggressively (Anderson, 2004; Anderson & Bushman, 2001; Bushman & Anderson, 2002). Thus depending on their past experience and the cultures in which they live, individuals learn (1) various ways of seeking to harm others (see Figure 10.3), (2) which people or groups are appropriate targets for aggression, (3) what actions by others justify retaliation or vengeance on their part, and (4) what situations or contexts are ones in which aggression is permitted or even approved. In short, the social learning perspective suggests that whether a specific person will aggress in a given situation depends on many factors, including this person's past experience, the current rewards associated with past or present aggression, and attitudes and values that shape this person's thoughts concerning the appropriateness and potential effects of such behavior.

Building on the social learning perspective, a newer framework known as the **general aggression model (GAM)** provides an even more complete account of the foundations of human aggression (Anderson, 1997; Anderson & Bushman, 2002b). According to this theory, a chain of events that may ultimately lead to overt aggression can be initiated by two major types of input variables—(1) factors relating to the current situation (situational factors) and (2) factors relating to the people involved (personal factors). Variables falling into the first category include frustration, some kind of provocation from another person

frustration-aggression hypothesis
The suggestion that frustration is a very powerful determinant of aggression.

general aggression model (GAM)
A modern theory of aggression suggesting that aggression is triggered by a wide range of input variables that influence arousal, affective stages, and cognitions.

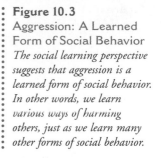

Figure 10.3
Aggression: A Learned Form of Social Behavior
The social learning perspective suggests that aggression is a learned form of social behavior. In other words, we learn various ways of harming others, just as we learn many other forms of social behavior.

(e.g., an insult), exposure to other people behaving aggressively (aggressive models, real or in the media), and virtually anything that causes individuals to experience discomfort—everything from uncomfortably high temperatures to a dentist's drill or even an extremely dull lecture. Variables in the second category (individual differences across people), include traits that predispose some individuals toward aggression (e.g., high irritability), certain attitudes and beliefs about violence (e.g., believing that it is acceptable and appropriate), a tendency to perceive hostile intentions in others' behavior, and specific skills related to aggression (e.g., knowing how to fight or how to use various weapons).

According to the GAM, these situational and individual (personal) variables lead to overt aggression through their impact on three basic processes: arousal—they may increase physiological arousal or excitement; affective states—they can arouse hostile feelings and outward signs of these (e.g., angry facial expressions); and cognitions—they can induce individuals to think hostile thoughts or can bring beliefs and attitudes about aggression to mind. Depending on individuals' interpretations (appraisals) of the current situation and restraining factors (e.g., the presence of police or the threatening nature of the intended target person), they then engage either in thoughtful action, which might involve restraining their anger, or impulsive action, which can lead to overt aggressive actions occur (see Figure 10.4 on page 342 for an overview of this theory.)

Bushman and Anderson (e.g., 2002) have expanded this theory to explain why individuals who are exposed to high levels of aggression, directly, in the actions of others, or in films and video games, may tend to become increasingly aggressive themselves. Repeated exposure to such stimuli serves to strengthen knowledge structures related to aggression—beliefs, attitudes, schemas, and scripts relevant to aggression (refer to Chapter 2). As these knowledge structures related to aggression grow stronger, it is easier for these to be activated by situational or personal variables. The result is that the people in question are truly primed for aggression.

The GAM is certainly more complex than earlier theories of aggression (e.g., the famous frustration-aggression hypothesis; Dollard et al., 1939). In addition, because it fully reflects recent progress in the field, it seems much more likely to provide an accurate view of the nature of human aggression than these earlier theories—and that, of course, is what scientific progress is all about!

> *Principles to Remember*
>
> Aggression does not stem from one or just a few factors. Rather, it is the result of a large number of variables operating together. Therefore, views like the famous frustration-aggression theory are truly misleading.

Figure 10.4
The GAM: A Modern Theory of Human Aggression

As shown here, the general aggression model (GAM) suggests that human aggression stems from many different factors. Input variables relating to the situation or person influence cognitions, affect, and arousal, and these internal states plus other factors, such as appraisal and decision mechanism, determine whether, and in what form, aggression occurs.

(*Source:* Based on suggestions by Bushman and Anderson, 2002.)

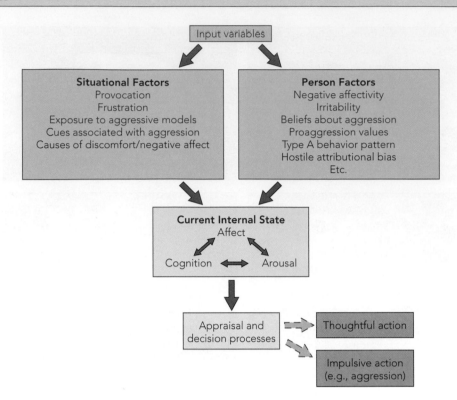

KeyPoints

- Aggression is the intentional infliction of harm on others. While most social psychologists reject the view that human aggression is strongly determined by genetic factors, evolutionary-oriented theorists claim that genetic factors play some role in such behavior.

- Drive theories suggest that aggression stems from externally elicited drives to harm or injure others. The frustration-aggression hypothesis is the most famous example of such theories.

- Modern theories of aggression, such as the general aggression model (GAM) recognize the impor-

tance in aggression of learning, various eliciting input variables, individual differences, affective states, and especially, cognitive processes.

Think About It

If aggression actually stems from many different factors rather than from just one or a few factors (e.g., frustration), does that fact make it harder or easier to control?

Causes of Human Aggression: Social, Cultural, Personal, and Situational

Think back to the last time you lost your temper. What made you blow your cool? Was it something another person said or did, such as a condescending remark, or something that made you feel jealous (e.g., Marshall & Brown, 2006)? Was it something about yourself—are you easily annoyed, do you perceive that others often treat you unfairly? Or was it something about the situation: Had you been drinking or was the weather hot and steamy? In fact, research findings indicate that all of these factors—plus many others—

can play a role in human aggression. To make understanding the broad range of these factors easier, we'll discuss them under four categories: social, cultural, personal, and situational factors that can sometimes trigger aggression.

Social Determinants of Aggression: Frustration, Provocation, and Heightened Arousal

Aggression, like other forms of social behavior, is often a response to something in the social world around us. Specifically, it often occurs in response to something other people have said or done. In other words, individuals aggress because the words or deeds of other people provoke them (i.e., anger, annoy, or irritate them). Here, we describe several ways in which this can—and often does—occur.

Frustration: Why Not Getting What You Want (or What You Expect) Can Sometimes Lead to Aggression

Suppose that you asked twenty people you know to name the single most important cause of aggression. What would they say? The chances are good that most would reply frustration. And if you asked them to define frustration, many would state: "the way I feel when something—or someone—prevents me from getting what I want or expect to get in some situation." This widespread belief in the importance of frustration as a cause of aggression stems, at least in part, from the famous frustration-aggression hypothesis mentioned in our discussion of drive theories of aggression (Dollard et al., 1939). In it is original form, this hypothesis made two sweeping assertions: (1) Frustration always leads to some form of aggression, and (2) aggression always stems from frustration. In short, the theory held that frustrated people always engage in some type of aggression and that all acts of aggression, in turn, result from frustration. Bold statements like these are appealing, but this doesn't imply that they are necessarily accurate. In fact, existing evidence suggests that both portions of the frustration-aggression hypothesis assign far too much importance to frustration as a determinant of human aggression. When frustrated, individuals do *not* always respond with aggression. On the contrary, they show many different reactions, ranging from sadness, despair, and depression on the one hand to direct attempts to overcome the source of their frustration on the other. In short, aggression is definitely not an automatic response to frustration.

Second, it is equally clear that not all aggression stems from frustration. People aggress for many different reasons and in response to many different factors. For example, professional boxers hit their opponents because they wish to win valued prizes—not because of frustration. Similarly, the agents of CTU on the television show *24* do not attack or torture terrorists because they have been frustrated by these people. Rather they do it out of a sense of duty and patriotism. In other words, they aggress for relatively instrumental reasons—to get what they want and not as a reactions to intense frustration. In these and many other cases, aggression stems from factors other than frustration. We'll consider some of these other causes of aggression.

In view of these facts (which are summarized in Figure 10.5 on page 344), few social psychologists now accept the idea that frustration is the only, or even the most important, cause of aggression. Instead, most believe that it is simply one of many factors that can potentially lead to aggression. We should add that frustration can serve as a powerful determinant of aggression under certain conditions—especially when it is viewed as illegitimate or unjustified (e.g., Folger & Baron, 1996). For instance, if a student believes that she deserves a good grade on a term paper but then receives a poor one, with no explanation, she may conclude that she has been treated very unfairly—that her legitimate needs have been thwarted. The result: She may have hostile thoughts, experience intense anger, and seek revenge against the perceived source of such frustration—in this case, her professor.

Figure 10.5
Frustration: Not the Major Cause of Aggression Most People Believe
Although many people continue to believe that frustration is a major cause of aggression, decades of careful research indicate that this view is incorrect. Aggression stems from many different factors—not solely from frustration; and aggression is not the inevitable result of being frustrated.

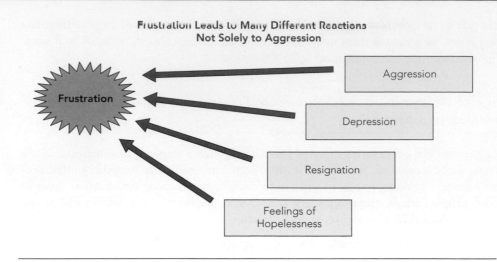

Frustration Leads to Many Different Reactions
Not Solely to Aggression

Frustration

Aggression

Depression

Resignation

Feelings of
Hopelessness

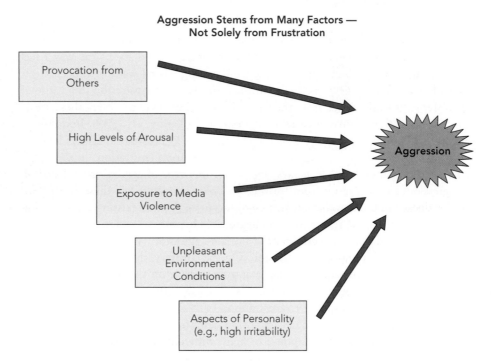

Aggression Stems from Many Factors —
Not Solely from Frustration

Provocation from
Others

High Levels of Arousal

Exposure to Media
Violence

Unpleasant
Environmental
Conditions

Aspects of Personality
(e.g., high irritability)

Aggression

Direct Provocation: When Aggression (or Even Teasing) Breeds Aggression

Major world religions generally agree in suggesting that, when provoked by another person, we should "turn the other cheek"; in other words, the most appropriate way to respond to being annoyed or irritated by another person is to do our best to ignore this treatment. In fact, however, research findings indicate that this is easier to say than to do, and that physical or verbal **provocation** from others is one of the strongest causes of human aggression. When we are on the receiving end of some form of aggression from others—criticism we consider unfair, sarcastic remarks, or physical assaults—we tend to reciprocate, returning as much aggression as we have received. Or, perhaps even more, especially if we are certain that the other person meant to harm us (Ohbuchi & Kambara, 1985).

What kinds of provocation produce the strongest push toward aggression? Existing evidence suggests that condescension—expressions of arrogance or disdain on the part of others are powerful (Harris, 1993). Harsh and unjustified criticism, especially criticism that attacks us rather than our behavior, is another powerful form of provocation, and when exposed to it, most people find it difficult to avoid getting angry and retaliating in some manner, either immediately or later on (Baron, 1993b). Still another form of provo-

provocation
Actions by others that tend to trigger aggression in the recipient, often because they are perceived as stemming from malicious intent.

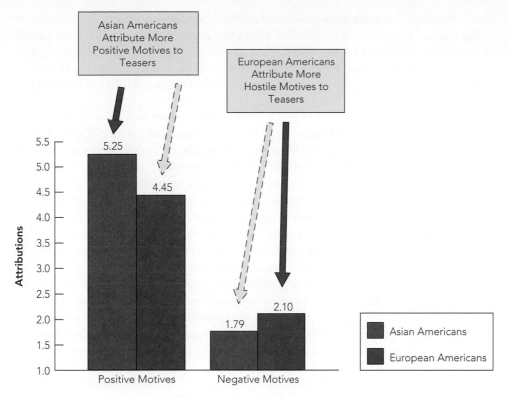

Figure 10.6
Teasing: Sometimes, a Social Cause of Aggression
Teasing is common in social interactions. If it is attributed to hostile motives—a desire to hurt or embarrass the recipient—it can serve as an important source of provocation. As shown here, though, people of European descent (European Americans) are more likely to perceive teasing as hostile than persons of Asian descent (Asian Americans), so cultural factors play a key role in determining the effects of teasing. Higher numbers mean attribution to positive motives; lower numbers mean attribution to hostile motives.

(*Source:* Based on data from Campos, Keltner, Beck, Gonzaga, & John, 2007.)

cation to which many people respond with annoyance is **teasing**—provoking statements that call attention to individual's flaws and imperfections, but can be, at the same time, somewhat playful in nature (e.g., Kowalski, 2001).

Teasing can range from mild, humorous remarks (e.g., "Hey, you look like your hair just went through an electric mixer!") and humorous nicknames (e.g., "Slim"—for an overweight person) to comments that seem more designed to hurt than amuse (e.g., "Is that really you or are you wearing a fat suit?"). Research findings indicate that the more individuals attribute teasing to hostile motives—a desire to embarrass or annoy them—the more likely they are to respond aggressively (Campos, Keltner, Beck, Gonzaga, & John, 2007). But large cultural differences exist in this regard. People from individualist cultures (e.g., the United States, Western Europe) are strongly concerned with establishing a sense of uniqueness and a positive public image. Those from collectivist cultures, in contrast (e.g., many Asian cultures), are less concerned with uniqueness and more concerned with getting along well with others and being part of the larger group. These differences in perspective suggest that people in individualist cultures should respond more negatively to teasing than people in collectivist cultures, and this prediction has recently been confirmed (Campos et al., 2007). When asked to describe instances of teasing in their own lives, individuals who identified themselves as Asian Americans reported more positive reactions to such events and attributed less hostility to teasing than did European Americans (see Figure 10.6). Because Asian cultures tend to be collectivist in orientation and U.S. culture is strongly individualist in nature, these findings suggest that cultural factors do indeed strongly determine how individuals react to teasing—as a form of provocation (in U.S. culture) or as a humorous exchange designed to enhance personal closeness (in Asian cultures).

Heightened Arousal: Emotion, Cognition, and Aggression

Suppose that you are driving to the airport to meet a friend. On the way there, another driver cuts you off, and you almost have an accident. Your heart pounds wildly and your

teasing
Provoking statements that call attention to the target's flaws and imperfections.

excitation transfer theory
A theory suggesting that arousal produced in one situation can persist and intensify emotional reactions occurring in later situations.

blood pressure shoots through the roof, but fortunately, no accident occurs. Now you arrive at the airport. You park and rush inside. When you get to the security check, an elderly man in front of you sets off the buzzer. He becomes confused and can't seem to understand that the security guard wants him to take off his shoes. You are irritated by this delay. In fact, you begin to lose your temper and mutter "What's wrong with him? Can't he figure it out?"

Now for the key question: Do you think that your recent near miss in traffic may have played any role in your sudden surge of anger? Could the emotional arousal from that incident have somehow transferred to the scene inside the airport? Growing evidence suggests that it could (Zillmann, 1988; 1994). Under some conditions, heightened arousal—whatever its source—can enhance aggression in response to provocation, frustration, or other factors. In fact, in various experiments, arousal stemming from such varied sources as participation in competitive games (Christy, Gelfand, & Hartmann, 1971), exercise (Zillmann, 1979), and even some types of music (Rogers & Ketcher, 1979) has been found to increase subsequent aggression. Why is this the case? A compelling explanation is offered by **excitation transfer theory** (Zillmann, 1983; 1988).

This theory suggests that because physiological arousal tends to dissipate slowly over time, a portion of such arousal may persist as a person moves from one situation to another. In the example, some portion of the arousal you experienced because of the near miss in traffic may still be present as you approach the security gate in the airport. Now when you encounter a minor annoyance, that arousal intensifies your emotional reactions to the annoyance. The result: You become enraged rather than just mildly irritated. Excitation theory further suggests that such effects are most likely to occur when the people involved are relatively unaware of the presence of residual arousal—a common occurrence because small elevations in arousal are difficult to notice (Zillmann, 1994). Excitation transfer theory also suggests that such effects are likely to occur when the people involved recognize their residual arousal but attribute it to events occurring in the present situation (Taylor, Helgeson, Reed, & Skokan, 1991). In the airport incident, for instance, your anger would be intensified if you recognized your feelings of arousal but attributed them to the elderly man's actions rather than the driver who nearly cut you off (see Figure 10.7.)

Figure 10.7
Excitation Transfer Theory
This theory suggests that arousal occurring in one situation can persist and intensify emotional reactions in later, unrelated situations. For instance, the arousal produced by a near miss in traffic can intensify feelings of annoyance stemming from delays at an airport security gate.

(*Source:* Based on suggestions by Zillmann, 1994.)

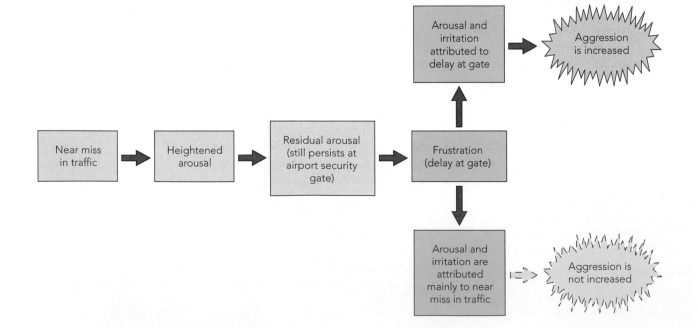

Exposure to Media Violence: Effects of Violence in Films, on Television, and in Video Games

Think about the films and television programs you have seen in recent weeks. How much aggression or violence did each contain? How often did characters in these movies or television shows hit, shoot at, or otherwise attempt to harm others? Probably, often because there is no doubt that violence is frequent in the popular offerings of the mass media (Bushman & Anderson, 2002a; Reiss & Roth, 1993; Waters, Block, Friday, & Gordon, 1993).

This fact raises an important question that social psychologists have studied for decades: Does exposure to such materials increase aggression among children or adults? Literally hundreds of studies have been performed to test this possibility, and the results seem clear: Exposure to media violence may indeed be one factor contributing to high levels of violence in countries where such materials are viewed by large numbers of people (e.g., Anderson, Berkowitz, et al., 2003; Paik & Comstock, 1994; Wood, Wong, & Cachere, 1991). In fact, in a summary of research findings in this area (Anderson et al., 2004), leading experts on this topic who have provided testimony in U.S. Senate hearings on media and violence offered the following basic conclusions:

1. Research on exposure to violent television, movies, video games, and music indicates that such materials significantly increase the likelihood of aggressive behavior by people exposed to them.

2. Such effects are both short term and long term in nature.

3. The magnitude of these effects is large—at least as large as the various medical effects considered to be important by physicians (e.g., the effect of aspirin on heart attacks).

In other words, social psychology's leading experts on the effects of media violence agree that these effects are real, lasting, and important—effects with important implications for society and for the safety and well-being of millions of people who are the victims of aggressive actions each year.

Many different types of research support these conclusions. For example, in short-term laboratory experiments, children or adults exposed to violent films and television programs have been found to show more aggression than others exposed to nonviolent films or programs (e.g., Bushman & Huesmann, 2001). Some of these studies are true classics in social psychology and had important effects on subsequent research. We describe them in detail in *Building the Science: Classics of Social Psychology* on pages 348–349.

Other research on the effects of media violence, in contrast, has employed longitudinal procedures, in which the same participants are studied for many years (e.g., Anderson & Bushman, 2002b; Huesmann & Eron, 1984; 1986). Results of such research, too, are clear: The more violent films or television programs participants watched as children, the higher their levels of aggression as teenagers or adults are—for instance, the higher the likelihood that they have been arrested for violent crimes. Such findings have been replicated in many different countries—Australia, Finland, Israel, Poland, and South Africa (Botha, 1990). Thus they appear to hold across different cultures. Further, such effects are not restricted only to actual programs or films; they appear to be produced by violence in news programs, by violent lyrics in popular music (e.g., Anderson, Carnagey, & Eubanks, 2003), and by violent video games (Anderson, 2004; Anderson & Bushman, 2001). For instance, in a study by Bartholow, Bushman, and Sestir (2006), individuals who reported that they had often played violent video games in the past directed more aggression against another person who had done nothing to provoke them than people who had rarely played such games. Aggression was measured in the context of a competitive reaction time task in which the slower player on each trial would receive a blast of loud noise, the intensity of which was set by the winner. As shown in Figure 10.9 on page 349, the more participants in the study had played violent video games in the past, the stronger the aggression they directed to their "opponent" on trials when they won.

BUILDING THE SCIENCE
CLASSICS OF SOCIAL PSYCHOLOGY

Bandura's Famous "Bobo Doll" Studies: Televised Violence Visits the Laboratory

Does exposure to violence in television programs increase aggression among young children? That was the question Albert Bandura and others addressed in the early 1960s—a time when social psychology was still, in many respects, a new and rapidly growing science. To address this question, Bandura's team of researchers (e.g., Bandura, Ross, & Ross, 1963a; 1963b) devised an ingenious approach. Instead of using actual television programs, they constructed their own TV shows in which an adult model was shown aggressing against a large inflated toy clown (a Bobo doll) in unusual ways. For instance, the model sat on the doll, punched it repeatedly in the nose, struck it on the head with a toy mallet, and kicked it about the room. This "program" or one in which the model showed no aggressive actions toward the Bobo doll was then shown to nursery school-age children.

Following exposure to one of the two programs, the children were placed in a room containing many toys, several of which had been used by the adult model in his or her attacks against the doll. They were allowed to play freely for twenty minutes, and during this period their behavior was carefully observed to see if, perhaps, they would show actions similar those of the model in the aggressive program. Results were clear: Young children exposed to the actions of an aggressive adult model showed strong tendencies to imitate these behaviors (see Figure 10.8). In contrast, those exposed to a nonaggres-

Figure 10.8
Bandura's "Bobo Doll" Studies: Early Evidence for the Effects of Televised Violence
In these famous studies, children saw a "television program" in which an adult model either attacked an inflated plastic doll (top) or sat quietly. When given a chance to play with the same toys, children imitated the actions of the aggressive model (middle, bottom). These findings suggested that exposure to violence in the media may lead to similar actions by viewers.

(Photos Copyright 1963, American Psychological Association; Reproduced with permission from Albert Bandura.)

sive adult model (the one who sat quietly in the room and didn't attack the inflated doll) did not show similar actions.

Bandura and his associates reasoned that the children had learned new ways of aggressing from the program they watched, and that in a similar manner, children could also learn new ways of aggressing against others and also learn that aggression is an acceptable form of behavior from watching actual television shows and films.

Although Bandura's research was criticized by other researchers—and the television industry—as demonstrating simply that children imitate certain kinds of play rather than aggression, this early research soon gripped the attention of many social psychologists and led to a large number of studies designed to address this and other issues. For instance, in one such study, Liebert and Baron (1972) exposed children to excerpts from a highly violent television show (*The Untouchables*) or to a nonaggressive but equally exciting film of a horse race. Then children in both groups were provided with a chance to either hurt or help another child by pushing red and green buttons. The children who watched the aggressive television program showed greater willingness to hurt the other child than those who watched the nonaggressive film. (The other child was imaginary, so no one was ever hurt in any way.)

In a sense, then, the early Bobo doll studies started a process in which social psychologists used more and more sophisticated research methods to answer the basic question with which Bandura began: Does exposure to media violence make viewers more likely to aggress? As we have already noted, the answer, unfortunately, appears to be a strong and clear yes.

As the experts on media violence mentioned above put it: "The cup of research knowledge about violence in the media is relatively full. . . . It . . . supports sustained concern about media violence and sustained efforts to curb its adverse effects" (Anderson, Berkowitz, et al., 2003, p. 105).

The Effects of Media Violence: Why Do They Occur?

By now, you may be wondering about a basic question: Why does exposure to media violence (of many different kinds) increase aggression among people exposed to it? A com-

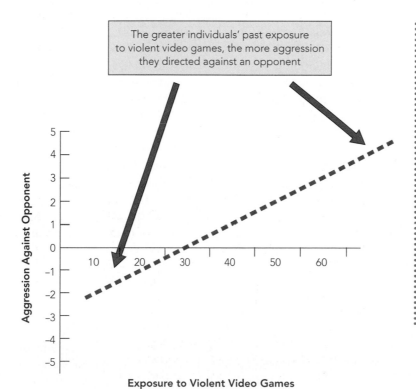

The greater individuals' past exposure to violent video games, the more aggression they directed against an opponent

Figure 10.9

Exposure to Violent Video Games: One Factor in Aggression
The more individuals had played violent video games in their past lives, the more aggressive they were toward an opponent in a competitive reaction time task. (On each trial, the "loser" received a blast of noise, and the intensity of this noise was set by the "winner.") These findings are consistent with the view that long-term exposure to media violence increases the tendency to aggress against others.

(*Source:* Based on data from Bartholow, Bushman, & Sestir, 2006).

pelling answer has been provided recently by Bushman and Anderson (2002), who suggest that the effects of media violence can be readily understood within the context of the GAM presented previously in this chapter. As you may recall, this model suggests that both personal and situational factors influence individuals' internal states—their feelings, thoughts, and arousal—and that these internal states, in turn, shape individuals' appraisal of a given situation and their decision as to how to behave in it—aggressively or nonaggressively. Bushman and Anderson suggest that repeated exposure to media violence can strongly affect cognitions relating to aggression, gradually creating a hostile expectation bias—a strong expectation that others will behave aggressively. This, in turn, causes individuals to be more aggressive themselves; after all, they perceive provocations from others everywhere, even when they really don't exist. Studies designed to test this reasoning have generated results consistent with it, so it appears that the GAM and the processes it describes do indeed play an important role in the effects of media violence.

The Effects of Media Violence: Neuroscience Evidence for the Impact of Desensitization

One other factor that may also play an important role is desensitization to violence. In other words, as a result of exposure to large amounts of violent content in television programs, films, and video games, individuals become less sensitive to violence and its consequences (Anderson, Carnagey, et al., 2003). Research findings suggest that such effects do occur and can contribute to increased aggression by persons exposed to media violence (e.g., Funk, Bechtoldt-Baldacci, Pasold, et al, 2004). Perhaps the most dramatic evidence for such desensitization, however, is provided by research using a social neuroscience perspective.

Actually, the research we described previously by Bartholow and others (2006) provides a clear example of this approach. As you may recall, individuals in that study reported on the extent to which they had played violent and nonviolent video games in the past and then participated in a competitive reaction time task in which they could determine the loudness of unpleasant sounds delivered to another person (who did not actually exist) when that person lost the competition. Before playing the competitive game, participants first viewed a series of neutral images (e.g., a man on a bicycle) and violent images (e.g., one person holding a gun to another person's head). Activity in their brains was recorded while they watched these images. In particular, activity that had been found in previous research to indicate the extent to which incoming emotion-provoking stimuli are being processed and categorized was carefully analyzed. (This is known as P300 activity—one kind of event-related brain potential, which are changes in brain activity that occur as certain kinds of information are processed). Presumably, if individuals have been desensitized to violent images by their past experience in playing video games, P300 activity would be smaller when they view violent images. In fact that's exactly what happened: Individuals who had previously played violent video games frequently showed smaller P300 reactions when viewing violent images than individuals who reported previously having played mainly nonviolent games. These findings suggest that exposure to media violence does indeed desensitize the people who view it. Other findings (e.g., Bartholow et al., 2006) indicate that the degree of such desensitization, in turn, predicts the likelihood that such people will aggress against others.

Overall, it appears that exposure to violence in films, television, or video games increases the tendency to aggress against others in several ways. First, as we just saw, it reduces individuals' emotional reactions to such events so that, in a sense, they perceive them as nothing out of the ordinary. Second, it strengthens beliefs, expectations, and other cognitive processes related to aggression. In other words, as a result of repeated exposure to violent movies, TV programs, or violent video games, individuals develop strong *knowledge structures* relating to aggression—structures reflecting and combining these beliefs, expectations, schemas, and scripts. When these knowledge structures are then activated by various events, such people feel, think, and act aggressively because this is what, in a sense, they have learned to do.

Whatever the precise underlying mechanisms, forty years of research on this issue suggests strongly that exposure to media violence can have harmful effects on society. So why, then, is there so much of it on television, in movies, and in video games? The answer, sad to relate, is that violence sells—people seem to find it exciting and enjoyable. Moreover, advertisers assume this is true and "put their money where the action is" (Bushman, 1998). In short, this is one more case in which economic motives take precedence over everything else. We know what to do, as a society, with respect to media violence: We should reduce it, if decreasing violence is our goal. But as long as people are willing to pay to see aggressive shows and films or buy violent games, there seems little chance this will happen. But we are optimists by nature so we can always hope!

Violent Pornography: When Sex and Aggression Mix— and Perhaps Explode!

When we lecture, we sometimes notice students in our classes who are gazing intently at the screens of their laptop computers. No, they are not taking notes—they seem to be largely unaware of what the professor is saying or doing. And occasionally, when I pass by their seats quietly, I notice that what they are watching is . . . pornography of some type. This doesn't happen often, but the fact that it happens at all brings an important point into focus: Pornographic images are now freely available to virtually everyone—including, unfortunately—children. And, disturbingly, some of this material includes violent content, in which victims—usually, but not always, women—are abused, exploited, and harmed in various ways (e.g., Linz, Fuson, & Donnerstein, 1990; Malamuth & Check, 1985).

If exposure to violence in the media can increase aggressive tendencies among people exposed to such content, it seems possible that exposure to violent pornography might also produce such effects. In fact, because pornography often generates high levels of arousal (both negative and positive emotions), it is possible that such effects might even be stronger than is true for media violence that does not contain sexual content. While there is currently much less evidence on this issue than on the effects of media violence generally, some findings suggest that violent pornography may indeed have negative effects. For instance, laboratory studies (e.g., Linz, Donnerstein, & Penrod, 1988) indicate that exposure to violent pornography can increase men's willingness to aggress against women. Perhaps even more disturbing, repeated exposure to such materials appears to produce the kind of desensitizing effect we described previously; in this case, such desensitization reduces emotional reactions to mistreatment or harm to sexual victims so that the people who view them and who have been desensitized no longer find such images highly disturbing. Finally, and most unsettling of all, exposure to violent pornography seems to encourage adoption of callous attitudes toward sexual violence, leading both women and men to accept dangerous myths about rape and other forms of sexual violence—for example, the myth that many women unconsciously want to be raped or that almost all victims of rape are promiscuous and place themselves in situations where they are likely to be sexually assaulted (Malamuth & Brown, 1994).

In sum, growing availability of pornography—and especially pornography that includes themes of sexual violence—appears to be a dangerous trend. No, not all people who are exposed to such materials become more willing to engage in such behavior themselves. But growing evidence suggests that the mixture of sex and violence contained in such pornography can be a dangerous and volatile one indeed! (Please read *Social Psychology: What It Tells Us About* . . . on page 352 for a discussion of the effects of yet another type of violence in the media—violent lyrics in popular music.

SOCIALPSYCHOLOGY

The Effects of Sexually Aggressive Song Lyrics

*"Don't put out? I'll put you out
Won't get out? I'll push you out . . .
Am I too nice? Buy you ice
Bitch, if you died, wouldn't buy you life . . ."*

("Superman," Eminem)

*"You're just a little boy
Think you're so cute, so coy
You must talk so big, to make up for smaller things
You're just a little boy
All you'll do is annoy . . ."*

("Can't Hold Us Down," Christina Aguilera)

Lyrics like these are far from rare in certain kinds of popular music, and as you probably know, these are relatively mild! Such lyrics express negative views toward the other sex and often present images of violence, especially during sexual relations. Disturbingly, songs containing such words are popular. For instance Eminem, one well-known singer famous for his aggressive lyrics, recently sold 7.4 million copies of a single album (*The Eminem Show*). Clearly, then, large numbers of people—especially young men and women (who typically report listening to between half an hour and one hour of music every day) are exposed to these songs and their highly aggressive lyrics on a regular basis. This raises an important question: What are the effects of long-term exposure to such words? Recent research by social psychologists suggests that these effects may be parallel to those of exposure to violent images in films, on television, and in video games.

For instance, in one carefully conducted series of studies, Fischer and Greitemeyer (2006) had male and female participants listen to either songs with neutral lyrics (songs that had no sexually aggressive content), misogynous songs (ones that expressed negative attitudes toward women and described sexual aggression against them), and men-hating songs (ones that contained lyrics expressing negative attitudes and aggression toward men). After exposure to these songs, they performed a word completion task designed to measure the extent to which these songs stimulated aggressive thoughts and ideas. Finally, they were told that the study was over but were asked to help with another experiment designed to examine the relationships between temperature and intellectual performance. They were told that as part of this study, another person would have to keep her or his arm in icy cold water—a very painful experience—and were asked to indicate how long this treatment should continue. The longer the time they suggested, the greater their aggression against this person (who, of course, did not really exist but was described to participants as being either a man or a woman).

As you can see from Figure 10.10, results indicated that as compared to songs with neutral lyrics, songs with misogynous lyrics increased aggression by men against a female victim, and songs with men-hating lyrics increased aggression by women against a male victim. In other words, the aggressive lyrics of these popular songs produced effects similar to those generated by other forms of media violence.

Cultural Factors in Aggression: "Cultures of Honor" and Sexual Jealousy

While aggression is often triggered by the words or deeds of other people, it can also stem from cultural factors—beliefs, norms, and expectations in a given culture suggesting that aggression is appropriate or perhaps even required under certain circumstances. Social psychologists have taken careful note of this fact in recent research on what is known as **cultures of honor**—cultures in which there are strong norms indicating that aggression is an appropriate response to insults to one's honor. This is a theme in many films about the old West, in which characters felt compelled to have a shoot-out with another person because their honor had somehow been sullied and is also seen in Asian films that present epic battles between warriors who possess seemingly magical powers (see Figure 10.11).

Why did such norms develop? Cohen and Nisbett (1994; 1997) suggest that they may be traced to the fact that in some geographic areas, wealth was once concentrated

cultures of honor
Cultures in which there are strong norms indicating that aggression is an appropriate response to insults to one's honor.

Figure 10.10

Effects of Sexually Aggressive Song Lyrics

Men exposed to sexually aggressive songs (misogynous) were more aggressive toward a female victim than men exposed to either neutral songs or ones with men-hating lyrics. Women exposed to songs with men-hating lyrics were more aggressive toward a male victim than women exposed to either neutral or misogynous lyrics. These findings suggest that the sexually aggressive lyrics found in many popular songs may, like violent images in films and movies, contribute to increased aggression among the people exposed to them.

(*Source:* Based on data from Fischer & Greitemeyer, 2006).

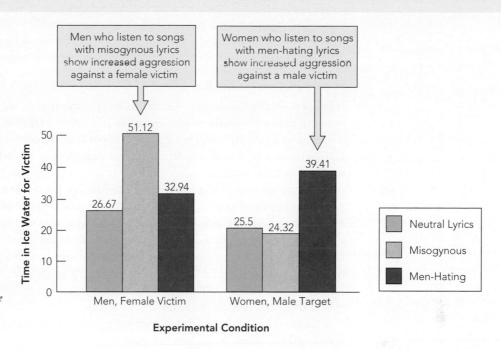

As noted by Fischer and Greitemeyer (2006), these findings are especially disturbing because they were produced by exposure to just a few songs; in real life, in contrast, people listen to these songs dozens or hundreds of times. So are violent lyrics in popular songs harmful? While representatives of the mass media often contend that this is a matter of opinion (just as defenders of the tobacco industry once made similar claims about the harmful effects of smoking), we believe that the scientific evidence is clear: Yes, such songs do produce harmful effects. But where we go from here—what we do about this fact—is more complex and can only be resolved through continuing and highly complex political processes.

mainly in assets that could readily be stolen (e.g., cattle and, sadly, slaves). For this reason, it became important for individuals to demonstrate that they would not tolerate such thefts or any other affront to their honor. The result? Norms condoning violence in response to insults to one's honor emerged and were widely accepted.

Recent findings indicate that such norms are definitely

Figure 10.11

Cultures of Honor: Norms Requiring Aggression

In cultures of honor, there are strong norms suggesting that insults to one's honor must be avenged through aggression. This theme is captured in the gunfights that featured prominently in many films about the Old West and, as shown here, in recent films about warriors in Asia.

not a thing of the past; on the contrary, they are alive and well in many parts of the world (e.g., Vandello & Cohen, 2003). For instance, in one recent study, Caucasian baseball pitchers were more likely to hit batters in situations in which their honor had been, in a sense, insulted: after another batter had hit a homerun or after one of their own team-mates had been hit by a pitched ball (Timmerman, 2007). While cultural beliefs con-doning or even requiring aggression in response to affronts to one's honor operate in many different contexts, their impact is especially apparent with respect to sexual jealousy.

Sexual Jealousy: One Key Effect of Concern with One's Honor

Infidelity—real or imagined—occurs in every society, even in ones that greatly restrict informal contact between women and men. In cultures of honor, such behavior by women is viewed as especially threatening to male honor (e.g., Baker, Gregware, & Cassidy, 1999) and can result in drastic responses—severe punishment for both the women and men involved in such contacts.

Even in cultures of honor where such actions are not condoned (e.g., cultures in South America), crimes of passion, in which husbands murder their wives or their wives' lovers, are condoned, at least to a degree. In these cultures, sexual infidelity by a wife or lover is viewed as the ultimate insult to a male's honor, so when men take action to restore their honor, it is viewed not merely as justified, but perhaps as actually required. As one saying from such a culture puts it: "Only blood can restore lost honor." This suggests that in cul-tures of honor, jealousy will be a powerful determinant of aggression—more powerful than it is in other cultures. Is this true?

Clear evidence on this issue is provided by research conducted by Vandello and Cohen (1999; 2003). These social psychologists reasoned that the code of male honor is espe-cially strong in Latin America and in the southern part United States. Thus situations that induce jealousy would be expected to produce stronger aggressive reactions by jealous peo-ple in those cultures than in others. Moreover, people in honor-oriented cultures should tend to be more accepting of such aggression than people in other cultures (e.g., Nisbett & Cohen, 1996).

To test these ideas, the researchers conducted several kinds of studies, but among these, perhaps the most interesting is one in which participants witnessed an interaction between a couple (both were assistants of the researchers) in which the female stated that she was planning to visit her ex-boyfriend's house. The male in the couple indicated that he did not want her to do that, and the exchange between them became increasingly heated until the male grabbed the woman's car keys and pushed her roughly against the wall. Then he left. At this point, the female turned to the participant, who had been pre-sent during this scene, and either expressed contrition, explaining that "My fiancé really cares about me, and I guess that's just how he shows it," or anger "That was my fiancé. He gets so jealous sometimes. . . . I'm getting so damn tired of this, you know?"

Later, participants, who were from the northern part of the United States, the south-ern part of the United States, or were of Hispanic descent, rated their impressions of the woman. As predicted, participants from the South and those who were of Hispanic Amer-ican descent rated her more favorably when she reacted with tolerance to her fiancé's mis-treatment than when she reacted with anger (see Figure 10.12). Participants from the North generally showed the opposite pattern. In other words, participants in the study who came from cultures of honor reacted favorably to the forgiving woman because she was showing the kind of reaction that would help to restore her partner's compromised honor.

Overall, the findings reported by Vandello and Cohen (2003) and others (Puente & Cohen, 2003) indicate that jealousy is indeed a powerful cause of aggression, and that, moreover, violence stemming from it—or from other factors that threaten a man's honor—are excused or condoned, at least to a degree, in cultures of honor. Clearly, then, cultural factors play a vital role in both the occurrence of aggression and in how it is perceived and evaluated.

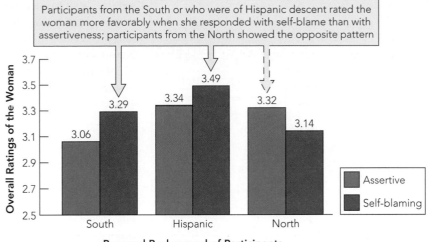

Participants from the South or who were of Hispanic descent rated the woman more favorably when she responded with self-blame than with assertiveness; participants from the North showed the opposite pattern

Figure 10.12
Sexual Jealousy in Cultures of Honor
Participants from the southern United States or participants who were of Hispanic American descent rated a woman who responded to mistreatment by her fiancé with contrition (e.g., blaming herself) more favorably than a woman who responded with anger or assertiveness. In contrast, participants from the northern United States showed the opposite pattern. These findings illustrate the powerful impact of cultures of honor on reactions to sexual jealousy.

(*Source:* Based on data from Vandello and Cohen, 2003.)

KeyPoints

- Contrary to the famous frustration-aggression hypothesis, all aggression does not stem from frustration, and frustration does not always lead to aggression. Frustration is a strong elicitor of aggression only under certain limited conditions.

- In contrast, provocation from others is a powerful elicitor of aggression. Even mild teasing can stimulate aggression, although such effects are stronger in certain cultures than others.

- Heightened arousal can increase aggression if it persists beyond the situation in which it was induced and is falsely interpreted as anger.

- Exposure to media violence has been found to increase aggression among viewers. This is a result of several factors, such as the priming of aggressive thoughts, a weakening of restraints against aggression, and also to desensitization to such materials.

- Exposure to violent pornography appears to increase the willingness of some people to engage in similar behavior and to generate callous attitudes toward various forms of sexual violence.

- Sexually aggressive lyrics in popular songs, too, have been found to increase aggression by men toward women and by women toward men.

Think About It

If media violence increases aggression, the solution seems simple: ban or restrict such content. But that raises complex issues concerning freedom of expression. In many societies, restricting such materials would be a violation of certain basic rights. Given this dilemma, what do you think should be done to reduce the potentially harmful effects of various kinds of violence in the media? Not needed at this point.

Personality and Aggression: Why Some People Are More Aggressive than Others

Are some people primed for aggression by their personal characteristics? Informal observation suggests that this is so. While some individuals rarely lose their tempers or engage in aggressive actions (see Figure 10.13 on page 356), others seem to be forever "losing it," with potentially serious consequences. In this section, we will consider several characteristics—

Figure 10.13
Are Some People More Likely to Aggress than Others? Absolutely!
Some people, like the "disgruntled employee of the month" shown here on the right, seem to possess personal characteristics that make them especially likely to aggress against others. Research findings indicate that such differences do exist and often play a role in the occurrence of overt aggression.

(*Source:* Universal Press Syndicate, February 20, 1999).

aspects of personality—that seem to play an important role in aggression. First, though, we'll begin with a brief discussion of how personality characteristics can influence aggression—and many other forms of behavior.

The TASS Model: Traits as Sensitivities to Various Situations

In everyday speech, we often talk about people as possessing discrete traits. For instance we might say, "She is friendly," "He is lazy," or "She is really smart." And as we saw in Chapter 3 in our discussion of the fundamental attribution error, we often go further, assuming that others' traits and characteristics largely determine their behavior. Social psychologists, in contrast, hold a somewhat different view. They note that situations are important, too, and that social behavior often derives from a complex interaction between situational factors and personal traits or other characteristics (e.g., Kammarath, Mendoza-Denton, & Mischel, 2005). One theory that takes careful account of this fact is known as the **TASS model**—the traits as situational sensitivities model. This model suggests that many aspects of personality function in a threshold-like manner: only when situational factors are strong enough to trigger them, do they influence behavior. (In contrast, a more traditional model of how personality factors influence behavior suggests that such factors are most likely to exert strong or clear effects in ambiguous or weak situations—ones that don't require people to behave in certain ways.)

When applied to aggression, the TASS model makes the following prediction: The tendency to behave aggressively (sometimes known as trait aggressiveness) will only influence overt behavior when situational factors are strong enough to activate it. For people high in this trait, even weak provocations will stimulate an aggressive reaction; for people low in this trait, in contrast, much stronger levels of provocation are required to trigger aggression. Evidence for this view has recently been reported by Marshall and Brown (2006). They first measured the trait aggressiveness of a large number of students and then placed them in a situation where they were exposed to either no provocation from another person, moderate provocation, or strong provocation. Then participants in all three groups were given an opportunity to aggress against this other person (by setting the intensity of bursts of noise this person would receive if she lost on a competitive reactions time task). The researchers predicted that for people high in trait aggressiveness, even a moderate level of provocation would trigger intense aggressive reactions; for people low in trait aggressiveness, however, a moderate provocation would trigger little or no aggression. Only a strong provocation would result in overt aggression. As shown in Figure 10.14, this is precisely what happened. People high in the tendency to aggress (high in trait aggressiveness) literally "exploded" when they received even a mild provocation from another person (a mildly negative evaluation of an essay they wrote). In contrast, people low in trait aggressiveness showed little or no reaction to a mild provocation, but they did respond with strong aggression when they received a powerful provocation (an unfairly negative evaluation of their work, that described it as "the worse I've ever read").

TASS model
The traits as situational sensitivities model. A view suggesting that many personality traits function in a threshold-like manner, influencing behavior only when situations evoke them.

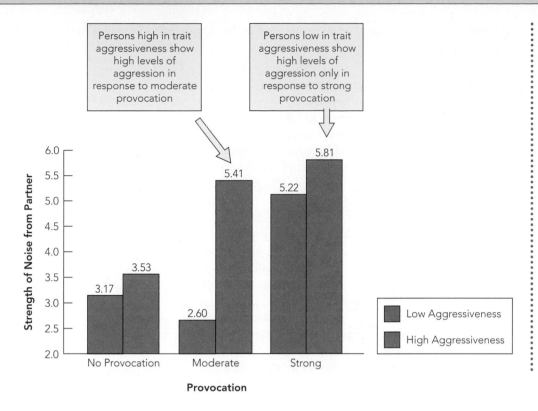

Persons high in trait aggressiveness show high levels of aggression in response to moderate provocation

Persons low in trait aggressiveness show high levels of aggression only in response to strong provocation

Low Aggressiveness

High Aggressiveness

Figure 10.14
Aggression: Often, It Stems from a Complex Interaction between Situational and Personal Factors

When mildly provoked, people high in trait aggressiveness showed high levels of aggression toward the person who annoyed them. In contrast, people low in trait aggressiveness did not show high levels of aggression unless they had been strongly provoked. These findings illustrate the fact that aggression, like many other forms of social behavior, reflects a complex interaction between situational and personal factors.

(*Source:* Based on data from Marshall & Brown, 2006).

These findings, and those of many other studies, indicate that personal dispositions and traits do indeed influence aggression—just as they play a role in many other forms of social behavior. But they don't do so directly, rather, they interact in complex ways with many situational factors, and it is the combination that often proves deadly.

The Type A Behavior Pattern: Why the *A* in Type A Could Stand for Aggression

Do you know anyone you could describe as (1) extremely competitive, (2) always in a hurry, and (3) especially irritable and aggressive? If so, this person shows the characteristics of what psychologists term the **type A behavior pattern** (Glass, 1977; Strube, 1989). At the opposite end of the continuum are people who do not show these characteristics—individuals who are not highly competitive, who are more relaxed and not always fighting the clock, and who do remain calm even in the face of strong provocation; such people are described as showing the **type B behavior pattern.**

Given the characteristics mentioned, it seems only reasonable to expect that type A people would tend to be more aggressive than type B people in many situations. In fact, the results of several experiments indicate that this is actually the case (Baron, Russell, & Arms, 1985; Carver & Glass, 1978; Gladue, 1991).

Additional findings indicate that type A people are truly hostile: They don't merely aggress against others because this is a useful means for reaching other goals, such as winning athletic contests or furthering their own careers. Rather, they are more likely than type B people to engage in what is known as **hostile aggression**—aggression in which the prime objective is inflicting some kind of harm on the victim (Strube, Turner, Cerro, Stevens, & Hinchey, 1984). In view of this fact, it is not surprising to learn that type A people are more likely than type B people to engage in such actions as child abuse or spouse abuse (Strube et al., 1984). In contrast, type A people are *not* more likely than type B people to engage in **instrumental aggression,** which is aggression performed primarily to attain other goals aside from harming the victim, goals such as control of valued resources or praise from others for behaving in a "tough" manner.

type A behavior pattern
A pattern consisting primarily of high levels of competitiveness, time urgency, and hostility.

type B behavior pattern
A pattern consisting of the absence of characteristics associated with the type A behavior pattern.

hostile aggression
Aggression in which the prime objective is inflicting some kind of harm on the victim.

instrumental aggression
Aggression in which the primary goal is not to harm the victim but rather attainment of some other goal—for example, access to valued resources.

Narcissism, Ego Threat, and Aggression: On the Dangers of Wanting to be Superior

Do you know the story of Narcissus? He was a character in Greek mythology who fell in love with his own reflection in the water and drowned trying to reach it. His name has now become a synonym for excessive self-love—for holding an over-inflated view of one's own virtues or accomplishments; and research findings indicate that this trait may be linked to aggression in important ways. Specifically, studies by Bushman and Baumeister (1998) suggest that people high in narcissism (ones who agree with items such as "If I ruled the world it would be a much better place" and "I am more capable than other people") react with exceptionally high levels of aggression to "slights" from others—feedback that threatens their inflated self-image. Why? Perhaps because such people have nagging doubts about the accuracy of their inflated egos and so react with intense anger toward anyone who threatens to undermine them. Alternatively, they may react strongly to even mild provocations because they believe that they are so much better than other people, and as a result, perceive even very mild critical comments from others as strong slurs on their inflated self-image. This latter possibility was investigated by McCullough and others (McCullough, Emmons, et al., 2003).

These researchers reasoned that narcissistic people perceive themselves as the victims of transgressions more often then nonnarcissitic people because of their inflated self-image. To test this prediction, they asked college students to complete a measure of narcissism and then to keep a diary for fourteen days in which they recorded the number of times in which other people offended them in some way. As expected, the higher participants scored in narcissism, the greater the number of transgressions by others they reported. This was especially true for one aspect of narcissism relating to exploiting others or being entitled to wonderful treatment by them (e.g., strong agreement with statements such as "I insist on getting the respect that is due me").

The finding that narcissism is one personal characteristic related to aggression has important implications because at the present time, many schools in the United States focus on building high self-esteem among their students. Up to a point, this may indeed be beneficial. But if such esteem-building tactics are carried too far and produce children whose opinions of themselves are unrealistically high (i.e., narcissistic), the result may actually be an increased potential for violence. Clearly, this is a possibility worthy of further, careful study.

Sensation Seeking and Aggression: Are People Who Like Lots of "Action" More Aggressive than Others?

Do you know anyone who gets bored easily, seeks lots of new experiences—especially exciting ones with an element of risk—and is generally uninhibited? If so, this person may be high in what social psychologists describe as sensation seeking or in the closely related trait of impulsivity (e.g., Zuckerman, 1994). And there are grounds for expecting such people to be higher than others in aggression, too. Why would this be the case? Again, the GAM (general aggression model) suggests some possible reasons. First, it may be that people high in sensation seeking or impulsiveness experience anger and hostile feelings more often than others. Their emotions are easily aroused, so they may have lower thresholds for becoming angry. Moreover, their tendencies to get bored and to seek exciting new experiences may lead them to have more hostile thoughts: After all, aggressive exchanges with others are exciting and dangerous. Is Jack Bauer, the agent in *24*, a high sensation seeker? In the light of research evidence concerning the characteristics of such people, this seems like a reasonable possibility. He does seem to crave excitement (why else would someone hold such a job?), and he does seem to lose his temper quite easily.

Evidence for these predictions has been reported by Joireman, Anderson, and Strathman (2003), who found that people high in sensation seeking show several tendencies related to aggression. First, they are attracted to situations that elicit aggression, which they find exciting and appealing. Second, they are indeed more likely to experience anger and hostility. And third, they are more likely to focus on the immediate rather than delayed consequences of their behavior. The overall result? They tend to show higher levels of both physical and verbal aggression than others. The moral of these findings is clear: Beware of people who seek thrills, excitement, and adventure—a heightened tendency to aggress may go along with this personal characteristic.

Gender Differences in Aggression: Do They Exist?

Are males more aggressive than females? Folklore suggests that they are, and research findings suggest that in this case, informal observation is correct: When asked whether they have ever engaged in any of a wide range of aggressive actions, males report a higher incidence of many aggressive behaviors than do females (Harris, 1994). On closer examination, however, the picture regarding gender differences in the tendency to aggress becomes more complex. On the one hand, males are generally more likely than females both to perform aggressive actions and to serve as the target for such behavior (Bogard, 1990; Harris, 1992; 1994). Further, this difference seems to persist throughout the lifespan, occurring even among people in their seventies and eighties (Walker, Richardson, & Green, 2000). On the other hand, the size of these differences appears to vary greatly across situations.

First, gender differences in aggression are much larger in the absence of provocation than in its presence. In other words, males are significantly more likely than females to aggress against others when they have not been provoked in any manner (Bettencourt & Miller, 1996). In situations in which provocation is present, and especially when it is intense (see Figure 10.15), such differences tend to disappear.

Second, the size—and even direction—of gender differences in aggression seems to vary greatly with the type of aggression in question. Research findings indicate that males are more likely than females to engage in various forms of direct aggression—actions aimed directly at the target and which clearly stem from the aggressor (e.g., physical assaults, pushing, shoving, throwing something at another person, shouting, making insulting remarks [Björkqvist, Österman, & Hjelt-Bäck, 1994a]). However females are more likely to engage in various forms of indirect aggression—actions that allow the aggressor to conceal his or her identity from the victim, and which, in some cases, make it difficult for the victim to know that they have been the target of intentional harm doing. Such actions include spreading vicious rumors about the target person, gossiping behind this person's back, telling others not to associate with the intended victim, making up stories to get them in trouble, and so on. Research findings indicate that gender differences with respect to indirect aggression are present among children as young as eight years old and increase through age fifteen (Björkqvist, Lagerspetz, & Kaukianinen, 1992; Österman et al., 1998); they seem to persist into adulthood as well (Björkqvist, Österman, & Hjelt-Bäck, 1994b; Green, Richardson, & Lago, 1996). Further, these differences have been observed in several different countries—Finland, Sweden, Poland, Italy, and Australia (Österman et al., 1998; Owens, Shute, & Slee, 2000), so they appear to be quite general in scope.

Third, recent findings indicate that for women and men, being aggressive can be a social "plus," conferring high status and appeal on the people who demonstrate it (Hawley, Card, & Little, 2007). This is especially true for individuals who combine aggression with high levels of actions meant to

Figure 10.15

Gender Differences in Aggression: Smaller Than You Think

While men are generally more aggressive than women, this difference tends to disappear in the face of strong provocation.

enhance relationships (e.g., high social skills, high levels of extraversion). Such people, described by Hawley and others as *bistrategic controllers*, combine high levels of aggression with prosocial, relationship-boosting actions. As a result, they are often successful in gaining access to valued rewards (e.g., high status, approval from others) and become popular with their peers. This pattern—which Hawley and others describe as "the bright side of bad behavior" (Hawley, Little, & Rodin, 2007)—is equally frequent among females and males, and this fact suggests, too, that gender differences in aggression have been overstated in the past. We discussed this fascinating research in more detail in Chapter 9, in *Making Sense of Common Sense: A Social Psychological Perspective*, which focused on the popular, but inaccurate view that aggression and helping (prosocial behavior) are opposites.

In sum, gender differences with respect to aggression do exist and can be observed in some contexts. But overall, such differences are both far smaller in magnitude and much more complex in nature than common sense suggests.

Situational Determinants of Aggression: The Effects of Heat and Alcohol

While aggression is often strongly influenced by social factors and personal traits, it is also affected by factors relating to the situation or context in which it occurs. Here, we'll examine two of the many *situational factors* that can influence it: high temperatures and alcohol.

In the Heat of Anger: Temperature and Aggression

Boiling mad; Hot-tempered; in a white-hot rage . . . Phrases like these suggest that there may well be a link between temperature and human aggression. And in fact, many people report that they often feel especially irritable and short-tempered on hot and steamy days. Is there really a link between climate and human aggression? Social psychologists have been studying this question for more than three decades, and during this period the methods they have used and the results they have obtained have become increasingly sophisticated. The most reasonable answer, we believe—one based on the results of careful research—is "yes, heat does increase aggression—but only up to a point." Beyond some level, aggression may actually decline as temperatures rise because people become so uncomfortable and fatigued that they are actually less likely to engage in any behavior, including overt aggression.

The earliest studies on this topic (e.g., Baron, 1972) were experiments conducted under controlled laboratory conditions, in which temperature was systematically varied as the independent variable. For instance, participants were exposed either to comfortably pleasant conditions (temperatures of seventy to seventy-two degrees Fahrenheit) or to uncomfortably hot conditions (temperatures of ninety-four to ninety-eight degree Fahrenheit) and were then given opportunities to aggress against another person. (In fact, they only believed they could harm this person; ethical considerations made it necessary to assure that no harm could actually take place.) Results were surprising: High temperature reduced aggression for both provoked and unprovoked people. The initial explanation of these findings was that the high temperatures were so uncomfortable, that participants focused on getting away from them, and this caused them to reduce their aggression. After all, aggression might lead to unfriendly encounters with the victim and this would prolong their misery.

This seemed reasonable—when they are very hot, people do seem to become lethargic and tend to concentrate on reducing their discomfort rather than on "evening the score" with others. However, these early studies suffered from important drawbacks that made it difficult to assess this interpretation. For instance, the exposure to the high temperatures lasted only a few minutes, while in the real world, this occurs over much longer periods. Subsequent studies, therefore, used very different methods (e.g., Anderson, 1989; Anderson & Anderson, 1996; Bell, 1992). Specifically, they examined long-term records of temperatures and police records of various aggressive crimes to determine whether the frequency of such crimes increased with rising temperatures. For instance, consider a careful study conducted by Anderson, Bushman, and Groom (1997).

These researchers collected average annual temperatures for fifty cities in the United States over a forty-five-year period (1950–1995). In addition, they obtained information on the rate of both violent crimes (aggravated assault, homicide) and property crimes (burglary, car theft), and another crime which has often been viewed as primarily aggressive in nature: rape. They then performed analyses to determine if temperature was related to theses crimes. In general, hotter years did indeed produce higher rates of violent crimes but did not produce increases in property crimes or rape. This was true even though the effect of many other variables that might also influence aggressive crimes (e.g., poverty, age distribution of the population) were eliminated. These findings, and those of related studies (e.g., Anderson, Anderson, & Deuser, 1996) suggest that heat is indeed linked to aggression.

Sophisticated as this research was, however, it did not fully resolve one key question: Does this relationship between heat and aggression have any limits? In other words, does aggression increase with heat indefinitely or only up to some point, beyond which aggression actually declines as temperatures continue to rise? As you may recall, that is the pattern obtained in initial laboratory studies on this topic.

Additional research by Rotton and Cohn (Cohn & Rotton, 1997; Rotton & Cohn, 2000) has carefully addressed this issue. These researchers reasoned that if people do indeed try to reduce their discomfort when they are feeling uncomfortable (e.g., when temperatures are extremely high), the relationship between heat and aggression should be stronger in the evening hours than at midday. Why? Because temperatures fall below their peak in the evening. In other words, a finer grained analysis would reveal a curvilinear relationship between heat and aggression during the day but a linear one at night. This is just what they found.

In sum, research on the effects of heat on aggression suggests that there is indeed a link between heat and aggression: When people get hot, they become irritable and may be more likely to lash out at others. However there may be limits to this relationship, stemming from the fact that after prolonged exposure to high temperatures, people become so uncomfortable that they are lethargic and focus on reducing their discomfort—not on attacking others. Short of these extreme conditions, however, there is a big grain of truth in the phrase "the heat of anger," and when temperatures rise, tempers may, too—with serious social consequences. That is certainly something to consider in the context of global warming and the real possibility that all of us will soon be exposed to uncomfortably hot outdoor temperatures more frequently than was true in the past.

Alcohol and Aggression: A Potentially Dangerous Mix

It is widely assumed by many that people become more aggressive when they consume alcohol. This idea is supported by the fact that bars and nightclubs are often the scene of violence. However, while alcohol is certainly consumed in these settings, other factors might be responsible for the fights—or worse—that often erupt: competition for desirable partners, crowding, and even cigarette smoke, which irritates many people (Zillmann, Baron, & Tamborini, 1981)—although, many places, even bars, are now smoke free. What does systematic research reveal about a possible link between alcohol and aggression? Interestingly, it tends to confirm the existence of such a link.

In several experiments, participants who consumed substantial doses of alcohol— enough to make them legally drunk—have been found to behave more aggressively and to respond to provocations more strongly than those who did not consume alcohol (e.g., Bushman & Cooper, 1990; Gustafson, 1992). Needless to say, participants in such research are always warned in advance that they may be receiving alcoholic beverages and only those who consent to such procedures actually take part (e.g., Pihl, Lau, & Assaad, 1997). But why does alcohol produce such effects? Does it simply eliminate inhibitions against act-

Figure 10.16
Alcohol: It Can Influence Aggression Even If It Is Not Consumed
Research findings indicate that cues related to alcohol (e.g., beer bottles, martini glasses, ads for specific brands of alcohol) can trigger aggression even if the alcohol itself is not consumed. This is because these cues can stimulate aggressive thoughts and images and these, in turn, increase actual aggression.

ing in an impulsive and possibly dangerous way? Or does it make people especially sensitive to provocations, so that they are more likely to behave aggressively (e.g., Gantner & Taylor, 1992)? In other words, does it lower their threshold for responding aggressively to provocations? All of these possibilities are reasonable and are supported by some evidence, but recent findings suggest that the effects of alcohol on aggression may stem, at least in part, from reduced cognitive functioning and what this does, in turn, to social perception.

Specifically, the findings of several studies (e.g., Bartholow, Pearson, Gratton, & Fabiani, 2003), indicate that alcohol impairs cognitive functions of higher orders, such as evaluation of stimuli and memory. This may make it harder for individuals to evaluate others' intentions (hostile or not hostile) and to evaluate the effects that various forms of behavior on their part, including aggression, may produce (e.g., Hoaken, Giancola, & Phil, 1998). For instance, people who have consumed alcohol show reductions in their capacity to process positive information about someone they initially dislike. This means that if such a person provoked them but then apologized, those who have consumed alcohol might be less able to process this information carefully and so would remain likely to aggress, despite the apology. This is speculation at present, but does seem to fit other findings concerning the impact of alcohol (e.g., Bartholow et al., 2003).

Quite apart from these effects, which stem from the impact of alcohol on the nervous system, there is also evidence indicating that alcohol can influence aggression simply because it has been associated with such behavior in the past. In other words, because alcohol and aggression have been linked in people's lives, cues associated with alcohol (e.g., pictures of beer bottles or martini glasses, or ads for specific brands of alcohol; see Figure 10.16 on page 362) may trigger aggression even if the alcohol itself is not consumed. Evidence for this possibility has been reported by Bartholow and Heinz (2006). In one study, they exposed participants either to alcohol ads (e.g., ads for Budweiser, Grey Goose vodka) or to neutral ads for paper towels and cheese. Then both groups read descriptions of another person and rated this individual on several dimensions. It was predicted that participants who had read the alcohol ads would perceive more hostility in ambiguous actions by the stranger than those who had read the neutral ads. This would be so because the alcohol ads would trigger thoughts and images related to aggression. This is precisely what happened. These findings indicate that alcohol (or just cues related to it) can trigger aggression even when it is not actually consumed, merely because it has often been associated with aggression in the past. This is yet one more reason why everyone should treat alcohol not as an aid to having a good time but as a potentially dangerous drug with serious—and dangerous—side effects.

> ### ✑ Principles to Remember
>
> Aggression is influenced by many different factors relating to the words and deeds of other people, personal traits, and situational factors. So beware of any suggestions that it is the result of one or just a few factors—for instance, "inherited tendencies toward violence," or "intense frustration." Such views are misleading, to say the least.

✑ KeyPoints

- In cultures of honor, norms requiring aggression as a response to threats to one's honor exist and exert powerful effects.

- Sexual jealousy poses a major threat to male honor in such cultures, with the result that male aggression in response to the sexual infidelity of women is condoned to a greater extent, and women who are accepting of such aggression are viewed more favorably than ones who are not.

- Personality traits interact with situational factors to influence aggression; only if the situational factors (e.g., provocation) are above threshold do these personal traits enhance aggression. But when situation is strong and clear (e.g., high provocation), individual differences are eliminated also.

- People showing the type A behavior pattern are more irritable and aggressive than people with the type B behavior pattern.

- People high in narcissism hold an overinflated view of their own worth. They react with exceptionally high levels of aggression to feedback that threatens their inflated egos. They also view themselves, more than other people, as victims of the transgressions from others, and this may contribute to their heightened aggression.

- People high in sensation seeking tend to be more aggressive than those low in sensation seeking because they are attracted to situations that elicit aggression and because they experience anger and hostile thoughts more often.

- Males are more aggressive overall than females, but this difference is highly dependent on the situation and is eliminated in the context of strong provocation. Males are more likely to use direct forms of aggression, but females are more likely to use indirect forms of aggression. Both women and men who combine aggression with skills that enhance relationships are popular, and this, too, suggests that gender differences in aggression are smaller and more complex than was suggested in the past.

- High temperatures tend to increase aggression but only up to a point. Beyond some level, aggression declines as temperatures rise.

- Consuming alcohol can increase aggression because this drug reduces individual's capacity to process some kinds of information. Even stimuli related to aggression (e.g., ads for beers or specific brands of vodka or gin) can increase aggression because these cues have been associated with aggression in the past.

Think About It

When they are uncomfortably hot, many people consume alcohol as a way of reducing their discomfort. That means that the aggression-enhancing effects of alcohol are pitted against the aggression-reducing effects of minimizing discomfort. Which effect do you think will win? In other words, will drinking alcohol under these conditions increase or reduce subsequent aggression?

Aggression in Ongoing Relationships: Bullying and Aggression at Work

Reports of instances in which people are attacked by total strangers are disturbing. Even more unsettling, however, are situations in which people are harmed by others they know well or with whom they have continuing relationships—family members, spouses, partners, schoolmates, coworkers. While such aggression takes many different forms, we'll focus here on two important topics: bullying (e.g., Ireland & Ireland, 2000; Smith & Brain, 2000), and workplace violence (Griffin & O'Leary, 2004).

Bullying: Singling Out Others for Repeated Abuse

Almost everyone has either experienced or observed the effects of **bullying**—a form of behavior in which aggression is primarily "one-way"—one person repeatedly assaults one or more others who have little or no power to retaliate (Olweus, 1993). In other words, in bullying relationships, one person does the aggressing, and the other is on the receiving end. While bullying has been studied primarily as something that occurs between children and teenagers, it is also common in other contexts too, such as workplaces and prisons (e.g., Ireland & Archer, 2002). Indeed, research findings indicate that fully 50 percent of people in prison are exposed to one or more episodes of bullying each week (Ireland & Ireland, 2000). In this discussion, therefore, we'll consider research on bullying in many different contexts.

Why Do People Engage in Bullying?

A basic question about bullying, of course, is why does it occur? Why do some individuals choose targets they then terrorize over and over again? While there is no simple answer to this question, two motives appear to play a key role: the motive to hold power over others and the motive to be part of a group that is "tough" and therefore high in status (e.g., Olweus, 1999; Roland, 2002). These motives are clearly visible in research conducted by Roland (2002). In this study, more than two thousand children in Norway answered questions designed to measure their desire to exercise power over others, their desire to be part of powerful groups, and their tendency to be unhappy or depressed. (Previous research had suggested that feeling depressed is another cause of bullying—it makes the bullies feel better.) A measure of bullying was obtained by asking the children to indicate how often they had bullied other children (never, now and then, weekly, and daily). Such self-reports of bullying have generally been found to be accurate when compared with teachers' ratings.

Results revealed some interesting gender differences. Among boys, both the desire to gain power and to be part of powerful groups were significantly related to bullying, while feeling depressed was not. For girls, all three motives were related to bullying. This suggests that for girls, at least, aggressing against someone who can't retaliate is one technique for countering the negative feelings of depression. While many other factors also play a role in bullying, the motives mentioned here have been found to be among the most important causes of such behavior.

The Characteristics of Bullies and Victims

Are bullies always bullies and victims always victims? While common sense suggests that these roles would tend to relatively fixed, research findings indicate that, in fact, they are not. Many people who are bullies in one context become a victim in other situations and vice versa. So there are various combinations to consider—those who appear to be pure bullies (people who are always and only bullies), pure victims (people who are always and only victims), and bully–victims (people who switch back and forth between these roles).

bullying
A pattern of behavior in which one individual is chosen as the target of repeated aggression by one or more others; the target person (the victim) generally has less power than those who engage in aggression (the bullies).

But what, aside from the motives for power and belonging we described previously, makes some people become bullies in the first place? Findings of careful research on bullying point to the following factors. First, bullies tend to believe that others act the way they do intentionally or because of lasting characteristics (Smorti & Ciucci, 2000). In contrast, victims tend to perceive others as acting as they do at least in part because they are responding to external events of conditions, including how others have treated them.

Another difference is that bullies (and also bully–victims) tend to be lower in self-esteem than other people. As a result, they aggress against others to build up their self-image. In addition, bullies tend to adopt a ruthless, manipulative approach to life and to dealing with other people (e.g., Andreou, 2000; Mynard & Joseph, 1997). They believe that others are not to be trusted, so they feel it is totally justified to break their word and take unfair advantage of others (e.g., to attack them when their guard is down).

Finally, bullies and bully–victims believe that the best way to respond to bullying is with aggression. They believe, more than other people, that being highly aggressive will bring them high levels of respect (Ireland & Archer, 2002).

Reducing the Occurrence of Bullying: Some Positive Steps

Bullying can have truly devastating effects on its victims. In fact, there have been several cases in which children who have been repeatedly bullied by their classmates have actually committed suicide (O'Moore, 2000), and similar results often occur in prisons, where people who are brutalized by their fellow inmates see death as the only way out. These distressing facts lead to the following question: What can be done to reduce or even eliminate bullying? Many research projects—some involving entire school or prison systems in several countries—have been conducted to find out, and the results have been at least moderately encouraging. Here is an overview of the main findings:

- First, bullying must been seen to be a serious problem by all involved parties—teachers, parents, students, prisoners, guards, fellow employees, and supervisors (if bullying occurs in works settings).

- If bullying occurs, people in authority (teachers, prison guards, supervisors) must draw attention to it and take an unequivocal stand against it.

- Potential victims must be provided with direct means for dealing with bullying; they must be told precisely what to do and who to see when bullying occurs.

- Outside help is often useful in identifying the cause of bullying and in devising programs to reduce it.

Programs that have emphasized these points have produced encouraging results. Overall, then, there appear to be grounds for optimism; bullying can be reduced, provided it is recognized as being a serious problem and steps to deal with it are implemented.

Workplace Aggression: Harming Others at Work

In recent years, the news has been filled with instances of workplace violence—dramatic events in which employees attack other employees or their bosses, sometimes with tragic results. Media attention to these events has created the impression that we face a rising tide of violence in workplaces and some statistics seem to confirm this view: More than eight hundred people are murdered at work each year in the United States alone (National Institute for Occupational and Safety Health, 1993). It's important to keep two facts in mind, however: (1) the large majority of violence occurring in work settings is performed by "outsiders"—people who do not work there but who enter a workplace to commit robbery or other crimes (see Figure 10.17 on page 366), and (2) recent surveys indicate that threats of physical harm or actual harm in work settings are actually quite rare—in fact,

Figure 10.17
Workplace Violence: A Closer Look

As shown here, most instances of workplace violence are performed by outsiders during robberies and other crimes. Few instances involve one employee physically attacking another.

(*Source:* Baron & Neuman, 1996.)

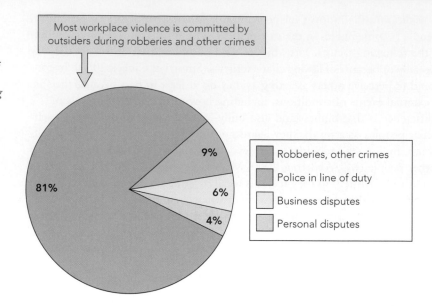

Most workplace violence is committed by outsiders during robberies and other crimes

81%

9%

6%

4%

- Robberies, other crimes
- Police in line of duty
- Business disputes
- Personal disputes

the chances of being killed at work (by outsiders or coworkers combined) are something like 1 in 450,000 (although this is considerably higher in some "high-risk occupations" such as taxi drivers or police [LeBlanc & Barling, 2004]). So, in contrast to what the news media suggest, available evidence indicates that workplace violence is relatively rare and is not the major problem it has sometimes been represented to be.

In contrast to workplace violence, **workplace aggression**—any form of behavior through which individuals seek to harm others in their workplace—is much more common (Griffin & O'Leary, 2004; Neuman & Baron, 2004). What is such aggression like? Growing evidence suggests that it is largely covert (i.e., hidden) rather than overt in nature. The reason for this is clear. In environments in which people interact with each other frequently, aggression is guided by a basic principle known as the **effect-danger ratio.** Specifically, when people engage in aggression against others who they will see every day (e.g., Björkqvist et al., 1994b), most will attempt to produce the greatest amount of harm to the victim possible (the effect), while at the same time minimizing the chances that they will be on the receiving end of retaliation (the danger). One useful way to do this is to aggress in subtle ways so that the victim can't be sure who caused the harm she or he is suffering and in fact, can't even tell whether the harm is the result of the actions of someone else or just as a result of impersonal factors, such as bad luck. For this reason, it is not at all surprising that most forms of aggression in work settings are subtle ones.

What specific forms of aggression do individuals actually use in workplaces? Research on this question suggests that three types of expressions of hostility—behaviors that are primarily verbal or symbolic in nature (e.g., belittling others' opinions or talking behind their backs)—are most common (e.g., Andersson & Pearson, 1999; Baron, Neuman, & Geddes, 1999):

- Obstructionism—behaviors designed to obstruct or impede the target's performance (e.g., failure to return phone calls or respond to memos, failure to transmit needed information, interfering with activities important to the target).

- Incivility—low-intensity deviant behavior with ambiguous intent to harm the target, in violation of workplace norms for mutual respect (e.g., sending a rude e-mail, excluding someone from a meeting, giving hostile looks or stares, or addressing a coworker inappropriately or unprofessionally [Pearson & Porath, 2004]).

- Overt aggression—behaviors that have typically been included under the heading "workplace violence" (e.g., physical assault, theft or destruction of property, threats of physical violence).

workplace aggression
Any form of behavior through which individuals seek to harm others in their workplace.

effect-danger ratio
A principle suggesting that in situations in which they interact frequently with potential victims, most people try—when engaging in aggression—to maximize the harm they produce while minimizing the danger of retaliation.

"Brodman, after giving it much thought, I've decided to let you go for no apparent reason."

Figure 10.18
Abusive Supervision: Often It Involves Unpredictable—and Unfair—Evaluations
While the boss shown here is not shouting angrily at his employee, he is definitely mistreating him and behaving in an aggressive manner. How would you like to be fired for no reason? And wouldn't you view that as an aggressive act by your boss? We're sure that you would. So abusive supervision, like other kinds of aggression, takes many different forms.

(*Source: The New Yorker,* February 6, 2006.)

Research findings indicate that while all three forms occur in work settings, the first two are much more frequent—as the effect-danger principle would predict (Baron & Neuman, 1996; Griffin & O'Leary, 2004).

What are the causes of workplace aggression? As is true of aggression in any context, many factors seem to play a role. However one that has emerged again and again in research on this topic is perceived unfairness (e.g., Skarlicki & Folger, 1997). When individuals feel that they have been treated unfairly by others in their organization—or by the organization itself—they experience intense feelings of anger and resentment and often seek to "even the score" by harming the people they hold responsible in some manner. In addition, aggression in work settings seems to be influenced by general societal norms concerning the acceptability of such behavior. For instance, one recent study (Dietz, Robinson, Folger, Baron, & Jones, 2003) found that the greater the incidence of violence in communities surrounding U.S. post offices was, the higher the rates of aggression within these branch offices was. It was as if acceptance of violence in the surrounding communities paved the way for similar behavior inside this organization.

Other factors that seem to play a role in workplace aggression relate to changes that have occurred recently in many workplaces: reductions in staff so that everyone has to do more work; unexpected layoffs; and increased use of part-time employees, which generates feelings of insecurity among regular employees who begin to fear for their own jobs. Because such changes have occurred with increasing frequency in recent years, it seems possible that the incidence of workplace aggression may be increasing for this reason. Now, before concluding this discussion, let's look at one especially disturbing form of workplace aggression—abusive supervision.

Abusive Supervision: Bosses Who Make Workplaces Unbearable

Have you ever had a boss who frequently shouted at you and other subordinates? Who ridiculed your work? Who always seemed to be in an irritable mood, and who seemed to evaluate your work in a totally unpredictable—and unfair—manner (see Figure 10.18)? If so, you may have experienced a specific kind of workplace aggression known as abusive supervision (Tepper, 2000). Unfortunately, this pattern is far from rare. About 10 percent of all employees report that they are currently being exposed to such treatment, and 30 percent report that they have had such a boss at some point in the past (Taylor, 2004).

Why do abusive bosses do it? Why, in a sense, do they act like bullies toward their subordinates? Unlike the bullies we have all encountered as children, abusive supervisors are not seeking power: They already have it. As a result, they don't search for weak or helpless victims the way child bullies do. Rather, they heap their abuse on everyone—all their subordinates. One social psychologist who has studied such bosses believes that they engage in abusive behavior partly to vent their own frustrations but mainly for the sheer pleasure of exercising their power and the gains in self-esteem this gives them (Hornstein, 2004).

When abusive supervision occurs—the effects are more serious than merely creating an unpleasant work environment. This kind of supervision damages not only the employees on the receiving end, but also the entire organization as well. For example, abusive supervision may reduce the willingness of employees to help one another at work (Tepper, Duffy, Hoobler, & Ensley, 2004). In sum, abusive supervision—aggression directed by bosses toward their subordinates—is all too common and makes going to work truly difficult for large numbers of people.

KeyPoints

- Bullying involves repeated aggression against individuals who, for various reasons, are unable to defend themselves against such treatment. Bullying occurs in many contexts, including schools, workplaces, and prisons. Few children are solely bullies or victims; more play both roles. Bullies and bully–victims appear to have lower self-esteem than children who are not involved in bullying.

- Workplace aggression takes many different forms, but it is usually covert in nature. It stems from a wide range of factors including perceptions of having been treated unfairly and many disturbing changes that have occurred in workplaces recently.

- Abusive supervision involves a continued pattern of aggression by bosses toward their subordinates. It has been found to harm not only the individuals, but also the entire workplace as well.

Think About It

If you had an abusive boss, what would you do to deal with this situation? Would you quit? Complain to other people in the company? Try to modify the boss's behavior in various ways? What techniques do you think would work best?

The Prevention and Control of Aggression: Some Useful Techniques

If there is one idea we hope you'll remember and take away with you from this chapter, here it is: Aggression is not an inevitable or unalterable form of behavior. On the contrary, because it stems from a complex interplay between cognitions, situational factors, and personal characteristics, it can be prevented or reduced. With that optimistic thought in mind, we'll now examine several techniques that, when used appropriately, can be highly effective in reducing the frequency or intensity of human aggression.

Punishment: Just Desserts or Deterrence?

punishment
Procedures in which aversive consequences are delivered to individuals when they engage in specific actions.

In most societies throughout the world, **punishment**—delivery of aversive consequences— is a major technique for reducing aggression. People who engage in such behavior receive large fines, are put in prison, and in some countries are placed in solitary confinement or receive physical punishment for their aggressive actions. In many cases, this involves spending time in prison, but in some locations, extreme cases of violence, such as mass murder, may result in capital punishment—legal execution of the convicted criminals. Why do so many societies punish aggressive acts? Basically, for two major reasons (e.g., Darley, Carlsmith, & Robinson, 2000).

First, there is a widespread belief that individuals who engage in acts of aggression viewed as inappropriate in their societies deserve to be punished. They have inflicted harm on others—and on society in general—and should suffer to make amends for this harm. This perspective suggests that the amount of punishment people receive should be matched to the magnitude of harm they have caused (e.g., breaking someone's arm should deserve less punishment than permanently harming them or killing them). In addition, the magnitude of punishment should take into account extenuating circumstances—for instance, was there some "good" motive for the aggressive action, such as self-defense or defense of one's family?

The second reason for punishing people who commit aggressive actions is to deter them (or others) from engaging in such behavior in the future. This basis for punishment implies that ease of detection of the crime should be given careful attention: If aggressive actions are hard to detect (e.g., they involve hidden or covert forms of harming others), they should be strongly punished because only strong punishment will deter people from engaging in actions they believe they can get away with. Similarly, public punishment would be expected to be more effective in deterring future crimes than private punishment, especially in cultures in which public shame is viewed as a truly negative outcome.

Which of these two perspectives are most important in determining the magnitude of punishment people feel is justified for specific aggressive acts or other offenses? Research by Carlsmith, Darley, and Robinson (2002) suggests that in general, the first perspective tends to dominate. So across many different contexts, most people seem to believe that the punishment should fit the crime.

There is still another rationale for using punishment to reduce aggressive behavior that we have not yet mentioned: Some kinds of punishment, at least, remove dangerous people from society (e.g., by placing them in prison), and in this way, protects future victims from possible harm. Is there any support for this view? In fact, statistics indicate that once people engage in violent crimes, they are likely to do so again. If that's true, then removing them from society can indeed help prevent additional acts of aggression against others (although, not against other prisoners). This is one rationale for giving people convicted of aggressive crimes long prison sentences, although it is rarely stated by judges or prosecuting attorneys.

Another important question relating to punishment is simple: Does it work? Can it reduce the tendency of specific people to engage in harmful acts of aggression? Here, existing evidence is relatively clear: Punishment can reduce aggression, but only if it meets four basic requirements: (1) it must be prompt—it must follow aggressive actions as quickly as possible; (2) it must be certain to occur—the probability that it will follow aggression must be high; (3) it must be strong—strong enough to be highly unpleasant to potential recipients; and (4) it must be perceived by recipients as justified or deserved.

Unfortunately, these conditions are typically not met in the criminal justice systems of many nations. In most societies, the delivery of punishment for aggressive actions is delayed for months or even years. Similarly, many criminals avoid arrest and conviction, so the certainty of punishment is low. The magnitude of punishment itself varies from one city, state, or even courtroom to another. And often, punishment does not seem to fit the crime—it does not seem to be justified or deserved. In such cases, the people who are punished may view such treatment as aggression against them—as a kind of provocation. And as we saw previously, provocation is a powerful trigger for aggression. In view of these facts, it is hardly surprising that the threat of punishment—even severe punishment— does not seem to be effective in deterring violent crime. The conditions necessary for it to be effective simply do not exist, and probably, given the nature of most legal systems, cannot exist. For this reason, we must conclude that the belief that severe punishments for aggressive crimes will successfully deter such behavior is wildly optimistic. But read on: Other techniques for reducing aggression, including several based on principles of social cognition, can be much more effective.

Self-Regulation: Internal Mechanisms for Controlling Aggression

From an evolutionary perspective, aggression can be viewed as adaptive behavior, at least in some situations. For instance, competition for desirable mates is often intense, and one way to "win" in such contests is through aggression against potential rivals. So, especially for males, strong tendencies to aggress against others can yield beneficial outcomes. On the other hand, living together in human society often requires restraining aggressive behavior. Lashing out at others in response to every provocation is definitely not adaptive and can greatly disrupt social life. For this reason, it is clear that we possess effective internal mechanisms for restraining anger and overt aggression (e.g., Baumeister, 1997; 2005). Such mechanisms are described by the term self-regulation (or self-control) and refer to our capacity to regulate many aspects of own behavior, including aggression.

Unfortunately, such self-regulation often requires lots of cognitive effort, so one reason why this internal system of restraint sometimes fails is that we simply don't have the resources required. In other words, aggression often erupts because we have invested so much cognitive effort in other tasks that we don't have enough left to perform this important but demanding function. Evidence for precisely this reasoning is provided by research conducted by DeWall, Baumeister, Stillman, and Gailliot (2007). In one especially interesting study, participants were told that the research was investigating the relationship between food-tasting preferences and written expression. They then wrote an essay which would, supposedly, be evaluated by another participant in the study. Next they tasted a snack of cheese and crackers that this other person had supposedly prepared for them.

At this point, the key manipulation of the study occurred. In a self-control depletion condition, a delicious-looking donut was placed in front of participants, and they were instructed to taste it. Just as they began, though, the experimenter stopped them, claiming that he had made an error and in that in fact, they should not taste the donut. The researchers predicted that the effort involved in resisting this delicious food would consume self-regulation resources. In a control condition, in contrast, a radish—not donut—was placed on the table in front of participants. Refraining from eating this food, the researchers predicted, would consume much smaller amounts of self-control resources.

Participants then received negative feedback from the partner on the essay they had written; this served as the provocation to aggression. Finally they were asked to prepare a snack for their partners by giving this person hot sauce and chips. Because the partner had previously indicated that he or she did not like spicy dishes, the amount of hot sauce they sent to this person provided a measure of aggression. (After all, eating it would cause the partner—who, in fact didn't really exist—considerable discomfort.)

As predicted, participants in the self-control depletion (donut) condition used more hot sauce than those in the control (radish) condition (see Figure 10.19). This was true despite the fact that participants in the depletion condition did not report greater anger. Their higher level of aggression, therefore, was as a result of the depletion of cognitive resources used in self-control. In several follow-up studies, similar results were found using different techniques for depleting self-control resources and for measuring aggression. In each case, when individuals had "used up" their cognitive resources, they were less able to restrain anger and aggression in response to provocations.

Interestingly, other research findings (e.g., Mauss, Evers, Wilhelm & Gross, 2006) indicate that self-control of aggressive impulses does not necessarily involve the use of cognitive resources. In fact, when individuals have positive implicit attitudes toward regulating their own emotions, they may be able to restrain aggression almost effortlessly—simply because they have positive attitudes toward exerting such emotional control. Further, it appears that one way in which individuals self-regulate their behavior so as to avoid aggress-

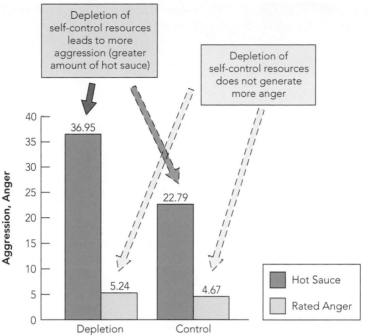

Depletion of self-control resources leads to more aggression (greater amount of hot sauce)

Depletion of self-control resources does not generate more anger

Figure 10.19
Restraining Aggression through Self-Regulation
Aggression is often restrained by self-regulatory processes that prevent its overt expression. When the cognitive resources needed for self-regulation are depleted, however, aggression is no longer blocked and can increase, as occurred in the depletion condition of the study shown here. However depletion of these cognitive resources does not necessarily increase anger.

(*Source:* Based on data from DeWall, Baumeister, Stillman, & Gailliot, 2007).

ing involves thinking prosocial thoughts—thinking about helping others and caring for them (see Chapter 9). The more readily people can bring such thoughts to mind when provoked or exposed to conditions that normally tend to trigger aggression, the less likely they are to behave in an aggressive manner (Meier, Robinson, & Wilkowski, 2006).

So where does this intriguing research leave us? With the suggestion that one effective means of reducing human aggression—perhaps an effective one—is strengthening the internal mechanisms that usually operate to control such behavior. We all possess these mechanisms, so the major task is making them stronger and ensuring that they are not overwhelmed by other demands on our cognitive resources. How can internal restraints against aggression be strengthened? In several different ways. For instance, exposure to other people who show restraint even in the face of strong provocation (nonaggressive models [e.g., Baron & Richardson, 1994]) might help, as would providing training designed to strengthen internal restraints. In addition, individuals can be taught to recognize when their cognitive resources are being "stretched" because those are the occasions on which inappropriate aggression is most likely to occur. For information on another potential means of reducing aggression—one that is widely viewed as highly effective—read *Making Sense of Common Sense: A Social Psychological Perspective* on page 372.

Forgiveness: Compassion Instead of Revenge

Almost everyone has experienced intense desires for revenge: Another person harms us in some manner, and we conclude that retaliating against them would be appropriate. Seeking to "pay them back" seems only natural, and we often feel it will make us feel better and—more importantly—restore our sense of justice.

But in fact, seeking revenge often has harmful effects for everyone concerned. People who seek it may feel better temporarily, but their actions may start the upward spiral of retaliation, revenge, and further retaliation that we described in our discussion of the effects of provocation. As a result, both parties are at increasing risk. For these reasons **forgiveness**—giving up the desire to punish someone who has hurt us and seeking, instead, to act in kind, helpful ways toward them—may be highly beneficial in many ways including the reduction

forgiveness
Giving up the desire to punish someone who has hurt us and seeking, instead, to act in kind, helpful ways toward them.

MAKING SENSE OF COMMON SENSE
A SOCIAL PSYCHOLOGICAL PERSPECTIVE
Catharsis: Does "Blowing Off Steam" Really Help?

When I was a little boy, my grandmother used to greet my temper tantrums by saying: "That's OK, get it out . . . don't keep it bottled up inside—that will hurt you." In other words, she was a true believer in the **catharsis hypothesis**—the view that if individuals vent their anger and hostility in nonharmful ways, their tendencies to engage in more dangerous types of aggression will be reduced (Dollard et al., 1939).

Is this actually true? Most people seem to believe that it is; for instance, newspaper columnists (including "Dear Abby") often urge people to express their aggressive emotions and thoughts as a means of reducing them. But systematic research on catharsis by social psychologists calls such advice into doubt: Widespread faith in the effectiveness of catharsis does not seem justified. On the contrary, it appears that so-called venting activities, such as watching, reading about, or imagining aggressive actions, or even engaging in "play" aggressive actions, such as punching a punching bag, are more likely to increase subsequent aggression than to reduce it (e.g., Bushman, 2001; Bushman, Baumeister, & Stack, 1999). A clear demonstration of this fact is provided by research conducted by Anderson, Carnagey, and others (2003).

These researchers reasoned that if catharsis really works, then exposure to songs with violent lyrics would allow people to vent aggressive thoughts or feelings, and as a result, they would show lower levels of hostility and lower levels of aggressive thoughts. However if catharsis does not work—and on the basis of previous findings, the researchers did not expect that it would—exposure to songs with violent lyrics might actually increase hostility and aggressive cognitions. To test these competing predictions, they conducted a series of studies in which participants listened to violent or nonviolent songs and then completed measures of their current feelings (hostile or friendly) and their aggressive cognitions (e.g., how much similarity they perceived between aggressive and ambiguous words—ones that could have both an aggressive and nonaggressive meaning, such as alley or police; how quickly they pronounced aggressive and nonaggressive words that appeared on a computer screen). Results of all the studies were consistent: After hearing songs with violent lyrics, participants showed an increase both in hostile feelings and in their aggressive thoughts. So catharsis definitely did not occur.

Why does "letting it out" fail to reduce aggression? For several reasons. First, anger may actually be increased when individuals think about wrongs they have suffered at the hands of others and imagine ways of harming these people. Second, watching aggressive scenes, listening to songs with aggressive lyrics, or merely thinking about revenge and other aggressive activities may activate even more aggressive thoughts and feelings. These, in turn, may color interpretations of actual social interactions so that ambiguous actions by others are more likely to be perceived as hostile ones and in which individuals behave more provocatively themselves. The result? Aggression is increased and not reduced as the catharsis hypothesis suggests. Third, even if catharsis did occur, the effects would probably be temporary; whatever made the people involved angry might well occur again, so any benefits would be short term at best.

Is there even a small grain of truth in the catharsis hypothesis? Perhaps only this: Giving vent to angry feelings may make individuals feel better emotionally. Anyone who has punched their own pillow or shouted angrily when alone in their own room has experienced such effects. But research findings indicate that such effects do not really reduce the long-term tendency to engage in aggressive actions. In fact, because reduced tension is pleasant, the long-term effects, again, may be a strengthening rather than weakening of aggressive impulses.

In short, systematic research by social psychologists suggests that in this case, commonsense beliefs about the effectiveness of catharsis (and suggestions to this effect by Freud and others), are not really justified. So resist the urging of those newspaper columnists, and do not put your faith in catharsis as a useful means for keeping your own anger—and aggression—in check.

of subsequent aggression (e.g., McCullough, Bellah, Kilpatrick, & Johnson, 2001). Recent findings (McCullough, Fincham, & Tsang, 2003) indicate that it may be easier to attain the first goal—giving up the desire for revenge—than to attain the second, forgiving this person to the point where we actually behave in positive ways toward him or her. But from the point of view of the present discussion, surrendering the desire for revenge may, in and of itself, be a useful step in terms of reducing subsequent aggression. Not only does it reduce the desire to strike back at the person who offended us, but it may also enhance our own psychological well-being, too. In this context, greeting cards that say "Please forgive me" or simply "I'm sorry" may actually have considerable value, if the messages they contain are accepted by the people who receive them (see Figure 10.20).

Figure 10.20
Forgiveness: One Effective Means of Reducing Aggression
Growing evidence suggests that forgiveness—giving up the desire to punish someone who has hurt us and seeking instead, to act in kind, helpful ways toward them—can be an effective means for reducing anger and aggression. Further, the closer we are to the person, the more inclined we are to offer forgiveness.

Benefits of this latter type are demonstrated clearly in research by Karremans, Van Lange, Ouwerkerk, and Kluwer (2003). These researchers asked participants in their study to remember an incident in which they were offended by another person. Then they completed a test which was described as a measure of their forgiveness for this person. The test was scored, and they were given feedback indicating either that they had forgiven the offender or that had not forgiven this person. Finally, participants completed additional measures of their current tension and their psychological well-being. Results indicated that those in the forgiveness condition (participants lead to believe that they had forgiven the offender) reported higher self-esteem and lower levels of negative affect than those in the no-forgiveness condition. Other findings showed that the benefits of forgiveness were stronger for relationships to which individuals are strongly committed than for ones to which they are less committed. In other words, the closer we are to someone who offends us, the more beneficial it is to forgive them.

How, precisely, does forgiveness work? What do people do to forgive those who have harmed them? One technique involves empathy; they try to understand the feelings, emotions, and circumstances that caused the offending person to harm them. Similarly, they make generous attributions about the causes of their enemies' behavior, concluding that they had good reasons for acting as they did, even though this produced negative outcomes. Perhaps most important of all, they avoid ruminating about past transgressions; once these are over, they put them out of their minds and concentrate on other things (McCullough, et al., 2001).

In sum, given the benefits that forgiveness may confer, this seems to be one social skill we should all try to develop. When we do, we may learn that there is indeed a large grain of truth in the proverb: "To err is human; to forgive, divine."

> **Principles to Remember**
> Aggression is a basic and frequent form of behavior, but it can be restrained or reduced. Several techniques are helpful, but they must be used carefully to be effective.

catharsis hypothesis
The view that providing angry people with an opportunity to express their aggressive impulses in relatively safe ways will reduce their tendencies to engage in more harmful forms of aggression.

KeyPoints

- Punishment can be effective in reducing aggression but only when it is delivered under certain conditions that are rarely met.

- The catharsis hypothesis appears to be mainly false. Engaging in vigorous activities may produce reductions in arousal, but these are only temporary. Similarly, the likelihood of subsequent aggression is not reduced by engaging in apparently "safe" forms of aggression.

- Aggression is often restrained by internal self-regulatory processes. If the cognitive resources needed by these processes are depleted, however, aggression is more likely to occur.

- Forgiveness—surrendering the desire for revenge—is effective in reducing aggression. In addition, it may contribute to our psychological well-being.

Think About It

Some people are better at controlling their tempers than others, even in the face of strong provocations. What factors do you think play a role in such differences? Are people who can control their own tempers better at self-regulatory mechanisms than people who cannot?

SUMMARY AND REVIEW

- Aggression is the intentional infliction of harm on others. Most social psychologists reject the view that human aggression is strongly determined by genetic factors, but many now believe that genetic factors play some role in such behavior. Drive theories suggest that aggression stems from externally elicited drives to harm or injure others. The frustration-aggression hypothesis is the most famous example of such theories. Modern theories of aggression, such as the general aggression model (GAM), recognize the importance of learning in aggression, various eliciting input variables, individual differences, affective states, and, especially, cognitive processes. While frustration does not always generate aggression, provocation from others is generally a strong determinant of aggression. Even mild teasing can stimulate aggression, although such effects are stronger in certain cultures than others. Heightened arousal can increase aggression if it persists beyond the situation in which it was induced and is falsely interpreted as anger.

- Exposure to media violence has been found to increase aggression among viewers. Similarly, exposure to violent pornography appears to increase the willingness to engage in similar behavior and generates callous attitudes toward various forms of sexual violence. Sexually aggressive lyrics in popular songs, too, have been found to increase aggression by men toward women and by women toward men.

- In cultures of honor, norms requiring aggression as a response to threats to one's honor exist and exert powerful effects. Sexual jealousy poses a major threat to male honor in such cultures, with the result that aggression in response to sexual infidelity is condoned to a greater extent, and women who are accepting of such aggression are viewed more favorably than ones who are not. Personality traits interact with situational factors to influence aggression; only if situational factors (e.g., provocation) are above threshold do these personal traits enhance aggression. Persons showing the type A behavior pattern are more irritable and aggressive than persons with the type B behavior pattern.

- People high in narcissism hold an overinflated view of their own worth. They react with exceptionally high levels of aggression to feedback from others who threaten their inflated egos. People high in sensation seeking tend to be more aggressive than others because they are attracted to situations that elicit aggression and because they experience anger and hostile thoughts more often than people lower on this dimension. Males are more aggressive overall than females, but this difference decreases in the context of strong provocation. Males are more likely to use direct forms of aggression, but females are more likely to use indirect forms of aggression.

- Uncomfortable heat increases aggression but only up to a point. Beyond some level, aggression declines as temperatures rise further. Consuming alcohol can increase aggression, especially among those who normally show low levels of aggression. Alcohol may exert these effects by reducing individuals' capacity to process some kinds of information and by changing their reactions to unexpected behaviors by others.

- Bullying involves repeated aggression against individuals who, for various reasons, are unable to defend themselves against such treatment. Bullying occurs in many contexts, including schools, workplaces, and prisons. Few children are solely bullies or victims; more play both roles. Bullies and bully–victims appear to have lower self-esteem than children who are not involved in bullying. Workplace aggression takes many different forms, but it is usually covert in nature. It stems from a wide range of factors including perceptions of having been treated unfairly and changes that have occurred in workplaces recently. Abusive supervision involves a continued pattern of aggression by bosses toward their subordinates. It has been found to harm not only the victims, but also the entire workplace as well.

- Many techniques for reducing aggression exist. Punishment can be effective in this respect but only when it is delivered under highly specified conditions. The catharsis hypothesis appears to be mainly false. Aggression is not reduced by engaging in apparently safe forms of aggression. Aggression is often restrained by internal self-regulatory processes. If the cognitive resources needed by these processes are depleted, however, aggression is more likely to occur. Forgiveness—surrendering the desire for revenge—is also effective in reducing aggression. In addition, it may contribute to our psychological well-being.

Key Terms

aggression (p. 338)

bullying (p. 364)

catharsis hypothesis (p. 372)

cultures of honor (p. 352)

drive theories (of aggression) (p. 339)

effect-danger ratio (p. 366)

excitation transfer theory (p. 346)

frustration-aggression hypothesis (p. 340)

forgiveness (p. 371)

general aggression model (GAM) (p. 340)

hostile aggression (p. 357)

instrumental aggression (p. 357)

provocation (p. 344)

punishment (p. 368)

TASS model (p. 356)

teasing (p. 345)

type A behavior pattern (p. 357)

type B behavior pattern (p. 357)

workplace aggression (p. 366)

Connections
INTEGRATING SOCIAL PSYCHOLOGY

In this chapter, you read about . . .	In other chapters, you will find related discussions of . . .
the role of cognitive and affective variables in aggression	the role of these factors in many other forms of social behavior . . . social cognition (Chapter 2), attitude change (Chapter 5), prejudice (Chapter 6), and helping (Chapter 9).
social factors that play a role in aggression	the effects of these factors on other forms of social behavior . . . social models (Chapter 9), attributions (Chapter 3), and arousal (Chapter 7).
personal characteristics that influence aggression	the role of these factors in several other forms of social behavior . . . social perception (Chapter 3), obedience (Chapter 8), helping behavior (Chapter 9), and leadership (Chapter 12).

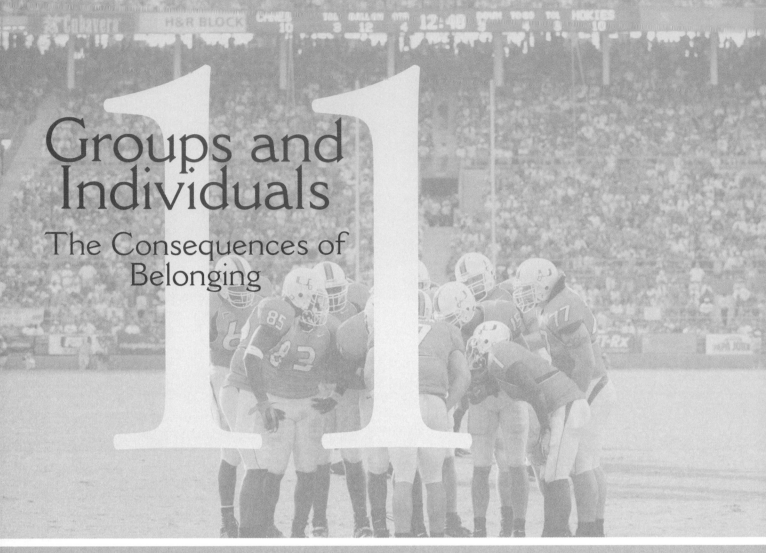

Groups and Individuals
The Consequences of Belonging

11

CHAPTER OUTLINE

- **Groups: When We Join . . . And When We Leave**
  Groups: Key Components
    SOCIAL PSYCHOLOGY: WHAT IT TELLS US
    ABOUT . . . IS YOUTUBE JUST A WEB SITE, OR IS
    IT A REAL GROUP?
  The Benefits—and Costs—of Joining

- **Effects of the Presence of Others: From Task Performance to Behavior in Crowds**
  Social Facilitation: Performing in the Presence of Others
    BUILDING THE SCIENCE: CLASSICS OF SOCIAL
    PSYCHOLOGY—DOES THE PRESENCE OF OTHERS
    HAVE AN EFFECT ON PERFORMANCE? ASK ANY
    COCKROACH!
  Social Loafing: Letting Others Do the Work
  Effects of Being in a Crowd

- **Coordination in Groups: Cooperation or Conflict?**
  Cooperation: Working with Others to Achieve Shared Goals

Conflict: Its Nature, Causes, and Effects
Resolving Conflicts: Some Useful Techniques

- **Perceived Fairness in Groups: Its Nature and Effects**
  Basic Rules for Judging Fairness: Distributive, Procedural, and Transactional Justice
  Reactions to Perceived Unfairness: Tactics for Dealing with Injustice

- **Decision Making by Groups: How It Occurs and the Pitfalls It Faces**
  The Decision-Making Process: How Groups Attain Consensus
  The Downside of Group Decision Making
    MAKING SENSE OF COMMON SENSE: A SOCIAL
    PSYCHOLOGICAL PERSPECTIVE—DOES
    BRAINSTORMING IN A GROUP RESULT IN MORE
    AND HIGHER QUALITY INVENTIVE IDEAS?

Belonging to groups has always been, for me, a natural part of life. I like being immersed with my "mates" as we struggle toward some common goal or feeling a sense of "oneness" with those with whom I share an identity—being accepted by other group members is assurance that I, in fact, do "belong." But is group life as "natural" and positive as I have always believed?

In all honesty, being a member of a group can bring some significant negatives to one's life. First of all, if it's a cohesive group—one where there are strong bonds among the members—it could be difficult to even get admitted, or it might result in some initiations that I would wish to avoid. And what if, after getting in, I discover that there are group norms I don't like? If I'm new to the group, my status is likely to be low, which would make it difficult for me to change the group's norms. Moreover, as a newcomer, my performance in the group may be evaluated by more established members, resulting in anxiety on my part. Some conflict is likely within almost any group, and managing potentially difficult interactions might be quite effortful—so, do I really have enough energy for all that? Is it possible I might put more effort into a group than the rewards I'd get from it? Realistically, some groups require major commitments of time, and, though it might seem selfish, I could end up questioning whether the benefit gained from membership is really enough to make belonging worthwhile.

Maybe it would simply be easier to work alone in my garden and talk to my cats, Gremlin and Giovanni, whenever I feel a need to express myself. Would life—if I didn't belong to any human groups—really be as relaxed as it appears in Figure 11.1?

Despite the potential hassles, maybe the "hermit thing" has less going for it than at first it might appear. Barbra Streisand claimed in a famous song that, "People who need people are the luckiest people in the world." Which view is right?

Figure 11.1
Life If We Didn't Belong to Groups: Alone but Simple?
People join groups for many reasons, but sometimes we may find ourselves wondering why we bother and if life alone might not be a whole lot simpler and more relaxed if we didn't.

(*Source:* Diana Chamberlain)

I must admit I'm inclined toward Barbra's view. I happily claim membership in a variety of different groups. I'm a member of a nation, various professional associations for social psychologists, a research group at the University of Kansas, a small gardening group, a family, and I am part of a group of friends where we cook for one another every Sunday night. Given that I want to stay in these groups, how can I avoid falling victim to the potential downsides of group membership? That is, with all those possibilities for negative outcomes, why do people join and stay in groups at all? Can we just dispense with them, or do groups critically shape who we are?

Maybe joining and staying in groups are natural inclinations—that we're somehow "programmed for group life." Some psychologists believe that we are **obligatorily interdependent**—that our evolutionary history is one of a necessary reliance on each other for collective knowledge and information sharing, and that, indeed, such group connectedness is essential to our survival as a species. Brewer and Caporael (2006) argue that interdependence among group members is the primary strategy for survival among humans, with the group providing a critical buffer between the individual and the physical habitat.

So how would this group-based fitness idea play out? The "selfish gene" notion (Dawkins, 1976) sees evolution as the passing on of genes by those organisms that survive to reproduce. If it is true that groups are highly important for survival, then those humans who had a greater affinity for group life would be more likely to pass on their genes to successive generations. That is, the genetic code for higher levels of group affinity, cooperation, and getting along with others, should be more likely to be passed along than, say, genes that carry a temperament that is a poor fit for group life.

A poor fit for group life, at least in our evolutionary history, would have been dangerous. It has always been the case that human infants cannot, for many years after birth, survive on their own, care for themselves, find food, or defend themselves from predators. For this reason, it really does take a village to raise a child. As humans grow to adulthood, they engage in activities essential to survival that can only be achieved by coordinated efforts—including mating, building shelter, hunting, and so on.

Thus the fit between individuals and the various groups to which they belong or interact with, can impede or enhance the chances of passing along their genes. Indeed, some of those genes may be ones directly related to how well they fit into groups. Brewer and Caporael (2006) see social coordination as central to the survival of the group because coordination and the security that it brings is what, ulti-

obligatory interdependence
Because of our evolutionary history, it is necessary that we rely on the group for survival as a species.

378

mately, makes reproduction even possible. That is, these theorists see human biology as the product of social organization and not the other way around.

What implications does an evolutionary perspective have for our attitudes toward groups in the here-and-now? Schachter (1959) concluded that the arousal of any strong emotion in humans tends to create the need to compare this reaction with others. This suggests that the complex emotional lives of humans may, in fact, be one of the causes of the human need for group affiliation. Indeed, it is under the most threatening or uncertain conditions that we seem to need our groups most. In these instances, for psychological security, we may increasingly identify with social groups (Hogg, 2007).

Thus we seem—by virtue of our genetic endowment—to survive and thrive best when we are connected to others. In fact, among the best predictors of level of happiness across persons is degree of connectedness to others (Argyle, 2001; Diener & Oishi, 2005; Lyubomirsky, King, & Diener, 2005). While we are born into some of our groups, such as our family or racial group, others are self-selected—we choose to join such groups as fraternities and sororities. Some groups are temporary and come into existence to accomplish a specific purpose, such as completing a team project, while others are longer lasting and less linked to specific goals (e.g., being a member of your university or student community). Some groups, such as a workplace organization, are joined explicitly because of the benefits they provide. For other groups, any material benefits of membership might be hard to see, although those groups can have considerable relevance for our identities (e.g., a peer or friendship group).

But even for those groups that we join because they are useful to us, we are often quite willing to defend them, and our membership in them, from criticism. Family, ethnic, and national pride are commonplace and often strong. Thus we have emotional connectedness to groups—we like them, like being in them, and often develop strong bonds with the people in them. Perhaps that is the point: If evolutionary psychology is to be believed, joining groups, and staying in them, is, at least in part, biologically determined, although it feels perfectly natural—as if we really *want* to belong and *freely choose* to join.

In this chapter we'll first consider whether there are different types of groups, when we join them and why, and what determines when we choose to quit them. Next, we'll examine the impact of what is, in some ways, the most basic group effect: the mere presence of others. As we'll see, the presence of others, even if we are not in a formal group with them, can affect our performance on many tasks and other important aspects of our behavior. Third, we'll briefly examine the nature of cooperation and conflict in groups—why these contrasting patterns emerge and the effects they produce. After that, we'll address the closely related question of perceived fairness in groups. Finally, we'll turn to decision making in groups, and the unexpected dangers this process can pose.

Groups: When We Join . . . And When We Leave

What is a group? Do we know one when we see it? Look at the photos in Figure 11.2. Which one shows a group? You would probably identify the photo on the right as a group, but the one on the left as a mere collection of persons waiting in line. Perhaps that is because you have a definition of the term **group** that is close to the one adopted by many social psychologists: people who perceive themselves to be bonded together in a coherent unit to some degree (Brown, 2000; Dasgupta, Banaji, & Abelson, 1999).

The basis of this perceived bond can differ in different types of groups (Prentice, Miller, & Lightdale, 1994). In **common-bond groups,** which tend to involve face-to-face interaction among members, the individuals in the group are bonded *to* each other. Examples of these kinds of groups include: the players on a sports team, friendship groups, and work teams. In contrast, in **common-identity groups** the members are linked via the category as a whole rather than each other, with face-to-face interaction often being entirely absent. Our national, linguistic, university, and gender groups, in which we might not even know personally all or even most of the other group members, are good examples of groups that we might identify with strongly but not because of the bonds we have with specific other individual members. As you'll see in this chapter, both of these types of group memberships can be important to people. Depending on what psychological need is salient at any given moment, different types of group memberships come to mind. For example, when affiliation needs are activated, intimate common-bond groups become accessible, whereas when identity needs are primed, social categories in which we share a common-identity with other members, are likely to become salient (Johnson et al., 2006).

Groups can and do differ dramatically in terms of their **entitativity**—the extent to which they are perceived as coherent wholes (Campbell, 1958). Entitativity can range from, at the low end, a mere collection of individuals who happen to be in the same place at the same time and who have little or no connection with one another, to at the high end, where members of intimate groups such as families share a name, a history, and an identity. As shown in Table 11.1, when people are asked to freely name different types of groups, there is considerable agreement about which types of groups are perceived to be high and low in entitativity (Lickel et al., 2000). Those groups that are rated as high in entitativity also tend to be groups that people rate as relatively important to them.

What determines whether, and to what extent, we perceive a group as an entity? Groups high in entitativity tend to have the following characteristics: (1) members interact with one another often, although not necessarily in a face-to-face setting (it could be over the Internet, for example), (2) the group is of consequence to its members, (3) members share common goals, and (4) they are similar to one another in important ways. The higher groups are on these dimensions, the more they will be seen by their members and nonmembers alike as forming coherent entities—real groups that can, and often do, exert powerful effects upon their members.

Highly entitative groups are more likely to be stereotyped than are groups low in entitativity (Yzerbyt, Corneille, & Estrada, 2001). People even use different language to describe entitative groups compared to those low in entitativity (Spencer-Rodgers, Hamilton, & Sherman, 2007). Specifically, abstract language is used to imply that high entitativity groups are enduring and that they possess distinct characteristics that differentiate them from other groups, whereas groups low in entitativity are seen as less distinctive and members are less likely to be characterized as sharing attributes. Perhaps, surprisingly, it is not the size of a group per se that matters for entitativity—some small and some large groups are perceived to be high in entitativity. It is behavioral features such as sharing of resources, reciprocating favors among group members, recognition of group authorities, and adherence to group norms that tend to result in greater entitativity rather than structural features of groups (Lickel, Rutchick, Hamilton, & Sherman, 2006). Let's look more

---

group
A collection of people who are perceived to be bonded together in a coherent unit to some degree.

common-bond groups
Groups that tend to involve face-to-face interaction and in which the individual members are bonded to each other.

common-identity groups
Face-to-face interaction is often absent, and the members are linked together via the category as a whole rather than each other.

entitativity
The extent to which a group is perceived as being a coherent entity.

 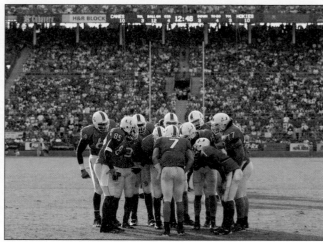

Figure 11.2

What Makes a Group a Group?

The photo on the left shows a collection of people who just happen to be in the same place—lining up to buy coffee—they are not part of a group. The photo on the right shows a real group in which the members interact with one another in a coordinated way and have shared goals and outcomes. Moreover, they feel that they are, in fact, part of a group.

Table 11.1　Are Entitativity and Importance of the Group Related?		
As can be seen here, some groups are seen as being high in entitativity (1 = not a group; 9 = very much a group) and others not. The perceived importance of a given group to its members was strongly correlated (r = 0.75) with how much of an entity it was perceived to be. *(Source:* Based on data from Lickel et al., 2000.)		
TYPE OF GROUP	**ENTITATIVITY**	**IMPORTANCE TO SELF**
Families	8.57	8.78
Friends/romantic partners	8.27	8.06
Religious groups	8.20	7.34
Music groups	7.33	5.48
Sports groups	7.12	6.33
Work groups	6.78	5.73
Ethnic groups	6.67	7.67
Common interest groups	6.53	5.65
National groups	5.83	5.33
Students in a class	5.76	4.69
Gender groups	4.25	3.00
Region of country	4.00	3.25
Physical attributes	3.50	2.50

closely at the issue of what constitutes a group and review the development of one in the context of the relatively recent phenomenon of online groups, specifically, YouTube, in *Social Psychology: What It Tells Us About . . .*

Groups: Key Components

Before turning to the specific ways in which groups affect various aspects of our behavior and thought, it is useful to consider several basic features of groups—ones that are present in virtually every group. These features are status, roles, norms, and cohesiveness.

SOCIALPSYCHOLOGY | WHAT IT TELLS US ABOUT . . .

Is YouTube Just a Website, or Is It a Real Group?

YouTube is a video-sharing website that has rapidly attracted a lot of attention (see Table 11.2). On YouTube, people watch videos that others have uploaded to the site, although there can be also interaction between any visitor (commenter) and other visitors who comment on that video and between visitors and those who upload videos. Does a sense of "we-ness" develop at YouTube so its members come to see themselves as constituting a real group?

After people view a given uploaded video, they are able to make comments about the video and rate it. Anyone visiting that video can see all the rest of the comments and make comments addressed to the blogger or to other commenters in the manner of a message board. In this way, people engage in shared admiration for, or disapproval of, the video, the blogger, or other commenters. Pet lovers and cooks (like myself) find their way to the animal videos and cooking demonstrations. People interested in politics watch clips from the Republican and Democratic primary debates in 2007, including YouTube interviews with the candidates that have generated millions of views and heated arguments among the commenters.

Like a lot of groups, the YouTube community has members that are both low and high identifiers. Some people who come to the site might be seen as casual visitors only, and they may not wish to interact with other visitors at all. Thus, while such people may recognize that YouTube is a site where they could potentially interact with other group members, they choose not to and are low-identified group members or may not even see themselves as belonging to the group at all. For those who do identify with the community, YouTube may be thought of as comprising a number of subgroups— loosely based on the different categories of videos that can be uploaded (e.g., comedy, people and blogs, news and politics, or pets and animals).

Viewers are often loyal to particular bloggers and may comment negatively about other bloggers, as if, within the larger YouTube community, an identity is formed around a blogger, as often happens with fans of particular musicians or actors. A shared goal of YouTubers appears to be interacting with particular bloggers and others who also like (or don't like) that blogger. In many video blogs, the blogger either simply talks to viewers about nothing, engages in skits or other humorous antics, or performs in some other way. These blogs are marked by high levels of amateurishness and are generally quite personalized—the person who made the video gives viewers a glimpse of her or his private life. In terms of content then, there are plenty of individual differences being expressed on YouTube, as there are in other groups. YouTube offers people a safe way to express themselves, and it is obvious from the comments that visitors admire YouTube bloggers who make even mildly entertaining videos. That is, certain bloggers attain status by being popular within the community as a whole.

Although many people find in YouTube a way to express their opinions or argue their political views, there are, no doubt, untold numbers who think arguing with another person in a message board or comments section is pointless. But those for whom YouTube is a gratifying experience, on either side of the lens, there is a shared loyalty to the YouTube community. People often criticize individual bloggers or particular videos but not the Web site's concept as a whole.

Status: Hierarchies in Groups

When the president of the United States, or any other nation for that matter, enters the room, everyone stands; and no one sits down until the president has taken a seat. Why? Although presidents are U.S. citizens like the rest of us, they occupy a special position within the group. Many groups have members who differ in **status**—position or rank within the group. Sometimes it is an official position as in the case of president, and sometimes it is not so explicit and instead is simply the "old-timers" in a group who are accorded higher status compared to "newcomers." People are often extremely sensitive to their status within a group because it is linked to a wide range of desirable outcomes—everything

status
The individual's position or rank within the group.

Table 11.2   The YouTube Community: Is It a Group?

YouTube is a phenomenon that has really taken off; it's a place where people interact with others, including with the videos the site is known for and verbally in blogs in which opinions are shared on everything from popular videos to political issues of the day.

YOUTUBE FUN FACTS

- Founded in February 2005.
- YouTube is a video-sharing Web site, where any person may upload videos for public or private sharing with others.
- Superficially, it is not unlike a library for videos, much as Photobucket is a storage bin for still photos.
- Videos occupy one of twelve categories, covering comedy, gadgets and games, music, news and politics, pets, and people and blogs.
- August 2006: YouTube announced that within eighteen months it would offer every music video ever made for viewing free of charge on its site.
- Sixty-five thousand videos are uploaded per hour, on average, onto the site.
- October 2006: YouTube sold to Google for over $1.5 billion in Google stock.
- May 2007: YouTube named one hundred popular video submitters as "Partners" (eligible for monetary compensation) in honor of their contributions to the site.

To honor the popularity of certain "YouTubers," YouTube held an awards contest in 2007. As noted in Table 11.2, YouTube offered one hundred of its most committed and popular bloggers "Partner" status and a share in advertising revenue. There was a huge outcry that this move would destroy the YouTube community because commenters said that monetary rewards would, in their view, ruin the YouTube experience, and many announced they would not watch the videos of any blogger who "turned pro."

The YouTube community is a real group, with considerable perceived entitativity for many members. YouTubers refer explicitly to the YouTube community as important to them, and the interaction between visitors and with bloggers is perceived to be the same as that happening in the real world. It is clear people try to protect, for themselves and others, the YouTube culture, and we-ness they specifically identify with, and they show remarkable cohesion when doing so. When a popular YouTuber indicated that he would be accepting YouTube's Partner designation, many commenters were clearly distraught and begged him not to do so, warning him, "accepting money will change you." The beauty of YouTube though is that, if money does change him, there are plenty of avid bloggers, uploading videos at a phenomenal rate, who are ready to replace him on the monitors, and in the hearts, of the YouTube community.

from salary to respect and deference from other group members. For this reason, groups often use status as a means of influencing the behavior of their members, with only "good" members—ones who follow the group's rules—receiving it.

Evolutionary psychologists attach considerable importance to status attainment within a group, noting that in many different species, including our own, high status confers important advantages on those who possess it. Specifically, people high in status have greater access than people lower in status to key resources relating to survival and reproduction, such as food and access to mates (Buss, 1999).

But how, precisely, do people acquire high status? Physical attributes, such as height, may play some role—taller men and women have a consistent edge, especially in the workplace (Judge & Cable, 2004). Those who are taller are held in higher esteem compared to shorter people; they are literally looked up to. Meta-analyses have revealed that taller people earn more in salary, are perceived as having more skills, and are more likely to be nominated as leader of groups relative to shorter people (Judge & Cable, 2004). Height even predicts who wins the U.S. presidency, within each election year's set of candidates. In fact, people judge those who have just won an election to be taller than they were before winning. In a Canadian voter study, the winner of an election (then Prime Minister Brian Mulroney) was judged as taller after the election, compared to judgments of his preelection height, while the losers were seen as shorter (Higham & Carment, 1992).

Factors relating to individuals' behavior also play a critical role in status acquisition. People who are seen as prototypical—by embodying the group's central attributes—are particularly likely to be accorded status and be selected as leader of a group (Haslam & Platow, 2001). Longevity or seniority in a group too can result in higher status—to the extent that it is seen as reflective of wisdom or knowledge of in-group ways (Haslam, 2004).

Once status within a group is obtained, people with high status actually behave differently than those with lower status. Guinote, Judd, and Brauer (2002) observed that high status group members are more "idiosyncratic and variable" in their behavior than are lower status group members. Indeed, there appears to be an awareness of the need to conform to group norms more strongly among those who are junior in a group and therefore have lower status (Jetten, Hornsey, & Adarves-Yorno, 2006). Across a number of different samples from professional to student groups in which status varied, people with high status report conforming less than do people with lower status. As shown in Figure 11.3, when surveyed about "how susceptible to group influence" they were, social psychologists who were senior in terms of number of years in a professional organization reported being less conforming than those who had few years in the organization or those who had just recently joined. By portraying themselves as open to group influence, low status group members may be helping to ensure they become as accepted in the organization as high status group members already feel they are. Thus there can be little doubt that differences in status are an important fact of life in most groups and have implications for how we perceive ourselves and actually behave.

Roles: Differentiation of Functions within Groups

Think of a group to which you belong or have belonged—anything from a sports team to a sorority or fraternity. Now consider this question: Did everyone in the group perform the same functions? Your answer is probably no. Different people performed different tasks and were expected to accomplish different things for the group. In short, they played different **roles.** Sometimes roles are assigned; for instance, a group may select different individuals to serve as its leader, treasurer, or secretary. In other cases, individuals gradually acquire certain roles without being formally assigned to them. Regardless of how roles are acquired, in many groups, someone often serves as the good listener, taking care of members' emotional needs, while another person tends to specialize in getting things done. People who fulfill the socio-emotional function in one group may, in another group, fulfill the task function, although different individuals tend to occupy each of these roles in any given group (Slater, 1955).

roles
The set of behaviors that individuals occupying specific positions within a group are expected to perform.

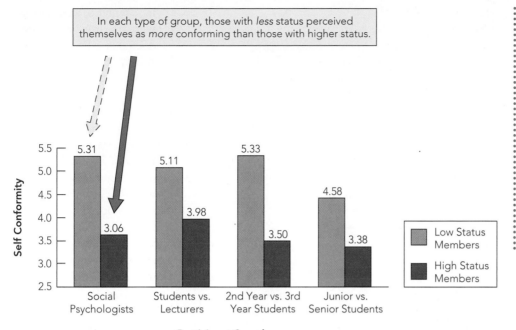

In each type of group, those with *less* status perceived themselves as *more* conforming than those with higher status.

Social Psychologists: 5.31 / 3.06
Students vs. Lecturers: 5.11 / 3.98
2nd Year vs. 3rd Year Students: 5.33 / 3.50
Junior vs. Senior Students: 4.58 / 3.38

Self Conformity

Low Status Members
High Status Members

Participant Sample

Figure 11.3
Status Matters for Conformity
As you can see, in every participant sample, those who were relatively high in status or more senior rated themselves personally as less conforming to the in-group's norms than did people who were lower in status or more junior members of their group. Status would appear to grant freedom to group members.

(*Source:* Based on data from Jetten, Hornsey, & Adarves-Yorno, 2006.)

To the extent that people internalize their social roles—those roles are linked to key aspects of the self-concept—they can have important implications for psychological well-being. Indeed, enacting a role well can lead people to feel that their behavior reflects their authentic self. Consider students in one study whose key self-perceptions were first measured and who were subsequently randomly assigned to fulfill a particular role in a class task (Bettencourt, Molix, Talley, & Sheldon, 2006). The behaviors called for when assigned to the "the idea generating" role are rather different than the behaviors required when assigned to the "the devil's advocate" role. The results showed that for those people whose traits were consistent with whichever role they were assigned, they perceived their behavior during the task as authentically reflecting themselves, exhibited more positive mood, and enjoyed the class task more than people for whom there was a discrepancy between their self-perceptions and the role they had enacted.

Other dramatic investigations of the effects of role assignment have observed profound effects on behavior—to the extent that the individual takes on the role and perceives it as part of their identity. In one famous instance—the Stanford prison study—male college students who had volunteered for a study of prison life were randomly assigned to either the role of guard or prisoner. The major purpose of the study was to find out whether, as a result of simply being placed in a role, participants would come to behave in ways that were consistent with that role (i.e., would they act like real guards and real prisoners [Haney, Banks, & Zimbardo, 1973])?

The answer was seemingly quick in coming. Over just a few days, with the investigator's encouragement in a person's role as prison warden, dramatic changes in the behavior of both the prisoners and the guards were evident. Although the prisoners were initially rebellious, they became increasingly passive and appeared to become depressed over the six days before the study was terminated, while the guards became increasingly brutal. Those in the guard role harassed the prisoners, forced them to derogate one another, and assigned them to tedious, senseless tasks. In short, participants came to act increasingly like actual prisoners and actual guards as the study progressed.

Was it simply being placed in the differing roles that exerted these powerful—and chilling—effects on behavior as Haney and others (1973) concluded? We cannot know the psychological processes that actually drove the behavioral changes that were exhibited because no data relevant to this question were collected in that study. However as we noted

Figure 11.4
Group Norms Dictate
Different Behaviors
*Members of different groups, or
those occupying different roles
within a group, are likely to be
guided by differing norms.
Sometimes, as shown here, the
norms may be so incompatible
that the two groups will find it
difficult to "work" together.*

(*Source: The New Yorker*
December 20, 1999.)

"*Only time will tell whether this merger makes sense or not.*"

in Chapter 8, a recent simulated prison study con-
ducted at a BBC studio in
Britain has obtained new
answers concerning the
question of when and why
role assignments affect our
behavior have begun to
emerge (see Reicher &
Haslam, 2006). The adult
participants in this study
were first given a battery of
psychological tests before
being randomly assigned
to the role of either prisoner or guard. In this
way, the investigators could
be sure that the people
assigned to each group did
not differ before the study
began in ways that might
affect their role behav-
ior (e.g., tendency toward
depression, authoritarian-
ism, social dominance).
Were the same behaviors
observed as occurred in the
Stanford prison study?

No, the dynamics were rather different. Over the course of the study, those assigned
to be guards failed to identify with their role, in part because of their concerns with being
liked by the prisoners and how others might perceive them when the study was over (and
it was televised). Aggression, on the part of the guards, was absent in this case. In contrast, the prisoners showed significant increases, as the study progressed, in the degree to
which they identified with their role and the other prisoners. Did this difference in identification with their assigned role make a difference for the behavior that was observed?
The answer was a definite yes. Because the guards did not identify with their role, they
failed to impose their authority collectively, and they were eventually overcome by the other
group whose members were highly identified with their group. Over the course of the
study, the guards also showed increased stress responses that the prisoners did not show—
both self-reported burnout and greater cortisol reactivity, which is a physiological indicator of stress (Haslam & Reicher, 2006). Those assigned to the prisoner role, however,
showed increasing identification with the other prisoners, developed a norm of rebellion,
and showed reductions in depression over the course of the study.

Collectively, what these simulated prison studies illustrate is that roles are not automatic determinants of behavior. Were it so, it would reflect an extremely mechanistic view
of people and their behavior—lacking little psychology about how we come to act as we
do in groups. Rather, an internalization process whereby we come to identify with, and
see ourselves in terms of, a role and identity must take place before our behavior will reflect
it. Once people do identify with a role and with others with whom that role is shared,
they will be guided by what they perceive to be the norms or appropriate ways of acting
for "people like us." Before we turn to the importance of norms and how they guide our
behavior in groups, ask yourself whether the norms of the two groups shown in Figure
11.4 are likely to be the same or likely to be so fundamentally incompatible that they cannot effectively work together.

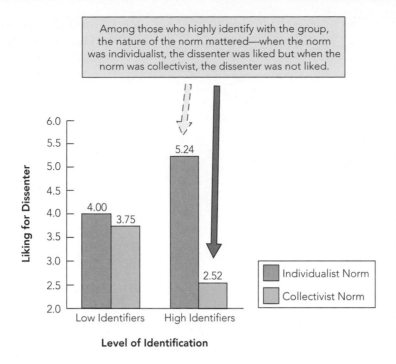

Among those who highly identify with the group, the nature of the norm mattered—when the norm was individualist, the dissenter was liked but when the norm was collectivist, the dissenter was not liked.

Figure 11.5
Responses to a Dissenting Group Member: It Depends on the Group Norm
Dissent, or disagreeing with other group members, can result in negative evaluations by those who highly identify with the group when the group's norm is collectivist and conflict is to be avoided. In contrast, when the group's norm is individualist, those who highly identify with the group are tolerant of dissenting group members. The norm of the group does not affect how low identifiers evaluate a dissenting fellow group member.

(*Source:* Based on data from Hornsey, Jetten, McAuliffe, & Hogg, 2006.)

Norms: The Rules of the Game

Groups can powerfully affect the behavior of their members via **norms**—implicit rules that inform us about how we ought to behave. Although we discussed the influence of norms on behavior in Chapter 9, here we want to consider how different norms can operate in different groups, and what happens when we deviate from what is normatively expected of us. An important norm that varies considerably across cultures but can also apply differentially to groups within a culture is **collectivism** versus **individualism.** In collectivist groups, the norm is to maintain harmony among group members, even if doing so might entail some personal costs; in such groups, disagreement and conflict among members are to be avoided. In contrast, in individualistic groups, the norm is to value standing out from the group and being different from others; individual variability is to be expected and disagreeing with the group is often seen as courageous. Therefore greater tolerance might be expected for those who deviate from group norms in individualist groups than in collectivist groups. Of course, people differ in how much they value being a member of a particular group. Considerable research has illustrated that when being a member of a particular group is important to our self-concept (we highly identify with it), we are more likely to be guided by its norms but ignore or even act contrary to its norms when we are not identified with that group (Jetten, Spears, & Manstead, 1997; Moreland & Levine, 2001). How then do people who are high or low in identification with an individualist or a collectivist group respond to someone who deviates from their group?

This question was addressed in a series of studies by Hornsey, Jetten, McAuliffe, and Hogg (2006). First, participants were selected who were either high or low in identification with their university. Then the norm of their student culture was described as being collectivist, with an emphasis on members achieving goals that will benefit the group as a whole rather than the student's personal goals, or as individualist, in which meeting personal goals is emphasized by members over achieving the goals of the student group as a whole. Responses to a student who was described as dissenting from the position of most students on an issue were then measured. As can be seen in Figure 11.5, among those who highly identify with their student group, a dissenter was liked when the norm was individualist, but that same dissenter was disliked when the norm was collectivist. Among those low in identification with the student group, the norm did not affect evaluations of

norms
Rules or expectations within a group concerning how its members should (or should not) behave.

collectivism
Groups in which the norm is to maintain harmony among group members, even if doing so might entail some personal costs.

individualism
In such groups the norm is to value standing out from the group and being different from others; individual variability is to be expected and disagreement among members is tolerated.

"Let's face it: you and this organization have never been a good fit."

Figure 11.6
Cohesive Groups Can Be Hard to Enter
As this dog is learning, fitting into a cohesive "cat-run" organization may be difficult, if not impossible.

(*Source: The New Yorker* December 18, 2000.)

the dissenting student. This research illustrates the potential costs of violating a group's norms—at least in the eyes of those who highly value that group.

Cohesiveness: The Force that Binds

Consider two groups. In the first, members like one another a great deal, strongly concur with the goals their group is seeking, and feel that they could not possibly find another group that would better satisfy their needs. They have formed a group identity and as a result are likely to perform their tasks well together. In the second, the opposite is true: Members don't like one another much, don't share common goals, and are actively seeking other groups which might offer them a better deal. They lack a shared identity and are less likely to successfully perform tasks together. The reason for this difference in the experiences and performances of these two groups is what social psychologists refer to as **cohesiveness**—all the forces that cause members to remain in the group (Ellemers, de Gilder, & Haslam, 2004). Cohesive groups have a sense of solidarity: They see themselves as homogenous, supportive of in-group members, cooperative with in-group members but less so with those defined as out-group members, oriented toward achieving group goals rather than individual goals, have high morale, and perform better than noncohesive groups (Hogg, 2007; Mullen & Cooper, 1994). As shown in Figure 11.6, out-group members may find it difficult to gain acceptance in cohesive groups—they may not "fit" the norms all that well. In fact, the presence of an out-group or other form of competitive threat tends to increase members' attraction and commitment to their own group (Hogg, 1992). It should not be surprising to find then that within nations that are at war, levels of cohesiveness dramatically increase.

In sum, several aspects of groups—status, roles, norms, and cohesiveness—play an important role in their functioning and in how they affect their members. We introduce these basic dimensions here because we'll refer to them in later sections of this chapter.

> **Principles to Remember**
> People's behavior in groups depends on the role they occupy and how much they identify with it, their status within the group, the group's norms, and whether it is a cohesive or noncohesive group.

The Benefits—and Costs—of Joining

If you consider how many different groups you belong to, you may be surprised at the length of the list—especially if you consider both common-bond (face-to-face) and common-identity (social categories) groups. While some people belong to more groups than others, despite the question posed in the opening of this chapter about whether being a hermit might be simpler, most of us are "joiners"—members of many different groups. In fact, sometimes we put forth a lot of effort to gain admittance to groups. Why, if we work hard to get in and the benefits of membership are so great, do we sometimes choose to leave groups? Withdrawing from a group to which we have belonged for months, years, or even decades can be a stressful experience. Here's what social psychologists have found out about why we join and the processes involved in leaving groups.

cohesiveness
All forces (factors) that cause group members to remain in the group.

KeyPoints

- Evolutionary theorists suggest that groups are necessary for human survival.

- Groups are composed of people who perceive themselves and are perceived by others as forming a coherent unit to some degree. The extent to which the group is perceived to form a coherent entity is known as entitativity.

- There are different kinds of groups: common-bond, in which the individual members have bonds with each other, and common-identity, in which the members are linked via the category as a whole.

- Groups or communities can form even without face to face interaction—such as online groups at YouTube.

- Basic aspects of groups involve status, roles, norms, and cohesiveness.

- People gain status in a group for many reasons, ranging from physical characteristics (e.g, height) to various aspects of their behavior. Status tends to be higher for those who are prototypical of the group, or have seniority within the group.

- The effects of roles on our behavior are often powerful, primarily when we have internalized the role as part of our identity.

- Deviating from group norms can affect how other group members, especially those who highly identify with the group, evaluate us. Norms can be collectivist or individualist.

- Another important feature of groups is their level of cohesiveness—the sum of all the factors that cause people to want to remain members.

Think About It

Think about the groups you belong to—do you play the same role and have similar status in each group or do those differ depending on whether the group membership is self-selected, temporary, one you highly identify with, or is a common-bond versus a common-identity group?

The Benefits of Joining: What Groups Do for Us

That people sometimes go through a lot to join a specific group is clear: Membership in many groups is by invitation only, and winning that invitation can be difficult. Perhaps more surprising is that once they gain admission, many people will stick with a group even when it experiences hard times. For instance, consider some sports fans and how they remain loyal to their team when it has a miserable season, even when it is the target of ridicule and gains a reputation as the worst of the worst. What accounts for this strong desire to join—and remain a part of—social groups? The answer, it appears, involves several different factors.

First, we often gain self-knowledge from belonging to various groups (Tajfel & Turner, 1986). Our membership in them tells us what kind of person we are—or perhaps, would like to be—so group membership becomes central to our self-concept. The result? We want in, and once we belong, we find it hard to imagine life outside this group because being a member helps make our life meaningful by defining to some extent who we are. Indeed, to be rejected by a group—even one we have recently joined—can be among the most painful of experiences (Williams, 2001). Being ostracized from just an online computer group can lower feelings of control and self-esteem both immediately after it occurs and continuing after even a forty-five-minute delay. Such harmful effects are particularly acute among people who are high in social anxiety and who fear rejection (Zadro, Boland, & Richardson, 2006).

Another obvious benefit of belonging to some groups is that they help us reach our goals. One important goal is attaining prestige. When an individual is accepted into a certain type of group—a highly selective school, an exclusive social club, a varsity sports team—self-esteem can increase. Just how important is this boost from joining and identifying with particular groups? As you can probably guess, the more an individual is seeking

Figure 11.7
Producing Social
Change: One Reason
Why People Join Groups
*One potential benefit
individuals obtain from
joining groups is social change.
For instance, by joining
together, members of oppressed
groups can often improve their
standing in, and treatment by,
society.*

self-enhancement—boost-
ing one's own public
image—the more impor-
tant will a group's status be
to that person and the more
strongly she or he will identify with it. In contrast, the
more a person is seeking
self-transcendence—to
contribute by helping others—the less important a
group's status will be that
person. This is precisely
what was found in research
by Roccas (2003). She first
measured students' desires for self-enhancement and self-transcendence. In addition, the perceived status of a group to which they belonged (in this case, their school) and their degree
of identification with this group were assessed. Results indicated that the stronger people's
desire for self-enhancement, the greater the link between the perceived status of the school
and identification with their school. In contrast, the stronger their desire for self-transcendence, the weaker the link was between school status and identification. In other words,
the group's status was more important to those seeking to boost their own image than for
those who were more concerned with a different goal—helping others.

People are also attracted to groups when they fit our goals—even if those goals are
relatively transient. Suppose you feel willing to take risks and try something new or, conversely, want to feel secure and feel a little cautious. How might these orientations affect
the kind of group you would join and value being in it? Would you prefer a relatively high
power group (that is able to exert influence and get things done) or a relatively low power
group with less of those capabilities? Recent research findings indicate that we like being
in a group best when that group matches our goal orientation (Sassenberg, Jonas, Shah,
& Brazy, 2007). Although people tend to like groups with greater power in general, this
is especially so when we are oriented toward greater risk, and we value lower power groups
when we are feeling more cautious and insecure.

Another important benefit of joining groups is that doing so often helps us to accomplish goals we could not achieve alone (i.e., social change). How can members of ethnic
minority groups, women, gays, or others that have been the target of oppression attain
equal rights? As we saw in Chapter 6, one way devalued groups cope with the discrimination they experience is to increasingly turn to and identify with their group. As a result
of recognizing shared grievances, people can develop a **politicized collective identity** and
engage in a power struggle on behalf of their group. As shown in Figure 11.7, by joining
together, people who have been the victims of prejudice gain "social clout" and can succeed in winning better treatment for their group (Simon & Klandermans, 2001). Indeed,
identification with such groups is a strong predictor of participation in public marches
and protests, initiating and signing petitions, boycotts against businesses that discriminate
against various minorities, and so on (Stürmer & Simon, 2004).

Clearly, then, we derive many benefits—some personal and some collective—from
belonging to and identifying with various groups. Indeed, it's apparent that we really can't
meet many of our most basic needs—social and otherwise—outside of groups.

**politicized collective
identity**
Recognizing shared grievances
and engaging in a power
struggle on behalf of one's
devalued group.

The Costs of Getting Accepted into a Group

Many groups erect high barriers to entry: They want only some people to join, and they
insist that those who do be highly motivated to enter. Steep initiation fees, substantial
efforts to prove one's credentials as being suitable, and long trial or probationary periods
are common methods of restricting group membership.

Social psychologists have addressed the question: What are the consequences of undergoing severe admission processes in terms of their impact on commitment to the group? Does paying a high price to secure membership in such selective groups require us to cognitively justify our time and effort in doing so and might that make it difficult to later admit that joining might have been a mistake? Moreover, could it be the case that the greater the discomfort (embarrassment, humiliation, or physical pain) we suffer during the admission process, the more cognitive dissonance will lead us to boost our perceptions of the group once we have gained admission?

To increase our commitment to a group because we have paid a heavy material or psychological price to join it might at first appear to be a rather strange idea. In a classic experiment, Aronson and Mills (1959) illustrated why this sometimes happens. To imitate differentially severe initiation rites, students in their study were asked to read either highly embarrassing material in front of a group, mildly embarrassing material, or they did not read any material. As we saw in Chapter 5, according to Festinger's (1957) cognitive dissonance theory, people feel discomfort when their attitudes and behavior are discrepant. When we have put forth considerable effort to achieve membership in a group, we may need to change our attitudes toward that group in a positive direction to justify our effortful behaviors. As a result, after going through an initiation to be admitted to a group and then learning that the group is unattractive after all, our commitment toward that group should actually increase. As these researchers predicted, liking for the group was greater as the severity of the initiation increased; the more embarrassing the material the students had to read, the more attractive they subsequently found this boring group.

The Costs of Membership: Why Groups Sometimes Splinter

As we discussed in the opening of this chapter, groups can seem like they are mixed blessings in life. While groups can help us to reach our goals, help to boost our status along the way, and form an important part of who we are, they also impose certain costs.

First, group membership often restricts personal freedom. Members of various groups are expected to behave in certain ways, and if they don't, the group may impose strong sanctions or may, ultimately, expel such violators from membership. For instance, in the United States, it is considered inappropriate for military officers to make public statements about politics. Even high-ranking generals who do so may be strongly reprimanded. In fact, during the Korean War, President Harry S. Truman removed an extremely famous general—Douglas McArthur—from command because he made such public statements.

Similarly, groups often make demands on members' time, energy, and resources, and they must meet these demands or surrender their membership. Some churches, for instance, require that their members donate 10 percent of their income to the church. People wishing to remain in these groups must comply or face expulsion. Finally, groups sometimes adopt positions or policies of which some members disapprove. Again, the dissenting members must remain silent, speak out and run the risk of strong sanctions, or withdraw. So group membership is not always a bed of roses; there are some real thorns hidden among the benefits, and members must often consider these carefully as they weigh the costs of group membership against its benefits.

Withdrawing from some groups can be a major step with lasting repercussions. For example, a person can give up their U.S. citizenship voluntarily at a U.S. Embassy by swearing an affidavit stating their desire to do so. People can also lose their U.S. passport and national rights if they take on the citizenship of another country, seek political office in another country, or otherwise assume an official role as representative of another nation. Although few people voluntarily make this choice—to rescind their citizenship—some young U.S. citizens did so as part of their objection to the war in Vietnam and to being drafted to fight in it. Although some nations allow dual citizenship, belonging to some groups can indeed prevent us from becoming members of other groups.

Such examples raise an intriguing question: Why might individuals take this ultimate action—exiting a group they once highly valued? One intriguing answer has been provided

*Less than twenty years ago, the
first women were ordained as
priests in the Church of
England. Some group members
found this change ideologically
intolerable and left the church,
while others saw the admission
of women to the priesthood as
enhancing their group identity.*

in a series of studies involving political parties and church groups (Sani, in press). When individuals identify with these sorts of groups, they often redraw the boundaries of their self-concept to include other group members (Aron & McLaughlin-Volpe, 2001). In other words, as far as they are concerned, other members of the group are categorized together with the self to in effect become "we." To the extent that people do identify themselves and others as part of the same category, then they may choose to withdraw from groups that they no longer see as meeting the definition of the we-ness they initially adopted. Thus individuals may decide to leave a group, and a group may splinter, when members conclude that some subset of the group has changed sufficiently that they can no longer be viewed as falling within the boundaries of their extended self-concept. This is particularly likely when differences in **ideology**—the philosophical and political values of a group—among different factions of the group become so disparate that some members cannot see themselves as part of the same group or sharing a social identity with other members of the group.

Evidence for this ideological splintering process among members of the Church of England was obtained by Sani (2005; Sani & Todman, 2003). In 1992, the Church of England changed their five-hundred-year tradition of allowing only males to enter the priesthood by adopting a new policy of accepting women as priests (see Figure 11.8). In 1994, the first women were ordained as priests, and as a result, hundreds of clergy who objected to this ideological change decided to leave the church. Why did they feel this drastic action was necessary? After all, they had been members and officials of this church for much of their lives and their identities were strongly bound up with it.

To investigate what led to this upheaval among members, these researchers asked over one thousand priests and deacons in the Church of England to express their views about the new policy of ordaining women as priests, the extent to which they felt this had changed the church greatly, how much they identified with the Church of England, the degree to which they felt emotionally distressed by the change, and whether they believed their views (if they were opposed to the policy change) would be heard. Results indicated that clergy who left the church did so because they felt this policy change altered fundamental doctrines so much that it was no longer the same organization as the one they originally joined and that it no longer represented their views. Further, they felt strongly that no one would pay attention to their dissenting opinions and that this left them no choice but to withdraw. As shown in Figure 11.9, perceiving their group identity as being subverted by this change resulted in emotional distress, reduced the perception that the church was an entitative group, and lowered identification with the church. These processes lead to a **schism**—splintering of the group into distinct factions that could not stay together united by a single identity. For those members who felt compelled to leave, the emotional distress experienced reflected the loss of this important identity and was akin to bereavement; because of this policy change, they perceived the original group that they had joined was effectively dead.

ideology
The philosophical and political values that govern a group.

schism
Splintering of a group into distinct factions following an ideological rift among members.

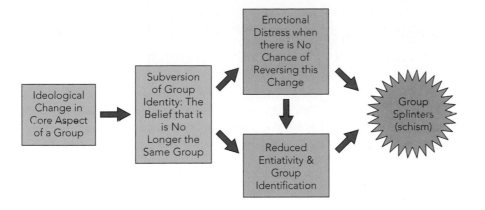

Figure 11.9
Why Groups Sometimes Splinter
Research (Sani, 2005; Sani & Todman, 2002) indicates that groups splinter when members perceive that the group has changed so much (subversion) that it is no longer the same entity (group) they originally joined, and when they conclude that no one will listen to their protests over this change (there is no chance of reversing it).

(*Source:* Based on suggestions by Sani, in press.)

This potential for splintering as groups undergo change is not restricted to religious groups. On the contrary, Sani (in press) notes that similar splits have occurred in many other groups—political parties, social movements, and in fact, can occur in any group that is based on shared beliefs and values. In other words, when groups splinter and many members leave, this is simply the final step in a process that has been unfolding for some time. Groups change, and when they do so to the extent that members feel that they can no longer identify with the group, the final outcome is inevitable: Some members will withdraw because, they believe, the group is no longer the same as the one they originally joined. Withdrawing is simply acknowledging what is already fact.

> **Principles to Remember**
> Belonging, one of the bedrock motivations of human life, can be rewarding, but membership in groups can also be costly.

KeyPoints

- Joining groups confers important benefits on members, including increased self-knowledge, progress toward important goals, enhanced status, and when a politicized collective identity is formed, a means of attaining social change.

- However group membership also exacts important costs, such as loss of personal freedom and heavy demands on time, energy, and resources.

- The desire to join exclusive and prestigious groups may be so strong that individuals are willing to undergo painful and dangerous initiations to become members. After doing so, people must justify to themselves their efforts to join the group and therefore show increased positive attitude change toward that group.

- Individuals withdraw from groups when they feel that the group's ideology has changed so much

that it no longer reflects their basic values or beliefs. When a schism or splintering of a group into distinct factions occurs, some members experience emotional distress, feel they can no longer identify with the group, and they no longer see the group as the cohesive one they originally joined.

Think About It

Have you ever thought about joining a fraternity or sorority? If so, what effects do you think experiencing hazing, in which established group members subject you to some forms of humiliation, might have on your commitment to the group?

Effects of the Presence of Others: From Task Performance to Behavior in Crowds

The fact that our behavior is often strongly affected by the groups to which we belong is far from surprising; after all, in these groups there are usually well-established norms that tell us how we are expected to behave as members. Perhaps much more surprising is the fact that often, we are strongly affected by the mere presence of others, even if we are not part of a formal group. You are probably already familiar with such effects from your own experience. For instance, suppose you are sitting alone in a room studying. You may sit any old way you find comfortable, including putting your feet up on the furniture. But if a stranger enters the room, all this may change. You will probably refrain from doing some things you might have done when alone, and you may change many other aspects of your behavior—even though you don't know this person and are not directly interacting with her or him (see Figure 11.10). So clearly, we are often affected by the mere physical presence of others. While such effects take many different forms, we'll focus here on two that are especially important: the effects of the presence of others on our performance of various tasks and the effects of being in a large crowd.

Figure 11.10
Effects of the Mere Presence of Others
Often, the mere presence of other people, even if they are total strangers, can strongly affect our behavior. For example, we change from casual slouching and feet on the furniture to a more "socially acceptable" posture.

(*Source:* Stephen Reysen)

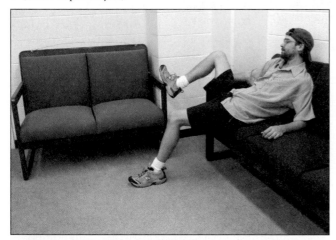

Social Facilitation: Performing in the Presence of Others

Sometimes, when we perform a task, we work totally alone; for instance, you might study alone in your room, and as I write this chapter, I am alone in my office. In many other cases, even if we are working on a task by ourselves, other people are present—for instance, you might study at an Internet café or in your room while your roommate sleeps or also studies. In other situations, we work on projects together with other people as part of a task-performing group. What are the effects of the presence of others on our performance in these various settings? Let's see what research findings suggest.

Imagine that you are a dancer and that you are preparing for your first important performance. You practice your routines alone for several hours each day, month after month. Finally, the big day arrives and you walk out onto the stage to find a huge audience seated there waiting to see you dance (see Figure 11.11). How will you do? Most of us can recall times when we have been nervous about performing in front of others; I can still remember the first time I ever lectured in a big undergraduate class. Evidence from several different studies confirms that the presence of others can affect our performance. A dramatic demonstration of such effects is provided by well-known research that we describe in the *Building the Science: Classics of Social Psychology* on page 396.

Can Having an Audience Distract Us?

Some have suggested that the presence of others, either as an audience or as coactors, can be distracting, and for this reason, it can produce cognitive overload (e.g., Baron, 1986). Because performers must divide their attention between the task and the audience, such increased cognitive load can result in a tendency to restrict one's attention so as to focus only on essential cues or stimuli while screening out nonessential ones. Several findings offer support for this view, known as

distraction-conflict theory. So, which is more important—increased arousal with an audience (Zajonc, 1965) or this tendency toward a narrowed attentional focus?

Huguet, Galvaing, Monteil, and Dumas (1999) attempted to resolve this issue by suggesting that any distraction could affect a performer. Yes, the presence of others generates increased arousal, but it may do so

Figure 11.11
How Does an Audience Affect Our Performance? *What happens when people perform in front of an audience—do they do better or worse than when they are alone? Social psychological research offers some intriguing answers concerning the effects of an audience on this dancer's performance.*

because of the cognitive demands of paying attention both to an audience and to the task being performed rather than as a result of their mere physical presence. So the presence of others may influence task performance by inducing a narrowed attention focus. Hetherington, Anderson, Norton, and Newson (2006) applied these ideas to understand the effects of others on eating as a function of distraction. Caloric intake was measured in male participants under differing distraction conditions. Both eating with friends and while watching TV increased eating. Because both friends and TV can be distracting, it can result in a greater focus on the food and thus lead to improved performance (i.e., greater caloric intake). In contrast, eating in the presence of strangers was less distracting, and therefore, caused no increased focus on food and no increased caloric intake. One advantage of this cognitive perspective is that it helps explain when and why animals and people are affected by the presence of an audience that differs in how distracting it is to the performer. After all, animals, too, (even cockroaches) can experience conflicting tendencies to work on a task and pay attention to an audience.

> **⌒Principles to Remember**
> An audience affects our performance differentially depending on the type of task (how well practiced at it we are) and how much we are distracted by the audience.

distraction-conflict theory
A theory suggesting that social facilitation stems from the conflict produced when individuals attempt, simultaneously, to pay attention to the other people present and to the task being performed.

⌒KeyPoints

- The mere presence of other people either as an audience or as coactors can influence our performance on many tasks. Such effects are known as social facilitation.

- The drive theory of social facilitation suggests that the presence of others is arousing and can either increase or reduce performance, depending on whether dominant responses in a given situation are correct or incorrect.

- The evaluation-apprehension view suggests that an audience disrupts performance because of the anxiety about being evaluated that can be experienced.

- The distraction-conflict perspective suggests that the presence of others induces conflicting tendencies to focus on the task being performed and on the audience or coactors. This can result both in increased arousal and narrowed attentional focus.

- Recent findings offer support for the view that several kinds of audiences produce narrowed attentional focus among people performing a task. Both the arousal and cognitive views of social facilitation can help explain why social facilitation occurs among animals and people.

Think About It
The potential that other people are watching us perform many tasks has increased—including surveillance by cameras in public places, such as stores and at traffic intersections. Do you think our behavior is likely to be improved or disrupted—depending on the extent to which we are aware that we are being watched?

BUILDING THE SCIENCE
CLASSICS OF SOCIAL PSYCHOLOGY

Does the Presence of Others Have an Effect on Performance? Ask Any Cockroach!

Almost forty years ago, Zajonc, Heingartner, and Herman (1969) conducted an interesting and, seemingly, zany experiment. They arranged to have cockroaches run a maze. That would have been strange enough for social psychologists, but these researchers added a curious twist to the roach maze: They constructed clear plastic boxes close enough to the maze so that a roach "audience" could observe the participants running the maze. With this setup the roaches in the maze would also know they were being watched; they would be aware of the presence of the onlooking audience.

As it turned out, those cockroaches who were being watched by other roaches ran the maze faster than cockroaches without an audience. Zajonc and others were intent on making a point about a group phenomenon called social facilitation, that is, the effects of the presence of others on performance. Although, as social psychologists, we typically study human, as opposed to cockroach, behavior, why did Zajonc and others choose to conduct an animal experiment of this type?

To understand why he did so, we need to go back to the first published experiment in social psychology. In 1898, Triplett noticed that cyclists tend to have faster times when riding in the presence of other cyclists compared to when riding alone (i.e., "against the clock"). To ensure his observation was correct, he conducted a study under controlled laboratory conditions. He instructed forty adolescents to wind a fishing reel as rapidly as possible. As hypothesized, they reeled faster in pairs than when they performed the task alone. Triplett concluded that it

was the presence of another contestant simultaneously participating in the race that "liberates latent energy not ordinarily available." Thus it appeared that it was the mere presence of others that caused increased performance. Later, Allport (1920) performed experiments using a different type of task that also supported Triplett's conclusion. Allport experimented with free association of thoughts in a business environment. When with a coworker, the number of associations generated increased relative to when the participant was not with a coworker. So, regardless of whether it was a physical or mental task, the presence of others seemed to facilitate performance.

Zajonc (1965) argued that the mere presence of others would only facilitate a well-learned response and that it could inhibit a less practiced or "new" response. Why? He noted that the presence of others increases physiological arousal (our bodies become more energized), and as a result, any dominant response will be facilitated. This means that we can focus better on something we know or have practiced when we're aroused, but that same physiological arousal will create problems when we're dealing with something new or complex. This reasoning—depicted in Figure 11.12—became known as the drive theory of social facilitation because it focuses on arousal or drive-based effects on performance. The presence of others will improve individuals' performance when they are highly skilled at the task in question (in this case their dominant responses would tend to be correct) but will interfere with performance when they are not highly skilled—for instance, when they are learning

Social Loafing: Letting Others Do the Work

You have probably had the experience of seeing a road or construction crew in which some appear to be working hard while others seem to be standing around not doing much at all. When it comes to a larger task, such as lifting a telephone pole, one in which everyone has to fully pitch in to accomplish the task, the question is: Will all of the workers exert equal effort? Probably not. Some will contribute by taking on as much of the load as they can, others will exert themselves moderately, and some may simply hang on and pretend to be lifting when, in fact, they are not (see Figure 11.13 on page 398).

This pattern is quite common in situations in which groups perform what are known as **additive tasks**—ones in which the contributions of each member are combined into a single group output. On such tasks, some people work hard while others goof off, doing

additive tasks
Tasks for which the group product is the sum or combination of the efforts of individual members.

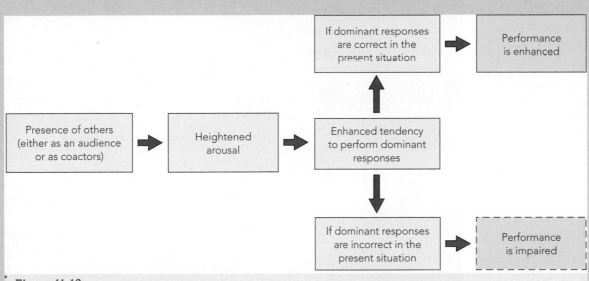

Figure 11.12
The Drive Theory of Social Facilitation
According to the drive theory of social facilitation (Zajonc, 1965), the presence of others, either as an audience or coactors, increases arousal and this, in turn, strengthens the tendency to perform dominant responses. If these responses are correct, performance is improved; if they are incorrect, performance is harmed.

to perform it (for their dominant responses would not be correct in that case).

Other researchers thought that people's performance might sometimes be disrupted by the presence of an audience because of apprehension about having their performance evaluated. This **evaluation apprehension** idea was studied by Cottrell, Wack, Sekerak and Rittle (1968). In fact, several of their experiments found that social facilitation did not occur when an audience was blindfolded or displayed no interest in watching the person performing the task, which lent support to this interpretation.

But Zajonc (1965) did not believe that the fear of potential evaluation was necessary for social facilitation to occur, which was why he performed the cockroach experiment. Given that we can assume that cockroaches do not evaluate the maze-running abilities of other cockroaches, it is safe to say that social facilitation does not require evaluation apprehension to work, at least for some species.

evaluation apprehension
Concern over being evaluated by others. Such concern can increase arousal and so contribute to social facilitation effects.

less than their share and less than they might do if working alone. Social psychologists refer to such effects as **social loafing**—reductions in motivation and effort that occur when individuals work collectively in a group compared to when they work individually as independent co-actors (Karau & Williams, 1993).

Social loafing has been demonstrated in many different task contexts. For example in one of the first, Latané, Williams, and Harkins (1979) asked groups of male students to clap or cheer as loudly as possible at specific times, supposedly so that the experimenter could determine how much noise people make in social settings. To make sure participants were not affected by the actual noise of other participants, they wore headphones, through which noise making was played at a constant volume. Furthermore, they could not see the other participants but were only told how many others they were shouting with. They performed these tasks in groups of two, four, or six people. Results indicated

social loafing
Reductions in motivation and effort when individuals work in a group compared to when they work individually.

Figure 11.13
Does Everyone Do Their Share of the Work? Not Always
When several people work together to accomplish a task, it is probable that they will not all exert the same amount of effort. Some will work quite hard, others will do less, and perhaps a few will do nothing at all while pretending to work hard! Social loafing in groups tends to reduce their output overall.

that although the total amount of noise rose as group size increased, the amount produced by each participant dropped. In other words, each person put out less and less effort as the size of the group increased.

Such effects are not restricted to simple and seemingly meaningless situations; on the contrary, they appear to be quite general in scope and occur with respect to many different tasks—cognitive ones and those involving physical effort (Weldon & Mustari, 1988; Williams & Karau, 1991). As anyone who has worked as a server in a restaurant knows, social loafing can occur when your tip is at stake! People leave proportionally less in tips as the size of the group increases, which may be one reason why a standard tip is often added to the tab by the restaurant when there are six or more in a party.

To ask whether social loafing occurs in school settings might elicit a "duh" response from students. Englehart (2006) suggests that social loafing can explain patterns of student participation, a problematic area for many teachers, as a function of the size of the class. In a larger class, students are more anonymous with regard to any teacher's ability to remember who more readily participated. Thus students may loaf with impunity. Students in larger classes may nevertheless participate if they are in a highly competitive environment. Moreover, if a topic is particularly relevant to the daily lives or concerns of students, their interest may undercut their inclination to loaf in larger classes. For the most part, however, social loafing is simply less likely to happen in smaller classes.

Price, Harrison, and Gavin (2006) assessed the contributions of various psychological factors to social loafing among students working in teams on a project over a three-month period. In their study, two major factors affected social loafing. First, if people felt dispensable to the group, they were more likely to loaf. Second, the more fairness that was perceived in the group generally, the less likely participants were to loaf. What determined these two perceptions—dispensability and fairness? When participants had substantial knowledge and skills relating to the task, they felt less dispensable. So, in effect, being able to offer task-relevant help to the group served to counteract loafing. In addition, people in the group were either more or less similar to each other on dimensions, such as age, sex, ethnicity, and marital status. This factor related to feelings of fairness. That is, if people felt dissimilar to other group members, they were less likely to feel fairly treated, and thus, were more likely to loaf. This may come about because, in fact, those who are "different" are marginalized in the group. However it arises though, dissimilarity from the other group members led participants to feel more dispensable, and thus more likely to loaf. So what can be done to reduce social loafing?

Reducing Social Loafing: Some Useful Techniques

The most obvious way of reducing social loafing involves making the output or effort of each participant readily identifiable (Williams, Harkins, & Latané, 1981). Under these conditions, people can't sit back and let others do their work, so social loafing is reduced. When people believe their contribution matters, and a strong performance on the part of the group will lead to a desired outcome, individuals also tend to try harder (Shepperd & Taylor, 1999). So, pooling contributions to a task—such as cowriting a paper—will be effective only to the extent that each writer's contributions is clear; even better is when each person feels uniquely skilled to write their own part.

Second, groups can reduce social loafing by increasing group members' commitment to successful task performance (Brickner, Harkins, & Ostrom, 1986). Pressures toward working hard will then serve to offset temptations to engage in social loafing. Third, social loafing can be reduced by increasing the apparent importance or value of a task (Karau & Williams, 1993). Fourth, social loafing is reduced when individuals view their contributions to the task as not redundant with those of others (Weldon & Mustari, 1988). Fifth, people are less likely to loaf if they are given some kind of standard of performance— either in terms of how much others are doing or their own past performance (Williams et al., 1981). Together, these steps can sharply reduce social loafing and the temptation to goof off at the expense of others.

Effects of Being in a Crowd

Have you ever attended a football or basketball game at which members of the crowd screamed insults, threw things at the referees, or engaged in other violent behavior they would probably never show in other settings? Most of us haven't because such extreme events are relatively rare, although, interestingly enough, this is part of the stereotype of how people behave in crowds, particularly those at sporting events. English soccer fans have become especially famous for **hooliganism**—incidents throughout Europe of serious disorder at matches involving England's team (Stott, Hutchison, & Drury, 2001). Such effects in crowds—in which there is a drift toward wild, unrestrained behavior—were initially termed **deindividuation** because they seemed to stem, at least in part, from the fact that when people are in a large crowd they tend to "to lose their individuality" and instead act as others do. More formally, the term *deindividuation* was used to indicate a psychological state characterized by reduced self-awareness and personal identity salience, brought on by external conditions, such as being an anonymous member of a large crowd.

Initial research on deindividuation (Zimbardo, 1976) seemed to suggest that being in a crowd makes people anonymous and therefore less responsible or accountable for their own actions, which, in turn, encourages unrestrained, antisocial actions. More recent evidence, though, indicates that deindividuation leads to greater normative behavior, not less. When we are part of a large crowd we are more likely to obey the norms of this group— whatever those may be (Postmes & Spears, 1998). For instance, at a sporting event, when norms in that situation suggest that it is appropriate to boo the opposing team, that is what many people—especially highly identified fans—will do. Certainly that seems to have been the norm that was active for "English hooligans" in the past. However recent evidence indicates that, as a result of social psychological intervention with police agencies, those norms can be changed (Stott, Adang, Livingstone, & Schreiber, 2007). As a result, at the Euro2004 matches, England's fans no longer defined hooliganism as characteristic of their fan group; they self-policed by marginalizing those few English fans who attempted to create conflict, and no violent incidents took place.

In a classic study demonstrating the importance of the nature of the norms operating

hooliganism
Negative stereotype about how people behave in crowds at sporting events, especially applied to incidents involving England's soccer fans.

deindividuation
A psychological state characterized by reduced self-awareness brought on by external conditions, such as being an anonymous member of a large crowd.

Figure 11.14
The Crowd: Conforming to Norms for Good or Ill
Crowds sometimes engage in actions that individual members would never dream of performing if they were alone. Those actions can range from dramatically destructive, as in the left photo, to peaceful, as in the right photo. Identifying with others in a crowd can strongly affect our behavior and encourage conformity to the norms governing that particular crowd.

in conditions of anonymity, Johnson and Downing (1979) had some groups of participants dress in hoods reminiscent of those worn by the Klu Klux Klan, while other participants wore clothing similar to nurses' uniforms. Half of the participants in each group wore a mask (the deindividuated condition), while faces were visible for others (the individuated condition). In the individuated condition, when the participants were given an opportunity to shock another person, those in the robes gave more intense shocks than those in the nurses' uniform. Did deindividuation intensify aggressive behavior in the robe condition? Yes, slightly, but the nurses' uniform substantially reduced the intensity of shock delivered under conditions of deindividuation.

Overall, then, being part of a large crowd and experiencing deindividuation does not necessarily lead to negative or harmful behaviors: It simply increases the likelihood that crowd members will follow the norms of the group. Those norms might be of showing respect and silently crying—behaviors demonstrated at the immense gatherings following Diana, Princess of Wales' death. Or, they could be norms of working together for a purpose—coordinating efforts to save people from crumbled buildings or praying and singing joyously together at huge Christian revival meetings. What is crucial is the norm and identity that is salient in a particular crowd. When people are in large crowds, as shown in Figure 11.14, what behavior they will exhibit—for good or ill—will depend on what norms are operating.

> **Principles to Remember**
> Behavior in groups is governed by group identities and the norms applicable to those identities. Crowds can result in violent or prosocial actions.

KeyPoints

- When individuals work together on an additive task, in which their contributions are combined, social loafing—reduced output by each group member—frequently occurs. Such loafing has been found on physical, cognitive, and verbal tasks among both adults and children.

- Social loafing can be reduced in several ways: by making outputs individually identifiable, by increasing commitment to the task and task importance, and by assuring that each members' contributions to the task are unique.

- When we are part of a large crowd, deindividuation—in which we are less aware of our personal self and morals—can occur. People therefore act more normatively in crowds based on what group identity is salient. Those norms can sanction either antisocial behavior or prosocial actions.

Think About It
Because the norms operating in a large group are so crucial to predicting whether people will act in either an antisocial or a prosocial fashion, how might we know—before placing ourselves in that setting—what norms are likely to operate in a specific crowd?

Coordination in Groups: Cooperation or Conflict?

Cooperation—helping that is mutual and both sides benefit—is common in groups working together to attain shared goals. As we discussed in the beginning of this chapter, by cooperating, people can attain goals they could never hope to reach by themselves. Surprisingly, though, cooperation does not always develop in groups. Sometimes people belonging to a group may perceive their personal interests as incompatible, and instead of coordinating their efforts, they may work against each other, often producing negative results for both sides. This is known as **conflict** and can be defined as a process in which individuals or groups perceive that others have taken, or will soon take, actions incompatible with their own interests. Conflict is indeed a process, for, as you probably know from your own experience, it has a nasty way of escalating—from simple mistrust, through a spiral of anger, to actions designed to harm the other side. When carried to extremes, the ultimate effects can be harmful to both sides. Let's see what social psychologists have learned about both patterns of behavior.

Cooperation: Working with Others to Achieve Shared Goals

Cooperation is often highly beneficial to the people involved. So, why don't group members always cooperate? One answer is straightforward: because some goals that people seek simply can't be shared. Several people seeking the same job or romantic partner can't combine forces to attain these goals; the rewards can go to only one. Likewise, if I want to look "good," I might not want to cooperate with others and have to share the glory—as shown in Figure 11.15. In such cases, cooperation may not allow people to maximize the likelihood of attaining all their goals, or their most important one, in a particular situation.

In many other situations, however, cooperation could develop but does not. This is precisely the kind of situation of most interest to social psychologists, who have tried to identify the factors that tip the balance either toward or away from cooperation.

Social Dilemmas: Where Cooperation Could Occur But Often Doesn't

Social dilemmas are situations in which each person can increase his or her individual gains by acting in purely selfish manner, but if all (or most) people do the same thing, the outcomes experienced by all are reduced (Komorita & Parks, 1994). A classic illustration of this kind of situation is known as the prisoner's dilemma—a situation faced by two suspects who have been caught by police. Here, either or both people can choose to cooperate (e.g., stay silent and not confess) or compete (e.g., "rat the other person out"). If both cooperate with each other, then they both experience large gains. If both compete, each person loses substantially. What happens if one chooses to compete while the other chooses to cooperate? In this case the one who competes experiences a moderate gain, while the trusting one loses. Social psychologists have used this type of situation to examine the factors that tip the balance toward trust and cooperation or mistrust and competition (Insko et al., 2001).

cooperation
Behavior in which groups work together to attain shared goals.

conflict
A process in which individuals or groups perceive that others have taken or will soon take actions incompatible with their own interests.

social dilemmas
Situations in which each person can increase his or her individual gains by acting in one way, but if all (or most) people do the same thing, the outcomes experienced by all are reduced.

Figure 11.15
Should You Cooperate with Coworkers or Compete with Them— That Is the Question! *Employees sometimes have to decide whether to cooperate (by working to attain a shared goal) or to compete (by valuing their own career advancement over the good of the group). Research findings indicate that many factors influence the choice people make in this kind of situation.*

Figure 11.16
Awareness of Sanction for Noncooperation Can Undermine Trust and Cooperation

At first, awareness that there are sanctions for noncooperation might serve to ensure people cooperate with others (left). However later responses to a new social dilemma may be less cooperative following exposure to sanctions for noncooperation because it serves to undermine trust in others (right).

(*Source:* Based on data from Mulder, van Dijk, De Cremer, & Wilke, 2006.)

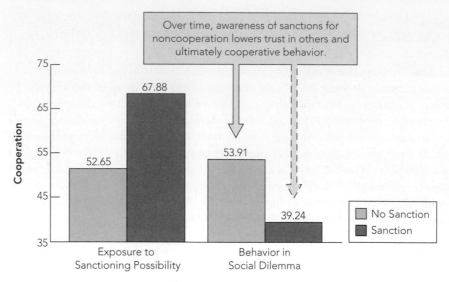

It might be reasonable to suppose that decreasing the attractiveness of competition should increase cooperation. One way to do this would be to increase the sanctions given in social dilemma for uncooperative choices. But doing so might change how people perceive such situations—from one involving trust in others to one based on economic self-interest. When seen as based in trust, cooperation should be higher than when the dilemma is seen as a situation in which people act on their own self-interests. To what degree, then, does the presence of sanctions for noncooperation undermine people's subsequent cooperative behavior—the exact opposite of its intended effect?

Mulder, van Dijk, De Cremer, and Wilke (2006) addressed this question by first telling their participants about a game that "other participants in a prior study" were said to have engaged in. All participants were told about a situation in which four group members had to decide whether to keep chips for themselves or donate them to the group. The total number of chips that were donated by the members to the group would be doubled in value by the experimenter and then equally divided among the members. This information phase of the study was included so that the presence of sanctioning for noncooperative group members could be varied. The crucial manipulation was whether a sanctioning system—applied to the two people who donated the least amount of chips—was said to have been operating or not. Later, when the participants took part in a different social dilemma in which no sanctioning was mentioned, the influence of exposure to the prior sanctioning system for noncooperation could be assessed. As you can see in Figure 11.16, prior exposure to the sanctioning for noncooperation subsequently lowered cooperation when the participants made their behavioral choices in a social dilemma. The reduction in cooperation among those exposed to a sanctioning system stemmed from changes in participants' perceptions of the extent to which they could trust that others will behave cooperatively.

Conflict: Its Nature, Causes, and Effects

Unfortunately, conflict is an all-too-common part of social life and can be extremely costly to both sides. We consider what factors cause such behavior, and perhaps even more importantly, what can be done to reduce it.

Our definition of conflict emphasizes the existence of incompatible interests and recognition of this fact by the parties involved. But conflict can sometimes occur when the two sides don't really have opposing interests—they may simply believe that these exist (De Dreu

& Van Lang, 1995; Tjosvold & DeDreu, 1997). In short, a growing body of evidence suggests that social factors play a strong a role in initiating conflicts.

One social factor that plays a role in this respect is what has been termed faulty attribution—errors concerning the causes of others' behavior (Baron, 1990a). When individuals find that their interests have been thwarted, they gen-

Figure 11.17
Destructive Criticism: One Social Cause of Conflict
When one person criticizes another harshly and without clear justification, the recipient may react with anger and a desire for revenge. The result is that the seeds for bitter and lasting conflict between them may be planted, a conflict that does not stem from incompatible interests.

erally try to determine why this occurred. Was it bad luck? A lack of planning on their part? Or was it the result of intentional interference by another person or group? If they conclude that the latter is true, then the seeds for an intense conflict may be planted—even if other people actually had nothing to do with the situation. In other words, erroneous attributions concerning the causes of negative outcomes can, and often do, play an important role in conflicts and sometimes cause them to occur when they could readily have been avoided.

Another social factor that plays an important role in conflict is what might be termed *faulty communication*—the fact that individuals sometimes communicate with others in a way that angers or annoys them. Have you ever been on the receiving end of harsh criticism—criticism you felt was unfair, insensitive, and not in the least helpful? The results of several studies indicate that feedback of this type, known as destructive criticism, can leave the recipient hungry for revenge and so set the stage for conflicts that, again, do not necessarily stem from incompatible interests (see Figure 11.17; e.g., Baron, 1990a; Cropanzano, 1993).

A third social cause of conflict involves the tendency to perceive our own views as objective and as reflecting reality but those of others as biased by their ideology (Keltner & Robinson, 1997; Oakes et al., 1994). As a result of this tendency, we magnify differences between our views and those of others and also exaggerate conflicts of interest between us. Research findings indicate that this tendency is stronger for groups or individuals who currently hold a dominant or powerful position (Keltner & Robinson, 1997). This, in turn, often leads to what is known as the status quo bias—a tendency for powerful groups defending the current status quo to be less accurate at intergroup perception than the groups that are challenging them. For instance, as we described in Chapter 6, they perceive their position as much more reasonable or objective than it is.

Finally, conflict within a group may stem from poor initial performance by the group. Poor performance and negative feedback about this performance may be threatening to group members and this, in turn, can lead them to blame each other for these poor results (recall our discussion of the self-serving bias in Chapter 3). To test these predictions, Peterson and Behfar (2003) assessed the amount of conflict master of business administration students experienced before and after they received grades on a team project. Course instructors provided information on the grades received by each team on class projects as a measure of performance feedback to the teams. Results indicated that, the more negative the feedback groups received, the greater the conflict they reported after receiving this information. In sum, then, conflict does not stem solely from opposing interests.

Resolving Conflicts: Some Useful Techniques

Because conflicts are often costly, the people involved usually want to resolve them as quickly as possible. What steps are most useful for reaching this goal? Two seem especially useful—bargaining and superordinate goals.

bargaining (negotiation)
A process in which opposing sides exchange offers, counteroffers, and concessions, either directly or through representatives.

Bargaining: The Universal Process

By far the most common strategy for resolving conflicts is **bargaining** or **negotiation** (Pruitt & Carnevale, 1993). In this process, opposing sides exchange offers, counteroffers, and concessions, either directly or through representatives. If the process is successful, a solution acceptable to both sides is attained, and the conflict is resolved. If, instead, bargaining is unsuccessful, costly deadlock may result and the conflict will intensify. What factors determine which of these outcomes occurs?

First, and perhaps most obviously, the outcome of bargaining is determined, in part, by the specific tactics adopted by the bargainers. Many of these are designed to accomplish a key goal: reduce the opponent's aspirations (i.e., hopes or goals), so that this person or group becomes convinced that it cannot get what it wants and should, instead, settle for something less favorable to their side. Tactics for accomplishing this goal include: (1) beginning with an extreme initial offer—one that is favorable to the side proposing it; (2) the "big-lie" technique—convincing the other side that one's break-even point is much higher than it is so, that they offer more than would otherwise be the case; for example, used car sales people may claim that they will lose money on the deal if the price is lowered when in fact this is false; and (3) convincing the other side that you can go elsewhere and get even better terms (Thompson, 1998).

A second and important determinant of the outcome of bargaining involves the overall orientation of the bargainers to the process (Pruitt & Carnevale, 1993). People taking part in negotiations can approach such discussions from either of two distinct perspectives. In one, they can view the negotiations as win–lose situations in which gains by one side are necessarily linked with losses for the other. Negotiations can also be approached as potential win–win situations, in which the interests of the two sides are not necessarily incompatible and in which the potential gains of both sides can be maximized.

This approach produces more favorable results in the long run and is typically what is used when negotiating international conflicts, such as the one between the Israelis and Palestinians. Such peace agreements, when achieved, are known as integrative agreements—ones that offer greater joint benefits than would be attained by simply splitting all differences down the middle. Consider a simple example of this: Two cooks are preparing recipes that call for an entire orange, and they have only one. What should they do? One possibility is to divide the orange in half. That leaves both with less than they need. Suppose, however, through discussion it is learned that one cook needs all the juice while the other needs all the peel. Here, a much better solution is possible: They can share the orange, each using the part most needed. Many techniques for attaining such integrative solutions exist; a few of these are summarized in Table 11.3.

Table 11.3 Tactics for Reaching Integrative Agreements

Many strategies can be useful in attaining integrative agreements—ones that offer better outcomes than simple compromise. Several of these are summarized here.

TACTIC	DESCRIPTION
Broadening the pie	Available resources are increased so that both sides can obtain their major goals.
Nonspecific compensation	One side gets what it wants; the other is compensated on an unrelated issue.
Logrolling	Each party makes concessions on low-priority issues in exchange for concessions on issues it values more highly.
Bridging	Neither party gets its initial demands, but a new option that satisfies the major interests of both sides is developed.
Cost cutting	One party gets what it desires, and the costs to the other party are reduced in some manner.

To achieve an integrative solution with another party, it often requires really listening to what is necessary for the other side and being concerned about what is of greatest importance to them. Indeed, one might need to address the other side's concern about "saving face." White, Tynan, Galinsky, and Thompson (2004) examined the impact of "sensitivity to loss of face" in a simulated negotiation among business students. When the seller of a business was committed to it, negotiations with the buyer were less successful when the seller was sensitive to losing face. This research illustrates how important it can be to avoid actions during bargaining that threaten an opponent and to take into account the other party's psychological needs.

Superordinate Goals: "We're All in This Together"

As we saw in Chapter 6, members of groups in conflict often divide the world into two opposing camps—"us" and "them." They perceive members of their own group (us) as quite different from, and usually better than, people belonging to other groups (them). These tendencies to magnify differences between one's own group and others and to disparage outsiders are powerful and often play a role in the occurrence and persistence of conflicts. Fortunately, they can be countered through the induction of **superordinate goals**—goals that both sides seek and that tie their interests together rather than driving them apart (Sherif et al., 1961). When opposing sides can be made to see that they share overarching goals, conflict is often sharply reduced and may, in fact, be replaced by overt cooperation.

superordinate goals
Goals that both sides to a conflict seek and that tie their interests together rather than driving them apart.

> ### Principles to Remember
> Choosing to cooperate with others often rests on the extent to which we trust those others. Conversely, conflict often stems from and can escalate when we do not trust others and perceive them as likely to act in ways that are incompatible with our interests.

KeyPoints

- Cooperation—working together with others to obtain shared goals—is a common aspect of social life. However cooperation does not develop in many situations in which it is possible, partly because such situations involve social dilemmas in which individuals can increase their own gains by defection.

- Having sanctions for noncooperation can change the extent to which people trust others and thereby lower the extent to which they engage in cooperation.

- Conflict often begins when individuals or groups perceive that others' interests are incompatible with their own interests. Social factors, such as faulty attributions, poor communication, the tendency to perceive our own views as objective, destructive criticism, and poor initial performance, can play a role in conflict.

- Conflict can be reduced in many ways, but bargaining and the induction of superordinate goals seem to be particularly effective.

Think About It

Are all bargaining strategies—even if effective—likely to be perceived as ethical? Getting the best deal for oneself or one's group can often involve being less than truthful to the other party.

Perceived Fairness in Groups: Its Nature and Effects

Have you ever been in a situation in which you felt that you were getting less than you deserved from some group to which you belong? If so, you probably experienced anger and resentment in response to such perceived unfairness or injustice (Cropanzano, 1993; Scher, 1997). If so, you may have taken some concrete action to rectify it and attempt to get whatever it was you felt you deserved. Social psychologists have conducted many studies to understand (1) the factors that lead individuals to decide they have been treated fairly or unfairly and (2) what they do about it—their efforts to deal with perceived unfairness (Adams, 1965). We'll now consider both questions.

Basic Rules for Judging Fairness: Distributive, Procedural, and Transactional Justice

Deciding whether we have been treated fairly in our relations with others can be quite tricky. First, we rarely have all the information needed to make such a judgment accurately (van den Bos & Lind, 2001). Second, even if we did, perceived fairness is in the eye of the beholder, so is subject to many forms of bias. Despite such complexities, research on perceived fairness in group settings indicates that, in general, we make these judgments by focusing on three distinct aspects or rules.

The first, known as **distributive justice (fairness),** involves the outcomes we and others receive. According to the equity rule, available rewards should be divided among group members in accordance with their contributions: The more they provide in terms of effort, experience, skills, and other contributions to the group, the more they should receive. For example, we expect people with more seniority in a group or organization to receive higher salaries than beginners; similarly, we expect people who have made major contributions toward reaching the group's goals to receive greater rewards than people who have contributed little. In short, we often judge fairness in terms of the ratio between the contributions group members have provided and the rewards they receive (Adams, 1965). We expect this ratio to be approximately the same for all members, and to the extent it is not, we perceive that distributive justice has been violated and that unfairness exists (Brockner & Wiesenfeld, 1996; Greenberg, 1993).

While people are concerned with the outcomes they receive, this is far from the entire story where judgments of fairness are concerned. In addition, people are also interested in the fairness of the procedures through which rewards have been distributed—what is known as **procedural justice** (Folger & Baron, 1996; Blader & Tyler, 2005). We base our judgments about it on factors such as: (1) the extent to which the procedures are applied in the same manner to all people; (2) there are opportunities for correcting any errors in distributions; (3) decision makers avoid being influenced by their own self-interest; and (4) the extent to which decisions are made in a manner compatible with the ethical and moral values held by the people affected.

Evidence that such factors really do influence our judgments concerning procedural justice has been obtained in many studies (Brockner et al., 1994; Blader & Tyler, 2005). For instance, in one investigation, when people perceived authorities as holding attitudes that are biased against them, and when they believed they lack "voice" (e.g., cannot complain or won't be listened to), the more they report procedural injustice (van Prooijen, van den Bos, Lind, & Wilke, 2006).

We also judge fairness in terms of the way information about outcomes and procedures is given to us. This is known as **transactional justice,** and two factors seem to play a key role in our judgments about it: the extent to which we are given clear and rational reasons for why rewards were divided as they were (Bies, Shapiro, & Cummings, 1988), and the courtesy or respect with which we are informed about these divisions (Greenberg, 1993; Tyler, Boeckmann, Smith, & Huo, 1997).

In sum, we judge fairness in several different ways—in terms of the rewards we have received (distributive justice), the procedures used to reach these divisions (procedural justice), and the style in which we are informed about these divisions (transactional justice). All three forms of justice can have strong effects on our behavior.

In many situations in which we ask the question "Am I being treated fairly?" we do not have sufficient information about the outcomes or procedures used to clearly apply rules of distributive and procedural justice. We don't know exactly what rewards others

---

distributive justice (fairness)
Refers to individuals' judgments about whether they are receiving a fair share of available rewards—a share proportionate to their contributions to the group or any social relationship.

procedural justice
Judgments concerning the fairness of the procedures used to distribute available rewards among group members.

transactional justice
Refers to the extent to which people who distribute rewards explain or justify their decisions and show respect and courtesy to those who receive the rewards.

have received (e.g., their salaries), and we may not know all the procedures or whether they were consistently followed when distributing rewards to group members. What do we do in such situations? Meta-analyses (Barsky & Kaplan, 2007) have revealed that we treat our feelings as a source of information and base our judgments on them, reasoning "If I feel good, this must be fair," or "If I feel bad, this must be unfair."

Reactions to Perceived Unfairness: Tactics for Dealing with Injustice

What do people do when they feel that they have been treated unfairly? As you probably know from your own experience, there are many options. First, if unfairness centers on rewards (distributive justice), people may focus on changing the balance between their contributions and their outcomes. For example, we may reduce our contributions or demand larger rewards. Employees who feel that they are being underpaid may do less on the job or request more benefits. If these tactics fail, they may protest, join a union and go on strike, or, ultimately, quit and look for another job.

When unfairness centers on procedures (procedural justice) or a lack of courteous treatment by the people who determine reward divisions (transactional justice), rather than on rewards themselves, people may adopt different tactics. Procedures can be harder to change than outcomes because they go on behind "closed doors" and may differ from announced policies in many ways. Similarly, changing the negative attitudes that lie behind insensitive treatment by bosses is a difficult, if not impossible, task. As a result, individuals who feel that they have been treated unfairly in these ways often turn to more covert (hidden) techniques for "evening the score." The evidence suggests that such feelings of unfairness lie behind many instances of employee theft and sabotage (Greenberg, 1997).

> ### Principles to Remember
>
> People care about fairness and justice. In fact, we may sometimes care more about how we are treated—procedural and transactional justice—than what outcome we receive.

KeyPoints

- Individuals wish to be treated fairly by the groups to which they belong. Fairness can be judged in terms of outcomes (distributive justice), in terms of procedures (procedural justice), or in terms of respectful treatment (transactional justice).

- When individuals feel that they have been treated unfairly, they often take steps to restore fairness. These can range from overt actions such as reducing their contributions, protesting, or use of covert actions, such as employee theft or sabotage.

- People may not have the necessary information to determine whether their outcomes or the procedures used are fair or not. When such information is unknown, people may use their feelings or mood as a basis for judging perceived fairness.

Think About It

How might our position within a group affect our behavioral responses to perceived unfairness?

Decision Making by Groups: How It Occurs and the Pitfalls It Faces

One of the most important activities that groups perform is **decision making**—deciding on one out of several possible courses of action. Governments, corporations, and many other organizations entrust key decisions to groups. Why? People seem to believe that groups reach better decisions than individuals. After all, they can pool the expertise of their members and avoid the biases and extreme decisions that might be made by individuals acting alone. But are such beliefs about group decision making accurate? Do groups really make better decisions than individuals?

In their efforts to address this issue, social psychologists have focused on three major questions: (1) How do groups actually make their decisions and reach a consensus? (2) Do decisions reached by groups differ from those made by individuals? (3) What accounts for the fact that groups sometimes make disastrous decisions? People seem to be implicitly aware that group decision making might have its pitfalls—given the number of jokes there are about groups. Consider the following: "What's a camel?" "It's a horse designed by a committee!" Here the idea is that a beautiful and elegant animal, such as a horse, in the hands of a group will be turned into a lumpy creature like the camel.

The Decision-Making Process: How Groups Attain Consensus

When groups first begin to discuss any issue, their members rarely start out in complete agreement. Rather, they come to the decision-making task with a range of views (Gigone & Hastie, 1997; Larson, Foster-Fishman, & Franz, 1998). After some period of discussion, however, groups usually do reach a decision. How is this accomplished, and can the final outcome be predicted from the views initially held by the members of the group?

The Decision Quality of Groups: Less or More Extreme?

Many suppose that groups are far less likely than individuals to make extreme decisions. Is that view correct? A large body of evidence indicates that groups are actually more likely to adopt extreme positions than if its members made those same decisions alone. Across many different kinds of decisions and many different contexts, groups show a pronounced tendency to shift toward views that are more extreme than the ones with which they initially began (Burnstein, 1983; Lamm & Myers, 1978). This is known as **group polarization,** and its major effects can be summarized as follows: Whatever the initial leaning or preference of a group before its discussions, this preference is strengthened during the group's deliberations. As a result, groups make more extreme decisions than individuals. Initial research on this topic (Kogan & Wallach, 1964) suggested that groups move toward riskier alternatives as they discuss important issues—a change described as the risky shift. But additional research showed that the shift was not always toward risk; the shift toward risk only happened in situations where the initial preference of the group leaned in that direction. The shift could be in the opposite direction—toward increased caution—if caution was the group's initial preference.

Why do groups tend to move, as shown in Figure 11.18, toward increasingly extreme views and decisions over the course of their discussions? Two major factors are involved. First, social comparison plays a role. If we all want to be above average, in which opinions are concerned, this implies holding views that are better than other group members. Being better would mean holding views that are more prototypical of the group's overall preference but even more so. So, for example, in a group of liberals, better would mean more liberal. Among a group of conservatives, it would mean more conservative.

A second factor involves the fact that during group discussion, most arguments favor the group's initial preference. As a result of hearing such arguments, persuasion occurs (pre-

decision making
Processes involved in combining and integrating available information to choose one out of several possible courses of action.

group polarization
The tendency of a group member to shift toward more extreme positions than those they initially held by the individual members as a result of group discussion.

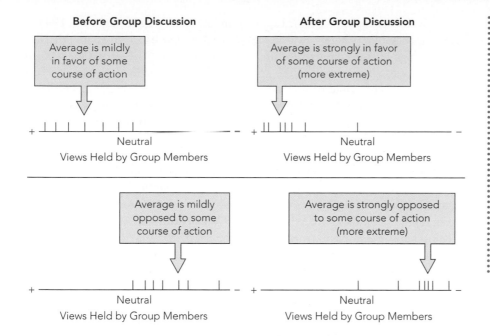

Figure 11.18
Group Polarization: How It Works
As shown here, group polarization involves the tendency for decision-making groups to shift toward views that are more extreme than the ones with which the groups initially began but in the same general direction. Thus if groups start out slightly in favor of one view or position, they often end up holding this view more strongly or extremely after discussion. This shift toward extremity can be quite dangerous in many settings.

sumably through the central route described in Chapter 5), and members shift, increasingly, toward the majority's view. As a result, the proportion of arguments favoring the group's initial preference increases, so that ultimately, members convince themselves that this must be the "right" view (Vinokur & Burnstein, 1974).

The Downside of Group Decision Making

The drift of many decision-making groups toward polarization is a serious problem—one that can interfere with their ability to make sound decisions—but this is not the only process that can exert such negative effects (Hinsz, 1995). Among the most important of these other processes are (1) groupthink, (2) groups' seeming inability to share and use information held by only some of their members, and (3) inhibitors to effective brainstorming.

Groupthink: When Cohesiveness is Dangerous

Previously we described how high levels of cohesiveness in groups have benefits: It can increase task motivation and make those groups more satisfying. But, like anything else, there can be too much of a good thing. When cohesiveness reaches extremely high levels, **groupthink** may develop. This is a strong tendency for decision-making groups to "close ranks" around a decision, to assume that the group can't be wrong, with pressure for all members to support the decision strongly, and to reject any information contrary to the decision. Research indicates that once groupthink develops, groups become unwilling to change their decisions, even when initial outcomes suggest that those decisions were poor ones (Haslam et al., 2006).

Consider the decisions of three U.S. presidents (John F. Kennedy, Lyndon B. Johnson, and Richard M. Nixon) to escalate the war in Vietnam. Each escalation brought increased U.S. casualties and no progress toward the goal of assuring the survival of South Vietnam as an independent country. Likewise, President George W. Bush and his cabinet chose to invade Iraq and then escalate the number of U.S. troops on the ground there, without critically considering the assumption that is now known to be incorrect (Saddam Hussein possessed weapons of mass destruction). According to Janis (1982), the social psychologist who originated the concept of groupthink, this process—and the fact that it encourages an unwillingness among members of cohesive groups to consider alternative courses of action—may well have contributed to these events.

groupthink
The tendency of the members of highly cohesive groups to assume that their decisions can't be wrong, that all members must support the group's decisions strongly, and that information contrary to it should be ignored.

Why does groupthink occur? Research findings (Kameda & Sugimori, 1993; Tetlock, Peterson, McGuire, Change & Feld, 1992) suggest that two factors are crucial. One of these is a high level of cohesiveness among group members. The second is emergent group norms—norms suggesting that the group is infallible, morally superior, and because of these factors, there should be no further discussion of the issues at hand: The decision has been made, and the only valid response is to support it as strongly as possible. Closely related to these effects is a tendency to reject any criticism by outside sources. Criticism from outsiders is viewed with suspicion and attributed negative motives. The result? It is largely ignored and may even tend to strengthen the group's cohesiveness because members rally to defend the group against perceived assaults by outsiders.

Such rejection of criticism on the part of outsiders has been reported by Hornsey and Imani (2004). They asked Australian college students to read comments supposedly made during an interview that were either positive ("When I think of Australians I think of them as being fairly friendly and warm people," or negative, "When I think of Australians I think of them as being fairly racist"). The comments were attributed either to another Australian (an in-group member), a person from another country who had never lived in Australia (inexperienced-out-group), or to a person from another country who had once lived in Australia and therefore had experience with Australians (experienced-out-group). Participants then evaluated the source of the comments and rated the extent to which this person's comments were designed to be constructive.

Hornsey and Imani (2004) reasoned that when the comments were negative, both the stranger and the comments would receive lower ratings when this person was an out-group member than an in-group member. Further, an out-group member's experience with the in-group (having lived in Australia) would not make any difference because this person was still not a member of the in-group. When the comments were positive, such effects were not expected to occur; after all, praise is acceptable no matter what its source.

As you can see from Figure 11.19, this is precisely what happened. When the stranger's comments were positive, whether this person was an Australian or not, made no difference. But when this person made negative comments, both the stranger and the comments were viewed more negatively when this person was from an out-group—regardless of degree of experience with Australia—than when this person was a member of the in-group. Further, when criticism of the in-group is voiced, if it is aired in front of an out-group audience, evaluations of the critic are even worse than if the criticism were voiced to the in-group only (Hornsey et al., 2005).

The Failure to Share Information Unique to Each Member

A second potential source of bias in decision-making groups involves the fact that such groups do not always pool their resources and share information and ideas unique to each member. In fact, research (Gigone & Hastie, 1997; Stasser, 1992) indicates such pooling of resources or information may be the exception rather than the rule. The result: The decisions they make tend to reflect the shared information (Gigione & Hastie, 1993). This is not a problem if such information points to the best decision. But consider what happens when information pointing to the best decision is not shared by most members. In such cases, the tendency of group members to discuss mainly the information they all already possess may prevent them from reaching the best decision.

> ### Principles to Remember
> A decision made by a group—simply because it was made by a group—is not of higher quality, or more accurate, than a decision made by an individual.

Brainstorming: Idea Generation in Groups

In our discussion of social facilitation, we considered the consequences of being observed by others for our performance on a variety of tasks. When groups work on creative tasks together they tend to produce different kinds of solutions than when working alone (Adarves-Yorno, Postmes, & Haslam, 2007). In **brainstorming**—a process whereby people meet as a group to generate new ideas—we might ask whether being in a group will

brainstorming
A process in which people meet as a group to generate new ideas freely.

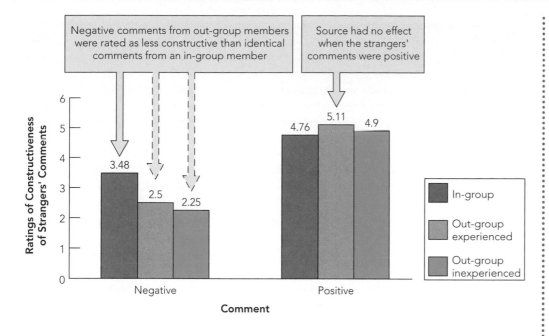

Negative comments from out-group members were rated as less constructive than identical comments from an in-group member

Source had no effect when the strangers' comments were positive

In-group
Out-group experienced
Out-group inexperienced

Negative: 3.48, 2.5, 2.25
Positive: 4.76, 5.11, 4.9

Ratings of Constructiveness of Strangers' Comments

Comment

Figure 11.19
Rejection of Criticism from Out-Group Members: One Reason Why Groups Sometimes Make Bad Decisions
When participants' in-group (Australians) was criticized, these comments were viewed more negatively when made supposedly by an out-group member than when made by a member of an in-group. Moreover, this was true even if the critic had lived in Australia for several years. These findings suggest that groups' tendency to reject criticism from outsiders may be one reason why they often make bad decisions.

(*Source:* Based on data from Hornsey & Imani, 2004.)

facilitate performance in terms of coming up with new ideas or perhaps, be distracting, and so produce the opposite effect. Does being in a group affect the quality—give us better ideas—and quantity—more overall ideas generated? We investigate this topic in *Making Sense of Common Sense: A Social Psychological Perspective* on p. 412.

KeyPoints

- It is widely believed that groups make better decisions than individuals. However research findings indicate that groups are often subject to group polarization, which leads them to make more extreme decisions than individuals. This occurs for two reasons: Members want to hold views that are more prototypical than others, which means more extreme than average, and because during group discussions members are persuaded by the arguments that other members make, and, therefore they subsequently move their own views in that direction.

- In addition, groups often suffer from groupthink—a tendency for highly cohesive groups to assume that they can do no wrong and that information contrary to the group's view should be rejected.

- Groups do tend to reject criticism from out-group members relative to identical criticism from in-group members. It is also more distressing to hear one's in-group criticized in front of an out-group compared to when the audience consists of other in-group members only.

- Group members often fail to share during discussion information that only some members possess.

Instead, discussions tend to focus on the information that all members share, so the decisions they make tend to reflect this shared information.

- Brainstorming—generating ideas in a group—does not result in more creativity than individuals in terms of quality of the ideas produced. This appears to be largely because group members fear their ideas will be viewed negatively, and they are unable to come up with new ideas while also trying to expand on others' ideas.

- Groups and individuals can arrive equally at creative solutions to problems, although groups are more strongly influenced by salient norms in terms of the techniques to use.

Think About It

If you found yourself in a group that was, in your view, rushing headlong into a bad decision, would you argue the content of the decision, or would you question the process that was leading to it? How might you go about doing this?

MAKING SENSE OF COMMON SENSE

A SOCIAL PSYCHOLOGICAL PERSPECTIVE

Does Brainstorming in a Group Result in More and Higher Quality Inventive Ideas?

You may have seen the television show, *Whose Line Is It Anyway?* The show was hosted by Drew Carey and features four talented comedians. If you watch it carefully, you'll note that the improvisational comedy sketches ("improv") require the performers to "feed off of" each other's creative ideas; the performers are experts at going along with the creative instincts of the other comics. Apart from the fun, the idea of taking off on others' ideas seems like it should result in higher quality comedy overall.

In corporate America there are situations in which such creative teamwork should also result in more and higher quality inventive ideas. In fact, advertising executives, always in need of fresh new ideas, invented brainstorming (Osborn, 1953). It is a group process with specific rules meant to encourage the generation of as many good ideas as possible—where any idea, however silly or impractical, is welcome and the emphasis is placed on producing lots of ideas, without criticism of any one of them. Like improv, participants should build on each other's ideas in brainstorming—feed off each other's creative thinking—so that the group's output will be more than the sum of the parts—were those individuals being creative alone. While brainstorming in a group can be more enjoyable than working by oneself, the question is: Does it in fact lead to superior outcomes?

People have generally assumed that brainstorming will result in more creative output than working as an individual (Stroebe, Diehl, & Abakoumkin, 1992). But in contrast to this commonsense expectation, brainstorming does not on the whole result in more creative ideas being generated than if the same folks worked alone. In fact, in an experiment, Mullen, Johnson, and Salas (1991) showed that brainstorming reduces both the quantity and quality of output compared with people working alone. So, why doesn't such a great idea in theory work in practice?

Being asked to come up with creative ideas can be threatening. While the rules of brainstorming officially preclude criticism, in practice that might not really be the case. For example, in one study (Collaros & Anderson, 1969), some individuals were told that other group members had considerable expertise regarding the topic; individuals so warned about their own relative lack of expertise were more likely to limit their creative input to the group. Thus, while group members may overtly follow the rule against criticizing an idea, evaluation apprehension may cause people to decide that others are negatively evaluating their ideas, thus limiting willingness to contribute.

Also, keep in mind that the original purpose behind brainstorming was idea production (i.e., generating a large numbers of ideas). Even more important than evaluation apprehension, then, is the problem of "production blocking." In a group setting, various members may be creating their own ideas, as another member is creating his or her own. If individuals abandon their own creations to listen to others, then the production of creative ideas becomes less efficient. Diehl and Stroebe (1991) showed that in face-to-face brainstorming groups, productivity was reduced because people are either in the middle of being creative or are waiting for an opportunity to respond to another person, during which time they may forget important details of their own idea.

More recently, Dugosh and Paulus (2005) investigated both cognitive and social aspects of brainstorming, particularly the effects of idea exposure. This is especially important because the benefits of brainstorming were supposed to be found in group members' exposure to others' creativity. These researchers considered whether exposure to common or unique ideas by other group members would result in similar quality ideas being generated by the other participants and whether people engage in social comparison during brainstorming. Some research has suggested that "performance matching" could lead to lowered motivations for idea output (i.e., everyone sort of "dumbing down" to conform to a low-output norm). Munkes and Diehl (2003) have suggested, however, that such social comparison ought to result in competition and raise the quality of the ideas generated. Dugosh and Paulus's study tested this idea by having some participants believe that the ideas they were exposed to were selected by a computer from an "idea database," whereas other participants were told that the ideas came from people similar to themselves.

Dugosh and Paulus (2005) found that exposure to more ideas did in fact result in more ideas being generated by participants in their study. Moreover, participants who were led to believe they were being exposed to people-generated ideas, as opposed to computer-selected ideas, produced more ideas; participants felt the need to be as creative as those "other people."

In general, people in creative idea-generating groups appear not to exhibit the same level of productive inventiveness as the comedians on *Whose Line Is It Anyway?* We may assume that those comics are extremely competitive and have little evaluation apprehension. But the entire success of the improvisational effort relies on a combination of feeding off of someone else's idea, all the while coming up with ideas of one's own—so where is the production blocking? The answer may lie in a simple difference between average brainstormers and those professional comedians who don't mind being silly in public—in fact, that's what they are paid for. In improv comedy, a high degree of competence (the ability to recognize a bad idea in oneself) may be matched by the fact that we are talking about comedy—silly ideas may even be funny. But in many brainstorming contexts, bad ideas may be generated and the comedic value of those ideas may be less appreciated. Classic brainstorming, as we've noted, puts a premium on not criticizing anyone's idea. This seems quite intuitive because people would certainly be more likely to come up with stimulating ideas, and probably more of them, if they were not constrained by the notion that their ideas are going to be viewed as silly by the other group members.

Nemeth, Personnaz, Personnaz, and Goncalo (2004), point out that dissent, debate, and competing views are widely valued as stimuli for creative ideas. These researchers gave two different instructions to brainstorming groups, either traditional instructions or instructions encouraging people to debate the merits of ideas. In general, debate instructions produced results superior to traditional instructions (although there was value in both types of instructions). The results held true in both the United States and France. Thus a central tenet of brainstorming, the lack of criticism of new ideas, seems, on balance, to add less in the way of stimulation of idea production than does the cognitive stimulation provided by honest dissent and debate.

As comedians performing improv will tell you, it is essential to "go with" whatever silliness another comedian feeds you; this "rule" often leads to utterly absurd situations (i.e., great humor). But when more serious ideas are needed, perhaps a more adversarial cognitive process leads to better results.

SUMMARY AND REVIEW

- Humans may be obligatorily interdependent; because of our evolutionary history we are reliant on the group for survival. Groups are collections of people who perceive themselves as forming a coherent unit to some degree. In common-bond groups, the members tend to be bonded with each other, whereas in common-identity groups, members tend to be linked via the category as a whole. The extent to which the group is perceived to form a coherent entity is known as entitativity.

- Basic aspects of groups involve status, roles, norms, and cohesiveness. People achieve high status—position or rank within a group—for many reasons, ranging from physical characteristics (e.g., height), how prototypical of the group they are, and various aspects of their behavior. To the extent that people internalize their social roles, where those roles are linked to aspects of their self-concept, they can have important implications for behavior and well-being. Being assigned to act as prisoner or guard in a prison simulation can result in behavioral changes to the extent that people identify with those roles and are guided by the norms associated with it. Cohesiveness—the factors that cause people to want to remain members—produces a sense of solidarity among members.

- Joining groups confers important benefits on members, including increased self-knowledge, progress toward important goals, enhanced status, and attaining social change. However group membership also exacts important costs, such as loss of personal freedom and heavy demands on time, energy, and resources. The desire to join exclusive and prestigious groups may be so strong that individuals are willing to undergo painful and dangerous initiations to become members. Undergoing severe initiation processes to obtain admission in a group frequently increases commitment to that group.

- Individuals often withdraw from groups when they feel that the group has changed so much that it no longer reflects their basic values or beliefs. When a group undergoes a schism—splintering into distinct factions—it can produce emotional distress in those who feel compelled to leave.

- The mere presence of other people either as an audience or as coactors can influence our performance on many tasks. Such effects are known as social facilitation. The drive theory of social facilitation suggests that the presence of others is arousing and can either increase or reduce performance, depending on whether dominant responses in a given situation are correct or incorrect. The distraction-conflict theory suggests that the presence of others induces conflicting tendencies to focus on the task being performed and on an audience or coactors. This can result both in increased arousal and narrowed attentional focus, explaining why social facilitation occurs in many species.

- When individuals work together on a task, social loafing—reduced output by each group member—sometimes occurs. Social loafing can be reduced in several ways: by making outputs individually identifiable, by increasing commitment to the task and task importance, and by assuring that each member's contributions to the task are unique.

- Being part of a large crowd has been stereotyped as inducing hooliganism—violent and antisocial incidents—as a result the reduction in self-awareness that occurs with deindividuation. Contrary to this idea, anonymity in a crowd actually induces more normative or conforming behavior. The norms operating in some crowds may be changed, and the likelihood of violence reduced. Deindividuation can intensify either aggressive or prosocial behavior, depending on what norms are operating in a particular crowd context.

- Cooperation—working together with others to obtain shared goals—is a common aspect of social life. However cooperation does not develop in many situations in which it is possible, partly because such situations involve social dilemmas in which individuals can increase their own gains at the expense of the other. Sanctioning for noncooperation though can decrease people's trust in the other and thereby undermine their subsequent willingness to cooperate.

- Conflict is a process that begins when individuals or groups perceive that others are incompatible with their interests. Conflict can also stem from social factors, such as faulty attributions, poor communication, the tendency to perceive our own views as objective, and destructive criticism. Conflict can be reduced in many ways, but bargaining and the induction of superordinate goals seem to be most effective.

- Individuals wish to be treated fairly by the groups to which they belong. Fairness can be judged in terms of outcomes (distributive justice), in terms of procedures (procedural justice), or in terms of courteous treatment (transactional justice). When individuals feel that they have been treated unfairly, they often take steps to restore fairness. These include overt actions, such as reducing one's efforts, protesting or the use of covert actions, such as theft or sabotage.

- Research findings indicate that groups are often subject to group polarization, which leads them to make more extreme decisions than individuals. In addition, groups often suffer from groupthink—a tendency to assume that they can't be wrong and that information contrary to the group's view should be rejected. Groups do tend to reject criticism from out-group members relative to identical criticism from in-group members. Groups often fail to share information that only some members possess, and this can lead to biased decisions.

- People tend to believe that brainstorming—a situation in which people attempt to generate new ideas in a group—will be more effective than individuals working alone. Research illustrates that this is generally not true, partly because people feel evaluation apprehension, and they are blocked from producing their own ideas by waiting for other group members to finish.

Key Terms

additive tasks (p. 396)

bargaining (negotiation) (p. 404)

brainstorming (p. 410)

cohesiveness (p. 388)

collectivism (p. 387)

common-bond groups (p. 380)

common-identity groups (p. 380)

conflict (p. 401)

cooperation (p. 401)

decision making (p. 408)

deindividuation (p. 399)

distraction-conflict theory (p. 395)

distributive justice (fairness) (p. 406)

entitativity (p. 380)

evaluation apprehension (p. 397)

group polarization (p. 408)

group (p. 380)

groupthink (p. 409)

hooliganism (p. 399)

ideology (p. 392)

individualism (p. 387)

norms (p. 387)

obligatory interdependent (p. 378)

politicized collective identity (p. 390)

procedural justice (p. 406)

roles (p. 384)

schism (p. 392)

social dilemmas (p. 401)

social loafing (p. 397)

status (p. 383)

superordinate goals (p. 405)

transactional justice (p. 406)

Connections
INTEGRATING SOCIAL PSYCHOLOGY

In this chapter, you read about . . .	In other chapters, you will find related discussions of . . .
the role of norms in the functioning of groups	the nature of norms and their role in social influence (Chapter 9), attitudes (Chapter 5), and aggression (Chapter 11).
the nature of cooperation and conflict and factors that affect their occurrence	other forms of behavior that either assist or harm others: discrimination (Chapter 6), helping behavior (Chapter 10), and aggression (Chapter 11).
individuals' concern with others' evaluations of their performance	the effects of others' evaluations on our self-concept (Chapter 4) and on our liking for others (Chapter 7).
perceived fairness	the effects of perceived fairness on many other forms of social behavior, such as discrimination (Chapter 6), helping (Chapter 10), aggression (Chapter 11), and its role in close relationships (Chapter 7).

Social Psychology
Applying Its Principles to Law, Health, and Business

CHAPTER OUTLINE

- **Social Psychology and the Legal System**
  Social Influence and the Legal System
  Social Cognition and the Legal System: Why
    Eyewitness Testimony Is Often Inaccurate
    BUILDING THE SCIENCE: CLASSICS OF SOCIAL
    PSYCHOLOGY—EARLY EVIDENCE THAT EVEN
    "EXPERT" EYEWITNESSES ARE INACCURATE:
    MUNSTERBERG'S INGENIOUS RESEARCH
  The Influence of Prejudice and Stereotypes on the
    Legal System

- **Social Psychology and Health**
  The Role of Attitudes in Personal Health:
    Promoting a Healthy Lifestyle
  Obesity: A Social Psychological Perspective on a
    Major Threat to Health
  Stress: Its Causes, Effects, and Control

- **Social Psychology and the World of Work**
  Work-Related Attitudes: The Nature and Effects
    of Job Satisfaction
    MAKING SENSE OF COMMON SENSE: A SOCIAL
    PSYCHOLOGICAL PERSPECTIVE—ARE HAPPY
    WORKERS PRODUCTIVE WORKERS? THE
    ATTITUDE-BEHAVIOR LINK REVISITED
  Organizational Citizenship Behavior: Prosocial
    Behavior at Work
  Leadership: Influence in Group Settings
    SOCIAL PSYCHOLOGY: WHAT IT TELLS US
    ABOUT . . . HOW TO MAKE A GOOD FIRST
    IMPRESSION IN JOB INTERVIEWS

In the 1970s and 1980s, New York, like many other U.S. cities, faced a growing crisis. Crime rose dramatically, to the point where ordinary citizens were afraid to walk through the streets of many neighborhoods and were reluctant to use the subway system to get around town. I grew up in New York, and in the 1950s and 1960s of my youth, it truly glittered. When I returned for visits in the 1970s and 1980s, however, it had definitely lost its luster. Graffiti and garbage were everywhere, and the streets were filled with aggressive beggars who simply would not accept no for an answer. My relatives urged me to take taxis instead of the subway, and burglaries, murder, and crimes of violence rose to truly frightening levels. In fact, it sometimes seemed as though the entire city was on the edge of collapse (see Figure 12.1 on page 418).

But then, starting in the early 1990s, the situation changed—dramatically. Crime statistics began to drop, at first slowly, but then rapidly; the public transportation system became safe, efficient, and relatively clean once again; and citizens returned—in increasing numbers—to the streets and parks of their neighborhoods. Overall, the city seemed to come back to life, and tourism, real estate, and culture all boomed.

What happened to produce these dramatic changes? Clearly, many factors played a role, but one of the most important was a newly revitalized police department. William J. Bratton, who had been chief of police in Boston, came to New York to head its department in 1994, and with the strong support of newly elected Mayor Rudolph Giuliani, quickly introduced changes that produced amazing results. He adopted a new strategy for policing the city's streets—one that emphasized partnership with local communities. This meant putting police back into the local neighborhoods and focusing increased efforts on preventing crime rather than merely responding to it when it occurred. Bratton also restructured the entire department, giving increased

Figure 12.1
Rescuing New York City: Did Social Psychological Principles Play a Role?
In the 1970s and 1980s, many major cities in the United States (including New York) were in serious decline. Crime had risen to frightening levels and the streets were no longer safe for ordinary citizens. Changes in the ways in which police departments operated made a major difference, and in a sense, gave New York and other cities back to their citizens. Although the individuals who made these changes were not social psychologists, several of the changes they instituted, and the effects these changes produced, are closely related to principles of social psychology.

responsibility and autonomy to each precinct commander—in a sense, creating seventy-six "mini" police departments in place of one. Each precinct now had control over its own resources and how to use them but had increased responsibility, too; each precinct was expected to protect the safety of the citizens within its boundaries. Other changes involved a new emphasis on taking actions that would prevent the return crime from an area once it had been driven away. This included: (1) obtaining accurate information on what was happening in each neighborhood, (2) developing techniques for rapid deployment of police when needed, (3) designing effective tactics for dealing with various tasks—for instance, handling drug pushers and users, and (4) vigorous follow-up actions to keep crime at low levels once it had been reduced. As the situation improved, morale in the police department rose, and citizens began to hold much more positive attitudes toward police officers. They gradually came to see the police as allies in the war against crime—people who were truly trying to help. These changed attitudes and perceptions increased public cooperation with the police still further and helped them to do their job with increasing success. Crime dropped even more, and optimism about the city's future rose. No, the situation did not become perfect, but it improved so much that people began to see safe streets, subways, and neighborhoods as "normal"—something to which they were entitled and which they expected to enjoy. We're happy to report, these changes have persisted—and perhaps even strengthened—in recent years. Crime has not returned to threaten the Big Apple as it did in past decades. Partly as a result of his major successes in New York, William Bratton was appointed chief of police by Los Angeles in 2002 and, since that time, has been applying the same principles to help that troubled city make similar gains.

ratton is not a social psychologist, and as far as we know, he did not use a textbook like this one to design changes in the New York City police department. But in fact, he holds a college degree, and we strongly suspect that he was exposed to the principles of social psychology in one—or perhaps several—different courses. In any case, it seems clear that both the changes he made and the effects they produced are closely related to basic principles of social psychology—principles covered in previous chapters of this book. For instance, consider the role of the public's attitudes toward the police. When Bratton took over as chief of police, these were negative: Many citizens viewed the police as adversaries—and corrupt ones, at that! (The department had been rocked by major scandals in the preceding years.) As a result, the public had little desire to cooperate with the police or help them to do their jobs. The changes he made, though, quickly altered these negative views and resulted in improved attitudes about the police—and a much stronger desire on the part of the public to assist them. So clearly, both attitudes and prosocial behavior—topics covered in previous chapters of this book—are directly relevant. So, too, are important aspects of social cognition and attribution. As we saw in a previous chapter, expectations often shape reality, so when the citizens of New York began to expect improved conditions, this helped create them. As crime rates began to drop, citizens also made increasingly favorable attributions about the police—they came to see them as doing their best and as really trying to help. These favorable attributions increased public cooperation with the police and made it still harder for criminals to "do their thing." The press, too, played a role: As crime dropped, an increasing number of articles supporting the police appeared in the city's newspapers and on local news reports; this exerted a form of social influence on residents of New York, further enhancing attitudes toward the police and building an atmosphere of hope. In addition, as crime dropped, cleaning crews could do their job without interference, and the city's appearance improved. This activated long-dormant social norms against throwing litter into the streets or placing graffiti on subway cars. As a result, the environment improved still further, and people began to take pride in their city once again.

We're certainly not suggesting that these were the only factors at work—many others, too, played a role (for instance, a shift in demographics, so that the proportion of teenagers and young people in the city declined). All we are suggesting is that this dramatic reversal of the long-term decline in New York and other large cities can be understood in the context of major principles of social psychology. In fact, we believe that these principles help us to understand how, and why, the positive outcomes described above were produced.

That's the major theme of the present chapter: ways in which the principles and findings of social psychology have been used, or are potentially useful, in efforts to solve important practical problems. As we have stated previously, we fervently believe that social psychology is much more than an interesting field that studies a wide range of fascinating topics. Rather, the findings and principles it uncovers have great potential for improving human life. Actually, there are so many ways in which social psychology's principles can be put to such practical use that we could not possibly examine all of them here. Instead, we'll focus on applications of social psychological knowledge in three major areas of life: (1) the legal system, (2) personal health, and (3) the world of work. For each, we'll examine research that is either based directly on the principles of social psychology or that can be understood in light of those principles. In other words, as its title suggests, this chapter is designed to serve as a kind of capstone for the book—and for your first course in social psychology; in it, we'll attempt to pull together many findings and principles covered in previous chapters and illustrate that these are not only interesting, but they are also exceptionally useful too!

Social Psychology and the Legal System

Figure 12.2

Justice: Is It Really Blind?

Ideally, justice should be blind to the background, characteristics, gender, and ethnic identity of individuals—everyone should be treated equally. In fact, however, this goal is easier to imagine than to attain.

Is justice really blind? It is shown this way (blindfolded) on many court buildings throughout the world (see Figure 12.2), and this is the ideal: All people should be equal before the law and treated in the same, impartial manner. After reading the chapters in this book, however, you probably realize that while this is an admirable ideal, it may be very hard to achieve in real life. As we saw in previous discussions, it is difficult, if not impossible, for us to ignore the words, behaviors, or personal characteristics of other people or to dismiss the preconceived ideas, beliefs, and stereotypes that we have developed over years from our thinking and decision making. So while we might wish that justice could be totally impartial and fair, we must recognize that making it—and our legal system—live up to these goals is a tall order. To move toward it, many social psychologists believe that we must first understand the potential sources of error and bias that either creep into the legal system or in some cases, are actively introduced by its key players—attorneys, judges, and police. Once we understand the possible risks, we may be able to take steps to correct these problems and reduce, if not totally eliminate them, from the system. The result? Justice could indeed be more fair and impartial, as we all desire. What are some of these potential pitfalls and how can we seek to reduce them? Because most of them involve the powerful impact of social influence, stereotypes, and also potential errors and biases in social cognition, we'll discuss them under these headings—which, of course, involve major topics and principles of social psychology.

Social Influence and the Legal System

In a sense, most legal proceedings—trials or interrogation of suspects in a crime—involve an element of social influence. During trials, for instance, attorneys attempt to persuade jurors and perhaps the presiding judge, of the guilt or innocence of the people on trial. And during interrogation of suspects, police often attempt to influence the individuals they question to confess—or at least, tell the full truth. Clearly, social influence is, potentially, a major factor in these activities, and this is widely recognized by attorneys, police, and other participants in the legal system. It is one reason why defense attorneys often urge their clients to dress conservatively and groom neatly: doing so can help them make a better impression on jurors and so, perhaps exert subtle influence on them in the direction of a favorable judgment. (As shown in Figure 12.3, however, such tactics don't always succeed.)

Social influence can also play an important role in events that happen before a case goes to trial. While this can occur in many different ways, three that are especially important are: (1) police interrogations, (2) lineups, and (3) media coverage of such cases.

Police Interrogations: Using Social Influence to Get at the Truth

After police take a suspect into custody, they interrogate this person in various ways to prepare the ground for further legal proceedings. How do they handle this important responsibility? Most of us would prefer that they adopt what is known as an *inquisitorial approach*—a search for the truth—rather than an *adversarial approach*—an approach in which they seek to prove guilt, perhaps by wringing a confession out of an unwilling defendant (Williamson, 1993). In other words, most of us prefer that the police seek to gather information rather than engage in powerful forms of persuasion or social influence, to force defendants to confess (see Chapter 8).

In fact, though, recent findings indicate that even if police do not engage in such actions, serious forms of bias can enter the process. Defendants, who find themselves in a highly stressful and emotionally charged setting, may sometimes become highly agitated and confused, with the result that they confess to crimes they did not commit And then, to make matters worse, jurors may tend to accept these confessions as accurate with the tragic result that innocent people are convicted and sent to prison for crimes committed by other, unknown individuals.

How can such distortions of the impartial and fair legal system we all desire be avoided? One possibility has involved the requirement that all interrogations of defendants by police be videotaped. This, it is assumed, will prevent police from using strong-arm tactics and will also, when shown to jurors, permit them to make judgments about whether a confession was coerced or not and whether it is true or false. On the basis of this reasoning, this requirement has been instituted in several countries (e.g., the United Kingdom) and in many states in the United States. But there is a serious problem with such procedures, one involving an effect we examined previously in this book: Our tendency to perceive whatever is the focus of our attention as being more important and more central to subsequent events than whatever is not the focus of our attention (see Chapter 3). For instance, if we observe two people holding a casual conversation, the one who is most directly in our view is the one we will perceive as being more influential—the one who exerted the greatest effect on the conversation.

Applying this principle to videotapes of police interrogations, Lassiter and others (e.g., Lassiter, Geers, Handley, Weiland, & Munhall, 2002) noted that many of these tapes focus solely on the defendant. As result, jurors may tend to view any confessions obtained as true and voluntary because the defendant is in the center of their attention. To test this prediction, Lassiter and his co-workers conducted a series of studies in which participants viewed videotapes of interrogations in which the suspect confessed. In one condition, the camera focused entirely on the suspect, while in another condition both the suspect and interrogator were shown. Everything else was held constant—the suspect's answers, the interrogator's questions, and so on. Results were dramatic: Participants rated the confessions in the first condition (only the suspect was shown) as more voluntary than those in the second, despite the fact that the suspect's words were identical. Further, they rated the suspects as more guilty and recommended harsher sentences in the suspect-only condition than in the condition where both suspect and interrogator were shown. Why does this occur? Further research (e.g., Lassiter, 2002) indicates that this has to do mainly with how we extract and initially register information from events we observe. Whatever serves as the focus of our attention becomes the center of our initial thoughts, and this, in turn, strongly affects our later judgments. Whatever the precise mechanism, however, these findings have important implications. They suggest that videotaping police interrogations can be beneficial—but only if the camera shows both the interrogator and the defendant. Focusing on the defendant (suspect) alone can lead jurors and others to overestimate the extent to which any confessions were offered voluntarily.

Another factor that can strongly affect the outcome of police interrogations is the location of such procedures—where they take place (Schooler & Loftus, 1986). For this reason, the investigators much prefer to conduct a formal investigation in an intimidating location, such as police headquarters, rather than in a nonthreatening location, such as the suspect's home or place of work. Both the location and the authority of the questioner (a government representative) reinforce the ordinary citizen's belief that the one asking the questions is an expert who possesses detailed knowledge of the case (Gudjonsson & Clark, 1986). The officer is in charge of what happens during the interview, and the person

"I got a haircut and a new suit just for this, Your Honor. I think forty-five years in the slammer shows damned little appreciation."

Figure 12.3
Social Influence: An Important Factor in the Legal System
Attorneys often advise their clients to dress and groom neatly to make a better impression on jurors and the presiding judge. Often, this helps, but as shown here, not always.

(*Source: The New Yorker.*)

being questioned is not supposed to interrupt or argue about what is said. As a result, once an answer is made, the witness is inclined to believe it, especially if the interrogator provides immediate reinforcement with a nod or by saying "good," or something like that. As will be described in a later section on eyewitness testimony, this can lead the person being questioned to believe and even remember the details of something that never happened.

Additional Aspects of Interrogation: How Social Influence Is Actually Used in Such Procedures

In seeking a confession, interrogators need not resort to heavy-handed methods because more subtle approaches can often be just as effective (Kassin & McNall, 1991). For example, in interacting with a suspect, an interrogator can minimize the strength of the evidence and the seriousness of the charge, perhaps blaming the victim rather than the suspect for what happened. When an interrogator minimizes the crime and seems supportive, there is an implicit promise that punishment will be relatively mild. Not only is this technique, which is based on ingratiation, effective (see Chapter 8), but it also avoids the legal problems associated with threatening a suspect. Jurors tend to discount a confession obtained by threats of punishment, but the minimization approach is perceived as acceptable. In fact though, while this "soft-sell technique" may seem to be noncoercive, it is simply a less obvious way to encourage compliance. In effect, the suspect confesses after being lulled into a false sense of security.

Other tactics of social influence, too, are used by interrogators. Kassin and Kiechel (1996) point out that police sometimes present suspects with false polygraph results, fake fingerprint data, inaccurate eyewitness identifications, and false information about the confession of a fellow-suspect—all in an attempt to persuade them to confess. The power of such procedures is clearly illustrated by research conducted by Kassin and Kiechel (1996), in which college students were led to believe that they were taking part in a laboratory experiment involving reaction time. Each participant interacted with a female assistant who read a list of letters; the participants' task was to respond by typing the letter on a keyboard. There was a special warning not to press the ALT key because this would cause the program to crash and the data to be lost. The pace of the study was set by the accomplice to be either fast, so that the participant would be less sure of what might have happened (high vulnerability) or slow (low vulnerability). After the experiment was underway, the computer suddenly ceased functioning, and the apparently upset experimenter rushed in and accused the participant of pressing the key despite the warning not to do so. "Did you hit the 'ALT' key?" To determine the effect of false evidence—one potential technique for generating false confessions—the accomplice either said that she had seen the participant hit the key or that she had not seen what happened. No one actually did hit that key, but the question was whether each individual would comply by signing a false confession, internalize the false confession by telling another student privately that he pressed the key, and confabulate by later recalling false details about the transgression that supposedly had occurred.

Results indicated that fully 69 percent of the participants signed the false confession, that 28 percent internalized their guilt, and that 9 percent produced confabulated details about their actions. These effects were stronger when the study pace was fast and when false evidence was present. In fact, when the study pace was fast, and false evidence was provided every participant confessed, most internalized their guilt, and over one-third falsely remembered details of their crime! So, not only does false evidence and uncertainty about what to do increase the likelihood of false confessions, these factors also increase the likelihood that people will believe their own false confessions and remember imaginary details about a crime they did not commit. As we have noted throughout this book, and especially in Chapter 8, social influence really is a powerful tool, and it can be turned to good or evil purposes, depending on who happens to be wielding it.

Lineups: How Subtle Social Pressure Sometimes Leads to Tragic Errors

One technique police often use to help identify suspects is the **lineup**—a procedure in which witnesses to a crime are shown several people, one or more who may be suspects in a case and asked to identify any that they recognize as the person who committed the crime. Witnesses may look either at the real people involved or at photos of them. Although these procedures are designed to get at the truth—to allow witnesses to identify the real criminals—they are clearly subject to several forms of bias related to social influence.

For instance, consider the way in which suspects are presented. In sequential lineups the suspects are presented one at a time, and witnesses indicate whether they recognize each one. In simultaneous lineups, in contrast, all the suspects are shown at once, and witnesses are asked to indicate which one (if any) they recognize (see Figure 12.4). Results of many studies indicate that sequential lineups are better in the sense that they reduce the likelihood that witnesses will make a serious kind of mistake—identify someone who did not commit the crime (Steblay, Dysart, Fulero, & Lindsay, 2001).

Perhaps the most disturbing findings concerning lineups relate to the impact of instructions to witnesses. Totally neutral instructions simply ask them to identify the person who committed the crime and don't indicate whether or not this person is present. In contrast, biased instructions suggest that the criminal is present and that their task as witnesses is to pick this person out from the others (e.g., Pozzulo & Lindsay, 1999). Such instructions expose witnesses to a subtle form of social influence: They may feel pressured to identify someone, even if no one they recognize is present.

Research by Pozzulo and Dempsey (2006) illustrates this danger quite clearly. They had both children and adults watch a videotape of a staged crime—one in which a woman's purse was stolen. Both groups were then shown a lineup consisting of photos of people who resembled the people who committed the crime. Simultaneous presentation of the photos was used. A key aspect of the study involved instructions to the participants. In one condition (neutral instructions), they were told that the criminal might or might not be present in the lineup. In the biased instructions condition, they were led to believe that this person was indeed present in the lineup. In fact, though, this person was not included in the lineup, so the key question was: Would the biased instructions lead participants to falsely identify someone—an innocent person—as the culprit? That's exactly what happened. As shown in Figure 12.5 on page 424, both adults and children were more likely to falsely identify an innocent person after hearing the biased instructions (ones leading them to conclude that the criminal was present) than after hearing the neutral instructions. These findings indicate that social influence is at work in police lineups and that stringent procedures should be adopted to avoid such effects; adherence to such procedures will increase the likelihood that witnesses can actually help in identifying the real criminals.

Figure 12.4
Lineups: Useful, but Susceptible to Several Forms of Bias
Police often use lineups to help identify the people who have committed various crimes. Such procedures are helpful but can be influenced by several sources of bias, including ones related to social influence. For instance, instructions suggesting that the criminal is present may lead to an increased tendency to falsely identify innocent victims.

Effects of Media Coverage on Perceptions of Defendants

Many legal proceedings—especially ones involving famous defendants or especially dramatic crimes—receive a great deal of coverage from the media. For instance, when Martha Stewart was put on trial in 2004, daily events during the trial appeared in hundreds of newspapers and in virtually every news program on television. Similar massive coverage occurs for other celebrities accused of crimes, and it seems clear that this can have powerful effects on the public's perceptions of defendants and can, in some cases, even influ-

lineup
A procedure in which witnesses to a crime are shown several people, one or more of whom may be suspects in a case, and asked to identify those that they recognize as the person who committed the crime.

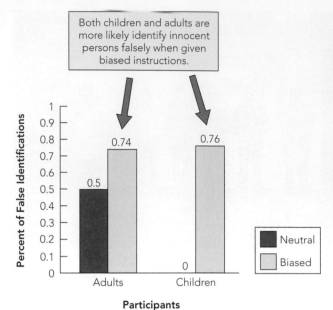

Figure 12.5
Instructions to Witnesses: An Important Factor in the Accuracy of Lineups
As shown here, when given instructions suggesting that the person who committed a crime was present in a lineup (actually, he was not), both children and adults showed increased tendency to identify someone falsely (an innocent person) as the criminal, as compared to instructions which clearly indicated that the guilty person might not be present in the lineup.

(*Source:* Based on data from Pozzulo & Dempsey, 2006.)

ence jurors. When a suspect is arrested, we quickly learn a great deal about that person, often with photos and videotapes of the accused wearing handcuffs, surrounded by officers of the law. Because such coverage does not tend to emphasize evidence pointing to the defendant's innocence, there is a strong tendency to form a negative impression of the suspect based on the primacy effect—the tendency for information we receive first to strongly influence our impressions of others (see Chapter 3). Moreover people tend to believe assertions made in the media (Gilbert, Tafarodi, & Malone, 1993). The result? Defendants are often viewed as guilty by the public, even before the trial begins. In effect, people are not psychologically acting in such a way as to meet the criteria of the law—"innocent, until proven guilty."

Because of these effects on public opinion (including the people who will eventually serve as jurors), pretrial publicity tends to benefit the prosecution and harm the defense. Moran and Cutler (1991) have documented just such effects of pretrial coverage on the assumption of guilt among potential jurors in actual cases. In general, the greater the amount of publicity about a crime there is, the greater the tendency of jurors to convict whoever is accused of committing it (Linz & Penrod, 1992). According to Moran (1993), government officials take advantage of these effects by providing as much crime information as possible to newspapers and television stations. The goal is for the public and potential jurors to form a negative impression of the defendant and thus support the government's case.

Research clearly indicates that media presentations affect the final verdict of many trials even if vigorous efforts are made to screen out jurors who have been exposed to news about the crime and to remind them of the importance of maintaining an open mind and an impartial attitude until they hear all of the evidence (Dexter, Cutler, & Moran, 1992). As we noted in Chapter 2 and elsewhere in this book, we are not always aware of the information, feelings, and other reactions that shape our decisions and judgments, so asking potential jurors whether they can be totally fair and impartial (a standard legal procedure), is almost like asking them "Do you understand every single factor that influences your ideas and your thinking (e.g., O'Connell, 1988)?"

One solution would be to change the law. For example, the United Sates allows publicity before and during trials, while Canada restricts such coverage to avoid "polluting" the jury. A simpler solution to the media problem is suggested by findings reported by Fein, McCloskey, and Tomlinson (1997). The biasing effects of pretrial publicity can be greatly weakened if the jurors are given reason to be suspicious about why incriminating evidence might have been given to the media. That is, this tactic shifts attention away from the content of the leaked evidence to the underlying motivation of those who leaked the evidence.

Social Influence and Judgments Concerning the Use of Deadly Force by Police

In recent years, there has been much concern over incidents in which police have shot—and sometimes killed—individuals who turned out to be unarmed. Clearly, police were unjustified in using deadly force in these cases—they engaged in what is known as **misuse of deadly force** (see Figure 12.6). But when, precisely, is such force justified, and when is it unjustified? How do ordinary citizens make such judgments? Research conducted by Perkins and Bourgeois (2006), offers at least a partial answer.

Participants in their studies were asked to read descriptions of the fatal shooting of a suspect. The descriptions varied with respect to the number of police officers involved (two or six) and in terms of the number of shots first (four, eight, sixteen, or thirty-two). Then, participants rated the extent to which the police actions constituted a misuse of deadly

misuse of deadly force
Refers to instances in which police use deadly (often lethal) force against suspected criminals, when in fact, such force is not necessary, and these people are not an actual threat to police or public safety.

force (from no misuse to absolute misuse of deadly force). On the basis of research on social influence, the researchers initially predicted that the greater the number of police present and the more shots fired, the more the use of force would be viewed as inappropriate. In fact, however, results provided support for only one of these predictions. The greater the number of shots fired, the more the use of deadly force was seen as inappropriate—just as expected. But the greater the number of police involved, the more justified deadly force was perceived to be. Why? Perhaps because when six individual police officers decide to fire at a suspect, observers conclude that this person must really have been doing something suspicious—or dangerous. In other words, a sub-

Figure 12.6
Deadly Force: When Do Police Misuse It?
Police are charged with protecting society from dangerous criminals, and sometimes, they must use deadly force to carry out this assignment. Sometimes, though, they may misuse such deadly force—employ it when it is actually not necessary. How do we determine whether deadly force is truly needed or is inappropriate? Research conducted by social psychologists provides at least a partial answer to this complex question.

tle form of social influence is at work: If a lot of police offices reacted in the same way, then our confidence that the suspect was acting in a dangerous or suspicious manner is strengthened because as we saw in Chapter 8 the impact of social influence increases as the number of people exerting it rises. To the extent this interpretation is accurate, this suggests yet another way—and a potentially important one—in which social influence can affect the legal system.

Social Cognition and the Legal System: Why Eyewitness Testimony Is Often Inaccurate

Eyewitness testimony—evidence given by people who have witnessed a crime—plays an important role in many trials. At first glance, this makes a great deal of sense: What better source of information about the events of a crime than the people who actually saw them? But there is an important "joker" in this deck: As we have seen over and over again, human perception, thought, and memory are far from perfect. On the contrary, all of these basic processes—building blocks of our understanding of the social world—are subject to a wide range of errors and distortions. This leads to an intriguing question: Are eyewitnesses really as accurate as we would like to believe? Or, like other aspects of social cognition, are they influenced by important forms of error and bias?

Unfortunately from the point of view of developing a totally fair, impartial, and accurate legal system, the answer is clear: They *must* be. In fact, though, witnesses often falsely identify innocent people as criminals (Wells, 1993), make mistakes about important details concerning a crime (Loftus, 2003), and sometimes report remembering events that did not actually take place (e.g., Zaragoza, Payment, Ackil, Drivdahl, & Beck, 2001). We should add immediately that these findings are not entirely new; in fact, as shown in *Building the Science: Classics of Social Psychology* on p. 426, these findings were reported in some of the first systematic research conducted by social psychologists.

Why do such errors occur? How can people actually present when a crime occurs make serious errors about it? The answer seems to center on several factors that, together, can produce distortions in memory—a key cognitive process that, as we noted in Chapter 2, forms the basis for many aspects of social thought (Wells, Memon, & Penrod, 2006).

One such source of error involves suggestibility—witnesses are sometimes influenced by leading questions and similar techniques used by attorneys or police officers as we described in the section on lineups. In addition, eyewitnesses often make errors with respect to source monitoring—eyewitnesses often attribute their memories to the wrong source. For instance, they identify a suspect in a lineup as the person who committed a crime because they remember having seen this individual before and assume it was at the

eyewitness testimony
Evidence given by persons who have witnessed a crime—plays an important role in many trials.

scene of the crime when, in fact, his or her face may be familiar because they saw it in an album of mug shots. Let's now take a look at some of the other major factors that make eyewitness testimony less accurate than we would wish.

The Role of Emotion: Affect and Cognition Revisited

In Chapter 2, we noted that our current feelings or emotions can often exert powerful effects on our thoughts, what we remember, and our decisions and judgments (e.g., Martin & Clore, 2001). In fact, witnesses quite often make mistakes, in part, because intense emotions tend to exert effects on their information processing. Such effects are especially likely to occur when a witness is the victim of a crime. Loftus (1992a) described a case in which a rape victim identified the wrong man as the rapist; this individual, though innocent, was convicted, imprisoned, and eventually released only when the actual rapist confessed. Unfortunately, errors of this type are far from rare; inaccurate eyewitnesses constitute the single most important factor in the wrongful conviction of innocent defendants, and strong emotions often contribute to such tragic mistakes (Wells, 1993; Wells, Luus, & Windschitl, 1994).

Time and Intervening Information

Another major obstacle to accuracy among eyewitnesses is the passage of time between witnessing an event and testifying about what was seen and heard (Loftus, 1992b). During that interval, the witness is almost always exposed to misleading postevent information from police questions, news stories, and the statements made by others. Such information becomes incorporated into what the witness remembers—it all blends together as part of what *seems* to be remembered. Inaccuracy occurs because eyewitnesses can no longer distinguish between what is actually remembered and events or experiences that have occurred since the crime.

BUILDING THE SCIENCE
CLASSICS OF SOCIAL PSYCHOLOGY

Early Evidence that Even "Expert" Eyewitnesses Are Inaccurate: Munsterberg's Ingenious Research

In 1907 the Model T had not yet been born (it didn't appear until 1908), the dark clouds of World War I had just begun to gather; and in most countries, women did not yet have the right to vote; truly, it was a different world. But Hugo Munsterberg, one of the first researchers in the newly emerging field of social psychology, was thinking in very modern terms. After examining research on memory and the effects of emotions on perception, and after discovering that his own reports of a theft in his home were filled with errors, Munsterberg (1907) found himself wondering: Are eyewitnesses to crimes really accurate? Or do the limits of their memory—and their emotions—lead them to serious errors? To find out, he conducted an ingenious study—one of the first in the history of social psychology.

During a meeting of a scientific association (one attended by legal experts, psychologists, and physicians), the proceedings were interrupted by a series of unusual events. Suddenly and unexpectedly a clown in a colorful costume burst into the room followed by a black man carrying a gun. The two individuals shouted at each other, one fell down, the other jumped on him, and a shot rang out. Then both men ran out of the room. Only the president of the association knew that these events had been arranged by Munsterberg. The other people present—scientists and doctors attending the conference—had no idea it was part of an experiment. They were then asked to write down exactly what had happened to help the police investigate this strange event.

Memory Distortion and Construction: Fuzzy-Trace Theory and Remembering What Never Happened

Now, we come to what is, perhaps, the most powerful and certainly the most dramatic source of error in eyewitness testimony: the limitations of human memory. While memory—our systems for storing and later retrieving information about the world—is truly amazing (e.g., it can store virtually unlimited amounts of information for years or even decades), it is far from perfect. In fact, memory is subject to many kinds of error. Perhaps the most important of these from the point of view of this discussion, however, involve what has often been termed memory construction—the development of memories for events that never took place or experiences that we never had. Where do these false memories—memories for events we never experienced—come from? The answer seems to be that often, they are somehow "planted" in our minds by the words or actions of others. Often, this is done unintentionally. For instance, some therapists urge their patients to look at old family photo albums to recover repressed memories of childhood sexual abuse (Figure 12.7). Research findings suggest that doing so may help to trigger long-forgotten memories, but it can also, under some conditions, lead to false memories about events that never happened (Lindsay, Hagen, Read, Wade, & Garry, 2004). Here's an example from my own life. When I was a child, my grandmother showed me an album containing photos of her parents. I never met them, but I generated false

Figure 12.7

Photos of the Past: Reliable Memory Cue—or the Basis for False Memories?
Nearly everyone likes to look at old photos of their family. Often, these help us to recall events from the past we want to remember. But growing evidence suggests that sometimes, this activity can lead us to construct memories for events that never happened or events we never experienced.

Despite the fact that the participants were all professionals trained to observe human behavior, and despite the fact that they wrote down their observations immediately after the event, their reports were found to be highly inaccurate. Only one witness provided a completely accurate description of what had occurred. Most others were moderately accurate at best; and more than half were quite inaccurate. What kind of errors did they make? Every conceivable kind. They reported many false details (e.g., that the black man wore a derby, a top hat, or some other covering on his head—he did not; that the clown's costume was one color when in fact it was another).

On the basis of these findings, Munsterberg (see Figure 12.8) concluded that witnesses to an event are truly inaccurate and can, at best, report about half of what they see. So yes, 1907 was a long time ago and the methods used by Munsterberg were far less sophisticated, in many respects, than the ones employed by researchers today. The conclusions he reached, however,

Figure 12.8

Hugo Munsterberg: An Early Researcher in Social Psychology
Hugo Munsterberg (1863–1916) conducted the first systematic study on the accuracy of eyewitnesses. His findings were so surprising that they stimulated research on this topic that is continuing even today.

have stood the test of time very well and have encouraged decades of research on eyewitness testimony and related topics. In this respect, we believe, his research definitely qualifies as a true classic of social psychology—early work that helped build the foundations of our modern field.

memories about having met them. I realized, in later years, that it was not possible for those memories to be true because they died long before I was born, but the memories—once created (probably from my grandmother's stories about her parents)—seemed completely real.

Another perspective on false memories is provided by what psychologists term **fuzzy-trace theory** (Reyna & Titcomb)—a theory about the relationship between memory and higher reasoning processes. According to this theory, when we make decisions and judgments, we often focus on the general idea or gist of information stored in memory and not on the information itself. One result is that we then remember information consistent with the gist of our real memories even though it is false. Fuzzy-trace theory leads to some intriguing predictions. For instance, it predicts that at first, the more often we are exposed to information we wish to remember, the more false memories about it we will have. This is because gist memories form quickly and are more stable than memories for specific facts or information. So up to some point, false memories are stronger than real ones. As repetitions continue, however, false memories are countered by accurate memories for specific information and tend to decrease (Seamon et al., 2002).

In sum, there are many reasons why eyewitnesses are not nearly as accurate as was once believed, and most of these relate to the ways in which we store, process, and later recall information about events and people. In this way, basic aspects of human cognition—and in particular, social cognition—play an important role. In other words, the findings and principles of social psychology provide important insights into a crucial aspect of the legal system—insights that, without these findings and principles—would not be available.

Increasing Eyewitness Accuracy

Before concluding, we should briefly note that while eyewitness testimony is not as accurate as we might wish, there are several techniques for improving it (e.g., Wells et al., 2006). One promising approach involves conducting improved interviews with witnesses—interviews that may enhance their ability to remember crucial information accurately (e.g., Geiselman & Fisher, 1997). In such cognitive interviews, eyewitnesses are asked to report everything they can remember; this provides them with multiple retrieval cues (aids to memory) and can increase accuracy of recall. In addition, they are sometimes asked to describe events from different perspectives and in several different orders—not just the one in which the events actually occurred. These and other steps seem to increase the accuracy of eyewitness testimony, but they are far from perfect, so the basic problem remains: Eyewitness testimony is not nearly as accurate as was once widely believed. For this reason, it is probably best to view it as an imperfect and potentially misleading source of information.

Other efforts have focused on improving police lineups as a technique for identifying guilty people. As we noted previously, lineups are subject to several sources of bias and error, but because social psychologists have uncovered these, steps can be taken to guard against them and increase their value and accuracy. In a sense, a lineup is analogous to a social psychological experiment (Wells & Luus, 1990). The officer conducting the lineup is the experimenter, the eyewitnesses are the research participants, the suspect is the primary stimulus, a witness's positive identification constitutes the response data, and the non-suspects, and the arrangement of the lineup constitute the research design. Also, the police have a hypothesis that the suspect is guilty. Finally, for either experiments or testimony, the data are stated in terms of probability because neither experiments nor lineups can provide absolute certainty. This analogy is useful because it suggests several ways in which police can improve the accuracy of lineups by adapting procedures routinely used by social psychologists. For example, a blank lineup control can be adopted; this means that a witness is first shown a lineup containing only innocent nonsuspects (Wells, 1984). If the witness fails to identify any of them, confidence in his or her accuracy is increased. If an innocent person is identified, the witness is informed and then cautioned about the danger of making a false identification, thus improving accuracy when actual lineups are presented. Other procedures that seem to increase the usefulness of lineups—or, at the least, reduce the chances that innocent people will be identified as the criminal—include choosing

fuzzy-trace theory
A theory suggesting that when we make decisions or judgments, we often focus on the general idea or gist of information stored in memory and not on the information itself. One result is that we then remember information consistent with the gist of our real memories even though it is false.

"fillers" (people who are not actually suspects) to be similar to the descriptions of the criminal given by eyewitnesses rather than to be similar in appearance to the actual suspect, using larger rather than smaller lineups, sequential rather than simultaneous lineups, and avoiding actions that inflate eyewitnesses' confidence in their own judgments. For instance, telling them whether they have chosen the suspect or a filler person in a lineup. Overall, research findings (e.g., Wells et al., 2006) indicate that all of these procedures can be helpful.

Additional approaches that improve accuracy include the presentation of pictures of the crime scene and of the victim to the witness before an identification is made (Cutler, Penrod, & Martens, 1987), avoiding even the hint of biased instructions (ones suggesting that the criminal is included in the lineup), and using a double-blind procedure, such as that used in social psychological experiments—procedures in which neither the witnesses nor the people presenting the lineup know who is the true suspect or even whether that person is included in the lineup. The goal, of course, is to increase the accuracy with which guilty people are identified, and once again, procedures regularly used by social psychologists in their research can prove helpful. Overall, then, we do know how to help eyewitnesses improve the accuracy of their testimony—research by social psychologists and by psychologists who are experts in memory—give us at least part of the answer. The really difficult task, however, is to get the legal system to adopt these recommended procedures. A few states and localities have actually accepted these recommendations and acted on them, but as noted recently by several experts on eyewitness identification (Wells et al., 2006), winning acceptance for truths—even ones established by science—is often a tricky business. In *Building the Science: Classics of Social Pychology* on page 426 we examine the research that started the systematic investigations of eyewitness testimony by social psychologists—a true classic of social psychology conducted by Hugo Munsterberg more than one hundred years ago.

The Influence of Prejudice and Stereotypes on the Legal System

If justice were truly blind—as we all wish, in principle, that it were—then it would be completely unaffected by race, gender, ethnic background, and other factors. In other words, decisions by judges and juries would be based entirely on evidence, and the characteristics of defendants would have no effect. Having read the chapters in this book on social cognition, attitudes, and prejudice, however, you probably already realize that this state of affairs—although desirable—is difficult, if not impossible, to attain. As human beings, each of us enters any social situation, including legal proceedings, with complex sets of attitudes, beliefs, values, and—unfortunately—stereotypes concerning various groups. These can then interact in many ways with information concerning the particular case in question and so influence the decisions we reach as jurors. How common are such effects? And what can be done to eliminate them? These are the issues to which we turn next (e.g., Levine & Wallach, 2001).

The Characteristics of Defendants and Jurors and How They Influence Legal Proceedings

Let's begin with the characteristics of defendants—the people on trial. These include race, gender, and ethnic background, and all these factors have been found to influence jury decisions and other outcomes. In the United States, African American defendants have generally been found to be at a disadvantage. For example, they are more likely than Caucasians to be convicted of murder and to receive the death penalty and to be proportionally overrepresented on death row.

Race, however, is not the only characteristic of defendants that can play a role in legal proceedings. In addition, their physical appearance (attractiveness), gender, and socioeconomic status are also important. For example, people accused of most major crimes are less likely to be found guilty if they are physically attractive, female, and of high rather than low socioeconomic status (Mazzella & Feingold, 1994). Attractiveness has been studied the

Figure 12.9
Defendant's Appearance:
A Factor that Shouldn't
Matter but Does!
*Research findings indicate that
attractive defendants have a
big "edge" in the courtroom:
They are convicted less often
and tend to receive lighter
sentences or smaller fines than
unattractive defendants.*

most, and in real and mock trials, attractive defendants have a major advantage over unattractive ones with respect to being acquitted, receiving a light sentence, and gaining the sympathy of the jurors (see Figure 12.9; Downs & Lyons, 1991; Quigley, Johnson, & Byrne, 1995; Wuensch, Castellow, & Moore, 1991).

In addition to race and attractiveness, another visible characteristic—gender—also plays an important role in legal proceedings. In general, female defendants tend to be treated more leniently by juries and courts than male defendants, but this depends on the specific crime. For instance, in cases involving assault, female defendants are actually more likely to be found guilty than male defendants, perhaps because assault is considered an even more unacceptable and unusual behavior for women than men (Cruse & Leigh, 1987). The gender of jurors, too, can be important. One of the consistent differences between male and female jurors is in reaction to cases involving sexual assault. In judging what occurred in cases of rape, men are more likely than women to conclude that the sexual interaction was consensual (Harris & Weiss, 1995). Schutte and Hosch (1997) analyzed the results of thirty-six studies of simulated cases of rape and child abuse. In responding to defendants accused of either crime, women were more likely than men to vote for conviction.

Jurors also appear to differ in the way they process information, and these differences can lead to more or less accurate decisions. For example, about one-third have already made up their minds about the trial by the time the opening arguments are made. As the trial progresses, 75 to 85 percent begin to favor one side over the other, and this bias affects how subsequent evidence is processed (Carlson & Russo, 2001). As we saw in Chapter 2, the confirmation bias may begin to operate, with the result that only information consistent with their initial opinion is noticed and remembered. The outcome is that jurors make up their minds with increasing certainty, even though they are not really paying careful attention to both sides.

Can the Effects of Prejudice on Legal Proceedings Be Reduced?

Our comments so far in this section seem to paint a picture in which the decisions reached by jurors and perhaps even judges are influenced by factors we all wish did not exert such effects. But don't despair: Growing evidence suggests that although the factors we have discussed do indeed influence outcomes, these effects may not be as large as was previously suspected, and may be overcome—at least to a considerable extent—by some aspects of legal processes.

Perhaps the clearest, and most encouraging evidence in this respect, is provided by research conducted by Bothwell, Piggott, Foley, and McFatter (2006). Taking account of past research on prejudice and stereotypes, these researchers reasoned that often, these cognitive factors operate at an automatic or unconscious level; they influence behavior but do so in subtle rather than overt ways, and the people who hold such views often state—vigorously—that they are not prejudiced. This suggests that such prejudiced views would be more likely to influence their private judgments than their public decisions as jurors. In other words, while specific jurors might well have subtle negative views about various racial or ethnic groups, these views would be more likely to find expression in their private judgments and thoughts than in their actual decisions as jurors (e.g., Hebl, Foster, Mannix, & Dovidio, 2002). Jury deliberations, which are often lengthy and detailed, might serve to reduce the impact of subtle and nonconscious forms of prejudice and so help make the process more fair.

To test this reasoning, Bothwell and others (2006) conducted research in which both students and prospective jurors in actual legal cases read about a sexual harassment suit in which a supervisor demanded sexual favors from a subordinate. Race of the supervisor and the subordinate (who had made the complaint) was varied, so that each could be either African American or Caucasian; gender, too, was a factor in the study, so that the supervisor and the subordinate could each be either a man or a woman. Participants read a case that presented one of these various combinations (e.g., an African American male supervisor and a Caucasian female subordinate; Caucasian female supervisor and an African America male subordinate, and so on). Participants then rated the responsibility of the person making the complaint and how much monetary compensation the victim should receive from the company. Results for these measures indicated that racial and gender prejudice exerted significant effects. For instance, the person making the complaint was held more responsible for what happened to him or her when the supervisor was African American than when this person was Caucasian. Similarly, they awarded less compensation when the supervisor was African American than when he or she was Caucasian. Participants reasoned—at the private level—that when the supervisor was African American, the subordinates "should have known better" than to go to this person's hotel room for a drink.

After making the private decisions and judgments, a mock trial was held in which jurors met and then recommended compensation for the victim. Here's the interesting—and encouraging—finding: At the end of the mock trials, the effects of race and gender largely disappeared. In other words, although the impact of these variables was present before actual jury deliberations, it was essentially eliminated by jury deliberations. For instance, as shown in Figure 12.8, as individuals, participants in the study privately awarded much less compensation to the victim of sexual harassment when the defendant (the supervisor) was African American than when he or she was Caucasian. After jury discussion, however, this difference totally disappeared (see Figure 12.10).

These findings, and those in related studies (e.g., Greene & Bornstein, 2003), suggest that while justice is certainly not entirely blind, the procedures used for reaching legal decisions can, at least sometimes, help to counter the impact of various characteristics of defendants, and perhaps of jurors, too. So while our existing system is far from perfect, it may operate more effectively than some experts have feared.

⌒Principles to Remember

Justice is definitely not blind. Many aspects of legal proceedings are influenced by cognitive, emotional, and social factors that can sometimes get in the way of totally fair and impartial outcomes.

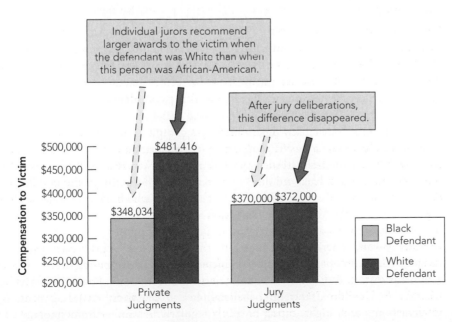

Figure 12.10
Are Jury Decisions Influenced by the Prejudice of Individual Jurors? Perhaps Not!
When participants in the study shown here made individual (private) recommendations for compensation to a victim of sexual harassment, they recommended larger awards when the defendant was Caucasian than when he or she was African-American. After jury deliberation, however, this difference—and others reflecting racial and gender prejudice—tended to disappear. These findings suggest that jury deliberations may help to reduce the impact of prejudices held by individual jurors.

(*Source:* Based on data from Bothwell, Pigott, Foley, & McFatter, 2006.)

KeyPoints

- Social influence plays an important role in many aspects of the legal system and can be observed with respect to police interrogations, lineups, and media coverage of crimes and trials.

- Most people prefer that police interrogators adopt an inquisitorial approach, in which they search for the truth, rather than an adversarial approach, in which they attempt to prove guilt.

- Research findings indicate that videotaping police interrogations reduces the use of abusive tactics by police, but it does not prevent jurors from viewing false confessions obtained under pressure as valid.

- Lineups can be helpful in identifying criminals, but they are susceptible to several forms of bias.

- Publicity in the media before a trial can have strong effects on public opinion about the guilt or innocence of the defendants and can even affect jurors' decisions.

- Eyewitnesses are not as accurate as is commonly believed. Several factors (e.g., intense emotion, the passage of time since the observed events, and errors in memory) all contribute to this fact.

- Individuals often construct false memories—memories for events that never happened. These mem- ories sometimes arise because we often focus on the general idea or gist of information stored in memory and not on the information itself. As a result, we remember information consistent with the gist of our real memories even though it is false.

- The accuracy of eyewitness testimony can be improved through the use of improved interviews and better lineup procedures.

- During trials, attorneys sometimes ask leading questions or present evidence that is inadmissible. Research findings indicate that jurors find it hard to ignore such information.

- Defendants' race, gender, and appearance often exert strong effects on the outcomes they experi- ence in legal proceedings, but such effects can sometimes be reduced by jury deliberations.

Think About It

If the findings of research conducted by social psychol- ogists offer clear recommendations for improving the fairness of the legal system, why have these suggestions not been adopted by police, courts, attorneys, and oth- ers? What can be done to encourage such adoption of these valuable research findings?

Social Psychology and Health

Why do people become ill? Your immediate reply is probably something like "Because they are exposed to bacteria or viruses." While that may be technically correct, it is becom- ing increasingly clear that organisms that produce disease are only part of the total pic- ture. Growing evidence from the field of **health psychology,** the branch of psychology that studies the relation between psychological variables and health, suggests that both health and illness are actually determined by a complex interaction among genetic, psy- chological, and social factors (Taylor, 2002). Yes, exposure to organisms that cause disease plays a role but so do health-related attitudes and beliefs and the kind of lifestyle we adopt. Do you smoke? Eat a balanced diet? Expose yourself to the sun in the middle of the day during the summer? Exercise regularly? Listen to music through earphones with the vol- ume turned way up? You already know that all of these behaviors can strongly affect our health—by either encouraging excellent health or the opposite.

Here's some sobering data concerning the potential role of our own behavior in our personal health. In one major study conducted over a ten-year period in Alameda County, California (Wiley & Camacho, 1980), a large group of adults were assessed concerning whether they followed certain (beneficial) health practices, including sleeping seven to eight hours each night, eating breakfast regularly, refraining from smoking, drinking

health psychology
The branch of psychology that studies the relation between psychological variables and health.

alcohol in moderation or not at all, maintaining their weight within normal limits, and exercising regularly (Wiley & Camacho, 1980). Results indicated many links between health-related behaviors and personal well-being. Most dramatic of all, those participants who reported practicing all or most of the health-promoting behaviors mentioned were much less likely to die during the study period than those who

Figure 12.11
Does Our Behavior Influence Our Health? Absolutely!
None of us will ever get a "newer model." The body we have is the only one we will ever have. The goal, then, is to keep it as healthy and vigorous as possible—and that means behaving in ways that help us reach this crucial goal.

practiced few or none of these behaviors. These findings, and those of many other studies, suggest that there is a strong link between the lifestyle we adopt and our health; the ad in Figure 12.11 emphasizes this important point, and the importance of taking care of the "model" (the body) we have. Because social psychology studies topics closely related to lifestyle such as attitudes and beliefs, different ways of coping with stress, and the personal characteristics that may play a role in our health (e.g., Dunkley, Zuroff, & Blankstein, 2003), it has much to contribute to our understanding of the factors that affect our health and well-being.

In this section, we'll consider applications of the findings and principles of social psychology to personal health. First, we'll examine the role of attitudes in personal health and how they can help encourage a lifestyle that promotes health and healthy behaviors. Next, we'll turn to a major threat health risk at the present time—rising rates of obesity. Here, we'll examine some of the social factors that play a role in this increasing problem and describe some possible solutions to it. Then, we'll examine one especially important factor in personal health—stress—examining its basic nature, some of its major causes, and several of its key effects.

The Role of Attitudes in Personal Health: Promoting a Healthy Lifestyle

How long will you live? And how healthy will you be during your life—especially during the later decades? At some point, nearly everyone wonders about these questions. When we are young—in our teens, twenties, or thirties—we rarely think about them. But as we grow older, we do so with increasing frequency, even if we remain in good health. The answers to these questions are complex and are only just beginning to emerge, but we are definitely making progress. Genetic factors clearly play some role; people whose parents and grandparents lived to ripe old ages are more likely to do so themselves than would be expected by chance alone. And research findings suggest that a group of genes found on a single human chromosome may well play some role in determining life span (Perls & Silver, 1999). But it is also clear that environmental factors, and especially, the lifestyle we adopt, matter, too. And in this respect, the attitudes we hold about health generally, or about our own health specifically, can be important. For instance, consider research by Levy et al. (2002).

These researchers conducted a longitudinal study stretching across more than twenty-two years, in which they measured individuals' self-perceptions of aging—their beliefs about what would happen to them as they grew older. Then they divided the participants into those who had mainly positive perceptions about their own aging and those who had

Figure 12.12
Self-Perceptions of Aging and Actual Longevity
As shown here, people who believed that they would age well actually lived longer than those who believed that as they aged, they would experience serious problems and deterioration. These findings can be viewed as illustrating the powerful effects of attitudes on personal health

(*Source:* Based on data from Levy, Slade, Kunkel, & Kasl, 2002.)

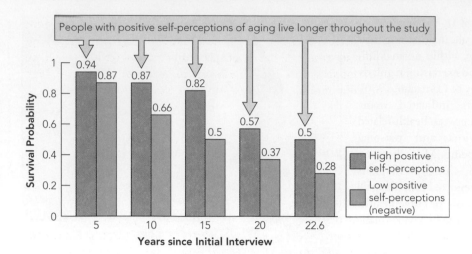

mainly negative ones. When they followed these individuals for more than two decades, they obtained an amazing result: Those with positive beliefs about aging were more likely to continue living throughout the study than those with negative beliefs about aging. In fact, those in the positive belief group lived on average seven-and-a-half years longer than with negative beliefs (see Figure 12.12).

What accounts for this difference? Further research indicated that it was as a result, at least in part, of what Levy et al. (2002) describe as the will to live. People with positive self-perceptions of aging tended to perceive their lives as hopeful, fulfilling, and worth living, while those with negative self-perceptions tended to perceive their lives as empty, worthless, and hopeless. Such self-perceptions may have caused the positive group to take better care of themselves—to live a more healthy lifestyle—with the result that they did, in fact, live longer. So, in a sense, individuals' attitudes and beliefs about aging influenced their behavior and that helped those with positive beliefs to actually live longer. Certainly this is an especially important kind of link between attitudes and behavior or between attitudes and important life outcomes.

Growing evidence suggests that as is often the case, attitudes concerning health don't always exert direct effects on health-generating behaviors (e.g., McAuley, Pena, & Jerome, 2001). Specifically, such effects appear to operate through both attributions (which we discussed in detail in Chapter 3) and self-efficacy—the belief, held by individuals, that they can accomplish what they set out to accomplish in a given area of life (Shields, Brawley, & Lindover, 2006). For instance, individuals are more likely to exercise and to complete exercise programs when they believe that they can actually reach this goal and when they perceive strong links between exercising and health benefits. If, in contrast, they don't believe that they can reach the goal of getting in shape, they are much more likely to give up and quit; in view of the effort required to exercise vigorously and regularly, that's hardly surprising.

More surprising, however, are recent findings indicating that the beneficial effects of exercise actually stem, at least in part, from believing in these effects. For instance, in a dramatic illustration of such effects, Crum and Langer (2007) told some maids in a large hotel that their regular job activities provided healthy exercise; others were not given this information. Several weeks later, the maids told that they were getting good exercise actually showed lowered blood pressure, reductions in weight, and a decrease in body fat. Apparently, just believing in the positive effects of exercise can help produce them, apart from the actual physiological effects of exercise themselves.

But what, precisely, is a healthy lifestyle? Probably, you already know quite a bit about this: It is a way of living in which we avoid behaviors potentially harmful to our health (e.g., excessive use of alcohol, smoking, unprotected sex, unprotected exposure to the sun [Glanz,

Geller, Shigaki, Maddock, & Isnec, 2002]) and seek early detection and effective treatment of illness when they occur. Because you have already heard many persuasive messages urging you to avoid various threats to your health and to seek early medical advice, we'll focus here on one topic that now looms as a truly major threat to the health of North Americans and people in many other countries: the growing worldwide epidemic of obesity.

Obesity: A Social Psychological Perspective on a Major Threat to Health

Recent statistics suggest that in the United States more than 66 percent of all adults are obese—they weigh far more than the ideal for their height and body frame. But you don't need statistics to demonstrate this fact, just go to any nearby shopping mall or theater and observe the crowd. You will soon have your own evidence that North Americans (and people in many other countries, too) are truly becoming "super-sized." Because obesity is clearly harmful to personal health—it increases the risk of heart disease, bone disease, and a host of other illnesses—two key questions arise: (1) What factors are responsible for this growing problem? And (2) what, if anything, can be done to reverse the trend?

Many different factors contribute to the fact that around the globe increasing numbers of people are gaining weight. First, genetic factors appear to be important. Consider the situation faced by our ancestors: periods of plenty alternated with periods of famine. Under these conditions, people who were efficient at storing excess calories as fat during times of plenty gained an important advantage: They were more likely to survive during famines and to have children. As a result, all of us living today have some tendency to gain weight when we overeat—much to our dismay!

Environmental factors, too, play an important role. In recent years, the size of portions of many foods has increased dramatically. Almost every time I eat at a restaurant, I find myself taking food home in a plastic container. Why? Is it because I eat less as I grow older? Perhaps. But more likely is the growing trend toward supersized portions: Restaurants—from fine ones to fast-food outlets—have increased the size of portions. Thirty years ago, a Coke or Pepsi was eight ounces, now, one-liter bottles (about thirty-two ounces) are being offered as a single serving. Similarly, McDonald's hamburgers were small and thin and contained about two hundred calories, now, most people purchase double cheeseburgers or Big Macs containing four or five hundred calories. Because people tend to eat their entire portion of food, no matter how big it is, this, too, may be a factor in the rising rate of obesity (see Figure 12.13).

In addition—and most central to this discussion—social factors, play an important role. First, people don't walk as much as they did in the past. In cities, fear of crime has stopped many people from walking to stores and other locations. Similarly, shopping malls

Figure 12.13
Supersized Portions in Restaurants: One Reason Why Many People, Too, Are Now Supersize?
The size of portions served in restaurants has increased dramatically in the past thirty years. Compare today's burger on the left with the original McDonald's hamburger held by Ray Kroc on the right. This may be one factor contributing to the growing number of people who are seriously overweight in the United States and, increasingly, in many other countries, too.

have brought a large number of stores to one location, with parking just outside the door. In the past, people had to walk many blocks to visit as many different shops—and often rode public transportation to reach them because parking was so difficult. Now, most people do their shopping at malls or in shopping centers where the stores are close together. And school buses tend to stop in front of every house, thus, assuring that even children have less opportunity to exercise than was true in the past.

Another social factor involves more enticing media campaigns for meals and snacks that are high in calories. Who can resist the foods shown in TV commercials, on billboards, and magazines? Fewer and fewer people, it seems, so caloric intake—and weight gain—is increased by this factor, too.

Yet another factor involves the fact that the sit-down dinner is fast disappearing. Instead of eating their meals together, a growing number of families eat at different times, often away from home. This can lead to a situation in which people snack all day; after all, there is no reason to save their appetites for a family meal. Research findings indicate that it is much harder for our built-in bodily mechanisms to regulate eating when it occurs in this manner, so this is yet another social factor that contributes to expanding waistlines.

Finally, consider social norms concerning weight: Thin is definitely "in," and most people report that they want to weigh less than they do. Yet, despite such attitudes, the number of extremely large people continues to increase. As it does, overweight individuals can, perhaps, take consolation from the fact that they are not alone. In sum, many social factors appear to play a role in the trend toward obesity occurring in many countries in recent years.

Antifat Attitudes

One other consequence of the "you-can't-be-too-thin" philosophy promoted by the media may, perhaps, be growing prejudice toward people who are quite obese. That such negative attitudes exist is indicated by the results of many recent studies. For instance, in one experiment with somewhat disturbing results (Hebl & Mannix, 2003), participants played the role of en employer choosing among several male job applicants. Part of the information they received about each applicant was a photo showing this person sitting next to a woman who was either of normal weight or overweight. Reflecting an antifat prejudice, the applicants were rated lower when they were shown sitting next to an overweight person than one of normal weight.

Additional findings indicate that antifat attitudes may derive, at least in part, from the widespread belief that people who are obese are responsible for their excess weight (Crandall et al., 2001). In fact, this is a general principle established by social psychologists: Prejudices often reflect underlying beliefs that people with some negative attribute are responsible for possessing it. In other words, we hold negative attitudes toward people whom, we believe, are responsible for having characteristics we evaluate negatively. Whatever its origins, it is clear that antifat prejudice is a fact of social life just at a time when the number of people to whom it can be applied is growing rapidly.

Stress: Its Causes, Effects, and Control

Have you ever felt that you were right at the edge of being overwhelmed by negative events in your life or by pressures you could no longer handle (see Figure 12.14)? If so, you are already quite familiar with **stress,** which is our response to events that disrupt, or threaten to disrupt, our physical or psychological functioning (Lazarus & Folkman, 1984; Taylor, 2002). Unfortunately, stress is a common part of modern life—something few of us can avoid altogether. Partly for this reason, and partly because it seems to exert negative effects on both physical health and psychological well-being, stress has become an important topic of research in psychology, and social psychologists have made major contributions to this work. We'll now review the key findings of this research, with special attention to

stress
Our response to events that disrupt, or threaten to disrupt, our physical or psychological functioning.

Figure 12.14
Stress: An All Too-
Common Part of
Modern Life
*Have you ever felt that you were
about to be overwhelmed? That
you could no longer cope with all
the demands in your life? If so,
you already know from personal
experience how unpleasant—and
how harmful to personal health—
persistent high levels of stress can be.*

its links to major principles of social psychology. Please note that stress has many other effects aside from ones on personal health—for instance, it can strongly influence performance on many tasks and key aspects of decision making. Here, though we'll focus on its impact on personal health.

Major Sources of Stress and Their Effects on Personal Health

What factors contribute to stress? Unfortunately, the list is a long one: Many conditions and events can add to our total stress quotient. Among the most important of these, though, are major stressful life events (e.g., the death of a loved one or a painful divorce) and the all-too-frequent minor hassles of everyday life. (Another major source of stress is events occurring at work, but because we cover applications of social psychology to business settings in a later section, we won't discuss those here.)

Death of a spouse, injury to one's child, failure in school or at work—unless we lead truly charmed lives, most of us experience traumatic events and changes at some time or other. What are their effects on us? This question was first investigated by Holmes and Rahe (1967), who asked a large group of people to assign arbitrary points (from one to one hundred) to various life events according to how much readjustment each had required. (A few examples: death of a spouse = one hundred points; getting fired = forty-seven points; taking out a car loan = seventeen points). Holmes and Rahe then related the total number of points accumulated by another group of individuals during a single year to changes in their personal health. The results were dramatic: The greater the number of stress points people accumulated, the greater was their likelihood of becoming seriously ill. Although this study had a number of flaws (e.g., the correlational design did not allow for causal inferences), it suggested that accumulated stress, rather than stress emanating for any specific stressor, is associated with health problems.

More recent research has begun to identify the specific effects of accumulated stress on health (McEwen, 1998). For example, in one study, Cohen and his colleagues (1998) asked a group of volunteers to describe stressful events they had experienced during the previous year and to indicate the temporal course (the onset and offset) of each event. The stressful events described by participants ranged from acute stressors that were brief in duration (e.g., a severe reprimand at work or a fight with a spouse) to more chronic ones that typically lasted a month or more and involved significant disruption of everyday routines (e.g., ongoing marital problems or unemployment). Then the researchers gave these people nose drops containing a low dose of a virus that causes the common cold. Results indicated that volunteers who reported experiencing chronic stressors were more likely to develop a cold than those who had experienced only acute stressors. Moreover, the longer the duration of the stressor, the greater was the risk for developing a cold.

While certain major life events, such as the death of a loved one, are dramatic and deeply disturbing, they occur only rarely. Does this mean that in general, our lives are a calm lake of tranquility? Hardly. As you know, daily life is filled with countless minor annoying sources of stress—termed *hassles*—that seem to make up for their relatively low intensity by their much higher frequency. That such daily hassles are an important cause of stress is suggested by the findings of several studies by Lazarus and others (e.g., DeLongis, Folkman, & Lazarus, 1988; Lazarus et al., 1981; Lazarus et al., 1985). These researchers developed a hassles scale on which individuals indicate the extent to which they have been "hassled" by common events during the past month. The items included in this scale deal with a wide range of everyday events, such as having too many things to do at once, misplacing or losing things, troublesome neighbors, and concerns over money.

While such events may seem relatively minor when compared with the life events discussed previously, they appear to be quite important. When scores on the hassles scale are related to reports of psychological symptoms, strong positive correlations are obtained (Lazarus et al., 1985). In short, the more stress people report as a result of daily hassles, the poorer their psychological well-being. You can assess the extent of your own exposure to daily hassles using the hassles scale provided in Table 12.1. Now, let's consider the ways in which stress influences personal health.

Table 12.1   The Daily Hassles Scale

By completing the items here, you can obtain an index of how much stress you experience from the hassles of daily life. (*Source:* Adapted from items developed by Lazarus, Opton, Nomikos, & Rankin, 1985.)

Daily Hassles: Directions: Listed here are a number of ways in which a person can feel hassled. As you read each hassle, use the following rating scale to rate how much a hassle each item is for you: 0 = none or did not occur; 1 = somewhat severe; 2 = moderately severe; 3 = extremely severe. Add up your total. The higher your score, the more likely your psychological well-being will be affected.

__ Auto maintenance	__ Concerns about money for emergencies	__ Fear of rejection
__ Being lonely	__ Concerns about news events	__ Feel conflicted over what to do
__ Care for pet	__ Concerns about owing money	__ Filling out forms
__ Concerns about accidents	__ Concerns about weight	__ Financial dealings with friends or acquaintances
__ Concerns about bodily functions	__ Customers or clients give you a hard time	__ Financial security
__ Concerns about getting credit	__ Cutting down on electricity, water, or other utilities.	__ Friends or relatives too far away
__ Concerns about health in general	__ Decisions about having children	__ Gossip
__ Concerns about inner conflicts	__ Difficulties seeing or hearing	__ Having to wait
__ Concerns about medical treatment	__ Difficulties with friends	__ Health of a family member
__ Concerns about meeting high standards	__ Fear of confrontation	__ Home maintenance (inside)
		__ Inability to express yourself

__ Inconsiderate smokers	__ Not getting enough rest	__ Side effects of medication
__ Legal problems	__ Not getting enough sleep	__ Silly practical mistakes
__ Menstrual (period) problems	__ Not seeing enough people	__ Smoking too much
__ Misplacing or losing things	__ Overloaded with family responsibilities	__ Social obligations
__ Nightmares	__ Personal use of drugs	__ Someone owes you money
__ Not enough money for basic necessities	__ Physical appearance	__ The weather
__ Not enough money for clothing	__ Physical illness	__ Thoughts about death
__ Not enough money for entertainment and recreation	__ Planning meals	__ Too many interruptions
__ Not enough money for food	__ Prejudice and discrimination from others	__ Too many responsibilities
__ Not enough money for health care	__ Preparing meals	__ Too many things to do
__ Not enough money for housing	__ Problems getting along with fellow workers	__ Too much time on hands
__ Not enough money for transportation	__ Problems with employees	__ Transportation problems
__ Not enough personal energy	__ Problems with your lover	__ Trouble making decisions
__ Not enough time for entertainment and recreation	__ Property, investments, or taxes	__ Trouble relaxing
__ Not enough time for family	__ Regrets over past decisions	__ Trouble with arithmetic skills
__ Not enough time to do the things you need to do	__ Rising prices of common goods	__ Trouble with reading, writing, or speaking ability
	__ Sexual problems that result from physical problems	__ Troubling thoughts about your future
	__ Shopping	__ Use of alcohol
		__ Wasting time
		__ Yardwork or outside home maintenance

How Does Stress Affect Health?

We hope that by now, you are convinced that stress plays an important role in personal health. But how, exactly, do these effects occur? While the precise mechanisms involved remain to be determined, growing evidence suggests that the process goes something like this: By draining our resources, inducing negative affect, and keeping us off balance physiologically, stress upsets our complex internal chemistry. In particular, it may interfere with efficient operation of our immune system—the mechanism through which our bodies recognize and destroy potentially harmful substances and intruders, such as bacteria, viruses, and cancerous cells. When functioning normally, the immune system is nothing short of amazing: Each day it removes or destroys many potential threats to our health.

Unfortunately, prolonged exposure to stress seems to disrupt this system. Chronic exposure to stress can reduce circulating levels of lymphocytes (white blood cells that fight

Figure 12.15
Stress and Illness: One Useful Model
One model of how stress affects our health suggests that it does so through both direct and indirect effects.

(*Source:* Based on suggestions by Baum, 1994.)

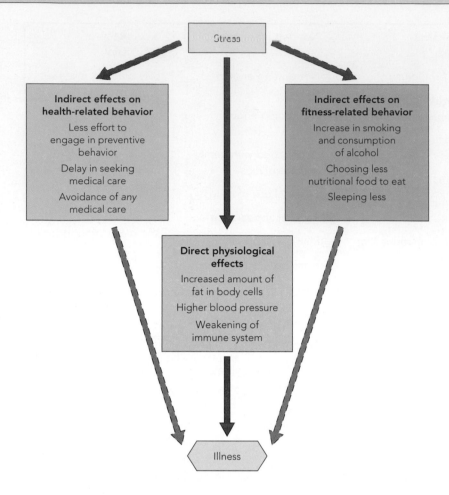

infection and disease) and increase levels of the hormone cortisol, a substance that suppresses aspects of our immune system (Kemeny, 2003).

One model of how stress can affect our health—a model proposed by a social psychologist—is illustrated in Figure 12.15, This model suggests that stress exerts both direct and indirect effects on us. The direct effects are the ones just described (e.g., on our immune system and other bodily functions). The indirect effects involve influences on the lifestyles we adopt—our health-related behaviors (e.g., whether we seek medical care promptly when we need it), and fitness-related behavior (e.g., the diet we choose, exercise, etc.). While this model may not include all the ways in which stress can affect our health, it offers a useful overview of several ways in which such effects may arise.

Coping with Stress

Because stress is an inescapable part of life, the key task we face is not trying to eliminate or avoid it but rather to cope with it effectively in ways that reduce its adverse effects while helping us deal with its causes. You are already familiar with several effective means for coping with stress such as improving your physical fitness (e.g., Brown, 1991) and eating a healthy diet—which can provide the added benefit of regulating your weight. Maintaining a stable weight is a very important outcome, one to which we'll return in a later section. Here, we'll focus on one strategy—that is closely related to social psychology and its knowledge about the social side of life: seeking **social support**—drawing on the emotional and other resources provided by others.

What do you do when you feel stressed? Many people turn to friends or family, seeking their advice, help, and sympathy. And research findings indicate that this can be a highly effective means of protecting our personal health from the ravages of stress (House,

social support
Drawing on the emotional and task resources provided by others as a means of coping with stress.

Figure 12.16
Pets Can Reduce Stress!
Research findings indicate that for many people, owning a pet can help to reduce stress.

Landis, & Umberson, 1988). Just being with those you like can be helpful; even monkeys seek contact with others in stressful situations (Cohen, Kaplan, Cunnick, Manuck, & Rabin, 1992). You may remember the discussion of similar instances of human affiliation in Chapter 7. As you might also guess on the basis of research on the effects of similarity, people who desire social support tend to turn to others who are similar to themselves in various ways (Morgan, Carder, & Neal, 1997). But you don't have to have contact with another person to experience such benefits; recent findings indicate that having a pet can help reduce stress (see Figure 12.16 [e.g., Allen, 2003]).

For instance, in one intriguing study (Allen, Shykoff, & Izzo, 2001), stockbrokers who lived alone, who described their work as stressful, and who all had high blood pressure were either randomly selected to receive a pet cat or dog from an animal shelter or to not receive a pet. Results indicated that the pets were an excellent source of social support, reducing stress among those who received them. In fact, when exposed to high levels of stress, those who had acquired pets cut their blood pressure increases by half compared to those who did not receive pets.

Why are pets so effective in this regard? One possibility is that they provide non-judgmental social support: They love their owners under all conditions. Whatever the precise reasons, it seems clear that pets can be an important aid in coping with stress—at least for people who enjoy having them.

In contrast, a lack of a reliable social support network can actually increase a person's risk of dying from disease, accidents, or suicide. People who are divorced or separated from their spouses often experience reduced functioning in certain aspects of their immune system, compared to individuals who are happily married (Kiecolt-Glaser et al., 1987; 1988).

Although it is clear that receiving social support is important to health, recent findings seem to indicate that providing social support to others may be just as important. In one revealing study, Brown, Nesse, Vinokur, & Smith (2003) isolated and compared the unique effects of giving and receiving social support on mortality in a sample of 846 elderly married people. The researchers initially measured the extent to which participants received and gave support to their spouse and to others (friends, relatives, neighbors) and then monitored mortality rates over a five-year period. Participants who reported providing high levels of support to others were significantly less likely to die over the five-year period than participants who had provided little or no support to others. By contrast, receiving social support, from one's spouse or from others, did not appear to affect mortality among people in this group. In short, these findings suggest it may be better to give than to receive, especially when it comes to personal health.

> **Principles to Remember**
> Personal health is strongly influenced by social factors, including our attitudes toward behaviors that promote health, social factors that promote obesity, and the ways in which we cope with stress (e.g., by seeking social support).

KeyPoints

- Attitudes can influence personal health in many ways—especially by promoting (or discouraging) healthy lifestyles.

- As is true of other attitudes, though, positive attitudes toward healthy behaviors don't always produce such actions—a sizeable attitude-behavior gap often exists.

- Obesity is increasing around the world and poses a major threat to personal health.

- Many factors play a role in this obesity trend, including social factors, such as the fact that cars are more widely available so people do less walking, a growing tendency for family members to eat separately—and hence, all day—and growing acceptance of obesity as a "normal" state for many people.

- Effective procedures for halting or reversing weight gain exist and do work for people who follow them carefully.

- Stress is our response to events that disrupt, or threaten to disrupt, our physical or psychological functioning. Stress stems from many causes including major life events and the hassles of daily life.

- Many tactics for coping with stress exist, but one of the most important involves social support—the emotional support and friendship provided by others.

Think About It

Nearly everyone knows what behaviors promote good health. So why is there a sizeable gap between these health promoting attitudes and actual behavior? What can be done to help close this gap?

Social Psychology and the World of Work

In an important sense, work settings are social settings, ones in which people interact with each other for many hours each day, often for months, years, or even decades. Given this basic fact, it seems clear that the principles and findings of social psychology are directly relevant to work settings and virtually everything that goes on in them. In fact, social psychology has long been applied to understanding many aspects of human behavior in work settings. Much of this research has been carried out by **industrial-organizational psychologists**—psychologists who specialize in studying all forms of behavior and cognition in work settings (e.g., Aamodt, 2007). But social psychologists, too, have been actively involved in this work—increasingly so in recent years (Haslam, van Knippenberg, Platow, & Ellemers, 2003). To give you an overview of such work, we'll focus here on several topics that illustrate clearly how the findings and principles of social psychology can be applied to practical questions concerning our working lives. Consistent with this basic theme, we'll first examine the role of attitudes in work settings, focusing on job satisfaction—people's attitudes toward their jobs (e.g., Weiss, 2002). Next, we'll turn to prosocial behavior at work—the many ways in which employees help each other on the job, and the factors that encourage (or discourage) such actions (e.g., Organ, 1988). Finally, we'll return to the role of influence in work (and other) settings by examining the nature of leadership. Leaders are often defined as the people in a group who are most influential, and as social psychologists, we find that definition to be a useful one (e.g., Avolio, 2007; Yukl, 2006).

Work-Related Attitudes: The Nature and Effects of Job Satisfaction

industrial-organizational psychologists
Psychologists who specialize in studying all forms of behavior and cognition in work settings.

As noted in Chapter 5, we are rarely neutral to the social world. On the contrary, we hold strong attitudes about many aspects of it. Jobs are no exception to this rule. If asked, most people can readily report their attitudes toward their jobs and also toward the organizations that employ them. Attitudes concerning one's own job or work are generally referred to by the term **job satisfaction** (e.g., Wanous, Reichers, & Hudy, 1997), while attitudes toward one's company are known as organizational commitment (e.g., Brown, 1996; Keller, 1997). Because job satisfaction is linked more directly to basic research on attitudes in social psychology, we'll focus on this topic here.

Job Satisfaction: Its Causes

Despite the fact that many jobs are repetitive and boring in nature, surveys involving literally hundreds of thousands of employees conducted over the course of several decades point to a surprising finding: Most indicate that they are quite satisfied with their jobs. In part, this may reflect the operation of cognitive dissonance (see Chapter 5). Because most people know that they have to continue working and know that there is often considerable effort—and risk—involved in changing jobs, stating that they are not satisfied with their current jobs would tend to generate dissonance. To avoid or reduce such reactions, therefore, many people find it easier to report high levels of job satisfaction and may then actually come to accept their own ratings as a true reflection of their views.

While most people report being relatively satisfied with their jobs, they do vary in this respect, with some reporting high levels and others reporting lower levels of job satisfaction. What factors influence such attitudes? Research on this issue indicates that two major groups of factors are important: organizational factors related to a company's practices or the working conditions it provides, and personal factors related to the characteristics of individual employees.

The organizational factors that influence job satisfaction contain few surprises: People report higher satisfaction when they feel that the reward systems in their companies are fair (when raises, promotions, and other rewards are distributed fairly; see Chapter 11), when they like and respect their bosses and believe these people have their best interests at heart, when they can participate in the decisions that affect them, when the work they perform is interesting rather than boring and repetitious, and when they are neither overloaded, with too much to do in a given amount of time, or underloaded, with too little to do (e.g., Callan, 1993; Melamed et al., 1993; Miceli & Lane, 1991). Physical working conditions, too, play a role: When they are comfortable, employees report higher job satisfaction than when these are uncomfortable (e.g., too hot, too noisy [Baron, 1994]).

More surprising, perhaps, are findings concerning the factors that do not exert strong effects on job satisfaction. For instance, while you might guess that job satisfaction would be strongly linked to pay, this is not the case (e.g., Landy & Conte, 2004). In fact, findings on personal happiness (such happiness is related, in part, to satisfaction with one's job or work), indicates that earning a high salary is not closely related to happiness (e.g., Diener & Lucas, 1999). More important than actual pay, it appears, is the question of fairness. As long as people feel that their pay is fair (in line with what they feel they deserve), their job satisfaction tends to be high.

Turning to personal factors, both seniority and status play a role: The longer people have been in a given job and the higher their status, the greater their satisfaction (Zeitz, 1990). Similarly, the greater the extent to which jobs are closely matched to individuals' personal interests, the greater their satisfaction is (Fricko & Beehr, 1992). In addition, several personal traits are closely related to job satisfaction. For instance, type A people tend to be more satisfied than type B people, despite their greater overall irritability (see Chapter 10). Perhaps this is so because jobs allow people to stay busy, and type A people, of course, like to be busy all the time! (See Figure 12.17 on page 444 for a summary of all these factors.)

On the other hand, another finding from research on job satisfaction may greatly surprise you—although, in fact, it is related to research on the evolutionary perspective in social psychology. Some studies (ones that are far from conclusive and still somewhat controversial) seem to suggest that genetic factors could play a role in job satisfaction. In other words, some people seem to have an inherited tendency to be either satisfied or dissatis-

job satisfaction
Attitudes individuals hold concerning their jobs.

Figure 12.17
Causes of Job
Satisfaction: A Summary
As shown here, job satisfaction is influenced by a number of organizational and personal factors. While some findings suggest genetic factors may play some role in influencing job satisfaction, the evidence pointing to this conclusion is far from conclusive.

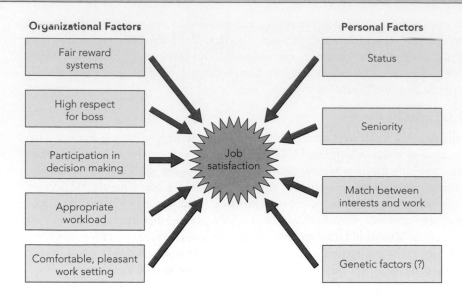

fied with their jobs. Needless to say, such effects are small, and situational factors relating to actual working conditions can certainly overwhelm general tendencies to be satisfied or dissatisfied with almost any job. But it does appear that overall some people seem to be reasonably happy with their jobs no matter what they are like, while others are unhappy even under favorable working conditions.

The first research pointing to such conclusions was conducted by Arvey, Bouchard, Segal, and Abraham (1989). These researchers measured current job satisfaction in thirty-four pairs of identical (monozygotic) twins who had been separated at an early age and then raised apart. Because such twins have identical genetic inheritance but have had different life experiences (being raised in different homes) the extent to which they report similar levels of job satisfaction provides information on the potential role of genetic factors in such attitudes. Results indicated that the level of job satisfaction reported by these pairs of twins correlated significantly and that these correlations were higher than was true for unrelated people who, of course, do not share the same genes. Additional findings indicated that as much as 30 percent of the variation in job satisfaction may stem from genetic factors. While these findings remain somewhat controversial (e.g., Cropanzano & James, 1990), they have been replicated in other studies (e.g., Arvey et al., 1989; Judge, 1992; Keller, Bouchard, Arvery, et al., 1992), so it does seem possible (although far from proven) that genetic factors play some role (almost certainly a small one) in job satisfaction. How, you are probably wondering, can this be so? How can genetic factors influence attitudes toward one's job? The answer involves the fact that genetic factors influence certain aspects of personality. Research findings (e.g., Judge et al., 2002) indicate that basic aspects of personality—ones that are known to be influenced by genetic factors (for instance, a general tendency to experience positive or negative moods [e.g., Watson & Clark, 1994]) are also significantly related to job satisfaction. Together, these findings suggest that genetic factors influence job satisfaction through their impact on these basic aspects of personality. In other words, genetic factors predispose specific people to experience positive moods or feelings, to be high in agreeableness (the tendency to trust others and cooperate with them), and other factors. These characteristics then lead them to experience—and express—high job satisfaction. Overall, genetic factors don't influence job satisfaction directly, rather, they exert their effects indirectly, by influencing key aspects of personality.

Evidence for this reasoning has recently been reported by Ilies and Judge (2003).

These researchers found that both the "big five" dimensions of personality and positive affectivity–negative affectivity (the tendency to experience positive or negative affect) did indeed help explain the effects of genetic factors on job satisfaction. While both factors were found to play a role, the effects of positive affectivity–negative affectivity were stronger. In a practical sense, these findings mean that genetic factors influence the tendency to experience positive feelings, such as enthusiasm, confidence, and cheerfulness (Watson, Wiese, Vaidya, & Tellgen, 1999) versus negative feelings, such as fear, hostility, and anger, and these tendencies, in turn, influenced job satisfaction. If you've ever known someone who seemed happy and cheerful in every situation or someone who was just the opposite, you get the picture. Yes, people are satisfied or dissatisfied with their jobs for lots of reasons. But in addition, it appears that some people—because of personality traits that are in part inherited—are more likely to express high satisfaction than others in almost any context.

In short, while working conditions, the nature of the jobs people perform, and many organizational factors combine to determine job satisfaction, these work-related attitudes are also strongly affected by personal traits or characteristics—ones people take with them from job to job and situation to situation. As a result, some people express a high level of satisfaction no matter where they work, while others express a low level no matter where they work. Which ones would you most like to have as coworkers? The answer seems clear! (Now that we've discussed the factors that influence job satisfaction—attitudes toward one's job—we'll turn to an important question: What are the effects of job satisfaction on performance and other aspects of employees' behavior? For a discussion of this question, read *Making Sense of Common Sense: A Social Psychological Perspective* below.)

MAKING SENSE OF COMMON SENSE
A SOCIAL PSYCHOLOGICAL PERSPECTIVE
Are Happy Workers Productive Workers? The Attitude-Behavior Link Revisited

Are happy workers—ones who like their jobs—productive workers? While common sense seems to suggest that they are, it's important to remember that job satisfaction is a special kind of attitude, and that although attitudes are often reflected in overt behavior, this is not always so (Greenberg & Baron, 2008). For instance, consider a subordinate who truly dislikes her boss: Will she express this attitude openly to the supervisor? Probably not because the costs are simply too high. In this and many other situations, attitudes exist but can't readily be expressed in overt behavior. This appears to be true for job satisfaction; it does indeed influence work performance but not to the same degree in every situation. Thus overall—across many different jobs and organizations—the relationship between job satisfaction and work performance is relatively weak—correlations in the range of 0.15 to 0.20 (Judge, et al., 2002). The strength of this relationship varies across different occupations—for instance it is stronger for scientists and engineers than for nurses—but

it is not strong for any occupation studied (Judge, Thoresen, Bono, & Patton, 2001).

Why isn't this relationship stronger? Because several factors tend to weaken or moderate the impact of job satisfaction on performance. One involves the fact that many jobs leave little room for variations in performance. If employees don't perform at some minimal level, they will lose their jobs. But if they perform much better than expected, they may find themselves waiting around for input from other people—input they need to do their own jobs. In short, limits in the range of possible performance tend to weaken the relationship between job satisfaction and job performance.

Still another possibility is that in some cases, job satisfaction results from good performance rather than vice versa. This possibility is easier to understand with respect to the performance of an entire organization rather than the performance of individuals. Imagine that because it adopts policies that have been found to enhance employees' per-

Continued on page 446

formance (e.g., involving them in important decisions, rewarding them for new accomplishments), employees do show good performance. This good performance, in turn, enhances the financial success of the company. Because it is successful, it can offer good benefits and increased pay and enjoy a good reputation. The result? Employees feel well treated and are proud to work for this company, and this leads them to experience—and report—high levels of job satisfaction. In fact, findings reported by Schneider, Hanges, Smith, and Salvaggio, (2004) provide support for this reasoning, so it seems to be accurate and helps explain why the link between job satisfaction and individual performance is weaker than might be expected (see Figure 12.18).

One more factor that affects the link between job satisfaction and performance is also worth mentioning. In Chapter 5, we noted that attitudes have three basic components—affective, cognitive, and behavioral. Interestingly, these three components are not always in complete alignment. For instance, it is possible to like someone but believe that they have a few negative characteristics. Similarly, it is possible to really like a job but to believe that it is not especially helpful to one's future career. What happens when the affective and cognitive components of an attitude are somewhat inconsistent? One outcome is that the attitudes in question are less predictive of overt behavior. Applying this to job satisfaction Schleicher, Watt, and Greguras (2004) suggested that the greater the affective-cognitive consistency (ACC) of job attitudes, the stronger is the link between these attitudes and on-the-job performance. To test this hypothesis, they measured both the affective and cognitive components of job satisfaction for a group of employed people working in a wide variety of industries. From this information, they calculated an index of ACC for each person. Ratings of the participants' actual job performance were obtained from their supervisors. Results were clear: For people whose ACC was high, job satisfaction was positively related to actual job performance. For persons whose ACC was low, in contrast, job satisfaction was not significantly related to job performance.

In sum, while job satisfaction is modestly related to individual performance—happy workers do perform slightly better, overall, than unhappy ones—this relationship is complex, and overall results are consistent with the findings of basic research in social psychology on attitudes and their effects on overt behavior.

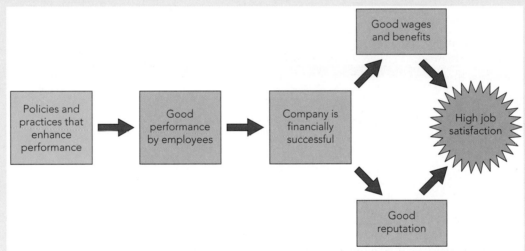

Figure 12.18
Why Good Performance May Lead to High Job Satisfaction Rather than Vice Versa
Enlightened policies on the part of a company (e.g., giving employees a voice in key decisions) may enhance employees' performance. This, in turn, contributes to the company's financial success and to its ability to offer good pay and benefits, as well as to its reputation. As a result, employees experience high job satisfaction. So in such cases, it is good performance that produces high job satisfaction rather than the other way round.

(*Source:* Based on findings reported by Schneider, Hanges, Smith, & Salvaggio, 2004.)

Organizational Citizenship Behavior: Prosocial Behavior at Work

In Chapter 9, we examined many aspects of prosocial behavior—helpful actions that benefit others but have no obvious benefits for the people who perform them. As we saw in that chapter, prosocial behavior stems from many different factors and can yield a wide range of effects. That such behavior often occurs in work settings, too, is obvious. If you have ever helped a coworker with their job, filled in for someone when they had to be absent, or switched vacation dates with another person to help them out, you already know that helping is quite common at work (see Figure 12.19). Let's take a brief look at what research on prosocial behavior in work settings has found with respect to its forms and the factors that affect whether, and how often, it occurs.

The Nature of Prosocial Behavior at Work: Some Basic Forms

While a number of different terms have been used to describe prosocial behavior in work settings (e.g., Van Dyne & LePine, 1998), most researchers refer to such behavior as **organizational citizenship behavior (OCB)**—prosocial

Figure 12.19
Prosocial Behavior at Work: Far from Rare
Employees who work together often help one another. Such prosocial behavior (known as organizational citizenship behavior) is not required by their jobs and is often not formally rewarded by the group or organization, but it is still quite common.

behavior occurring within an organization that may or may not be rewarded by that organization (e.g., Organ, 1997; Podsakoff, MacKenzie, et al., 2000). In general, such behaviors are ones that are not required by the helper's job and are not recognized by the formal reward systems (e.g., through a bonus or a raise in pay). As we'll note, though, helping others is often recognized by organizations and can result in important rewards to the people who engage in it (Allen, 2006). While individuals can help others at work in many different ways, research findings indicate that most of these actions fall under of the following five categories:

- Altruism: Helping others to perform their jobs (note that social psychologists do not use the term *altruism* in this way).

- Conscientiousness: Going beyond the minimum requirements of a job or doing more than is required. For instance, an employee who prides themself on never missing a day of work or on taking short breaks is showing conscientiousness.

- Civic virtue: Participating in and showing concern for the "life" of the organization. Two examples: attending voluntary meetings or social occasions and reading memos rather than throwing them in the trash.

- Sportsmanship: Showing willingness to tolerate unfavorable conditions without complaining. If an employee decides to "grin and bear it" rather than complain, she or he is showing this type of OCB.

- Courtesy: Making efforts to prevent interpersonal problems with others. For instance, "turning the other cheek" when annoyed by another person at work or behaving courteously toward them even when they are rude.

Helping Others at Work as a Social Dilemma

As we noted in Chapter 9, there are many different motives for helping others, ranging from empathy and pleasure at making someone feel good to boosting our own status (Hardy & Van Vugt, 2006). An additional way of looking at OCB is to view it as a social dilemma—a situation in which short-term personal interests are at odds with long-term collective interests. When people offer help to fellow employees—especially when this is voluntary and not an official part of their jobs—their actions reflect one kind of social dilemma known as a social fence; there is a trade-off between short-term individual costs (the effort involved in helping the other person) and the long-term collective benefits—positive outcomes for the work group or entire organization. In contrast, the decision to engage in noncomplaince behaviors (NCBs; e.g., the decision not to help the other person or to do something that is contrary to the group or organization's values, such as neglecting one's job or showing substandard performance) represents another kind of social dilemma—one known a social delayed trap; here, there are short-term individual benefits but long-term collective costs.

organizational citizenship behavior (OCB)
Help people give each other at work that is not a required part of their jobs.

Are OCBs viewed as a social dilemma? Evidence reported by Joireman, Kadmar, Daniels, and Duell (2006) indicates that they are: Most people do in fact view helping others as actions involving short-term costs but long-term potential benefits for the work group or organization, but they view NCBs as showing exactly the opposite pattern. So, the decision to engage in OCB is, in part, one of balancing personal interests and those of the group.

Helping at Work: Other Factors that Influence Its Occurrence

Other factors, too, have been found to influence prosocial behavior at work. One of these involves social identity—a concept we discussed in Chapter 4. This refers to the extent to which employees identify with the companies for which they work—the extent to which they feel that their company is a group to which they belong. The stronger such social identity, the more likely employees are to engage in various forms of citizenship behavior (Haslam, Branscombe, & Bachmann, 2003). Another important factor in helping at work—perhaps by far the most important one—is the belief, among employees, that they are being treated fairly. This can involve fairness outcomes received (distributive justice— do people get rewards that reflect the size of their contributions?), the procedures used to determine these outcomes (procedural justice—are the procedures used to determine who gets what fair?), and the style or manner in which outcomes are delivered (interactional justice—do the people who distribute rewards treat the recipients openly and with courtesy? [e.g., Greenberg & Lind, 2000]). All three forms are important, and all play a role in willingness to help others by going "beyond the call of duty." In other words, the greater the extent to which employees feel that they are being treated in these ways, the greater the tendency to help others in many ways.

One additional factor that influences OCB is employees' perceptions of the breadth of their jobs—what behaviors are required and which are voluntary. The more broadly employees define their jobs, the more likely they are to engage in instances of OCB (Morrison, 1994; Van Dyne & LePine, 1998). For instance, if a professor believes that helping other professors by taking over their classes when they are out of town is part of her job—this is simply the "right thing to do"—she may be much more willing to engage in such behavior than if she believes that this is definitely not part of her job and not her responsibility.

Finally, the frequency of OCB seems to be influenced by attitudes held by employees about their organizations—attitudes generally known as organizational commitment. The more favorable these are, the higher the frequency of OCB.

In sum, many factors seem to influence the occurrence of OCB at work, just as many factors influence such behavior in other settings. Whatever the specific causes, it is clear that a high incidence of helpful, considerate behavior can not only make work settings more pleasant; they can also enhance performance and behaviors that help the organization prosper, too (e.g., Simons & Roberson, 2003).

The Effects of Helping at Work: Beneficial for Both Organizations and Individuals

Have you ever heard the old saying "What goes around comes around?" It suggests that reciprocity is a key principle of life: What we do for others is often what we get back. If that's true, then it is reasonable to predict that the more we help others at work—the more OCBs we perform—the more likely we are to be helped in return. Not surprisingly, research findings tend to confirm this pattern. Moreover, OCB seems to be somewhat "contagious." The greater the extent to which it occurs in an organization, the more it becomes part of the accepted norms or culture, and this encourages its occurrence in a positive upward spiral.

Perhaps even more important, the incidence of OCB in an organization does seem to have important effects on the performance of groups or even entire organizations. Many studies indicate that the higher the frequency of OCB in an organization, the better its performance, both in terms of quality and quantity, the higher its operating efficiency, and even the greater its sales are (e.g., Podsakoff et al., 2000).

In addition, a high level of OCB tends to make an organization a more attractive place in which to work. This makes it easier to hire excellent employees and that, of course, is a key ingredient in an organization's success (e.g., Podsakoff & MacKenzie, 1997). OCB can also have a positive impact on the satisfaction and organizational commitment of employees, and that, too, can contribute to improved performance.

But helping others doesn't only assist these people and the organization. Research findings indicate that it may also produce positive outcomes for the people who help. Specifically, employees who often help others at work soon acquire the reputation of being a "team player" and a "good citizen," and as a result, they are often recommended for raises and promotions by their supervisors more often than other employees (e.g., Allen, 2006). Such benefits seem to be greater for men than women—perhaps because women are *expected* to be more helpful—but they do occur for both genders. So, reciprocity does seem to operate at the group or organizational level as well as between individuals, and people who are helpful to others are often rewarded, one way or another, for their prosocial, helpful actions.

Leadership: Influence in Group Settings

Leadership; the word itself conjures up images of heroic figures leading their followers toward something better—victory, prosperity, happiness, social justice—choose the label you prefer. But what, precisely, is **leadership**? Researchers in several different fields, including social psychology, have considered this question for decades, and the result is that at present, there is general agreement that leadership involves influence—influencing others in a group (or organization) by establishing a direction for collective effort and then encouraging the activities needed to move in that direction (Yukl, 2006; Zaccaro, 2007). Consistent with that definition, being a leader involves exerting influence—changing the behavior and thoughts of other members of the group so that they work together to attain the group's common goals.

Research on leadership has been part of social psychology and related fields for many years (e.g., Avolio, 2007; Sternberg, 2007). Here, we'll consider key aspects of the findings of research on this topic in terms of (1) Why do some individuals, but not others, become leaders? (2) What leaders actually do—how do they fill this role in their groups? And (3) what is the difference between two important forms of leadership—transactional and transformational leadership?

Why Do Some Persons but Not Others Become Leaders?

Are some people born to lead? Common sense suggests that this is so. Famous leaders, such as Alexander the Great, Queen Elizabeth I, and Abraham Lincoln seem to differ from ordinary people in several respects. Such observations led early researchers to formulate the **great person theory of leadership**—the view that great leaders possess certain traits that set them apart from most human beings, traits that are possessed by all such leaders, no matter when or where they lived.

These are intriguing ideas, but early research designed to test them was not encouraging. Try as they might, researchers could not come up with a short list of key traits shared by all great leaders (Yukl, 1998). In recent years, however, this situation has changed greatly. More sophisticated research methods coupled with a better understanding of the basic dimensions of human personality have led many researchers to conclude that leaders do indeed differ from other persons in several important ways (Kirkpatrick & Locke, 1991). Specifically, modern theories of leadership suggest that leader characteristics—their cognitive abilities, aspects of their personality, their motives, values, social skills, expertise, and problem-solving skills—all play a role in leadership. However these characteristics don't operate in isolation from situations, rather they interact with situational factors so that some characteristics (motives, skills, and personality traits) are beneficial under some circumstances but are not helpful under others. For example, an individual who is good at solving everyday practical problems and is highly organized (high in conscientiousness—one of the big five dimensions of personality) might be successful as a leader under conditions where a dramatic hero or heroine is not needed—for instance, in dealing with routine problems and running a stable group or organization. In contrast, a leader who is

leadership
Influencing others in a group (or organization) by establishing a direction for collective effort and then managing the collective activities needed to move in that direction.

great person theory of leadership
The view that leaders possess certain traits that set them apart from other people and that are possessed by all leaders no matter where or when they live.

Figure 12.20
Modern Theories of
Leadership
*Modern views of leadership
recognize that it involves
exerting influence on others,
and that this, in turn, depends
on both personal characteristics
of leaders and situational
factors. Leadership, in other
words, is a very complex process
that involves many aspects of
social behavior and social
thought.*

(*Source:* Based on suggestions by
Zaccaro, 2007.)

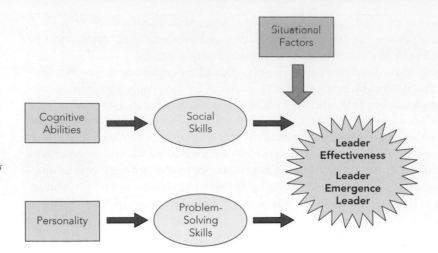

charismatic, has tremendous ambition, and is outstanding at communicating with others—and so inspiring them—might be more successful in situations that require these characteristics—for instance, a military campaign or as a highly competitive sport. One recent theory of leadership that clearly illustrates this approach suggests that some characteristics possessed by individual leaders (e.g., their motives, cognitive abilities, and personality) influence other attributes (problem-solving skills, expertise, and social skills) and that these, in turn, then influence important outcomes, such as who becomes a leader, how successful they are in this role, and how far they advance in their careers (Zaccaro, 2007). The theory also notes, however, that such effects emerge only through complex interactions between these characteristics and situational factors (see Figure 12.20).

While many different characteristics and traits play a role in leader's effectiveness, we should note that one stands out as perhaps the most important: the ability to respond appropriately to changing conditions and shifting requirements. In other words, the most successful leaders are often those who are most flexible and adaptable; they can meet each new challenge and so lead their groups to the goals they desire (Zaccaro, 2007).

So, are some people more suited for leadership than others? The answer appears to be yes, at least to some extent. People who possess certain traits are more likely to become leaders and to succeed in this role than people who do not possess these traits or possess them to a lesser degree. It is also clear, however, that leaders do not operate in a social vacuum. On the contrary, different groups, facing different tasks and problems, seem to require different types of leaders—or at least leaders who demonstrate contrasting styles (Avolio, 2007; House & Podsakoff, 1994; Locke, 1991). In sum, leader traits—or leader attributes as they are now generally termed—do indeed matter but are only part of the total picture. What else is important? We have already mentioned situational factors—the kind of situations leaders face. For instance, research findings indicate that organizations facing difficult conditions (companies in crisis) are more likely to choose women to be their leaders than companies that face more ordinary conditions (Ryan & Haslam, 2007). Why? Apparently, partly, because they are assumed to possess traits that will help them deal with crisis (e.g., being understanding, intuitive, and cheerful) and those characteristics—although usually not seen as contributing to excellent leadership—may be viewed in this manner in crisis situations. Whatever the precise reasons, these findings indicate that situational factors play an important role in leadership, strongly influencing who becomes a leader and leaders' success in this role. In addition, two other factors have been found to be important: leader's behavior and their relations with followers.

What Do Leaders Do? Basic Dimensions of Leader Behavior

All leaders are definitely not alike. They may share certain traits to a degree, but they differ greatly in terms of their approach to leadership and the behaviors they show in this role (e.g., George, 1995; Peterson, 1997; Sternberg, 2007). While there are probably as

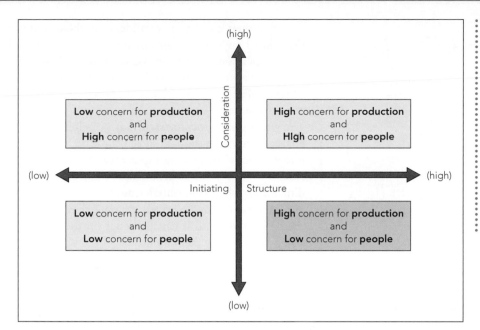

Figure 12.21
Leader Behavior: Two Basic Dimensions
Leaders' behavior has been found to vary along the two dimensions shown here: consideration, which involves concern for people and good relations with them, and initiating structure, which involves concern for production and task completion. These dimensions are largely independent, so any leader can be high or low on each.

many different styles of leadership as there are leaders, research on leader behavior suggests that in fact, most leaders can be placed along a small number of dimensions relating to their overall approach to leadership. Two such dimensions emerged in early research on leadership (e.g., Weissenberg & Kavanagh, 1972) and have been confirmed over and over again. The first is known as **initiating structure (production orientation).** Leaders high on this dimension are primarily concerned with getting the job done. They engage in actions such as organizing work, urging subordinates to follow the rules, setting goals, and making leader and subordinate roles explicit. In contrast, leaders low on this dimension engage in such actions to a lesser degree.

The second dimension is known as **consideration (person orientation).** Leaders high on this dimension focus on establishing good relations with their subordinates and on being liked by them. They engage in such actions as doing favors for subordinates, explaining things to them, and watching out for their welfare. Leaders low on this dimension, in contrast, do not really care how well they get along with their subordinates (see Figure 12.21 for an overview of these two basic dimensions of leader behavior).

Is either of these two styles superior? Not really. Both offer a mixed pattern of advantages and disadvantages. High consideration (high concern with people) can lead to improved group morale, but because such leaders do not like to tell subordinates what to do or give them negative feedback, efficiency sometimes suffers. In contrast, when leaders are high on initiating structure, efficiency may be high but subordinates may conclude that the leader does not really care about them, and their commitment to the organization may suffer. Overall, though, it appears that leaders who are high on both dimensions may have an edge in many situations. In other words, leaders who are concerned with establishing good relations with their subordinates and, at the same time, with maintaining productivity may often prove superior to leaders showing other patterns of behavior.

Two other important aspects of leader behavior that have been uncovered by careful research involve the extent to which leaders make all the decisions themselves or allow participation by group members (an autocratic-participative dimension) and the extent to which leaders try to "run the show" by closely directing the activities of all group members—a directive-permissive dimension (Muczyk & Reimann, 1987; Peterson, 1997). If you think back over your own experiences, you can probably recall leaders who were high or low on both of these dimensions. For instance, in a summer job I once held, the manager of the department was definitely on the directive end of the directive-permissive dimension: He was constantly looking over our shoulders and telling us how to do virtually everything. Many employees dislike this kind of micromanagement because it sug-

initiating structure (production orientation)
A key dimension of leader behavior; leaders high on this dimension are primarily concerned with getting the job done (i.e., with production).

consideration (person orientation)
A key dimension of leader behavior; leaders high on this dimension focus on establishing good relations with their subordinates and on being liked by them.

"We may need a clearer message."

Figure 12.22
There Are No Leaders without Followers!
The "leader" in this cartoon is seeking to exert influence, but as you can see from the signs carried by the people in the audience, they are not following his suggestions. In fact, they don't even seem to know what these are! So, he is really not a leader.

(*Source:* The *New Yorker*, March 19, 2007.)

gests that their boss has no confidence in them; and in fact, that's just how I felt. Again, being high or low in each of these dimensions is not necessarily good or bad from the point of view of leader effectiveness—this depends on the situation. For instance, under emergency conditions, when decisions have to be taken quickly, as in a hospital emergency room, an autocratic style may be helpful; under more relaxed conditions, though, most people prefer participative leaders who let them have input into the decision-making situation. The same is true for the directive–permissive dimension; when subordinates are new at their jobs, they need direction from the leader, but once they have mastered their jobs, though, it is usually better for the leader to take a step back and let them alone.

Leaders and Followers: Two Sides of the Same Coin

In a sense, there is no influence without two parties: the one who does the influencing and the one who is influenced. Further, influence is rarely one-way: Usually, even the individuals who exert influence are affected in some way by those whose behavior or attitudes they seek to change; that is a well-established principle of social psychology (e.g., Cialdini, 2006). Yet, so far, we have focused entirely on leaders, while ignoring followers and their important role. In a crucial sense, of course, followers are the core of leadership. Without them, there really is no such thing as leadership. So, is the leader shown in Figure 12.22 really a leader? Because the people in the audience are not really listening to his message (whatever that is), probably not.

The importance of followers is given full consideration in modern theories of leadership. For instance, two experts on leadership (Hackman & Wageman, 2007) suggest that leaders and followers are both essential parts of the leadership relationship, and that all theories of leadership should note that both play a crucial role and that both (followers and leaders) exert influence and receive it. Further, leaders don't have the same kind of relations with all of their followers and often differentiate between those with whom they have close and cordial relations and other followers with whom they have more distant relations (e.g., Graen and Uhl-Bien, 1995). In sum, the crucial role of followers is now widely recognized. In fact, no one is actually a leader unless they have people willing to accept influence from them—or, as Andre Maurois put it: "The most important quality in a leader is that of being acknowledged as such."

Transactional and Transformational Leaders: Different Approaches, Different Effects

Have you ever seen films of Margaret Thatcher? Nelson Mandela? Gandhi? (See Figure 12.23.) If so, you may have noticed that there seemed to be something special about these leaders. As you listened to their speeches, you may have found yourself being moved by their words and stirred by the vision of the future they presented. If so, you are not alone: These leaders exerted powerful effects on many millions of people and by doing so, changed their societies. Leaders who accomplish such feats are termed **transformational leaders** (House & Howell, 1992; Kohl, Steers, & Terborg, 1995). Such leaders are often viewed as being charismatic—they exert such profound effects on their followers that it almost seems as though they wield some kind of magic power. In fact, though, careful research by social psychologists suggests that there is nothing mystical about their impact. Rather, it stems from four characteristics that they demonstrate to a high degree: idealized influence—they are admired and trusted by their followers; inspirational motivation—they know how to inspire people by offering them meaning and challenge in their work, often through the presentation of stirring visions of a glorious future; intellectual stimulation—they stimulate their followers to be innovative and creative by questioning existing assumptions and reframing problems in new ways; and individualized consideration—they pay attention to their followers' needs for achievement and growth by acting as a mentor (e.g., Antonakis, 2001; Avo-

transformational leaders
Leaders who, because of several characteristics, exert profound effects on their followers.

lio, Bass, & Jung, 1999). Together, these four components provide transformational leaders with tremendous influence over their followers. They can boost followers' motivation and performance to high levels, command great allegiance and respect, and induce followers to undertake difficult or even dangerous tasks (Avolio & Bass, 2002; Bass, Avolio, Jung, & Berson, 2003; DeGroot, Kiker, & Cross, 2000).

In addition, other findings suggest that transformational leaders also demonstrate high levels of self-confidence, excellent communication skills, and an exciting personal style (House, Spangler, & Woycke, 1991). And leaders are more likely to be seen as charismatic when they behave in a way that affirms their membership in the group (e.g., Haslam et al., 2001). In other words, leaders are seen as being charismatic to the extent that they are perceived by their followers as "doing it for us"—behaving in ways that promote the welfare of the group (e.g., Haslam & Reicher, 2006). Finally, transformational leaders are often masters of impression management, a process we described in Chapter 3. When this skill is added to the traits and behaviors previously mentioned and combined with transformational leaders' use of vision and reframing of problems, the ability of such leaders to influence large numbers of followers (for good or ill) loses its mystery. One more point: Findings suggest that in fact, transformational leaders produce two seemingly contradictory effects on followers. On the one hand they make them dependent on them, and on the other, they empower them, increasing their followers' feelings of self-efficacy and self-esteem (Kark, Shamir, & Chen, 2003). How can both of these effects occur? Because, apparently, transformational (charismatic) leaders induce high levels of identification with themselves personally and high levels of identification with the group they lead. As a result, when followers do what transformational leaders want them to do, they feel closer to this person and simultaneously feel closer to or more identified with their group, which, in turn, boosts their self-esteem. This is why the followers of transformational leaders, whether they are great political leaders or the leaders of cults, feel powerful allegiance to the leader yet at the same time also believe that the leader has somehow increased their personal freedom and self-esteem.

In contrast to transformational leaders, **transactional leaders** are the kind we are more likely to meet in our everyday lives. They, too, exert strong influence over their followers, but they do it in a different way. Such leaders work largely within the system by offering praise, rewards, and resources for good performance but negative outcomes (e.g., disciplinary actions) for poor performance. They build motivation among followers by clarifying key goals and providing recognition for achieving them rather than through inspirational appeals or stirring visions. Yet transactional leaders can be highly effective; they can boost the motivation, morale, and productivity of their followers and keep things "humming along" in situations where neither the work being performed nor the goals being sought are highly inspiring—in others words, in most ordinary work settings (e.g., Goodwin, Wofford, & Whittington, 2001).

Clearly, transactional and transformational leaders differ sharply in style; and this, in turn, leads to an intriguing question: Is either type better from the point of view of maximizing a group's performance? To find out, Waldman and his colleagues (Waldman et al., 2001) asked several hundred high-level executives in more than one hundred different companies to rate the CEO (leader) of their company in terms of both styles of leadership. These ratings were then related to the companies' financial performance (how successful they were financially). An additional aspect of the study involved the extent to which the companies faced an uncertain and unpredictable environment. Waldman et al. (2001) reasoned that charismatic (transformational) leaders would do better in uncertain and rapidly changing environments because such leaders would be more effective than transactional leaders in

Margaret Thatcher

Nelson Mandela

Gandhi

Franklin D. Roosevelt

Figure 12.23
Transformational Leaders: Leaders Who Truly Changed the World—or at Least, Their Societies
Transformational leaders are leaders who because of certain characteristics are able to exert powerful effects on their followers and often, on their societies or the entire world.

transactional leaders
Leaders who direct their groups by rewarding them for desired behavior, by taking action to correct mistakes or departures from existing rules. Such leaders generally strengthen existing structures and strategies within an organization.

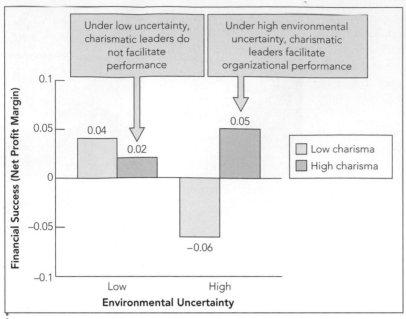

Figure 12.24

Charismatic Leaders: When Do They Facilitate Organizational Performance?

When organizations faced rapidly changing and unpredictable environments, they performed significantly better when their leaders were high in charisma than low in charisma. When organizations faced stable, predictable environments, in contrast, leaders' charisma did not strongly affect organizational performance.

(*Source:* Based on data from Waldman, Ramiriz, House, & Puranam, 2001.)

> ✑ **Principles to Remember**
>
> Work settings are truly social settings—ones in which the principles and findings of social psychology are directly applicable.

gaining high commitment and effort from employees. But this advantage would disappear in more stable environment.

As you can see from Figure 12.24, results confirmed this prediction. Whether leaders were low or high in charisma did not matter much in stable, unchanging environments. But in rapidly changing and chaotic environments, companies whose leaders were high in charisma outperformed those whose leaders were low in charisma. Interestingly, the extent to which leaders were low or high in transactional leadership style did not influence the companies' financial performance.

In sum, several decades of research employing a wide range of participants and many different measures of group performance indicate that leaders, and their specific style of performing this role, do indeed matter. While there does not appear to be one single style of leadership that is always best, it is clear that some styles are preferred by most group members and that depending on the circumstances faced by a group, some leaders are more likely than others to facilitate performance. So what's the final message in this research? That choosing the right leader is a crucial task for all groups because it can strongly shape the group's morale, motivation, and performance.

Throughout this chapter, we have emphasized the relevance of social psychology—its principles and findings—to the world of work. To emphasize that theme once again, we describe one more such link in *Social Psychology: What It Tells Us About . . .* below.

SOCIALPSYCHOLOGY

WHAT IT TELLS US ABOUT . . .

How to Make a Good First Impression in Job interviews

Everyone wants to make a good first impression, so we try to do our best in this respect when we meet other people for the first time. As we saw in Chapter 3, social psychologists have identified a number of factors that are highly effective in making favorable first impressions on others. Good first impressions are useful in many contexts but are especially important in job interviews; each applicant often gets only a few minutes to convince the interviewer she or he is the right person for the job. What can you do to "shine" in this important context? Here is what the results of careful research on impression management suggests:

- Flattery will (often) get you everywhere: As we saw in our discussion of ingratiation, flattering others—making statements that praise them, their company, or their accomplishments—can be useful, as long as you don't overdo it (Kilduff & Day, 1994). If your praise is too excessive, the interviewer won't buy it, and it may backfire.

- Be prepared: Learn about the company for which you are interviewing and the nature of the job for which you are applying. Then let the interviewer know that you have, in fact, done your homework. Nothing creates a negative impression faster than being completely clueless about a company or a specific job.

- Look your best: Mae West, a Hollywood star of the 1930s, once remarked: "Look your best; who said love is blind?" As we have seen, personal appearance does matter, so do everything you can enhance your appearance when you come for an interview. Again, don't overdo it; for instance, don't apply a "killer" dose of perfume, don't wear too much make-up, and don't overdress. But being neat and well groomed will indicate to the interviewer that you take the interview seriously, and this will usually count in your favor.

- Emphasize your strengths: No one is good at everything, so if you claim to be perfect or nearly perfect in everything, the interviewer will not be impressed. But if you emphasize the things you do best, your experience, and provide specific examples of how you used these skills and talents, you will be on the way to generating a positive first impression.

- Agree with the interviewer as much as possible: No one likes to be contradicted, and as we noted previously, similarity is a major cause of liking between people. So, if you disagree with the interviewer, bite your tongue and do not call attention to this fact. Focus, instead, on agreeing with this person as much as possible. This, too, will help to boost the first impression you make.

- Be realistic: If you get to the point of discussing salary and other benefits with the interviewer, be sure to be realistic. While it is good to be confident and to expect all that you deserve, asking for more than the "going rate" can be a big mistake. It may suggest to the interviewer that you have an overinflated view of yourself or will be demanding once hired. But if, instead, your requests are reasonable ones, the interviewer will perceive you as someone who is in touch with reality, and this, too, will boost her or his first impression of you.

If you keep these points in mind, you will start off on the right foot in many job interviews, and that is usually an important first step toward getting the job you want.

KeyPoints

- Work settings are social settings, so many findings and principles of social psychology are directly relevant to them.

- Job satisfaction refers to individuals' attitudes toward their jobs. Job satisfaction is influenced by organizational factors, such as working conditions and the fairness of reward systems, and personal factors, such as seniority, status, and specific personality traits. Recent findings suggest that job satisfaction is often highly stable over time for many people and that it may be influenced by genetic factors.

- The relationship between job satisfaction and task performance is relatively weak, partly because many factors other than these work-related attitudes influence performance.

- Recent findings indicate that good performance may contribute to job satisfaction rather than vice versa.

- Individuals often engage in prosocial behavior at work. This is known as OCB and can take many different forms.

- OCB is influenced by several factors, but among these, perceived fairness in the group or organization may be the most important.

- Individuals who engage in prosocial behavior are not formally rewarded by their organizations for such actions but may ultimately receive major rewards for doing so (raises or promotions).

- Leadership refers to the process through which one member of a group (its leader) influences other group members toward the attainment of shared group goals.

- While the great person theory of leadership has been shown to be false, recent findings suggest that leaders do indeed differ from other people with respect to several traits. Among these, the most important may be flexibility or adaptability.

- In addition, leaders vary with respect to their behavior or style. Classic research in social psychology suggested that leaders vary in terms of two basic dimensions: consideration and initiating structure. In addition, leaders vary along two other key dimensions: autocratic-participative and directive-permissive.

- Transformational (charismatic) leaders exert profound effects on their followers and often change their societies. Research on the nature of such leadership suggests that it stems from certain behaviors by leaders, such as stating a clear vision, framing the group's goals in ways that magnify their importance, and possession of a stirring personal style.

- In contrast, transactional leaders exert influence through such steps as clarifying goals and rewarding good performance. They operate within the system rather than by changing it.

- Recent research suggests that transformational leaders may produce better group performance in environments that are changing rapidly, but they are not superior to transactional leaders in more stable environments.

Think About It

The belief that leaders are of crucial importance is popular. But do leaders really matter so much? What do you think? Are there times or conditions in which their role is only a minor one? Why would this be so?

SUMMARY AND REVIEW

- Social influence plays an important role in many aspects of the legal system and can be observed with respect to police interrogations, lineups, and media coverage of crimes and trials. Research findings indicate that videotaping police interrogations reduces the use of abusive tactics by police, but they do not prevent jurors from viewing false confessions, obtained under pressure, as valid. Lineups can be helpful in identifying criminals, but they are susceptible to several forms of bias. Publicity in the media before a trial can have strong effects on public opinion about the guilt or innocence of the defendant and can even affect jurors' decisions. Eyewitnesses are not as accurate as is commonly believed. Several factors (e.g., intense emotion, the passage of time since the observed events, and errors in memory) contribute to this fact. Individuals often construct false memories—memories for events that never happened. These memories sometimes arise because we focus on the general idea or gist of information stored in memory and not on the information itself. As a result, we remember information consistent with the gist of our real memories even though it is false. The accuracy of eyewitness testimony can be improved through the use of improved interviews and better lineup procedures. Defendants' race, gender, and appearance often exert strong effects on the outcomes they experience in legal proceedings.

- Attitudes can influence personal health in many ways—especially by promoting healthy lifestyles. As is true of other attitudes, though, positive attitudes toward healthy behaviors don't always produce such actions—a sizeable attitude-behavior gap often exists. Obesity is increasing around the world and poses a major threat to personal health.

- Many factors play a role in this obesity trend, including social factors as the fact that because of the advent of shopping malls and other changes, people do less walking, a growing tendency for family members to eat separately—and hence, eat all day—and growing acceptance of obesity as a normal state for many people. Effective procedures for halting or reversing weight gain exist, and do work for people who follow them carefully.

- Stress is our response to events that disrupt, or threaten to disrupt, our physical or psychological functioning. Stress stems from many causes including major life events and the hassles of daily life. Many tactics for coping with stress exist, but one of the most important involves social support—emotional support and friendship from others.

- Work settings are social settings, so many findings and principles of social psychology are directly relevant to them. Job satisfaction refers to individuals' attitudes toward their jobs. Job satisfaction is influenced by organizational factors, such as working conditions and the fairness of reward systems, and personal factors, such as seniority, status, and specific personality traits. Recent findings suggest that job satisfaction is often highly stable over time and that it may be influenced by genetic factors. The relationship between job satisfaction and task performance is relatively weak, partly because many factors other than these work-related attitudes influence performance. Recent findings indicate that good performance may contribute to job satisfaction rather than vice versa.

- Individuals often engage in prosocial behavior at work. This is known as organizational citizenship behavior

(OCB), and can take many different forms. OCB is influenced by several factors, but among these, perceived fairness in the group or organization may be the most important. Individuals who engage in prosocial behavior are not formally rewarded by their organizations for such actions, but they may ultimately receive major rewards for doing so (raises or promotions).

- Leadership refers to the process through which one member of a group (its leader) influences other group members toward the attainment of shared group goals. While the great person theory of leadership has been shown to be false, research findings suggest that leaders do indeed differ from other people with respect to several traits. Leaders vary with respect to their behavior or style. Classic research in social psychology suggested that leaders vary in terms of two basic dimensions: consideration and initiating structure. In addition, leaders vary along two other key dimensions: autocratic-participative and directive-permissive. Transformational (charismatic) leaders exert profound effects on their followers and often change their societies. Research on the nature of such leadership suggests that it stems from certain behaviors by leaders, such as stating a clear vision, framing the group's goals in ways that magnify their importance, and possession of a stirring personal style. In contrast, transactional leaders exert influence through such steps as clarifying goals and rewarding good performance. They operate within the system rather than by changing it. Research findings suggest that transformational leaders may produce better group performance in environments that are changing rapidly but that they are not superior to transactional leaders in more stable environments.

Key Terms

consideration (person orientation) (p. 451)

eyewitness testimony (p. 425)

fuzzy-trace theory (p. 426)

great person theory of leadership (p. 449)

health psychology (p. 432)

industrial-organizational psychologists (p. 442)

initiating structure (production orientation) (p. 451)

job satisfaction (p. 443)

leadership (p. 449)

lineup (p. 423)

misuse of deadly force (p. 424)

organizational citizenship behavior (OCB) (p. 447)

social support (p. 440)

stress (p. 436)

transactional leaders (p. 453)

transformational leaders (p. 452)

Connections
INTEGRATING SOCIAL PSYCHOLOGY

In this chapter, you read about . . .	In other chapters, you will find related discussions of . . .
how the media may influence legal proceedings	how the media influence aggression and other forms of social behavior (Chapter 10).
how memory distortion and construction reduce the accuracy of eyewitnesses	how errors in memory influence social thought and judgments (Chapters 2, 3, and 4).
how the attractiveness, race, and gender of defendants and jurors influences legal proceedings	the role of attractiveness, gender, and race in many other contexts (e.g., Chapters 6 and 7.)
how personal characteristics can influence personal health	the role of personal characteristics in many aspects of social behavior and thought (almost all chapters of this book).

Glossary

above average effect: The tendency for people to rate themselves as above the average on most positive social attributes.

action identification: The level of interpretation we place on an action; low-level interpretations focus on the action itself, whereas higher-level interpretations focus on its ultimate goals.

actor-observer effect: The tendency to attribute our own behavior mainly to situational causes but the behavior of others mainly to internal (dispositional) causes.

adaptive response: Any physical characteristic or behavioral tendency that enhances the odds of reproductive success for an individual or for other individuals with similar genes.

additive tasks: Tasks for which the group product is the sum or combination of the efforts of individual members.

affect: Our current feelings and moods.

affect infusion model: A theory explaining how affect influences social thought and social judgments.

affect-centered model of attraction: A conceptual framework in which attraction and low interpersonal trust are the hallmark signs. This is the most insecure and least adaptive attachment style.

aggression: Behavior directed toward the goal of harming another living being who is motivated to avoid such treatment.

altruistic personality: A cluster of traits (e.g., high in empathy, belief in a just world) that predisposes individuals to behave in a prosocial manner.

anchoring and adjustment heuristic: A heuristic that involves the tendency to use a number of value as a starting point to which we then make adjustments.

appearance anxiety: Apprehension or worry about whether one's physical appearance is adequate and about the possible negative reactions of other people.

appearance-rejection sensitivity: From time to time these people worry about their appearance and fear that others may snub them because they don't quite measure up on this dimension.

assumed similarity: The extent to which two people believe they are similar.

asynchronous communication: Use of text, which allows greater control over what we say to others; visual and voice cues are absent.

attachment style: The degree of security experienced in interpersonal relationships. Differential styles initially develop in the interactions between infant and caregiver when the infant acquires basic attitudes about self worth and interpersonal trust.

attitude accessibility: The ease with which we can remember specific attitudes and bring them into consciousness.

attitude certainty: The tendency to believe we know our attitude position: both in terms of clarity and feeling it is the correct one to hold.

attitude similarity: The extent to which two individuals share the same attitudes.

attitude-to-behavior process model: A model of how attitudes guide behavior that emphasizes the influence of attitudes and stored knowledge of what is appropriate in a given situation on an individual's definition of the present situation. This definition, in turn, influences overt behavior.

attitude: Evaluation of various aspects of the social world.

attribution: The process through which we seek to identify the causes of others' behavior and so gain knowledge of their stable traits and dispositions.

autobiographical memory: Concerned with memory of the ourselves in the past, sometimes over the life course as a whole.

autokinetic phenomenon: The apparent movement of a single, stationary source of light in a dark room. Often used to study the emergence of social norms and social influence.

automatic processing: This occurs when, after extensive experience with a task or type of information, we reach the stage where we can perform the task or process the information in a seemingly effortless, automatic, and nonconscious manner.

availability heuristic: A strategy for making judgments on the basis of how easily specific kinds of information can be brought to mind.

balance theory: The formulations of Heider and of Newcomb that specify the relationships among (1) an individual's liking for another person, (2) their attitude about a given topic, and (3) the other person's attitude about the same topic. Balance (liking plus agreement) results in a positive emotional state. Imbalance (liking plus disagreement) results in a negative state and a desire to restore balance. Nonbalance (disliking plus either agreement or disagreement) leads to indifference.

bargaining (negotiation): A process in which opposing sides exchange offers, counteroffers, and concessions, either directly or through representatives.

big five dimensions of personality: Basic dimensions of personality in which individuals stand along several of these dimensions (e.g., extroversion, agreeableness, neuroticisim) and is often apparent in their behavior.

bilateral symmetry: When the left and the right side of the body (or parts of a body) are alike.

body language: Cues provided by the position, posture, and movement of others' bodies or body parts.

bona fide pipeline: A technique that uses priming to measure implicit racial attitudes.

brainstorming: A process in which people meet as a group to generate new ideas freely.

bullying: A pattern of behavior in which one individual is chosen as the target of repeated aggression by one or more others; the target person (the victim) generally has less power than those who engage in aggression (the bullies).

catharsis hypothesis: The view that providing angry people with an opportunity to express their aggressive impulses in relatively safe ways will reduce their tendencies to engage in more harmful forms of aggression.

central route (to persuasion): Attitude change resulting from systematic processing of information presented in persuasive messages.

classical conditioning: A basic form of learning in which one stimulus, initially neutral, acquires the capacity to evoke reactions through repeated pairing with another stimulus. In a sense, one stimulus becomes a signal for the presentation or occurrence of the other.

close friendship: A relationship in which two people spend a great deal of time together, interact in a variety of situations, and provide mutual emotional support.

cognitive dissonance: An internal state that results when individuals notice inconsistency between two or more attitudes or between their attitudes and their behavior.

cohesiveness: The extent to which we are attracted to a social group and want to belong to it; all forces (factors) that cause group members to remain in the group.

collective guilt: The emotion that can be experienced when we are confronted with the harmful actions done by our in-group against an out-group. It is most likely to be experienced when the harmful actions are seen as illegitimate.

collectivism: Groups in which the norm is to maintain harmony among group members, even if doing so might entail some personal costs.

common in-group identity model: A theory suggesting that to the extent individuals in different groups view themselves as members of a single social entity, intergroup bias will be reduced.

common-bond groups: Groups that tend to involve face-to-face interaction and in which the individual members are bonded to each other.

common-identity groups: Face-to-face interaction is often absent, and the members are linked together via the category as a whole rather than each other.

communal behavior: Benevolent acts in a relationship that "cost" the one who performs those acts and benefit the partner and the relationship itself.

companionate love: Love that is based on friendship, mutual attraction, shared interests, respect, and concern for one another's welfare.

compliance: A form of social influence involving direct requests from one person to another.

conditioned stimulus: The stimulus that comes to stand for or signal a prior unconditioned stimulus.

conflict: A process in which individuals or groups perceive that others have taken or will soon take actions incompatible with their own interests.

conformity: A type of social influence in which individuals change their attitudes or behavior to adhere to existing social norms.

consensus: The extent to which other people react to some stimulus or even in the same manner as the person we are considering.

consideration (person orientation): A key dimension of leader behavior; leaders high on this dimensions focus on establishing good relations with their subordinates and on being liked by them.

consistency: The extent to which an individual responds to a given stimulus or situation in the same way on different occasions (i.e., across time).

consummate love: In Sternberg's triangular model of love, a complete and ideal love that combines intimacy, passion, and decision (commitment).

contact hypothesis: The view that increased contact between members of various social groups can be effective in reducing prejudice between them.

cooperation: Behavior in which groups work together to attain shared goals.

correlational method: A method of research in which a scientist systematically observes two or more variables to determine whether changes in one are accompanied by changes in the other.

correspondence bias (fundamental attribution error): The tendency to explain others' actions as stemming from dispositions even in the presence of clear situational causes.

correspondent inference: A theory describing how we use others' behavior as a basis for inferring their stable dispositions.

counterfactual thinking: The tendency to imagine other outcomes in a situation than the ones that actually occurred ("What might have been.")

cultures of honor: Cultures in which there are strong norms indicating that aggression is an appropriate response to insults to one's honor.

deadline technique: A technique for increasing compliance in which target people are told that they have only limited time to take advantage of some offer or to obtain some item.

debriefing: Procedures at the conclusion of a research session in which participants are given full information about the nature of the research and the hypothesis or hypotheses under investigation.

deception: A technique whereby researchers withhold information about the purposes or procedures of a study from people participating in it.

decision (commitment): In Sternberg's triangular model of love, these are the cognitive processes involved in deciding that you love another person and are committed to maintain the relationship.

decision making: Processes involved in combining and integrating available information to choose one out of several possible courses of action.

deindividuation: A psychological state characterized by reduced self-awareness brought on by external conditions, such as being an anonymous member of a large crowd.

dependent variable: The variable that is measured in an experiment.

descriptive norms: Norms simply indicating what most people do in a given situation.

diffusion of responsibility: A principle suggesting that the greater the number of witnesses to an emergency the less likely victims are to receive help. This is because each bystander assumes that someone else will do it.

discrimination: Differential (usually negative) behaviors directed toward members of different social groups.

dismissing attachment style: A style characterized by high self-esteem and low interpersonal trust. This is a conflicted and somewhat insecure style in which the individual feels that they deserve a close relationship but is frustrated because of mistrust of potential partners. The result is the tendency to reject the other person at some point in the relationship to avoid being the one who is rejected.

distinctiveness: The extent to which an individual responds in the same manner to different stimuli or events.

distraction-conflict theory: A theory suggesting that social facilitation stems from the conflict produced when individuals attempt, simultaneously, to pay attention to the other people present and to the task being performed.

distributive justice (fairness): Refers to individuals' judgments about whether they are receiving a fair share of available rewards; a share proportionate to their contributions to the group or any social relationship.

door-in-the-face technique: A procedure for gaining compliance in which requesters begin with a large request and then, when this is refused, retreat to a smaller one (the one they actually desired all along).

downward social comparison: A comparison of the self to another who does less well than or is inferior to us.

drive theories (of aggression): Theories suggesting that aggression stems from external conditions that arousal the motive to harm or injure others. The most famous of these is the frustration-aggression hypothesis.

eating disorders: Serious forms of mental disorder in which individuals engage in unhealthy, and sometimes dangerous, efforts to control their body weight. Research findings indicate that social influence exerted by the media may play an important role in these disorders.

effect-danger ratio: A principle suggesting that in situations in which they interact frequently with potential victims, most people try—when engaging in aggression—to maximize the harm they produce while minimizing the danger of retaliation.

ego depletion: When our capacity to self-regulate has been reduced because of prior expenditures of limited resources.

elaboration likelihood model (ELM): A theory suggesting that persuasion can occur in either of two distinct ways, differing in the amount of cognitive effort or elaboration it requires.

empathic joy hypothesis: The view is that helpers respond to the needs of a victim because they want to accomplish something, and doing so is rewarding in and of itself.

empathy: Emotional reactions that are focused on or oriented toward other people and include feelings of compassion, sympathy, and concern.

empathy-altruism hypothesis: The suggestion that some prosocial acts are motivated solely by the desire to help someone in need.

enemyship: This refers to a personal relationship based on hatred and malice in which one person wishes to produce another person's downfall and attempts to sabotage that person's life progress.

entitativity: The extent to which a group is perceived as being a coherent entity.

essence: Typically some biologically based feature that is used to distinguish one group and another; frequently can serve as justification for the differential treatment of those groups.

evaluation apprehension: Concern over being evaluated by others. Such concern can increase arousal and so contribute to social facilitation effects.

evolutionary psychology: A new branch of psychology that seeks to investigate the potential role of genetic factors in various aspects of human behavior.

excitation transfer theory: A theory suggesting that arousal produced in one situation can persist and intensify emotional reactions occurring in later situations.

experimentation (experimental method): A method of research in which one or more factors (the independent variables) are systematically changed to determine whether such variations affect one or more other factors (dependent variables).

explicit attitudes: Consciously accessible attitudes that are controllable and easy to report.

eyewitness testimony: Evidence given by persons who have witnessed a crime—plays an important role in many trials.

fear appeals: Attempting to change people's behaviors by use of a message that induces fear.

fearful-avoidant attachment style: A style characterized by low self-esteem and low interpersonal trust. This is the most insecure and least adaptive attachment style.

foot-in-the-door technique: A procedure for gaining compliance in which requesters begin with a small request and then, when this is granted, escalate to a larger one (the one they actually desired all along).

forewarning: Advance knowledge that one is about to become the target of an attempt at persuasion. Forewarning often increases resistance to the persuasion that follows.

forgiveness: Giving up the desire to punish someone who has hurt us and seeking, instead, to act in kind, helpful ways toward them.

frustration-aggression hypothesis: The suggestion that frustration is a powerful determinant of aggression.

fundamental attribution error (correspondence bias): The tendency to overestimate the impact of dispositional cues on others' behavior.

fuzzy-trace theory: A theory suggesting that when we make decisions or judgments, we often focus on the general idea or gist of information stored in memory and not on the information itself. One result is that we then remember information consistent with the gist of our real memories even though it is false.

gender stereotypes: Stereotypes concerning the traits possessed by females and males and that distinguish the two genders from each other.

general aggression model (GAM): A modern theory of aggression suggesting that aggression is triggered by a wide range of input variables that influence arousal, affective stages, and cognitions.

generativity: Refers to an adult's interest in and commitment to the well-being of future generations.

glass ceiling: Barriers based on attitudinal or organizational bias that prevent qualified females from advancing to top-level positions.

great person theory of leadership: The view that leaders possess certain traits that set them apart from other people and that are possessed by all leaders no matter where or when they live.

group: A collection of people who are perceived to be bonded together in a coherent unit to some degree.

groupthink: The tendency of the members of highly cohesive groups to assume that their decisions can't be wrong, that all members must support the group's decisions strongly, and that information contrary to it should be ignored.

group polarization: The tendency of a group member to shift toward more extreme positions than those they initially held by the individual members as a result of group discussion.

habit: Repeatedly performing a specific behavior so responses become relatively automatic whenever that situation is encountered.

health psychology: The branch of psychology that studies the relation between psychological variables and health.

heuristic processing: Processing of information in a peruasive message that involves the use of simple rules of thumb or mental shortcuts.

heuristics: Simple rules for making complex decisions or drawing inferences in a rapid manner and seemingly effortless manner.

hooliganism: Negative stereotype about how people behave in crowds at sporting events, especially applied to incidents involving England's soccer fans.

hostile aggression: Aggression in which the prime objective is inflicting some kind of harm on the victim.

hypocrisy: Publicly advocating some attitudes or behavior and then acting in a way that is inconsistent with these attitudes or behavior.

hypothesis: An as yet unverified prediction concerning some aspect of social behavior or social thought.

identity interference: When two important social identities are perceived as in conflict such that acting on the basis of one identity interferes with performing well based on the other identity.

ideology: The philosophical and political values that govern a group.

implementation plan: A plan for how to implement our intentions to carry out some action.

implicit associations: Links between group membership and trait associations or evaluations that the perceiver may be unaware of. They can be activated automatically based on the group membership of a target.

implicit attitudes: Unconscious associations between objects and evaluative responses.

implicit personality theories: Beliefs about what traits or characteristics tend to go together.

impression formation: The process through which we form impressions of others.

impression management (self-presentation): Efforts by individuals to produce favorable first impressions on others.

incidental feelings: Those feelings induced separately or before a target is encountered, as a result those feelings are irrelevant to the group being judged but can still affect judgments of the target.

independent self-concept: In individualistic cultures, the expectation is that people will develop a self-concept as separate from or independent of others. Men are expected to have an independent self-concept more so than women.

independent variable: The variable that is systematically changed (i.e., varied) in an experiment.

individualism: In such groups the norm is to value standing out from the group and being different from others; individual variability is to be expected and disagreement among members is tolerated.

individuation: The need to be distinguishable from others in some respects.

induced or forced compliance: Situations in which individuals are somehow induced to say or do things inconsistent with their true attitudes.

industrial-organizational psychologists: Psychologists who specialize in studying all forms of behavior and cognition in work settings.

information overload: Instances in which our ability to process information is exceeded.

informational social influence: Social influence based on the desire to be correct (i.e., to possess accurate perceptions of the social world).

informed consent: A procedure in which research participants are provided with as much information as possible about a research project before deciding whether to participate in it.

ingratiation: When we try to make others like us by conveying that we like them; praising others to flatter them.

in-group: The social group to which we perceive ourselves as belonging ("us").

initiating structure (production orientation): A key dimension of leader behavior; leaders high on this dimension are primarily concerned with getting the job done (i.e., with production).

injunctive norms: Norms specifying what ought to be done; what is approved or disapproved behavior in a given situation.

instrumental aggression: Aggression in which the primary goal is not to harm the victim but rather attainment of some other goal—for example, access to valued resources.

instrumental conditioning: A basic form of learning in which responses that lead to positive outcomes or which permit avoidance of negative outcomes are strengthened.

interdependence: Refers to an interpersonal association in which two people influence each others' lives. They often focus their thoughts on one another and regularly engage in joint activities.

interdependent self-concept: In collectivist cultures, the expectation is that people will develop a self-concept in terms of one's connections or relationships with others. Women are expected to have an interdependent self-concept more so than men.

intergroup comparisons: Judgments that result from comparisons between our group and another group.

interpersonal attraction: A person's attitude about another person. Attraction is expressed along a dimension that ranges from strong feelings of liking to strong feelings of dislike.

interpersonal trust: An attitudinal dimension underlying attachment styles that involves the belief that other people are generally trustworthy, dependable, and reliable as opposed to the belief that others are generally untrustworthy, undependable, and unreliable. This is the most successful and most desirable attachment style.

intimacy: In Sternberg's triangular model of love, the closeness felt by two people; the extent to which they are bonded.

intragroup comparisons: Judgments that result from comparisons between individuals who are members of the same group.

introspection: To privately contemplate "who we are." It is a method for attempting to gain self-knowledge.

job satisfaction: Attitudes individuals hold concerning their jobs.

kin selection theory: A theory suggesting that a key goal for all organisms—including human beings—is getting our genes into the next generation; one way in which individuals can reach this goal is by helping others who share their genes.

leadership: Influencing others in a group (or organization) by establishing a direction for collective effort and then managing the collective activities needed to move in that direction.

less-leads-to-more effect: The fact that offering individuals small rewards for engaging in counterattitudinal behavior often produces more dissonance, and so more attitude change, than offering them larger rewards.

lineup: A procedure in which witnesses to a crime are shown several people, one or more of whom may be suspects in a case and asked to identify those that they recognize as the person who committed the crime.

linguistic style: Aspects of speech apart from the meaning of the words employed.

loneliness: The unpleasant emotional and cognitive state based on desiring close relationships but being unable to attain them.

love: A combination of emotions, cognitions, and behaviors that often play a crucial role in intimate relationships.

lowball procedure: A technique for gaining compliance in which an offer or deal is changed to make it less attractive to the target person after this person has accepted it.

magical thinking: Thinking involving assumptions that don't hold up to rational scrutiny—for example, the belief that things that resemble one another share fundamental properties.

mediating varible: A variable that is affected by an independent variable and then influences a dependent variable. Mediating varibles help explain why or how specific varibles influence social behavior or thought in certain ways.

mere exposure: By having seen before, but not necessarily remembering having done so, attitudes toward an object can become more positive.

microexpressions: Fleeting facial expressions lasting only a few tenths of a second.

minimal groups: When we are categorized into different groups based on some "minimal" criteria we tend to favor others who are categorized in the same group as ourselves compared to those categorized as members of a different group.

misuse of deadly force: Refers to instances in which police use deadly (often lethal) force against suspected criminals, when in fact, such force is not necessary, and these people are not an actual threat to police or public safety.

modern racism: More subtle beliefs than blatant feelings of superiority. It consists primarily of thinking minorities are seeking and receiving more benefits than they deserve and a denial that discrimination affects their outcomes.

mood congruence effects: The fact that we are more likely to store or remember positive information when in a positive mood and negative information when in a negative mood.

mood dependent memory: The fact that what we remember while in a given mood may be determined, in part, by what we learned when previously in that mood.

moral integrity: Refers to the extent to which individuals care about considerations of goodness and fairness when they act; moral integrity frequently involves accepting some sacrifice of self-interest to do "the right thing."

multicultural perspective: A focus on understanding the cultural and ethnic factors that influence social behavior.

narcissism: A personality disposition characterized by unreasonably high self-esteem, a feeling of superiority, a need for admiration, sensitivity to criticism, a lack of empathy, and exploitative behavior.

need for affiliation: The basic motive to seek and maintain interpersonal relationships.

negative state-relief model: The proposal that prosocial behavior is motivated by the bystander's desire to reduce his or her own uncomfortable negative emotions or feelings.

negativity bias: Refers to the fact that we show greater sensitivity to negative information than to positive information.

noncommon effects: Effects produced by a particular cause that could not be produced by any other apparent cause.

nonverbal communication: Communication between individuals that does not involve the content of spoken language. It relies instead on an unspoken language of facial expressions, eye contact, and body language.

normative focus theory: A theory suggesting that norms will influence behavior only to the extent that they are focal for the people involved at the time the behavior occurs.

normative social influence: Social influence based on the desire to be liked or accepted by other people.

norms: Rules or expectations within a group concerning how its members should (or should not) behave.

obedience: A form of social influence in which one person simply orders one or more others to perform some action(s).

objective scales: Those with measurement units that are tied to external reality so that they mean the same thing regardless of category membership (e.g., dollars earned, feet and inches, chosen or rejected).

obligatory interdependence: Because of our evolutionary history, it is necessary that we rely on the group for survival as a species.

observational learning: A basic form of learning in which individuals acquire new forms of behavior as a result of observing others.

optimistic bias: Our predisposition to expect things to turn out well overall.

organizational citizenship behavior (OCB): Help people give each other at work that is not a required part of their jobs.

out-group: Any group other than the one to which we perceive ourselves belonging.

overconfidence barrier: The tendency to have more confidence in the acacuracy of our own judgments than is reasonable.

paralinguistic cues: Visual or voice cues during communication that typically assist in deciphering the meaning of a message.

passion: In Sternberg's triangular model of love, the sexual motives and sexual excitement associated with a couple's relationship.

passionate love: An intense and often unrealistic emotional response to another person. When this emotion is experienced, it is usually perceived as an indication of true love, but to outside observers it appears to be infatuation.

peripheral route (to persuasion): Attitude change that occurs in response to peripheral persuasion cues, which is often based on information concerning the expertise or status of would-be persuaders.

perseverance effect: The tendency for beliefs and schemas to remain unchanged even in the face of contradictory information.

personal-versus-social identity continuum: This signifies the two distinct ways that we can categorize ourselves. At the personal level, we can be thought of as a unique individual, whereas at the social identity level, we think of the self as a member of a group.

persuasion: Efforts to change others' attitudes through the use of various kinds of messages.

physical attractiveness: The combination of characteristics that are evaluated as beautiful or handsome at the positive extreme and as unattractive at the negative extreme.

planning fallacy: The tendency to make optimistic predictions concerning how long a given task will take for completion.

playing hard to get: A technique that can be used for increasing compliance by suggesting that a person or object is scarce and hard to obtain.

pluralistic ignorance: When we collectively misunderstand what attitudes others hold and believe erroneously that others have different attitudes than us; refers to the fact that because none of the bystanders respond to an emergency, no one knows for sure what is happening and each depends on the others to interpret the situation.

politicized collective identity: Recognizing shared grievances and engaging in a power struggle on behalf of one's devalued group.

positive illusions: Beliefs we hold about ourselves that are not entirely accurate, that we can do more than is the case, that negative events aren't as likely to befall us as they are others, and the chances for success are higher for the self than others.

possible selves: Image of how we might be in the future—either a "dreaded" potential to be avoided or "desired" potential that can be strived for.

prejudice: Negative emotional responses based on group membership.

preoccupied attachment style: A style characterized by low self-esteem and high interpersonal trust. This is a conflicted and somewhat insecure style in which the individual strongly desires a close relationship but feels that they are unworthy of the partner and is thus vulnerable to being rejected.

prevention focus: When people are concerned about avoiding losses and focused on preventing negative events from occurring.

priming: It is a situation that occurs when stimuli or events increase the availability in memory or consciousness of specific types of information held in memory.

procedural justice: Judgments concerning the fairness of the procedures used to distribute available rewards among group members.

promotion focus: When people are concerned with promoting or gaining outomes; when they focus on not missing an opportunity to benefit.

proportion of similarity: The number of specific indicators that two people are similar divided by the number of specific indicators that two people are similar plus the number of specific indicators that they are dissimilar.

prosocial behavior: Actions by individuals that help others with no immediate benefit to the helper.

provocation: Actions by others that tend to trigger aggression in the recipient, often because they are perceived as stemming from malicious intent.

proximity: In attraction research, the physical closeness between two individuals with respect to where they live, where they sit in a classroom, where they work, and so on. The smaller the physical distance, the greater the probability that the two people will come into repeated contact experiencing repeated exposure to one another, positive affect, and the development of mutual attraction.

punishment: Procedures in which aversive consequences are delivered to individuals when they engage in specific actions.

reactance: Negative reactions to threats to one's personal freedom. Reactance often increases resistance to persuasion and can even produce negative attitude change or opposite to what was intended.

realistic conflict theory: The view that prejudice stems from direct competition between various social groups over scarce and valued resources.

recategorization: Shifts in the boundaries between our in-group ("us") and some out-group ("them"). As a result of such recategorization, people formerly viewed as out-group members may now be viewed a belonging to the in-group and consequently are viewed more positively.

reference groups: Groups of people with whom we identify and whose opinions we value.

repeated exposure: Zajonc's finding that frequent contact with any mildly negative, neutral, or positive stimulus results in an increasingly positive evaluation of that stimulus.

representativeness heuristic: A strategy for making judgments based on the extent to which current stimuli or events resemble other stimuli or categories.

repulsion hypothesis: Rosenbaum's provocative proposal that attraction is not increased by similar attitudes but is simply decreased by dissimilar attitudes. This hypothesis is incorrect as stated, but it is true that dissimilar attitudes tend to have negative effects that are stronger than the positive effects of similar attitudes.

respect: Being seen positively and as having worth.

risk averse: We weigh possible losses more heavily than equivalent potential gains. As a result, we respond more negatively to changes that are framed as potential losses than positively to changes that are framed as potential gains.

roles: The set of behaviors that individuals occupying specific positions within a group are expected to perform.

salience: When someone or some object stands out from its background or is the focus of attention.

schemas: Mental frameworks centering on a specific theme that help us to organize social information.

schism: Splintering of a group into distinct factions following an ideological rift among members.

secure attachment style: A style characterized by high self-esteem and high interpersonal trust. This is the most successful and most desirable attachment style.

selective avoidance: A tendency to direct attention away from information that challenges existing attitudes. Such avoidance increases resistance to persuasion.

self-control: Foregoing short-term rewards and instead waiting for long-term rewards.

self-deprecating: Putting ourselves down or implying that we are not as good as someone else.

self-efficacy: The belief that we can achieve a goal as a result of our own actions.

self-esteem: The degree to which we perceive ourselves positively or negatively; our overall attitude toward ourselves. It can be measured explicitly or implicitly.

self-evaluation maintenance model: This perspective suggests that to maintain a positive view of ourselves, we distance ourselves from others who perform better than we do on valued dimensions and move closer to others who perform worse than us. This view suggests that doing so will protect our self-esteem.

self-fulfilling prophecy: Predictions that, in a sense, make themselves come true.

self-interest (egoism): The view that a large portion of human behavior is based on seeking whatever provides us with the most satisfaction; we seek rewards and try to avoid punishments.

self-promotion: Attempting to present ourselves to others as having positive attributes.

self-reference effect: Refers to the fact that we seem to orient ourselves toward stimuli that are associated with us. We show a preference for objects owned by and reflective of ourselves.

self-regulation: Limited capacity to engage our willpower and control our own thinking and emotions.

self-serving bias: The tendency to attribute positive outcomes to internal causes (e.g., one's own traits or characteristics) but negative outcomes or events to external causes (e.g., chance, task difficulty).

self-verification perspective: Theory that addresses the processes by which we lead others to agree with our views of ourselves; wanting others to agree with how we see ourselves.

shifting standards: When we use one group as the standard but shift to another group as the comparison standard when judging members of a different group.

similarity-dissimilarity effect: The consistent finding that people respond positively to indications that another person is similar to themselves and negatively to indications that another person is dissimilar from themselves.

singlism: Negative stereotyping and discrimination directed toward people who are single.

social categorization: The tendency to divide the social world into separate categories: our in-group ("us") and various out-groups ("them").

social cognition: The manner in which we interpret, analyze, remember, and use information about the social world.

social comparison: The process through which we compare ourselves to others to determine whether our view of social reality is, or is not, correct.

social comparison theory: Festinger (1954) suggested that people compare themselves to others because for many domains and attributes there is no objective yardstick to evaluate ourselves against, and other people are therefore highly informative.

social dilemmas: Situations in which each person can increase their individual gains by acting in one way, but if all (or most) people do the same thing, the outcomes experienced by all are reduced.

social exclusion: Conditions in which individuals feel that they have been excluded from some social group.

social facilitation: Effects on performance resulting from the presence of others.

social identity theory: Addresses how we respond when our group identity is salient. Suggests that we will move closer to positive others with whom we share an identity but distance from other ingroup members who perform poorly or otherwise make our social identity negative.

social influence: Efforts by one or more individuals to change the attitudes, beliefs, perceptions, or behaviors of one or more others.

social learning: The process through which we acquire new information, forms of behavior, or attitudes from other people.

social learning view (of prejudice): The view prejudice is acquired through direct and vicarious experiences in much the same manner as other attitudes.

social loafing: Reductions in motivation and effort when individuals work in a group compared to then they work individually.

social neuroscience: An area of research in social psychology that seeks knowledge about the neural and biological bases of social processes.

social norms: Rules indicating how individuals are expected to behave in specific situations.

social perception: The process through which we seek to know and understand other people.

social psychology: The scientific field that seeks to understand the nature and causes of individual behavior and thought in social situations.

social rejection: Rejection by one individual of another individual, not on the basis of what they have done, but on the basis of prejudice, stereotypes, and biases.

social support: Drawing on the emotional and task resources provided by others as a means of coping with stress.

spreading of alternatives: When individuals make a decision between two options they tend to reduce the positivity of the item they did not choose and increase the positivity of the item they did choose.

staring: A form of eye contact in which one person continues to gaze steadily at another regardless of what the recipient does.

status: The individual's position or rank within the group.

stereotype threat: Can occur when people believe that they might be judged in light of a negative stereotype about their group or that, because of their performance, they may in some way confirm a negative stereotype of their group.

stereotypes: Beliefs about social groups in terms of the traits or characteristics that they are believed to share. Stereotypes are cognitive frameworks that influence the processing of social information.

stigma consciousness: A readiness to perceive negative outcomes as a result of our devalued group membership.

stress: Our response to events that disrupt, or threaten to disrupt, our physical or psychological functioning.

subjective scales: Response scales that are open to interpretation and lack an externally grounded referent, including scales labeled from good to bad or weak to strong. They are said to be subjective because they can take on different meanings depending on the group membership of the person being evaluated.

subliminal: Stimuli shown to participants so rapidly that they cannot be recognized or identified by them.

subliminal conditioning: Classical conditioning of attitudes by exposure to stimuli that are below individuals' threshhold of conscious awareness.

subtype: A subset of a group that is not consistent with the stereotype of the group as a whole.

superordinate goals: Those that can only be achieved by cooperation between groups; goals that both sides to a conflict seek and that tie their interests together rather than driving them apart.

survey method: A method of research in which a large number of people answer questions about their attitudes or behavior.

symbolic social influence: Social influence resulting from the mental representation of others or our relationships with them.

systematic observation: A method of research in which behavior is systematically observed and recorded.

systematic processing: Processing of information in a persuasive message that involves careful consideration of message content and ideas.

TASS model: The traits as situational sensitivities model. A view suggesting that many personality traits function in a threshold-like manner, influencing behavior only when situations evoke them.

teasing: Provoking statements that call attention to the target's flaws and imperfections.

terror management: Our efforts to come to terms with certainty of our own death and its unsettling implications.

that's-not-all technique: A technique for gaining compliance in which requesters offer additional benefits to target people before they have decided whether to comply with or reject specific requests.

theories: Efforts by scientists in any field to answer the question "Why?" Theories involve attempts to understand why certain events or process occur as they do.

theory of planned behavior: An extension of the theory of reasoned action, suggesting that in addition to attitudes toward a given behavior and subjective norms about it, individuals also consider their ability to perform the behavior.

theory of reasoned action: A theory suggesting that the decision to engage in a particular behavior is the result of a rational process in which behavioral options are considered, consequences or outcomes of each are evaluated, and a decision is reached to act or not to act. That decision is then reflected in behavioral intentions, which strongly influence overt behavior.

thought suppression: Our efforts to prevent certain thoughts from enetering consciousness.

threat: It primarily concerns fear that our group interests will be undermined or our self-esteem is in jeopardy.

tokenism: Tokenism can refer to hiring based on group membership. It can concern a numerically infrequent presence of members of a particular category or it can also refer to instances where individuals perform trivial positive actions for members of out-groups that are later used as an excuse for refusing more meaningful beneficial actions for members of these groups.

transactional justice: Refers to the extent to which people who distribute rewards explain or justify their decisions and show respect and courtesy to those who receive the rewards.

transactional leaders: Leaders who direct their groups by rewarding them for desired behavior, by taking action to correct mistakes or departures from existing rules. Such leaders generally strengthen existing structures and strategies within an organization.

transformational leaders: Leaders who, because of several characteristics, exert profound effects on their followers.

triangular model of love: Sternberg's conceptualization of love relationships.

trivialization: A technique for reducing dissonance in which the importance of attitudes or behavior that are inconsistent with each other is cognitively reduced.

type A behavior pattern: A pattern consisting primarily of high levels of competitiveness, time urgency, and hostility.

type B behavior pattern: A pattern consisting of the absence of characteristics associated with the type A behavior pattern.

unconditioned stimulus: A stimulus that evokes a positive or negative response without substantial learning.

unpriming: Refers to the fact that the effects of the schemas tend to persist until they are somehow expressed in thought or behavior and only then do their effects decrease.

unrequited love: Love felt by one person for another who does not feel love in return.

upward social comparison: A comparison of the self to another who does better than or is superior to us.

within-group comparisons: Making comparisons between a target and other members of that same category only.

workplace aggression: Any form of behavior through which individuals seek to harm others in their workplace.

References

Aamodt, M. G. (2007). *Industrial-organizational psychology: An applied approach* (5th ed.). Pacific Grove, CA: Wadsworth.

Aarts, H., Custer, R., & Wegner, D.M. (2005). On the inference of personal authorship: Enhancing experienced agency by priming effect information. *Consciousness and Cognition, 14,* 439-458.

Aarts, H., & Dijksterhuis, A. (2003). The silence of the library: Environment, situational norms, and social behavior. *Journal of Personality and Social Psychology, 84,* 18–24.

Adams, G. (2005). The cultural grounding of personal relationships: Enemyship in North American and West African worlds. *Journal of Personality and Social Psychology, 88,* 948–968.

Adams, G., Anderson, S. L., & Adonu, J. K. (2004). The cultural grounding of closeness and intimacy. In D. Mashek & A. Aron (Eds.), *The handbook of closeness and intimacy* (pp. 321–330). Mahwah, NJ: Erlbaum.

Adams, G., Biernat, M., Branscombe, N. R., Crandall, C. S., & Wrightsman, L. S. (2007). Beyond prejudice: Toward a sociocultural psychology of racism and oppression. In G. Adams, M. Biernat, N. R. Branscombe, C. S. Crandall, & L. S. Wrightsman (Eds.), *Commemorating Brown: The social psychology of racism and discrimination.* Washington, DC: American Psychological Association.

Adams, G., Garcia, D. M., Purdie-Vaughns, V., & Steele, C. M. (2006). The detrimental effect of a suggestion of sexism in an instruction situation. *Journal of Experimental Social Psychology, 42,* 602–615.

Adams, J. S. (1965). Inequity in social exchange. In L. Berkowitz (Ed.), *Advances in experimental social psychology* (Vol. 2, pp. 267–299). New York: Academic Press.

Adarves-Yorno, I., Postmes, T., & Haslam, S. A. (2007). Creative innovation or crazy irrelevance? The contribution of group norms and social identity to creative behavior. *Journal of Experimental Social Psychology, 43,* 410–416.

Ajzen, I. (1987). Attitudes, traits, and actions: Dispositional prediction of behavior in personality and social psychology. In L. Berkowitz (Ed.), *Advances in experimental social psychology* (Vol. 20). San Diego, CA: Academic Press.

Ajzen, I. (1991). The theory of planned behavior: Special issue: Theories of cognitive self-regulation. *Organizational Behavior and Human Decision Processes, 50,* 179–211.

Ajzen, I. (2001). Nature and operation of attitudes. *Annual Review of Psychology, 52,* 27–58.

Ajzen, I., & Fishbein, M. (1980). *Understanding attitudes and predicting social behavior.* Englewood Cliffs, NJ: Prentice-Hall.

Ajzen, I., & Fishbein, M. (2005). The influence of attitudes on behavior. In D. Albarracin, B. T. Johnson, & M. P. Zanna (Eds.), *The handbook of attitudes* (pp. 173–221). Mahwah, NJ: Lawrence Erlbaum.

Alagna, F. J., Whitcher, S. J., & Fisher, J. D. (1979). Evaluative reactions to interpersonal touch in a counseling interview. *Journal of Counseling Psychology, 26,* 465–472.

Albarracin, D., Johnson, B. T., Fishbein, M., & Muellerleile, P. A. (2001). Theories of reasoned action and planned behavior as models of condom use: A meta-analysis. *Psychological Bulletin, 127,* 142–161.

Alicke, M. D., Vredenburg, D. S., Hiatt, M., & Govorun, O. (2001). The better than myself effect. *Motivation and Emotion, 25,* 7–22.

Allen, K. (2003). Are pets a healthy pleasure? The influence of pets on blood pressure. *Current Directions in Cognitive Science, 12,* 236–239.

Allen, K., Shykoff, B. E., & Izzo, J. L. (2001). Pet ownership, but not ACE inhibitor therapy, blunts home blood pressure responses to mental stress. *Hypertension, 38,* 815–820.

Allen, T. D. (2006). Rewarding good citizens: The relationship between citizenship behavior, gender, and organizational rewards. *Journal of Applied Social Psychology, 36,* 120–143.

Allgeier, E. R., & Wiederman, M. W. (1994). How useful is evolutionary psychology for understanding contemporary human sexual behavior? *Annual Review of Sex Research, 5,* 218–256.

Allport, F. H. (1920). The influence of the group upon association and thought. *Journal of Experimental Psychology, 3,* 159–182.

Amato, P. R. (1986). Emotional arousal and helping behavior in a real-life emergency. *Journal of Applied Social Psychology, 16,* 633–641.

American Psychiatric Association. (1994). *Diagnostic and statistical manual of mental disorders* (4th ed.). Washington, DC: American Psychiatric Association.

Ames, D. R., Flynn, F. J., & Weber, E. U. (2004). It's the thought that counts: On perceiving how helpers decide to lend a hand. *Personality and Social Psychology Bulletin, 30,* 461–474.

Andersen, S. M., & Baum, A. (1994). Transference in interpersonal relations: Inferences and affect based on significant-other representations. *Journal of Personality, 62,* 459–497.

Anderson, C. A. (1989). Temperature and aggression: Effects on quarterly, yearly, and city rates of violent and nonviolent crime. *Journal of Personality and Social Psychology, 52,* 1161–1173.

Anderson, C. A. (1997). Effects of violent movies and trait hostility on hostile feelings and aggressive thoughts. *Aggressive Behavior, 23,* 161–178.

Anderson, C. A. (2004). The influence of media violence on youth. Paper presented at the annual convention of the Association for Psychological Science, Los Angeles, CA.

Anderson, C. A., & Anderson, K. B. (1996). Violent crime rate studies in philosophical context: A destructive testing approach to heat and Southern culture of violence effects. *Journal of Personality and Social Psychology, 70,* 740–756.

Anderson, C. A., Anderson, K. B., & Deuser, W. E. (1996). Examining an affective aggression framework: Weapon and temperature effects on aggressive thoughts, affect, and attitudes. *Personality and Social Psychology Bulletin, 22,* 366–376.

Anderson, C. A., Berkowitz, L., Donnerstein, E., Huesmann, L. R. Johnson, J., Linz, D., et al. (2003). The influence of media violence on youth. *Psychological Science in the Public Interest, 4,* 81–110.

Anderson, C. A., & Bushman, B. J. (2001). Effects of violent video games on aggressive behavior, aggressive cognition, aggressive affect, physiological arousal, and prosocial behavior: A meta-analytic review of the scientific literature. *Psychological Science, 12,* 353–359.

Anderson, C. A., & Bushman, B. J. (2002). Human aggression. *Annual Review of Psychology, 53,* 27–51.

Anderson, C. A., Bushman, B. J., & Groom, R. W. (1997). Hot years and serious and deadly assault: Empirical tests of the heat hypothesis. *Journal of Personality and Social Psychology, 73,* 1213–1223.

Anderson, C. A., Carnagey, N. L., & Eubanks, J. (2003). Exposure to violent media: The effects of songs with violent lyrics on aggressive thoughts and feelings. *Journal of Personality and Social Psychology, 84,* 960–971.

Anderson, C. A., Carnagey, N. L., Flanagan, M., Benjamin, A. J., Eubanks, J., & Valentine, J. C. (2004). Violent video games: Specific effects of violent content on aggressive thoughts and behavior. In M. Zanna (Ed.), *Advances in experimental social psychology* (Vol. 36). New York: Elsevier.

Anderson, C. A., Miller, R. S., Riger, A. L., Dill, J. C., & Sedikides, C. (1994). Behavioral and characterological attributional styles as predictors of depression and loneliness: Review, refinement, and test. *Journal of Personality and Social Psychology, 66,* 549–558.

Anderson, C. A., Berkowitz, L., Donnerstein, E., Huesmann, L. R., Johnson, J. D., Linz, D., Malamuth, N. M., & Wartella, E. (2004). The influence of media violence on youth. *Psychology in the Public Interest, 4,* 81–110.

Anderson, N. H. (1965). Averaging versus adding as a stimulus combination rule in impression formation. *Journal of Experimental Social Psychology, 70,* 394–400. serial presentation. *Journal of Personality and Social Psychology, 10,* 354–362.

Anderson, V. L. (1993). Gender differences in altruism among holocaust rescuers. *Journal of Social Behavior and Personality, 8,* 43–58.

Andreoletti, C., Zebrowitz, L. A., & Lachman, M. E. (2001). *Personality and Social Psychology Bulletin, 27,* 969–981.

Andreou, E. (2000). Bully/victim problems and their association with psychological constructs in 8- to 12-year-old Greek schoolchildren. *Aggressive Behavior, 26,* 49–58.

Angier, N. (2002, July 23). Why we're so nice: We're wired to cooperate. *The New York Times,* F1, F8.

Angier, N. (2003, July 8). Opposites attract? Not in real life. *The New York Times,* F1, F6.

Antonakis, J. (2001). *The validity of the transformational, transactional, and laissez-fair leadership model as measured by the Multifactor Leadership Questionnaire (MLQ 5X).* Unpublished doctoral dissertation.

Apanovitch, A. M., McCarthy, D., & Salovey, P. (2003). Using message framing to motivate HIV testing among low-income, ethnic minority women. *Health Psychology, 22,* 60–67.

Aquino, K., Reed, A., Thau, S., & Freeman, D. (2006). A grotesque and dark beauty: How moral identity and mechanisms of moral disengagement influence cognitive and emotional reactions to war. *Journal of Experimental Social Psychology, 43,* 385–392.

Archibald, F. S., Bartholomew, K., & Marx, R. (1995). Loneliness in early adolescence: A test of the cognitive discrepancy model of loneliness. *Personality and Social Psychology Bulletin, 21,* 296–301.

Argyle, M. (2001). *The psychology of happiness.* London: Routledge.

Aronson, E., & Mills, J. (1959). The effect of severity of initiation on liking for a group. *Journal of Abnormal and Social Psychology, 59,* 177–181.

Arriaga, X. B., Reed, J. T., Goodfriend, W., & Agnew, C. R. (2006). Relationship perceptions and persistence: Do fluctuations in perceived partner commitment undermine dating relationships? *Journal of Personality and Social Psychology, 91,* 1045–1065.

Aristotle. (1932). *The rhetoric* (L. Cooper, Trans.). New York: Appleton-Century-Crofts. (Original work published c. 330 B.C.)

Arkes, H. R., & Tetlock, P. E. (2004). Attributions of implicit prejudice, or "Would Jesse Jackson 'Fail' the Implicit Association Test?" *Psychological Inquiry, 15,* 257–278.

Armor, D. A., & Taylor, S. E. (2002). When predictions fail: The dilemma of unrealistic optimism. In T. Gilovich, D. Griffin, & D. Kahneman (Eds.), *Heuristics and biases: The psychology of intuitive judgment* (pp. 334–347). New York: Cambridge University Press.

Aron, A., & McLaughlin-Volpe, T. (2001). Including others in the self: Extensions to own and partner's group membership. In C. Sedikides & M. B. Brewer (Eds.), *Individual self, relational self, collective self* (pp. 89–108). Philadelphia: Psychology Press.

Aron, A., & Westbay, L. (1996). Dimensions of the prototype of love. *Journal of Personality and Social Psychology, 70,* 535–551.

Aron, A., Aron, E. N., & Allen, J. (1998). Motivations for unreciprocated love. *Personality and Social Psychology Bulletin, 24,* 787–796.

Aron, A., Paris, M., & Aron, E. N. (1995). Falling in love: Prospective studies of self-concept change. *Journal of Personality and Social Psychology, 69,* 1102–1112.

Aron, A., Dutton, D. G., Aron, E. N., & Iverson, A. (1989). Experiences of falling in love. *Journal of Social and Personal Relationships, 6,* 243–257.

Aronoff, J., Woike, B. A., & Hyman, L. M. (1992). Which are the stimuli in facial displays of anger and happiness? Configurational bases of emotion recognition. *Journal of Personality and Social Psychology, 62,* 1050–1066.

Aronson, J., Lustina, M. J., Good, C., Keough, K., Steele, C. M., & Brown, J. (1999). When white men can't do math: Necessary and sufficient factors in stereotype threat. *Journal of Experimental Social Psychology, 35,* 29–46.

Arriaga, X. B., & Agnew, C. R. (2001). Being committed: Affective, cognitive, and conative components of relationship commitment. *Personality and Social Psychology Bulletin, 27,* 1190–1203.

Arvey, R. D., Bouchard, T. J., Jr., Segal, N. L., & Abraham, L. M. (1989). Job satisfaction: Genetic and environmental components. *Journal of Applied Psychology, 74,* 187–192.

Arvey, R. D., McCall, P. B., Bouchard, T. J., Tabuman, P., & Cavanagh, M. A. (1994). Genetic influences on job satisfaction and work values. *Personality and Individuial Differences, 17,* 21-33.

Asch, S. (1946). Forming impressions of personality. *Journal of Abnormal and Social Psychology, 41,* 258–290.

Asch, S. E. (1951). Effects of group pressure upon the modification and distortion of judgment. In H. Guetzkow (Ed.), *Groups, leadership, and men.* Pittsburgh: Carnegie.

Asch, S. E. (1955). Opinions and social pressure. *Scientific American, 193*(5), 31–35.

Asch, S. E. (1956). Studies of independence and conformity: A minority of one against unanimous majority. *Psychological Monographs, 70* (Whole No. 416).

Asendorpf, J. B. (1992). A Brunswickean approach to trait continuity: Application to shyness. *Journal of Personality, 60,* 55–77.

Asher, S. R., & Paquette, J. A. (2003). Loneliness and peer relations in childhood. *Current Directions in Psychological Science, 12,* 75–78.

Ashmore, R. D., Deaux, K., & McLaughlin-Volpe, T. (2004). An organizing framework for collective identity: Articulation and significance of multidimensionality. *Psychological Bulletin, 130,* 80–114.

Ashmore, R. D., Solomon, M. R., & Longo, L. C. (1996). Thinking about fashion models' looks: A multidimensional approach to the structure of perceived physical attractiveness. *Personality and Social Psychology Bulletin, 22,* 1083–1104.

Aune, K. S., & Wong, N. C. H. (2002). Antecedents and consequences of adult play in romantic relationships. *Personal Relationships, 9,* 279–286.

Averill, J. R., & Boothroyd, P. (1977). On falling in love: Conformance with romantic ideal. *Motivation and Emotion, 1,* 235–247.

Avolio, B. J. (2007). Promoting more integrative strategies for leadership theory-building. *American Psychologist, 62,* 25–33.

Avolio, B. J. (1999). *Full leadership development: Building the vital forces in organizations.* Thousand Oaks, CA: Sage.

Avolia, B. J., & Bass, B. M. (2002) (Eds). *Developing potential across a full range of leadership.* Wahwah, NJ: Erlbaum.

Avolio, B. J., Bass, B. M., & Jung, D. (1999). Reexamining the components of transformational and transactional leadership using the Multifactor Leadership Questionnaire. *Journal of Occupational and Organizational Psychology, 7,* 441–462.

Azar, B. (1997, November). Defining the trait that makes us human. *APA Monitor, 1,* 15.

Azar, O. H. (2007). The social norm of tipping: A review. *Journal of Applied Social Psychology, 137,* 380–402.

Baddeley, A. D. (1990). *Human memory.* Boston: Allyn & Bacon.

Baker, N. V., Gregware, P. R., & Cassidy, M. A. (1999). Family killing fields: Honor rationales in the murder of women. *Violence Against Women, 5,* 164–184.

Baldwin, D. A. (2000). Interpersonal understanding fuels knowledge acquisition. *Current Directions in Psychological Science, 9,* 40–45.

Baldwin, M. W., Carrell, S. E., & Lopez, D. F. (1990). Priming relationship schemas: My advisor and the Pope are watching me from the back of my mind. *Journal of Experimental Social Psychology, 26,* 435–454.

Baldwin, M. W., & Holmes, J. G. (1987). Salient private audiences and awareness of the self. *Journal of Personality and Social Psychology, 52,* 1087–1098.

Banaji, M., & Hardin, C. (1996). Automatic stereotyping. *Psychological Science, 7,* 136–141.

Bandura, A. (1990). Selective activation and disengagement of moral control. *Journal of Social Issues, 46,* 27–46.

Bandura, A. (1997). *Self-efficacy: The exercise of control.* New York: W. H. Freeman.

Bandura, A. (1977). Self-efficacy: Toward a unifying theory of behavioral change. *Psychological Review, 84,* 191–215.

Bandura, A. (1999). Moral disengagement in the perpetration of inhumanities. *Personality and Social Psychology Review, 3,* 193–209.

Bandura, A., Ross, D., & Ross, S. (1963a). Imitation of film-mediated aggressive models. *Journal of Abnormal and Social Psychology, 66,* 3–11.

Bandura, A., Ross, D., & Ross, S. (1963b). Vicarious reinforcement and imitative learning. *Journal of Abnormal and Social Psychology, 67,* 601–607.

Bargh, J. A. (1999). The unbearable automaticity of being. *American Psychologist, 54,* 462–479.

Bargh, J. A., & Chartrand, T. L. (2000). Studying the mind in the middle: A practical guide to priming and automaticity research. In H. Reis & C. Judd (Eds.), *Handbook of research methods in social psychology* (pp. 253–285). New York: Cambridge University Press.

Bargh, J. A., Chen, M., & Burrows, L. (1996). Automaticity of social behavior: Direct effects of trait construct and stereotype activation on action. *Journal of Personality and Social Psychology, 71,* 230–234.

Bargh, J. A., Gollwitzer, P. M., Lee-Chai, A., Barndollar, K., & Trotschel, R. (2001). The automated will: Nonconscious activation and pursuit of behavioral goals. *Journal of Personality and Social Psychology, 18,* 1014–1027.

Bar-Heim, Y., Ziv, T., Lamy, D., & Hodes, R. M. (2006). Nature and nurture in own-race face processing. *Psychological Science, 17,* 159–163.

Baron, R. A. (1972). Aggression as as function of ambient temperature and prior anger arousal. *Journal of Personality and Social Psychology, 21,* 183-189.

Baron, R. A. (1989a). Applicant strategies during job interviews. In G. R. Ferris & R. W. Eder (Eds.), *The employment interview: Theory, research, and practice* (pp. 204–216). Newbury Park, CA: Sage.

Baron, R. A. (1989b). Personality and organizational conflict: The Type A behavior pattern and self-monitoring. *Organizational Behavior and Human Decision Processes, 44,* 281–297.

Baron, R. A. (1990). Attributions and organizational conflict. In S. Graha & V. Folkes (Eds.), *Attribution theory: Applications to achievement, mental health, and interpersonal conflict* (pp. 185–204). Hillsdale, NJ: Erlbaum.

Baron, R. A. (1993a). Effects of interviewers' moods and applicant qualifications on ratings of job applicants. *Journal of Applied Social Psychology, 23,* 254–271.

Baron, R. A. (1993b). Reducing aggression and conflict: The incompatible response approach, or why people who feel good usually won't be bad. In G. C. Brannigan & M. R. Merrens (Eds.), *The undaunted psychologist* (pp. 203–218). Philadelphia: Temple University Press.

Baron, R. A. (1993c). Criticism (informal negative feedback) as a source of perceived unfairness in organizations: Effects, mechanisms, and countermeasures. In R. Cropanzano (Ed.), *Justice in the workplace: Approaching fairness in human resource management* (pp. 155–170). Hillsdale, NJ: Erlbaum.

Baron, R. A. (1994). The physical environment of work settings: Effects of task performance, interpersonal relations, and job satisfaction. In M. Staw & L. L. Cummings (Eds.), *Research in organizational behavior* (Vol. 16, pp. 1–46). Greenwich, CT: JAI Press.

Baron, R. A. (1997). The sweet smell of helping: Effects of pleasant ambient fragrance on prosocial behavior in shopping malls. *Personality and Social Psychology Bulletin, 23,* 498–503.

Baron, R. A. (In press). The role of affect in the entrepreneurial process. *Academy of Management Journal.*

Baron, R. A., & Markman, G. D. (2004). Toward a process view of entrepreneurship: The changing impact of individual level variables across phases of new venture development. In M. A. Rahim, R. T. Golembiewski, & K. D. Mackenzie (Eds.), *Current topics in management* (Vol. 9). New Brunswick, NJ: Transaction Publishers.

Baron, R. A., & Richardson, D. R. (1994). *Human aggression* (2nd ed.). New York: Plenum.

Baron, R. A., & Shane, S. A. (2007). *Entrepreneurship: A process perspective* (2nd ed.). Cincinnati: Southwest-Thomson.

Baron, R. A., & Thomley, J. (1994). A whiff of reality: Positive affect as a potential mediator of the effects of pleasant fragrances on task performance and helping. *Environment and Behavior, 26,* 766–784.

Baron, R. A., Neuman, J. H., & Geddes, D. (1999). Social and personal determinants of workplace aggression: Evidence for the impact of perceived injustice and the Type A behavior pattern. *Aggressive Behavior, 25,* 4, 281–296.

Baron, R. A., Russell, G. W., & Arms, R. L. (1985). Negative ions and behavior: Impact on mood, memory, and aggression among Type A and Type B persons. *Journal of Personality and Social Psychology, 48,* 746–754.

Baron, R. S. (1986). Distraction/conflict theory: Progress and problems. In L. Berkwoitz (Ed.), *Advances in experimental social psychology* (Vol. 19, pp. 1–40). Orlando: Academic Press.

Baron, R. S., Vandello, U. A., & Brunsman, B. (1996). The forgotten variable in conformity research: Impact of task importance on social influence. *Journal of Personality and Social Psychology, 71,* 915–927.

Barrick, M. R., Stewart, G. L., & Piotrowski, M. (2002). Personality and job performance: Test of the mediating effects of motivation among sales representatives. *Journal of Applied Psychology, 87,* 43–51.

Barsky, A., & Kaplan, S. A. (2007). If you feel bad, it's unfair: A quantitative synthesis of affect and organizational justice perceptions. *Journal of Applied Psychology, 92,* 286–295.

Bar-Tal, D. (1990). Causes and consequences of delegitimization: Models of conflict and ethnocentrism. *Journal of Social Issues, 46,* 65–81.

Bar-Tal, D. (2003). Collective memory of physical violence: Its contribution to the culture of violence. In E. Cairns & M. D. Roe (Eds.), *The role of memory in ethnic conflict* (pp. 77–93). New York: Palgrave Macmillan.

Bartholomew, K., & Horowitz, L. M. (1991). Attachment styles among young adults: A test of a four category model. *Journal of Personality and Social Psychology, 61,* 226–244.

Bartholow, B. D., Bushman, B. J., & Sestir, M. A. (2006). Chronic violent video game exposure and desensitization to violence: Behavioral and event-related brain potential data. *Journal of Experimental Social Psychology, 42,* 532–539.

Bartholow, B. D., Dickter, C. L., & Sestir, M. A. (2006). Stereotype activation and control of race bias: Cognitive control of inhibition and its impairment by alcohol. *Journal of Personality and Social Psychology, 90,* 272–287.

Bartholow, B. D., & Heinz, A. (2006). Alcohol and aggression without consumption: Alcohol cues, aggressive thoughts, and hostile perception bias. *Psychological Science, 17,* 30–37.

Bartholow, B. D., Pearson, M. A., Gratton, G., & Fabiani, M. (2003). Effects of alcohol on person perception: A social cognitive neuroscience approach. *Journal of Personality and Social Psychology, 85,* 627–638.

Bass, B. M., Avolio, B. J., Jung, D. I., & Berson, Y. (2003). Predicting unit performance by assessing transformational and transactional leadership. *Journal of Applied Psychology, 88,* 207–218.

Bassili, J. N. (2003). The minority slowness effect: Subtle inhibitions in the expression of views not shared by others. *Journal of Personality and Social Psychology, 84,* 261–276.

Batson, C. D., & Oleson, K. C. (1991). Current status of the empathy–altruism hypothesis. In M. S. Clark (Ed.), *Prosocial behavior* (pp. 62–85). Newbury Park, CA: Sage.

Batson, C. D., Early, S., & Salvarani, G. (1997). Perspective taking: Imagining how another feels versus imagining how you would feel. *Personality and Social Psychology Bulletin, 23,* 751–758.

Batson, C. D., Kobrynowicz, D., Dinnerstein, J. L., Kampf, H.C., & Wilson, A. D. (1997). In a very different voice: Unmasking moral hypocrisy. *Journal of Personality and Social Psychology, 72,* 1335-1348.

Batson, C. D., & Thompson, E. R. (2001). Why don't moral people act morally? Motivational considerations. *Current Directions in Psychological Science, 10,* 54–57.

Batson, C. D., Thompson, E. R., & Chen, H. (2002). Moral hypocrisy: Addressing some alternatives. *Journal of Personality and Social Psychology, 83,* 330–339.

Batson, C. D., Tsang, J., & Thompson, E. R. (2000). *Weakness of will: Counting the cost of being moral.* Unpublished manuscript, University of Kansas, Lawrence.

Batson, C. D., Klein, T. R., Highberger, L., & Shaw, L. L. (1995). Immorality from empathy-induced altruism: When compassion and justice conflict. *Journal of Personality and Social Psychology, 68,* 1042–1054.

Batson, C. D., Duncan, B. D., Ackerman, P., Buckley, T., & Birch, K. (1981). Is empathic emotion a source of altruistic motivation? *Journal of Personality and Social Psychology, 40,* 290–302.

Batson, C. D., O'Quin, K., Fultz, J., Vanderplas, M., & Isen, A. M. (1983). Influence of self-reported distress and empathy on egoistic versus altruistic motivation to help. *Journal of Personality and Social Psychology, 45,* 706–718.

Batson, C. D., Thompson, E. R., Seuferling, G., Whitney, H., & Strongman, J. A. (1999). Moral hypocrisy: Appearing moral to oneself without being so. *Journal of Personality and Social Psychology, 77,* 525–537.

Batson, C. D., Batson, J. G., Todd, R. M., Brummett, B. H., Shaw, L. L., & Aldeguer, C. M. R. (1995). Empathy and the collective good: Caring for one of the others in a social dilemma. *Journal of Personality and Social Psychology, 68,* 619–631.

Batson, C. D., Ahmed, N., Yin, J., Bedell, S. J., Johnson, J. W., Templin, C. M., & Whiteside, A. (1999). Two threats to the common good: Self-interested egoism and empathy-induced altruism. *Personality and Social Psychology Bulletin, 25,* 3–16.

Batson, C. D., Lishner, D. A., Carpenter, A., Dulin, L., Harjusola-Webb, S., Stocks, E. L., Gale, S., Hassan, O., & Sampat, B. (2003). ". . . As you would have them do unto you.": Does imagining yourself in the other's place stimulate moral action? *Personality and Social Psychology Bulletin, 29,* 1190–1201.

Baum, A. (1994). Behavioral, biological, and environmental interactions in disease processes. In S. Blumenthal, K. Matthews, & S. Weiss (Eds.), *New research frontiers in behavioral medicine: Proceedings of the national conference* (p. 62). Washington, DC: NIH Publications.

Baumeister, R. F. (1991). *Escaping the self.* New York: Basic Books.

Baumeister, R. F. (1997). *Evil: Inside human violence and cruelty.* New York: W.H. Freeman.

Baumeister, R. F. (1998). The self. In D. T. Gilbert, S. T. Fiske, & G. Lindzey (Eds.), *Handbook of social psychology* (4th ed., Vol. 1, pp. 680–740). New York: McGraw-Hill.

Baumeister, R. F. (2005). *The cultural animal: Human nature, meaning, and social life.* New York: Oxford University Press.

Baumeister, R. F., & Leary, M. R. (1995). The need to belong: Desire for interpersonal attachments as a fundamental human motivation. *Psychological Bulletin, 117,* 497–529.

Baumeister, R. F., & Twenge, J. M. (2003). The social self. In T. Millon & M. J. Lerner (Eds.), *Handbook of psychology: Personality and social psychology.* (Vol. 5, pp. 327–352). New York: John Wiley.

Baumeister, R. F., Twenge, J. M., & Nuss, C. K. (2002). Effects of social exclusion on cognitive processes: Anticipated aloneness reduces intelligent thought. *Journal of Personality and Social Psychology, 83,* 817–827.

Baumeister, R. F., Campbell, D. J., Krueger, J. I., & Vohs, K. D. (2003). Does high self-esteem cause better performance, interpersonal success, happiness, or healthier lifestyles? *Psychological Science in the Public Interest, 4,* 1–44.

Baumeister, R. F., Campbell, J. D., Krueger, J. I., & Vohs, K. D. (2005). Exploding the self-esteem myth. *Scientific American, 292,* 84–92.

Baxter, L. A. (1990). Dialectical contradictions in relationship development. *Journal of Social and Personal Relationships, 7,* 69–88.

BBC News. (2004). Quarter of students cheating. Retrieved March 12, 2007 from http://news.bbc.co.uk/1/hi/education.

Beall, A. E., & Sternberg, R. J. (1995). The social construction of love. *Journal of Social and Personal Relationships, 12,* 417–438.

Beauvois, J. L., & Dubois, N. (1988). The norm of internality in the explanation of psychological events. *European Journal of Social Psychology, 18,* 299–316.

Bell, B. (1993). Emotional loneliness and the perceived similarity of one's ideas and interests. *Journal of Social Behavior and Personality, 8,* 273–280.

Bell, B. E. (1995). Judgments of the attributes of a student who is talkative versus a student who is quiet in class. *Journal of Social Behavior and Personality, 10,* 827–832.

Bell, P. A. (1992). In defense of the negative affect escape model of heat and aggression. *Psychological Bulletin, 111,* 342–346.

Bell, R. A. (1991). Gender, friendship network density, and loneliness. *Journal of Social Behavior and Personality, 6,* 45–56.

Benjamin, E. (1998, January 14). Storm brings out good, bad and greedy. Albany *Times Union,* pp. A1, A6.

Benoit, W. L. (1998). Forewarning and persuasion. In M. Allen & R. Priess (Eds.), *Persuasion: Advances through meta-analysis* (pp. 159–184). Cresskill, NJ: Hampton Press.

Ben-Porath, D. D. (2002). Stigmatization of individuals who receive psychotherapy: An interaction between help-seeking behavior and the presence of depression. *Journal of Social and Clinical Psychology, 21,* 400–413.

Benson, P. L., Karabenick, S. A., & Lerner, R. M. (1976). Pretty pleases: The effects of physical attractiveness, race, and sex on receiving help. *Journal of Experimental Social Psychology, 12,* 409–415.

Berg, J. H., & McQuinn, R. D. (1989). Loneliness and aspects of social support networks. *Journal of Social and Personal Relationships, 6,* 359–372.

Berkowitz, L. (1989). Frustration-aggression hypothesis: Examination and reformulation. *Psychological Bulletin, 106,* 59–73.

Berkowitz, L. (1993). *Aggression: Its causes, consequences, and control.* New York: McGraw-Hill.

Bernieri, F. J., Gillis, J. S., Davis, J. M., & Grahe, J. E. (1996). Dyad rapport and the accuracy of its judgment across situations: A lens model analysis. *Journal of Personality and Social Psychology, 71,* 110–129.

Berry, D. S., & Hansen, J. S. (1996). Positive affect, negative affect, and social interaction. *Journal of Personality and Social Psychology, 71,* 796–809.

Berscheid, E., & Hatfield, E. (1974). A little bit about love. In T. L. Huston (Ed.), *Foundations of interpersonal attraction* (pp. 355–381). New York: Academic Press.

Berscheid, E., & Reis, H. T. (1998). Attraction and close relationships. In D. T. Gilbert, S. T. Fiske, & G. Lindzey (Eds.), *The handbook of social psychology* (4th ed., Vol. 2, pp. 193–281). New York: McGraw-Hill.

Bersoff, D. M. (1999). Why good people sometimes do bad things: Motivated reasoning and unethical behavior. *Personality and Social Bulletin, 25,* 28–39.

Bettencourt, B. A., & Miller, N. (1996). Gender differences in aggression as a function of provocation: A meta-analysis. *Psychological Bulletin, 119,* 422–447.

Bettencourt, B. A., Molix, L., Talley, A. E., & Sheldon, K. M. (2006). Psychological need satisfaction through social roles. In T. Postmes & J. Jetten (Eds.), *Individuality and the group: Advances in social identity* (pp. 196–214). London: Sage.

Bierhoff, H. W., Klein, R., & Kramp, P. (1991). Evidence for the altruistic personality from data on accident research. *Journal of Personality, 59,* 263–280.

Biernat, M. (2005). *Standards and expectancies: Contrast and assimilation in judgments of self and others.* New York: Psychology Press.

Biernat, M., & Thompson, E. R. (2002). Shifting standards and contextual variation in stereotyping. *European Review of Social Psychology, 12,* 103–137.

Biernat, M., Eidelman, S., & Fuegan, K. (2002). Judgment standards and the social self: A shifting standards perspective. In J. P. Forgas & K. D. Williams (Eds.), *The social self: Cognitive, interpersonal, and intergroup perspectives* (pp. 51–72). Philadelphia: Psychology Press.

Bies, R. J., Shapiro, D. L., & Cummings, L. L. (1988). Causal accounts and managing organizational conflict: Is it enough to say it's not my fault? *Communication Research, 15,* 381–399.

Birchmeier, Z., Joinson, A. N., & Dietz-Uhler, B. (2005). Storming and forming a normative response to a deception revealed online. *Social Science Computer Review, 23,* 108–121.

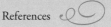

Bizer, G. Y., Tormala, Z. L., Rucker, D. D., & Petty, R. E. (2006). Memory-based versus on-line processing: Implications for attitude strength. *Journal of Experimental Social Psychology, 42,* 646–653.

Björkqvist, K., Lagerspetz, K. M., & Kaukiainen, A. (1992). Do girls manipulate and boys fight? Developmental trends in regard to direct and indirect aggression. *Aggressive Behavior, 18,* 117–127.

Björkqvist, K., Österman, K., & Hjelt-Bäck, M. (1994a). Aggression among university employees. *Aggressive Behavior, 20,* 173–184.

Björkqvist, K., Österman, K., & Lagerspetz, K. M. J. (1994b). Sex differences in covert aggression among adults. *Aggressive Behavior, 20,* 27–33.

Blader, S. L., & Tyler, T. R. (2005). How can theories of organizational justice explain the effects of fairness? In J. Greenberg & J. A. Colquitt (Eds.), *Handbook of organizational justice* (pp. 329–354). Mahwah, NJ: Lawrence Erlbaum.

Blair, I. V. (2002). The malleability of automatic stereotypes and prejudice. *Personality and Social Psychology Review, 6,* 242–261.

Blazer, D. G., Kessler, R. C., McGonagle, K. A., & Swartz, M. S. (1994). The prevalence and distribution of major depression in a national community sample: The National Comorbidity Survey. *American Journal of Psychiatry, 151,* 979–986.

Bless, H. (2001). The consequences of mood on the processing of social information. In A. Tesser & N. Schwarz (Eds.), *Blackwell handbook in social psychology* (pp. 391–412). Oxford, England: Blackwell Publishers.

Bobo, L. (1983). Whites' opposition to busing: Symbolic racism or realistic group conflict? *Journal of Personality and Social Psychology, 45,* 1196–1210.

Bodenhausen, G. F. (1993). Emotion, arousal, and stereotypic judgment: A heuristic model of affect and stereotyping. In D. Mackie & D. Hamilton (Eds.), *Affect, cognition, and stereotyping: Intergroup processes in intergroup perception* (pp. 13–37). San Diego, CA: Academic Press.

Boer, F., Westenberg, M., McHale, S. M., Updegraff, K. A., & Stocker, C. M. (1997). The factorial structure of the Sibling Relationship Inventory (SRI) in American and Dutch samples. *Journal of Social and Personal Relationships, 14,* 851–859.

Bogard, M. (1990). Why we need gender to understand human violence. *Journal of Interpersonal Violence, 5,* 132–135.

Bohner, G., Jarvis, C. I., Eyssel, F., & Siebler, F. (In press). The causal impact of rape myth acceptance on men's rape proclivity: Comparing sexually coercive and noncoercive men. *European Journal of Social Psychology.*

Bohner, G., Siebler, F., & Schmelcher, J. (2006). Social norms and the likelihood of raping: Perceived rape myth acceptance of others affects men's rape proclivity. *Personality and Social Psychology Bulletin, 32,* 286–297.

Bolino, M. C., & Turnley, W. H. (1999). Measuring impression management in organizations: A scale development based on the Jones and Pittman taxonomy. *Organizational Research Methods, 2,* 187–206.

Bond, M. H. (1996). Chinese values. In M. H. Bond (Ed.), *The handbook of Chinese psychology* (pp. 208–226). Oxford, England: Oxford University Press.

Bond, R., & Smith, P. B. (1996). Culture and conformity: A meta-analysis of studies using Asch's (1952b, 1956) line judgment task. *Psychological Bulletin, 119,* 111–137.

Bornstein, R. F., & D'Agostino, P. R. (1992). Stimulus recognition and the mere exposure effect. *Journal of Personality and Social Psychology, 63,* 545–552.

Bossard, J. H. S. (1932). Residential propinquity as a factor in marriage selection. *American Journal of Sociology, 38,* 219–224.

Bosson, J. K., Haymovitz, E. L., & Pinel, E. C. (2004). When saying and doing diverge: The effects of stereotype threat on self-reported versus non-verbal anxiety. *Journal of Experimental Social Psychology, 40,* 247–255.

Botha, M. (1990). Television exposure and aggression among adolescents: A follow-up study over 5 years. *Aggressive Behavior, 16,* 361–380.

Bothwell, R. K., Pigott, M. A., Foley, L. A., & McFatter, R. M. (2006). Racial bias in juridic judgment at private and public levels. *Journal of Applied Social Psychology, 36,* 2134–2149.

Bowlby, J. (1969). *Attachment and loss: Vol. 1. Attachment.* New York: Basic Books.

Bowlby, J. (1973). *Attachment and loss: Vol. 2. Separation.* New York: Basic Books.

Bowlby, J. (1982). *Attachment and loss: Vol. 1. Attachment* (2nd ed.). New York: Basic Books.

Branscombe, N. R. (2004). A social psychological process perspective on collective guilt. In N. R. Branscombe & B. Doosje (Eds.), *Collective guilt: International perspectives* (pp. 320–334). New York: Cambridge University Press.

Branscombe, N. R., & Miron, A. M. (2004). Interpreting the ingroup's negative actions toward another group: Emotional reactions to appraised harm. In L. Z. Tiedens & C. W. Leach (Eds.), *The social life of emotions* (pp. 314–335). New York: Cambridge University Press.

Branscombe, N. R., & Wann, D. L. (1994). Collective self-esteem consequences of outgroup derogation when a valued social identity is on trial. *European Journal of Social Psychology, 24,* 641–657.

Branscombe, N. R., Schmitt, M. T., & Harvey, R. D. (1999). Perceiving pervasive discrimination among African-Americans: Implications for group identification and well-being. *Journal of Personality and Social Psychology, 77,* 135–149.

Branscombe, N. R., Schmitt, M. T., & Schiffhauer, K. (2007). Racial attitudes in response to thoughts of White privilege. *European Journal of Social Psychology, 37,* 203–215.

Branscombe, N. R , Slugoski, B., & Kappen, D. M. (2004). The measurement of collective guilt: What it is and what it is not. In N. R. Branscombe & B. Doosje (Eds.), *Collective guilt: International perspectives* (pp. 16–34). New York: Cambridge University Press.

Branscombe, N. R., Wann, D. L., Noel, J. G., & Coleman, J. (1993). Ingroup or outgroup extremity: Importance of the threatened identity. *Personality and Social Psychology Bulletin, 19,* 381–388.

Brauer, M. (2001). Intergroup perception in the social context: The effects of social status and group membership on perceived out-group homogeneity and ethnocentrism. *Journal of Experimental Social Psychology, 37,* 15–31.

Braza, P., Braza, F., Carreras, M. R., & Munoz, J. M. (1993). Measuring the social ability of preschool children. *Social Behavior and Personality, 21,* 145–158.

Brehm, J. W. (1966). *A theory of psychological reactance.* New York: Academic Press.

Brennan, K. A., & Bosson, J. K. (1998). Attachment-style differences in attitudes toward and reactions to feedback from romantic partners: An exploration of the relational bases of self-esteem. *Personality and Social Psychology Bulletin, 24,* 699–714.

Brewer, M. B., & Brown, R. (1998). Intergroup relations. In D. T. Gilbert, S. T. Fiske, & G. Lindzey (Eds.), *The handbook of social psychology* (4th ed., Vol. 2, pp. 554–594). New York: McGraw-Hill.

Brewer, M. B., & Caporael, L. R. (2006). An evolutionary perspective on social identity: Revisiting groups. In M. Schaller, J. A. Simpson & D. T. Kenrick (Eds.), *Evolution and social psychology: Frontiers of social psychology* (pp. 143–161). Madison, CT: Psychosocial Press.

Brickner, M., Harkins, S., & Ostrom, T. (1986). Personal involvement: Thought provoking implications for social loafing. *Journal of Personality and Social Psychology, 51,* 763–769.

Bringle, R. G., & Winnick, T. A. (1992, October). *The nature of unrequited love.* Paper presented at the first Asian Conference in Psychology, Singapore.

Brinol, P., Rucker, D. D., Tormala, Z. L., & Petty, R. E. (2004). Individual differences in resistance to persuasion: The role of beliefs and meta-beliefs. In E. S. Knowles & J. A. Linn (Eds.), *Resistance to persuasion* (pp. 83–104). Mahwah, NJ: Lawrence Erlbaum.

Brockner, J., Konovsky, M., Cooper-Schneider, R., Folger, R., Martin, C., & Bies, R. J. (1994). Interactive effects of procedural justice and outcome negativity on victims and survivors of job loss. *Academy of Management Journal, 37,* 397–409.

Brockner, J. M., & Wiesenfeld, B. M. (1996). An integrative framework for explaining reactions to decisions: Interactive effects of outcomes and procedures. *Psychological Bulletin, 120,* 189–208.

Broemer, P. (2004). Ease of imagination moderates reactions to differently framed health messages. *European Journal of Social Psychology, 34,* 103–119.

Brooks-Gunn, J., & Lewis, M. (1981). Infant social perception: Responses to pictures of parents and strangers. *Developmental Psychology, 17,* 647–649.

Brothers, L. (1990). The neural basis of primate social communication. *Motivation and Emotion, 14,* 81–91.

Brown, J. D. (1991). Staying fit and staying well: Physical fitness as a moderator of life stress. *Journal of Personality and Social Psychology, 60,* 555–561.

Brown, J. D., & Rogers, R. J. (1991). Self-serving attributions: The role of physiological arousal. *Personality and Social Psychology Bulletin, 17,* 501–506.

Brown, L. M. (1998). Ethnic stigma as a contextual experience: Possible selves perspective. *Personality and Social Psychology Bulletin, 24,* 165–172.

Brown, R. (2000). Social identity theory: Past achievements, current problems and future challenges. *European Journal of Social Psychology, 30,* 745–778.

Brown, R. P., Charnsangavej, T., Keough, K. A., Newman, M. L., & Rentfrow, P. J. (2000). Putting the "affirm" into affirmative action: Preferential selection and academic performance. *Journal of Personality and Social Psychology, 79,* 736–747.

Brown, S. L., Nesse, R. M., Vinokur, A. D., & Smith, D. M. (2003). Providing social support may be more beneficial than receiving it. *Psychological Science, 14,* 320–327.

Brown, S. P. (1996). A meta-analysis and review of organizational research on job involvement. *Psychological Bulletin, 120,* 235–255.

Bryan, J. H., & Test, M. A. (1967). Models and helping: Naturalistic studies in aiding behavior. *Journal of Personality and Social Psychology, 6,* 400–407.

Budesheim, T. L., & Bonnelle, K. (1998). The use of abstract trait knowledge and behavioral exemplars in causal explanations of behavior. *Personality and Social Psychology Bulletin, 24,* 575–587.

Budson, A. E., & Price, B. H. (2005). Memory dysfunction. *New England Journal of Medicine, 352,* 692–699.

Buehler, R., & Griffin, D. (1994). Change-of-meaning effects in conformity and dissent: Observing construal processes over time. *Journal of Personality and Social Psychology, 67,* 984–996.

Buehler, R., Griffin, D., & MacDonald, H. (1997). The role of motivated reasoning in optimistic time predictions. *Personality and Social Psychology Bulletin, 23,* 238–247.

Buehler, R., Griffin, D., & Ross, M. (1994). Exploring the "planning fallacy": Why people underestimate their task completion times. *Journal of Personality and Social Psychology, 67,* 366–381.

Burger, J. M. (1986). Increasing compliance by improving the deal: The that's-not-all technique. *Journal of Personality and Social Psychology, 51,* 277–283.

Burger, J. M. (1992). *Desire for control: Personality, social, and clinical perspectives.* New York: Plenum.

Burger, J. M. (1995). Individual differences in preference for solitude. *Journal of Research in Personality, 29,* 85–108.

Burger, J. M., & Cornelius, T. (2003). Raising the price of agreement: Public commitment and the low-ball compliance procedure. *Journal of Applied Social Psychology, 33,* 923–934.

Burger, J. M., Messian, N., Patel, S., del Pardo, A., & Anderson, C. (2004). What a coincidence! The effects of incidental similarity on compliance. *Personality and Social Psychology Bulletin, 30,* 35–43.

Burnstein, E. (1983). Persuasion as argument processing. In M. Brandstatter, J. H. Davis, & G. Stocker-Kriechgauer (Eds.), *Group decision processes.* London: Academic Press.

Burnstein, E., Crandall, C., & Kitayama, S. (1994). Some neo-Darwinian rules for altruism: Weighing cues for inclusive fitness as a function of the biological importance of the decision. *Journal of Personality and Social Psychology, 67,* 773–789.

Burrus, J., & Roese, N. J. (2006). Long ago it was meant to be: The interplay between time, construal, and fate beliefs. *Personality and Social Psychology Bulletin, 32,* 1050–1058.

Bushman, B. J. (1988). The effects of apparel on compliance: A field experiment with a female authority figure. *Personality and Social Psychology Bulletin, 14,* 459–467.

Bushman, B. J. (1998). Effects of television violence on memory for commercial messages. *Journal of Experimental Psychology: Applied, 4,* 1–17.

Bushman, B. J. (2001). Does venting anger feed or extinguish the flame? Catharsis, rumination, distraction, anger, and aggressive responding. Manuscript under review.

Bushman, B. J., & Anderson, C. A. (2002). Violent video games and hostile expectations: A test of the general aggression model. *Personality and Social Psychology Bulletin, 24,* 949–960 and *Social Psychology Bulletin, 28,* 1679–1686.

Bushman, B. J., & Baumeister, R. F. (1998). Threatened egotism, narcissism, self-esteem, and direct and displaced aggression: Does self-love or self-hate lead to violence? *Journal of Personality and Social Psychology, 75,* 219–229.

Bushman, B. J., & Cooper, H. M. (1990). Effects of alcohol on human aggression: An integrative research review. *Psychological Bulletin, 107,* 341–354.

Bushman, B. J., & Huesmann, L. R. (2001). Effects of televised violence on aggression. In D. Singer & J. Singer (Eds.), *Handbook of children and the media* (pp. 223–254). Thousands Oaks, CA: Sage.

Bushman, B. J., Baumeister, R. F., & Stack, A. D. (1999). Catharsis messages and anger-reducing activities. *Journal of Personality and Social Psychology, 76,* 367–376.

Buss, D. M. (1994). The strategies of human mating. *American Scientist, 82,* 238–249.

Buss, D. M. (1998). *Evolutionary psychology.* Boston: Allyn & Bacon.

Buss, D. M. (2004). *Evolutionary psychology: The new science of the mind.* (2nd ed.). Boston: Allyn and Bacon.

Buss, D. M., & Shackelford, T. K. (1997). From vigilance to violence: Mate retention tactics in married couples. *Journal of Personality and Social Psychology, 72,* 346–361.

Buss, D. M., Larsen, R. J., Westen, D., & Semmelroth, J. (1992). Sex differences in jealousy: Evolution, physiology, and psychology. *Psychological Science, 3,* 251–255.

Buston, P. M., & Emlen, S. T. (2003). Cognitive processes underlying human mate choice: The relationship between self-perception and mate preferences in Western society. *The Proceedings of the National Academy of Sciences, 100,* 8805–8810.

Buunk, B. P., & Prins, K. S. (1998). Loneliness, exchange orientation, and reciprocity in friendships. *Personal Relationships, 5,* 1–14.

Buunk, B. P., Dukstra, P., Fetchenhauer, D., & Kenrick, D. T. (2002). Age and gender differences in mate selection criteria for various involvement levels. *Personal Relationships, 9,* 271–278.

Byrne, B. M., & Shavelson, R. J. (1996). On the structure of social self-concept for pre-, early, and late adolescents: A test of the Shavelson, Hubner, and Stanton (1976) model. *Journal of Personality and Social Psychology, 70,* 599–613.

Byrne, D. (1961a). The influence of propinquity and opportunities for interaction on classroom relationships. *Human Relations, 14,* 63–69.

Byrne, D. (1961b). Interpersonal attraction and attitude similarity. *Journal of Abnormal and Social Psychology, 62,* 713–715.

Byrne, D. (1971). *The attraction paradigm.* New York: Academic Press.

Byrne, D. (1991). Perspectives on research classics: This ugly duckling has yet to become a swan. *Contemporary Social Psychology, 15,* 84–85.

Byrne, D. (1992). The transition from controlled laboratory experimentation to less controlled settings: Surprise! Additional variables are operative. *Communication Monographs, 59,* 190–198.

Byrne, D. (1997a). An overview (and underview) of research and theory within the attraction paradigm. *Journal of Social and Personal Relationships, 14,* 417–431.

Byrne, D., & Blaylock, B. (1963). Similarity and assumed similarity of attitudes among husbands and wives. *Journal of Abnormal and Social Psychology, 67,* 636–640.

Byrne, D., & Nelson, D. (1965). Attraction as a linear function of proportion of positive reinforcements. *Journal of Personality and Social Psychology, 1,* 659–663.

Byrne, R. L. (2001, June 1). *Good safety advice.* Internet.

Cacioppo, J. T., Gardner, W. L., & Berntson, G. G. (1997). Beyond bipolar conceptualizations and measures: The case of attitudes and evaluative space. *Personality and Social Psychology Review, 1,* 3–25.

Cacioppo, J. T., Hawkley, L. C., & Berntson, G. G. (2003). The anatomy of loneliness. *Current Directions in Psychological Science, 12,* 71–74.

Cacioppo, J. T., Berntson, G. G., Long, T. S., Norris, C. J., Rickhett, E., & Nusbaum, H. (2003). Just because you're imaging the brain doesn't mean you can stop using your head: A primer and set of first principles. *Journal of Personality and Social Psychology, 85,* 650–661.

Cacioppo, J. T., Hawkley, L. C., Berntson, G. G., Ernst, J. M., Gibbs, A. C., Stickgold, R., & Hobson, J. A. (2002). Do lonely days invade the nights? Potential social modulation of sleep efficiency. *Psychological Science, 13,* 384–387.

Cadenhead, A. C., & Richman, C. L. (1996). The effects of interpersonal trust and group status on prosocial and aggressive behaviors. *Social Behavior and Personality, 24,* 169–184.

Callahan, D. (2004). *The cheating culture: Why more Americans are doing wrong to get ahead.* Orlando, FL: Harcourt.

Callan, V. J. (1993). Subordinate manager communication in different sex-dyads: Consequences for job satisfaction. *Journal of Occupational and Organizational Psychology, 66,* 13–27.

Campbell, D. T. (1958). Common fate, similarity, and other indices of the status of aggregates of persons as social entities. *Behavioral Science, 4,* 14–25.

Campbell, L., Simpson, J. A., Kashy, D. A., & Fletcher, G. J. O. (2001). Ideal standards, the self, and flexibility of ideals in close relationships. *Personality and Social Psychology Bulletin, 27,* 447–462.

Campbell, W. K. (1999). Narcissism and romantic attraction. *Journal of Personality and Social Psychology, 77,* 1254–1270.

Campbell, W. K., & Foster, C. A. (2002). Narcissism and commitment to romantic relationships: An investment model analysis. *Personality and Social Psychology Bulletin, 28,* 484–495.

Campos, B., Keltner, D., Beck, J. M., Gonzaga, G. C., & John, O. P. (2007). Culture and teasing: The relational benefits of reduced desire for positive self-differentiation. *Personality and Social Psychology Bulletin, 33,* 3–16.

Cann, A., Calhoun, L. G., & Banks, J. S. (1995). On the role of humor appreciation in interpersonal attraction: It's no joking matter. *Humor: International Journal of Humor Research.*

Caplan, S. E. (2005). A social skill account of problematic internet use. *Journal of Communication, 55,* 721–736.

Caprara, G. V., Barbaranelli, C., Pastorelli, C., Bandura, A., & Zimbardo, P. G. (2000). Prosocial foundations of children's academic achievement. *Psychological Science, 11,* 302–306.

Carey, M. P., Morrison-Beedy, D., & Johnson, B. T. (1997). The HIV-Knowledge Questionnaire: Development and evaluation of a reliable, valid, and practical self-administered questionnaire. *AIDS and Behavior, 1,* 61–74.

Carlsmith, K. M., Darley, J. M., & Robinson, P. H. (2002). Why do we punish? Deterrence and just deserts as motives for punishment. *Journal of Personality and Social Psychology, 83,* 284–299.

Carlson, K. A., & Russo, J. E. (2001). Biased interpretation of evidence by mock jurors: A meta-analysis. *Journal of Experimental Psychology: Applied, 7,* 91–103.

Carpenter, S. (2001a, July/August). They're positively inspiring. *Monitor on Psychology,* 74–76.

Carvallo, M., & Gabriel, S. (2006). No man is an island: The need to belong and dismissing avoidant attachment style. *Personality and Social Psychology Bulletin, 32,* 697–709.

Carver, C. S., & Glass, D. C. (1978). Coronary-prone behavior pattern and interpersonal aggression. *Journal of Personality and Social Psychology, 376,* 361–366.

Cash, T. F., & Duncan, N. C. (1984). Physical attractiveness stereotyping among black American college students. *Journal of Social Psychology, 122,* 71–77.

Cashdan, E. (1998). Are men more competitive than women? *British Journal of Social Psychology, 37,* 213–229.

Caspi, A., & Herbener, E. S. (1990). Continuity and change: Assortative marriage and the consistency of personality in adulthood. *Journal of Personality and Social Psychology, 58,* 250–258.

Caspi, A., Herbener, E. S., & Ozer, D. J. (1992). Shared experiences and the similarity of personalities: A longitudinal study of married couples. *Journal of Personality and Social Psychology, 62,* 281–291.

Castano, E., Paladino M. P., Coull, A., & Yzerbyt, V. Y. (2002). Protecting the ingroup stereotype: Ingroup identification and the management of deviant ingroup members. *British Journal of Social Psychology, 41,* 365–385.

Castelli, L., Zogmaister, C., & Smith, E. R. (2004). On the automatic evaluation of social exemplars. *Journal of Personality and Social Psychology, 86,* 373–387.

Catalyst (2002). *2002 Catalyst census of women corporate officers and top earners of the Fortune 500.* New York: Catalyst.

Caughlin, J. P., Huston, T. L., & Houts, R. M. (2000). How does personality matter in marriage? An examination of trait anxiety, interpersonal negativity, and marital satisfaction. *Journal of Personality and Social Psychology, 78,* 326–336.

Center for American Women and Politics (2005). *Sex differences in voter turnout.* Retrieved June 28, 2007 from the Eagleton Institute of Politics, Rutgers University Web site: http://www.cawp.rutgers.edu/Facts/Elections/Womensvote2004.html

Cesario, J., Plaks, J. E., & Higgins, E. (2006). Automatic social behavior as motivated preparation to interact. *Journal of Personality and Social Psychology, 90,* 893–910.

Chaiken, S., & Trope, Y. (1999). *Dual-process theories in social psychology.* New York: Guilford Press.

Chaiken, S., Liberman, A., & Eagly, A. H. (1989). Heuristic and systematic processing within and beyond persuasion context. In J. S. Uleman & J. A. Bargh (Eds.), *Unintended thought* (pp. 212–252). New York: Guilford.

Chajut, E., & Algom, D. (2003). Selective attention improves under stress: Implications for theories of social cognition. *Journal of Personality and Social Psychology, 85,* 231–248.

Chaplin, W. F., Phillips, J. B., Brown, J. D., Clanton, N. R., & Stein, J. L. (2000). Handshaking, gender, personality, and first impressions. *Journal of Personality and Social Psychology, 79,* 110–117.

Chartrand, T. L., & Bargh, J. A. (1999). The Chameleon effect: The perception-behavior link and social interaction. *Journal of Personality and Social Psychology, 76,* 893–910.

Chartrand, T. L., Maddux, W. W., & Lakin, J. L. (2004). Beyond the perception-behavior link: The ubiquitous utility and motivational moderators of non-conscious mimicry. In R. Hassin, J. Uleman, & J. A. Bargh (Eds.), *Unintended thought 2: The new unconscious.* New York: Oxford University Press.

Chen, F. F., & Kenrick, D. T. (2002). Repulsion or attraction? Group membership and assumed attitude similarity. *Journal of Personality and Social Psychology, 83,* 11–125.

Chen, M., & Bargh, J. A. (1997). Nonconscious behavioral confirmation processes: The self-fulfilling consequences of automatic stereotype activation. *Journal of Experimental Social Psychology, 33,* 541–560.

Chen, S., Chen, K., & Shaw, L. (2004). Self-verification motives at the collective level of self-definition. *Journal of Personality and Social Psychology, 86,* 77–94.

Cheverton, H. M., & Byrne, D. (1998, February). *Development and validation of the Primary Choice Clothing Questionnaire.* Presented at the meeting of the Eastern Psychological Association, Boston.

Choi, I., & Nisbett, R. E. (1998). Situational salience and cultural differences in the correspondence bias and actor-observer bias. *Personality and Social Psychology Bulletin, 24,* 949–960.

Christy, P. R., Gelfand, D. M., & Hartmann, D. P. (1971). Effects of competition-induced frustration on two classes of modeled behavior. *Developmental Psychology, 5,* 104–111.

Cialdini, R. B. (1994). *Influence: Science and practice* (3rd ed.). New York: Harper Collins.

Cialdini, R. B. (2000). *Influence: Science and practice* (4th ed.). Boston: Allyn & Bacon.

Cialdini, R. B. (2006). *Influence: The psychology of persuasion.* New York: Collins

Cialdini, R., Brown, S., Lewis, B., Luce, C., & Neuberg, S. (1997). Reinterpreting the empathy-altruism relationships: When one into one equals oneness. *Journal of Personality and Social Psychology, 67,* 773–789.

Cialdini, R. B., & Petty, R. (1979). Anticipatory opinion effects. In B. Petty, T. Ostrom, & T. Brock (Eds.), *Cognitive responses in persuasion.* Hillsdale, NJ: Erlbaum.

Cialdini, R. B., Reno, R. R., & Kallgren, C. A. (1990). A focus theory of normative conduct : Recycling the concept of norms to reduce littering in public places. *Journal of Personality and Social Psychology, 91,* 105-1026.

Cialdini, R. B., & Trost, M. R. (1998). Social influence: Social norms, conformity, and compliance. In D. T. Gilbert, S. T. Fiske, & G. Lindzey (Eds.), *The handbook of social psychology* (Vol. 2, pp. 151–192). Boston: McGraw-Hill.

Cialdini, R. B., Baumann, D. J., & Kenrick, D. T. (1981). Insights from sadness: A three-step model of the development of altruism as hedonism. *Developmental Review, 1,* 207–223.

Cialdini, R. B., Kallgren, C. A., & Reno, R. R. (1991). A focus theory of normative conduct. *Advances in Experimental Social Psychology, 24,* 201–234.

Cialdini, R. B., Kenrick, D. T., & Baumann, D. J. (1982). Effects of mood on prosocial behavior in children and adults. In N. Eisenberg-Berg (Ed.), *Development of prosocial behavior.* New York: Academic Press.

Cialdini, R. B., Cacioppo, J. T., Bassett, R., & Miller J. A. (1978). A low-ball procedure for producing compliance: Commitment then cost. *Journal of Personality and Social Psychology, 36,* 463–476.

Cialdini, R. B., Schaller, M., Houlainham, D., Arps, K., Fultz, J., & Beaman, A. L. (1987). Empathy-based helping: Is it selflessly or selfishly motivated? *Journal of Personality and Social Psychology, 52,* 749–758.

Cialdini, R. B., Vincent, J. E., Lewis, S. K., Catalan, J., Wheeler, D., & Darby, B. L. (1975). Reciprocal concessions procedure for inducing compliance: The door-in-the-face technique. *Journal of Personality and Social Psychology, 31,* 206–215.

Ciavarella, M. A., Bucholtz, A. K., Riordan, C. M., Gatewood, R. D., & Stokes, G. S. (2004). The big five and venture success: Is there a linkage? *Journal of Business Venturing, 19,* 465–484.

Clark, L. A., Kochanska, G., & Ready, R. (2000). Mothers' personality and its interaction with child temperament as predictors of parenting behavior. *Journal of Personality and Social Psychology, 79,* 274–285.

Clark, M. S., & Grote, N. K. (1998). Why aren't indices of relationship costs always negatively related to indices of relationship quality? *Personality and Social Psychology Review, 2,* 2–17.

Clark, M. S., Ouellette, R., Powel, M. C., & Milberg, S. (1987). Recipient's mood, relationship type, and helping. *Journal of Personality and Social Psychology, 53,* 94–103.

Clary, E. G., & Snyder, M. (1999). The motivations to volunteer: Theoretical and practical considerations. *Current Directions in Psychological Science, 8,* 156–159.

Clore, G. L., Schwarz, N., & Conway, M. (1993). Affective causes and consequences of social information processing. In R. S. Wyer & T. K. Srull (Eds.), *Handbook of social cognition* (2nd ed.). Hilldsale, NJ: Erlbaum.

Cohen, D., & Nisbett, R. E. (1994). Self-protection and the culture of honor: Explaining southern violence. *Personality and Social Psychology Bulletin, 20,* 551–567.

Cohen, D., & Nisbett, R. E. (1997). Field experiments examining the culture of honor: The role of institutions in perpetuating norms about violence. *Personality and Social Psychology Bulletin, 23,* 1188–1199.

Cohen, J. D. (2005). The vulcanization of the human brain: A neural perspective on interactions between cognition and emotion. *Journal of Economic Perspectives, 19,* 3–24.

Cohen, S., Kaplan, J. R., Cunnick, J. E., Manuck, S. B., & Rabin, B. S. (1992). Chronic social stress, affiliation, and cellular immune response in non-human primates. *Psychological Science, 3,* 301–304.

Cohen, S., Frank, E., Doyle, W. J., Skoner, D. P., Rabin, B. S., & Gwalatney, J. M. (1998). Types of stressors that increase susceptibility to the common cold in healthy adults. *Health Psychology, 3,* 214–223.

Cohen, T. R., Montoya, R. M., & Insko, C. A. (2006). Group morality and intergroup relations: Cross-cultural and experimental evidence. *Personality and Social Psychology Bulletin, 32,* 1559–1572.

Cohn, E. G., & Rotton, J. (1997). Assault as a function of time and temperature: A moderator-variable time-series analysis. *Journal of Personality and Social Psychology, 72,* 1322–1334.

Collaros, P. A., & Anderson, L. R. (1969). Effect of perceived expertness upon creativity of members of brainstorming groups. *Journal of Applied Psychology, 53,* 159–63.

Coles, R. (1997). *The moral intelligence of children.* New York: Random House.

Collins, M. A., & Zebrowitz, L. A. (1995). The contributions of appearance to occupational outcomes in civilian and military settings. *Journal of Applied Social Psychology, 25,* 129–163.

Collins, N. L., & Feeney, B. C. (2000). A safe haven: An attachment theory perspective on support seeking and caregiving in intimate relationships. *Journal of Personality and Social Psychology, 78,* 1053–1073.

Condon, J. W., & Crano, W. D. (1988) Inferred evaluation and the relation between attitude similarity and interpersonal attraction. *Journal of Personality and Social Psychology, 54,* 789–797.

Coniff, R. (2004, January). Reading faces. *Smithsonian,* 44–50.

Correia, I., Vala, J., & Aguiar, P. (2007). Victim's innocence, social categorization, and the threat to the belief in a just world. *Journal of Experimental Social Psychology, 43,* 31–38.

Correll, J., Urland, G. R., & Ito, T. A. (2006). Event-related potentials and the decision to shoot: The role of threat perception and cognitive control. *Journal of Experimental Social Psychology, 42,* 120–128.

Cottrell, C. A., & Neuberg, S. L. (2005). Different emotional reactions to different groups: A sociofunctional threat-based approach to "prejudice." *Journal of Personality and Social Psychology, 88,* 770–789.

Cottrell, C. A., Neuberg, S. L., & Li, N. P. (2007). What do people desire in others? A sociofunctional perspective on the importance of different valued characteristics. *Journal of Personality and Social Psychology, 92,* 208–231.

Cottrell, N. B., Wack, K. L., Sekerak, G. J., & Rittle, R. (1968). Social facilitation of dominant responses by the presence of an audience and the mere presence of others. *Journal of Personality and Social Psychology, 9,* 245–250.

Cozzarelli, C., Karafa, J. A., Collins, N. L., & Tagler, M. J. (2003). Stability and change in adult attachment styles: Associations with personal vulnerabilities, life events, and global construals of self and others. *Journal of Social and Clinical Psychology, 22,* 315–346.

Cramer, R. E., McMaster, M. R., Bartell, P. A., & Dragma, M. (1988). Subject competence and minimization of the bystander effect. *Journal of Applied Social Psychology, 18,* 1133–1148.

Crandall, C. S. (1988). Social contagion of binge eating. *Journal of Personality and Social Psychology, 55,* 588–598.

Crandall, C. S. (2004). Social contagion of binge eating. In R. M. Kowalski & M. R. Leary (Eds.), *The interface of social and clinical psychology: Key readings* (pp. 99–115). New York: Psychology Press.

Crandall, C. S., Eshleman, A., & O'Brien, L. T. (2002). Social norms and the expression and suppression of prejudice: The struggle for internalization. *Journal of Personality and Social Psychology, 82,* 359–378.

Crangle, C. E. (2007). Gender equity at Stanford University: A story behind the statistics. In F. J. Crosby, M. S. Stockdale, & S. A. Ropp (Eds.), *Sex discrimination in the workplace* (pp. 69–81). Malden, MA: Blackwell.

Crano, W. D. (1995). Attitude strength and vested interest. In R. E. Petty & J. A. Krosnick (Eds.), *Attitude strength: Antecedents and consequences* (Vol. 4, pp. 131–157). Hillsdale, NJ: Erlbaum.

Creighton, M. (1904). *Life,* p. 77.

Crites, S. L., & Cacioppo, J. T. (1996). Electrocortical differentiation of evaluative and nonevaluative categorizations. *Psychological Science, 7,* 318–321.

Crocker, J., & Major, B. (1989). Social stigma and self-esteem: The self-protective properties of stigma. *Psychological Review, 96,* 608–630.

Crocker, J., & Wolfe, C. T. (2001). Contingencies of self-worth. *Psychological Review, 108,* 593–623.

Crocker, J., Cornwell, B., & Major, B. (1993). The stigma of overweight: Affective consequences of attributional ambiguity. *Journal of Personality and Social Psychology, 64,* 60–70.

Cropanzano, R. (Ed.). (1993). *Justice in the workplace* (pp. 79–103). Hillsdale, NJ: Erlbaum.

Crosby, F. J. (2004). *Affirmative action is dead: Long live affirmative action.* New Haven, CT: Yale University Press.

Cruse, D. F., and Leigh, B. C. "Adam's Rib" revisited: Legal and non-legal influences on the processing of trial testimony. *Social Behavior,* 1987, *2,* 221-230

Crutchfield, R. A. (1955). Conformity and character. *American Psychologist, 10,* 191–198.

Cuddy, A. J., Fiske, S. T., & Glick, P. (2007). The BIAS map: Behaviors from intergroup affects and stereotypes. *Journal of Personality and Social Psychology, 92* (4), 631–648.

Cunningham, M. R. (1979). Weather, mood, and helping behavior: Quasi-experiments with the sunshine Samaritan. *Journal of Personality and Social Psychology, 37,* 1947–1956.

Cunningham, M. R. (1986). Measuring the physical in physical attractiveness: Quasi-experiments on the sociobiology of female facial beauty. *Journal of Personality and Social Psychology, 50,* 925–935.

Cunningham, M. R., Roberts, A. R., Wu, C.-H., Barbee, A. P., & Druen, P. B. (1995). "Their ideas of beauty are, on the whole, the same as ours": Consistency and variability in the cross-cultural perception of female physical attractiveness. *Journal of Personality and Social Psychology, 68,* 261–279.

Cunningham, M. R., Shaffer, D. R., Barbee, A. P., Wolff, P. L., & Kelley, D. J. (1990). Separate processes in the relation of elation and depression to helping: Social versus personal concerns. *Journal of Experimental Social Psychology, 26,* 13–33.

Cunningham, W. A., Johnson, M. K., Gatenby, J. C., Gore, J. C., & Banaji, M. R. (2003). Neural components of social evaluation. *Journal of Personality and Social Psychology, 85,* 639–649.

Cutler, B. L., Penrod, S. D., & Martens, T. K. (1987). Improving the reliability of eyewitness identification: Putting content into context. *Journal of Applied Psychology, 72,* 629–637.

Darley, J. M. (1993). Research on morality: Possible approaches, actual approaches. *Psychological Science, 4,* 353–357.

Darley, J. M. (1995). Constructive and destructive obedience: A taxonomy of principal-agent relationships. *Journal of Social Issues, 125,* 125–154.

Darley, J. M., & Batson, C. D. (1973). From Jerusalem to Jericho: A study of situational dispositional variables in helping behavior. *Journal of Personality and Social Psychology, 27,* 100–108.

Darley, J. M., & Latané, B. (1968). Bystander intervention in emergencies: Diffusion of responsibility. *Journal of Personality and Social Psychology, 8,* 377–383.

Darley, J. M., Carlsmith, K. M., & Robinson, P. H. (2000). Incapacitation and just desserts as motives for punishment. *Law and Human Behavior, 24,* 659–684

Dasgupta, N., & Asgari, S. (2004). Seeing is believing: Exposure to counterstereotypic women leaders and its effect on the malleability of automatic gender stereotyping. *Journal of Experimental Social Psychology, 40,* 642–658.

Dasgupta, N., Banji, M. R., & Abelson, R. P. (1999). Group entiativity and group perception: Association between physical features and psychological judgment. *Journal of Personality and Social Psychology, 75,* 991–1005.

Daubman, K. A. (1993). *The self-threat of receiving help: A comparison of the threat-to-self-esteem model and the theat-to-interpersonal-power model.* Unpublished manuscript, Gettysburg College, Gettysburg, PA.

Daubman, K. A. (1995). Help which implies dependence: Effects on self-evaluations, motivation, and performance. *Journal of Social Behavior and Personality, 10,* 677–692.

Davila, J., & Cobb, R. J. (2003). Predicting change in self-reported and interviewer-assessed adult attachment: Tests of the individual difference and life stress models of attachment change. *Personality and Social Psychology Bulletin, 29,* 859–870.

Davis, M. H., Hall, J. A., & Meyer, M. (2003). The first year: Influences on the satisfaction, involvement, and persistence of new community volunteers. *Personality and Social Psychology Bulletin, 29,* 248–260.

Davis, M. H., Luce, C., & Kraus, S. J. (1994). The heritability of characteristics associated with dispositional empathy. *Journal of Personality, 62,* 369–391.

Dawkins, R. (1976). *The selfish gene.* New York: Oxford University Press.

Deaux, K., & LaFrance, M. (1998). Gender. In D. T. Gilbert, S. T. Fiske, & G. Lindzey (Eds.), *The handbook of social psychology* (4th ed., Vol. 1, pp. 788–827). New York: McGraw-Hill.

De Bruin, E. N. M., & Lange, P. A. M., van (2000). What people look for in others: Influences on the perceiver and the perceived in information selection. *Personality and Social Psychology Bulletin, 26,* 206-219.

DeDreu, C. K. W., & Van Lange, P. A. M. (1995). Impact of social value orientation on negotiator cognition and behavior. *Personality and Social Psychology Bulletin, 21,* 1178–1188.

DeGroot, T., Kiker, D. S., & Cross, T. C. (2000). A meta-analysis to review organizational outcomes related to charismatic leadership. *Canadian Journal of Administrative Sciences, 17,* 356–371.

DeHart, T., & Pelham, B. W. (2007). Fluctuations in state implicit self-esteem in response to daily negative events. *Journal of Experimental Social Psychology, 43,* 157–165.

DeHart, T., Pelham, B. W., & Tennen, H. (2006). What lies beneath: Parenting style and implicit self-esteem. *Journal of Experimental Social Psychology, 42,* 1–17.

De Houwer, J., Thomas, S., & Baeyens, F. (2001). Associative learning of likes and dislikes: A review of 25 years of research on human evaluative conditioning. *Psychological Bulletin, 127,* 853–869.

DeJong, W., & Musilli, L. (1982). External pressure to comply: Handicapped versus nonhandicapped requesters and the foot-in-the-door phenomenon. *Personality and Social Psychology Bulletin, 8,* 522–527.

DeLongis, A., Folkman, S., & Lazarus, R. S. (1988). The impact of daily stress on health and mood: Psychological and social resources as mediators. *Journal of Personality and Social Psychology, 54,* 486–595.

DePaulo, B. M. (2006). *Singled out: How singles are stereotyped, stigmatized, and ignored, and still live happily ever after.* New York: St. Martin's Press.

DePaulo, B. M., Brown, P. L., Ishii, S., & Fisher, J. D. (1981). Help that works: The effects of aid on subsequent task performance. *Journal of Personality and Social Psychology, 41,* 478–487.

DePaulo, B. M., & Kashy, D. A. (1998). Everyday lies in close and casual relationships. *Journal of Personality and Social Psychology, 74,* 63–79.

DePaulo, B. M., Lindsay, J. J., Malone, B. E., Muhlenbruck, L., Chandler, K., & Cooper, H. (2003). Cues to deception. *Psychological Bulletin, 129,* 74–118.

DePaulo, B. M., & Morris, W. L. (2006). The unrecognized stereotyping and discrimination against singles. *Current Directions in Psychological Science, 15,* 251–254.

DeSteno, D. (2004). *New perspectives on jealousy: An integrative view of the most social of social emotions.* Paper presented at the meeting of the American Psychological Society, Chicago, IL.

DeSteno, D., Dasgupta, N., Bartlett, M. Y., & Cajdric, A. (2004). Prejudice from thin air: The effect of emotion on automatic intergroup attitudes. *Psychological Science, 15,* 319–324.

DeSteno, D., Valdesolo, P., & Bartlett, M. Y. (2006). Jealousy and the threatened self: Getting to the heart of the green-eyed monster. *Journal of Personality and Social Psychology, 91,* 626–641.

Deutsch, M., & Gerard, H. B. (1955). A study of normative and informational social influences upon individual judgment. *Journal of Abnormal and Social Psychology, 51,* 629–636.

Devine, P. G., Plant, E. A., & Blair, I. V. (2001). Classic and contemporary analyses of racial prejudice. In R. Brown & S. Gaertner (Eds.), *Blackwell handbook of social psychology: Intergroup processes* (pp. 198–217). Oxford, UK: Blackwell.

De Wall, C. N., Baumeister, R. F., Stillman, T. F., & Gailliot, M. T. (2007). Violence restrained: Effects of self-regulation and its depletion on aggression. *Journal of Experimental Social Psychology, 43,* 62–76.

Dexter, H. R., Cutler, B. L., & Moran, G. (1992). A test of voir dire as a remedy for pretrial publicity. *Journal of Applied Social Psychology, 22,* 819-832.

Diehl, M., & Stroebe, W. (1991). Productivity loss in idea-generating groups: Tracking down the blocking effect. *Journal of Personality and Social Psychology, 61,* 392–403.

Diener, E., & Lucas, R. R. (1999). Personality and subjective well-being. In E. Kahneman, E. Diener, & N. Schwarz (Eds.), *Well-being: The foundations of hedonic psychology* (pp. 434–450). New York: Russell Stage Foundation.

Diener, E., & Oishi, S. (2005). The nonobvious social psychology of happiness. *Psychological Inquiry, 16,* 162–167.

Diener, E., Wolsic, B., & Fujita, F. (1995). Physical attractiveness and subjective well-being. *Journal of Personality and Social Psychology, 69,* 120–129.

Dietrich, D. M., & Berkowitz, L. (1997). Alleviation of dissonance by engaging in prosocial behavior or receiving ego-enhancing feedback. *Journal of Social Behavior and Personality, 12,* 557–566.

Dietz, J., Robinson, S. A., Folger, R., Baron, R. A., & Jones, T. (2003). The impact of societal violence and organizational justice climate on workplace aggression. *Academy of Management Journal, 46,* 317–326.

Dijksterhuis, A. (2004). I like myself but I don't know why: Enhancing implicit self-esteem by subliminal evaluative conditioning. *Journal of Personality and Social Psychology, 86,* 345–355.

Dijksterhuis, A., & Bargh, J. A. (2001). The perception-behavior expressway: Automatic effects of social perception and social behavior. In M. P. Zanna (Ed.), *Advances in experimental social psychology* (Vol. 33, pp. 1–40). San Diego: Academic Press.

Dijksterhuis, A., & Nordgren, L. F. (2007). A theory of unconscious thought. *Perspectives on Psychological Science.*

Dijksterhuis, A., & van Knippenberg, A. (1996). The knife that cuts both ways: Facilitated and inhibited access to traits as a result of stereotype-activation. *Journal of Experimental Social Psychology, 32,* 271–288.

Dijksterhuis, A., & van Olden, Z. (2006). On the benefits of thinking unconsciously: Unconscious thought can increase post-choice satisfaction. *Journal of Experimental Social Psychology, 42,* 627–631.

Dion, K. K., Berscheid, E., & Hatfield (Walster), E. (1972). What is beautiful is good. *Journal of Personality and Social Psychology, 24,* 285–290.

Dion, K. K., & Dion, K. L. (1991). Psychological individualism and romantic love. *Journal of Social Behavior and Personality, 6,* 17–33.

Dion, K. L., & Earn, B. M. (1975). The phenomenology of being a target of prejudice. *Journal of Personality and Social Psychology, 32,* 944–950.

Dittmann, M. (2003, November). Compassion is what most find attractive in mates. *Monitor on Psychology, 10,* 12.

Dollard, J., Doob, L., Miller, N., Mowerer, O. H., & Sears, R. R. (1939). *Frustration and aggression.* New Haven, CT: Yale University Press.

Doosje, B., & Branscombe, N. R. (2003). Attributions for the negative historical actions of a group. *European Journal of Social Psychology, 33,* 235–248.

Dovidio, J. F., Evans, N., & Tyler, R. B. (1986). Racial stereotypes: The contents of their cognitive representations. *Journal of Experimental Social Psychology, 22,* 22–37.

Dovidio, J. F., & Gaertner, S. L. (1999). Reducing prejudice: Combating intergroup biases. *Current Directions in Psychological Science, 8,* 101–105.

Dovidio, J. F., Gaertner, S. L., & Validzic, A. (1998). Intergroup bias: Status differentiation and a common ingroup identity. *Journal of Personality and Social Psychology, 75,* 109–120.

Dovidio, J. F., Brigham, J., Johnson, B., & Gaertner, S. (1996). Stereotyping, prejudice, and discrimination: Another look. In N. Macrae, C. Stangor, & M. Hwestone (Eds.), *Stereotypes and stereotyping* (pp. 1276–1319). New York: Guilford.

Dovidio, J. F., Gaertner, S. L., Isen, A. M., & Lowrance, R. (1995). Group representations and intergroup bias: Positive affect, similarity, and group size. *Personality and Social Psychology Bulletin, 21,* 856–865.

Downs, A. C., & Lyons, P. M. (1991). Natural observations of the links between attractiveness and initial legal judgments. *Personality and Social Psychology Bulletin, 17,* 541–547.

Duan, C. (2000). Being empathic: The role of motivation to empathize and the nature of target emotions. *Motivation and Emotion, 24,* 29–49.

Dubois, N., & Beauvois, J. L. (1996). Internality, academic status and intergroup attributions. *European Journal of Psychology of Education, 11,* 329–341.

Duck, J. M., Hogg, M. A., & Terry, D. J. (1999). Social identity and perceptions of media persuasion: Are we always less influenced than others? *Journal of Applied Social Psychology, 29,* 1879–1899.

Duck, S., Pond, K., & Leatham, G. (1994). Loneliness and the evaluation of relational events. *Journal of Social and Personal Relationships, 11,* 253–276.

Duggan, E. S., & Brennan, K. A. (1994). Social avoidance and its relation to Bartholomew's adult attachment typology. *Journal of Social and Personal Relationships, 11,* 147–153.

Dugosh, K. L., & Paulus, P. B. (2005). Cognitive and social comparison processes in brainstorming. *Journal of Experimental Social Psychology, 41,* 313–320.

Duncan, J., & Owen, A. W. (2000). Common regions of the human frontal lobe recruited by diverse cognitive demands. *Trends in Cognitive Science, 23,* 475–483.

Dunkley, D. M., Zuroff, D. C., & Blankstein, K. R. (2003). Self-critical perfectionism and daily affect: Dispositional and situational influences on stress and coping. *Journal of Personality and Social Psychology, 84,* 234–252.

Dunn, J. (1992). Siblings and development. *Current Directions in Psychological Science, 1,* 6–11.

Dutton, D. G., & Aron, A. P. (1974). Some evidence for heightened sexual attraction under conditions of high anxiety. *Journal of Personality and Social Psychology, 30,* 510–517.

Eagly, A. H. (1987). *Sex differences in social behavior: A social-role interpretation.* Hillsdale, NJ: Erlbaum.

Eagly, A. H. (2007). Female leadership advantage and disadvantage: Resolving the contradictions. *Psychology of Women Quarterly, 31,* 1–12.

Eagly, A. H., & Carli, L. (1981). Sex of researchers and sex-typed communications as determinants of sex differences in influence-ability: A meta-analysis of social influence studies. *Psychological Bulletin, 90,* 1–20.

Eagly, A. H., & Chaiken, S. (1993). *The psychology of attitudes.* Orlando, FL: Harcourt Brace Jovanovich.

Eagly, A. H., & Chaiken, S. (1998). Attitude structure and function. In G. Lindsey, S. T., Fiske, & D. T. Gilbert (Eds.), *Handbook of social psychology* (4th ed.). New York: Oxford University Press and McGraw-Hill.

Eagly, A. H., & Chaiken, S. (2005). Attitude research in the 21st century: The current state of knowledge. In D. Albarracin, B. T. Johnson, & M. P. Zanna (Eds.), *The handbook of attitudes* (pp. 743–767). Mahwah, NJ: Lawrence Erlbaum.

Eagly, A. H., Chaiken, S., & Wood, W. (1981). An attributional analysis of persuasion. In J. H. Harvey, W. Ickes, & R. F. Kidd (Eds.), *New directions in attribution research* (pp. 37–62). Hillsdale, NJ: Lawrence Erlbaum.

Eagly, A. H., & Karau, S. J. (2002). Role congruity theory of prejudice toward female leaders. *Psychological Review, 109,* 573–598.

Eagly, A. H., & Mladinic, A. (1994). Are people prejudiced against women? Some answers from research on attitudes, gender stereotypes, and judgments of competence. In W. Sroebe & M. Hewstone (Eds.), *European review of social psychology* (Vol. 5, pp. 1–35). New York: Wiley.

Eagly, A. H., Makhijani, M. G., & Klonsky, B. G. (1992). Gender and the evaluation of leaders: A meta-analysis. *Psychological Bulletin, 111,* 3–22.

Eagly, A. H., Chen, S., Chaiken, S., & Shaw-Barnes, K. (1999). The impact of attitudes on memory: An affair to remember. *Psychological Bulletin, 124,* 64–89.

Eagly, A. H., Kulesa, P., Brannon, L. A., Shaw, K., & Hutson-Comeaux, S. (2000). Why counterattitudinal messages are as memorable as proattitudinal messages: The importance of active defense against attack. *Personality and Social Psychology Bulletin, 26,* 1392–1408.

Eibach, R. P., & Keegan, T. (2006). Free at last? Social dominance, loss aversion, and White and Black Americans' differing assessments of racial progress. *Journal of Personality and Social Psychology, 90,* 453–467.

Eich, E. (1995). Searching for mood dependent memory. *Psychological Science, 6,* 67–75.

Eisenman, R. (1985). Marijuana use and attraction: Support for Byrne's similarity-attraction concept. *Perceptual and Motor Skills, 61,* 582.

Eisenstadt, D., & Leippe, M. R. (1994). The self-comparison process and self-discrepant feedback: Consequences of learning you are what you thought you were not. *Journal of Personality and Social Psychology, 67,* 611–626.

Ekman, P. (2001). *Telling lies: Clues to deceit in the marketplace, politics, and marriage* (3rd ed.). New York: Norton.

Ekman, P., & Friesen, W. V. (1975). *Unmasking the face.* Englewood Cliffs, NJ: Prentice-Hall.

Ekman, P., O'Sullivan, M., & Frank, M. G. (1999). A few can catch a liar. *Psychological Science, 10,* 263–266.

Ekman, P. (2003). *Emotions revealed.* New York: Times Books.

Elfenbein, H .A., & Ambady, N. (2002). On the universality and cultural specificity of emotion.

Ellemers, N. (2001). Individual upward mobility and the perceived legitimacy of intergroup relations. In J. T. Jost & B. Major (Eds.), *The psychology of legitimacy* (pp. 205–222). New York: Cambridge University Press.

Ellemers, N., de Gilder, D., & Haslam, S. A. (2004). Motivating individuals and groups at work: A social identity perspective on leadership and group performance. *Academy of Management Review, 29,* 459–478.

Elliot, A. J., & Devine, P. G. (1994). On the motivational nature of cognitive dissonance: Dissonance as psychological discomfort. *Journal of Personality and Social Psychology, 67,* 382–394.

Elliot, A. J., & Reis, H. T. (2003). Attachment and exploration in adulthood. *Journal of Personality and Social Psychology, 5,* 317–331.

Ellsworth, P. C., & Carlsmith, J. M. (1973). Eye contact and gaze aversion in aggressive encounter. *Journal of Personality and Social Psychology, 33,* 117–122.

Englehart, J. M. (2006). Teacher perceptions of student behavior as a function of class size. *Social Psychology of Education, 9,* 245–272.

Englich, B., Mussweiler, T., & Strack, F. (2006). Playing dice with criminal sentences: The influence of irrelevant anchors on experts' judicial decision making. *Personality and Social Psychology Bulletin, 32,* 188–200.

Epley, N., & Dunning, D. (2000). Feeling "holier than thou": Are self-serving assessments produced by errors in self- or social prediction? *Journal of Personality and Social Psychology, 79,* 861–875.

Epley, N., & Gilovich, T. (2006). The anchoring-and-adjustment heuristic: Why the adjustments are insufficient. *Psychological Science, 17,* 311–318.

Epley, N., & Huff, C. (1998). Suspicion, affective response, and educational benefit as a result of deception in psychology research. *Personality and Social Psychology Bulletin, 24,* 759–768.

Erez, A., & Isen, A.I. (2002). The influence of positive affect on the components of expectancy motivation. *Journal of Applied Psychology, 87,* 1055–1067.

Erwin, P. G., & Letchford, J. (2003). Types of preschool experience and sociometric status in the primary school. *Social Behavior and Personalty, 31,* 129–132.

Esses, V. M., Jackson, L. M., Nolan, J. M., & Armstrong, T. L. (1999). Economic threat and attitudes toward immigrants. In S. Halli & L. Drieger (Eds.), *Immigrant Canada: Demographic, economic and social challenges* (pp. 212–229). Toronto: University of Toronto Press.

Estrada, C. A., Isen, A. M., & Young, M. J. (1995). Positive affect improves creative problem solving and influences reported source of practice satisfaction in physicians. *Motivation and Emotion, 18,* 285–300.

Etcoff, N. (1999). *Survival of the prettiest: The science of beauty.* New York: Doubleday.

Etcoff, N. L., Ekman, P., Magee, J. J., & Frank, M. G. (2000). Lie detection and language comprehension. *Nature, 40,* 139.

Ethier, K. A., & Deaux, K. (1994). Negotiating social identity when contexts change: Maintaining identification and responding to threat. *Journal of Personality and Social Psychology, 67,* 243–251.

Falomir-Pichastor, J. M., Munoz-Rojas, D., Invernizzi, F., & Mugny, G. (2004). Perceived in-group threat as a factor moderating the influence of in-group norms on discrimination against foreigners. *European Journal of Social Psychology, 34,* 135–153.

Faulkner, S. J., & Williams, K. D. (1999, April). *After the whistle is blown: The aversive impact of ostracism.* Paper presented at the meeting of the Midwestern Psychological Association, Chicago.

Fazio, R. H. (2000). Accessible attitudes as tools for object appraisal: The costs and benefits. In G. R. Maio & J. M. Olson (Eds.), *Why we evaluate: Functions of attitudes* (pp. 1–26). Mahwah, NJ: Erlbaum.

Fazio, R. H., & Hilden, L. E. (2001). Emotional reactions to a seemingly prejudiced response: The role of automatically activated racial attitudes and motivation to control prejudiced reactions. *Personality and Social Psychology Bulletin, 27,* 538–549.

Fazio, R. H., & Olson, M. A. (2003). Implicit measures in social cognition research: Their meaning and uses. *Annual Review of Psychology, 54,* 297–327.

Fazio, R. H., & Roskos-Ewoldsen, D. R. (1994). Acting as we feel: When and how attitudes guide behavior. In S. Shavitt & T. C. Brock (Eds.), *Persuasion* (pp. 71–93). Boston: Allyn and Bacon.

Fazio, R. H., Ledbetter, J. E., & Towles-Schwen, T. (2000). On the costs of accessible attitudes: Detecting that the attitude object has changed. *Journal of Personality and Social Psychology, 78,* 197–210.

Feagin, J. R., & McKinney, K. D. (2003). *The many costs of racism.* Lanham, MD: Rowman & Littlefield.

Fehr, B. (1999). Laypeople's conceptions of commitment. *Journal of Personality and Social Psychology, 76,* 90–103.

Fehr, B. (2004). Intimacy expectations in same-sex friendships: A prototype interaction-pattern model. *Journal of Personality and Social Psychology, 86,* 265–284.

Fehr, B., & Broughton, R. (2001). Gender and personality differences in conceptions of love: An interpersonal theory analysis. *Personal Relationships, 8,* 115–136.

Fein, S., McCloskey, A. L., & Tomlinson, T. M. (1997). Can the jury disregard that information? The use of suspicion to reduce the prejudicial effects of pretrial publicity and inadmissible testimony. *Personality and Social Psychology Bulletin, 23,* 1215–1226.

Feingold, A. (1992). Good-looking people are not what we think. *Psychological Bulletin, 111,* 304–341.

Feldman, R. S., Forrest, J. A., & Happ, B. R. (2002). Self-presentation and verbal deception: Do self-presenters lie more? *Basic and Applied Social Psychology, 24,* 163–170.

Felmlee, D. H. (1995). Fatal attractions: Affection and disaffection in intimate relationships. *Journal of Social and Personal Relationships, 12,* 295–311.

Felmlee, D. H. (1998). "Be careful what you wish for . . .": A quantitative and qualitative investigation of "fatal attractions." *Personal Relationships, 5,* 235–253.

Femlee, D., & Sprecher, S. (2000). Close relationships and social psychology: Intersections and future paths. *Social Psychology Quarterly, 63,* 365–376.

Ferreira, M. B., Garcia-Marques, L., Sherman, S. J., & Sherman, J. W. (2006). Automatic and controlled components of judgment and decision making. *Journal of Personality and Social Psychology, 91,* 797–813.

Feshbach, S. (1984). The catharsis hypothesis, aggressive drive, and the reduction of aggression. *Aggressive Behavior, 10,* 91–101.

Festinger, L. (1954). A theory of social comparison processes. *Human Relations, 7,* 117–140.

Festinger, L., & Carlsmith, J. M. (1959). Cognitive consequences of forced compliance. *Journal of Abnormal and Social Psychology, 58,* 203–210.

Festinger, L., Riecken, H. W., & Schachter, S. (1956). *When prophecy fails.* Minneapolis: University of Minnesota Press.

Festinger, L., Schachter, S., & Back, K. (1950). *Social pressures in informal groups: A study of a housing community.* New York: Harper.

Fichten, C. S., & Amsel, R. (1986). Trait attributions about college students with a physical disability: Circumplex analyses and methodological issues. *Journal of Applied Social Psychology, 16,* 410–427.

Fiedler, K., Messner, C., & Bluemke, M. (2006). Unresolved problems with the "I", the "A", and the "T": A logical and psychometric critique of the Implicit Association Test (IAT). *European Review of Social Psychology, 17,* 74–147.

Fink, B., & Penton-Voak, I. (2002). Evolutionary psychology of facial attractiveness. *Current Directions in Psychological Science, 11,* 154–158.

Fischer, P., & Greitemeyer, T. (2006). Music and aggression: The impact of sexual-aggressive song lyrics on aggression-related thoughts, emotions, and behavior toward the same and the opposite sex. *Personality and Social Psychology Bulletin 32,* 1165–1176.

Fischman, J. (1986, January). Women and divorce: Ten years after. *Psychology Today,* 15.

Fisher, J. D., & Byrne, D. (1975). Too close for comfort: Sex differences in response to invasions of personal space. *Journal of Personality and Social Psychology, 32,* 15–21.

Fisher, J. D., Nadler, A., & Whitcher-Alagna, S. (1982). Recipient reactions to aid. *Psychological Bulletin, 91,* 27–54.

Fiske, S. T. (1993). Social cognition and social perception. In L. W. Porter & M. R. Rosenzweig (Eds.), *Annual Review of Psychology, 44,* 155–194.

Fiske, S. T. (2000). Interdependence and the reduction of prejudice. In S. Oskamp (Ed.), *Reducing prejudice and discrimination* (pp. 115–135). Mahwah, NJ: Erlbaum.

Fiske, S. T., & Berdahl, J. (2007). Social power. In A. Kruglanski & E. T. Higgins (Eds.), *Social psychology: A handbook of basic principles* (2nd ed.). New York: Guilford Press.

Fiske, S. T., & Stevens, L. E. (1993). What's so special about sex? Gender stereotyping and discrimination. In S. Oskamp & M. Costanzo (Eds.), *Gender issues in contemporary society* (pp. 173–196). Newbury Park, CA: Sage.

Fiske, S. T., Lin, M. H., & Neuberg, S. L. (1999). The continuum model: Ten years later. In S. Chaiken & Y. Trope (Eds.), *Dual process theories in social psychology* (pp. 231–254). New York: Guilford.

Fiske, S. T., Cuddy, A. J. C., Glick, P., & Xu, J. (2002). A model of (often mixed) stereotype content: Competence and warmth respectively follow from perceived status and competition. *Journal of Personality and Social Psychology, 82,* 878–902.

Fitzsimmons, G. M., & Bargh, J. A. (2003). Thinking of you: Nonconscious pursuit of interpersonal goals associated with relationships partners. *Journal of Personality and Social Psychology, 84,* 148–164.

Fitzsimons, G. M., & Kay, A. C. (2004). Language and interpersonal cognition: Causal effects of variations in pronoun usage on perceptions of closeness. *Personality and Social Psychology Bulletin, 30,* 547–557.

Fleming, M. A., & Petty, R. E. (2000). Identity and persuasion: An elaboration likelihood approach. In D. J. Terry & M. A. Hogg (Eds.), *Attitudes, behavior, and social context* (pp. 171–199). Mahwah, NJ: Erlbaum.

Fletcher, G. J. O., Simpson, J. A., & Thomas, G. (2000). Ideals, perceptions, and evaluations in early relationship development. *Journal of Personality and Social Psychology, 79,* 933–940.

Fletcher, G. J. O., Simpson, J. A., Thomas, G., & Giles, L. (1999). Ideals in intimate relationships. *Journal of Personality and Social Psychology, 76,* 72–89.

Flynn, F. J., Reagans, R. E., Amanatullah, E. T., & Ames, D. R. (2006). Helping one's way to the top: Self-monitors achieve status by helping others and knowing who helps them. *Journal of Personality and Social Psychology, 91,* 1123–1137.

Folger, R., & Baron, R. A. (1996). Violence and hostility at work: A model of reactions to perceived injustice. In G. R. VandenBos and E. Q. Bulato (Eds.), *Violence on the job: Identifying risks and developing solutions* (pp. 51–85). Washington, DC: American Psychological Association.

Foltz, C., Barber, J. P., Weinryb, R. M., Morse, J. Q., & Chittams, J. (1999). Consistency of themes across interpersonal relationships. *Journal of Social and Clinical Psychology, 18,* 204–222.

Forgas, J. P. (1995a). Mood and judgment: The affect infusion model (AIM). *Psychological Bulletin, 117,* 39–66.

Forgas, J. P. (1995b). Strange couples: Mood effects on judgments and memory about prototypical and atypical targets. *Personality and Social Psychology Bulletin, 21,* 747–765.

Forgas, J. P. (1998). Asking nicely? The effects of mood on responding to more or less polite requests. *Personality and Social Psychology Bulletin, 24,* 173–185.

Forgas, J. P. (Ed.). (2000). *Feeling and thinking: Affective influences on social cognition.* New York: Cambridge University Press.

Forge, K. L., & Phemister, S. (1987). The effect of prosocial cartoons on preschool children. *Child Study Journal, 17,* 83–88.

Forrest, J. A., & Feldman, R. S. (2000). Detecting deception and judge's involvement; lower task involvement leads to better lit detection. *Personality and Social Psychology Bulletin, 26,* 118–125.

Fowers, B., Lyons, E., Montel, K., & Shaked, N. (2001). Positive illusions about marriage among married and single individuals. *Journal of Family Psychology,* 95–109.

Fox, R. L., & Oxley, Z. M. (2003). Gender stereotyping in state executive elections: Candidate selection and success. *Journal of Politics, 65,* 833–850.

Frable, D. E., Blackstone, T., & Scherbaum, C. (1990). Marginal and mindful: Deviants in social interactions. *Journal of Personality and Social Psychology, 59,* 140–149.

Fraley, R.C. (2000). Attachment continuity from infancy to adulthood: Meta-analysis and dynamic modeling of developmental mechanisms. *Dissertation Abstracts International: Section B: The Sciences & Engineering, 60* (n8-B):4273.

Fraley, R. C., & Shaver, P.R. (2000). Adult romantic attachment: Theoretical developments, emerging controversies, and unanswered questions. *Review of General Psychology, 4,* 132–154

Franiuk, R., Cohen, D., & Pomeratz, E. M. (2002). Implicit theories of relationships: Implications for relationship satisfaction and longevity. *Personal Relationships, 9,* 345–367.

Frank, E., & Brandstatter, V. (2002). Approach versus avoidance: Different types of commitment to intimate relationships. *Journal of Personality and Social Psychology, 82,* 208–221.

Fredrickson, B. L. (1995). Socioemotional behavior at the end of college life. *Journal of Social and Personal Relationships, 12,* 261–276.

Freedman, J. L., & Fraser, S. C. (1966). Compliance without pressure: The foot-in-the-door technique. *Journal of Personality and Social Psychology, 4,* 195–202.

Fricko, M. A. M., & Beehr, T. A. (1992). A longitudinal investigation of interest congruence and gender concentration as predictors of job satisfaction. *Personnel Psychology, 45,* 99–117.

Friedman, H. S., Riggio, R. E., & Casella, D. F. (1988). Nonverbal skill, personal charisma, and initial attraction. *Personality and Social Psychology Bulletin, 14,* 203–211.

Fritzsche, B. A., Finkelstein, M. A., & Penner, L. A. (2000). To help or not to help: Capturing individuals' decision policies. *Social Behavior and Personality, 28,* 561–578.

Fry, D. P. (1998). Anthropological perspectives on aggression: Sex differences and cultural variation. *Aggressive Behavior, 24,* 81–95.

Fuegen, K., & Biernat, M. (2002). Reexamining the effects of solo status for women and men. *Personality and Social Psychology Bulletin, 28,* 913–925.

Fuegen, K., & Brehm, J. W. (2004). The intensity of affect and resistance to social influence. In E. S. Knowles & J. A. Linn (Eds.), *Resistance and persuasion* (pp. 39–63). Mahwah, NJ: Erlbaum.

Fujita, K., Trope, Y., Liberman, N., & Levin-Sagi, M. (2006). Construal levels and self-control. *Journal of Personality and Social Psychology, 90,* 351–367.

Fultz, J., Shaller, M., & Cialdini, R. B. (1988). Empathy, sadness, and distress: Three related but distant vicarious affective responses to another's suffering. *Personality and Social Psychology Bulletin, 14,* 312–325.

Funk, J. B., Bechtoldt-Baldacci, H., Pasold, T., & Baumgartner, J. (2004). Violence exposure in real-life, video games, television, movies, and the internet: Is there desensitization? *Journal of Adolescence, 27,* 23–39.

Furr, R. M., & Funder, D. C. (1998). A multimodal analysis of personal negativity. *Journal of Personality and Social Psychology, 74,* 1580–1591.

Gabaix, X. & Laibson, L. (2006). Shrouded attributes, consumer myopia, and information suppression in competitive markets. *Quarterly Journal of Economics, 121.* 505–540.

Gaertner, S. L., Rust, M. C., Dovidio, J. F., Bachman, B. A., & Anastasio, P. A. (1994). The contact hypothesis: The role of common ingroup identity on reducing intergroup bias. *Small Group Research, 25,* 224–249.

Gaertner, S. L., Mann, J., Murrell, A., & Dovidio, J. F. (1989). Reducing intergroup bias: The benefits of recategorization. *Journal of Personality and Social Psychology, 57,* 239–249.

Gaertner, S. L., Mann, J. A., Dovidio, J. F., Murrell, A. J., & Pomare, M. (1990). How does cooperation reduce intergroup bias? *Journal of Personality and Social Psychology, 59,* 692–704.

Gallucci, G. (2003). I sell seashells by the seashore and my name is Jack: Comment on Pelham, Mirenberg, and Jones (2002). *Journal of Personality and Social Psychology, 85,* 789–799.

Galton, F. (1952). *Hereditary genius: An inquiry into its laws and consequences.* New York: Horizon. (Original work published 1870.)

Gantner, A. B., & Taylor, S. P. (1992). Human physical aggression as a function of alcohol and threat of harm. *Aggressive Behavior, 18,* 29–36.

Garcia, D. M., Horstman Reser, A., Amo, R. B., Redersdorff, S., & Branscombe, N. R. (2005). Perceivers' responses to in-group and out-group members who blame a negative outcome on discrimination. *Personality and Social Psychology Bulletin, 31,* 769–780.

Garcia, S. M., Weaver, K., Moskowitz, G. B., & Darley, J. M. (2002). Crowded minds: The implicit bystander effect. *Journal of Personality and Social Psychology, 83,* 843–853.

Garcia-Marques, T., Mackie, D. M., Claypool, H. M., & Garcia-Marques, L. (2004). Positivity can cue familiarity. *Personality and Social Psychology Bulletin, 30,* 585–593.

Gardner, R. M., & Tockerman, Y. R. (1994). A computer–TV methodology for investigating the influence of somatotype on perceived personality traits. *Journal of Social Behavior and Personality, 9,* 555–563.

Gawronski, G. (2003). Implicational schemata and the correspondence bias: On the diagnostic value of situationally constrained behavior. *Journal of Personality and Social Psychology 84,* 1154–1171.

Geary, D. C., Vigil, J., & Byrd-Craven, J. (2004). Evolution of human mate choice. *Journal of Sex Research, 41,* 27–42.

Geiselman, R. E., & Fisher, R. P. 1997. Ten years of cognitive interviewing. In D. G. Payne & F. G. Conrad (Eds.), *Intersections of basic and applied research* (pp. 291-310). Mahwah, N. J.: Erlbaum.

George, M. S., Ketter, T. A., Parekh-Priti, I., Horwitz, B., et al. (1995). Brain activity during transient sadness and happiness in healthy women. *American Journal of Psychiatry, 152,* 341–351.

Gerard, H. B., Wilhelmy, R. A., & Conolley, E. S. (1968). Conformity and group size. *Journal of Personality and Social Psychology, 8,* 79–82.

Gibbons, D., & Olk, P. M. (2003). Individual and structural origins of friendship and social position among professionals. *Journal of Personality and Social Psychology, 84,* 340–351.

Gibbons, F. X., Eggleston, T. J., & Benthin, A. C. (1997). Cognitive reactions to smoking relapse: The reciprocal relation between dissonance and self-esteem. *Journal of Personality and Social Psychology, 72,* 184–195.

Gigone, D., & Hastie, R. (1993). The common knowledge effect: Information sharing and group judgment. *Journal of Personality and Social Psychology, 65,* 959–974.

Gigone, D., & Hastie, R. (1997). The impact of information on small group choice. *Journal of Personality and Social Psychology, 72,* 132–140.

Gilbert, D. T. (2002). Inferential correction. In T. Gilovich, D. W. Griffin, & D. Kahneman (Eds.), *Heuristics and biases: The psychology of intuitive judgment* (pp. 167–184) New York: Cambridge University Press.

Gilbert, D. T., & Malone, P. S. (1995). The correspondence bias. *Psychological Bulletin, 117,* 21–38.

Gilbert, D. T., & Wilson, T. D. (2000). Miswanting: Some problems in the forecasting of future affective states. In J. Forgas (Ed.), *Feeling and thinking: The role of affect in social cognition.* New York: Cambridge University Press.

Gilbert, D. T., Tafarodi, R. W., & Malone, P. S. (1993). You can't not believe everything you read. *Journal of Personality and Social Psychology, 65,* 221–233.

Gilovich, T., Medvec, V. H., & Savitsky, K. (2000). The spotlight effect in social judgment: An egocentric bias in estimates of the salience of one's own actions and appearance. *Journal of Personality and Social Psychology, 78,* 211–222.

Giner-Sorolla, R. (2001). Affective attitudes are not always faster: The moderating role of extremity. *Personality and Social Psychology Bulletin, 27,* 666–677.

Ginsburg, H. J., Ogletree, S. M., Silakowski, T. D., Bartels, R. D., Burk, S. L., & Turner, G. M. (2003). Young children's theories of mind about empathic and selfish motives. *Social Behavior and Personality, 31,* 237–244.

Gladue, B. A. (1991). Aggressive behavioral characteristics, hormones, and sexual orientation in men and women. *Aggressive Behavior, 17,* 313-326.

Gladue, B. A., & Delaney, H. J. (1990). Gender differences in perception of attractiveness of men and women in bars. *Personality and Social Psychology Bulletin, 16,* 378–391.

Glanz, K., Geller, A. C., Shigaki, D., Maddock, J. E., & Isnec, M. R. (2002). A randomized trial of skin cancer prevention in aquatics settings: The pool cool program. *Health Psychology, 21*(6), 579–587.

Glaser, J., & Salovey, P. (1998). Affect in electoral politics. *Personality and Social Psychology Review, 2,* 156–172.

Glass, D. C. (1977). *Behavior patterns, stress, and coronary disease.* Hillsdale, NJ: Erlbaum.

Gleicher, F., Boninger, D., Strathman, A., Armor, D., Hetts, J., & Ahn, M. (1995). With an eye toward the future: Impact of counterfactual thinking on affect, attitudes, and behavior. In N. J. Roses & J. M. Olson (Eds.), *What might have been: The social psychology of counterfactual thinking.* (pp. 283–304). Mahwah, NJ: Erlbaum.

Glick, P. (2002). Sacrificial lambs dressed in wolves' clothing: Envious prejudice, ideology, and the scapegoating of Jews. In *Understanding genocide: The social psychology of the Holocaust* (pp. 113–142). New York: Oxford University Press.

Goethals, G. R., & Darley, J. (1977). Social comparison theory: An attributional approach. In J. M. Suls & R. L. Miller (Eds.), *Social comparison processes: Theoretical and empirical perspectives* (pp. 259–278). Washington, DC: Hemisphere.

Goffman, E. (1959). *The presentation of self in everyday life.* New York: Doubleday.

Goldenberg, J. L., Pyszczynski, T., Greenberg, J., McCoy, S. K., & Solomon, S. (1999). Death, sex, love, and neuroticism: Why is sex such a problem? *Journal of Personality and Social Psychology, 77,* 1173–1187.

Gollwitzer, P. M. (1999). Implementation intentions: Strong effects of simple plans. *American Psychologist, 54,* 493–503.

Goodwin, R., Cook, O., & Yung, Y. (2001). Loneliness and life satisfaction among three cultural groups. *Personal Relationships, 8,* 225–230.

Goodwin, S. A., Gubin, A., Fiske, S. T., & Yzerbyt, V. (2000). Power can bias impression processes: Stereotyping subordinates by default and by design. *Group Processes and Intergroup Relations, 3,* 227–256.

Goodwin, V. L., Wofford, J. C., & Whittington, J. L. (2001). A theoretical and empirical extension to the transformational leadership construct. *Journal of Occupational Behavior, 22,* 759–774.

Gordon, R. A. (1996). Impact of ingratiation in judgments and evaluations: A meta-analytic investigation. *Journal of Personality and Social Psychology, 71,* 54–70.

Gould, S. J. (1996, September). The Diet of Worms and the defenestration of Prague. *Natural History,* 18–24, 64, 66–67.

Graen, G. B., & Uhl-bien, M. (1995). Relationship-based approach to leadership: Development of leader-member exchange (LMX) theory of leadership over 25 years: Applying a multi-level multi-domain perspective. *Leadership Quarterly, 6,* 219–247.

Graham, S., & Folkes, V. (Eds.). (1990). *Attribution theory: Applications to achievement, mental health, and interpersonal conflict.* Hillsdale, NJ: Erlbaum.

Green, J. D., & Campbell, W. K. (2000). Attachment and exploration in adults: Chronic and contextual accessibility. *Personality and Social Psychology Bulletin, 26,* 452–461.

Green, L. R., Richardson, D. R., & Lago, T. (1996). How do friendship, indirect, and direct aggression relate? *Aggressive Behavior, 22,* 81–86.

Greenbaum, P., & Rosenfield, H. W. (1978). Patterns of avoidance in responses to interpersonal staring and proximity: Effects of bystanders on drivers at a traffic intersection. *Journal of Personality and Social Psychology, 36,* 575–587.

Greenberg, J. (1993). Justice and organizational citizenship: A commentary on the state of the science. *Employee Responsibilities and Rights Journal, 6,* 249-256.

Greenberg, J. (1997). A social influence model of employee theft: Beyond the fraud triangle. In R. J. Lewicki, R. J. Bies, & B. H. Sheppard (Eds.), *Research on negotiation in organizations* (Vol. 6, pp. 29–52). Greenwich, CT: JAI Press.

Greenberg, J., & Baron, R. A. (2008). *Behavior in organizations* (9th ed.). Upper Saddle River, NJ: Prentice-Hall.

Greenberg, J., & Baron, R. A. (2007). *Behavior in organizations* (9th ed.). Upper Saddle River, NJ: Prentice-Hall.

Greenberg, J., & Lind, E. A. (2000). The pursuit of organizational justice: From conceptualization to implication to application. In C. L. Cooper & E. A. Locke (Eds.), *Industrial/organizational psychology: What we know about theory and practice.* (pp. 72–107). Oxford, England: Blackwell.

Greene, E., & Bornstein, E. H. (2003). *Determining damages: The psychology of jury awards* Washington, DC: American Psychological Association

Greenwald, A. G. (2002). Constructs in student ratings of instructors. In H. I. Braun & D. N. Douglas (Eds.), *The role of constructs in psychological and educational measurement* (pp. 277–297). Mahwah, NJ: Erlbaum.

Greenwald, A. G., & Banaji, M. R. (1995). Implicit social cognition: Attitudes, self-esteem, and stereotypes. *Psychological Review, 102,* 4–27.

Greenwald, A. G., Banaji, M. R., Rudman, L. A., Farnham, S. D., Nosek, B. A., & Mellott, D. S. (2002). A unified theory of implicit attitudes, stereotypes, self-esteem, and self-concept. *Psychological Review, 109*, 3–25.

Greenwald, A. G., McGhee, D. E., & Schwarz, J. L. K. (1998). Measuring individual differences in implicit cognition: The Implicit Association Test. *Journal of Personality and Social Psychology, 74*, 1464–1480.

Grube, J. A., & Piliavin, J. A. (2000). Role identity, organizational experiences, and volunteer performance. *Personality and Social Psychology Bulletin, 26*, 1108–1119.

Guagnano, G. A. (1995). Locus of control, altruism and agentic disposition. *Population and Environment, 17*, 63–77.

Gudjonsson, G. H., & Clark, N. K. (1986). Suggestibility in police interrogation: A social psychological model. *Social Behavior, 1*, 83–104.

Guimond, S. (2000). Group socialization and prejudice: The social transmission of intergroup attitudes and beliefs. *European Journal of Social Psychology, 30*, 335–354.

Guimond, S., Branscombe, N. R., Brunot, S., Buunk, B. P., Chatard, A., Désert, M., et al. (2007). Culture, gender, and the self: Variations and impact of social comparison processes. *Journal of Personality and Social Psychology, 92*, 1118–1134.

Guinote, A., Judd, C. M., & Brauer, M. (2002). Effects of power on perceived and objective group variability: Evidence that more powerful groups are more variable. *Journal of Personality and Social Psychology, 82*, 708–721.

Gulli, C., Kohler, N., & Patriquin, M. (2007, February 9). The great university cheating scandal. *Maclean's*. Retrieved 12, March, 2007 at www.macleans.ca/article.jsp?content=20070209_174847_6984&source=srch.

Gump, B. B., & Kulik, J. A. (1997). Stress, affiliation, and emotional contagion. *Journal of Personality and Social Psychology, 72*, 305–319.

Gustafson, R. (1990). Wine and male physical aggression. *Journal of Drug Issues, 20*, 75–86.

Hackman, J. R., & Wageman, R. (2007). Asking the right questions about leadership. *American Psychologist, 62*, 43–47.

Hahn, J., & Blass, T. (1997). Dating partner preferences: A function of similarity of love styles. *Journal of Social Behavior and Personality, 12*, 595–610.

Halberstadt, J., & Rhodes, G. (2000). The attractiveness of nonface averages: Implications for an evolutionary explanation of the attractiveness of average faces. *Psychological Science, 11*, 285–289.

Halbertal, T. H., & Koren, I. (2006). Between "being" and "doing": Conflict and coherence in the identity formation of gay and lesbian Orthodox Jews. In D. P. McAdams, R. Josselson, & A. Lieblich (Eds.), *Identity and story: Creating self in narrative* (pp. 37–61). Washington, DC: American Psychological Association.

Hall, J. A., & Matsumoto, D. (2004). Gender differences in judgments of multiple emotions from facial expressions. *Emotion, 3*, 201–206.

Hall-Elston, C., & Mullins, L. C. (1999). Social relationships, emotional closeness, and loneliness among older meal program participants. *Social Behavior and Personality, 27*, 503–518.

Hamilton, G. V. (1978). Obedience and responsibility: A jury simulation. *Journal of Personality and Social Psychology, 36*, 126–146.

Hamilton, V. L., & Sanders, J. (1995). Crimes of obedience and conformity in the workplace: Surveys of Americans, Russians, and Japanese. *Journal of Social Issues, 51*, 67–88.

Haney, C., Banks, W., & Zimbardo, P. (1973). Interpersonal dynamics in a simulated prison. *International Journal of Criminology, 1*, 69–97.

Hanko, K., Master, S., & Sabini, J. (2004). Some evidence about character and mate selection. *Personality and Social Psychology Bulletin, 30*, 732–742.

Hansen, N., & Sassenberg, K. (2006). Does social identification harm or serve as a buffer? The impact of social identification on anger after experiencing social discrimination. *Personality and Social Psychology Bulletin, 32*, 983–996.

Hardy, C. L., & Van Vugt, M. (2006). Nice guys finish first: The competitive altruism hypothesis. *Personality and Social Psychology Bulletin, 32*, 1402–1413.

Hareli, S., & Weiner, B. (2000). Accounts for success as determinants of perceived arrogance and modesty. *Motivation and Emotion, 24*, 215–236.

Harker, L., & Keltner, D. (2001). Expressions of positive emotion in women's college yearbook pictures and their relationship to personality and life outcomes across adulthood. *Journal of Personality and Social Psychology, 80*, 112–124.

Harmon-Jones, E. (2000). Cognitive dissonance and experienced negative affect: Evidence that dissonance increases experienced negative affect even in the absence of aversive consequences. *Personality and Social Psychology Bulletin, 26*, 1490–1501.

Harmon-Jones, E., & Allen, J. J. B. (2001). The role of affect in the mere exposure effect: Evidence from psychophysiological and individual differences approaches. *Personality and Social Psychology Bulletin, 27*, 889–898.

Harmon-Jones, E., & Devine, P. G. (2003). Introduction to the special section on social neuroscience: Promise and caveats. *Journal of Personality and Social Psychology, 85*, 589–593.

Harris, C. R. (2003). A review of sex differences in sexual jealousy, including self-report data, psychophysiological responses, interpersonal violence, and morbid jealousy. *Personality and Social Psychology Review, 7,* 102–128.

Harris, L. R., & Weiss, D. J. (1995). Judgments of consent in simulated rape cases. *Journal of Social Behavior and Personality, 10,* 79–90.

Harris, L. T., & Fiske, S. T. (2006). Dehumanizing the lowest of the low. *Psychological Science, 17,* 847–853.

Harris, L. T., Todorov, A., & Fiske, S. T. (2005). Attributions on the brain: Neuro-imaging dispositional inferences, beyond theory of mind. *NeuroImage, 28,* 763–769.

Harris, M. B. (1992). Sex, race, and experiences of aggression. *Aggressive Behavior, 18,* 201–217.

Harris, M. B. (1993). How provoking! What makes men and women angry? *Journal of Applied Social Psychology, 23,* 199–211.

Harris, M. B. (1994). Gender of subject and target as mediators of aggression. *Journal of Applied Social Psychology, 24,* 453–471.

Harris, M. B., Harris, R. J., & Bochner, S. (1982). Fat, four-eyed, and female: Stereotypes of obesity, glasses, and gender. *Journal of Applied Social Psychology, 12,* 503–516.

Harrison, M. (2003). "What is love?" Personal communication.

Haslam, S. A. (2001). *Psychology in organizations: The social identity approach.* London: Sage.

Haslam, S. A. (2004). *Psychology in organizations: The social identity approach* (2nd ed.). London: Sage.

Haslam, S. A., Branscombe, N. R., & Bachmann, S. (2003). Why consumers rebel: Social identity and the etiology of adverse reactions to service failure. In Haslam, S. A., van Knippenberg, D., Platow, M. J., & Ellemers, N. (Eds.), *Social identity at work* (pp. 293–309). New York: Psychological Press.

Haslam, S. A., & Platow, M. J. (2001). The link between leadership and followership: How affirming social identity translates vision into action. *Personality and Social Psychology Bulletin, 27,* 1469–1479.

Haslam, S. A., & Reicher, S. D. (2006). Stressing the group: Social identity and the unfolding dynamics of responses to stress. *Journal of Applied Psychology, 91,* 1037–1052.

Haslam, S. A., Ryan, M. K., Postmes, T., Spears, R., Jetten, J., & Webley, P. (2006). Sticking to our guns: Social identity as a basis for the maintenance of commitment to faltering organizational projects. *Journal of Organizational Behavior, 27,* 607–628.

Haslam, S. A., & Wilson, A. (2000). In what sense are prejudicial beliefs personal? The importance of an in-group's shared stereotypes. *British Journal of Social Psychology, 39,* 45–63.

Haslam, S. A., van Knippenberg, D., Platow, M. J., & Ellemers, N. (2003). *Social identity at work: Developing theory and organizational practice.* New York: Psychological Press.

Haslam, S. A. (2001). *Psychology in organizations: The social identity approach.* London: Sage.

Hassin, R., & Trope, Y. (2000). Facing faces: Studies on the cognitive aspects of physiognomy. *Journal of Personality and Social Psychology, 78,* 837–852.

Hatfield, E. (1987). Passionate and companionate love. In RJ. Sternberg & M. I. Barnes (Eds.)., *The psychology of love,* (pp. 191-216). New Haven, CT: Yale University Press.

Hatfield, E., & Rapson, R. L. (1993). Historical and cross-cultural perspectives on passionate love and sexual desire. *Annual Review of Sex Research, 4,* 67–97.

Hatfield, E., & Sprecher, S. (1986a). *Mirror, mirror . . . : The importance of looks in everyday life.* Albany, NY: S. U. N. Y. Press.

Hatfield, E., & Sprecher, S. (1966b). Measuring passionate lives in intimate relations. *Journal of Adolescence, 9,* 383-410.

Hatfield, E., & Walster, G. W. (1981). *A new look at love.* Reading, MA: Addison-Wesley.

Haugtvedt, C. P., & Wegener, D. T. (1994). Message order effects in persuasion: An attitude strength perspective. *Journal of Consumer Research, 21,* 205–218.

Hawkley, L. C., Burleson, M. H., Berntson, G. G., & Cacioppo, J. T. (2003). Loneliness in everyday life: Cardiovascular activity, psychosocial context, and health behaviors. *Journal of Personality and Social Psychology, 85,* 105–120.

Hawley, P. H., Card, N., & Little, T. D., (2007). The allure of a mean friend: Relationship quality and processes of aggressive adolescents with prosocial skills. *International Journal of Behavioral Development, 32,* 21–32.

Hawley, P. H., Little, T. D., & Rodin, P. C., (Eds). (2007). *Aggression and adaptation: The bright side of bad behavior.* Mahwah, NJ: Lawrence Erlbaum.

Hayden, S. R., Jackson, T. T., & Guydish, J. N. (1984). Helping behavior of females: Effects of stress and commonality of fate. *Journal of Psychology, 117,* 233–237.

Hebl, M. R., & Mannix, L. M. (2003). The weight of obesity in evaluating others: A mere proximity effect. *Personality and Social Psychology, 29,* 28–38.

Heider, F. (1958). *The psychology of interpersonal relations.* New York: Wiley.

Heilman, M. E. (2001). Description and prescription: How gender stereotypes prevent women's ascent up the organizational ladder. *Journal of Social Issues, 57,* 657–674.

Heilman, M. E., Block, C. J., & Lucas, J. A. (1992). Presumed incompetent? Stigmatization and affirmative action efforts. *Journal of Applied Psychology, 77,* 536–544.

Heilman, M. E., & Okimoto, T. G. (2007). Why are women penalized for success at male tasks?: The implied communality deficit. *Journal of Applied Psychology, 92,* 81–92.

Hendrick, C., & Hendrick, S. S. (1986). A theory and method of love. *Journal of Personality and Social Psychology, 50*, 392–402.

Hendrick, C., Hendrick, S. S., Foote, F. H., & Slapion-Foote, M. J. (1984). Do men and women love differently? *Journal of Social and Personal Relationships, 1*, 177–195.

Hendrick, S. S., & Hendrick, C. (2002). Linking romantic love with sex: Development of the Perceptions of Love and Sex Scale. *Journal of Social and Personal Relationships, 19*, 361–378.

Herek, G. M., Gillis, J. R., & Cogan, J. C. (1999). Psychological sequelae of hate-crime victimization among lesbian, gay, and bisexual adults. *Journal of Consulting and Clinical Psychology, 67*, 945–951.

Herrera, N. C., Zajonc, R. B., Wieczorkowska, G., & Cichomski, B. (2003). Beliefs about birth rank and their reflection in reality. *Journal of Personality and Social Psychology, 85*, 142–150.

Hetherington, M. M., Anderson, A. S., Norton, G. N., & Newson, L. (2006). Situational effects on meal intake: A comparison of eating alone and eating with others. *Physiology and Behavior, 88*, 498–505.

Higgins, E. T., & Kruglanski, A. W. (Eds.). (1996). *Social psychology: Handbook of basic principles.* New York: Guilford Press.

Higgins, E. T., & Spiegel, S. (2004). Promotion and prevention strategies for self-regulation: A motivated cognition perspective. In R. F. Baumeister & K. D. Vohs (Eds.), *Handbook of self-regulation: Research, theory, and applications* (pp. 171–187). New York: Guilford.

Higgins, N. C., & Shaw, J. K. (1999). Attributional style moderates the impact of causal controlability information on helping behavior. *Social Behavior and Personality, 27*, 221–236.

Higham, P. A., & Carment, W. D. (1992). The rise and fall of politicians: The judged heights of Broadbent, Mulroney and Turner before and after the 1988 Canadian federal election. *Canadian Journal of Behavioral Science, 24*, 404–409.

Hilton, D. J. (1998). *Psychology and the city: Applications to trading, dealing, and investment analysis.* London: Center for the Study of Financial Innovation.

Hilton, N. Z., Harris, G. T., & Rice, M. E. (2000). The functions of aggression by male teenagers. *Journal of Personality and Social Psychology, 79*, 988–994.

Hinsz, V. B. (1995). Goal setting by groups performing an additive task: A comparison with individual goal setting. *Journal of Applied Social Psychology, 25*, 965–990.

Hoaken, P. N. S., Giancola, P. R., & Pihl, R. O. (1998). Executive cognitive functions as mediators of alcohol-related aggression. *Alcohol and Alcoholism, 33*, 45–53.

Hoffer, E. (1953). *The passionate state of mind and other aphorisms.* Cutchogue, NY: Buccaneer Books.

Hogg, M. A. (1992). *The social psychology of group cohesiveness: From attraction to social identity.* Hertfordshire, UK: Harvester Wheatsheaf.

Hogg, M. A. (2007). Organizational orthodoxy and corporate autocrats: Some nasty consequences of organizational identification in uncertain times. In C. Bartel, S. Blader & A. Wrzesniewski (Eds.), *Identity and the modern organization* (pp. 35–59). Mahwah, NJ: Erlbaum.

Holmes, J. G. (2002). Interpersonal expectations as the building blocks of social cognition: An interdependence theory perspective. *Personal Relationships, 9*, 1–26.

Holmes, T. H., & Rahe, R. H. (1967). The social readjustment rating scale. *Journal of Psychosomatic Research, 22*, 213–218.

Hope, D. A., Holt, C. S., & Heimberg, R. G. (1995). Social phobia. In T. R. Giles (Ed.), *Handbook of effective psychotherapy* (pp. 227–251). New York: Plenum.

Hopkins, A. B. (2007). Opposing views, strongly held. In F. J. Crosby, M. S. Stockdale, & S. A. Ropp (Eds.), *Sex discrimination in the workplace* (pp. 59–67). Malden, MA: Blackwell.

Horgan, T. G., Schmid Mast, M., Hall, J. A., & Carter, J. D. (2004). Gender differences in memory for the appearance of others. *Personality and Social Psychology Bulletin, 30*, 185–196.

Hornsey, M. J., de Bruijn, P., Creed, J., Allen, J., Ariyanto, A., & Svensson, A. (2005). Keeping it in-house: How audience affects responses to group criticism. *European Journal of Social Psychology, 35*, 291–312.

Hornsey, M. J., & Hogg, M. A. (2000). Intergroup similarity and subgroup relations: Some implications for assimilation. *Personality and Social Psychology Bulletin, 26*, 948–958.

Hornsey, M. J., & Imani, A. (2004). Criticizing groups from the inside and the outside: An identity perspective on the intergroup sensitivity effect. *Personality and Social Psychology Bulletin, 30*, 365–383.

Hornsey, M. J., Jetten, J., McAuliffe, B. J., & Hogg, M. A. (2006). The impact of individualist and collectivist group norms on evaluations of dissenting group members. *Journal of Experimental Social Psychology, 42*, 57–68.

Hornstein, H. (2004). *Brutal bosses and their prey.* New York: Columbia University Press.

House, J. S., Landis, K. R., & Umberson, D. (1988). Social relationships and health. *Science, 241*, 540–545.

House, R. J., & Howell, J. M. (1992). Personality and charismatic leadership. *Leadership Quarterly, 3*, 81–108.

House, R. J., & Podsakoff, P. M. (1994). Leadership effectiveness: Past perspectives and future directions for research. In J. Greenberg (Ed.), *Organizational behavior: The state of the science* (pp. 45–82). Hillsdale, NJ: Erlbaum.

House, R. J., Spangler, W. D., & Woycke, J. (1991). Personality and charisma in the U.S. presidency: A psychological theory of leader effectiveness. *Administrative Science Quarterly, 36*, 364–396.

Hovland, C. I., & Weiss, W. (1951). The influence of source credibility on communication effectiveness. *Public Opinion Quarterly, 15,* 635–650.

Hovland, C. I., Janis, I. L., & Kelley, H. H. (1953). *Communication and persuasion: Psychological studies of opinion change.* New Haven, CT: Yale University Press.

Huang, I.-C. (1998). Self-esteem, reaction to uncertainty, and physician practice variation: A study of resident physicians. *Social Behavior and Personality, 26,* 181–194.

Huesmann, L. R., & Eron, L. D. (1984). Cognitive processes and the persistence of aggressive behavior. *Aggressive Behavior, 10,* 243–251.

Huesmann, L. R., & Eron, L. D. (1986). *Television and the aggressive child: A cross-national comparison.* Hillsdale, NJ: Erlbaum.

Hugenberg, K., & Bodenhausen, G. V. (2003). Facing prejudice: Implicit prejudice and the perception of facial threat. *Psychological Science, 14,* 640–643.

Hughes, S. M., Harrison, M. A., & Gallup, G. G., Jr. (2002). The sound of symmetry: Voice as a marker of developmental instability. *Evolution and Human Behavior, 23,* 173–180.

Huguet, P., Galvaing, M. P., Monteil, J. M., & Dumas, F. (1999). Social presence effects in the Stroop task: Further evidence for an attentional view of social facilitation. *Journal of Personality and Social Psychology, 77,* 1011–1025.

Hummert, M. L., Crockett, W. H., & Kemper, S. (1990). Processing mechanisms underlying use of the balance scheme. *Journal of Personality and Social Psychology, 58,* 5–21.

Hunt, A. McC. (1935). A study of the relative value of certain ideals. *Journal of Abnormal and Social Psychology, 30,* 222–228.

Huston, T. L. (2006). Positive illusions in marital relationships: A 13-year longitudinal study. *Personality and Social Psychology Bulletin, 32,* 1579–1594.

Huston, T. L., Caughlin, J. P., Houts, R. M., Smith, S. E., & George, L. J. (2001). The connubial crucible: Newlywed years as predictors of marital delight, distress, and divorce. *Journal of Personality and Social Psychology, 80,* 237–252.

Ickes, W., Hutchison, J., & Mashek, D. (2004). Closeness as intersubjectivity: Social absorption and social individuation. In D. Mashek and A. Aron (Eds.), *The handbook of closeness and intimacy* (pp. 357–373). Mahwah, NJ: Erlbaum.

Illies, R., & Judge, T. A. (2003). On the heritability of job satisfaction: The mediating role of personality. *Journal of Applied Psychology, 88,* 750–759.

Insel, T. R. & Carter, C. S. (1995, August). The monogamous brain. *Natural History,* 12–14. Jones, Carpenter, & Quintana. (1985).

Insko, C. A. (1985). Balance theory, the Jordan paradigm, and the West tetrahedron. In L. Berkowitz (Ed.), *Advances in experimental social psychology.* New York: Academic Press.

Inzlicht, M., & Ben-Zeev, T. (2000). A threatening intellectual environment: Why females are susceptible to experiencing problem-solving deficits in the presence of males. *Psychological Science, 11,* 365–371.

Ireland, C. A., & Ireland, J. L. (2000). Descriptive analysis of the nature and extent of bullying behavior in a maximum security prison. *Aggressive Behavior, 26,* 213–222.

Ireland, J. L., & Archer, J. (2002). The perceived consequences of responding to bullying with aggression: A study of male and female adult prisoners. *Aggressive Behavior, 28,* 257–272.

Isen, A. M. (1984). Toward understanding the role of affect in cognition. In S. R. Wyer & T. K. Srull (Eds.), *Handbook of social cognition* (Vol. 3, pp. 179–236). Hillsdale, NJ: Erlbaum.

Isen, A. M. (2000). Positive affect and decision making. In M. Lewis & J. M. Haviland-Jones (Eds.), *Handbook of emotions* (2nd ed., pp. 417–435). New York: Guilford Press.

Isen, A. M. (2002). Missing in Action in the AIM: Positive Affect's Facilitation of Cognitive Flexibility, Innovation, and Problem Solving. *Psychological Inquiry, 13*(1): 57–65.

Isen, A.M. & Labroo, A.A. (2003). "Some Ways in Which Positive Affect Facilitates Decision Making and Judgment." In S. Schneider & J. Shanteau (Eds.) *Emerging Perspectives on Judgment and Decision Research.* NY, Cambridge: 365–393.

Isen, A. M., & Levin, P. A. (1972). Effect of feeling good on helping: Cookies and kindness. *Journal of Personality and Social Psychology, 21,* 384–388.

Istvan, J., Griffitt, W., & Weidner, G. (1983). Sexual arousal and the polarization of perceived sexual attractiveness. *Basic and Applied Social Psychology, 4,* 307–318.

Ito, T. A., Chiao, K. W., Devine, P. G., Lorig, T. S., & Cacioppo, J. T. (2006). The influence of facial feedback on race bias. *Psychological Science, 17,* 256–261.

Izard, C. (1991). *The psychology of emotions.* New York: Plenum.

Jackman, M. R. (1994). *The velvet glove: Paternalism and conflict in gender, class, and race relations.* Berkeley, CA: University of California Press.

Jackson, L. M., & Esses, V. M. (1997). Of scripture and ascription: The relation between religious fundamentalism and intergroup helping. *Personality and Social Psychology Bulletin, 23,* 893–906.

Jackson, L. M., Esses, V. M., & Burris, C. T. (2001). Contemporary sexism and discrimination: The importance of respect for men and women. *Personality and Social Psychology Bulletin, 27,* 48–61.

Jackson, T., Soderlind, A., & Weiss, K. E. (2000). Personality traits and quality of relationships as predictors of future loneliness among American college students. *Social Behavior and Personality, 28,* 463–470.

Jacobi, L., & Cash, T. F. (1994). In pursuit of the perfect appearance: Discrepancies among self-ideal percepts of multiple physical attributes. *Journal of Applied Social Psychology, 24,* 379–396.

Jacobs, J. A., & Steinberg, R. (1990). Compensating differentials and the male-female wage gap: Evidence from the New York state comparable worth study. *Social Forces, 69,* 439–468.

Janis, I. L. (1982). *Victims of groupthink* (2nd ed.). Boston: Houghton Mifflin.

Janis, I., & Feshbach, S. (1953). Effects of fear-arousing communications. *Journal of Abnormal and Social Psychology, 48,* 78–92.

Jarrell, A. (1998, October 4). Date that calls for judicious attire. *New York Times,* 9-1–9-2.

Jellison, J. M., & Green, J. (1981). A self-presentation approach to the fundamental attribution error: The norm of internality. *Journal of Personality and Social Psychology, 40,* 643–649.

Jensen-Campbell, L. A., West, S. G., & Graziano, W. G. (1995). Dominance, prosocial orientation, and female preferences: Do nice guys really finish last? *Journal of Personality and Social Psychology, 68,* 427–440.

Jetten, J., Branscombe, N. R., Schmitt, M. T., & Spears, R. (2001). Rebels with a cause: Group identification as a response to perceived discrimination from the mainstream. *Personality and Social Psychology Bulletin, 27,* 1204–1213.

Jetten, J., Hornsey, M. A., & Adarves-Yorno, I. (2006).When group members admit to being conformist: The role of relative intragroup status in conformity self-reports. *Personality and Social Psychology Bulletin, 32,* 162–173.

Jetten, J, McAuliffe, B.J., Hornsey, M.J., & Hogg, M.A. (2006). Differentiation between and within groups: The influence of individualist and collectivist group norms. *European Journal of Social Psychology, 36,* 825-843.

Jetten, J., & Postmes, T. (2006). "I did it my way." Collective expressions of individualism. In T. Postmes & J. Jetten (Eds.), *Individuality and the group: Advances in social identity* (pp. 116–136). London: Sage.

Jetten, J., Spears, R., & Manstead, A. S. R. (1997). Strength of identification and intergroup differentiation: The influence of group norms. *European Journal of Social Psychology, 27,* 603–609.

Johnson, A. L., Crawford, M. T., Sherman, S. J., Rutchick, A. M., Hamilton, D. L., Ferreira, M. B., et al. (2006). A functional perspective on group memberships: Differential need fulfillment in a group typology. *Journal of Experimental Social Psychology, 42,* 707–719.

Johnson, B. T. (1994). Effects of outcome-relevant involvement and prior information on persuasion. *Journal of Experimental Social Psychology, 30,* 556–579.

Johnson, J. C., Poteat, G. M., & Ironsmith, M. (1991). Structural vs. marginal effects: A note on the importance of structure in determining sociometric status. *Journal of Social Behavior and Personality, 6,* 489–508.

Johnson, J. D., & Lecci, L. (2003). Assessing anti-White attitudes and predicting perceived racism: The Johnson-Lecci scale. *Personality and Social Psychology Bulletin, 29,* 299–312.

Johnson, J. D., Simmons, C., Trawalter, S., Ferguson, T., & Reed, W. (2003). Observer race and White anti-Black bias: Factors that influence and mediate attributions of "ambiguously racist" behavior. *Personality and Social Psychology Bulletin, 29,* 609–622.

Johnson, M. K., & Sherman, S. J. (1990). Constructing and reconstructing the past and the future in the present. In E. T. Higgins & R. M. Sorrentino (Eds.), *Handbook of motivation and social cognition: Foundations of social behavior* (pp. 482–526). New York: Guilford.

Johnson, R. D., & Downing, L. L. (1979). Deindividuation and valence of cues: Effects on prosocial and antisocial behavior. *Journal of Personality and Social Psychology, 37,* 1532–1538.

Johnston, V. S., & Oliver-Rodriguez, J. C. (1997). Facial beauty and the late positive component of event-related potentials. *Journal of Sex Research, 34,* 188–198.

Johnstone, B., Frame, C. L., & Bouman, D. (1992). Physical attractiveness and athletic and academic ability in controversial–aggressive and rejected–aggressive children. *Journal of Social and Clinical Psychology, 11,* 71–79.

Joireman, J., Anderson, J., & Strathman, A. (2003). The aggression paradox: Understanding links among aggression, sensation seeking, and the consideration of future consequences. *Journal of Personality and Social Psychology, 84,* 1287–1302.

Joireman, J., Kamdar, D., Daniels, D., & Duell, B. (2006). Good citizens to the end? It depends: Empathy and concern with future consequences moderate the impact of a short-term time horizon on organizational citizenship behaviors. *Journal of Applied Psychology, 91,* 1307–1320.

Jonas, K. J., & Sassenberg, K. (2006). Knowing how to react: Automatic response priming from social categories. *Journal of Personality and Social Psychology, 90,* 709–721.

Jones, E. E. (1964). *Ingratiation: A social psychology analysis.* New York: Appleton-Century-Crofts.

Jones, E. E. (1979). The rocky road from acts to dispositions. *American Psychologist, 34,* 107–117.

Jones, E. E., & Davis, K. E. (1965). From acts to disposition: The attribution process in person perception. In L. Berkowitz (Ed.), *Advances in experimental social psychology* (Vol. 2, pp. 219–266). New York: Academic Press.

Jones, E. E., & Harris, V. A. (1967). The attribution of attitudes. *Journal of Experimental Social Psychology, 3,* 1–24.

Jones, E. E., & McGillis, D. (1976). Corresponding inferences and attribution cube: A comparative reappraisal. In J. H. Har, W. J. Ickes, & R. F. Kidd (Eds.), *New directions in attribution research* (Vol. 1). Morristown, NJ: Erlbaum.

Jones, E. E., & Nisbett, R. E. (1971). *The actor and the observer: Divergent perceptions of the causes of behavior.* Morristown, NJ: General Learning Press.

Jones, J. H. (1997, August 25 and September 1). Dr. Yes. *New Yorker,* 98–110, 112–113.

Judd, C. M., Ryan, C. S., & Parke, B. (1991). Accuracy in the judgment of in-group and out-group variability. *Journal of Personality and Social Psychology, 61,* 366–379.

Judge, T. A. (1992). The dispositional perspective in human resources research. *Research in Personnel and Human Resources Management, 10,* 31–72.

Judge, T. A., & Cable, T. A. (2004). The effect of physical height on workplace success and income: Preliminary test of a theoretical model. *Journal of Applied Psychology, 89,* 428–441.

Judge, T. A., Thoresen, C. J., Bono, J. E., & Patton, G. K. (2001). The job satisfaction–performance relationship: A qualitative and quantitative review. *Psychological Bulletin, 127,* 376–407.

Kahneman, D., & Miller, D. T. (1986). Norm theory: Comparing reality to its alternatives. *Psychological Review, 93,* 136–153.

Kahneman, D. & Tversky, A. (1982). Judgment under uncertainty: Heuristics and biases. In D. Kahneman P,. Slovic, & A. Tversky (Eds.). *Judgment under uncertainty: Heuristics and biases* (pp. 3–22). Cambridge, England: Cambridge Univeristy Press.

Kahneman, D., & Tversky, A. (1984). Choices, values, and frames. *American Psychologist, 39,* 341–350.

Kaiser, C. R., & Miller, C. T. (2001). Stop complaining! The social costs of making attributions to discrimination. *Personality and Social Psychology Bulletin, 27,* 254–263.

Kallgren, C. A., Reno, R. R., & Cialdini, R. B. (2000). A focus theory of normative conduct: When norms do and do not affect behavior. *Personality and Social Psychology Bulletin, 26,* 1002–1012.

Kameda, T., & Sugimori, S. (1993). Psychological entrapment in group decision making: An assigned decision rule and a groupthink phenomenon. *Journal of Personality and Social Psychology, 65,* 282–292.

Kammarath, L. K., Mendoza-Denton, R., & Mischel, W. (2005). Incorporating if . . . then . . . personality signatures in person perception: Beyond the person-situation dichotomy. *Journal of Personality and Social Psychology, 88,* 605–618.

Kandel, D. B. (1978). Similarity in real-life adolescent friendship pairs. *Journal of Personality and Social Psychology, 36,* 306–312.

Karau, S. J., & Williams, K. D. (1993). Social loafing: A meta-analytic review and theoretical integration. *Journal of Personality and Social Psychology, 65,* 681–706.

Kark, R., Shamir, B., & Chen, G. (2003). The two faces of transformational leadership: Empowerment and dependency. *Journal of Applied Psychology, 88,* 246–255.

Karraker, K. H., & Stern, M. (1990). Infant physical attractiveness and facial expression: Effects on adult perceptions. *Basic and Applied Social Psychology, 11,* 371–385.

Karremans, J. C., Van Lange, P. A. M., Ouwerkerk, J. W., & Kluwer, E. S. (2003). When forgiving enhances psychological well-being: The role of interpersonal commitment. *Journal of Personality and Social Psychology, 84,* 1011–1026.

Kashy, D. A., & DePaulo, B. M. (1996). Who lies? *Journal of Personality and Social Psychology, 70,* 1037–1051.

Kassin, S. M., & Kiechel, K. L. (1996). The social psychology of false confessions: Compliance, internalization, and confabulation. *Psychological Science, 7,* 125–128.

Kassin, S. M., & McNall, K. (1991). Police interrogations and confessions: Communicating promises and threats by pragmatic implication. *Law and Human Behavior, 15,* 233–251.

Katz, J., & Beach, S. R. H. (2000). Looking for love? Self-verification and self-enhancement effects on initial romantic attraction. *Personality and Social Psychology Bulletin, 26,* 1526–1539.

Kawakami K., & Dovidio, J. F. (2001). The reliability of implicit stereotyping. *Personality and Social Psychology Bulletin, 27,* 212–225.

Kawakami, K., Dion, K. L., & Dovidio, J. F. (1998). Racial prejudice and stereotype activation. *Personality and Social Psychology Bulletin, 24,* 407–416.

Kawakami K., Dovidio, J. F., Moll, J., Hermsen, S., & Russn, A. (2000). Just say no (to stereotyping): Effects of training in the negation of stereotypic associations on stereotype activation. *Journal and Personality and Social Psychology, 78,* 871–888.

Keller, L. M., Bouchard, T. J., Jr., Arvey, R. D., Segal, N. L., & Dawis, R. V. (1992). Work values: Genetic and environmental influences. *Journal of Applied Psychology, 77,* 79–88.

Keller, R. T. (1997). Job involvement and organizational commitment as longitudinal predictors of job performance: A study of scientists and engineers. *Journal of Applied Psychology, 82,* 539–545.

Kelley, H. H. (1972). Attribution in social interaction. In E. E. Jones et al. (Eds.), *Attribution: Perceiving the causes of behavior.* Morristown, NJ: General Learning Press.

Kelley, H. H., & Michela, J. L. (1980). Attribution theory and research. *Annual Review of Psychology, 31,* 57–501.

Kelly, A. E., & Kahn, J. H. (1994). Effects of suppression of personal intrusive thoughts. *Journal of Personality and Social Psychology, 66,* 998–1026.

Kelman, H. C. (1967). Human use of human subjects: The problem of deception in social psychological experiments. *Psychological Bulletin, 67,* 1–11.

Keltner, D., & Robinson, R. J. (1997). Defending the status quo: Power and bias in social conflict. *Personality and Social Psychology Bulletin, 23,* 1066–1077.

Keltner, D., Young, R. C., Heerey, E. A., Oemig, C., & Monarch, N. D. (1998). Teasing in hierarchical and intimate relations. *Journal of Personality and Social Psychology, 75,* 1231–1247.

Kemeny, M. E. (2003). The psychobiology of stress. *Current Directions in Psychological Science, 12,* 124–129.

Kenealy, P., Gleeson, K., Frude, N., & Shaw, W. (1991). The importance of the individual in the 'causal' relationship between attractiveness and self-esteem. *Journal of Community and Applied Social Psychology, 1,* 45–56.

Kenrick, D. T., & Gutierres, S. E. (1980). Contrast effects and judgments of physical attractiveness: When beauty becomes a social problem. *Journal of Personality and Social Psychology, 38,* 131–140.

Kenrick, D. T., Montello, D. R., Gutierres, S. E., & Trost, M. R. (1993). Effects of physical attractiveness on affect and perceptual judgments: When social comparison overrides social reinforcement. *Personality and Social Psychology Bulletin, 19,* 195–199.

Kenrick, D. T., Neuberg, S. L., Zierk, K. L., & Krones, J. M. (1994). Evolution and social cognition: Contrast effects as a function of sex, dominance, and physical attractiveness. *Personality and Social Psychology Bulletin, 20,* 210–217.

Kenrick, D. T., Sundie, J. M., Nicastle, L. D., & Stone, G. O. (2001). Can one ever be too wealthy or too chaste? Searching for nonlinearities in mate judgement. *Journal of Personality and Social Psychology, 80,* 462–471.

Kenworthy, J. B., & Miller, N. (2001). Perceptual asymmetry in consensus estimates of majority and minority members. *Journal of Personality and Social Psychology, 80,* 597–612.

Kernis, M. H., Cornell, D. P., Sun, C. R., Berry, A. J., & Harlow, T. (1993). There's more to self-esteem than whether it is high or low: The importance of stability of self-esteem. *Journal of Personality and Social Psychology, 65,* 1190–1204.

Kiecolt-Glaser, J. K., Fisher, L., Ogrocki, P., Stout, J. C., Speicher, C. E., & Glaser, R. (1987). Marital quality, marital disruption, and immune function. *Psychosomatic Medicine, 49,* 13–34.

Kiecolt-Glaser, J. K., Kennedy, S., Malkoff, S., Fisher, L., Speicher, C. E., & Glaser, R. (1988). Marital discord and immunity in males. *Psychosomatic Medicine, 50,* 213–229.

Kilduff, M., & Day, D. V. (1994). Do chameleons get ahead? The effects of self-monitoring on managerial careers. *Academy of Management Journal, 37,* 1047–1060.

Kilham, W., & Mann, L. (1974). Level of destructive obedience as a function of transmitter and executant roles in the Milgram obedience paradigm. *Journal of Personality and Social Psychology, 29,* 696–702.

Killeya, L. A., & Johnson, B. T. (1998). Experimental induction of biased systematic processing: The directed through technique. *Personality and Social Psychology Bulletin, 24,* 17–33.

Kirkpatrick, S. A., & Locke, E. A. (1991). Leadership: Do traits matter? *Academy of Management Executive, 5*(2), 48–60.

Kitzmann, K. M., Cohen, R., & Lockwood, R. L. (2002). Are only children missing out? Comparison of the peer-related social competence of only children and siblings. *Journal of Social and Personal Relationships, 19,* 299–316.

Klar, Y. (2002). Way beyond compare: The nonselective superiority and inferiority biases in judging randomly assigned group members relative to their peers. *Journal of Experimental Social Psychology, 38,* 331–351.

Klein, S. B., & Loftus, J. (1993). Behavioral experience and trait judgments about the self. *Personality and Social Psychology Bulletin, 16,* 740–745.

Klein, S. B., Loftus, J., & Plog, A. E. (1992). Trait judgments about the self: Evidence from the encoding specificity paradigm. *Personality and Social Psychology Bulletin, 18,* 730–735.

Kleinke, C. L. (1986). Gaze and eye contact: A research review. *Psychological Bulletin, 100,* 78–100.

Klinesmith, J., Kasser, T., & McAndrew, F. T. (2006). Guns, testosterone, and aggression. *Psychological Science, 17,* 568–571.

Klohnen, E. C., & Bera, S. (1998). Behavioral and experiential patterns of avoidantly and securely attached women across adulthood: A 31-year longitudinal perspective. *Journal of Personality and Social Psychology, 74,* 211–223.

Klohnen, E. C., & Luo, S. (2003). Interpersonal attraction and personality: What is attractive—self similarity, ideal similarity, complementarity, or attachment security? *Journal of Personality and Social Psychology, 85,* 709–722.

Knee, C. R. (1998). Implicit theories of relationships: Assessment and prediction of romantic relationship initiation, coping, and longevity. *Journal of Personality and Social Psychology, 74,* 360–370.

Koch, W. (1996, March 10). Marriage, divorce rates indicate Americans are hopelessly in love. *Albany Times Union,* p. A11.

Kochanska, G., Friesenborg, A. F., Lange, L. A., & Martel, M. M. (2004). Parents' personality and infants' temperament as contributors to their emerging relationship. *Journal of Personality and Social Psychology, 86,* 744–759.

Koehler, J. J. (1993). The base rate fallacy myth. *Psychology, 4.*

Kogan, N., & Wallach, M. A. (1964). *Risk-taking: A study in cognition and personality.* New York: Henry Holt.

Kohl, W. L., Steers, R., & Terborg, Jr. (1995). The effects of transformational leadership on teacher attitudes and student performance in Singapore. *Journal of Organizational Behavior, 73,* 695–702.

Komorita, M., & Parks, G. (1994). Interpersonal relations: Mixed-motive interaction. *Annual Review of Psychology, 46,* 183–207.

Koole, S. L., Greenberg, J., & Pyszczynski, T. (2006). Introducing science to the psychology of the soul: Experimental existential psychology. *Current Directions in Psychological Science, 15,* 211–216.

Kowalski, R. M. (1993). Interpreting behaviors in mixed-gender encounters: Effects of social anxiety and gender. *Journal of Social and Clinical Psychology, 12,* 239–247.

Kowalski, R. M. (1996). Complaints and complaining: Functions, antecedents, and consequences. *Psychological Bulletin, 119,* 179–196.

Kowalski, R. M. (2001). The aversive side of social interaction revisited. In R. M. Kowalski (Ed.), *Behaving badly: Aversive behaviors in interpersonal relationships* (pp. 297–309). Washington, DC: American Psychological Association.

Kozak, M. N., Marsh, A. A., & Wegner, D. M. (2006). What do I think you're doing? Action identification and mind attribution. *Journal of Personality and Social Psychology, 90,* 543–555.

Kraus, S. J. (1995). Attitudes and the prediction of behavior: A meta-analysis of the empirical literature. *Personality and Social Psychology Bulletin, 21,* 58–75.

Kray, L. J., Galinsky, A. D., & Wong, E. M. (2006). Thinking within the box: The relational processing style elicited by counterfactual mind-sets. *Journal of Personality and Social Psychology, 91,* 33–48.

Krosnick, J. A., Betz, A. L., Jussim, L. J., & Lynn, A. R. (1992). Subliminal conditioning of attitudes. *Personality and Social Psychology Bulletin, 18,* 152–162.

Kruger, J., Epley, N., Parker, J., & Ng, Z. W. (2005). Egocentrism over e-mail: Can we communicate as well as we think? *Journal of Personality and Social Psychology, 89,* 925–936.

Kulik, J. A., Mahler, H. I. M., & Moore, P. J. (1996). Social comparison and affiliation under threat: Effects on recovery from major surgery. *Journal of Personality and Social Psychology, 71,* 967–979.

Kunda, Z. (1999). *Social cognition: Making sense of people.* Cambridge, MA: MIT Press.

Kunda, Z., & Oleson, K. C. (1995). Maintaining stereotypes in the face of disconfirmation: Constructing grounds for subtyping deviants. *Journal of Personality and Social Psychology, 68,* 565–579.

Kurzban, R., & Neuberg, S. L. (2005). Managing ingroup and outgroup relationships. In D. M. Buss (Ed.), *Handbook of evolutionary psychology,* (pp. 653–675). New York: John Wiley.

Kwan, L. A., (1998). *Attitudes and attraction: A new view of how to diagnose the moderating effects of personality.* Unpublished master's thesis, National Universsity of Singapore.

Lalonde, R. N., & Silverman, R. A. (1994). Behavioral preferences in response to social injustice: The effects of group permeability and social identity salience. *Journal of Personality and Social Psychology, 66,* 78–85.

Lamm, H., & Myers, D. G. (1978). Group-induced polarization of attitudes and behavior. In L. Berkowitz (Ed.), *Advances in experimental social psychology.* New York: Academic Press.

Landau, M. J., Solomon, S., Greenberg, J., Cohen, F., Pyszczynski, T., Arndt, J., et al. (2004). Deliver us from evil: The effects of mortality salience and reminders of 9/11 on support for President George W. Bush. *Personality and Social Psychology Bulletin, 30,* 1136–1150.

Landy, F. F., & Conte, J. M. (2004). *Work in the 21st century.* New York: McGraw-Hill.

Langer, E. (1984). *The psychology of control.* Beverly Hills, CA: Sage.

Langlois, J. H., & Roggman, L. A. (1990). Attractive faces are only average. *Psychological Science, 1,* 115–121.

Langlois, J. H., Roggman, L. A., & Musselman, L. (1994). What is average and what is not average about attractive faces? *Psychological Science, 5,* 214–220.

LaPiere, R. T. (1934). Attitude and actions. *Social Forces, 13,* 230–237.

Larson, J. R., Jr., Foster-Fishman, P. G., & Franz, T. M. (1998). Leadership style and the discussion of shared and unshared information in decision-making groups. *Personality and Social Psychology Bulletin, 24,* 482–495.

Lassiter, G. D. (2002). Illusory causation in the courtroom. *Current Directions in Psychological Science, 11,* 204–208.

Lassiter, G. D., Geers, A. L., Handley, I. M., Weiland, P. E., & Munhall, P. M. (2002). Videotaped interrogations and confessions: A simple change in camera perspective alters verdicts in simulated trials. *Journal of Applied Psychology, 87,* 867–874.

Latané, B., & Darley, J. M. (1968). Group inhibition of bystander intervention in emergencies. *Journal of Personality and Social Psychology, 10,* 215–221.

Latané, B., & Darley, J. M. (1970). *The unresponsive bystander: Why doesn't he help?* New York: Appleton-Century-Crofts.

Latané, B., & L'Herrou, T. (1996). Spatial clustering in the conformity game: Dynamic social impact in electronic groups. *Journal of Personality and Social Psychology, 70,* 1218–1230.

Latané, B., Williams, K., & Harkins, S. (1979). Many hands make light the work: The causes and consequences of social loafing. *Journal of Personality and Social Psychology, 37,* 822–832.

Lau, S., & Gruen, G. E. (1992). The social stigma of loneliness: Effect of target person's and perceiver's sex. *Personality and Social Psychology Bulletin, 18,* 182–189.

Laurenceau, J.-P., Barrett, L. F., & Pietromonaco, P. R. (1998). Intimacy as an interpersonal process: The importance of self-disclosure, partner disclosure, and perceived partner responsiveness in interpersonal exchanges. *Journal of Personality and Social Psychology, 74,* 1238–1251.

Lazarus R. A. & Folkman, S. (1984). *Stress appraisal and coping.* New York Springer.

Lazarus, R. S., Opton, E. M., Nomikos, M. S., & Rankin, N. O. (1985). The principle of short-circuiting of threat: Further evidence. *Journal of Personality, 33,* 622–635.

LeBlanc, M. M., & Barling, J. (2004). Workplace aggression. *Current Directions in Psychological Science, 13,* 9–12.

Lee, A. Y. (2001). The mere exposure effect: An uncertainty reduction explanation revisited. *Personality and Social Psychology Bulletin, 27,* 1255–1266.

Lee, Y. T., & Seligman, M. E. P. (1997). Are Americans more optimistic than the Chinese? *Personality and Social Psychology Bulletin, 23,* 32–40.

Lehman, T. C., Daubman, K. A., Guarna, J., Jordan, J., & Cirafesi, C. (1995, April). *Gender differences in the motivational consequences of receiving help.* Paper presented at the meeting of the Eastern Psychological Association, Boston.

Lehmiller, J. J., & Agnew, C. R. (2006). Marginalized relationships: The impact of social disapproval on romantic relationships commitment. *Personality and Social Psychology Bulletin, 32,* 40–51.

Leippe, M. R., & Eisenstadt, D. (1994). Generalization of dissonance reduction: Decreasing prejudice through induced compliance. *Journal of Personality and Social Psychology, 67,* 395–413.

Lemley, B. (2000, February). Isn't she lovely? *Discover,* 42–49.

Lemonick, M. D., & Dorfman, A. (2001, July 23). One giant step for mankind. *Time,* 54–61.

Leventhal, H., Watts, J. C., & Pagano, F. (1967). Effects of fear and instructions on how to cope with danger. *Journal of Personality and Social Psychology, 6,* 313-321.

Levine, M., & Wallach, L. (2002). *Psychological problems, social issues, and the law.* Boston: Allyn & Bacon, Inc.

Levine, R. V., Martinez, T. S., Brase, G., & Sorenson, K. (1994). Helping in 36 U.S. cities. *Journal of Personality and Social Psychology, 67,* 69–82.

Levy, B., & Langer, E. (1994). Aging free from negative stereotypes: Successful memory in China and among the American deaf. *Journal of Personality and Social Psychology, 66,* 989–997.

Levy, B. R., Slade, M. D., Kunkel, S. R., & Kasl, S. V. (2002). Longevity increased by positive self-perceptions of aging. *Journal of Personality and Social Psychology, 83,* 261–270.

Leyens, J.-P., Desert, M., Croizet, J.-C., & Darcis, C. (2000). Stereotype threat: Are lower status and history of stigmatization preconditions of stereotype threat? *Personality and Social Psychology Bulletin, 26,* 1189–1199.

Li, N. P., Bailey, J. M., Kenrick, D. T., & Linsenmeier, J. A. W. (2002). The necessities and luxuries of male preferences: Testing the tradeoffs. *Journal of Personality and Social Psychology, 82,* 947–955.

Li, N. P., & Kenrick, D. T. (2006). Sex similarities and differences in preferences for short-term mates: What, whether, and why. *Journal of Personality and Social Psychology, 90,* 468–489.

Liberman, A., & Chaiken, S. (1992). Defensive processing of personally relevant health messages. *Personality and Social Psychology Bulletin, 18,* 669–679.

Liberman, N., Idson, L. C., Camacho, C. J., Higgins, E. G. (1999). Promotion and prevention choices between stability and change. *Journal of Personality and Social Psychology, 77,* 1135–1145.

Lickel, B., Hamilton, D. L., & Sherman, S. J. (2001). Elements of a lay theory of groups: Types of groups, relational styles, and the perception of group entitativity. *Personality and Social Psychology Review, 5,* 129–140.

Lickel, B., Hamilton, D. L., Wieczorkowski, G., Lewis, A., Sherman, S. J., & Uhles, A. N. (2000). Varieties of groups and the perception of group entiativity. *Journal of Personality and Social Psychology, 78,* 223–246.

Lickel, B., Rutchick, A. M., Hamilton, D. L., & Sherman, S. J. (2006). Intuitive theories of group types and relational principles. *Journal of Experimental Social Psychology, 42,* 28–39.

Liden, R. C., & Mitchell, T. R. (1988). Ingratiatory behaviors in organizational settings. *Academy of Management Review, 13,* 572–587.

Liebert, R. M., & Baron, R. A. (1972). Some immediate effects of televised violence on children's behavior. *Developmental Psychology, 6,* 469–475.

Lin, M.-C., & Haywood, J. (2003). Accommodation predictors of grandparent-grandchild relational solidarity in Taiwan. *Journal of Social and Personal Relationships, 20,* 537–563.

Linden, E. (1992). Chimpanzees with a difference: Bonobos. *National Geographic, 18*(3), 46–53.

Lindsay, D. S., Hagen, L., Read, J. D., Wade, K. A., & Garry, M. (2004). True photographs and false memories. *Psychological Science, 15,* 149–154.

Lindsey, E. W., Mize, J., & Pettit, G. S. (1997). Mutuality in parent–child play: Consequences for children's peer competence. *Journal of Social and Personal Relationships, 14,* 523–538.

Linz, D., & Penrod, S. (1992). Exploring the first and sixth amendments: Pretrial publicity and jury decision making. In D. K. Kagehiro & W. S. Laufer (Eds.), *Handbook of psychology and law.* New York: Springer-Verlag.

Linz, D., Donnerstein, E., & Penrod, S. (1988). Effects of long-term exposure to violent and sexually degrading depictions of women. *Journal of Personality and Social Psychology, 55,* 758–768.

Linz, D., Fuson, I. A., & Donnerstein, E. (1990). Mitigating the negative effects of sexually violent mass communications through pre-exposure briefings. *Communication Research, 17,* 641–674.

Locke, E. A. (1991). *The essence of leadership.* New York: Lexington Books.

Locke, V., & Johnston, L. (2001). Stereotyping and prejudice: A social cognitive approach. In M. Augoustinos & K. J. Reynolds (Eds.), *Understanding prejudice, racism, and social conflict* (pp. 107–125). London: Sage.

Locke, V., & Walker, I. (1999). Stereotyping, processing goals, and social identity: Inveterate and fugacious characteristics of stereotypes. In D. Abrams & M. A. Hogg (Eds.), *Social identity and social cognition* (pp. 164–182). Oxford: Blackwell.

Lockwood, P., & Kunda, Z. (1999). Increasing the salience of one's best selves can undermine inspiration by outstanding role models. *Journal of Personality and Social Psychology, 76,* 214–228.

Loftus, E. F. (1992). *Witness for the defense.* New York: St. Martin's Press.

Loftus, E. F. (2003). Make-believe memories. *American Psychologist, 58,* 867–873.

Long, C. R., Seburn, M., Averill, J. R., & More, T. A. (2003). Solitude experiences: Varieties, settings, and individual differences. *Personality and Social Psychology Bulletin, 29,* 578–583.

Lonnqvist, J. E., Leikas, S., Paunonen, S., Nissinen, V., & Verkasalo, M. (2006). Conformism moderates the relations between values, anticipated regret, and behavior. *Personality and Social Psychology Bulletin, 32,* 1469–1481.

Lopez, F. G., Gover, M. R., Leskela, J., Sauer, E. M., Schirmer, L., & Wyssmann, J. (1997). Attachment styles, shame, guilt, and collaborative problem-solving orientations. *Personal Relationships, 4,* 187–199.

Lord, C. G., & Saenz, D. S. (1985). Memory deficits and memory surfeits: Differential cognitive consequences of tokenism for tokens and observers. *Journal of Personality and Social Psychology, 49,* 918–926.

Lorenz, K. (1966). *On aggression.* New York: Harcourt, Brace, & World.

Lorenz, K. (1974). *Civilized man's eight deadly sins.* New York: Harcourt, Brace, Jovanovich.

Lowery, B. S., Unzueta, M. M., Goff, P. A., & Knowles, E. D. (2006). Concern for the in-group and opposition to affirmative action. *Journal of Personality and Social Psychology, 90,* 961–974.

Lundberg, J. K., & Sheehan, E. P. (1994). The effects of glasses and weight on perceptions of attractiveness and intelligence. *Journal of Social Behavior and Personality, 9,* 753–760.

Lyubomirsky, S., King, L., & Diener, E. (2005). The benefits of frequent positive affect: Does happiness lead to success? *Psychological Bulletin, 131,* 803–855.

Lyness, K. S., & Heilman, M. E. (2006). When fit is fundamental: Performance evaluations and promotions of upper-level female and male managers. *Journal of Applied Psychology, 91,* 777–785.

Ma, H. K., Shek, D. T. L., Cheung, P. C., & Tam, K. K. (2002). A longitudinal study of peer and teacher influences on prosocial and antisocial behavior of Hong Kong Chinese adolescents. *Social Behavior and Personality, 30,* 157–168.

Maass, A., Cadinu, M., Guarnieri, G., & Grasselli, A. (2003). Sexual harassment under social identity threat: The computer harassment paradigm. *Journal of Personality and Social Psychology, 85,* 853–870.

Maass, A., & Clark, R. D. III (1984). Hidden impact of minorities: Fifteen years of minority influence research. *Psychological Bulletin, 95,* 233–243.

Macaulay, J. (1970). A shill for charity. In J. Macaulay & L. Berkowitz (Eds.), *Altruism and helping behavior* (pp. 43–59). New York: Academic Press.

MacDonald, T. K., Zanna, M. P., & Fong, G. T. (1995). Decision making in altered states: Effects of alcohol on attitudes toward drinking and driving. *Journal of Personality and Social Psychology, 68,* 973–985.

Mack, D., & Rainey, D. (1990). Female applicants' grooming and personnel selection. *Journal of Social Behavior and Personality, 5,* 399–407.

Mackie, D. M., & Smith, E. R. (2002). Beyond prejudice: Moving from positive and negative evaluations to differentiated reactions to social groups. In D. M. Mackie & E. R. Smith (Eds.), *From prejudice to intergroup emotions: Differentiated reactions to social groups* (pp. 1–12). New York: Psychology Press.

Mackie, D. M., & Worth, L. T. (1989). Cognitive deficits and the mediation of positive affect in persuasion. *Journal of Personality and Social Psychology, 57,* 27–40.

MacKinnon, I. (2007). Model purse on anorexics makes weight vital statistics. *Times* Online, Retrieved February 21, 2007, from timesonline.co.uk/to1/news/world/artic.e407053.ece.

Macrae, C. N., Milne, A. B., & Bodenhausen, G. V. (1994). Stereotypes as energy-saving devices: A peek inside the cognitive toolbox. *Journal of Personality and Social Psychology, 66,* 37–47.

Macrae, C. N., Mitchell, J. P., & Pendry, L. F. (2002). What's in a forename? Cue familiarity and stereotypical thinking. *Journal of Experimental Social Psychology, 38,* 186–193.

Macrae, C. N., Bodenhausen, G. V., Milne, A. B., & Ford, R. (1997). On the regulation of recollection: The intentional forgetting of sterotypical memories. *Journal of Personality and Social Psychology, 72,* 709–719.

Maddux, W. W., Barden, J., Brewer, M. B., & Petty, R. E. (2005). Saying no to negativity: The effects of context and motivation to control prejudice on automatic evaluative responses. *Journal of Experimental Social Psychology, 41,* 19–35.

Madell, D. E., & Muncer, S. J. (2007). Control over social interactions: An important reason for young people's use of the internet and mobile phones for communication? *Cyber Psychology and Behavior, 10,* 137–140.

Madon, S., Jussim, L., & Eccles, J. S. (1997). In search of the powerful self-fulfilling prophecy. *Journal of Personality and Social Psychology, 72,* 791–809.

Maeda, E., & Ritchie, L. D. (2003). The concept of *shinyuu* in Japan: A replication of and comparison to Cole and Bradac's study on U.S. friendship. *Journal of Social and Personal Relationships, 20,* 579–598.

Maheswaran, D., & Chaiken, S. (1991). Promoting systematic processing in low-motivation settings: Effect of incongruent information on processing and judgment. *Journal of Personality and Social Psychology, 61,* 13–25.

Maio, G. R., Esses, V. M., & Bell, D. W. (1994). The formation of attitudes toward new immigrant groups. *Journal of Applied Social Psychology, 24,* 1762–1776.

Maio, G. R., Fincham, F. D., & Lycett, E. J. (2000). Attitudinal ambivalence toward parents and attachment style. *Personality and Social Psychology Bulletin, 26,* 1451–1464.

Maio, G. R., & Thomas, G. (2007). The epistemic-teleologic model of deliberate self-persuasion. *Personality and Social Psychology Review, 11,* 46–67.

Major, B. (1994). From social inequality to personal entitlement: The role of social comparisons, legitimacy appraisals, and group membership. In M. P. Zanna (Ed.), *Advances in experimental social psychology* (Vol. 26, pp. 293–348). San Diego, CA: Academic Press.

Major, B., Barr, L., Zubek, J., & Babey, S. H. (1999). Gender and self-esteem: A meta-analysis. In W. B. Swann, J. H. Langlois, & L. A. Gilbert (Eds.), *Sexism and stereotypes in modern society* (pp. 223–253). Washington, DC: American Psychological Association.

Malamuth, N. M., & Brown, L. M. (1994). Sexually aggressive men's perceptions of women's communications: Testing three explanations. *Journal of Personality and Social Psychology 67,* 699–712.

Malamuth, N. M., & Check, J. V. P. (1985). The effects of aggressive pornography on beliefs in rape myths: Individual differences. *Journal of Research in Personality, 19,* 299–320.

Manning, J. T., Koukourakis, K., & Brodie, D. A. (1997). Fluctuating asymmetry, metabolic rate and sexual selection in human males. *Evolution and Human Behavior, 18,* 15–21.

Marcus, B., Machilek, F., & Schütz, A. (2006). Personality in cyberspace: Personal web sites as media for personality expressions and impressions. *Journal of Personality and Social Psychology, 90,* 1014–1031.

Marcus, D. K., & Miller, R. S. (2003). Sex differences in judgments of physical attractiveness: A social relations analysis. *Personality and Social Psychology Bulletin, 29,* 325–335.

Markey, P. M., Funder, D. C., & Ozer, D. J. (2003). Complementarity of interpersonal behaviors in dyadic interactions. *Personality and Social Psychology Bulletin, 29,* 1082–1090.

Markman, G. D., Balkin, D. B., & Baron R. A. (2002). Inventors and new venture formation: The effects of general self-efficacy and regretful thinking. *Entrepreneurship Theory & Practice, 27,* 149–165.

Markus, H., & Nurius, P. (1986). Possible selves. *American Psychologist, 41,* 954–969.

Marques, J. M., Abrams, D., & Serôdio, G. S. (2001). Being better by being right: Subjective group dynamics and derogation of in-group deviants when generic norms are undermined. *Journal of Personality and Social Psychology, 81,* 436–447.

Marshall, M. A., & Brown, J. D. (2006). Trait aggressiveness and situational provocation: A test of the traits as situational sensitivities (TASS) model. *Personality and Social Psychology Bulletin, 32,* 1100–1113.

Martens, A., Johns, M., Greenberg, J., & Schimel, J. (2006). Combating stereotype threat: The effect of self-affirmation on women's intellectual performance. *Journal of Experimental Social Psychology, 42,* 236-243.

Martin, L. L., & Clore, G. L. (Eds.). (2001). *Mood and social cognition: Contrasting theories.* Mahwah, NJ: Erlbaum.

Martin, P. Y., Hamilton, V. E., McKimmie, B. M., Terry, D. J., & Martin, R. (2007). Effects of caffeine on persuasion and attitude change: The role of secondary tasks in manipulating systematic message processing. *European Journal of Social Psychology, 37,* 320–338.

Marx, D. M., & Stapel, D. A. (2006). It depends on your perspective: The role of self-relevance in stereotype-based underperformance. *Journal of Experimental Social Psychology, 42,* 768–775.

Maslach, C., Santee, R. T., & Wade, C. (1987). Individuation, gender role, and dissent: Personality mediators of situational forces. *Journal of Personality and Social Psychology, 53,* 1088–1094.

Matsumoto, D., & Willingham, B. (2006). The thrill of victory and the agony of defeat: Spontaneous expressions of medal winners of the 2004 Athens Olympic games. *Journal of Personality and Social Psychology, 91,* 568-581.

Matsushima, R., & Shiomi, K. (2002). Self-disclosure and friendship in junior high school students. *Social Behavior and Personality, 30,* 515–526.

Maurois, A. (1940). *The art of living.* The English Universities Press, UK.

Mauss, I. B., Evers, C., Wilhelm, F. H., & Gross, J. J. (2006). How to bite your tongue without blowing your top: Implicit evaluation of emotion regulation predicts affective responding to anger provocation. *Personality and Social Psychology Bulletin, 32,* 589–602.

May, J. L., & Hamilton, P. A. (1980). Effects of musically evoked affect on women's interpersonal attraction and perceptual judgments of physical attractiveness of men. *Motivation and Emotion, 4,* 217–228.

Mayo, C., & Henley, N. M. (Eds.). (1981). *Gender and nonverbal behavior.* Seacaucaus, NJ: Springer-Verlag.

Mazzella, R., & Feingold, A. (1994). The effects of physical attractiveness, race, socioeconomic status, and gender of defendants and victims on judgments of mock jurors: A meta-analysis. *Journal of Applied Social Psychology, 24,* 1315–1344.

McAdams, D. P., Diamond, A., Aubin, E. de S., & Mansfield, E. (1997). Stories of commitment: The psychosocial construction of generative lives. *Journal of Personality and Social Psychology, 72,* 678–694.

McAuley, E., Pen, M., & Jerome, G. (2001). Self-efficacy as a determinant and an outcome of exercise. In G. C. Roberts (Ed.), *Advances in motivation in sport and exercises* (pp. 235–261). Champaign, IL: Human Kinetics Publishers.

McCall, M. (1997). Physical attractiveness and access to alcohol: What is beautiful does not get carded. *Journal of Applied Social Psychology, 23,* 453–562.

McClure, S., Laibson, D Loewenstein, G., & Cohen, J. D. (2004). Separate neural systems value immediate and delayed monetary rewards, *Science* 306, October 15, 2004.

McConahay, J. B. (1986). Modern racism, ambivalence, and the Modern Racism Scale. In J. F. Dovidio & S. L. Gaertner (Eds.), *Prejudice, discrimination, and racism* (pp. 91–125). New York: Academic Press.

McCullough, M. E., Fincham, F. D., & Tsang, J. A. (2003). Forgiveness, forbearance, and time: The temporal unfolding of transgression-related interpersonal motivations. *Journal of Personality and Social Psychology, 84,* 540–557.

McCullough, M. E., Bellah, C. G., Kilpatrick, S. D., & Johnson, S. L. (2001). Vengefulness: Relationships with forgiveness, rumination, well-being, and the Big Five. *Personality and Social Psychology Bulletin, 27,* 601–610.

McDonald, H. E., & Hirt, E. R. (1997). When expectancy meets desire: Motivational effects in reconstructive memory. *Journal of Personality and Social Psychology, 72,* 5–23.

McDonald, R. D. (1962). *The effect of reward–punishment and affiliation need on interpersonal attraction.* Unpublished doctoral dissertation, University of Texas.

McEwen, B. S. (1998). Protective and dangerous effects of stress mediators. *New England Journal of Medicine, 338,* 171–179.

McGonagle, K. A., Kessler, R. C., & Schilling, E. A. (1992). The frequency and determinants of marital disagreements in a community sample. *Journal of Social and Personal Relationships, 9,* 507–524.

McGuire, S., & Clifford, J. (2000). Genetic and environmental contributions to loneliness in children. *Psychological Science, 11,* 487–491.

McGuire, S., McHale, S. M., & Updegraff, K. A. (1996). Children's perceptions of the sibling relationship in middle childhood: Connections within and between family relationships. *Personal Relationships, 3,* 229–239.

McHoskey, J. W. (1999). Machiavellianism, intrinsic versus extrinsic goals, and social interest: A self-determination theory analysis. *Motivation and Emotion, 23,* 267–283.

McKelvie, S. J. (1993a). Perceived cuteness, activity level, and gender in schematic babyfaces. *Journal of Social Behavior and Personality, 8,* 297–310.

McKelvie, S. J. (1993b). Stereotyping in perception of attractiveness, age, and gender in schematic faces. *Social Behavior and Personality, 21,* 121–128.

McLaughlin, L. (2001, April 30). Happy together. *Time,* 82.

McNulty, J. K., & Karney, B. R. (2004). Positive expectations in the early years of marriage: Should couples expect the best or brace for the worst? *Journal of Personality and Social Psychology, 86,* 729–743.

Mead, G. H. (1934). *Mind, self, and society.* Chicago: University of Chicago Press.

Medvec, V. H., & Savitsky, K. (1997). When doing better means feeling worse: The effects of categorical cutoff points on counterfactual thinking and satisfaction. *Journal of Personality and Social Psychology, 72,* 1284–1296.

Medvec, V. H., Madey, S. F., & Gilovich, T. (1995). When less is more: Counterfactual thinking and satisfaction among Olympic athletes. *Journal of Personality and Social Psychology, 69,* 603–610.

Mehrabian, A., & Piercy, M. (1993). Affective and personality characteristics inferred from length of first names. *Personality and Social Psychology Bulletin, 19,* 755–758.

Meier, B. P., Robinson, M. D., & Clore, G. L. (2004). Why good guys wear white. Automatic interferences about stimulus valence based on brightness. *Psychological Science, 15,* 82–87.

Meier, B. P., Robinson, M. D., & Wilkowski, B. M. (2006). Turning the other cheek: Agreeableness and the regulation of aggression-related primes. *Psychological Science, 17,* 136–142.

Melamed, S., Ben-Avi, I., Luz-J., & Green, G. S. (1993). Repetititve work, work underload and coronary heart disease among blue collars workers. *Journal of Psychosomatic Research, 39,* 19–29.

Meleshko, K. G. A., & Alden, L. E. (1993). Anxiety and self-disclosure: Toward a motivational model. *Journal of Personality and Social Psychology, 64,* 1000–1009.

Mendoza-Denton, R., Ayduk, O., Mischel, W., Shoda, Y., & Testa, A. (2001). Person X situation interactionism in self-encoding (*I am . . . When . . .*): Implications for affect regulation and social information processing. *Journal of Personality and Social Psychology, 80,* 533–544.

Meyers, S. A., & Berscheid, E. (1997). The language of love: The difference a preposition makes. *Personality and Social Psychology Bulletin, 23,* 347–362.

Miceli, M. P., & Lane, M. C. (1991). Antecedents of pay satisfaction: A review and extension. In K. Rowland & O. R. Ferris (Eds.), *Research in personnel and human resources management* (Vol. 9, pp. 235–309). Greenwich, CT: JAI Press.

Mikulincer, M. (1998). Adult attachment style and individual differences in functional versus dysfunctional experiences of anger. *Journal of Personality and Social Psychology, 74,* 513–524.

Mikulincer, M., Gillath, O., Halevy, V., Avihou, N., Avidan, S., & Eshkoli, N. (2001). Attachment theory and reactions to others' needs: Evidence that activation of the sense of attachment security promotes empathic responses. *Journal of Personality and Social Psychology, 81,* 1205–1224.

Miles, S. M., & Carey, G. (1997). Genetic and environmental architecture of human aggression. *Journal of Personality and Social Psychology, 72,* 207–217.

Milgram, S. (1963). Behavior study of obedience. *Journal of Abnormal and Social Psychology, 67,* 371–378.

Milgram, S. (1965a). Liberating effects of group pressure. *Journal of Personality and Social Psychology, 1,* 127–134.

Milgram, S. (1965b). Some conditions of obedience and disobedience to authority. *Human Relations, 18,* 57–76.

Milgram, S. (1974). *Obedience to authority.* New York: Harper.

Miller, D. A., Smith, E. R., & Mackie, D. M. (2004). Effects of intergroup contact and political predispositions on prejudice: Role of intergroup emotions. *Group Processes and Intergroup Relations, 7,* 221–237.

Miller, D. T., & McFarland, C. (1987). Pluralistic ignorance: When similarity is interpreted as dissimilarity. *Journal of Personality and Social Psychology, 53,* 298–305.

Miller, D. T., Monin, B., & Prentice, D. A. (2000). Pluralistic ignorance and inconsistency between private attitudes and public behaviors. In D. J. Terry & M. A. Hogg (Eds.), *Attitudes, behavior, and social context* (pp. 95–113). Mahwah, NJ: Erlbaum.

Miller, D. T., & Ross, M. (1975) Self-serving biases in the attribution of causality: Fact or fiction? *Psychological Bulletin, 82,* 213–225.

Miller, J. E., Niehuis, S., & Huston, T. L. (2006). Positive illusions in marital relationships: A 13-year longitudinal study. *Personality and Social Psychology Bulletin, 32,* 1579–1594.

Miller, L. C., Putcha-Bhagavatula, A., & Pedersen, W. C. (2002, June). Men's and women's mating preferences: Distinct evolutionary mechanisms? *Current Directions in Psychological Science, 11,* 88–93.

Miller, P. J. E., Caughlin, J. P., & Huston, T. L. (2003). Trait expressiveness and marital satisfaction: The role of idealization processes. *Journal of Marriage and Family, 65,* 978–995.

Miller, P. J. E., Niehuis, S., & Huston, T. L. (2006). Positive illusions in marital relationships: A 13-year longitudinal study. *Personality and Social Psychology Bulletin, 32,* 1579–1594.

Miller, P. J. E., & Rempel, J. K. (2004). Trust and partner-enhancing attributions in close relationships. *Personality and Social Psychology Bulletin, 30,* 695–705.

Miron, A. M., Branscombe, N. R., & Schmitt, M. T. (2006). Collective guilt as distress over illegitimate intergroup inequality. *Group Processes and Intergroup Relations, 9,* 163–180.

Mitchell, D. B. (2006). Nonconscious priming after 17 years: Invulnerable implicit memory? *Psychological Science, 17,* 925–929.

Monin, B. (2003). The warm glow heuristic: When liking leads to familiarity. *Journal of Personality and Social Psychology, 85,* 1035–1048.

Monin, B., & Miller, D. T. (2001). Moral credentials and the expression of prejudice. *Journal of Personality and Social Psychology, 81,* 33–43.

Monteith, M. J., Ashburn-Nardo, L., Voils, C. I., & Czopp, A. M. (2002). Putting the brakes on prejudice: On the development and operation of cues for control. *Journal of Personality and Social Psychology, 83,* 1029–1050.

Monteith, M. J., & Spicer, C. V. (2000). Contents and correlates of Whites' and Blacks' racial attitudes. *Journal of Experimental Social Psychology, 36,* 125–154.

Monteith, M. J., Devine, P. G., & Zuwerink, J. R. (1993). Self-directed versus other-directed affect as a consequence of prejudice-related discrepancies. *Journal of Personality and Social Psychology, 64,* 198–210.

Montepare, J. M., & Zebrowitz-McArthur, L. (1988). Impressions of people created by age-related qualities of their gates. *Journal of Personality and Social Psychology, 55,* 547–556.

Moore, T. (1993, August 16). Millions of volunteers counter image of a selfish society. *Albany Times Union,* p. A-2.

Moran, G. (1993, February 23). Personal communication.

Moran, G., & Cutler, B. L. (1991). The prejudicial impact of pretrial publicity. *Journal of Applied Social Psychology, 21,* 345–367.

Moreland, R. L., & Beach, S. R. (1992). Exposure effects in the classroom: The development of affinity among students. *Journal of Experimental Social Psychology, 28,* 255–276.

Moreland, R. L., & Levine, J. M. (2001). Socialization in organizations and work groups. In M. Turner (Ed.), *Groups at work: Theory and research* (pp. 69–112). Mahwah, NJ: Erlbaum.

Morey, N., & Gerber, G. L. (1995). Two types of competitiveness: Their impact on the perceived interpersonal attractiveness of women and men. *Journal of Applied Social Psychology, 25,* 210–222.

Morgan, D., Carder, P., & Neal, M. (1997). Are some relationships more useful than others? The value of similar others in the networks of recent widows. *Journal of Social and Personal Relationships, 14,* 745–759.

Morris, M. W., & Pang, K. (1994). Culture and cause: American and Chinese attributions for social and physical events. *Journal of Personality and Social Psychology, 67,* 949–971.

Morrison, E. W. (1994). Role definitions and organizational citizenship behavior: The importance of employees' perspective. *Academy of Management Journal, 37,* 1543–1567.

Morrison, E. W., & Bies, R. J. (1991). Impression management in the feedback-seeking process: A literature review and research agenda. *Academy of Management Review, 16,* 322–341.

Moscovici, S. (1985). Social influence and conformity. In G. Lindzey & E. Aronson (Eds.), *Handbook of social psychology* (3rd ed.). New York: Random House.

Mount, M. K., & Barrick, M. R. (1995). The Big Five personality dimensions: Implications for research and practice in human resources management. In K. M. Rowland & G. Ferris (Eds.), *Research in personnel and human resources management* (Vol. 13, pp. 153–200). Greenwich, CT: JAI Press.

Muczyk, J. P., & Reimann, B. C. (1987). The case for directive leadership. *Academy of Management Review, 12,* 637–647.

Mugny, G. (1975). Negotiations, image of the other and the process of minority influence. *European Journal of Social Psychology, 5,* 209–229.

Mulder, L. B., van Dijk, E., De Cremer, D., & Wilke, H. A. M. (2006). Undermining trust and cooperation: The paradox of sanctioning systems in social dilemmas. *Journal of Experimental Social Psychology, 42,* 147–162.

Mullen, B., & Cooper, C. (1994). The relation between group cohesiveness and performance: An integration. *Psychological Bulletin, 115,* 210–227.

Mullen, B., Johnson, C., & Salas, E. (1991). Productivity loss in brainstorming groups: A meta-analytic integration. *Basic and Applied Social Psychology, 12,* 3–23.

Munkes, J., & Diehl, M. (2003). Matching or competition? Performance comparison processes in an idea generation task. *Group Processes and Intergroup Relations, 6,* 305–320.

Munsterberg, H. (1907). *On the witness stand: Essays in psychology and crime.* New York: McClure.

Murray, L., & Trevarthen, C. (1986). The infant's role in mother-infant communications. *Journal of Child Language, 13,* 15–29.

Murray, S. L., Griffin, D. W., Rose, P., and Bellavia, G. (2006). For better or worse? Self-esteem and the contingencies of acceptance in marriage. *Personality and Social Psychology Bulletin, 32,* 866-880.

Murray, S. L., & Holmes, J. G. (1997). A leap of faith? Positive illusions in romantic relationships. *Personality and Social Psychology Bulletin, 23,* 586–604.

Murray, S. L., & Holmes, J. G. (1999). The (mental) ties that bind: Cognitive structures that predict relationship resilience. *Journal of Personality and Social Psychology, 77,* 1228–1244.

Murray, S. L., Holmes, J. G., & Griffin, D. W. (2000). Self-esteem and the quest for felt security: How perceived regard regulates attachment processes. *Journal of Personality and Social Psychology, 78,* 478–498.

Murray, S. L., Holmes, J. G., Dolderman, D., & Griffin, D. W. (2000). What the motivated mind sees: Comparing friends' perspectives to married partners views of each other. *Journal of Experimental Social Psychology, 36,* 600–260.

Murray, S. L., Holmes, J. G., Griffin, D. W., Bellavia, G., & Rose, P. (2001). The mismeasure of love: How self-doubt contaminates relationship beliefs. *Personality and Social Psychology Bulletin, 27,* 423–436.

Murray, S. L., Rose, P., Holmes, J., Derrick, J. H., Podchaski, E., Bellavia, G., et al. (2005). Putting the partner within reach: A relational perspective on felt security. *Journal of Personality and Social Psychology, 88,* 327–347.

Mynard, H., & Joseph, S. (1997). Bully victim problems and their association with Eysenck's personality dimensions in 8 to 13 year olds. *British Journal of Educational Psychology, 67,* 51–54.

Nadler, A., Fisher, J. D., & Itzhak, S. B. (1983). With a little help from my friend: Effect of a single or multiple acts of aid as a function of donor and task characteristics. *Journal of Personality and Social Psychology, 44,* 310–321.

Nadler, A., & Halabi, S. (2006). Intergroup helping as status relations: Effects of status stability, identification, and type of help on receptivity to high-status group's help. *Journal of Personality and Social Psychology, 91,* 97–110.

Nario-Redmond, M. R., & Branscombe, N. A. (1996). It could have better and it might have been worse: Implications for blame assignment in rape cases. *Basic and Applied Social Psychology, 18,* 347–366.

National Institute for Occupational Safety and Health, Center for Disease Control and Prevention. "Homicide in the workplace." Document #705003, December 5, 1993.

Nemeth, C. J., Personnaz, B., Personnaz, M., & Goncalo, J. A. (2004). The liberating role of conflict in group creativity: A study in two countries. *European Journal of Social Psychology, 34,* 365–374.

Neuman, J. H., & Baron, R. A. (2004). Aggression in the workplace: A social-psychological perspective. In S. Fox & P. E. Spector (Eds.), *Counterproductive workplace behavior: An integration of both actor and recipient perspectives on causes and consequences.* Washington, DC: American Psychological Association.

Newby-Clark, I. R., & Ross, M. (2003). Conceiving the past and future. *Personality and Social Psychology Bulletin, 29,* 807–818.

Newcomb, T. M. (1956). The prediction of interpersonal attraction. *Psychological Review, 60,* 393–404.

Newcomb, T. M. (1961). *The acquaintance process.* New York: Holt, Rinehart and Winston.

Newsom, J. T. (1999). Another side to caregiving: Negative reactions to being helped. *Current Directions in Psychological Science, 8,* 183–187.

Neyer, F. J., & Lang, F. R. (2003). Blood is thicker than water: Kinship orientation across adulthood. *Journal of Personality and Social Psychology, 84,* 310–321.

Nida, S. A., & Koon, J. (1983). They get better looking at closing time around here, too. *Psychological Reports, 52,* 657–658.

Nisbett, R. E. (1990). Evolutionary psychology, biology, and cultural evolution. *Motivation and Emotion, 14,* 255–264.

Nisbett, R. E., Caputo, C., Legbant, P., & Marecek, J. (1973). Behavior as seen by the actor and as seen by the observer. *Journal of Personality and Social Psychology, 27,* 154–164.

Nisbett, R. E., & Wilson, T. D. (1977). Telling more than we can know: Verbal reports on mental processes. *Psychological Review, 84,* 231–259.

Noel, J. G., Wann, D. L., & Branscombe, N. R. (1995). Peripheral ingroup membership status and public negativity toward outgroups. *Journal of Personality and Social Psychology, 68,* 127–137.

Norenzayan, A., & Hansen, G. (2006). Belief in supernatural agents in the face of death. *Personality and Social Psychology Bulletin, 32,* 174–187.

Norton, M. I., Frost, J. H., & Ariely, D. (2006). Less is more: The lure of ambiguity, or why familiarity breeds contempt. *Journal of Personality and Social Psychology, 92,* 97–105.

Norton, M. I., Sommers, S. R., Apfelbaum, E. P., Pura, N., & Ariely, D. (2006). Color blindness and interracial interaction: Playing the political correctness game. *Psychological Science, 17,* 949–953.

Nussbaum, S., Trope, Y., & Liberman, N. (2003). Creeping dispositionism: The temporal dynamics of behavior prediction. *Journal of Personality and Social Psychology 84,* 485–497.

Nyman, L. (1995). The identification of birth order personality attributes. *The Journal of Psychology, 129,* 51–59.

O'Connell, P. D. (1988). Pretrial publicity, change of venue, public opinion polls: A theory of procedural justice. *University of Detroit Law Review, 65,* 169–197.

O'Connor, S. C., & Rosenblood, L. K. (1996). Affiliation motivation in everyday experience: A theoretical comparison. *Journal of Personality and Social Psychology, 70,* 513–522.

O'Leary, S. G. (1995). Parental discipline mistakes. *Current Directions in Psychological Science, 4,* 11–13.

O'Moore, M. N. (2000). Critical issues for teacher training to counter bullying and victimization in Ireland. *Aggressive Behavior, 26,* 99–112.

Oskamp, S., & Schultz, P. W. (2005). *Attitudes and opinions* (3rd ed.). Mahwah, NJ: Lawrence Erlbaum.

O'Sullivan, C. S., & Durso, F. T. (1984). Effects of schema-incongruent information on memory for stereotypical attributes. *Journal of Personality and Social Psychology, 47,* 55–70.

O'Sullivan, M. (2003). The fundamental attribution error in detecting deception: The boy-who-cried-wolf effect. *Personality and Social Psychology Bulletin, 29,* 1316–1327.

Oakes, P. J., & Reynolds, K. J. (1997). Asking the accuracy question: Is measurement the answer? In R. Spears, P. J. Oakes, N. Ellemers, & S. A. Haslam (Eds.), *The social psychology of stereotyping and group life* (pp. 51–71). Oxford: Blackwell.

Oakes, P. J., Haslam, S. A., & Turner, J. C. (1994). *Stereotyping and social reality.* Oxford: Blackwell.

Oberlander, E. (2003, August). Cross-disciplinary perspectives on attachment processes. *American Psychological Society, 16,* 23, 35.

Oettingen, G. (1995). Explanatory style in the context of culture. In G. M. Buchanan & M. E. P. Seligman (Eds.), *Explanatory style.* Hillsdale, NJ: Erlbaum.

Oettingen, G., & Seligman, M. E. P. (1990). Pessimism and behavioral signs of depression in East versus West Berlin. *European Journal of Social Psychology, 201,* 207–220.

Ohbuchi, K., & Kambara, T. (1985). Attacker's intent and awareness of outcome, impression management, and retaliation. *Journal of Experimental Social Psychology, 21,* 321–330.

Ohman, A., Lundqvist, D., & Esteves, F. (2001). The face in the crowd revisited: Threat advantage with schematic stimuli. *Journal of Personality and Social Psychology, 80,* 381–396.

Okun, M. A., & Sloane, E. S. (2002). Application of planned behavior theory to predicting volunteer enrollment by college students in a campus-based program. *Social Behavior and Personality, 30,* 243–250.

Olson, J. M., & Maio, G. R. (2003). Attitudes in social behavior. In T. Millon & M. J. Lerner (Eds.), *Handbook of psychology: Personality and social psychology* (Vol. 5., pp. 299–325). New York: Wiley.

Olson, M. A., & Fazio, R. H. (2001). Implicit attitude formation through classical conditioning. *Psychological Science, 12,* 413–417.

Olweus, D. (1999). Sweden. In P. K. Smith, Y. Morita, J. Junger-Tas, D. Olweus, R. F. Catalano, & P. Slee (Eds.), *The nature of school bullying: A cross-national perspective* (pp. 7–27). New York: Routledge.

Omoto, A. M., & Snyder, M. (1995). Sustained helping without obligation: Motivation, longevity of service, and perceived attitude change among AIDS volunteers. *Journal of Personality and Social Psychology, 68,* 671–686.

Onishi, M., Gjerde, P. F., & Block, J. (2001). Personality implications of romantic attachment patterns in young adults: A multi-method, multi-informant study. *Personality and Social Psychology Bulletin, 27,* 1097–1110.

Orbell, S., Blair, C., Sherlock, K., & Conner, M. (2001). The theory of planned behavior and ecstasy use: Roles for habit and perceived control over taking versus obtaining substances. *Journal of Applied Social Psychology, 31,* 31–47.

Organ, D. (1988). *Organizational citizenship behavior: The good-soldier syndrome.* Lexington, MA: Lexington Books.

Organ, D. W. (1997). Organizational citizenship behavior: It's construct clean-up time. *Human Performance, 10,* 85–98.

Orpen, C. (1996). The effects of ingratiation and self promotion tactics on employee career success. *Social Behavior and Personality, 24,* 213–214.

Osborn, A. F. (1953). *Applied Imagination.* New York: Scribner.

Osborne, J. W. (2001). Testing stereotype threat: Does anxiety explain race and sex differences in achievement? *Contemporary Educational Psychology, 26,* 291–310.

Owens, L., Shute, R., & Slee, P. (2000). "Guess what I just heard!": Indirect aggression among teenage girls in Australia. *Aggressive Behavior, 26,* 57–66.

Paik, H., & Comstock, G. (1994). The effects of television violence on antisocial behavior: A meta-analysis. *Communication Research, 21,* 516–546.

Palmer, J., & Byrne, D. (1970). Attraction toward dominant and submissive strangers: Similarity versus complementarity. *Journal of Experimental Research in Personality, 4,* 108–115.

Paolini, S., Hewstone, M., Cairns, E., & Voci, A. (2004). Effects of direct and indirect cross-group friendships on judgments of Catholics and Protestants in Northern Ireland: The mediating role of an anxiety-reduction mechanism. *Personality and Social Psychology Bulletin, 30,* 770–786.

Park, B., Wolsko, C., & Judd, C. M. (2001). Measurement of subtyping in stereotype change. *Journal of Experimental Social Psychology, 37,* 325–332.

Park, J., & Banaji, M. R. (2000). Mood and heuristics: The influence of happy and sad states on sensitivity and bias in stereotyping. *Journal of Personality and Social Psychology, 78,* 1005–1023.

Park, L. E. (2007). Appearance-based rejection sensitivity: Implications for mental and physical health, affect, and motivation. *Personality and Social Psychology Bulletin, 33,* 290–504.

Park, L. E., & Pelham, B. W. (2006). Self versus others' ratings of physical attractiveness. Unpublished raw data.

Patrick, H., Neighbors, C., & Knee, C. R. (2004). Appearance-related social comparisons: The role of contingent self-esteem and self-perceptions of attractiveness. *Personality and Social Psychology Bulletin, 30,* 501–514.

Paulhus, D. L., Bruce, M. N., & Trapnell, P. D. (1995). Effects of self-presentation strategies on personality profiles and their structure. *Personality and Social Psychology Bulletin, 21,* 100–108.

Pavalko, E. K., Mossakowski, K. N., & Hamilton, V. J. (2003). Does perceived discrimination affect health? Longitudinal relationships between work discrimination and women's physical and emotional health. *Journal of Health and Social Behavior, 43,* 18–33.

Pearson, C. M., & Porath, C. L. (2004). On incivility, its impact, and directions for future research. In R. W. Griffin & A. M. O'Leary-Kelly (Eds.), *The dark side of organizational behavior* (pp. 403–425). San Francisco, CA: Jossey-Bass.

Pelham, B. W., Mirenberg, M. C., & Jones, J. T. (2002). Why Susie sells seashells by the seashore: Implicit egotism and major life decisions. *Journal of Personality and Social Psychology, 82,* 469–487.

Pennebaker, J. W., Dyer, M. A., Caulkins, R. S., Litowicz, D. L., Ackerman, P. L., & Anderson, D. B. (1979). Don't the girls all get prettier at closing time: A country and western application to psychology. *Personality and Social Psychology Bulletin, 5,* 122–125.

Penner, L. A., Dovidio, J. F., Piliavin, J. A., & Schroeder, D. A. (2005). Prosocial behavior: Multilevel perspective. *Annual Review of Psychology, 46,* 365–392.

Penner, L. A., & Finkelstein, M. A. (1998). Dispositional and structural determinants of volunteerism. *Journal of Personality and Social Psychology, 74,* 525–537.

Pentony, J. F. (1995). The effect of negative campaigning on voting, semantic differential, and thought listing. *Journal of Social Behavior and Personality, 10,* 631–644.

Perkins, J. E., & Bourgeois, M. J. (2006). Perceptions of police use of deadly force. *Journal of Applied Social Psychology, 36,* 161–177.

Perls, T. T., & Silver, M. H. (1999). *Living to 100: Lessons in living to your maximum potential at any age.* New York: Basic Books.

Peterson, R. S. (1997). A directive leadership style in group decision making can be both a virtue and vice: Evidence from elite and experimental groups. *Journal of Personality and Social Psychology, 72,* 1107–1121.

Peterson, R. S., & Behfar, K. J. (2003). The dynamic relationship between performance feedback, trust, and conflict in groups: A longitudinal study. *Organizational Behavior and Human Decision Processes, 92,* 102–112.

Peterson, V. S., & Runyan, A. S. (1993). *Global gender issues.* Boulder, CO: Westview Press.

Petrocelli, J. V., Tormala, Z. L., & Rucker, D. D. (2007). Unpacking attitude certainty: Attitude clarity and attitude correctness. *Journal of Personality and Social Psychology, 92,* 30–41.

Pettigrew, T. F. (1981). Extending the stereotype concept. In D. L. Hamilton (Ed.), *Cognitive processes in stereotyping and intergroup behavior* (pp. 303–331). Hillsdale, NJ: Erlbaum.

Pettigrew, T. F. (1997). Generalized intergroup contact effects on prejudice. *Personality and Social Psychology Bulletin, 23,* 173–185.

Pettigrew, T. W. (2007). Still a long way to go: American Black-White relations today. In G. Adams, M. Biernat, N. R. Branscombe, C. S. Crandall, & L. S. Wrightsman (Eds.), *Commemorating Brown: The social psychology of racism and discrimination.* Washington, DC: American Psychological Association.

Pettijohn, T. E. F., II, & Jungeberg, B. J. (2004). Playboy playmate curves: Changes in facial and body feature preferences across social and economic conditions. *Personality and Social Psychology Bulletin, 30,* 1186–1197.

Petty, R. E., & Cacioppo, J. T. (1986). The elaboration likelihood model of persuasion. In L. Berkowitz (Ed.), *Advances in experimental social psychology* (Vol. 19, pp. 123–205). New York: Academic Press.

Petty, R. E., & Cacioppo, J. T. (1990). Involvement and persuasion: Tradition versus integration. *Psychological Bulletin, 107,* 367–374.

Petty, R. E., Wheeler, C., & Tormala, Z. L. (2003). Persuasion and attitude change. In T. Millon & M. J. Lerner (Eds.), *Handbook of psychology: Personality and social psychology* (Vol. 5, pp. 353–382). New York: Wiley.

Petty, R. J., & Krosnick, J. A. (Eds.). (1995). *Attitude strength: Antecedents and consequences* (Vol. 4). Hillsdale, NJ: Erlbaum.

Phelps, E. A., O'Connor, K. J., Gatenby, J. C., Gore, J. C., Grillon, C., & Davis, M. (2001). Activation of the left amygdala to a cognitive representation of fear. *Nature Neuroscience, 4,* 437–441.

Pickett, C. L., Gardner, W. L., & Knowles, M. (2004). Getting a cue: The need to belong and enhanced sensitivity to social cues. *Personality and Social Psychology Bulletin, 30,* 1095–1107.

Pihl, R. O., Lau, M. L., & Assad, J. M. (1997). Aggressive disposition, alcohol, and aggression. *Aggressive Behavior, 23,* 11–18.

Pinel, E. C. (2004). You're just saying that because I'm a woman: Stigma consciousness and attributions to discrimination. *Self and Identity, 3,* 39–51.

Pines, A. (1997). Fatal attractions or wise unconscious choices: The relationship between causes for entering and breaking intimate relationships. *Personal Relationship Issues, 4,* 1–6.

Pinker, S. (1998). *How the mind works.* New York: Norton.

Pittman, T. S. (1993). Control motivation and attitude change. In G. Weary, F. Gleicher, & empirical review. *Psychological Bulletin, 130,* 435–468.

Plant, E. A., & Butz, D. A. (2006). The causes and consequences of an avoidance-focus for interracial interactions. *Personality and Social Psychology Bulletin, 32,* 833–846.

Plant, E. A., & Devine, P. G. (1998). Internal and external motivation to respond without prejudice. *Journal of Personality and Social Psychology, 75,* 811–832.

Podsakoff, P. & MacKenzie, S.B. (1997). Impact of organizational citizenship behavior on organizational performance: A review and suggestions for future research. *Human Performance, 10,* 133–152.

Podsakoff, P. M., MacKenzie, S. B., Paine, J. B., & Bachrach, D. G. (2000). Organizational citizenship behaviors: A critical review of the theoretical and empirical literature and suggestions for future research. *Journal of Management, 26,* 513–563.

Polivy, J., & Herman, C. P. (2000). The false-hope syndrome: Unfulfilled expectations of self-change. *Current Directions in Psychological Science, 9,* 128–131.

Pollak, K. I., & Niemann, Y. F. (1998). Black and white tokens in academia: A difference in chronic versus acute distinctiveness. *Journal of Applied Social Psychology, 28,* 954–972.

Postmes, T., & Branscombe, N. R. (2002). Influence of long-term racial environmental composition on subjective well-being in African Americans. *Journal of Personality and Social Psychology, 83,* 735–751.

Postmes, T., & Spears, R. (1998). Deindividuation and antinormative behavior: A meta-analysis. *Psychological Bulletin, 123,* 238–259.

Powell, A. A., Branscombe, N. R., & Schmitt, M. T. (2005). Inequality as "ingroup privilege" or "outgroup disadvantage": The impact of group focus on collective guilt and interracial attitudes. *Personality and Social Psychology Bulletin, 31,* (4), 508-521.

Pozzulo, J., D., & Demopsey, J. (2006). Biased lineup instructions: Examining the effect of pressure on children's andadultas' eyewitness identification accuracy. *Journal of Applied Social Psychology, 36,* 1381–1394.

Pozzulo, J. D., & Lindsay, R. C. L. (1999). Elimination lineups: An improved identification for child eyewitnesses. *Journal of Applied Psychology, 84,* 167–176.

Prentice, D. A., & Miller, D. T. (1992). When small effects are impressive. *Psychological Bulletin, 112,* 160–164.

Prentice, D. A., Miller, D. T., & Lightdale, J. R. (1994). Asymmetries in attachments to groups and to their members: Distinguishing between common-identity and common-bond groups. *Personality and Social Psychology Bulletin, 20,* 484–493.

Price, K. H., Harrison, D. A., & Gavin, J. H. (2006). Withholding inputs in team contexts: Member composition, interaction processes, evaluation structure, and social loafing. *Journal of Applied Psychology, 91,* 1375–1384.

Pronin, E., & Ross, L. (2006). Temporal differences in trait self-ascription: When the self is seen as an other. *Journal of Personality and Social Psychology, 90,* 197–209.

Pronin, E., Steele, C. M., & Ross, L. (2004). Identity bifurcation in response to stereotype threat: Women and mathematics. *Journal of Experimental Social Psychology, 40,* 152–168.

Pronin, E., Wegner, D. M., McCarthy, K., & Rodriguez, S. (2006). Everyday magical powers: The role of apparent mental causation in the overestimation of personal influence. *Journal of Personality and Social Psychology, 91,* 218–231.

Pruitt, D. G., & Carnevale, P. J. (1993). *Negotiation in social conflict.* Pacific Grove, CA: Brooks/Cole.

Pryor, J. B., Reeder, G. D., Yeadon, C., & Hesson-McInnis, M. (2004). A dual-process model of reactions to perceived stigma. *Journal of Personality and Social Psychology, 87,* 436–452.

Puente, S., & Cohen, D. (2003). Jealousy and the meaning (or nonmeaning) of violence. *Personality and Social Psychology Bulletin, 29,* 449–460.

Pullium, R. M. (1993). Reactions to AIDS patients as a function of attributions about controllability and promiscuity. *Social Behavior and Personality, 21,* 297–302.

Queller, S., & Smith, E. R. (2002). Subtyping versus bookkeeping in stereotype learning and change: Connectionist simulations and empirical findings. *Journal of Personality and Social Psychology, 82,* 300–313.

Quigley, B. M., Johnson, A. B., & Byrne, D. (1995, June). *Mock jury sentencing decisions: A meta-analysis of the attractiveness–leniency effect.* Paper presented at the meeting of the American Psychological Society, New York.

Quinn, J. M., & Wood, W. (2004). Forewarnings of influence appeals: Inducing resistance and acceptance. In E. S. Knowles & J. A. Linn (Eds.), *Resistance and persuasion* (pp. 193–213). Mahwah, NJ: Erlbaum.

Ray, G. E., Cohen, R., Secrist, M. E., & Duncan, M. K. (1997). Relating aggressive victimization behaviors to children's sociometric status and friendships. *Journal of Social and Personal Relationships, 14,* 95–108.

Read, S. J., & Miller, L. C. (1998). *Connectionist and PDP models of social reasoning and social behavior.* Mahwah, NJ: Erlbaum.

Redersdorff, S., Martinot, D., & Branscombe, N. R. (2004). The impact of thinking about group-based disadvantages or advantages on women's well-being: An experimental test of the rejection-identification model. *Current Psychology of Cognition, 22,* 203–222.

Reicher, S., & Haslam, S. A. (2006). Rethinking the psychology of tyranny: The BBC prison study. *British Journal of Social Psychology, 45,* 1–40.

Reisenzein, R., Bordgen, S., Holtbernd, T., & Matz, D. (2006). Evidence for strong dissociation between emotion and facial displays: The case of surprise. *Journal of Personality and Social Psychology, 91,* 295–315.

Reisman, J. M. (1984). Friendliness and its correlates. *Journal of Social and Clinical Psychology, 2,* 143–155.

Reiss, A. J., & Roth, J. A. (Eds.). (1993). *Understanding and preventing violence.* Washington, DC: National Academy Press.

Reno, R. R., Cialdini, R. B., & Kallgren, C. A. (1993). The transsituational influence of social norms. *Journal of Personality and Social Psychology, 64,* 104–112.

Rensberger, B. (1993, November 9). Certain chemistry between vole pairs. *Albany Times Union,* pp. C-1, C-3.

Reskin, B., & Padavic, I. (1994). *Women and men at work.* Thousand Oaks, CA: Pine Forge Press.

Rhodes, G., & Tremewan, T. (1996). Averageness, exaggeration, and facial attractiveness. *Psychological Science, 7,* 105–110.

Richard, F. D., Bond, C. F., Jr., & Stokes-Zoota, J. J. (2001). "That's completely obvious . . . and important." Lay judgments of social psychological findings. *Personality and Social Psychology Bulletin, 27,* 497–505.

Richards, Z., & Hewstone, M. (2001). Subtyping and subgrouping: Processes for the prevention and promotion of stereotype change. *Personality and Social Psychology Review, 5,* 52–73.

Richson, J. A., & Shelton, J. N. (2003). When prejudice does not pay: Effects of interracial contact on executive function. *Psychological Science, 14,* 287–290.

Robbins, T. L., & DeNisi, A. S. (1994). A closer look at interpersonal affect as a distinct influence on cognitive processing in performance evaluations. *Journal of Applied Psychology, 79,* 341–353.

Robins, R. W., Hendin, H. M., & Trzesniewski, K. H. (2001). *Personality and Social Psychology Bulletin, 27,* 151–161.

Robins, R. W., Spranca, M. D., & Mendelsohn, G. A. (1996). The actor–observer effect revisited: Effects of individual differences and repeated social interactions on actor and observer attribution. *Journal of Personality and Social Psychology, 71,* 375–389.

Robinson, L. A., Berman, J. S., & Neimeyer, R. A. (1990). Psychotherapy for the treatment of depression: A comprehensive review of controlled outcome research. *Psychological Bulletin, 108,* 30–49.

Robinson, R. J., Keltner, D., Ward, A., & Ross, L. (1995). Actual versus assumed differences in construal: "Naive realism" in intergroup perception and conflict. *Journal of Personality and Social Psychology, 68,* 404-417.

Roccas, S. (2003). Identification and status revisited: The moderating role of self-enhancement and self-transcendence values. *Personality and Social Psychology Bulletin, 29,* 726–736.

Roccas, S., & Brewer, M. B. (2002). Social identity complexity. *Personality and Social Psychology Review, 6,* 88–106.

Rochat, F., & Modigliani, A. (1995). The ordinary quality of resistance: From Milgram's laboratory to the village of Le Chambon. *Journal of Social Issues, 5,* 195–210.

Roese, N. J., & Olson, J. M. (1997). Counterfactual thinking: The intersection of affect and function. In M. P. Zanna (Ed.), *Advances in experimental social psychology, 29* (pp. 1–59). New York: Academic Press.

Rogers, R. W. (1980). *Subjects' reactions to experimental deception.* Unpublished manuscript, University of Alabama, Tuscaloosa.

Rogers, R. W., & Ketcher, C. M. (1979). Effects of anonymity and arousal on aggression. *Journal of Psychology, 102,* 13–19.

Rokach, A., & Neto, F. (2000). Coping with loneliness in adolescence: A cross-cultural study. *Social Behavior and Personality, 28,* 329–342.

Roland, E. (2002). Aggression, depression, and bullying others. *Aggressive Behavior, 28,* 198–206.

Rosenbaum, M. E. (1986). The repulsion hypothesis: On the nondevelopment of relationships. *Journal of Personality and Social Psychology, 51,* 1156–1166.

Rosenberg, M. (1965). *Society and the adolescent self-image.* Princeton, NJ: Princeton University Press.

Rosenhan, D. L., Salovey, P., & Hargis, K. (1981). The joys of helping: Focus of attention mediates the impact of positive affect on altruism. *Journal of Personality and Social Psychology, 40,* 899–905.

Rosenthal, R. (1994). Interpersonal expectancy effects: A thirty year perspective. *Current Direction in Psychological Science, 3,* 176–179.

Rosenthal, R., & DePaulo, B. M. (1979). Sex differences in accommodation in nonverbal communication. In R. Rosenthal (Ed.), *Skill in nonverbal communication: Individual differences* (pp. 68–103). Cambridge, MA: Oelgeschlager, Gunn & Hain.

Rosenthal, R., & Jacobson, L. (1968). *Pygmalion in the classroom: Teacher expectation and student intellectual development.* New York: Holt, Rinehart, & Winston.

Ross, L. (1977). The intuitive scientist and his shortcoming. In L. Berkowitz (Ed.), *Advances in experimental social psychology* (Vol. 10, pp. 174–221). New York: Academic Press.

Ross, M., & Wilson, A. E. (2003). Autobiographical memory and conceptions of self: Getting better all the time. *Current Directions in Psychological Science, 12,* 66–69.

Rotenberg, K. J. (1997). Loneliness and the perception of the exchange of disclosures. *Journal of Social and Clinical Psychology, 16,* 259–276.

Rotenberg, K. J., & Kmill, J. (1992). Perception of lonely and non-lonely persons as a function of individual differences in loneliness. *Journal of Social and Personal Relationships, 9,* 325–330.

Rothman, A. J., & Hardin, C. D. (1997). Differential use of the availability heuristic in social judgment. *Personality and Social Psychology Bulletin, 23,* 123–138.

Rotton, J., & Cohn, E. G. (2000). Violence is a curvilinear function of temperature in Dallas: A replication. *Journal of Personality and Social Psychology, 78,* 1074–1081.

Rotton, J., & Kelley, I. W. (1985). Much ado about the full moon: A meta-analysis of lunar-lunacy research. *Psychological Bulletin, 97,* 286–306.

Rowatt, W. C., Cunningham, M. R., & Druen, P. B. (1998). Deception to get a date. *Personality and Social Psychology Bulletin, 24,* 1228–1242.

Rowe, P. M. (1996, September). On the neurobiological basis of affiliation. *APS Observer,* 17–18.

Rozin, P., & Nemeroff, C. (1990). The laws of sympathetic magic: A psychological analysis of similarity and contagion. In W. Stigler, R. A. Shweder, & G. Herdt (Eds.), *Cultural psychology: Essays in comparative human development* (pp. 205–232). Cambridge, England: Cambridge University Press.

Rozin, P., Lowery, L., & Ebert, R. (1994). Varieties of disgust faces and the structure of disgust. *Journal of Personality and Social Psychology, 66,* 870–881.

Rubin, J. Z. (1985). Deceiving ourselves about deception: Comment on Smith and Richardson's "Amelioration of deception and harm in psychological research." *Journal of Personality and Social Psychology, 48,* 252–253.

Ruder, M., & Bless, H. (2003). Mood and the reliance on the ease of retrieval heuristic. *Journal of Personality and Social Psychology, 85,* 20–32.

Rudman, L. A., & Fairchild, K. (2004). Reactions to counter stereotypic behavior: The role of backlash in cultural stereotype maintenance. *Journal of Personality and Social Psychology, 87,* 157–176.

Ruiz, J. M., Matthews, K. A., Scheier, M. F., & Schulz, R. (2006). Does who you marry matter for your health? Influence of patients' and spouses' personality on their partners' psychological well-being following coronary artery bypass surgery. *Journal of Personality and Social Psychology, 91,* 255–267.

Rusbult, C. E., & Zembrodt, I. M. (1983). Responses to dissatisfaction in romantic involvements: A multidimensional scaling analysis. *Journal of Experimental Social Psychology, 19,* 274–293.

Rusbult, C. E., Martz, J. M., & Agnew, C. R. (1998). The Investment Model Scale: Measuring commitment level, satisfaction level, quality of alternatives, and investment size. *Personal Relationships, 5,* 467–484.

Rusbult, C. E., Morrow, G. D., & Johnson, D. J. (1987). Self-esteem and problem-solving behavior in close relationships. *British Journal of Social Psychology, 26,* 293–303.

Ruscher, J. B., & Hammer, E. D. (1994). Revising disrupted impressions through conversation. *Journal of Personality and Social Psychology, 66,* 530–541.

Rushton, J. P. (1989). Genetic similarity, human altruism, and group selection. *Behavioral and Brain Sciences, 12,* 503–559.

Russell, J. A. (1994). Is there universal recognition of emotion from facial expressions? A review of cross-cultural studies. *Psychological Bulletin, 115,* 102–141.

Rutkowski, G. K., Gruder, C. L., & Romer, D. (1983). Group cohesiveness, social norms, and bystander intervention. *Journal of Personality and Social Psychology, 44,* 542–552.

Ruvolo, A. P., Fabin, L. A., & Ruvolo, C. M. (2001). Relationship experiences and change in attachment characteristics of young adults: The role of relationship breakups and conflict avoidance. *Personal Relationships, 8,* 265–281.

Ryan, M. K., David, B., & Reynolds, K. J. (2004). Who cares? The effect of gender and context on the self and moral reasoning. *Psychology of Women Quarterly, 28,* 246–255.

Ryan, M. K., & Haslam, S. A. (2007). The glass cliff: Exploring the dynamics surrounding the appointment of women to precarious leadership positions. *Academy of Management Journal, 32,* 549–572.

Ryckman, R. M., Robbins, M. A., Kaczor, L. M., & Gold, J. A. (1989). Male and female raters' stereotyping of male and female physiques. *Personality and Social Psychology Bulletin, 15,* 244–251.

Ryff, C. D., & Singer, B. (2000). Interpersonal flourishing: A positive health agenda for the new millennium. *Personality and Social Psychology Review, 4,* 30–44.

Sadker, M., & Sadker, D. (1994). *Failing at fairness: How America's schools cheat girls.* New York: Charles Scribners Sons.

Sadler, P., & Woody, E. (2003). Is who you are who you're talking to? Interpersonal style and complementarity in mixed-sex interactions. *Journal of Personality and Social Psychology, 84,* 80–96.

Sahdra, B., & Ross, M. (2007). Group identification and historical memory. *Personality and Social Psychology Bulletin, 33,* 384–395.

Salmela-Aro, K., & Nurmi, J.-E. (1996). Uncertainty and confidence in interpersonal projects: Consequences for social relationships and well-being. *Journal of Social and Personal Relationships, 13,* 109–122.

Salovey, P., Mayer, J. D., & Rosenhan, D. L. (1991). Mood and helping: Mood as a motivator of helping and helping as a regulator of mood. In M. S. Clark (Ed.), *Prosocial behavior* (pp. 215–237). Newbury Park, CA: Sage.

Sanchez, D. T., Crocker, J., & Boike, K. R. (2005). Doing gender in the bedroom: Investing in gender norms and the sexual experience. *Personality and Social Psychology Bulletin, 31,* 1445–1455.

Sanchez, D. T., Kiefer, A. K., & Ybarra, O. (2006). Sexual submissiveness in women: Costs for sexual autonomy and arousal. *Personality and Social Psychology Bulletin, 32,* 512–524.

Sanfey, A. G. Rilling, J. K., Aronson, J. A., Nystrom L. E. & Cohen, J. D. (2003). The neural basis of economic decision making in the ultimatum game. *Science, 300,* 1755–1757.

Sangrador, J. L., & Yela, C. (2000). 'What is beautiful is loved': Physical attractiveness in love relationships in a representative sample. *Social Behavior and Personality, 28,* 207–218.

Sani, F. (2005). When subgroups secede: Extending and refining the social psychological model of schism in groups. *Personality and Social Psychology Bulletin, 31,* 1074-1086.

Sani, F. (In press). Why groups fall apart: A social psychological model of the schismatic process. In F. Butera & J. Levine (Eds.), *Hoping and coping: How minorities manage their social environments.* New York: Cambridge University Press.

Sani, F., & Todman, J. (2002). Should we stay or should we go? A social psychological model of schisms in groups. *Personality and Social Psychology Bulletin, 28,* 1647–1655.

Sanitioso, R. B., & Wlodarski, R. (2004). In search of information that confirms a desired self-perception: Motivated processing of social feedback and choice of social interactions. *Personality and Social Psychology Bulletin, 30,* 412–422.

Sanna, L. J. (1997). Self-efficacy and counterfactual thinking: Up a creek with and without a paddle. *Personality and Social Psychology Bulletin, 23,* 654–666.

Sanna, L. J., & Pusecker, P. A. (1994). Self-efficacy, valence of self-evaluation, and performance. *Personality and Social Psychology Bulletin, 20,* 82–92.

Sassenberg, K., Jonas, K. J., Shah, J. Y., & Brazy, P. C. (2007). Why some groups just feel better: The regulatory fit of group power. *Journal of Personality and Social Psychology, 92,* 249–267.

Schachter, S. (1951). Deviation, rejection, and communication. *Journal of Abnormal and Social Psychology, 46,* 190–207.

Schachter, S. (1959). *The psychology of affiliation.* Stanford, CA: Stanford University Press.

Schachter, S. (1964). The interaction of cognitive and physiological determinants of emotional state. In L. Berkowitz (Ed.), *Advances in experimental social psychology* (Vol. 1, pp. 48–81). New York: Academic Press.

Schein, V. E. (2001). A global look at psychological barriers to women's progress in management. *Journal of Social Issues, 57,* 675–688.

Scher, S. J. (1997). Measuring the consequences of injustice. *Personality and Social Psychology Bulletin, 23,* 482–497.

Schleicher, D. J., Watt, J. D., & Greguras, G. J. (2004). Reexamining the job satisfaction-performance relationships: The complexity of attitudes. *Journal of Applied Psychology, 89,* 165–177.

Schmid Mast, M., & Hall, U. A. (2006). Women's advantage at remembering others' appearance: A systematic look at the why and when of a gender difference. *Personality and Social Psychology Bulletin, 32,* 353–364.

Schmitt, D. P. (2004). Patterns and universals of mate poaching across 53 nations: The effects of sex, culture, and personality on romantically attracting another person's partner. *Journal of Personality and Social Psychology, 86,* 560–584.

Schmitt, D. P., & Buss, D. M. (2001). Human mate poaching: Tactics and temptations for infiltrating existing mateships. *Journal of Personality and Social Psychology, 80,* 894–917.

Schmitt, M. T., & Branscombe, N. R. (2002b). The causal loci of attributions to prejudice. *Personality and Social Psychology Bulletin, 28,* 484–492.

Schmitt, M. T., Branscombe, N. R., Kobrynowicz, D., & Owen, S. (2002). Perceiving discrimination against one's gender group has different implications for well-being in women and men. *Personality and Social Psychology Bulletin, 28,* 197-210.

Schmitt, M. T., Branscombe, N. R., & Postmes, T. (2003). Women's emotional responses to the pervasiveness of gender discrimination. *European Journal of Social Psychology, 33,* 297–312.

Schmitt, M. T., Ellemers, N., & Branscombe, N. R. (2003). Perceiving and responding to gender discrimination at work. In S. A. Haslam, D. van Knippenberg, M. Platow, & N. Ellemers (Eds.), *Social identity at work: Developing theory for organizational practice* (pp. 277–292). Philadelphia, PA: Psychology Press.

Schmitt, M. T., Silvia, P. J., & Branscombe, N. R. (2000). The intersection of self-evaluation maintenance and social identity theories: Intragroup judgment in interpersonal and intergroup contexts. *Personality and Social Psychology Bulletin, 26,* 1598–1606.

Schneider, B., Hanges, P. J., Smith, D. B., & Salvaggio, A. N. (2004). Which comes first: Employee attitudes or organizational financial and market performance? *Journal of Applied Psychology, 88,* 836–851.

Schooler, J. W., & Loftus, E. F. (1986). Individual differences and experimentation: Complementary approaches to interrogative suggestibility. *Social Behavior, 1,* 105–112.

Schubert, T. W. (2004). The power in your hand: Gender differences in bodily feedback from making a fist. *Personality and Social Psychology Bulletin, 30,* 757–769.

Schul, Y., & Vinokur, A. D. (2000). Projection in person perception among spouses as a function of the similarity in their shared experiences. *Personality and Social Psychology Bulletin, 26,* 987–1001.

Schumacher, M., Corrigan, P. W., & Dejong, T. (2003). Examining cues that signal mental illness stigma. *Journal of Social and Clinical Psychology, 22,* 467–476.

Schusterman, R. J., Reichmuth, C. J., & Kastak, D. (2000). How animals classify friends and foes. *Current Directions in Psychological Science, 9,* 1–6.

Schutte, J. W., & Hosch, H. M. (1997). Gender differences in sexual assault verdicts: A meta-analysis. *Journal of Social Behavior and Personality, 12,* 759–772.

Schwarz, N., & Bohner, G. (2001). The construction of attitudes. In A. Tesser & N. Schwarz (Eds.), *Blackwell handbook of social psychology: Intrapersonal processes* (pp. 436–457). Oxford, UK: Blackwell.

Schwarz, N., Bless, H., Strack, F., Klumpp, G., Rittenauer-Schatka, G., & Simons, A. (1991). Ease of retrieval as information: Another look at the availability heuristic. *Journal of Personality and Social Psychology, 61,* 195–202.

Schwarzer, R. (1994). Optimism, vulnerability, and self-beliefs as health-related cognitions: A sytematic overview. *Psychology and Health, 9,* 161–180.

Scutt, D., Manning, J. T., Whitehouse, G. H., Leinster, S. J., & Massey, C. P. (1997). The relationship between breast symmetry, breast size and occurrence of breast cancer. *British Journal of Radiology, 70,* 1017–1021.

Seamon, J. G., Lee, I. A., Toner, S. K., Wheeler, R. H., Goodkind, M. S. & Birch, A. D. (2002). Thinking of critical words during study is unnecessary for false memory in the Deese, Roediger, and McDermott procedure. *Psychological Science, 13,* 526–531.

Sears, D. O. (2007).. The Americn color line fifty years after Brown v. Board: Many "Peoples of color" or Black exceptionalism? In G. Adams, M. Biernat, N. R. Branscombe, C. S. Crandall, & L. S. Wrightsman (Eds.), *Commemorating Brown: The social psychology of racism and discrimination.* Washington, DC: American Psychological Association.

Sedikides, C., & Anderson, C. A. (1994). Causal perception of intertrait relations: The glue that holds person types together. *Personality and Social Psychology Bulletin, 21,* 294–302.

Sedikides, C., & Gregg, A. P. (2003). Portraits of the self. In M. A. Hogg & J. Cooper (Eds.), *The Sage handbook of social psychology* (pp. 110–138). Thousand Oaks, CA: Sage.

Seery, M. D., Blascovich, J., Weisbuch, M., & Vick, B. (2004). The relationship between self-esteem level, self-esteem stability, and cardiovascular reactions to performance feedback. *Journal of Personality and Social Psychology, 87,* 133–145.

Segal, M. M. (1974). Alphabet and attraction: An unobtrusive measure of the effect of propinquity in a field setting. *Journal of Personality and Social Psychology, 30,* 654–657.

Selim, J. (2004, May). Who's a little bitty artist? Yes, you are! *Discover,* 16.

Seta, C. E., Hayes, N. S., & Seta, J. J. (1994). Mood, memory, and vigilance: The influence of distraction on recall and impression formation. *Personality and Social Psychology Bulletin, 20,* 170–177.

Settles, I. H. (2004). When multiple identities interfere: The role of identity centrality. *Personality and Social Psychology Bulletin, 30,* 487–500.

Shah, J. (2003). Automatic for the people; How representations of significant others implicitly affect goal pursuit. *Journal of Personality and Social Psychology, 84,* 661–681.

Shams, M. (2001). Social support, loneliness and friendship preference among British Asian and non-Asian adolescents. *Social Behavior and Personality, 29,* 399–404.

Shanab, M. E., & Yahya, K. A. (1977). A behavioral study of obedience in children. *Journal of Personality and Social Psychology, 35,* 530–536.

Shane, S. (2003). *A general theory of entrepreneurship: The individual-opportunity nexus approach to entrepreneurship.* Aldershot, United Kingdom: Eward Elgar.

Shannon, M. L., & Stark, C. P. (2003). The influence of physical appearance on personnel selection. *Social Behavior and Personality, 31,* 613–624.

Sharp, D., Adair, J. G., & Roese, N. J. (1992). Twenty years of deception research: A decline in subjects' trust? *Personality and Social Psychology Bulletin, 18,* 585–590.

Sharp, M. J., & Getz, J. G. (1996). Substance use as impression management. *Personality and Social Psychology Bulletin, 22,* 60–67.

Shaver, P. R., & Brennan, K. A. (1992). Attachment styles and the "big five" personality traits: Their connections with each other and with romantic relationship outcomes. *Personality and Social Psychology Bulletin, 18,* 536–545.

Shaver, P. R., Morgan, H. J., & Wu, S. (1996). Is love a "basic" emotion? *Personal Relationships, 3,* 81–96.

Shaver, P. R., Murdaya, U., & Fraley, R. C. (2001). The structure of the Indonesian emotion lexicon. *Asian Journal of Social Psychology, 4,* 201–224.

Shaw, J. I., Borough, H. W., & Fink, M. I. (1994). Perceived sexual orientation and helping behavior by males and females: The wrong number technique. *Journal of Psychology and Human Sexuality, 6,* 73–81.

Sheldon, W. H., Stevens, S. S., & Tucker, W. B. (1940). *The varieties of human physique.* New York: Harper.

Shepperd, J. A., Ouellette, J. A., & Fernandez, J. K. (1996). Abandoning unrealistic optimistic performance estimates and the temporal proximity of self-relevant feedback. *Journal of Personality and Social Psychology, 70,* 844–855.

Shepperd, J. A., & Taylor, K. M. (1999). Social loafing and expectancy-value theory. *Personality and Social Psychology Bulletin, 25,* 1147–1158.

Sherif, M., Harvey, D. J., White, B. J., Hood, W. R., & Sherif, C. W. (1961). *The Robbers' cave experiment.* Norman, OK: Institute of Group Relations.

Sherif, M. A. (1937). An experimental approach to the study of attitudes. *Sociometry, 1,* 90–98.

Sherman, J. W., & Klein, S. B. (1994). Development and representation of personality impressions. *Journal of Personality and Social Psychology, 67,* 972–983.

Sherman, M. D., & Thelen, M. H. (1996). Fear of intimacy scale: Validation and extension with adolescents. *Journal of Social and Personal Relationships, 13,* 507–521.

Sherman, S. S. (1980). On the self-erasing nature of errors of prediction. *Journal of Personality and Social Psychology, 16,* 388–403.

Shields, C. A., Brawley, L. R., & Lindover, T. I. (2006). Self-efficacy as a mediator of the relationship between causal attributions and exercise behavior. *Journal of Applied Social Psychology, 36,* 2785–2802.

Sidanius, J., & Pratto, F. (1999). *Social dominance.* New York: Cambridge University Press.

Sigall, H. (1997). Ethical considerations in social psychological research: Is the bogus pipeline a special case? *Journal of Applied Social Psychology, 27,* 574–581.

Sigelman, C. K., Thomas, D. B., Sigelman, L., & Robich, F. D. (1986). Gender, physical attractiveness, and electability: An experimental investigation of voter biases. *Journal of Applied Social Psychology, 16,* 229–248.

Sigelman, L., & Welch, S. (1991). *Black Americans' view of racial inequality: The dream deferred.* New York: Cambridge University Press.

Sillars, A. L., Folwell, A. L., Hill, K. C., Maki, B. K., Hurst, A. P., & Casano, R. A. (1994). *Journal of Social and Personal Relationships, 11,* 611–617.

Simon, B. (2004). *Identity in modern society: A social psychological perspective.* Oxford: Blackwell.

Simon, B., & Klandermans, B. (2001). Politicized collective identity: A social psychological analysis. *American Psychologist, 56,* 319–331.

Simon, L., Greenberg, J., & Brehm, J. (1995). Trivialization: The forgotten mode of dissonance reduction. *Journal of Personality and Social Psychology, 68,* 247–260.

Simons, T., & Roberson, Q. (2003). Why managers should care about fairness: The effects of aggregate justice perceptions on organizational outcomes. *Journal of Applied Psychology, 88,* 432–443.

Simpson, J. A. (1987). The dissolution of romantic relationships: Factors involved in relationship stability and emotional stress. *Journal of Personality and Social Psychology, 53,* 683–692.

Simpson, J. A., Ickes, W., & Blackstone, T. (1995). When the head protects the heart: Empathic accuracy in dating relationships. *Journal of Personality and Social Psychology, 69,* 629–641.

Sinclair, S., Dunn, E., & Lowery, B. S. (2005). The relationship between parental racial attitudes and children's implicit prejudice. *Journal of Experimental Social Psychology, 41,* 283–289.

Singh, R., & Ho, S. Y. (2000). Attitudes and attraction: A new test of the attraction, repulsion and similarity–dissimilarity asymmetry hypotheses. *British Journal of Social Psychology, 39,* 197–211.

Sistrunk, F., & McDavid, J. W. (1971). Sex variable in conforming behavior. *Journal of Personality and Social Psychology, 17,* 200–207.

Sivacek, J., & Crano, W. D. (1982). Vested interest as a moderator of attitude-behavior consistency. *Journal of Personality and Social Psychology, 43,* 210-221

Skarlicki, D. P., & Folger, R. (1997). Retaliation in the workplace: The roles of distributive, procedural, and interactional justice. *Journal of Applied Psychology, 821,* 434–443.

Skinner, B. F. (1938). *The behavior of organisms: An experimental analysis.* Oxford, UK: Appleton-Century.

Slater, P. E. (1955). Role differentiation in small groups. *American Sociological Review, 20,* 300–310.

Smeaton, G., Byrne, D., & Murnen, S. K. (1989). The repulsion hypothesis revisited: Similarity irrelevance or dissimilarity bias? *Journal of Personality and Social Psychology, 56,* 54–59.

Smith, A. E., Jussim, L., & Eccles, J. S. (1999). Do self-fulfilling prophecies accumulate, dissipate, or remain stable over time? *Journal of Personality and Social Psychology, 77,* 548–565.

Smith, D. E., Gier, J. A., & Willis, F. N. (1982). Interpersonal touch and compliance with a marketing request. *Basic and Applied Social Psychology, 3,* 35–38.

Smith, E. R., & Zarate, M. A. (1992). Exemplar-based model of social judgment. *Psychological Review, 99,* 3–21.

Smith, K. D., Keating, J. P., & Stotland, E. (1989). Altruism reconsidered: The effect of denying feedback on a victim's status to empathetic witnesses. *Journal of Personality and Social Psychology, 57,* 641–650.

Smith, N. K., Larsen, J. T., Chartrand, T. L., Cacioppo, J. T., Katafiasz, H. A., & Moran, K. E. (2006). Being bad isn't always good: Affective context moderates the attention bias toward negative information. *Journal of Personality and Social Psychology, 90,* 210–220.

Smith, P. B., & Bond, M. H. (1993). *Social psychology across cultures.* Boston: Allyn & Bacon.

Smith, P. K., & Brain, P. (2000). Bullying in schools; lessons from two decades of research. *Aggressive Behavior, 26,* 1–9.

Smith, S. S., & Richardson, D. (1985). On deceiving ourselves about deception: Reply to Rubin. *Journal of Personality and Social Psychology, 48,* 254–255.

Smorti, A., & Ciucci, E. (2000). Narrative strategies in bullies and victims in Italian schoolchildren. *Aggressive Behavior, 26,* 33–48.

Sorrentino, R. M., Otsubo, Y., Yasunaga, S., Nezlek, J., Kouhara, S., & Shuper, P. (2005). Uncertainty orientation and social behavior: Individual differences within and across cultures. In R. M. Sorrentino, D. Cohen, J. M. Olson, & M. P. Zanna (Eds.), *Cultural and social behavior: The Ontario symposium* (Vol. 10, pp. 181–206). Mahwah, NJ: Erlbaum.

Sparrow, B., & Wegner, D. M. (2006). Unpriming: The deactivation of thoughts through expression. *Journal of Personality and Social Psychology, 9,* 1009–1019.

Sparrowe, R. T., Soetjipto, B. W., & Kraimer, M. L. (2006). Do leaders' influence tactics relate to members' helping behavior? It depends on the quality of the relationships. *Academy of Management Journal, 49,* 1194–1208.

Spears, R., Doosje, B., & Ellemers, N. (1999). Commitment and the context of social perception. In N. Ellemers, R. Spears, & B. Doosje (Eds.), *Social identity: Context, commitment, content* (pp. 59–83). Oxford: Blackwell.

Spears, R., Jetten, J., & Doosje, B. (2001). The (il)legitimacy of ingroup bias: From social reality to social resistance. In J. T. Jost & B. Major (Eds.), *The psychology of legitimacy* (pp. 332–362). New York: Cambridge University Press.

Spencer, S. J., Steele, C. M., & Quinn, D. M. (1999). Stereotype threat and women's math performance. *Journal of Experimental Social Psychology, 35,* 4–28.

Spencer-Rodgers, J., Hamilton, D. L., & Sherman, S. J. (2007). The central role of entitativity in stereotypes of social categories and task groups. *Journal of Personality and Social Psychology, 92,* 369–388.

Sprafkin, J. N., Liebert, R. M., & Poulous, R. W. (1975). Effects of a prosocial televised example on children's helping. *Journal of Personality and Social Psychology, 48,* 35–46.

Sprecher, S., & Regan, P. C. (2002). Liking some things (in some people) more than others: Partner preferences in romantic relationships and friendships. *Journal of Social and Personal Relationships, 19,* 463–481.

Stangor, C., & McMillan, D. (1992). Memory for expectancy-congruent and expectancy-incongruent information: A review of the social and social developmental literatures. *Psychological Bulletin, 111,* 42–61.

Stangor, C., Sechrist, G. B., & Jost, T. J. (2001). Changing racial beliefs by providing consensus information. *Personality and Social Psychology Bulletin, 27,* 486–496.

Stasser, G. (1992). Pooling of unshared information during group discussion. In S. Worchel, W. Wood, & J. H. Simpson (Eds.), *Group process and productivity* (pp. 48–67). Newbury Park, CA: Sage.

Steblay, N. M., Dysart, J., Fulero, S., & Lindsay, R. C. L. (2001). Eyewitness accuracy rates in sequential and simultaneous lineup presentations: A met-analytic comparison. *Law and Human Behavior, 25,* 459–473.

Steele, C. M. (1988). The psychology of self-affirmation: Sustaining the integrity of the self. In L. Berkowitz (Ed.), *Advances in experimental social psychology* (pp. 261–302). Hillsdale, NJ: Erlbaum.

Steele, C. M. (1997). A threat in the air: How stereotypes shape the intellectual identities and performance of women and African-Americans. *American Psychologist, 52,* 613–629.

Steele, C. M., & Aronson, J. (1995). Stereotype threat and the intellectual test performance of African Americans. *Journal of Personality and Social Psychology, 69,* 797–811.

Steele, C. M., & Lui, T. J. (1983). Dissonance processes as self-affirmation. *Journal of Personality and Social Psychology, 45,* 5–19.

Steele, C. M., Spencer, S. J., & Aronson, J. (2002). Contending with group image: The psychology of stereotype and social identity threat. *Advances in Experimental Social Psychology, 34,* 379–439.

Steele, C. M., Spencer, S. J., & Lynch, M. (1993). Self-image resilience and dissonance: The role of affirmational resources. *Journal of Personality and Social Psychology, 64,* 885–896.

Sternberg, R. J. (1986). A triangular theory of love. *Psychological Review, 93,* 119-135.

Sternberg, R. J. (1996). Love stories. *Personal Relationships, 3,* 59–79.

Sternberg, R. J. (2007). A systems model of leadership: WICS. *American Psychologist, 62,* 34–42.

Stuermer, S., Snyder, M., & Omoto, A. M. (2005). Prosocial emotions and helping: The moderating role of group membership. *Journal of Personality and Social Psychology, 88,* 532–546.

Stuermer, S., Snyder, M., Kropp, A., & Siem, B. (2006). Empathy-motivated helping: The moderating role of group membership. *Personality and Social Psychology Bulletin, 32,* 943–956.

Stevens, C. K., & Kristof, A. L. (1995). Making the right impression: A field study of applicant impression management during job interviews. *Journal of Applied Psychology, 80,* 587–606.

Stevens, L. E., & Fiske, S. T. (2000). Motivated impressions of a powerholder: Accuracy under task dependency and misperception under evaluation dependency. *Personality and Social Psychology Bulletin, 26,* 907–922.

Stewart, T. L., Vassar, P. M., Sanchez, D. T., & David, S. E. (2000). Attitudes toward women's societal roles moderates the effect of gender cues on target individuation. *Journal of Personality and Social Psychology, 79,* 143–157.

Stice, E. (2002). Risk and maintenance factors for eating pathology: A meta-analytic review. *Psychological Bulletin, 128,* 825–848.

Stone, A. A., Neale, J. M., Cox, D. S., Napoli, A., Valdimarsdottir, H., & Kennedy-Moore, E. (1994). Daily events are associated with a secretory immune response to an oral antigen in men. *Health Psychology, 13,* 440–446.

Stone, J., Lynch, C. I., Sjomeling, M., & Darley, J. M. (1999). Stereotype threat effects on Black and White athletic performance. *Journal of Personality and Social Psychology, 77,* 1213–1227.

Stone, J., Wiegand, A. W., Cooper, J., & Aronson, E. (1997). When exemplification fails: Hypocrisy and the motives for self-integrity. *Journal of Personality and Social Psychology, 72,* 54–65.

Stott, C. J., Adang, O., Livingstone, A., & Schreiber, M. (2007). Variability in the collective behaviour of England fans at Euro2004: 'Hooliganism,' public order policing and social change. *European Journal of Social Psychology, 37,* 75–100.

Stott, C. J., Hutchison, P., & Drury, J. (2001). 'Hooligans' abroad? Inter-group dynamics, social identity and participation in collective 'disorder' at the 1998 World Cup Finals. *British Journal of Social Psychology, 40,* 359–384.

Stritzke, W. G., Nguyen, A., & Durkin, K. (2004). Shyness and computer-mediated communication: A self-presentational theory perspective. *Media psychology, 6,* 1–22.

Stroebe, W., Diehl, M., & Abakoumkin, G. (1992). The illusion of group effectivity. *Personality and Social Psychology Bulletin, 18,* 643–650.

Stroh, L. K., Langlands, C. L., & Simpson, P. A. (2004). Shattering the glass ceiling in the new millenium. In M. S. Stockdale and F. J. Crosby (Eds.), *The psychology and management of workplace diversity* (pp. 147–167). Malden, MA: Blackwell.

Strube, M. J. (1989). Evidence for the Type in Type A behavior: A taxonometric analysis. *Journal of Personality and Social Psychology, 56,* 972–987.

Strube, M., Turner, C. W., Cerro, D., Stevens, J., & Hinchey, F. (1984). Interpersonal aggression and the Type A coronary-prone behavior pattern: A theoretical distinction and practical implications. *Journal of Personality and Social Psychology, 47,* 839–847.

Stukas, A. A., Snyder, M., & Clary, E. G. (1999). The effects of "mandatory volunteerism" on intentions to volunteer. *Psychological Science, 10,* 59–64.

Sturmer, S., & Simon, B. (2004). The role of collective identification in social movement participation: A panel study in the context of the German gay movement. *Personality and Social Psychology Bulletin, 30,* 263–277.

Sullivan, B. A., O'Connor, K. M., & Burris, E. R. (2006). Negotiator confidence: The impact of self-efficacy on tactics and outcomes. *Journal of Experimental Social Psychology, 42,* 567–581.

Suls, J., & Rosnow, J. (1988). Concerns about artifacts in behavioral research. In M. Morawski (Ed.), *The rise of experimentation in American psychology* (pp. 163–187). New Haven, CT: Yale University Press.

Swann, W. B. (2005). The self and identity negotiation. *Interaction Studies: Social Behavior and Communication in Biological and Artificial Systems, 6,* 69–83.

Swann, W. B., Chang-Schneider, C., & McClarty, K. L. (2007). Do people's self-views matter? Self-concept and self-esteem in everyday life. *American Psychologist, 62,* 84–94.

Swann, W. B., Jr., & Gill, M. J. (1997). Confidence and accuracy in person perception: Do we know what we think we know about our relationship partners? *Journal of Personality and Social Psychology, 73,* 747–757.

Swann, W. B., Jr., Rentfrow, P. J., & Gosling, S. D. (2003). The precarious couple effect: verbally inhibited men + critical, disinhibited women = bad chemistry. *Journal of Personality and Social Psychology, 85,* 1095–1106.

Swap, W. C. (1977). Interpersonal attraction and repeated exposure to rewarders and punishers. *Personality and Social Psychology Bulletin, 3,* 248–251.

Swim, J. K., & Campbell, B. (2001). Sexism: Attitudes, beliefs, and behaviors. In R. Brown & S. Gaertner (Eds.), *Blackwell handbook of social psychology: Intergroup processes* (pp. 218–237). Oxford, UK: Blackwell.

Swim, J. K., Aikin, K. J., Hall, W. S., & Hunter, B. A. (1995). Sexism and racism: Old-fashioned and modern prejudices. *Journal of Personality and Social Psychology, 68,* 199–214.

Tajfel, H. (1978). *The social psychology of the minority.* New York: Minority Rights Group.

Tajfel, H. (1981). Social stereotypes and social groups. In J. C. Turner & H. Giles (Eds.), *Intergroup behavior* (pp. 144–167). Chicago, IL: University of Chicago Press.

Tajfel, H. (1982). *Social identity and intergroup relations.* Cambridge, England: Cambridge University Press.

Tajfel, H., Billig, M., Bundy, R., & Flament, C. (1971). Social categorization and intergroup behaviour. *European Journal of Social Psychology, 1,* 149–178.

Tajfel, H., & Turner, J. C. (1986). The social identity theory of intergroup behavior. In S. Worchel & W. G. Austin (Eds.), *The social psychology of intergroup relations* (2nd ed., pp. 7–24). Monterey, CA: Brooks-Cole.

Tan, D. T. Y., & Singh, R. (1995). Attitudes and attraction: A developmental study of the similarity–attraction and dissimilarity–repulsion hypotheses. *Personality and Social Psychology Bulletin, 21* 975–986.

Taylor, E. (2004). Workplace focus: Working for a bully. *East Valley Tribune,* p. 19.

Taylor, K. M., & Shepperd, J. A. (1998). Bracing for the worst: Severity, testing, and feedback timing as moderators of the optimistic bias. *Personality and Social Psychology Bulletin, 24,* 915–926.

Taylor, S. E. (1989). *Positive illusions: Creative self-deception and the healthy mind.* New York: Basic Books.

Taylor, S. E. (2002). *Health psychology* (5th ed.). New York: McGraw-Hill.

Taylor, S. E., & Brown, J. D. (1988). Illusion and well-being: A social psychological perspective on mental health. *Psychological Bulletin, 103,* 193–210.

Taylor, S. E., Helgeson, V. S., Reed, G. M., & Skokan, L. A. (1991). Self-generated feelings of control and adjustment to physical illness. *Journal of Social Issues, 47,* 91–109.

Taylor, S. E., Lerner, J. S., Sherman, D. K., Sage, R. M., & McDowell, N. K. (2003). Are self-enhancing cognitions associated with healthy or unhealthy biological profiles? *Journal of Personality and Social Psychology, 85,* 605–615.

Tepper, B. J. (2000). Consequences of abusive supervision. *Academy of Management Journal, 43,* 178–190.

Tepper, B. J., Duffy, M. K., Hoobler, J., & Ensley, M. D. (2004). Moderators of the relationships between coworkers' organizational citizenship behavior and fellow employees- attitudes. *Journal of Applied Psychology, 89,* 455–465.

Terman, L. M., & Buttenwieser, P. (1935a). Personality factors in marital compatibility: I. *Journal of Social Psychology, 6,* 143–171.

Terman, L. M., & Buttenwieser, P. (1935b). Personality factors in marital compatibility: II. *Journal of Social Psychology, 6,* 267–289.

Terry, D. J., & Hogg, M. A. (1996). Group norms and the attitude-behavior relationship: A role for group identification. *Personality and Social Psychology Bulletin, 22,* 776–793.

Terry, D. J., Hogg, M. A., & Duck, J. M. (1999). Group membership, social identity, and attitudes. In D. Abrams & M. A. Hogg (Eds.), *Social identity and social cognition* (pp. 280–314). Oxford: Blackwell.

Terry, R. L., & Krantz, J. H. (1993). Dimensions of trait attributions associated with eyeglasses, men's facial hair, and women's hair length. *Journal of Applied Social Psychology, 23,* 1757–1769.

Tesser, A. (1988). Toward a self-evaluation maintenance model of social behavior. *Advances in Experimental Social Psychology, 21,* 181–227.

Tesser, A., & Martin, L. (1996). The psychology of evaluation. In E. T. Higgins & A. W. Kruglanski (Eds.), *Social psychology: Handbook of basic principles* (pp. 400–423). New York: Guilford Press.

Tesser, A., Martin, L. L., & Cornell, D. P. (1996). On the substitutability of the self-protecting mechanisms. In P. Gollwitzer & J. Bargh (Eds.), *The psychology of action* (pp. 48–68). New York: Guilford.

Tetlock, P. E., Peterson, R. S., McGuire, C., Change, S., & Feld, P. (1992). Assessing political group dynamics: A test of the groupthink model. *Journal of Personality and Social Psychology, 63,* 403–425.

Thompson, J. K., & Stice, E. (2001). Thin-ideal internalization: Mounting evidence for a new risk factor for body-image disturbance and eating pathology. *Current Directions in Psychological Science, 10,* 181–183.

Thompson, L. (1998). *The mind and heart of the negotiator.* Upper Saddle River, NJ: Prentice-Hall.

Tice, D. M., Bratslavsky, E., & Baumeister, R. F. (2000). Emotional distress regulation takes precedence over impulse control: If you feel bad, do it! *Journal of Personality and Social Psychology, 80,* 53–67.

Tice, D. M., Butler, J. L., Muraven, M. B., & Stillwell, A. M. (1995). When modesty prevails: Differential favorability of self-presentation to friends and strangers. *Journal of Personality and Social Psychology, 69,* 1120–1138.

Tidwell, M.-C. O., Reis, H. T., & Shaver, P. R. (1996). Attachment, attractiveness, and social interaction: A diary study. *Journal of Personality and Social Psychology, 71,* 729–745.

Tiedens, L. Z., & Fragale, A. R. (2003). Power moves: Complementarity in dominant and submissive nonverbal behavior. *Journal of Personality and Social Psychology, 84,* 558–568.

Timmerman, T. A. (2007). "It was a thought pitch": Personal, situational, and target influences on hit-by-pitch events across time. *Journal of Applied Psychology, 92,* 876-884.

Tjosvold, D., & DeDreu, C. (1997). Managing conflict in Dutch organizations: A test of the relevance of Deutsch's cooperation theory. *Journal of Applied Social Psychology, 27,* 2213–2227.

Todorov, A., Mandisodza, A. N., Goren, A., & Hall, C. C. (2005). Inferences of competence from faces predict election outcomes. *Science, 308,* 1623–1626.

Toi, M., & Batson, C. D. (1982). More evidence that empathy is a source of altruistic motivation. *Journal of Personality and Social Psychology, 43,* 281–292.

Tormala, Z. L., & Petty, R. E. (2004). Resistance to persuasion and attitude certainty: The moderating role of elaboration. *Personality and Social Psychology Bulletin, 30,* 1446–1457.

Tormala, Z. L., Petty, R. E., & Brinol, P. (2002). Ease of retrieval effects in persuasion: A self-validation analysis. *Personality and Social Psychology Bulletin, 28,* 1700–1712.

Towles-Schwen, T., & Fazio, R. H. (2001). On the origins of racial attitudes: Correlates of childhood experiences. *Personality and Social Psychology Bulletin, 27,* 162–175.

Towles-Schwen, T., & Fazio, R. H. (2003). Choosing social situations: The relation between automatically activated racial attitudes and anticipated comfort interacting with African Americans. *Personality and Social Psychology Bulletin, 29,* 170-182.

Trafimow, D., Silverman, E., Fan, R., & Law, J. (1997). The effects of language and priming on the relative accessibility of the private self and collective self. *Journal of Cross-Cultural Psychology, 28,* 107–123.

Trevarthen, C. (1993). The function of emotions in early infant communication and development. In J. Nadel & L. Camaioni (Eds.), *New perspectives in early communication development* (pp. 48–81). London: Routledge.

Triandis, H. C. (1990). Cross-cultural studies of individualism and collectivism. In J. J. Berman (Ed.), *Nebraska symposium on motivation, 1989* (pp. 41–133). Lincoln: University of Nebraska Press.

Triplett, N. (1898). The dynamogenic factors in pacemaking and competition. *American Journal of Psychology, 9,* 507–533.

Trobst, K. K., Collins, R. L., & Embree, J. M. (1994). The role of emotion in social support provision: Gender, empathy, and expressions of distress. *Journal of Social and Personal Relationships, 11,* 45–62.

Trope, Y., & Liberman, N. (2003). Temporal construal. *Psychological Review, 110,* 401–421.

Tyler, J. M., & Feldman R. S. (2004). Cognitive demand and self-presentation efforts: The influence of situational importance and interactions goal. *Self and Identity, 3,* 364–377.

Turner, J. C. (1991). *Social influence.* Pacific Grove, CA: Brooks/Cole.

Turner, J. C. (2006). Tyranny, freedom and social structure: Escaping our theoretical prisons. *British Journal of Social Psychology, 45,* 41–46.

Turner, J. C., & Onorato, R. S. (1999). Social identity, personality, and the self-concept: A self-categorization perspective. In T. R. Tyler, R. M. Kramer & O. P. John (Eds.), *The psychology of the social self* (pp. 11–46). Mahwah, NJ: Erlbaum.

Turner, J. C., Hogg, M. A., Oakes, P. J., Reicher, S. D., & Wetherell, M. S. (1987). *Rediscovering the social group: A self-categorization theory.* Oxford, UK: Blackwell.

Twenge, J. M., Baumeister, R. F., DeWall, C. N., Ciarocco, N. J., & Bartels, J. M. (2007). Social exclusion decreases prosocial behavior. *Journal of Personality and Social Psychology, 92,* 56–66.

Twenge, J. M., & Manis, M. M. (1998). First-name desirability and adjustment: Self-satisfaction, others' ratings, and family background. *Journal of Applied Social Psychology, 24,* 41–51.

Tykocinski, O. E. (2001). I never had a chance: Using hindsight tactics to mitigate disappointments. *Personality and Social Psychology Bulletin, 27,* 376–382.

Tyler, J. M., Feldman, R. S., & Reichert, A. (2006). The price of deceptive behavior: Disliking and lying to people who lie to us. *Journal of Experimental SociPsychology, 42,* 69-77.

Tyler, T. R., & Blader, S. (2000). *Cooperation in groups: Procedural justice, social identity and behavioral engagement.* Philadelphia, PA: Psychology Press.

Tyler, T. R., Boeckmann, R. J., Smith, H. J., & Huo, Y. J. (1997). *Social justice in a diverse society.* Boulder, CO: Westview.

Unger, L. S., & Thumuluri, L. K. (1997). Trait empathy and continuous helping: The case of volunteerism. *Journal of Social Behavior and Personality, 12,* 785–800.

Ungerer, J. A., Dolby, R., Waters, B., Barnett, B., Kelk, N., & Lewin, V. (1990). The early development of empathy: Self-regulation and individual differences in the first year. *Motivation and Emotion, 14,* 93–106.

Urbanski, L. (1992, May 21). Study uncovers traits people seek in friends. *The Evangelist,* 4.

U.S.Bureau of Labor Statistics. (2007). *Volunteering in the United States, 2006.* Washington DC: Bureau of Labor Statistics.

U.S. Bureau of Labor Statistics. (2006). *Women in the labor force: A databook.* Report 996. Retrieved May 21, 2007, from www.bls.gov/news.release/pdf/atus.pdf.

U.S. Department of Justice. (2003). *Sourcebook of criminal justice statistics.* Washington, DC: U.S. Government Printing Office.

Vallone, R. Ross, L., Lepper, M. (1985). Social status, cognitive alternative, and intergroup relations. In H. Tajfel (Ed.), *Differentiation between social groups* (pp. 201–226). London: Academic Press.

Van Boven, L., White, K., Kamada, A., & Gilovich, T. (2003). Intuitions about situational correction in self and others. *Journal of Personality and Social Psychology, 85,* 249–258.

Van den Bos, K., & Lind, E. W. (2001). Uncertainty management by means of fairness judgments. In M. P. Zanna (Ed.), *Advances in experimental social psychology* (Vol. 34, pp. 1–60). San Diego, CA: Academic Press.

Van Dyne, L., & LePine, J. A. (1998). Helping and voice extra-role behaviors: Evidence of construct and predictive validity. *Academy of Management Journal, 41,* 108–119.

Van Overwalle, F. (1997). Dispositional attributions require the joint application of the methods of difference and agreement. *Personality and Social Psychology Bulletin, 23,* 974–980.

Van Overwalle, F. (1998). Causal explanation as constraint satisfaction: A critique and a feedforward connectionist alternative. *Journal of Personality and Social Psychology, 74,* 312–328.

Van Prooijen, J. W., van den Bos, K., Lind, E. A., & Wilke, H. A. M. (2006). How do people react to negative procedures? On the moderating role of authority's biased attitudes. *Journal of Experimental Social Psychology, 42,* 632–645.

Vandello, J. A., & Cohen, D. (2003). Male honor and female fidelity: Implicit cultural scripts that perpetuate domestic violence. *Journal of Personality and Social Psychology, 84,* 997–1010.

Vanderbilt, A. (1957). *Amy Vanderbilt's complete book of etiquette.* Garden City, NY: Doubleday.

Van Vugt, M., & Van Lange, P. A. M. (In press). Psychological adaptations for prosocial behavior: The altruism puzzle. In M. Schaller, D. Kenrick, & J. Simpson (Eds.), *Evolution and social psychology.* New York: Psychology Press.

Vasquez, M. J. T. (2001). Leveling the playing field—Toward the emancipation of women. *Psychology of Women Quarterly, 25,* 89–97.

Vertue, F. M. (2003). From adaptive emotion to dysfunction: An attachment perspective on social anxiety disorder. *Personality and Social Psychology Review, 7,* 170–191.

Vinokur, A., & Burnstein, E. (1974). Effects of partially shared persuasive arguments on group-induced shifts: A group problem-solving approach. *Journal of Personality and Social Psychology, 29,* 305–315.

Vinokur, A. D., & Schul, Y. (2000). Projection in person perception among spouses as a function of the similarity in their shared experiences. *Personality and Social Psychology Bulletin, 26,* 987–1001.

Visser, P. S., Krosnick, J. A., & Simmons, J. P. (2003). Distinguishing the cognitive and behavioral consequences of attitude and certainty: A new approach to testing the common-factor hypothesis. *Journal of Experimental Social Psychology, 39,* 118–141.

Vogt, D. S., & Colvin, C. R. (2003). Interpersonal orientation and the accuracy of personality judgments. *Journal of Personality, 71,* 267–295.

Vohs, K. D., & Heatherton, T. F. (2000). Self-regulatory failure: A resource-depletion approach. *Psychological Science, 11,* 249–254.

Vonk, R. (1998). The slime effect: Suspicion and dislike of likeable behavior toward superiors. *Journal of Personality and Social Psychology, 74,* 849–864.

Vonk, R. (1999). Differential evaluations of likeable and dislikeable behaviours enacted towards superiors and subordinates. *European Journal of Social Psychology, 29,* 139–146.

Vonk, R. (2002). Self-serving interpretations of flattery: Why ingratiation works. *Journal of Personality and Social Psychology, 82,* 515–526.

Vonofakou, C., Hewstone, M., & Voci, A. (2007). Contact with out-group friends as a predictor of meta-attitudinal strength and accessibility of attitudes toward gay men. *Journal of Personality and Social Psychology, 92,* 804–820.

Vorauer, J. D., Hunter, A. J., Main, K. J., & Roy, S. A. (2000). Meta-stereotype activation: Evidence from indirect measures for specific evaluative concerns experienced by members of dominant groups in intergroup interaction. *Journal of Personality and Social Psychology, 78,* 690–707.

Waldman, D. A., Ramiriz, G. G., House, R. J., & Puranam, P. (2001). Does leadership matter? CEO leadership attributes and profitability under conditions of perceived environmental uncertainty. *Academy of Management Journal, 44,* 134–143.

Walker, S., Richardson, D. S., & Green, L. R. (2000). Aggression among older adults: The relationship of interaction networks and gender role to direct and indirect responses. *Aggressive Behavior, 26,* 145–154.

Walster, E., & Festinger, L. (1962). The effectiveness of "overheard" persuasive communication. *Journal of Abnormal and Social Psychology, 65,* 395–402.

Walster, E., Walster, G. W., Piliavin, J., & Schmidt, L. (1973). "Playing hard-to-get": Understanding an elusive phenomenon. *Journal of Personality and Social Psychology, 26,* 113–121.

Walther, E. (2002). Guilty by mere association: Evaluative conditioning and the spreading attitude effect. *Journal of Personality and Social Psychology, 82,* 919–934.

Wann, D. L., & Branscombe, N. R. (1993). Sports fans: Measuring degree of identification with their team. *International Journal of Sport Psychology, 24,* 1–17.

Wanous, J. P., Reiches, A. E., & Hudy, M. J. (1997). Overall job satisfaction: How good are single-item measures? *Journal of Applied Psychology, 82,* 247–252.

Waters, H. F., Block, D., Friday, C., & Gordon, J. (1993, July 12). Networks under the gun. *Newsweek,* 64–66.

Watson, D., Wiese, D., Vaidya, J., & Tellgen, A. (1999). The two general activation systems of affect: Structural findings, evolutionary considerations, and psychological evidence. *Journal of Personality and Social Psychology, 76,* 805–819.

Watts, B. L. (1982). Individual differences in circadian activity rhythms and their effects on roommate relationships. *Journal of Personality, 50,* 374–384.

Wayne, J. H., Riordan, C. M., & Thomas, K. M. (2001). Is all sexual harassment viewed the same? Mock juror decisions in same- and cross-gender cases. *Journal of Applied Social Psychology, 86,* 179–187.

Wayne, S. J., & Ferris, G. R. (1990). Influence tactics, and exchange quality in supervisor–subordinate interactions: A laboratory experiment and field study. *Journal of Applied Psychology, 75,* 487–499.

Wayne, S. J., & Kacmar, K. M. (1991). The effects of impression management on the performance appraisal process. *Organizational Behavior and Human Decision Processes, 48,* 70–88.

Wayne, S. J., & Liden, R. C. (1995). Effects of impression management on performance ratings: A longitudinal study. *Academy of Management Journal, 38,* 232–260.

Wayne, S. J., Liden, R. C., Graf, I. K., & Ferris, G. R. (1997). The role of upward influence tactics in human resource decisions. *Personnel Psychology, 50,* 979–1006.

Webb, T. L., & Sheeran, P. (2007). *How do implementation intentions promote goal attainment? A test of component processes. Journal of Experimental Social Psychology, 43,* 295-302.

Wegener, D. T., & Carlston, D. E. (2005). Cognitive processes in attitude formation and change. In D. Albarracin, B. T. Johnson, & M. P. Zanna (Eds.), *The handbook of attitudes* (pp. 493–542). Mahwah, NJ: Lawrence Erlbaum.

Wegener, D. T., Petty, R. E., Smoak, N. D., & Fabrigar, L. R. (2004). Multiple routes to resisting attitude change. In E. S. Knowles & J. A. Linn (Eds.), *Resistance and persuasion* (pp. 13–38). Mahwah, NJ: Erlbaum.

Wegner, D. M. (1992b). You can't always think what you want: Problems in the suppression of unwanted thoughts. In M. Zanna (Ed.), *Advances in experimental social psychology* (Vol. 25, pp. 193–225). San Diego, CA: Academic Press.

Wegner, D. M. (1994). Ironic processes of mental control. *Psychological Review, 101,* 34–54.

Wegner, D. M. (2003). Thought suppression and mental control. In *Encyclopedia of cognitive science,* (pp. 395-397). London: Macmillan.

Wegner, D. M., & Gold, D. B. (1995). Fanning old flames: Emotional and cognitive effects of suppressing thoughts of a past relationship. *Journal of Personality and Social Psychology, 68,* 782–792.

Wegner, D. M., & Zanakos, S. (1994). Chronic thought suppression. *Journal of Personality, 62,* 615–640.

Wegner, D. T., & Petty, R. E. (1994). Mood management across affective states: The hedonic contingency hypothesis. *Journal of Personality and Social Psychology, 66,* 1034–1048.

Weinberg, B. A., & Bealer, B. K. (2002). *The caffeine advantage.* New York: Free Press.

Weiner, B. (1980). A cognitive (attribution) emotion–action model of motivated behavior: An analysis of judgments of help-giving. *Journal of Personality and Social Psychology, 39,* 186–200.

Weiner, B. (1985). An attributional theory of achievement motivation and emotion. *Psychological Review, 92,* 548–573.

Weiner, B. (1993). On sin versus sickness: A theory of perceived responsibility and social motivation. *American Psychologist, 48,* 957–965.

Weiner, B. (1995). *Judgments of responsibility: A foundation for a theory of social conduct.* New York: Guilford.

Weisberg, J. (1990, October 1). Fighting words. *The New Republic, 42.*

Weiss, H. M. (2002). Deconstructing job satisfaction: Separating evaluations, beliefs, and affective experiences. *Human Resource Management Review, 12,* 173–194.

Weissenberg, P., & Kavanagh, M. H. (1972). The independence of initiating structure and consideration: A review of the evidence. *Personnel Psychology, 25,* 119–130.

Weldon, E., & Mustari, L. (1988). Felt dispensability in groups of coactors: The effects of shared responsibility and explicit anonymity on cognitive effort. *Organizational Behavior and Human Decision Processes, 41,* 330–351.

Wells, G. L. (1984). The psychology of lineup identification. *Journal of Applied Social Psychology, 14,* 89–103.

Wells, G. L. (1993). What do we know about eyewitness identification? *American Psychologist, 48,* 553–571.

Wells, G. L., & Luus, C. A. E. (1990). Police lineups as experiments: Social methodology as a framework for properly conducted lineups. *Personality and Social Psychology Bulletin, 16,* 106–117.

Wells, G. L., Luus, C. A. E., & Windschitl, P. D. (1994). Maximizing the utility of eyewitness identification evidence. *Current Directions in Psychological Science, 3,* 194–197.

Wells, G. L., Memon, A., & Penrod, S. D. (2006). Eyewitness evidence: Improving its probative value. *Psychological Science in the Public Interest, 7,* 45–75.

Werth, L., & Foerster, J. (2007). How regulatory focus influences consumer behavior. *European Journal of Social Psychology, 37,* 33–51.

Wheeler, L., & Kim, Y. (1997). What is beautiful is culturally good: The physical attractiveness stereotype has different content in collectivistic cultures. *Personality and Social Psychology Bulletin, 23,* 795–800.

Wheeler, S. C., Brinol, P., & Hermann, A. D. (2007). Resistance to persuasion as self-regulation: Ego-depletion and its effects on attitude change processes. *Journal of Experimental Social Psychology, 43,* 150–156.

Whiffen, V. E., Aube, J. A., Thompson, J. M., & Campbell, T. L. (2000). Attachment beliefs and interpersonal contexts associated with dependency and self-criticism. *Journal of Social and Clinical Psychology, 19,* 184–205.

White, J. B., Tynan, R., Galinsky, A. D., & Thompson, L. (2004). Face threat sensitivity in negotiation: Roadblock to agreement and joint gain. *Organizational Behavior and Human Decision Processes, 94,* 102–124.

White, K., Lehman, D. R., & Cohen, D. (2006). Culture, self-construal, and affective reactions to successful and unsuccessful others. *Journal of Experimental Social Psychology, 42,* 582–592.

Wiederman, M. W., & Allgeier, E. R. (1996). Expectations and attributions regarding extramarital sex among young married individuals. *Journal of Psychology & Human Sexuality, 8,* 21–35.

Wiley, J. A., & Camacho, T. C. (1980). Life-style and future health: Evidence from the Alameda County study. *Preventive Medicine, 9,* 1–21.

Williams, C. L. (1992). The glass escalator: Hidden advantages for men in the "female" professions. *Social Problems, 39,* 253–267.

Williams, J. E., & Best, D. L. (1990). *Sex and psyche: Gender and self viewed cross-culturally.* Newbury Park, CA: Sage.

Williams, K. B., Radefeld, P. A., Binning, J. F., & Suadk, J. R. (1993). When job candidates are "hard-" versus "easy-to-get": Effects of candidate availability on employment decisions. *Journal of Applied Social Psychology, 23,* 169–198.

Williams, K. D. (2001). *Ostracism: The power of silence.* New York: Guilford Press.

Williams, K. D., & Karau, S. J. (1991). Social loafing and social compensation: The effects of expectations of co-worker performance. *Journal of Personality and Social Psychology, 61,* 570–581.

Williams, K. D., Harkins, S., & Latané, B. (1981). Identifiability as a deterrent to social loafing: Two cheering experiments. *Journal of Personality and Social Psychology, 40,* 303–311.

Williamson, G. M., & Schulz, R. (1995). Caring for a family member with cancer: Past communal behavior and affective reactions. *Journal of Applied Social Psychology, 25,* 93–116.

Williamson, T. M. (1993). From interrogation to investigative interviewing: Strategic trends in police questioning. *Journal of Community and Applied Social Psychology, 3,* 89–99.

Willingham, D. T., & Dunn, E. W. (2003). What neuroimaging and brain localization can do, cannot, and should not do for social psychology. *Journal of Personality and Social Psychology, 85,* 662–671.

Willis, J., & Todorov, A. (2006). First impression: Making up your mind after a 100-ms. exposure to a face. *Psychological Science, 17,* 592–598.

Wilson, A. E., & Ross, M. (2001). From chump to champ: People's appraisals of their earlier and present selves. *Journal of Personality and Social Psychology, 80,* 572-584.

Wilson, D. W. (1981). Is helping a laughing matter? *Psychology, 18,* 6–9.

Wilson, J. P., & Petruska, R. (1984). Motivation, model attributes, and prosocial behavior. *Journal of Personality and Social Psychology, 46,* 458–468.

Wilson, T. D., Centerbar, D. B., Kermer, D. A., & Gilbert, D. T. (2005). The pleasures of uncertainty: Prolonging positive mood in ways people do not anticipate. *Journal of Personality and Social Psychology, 88,* 5–21.

Wilson, T. D., & Kraft, D. (1993). Why do I love thee?: Effects of repeated introspections about a dating relationship on attitudes toward the relationship. *Personality and Social Psychology Bulletin, 19,* 409–418.

Winograd, E., Goldstein, F. C., Monarch, E. S., Peluso, J. P., & Goldman, W. P. (1999). The mere exposure effect in patients with Alzheimer's disease. *Neuropsychology, 13,* 41–46.

Wisman, A., & Koole, S. L. (2003). Hiding in the crowd: Can mortality salience promote affiliation with others who oppose one's world view? *Journal of Personality and Social Psychology, 84,* 511–526.

Witt, L. A., & Ferris, G. B. (2003). Social skill as moderator of the conscientiousness-performance relationship: Convergent results across four studies. *Journal of Applied Psychology, 88,* 808–820.

Wohl, M. J. A., & Branscombe, N. R. (2005). Forgiveness and collective guilt assignment to historical perpetrator groups depend on level of social category inclusiveness. *Journal of Personality and Social Psychology, 88,* 288–303.

Wood, G. S. (2004, April 12 & 19). Pursuits of happiness. *The New Republic,* 38–42.

Wood, J. V. (1989). Theory and research concerning social comparisons of personal attributes. *Psychological Bulletin, 106,* 231–248.

Wood, J. V., & Wilson, A. E. (2003). How important is social comparison? In M. R. Leary & J. P. Tangney (Eds.), *Handbook of self and identity* (pp. 344–366). New York: Guilford Press.

Wood, W., Quinn, J. M., & Kashy, D. A. (2002). Habits in everyday life: Thought, emotion, and action. *Journal of Personality and Social Psychology, 83,* 1281–1297.

Wood, W., & Quinn, J. M. (2003). Forewarned and forearmed? Two meta-analytic syntheses of forewarning of influence appeals. *Psychological Bulletin, 129,* 119–138.

Wood, W., Wong, F. Y., & Cachere, J. G. (1991). Effects of media violence on viewers' aggression in unconstrained social interaction. *Psychological Bulletin, 109,* 371–383.

Wright, S. C. (2001). Strategic collective action: Social psychology and social change. In R. Brown & S. Gaertner (Eds.), *Blackwell handbook of social psychology: Intergroup processes* (pp. 409–430). Oxford: Blackwell.

Wright, S. C., Taylor, D. M., & Moghaddam, F. M. (1990). Responding to membership in a disadvantaged group: From acceptance to collective protest. *Journal of Personality and Social Psychology, 58,* 994–1003.

Wright, S. C., Aron, A., McLaughlin-Volpe, T., & Ropp, S. A. (1997). The extended contact effect: Knowledge of cross-group friendships and prejudice. *Journal of Personality and Social Psychology, 73,* 73–90.

Wuensch, K. L., Castellow, W. A., & Moore, C. H. (1991). Effects of defendant attractiveness and type of crime on juridic judgment. *Journal of Social Behavior and Personality, 6,* 713–724.

Wyer, R. S., Jr., & Srull, T. K. (Eds.). (1994). *Handbook of social cognition* (2nd ed., Vol. 1). Hillsdale, NJ: Erlbaum.

Wyer, R. S., Jr., Budesheim, T. L., Lambert, A. J., & Swan, S. (1994). Person memory judgment: Pragmatic influences on impressions formed in a social context. *Journal of Personality and Social Psychology, 66,* 254–267.

Yee, N., Bailenson, J. N., Urbanek, M., Chang, F., & Merget, D. (2007). The unbearable likeness of being digital: The persistence of nonverbal social norms in online virtual environments. *Cyber Psychology and Behavior, 10,* 115–121.

Yoder, J. D., & Berendsen, L. L. (2001). "Outsider within" the firehouse: African American and white women firefighters. *Psychology of Women Quarterly, 25,* 27–36.

Young, L. V. (2005). Service and disservice. In R. L. Taylor & W. E. Rosenbach (Eds.), *Military leadership: In pursuit of excellence* (5th ed., pp. 139–142). Boulder, CO: Westview Press.

Yukl, G., & Falbe, C. M. (1991). Importance of different power sources in downward and lateral relations. *Journal of Applied Psychology, 76,* 416–423.

Yukl, G. A. (1998). *Leadership in organizations* (4th ed.). Englewood Cliffs, NJ: Prentice-Hall.

Yukl, G. A. (2006). *Leadership in organizations* (6th ed.). Upper Saddle River, NJ: Prentice-Hall.

Yzerbyt, V. Y., Corneille, O., & Estrada, C. (2001). The interplay of subjective essentialism and entitativity in the formation of stereotypes. *Personality and Social Psychology Review, 5,* 141–155.

Yzerbyt, V., Rocher, S., & Schadron, G. (1997). Stereotypes as explanations: A subjective essentialist view of group perception. In R. Spears, P. J. Oakes, N. Ellemers, & S. A. Haslam (Eds.), *The social psychology of stereotyping and group life* (pp. 20–50). Oxford: Blackwell.

Zaccaro, S. J. (2007). Trait-based perspective on leadership. *American Psychologist, 62,* 6–16.

Zadro, L., Boland, C., & Richardson, R. (2006). How long does it last? The persistence of the effects of ostracism in the socially anxious. *Journal of Experimental Social Psychology, 42,* 692–697.

Zajonc, R. B. (1965). Social facilitation. *Science, 149,* 269–274.

Zajonc, R. B. (1968). Attitudinal effects of mere exposure [monograph]. *Journal of Personality and Social Psychology, 9,* 1–27.

Zajonc, R. B. (2001). Mere exposure: A gateway to the subliminal. *Current Directions in Psychological Science, 10,* 224–228.

Zajonc, R. B., Heingartner, A., & Herman, E. M. (1969). Social enhancement and impairment of performance in the cockroach. *Journal of Personality and Social Psychology, 13,* 83–92.

Zajonc, R. B., Adelmann, P. K., Murphy, S. T., & Niedenthal, P. M. (1987). Convergence in the physical appearance of spouses. *Motivation and Emotion, 11,* 335–346.

Zaragoza, M. S., Payment, K. E., Ackil, U. K., Drivdahl, S. B., & Beck, M. (2001). Interviewing witnesses: Forced confabulation and confirmative feedback increase false memories. *Psychological Science, 12,* 473–478.

Zarate, M. A., Garcia, B., Garza, A. A., & Hitlan, R. T. (2004). Cultural threat and perceived realistic conflict as dual predictors of prejudice. *Journal of Experimental Social Psychology, 40,* 99–105.

Zebrowitz, L. A. (1997). *Reading faces.* Boulder, CO: Westview Press.

Zebrowitz, L. A., Collins, M. A., & Dutta, R. (1998). The relationship between appearance and personality across the life span. *Personality and Social Psychology Bulletin, 24,* 736–749.

Zeitz, G. (1990). Age and work satisfaction in a government agency: A situational perspective. *Human Relations, 43,* 419–438.

Zillmann, D. (1979). *Hostility and aggression.* Hillsdale, NJ: Erlbaum.

Zillmann, D. (1983). Transfer of excitation in emotional behavior. In J. T. Cacioppo & R. E. Petty (Eds.), *Social psychophysiology: A sourcebook* (pp. 215–240). New York: Guilford Press.

Zillmann, D. (1988). Cognition–excitation interdependencies in aggressive behavior. *Aggressive Behavior, 14,* 51–64.

Zillmann, D. (1994). Cognition–excitation interdependencies in the escalation of anger and angry aggression. In M. Potegal & J. F. Knutson (Eds.), *The dynamics of aggression.* Hillsdale, NJ: Erlbaum.

Zillmann, D., Baron, R. A., & Tamborini, R. (1981). The social costs of smoking: Effects of tobacco smoke on hostile behavior. *Journal of Applied Social Psychology, 11,* 548–561.

Zimbardo, P. G. (2007). *The Lucifer effect: How good people turn evil.* New York: Random House.

Zimbardo, P. G., Haney, C., Banks, C., & Jaffe, D. (1973, April 8). A Pirandellian prison: The mind is a formidable jailer. *New York Times Magazine,* pp. 38–60.

Zoglin, R. (1993). The shock of the blue. *Time, 142*(17), 71–72.

Zukerman, M. (1994). *Behavioral expressions and biosocial bases of sensation seeking.* New York: Cambridge University Press.

Zuckerman, M., & O'Loughlin, R. E. (2006). Self-enhancement by social comparison: A prospective analysis. *Personality and Social Psychology Bulletin, 32,* 751–760.

Name Index

Aamodt, M. G., 442
Aarts, H., 94, 278
Abrams, D., 115
Adair, J. G., 32
Adams, G., 113, 186, 191, 244, 245
Adams, J. S., 406
Adarves-Yorno, I., 410
Adorno, 20
Agnew, C. R., 244, 265, 266
Agosti, V., 96
Agular, P., 187
Ahn, M., 59
Aikin, K. J., 211
Ajzen, I., 149, 162, 163
Alagna, F. J., 79
Albarracin, D., 162
Alden, L. E., 251
Algom, D., 44
Alicke, M. D., 136
Allen, J. J. B., 232
Allen, K., 441, 447, 449
Allgeier, E. R., 256
Allport, F. H., 19, 396
Amato, P. R., 321
Ambady, N., 77
American Psychiatric Association, 262
Ames, D. R., Flynn, F. J., 327
Amo, R. B., 195
Amsel, R., 236
Anastasio, P. A., 216
Andersen, S. M., 233
Anderson, 366
Anderson, C. A., 10, 100, 249, 320, 338, 340, 347, 348, 360, 361, 372
Anderson, K. B., 360
Anderson, L. R., 412
Anderson, N. H., 101
Anderson, V. L., 323
Andreoletti, C., 233
Andreou, E., 365
Angier, N., 239
Antonakis, J., 452
Apanovich, A. M., 168
Apfelbaum, E. P., 211
Aquino, K., 213
Archer, J., 364, 365
Archibald, F. S., 249
Argyle, M., 379
Ariely, D., 7, 211
Aristotle, 238
Arkes, H. R., 149
Armor, D. A., 59, 137
Armstrong, T. L., 206
Arndt, J., 205
Aron, A. P., 219, 255, 256, 257, 392
Aronoff, J., 78
Aronson, E., 180, 391

Aronson, J. A., 67, 140, 141, 142
Arriaga, X. B., 244, 252, 266
Arvey, R. D., 444
Asch, S. E., 20, 98, 275, 276, 278
Asendorpf, J. B., 250
Asgari, S., 113
Ashburn-Nardo, L., 188
Asher, S. R., 249
Ashmore, R. D., 126, 234
Aune, K. S., 252
Averill, J. R., 256
Avolio, B. J., 442, 449, 450, 451, 453
Ayduk, O., 121
Azar, B., 321, 323
Azar, O. H., 275
Azuma, 58

Babey, S. H., 131, 132
Bachman, B. A., 216
Baddeley, A. D., 64
Baeyens, F., 151
Baker, N. V., 354
Baldwin, D. A., 226
Baldwin, M. W., 153, 294
Balkin, D. B., 127
Banaji, M. R., 49, 65, 212
Bandura, A., 127, 137, 154, 213, 331, 340, 349
Barden, J., 188
Bargh, J. A., 38, 45, 49, 50, 165, 274, 294, 295
Bar-Haim, Y., 17
Baron, R. A., 10, 55, 63, 64, 68, 127, 137, 277, 280, 320, 343, 344, 350, 357, 360, 366, 367, 403, 406, 443, 445
Baron, R. S., 394
Barr, L., 131, 132
Barrick, M. R., 107
Barsky, A., 407
Bar-Tal, D., 206, 213
Bartholomew, K., 247
Bartholow, B. D., 204, 347, 350, 362, 363
Bartlett, M. Y., 203
Bass, B. M., 453
Bassili, J. N., 30
Batson, C. D., 180, 307, 321, 322, 331, 332
Baum, A., 233, 440
Baumeister, R. F., 41, 66, 67, 126, 131, 135, 226, 227, 338, 358, 370
Baxter, L. A., 264
BBC News, 147
Beach, S. R. H., 232, 253
Bealer, B. K., 171
Beall, A. E., 255
Beaman, A. L., 290
Beauvois, J. L., 195

Beehr, T. A., 443
Behfar, K. J., 403
Beike, D. R., 58
Bell, B. E., 236, 249
Bell, D. W., 155
Bell, P. A., 360
Bell, R. A., 251
Benjamin, E., 227
Benoir, W. L., 167
Ben-Porath, D. D., 228
Benson, P. L., 318
Benthin, A. C., 180
Ben-Zeev, T., 141
Bera, S., 247
Berdahl, J., 84
Berendsen, L. L., 123, 194
Berg, J. H., 249
Berkowitz, L., 308, 339, 340
Berman, J. S., 96
Bernieri, F. J., 236
Berntson, G. G., 15
Berry, A. J., 131
Berry, D. S., 229
Berscheid, E., 244, 255
Bersoff, D. M., 331
Best, D. L., 131
Bettencourt, B. A., 359, 385
Betz, A. L., 151
Bierhoff, H. W., 325
Biernat, M., 123, 134, 186, 191, 194, 196
Bies, R. J., 104, 406
Birchmeier, Z., 115
Bizer, G. Y., 149
Björkqvist, K., 359, 366
Blackstone, T., 139
Blader, S. L., 114, 406
Blair, C., 163
Blair, I. V., 76, 149, 188, 211
Blascovich, J., 131
Blass, T., 257
Blaylock, B., 262
Blazer, D. G., 96
Bless, H., 17, 47, 68
Block, C. J., 194
Bluemke, M., 149
Bobo, L., 206
Bodenhausen, G. F., 200
Bodenhausen, G. V., 200, 202
Boer, F., 248
Bogard, M., 359
Bohner, G., 148, 284
Bond, M. H., 10, 136, 277
Bond, R., 278, 285
Boninger, D., 59
Bonnelle, K., 102
Boothroyd, P., 256
Bordgen, S., 76
Bornstein, E. H., 431
Bornstein, R. F., 152

Bossard, J. H. S., 232
Bosson, J. K., 141, 142, 247
Botha, M., 347
Bothwell, R. K., 430, 431
Bourgeois, M. J., 424
Bowlby, J., 246, 247
Brain, P., 364
Brandstatter, V., 261
Brannon, L. A., 173
Branscombe, N. R., 59, 92, 113,
     115, 122, 123, 135, 136,
     139, 141, 153, 186, 189,
     191, 193, 194, 195, 196,
     202, 205, 212, 217
Bratslavsky, E., 41, 66, 67
Brauer, M., 201
Braza, P., 250
Brehm, J. W., 172, 177
Brennan, K. A., 247, 250
Brentson, G. G., 54
Brewer, M. B., 122, 188, 202, 378
Brickner, M., 399
Brigham, J., 165
Bringle, R. G., 256
Brinol, P., 174, 175
Brockner, J. M., 406
Broemer, P., 167
Brooks-Gunn, J., 232
Brothers, L., 321
Broughton, R., 257
Brown, J. D., 79, 93, 137, 141,
     142, 342, 356, 357, 440
Brown, L. M., 278, 351
Brown, R. P., 194, 202, 380
Brown, S. L., 441
Brown, S. P., 443
Bruce, M. N., 104
Bruder, G. E., 96
Brunol, P., 161
Brunot, S., 122
Bryan, J. H., 319
Buckley, T., 227
Budesheim, T. L., 101, 102
Budson, A. E., 41
Buehler, R., 8, 55, 56, 57, 137,
     280
Bundy, R., 208
Burger, J. M., 249, 285, 290,
     291, 292
Burnstein, E., 408, 409
Burris, C. T., 193
Burris, E. R., 127
Burrows, L., 49, 50
Burrus, J., 75, 88
Bushman, B. J., 10, 78, 300,
     320, 338, 340, 347, 348,
     351, 358, 361, 372
Buss, D. M., 11, 12, 256, 258,
     384
Buston, P. M., 239
Butler, J. L., 105
Buttenwieser, P., 261
Butz, D. A., 202
Buunk, B. P., 122, 250, 254
Byrne, B. M., 122, 228
Byrne, D., 104, 227, 229, 231,
     236, 239, 240, 241, 262, 317

Cable, T. A., 384
Cacioppo, J. T., 15, 53-54, 55,
     148, 169, 170, 249

Cadenhead, A. C., 325
Cadinu, M., 193
Cairns, E., 216
Cajdric, A., 203
Callan, V. J., 443
Camacho, T. C., 432, 433
Campbell, B., 188, 211
Campbell, D. T., 380
Campbell, J. D., 131
Campbell, L., 253
Campbell, W. K., 247, 262
Campos, B., 345
Cann, A., 241
Caplan, S. E., 116
Caporael, L. R., 378
Caprara, G. V., 321
Caputo, C., 90, 91
Carey, G., 87
Carey, M. P., 179
Carli, L., 287
Carlsmith, J. M., 78, 178
Carlsmith, K. M., 369
Carlson, K. A., 430
Carlston, D. E., 165
Carment, W. D., 384
Carnevale, P. J., 404
Carpenter, S., 323
Carter, J. D., 83
Carvallo, M., 17, 228, 247
Carver, C. S., 357
Cash, T. F., 234, 253
Cashdan, E., 84
Caspi, A., 256
Castelli, L., 17
Castro, V. S., 216
Catalyst, 192
Caughlin, J. P., 262
Center for the American Woman
     and Politics, 192
Centerbar, D. B., 68
Cesario, J., 50
Chagut, E, 44
Chaiken, S., 90, 149, 161, 166,
     167, 169, 173
Chandler, K., 75, 76, 80
Chang-Schneider, C., 129
Chaplin, W. F., 79, 236
Charnsangavej, T., 194
Chartrand, T. L., 55, 165
Chatard, A., 122
Chen, F. F., 241
Chen, K., 114
Chen, M., 45, 49, 50
Chen, S., 114, 173
Cheverton, H. M., 236
Chiao, K. W., 53
Choi, I., 92
Christ, O., 216
Christy, P. R., 346
Cialdini, R. B., 172, 273, 274,
     278, 279, 285, 289, 291,
     292, 308, 310, 321, 452
Cichomski, B., 100
Ciucci, E., 365
Clanton, N. R., 79
Clark, 444
Clark, L. A., 247
Clark, M. S., 264, 318
Clark, N. K., 421
Clark, R. D. III, 277
Clary, E. G., 329

Claypool, H. M., 64
Clifford, J., 249-250
Clore, G. L., 64, 426
Cobb, R. J., 247
Cogan, J. C., 196
Cohen, D., 136, 352, 354, 355
Cohen, F., 205
Cohen, J. D., 49, 67, 69
Cohen, S., 437, 441
Cohn, E. G., 10, 361
Coleman, J., 115
Coles, R., 323
Collaros, P. A., 412
Collins, M. A., 233
Collins, N. L., 227
Colvin, C. R., 83
Condon, J. W., 242
Coniff, R., 81
Conner, M., 163
Conte, J. M., 443
Conway, M., 64
Cooper, C., 388
Cooper, H. M., 75, 76, 80, 361
Cooper, J., 180
Corneille, O., 202
Cornelius, T., 291
Cornell, D. P., 131, 177
Cornwell, B., 196
Correia, I., 187
Correll, J., 204
Cottrell, C. A., 202, 242
Cottrell, N. B., 397
Cox, D. S., 180
Cozzarelli, C., 247
Cramer, R. E., 316
Crandall, C. S., 124, 186, 188,
     191, 202, 209, 278, 436
Crano, W. D., 159, 242
Creighton, M., 334
Cringle, C. E., 196
Crites, S. L., 148
Crocker, J., 134, 195, 196
Croizet, J. -C., 142
Cropanzano, R. (Ed.)., 403, 405,
     444
Crosby, F. J., 189
Crum, 434
Cruse, D.F., 430
Crutchfield, R. A., 277, 287
Cuddy, A. J., 14, 191
Cunningham, M. R., 104, 234,
     320, 321
Cunningham, W. A., 49
Custer, R., 94
Cutler, B. L., 424, 428
Czopp, A. M., 188

D'Agostino, P. R., 152
Darcis, C., 142
Darley, J. M., 31, 134, 142, 300,
     313, 314, 316, 317, 321, 368
Dasgupta, N., 113, 203, 380
Daubman, K. A., 285, 327
David, B., 122
David, S. E., 191
Davila, J., 247
Davis, K. E., 85, 86
Davis, M. H., 49, 323, 329
Dawkins, R., 378
Day, D. V., 104, 454
De Houwer, J., 151

Deaux, K., 125, 126, 191
DeBruin, E. N. M., 101
DeDreu, C. K. W., 403
DeGroot, T., 453
DeHart, T., 17, 130
DeJong, W., 291
Delaney, H. J., 235
DeLongis, 438
Demopsey, J., 423, 424
DeNisi, A. S., 64
DePaulo, B. M., 75, 76, 80, 83, 115, 198, 199, 248, 327
Désert, M., 122, 142
DeSteno, D., 203, 258, 259
Deutsch, M., 19, 277, 280
Devine, P. G., 14, 53, 177, 188, 211, 217
DeWall, C. N., 370, 371
Dexter, H. R., 424
Dickter, C. L., 204
Diehl, M., 412, 413
Diener, E., 234, 379, 443
Dietrich, D. M., 308
Dietz, J., 367
Dietz-Uhler, B., 115
Dijksterhuis, A., 130, 204
Dion, K. K., 233
Dion, K. L., 196, 204, 233
Dittmann, M., 251
Djiksterhuis, A., 50, 52
Dolderman, D., 102
Dollard, J., 340, 343, 372
Donnerstein, J. L., 180
Donovan, S., 96
Doosje, B., 92, 201, 209
Dorfman, A., 256
Dovidio, J. F., 165, 200, 204, 212, 216, 217, 218
Downing, L. L., 400
Downs, A. C., 430
Druen, P. B., 104
Duan, C., 321
Dubois, N., 195
Duck, J. M., 155
Duck, S., 251
Duggan, E. S., 250
Dugosh, K. L., 412, 413
Duncan, J., 49
Duncan, N. C., 234
Dunkley, D. M., 433
Dunn, E. W., 15, 215
Dunn, J., 247
Dunning, D., 331
Durkin, K., 115
Durso, F. T., 200
Dutton, D. G., 256

Eagly, A. H., 84, 113, 149, 161, 166, 169, 173, 191, 192, 193, 200, 281, 287
Earn, B. M., 196
Ebert, R., 76
Eccles, J. S., 44
Eggleston, T. J., 180
Eibach, R. P., 189
Eich, E., 64
Eidelman, S., 134
Eisenberg, 321
Eisenman, R., 241
Eisenstadt, D., 130, 179
Ekman, P., 75, 77, 80, 84

Elfenbein, H. A., 77
Ellemers, N., 194, 195, 209, 388
Elliot, A. J., 177, 247
Ellsworth, P. C., 78
Emlen, S. T., 239
Englehart, J. M., 398
Englich, B., 47
Epley, N., 31, 32, 48, 116, 331
Erez, A., 65
Eron, L. D., 347
Erwin, P. G., 250
Eshleman, A., 188, 202, 209
Esses, V. M., 155, 193, 206, 318
Esteves, F., 54
Estrada, C. A., 64, 202
Etcoff, N. L., 80, 253
Ethier, K. A., 125
Evans, N., 200

Fabrigar, L. R., 161
Fairchild, K., 205, 281
Falbe, C. M., 298
Fan, R., 122
Faulkner, S. J., 227
Fazio, R. H., 17, 148, 149, 158, 159, 164, 204, 213, 215, 229
Feagin, J. R., 215
Feeney, B. C., 227
Fehr, B., 246, 257
Fein, S., 424
Feingold, A., 233, 429
Feldman, R. S., 75, 80, 81
Felmlee, D. H., 245, 264
Ferguson, T., 188
Fernandez, J. K., 55
Ferreira, M. B., 49
Ferris, G. B., 104
Ferris, G. R., 104
Feshbach, S., 167, 339
Festinger, L., 19, 20, 134, 135, 154, 166, 167, 178, 232, 241, 391
Fichten, C. S., 236
Fiedler, K., 149
Fink, B., 234
Finkelstein, M. A., 330
Fischer, P., 338, 352, 353
Fischman, J., 266
Fishbein, M., 162, 163
Fisher, J. D., 79, 229, 327
Fisher, R. P., 427
Fiske, S. T., 14, 15, 40, 84, 101, 102, 122, 191, 201
Fitzsimmons, G. M., 248, 274, 295
Flament, C., 208
Fleming, M. A., 155
Fletcher, G. J. O., 252, 253
Flynn, F. J., 310
Folger, R., 343, 367, 406
Folkes, V., 85, 96
Foltz, C., 246
Fong, G. T., 163
Ford, R., 200
Forgas, J. P. (Ed.)., 39, 63, 65, 320
Forge, K. L., 320
Forrest, J. A., 75, 80
Förster, J., 149
Forsyth, 20

Foster, C. A., 262
Fowers, B., 264
Fox, R. L., 193
Frable, D. E., 139
Fragale, A. R., 240
Fraley, R. C., 77, 247
Franiuk, R., 253
Frank, E., 261
Frank, M. G., 80, 84
Fraser, S. C., 290
Fredrickson, B. L., 248, 249
Freedman, J. L., 290
Freeman, D., 213
Fricko, M. A. M., 443
Friedman, H. S., 236
Friesen, W. V., 77
Fritzsche, B. A., 317
Frost, J. H., 7
Fry, D. P., 339
Fuegen, K., 123, 134, 172, 194
Fujita, K., 127
Funder, D. C., 251
Funk, J. B., 350
Furr, R. M., 251

Gabaix, X., 67
Gabriel, S., 228, 247
Gaertner, S. L., 165, 212, 216, 217
Galinsky, A. D., 59, 60
Gallucci, G., 17
Gantner, A. B., 362
Garcia, B., 206
Garcia, D. M., 113, 195
Garcia, S. M., 313
Garcia-Marques, I., 49, 64
Garcia-Marques, T., 64
Gardner, R. M., 227, 236
Gardner, W. L., 54, 80
Garza, A. A., 206
Gatenby, J. C., 49
Gawronski, G., 101
Geiselman, R. E., 427
George, M. S., 450
Gerard, H. B., 277, 278, 280
Gerber, G. L., 236
Getz, J. G., 103
Gibbons, D., 249
Gibbons, F. X., 180
Gier, J. A., 79
Gigone, D., 408, 410
Gilbert, D. T., 68, 89, 90, 118, 424
Gill, M. J., 10
Gillis, J. R., 196
Gilovich, T., 48, 59, 92
Giner-Sorolla, R., 159
Ginsburg, H. J., 323
Gladue, B. A., 235, 257
Gladwell, M., 46
Glaser, J., 229
Glass, D. C., 357
Gleicher, F., 59
Glick, P., 14, 191, 202
Goethals, G. R., 134
Goff, P. A., 189
Goffman, E., 153
Gold, D. B., 60, 61
Goldenberg, J. L., 255
Goldinger, S. D., 58
Goldman, W. P., 152

Goldstein, F. C., 152
Gollwitzer, P. M., 163
Good, C., 141, 142
Goodwin, R., 249
Goodwin, S. A, 201
Goodwin, V. L., 453
Gordon, R. A., 242, 290
Gore, J. C., 49
Goren, A., 99
Gould, S. J., 242
Govorun, O., 136
Graen, G. B., 452
Graf, I. K., 104
Graham, S., 85, 96
Grasselli, A., 193
Green, J. D., 90, 195, 247
Green, L. R., 359
Greenbaum, P., 78
Greenberg, J., 93, 140, 177, 205,
   406, 407, 445
Greene, E., 431
Greenwald, A. G., 136, 148, 204,
   212
Gregg, A. P., 134
Greitemeyer, T., 338, 352, 353
Griffin, D. W., 8, 55, 56, 57,
   102, 137, 280, 364, 366, 367
Grillon, C., 49
Groom, R. W., 10
Grote, N. K., 264
Grube, J. A., 329
Gruen, G. E., 249
Guagnano, G. A., 330
Guarnieri, G., 193
Gubin, A., 201
Gudjonsson, G. H., 421
Guimond, S., 122, 215
Guinote, A., 384
Gulli, C., 147
Gump, B. B., 227
Gustafson, R., 361
Gutierres, S. E., 235

Hackman, J. R., 452
Hahn, J., 257
Halberstadt, J., 235
Hall, C. C., 99
Hall, J. A., 83
Hall, U. A., 83, 84
Hall, W. S., 211
Hall-Elston, C., 250
Hamilton, D. L., 123
Hamilton, G. V., 301
Hamilton, P. A., 229
Hamilton, V. E., 171, 172
Hamilton, V. J., 131
Hamilton, V. L., 285
Hammer, E. D., 101
Haney, C., 385
Hanko, K., 254
Hansen, G., 62
Hansen, J. S., 229
Hansen, N., 133
Happ, B. R., 80
Hardin, C. D., 47
Hardy, C. L., 309, 447
Hareli, S., 236
Harker, L., 229
Harlow, T., 131
Harmon-Jones, E., 14, 179, 232
Harris, C. R., 258

Harris, L. R., 430
Harris, L. T., 14, 15
Harris, M. B., 344, 359
Harris, V. A., 90, 91
Harrison, M., 255
Harvey, D. J., 207, 216
Harvey, R. D., 196
Haslam, S. A., 120, 200, 201,
   209, 219, 283, 384, 386,
   409, 442, 448, 450, 453
Hassin, R., 9
Hastie, R., 408, 410
Hatfield, E., 233, 255, 256
Haugtvedt, C. P., 160
Hawkley, L. C., 15, 249
Hawley, P. H., 334, 359, 360
Hayden, S. R., 318
Hayes, N. S., 63
Haymovitz, E. L., 141, 142
Haywood, J., 247
Heatherton, T. F., 128
Hebl, M. R., 430, 436
Heider, F., 85, 241
Heilman, M. E., 192, 193, 194
Heinz, A., 363
Hendin, H. M., 129
Hendrick, C., 252, 257
Hendrick, S. S., 252, 257
Henley, N. M., 83
Herbener, E. S., 256
Herek, G. M., 196
Herman, C. P., 126
Hermann, A. D., 175
Hermsen, S., 204, 218
Herrera, N. C., 100
Hetherington, M. M., 395
Hetts, J., 59
Hewstone, M., 43, 200, 216
Hiatt, M., 136
Higgins, E. T., 38, 50, 148
Higgins, N. C., 319
Higham, P. A., 384
Hilden, L. E., 17, 204, 213
Hilton, N. Z., 339
Hinsz, V. B., 409
Hirt, E. R., 63
Hitlan, R. T., 206
Ho, S. Y., 241
Hoaken, P. N. S., 362
Hodes, R. M., 17
Hoffer, E., 293
Hogg, M. A., 154, 155, 202,
   210, 379, 388
Holmes, J. G., 102, 153, 245,
   253
Holmes, T. H., 437
Holtbernd, T., 76
Hood, W. R., 207, 216
Hope, D. A., 251
Hopkins, A. B., 196
Horgan, T. G., 83
Hornsey, M. J., 210, 387, 410,
   411
Hornstein, H., 368
Horowitz, L. M., 247
Horstman Reser, A., 195
Hosch, H. M., 430
House, J. S., 440
House, R. J., 450, 452, 453
Hovland, C. I., 165, 166
Howell, J. M., 452

Huesmann, L. R., 347
Huff, C., 31, 32
Hugenberg, K., 202
Hughes, S. M., 253
Huguet, P., 395
Hummert, M. L., 241
Hunt, A. McC., 238
Hunter, A. J., 202
Hunter, B. A., 211
Huston, T. L., 103
Hutson-Comeaux, S., 173
Hyman, L. M., 78

Ickes, W., 264
Imani, A., 410, 411
Insel, T. R. & Carter, C. S., 256
Insko, C. A., 280, 401
Inzlicht, M., 141
Ireland, C. A., 364
Ireland, J. L., 364, 365
Isen, A. M., 63, 64, 65, 68, 256,
   320, 321
Ito, T. A., 53, 204
Izard, C., 76

Jackman, M. R., 188
Jackson, J. S., 216
Jackson, L. M., 193, 206, 318
Jackson, T., 249
Jacobi, L., 253
Jacobs, J. A., 192
Jacobson, L., 44
James, 444
Janis, I. L., 165, 167, 409
Jarrell, A., 236
Jellison, J. M., 90, 195
Jensen-Campbell, L. A., 236
Jetten, J., 123, 201, 202, 285,
   384, 385, 387
Johns, M., 140
Johnson, A. L., 380
Johnson, B. T., 10, 162, 165,
   172, 179
Johnson, J. C., 250
Johnson, J. D., 188, 201
Johnson, M. K., 49, 56
Johnson, R. D., 400
Johnston, L., 200
Johnston, V. S., 234
Johnstone, B., 234
Joinson, A. N., 115
Joireman, J., 358, 448
Jonas, K. J., 51
Jones, E. E., 85, 86, 89, 90, 91,
   93, 290
Jones, J. T., 16, 17
Jones, N., 20
Joseph, S., 365
Jost, T. J., 219
Judd, C. M., 76, 200
Judge, T. A., 384, 444, 445
Jungeberg, B. J., 13
Jussim, L. J., 44, 151

Kacmar, K. M., 104
Kahn, J. H., 61
Kahneman, D., 133, 188
Kahneman, P., 46
Kaiser, C. R., 195
Kamada, A., 92
Kambara, T., 344

Kameda, T., 410
Kammarath, L. K., 356
Kampf, H. C., 180
Kandel, D. B., 241
Kaplan, S. A., 407
Kappen, D. M., 212
Karau, S. J., 84, 193, 397, 398, 399
Kark, R., 453
Karney, B. R., 264
Karraker, K. H., 233
Karremans, J. C, 373
Kashy, D. A., 80, 115, 165, 248
Kasser, T., 28
Kassin, S. M., 422
Katafiasz, H. A, 55
Katz, J., 253
Kavanagh, M. H., 451
Kawakami, K., 204, 212, 218
Kay, A. C., 248
Keegan, T., 189
Keller, L. M., 444
Keller, R. T., 443
Kelley, H. H., 19, 165
Kelley, I. W., 10
Kelly, A. E., 61
Kelly, H. H., 86, 87, 90, 93
Kelman, H. C., 31
Keltner, D., 158, 229, 251, 403
Kemeny, M. E., 440
Kenealy, P., 234
Kennedy-Morre, E., 180
Kenrick, D. T., 11, 235, 241, 254
Kenworthy, J. B., 287
Keough, K. A., 141, 142, 194
Kermer, D. A., 68
Kernis, M. H., 131
Kessler, R. C., 96
Ketcher, C. M., 346
Kiechel, K. L., 422
Kiecolt-Glaser, J. K., 441
Kilduff, M., 104, 454
Kilham, W., 299, 301
Killeya, L. A., 10
Kim, Y., 100
Kirkpatrick, S. A., 449
Kitayama, S., 311
Kitzmann, K. M., 248
Klandermans, B., 390
Klar, Y., 136
Kleider, H. M., 58
Klein, S. B., 101, 102
Kleinke, C. L., 78
Klinesmith, J., 28
Klohnen, E. C., 241, 247, 252
Klonsky, B. G., 193
Klumpp, G., 47
Kmill, J., 249
Knee, C. R., 121, 253
Knowles, E. D., 189
Knowles, M., 80
Ko, S. J., 76
Kobrynowicz, D., 180, 196
Koch, W., 266
Kochanska, G., 246
Koehler, J. J., 46
Kogan, N., 408
Kohl, W. L., 452
Kohler, N., 147
Komorita, M., 401

Koole, S. L., 226, 227
Kouhara, S., 137
Kowalski, R. M., 195, 251, 345
Kozak, M. N., 89
Kraft, D., 117
Krantz, J. H., 103
Kraus, S. J., 158
Kray, L. J., 58, 60
Kristof, A. L., 104
Krosnick, J. A., 151, 159, 161, 229
Krueger, J. I., 131
Kruger, J., 116
Kruglanski, A. W., 38
Kulesa, P., 173
Kulik, J. A., 227
Kunda, Z., 39, 41, 43, 54, 126, 200
Kurzban, R., 242
Kwan, L.A., 241

Labroo, A. A., 63, 256
LaFrance, M., 191
Laibson, D., 69
Laibson, L., 67
Lalonde, R. N., 194
Lambert, A. J., 101
Lamm, H., 408
Lamy, D., 17
Landau, M. J., 205
Landy, F. F., 443
Lane, M. C., 443
Lang, F. R., 311
Lange, P. A. M., 101
Langer, E., 140, 434
Langlands, C. L., 193
Langlois, J. H., 234, 235
LaPiere, R. T., 157
Larsen, J. T., 55
Larson, J. R., 408
Lassiter, G. D., 421
Latané, B., 31, 278, 313, 314, 316, 317, 397
Lau, S., 249
Laurenceau, J. P., 248
Law, J., 122
Lazarus R.A, 436, 438
Leary, M. R., 226
Lecci, L., 201
Ledbetter, J. E., 159
Lee, A. Y., 232
Lee, Y. T., 93
Legbant, P., 90, 91
Lehman, D. R., 136
Lehman, T. C., 327
Lehmiller, J. J., 244, 265
Leigh, B.C., 430
Leippe, M. R., 130, 179
Leite, P., 96
Lemley, B., 235
Lemonick, M. D., 256
LePine, J. A., 447, 448
Lepper, M., 55
Lerner, J. S., 14
Letchford, J., 250
Leventhal, H., 167
Levin, P. A., 68, 320
Levine, M., 429
Levine, R. V., 316
Levin-Sagi, M., 127
Levy, B. R., 140, 433, 434

Lewin, K., 19
Lewis, M., 232
Leyens, J. P., 142
L'Herrou, T., 278
Li, N. P., 11, 253
Liberman, A., 167, 169
Liberman, N., 88, 90, 127
Lickel, B., 123, 380
Liden, R. C., 103, 104, 290
Liebert, R. M., 350
Lin, M. H., 101, 102
Lin, M.-C., 247
Lind, E. W., 406
Linden, E., 21
Lindsay, D. S., 426
Lindsay, J. J., 75, 76, 80
Lindsay, R. C. L., 423
Lindsey, E. W., 247
Linz, D., 351, 424
Lippitt, 19
Locke, E. A., 449, 450
Locke, V., 200
Lockwood, P., 126
Loewenstein, G., 69
Loftus, E. F., 421, 425, 426
Loftus, J., 101, 102
Long, C. R., 249
Lonnqvist, J. E., 277
Lopez, F. G., 247
Lord, C. G., 139
Lorenz, K., 338
Lorig, T. S., 53
Lowery, B. S., 189, 215
Lowery, L., 76
Lucas, J. A., 194
Lucas, J. R., 443
Lui, T. J., 177
Lundberg, J. K., 236
Lundqvist, D., 54
Luo, S., 241, 252
Lustina, M. J., 141, 142
Luus, C. A. E., 427
Lynch, C. I., 142
Lynch, M., 177
Lyness, K. S., 193
Lynn, A. R., 151
Lyons, P. M., 430
Lyubomirsky, S., 379

Ma, H. K., 322
Maass, A., 193, 277
McAdams, D. P., 330
McAndrew, F. T., 28
Macaulay, J., 319
McAuley, E., 434
McCall, M., 9
McCarthy, D., 168
McCarthy, K., 95
McClarty, K. L., 129
McClure, S., 69
McConahay, J. B., 211
McCullough, M. E., 358, 373
McDavid, J. W., 287
MacDonald, H. E., 57, 63
MacDonald, T. K., 163
McDonald, R. D., 229
McDougall, W., 19
McDowell, N. K., 14
McEwen, B. S., 437
McFarland, C., 58
McGhee, D. E., 148

McGillis, D., 85
McGonagle, K. A., 96, 264
McGuire, S., 248, 249-250
Machilek, F., 115
McHoskey, J. W., 325
Mack, D., 236
McKelvie, S. J., 234, 236
MacKenzie, S.B., 449
Mackie, D. M., 64, 65, 68, 202
McKimmie, B. M., 171, 172
McKinney, K. D., 215
MacKinnon, I., 296
McLaughlin-Volpe, T., 126, 219, 392
McMillan, D., 40, 41
McNulty, J. K., 264
McQuinn, R. D., 249
Macrae, C. N., 200, 236
Maddux, W. W., 188
Madell, D. E., 116
Madey, S. F., 59
Madson, S., 44
Maeda, E., 248
Magee, J. J., 80
Maheswaran, D., 169
Main, K. J., 202
Maio, G. R., 148, 155, 158, 247
Maisonneuve, 231
Major, B., 131, 132, 134, 195, 196
Makhijani, M. G., 193
Malamuth, N. M., 351
Malone, B. E., 75, 76, 80
Malone, P. S., 89, 90
Mandisodza, A. N., 99
Maner, 233
Manis, M. M., 9
Mann, J. A., 217
Mann, L., 299, 301
Manning, J. T., 253
Mannix, L. M., 436
Manstead, A. S. R., 202
Marcus, B., 115
Marcus, D. K., 234
Marecek, J., 90, 91
Markey, P. M., 240
Markman, G. D., 127
Marques, J. M., 115
Marsh, A. A., 89
Marshall, M. A., 342, 356, 357
Martens, A., 140
Martin, L. L., 11, 177, 426
Martin, P. Y., 171, 172
Martin, R., 171, 172
Martinot, D., 193
Marx, D. M., 141
Maslach, C., 285
Matsumoto, D., 77, 83
Matsushima, R., 248
Matz, D., 76
Mauss, I. B., 370
May, J. L., 229
Mayo, C., 83
Mazzella, R., 429
Mead, G. H., 131
Medvec, V. H., 59
Mehrabian, A., 236, 237
Meier, B. P., 236, 371
Melamed, S., 443
Meleshko, K. G. A., 251
Mendelsohn, G. A., 90
Mendoza-Denton, R., 121

Mercier, M. A., 96
Messner, C., 149
Meyers, S. A., 255
Miceli, M. P., 443
Michela, J. L., 86
Mikulincer, M, 247, 323
Miles, S. M., 87
Milgram, S., 20, 298, 299
Miller, C. T., 195
Miller, D. A., 202
Miller, D. T., 58, 93, 132, 133, 158, 194
Miller, J. E., 103, 226
Miller, L. C., 85, 254
Miller, N., 287, 359
Miller, P. J. E., 96, 263
Miller, R. S., 234
Mills, J., 391
Milne, A. B., 200
Mirenberg, M. C., 16
Miron, A. M., 202, 212
Mischel, W., 121
Mitchell, D. B., 41
Mitchell, T. R., 290
Mladinic, A., 192
Modigliani, A., 301
Moghaddam, F. M., 194
Moll, J., 204, 218
Monarch, E. S., 152
Mondloch, 226
Monin, B., 158, 194, 232
Monteith, M. J., 188, 201, 217
Montepare, J. M., 236
Moore, T., 328
Moran, G., 424
Moran, K. E., 55
Moreland, R. L., 232
Morey, N., 236
Morgan, D., 441
Morris, M. W., 90
Morris, W. L., 198, 199
Morrison, E. W., 104, 448
Morrison-Beedy, D., 179
Moscovici, S., 286
Mossakowski, K. N., 131
Mount, M. K., 107
Muczyk, J. P., 451
Muellerleile, P. A., 162
Mugny, G., 286
Muhlenbruck, L., 75, 76, 80
Mulder, L. B., 402
Mullen, B., 388, 412
Mullins, L. C., 250
Muncer, S. J., 116
Munkes, J., 413
Muraven, M. B., 105
Murdaya, U., 77
Murray, L., 246
Murray, S. L., 102, 253, 262, 265
Murrell, A. J., 217
Musilli, L., 291
Mussweiler, T., 47
Mustari, L., 398, 399
Myers, D. G., 408
Mynard, H., 365

Nadler, A., 327
Napoli, A., 180
Nario-Redmond, M. R., 59
National Institute for
   Occupational Safety and

Health, Center for Disease
   Control and Prevention, 365
Neale, J. M., 180
Neighbors, C., 121
Neimeyer, R. A., 96
Nelson, D., 240
Nemeroff, C., 61
Nemeth, C. J., 413
Neto, F., 249
Neuberg, S. L., 101, 102, 202, 242
Neuman, J. H., 366, 367
Newby-Clark, I. R., 57
Newcomb, T. M., 238, 241
Newman, M. L., 194
Newsom, J. T., 326
Neyer, F. J., 311
Nezlek, J., 137
Ng, Z-W., 116
Nguyen, A., 115
Niehuis, S., 103
Niemann, Y. F., 123
Nisbett, R. E., 11, 90, 91, 92, 93, 117, 352, 354
Noel, J. G., 115, 153, 278
Nolan, J. M., 206
Nordgren, L. F., 52
Norenzayan, A., 62
Norton, M. I., 7, 211
Nurmi, J.-E., 251
Nussbaum, S., 90
Nyman, L., 100
Nystrom, L. E., 67

OÆLeary, S. G., 364, 366, 367
Oakes, P. J., 120, 121, 200, 202, 209, 403
Oberlander, E., 246
O'Brien, L. T., 188, 202, 209
O'Connell, P. D., 424
O'Connor, K. J., 49
O'Connor, K. M., 127
O'Connor, S. C., 227
Oettingen, G., 93
Ohbuchi, K., 344
Ohman, A., 54
Oishi, S., 379
Okimoto, T. G., 193
Okun, M. A., 330
O'Leary, S. G., 247
Oleson, K. C., 43, 200, 307, 321
Oliver-Rodriguez, J. C., 234
Olk, P. M., 249
O'Loughlin, R. E., 136
Olson, J. M., 59, 148, 158
Olson, M. A., 148, 229
Olweus, D., 364
O'Moore, M. N., 365
Omoto, A. M., 329
Onishi, M., 247
Onorato, R. S., 123
Orbell, S., 163
Organ, D., 442, 447
Orpen, C., 242
Osborn, A. F., 412
Osborne, J. W., 141
Oskamp, S., 153
Österman, K, 359
O'Sullivan, C. S., 200
O'Sullivan, M., 17, 80, 84
Otsubo, Y., 137

Ouellette, J. A., 55
Owen, A. W., 49, 196
Owens, L., 359
Oxley, Z. M., 193

Padavic, I., 134
Pagano, F, 167
Palmer, J., 239
Pang, K., 90
Paolini, S., 216
Paquette, J. A., 249
Park, J., 65
Park, L. E., 237, 238
Parke, B., 200
Parker, J., 116
Parks, G., 401
Patrick, H., 121
Patriquin, M., 147
Paulhus, D. L., 104
Paulus, P. B., 412, 413
Pavalko, E. K., 131
Pearson, 366
Pelham, B. W., 16, 17, 130, 237,
    238
Peluso, J. P., 152
Pennebaker, J. W., 235
Penner, L. A., 326, 330
Penrod, S., 424
Penton-Voak, I., 234
Pentony, J. F., 230
Perkins, J. E., 424
Perls, T. T., 433
Peterson, R. S., 450
Peterson, V. S., 192
Petrocelli, J. V., 160
Petruska, R., 315
Pettigrew, T. F., 215, 216, 219
Pettigrew, T. W., 215
Pettijohn, T. E. F., II, 13
Petty, R., 172
Petty, R. E., 65, 68, 148, 149,
    155, 158, 161, 165, 169,
    170, 174, 188
Petty, R. J., 159, 161
Petzel, T., 216
Phelps, E. A., 49
Phemister, S., 320
Phillips, J. B., 79
Pickett, C. L., 80
Piercy, M., 236, 237
Pihl, R. O., 361
Piliavin, J. A., 329
Pinel, E. C, 113, 141, 142
Pines, A., 264
Pinker, S., 310
Piotrowski, M., 107
Pittman, T. S., 85
Plaks, J. E., 50
Plant, E. A., 188, 202, 211, 217
Platow, M. J., 384
Plog, A. E., 101, 102
Podsakoff, P. M., 447, 448, 449,
    450
Polivy, J., 126
Pollak, K. I., 123
Pomare, M., 217
Pontari, B. A., 105, 106
Postmes, T., 123, 139, 141, 285,
    399
Powell, A. A., 217
Pozzulo, J. D., 423, 424

Pratto, F., 214
Prentice, D. A., 132, 158, 380
Price, B. H., 41
Price, K. H., 398
Prins, K. S., 250
Pronin, E., 95, 119, 126, 127,
    141
Pruitt, D. G., 404
Pryor, J. B., 322
Puente, S., 354
Pullium, R. M., 329
Pura, N., 211
Purdie-Vaughns, V., 113
Pyszczynski, T., 93, 205

Queller, S., 200
Quigley, B. M., 430
Quinn, D. M., 140
Quinn, J. M., 165, 172, 173
Quitkin, F. M., 96

Rahe, R. H., 437
Rainey, D., 236
Rapson, R. L., 255
Ray, G. E., 250
Read, S. J., 85
Redersdorff, S., 193, 195
Reed, A., 213
Reed, W., 188
Regan, P. C., 252, 255
Reicher, S. D., 202, 283, 386,
    453
Reichert, A., 81
Reimann, B. C., 451
Reis, H. T., 244, 247
Reisenzein, R., 76
Reiss, A. J., 347
Rempel, J. K., 96
Reno, R. R., 278
Rensberger, B., 256
Rentfrow, P. J., 194
Reskin, B., 134
Reyna, 426
Reynolds, K. J., 121, 122
Rhodes, G., 235
Richard, F. D., 301
Richards, Z., 43, 200
Richardson, D., 32
Richman, C. L., 325
Richson, J. A., 17
Riecken, H. W., 178
Rilling, J. K., 67
Ritchie, L. D., 248
Rittenauer-Schatka, G., 47
Robbins, T. L., 64
Roberson, Q., 448
Robins, R. W., 90, 129
Robinson, L.A., 96
Robinson, R. J., 158, 403
Roccas, S., 122, 390
Rochat, F., 301
Rocher, S., 200
Rodriguez, S., 95
Roese, N. J., 32, 59, 75, 88
Rogers, R. J., 93
Rogers, R. W., 32, 346
Roggman, L. A., 234
Rokach, A., 249
Roland, E., 364
Ropp, S. A., 219
Rosenbaum, M. E., 241

Rosenberg, M., 129
Rosenblood, L. K., 227
Rosenfield, H. W., 78
Rosenhan, D. L., 321
Rosenthal, R., 44-45, 83
Roskos-Ewoldsen, D. R., 158,
    164
Rosnow, J., 31
Ross, I., 93, 141
Ross, L., 55, 119, 126, 127, 158
Ross, M., 8, 55, 56, 57, 93, 126,
    137, 213
Rotenberg, K. J., 249, 251
Roth, J. A., 347
Rothman, A. J., 47
Rotton, J., 10, 361
Rowatt, W. C., 104
Rowe, P. M., 226
Roy, S. A., 202
Rozin, P., 61, 76
Rubin, J. Z., 32, 255
Rucker, D. D., 149, 160, 174
Ruder, M., 17, 47, 68
Rudman, L. A., 205, 281
Ruiz, J. M., 260, 262
Runyan, A. S., 192
Rusbult, C. E., 266
Ruscher, J. B., 101
Russell, J. A., 77
Russn, A., 204, 218
Russo, J. E., 430
Rust, M. C., 216
Rutkowski, G. K., 316
Ruvolo, A. P., 247
Ryan, C. S., 200
Ryan, M. K., 122, 450
Ryckman, R. M., 236

Sadker, D., 45
Sadker, M., 45
Sadler, P., 240
Saenz, D. S., 139
Sage, R. M., 14
Sahdra, B., 213
Salmela-Aro, K., 251
Salovey, P., 168, 229, 320
Sanchez, D. T., 191, 281
Sanders, J., 285
Sanfey, A. G., 67
Sangrador, J. L., 258
Sani, F., 392
Sanitioso, R. B., 136
Sanna, I. J., 59
Sassenberg, K., 51, 133, 390
Savitsky, K., 59
Schachter, S., 19, 20, 65, 178,
    227, 239, 379
Schein, V. E., 192
Scher, S. J., 405
Scherbaum, C., 139
Schiffhauer, K., 189
Schimel, J., 140
Schleicher, D. J., 446
Schlenker, B. R., 105, 106
Schmid Mast, M., 83, 84
Schmitt, 196
Schmitt, D. P., 11
Schmitt, M. T., 113, 123, 135,
    139, 189, 194, 196, 202, 217
Schooler, J. W., 421
Schradron, G., 200

Schubert, T. W., 79
Schul, Y., 101
Schultz, P. W., 153
Schulz, R., 328
Schumacher, M., 236
Schusterman, R. J., 232
Schutte, J. W., 430
Schütz, A., 115
Schwartz, J. L. K., 148
Schwarz, N., 47, 64, 148
Schwarzer, R., 55
Scutt, D., 253
Seamon, J.G., 427
Sears, D. O., 211
Sechrist, G. B., 219
Sedikides, C., 100, 134
Seery, M. D., 131
Segal, M. M., 231
Seligman, M. E. P., 93
Selim, J., 246
Serôdio, G. S., 115
Sestir, M. A., 204
Seta, C. E., 63
Seta, J. J., 63
Settles, I. H., 122
Shackelford, T. K., 11
Shah, J., 10, 294, 295
Shams, M., 249
Shanab, M. E., 299
Shane, S. A., 55, 137
Shannon, M. L., 236
Sharp, D., 32
Sharp, M. J., 103
Shavelson, R. J., 122, 228
Shaver, P. R., 77, 247, 255
Shaw, J. I., 318
Shaw, J. K., 319
Shaw, K., 173
Shaw, L., 114
Shaw-Barnes, K., 173
Sheehan, E. P., 236
Sheeran, P., 162
Sheldon, W. H., 236
Shelton, J. N., 17
Shepperd, J. A., 55, 167, 399
Sherif, C. W., 207, 216
Sherif, J., 19
Sherif, M. A., 207, 216, 277, 405
Sherlock, K., 163
Sherman, D. K., 14
Sherman, J. W., 49, 102
Sherman, M. D., 250
Sherman, S. J., 49, 56, 123
Sherman, S. S., 301
Shields, C. A., 434
Shiomi, K., 248
Shoda, Y., 121
Shuper, P., 137
Sidanius, J., 214
Sigall, H., 31
Sigelman, C. K., 234
Sigelman, L., 188
Sillars, A. L., 264
Silver, M. H., 433
Silverman, E., 122
Silverman, R. A., 194
Silvia, P. J., 135
Simmons, C., 188
Simmons, J. P., 159
Simon, B., 390

Simon, L., 177
Simons, A., 47
Simons, B., 123
Simons, T., 448
Simpson, J. A., 253, 266
Simpson, P. A., 193
Sinclair, S., 215
Singer, 246
Singh, R., 241
Sistrunk, F., 287
Sivacek, J., 159
Sjomeling, M., 142
Skarlicki, D. P., 367
Skinner, B. F., 178
Slater, P. E., 384
Sloane, E. S., 330
Slugoski, B., 212
Smeaton, G., 241
Smith, A. E., 44
Smith, D. E., 79
Smith, E. R., 17, 101, 200, 202
Smith, K. D., 308
Smith, N. K., 55
Smith, P. B., 10, 278, 285
Smith, P. K., 364
Smith, S. S., 32
Smoak, N. D., 161
Smorti, A., 365
Snyder, M., 329
Solomon, S., 93, 205
Sommers, S. R., 211
Sorrentino, R. M., 137
Sparrow, B., 41, 42
Sparrowe, R. T., 274
Spears, R., 123, 201, 202, 209, 399
Spencer, S. J., 140, 141, 177
Spencer-Rodgers, J., 380
Spicer, C. V., 201
Spiegel, S., 148
Sprafkin, J. N., 319
Spranca, M. D., 90
Sprecher, S., 233, 245, 252, 255
Srull, T. K., 40, 200
Stangor, C., 40, 41, 219
Stapel, D. A., 141
Stark, C. P., 236
Stasser, G., 410
Steblay, N. M., 423
Steele, C. M., 113, 140, 141, 142, 177, 316
Stein, J. L., 79
Steinberg, R., 192
Stern, M., 233
Sternberg, R. J., 255, 256, 257, 449, 450
Stevens, C. K., 104
Stevens, L. E., 102, 122
Stewart, G. L., 107
Stewart, M. M., 96
Stewart, T. L., 191
Stice, E., 296
Stillwell, A. M., 105
Stone, A. A., 180
Stone, J., 142, 180
Stott, C. J., 399
Strack, F., 47
Strathman, A., 59
Stritzke, W. G., 115
Stroebe, W., 412
Stroh, L. K., 193

Strube, M. J., 357
Stuermer, S., 322
Stukas, A. A., 330
Sturmer, S., 390
Sugimori, S., 410
Sullivan, B. A., 127
Suls, J., 31
Sun, C. R., 131
Swan, S., 101
Swann, W. B., Jr., 10, 114, 129, 240
Swap, W. C., 232
Swartz, M. S., 96
Swim, J. K., 188, 211

Tajfel, H., 120, 123, 135, 200, 205, 207, 208, 389
Tamiko, 58
Tan, D. T. Y., 241
Taylor, D. M., 194
Taylor, K. M., 167, 399
Taylor, S. E., 14, 137, 346, 367, 432
Taylor, S. P., 362
Tennen, H., 130
Tepper, B. J., 367, 368
Terman, L. M., 261
Terry, D. J., 154, 155, 171, 172
Terry, R. L., 103
Tesser, A., 11, 135, 177
Test, M. A., 319
Testa, A., 121
Tetlock, P. E., 149, 410
Thau, S., 213
Thelen, M. H., 250
Thibaut, J., 19
Thomas, G., 148
Thomas, S., 151
Thomley, J., 320
Thompson (Which one), 405
Thompson, E. R., 191, 331
Thompson, J. K., 296
Thompson, L., 404
Thumuluri, L. K., 330
Tice, D. M., 41, 66, 67, 105, 248
Tidwell, M.-C. O., 247
Tiedens, L. Z., 240
Timmerman, T.A., 354
Titcomb, 426
Tjosvold, D., 403
Tockerman, Y. R., 236
Todman, J., 392
Todorov, A., 14, 99, 100, 107
Toi, M., 307
Tormala, Z. L., 148, 149, 158, 160, 161, 165, 169, 174
Towles-Schwen, T., 159, 213, 215
Trafimow, D., 122
Trapnell, P. D., 104
Trawalter, S., 188
Tremewan, T., 235
Trevarthen, C., 246
Triandis, H. C., 90
Trobst, K. K., 323
Trope, Y., 9, 88, 90, 127
Trost, M. R., 279
Trzesniewski, K. H., 129
Turner, J. C., 120, 123, 135, 155, 166, 200, 202, 205,

207, 209, 277, 278, 284, 301, 389
Tversky, A., 46, 188
Twenge, J. M., 9, 323, 324, 325
Tykocinski, O. E., 60
Tyler, J. M., 80, 81
Tyler, R. B., 200
Tyler, T. R., 114, 406

Uhl-bien, M., 452
Unger, L. S., 330
Ungerer, J. A., 321
Unzueta, M. M., 189
Urbanski, L., 248
Urland, G. R., 204
U.S. Bureau of Labor Statistics, 192, 328
U.S. Department of Justice, 258

Vala, J., 187
Valdimarsdottir, H., 180
Validzic, A., 216
Vallone, R., 55
Van Boven, L., 92
Van den Bos, K., 406
Van Dick, R., 216
Van Dyne, L., 447, 448
Van Knippenberg, A., 204
Van Lange, P. A. M., 308, 403
Van Olden, Z., 52
Van Overwalle, F., 85, 90
Van Prooijen, J. W., 406
Van Vugt, M., 308, 309, 447
Vandello, J. A., 354, 355
Vanderbilt, A., 79
Vasquez, M. J. T., 134
Vassar, P. M., 191
Vertue, F. M., 250
Vick, B., 131
Vinokur, A. D., 101, 409
Visser, P. S., 159
Voci, A., 216
Vogt, D. S., 83
Vohs, K. D., 128, 131
Voils, C. I., 188
Vonk, R., 104, 114, 242
Vonofakou, C., 216
Vorauer, J. D., 202
Vredenburg, D. S., 136

Wageman, R., 452
Wagner, U., 216
Waldman, D. A., 453, 454
Walker, I., 200
Walker, S., 359
Wallach, L., 429
Wallach, M. A., 408

Walster, E., 166, 293
Walster, G. W., 256
Walther, E., 151
Wann, D. L., 115, 136, 153, 205
Wanous, J. P., 443
Ward, A., 158
Waters, H. F., 347
Watson, D., 444, 445
Watts, B. L., 167, 241
Wayne, S. J., 103, 104, 290
Webb, T. L., 162
Wegener, D. T., 160, 161, 165
Wegner, D. M., 41, 42, 60, 61, 89, 94, 95
Wegner, D. T., 65, 68
Weinberg, B. A., 171
Weiner, B., 87, 88, 138, 236
Weisberg, J., 230
Weisbuch, M., 131
Weiss, D. J., 430
Weiss, H. M., 442
Weiss, W., 166
Weissenberg, P., 451
Welch, S., 188
Weldon, E., 398, 399
Wells, G. L., 425, 426, 427, 428
Werth, L., 149
Westbay, L., 257
Wetherell, M. S., 202
Wheeler, C., 148, 165, 169
Wheeler, I., 100
Wheeler, S. C., 175
Whitcher, S. J., 79
White, 19
White, B. J., 207, 216
White, K., 92, 136
Wieczorkowska, G., 100
Wiederman, M. W., 256
Wiegand, A. W., 180
Wiesenfeld, B. M., 406
Wiley, J. A., 432, 433
Williams, C. L., 193
Williams, J. F., 131
Williams, K. B., 293
Williams, K. D., 130, 227, 389, 397, 398, 399
Williamson, G. M., 328
Williamson, T. M., 420
Willingham, B., 77
Willingham, D. T., 15
Willis, F. N., 79, 99, 100, 107
Wilson, A., 219
Wilson, A. D., 180
Wilson, A. E., 126, 135
Wilson, D. W., 320
Wilson, J. P., 315
Wilson, T. D., 68, 117, 118

Winnick, T. A., 256
Winograd, E., 152
Wisman, A., 227
Witt, L. A., 104
Wlodarski, R., 136
Wohl, M. J. A., 217
Woike, B. A., 78
Wolf, C., 216
Wolsko, C., 200
Wong, E. M., 59, 60
Wong, N. C. H., 252
Wood, G. S., 254
Wood, J. V., 134, 135
Wood, W., 165, 166, 172, 173
Woody, E., 240
Worth, L. T., 65, 68
Wright, S. C., 194, 219
Wrightsman, L. S., 186, 191
Wuensch, K. L., 430
Wyer, R. S., Jr., 40, 101, 200

Xu, J., 191

Yahya, K. A., 299
Yasunaga, S., 137
Yela, C., 258
Yoder, J. D., 123, 194
Young, L. V., 124
Young, M. J., 64
Yukl, G. A., 298, 442, 449
Yzerbyt, V. Y., 200, 201, 202, 380

Zaccaro, S. J., 449, 450
Zadro, L., 389
Zajonc, R. B., 100, 232, 241, 395, 396, 397
Zanakos, S., 61
Zanna, M. P., 163
Zaragoza, M. S., 425
Zarate, M. A., 101, 206
Zebrowitz, I. A., 75
Zebrowitz, L. A., 233, 234, 236
Zebrowitz-McArthur, L., 236
Zeitz, G., 443
Zembrodt, I. M., 266
Zillmann, D., 340, 346, 361
Zimbardo, P. G., 273, 281, 282, 299, 399
Ziv, T., 17
Zoglin, R., 242
Zogmaister, C., 17
Zubek, J., 131, 132
Zuckerman, M., 136
Zukerman, M., 358
Zuwerink, J. R., 217

Subject Index

abortion, 158, 173
above average effect, 136
abstractions in impression formation, 101–102
Abu Ghraib Prison, 212–213, 212f, 283, 300
abuse
  bullying, 364–365
  in prison studies, 282–283, 283f, 385–386
  of prisoners, 212–213, 212f
  workplace, 367–368, 367f
academic outcomes
  self-concept related to, 125–127, 129–130, 136
  sexism and, 113
  stereotype threat and, 140–141
accidents, 43–44, 45f, 57–58. see also automobile accidents
accuracy
  attitude certainty and, 160–161
  as core value, 6, 29
  eyewitness testimony, 425–429
  social perception and, 101–102, 104f
acquired immune deficiency syndrome (AIDS), 125, 155, 179–180, 329
acting techniques for self-characterization, 119
action identification (attribution), 89
actions
  negative, 202
  overt, 14
  partner's, 103
  personal, 88–89
  reacting to others, 9, 9f, 19
  reasoned, 162–163
actor-observer effect, 92–93
adaptive response, 242
addictiveness, product promotions and, 158–159
additive tasks, 396–397
admiration, 115
advertisements
  attitudes and, 149–150, 150f, 151f
  as persuasion, 165–166, 166f, 168–169, 172
advice, 104
affect
  attraction and, 228–230, 229f, 230f
  definition of, 39
  empathy and, 321–323
  eyewitness testimony and, 426
  neuroscience of, 14, 17, 49, 67, 69
  nonverbal cues affecting, 76
  social cognition and, 63–69, 65f, 66f
  social groups and, 202–204, 203f, 204f
affective states, 66–67, 66f
affiliation, 226–228
affirmative action, 189
age, social importance of, 18
aggression
  causes, 342–348, 350–355
  first impression of, 99

low self-esteem and, 131
  mediating variables of, 27, 28f
  personality and, 355–360
  prevention/control, 368–373
  prosocial behavior vs., 333–334
  research on, 20
  roots of violence, 338–342
  situational determinants, 360–363
  societal variations of, 8
  workplace, 364–368
aging expectations, 434
agreeableness, importance of, 243
AIDS (acquired immune deficiency syndrome), 125, 155, 179–180, 329
Al Qaeda, 187, 187f
alcohol consumption
  aggression and, 361–363, 362f
  attitudes about, 153, 158–160, 163, 168, 168f
  prosocial behavior and, 316
  thought suppression and, 61
altruistic personality, 325–326, 330
Alzheimer's disease, 152
ambivalence, 160–161
American Revolutiony War, 287, 301
amulets, 245f
amygdala, 49
anchoring and adjustment heuristic, 47–48, 48f
anger
  facial expressions, 76, 77
  prejudice and, 202–203, 203f, 204f
  staring as sign of, 78
anonymity of crowds, 399–400
antidiscriminatory norms, 152, 152f
antifat attitudes, 436
"anti-out-group", 216
appeal, personal, 103–104, 105f
appearance. see physical appearance
appearance-rejection sensitivity, 236–238, 237f
approval, 156–158, 158f, 163
Arab Americans, 185–186
argument strength (persuasion), 169–170, 169f, 172, 175, 175f
Armenians, torture of, 299
arousal
  aggression, 345–346, 358–359
  emotional, 379
  romantic, 252, 255
Asch, Solomon, 275–277
associated effect of emotions, 229
associations, 150–152, 151f, 152f, 203–204
assumed similarity, 262
asynchronous communication, 116–117
atheists, 124
athletes, 59, 121, 129, 142
atomic submarines, 166
attachment styles
  overview, 246–248, 256

dismissing avoidant, 227–228, 228f, 247, 250, 262
  fearful-avoidant, 247, 250, 262
  preoccupied, 247, 262
  secure, 247, 262, 266, 323
attention, 54–55, 200, 203, 204f
attitude-behavior consistency, 156–158, 158f, 159f, 161, 176–177
attitude-behavior link, 445–446
attitude-discrepant behavior, 176–179, 179f
attitudes, 146–183
  behavior and, 148–150, 149f, 156–162, 162–165, 164f, 211
  certainty, 156–158, 158–159, 159f, 160–161
  clarity, 160–161
  classical conditioning of, 150–152, 151f, 152f
  cognitive dissonance and, 150, 176–181
  correctness, 160–161
  defending, 160–161, 172–174, 174f
  definition of, 148
  explicit vs. implicit, 148
  expression of, 158, 211
  extreme, 159–160, 159f
  formation of, 150–156
  implicit processes and, 17
  measurement of, 148–149
  persuasion and, 150f, 165–170, 170–176
  persuasion influence on, 149–150
  similarity and, 238–239, 240
  strength of, 158–159, 159f
  toward self, 129–133
attitude-to-behavior process model, 164–165, 164f
attraction. see also physical appearance
  biological factors of, 11–13
  close relationships, 244–245
  of communicators, 166–167, 167f
  external determinants, 230–238
  impressions of, 31, 99
  interdependent relationships, 245–251
  internal determinants, 226–230
  interpersonal, 20
  legal proceedings and, 429–430
  marriage, 260–267
  prosocial behavior and, 318
  romance, 252–259
  similarity, 238–244
attribution
  action identification and, 89
  causal, 86–88, 87–88, 87f
  definition of, 75
  depression and, 96–97, 96f
  fate vs. personal actions in, 88–89, 88f
  faulty, 403
  fundamental error sources of, 89–96
  of harm, 138–139, 139f
  research on, 20
  theories of, 85–89, 87f, 96

audience distraction, 394–395, 396–397
audiences
    goals of, 149–150, 150f, 153, 158f
    impact on task performance, 19
    persuasion and, 165–168, 167f, 168f
authority, 289
autobiographical memory, 126
autokinetic phenomenon, 277
automatic processing
    benefits of, 51–53, 52f
    vs. controlled processing, 48
    definition of, 49
    social behavior and, 49–51, 51f
automatic social behavior, 49–51, 51f
automaticity (normative behavior), 279
automobile accidents
    attitudes and, 163, 167, 168f
    counterfactual thinking and, 57–58
    information overload and, 43–44, 45f
    seat belts, 167, 179–180
    SUVs vs. smaller cars, 46
automobile sales, 37, 47, 161, 176
availability heuristic, 46–47
avoidance, selective, 173
awareness of the unusual, 314, 315f

babies' facial recognition, 17, 18f
"baby talk", 246
balance theory, 241
Bandura, Albert, 349
bargaining (negotiation), 404–405
base rates, 46
BBC prison study, 283, 386
beauty. see physical appearance
"beer goggles", 235
behavior. see also social behavior
    attitude-consistent, 158f, 159f
    attitude-discrepant, 176–179, 179f
    attitudes and, 156–165
    attraction and, 235
    entitativity and, 380
    interpretation of, 65
    motives for, 10, 98, 100, 102
    planned, 162–163
    prediction of, 148–150, 149f
    self-theories of, 119
    social psychology and, 8–13
    status and, 384
    stereotype threat impact on, 140–142
behavioral exemplars, 101–102
beliefs
    about self, 137, 174, 177
    in God, 124
    group stereotypes and, 191–192, 191t, 219
    in supernatural powers, 62
bias. see also prejudice
    correspondence (fundamental attribution error), 89–94
    glass ceiling effect and, 193
    in information processing, 8, 81
    negativity, 54–55
    optimistism, 55–57, 59f
    self-serving, 93–94, 94f, 136–137
    situation-specific, 57–61, 62f
biased instructions, 423, 424f
bilateral symmetry, 253
binge eating, 124
biological factors. see genetic factors
birth order, 100
bistrategic controllers, 360
blame, 195–196, 319–320

bloggers, 382–383
blood pressure, 441
body language communication, 76, 78–79, 79f
body piercings, 123, 125, 125f, 163
bona fide pipeline, 212–213
brain, 14–15, 49, 67, 69
brainstorming, 410–411, 412–413
Bratton, William J., 417–419
breakup of relationships, 247
Brown v. Topeka Board of Education, 215
bullying. see abuse
Bush, George W., 58, 161, 205

caffeine drinks, 171–172, 171f
caloric intake, 436
cars. see automobile entries
Castro, Fidel, 93
catharsis hypothesis, 372
causal attribution, 86–88
causation/causality
    attribution, 86–88, 87f
    correlation vs., 24, 24f, 30
    mediating variables in, 27–28, 28f
caution, empathy and, 324–325
cell phones, use while driving, 43
central route to persuasion, 168–169, 169f
central traits, 98–99, 101
CEO (chief executive officer) positions, 192–193, 192f
character traits. see personality traits
characteristics, positive, 242–244
cheating, 147–148, 149f, 177
Cheney, Dick/Mary, 124, 124f
chief executive officer (CEO) positions, 192–193, 192f
childhood friendships, 248
children
    media violence, 349–350, 349f
    parents, interaction with, 246–247, 246f
choices, affect and, 66–67, 66f
Church of England, 392, 392f
cigarette smoking, 158–159, 167, 179
classical conditioning, 130, 150–152, 151f, 152f, 229
close relationships, 244–245, 248–251, 249f
clothing, 235
cockroaches, 397f
coercion, 179
coffee, 171–172, 171f
cognition
    affect and, 64–65, 66f
    affect influence on, 65f
    behavior and, 14
    eyewitness testimony and, 426
    in impression management, 105–106
    neuroscience of, 49, 67, 69
    performance deficits impact on, 139–140, 140f
    social. see social cognition
cognitive dissonance
    attitude change and, 177, 179, 179f
    behavior change and, 179–180, 180f
    classic studies on, 178
    definition of, 20, 176–177
    group admission and, 391
cognitive framework. see schemas
cognitive processes
    overview, 9–10
    automatic and controlled, 38f, 49–53
    in impression formation, 101–102

loneliness reduction, 251
    underlying persuasion, 168–170, 169f
cohesiveness, 278, 388, 409–410
collective guilt, 212–213, 217–218, 218f
collective identity, 390
collectivism, 387–388
collectivist cultures, 285, 345
college students, romance and, 252
colors, clothing, 235
commitment, 59, 261, 289, 290–291
common in-group identity model, 216–217
common sense, 7–8, 16, 33
common-bond groups, 380
common-identity groups, 380
communication. see also nonverbal communication
    asynchronous vs. synchronous, 116–117
    faulty, 403
    persuasion and, 165–166, 167f
Communist Party, 166
community violence, 367
companies in crisis, 450
companionate love, 256
comparison
    intragroup vs. intergroup, 120–121, 121f
    of performance, 135–136, 136f
    of self. see social comparison
compassion, 373
competence
    first impression of, 99
    as prejudice dimension, 15, 194, 195f
    stereotype beliefs about, 191–192, 191t
competition
    cooperation vs., 401–402, 401f
    intergroup, 206–207, 206f, 207f
competitive altruism, 308–310, 309f, 310f
complementarity, 239–240
complexity, implicit processes and, 17
compliance
    overview, 288–293, 289f
    definition of, 273, 274
    group membership requirements, 391
    induced, 177, 179, 179f
compliance professionals, 288–289
composite faces, 234–235, 235f
condescension, 344
conditioned stimulus, 150–151, 151f
conditioning
    classical, 130, 150–152, 151f, 152f, 229
    instrumental, 153–154
    operant, 178
    self-esteem and, 130
    subliminal, 152
confessions, 421–422
conflicts
    overview, 402–405
    definition of, 401
    within marriage, 264
    theory, 206–207, 206f, 207f
conformity
    overview, 274–281, 275f, 284–287
    definition of, 273
    research on, 19, 20
    status and, 384
confounding variables, 26–27, 26f
conscious awareness, 130
conscious choice, 66–67, 66f
conscious thought. see cognition
consensus in causal attribution, 86–88, 87f
consent, informed, 32
consideration (person orientation), 451

consistency
  attitude-behavior, 156–158, 158*f*, 159*f*, 161, 176–177
  in causal attribution, 86–88, 87*f*
  compliance and, 290–291
  as core value, 20, 29–30
consummate love, 257, 258
contact hypothesis of prejudice, 215–216
contempt, attraction vs., 232*f*
context, 149–150, 150*f*, 235, 243*t. see also* cultural context; social context
contrast effect, 235
controllability, 87–88, 127–128
controlled processing, 48, 60–61
cooperation, 243, 401–402, 401*f*
coordination, 401–405
core values, 6–7
correlation, 23–24, 24*f*, 30
correspondence bias, 89–96, 92*f*, 93*f*, 94*f*, 95*f*
correspondent inference, 85
cortisol (hormone), 439–440
cost-benefit analysis of research, 31
counterarguments, 160–161, 172–174, 174*f*
counterfactual thinking, 57–60
couples, 102–103, 104*f. see also* marriage
court decisions, heuristics for, 47–48, 48*f*
courtship, 8
creativity, affect and, 64, 69, 135
credibility, 166
crimes of passion, 354
criminal justice systems, 369
criticism, 344, 403, 410, 411*f*
cultural context
  aggression and, 359
  of attitudes, 148–150, 152
  clothing colors, 235
  of correspondence bias, 90–92
  diversity of, 18
  honor, 252–255, 259, 353*f*
  individualism, 285
  mate criteria, 254
  media violence, 347
  of nonverbal communication, 77, 79, 79*f*
  physical attraction, 252
  protection against enemies, 245
  of relationships, 245
  of self-definition, 121–123
  of self-esteem, 131–132
  social behavior and, 9–10, 11*f*
  stigmatized identity dependence on, 140, 140*f*
  teasing, 345, 345*f*
culture, definition of, 10
cultures of honor, 252–255, 353*f*
cyberspace, 104, 111–113, 112*f*, 114*f*

Daily Hassles Scale, 438–439
dating, 104–105, 105*f*, 106–107, 107*f*
deactivation of schemas, 41–42, 42*f*
deadlines, compliance and, 293, 293*f*
deadly force by police, 424–425
death, certainty of, 62
debriefing, 32
deception, 31–33, 80–84, 84*f*, 115
decision making. *see also* automatic processing; heuristics
  affect and, 64–65, 67
  complex, 43–44, 45*f*
  in groups, 408–411
  prosocial behavior, 317
  in triangular model of love, 257, 258
  at work, 451–452

defensiveness, self-esteem and, 131
dehumanization, 15, 16*f*
deindividuation, 399
deliberation in spontaneous reactions, 164–165, 164*f*
dependent variable, 25
depression, 96–97, 96*f*, 364
derogation, 205, 205*f*, 206*f*, 212–213, 212*f*
descriptive norms, 278
desegregation, 215–216
desensitization to violence, 348, 350, 351
destructive obedience, 299–301
deterrence, 369
devaluation of women, 131–133
diet/dieting, 128, 153, 155, 157
differential respect, 193
direct aggression, 359
disability, social importance of, 18
disagreements within marriage, 264
disappointment, counterfactual thinking and, 59–60
disapproval
  attitudes and, 156–158, 158*f*, 163
  self-definition related to, 123, 125
disaster-induced interactions, 227
discrimination
  attitude formation and, 152, 152*f*, 157
  body piercings and, 123, 125
  definition of, 188, 190, 202
  empathy and, 325
  group membership and, 188–189, 190*f*
  racial, 195–196, 211
  sex-related. *see* gender discrimination
  single people and, 198–199, 199*f*
disgust, 15, 76, 202–203, 203*f*
disliking, 7, 15–16, 135, 148, 194–195. *see also* prejudice
dismissing avoidant attachment style, 227–228, 228*f*, 247, 250, 262
dispositional causes, 90–92, 93–94, 94*f*
dispositions, personality, 262
dissimilarity, 7, 240–242
dissonance, 20, 177, 179
distinctiveness, 86–88, 87*f*, 210–211, 210*f*
distortions in social cognition, 42–43
distraction-conflict theory, 394–395
distress, feelings of, 66–67, 66*f*
distributive justice (fairness), 406
diversity, 18
divorce, 264–266
dominance, submission vs., 240
door-in-the face, 292
downside of being helped, 326–327
downward social comparison, 133–134, 135–136
dress style, 103
drive theories of aggression, 339–340, 340*f*, 343
drive theory of social facilitation, 396–397, 397*f*
driving accidents. *see* automobile accidents
drug abuse, 61, 131, 163–164

ease-of-use heuristic, 46–47, 68
eating disorders, 296–297, 297*f*
economic theory, 67
ecstasy (drug), 164
effect-danger ratio, 366, 367
efficient thought. *see* automatic processing
egalitarianism, 217–218
ego depletion, 175, 175*f*

ego threat, 358
elaboration-likelihood model (ELM), 169–171, 169*f*
e-mail, 116, 116*f*
emergency responses, 313–317, 317*f*, 321, 328–331
emotional arousal, 252, 255, 345–346
emotions
  attraction and, 228–229
  body language and, 78–79, 79*f*
  distress, 66–67, 66*f*
  in e-mail communication, 116, 116*f*
  eyewitness testimony and, 426
  in facial expressions, 76–76, 77*f*, 78*f*
  insight into, 119
  neuroscience of, 14, 67
  performance impact on, 138–139, 139*f*
  persuasion and, 167–168, 168*f*
  prejudice and, 202–203, 203*f*, 209
  prosocial behavior and, 320–321
  recognition of, 19
  two-factor theory of, 65
empathic joy hypothesis, 308, 309*f*
empathy/altruism, 306–307, 307*f*, 321–323, 321*f*
employment. *see* job hunting
encoding, schemas impact on, 40
enemyship, 245
Enron, 271–272, 273
entitativity, 380–382, 381*t*
entrepreneurs, 137
"envious prejudice", 191
environmental conditions, prosocial behavior and, 320–321
environmental psychology, 20
envy, 202–203, 203*f*
error. *see* bias
error sources, 46, 54–63, 60*f*, 89–96
essences, 202
ethics, 32, 84, 84*f*
ethnicity
  attitudes and, 148–149, 152, 157
  discrimination related to, 195–196, 211, 213
  prejudice and, 202, 204, 206, 215, 218–219, 219*f*
  racial equality and, 188–189, 190*f*
  self-definition and, 122–123, 125–126
  self-esteem and, 140
  self-serving bias and, 93, 136
  social importance of, 18, 125
  stereotyping and, 141–142, 219
  teasing and, 344
  volunteering and, 329
euthanasia, 171
evaluation
  of groups, 196–197, 197*f*
  of self, 133–136, 133–138, 134*f*, 136–137, 136*f*, 137, 138–142
  of social world, 146–183. *see also* attitudes
evaluation apprehension, 397
evolutionary psychology, 10–13, 12*f*
exams, cheating, 147–148, 149*f*, 177
excitation transfer theory, 345–346, 346*f*
experimental method, 25–27, 26*f*
experimentation, 19, 24
expert opinion, 57
explicit attitudes, 148
exposure effect, 232
expressions
  facial, 76–76, 77*f*, 78*f*
  online communication, 116, 116*f*

external determinants, 230–238
external validity, 27
extraversion, 243
"Extreme Makeover", 126, 127*f*
extroverts, 80, 105–106
eye contact communication, 76, 78, 81
eyewitness testimony, 425–429

face-to-face contacts, 107, 115–116
facial expressions, 19, 76–77, 77*f*, 78*f*, 81
facial recognition, 17, 18*f*
facial types, 234, 234*f*
failure, 93–94, 94*f*, 138–140, 139*f*, 140*f*
fairness perceptions, 367, 398, 405–407, 443
familiarity, 7, 232
families, attitude formation and, 153–154,
    215, 246–248
fate attribution, 88–89, 88*f*
fatigue, thought suppression and, 61
favoritism, 248
fear
    facial expressions, 76
    persuasion and, 167–168, 168*f*
    prejudice and, 202–203, 203*f*
fearful-avoidant attachment style, 247, 250,
    262
federal funding for research, 32
feedback, 104
feelings
    incidental, 203
    influences on, 17, 64–67, 65*f*, 66*f*
    introspection, 118
    neuroscience of, 14, 49
    nonverbal cues affecting, 76
    social cognition and, 39, 63–69
female political candidates, 234
"feminine intuition", 83
films, violent, 347
first impressions
    cognitive perspective of, 101–102
    motives for forming, 20, 98–99, 102
    rapid formation of, 80, 99–100, 99*f*
    schemas for, 100–101
    speed dating and, 106–107
flattery, 104, 242, 290
food. *see* diet/dieting
foot-in-the-door, 290–291, 290*f*
forewarning, 172–173
forgiveness, 371, 373, 373*f*
fraternities, 153
freedom, personal, 170, 172
Freud, Sigmund, 338
friendships
    attitude formation and, 153–154, 157
    close, 248–251
    compliance and, 289, 290
    prejudice and, 15
    romance vs., 252–253
frustration, aggression and, 340, 343–344, 344*f*
frustration-aggression hypothesis, 340
fundamental attribution error, 89–96, 92*f*,
    93*f*, 94*f*, 95*f*
future
    automatic social processing for, 50–51, 51*f*
    introspective predictions about, 118
    possible selves in the, 126–127, 127*f*
    predictions about, 55–57
fuzzytrace theory, 426

GAM (general aggression model), 340–342,
    342*f*, 348, 358–359

game playing in relationships, 247, 256–257
gender. *see also* men; women
    aggression and, 339, 359–360, 359*f*
    attitude formation and, 153–155, 155*f*
    bullying, 364
    close friendships and, 248–249
    companies in crisis, 450
    conformity, 287
    eating disorders, 296–297, 297*f*
    empathy and, 323, 324*f*
    "feminine intuition", 83
    legal proceedings and, 429, 430
    love styles, 257
    mating criteria, 254
    parent-child resemblance and, 12, 12*f*
    self-perception, 122–123, 123*f*, 131–133, 132*f*
    sexual norms, 281, 281*f*
    sexually aggressive lyrics, 351, 352*f*
    social behavior and, 18, 20
    social perception and, 76, 79, 84–86
    stereotyping, 140–141, 205
    values differences, 131–133, 140–141
    women clergy, 392, 392*f*
gender discrimination
    academic outcomes and, 113
    emotional consequences of, 139
    in employment, 131–132, 192–193, 192*f*
    hate groups, 188
    self perceptions in, 113, 113*f*
    token women, 194–195
gender stereotypes
    beliefs concerning, 191–192, 191*t*
    differential respect and, 193
    glass ceiling and, 192–193, 192*f*
    self perceptions in, 113, 113*f*
    token women and, 194–195, 194*f*, 195*f*
general aggression model (GAM), 340–342,
    342*f*, 348, 358–359
generativity, 330–331
genetic factors
    aggression and, 338–339
    in altruism, 310–311
    empathy and, 323
    evolutionary mechanisms, 11, 12*f*, 13
    job satisfaction, 443–445
    in loneliness, 249–250
    in physical attraction, 253
    of social behavior, 10–13, 12*f*, 19
genocide, 92, 92*f*
Genovese, Kitty, 312
German atrocities. *see* Nazi Germany
Gestalt psychology, 98
gestures, communication through, 78–79, 79*f*,
    115
gist memories, 426–427
glass ceiling, 192–193, 192*f*
global positioning systems (GPS), 44, 45*f*
global warming, 361
goals, superordinate, 207, 208, 217
great person theory of leadership, 449
grooming, personal, 103
group membership. *see also* prejudice
    disliking based on, 187–188, 202, 209,
        209*t*
    distinctiveness, 210–211, 210*f*
    individual perceptions of, 216–217
    unjust circumstances attributed to,
        195–196
groups
    overview, 380–388, 381*f*
    actions toward. *see* discrimination

attitude formation and, 153–155, 155*f*
behavior in, 9, 19–20
brain storming, 412–413
conformity, 278, 280–284
coordination, 401–405
decision making, 408–411
effects of others, 394–395
fairness perceptions, 405–407
feelings toward. *see* prejudice
fundamental attribution error about, 92,
    92*f*
harmful behavior, 212–213, 212*f*
inequality perceptions of, 188–189, 190*f*
joining, 388, 389–393
polarization, 408, 409*f*
pressure, 275–277, 276*f*, 280–284
ratings, 196–197, 197*f*
self-comparison related to, 120–121,
    135–136
social comparison and, 134–135, 136*f*
social loafing, 395–400, 398*f*
stereotyping and, 140–142, 191–197, 195*f*
subset of, 200
groupthink, 409–410
guilt, 212–213, 217–218, 218*f*
gullibility, 173
gun control, 160

habit formation, 165
handshakes, 79–80, 235
happiness
    facial expressions, 76, 77
    introspective predictions of, 118
    marital, 261–266
    pros and cons of, 68
    romance and, 102–103, 104*f*
hate groups, 189, 189*f*, 211
health
    cognitive behavioral change and, 179–180
    loneliness and, 248
    marital partner's impact, 262
    as mating criterion, 254
    persuasion and, 167–168
    social psychology and, 432–441
    unrealistic expectations, 137
heat (temperature), aggression and, 360–361
height, 235
heuristic processing, 168–170, 169*f*
heuristics
    anchoring and adjustment, 47–48, 48*f*
    availability, 46–47
    definition of, 39
    information overload and, 43–44, 45*f*
    mood influence on, 64–65, 68
    persuasive intent and, 173
    representativeness, 46
    social cognition and, 43–48
hijackers, 186
"hippie" identity, 125
Hispanics, 354
HIV (human immunodeficiency virus), 155,
    168
"holier than thou" self-assessments, 331
Holocaust, 92, 92*f*, 191, 208, 217
homicides, 258, 365–366
homosexuality
    marginalization, 265
    prejudice and, 186, 211
    social identity and, 124, 124*f*
    social interactions and, 50–51, 51*f*
honesty in self-presentation, 115

hooliganism, 399
hostility, 131, 357. *see also* aggression
hot weather, aggression and, 360–361
human immunodeficiency virus (HIV), 155, 168
human study participants, 20, 26, 31–32
humor, 116, 243
Hussein, Saddam, 58
hypocrisy, 180, 180*f*
hypothesis, 23–24, 28

IAT (Implicit Association Test), 148–149
ideal partners, 242–244
idealism, romantic, 253, 263
identity
    group, 216–217, 386
    "nonmainstream", 125, 125*f*
    online, 111–113, 114*f*, 115–116, 116*f*
    personal vs. social, 120–129, 121*f*. *see also* social identity
    stigmatized, 140, 140*f*
ideology, 392
illusions
    marital happiness, 263, 263*f*
    positive, 137
    romantic, 253
    social perception and, 101–102, 104*f*
imaging techniques, 14
Imams, 185
imbalance, 241
immigrants, prejudice and, 186, 206
immune system, 14, 439–440
implementation plan, 163
implicit (nonconscious) processes, 16–17, 18*f*, 130
Implicit Association Test (IAT), 148–149
implicit attitudes, 148
implicit personality theories, 100–101
impression formation, 10, 75, 80, 97–103, 99*f*, 104*f*
impression management (self-presentation)
    overview, 103–108
    cognitive load and, 105–106
    compliance and, 290
    description of, 75, 103
    online, 111–112, 112*f*, 114*f*, 115–116, 116*f*
    self-esteem and, 130
    tactics of, 103–104, 105*f*, 114–117
impulsiveness, 66–67, 66*f*
Imus, Don, 157
incidental feelings, 203
incidental similarity, 290
inconsistency
    attitude-behavior, 156–158, 158*f*, 159*f*, 161, 176–177
    human dislike of, 20, 29–30
independence, personal, 170, 172
independent variable, 25–27, 26*f*
indirect aggression, 359
individualism
    collectivism vs., 387–388
    research balance with, 31–32
    in resisting persuasion, 170, 172, 174
    self-comparison related to, 120–121
    in social comparison, 134–135, 136*f*
    of social psychology, 8
individualistic cultures, 285, 345
individuation, 285–286
induced compliance, 177, 179, 179*f*
industrial-organizational psychologists, 442

inequality
    glass ceiling and, 192–193, 192*f*
    group perceptions of, 188–189, 190*f*, 217, 218
infancy, relationships, 246–247
inferences, 10, 85, 98, 100, 119. *see also* heuristics
infidelity, 354
influence. *see* personal influence; social influence
information. *see also* social cognition
    bias in, 8, 68, 81, 93
    ignoring, 173–174, 174*f*
    overload, 43–44, 45*f*, 61
    processing, 99–101
    selectivity of, 173
informational social influence, 280
informed consent, 32
ingratiation, 114, 289, 290
in-groups, 202–206, 204*f*, 208–210, 208*f*, 213, 216–217, 388
inheritance. *see* genetic factors
initiating structure (production orientation), 451
injunctive norms, 278
injustice, response to, 407
The Insider (movie), 159
instant messaging, 115–116
instincts, 19, 338–339
institutional review board, 32
instrumental aggression, 357
instrumental conditioning, 153–154
integrative agreements, 404–405, 404*f*
intelligence in relationships, 243
intention-behavior relationship, 162–164, 163*f*
interactions. *see* social interactions
interchannel discrepancies, 81
interdependent relationships, 245–251
intergroup comparisons, 121, 134–135, 136*f*
intergroup competition/conflict, 206–207, 206*f*, 207*f*
internal determinants, 226–230
Internet
    dating services, 104, 254, 254*f*
    hate groups, 189, 189*f*, 211
    pop up ads, 165, 168
    self presentation on, 115–116, 116*f*
    self-identity and, 111–113, 112*f*, 114*f*
    surveys, 22, 22*f*
interpersonal attraction, research on, 20
interpersonal comparison, 134–135, 136*f*
interpersonal relationships, 101–102, 104*f*
interpersonal trust, 246–247
intervening information, 426
intimacy, 248, 252, 257
intragroup comparisons, 120, 122–123, 123*f*
introspection, 117–118
introversion, 105–106
intuition, 83
IQ tests, 44–45
Iraq War, 58–59, 59*f*, 161, 409
irrationality, 94–96, 95*f*
Islam, 185
Israeli-Palestinian conflict, 206, 206*f*

jealousy, 258–259, 259*f*, 354–355, 355*f*
Jews
    German atrocities against, 92, 92*f*, 191, 208, 217
    rescue of, 323, 324*f*

job hunting
    interviews, 64, 105–106, 454–455
    playing hard to get, 293
    workplace satisfaction, 442–446, 444*f*, 446*f*
joining (groups), 388, 389–395
joy, expression of, 76
judgments
    heuristics in, 46
    in impression formation, 101–102
    schemas impact on, 40–41
    social, 62, 111–113, 112*f*, 122–123
just world, 195–196
justice, 420, 420*f*
justification in cognitive dissonance, 179

kin selection theory, 310–311, 322

Latin America, 354
laziness, 148
leadership
    tokenism impact on, 195, 195*f*
    at work, 449–454, 450*f*, 452*f*
learning, 150–156, 154*f*, 215
legal decisions, 47–48, 48*f*
legal systems, 369, 420–431
Legally Blonde (movie), 3–5, 4*f*
legitimization of prejudice, 209, 209*t*
less-leads-to-more effect, 179
libido. *see* sex
lies, recognition of, 80–84, 84*f*
lifestyle, 433–435, 433*f*
likeability, 99
liking, 16, 104, 135, 148
limbic system, 49, 67, 69
lineups, police, 423, 423*f*
linguistic style, 81
logic, 49, 54, 62, 67
logical love, 257
loneliness, 249–251, 250*f*
long-term relationships, 101–102, 104*f*
"looking good", 103, 106, 107
Los Angeles police, 418
love, 20, 101–102, 104*f*, 254–258
lowball procedure, 291, 291*f*

Machiavellianism personality, 325
magical thinking, 61–62, 62*f*, 94–96, 95*f*, 127
magnetic resonance imaging (MRI), 14, 67
male political candidates, 234
management positions, 192–193, 192*f*
manipulation, 229
marginalization, 194, 265, 398–399
marriage
    arranged, 254
    attraction, 260–267
    cultural differences, 260*f*
    expectations, 245
    protection as social institution, 199, 199*f*
    similarity and, 238
    social perception of, 102–103
    stereotypes and, 198, 198*t*
    variations of, 8
mate selection, 11–13, 238, 242–244, 253–258, 254*f*
media
    persuasion, 165, 166*f*, 168, 173
    pretrial publicity, 423–424
    prosocial models, 319–320, 323
    tobacco campaigns, 158–159
mediating variables, 28, 28*f*
medical diagnosis errors, 47

memories
  accuracy, 426–427, 428–429
  autobiographical, 126
  harmful behaviors and, 213
  implicit processes impact on, 17
  mood effects on, 63–64, 65*f*
  schemas impact on, 40–41
men, 131–133, 132*f*, 191, 191*t. see also*
  gender
mental abstractions in impression formation,
  101–102
mental framework. *see* schemas
mental shortcuts, 48, 64, 68
mere exposure, 152
messages, 166–168, 169*f*, 172–174, 174*f*
"method-acting", 119
microexpressions, 80
Milgram, Stanley, 298–299
minimal groups, 203
minorities
  influence of, 286–287, 286*f*
  racial equality, 188–189, 190*f*
  students, 44–45, 189, 190*f*, 195–196
minority slowness effect, 30–31
misuse of deadly force, 424
models' body mass, legislation, 296
monogamy, 245, 256
mood
  cognition and, 64–67, 65*f*, 66*f*
  congruence effects, 64, 65*f*
  good, 68
  helping correlation to, 24*f*, 68
  implicit processes impact on, 17
  neuroscience of, 49
  prejudice impact on, 138–139, 139*f*
  prosocial behavior and, 320
  social cognition and, 39, 63–69
mood dependent memory, 64, 65*f*
moral hypocrisy, 331
moral integrity, 331
moral intelligence, 323
morality, 331–332
motives
  for behavior, 10, 98, 100, 102, 306–311,
    331*f*
  insight into, 119, 137
  interpretation of, 65
MRI (magnetic resonance imaging), 14, 67
multicultural perspective, 18, 152. *see also*
  cultural context
Munsterberg, Hugo, 428–429
Muslims, 185, 187*f*, 212

name stereotyping, 235, 236*t*
narcissism, 262, 358
naturalistic observation, 21
Nazi Germany
  attrocities against Jews, 92, 92*f*, 191, 208,
    217
  death camps, 298, 299
  rescue of Jews, 323, 324*f*
NCBs (noncompliance behaviors), 447
need for affiliation, 227, 228
negation training (prejudice reduction),
  218–219, 219*f*
negative emotions
  attitude and, 148, 150–152, 152*f*
  low self-esteem and, 131
  persuasion aimed at, 167, 168*f*
  prosocial behavior and, 119

  toward social group, 202–204, 203*f*,
    204*f*
negative state-relief model, 308, 309*f*, 321
negativity bias, 54–55
negotiation (bargaining), 404–405
netiquette, 111
neural systems for social information
  processing, 49, 67, 69
neurobiological basis for affiliation, 226
neuroimaging techniques, 14
neuroscience. *see* social neuroscience
New Year's resolutions, 126
New York City police, 417–418, 419
noncommon effects, 85–86
noncompliance behaviors (NCBs), 447
nonconscious (implicit) processes, 16–17, 18*f*,
  130
"nonmainstream" identity, 125, 125*f*
nonverbal communication, 75–84, 77*f*, 78*f*,
  79*f*, 84*f*
normative focus theory, 278
normative social influence, 280
norms
  conformity and, 274–275, 275*f*, 278–279
  of crowds, 399–400, 400*f*
  group, 386–387, 386*f*, 387–388, 387*f*,
    388*f*, 410
  social. *see* social norms
  subjective, 163–164
Nowak, Lisa (astronaut), 258
nuclear power plants, 160

obedience, 20, 273, 274, 298–301, 299*f*, 301*f*
obesity, 435–436
objectivity, 6, 30, 197, 197*f*
obligatory interdependence, 378
observable characteristics, 233–238
observation
  in impression formation, 101–102
  in learning, 154–155, 154*f*
  in research, 7
  self-knowledge and, 119, 119*f*
  systematic, 21
OCB (organizational citizenship behavior),
  447–449
online presence
  dating, 104, 254, 254*f*
  identity, 111–113, 114*f*, 115–116, 116*f*
only children, 248
open-mindedness, 6, 30
operant conditioning, 178
Oppenheimer, Robert J., 166
opposites, attraction and, 239–240
optimism, 55–57, 56*f*, 137
optimistic bias, 55–59, 56*f*, 59*f*
organizational citizenship behavior (OCB),
  447–449
organizational factors (employment), 443, 444*f*
other persons. *see also* social perception
  actions/characteristics of, 9, 9*f*
  in impression management, 103, 103–104,
    105*f*
  interpretation of behavior of, 65
  perception and understanding, 72–109
  positive regard for, 114
  self–definition related to, 123, 125–126,
    125*f*
  self-knowledge gained from, 119, 119*f*
out-groups
  cohesiveness and, 388

  prejudice and, 195–196, 202–204, 204*f*,
    210
  social categorization and, 208–210, 208*f*,
    216, 216–217
overconfidence barrier, 55

P300 activity, 350
Palestinian-Israeli conflict, 206, 206*f*
paralinguistic cues, 115
parent-child resemblance, 12, 12*f*
parents
  attitude formation and, 153
  children, interaction with, 246–247, 246*f*
  elder care, 245
  as models, 323
  prejudice formation and, 215
passion in triangular model of love, 257
passionate love, 255–256, 255*f*
Passionate Love Scale, 255
peace agreements, 404
peers, 15, 153–154, 157, 323
Pelosi, Nancy, 194, 194*f*
Pentagon, terrorist attacks on, 186
perception. *see also* social perception
  attitudes and, 160–161, 163
  individual, 216–217
  of inequality, 188–189, 190*f*, 217, 218
performance, 403, 448. *see also* academic
  outcomes; task performance
performance distractions, 394–395, 396–397
peripheral route to persuasion, 168–169,
  169*f*
peripheral traits, 98–99
perseverance effect, 43
personal appeal, 103–104, 105*f*
personal control, 285
personal factors
  of attitude strength, 159, 159*f*, 161
  employment, 443, 444*f*
  in impression management, 103
personal freedom, 170, 172
personal influence, 94–96, 95*f*, 126–127,
  127–128
personal space, 229
personal-versus-social identity continuum,
  120, 121*f*
personality dispositions, 262
personality traits
  aggression, 355–360, 356*f*
  central vs. peripheral, 98–99
  empathy and, 325–327
  handshake as revealing of, 79–80
  implicit theories of, 100–101
  social behavior and, 20, 98–99
persuasion
  attitude change and, 149–150, 150*f*,
    165–170, 170–176
  audiences and, 165–168, 167*f*, 168*f*
  caffeine effects on, 171–172, 171*f*
  cognitive processes underlying, 168–170
  communicators and, 165–166, 167*f*
  credibility and, 166
  definition of, 165, 166*f*
  elaboration-likelihood model of, 169–170,
    169*f*
  fear appeals, 167–168, 168*f*
  intentions, 172–173
  messages and, 166–167
PET (positron emission tomography), 14
pets, 441, 441*f*

physical appearance
    attraction/attractiveness, 31, 233–235,
      236–238
    biological factors of, 11–13
    categories of, 234f
    deception and, 31
    legal proceedings and, 429
    prosocial behavior and, 318
    reacting to others, 9, 9f
    remembering, 83–84
    self-esteem and, 28
physical health. see health
physical world, social behavior and, 10, 15, 20
physiological response to threats, 131
physique, 235
planned behavior theory, 162–163
planning fallacy, 55–57, 56f
playing hard to get, 293
pluralistic ignorance, 314–316
polarization, 408
police departments, 417–419
police interrogations, 420–422
politeness, 50, 148
political candidates, 234, 235, 283–284
political views, 20, 153, 158, 169
politicized collective identity, 390
polls in research, 22
polygamy, 245
popular culture, 7
pornography, 351–352
portion sizes, 435, 435f
positive emotions, 167–168
positive illusions, 137
positive reactions, 148, 150–152, 152f
positron emission tomography (PET), 14
possessive love, 257
possible selves, 126–127, 127f
posture communication, 78–79
power, group/social, 84, 201
praise/praising, 114
Pravda, 166
predictions, 23, 29–30, 29f, 55–57, 105–106
preferences
    affect impact on, 67, 68, 69
    automatic decisions on, 52, 52f
    mate, 11–13
    nonconscious influences on, 17, 18f
prefrontal cortex, 49, 67
prejudice, 202–220. see also bias
    in action, 211–213. see also discrimination
    attitude formation and, 152, 152f, 157
    competition for resources and, 206–207,
      206f, 207f
    contact hypothesis of, 215–216
    countering and reducing, 214–220, 390
    definition of, 187, 190
    development of, 202–204, 203f, 204f
    dimensions of, 14–15
    envy, 191
    group membership and, 187–188, 202
    in legal proceedings, 430–431
    legitimization of, 209, 209t
    neutral face of, 15, 16f
    origins of, 204–211
    racial, 185, 202, 203f, 204. see also racism
    schemas impact on, 44, 50–51, 51f, 65
    self as target of, 138–142, 217
    self-esteem and, 131, 195–196, 204–206,
      205f, 206f
    social learning view of, 215

against women, 131, 194–195
preoccupied attachment style, 247, 262
prevention, aggression, 368–373
prevention focus, 149–150, 150f
pride, 131
priming of schemas, 41–42
prison studies, 282–283, 283f, 385–386
private acceptance, 277
procedural justice, 406
pro-choice, 158, 173
product promotions
    addictiveness and, 158–159
    attitude change and, 149–150, 150f, 151f
    observational learning with, 154–155, 155f
    as persuasion, 165–166, 166f, 168–169
professions, self-definition and, 126–127, 132
pro-life, 158, 173
promotion focus, 149–150, 150f
property crimes, 361
proportion of similarity, 240–241, 240f
"props" (impression management), 103, 105f
prosocial behavior
    commitment to prosocial acts, 328–334
    in emergencies, 312–317
    influences, 318–327
    models of, 319f
    mood correlation, 24f, 68
    motives, 306–311, 329–331, 330t
    at work, 446–449
protection against enemies, 245, 245f
provocation, 344–345, 359, 362, 369
proximity, 230–232, 231f, 249f
psychological presence, 294–295
psychology. see also social psychology
    environmental, 20
    evolutionary, 10–13, 12f
    Gestalt, 98
punishments, 153–154, 178, 368–370

quotas (gender), 194–195, 195f

race
    classification, 202
    equality, 188–189, 190f
    legal proceedings and, 429
    preference, 17, 18f
racial attitudes, 148–149, 152, 157, 212–213,
    329, 344
racism
    blame vs. responsibility for, 195–196
    collective guilt reduction of, 217–218, 218f
    development of, 202, 203f, 204, 215
    group perceptions of, 188–189, 190f, 191
    modern, 211
rape myths, 284, 351
rappers, 186
rationality, 54, 54–57, 67
reactance, 170, 172
reactions/reacting
    to actions of others, 9, 9f, 75–74
    affective, 202–204, 203f, 204f
    attitude and, 148, 150–152, 152f
    behavioral, 164–165, 164f
    implicit processes and, 17
    in positive impressions, 103–104
realistic conflict theory, 206
realistic self beliefs, 137
reasoned action theory, 162–163
reason/reasoning, 49, 54, 67, 162–164, 163f
rebound effect (thought suppression), 61

recall. see memories
recategorization, 216–217
reciprocal liking, 242–244
reciprocity
    in altruism, 310
    assistance and, 327
    compliance and, 289, 292, 292f
    mutual liking, 242
    in workplace settings, 448
reference groups, attitudes and, 154–155, 155f
rejection, 115, 123, 125, 236–238
religious orientation, 18, 124, 152, 185, 213
repeated exposure
    to aggression, 341
    to media violence, 348
    proximity and, 231–232, 231f, 232f
representativeness heuristic, 46
reproductive success
    agression and, 338
    in altruism, 310
    groups and, 378–379
    love and, 256
    physical attraction and, 253
    resources and, 254
repulsion hypothesis, 241
research
    core values for, 6–7
    correlation methods, 23–24, 24f
    ethics of, 32
    experimental methods, 25–27, 26f
    individual rights and, 31–32
    observations, 7, 21
    proposals, 31–32
    surveys, 22–23, 22f
resistance, 284–286, 284f, 300–301
resources as mating criterion, 254
retrieval
    ease of, 46–47
    mood effects on, 63–64, 65f
    schemas impact on, 40–41
revenge, 373
rewards
    affect and preference for, 67, 69
    attitude formation and, 153–154
    cognitive dissonance and, 178–179
    social behavior and, 20
Rice, Condoleeza, 194, 194f
Richards, Michael, 157
risk averse, 188
risky shifts (decision making), 408
rivalry, sibling, 248
Robber's Cave boys camp, 207, 207f, 216–217
Rocky IV (movie), 205
role differentiation, 384–386
romance
    attraction, 252–259
    mate preference and, 11–13
    research on, 20
    social perception and, 102–103, 104f
"Romeo-and-Juliet" effect, 266
Rosenberg Self-Esteem Scale, 129–130,
    130f
rudeness, 50, 148

sabotage, self-esteem, 205, 206f
sadness, facial expressions, 76, 77
safe sex, 155, 162, 179–180
safety judgment errors, 46, 163, 167
salience, 120, 122–123, 123f, 219
same-sex relationships. see homosexuality

sanctions for noncooperation, 402, 402f
sarcasm, online communication, 116
scarcity, 235, 293
schemas
  activation of, 41–42
  affect influence and, 65
  definition of, 39–40, 40f
  impression formation and, 100–101
  persistence of, 42–43, 43
  priming/unpriming of, 41–42, 42f
  romantic, 252–253, 253f
  self-confirmation of, 44–45, 44f
  social cognition and, 38–43
  stereotypes as, 200
schisms, 392
science, definition of, 6, 7f
scientific approach, 7–8, 29–30, 29f
seat belts, 167, 179–180
secure attachment, 246, 247, 262, 266, 323
segregation, 215–216
selection (evolutionary), 11, 12f
selective altruism, 307, 307f
selective avoidance, 173
selective exposure, 173
self, 110–145. *see also* social comparison
  attitudes toward, 129–133
  evaluation of, 133–138
  knowing, 117–119
  managing in social contexts, 110–117
  "observer" perspective of, 119, 119f
  positive illusions about, 137
  as prejudice target, 138–142, 217
  thinking about, 120–129
self image
  affirmation, 177
  assessment, 114, 136–137
  beliefs, 137, 174, 177
  categorization, 135
  characterization, 17
  confirmation, 44–45, 44f
  construal, low vs. high, 127–128
  definition of, 120–121, 121–123
  depreciating, 115
  description of, 103–104, 120–121
  doubt, 130
  efficacy, 127, 137
  enhancement, 103–104, 105f, 389–390
  evolution of, 127–128
  favorable public perceptions, 114, 119
  gendered, 122–123, 123f
  maintenance, 135
  situation-dependent, 121–123
  social identity vs., 120–121
  stereotyping, 140–142
  tokenism impact, 195, 195f
self-esteem
  overview, 129–133
  aggression and, 358
  appearance and, 234
  assistance and, 326
  bullying and, 365
  definition of, 129
  evolution of, 246–247
  gender differences of, 131–133, 132f
  group admission, 389–390
  high, 131
  jealousy and, 258–259
  measurement of, 129–130, 130f
  prejudice impact on, 195–196
  sexual norms and, 281
  social comparison and, 133–134, 134f

success as criterion, 265
  tokenism impact on, 195, 195f
self-failure, 126, 130
self-fulfilling prophecies, 44–45, 44f
self-help books, 117, 118f
self-image, 17, 135, 217
self-inferences, 119
self-inspection, 117–118
self-interest, 166, 331
self-knowledge, 117–118, 119, 119f
selfless love, 257
self-perception
  gendered, 122–123, 123f
  leading others to agree with, 114
  personal vs. social, 120–121, 134–135
  positive, 136–137
  situation-dependent, 121–123
self-portrayal, 103–104
self-presentation, 103–108. *see also* impression
  management
self-promotion, 114, 290
self-regulation, 175, 175f, 370–371, 371f
self-serving bias, 93–94, 94f, 136–137
self-theories of behavior, 119
self-transcendence, 390
self-verification perspective, 114
Sendler, Irena, 324f
seniority, 384
sensation seeking, 358
sentences, legal, 47–48, 48f
separation (relationships), 249
September 11, 2001, 185–187, 187f, 205, 314
SES (socioeconomic status), 18, 429
sex
  aggression and, 351–355, 353f, 355f
  attitude formation, 153–154
  gender norms/pleasure, 281, 281f
  passionate love and, 255
  rape, 284, 351, 361, 430
  romance and, 252
  safe, 155, 163, 179–180
sexism/sex discrimination. *see* gender
  discrimination
sexual orientation
  marginalization, 265
  social identity and, 124, 124f, 142
  social importance of, 18, 186, 211
  social interactions and, 50–51, 51f
sexually aggressive lyrics, 351, 352f
Shepard, Matthew, 211
Sherif, Muzafer, 277
shifting standards for group ratings, 196–197,
  197f
sibling relationships, 247–248, 248f
similarity
  attraction/attractiveness, 238–244, 239f
  compliance and, 290
  in marriage, 261–262
  prosocial behavior and, 318
similarity-dissimilarity effect, 240
single people, 198–199, 198t, 199f
singlism, 198
situations
  affiliation influences, 227
  attitudes and, 149–150, 152, 158
  bias specific to, 57–61, 62f
  norms, 279, 279f
  with potential harm, 138–139, 139f
  self-definition and, 121–123, 123f
  self-esteem and, 130, 130f
  unjust, 195–196

skepticism, 6, 30
skill acquisition, 139–140, 140f
sleep problems, 248
slogans, 149
smoking, attitudes about, 158–159, 167, 179
snacking, 436
social behavior
  automatic, 49–51, 51f
  biological factors influence on, 10–13, 12f
  cognitive processes and, 9–10, 14
  cultural context and, 9–10, 11f
  deception, 81–83, 84f
  implicit processes and, 16–17, 18f
  social life, 3, 4f
social change
  conditions for, 283–284
  group membership for, 390f
  for racial equality, 188–189, 190f
social cognition, 36–71
  affect and, 39, 63–69
  attitude as essential to, 148–149
  automatic and controlled processing in, 38f,
    49–53
  definition of, 38
  error sources in, 54–63
  heuristics and, 39, 43–48
  optimistic conclusions about, 62
  prejudice influence on, 203, 204f
  schemas and, 38–43, 40f, 42f
  stereotypes and, 200
  thought processes in, 9–10, 14
social comparison
  affiliation for, 227
  attitude formation and, 153–154
  bias in, 133–138
  decision making and, 408
  downward vs. upward, 133–134, 135–136
  evaluation dynamics in, 133–136, 134f,
    136f
  intragroup vs. intergroup, 120–121
  realistic vs. unrealistic, 137
  self-serving biases in, 136–137
  situation-dependent, 121–123, 123f
  stereotyping and, 140–142
social comparison theory, 133–134, 241–242
social contact optimization, 227
social context, 110–117, 121–123, 123f,
  156–158, 158f
social dilemmas, 401–402
social diversity, 18
social exclusion, 227, 323–324, 325f, 389
social facilitation, 394–395, 396–397
social fence, 447
social groups. *see* groups
social identity
  cognitive deficit and, 139–140, 140f
  conflict among, 124
  continuum theory of, 120–121, 121f
  gendered, 122–123, 123f
  online, 111–113, 114f, 115–116, 116f
  others' treatment and, 123, 125–126,
    125f
  over time, 119, 119f, 126–127, 127f
  personal identity vs., 120–129
  prejudice and, 196, 207, 209–211, 210f
  prosocial behavior and, 448
  self control of, 127–128
  situation-dependent, 121–123, 123f
  visual indicators of, 123, 125–126,
    125f
social identity theory, 120, 121f, 135

social influence
    overview, 273–274, 273f, 284–287
    affect-attraction relationship and, 229–230
    compliance, 288–293, 289f
    conformity, 274–281
    legal systems and, 420–425, 421f
    mood susceptibility to 66, 94–96, 95f
    obedience, 298–301, 299f, 301f
    prejudice reduction and, 219–220
    symbolic social influence, 294–297
social interactions
    overview, 9, 9f
    online, 111–13, 112f, 115–116, 116f
social learning, 150, 150–156, 215, 340, 341f
social loafing, 395–400, 398f
social models, 319–320, 319f
social neuroscience
    affect and, 14, 17, 67, 69
    description of, 14–15
    of information processing, 49
    of prejudice, 15, 16f
social norms
    overview, 274–275, 275f, 278–279
    antidiscriminatory, 152, 152f
    research on, 19
social perception, 72–109
    attribution in, 85–97
    gender differences in, 76, 79, 84–86
    impression management and, 103–108
    machine for, 75, 75f
    nonverbal communication in, 75–82
    stereotypes in, 20, 76
    theory in, 28–30, 29f
social psychology
    causes of social behavior/thought, 8–13
    definition of, 6
    history of, 19–21
    modern trends in, 14–18
    practical applications of, 32–33
    research methodology for, 21–28, 28f,
        31–32
    scientific nature of, 6–8, 21, 29–30
    summary review of, 3–5, 34–35
social psychology applications
    overview, 419
    health, 432–441
    legal systems, 420–431
    work world, 442–455
social skills
    appearance and, 234
    improving, 251
    loneliness and, 250
social status
    group hierarchy of, 201, 210–211, 210f
    high, 194–195, 194f, 195f
social support, 440–441
social thought. see social cognition
social validation, 289
socioeconomic status (SES), 18, 429
"soft-sell technique" (in confessions), 422
solidarity, 388
sororities, 153
sorrow, facial expressions, 76
speed dating, 106–107, 107f
splintering (groups), 392–393, 393f
spontaneous behavioral reactions, 164–165,
    164f
sport utility vehicle (SUV), safety of, 46
sports, 59, 121, 129, 142
sports figures, 166
"sports intelligence", 142

"standard-acting" (self-characterization), 119
Stanford prison study, 282, 385, 386
staring (communication), 78
status
    aggression and, 359–360
    assistance and, 326
    group, 283–284, 389–390
    prosocial behavior/aggression, 334
    social influence and, 287
status quo bias, 403
stereotypes/stereotyping, 190–201. see also
        gender stereotypes
    absence of, 196–197, 197f
    appearance and, 233–234
    attitudes and, 149
    blame vs. responsibility for, 195–196
    changes in, 200–201
    cognitive consequences of, 140, 140f, 200
    definition of, 188, 190–191
    entitativity and, 380
    formation of, 200
    glass ceiling and, 192–193, 192f
    "just say no" to, 218–219, 219f
    names and, 235, 236t
    operation of, 200
    schemas impact on, 43, 50–51, 51f, 65
    single people as, 198–199, 198t, 199f
    threats, 140–142, 141–142
    tokenism and, 194–195, 194f, 195f
    use of, 200
Stewart, Martha, 423
stigma consciousness, 113
stigmatized identity, 140, 140f
stimulus, conditioned vs. unconditioned,
    150–151, 151f
stress, 436–441, 437f, 438–439t
student associations, 125
students
    above average estimations of, 135, 137
    attitude formation and, 153–155, 158–160
    cheating by, 147–148, 149f, 177
    self-identity of, 121, 124, 125–126
students, ethnic minority. see also minorities
subgroup prejudice, 210–211, 210f
subjective norms, 163–164
subjective scales, 197, 197f
subliminal conditioning, 130, 152
submission, dominance vs., 240
subordination, group, 201
subtype, 200
success
    as marital acceptance criterion, 265
    realistic vs. unrealistic assessment of, 137
    self–serving bias in, 93–94, 94f, 136–137
    token women and, 194–195, 194f, 195f
suicide, 365
sunk costs, 59
superiority, 131, 210–211, 210f
supernatural powers, 62
superordinate goals, 207, 208, 217, 405
superstitions, 62
survey method, 22–23, 22f
SUV (sport utility vehicle), safety of, 46
symbolic social influence, 274, 294–297, 295f
systematic observation, 21
systematic processing, 168–169, 169f

task performance
    audiences' impact on, 19
    counterfactual thinking and, 60
    self-definition related to, 126–127

social comparison of, 133–136, 136–137,
    136f
    stereotyping and, 140–142
    unfavorable, 138–139, 139–141, 139f, 140f
TASS (traits as situational sensitivities model),
    356–357, 357f
teasing, 345, 345f
television
    attitude formation and, 149, 154, 154f, 157
    commercials, 165, 168, 172–173
    prosocial models, 319–320, 323
    violence, 339f, 347
temper, 355–356
temperature (heat), 360–361
temptation, 66–67, 66f, 127–128
Terman, Lewis M., 261
terror management, 62
terrorism
    low self-esteem and, 131, 205
    prejudice and, 185–186, 187f
    war on, 58–59, 59f, 212
text messaging, 115–116
that's-not-all technique, 292, 292f
theories. see specific theories
thought suppression, 60, 60–61, 60f
thought/thought processes. see also automatic
        processing; cognition; social cognition
    about self, 120–129
    attitude and, 148–149
    influence of, 94–96, 95f
    neuroscience of, 14
    nonconscious, 16–17, 18f
threats
    attitude formation and, 152, 152f
    prejudice originating from, 185–186, 187f,
        204–207, 210
    to self-esteem, 131, 204–206, 205f, 206f
    stereotyping and, 140–142, 191
    to subgroup identity, 210–211, 210f
tipping (in restaurants), 275, 275f, 398
tobacco products, 158–159, 167, 179
tokenism, 194–195, 194f, 195f
touching as communication, 79–80
tragedy, 59–60
traits, stereotypic, 191–193, 191t, 198, 198t,
    200, 219–220
traits as situational sensitivities model (TASS),
    356–357, 357f
transactional justice, 406–407
transactional leaders, 453–454, 454f
transformational leaders, 452–454, 453f,
    454f
triangular model of love, 257, 257f
trivialization, 177
trust, interpersonal, 246–247
trustworthiness, 99, 243
truth vs. lies, 80–84, 84f
Turkish troops' massacres, 299
TV. see television
two-factor theory of emotion, 65
type A behavior pattern, 357

"ultimatum paradigm", 67
unconditioned stimulus, 150–151
unconscious thought
    benefits of, 51–53, 52f
    vs. controlled processing, 48
    definition of, 49
    social behavior and, 49–51, 51f
underadaptive response, 242
unpriming of schemas, 41–42, 42f

unrequited love, 256
upward social comparison, 133–134, 135–136
U.S. presidency, 384
us-versus-them effect, 208–211, 208f

validity, external, 27
values, 114, 131–133, 140–141, 318
variables
    confounding, 26, 26f
    in correlational research, 23–24, 30
    in experimentation, 25–27, 26f
    mediating, 28, 28f
vested interests, 159–160
video games, 347–348, 348f
videotapes/videotaping, 180, 421
Vietnam War, 409
violence
    crimes, 361
    discrimination and, 212–213, 212f
    low self-esteem and, 131

media and, 347–351
pornography and, 351–352
roots of, 338–342
variations of, 8
workplace, 365–367, 366f
visual indicators (social identity), 123,
    125–126, 125f
voice pitch/tone, 76, 115, 116
volunteering, 328–331

walking, 235, 435–436
wealth (mating criterion), 254
weather, aggression and, 360–361
websites
    beauty enhancement, 235
    racist, 189, 189f
    self-identity and, 111–113, 112f, 114f
    self-presentation on, 115–116, 116f
well-being, 137, 138–139, 139f, 196
whistle-blower, 159
Wigand, Jeffrey, 159

will to live, 434
women. see also gender
    glass ceiling and, 192–193, 192f
    "good wife" stereotype, 113, 113f
    self-esteem level, 131–133, 132f
    situation-dependent self–construal of,
        122–123, 123f
    stereotypes of, 140–141, 191, 191t
    token, 194–195, 194f, 195f
    workplace discrimination against, 131–132,
        188, 193
women clergy, 392, 392f
workplace aggression, 365–367, 366f
workplace social psychology applications,
    442–455
World Trade Center, 186–187, 187f
World War II, 92, 92f, 165–166

YouTube, 282, 383t

zero-sum outcome of racism, 189

Photo Credits

CHAPTER 1

Pages 2, 3: Age Fotostock; 4 (left): Tracy Bennett/MGM/Picture Desk/Kobal Collection; 4 (right): Tracy Bennett/MGM/Picture Desk/Kobal Collection; 7 (left): Photo Researchers; 7 (right): Trevor Wood/Stone/Getty Images; 9 (top): Age Fotostock; 9 (bottom): Michelle D. Bridwell/PhotoEdit; 11 (top): Kayte Deioma/PhotoEdit; 11 (bottom): Peter Correz/Stone/Getty Images; 19: Archives of the History of Psychology 1.9; 22: ratemyprofessor.com page and photo courtesy of Robert A. Baron; 32: Photo Courtesy of Robert A. Baron;

CHAPTER 2

Pages 36, 37: Veer; 40 (left): Fancy Photography/Veer; 40 (right) Veer; 44: Bob Daemmrich Photography; 45: Paul Chinn/San Francisco Examiner/AP Images; 56 (top): Michael Dwyer/Stock Boston; 56 (bottom): Michael Dwyer/AP Images; 59: Hussein Malla/AP Images; 60: M. Antman/The Image Works; 62: Dave King/DK; 66: Jutta Klee/Corbis;

CHAPTER 3

Pages 72, 73: Michael A. Keller/Masterfile; 77 (left): Photo Courtesy of Robert A. Baron; 77 (right): Photo Courtesy of Robert A. Baron; 79 (left): Photo Courtesy of Robert A. Baron; 79 (middle): Photo Courtesy of Robert A. Baron; 79 (right): Photo Courtesy of Robert A. Baron; 82: David J. Phillip/AP Images; 94: Tony Freeman/PhotoEdit; 104: Michael A. Keller/Masterfile; 105 (left): Arnaldo Magnani/Getty Images; 105 (right): SuperStock/Alamy Images; 107: Jonathan Player/New York Times Agency;

CHAPTER 4

Pages 110, 111: Hans Neleman/Getty Images; 112: Stanley L. Rowin/Creative Eye/MIRA.com; 113: Lambert/Hulton Archives/Getty Image; 116: Photo Courtesy of Nyla Branscombe; 118: Tony Freeman/PhotoEdit; 124: J. Scott Applewhite/AP Images; 125: Yellow Dog Productions/Image Bank/Getty Images; 127 (left): Adam Larkey/ABC; 127 (right): Garth Vaughan/ABC; 130 (left): Kai Pfaffenbach/Corbis/Reuters; 130 (right): Mike Segar/Corbis/Reuters; 132 (top): M. Thomsen/Zefa/Corbis; 132 (bottom): Michael Newman/PhotoEdit; 140 (left): Michael Newman/PhotoEdit; 140 (right): Hans Neleman/Getty Images;

CHAPTER 5

Pages 146, 147: Stephen Welstead/LWA/Corbis; 149 (left): Courtesy of MacLean's Magazine; 149 (right): M. Thomsen/Zefa/Corbis; 151: Bill Aron/PhotoEdit; 152: Shaun Best/Reuters; 154 (top): Adam Larkey/ABC; 154 (bottom): Frank Micelotta/Getty Images; 158: PhotoCourtesy of Nyla Branscombe; 164: Stephen Welstead/LWA/Corbis; 166 (left): Jeff Greenberg/PhotoEdit; 166 (right): Michael Newman/PhotoEdit; 168: David Young-Wolff/PhotoEdit; 171: Peter Griffith/Masterfile; 180: Spencer Grant/PhotoEdit;

CHAPTER 6

Pages 184, 185: AP Images; 187 (top left): Nasser Shiyoukhi/AP Images; 187 (top right): Ralph Orlowski/Reuters; 187 (bottom): Masatomo Kuriya/Bettmann/Corbis; 189 (left): The Insurgent; 189 (right): AP Images; 194 (left): Dennis Cook/AP Images; 194 (right): Susan Walsh/AP Images; 199: Photo Photo Courtesy of Nyla Branscombe; 206: Oded Balilty/AP Images; 207: Archives of the History of American Psychology; 208 (left): Peggy Guggenheim Collection/ Venice/Dagli Orti/Picture Desk/Kobal Collection; 208 (right): The Art Archive/Bauhaus Archive/Eileen Tweedy/Picture Desk/Kobal Collection; 212: AP Images;

CHAPTER 7

Pages 224, 225: C. Devan/Zefa/Corbis; 229: The Granger Collection; 230: NewsCom; 231: Kelly-Mooney/Corbis; 233: C. Devan/Zefa/Corbis; 234 (left): Rufus F. Folkks/Corbis; 234 (right): James Devaney/WireImage/Getty Images; 235: Courtesy of Dr. Judith H. Langlois, Charles and Sarah Seay Regents Professor, Department of Psychology, Univerity of Texas, Austin; 239: Alex Wong/Getty Images; 245: Ellen Howdon/DK; 246 (left): Corbis RF; 246 (right): Simon Jarratt/Corbis; 248: Photo Courtesy of Robert A. Baron; 249: Photo Courtesy of Robert A. Baron; 255 (top): Phillip Jarrell/Getty Images; 255 (bottom): Stockbyte/Getty Images; 260 (top left): Najlah Feanny/Corbis; 260 (top right): Eurekaimages.com/Alamy Images; 260 (bottom): Danita Delimont/Alamy Images; 263: Reggie Casagrande/Getty Images;

CHAPTER 8

Pages 270, 271: Eric Lee/Lawrence Bender Productions/ Picture Desk/Kobal Collection; 275 (top): Jupiterimages/Creatas/Alamy Images; 275 (bottom): Sergio Dionisio/AP Images; 284 (left): Bonnie Kamin/PhotoEdit; 284 (right): Bonnie Kamin/PhotoEdit; 286: Eric Lee/Lawrence Bender Productions/ Picture; 290: Jeff Greenberg/The Image Works; 292: Michael Newman/PhotoEdit; 293: Rhoda Sidney/Stock Boston; 297 (a): Gregg DeGuire/Wireimage/Getty Images; 297 (b): Frederick M. Brown/Getty Images; 297 (c): Mark Savage/Corbis; 297 (d): Evan Agostini/Getty Images; 299: Courtesy of Alexandra Milgram;

CHAPTER 9

Pages 304, 305: Gabe Palmer/Corbis; 307: Finbarr O'Reilly/Reuters/NewsCom; 309: Photo Courtesy of Robert A. Baron; 315 (left): Jim Zuckerman/Corbis; 315 (right): Jim Zuckerman/Corbis; 316: Gabe Palmer/Corbis; 319: Alex Segre/Alamy Images; 320: Susan Van Etten/PhotoEdit; 321: Norbert Schaefer/Corbis; 324: Stach Antkowiak/AFP/Getty Images; 328: Bill Haber/AP Images;

CHAPTER 10

Pages 336, 337: Corbis/Reuters; 339: FOX-TV/Picture DeskKobal Collection; 341 (top left): Michael Newman/PhotoEdit; 341 (top right): Abreu Cesar Lucas/Image Bank/Getty Images; 341 (bottom left): Corbis/Reuters; 341 (bottom right): Dex Images/Corbis; 349: Courtesy of Albert Bandura; 353: Bejing New Picture/Elite Group/Picture Desk/Kobal Collection; 359: Rick Gomez/Corbis; 362 (top left): TongRo Image Stock/Brank X/Corbis; 362 (bottom left): IndexOpen; 362 (right): Michael Newman/PhotoEdit;373: David Young-Wolff/PhotoEdit;

CHAPTER 11

Pages 376, 377: David Bergman/Corbis; 378: Photo Courtesy Nyla Branscombe; 381 (left): Jeff Greenberg/Alamy Images; 381 (right): David Bergman/Corbis; 390: Mark Wilson/Getty Images; 392: Photofusion Picture Library/Alamy Images; 394: Photo Courtesy of Nyla Branscombe; 395: Jeff GreenbergPhotoEdit; 398: David Young-Wolff/PhotoEdit; 400 (left):Julian Martin/EFE/AP Images; 400 (right): Steve Liss/Time Life/Getty Images; 401:Getty RF; 403: Darrin Klimek/Getty Images;

CHAPTER 12

Pages 416, 417: Helen King/Corbis; 418 (left): Gerard Rancinan/Sygma/Corbis; 418 (right): Bo Zaunders/Corbis; 420: Alan Schein/Bettmann/Corbis; 423: James Shaffer/PhotoEdit; 425: Ace Stock Limited/Alamy Images; 427: Don Mason/Corbis; 429: Courtesy of the Library of Congress; 430 (left): Damian Dovarganes/AP Images; 430 (right): Steve Grayson/Pool/Getty Images; 433: Philip North-Coombes/Stone/Getty Images; 435 (left): Adrian Burke/Corbis; 435 (right): AP Images; 437 (left): Roger Bamber/Alamy Images; (right): Helen King/Corbis; 441 (left): Photo Courtesy of Robert A. Baron; 441 (right): Don Mason/Corbis; 447: Michael Newman/PhotoEdit; 453 (top left): Corbis/Bettmann; 453 (top right): Hans Gedda/Sygma/Corbis; 453 (bottom left): Hulton-Deutsch/Bettmann/Corbis; 453 (bottom right): Oscar White/Corbis;